WORLD ENCYCLOPEDIA OF 20TH CENTURY MURDER

Jay Robert Nash

BCA
LONDON · NEW YORK · SYDNEY · TORONTO

This edition published 1992 by BCA
by arrangement with
HEADLINE BOOK PUBLISHING PLC

CN 1587

First published in Great Britain
by HEADLINE BOOK PUBLISHING PLC

10 9 8 7 6 5 4 3 2 1

Printed and bound in Great Britain by
BPCC Hazells Ltd
Member of BPCC Ltd

BOOKS BY JAY ROBERT NASH

FICTION

On All Fronts
A Crime Story
The Dark Fountain
The Mafia Diaries

NONFICTION

Dillinger: Dead or Alive?
Citizen Hoover
Bloodletters and Badmen
Hustlers and Con Men
Darkest Hours
Among the Missing
Murder, America
Almanac of World Crime
Look for the Woman
People to See
The True Crime Quiz Book
The Innovators
Zanies
The Crime Movie Quiz Book
Open Files
The Toughest Movie Quiz Book Ever
The Dillinger Dossier
Murder Among the Mighty
Jay Robert Nash's Crime Chronology

REFERENCE

The Motion Picture Guide (12 vols.)
The Encyclopedia of World Crime (6 vols.)

THEATER

The Way Back
Last Rites for the Boys (1947)

POETRY

Lost Natives & Expatriates

FOREWORD

The *World Encyclopedia of 20th Century Murder* goes far beyond a staggering chronicle of slayings. More than a thousand murder entries (and more than 400 illustrations) will be found in this volume, representing all manner of slayers and all types of homicides, with varying degrees of motivation and method. From the lone, sensational jealousy killing of Stanford White in 1906 by Pittsburgh millionaire Harry K. Thaw, to the perverse slayings of British sex murderer John Christie and the latter day serial killer Ted Bundy, each case represents a different and, for the most part, unique story. In most instances, in-depth background information is provided, detailing childhood history, work, and marital experience and, most importantly, the social history of murderers who have shocked one generation after another with their crimes.

Within these hundreds of pages, the reader will discover all manner of killers—male and female, adult and child, and from all nations representing the rich and the poor, the comfortable and the desperate. International in scope, this volume seeks to explain, as much as the facts and intensive study will permit, the reasons behind the killing or killings that made headlines and impacted society. Often as not, the motivation remains unclear, sometimes utterly mystifying. In other slayings, the motivation is given through the killer's own confessions.

Those cases selected for this work encompass the globe and have been chosen according to the importance of each entry. By dint of sheer numbers, all mass murderers and serial killers of note have been included—Albert DeSalvo, Richard Speck, John Wayne Gacy, Juan Corona, Dean Corll. Scores of spectacular cases are offered, such as that of Dr. Crippen, who murdered his henpecking wife, piecemealed her body, and then fled with his mistress (disguised as a boy) by fast steamer from England to Canada in 1910. Crippen's tragic tale of domestic homicide and frantic flight to a new life made headlines in Europe and the U.S., this being the first case in which a killer was tracked down and identified by wireless communications (and a faster ship carrying a dedicated inspector of Scotland Yard).

The reader will also find within these pages the sensational tales of such killers as Johann Otto Hoch, an American bluebeard who may have murdered as many as fifty women in murder-for-profit schemes; the cannibal killers Albert Fish, Ed Gein, Fritz Haarmann; Jack Henry Abbott, a dedicated prison murderer whose literary talents brought him to freedom and more murder in New York; the notorious British killers John Haigh, the "Acid Bath" murderer, and George Joseph Smith, the infamous "Brides of the Bath" slayer; the French mass murderers, Landru (the original Bluebeard), Dr. Petiot, and Gaston Dominici.

Female slayers are also terrifyingly present: Belle Gunness of Indiana, who advertised in lonelyhearts columns for suitors and then murdered them by the dozen; the British bar girl Ruth Ellis, who killed her unfaithful lover and was hanged for it; the French writer Hera Myrtel, who murdered her husband in order to devote herself to her literary career and her lovers. Included are cases of teenagers and even children who murdered with motives as petty as losing a game or making a chance remark.

The scope of the *World Encyclopedia of 20th Century Murder* is designed to offer readers a worldwide view of homicide which covers all types of killers and all manner of murders in order to better understand a social problem that has spread to almost epidemic proportions, reaching into all levels of society and throughout all lands. The serial killer or mass murderer, for instance, is no longer a social phenomenon surfacing sporadically within a decade, but a nearly commonplace lethal creature whose presence has increased to alarming proportions as social units and concepts—the family, organized religion, the perception of law and order—have woefully decreased in importance. This is much in evidence, the reader will note, when addressing the modern-day killer.

One can no longer take comfort in viewing murder as a distant threat to oneself and one's family. It is now a reality living down the block, lurking around the corner, making all vulnerable to the unthinkable. Murder has been made convenient to the professional criminal who, when planning a robbery or similar type crime, also plans murder, if necessary, to accomplish his ends knowing that, if caught, he or she can legally plea-bargain or make another type of deal with prosecutors to escape the maximum punishment for murder. The legal process of appeals in the schedule-jammed courts around the world also aids the killer who can go on living for a decade or more, at public expense, following a conviction and death sentence.

In the early part of this century, murderers received a trial within a month of being charged, and sentences often followed upon convictions by a matter of days. Appeals took only one week to a month and executions were then promptly exercised. Mistakes were made in this overly expeditious process, enough to warrant the necessity of more time for more examination of individual cases. That

time, the killer's time, ironically borrowed from the victim, now seems interminably and unjustly extended, an agonizingly slow process of justice (or no justice at all in the end) known too well by would-be killers.

Murderers in the United States, more so than any other country, make up the greater portion of this work, in that more murders are committed in the U.S. each year (an average of 10,000 by handguns alone) than anywhere else and on a horrific scale that often rivals massacre. Often as not, this is a condition which has been brought about in recent decades because of the permissive acquisition and use of firearms, but it can also be attributed to an attitude of general unconcern by a public less willing than in times past to bring about change and reform.

As anyone studying this work will discover, civilized society can no longer reasonably view its killers as social pariahs, strangers in distant lands, as separate from normal society as is the moon from the earth. They are a real and present danger, increasing in numbers, reaching with lethal destructiveness into all our lives. They are truly among us.

Jay Robert Nash
1991

ACKNOWLEDGMENTS

Grateful acknowledgment is given to the thousands of persons who, over the years, have assisted the author in obtaining valuable source information, research materials of all kinds, photos, illustrations, trial reports, and tracts. Without the splendid and wonderful cooperation of these persons and organizations, this work would not have come into existence. Organizations deserving special recognition in this area include correctional facilities, criminal investigation agencies, government offices, historical societies, libraries, newspaper and other media, and police departments worldwide.

Some of the most helpful include:

CORRECTIONAL FACILITIES: Alabama Dept. of Corrections (Montgomery, Ala.); Arizona Dept. of Corrections (Phoenix, Ariz., Jo Stephens); Bay State Correctional Center (Norfolk, Mass., Deodato Arruda); Bureau of Prisons (Washington, D.C., Helen Butler, Tina Cloyd); California Dept. of Corrections (Sacramento, Calif., Lisa Korb); Connecticut Dept. of Correction (Hartford, Conn.); Delaware Dept. of Correction (Smyrna, Del., Kathryn Pippin); District of Columbia Dept. of Corrections (Washington, D.C., Pat Wheeler); Federal Bureau of Prisons - North Central Region (Kansas City, Mo.); Florida Dept. of Corrections (Tallahassee, Fla.); Georgia Dept. of Corrections (Atlanta, Ga.); Illinois Dept. of Corrections (Springfield, Ill.); Indiana Dept. of Corrections (Indianapolis, Ind.); Kansas Dept. of Corrections (Topeka, Kan., Thomas J. Sloan); Kentucky Corrections Cabinet Dept. of Adult Correctional Institutions; Lackawanna County Prison (Scranton, Pa.); Maryland Dept. of Public Safety and Correctional Services; Massachusetts Dept. of Probations and Records (Boston, Mass.); Minnesota Dept. of Corrections (St. Paul, Minn.); Missouri Dept. of Corrections and Human Resources; Nevada Dept. of Prisons (Carson City, Nev.); New York State Dept. of Corrections (Albany, N.Y., Kelly Priess); New Jersey Dept. of Corrections (Trenton, N.J.); North Carolina Dept. of Corrections (Raleigh, N.C., David Guth); Ohio Department of Rehabilitation and Correction (Columbus, Ohio); Oklahoma Dept. of Corrections (Oklahoma City, Okla., Michelle Matthews); Olmstead County (Minn.) Dept. of Corrections; Pennsylvania Dept. of Corrections (Harrisburg, Pa., Kenneth G. Robinson); South Carolina Dept. of Corrections (Columbia, S.C., Judy Bode); Tennessee Dept. of Corrections (Nashville, Tenn., William C. Haynes, Jr.); Texas Dept. of Corrections (Huntsville, Texas); U.S. Medical Center for Federal Prisoners (Springfield, Ill.); Leavenworth (Kan.) Penitentiary; Marion (Ill.) Penitentiary; Utah Dept. of Corrections (Salt Lake City, Utah).

COURT OFFICIALS: Nell E. Anderson (Clerk of the District Court, Teller County, Cripple Creek, Colo.); Tom Bigbee (Record Planning Commission, Canton, Ala.); C. Edward Bourassa (Register of Probate, Hillsborough County Probate Court, Nashua, N.H.); Richard P. Brinker (Clerk, Probate Division of Circuit Court of Miami, Fla.); Arlene D. Connors (Deputy Register in Probate, Milwaukee County, Milwaukee, Wis.); John J. Corcoran (Acting County Clerk, Los Angeles, Calif.); Susan Cottrell (Deputy, San Diego, Calif.); Virginia Crane (Deputy Court Clerk, Neptune, N.J.); John T. Curry (Circuit Clerk, Probate Division, Macon County, Ill.); Director of Licensing, Public Service Level, Minneapolis, Minn.; B.J. Dunavant (Clerk of the Probate Court, Shelby County, Memphis, Tenn.); Bremer Ehrler (Clerk, Jefferson County Court, Probate Division, Louisville, Ky.); C. Fatni (Record Clerk, Surrogate's Court, Kings County, N.Y.); Mildred Fulton (County Clerk, Cherokee County, Rusk, Texas); Mildred Gonder (Deputy Clerk, Probate Court, New Albany, Ind.); Harriet L. Gosnell (Trust Officer, People's Bank of Bloomington, Ill.); Jackie Griffin (Chief Deputy, Ellis County, Texas); Carole J. Hals (Deputy Clerk, County Court, Probate Division, Stark, Minn.); James B. Kelley, Jr. (Register, Probate Court, Taunton, Mass.); Julia Kowrak (Register of Wills, City Hall, Philadelphia, Pa.); Leland Larrison (Clerk, Probate Court, Terre Haute, Ind.); Madelina S. Marting (Deputy Clerk, Putnam County, N.J.); Sarah Montjoy (Deputy Clerk, Jefferson County Court, Probate Division, Louisville, Ky.); Olmsted County Court, Probate Division (Minn.); Carl M. Olsen (Deputy Clerk, San Francisco, Calif.); Mrs. Lana J. Olson (Register of Probate, Luce County, Newberry, Mich.); Lorna Pierce (Secretary to Judge Donald Gunn, Probate Court of St. Louis, Mo.); Probate Court, Port Arthur, Texas, Probate Court; Providence, R.I., Probate Court ; William J. Regan (Judge of the Surrogates Court, Buffalo, N.Y.); Elisabeth F. Sachse (Deputy Clerk of Court, Baton Rouge, La.); St. Joseph County Health Department (South Bend, Ind.); San Mateo County Sheriff's Office (Hall of Justice, Redwood City, Calif.); Joan R. Saunder (Deputy Register of Wills, Clerk of the Probate; Division, Washington, D.C.); Jean Smith (Deputy Clerk of Court, Watonwan County, St. James, Minn.); Nancy M. Spaulding (Chief Clerk, Schoharie, N.Y.); Storey County (Nev.) Probate Clerk; Surrogates Court of Essex, N.J.; Irene Thuringer (Deputy Clerk, Probate Dept., Pima County, Tucson, Ariz.); John M. Walker (Chief of Public Services, Los Angeles, Calif.); David M. Warren (Assistant Chief Deputy, Probate Courts Department, Harris County, Houston, Texas); R.D. Zumwalt (County Clerk, San Diego, Calif.).

CRIMINAL INVESTIGATION AGENCIES: Atlanta, Ga., U.S. Attorney's Office; Boston, Mass., U.S. Attorney's Office; Boston, Mass., District Attorney's Office; Brooklyn (N.Y.) District Attorney's Office; Bryan, Texas, District Attorney's Office (Bill Turner); Chicago, Ill., U.S. Attorney's Office; Columbus, Ohio, U.S. Attorney's Office; Cook County State's Attorney's Office (Chicago, Ill., Merle Aguilar); Cook County State's Attorney-Criminal Records Dept. (Chicago, Ill.); Danville, Ill. U.S. Attorney's Office (Rick Cox); Denver, Colo., District Attorney's Office (Dave Heckenbach, Assisant D.A.); Ft. Smith, Ark., District Attorney's Office (Steven Snyder, Assistant D.A.); Franklin County Prosecutor's Office (Columbus, Ohio, Thomas Tornabene); Geneva, Ill., State's Attorney's Office; Hamilton County (Ohio) Prosecutor's Office; Lee County State's Attorney's Office (Ft. Myers, Fla.); Livingston County, Ill., District Attorney's Office; Los Angeles City Attorney's Office (Mike Qualls); Los Angeles, Calif., District Attorney's Office (Grace Denton); Manhattan District Attorney's Office (New York, N.Y.); Montgomery County District Attorney's Office (Cheltenham, Pa.); New Bedford, Mass., District Attorney's Office; New Orleans, La., U.S. Attorney's Office; Reno, Nev., District Attorney's Office; San Jose, Calif., District Attorney's Office; Shiawassee City, Mich., District Attorney's Office; Suffolk County (N.Y.) Assistant District Attorney's Office (Jermyn Ray); Westchester County District Attorney's Office (N.Y.); Will County State's Attorney's Office (Joliet, Ill.).

GOVERNMENT OFFICES: Camden County (N.C.) Clerk's Office; Crown Point, Ind., Mayor's Office; Dept. of Treasury, Public Affairs Office (Washington, D.C., Robert R. Snow); FBI, Special Productions Branch (Washington, D.C., Melanie McElhinney); Federal Bureau of Investigations (Washington, D.C.); Hamilton County Clerk's Office (Cincinnati, Ohio); Municipal References & Resource Center of New York City (New York, N.Y., Devra Zetlan); Shiawassee County (Mich.) Clerk's Office; Tallahassee, Fla., City Clerk's Office (Becky Pippin); U.S. Information Agency (Washington, D.C., Scott Righetti).

HISTORICAL SOCIETIES: Anoka (Minn.) County Historical Society; Arizona State Historical Society (Tucson, Ariz.); Blair County Historical Society (Altoona, Pa., Sylva L. Emerson, Curator); California Historical Society (Los Angeles, Calif., Peter Evans); Chicago Historical Society; Colorado State Historical Society (Denver, Colo.); Connecticut Historical Society (Hartford, Conn.); Detroit Historical Society; Historical Society of Pennsylvania (Philadelphia, Pa.); Historical Society of Pennsylvania (Pittsburgh, Pa.); Illinois Historical Society (Chicago, Ill.); Illinois State Historical Society (Springfield, Ill.); Kansas State Historical Society (Topeka, Kan.); Kentucky Historical Society (Frankfort, Ky.); Massachusetts Historical Society (Boston, Mass.); Minnesota Historical Society (St. Paul, Minn.); Missouri State Historical Society (Columbia, Mo.); New Jersey Historical Society (Newark, N.J.); New York Historical Society (New York, N.Y., Mariam Touba); Oregon Historical Society (Portland, Ore.); Virginia Historical Society (Richmond, Va.); Wyoming State Historical Society (Cheyenne, Wyo.).

LIBRARIES: Alachua County Library District (Gainesville, Fla., Phillis Filer); Boston Public Library; Bridgeport Public Library (Bridgeport, Conn., Louise Minervino); Broward County Library (Ft. Lauderdale, Fla., Juanita Alpuche, Allison M. Ellis); California State Library (Sacramento, Calif.); Chicago Public Library (Chicago, Ill.); Columbia University Law Library (New York, N.Y.); Deerfield Public Library (Deerfield, Ill., Jack Hicks); Denver Public Library (Denver, Colo., James H. Davis, Picture Librarian); Detroit Public Library; Drug Enforcement Administration Library (Washington, D.C., Edith A. Crutchfield); Harvard Law School Library (Cambridge, Mass.); Illinois State Library (Springfield, Ill.); Indiana State Library (Indianapolis, Ind.); John Crerar Library (Chicago, Ill.); Library of Congress (Washington, D.C., Dan Burney); Metropolitan Library System (Oklahoma City, Okla.); Monroe County Law Library (Monroe, Mich., Judge Sullivan); New Orleans Public Library (New Orleans, La.); New York City Public Library (New York, N.Y.); New York State Law Library (Albany, N.Y.); Newberry Library (Chicago, Ill.); North Carolina State Library (Raleigh, N.C.); Northwestern University Law Library (Chicago, Ill.); Scotland Yard Library (London, England); Special Collections Library, Northwestern University (Evanston, Ill., Russell Maylone); University of California Library (Berkeley, Calif., William F. Roberts, Reference Librarian); University of Chicago Library (Chicago, Ill.); University of Missouri Law Library (Columbia, Mo.); University of Missouri Library (Columbia, Mo.); University of Oklahoma (Norman, Okla., Jack D. Haley, Assistant Curator, Western History Collections); University of Wisconsin Criminal Justice Reference and Information Center (Madison, Wis., Sue L. Center, Dir.); Wisconsin Dept. of Justice, Law Library (Madison, Wis., Michael F. Bemis); Yale University Law Library (New Haven, Conn., Robert E. Brooks, Reference; Jo Anne Giammattei, Acquisitions).

MISSING PERSONS BUREAUS: Chicago Police Dept. (Chicago, Ill., Lts. Bill Bodner, John Doyle, Bill Frost); New York Police Department (New York, N.Y., Detective John Griffin).

NEWSPAPERS/MEDIA: *Adam Smith's Money World* (New York, N.Y., Anne Hansen); Albuquerque (N.M.) *Journal;* Arizona *Daily Star* (Tucson, Ariz.); Arizona *Republic* (Phoenix, Ariz.); Arkansas *Democrat* (Booneville, Ark.); Atlanta (Ga.) *Constitution* (Diane Hunter); Baltimore (Md.) *Sun*; Bangor (Maine) *Daily News;* Boston (Mass.) *Herald* (Betsy Warrior); Boston (Mass.) *Globe* (William Boles); Capital News Service (Los Angeles, Calif., Jerry Goldberg); Charleston (W. Va.) *Gazette* (Ron Miller); *Chicago Sun Times* (Chicago, Ill.); *Chicago Tribune* (Chicago, Ill.); Cincinnati (Ohio) *Enquirer; Clarion-Ledger* (Jackson, Miss.); Cleveland (Ohio) *Plain Dealer* (Eileen M. Lentz); *Daily Northwestern* (Oshkosh, Wis.); *Daily Oklahoman* (Oklahoma City, Okla.); Dallas (Texas) *Morning News;* Dayton (Ohio) *Daily News;* Detroit (Mich.) *Free Press;* Detroit (Mich.) *News;* Gallatin (Tenn.)

Examiner (John Cannon); Greenville (S.C.) *News;* Houston (Texas) *Post;* Houston (Texas) *Chronicle* (Sherry Adams); Indianapolis (Ind.) *Star* (Nadine Moore); Japan *Times* (Tokyo, Japan, Shigeo Shimada); Las Vegas (Nev.) *Sun* (Jenny Scarantino); Los Angeles (Calif.) *Times* (Renee Nembhard); Louisville (Ky.) *Courier-Journal* (Patrick Chapman); Miami (Fla.) *Herald* (Liz Donovan, Nora Paul); *Morning Call* (Allentown, Pa., Lynn M. Dubbs); New York (N.Y.) *Daily News* (Faigi Rosenthal); New York (N.Y.) *Times* (Tom Wicker); *Newsday* (Garden City, N.Y., Elizabeth Whisnant); Omaha (Neb.) *World Herald;* Philadelphia (Pa.) *Inquirer;* Pittsburgh (Pa.) *Post Gazette;* Portland (Ore.) *Oregonian* (Sandra Macomber); *Press Telegram* (Long Beach, Calif., George Choma); Providence (R.I.) *Journal;* Reno (Nev.) *Gazette-Journal* (Carole Keith, Nan Spina); *Rocky Mountain News* (Denver, Colo.); St. Louis (Mo.) *Post-Dispatch* (Mike Marler); Salt Lake *Tribune* (Salt Lake City, Utah); San Antonio (Texas) *Express-News* (Judy Zipp); San Diego (Calif.) *Union;* San Francisco (Calif.) *Chronicle* (Nikki Bengal); San Francisco (Calif.) *Examiner;* Seattle (Wash.) *Times;* Seattle (Wash.) *Post-Intelligencer;* Selma (Ala.) *Times Journal* (Nicki Davis Maud); *Spokesman-Review* (Spokane, Wash.); Tampa *Tribune* (Tampa Bay, Fla.); *The State* (Columbia, S.C., Dargan Richards); *Times News* (Cumberland, Md., Linda Shuck); Topeka (Kan.) *Capital-Journal;* Trenton (N.J.) *Times;* Tucson (Ariz.) *Daily Citizen;* Tulsa (Okla.) *Daily World;* Wichita (Kan.) *Eagle Beacon;* Winnipeg *Free Press* (Winnipeg, Manitoba, Canada); WTEN-TV (Albany, N.Y., David A. Lamb).

POLICE DEPARTMENTS: Aurora (Ill.) Police Dept.; Baltimore (Md.) Police Dept. (Dennis S. Hill, Dir. Public Info. Div.); Boston (Mass.) Police Dept. (Allison Woodhouse, Research & Analysis); Brooklyn Organized Crime Strike Force (Brooklyn, N.Y.); Chicago (Ill.) Police Dept. (Dennis Bingham, Public Information; Tina Vicini, Dir. News Affair Div.); Chicago (Ill.) Police Dept. Academy (Sgt. Anthony Consieldi); Dallas (Texas) Police Dept. (Capt. J.E. Ferguson); Deerfield (Ill.) Police Dept. (Richard Brandt, Chief of Police, Thomas A. Creighton, Youth Dir.); Indianapolis (Ind.) Police Dept. (Maj. Robert L. Snow); Los Angeles (Calif.) Police Dept. (Stephen F. Hatfield, Public Information Dir.); Metropolitan Police Dept. (St. Louis, Mo.); Miami (Fla.) Police Dept. (Maj. Dean De Jong); Minneapolis (Minn.) Police Dept. (Ted Faul, Deputy Chief of Services; J.E. Bender, Officer); New Scotland Yard (London, England, Annette Eastgate, Robin Goodfellow, Steve Wilmot); Oshkosh (Wis.) Police Dept.; Pennsylvania State Police Troop H; Philadelphia (Pa.) Police Dept. (Mary Ann Edmunds); Portland (Ore.) Police Dept. (Candy Hill Turay); San Diego (Calif.) Police Dept. (Pliny Castanien); Washington, D.C., Police Dept.

NON-GOVERNMENT AGENCIES: Alcatraz Ferry (San Francisco, Calif.); Chicago Crime Commission (Chicago, Ill.).

OTHER CONTRIBUTORS: American Red Cross (Washington, D.C., Margaret O'Connor); Amnesty Int'l (New York, N.Y., Janice Christianson); Chinese Consulate's Office (New York, N.Y.); Joseph Dillman, Registered Pharmacist (Libertyville, Ill.); Japanese Consulate's Office (Chicago, Ill.); Korean Consulate's Office (Chicago, Ill.); Yuri Morozov, Translator; Northwestern University Language Dept. (Evanston, Ill., Rolf Erickson); Anthony J. Pellicano, Private Detective (Los Angeles, Calif.); Pinkerton's, Inc. (New York, N.Y., G.F. O'Neill); Salvation Army (Chicago, Ill., Col. Lloyd Robb); Seaman's Institute of New York City (New York, N.Y., Barbara Clauson).

HOW TO USE THIS ENCYCLOPEDIA

ALPHABETICAL ORDER

Each entry name in the *World Encyclopedia of 20th Century Murder* is bold-faced and listed alphabetically. Biographical entries are alphabetized by the subject's last name. Everything preceding the comma is treated as a unit when alphabetizing. Hyphens, diacritical marks, periods following initials, and spaces do not influence its alphabetization. Names with prefixes such as **de**, **von**, or **le** are listed under the most common form of the name. Names beginning in **Mc** or **M'** are treated as if spelled **Mac**. Asian names, in which the family name comes first, are alphabetized by the family name, omitting the comma. Identical names are alphabetized chronologically. When the names of two or more people head an entry, it is usually alphabetized according to the most prominent person's last name.

ENTRY HEADINGS

Entries appear in boldface and are categorized alphabetically under the name of the offender. Parenthetical remarks immediately following an entry name indicate an alternate spelling, that person's original or maiden name, or the entry's alias if preceded by **AKA:**. These names also appear in boldface.

Following the name are **date(s)** relevant to that entry. The letter **b.** preceding the date signifies that only the person's date of birth is known, while the letter **d.** signifies that only the person's date of death is known. The letter **c.** (circa) signifies that the date which immediately follows is approximate. In some cases **prom.** (prominent) is used to denote the year(s) in which that entry was noteworthy.

The **country** designation in each entry heading refers to the country in which the crime was committed or the country in which persons in the field of crime are known professionally. Entries where crimes are committed in more than three countries or committed on the high seas are designated as Int'l. (International).

A number of entries may include more than one person if the criminals or professionals worked together. When the relevant dates of a **multiple name entry** coincide, one date will follow the last person named in the entry heading.

REFERENCES

Cross references immediately following an entry refer the reader to entries containing additional information relevant to the case, person, place, or event being consulted. Direct references are also used frequently throughout to lead the readers from a well known name (alias, victim, event) to the name under which that entry appears (**Hooded Man, The,** See: **McKay, George**).

KEY TO ABBREVIATIONS

Afg.	=	Afghanistan
Ala.	=	Alabama
Alb.	=	Albania
Alg.	=	Algeria
Arg.	=	Argentina
Ariz.	=	Arizona
Ark.	=	Arkansas
Aus.	=	Australia
Aust.	=	Austria
Bav.	=	Bavaria
Belg.	=	Belgium
Ber.	=	Bermuda
Bol.	=	Bolivia
Braz.	=	Brazil
Brit.	=	Britain/England including Wales
Bul.	=	Bulgaria
Calif.	=	California
Can.	=	Canada
Col.	=	Colombia
Colo.	=	Colorado
Conn.	=	Connecticut
Cos.	=	Costa Rica
Czech.	=	Czechoslovakia
Del.	=	Delaware
Den.	=	Denmark
Dom.	=	Dominican Republic
Ecu.	=	Ecuador
El Sal.	=	El Salvador
Eth.	=	Ethiopia
Fin.	=	Finland
Fla.	=	Florida
Fr.	=	France
Ga.	=	Georgia
Ger.	=	Germany
Gr.	=	Greece
Guat.	=	Guatemala
Hond.	=	Honduras
Hung.	=	Hungary
Ice.	=	Iceland
Ill.	=	Illinois
Ind.	=	Indiana
Indo.	=	Indonesia
Int'l.	=	International
Ire.	=	Ireland
Isr.	=	Israel
Jam.	=	Jamaica
Jor.	=	Jordan
Kan.	=	Kansas
Kor.	=	Korea
Ky.	=	Kentucky
La.	=	Louisiana
Leb.	=	Lebanon
Lux.	=	Luxembourg
Mac.	=	Macedonia
Mass.	=	Massachusetts
Md.	=	Maryland
Mex.	=	Mexico
Mich.	=	Michigan
Mid. East	=	Middle East
Minn.	=	Minnesota
Miss.	=	Mississippi
Mo.	=	Missouri
Mont.	=	Montana
Mor.	=	Morocco
N. Zea.	=	New Zealand
N.C.	=	North Carolina
N.D.	=	North Dakota
N.H.	=	New Hampshire
N.J.	=	New Jersey
N.M.	=	New Mexico
N.Y.	=	New York
Neb.	=	Nebraska
Neth.	=	Netherlands
Nev.	=	Nevada
Nic.	=	Nicaragua

Nig.	=	Nigeria
Nor.	=	Norway
Okla.	=	Oklahoma
Ore.	=	Oregon
P.R.	=	Puerto Rico
Pa.	=	Pennsylvania
Pak.	=	Pakistan
Pan.	=	Panama
Para.	=	Paraguay
Per.	=	Persia
Phil.	=	Philippines
Pol.	=	Poland
Port.	=	Portugal
R.I.	=	Rhode Island
Rom.	=	Romania
Roman.	=	Roman Empire
Rus.	=	Russia (prior to 1918)
S. Afri.	=	South Africa
S.C.	=	South Carolina
S.D.	=	South Dakota
Saud.	=	Saudi Arabia
Scot.	=	Scotland
Sen.	=	Senegal
Si.	=	Sicily
Sing.	=	Singapore
Sri.	=	Sri Lanka
Sudan	=	Sudan
Swed.	=	Sweden
Switz.	=	Switzerland
Tai.	=	Taiwan
Tan.	=	Tanzania
Tenn.	=	Tennessee
Thai.	=	Thailand
trans.	=	translator
Tun.	=	Tunisia
Turk.	=	Turkey
U.A.E.	=	United Arab Emirates
U.K.	=	United Kingdom
U.S.	=	United States of America
U.S.S.R.	=	Union of Soviet Socialist Republics (after 1918)
Urug.	=	Uruguay
Va.	=	Virginia
Venez.	=	Venezuela
Viet.	=	Vietnam
Vt.	=	Vermont
W.Va.	=	West Virginia
Wash.	=	Washington
Wis.	=	Wisconsin
Wyo.	=	Wyoming
Yug.	=	Yugoslavia

A

Abbott, Jack Henry (AKA: **Jack Eastman**), 1944- , U.S. A man who spent most of his adult life in prison, Abbott committed his first murder in 1966 and, after novelist Norman Mailer worked for his release, killed a second time in 1981. At first, this convict, dedicated wholly to violence, was celebrated by New York's literati for penning a prison journal successfully published by Random House. Like many another criminal before him, Abbott, upon his 1981 release, was adopted by such literary lights as Norman Mailer, his sponsor, and Jerzy Kosinski. He was invited to smart cocktail parties where the rich and famous fawned over him. He was heralded as a "great writer" and an "insightful philosopher." But what Jack Henry Abbott really was, always had been, was a man who would kill anyone over the slightest annoyance. This he did, at the height of his brief literary fame, oblivious to his so-called rehabilitation: a cold-blooded, conscious murder that proved how dangerous it really was for amateur criminologists to meddle with crime.

A habitual criminal, Abbott spent all but nine months of his adult life in prison. He was convicted of forgery, bank robbery, and murder. In 1953, at age nine, Abbott proved so incorrigible in foster homes that he was sent to reform school in Utah. Released at age eighteen, Abbott was arrested and convicted of passing bad checks and sent to Utah State Penitentiary where he killed a fellow inmate in 1966. Tried for this murder, Abbott claimed self-defense and said that he had been the victim of a violent homosexual attack. When that ploy did not appear to affect the court, Abbott assumed the role of the lunatic, throwing a pitcher of water at the judge and claiming insanity. A court psychiatrist examined him and reported that Abbott was fit to stand trial. He was found Guilty and sentenced to fourteen years.

In 1971, Abbott escaped from Utah State Penitentiary and was at large for six weeks, during which time he robbed a Denver bank and, upon his recapture, became a federal prisoner. While serving time in a maximum security prison, Abbott read voraciously, consuming scores of books on philosophy, enmeshing himself in the credos of Karl Marx and becoming an avowed Marxist. Abbott read a 1977 newspaper story about Norman Mailer writing a book (*The Executioner's Song*) on Gary Gilmore, who was condemned for murder and awaiting execution in Utah State Penitentiary. Mailer, like his New York contemporary, Truman Capote, was suddenly departing mainstream literature to enter the world of criminology.

It was to Mailer, a powerful influence in the media, that Abbott began addressing his letters, which were fifteen-page, hand-written missives to the author. The clever Abbott, obviously realizing that Mailer was a complete novice in perceiving prison life, offered to aid him in that understanding by detailing his own experiences as a long-term, "state-raised" prisoner.

He intrigued the author by spewing forth tales of dark violence, writing in a clinically descriptive style reminiscent of Mailer's own early works, particularly certain passages from *The Naked and the Dead*, which had certainly not gone unnoticed in Abbott's endless rummaging through prison libraries. The prisoner's literary nightmares described fourteen years of solitary confinement: unbelievable cruelty on the part of prison guards who beat him, tortured him with antipsychotic drugs, sadistically gassed him, starved him so that he was forced to sustain himself by eating cockroaches in his cell, and placed him in strip-and-search cells where he had to stand naked, chained by one arm to his bed.

Abbott's relentless correspondence fed on hatred and violence, intriguing an author whose own interest in violence had always been intense. Mailer took Abbott's letters to the editors of the elitist *New York Review of Books*, and, at his urging in June 1980, an article praising Abbott's writing style appeared in that publication, along with a sample of the letters. This article was read with great interest by Errol McDonald, an editor at Random House. Within two months, McDonald had placed Abbott under a book contract which called for a $12,000 advance, and began organizing the killer's book, which was entitled *In the Belly of the Beast*. Almost immediately, Abbott began to energetically lobby for a parole. The Federal Bureau of Prisons made the first step easier by returning Abbott to Utah State Penitentiary to serve out his remaining time there. Once inside the walls of that institution, an automatic parole was considered. Mailer and others were influential, if not decisive, in their pleas that Abbott be released. Mailer wrote to the parole board that Abbott was really "a powerful and important American writer," urging a positive decision and offering the killer a job as his research assistant. McDonald, the Random House editor, also wrote to prison authorities, saying that he believed Abbott "could support himself as a professional writer if he were released from prison and that he could very well have a bright future."

The parole campaign was successful and Abbott was released on June 5, 1981, transferred from prison to a halfway house in Manhattan's Lower East Side. When the killer's plane arrived in New York, Norman Mailer was on hand to greet him. Almost at the same time, reviews of Abbott's recently released book gushed torrents of praise upon the killer. Wrote Colgate University Professor Terrence Des Pres in the New York *Times* Book Section: "...awesome, brilliant, perversely ingenious; its impact is indelible and, as an articulation of penal nightmare it is completely compelling." New York's literati welcomed the killer with warm embraces, celebrating his published achievement with a number of cocktail parties and smart gatherings at which Abbott was lionized. Great things were predicted for him. He would become a literary giant of the century. His books would be read as credo by anyone needing to know about prison life. Moreover, some even said, Abbott represented the new wave of American literature and was, in fact, its leader. Other than Mailer, many New York literary lions heaped praise on Abbott's work, and these included the brilliant writer Jerzy Kosinski of *Being There* fame. (Kosinski would later regret endorsing the lethal Abbott, being one of the few in the clique of the killer's admirers who later concluded that the Abbott episode was a fraud, likening the literary laurels placed upon Abbott's head to the literati's support of the Black Panthers in the 1960s.)

Abbott worked briefly for Mailer by doing some scanty research, but he spent most of his time drifting aimlessly about the city, a misplaced creature who paradoxically spent time with the elite and powerful of New York one hour, and the next walking about the worst area of the city, the Lower East Side, peopled with prostitutes, pimps, drug pushers, and hardened criminals like himself. Besides Mailer and Kosinski, Abbott found himself in the company of such sterling personalities as author Jean Malaquais, literary agent Scott Meredith, and Robert Silvers, editor of the *New York Review of Books*. He impressed them to no end with his knowledge of Sartre and Camus, existentialists like himself, he said. He knew just what names and quotations would lure these Establishment personalities closer to his web, manipulating them with ease, calling loudly for entrees from their own menus, chewing voraciously upon the fat of their own philosophical beliefs, and thanking them for allowing him, Jack Henry Abbott, convicted killer, to dine at their table.

Surrounded by the protecting arms of New York's literary sachems, Abbott undoubtedly felt that his future was secure. Now he lobbied discreetly for an even loftier position, one which would afford him continuous recognition and financial support, not as a reformed criminal but as a misunderstood literary giant. He expected his new friends to arrange a fellowship for him at the prestigious MacDowell Colony for accomplished artists in picturesque Petersborough, N.H. Here he would preside over the novice writer, the impressionable artist, dictating the thoughts of youthful, adoring followers. None of this, thankfully, was to be.

On the morning of July 18, 1981, Abbott, accompanied by two women, entered a small, all-night eatery, the BoniBon, on Second Avenue and Fifth Street. It was 5 a.m.

After Abbott and the women took their seats, 22-year-old Richard Adan, a struggling Cuban-born actor working as a waiter, approached the table to take their order. Adan had recently appeared on public TV in Spain in a series of dramatic roles that had given his career a boost. His newly completed play about the Lower East Side was soon to be produced by an experimental stage group and the youth, known always to be polite and pleasant, was looking eagerly forward to a blossoming career in the theater. Adan had recently married a young choreographer-actress whose father had given him a job as a waiter in his restaurant so the young couple could make ends meet.

Abbott asked Adan where the washroom was located. Adan, according to customers in the restaurant, courteously explained that it was an employee-only washroom and that insurance restrictions prevented customers from using it. Abbott became incensed and began using abusive language. According to witnesses, Adan asked him to go outside with him to try to settle the argument so as not to disturb the other customers. Abbott later claimed that Adan was threatening him, but it was Abbott who did the threatening. Once outside the restaurant, Abbott drew a knife with a medium-length blade and with one powerful thrust, drove the blade into Adan's heart. Another waiter, just at that moment, looked out of one of the restaurant's windows to see the young waiter jumping up and down, gushing blood. Abbott then returned to one of the women with him, college student Susan Roxas, and shouted, "Let's get out of here. I just killed a man!"

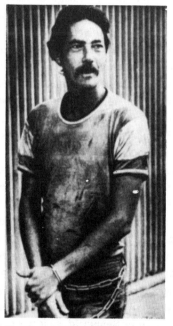

Convict and killer Jack Henry Abbott, chained in Louisiana and en route to his 1981 murder trial.

With that, Jack Henry Abbott, acclaimed author, vanished. It is revealing to quote Abbott's own work, where he describes how he knifed a fellow prisoner to death fifteen years earlier, a methodical, cold-blooded act that was duplicated with the same precision in his 1981 murder of Richard Adan: "The enemy is smiling and chatting away about something. He thinks you're his fool; he trusts you. You see the spot. It's a target between the second and third button on his shirt. As you calmly talk and smile, you move your left foot to the side to step across his right-side body length. A light pivot toward him with your right shoulder and the world turns upside down; you have sunk the knife to its hilt into the middle of his chest."

For two months Abbott eluded police and federal agents who were searching for him nationwide. Using the considerable advances from his book, Abbott managed to get to Mexico and hole up near the Guatemalan border; but after some weeks, not being able to speak Spanish or find work that would cloak his activities, he moved back to the U.S., to Louisiana. He was spotted in the Latin Quarter of New Orleans several times but whenever officers appeared, he had just departed his lodgings, almost as if he had been informed that authorities were closing in on him. Investigators interviewed the prostitutes of the Quarter and one streetwalker identified Abbott's photo, telling police that the much-wanted killer was looking for work in the Louisiana oil fields. Officers tracked the elusive killer through the oil towns of Algiers, Harvey, and Marrero, searching through the murky bunkhouses where hundreds of nameless itinerant workers lived, but at every turn they missed their man, sometimes only by minutes. Abbott seemed to have a sixth sense about lawmen closing in on him and would, according to fellow workers, suddenly quit whatever he was doing, grab his meager belongings, and depart. In mid-September 1981, New York Police Detective William Majeski, who had arrived at the BoniBon restaurant after the Adan killing to take charge of the investigation and had trailed Abbott with other officers to New Orleans, learned that the fugitive was using a social security card with the alias of Jack Eastman.

Abbott had selected an anonymous world into which he hoped to disappear. The boom town oil fields of Louisiana collected thousands of roughnecks and roustabouts, many with criminal records, men like Abbott, who sought obscurity. Mixing with these tough, taciturn men were illegal aliens from Mexico, refugees from Vietnam, the flotsam and jetsam of the world, as it were, men who worked for $4 an hour, sixteen hours a day, and paid a third of their salary to the company to sleep in filthy bunkhouses and eat from open-air canteens. The rest of their money they would give to the whores who visited these camps in droves.

On Sept. 23, 1981, following a tip from Detective Carl Parsiola of St. Mary's Parish, James Riley, an intelligence agent of the sheriff's department, accompanied by Dan Dossett of the Morgan City Police, and other officers, located Abbott working in the fields of the Ramos Oil Company. He was unloading pipe from trucks that clogged the roads. Overhead helicopters buzzed about on company work and the nearby bayous belched smoke from tugs pulling freight. Where years before there had been wilderness, this area was now cluttered with humanity and the officers were concerned that their man would once again escape. Carefully, Riley, Dossett, and the others moved

toward Abbott, pretending to be workers. When they saw him raise his arms to comb his hair, the lawmen rushed forward, eight shotguns leveled at him. Abbott was ordered to keep his hands in the air as officers moved forward to handcuff him. He said nothing, remaining motionless, offering no resistance. He wore cheap blue jeans and a T-shirt that were coated with oil; his boots were crusted with caked oil and were falling apart. Returned to New York and held at Riker's Island, Abbott was tried before Judge Irving Lang of the Manhattan State Supreme Court. He was defended by criminal attorney Ivan Fisher and prosecuted by James Fogel. Early on, Abbott displayed anxiety and nervousness, a pose unlike his earlier aloof attitudes.

In his own words, Abbott characterized the death of Adan as the result of a "tragic misunderstanding," a literary understatement without parallel. He went on to explain that he acted in self-defense, believing that Adan intended to attack him, the same plea that Abbott had employed when stabbing a fellow prison inmate to death in 1966. To that claim, a spectator in court rose and shouted, "You intended to do it, you scum!" This cry came from Henry Howard, the father-in-law of the dead Adan. Judge Lang ordered Howard removed from court, but he waited outside the courtroom throughout the trial, frustrated by his inability to see justice done.

The prosecution provided several witnesses, but one, Wayne Larsen, a 35-year-old Vietnam veteran, proved damning to Abbott's self-defense tactic. Larsen was standing at the corner of Second Avenue and Fifth Street and watched as Abbott attacked Adan. He testified that Adan was walking away from Abbott when Abbott drew his knife and raised it. He recalled that when Abbott struck Adan there was an impacting sound that "still rings in my ears." Even though Adan was mortally wounded and helpless, Abbott, according to Larsen, acted as if he had merely scratched his victim, cursing Adan and screaming, "Do you still want to continue this?" Adan had made no move toward Abbott and, according to Larsen, was trying to back away from his assailant. Abbott "made a beeline" for the back-pedaling Adan and lunged forward to make sure he killed his man and, in Larsen's words, Abbott's knife blow to Adan's chest was so powerful "that the hair swung back on his (Abbott's) head."

Abbott sat trembling in court, clutching a handkerchief. He wore glasses and his hair was combed in a meticulous pompadour. Immediately following Larsen's testimony, Abbott asked that he be allowed to leave the courtroom. "The testimony was extremely upsetting to him, reliving the event," lawyer Fisher later stated. Abbott's request was granted, although the paradox was evident. Abbott had graphically described his murder of another human being without a gnat-sting of remorse in his best-selling book but he was visibly upset by the retelling of his murder of Adan.

The victim, however, was offered up by Abbott to be not Adan, but Abbott. He again recited the litany of his prison sufferings, the endless abuse that was heaped upon him by an unthinking, inhumane prison system, the very rationale that had brought about his much-influenced parole. Abbott wanted it both ways, first to be released from prison for what the prison system had done to him, then excused from another murder outside of prison and shielded from being returned to that system because of what the prison system had done. If nothing else, Abbott was certainly angling for a minimum sentence, after having been found guilty of first degree manslaughter.

Prosecutor Fogel was having none of it, calling for a maximum sentence, a life term. "This is a killer," Fogel argued before the bench, "a killer by habit, a killer by inclination, a killer by philosophy, and a killer by desire."

Fisher clung to Abbott's own lifelong defense, stating that his client had been warped by a lifetime of prison. "He was mistreated for so long and in so horrible a way. If it was, in fact, the poison of prison that brought about these events, how can it be urged that a lot more is the cure?"

Judge Lang had earlier ruled that Abbott's previous convictions had qualified him as a "persistent violent felon." When he asked the defendant if he had anything to say before sentence was pronounced, Abbott mumbled, "No." Judge Lang then stated that the conviction of Abbott was in part "an indictment of a prison system which brutalized instead of rehabilitating...It's perfectly clear that the defendant could not cope with the reality of a non-prison existence." Judge Lang then sentenced Abbott to fifteen years to life, a minimum sentence. He would be returned to Utah State Penitentiary to serve out his remaining eight years for earlier convictions before serving the New York sentence of fifteen years.

Norman Mailer went before the court and implored leniency, stating, "Culture is worth a little risk. A major sentence would destroy him." Even though Abbott did not receive the maximum sentence, Mailer, following the sentencing, was disgruntled, saying that Judge Lang's sentence was so long as to be "killing." Complained the 59-year-old author, "At the point he gets out, he'll be as old as I am now." Adan's father-in-law, Henry Howard, heard the news of the sentence and was filled with rage. "In twenty-four years," he said, "Jack Abbott will be back on the street and he will kill again. Why are his rights better than Richard Adan's rights?"

This was a question answered obliquely and rather callously by Abbott's attorney, Ivan Fisher, who was quoted as saying, in responding to questions about Adan's family being entitled to the profits from Abbott's book (then estimated to be about $500,000), "If you kill a brain surgeon

you're in much more trouble than if you kill a waiter working nights at the BoniBon Restaurant. That's not my judgment, that's the law."

Before being led back to prison, Abbott, through Fisher, announced plans to sue the State of New York for $10 million for "the mental anguish and threats to his life" while he was a prisoner on Riker's Island. Meanwhile, Abbott's book soared to best-seller status, selling more than 40,000 hardbound copies through Random House. At the time, dramatic rights to Abbott's savage tale had been purchased by a film company headed by comic Alan King in the amount of $250,000. See: **Gilmore, Gary.**

Abdullah, Mohammed (Joseph Howk, Jr.), 1939-, U.S. A voracious reader since early childhood, Howk graduated at the head of his high school class at age fifteen. Though brilliant, he was a much disturbed boy, later claiming racial differences in his family caused him to develop deep mental trauma, his mother being black, his father white. His 140-plus IQ did not balance with the many irrational acts he committed, attempting to hang himself at age nine, trying to burn down his parents' Long Beach, Calif., home at age sixteen.

At that time Howk was taken to the Camarillo State Hospital and was diagnosed schizoid after extensive examinations. Although therapy was recommended, no psychiatric treatments were undertaken. The boy experimented with various religions, finally becoming a Catholic. He dropped this in favor of embracing the Nazi credo at age fifteen. He argued with his teachers over Aryan supremacy until he quit Long Beach City College since the school philosophy was at odds with his own. By seventeen Howk had discarded his ardent Nazi beliefs and dedicated himself to Mohammedanism. He was now a radical follower of Islam and changed his name to Mohammed Abdullah.

When Abdullah entered the University of California at Berkeley in 1958, he advertised his chosen religion, wearing a fez at all times and spouting Islamic credos, practicing Islamic customs. In one of the many coffee shops that catered to the waning beatnik clans, Abdullah met 34-year-old Martin Horowitz, a social dropout, an eccentric drifter who himself had psychiatric problems. Horowitz shared his offbeat philosophies with Abdullah who tagged along after his mentor until meeting statuesque Sonja Lillian Hoff, another student at Berkeley, majoring in home economics with her eye on future social work. The attractive girl was utterly fascinated with minority groups and Abdullah and his strange ways intrigued her.

The couple eventually fell in love but Abdullah's jittery

possessiveness soon disturbed the relationship. He could not stand to see the girl even talking to other male students. Abdullah told Sonja about his obsessive love for her and she showed considerable understanding, too much for her own good. After seeing the girl in casual conversation with another male student, Abdullah wrote in his diary (on Apr. 6, 1960), "Tonight I tried to kill myself but Sonja put herself between my knife and my throat." He added, "Next time I suspect her of liking another man, I shall kill her quickly and without warning."

Abdullah did catch the girl with another man but only threatened to murder her. So alarmed was the girl that this time she contacted police and Abdullah was ordered off campus. The girl began dating an Iranian student and Abdullah again threatened to kill her. She left Berkeley but made the error of returning to work a summer job. Abdullah saw her working in a restaurant as a waitress and implored her to come to his apartment for a reconciliation. (He had secretly planned, as noted in his diary, to lure her to the apartment where he would slit her throat and then commit suicide.) The girl told Abdullah never to contact her again.

Going to his one friend, Horowitz, Abdullah obtained a loaded .38-caliber pistol. Horowitz later stated that he loaned the weapon to his friend to "soothe his tensions," but later still, Abdullah claimed he purchased the weapon himself. Armed, the incensed Abdullah went to the Berkeley library on July 13, 1960, and typed a letter explaining his pain at being rejected and how he intended to murder Sonja Hoff: "I have stolen a pistol to kill my beloved and myself." He then approached the girl as she was studying and asked her to step outside. She agreed, an inexplicable move on her part in that she was once again being confronted by a man who had repeatedly threatened to kill her.

On the steps of the library, Abdullah yanked forth his pistol and, without a word to the girl he loved, shot Sonja Hoff in the head. She died instantly. Abdullah stood over her for some minutes while students and passersby stood riveted in shock. He fired another bullet at the prone girl but it missed. Then he calmly put the gun to his own head and fired a bullet into his skull.

The killer, however, survived even though the bullet remained lodged in his brain. He was blinded in one eye but was well enough by Jan. 3, 1961, to stand trial for murder. Abdullah was quickly found Guilty and was sentenced to die in San Quentin's gas chamber. Horowitz, the willing hand who had provided the murder weapon, was also tried and was convicted of manslaughter. When a ten-year sentence was pronounced, Horowitz went to pieces, sobbing wildly in court.

Mohammed Abdullah was a happy man as he awaited execution, telling his prison guards that he was sure Allah would give him Sonja once they were united in the hereafter. This heavenly reward was, however, denied to the zealot killer when California's Governor Edmund G. "Pat" Brown commuted the sentence to life imprisonment without parole. The governor's reason was that Abdullah had been insane throughout his life.

Acevedo, Louis, 1956- , U.S. Acevedo and Shelley Sperling had been a couple throughout their teenage years. But when the 18-year-old honor roll student went away to Marist College in Poughkeepsie, N.Y., her life began to change and she decided to end the relationship. Acevedo, however, would not accept the rejection. In September 1974 she agreed to meet him at a waterworks next to the campus, expecting a final talk. Instead, Acevedo struck her with a brick, fracturing her skull and severely injuring the hand she used to protect herself. He was charged with felony assault and released on $10,000 bail. Later, after a grand jury indicted him for attempted murder, he remained free on the same bail.

College authorities told a terrified Sperling to "phone for help" if Acevedo ever confronted her on campus, and security guards at Marist College were alerted to watch out for him. The former boyfriend, who worked as a part-time therapy aide at an institution for the mentally retarded, kept a gun in his locker. That fact, known to several of his acquaintances and friends, went unreported. On Feb. 18, 1975, Acevedo waited for Sperling outside the college cafeteria. When she saw him, she ran to a telephone and was dialing for help when he shot her dead.

Acid Bath Murders, See: Haigh, George John.

Ackerman, Bradley, 1964- , U.S. Ackerman and Julie Alban of Long Beach, Calif., had grown up in the same affluent neighborhood; their families lived across the street from each other. On June 8, 1988, after they had dated for about ten months, Ackerman asked her to marry him. She refused. Later that evening, as Alban lay sleeping in her parents' home, Ackerman entered her bedroom and shot her in the back. He then shot himself but later recovered from his wound. Alban was paralyzed for life.

Ackerman, the stepson of Daniel Ridder, chairman of the Long Beach *Press-Telegram*, was tried for first-degree murder. Defense counsel, Anthony Murray, arguing that his client was severely depressed over both a recent $30,000 gambling debt and failure to fulfill his early promise as a tennis player, reported Ackerman had taken thirty pills in an attempt to kill himself. Kenneth Lamb, the deputy district attorney who tried the case, told jurors that Ackerman's precision in firing the .38-caliber pistol did not indicate that he was suffering from a Valium blackout, and said the rejected suitor had invented that defense to escape responsibility. Ackerman was found guilty of a willful, premeditated attempt at first-degree murder and sentenced to life imprisonment. Lamb called the verdict "justified," pointing out that Ackerman had sentenced Alban to "death and, failing that, he sentenced her to life in a wheelchair."

Adamic, Louis, 1913-51, U.S. A Yugoslavian nationalist who came to America at age fourteen, Adamic became a successful and prominent U.S. writer. At age thirty-eight, he was found dead in his 100-year-old New Jersey farmhouse. Adamic arrived in the U.S. in 1927 and worked as a newsboy, then became a soldier, a sailor, a factory worker, and a restaurant helper. Turning to writing, he based one of his books, *Laughing in the Jungle*, on his experiences as a hobo, and produced several others about politics and the immigrant's status in America. *The Native's Return*, written after he visited his beloved Yugoslavia on a Guggenheim Fellowship, was his first bestseller. He then moved to an old farmhouse in Riegelsville, N.J., continuing as a supporter of the head of Yugoslavia, Marshall Tito, and campaigning briefly for American Progressive Party candidate Henry Wallace in the 1948 U.S. election. Adamic's name came up that same year before the House Un-American Activities Committee, when he was accused of membership in left-wing organizations. Neighbors said the Adamics had become reclusive over the last few years; their house appeared to be locked up and deserted. In fact, Adamic and his wife had moved to California, apparently after threats as a result of his work over a three-year period on a book called *The Eagle and the Roots*, a study promoting Yugoslavia as a bastion of democracy holding out against encroaching Russian Communism. The book was said to be critical of both Russia and the U.S., and was an ardent defense of Tito. Anton Smole, Yugoslav correspondent in San Francisco and a longtime friend, said Adamic had told him of several threats, including one in California when two men stopped him on the street, demanding to see his new book. When the author refused he was beaten unconscious. He moved back to New Jersey shortly thereafter, without his wife, and continued the final work on his book for six weeks.

On Sept. 4, 1951, a paper-mill technician on his way to work at 4 a.m. noticed a glare in the New Jersey hills near Adamic's farmhouse. When firemen arrived from two miles away, the farmhouse garage and studio had burned to the ground. The firemen put out the fire and went inside, discovering a litter of oily rags in the unswept rooms and an unburned wall of the garage soaked with oil. In a second-floor bedroom they found Adamic's body, a .22 Mossberg rifle lying in his lap, and a single bullet wound above his right ear. A Hunterdon County medical examiner returned a tentative verdict of suicide.

Police investigated the possibility of murder, based on threats Adamic had told Smoles and other friends about, demanding he quit work on his last book. According to Adamic's brother-in-law, Harold Sanders, Adamic's wife thought the death was suicide. Sanders said, "He was working too hard, was upset by world conditions, and was under great stress." The FBI investigated the case briefly, dropping it when no angles were found to follow up on. On Aug. 7, 1957, a rusty tin box containing $12,350 in disintegrating large-denomination bills was found in the walls of the burned farmhouse. The package, wrapped in brown paper, had "1950" written on it. At the time of Adamic's death his wife estimated the value of his estate at $5,000. Based on the date and the fact that Adamic had built the wall in which the box was discovered, it is believed that the author had hidden the money.

Adams, Louis, prom. 1932, U.S. The crowning of Mark Adams as "King of all the Gypsies in the World" was to be a festive celebration. In December 1931, Adams, a farmer in California's San Fernando Valley, invited an army of Gypsy fortune tellers, silversmiths, and card readers from across the U.S., to witness his coronation and feast on barbecued steer. The week-long party came to an abrupt end, however, when Mark's brother Louis Adams murdered his estranged wife from Chicago in front of their nine children. Despondent over their recent separation, Louis decided to take matters into his own hands. He was immediately arrested and jailed.

Adams, Millicent, 1942- , U.S. Socialite Millicent Adams, a post-debutante Bryn Mawr student, raised in upper-class comfort in Philadelphia, Pa., met engineering student Axel Schmidt and killed him when he jilted her for another more socially prominent woman. Schmidt was certainly a dedicated social climber, and his cruel treatment of Adams caused her first to think of suicide, or so she later claimed. But her destructive plan was one that evolved out of practice, not whim, since she bought a St. Bernard, took it to an unused servant's room in her family home and shot it with a .22-caliber Smith & Wesson which she had recently purchased. This scenario was enacted, it was later reported, to make sure that the weapon would work on its intended victim, herself.

Yet, when Adams went to bed with Schmidt for the last time in October 1962, the scorned woman turned the gun on Schmidt, not herself, shooting and killing him with a single, well-aimed bullet. Attorneys for Adams claimed that she had suffered a fit of temporary insanity. Adams pled guilty to manslaughter, but there was a condition. If the court gave her a ten-year probational sentence, Adams would commit herself to a mental health center. The court surprisingly accepted this arrangement.

Adams gave birth to a child, Lisa, whose father was the man she had slain and she was allowed to visit the girl on weekends. At the end of three years, Adams was released and labelled "rehabilitated." She relocated to the West Coast where she moved in with wealthy relatives. Millicent Adams did not pay dearly for committing homicide; some might have labelled it a slight inconvenience for having done away with a trifling lover.

Adams, William Nelson, 1902- , Brit. The case of 17-year-old William Adams and his murder of 60-year-old George Jones, is more than a curious one. On the evening of June 10, 1919, Adams, who had befriended the older man who had given him lodging in his room and bought him meals and drinks, was drinking with Jones and another man, Charlie Smith, in a Tooting pub. The trio left the pub late that night en route to Sutton when Adams stabbed Jones six times with a shoemaker's awl, three times in the throat and three times in the chest. Jones was later found half alive, wearing only his trousers and vest, his shirt wrapped awkwardly about his chest and neck as if someone had attempted to stop the flow of blood. Jones lived for three days and told police that he had no idea why Adams would want to hurt him, saying, "I had done nothing to him."

When Adams was finally arrested, he told another story, one with bizarre implications. He admitted that Jones had taken him in but had requested that Adams perform a special service in gratitude for his kindness—that the youth kill him. "I've done you a good turn," Adams quoted Jones as having said. "Now you do one for me. Will you kill me?" Adams went on to say that Jones was "worried out of his life" because he was facing a tax bill he could not pay. Adams said he would think about it and did, waiting a week until attacking Jones at the victim's own request in a Sutton park. He described how Jones removed his coat and hat, lying on the grass and handing the awl to Jones, saying, "The best way is to stab me in the left side of the neck."

Adams more or less hesitated but Jones kept urging him on. Charlie Smith, a man never found by police, watched the whole strange scene without participating. Finally, Adams worked up his nerve, he claimed, and stabbed the victim several times, but then tried to staunch the flow of blood by wrapping Jones's shirt around his wounds. He then took the victim's money and left the scene with Smith. Jones died on June 13, 1919, and Adams was charged with committing a homicide he labelled a "murder by request." The jury, listening to Adams's odd story at the Guildford Assizes in July 1919, dismissed the cry of the defendant that he was "only trying to oblige the old gentleman" and found him Guilty. Adams was sentenced to death, but Edward Shortt, then Home Secretary, commuted the prisoner's sentence to life imprisonment.

Adamson, John Harvey, 1944- , U.S. When an investigative reporter with information on Arizona land fraud and rampant underworld corruption in that state was killed by a car bomb in Phoenix in 1976, a $100,000 special prosecution fund was established to investigate the slaying. Adamson, a 32-year-old former tow-truck operator and sometime dog breeder, phoned Pulitzer prize-nominated investigative reporter Don Bolles on June 2, 1976, to say he would give Bolles information linking top Arizona Republicans to land fraud schemes. When Bolles rushed over to meet Adamson at the Phoenix Hotel, he found he had apparently been stood up.

Investigative reporter Don Bolles, murdered for his news probes.

Returning to his car, the reporter was blown up by a crude dynamite bomb that exploded as he got into the vehicle.

Hanging on for eleven days and through six operations, losing both legs and his right arm, Bolles died on June 13, 1976. His last words were: "Mafia...Emprise ...They finally got me...John Adamson, find him." Two hours later, Adamson was arrested and charged with murder. At a preliminary hearing held under strict security on June 21 at the Maricopa County Superior Court, Adamson pleaded Not Guilty. The prosecution's two main witnesses were Robert Lettiere, an ex-convict who described driving to a parking lot with Adamson to look for Bolles's car five days before the fatal bombing, and Gail Owens, a former girlfriend of Adamson's who had been with him when he bought a remote control device which he described as a gift for friend.

After a series of delays, including mistrials and moving the trial site due to pretrial publicity, Adamson pleaded guilty to planting the bomb. He escaped the death penalty in exchange for testimony against Max Dunlap and James Robison. According to Adamson, Dunlap, a wealthy contractor, and Robison, a plumber, detonated the bomb with a remote control radio transmitter used in model airplanes. Dunlap had also promised to help Adamson escape to Mexico after the killing, and to take care of his wife and child. Millionaire Arizona landowner and businessman Kemper

John Harvey Adamson, found guilty of Bolles' murder.

Marley, Sr., angry about an article Bolles had written about Marley's alleged troubles with the law in 1942, found his name linked with Dunlap in Adamson's testimony. Dunlap and Robison were convicted of the murder of Bolles and were sentenced to death on Jan. 10, 1977, in Maricopa County Superior Court. Adamson is serving a twenty-year sentence for his part in the crime.

On Feb. 1, 1980, the Arizona Supreme Court overturned the convictions of Dunlap and Robison, on the grounds they were denied their constitutional right to face their accuser, Adamson. The Court further stated that Adamson had refused to answer certain questions and that the trial judge, Howard Thompson, had erred by denying a motion of the defense to strike all of Adamson's related testimony after Thompson declined to force him to answer.

In November 1980 Adamson was sentenced to die in the gas chamber for Bolles's murder. During the new proceedings, Adamson said in a shaking voice that he had fulfilled his agreement to testify against people who once were close associates and that was "a personal punishment far greater than any court could impose." In December 1988 a federal appeals court overturned Adamson's death sentence. The U.S. Court of Appeals for the Ninth Circuit in San Francisco ruled that Adamson had been improperly sentenced by the Arizona Supreme Court because the trial judge had initially ruled that a prison term was the appropriate sentence for the murder. Later, the court imposed the death penalty only after Adamson violated a plea

agreement requiring him to testify against Robison and Dunlap. The death penalty, the court said, also violated the right to a jury trial by allowing the judge to decide whether murder is a capital crime.

Adamson, Joy, See: **Ekai, Paul Wakwaro.**

Agostini, Antonio (The Pajama Girl Murder), prom. 1934, Aus. An Italian immigrant working in Sydney, Agostini was married to an assertive, hard-drinking Englishwoman, Linda Platt, in 1930. The couple lived a meager existence on Agostini's small salary. He worked at odd jobs, mostly in restaurants as a waiter, and his income, or the lack of it, caused his wife to drink heavily and, according to Agostini's later statements, become abusive. To improve their lifestyle the couple moved to Melbourne where Linda Platt Agostini was last seen alive in August 1934. After that she vanished. When her friends or relatives inquired about her, Agostini merely shrugged, saying that she had run off with a lover. This raised few eyebrows for Mrs. Agostini, an attractive woman with a voluptuous figure, was known to play the field even after her marriage.

On Sept. 1, 1934, a farmer cleaning a culvert six miles from Albury (located between Melbourne and Sydney) found the body of a young woman. She was badly burned and her head showed vicious head wounds. Her curvacious body was adorned with only pajamas embroidered with a Chinese dragon. When coroner physicians examined the corpse closer they quickly discovered a bullet wound below the right eye. Parts of the skull had been dealt severe blows so that the bone had collapsed. There were burns over the body which conformed with the patches of oil discovered at the burial site. Someone had murdered this woman and then had attempted to destroy the body by soaking it in oil and burning it.

The corpse was first identified by no less than six people as Mrs. Anna Philomena Morgan Coots, the wife of a Sydney writer who had been reported missing. The medical examiners and the police were content to label the body such, and marked the "Coots" murder as solved, yet there was some doubt among the authorities as to the real identity of the dead woman, particularly when Mrs. Coots's mother, Mrs. Jeanette Routledge, viewed the corpse and stated, "I am certain that this is not my daughter." Mrs. Coots's grandmother, her landlady, and several close friends insisted otherwise, that, indeed, the corpse was Anna Coots. Authorities decided not to bury the murder victim under that name. They would wait for developments and other leads. The corpse was placed in a metal coffin which was filled with a special preservative, formalin, an aqueous solution of formaldehyde which will provide indefinite preservation of organic tissues. The body was stored in a basement area of Sydney University's Pathological Museum and there it waited until the police decided whether or not to bury it. The wait lasted for ten years.

During that time a curious police sergeant named King came to visit the corpse and peer at it as it swam in the formalin. (One report had it that the streetcars rumbling by outside caused the corpse to "bob like an apple" in the preservative fluid.) King reported to his superiors that he believed the woman was none other than a friend of his wife's, Linda Platt Agostini, someone the Kings had not seen since early 1931. He was sure of his identification, however, because of the unusually shaped ears on the corpse. They were pointed and had no lobes, something King had noticed about Mrs. Agostini when first meeting her. King made his statement in 1938 at a second inquest which was publicized. An amateur sleuth and medical criminologist, Dr. Palmer Benbow, decided to investigate. He convinced authorities to allow him to examine the corpse and the scanty evidence unearthed by the police.

There was not much to examine—the corpse, wrinkling in formalin, a bag which had been soaked with oil, a piece of toweling. When peering at the toweling under his microscope, Benbow noticed something the police had

Antonio Agostini, wife killer.

not discovered or, if they had, had ignored. There were laundry marks on the towel. These marks led the doctor to a shack outside of Albury and there he found an old bed with a metal frame which had been painted. Benbow matched flecks of paint from the frame of this bed to those found on the corpse, and matched fibres from a woolen blanket he found to those found in the dead woman's hair. He began interviewing residents in the area but suddenly Dr. Benbow's one-man investigation came to an abrupt halt. He later claimed that police had obstructed his work and that witnesses suddenly had nothing more to say to him after being visited by certain authorities. Oddly, Benbow's half-completed investigation aimed itself at establishing the corpse as that of Anna Morgan Coots, not Linda Agostini.

Edith Flemington, Linda's mother through an earlier marriage, had been contacted as early as 1935 when her daughter reportedly ran away to blissful oblivion with an unknown lover. For almost ten years Mrs. Flemington had been writing authorties around the world from her home in Littlehampton, Sussex, England, trying to find her daughter or her daughter's remains. The police in Sydney had sent her a photo of the corpse in the preservative fluid, but she had originally denied the remains as being that of her daughter. (Formalin usually causes the body to shrink and wrinkles to appear on the face, slightly disfiguring features.) But Mrs. Flemington did recognize the photo of the pajamas the dead woman had been wearing, yellow silk pajamas with a green dragon embroidered on the back

Linda Agostini, the victim known as The Pajama Girl.

which, Mrs. Flemington later recalled, had been given to Linda by her sister as a wedding gift.

Mrs. Flemington wrote many letters to the Sydney police describing her daughter and how she had clerked in London stores, been a movie usher and a hairdresser on the Red Star Line which is how she wound up in Australia. She wrote about her son-in-law, Agostini, and how he was not a "reliable type," a would-be silk merchant and part-time waiter, how, on one occasion, instead of buying her daughter an engagement ring, Agostini bought her a one-passage home which Linda never used. In her last letter to the Sydney police, Mrs. Flemington said that though she had failed to recognize the body in the formalin as her daughter she had had strange dreams as of late, seeing her daughter "afloat" in a dark, small area.

Then, in March 1944, Antonio Agostini, who had been interred in an alien prison camp during the war, came under suspicion once again. W.J. Mackay, the newly-appointed police commissioner for New South Wales, intended to clear up the matter once and for all. He had read Mrs. Flemington's last letter and examined the yellowing notes of Dr. Benbow. Mackay, leafing through the thick police files, noticed the name of a dentist who had worked on Linda's teeth, but oddly enough, the dentist had not been asked to compare his charts of Linda Agostini with the teeth of the dead woman. The dentist was called in and the teeth were compared. There was no doubt in the dentist's mind that the deceased was his former patient. Mackay next ordered physicians to take the corpse from the formalin bath and reconstruct it as best as possible. Then he brought in friends and relatives of both Mrs. Coots and Mrs. Agostini. The identification for Mrs. Agostini was the strongest, and Agostini was brought from his prison camp.

The short, balding, and near-sighted Agostini had been interrogated in 1935 by police who had accepted his story about his wife running off with another man. Mackay disregarded that tale and began to pump the little waiter. He soon changed his story. Yes, the pickled corpse was the late Mrs. Agostini, the little man admitted. He added, as he casually chain-smoked in front of the commissioner, that he had killed his wife but not intentionally. On Aug. 28, 1934 they both went to bed drunk but Linda woke up before dawn, he said. She was raving about another woman coming to see him at the restaurant where he worked. (Agostini insisted that his wife was jealous of him to the point of being neurotic.) Somehow she had gotten hold of a gun and was waving it at Agostini, he said, and he tried to take it away from her. In the struggle the gun went off and she was killed by the fatal shot. He panicked and attempted to carry the body downstairs, but it fell from his grasp and during its fall the terrible wounds to the head were inflicted on the stairs. He then drove out to the culvert and stuffed the body inside.

Much of Agostini's statements didn't make sense. If the death was accidental why had he attempted to burn the corpse beyond recognition.

Dr. Palmer Benbow

Agostini insisted that he had not done so, that, perhaps some other person finding the corpse had tried to burn it so as not to be blamed for a murder. More revealing was the report from the original examining physicians who stated that the head wounds found on the body were made *before* the bullet had been fired and that the blows to the skull caused the actual death of Linda Agostini. This, of course, pointed to a beating administered by Agostini. He was charged with murdering his wife and placed on trial on June 9, 1944. No matter how much the prosecution pressured Agostini, the little man would not budge. The killing was accidental, he insisted.

The jury undoubtedly believed the quiet little waiter. Agostini was convicted of manslaughter and sent to serve a six-year sentence at hard labor. He was released in 1950 and was promptly deported to his native Italy where he disappeared. By that time, the body of Linda Platt Agostini had finally found rest, having been buried in July 1944, in Melbourne's Preston Cemetery. There are those today who still insist that the corpse is that of Mrs. Coots who was never found and that there were actually *two murders* occuring on the same day and in the same area. One of the killers was brought to justice and the other, since only one corpse was unearthed, remained at large and unknown.

Ahearn, Danny, prom. 1930-40s, U.S. Growing up on New York's Lower East Side, Danny Ahearn admired gangsters, studied them carefully, and then joined their ranks as a teenager. Although Ahearn had extensive experience as a robber, gambler, and con man, his main profession was killing for hire. Arrested in New York twenty-two times on major charges, Ahearn was released twenty times. Tried twice for murder, he was released both times for lack of evidence. Reportedly after his final arrest, he gave a long, detailed interview in which he described the techniques and etiquettes of his trade. "For a man to commit murder," he explained, "he's got to have no heart." He advised professional assassins to have patience, study their intended victims carefully, keep a cool head, and stay on good terms with the police, reasoning that "They got to make a buck. They're human, too. Treat 'em nice. Then, if you get into trouble you may be able to do business with 'em." Ahearn recommended several standard murder methods such as placing dynamite in the starter of the victim's car or blowing up his house. Women were useful to lure the victims to isolated areas, or to get the target in compromising positions in bedrooms where they would be easy prey. He emphasized working with the police and making connections with them to set up favorable conditions for favors and exchanges.

When hired to kill a woman, Ahearn advised romancing her in nightclubs, then taking her to her apartment and gaining her confidence and affection, so one could later invite her on a vacation, perhaps in the mountains. To avoid trouble, the killer should make sure she writes a letter to her family saying she is going away. Every day of the vacation, he advised, dig part of a ditch in the woods. When the grave is finished, take her for a walk in the woods, knock her on the head, and bury her alive, Ahearn suggests. He suggested that a killer always carry around some poison in order to be prepared, and try, when possible, to leave a gun planted on the victim's body, because, he said, "Police don't interest themselves too much in the case where gangsters are killed."

Akulonis, Peter, d.1953, U.S. A quiet, reserved man who did chores for his elderly mother and worked hard for his livelihood, Akulonis came unravelled one day and murdered his entire family. As a youth in Lawrence, Maine, Akulonis was a troubled poor boy, partly deaf, with some facial paralysis, who rebelled by committing acts of petty crime. In the 1930s he changed his ways, marrying, fathering two sons, and becoming a hard-working boilermaker in a tank works. For years Akulonis kept to himself, raising his family. A co-worker talked about the factory: "The noise in here drives you bugs after a while, but he never come off his machine to talk to anybody. He was a bandit for work." Around the Christmas holiday of 1952, things began to change for Akulonis. He sat alone at lunch, complaining once to a friend with a new car, "How can you afford that when I drive a pile of junk? All I do is work and go home...I'm not getting anything out of life." He asked another man at the shop if he thought he was "crazy or something," and soon he began picking fights. Finally he quit and started to drink.

In mid-April Akulonis went to his four-room apartment in the afternoon, picked up a carpenter's ax, and killed his wife with a single blow, turning then on his 4-year-old son, Michael, whom he brutally murdered and mutilated. Going to his brother Alphonse's house, the killer herded his mother and two young nephews into a room and hacked them to death. When the brother returned, Akulonis met him in the kitchen and killed him, too. Picking up his 11-year-old son, Peter, Jr., at school, Akulonis drove the boy to some nearby woods, then shot him in the face with a .22 rifle, newly purchased from Sears Roebuck and Co. He returned to his car—a recent loan from his remaining brother Raymond—and drove it to the Cambridge factory where Raymond worked. Raymond got behind the wheel while Akulonis sat in the back. Two other workers along for the ride said they noticed nothing unusual about his behavior. The police, called by Alphonse's widow, were waiting at Raymond's house when the car pulled up. As the officers leaped out of their car, Akulonis shot Raymond through the head, then turned the rifle on himself. A note found in his pocket read, "I love Michael more than life. I loved Mom, Paul, Jimmy, Sis, Peter, Ray."

Alarcon, Nestor Mencias, prom. 1970, Mex. Nestor Alarcon, a 26-year-old Mexican peasant, was hired to kill Isabel Garcia by his employer, Senora Martinez Anguilar. Garcia was having an affair with Senora Anguilar's husband. Senora Anguilar first paid a witchdoctor to put a spell on Isabel Garcia, but when this failed to end the affair she offered Alarcon fifty-five pesos to kill the woman. "That's a lot of money for a man like me," he said later. He hacked Garcia to death with a machete, then turned on her 9-year-old daughter.

Police had closed the books on the case when Alarcon drew attention to himself by leaving town. He was picked up for routine questioning and confessed to murdering Garcia. He told police that Senora Anguilar put him up to it, but reneged on her part of the agreement after learning that Alarcon had also killed the girl. Alarcon later said he committed the murder because he felt obligated to carry out the orders of his employer.

Albanese, Charles, 1937- , U.S. In the fall of 1980 Fox Lake, a popular vacation spot near Chicago, was shocked by the deaths of two elderly residents, the first of many over the next sixteen months in a bizarre scheme to seize control of the estates of two wealthy families. If the plan succeeded, Charles Albanese, a prominent Chicago-area businessman driven to obtain wealth and power, would inherit the estates. But first he had to poison up to six of his relatives.

In August 1980 he implemented his heinous plan. Mary Lambert, the 87-year-old grandmother of Albanese's wife Virginia, died of an apparent heart attack on Aug. 6. Twelve days later Virginia's mother, 69-year-old Marion K. Mueller, died the same way. Described as healthy women, their sudden deaths within two weeks panicked friends and family into believing their local water supply was contaminated. Tests of the water proved negative.

Virginia Albanese inherited $150,000 from the two deceased. An investigation into the deaths uncovered that in May Charles Albanese had persuaded Lambert to leave her estate to her daughter, Mueller, in the event of her death, aware that his wife would receive the inheritance when Mueller died, and that she had previously willed her property to him.

The deaths were reinvestigated in 1981 when, on May 16, Charles' father, 69-year-old Michael J. Albanese, Sr., died of an unknown illness. His death left the family-owned trophy company and an estate worth $267,373 to his sons, Charles and Michael A. Albanese, Jr., and would revert to Charles at the death of Michael, Jr. In addition, Michael Sr., left his wife Clare a $200,000 life insurance policy paid in full at the time of his death. Should she die, Charles would become her beneficiary.

Authorities reopened the cases of Lambert and Mueller when they learned that all three dead persons were related and that the junior Albanese was ill with symptoms his father had shown before his death. An inquiry into the death of the senior Albanese finally showed signs of arsenic in his system. Doctors examined Michael, Jr., and found arsenic as well. The bodies of Lambert and Mueller, exhumed and autopsied, also showed arsenic in their systems. All of the evidence by now pointed to Charles Albanese, who was in line to inherit more than half a million dollars from both families.

Police took Albanese into custody as he, his wife, and his mother were leaving for a vacation in Jamaica. Police feared the two women would have been murdered there as they were the only remaining barriers to the wealth Albanese sought. A jury convicted Albanese on three counts of murder in the poisoning deaths of Mary Lambert, Marion Mueller, and Michael Albanese, Sr. Sentenced to death, he awaits punishment on death row. Albanese and his lawyers have appealed the sentence and on Sept. 29, 1988, the Illinois Supreme Court denied their appeal and scheduled Albanese to die in the electric chair on Jan. 25, 1989.

Alcott, John James, 1925-53, Brit. The murder for which Alcott was executed was much contested by his defense counsel who maintained that the killer was insane or, at least, a hysteric who had no idea that he was taking a human life. Though little is known of Alcott's early life, he later admitted that as a youth he got along poorly with his father. When his father later went into the army and served overseas during WWII, Alcott would go into the British countryside and wander for days, living off vegetables filched from farms, and sitting by small fires at night, brooding about his father. During Alcott's trial for murder in 1952, his defense counsel claimed that these early-day wanderings and remorse over an absent father were that of a mentally unbalanced child. The portrait was not unlike one drawn by Viennese psychoanalyst, Dr. Wilhelm Stekel, who had years earlier typified such conduct as that of the neurotic whom he labelled "the unconscious criminal." Stekel claimed that boys resentful of harsh fathers often harbor a secret and deep death wish for such parents. In the case of Alcott, the inference was made, he substituted other victims for his father, killing without conscience, without social sense, without a concept of law and order.

Alcott's teenage years were uneventful except that he did buy a bicycle he knew was stolen and for this offense was sent to a correctional school where he became a model student. He later stole a bicycle and then decided not to keep it, selling it. The sale brought him to the attention of the police and he was returned to the school for a short period. No other illegal incidents occurred in the young man's life until he was sent to Germany after enlisting in the British Army. He later claimed he suffered a series of blackouts while in the service, one following a minor traffic accident. Following the accident, he found himself wandering about the German countryside and being joined by a nomadic Czech who was trying to reach France. The pair stopped at a small lodging house where a night watchman offered them coffee then, inexplicably, according to Alcott, whirled about and threw the scalding coffee at the uniformed Alcott, screaming, "You English bastards take a man's last drink!"

Alcott jumped at the watchman, smashing his face with his fists while, according to Alcott, his Czech friend leapt forward with an empty whiskey bottle in one hand and a fire extinguisher in the other and crashed both of these down upon the watchman's head, sending him unconscious to the floor. The Czech, Alcott stated, hated all Germans after having spent years in a concentration camp during WWII. Both men fled the lodging house, unaware that the watchman was dead. They were picked up a few days later and Alcott was tried before a court-martial, charged with murder. He was found Guilty but, strangely enough, received a pardon and was discharged from the British Army under the term "Services No Longer Required," a discharge invariably reserved for those with poor military records. The reason why Alcott was pardoned for this murder was never explained, and no amount of prodding from civil authorities could later produce information on the murder from army officials.

After resuming civilian life, Alcott became a fireman and married, living quietly at Hither Green. In early August 1952, Alcott and his wife planned to vacation in France. Alcott told his wife that he would pick up his holiday pay but he traveled to Aldershot where he took a room in a boarding house and spent several days shopping for clothes in the area and visiting the station house at Ash Vale Station. There he introduced himself to the railway clerk, Geoffrey Dean, age twenty-eight, married and with a small child, telling Dean that he was a fellow railway worker. He returned to talk to Dean several times and undoubtedly noticed the considerable sums of money from fares that Dean periodically counted and stored in the station house safe. Shortly before 8 p.m. on Aug. 22, 1952, Dean turned over tickets and a date stamp to a night porter and told him he would be staying a little later in the office to perform some cleanup work. The station door was locked and a sign on the door told customers to purchase tickets from the porter. An army sergeant went to the station door and heard what he later described as possible scuffling noises and the voices of two men talking. He read the sign and went in search of the night porter. About an hour later another porter noticed a light on in the station office and knocked at the door. He got no response and looked into the window to see Dean sprawled on the floor, blood seeping from his body. Police were called, broke in the door, and found the murdered Dean with more than twenty stab wounds, several in the heart, the lungs, and even in his legs. Powerful blows had actually crushed some of the victim's bones. The safe was standing open and approximately £168 had been stolen.

Police began a thorough search of all the inns and boarding houses in the area, asking about strangers. One boarding house yielded an empty first-floor room where a young man had stayed. Found was a jacket with blood stains and in the pockets a wallet containing two ten-shilling notes which had blood spots and, most revealing, a passport bearing the name of John James Alcott. Police were posted at the house and some hours later they arrested Alcott as soon as he entered his room. He took little time in showing officers a chimney where he had hidden a knife in a leather sheaf. Inside his pockets were documents from the station house safe and £109. Alcott seemed carefree about being charged with Dean's murder, and all during the time he awaited trial he concerned himself with his wife's welfare and how she would manage financially without him.

At his trial, held at Surrey Assizes in Kingston on Nov. 18, 1952, Alcott showed a strange indifference to his predicament while his lawyers argued that he was certainly insane. He himself claimed that he had suffered another blackout, like those he had experienced in his military service and that the victim, as far as he could remember, was "a decent fellow." He didn't know why he was in Aldershot or why he went to the station house or why he suddenly murdered a man he had been having pleasant conversations with for several days. He explained that he must have blacked out because when he "came to" he was holding the bloody knife and the stolen money and realized that he was in trouble and that is why he hid the murder weapon. Alcott told the court that he "had gone berserk." Why then, if he had only a blind and inexplicable urge to murder had he taken the money, Alcott was asked. "Perhaps I did it because it had been there staring me in the face," he replied. "I could have taken two or three pounds at any time I had liked without his knowing it. It would have been easy, looking back at it."

The prosecution, however, presented a convincing argument that all of Alcott's blackouts, his loss of memory, and insane acts were feigned, that all of this was a back-up plan should he be caught after committing a pre-meditated robbery and murder. It was shown how Alcott

visited the station house a day before the murder and placed a call from there to another station house to inquire about the health of a fellow railway worker who had been accidentally scalded by hot cinders Alcott himself had been shoveling weeks earlier. He told Dean at the time of this call—which was to establish himself as a fellow railway worker to be trusted—that he expected a return call at the station house which would let him know about the injured worker. This was his ruse to excuse a return to the station house the following evening. Moreover, Alcott had purchased an entire new set of clothes—from coat, pants, shirt, to shoes—and these he intended to wear when fleeing the area after the robbery-murder, dumping the "murder clothes." The bloody pants and shoes Alcott had been wearing were found in bushes near the boarding house, and it was reported that these were the very items Alcott was hiding just before he was arrested on his return to the boarding house to retrieve his bloody jacket in order to hide it elsewhere.

The murder weapon was the knife Alcott had hidden in the chimney, one which he had purchased in Aldershot for the very purpose of killing Dean. He later claimed that he had bought the knife as a gift for a young brother and just happened to have the weapon in his pocket when he suffered his impulse to kill the station clerk. The jury did not accept the posture of insanity, nor did the accused man's background conform to the McNaghten Rules on insanity. Alcott was convicted of murder and Mr. Justice Finnemore sentenced him to death. Alcott's relentless attorneys doggedly sought to appeal the case on grounds of insanity. Their request for appeal was denied and Alcott was executed on Jan. 2, 1953.

Aldridge, Alfred Scott, prom. 1929-31, U.S. As a result of the 1929 trial in Washington, D.C., of Alfred Aldridge, a black man charged with the murder of a white police officer, lawyers were given the right to dismiss prospective jurors during the selection of the jury based on their racial prejudice.

Represented by court-appointed attorney James Reilly, Aldridge was charged with the murder of police officer Harry J. MacDonald. To ensure that his client received a fair trial, Reilly asked prospective jurors if they were prejudiced toward blacks. The presiding judge maintained that his questions were improper, prohibited him from continuing, and quickly began the trial. In the end, Aldridge was convicted and sentenced to death. Reilly immediately appealed to the U.S. Supreme Court.

Just one week before Aldridge was to be executed, the high court barred his execution and saved him from death.

The Supreme Court maintained that lawyers have the right to ask questions regarding a prospective juror's beliefs on race in order to protect their own client's inherent right to a fair trial. For the first time, lawyers won the right to reject jurors based on their racial prejudice.

Alexander, Frank, 1954-   , and **Alexander, Harald,** 1931- , Canary Is. The Alexanders, a reclusive German family, were religious fanatics who believed that only a select few of their religious cult were free of Satan's control and that all others were instruments of the Devil to be purged by violence if the "chosen one" of their cult so decreed. This is exactly what happened to the Alexanders in 1970 when 16-year-old Frank Alexander decided that his mother and sisters were possessed of the Devil and had to be murdered. A horrific slaughter followed in which Frank and his equally zealous father Harald destroyed their loved ones in the name of God. Their grisly acts they later excused as part of their religious beliefs.

The Alexanders had originated in Dresden and later moved to Hamburg where Harald Alexander became the ardent disciple of George Riehle, a religious zealot who was, in turn, the self-designated leader of the Lorber Society. Jacob Lorber (1800-64) had founded this religious group in the early part of the nineteenth century, a severe spiritual organization that taught unflinching self-denial and upheld the beliefs that all non-members were basically evil. Riehle became a member of this small sect, which never numbered more than a few hundred members through the decades, and sometime in the 1930s, Riehle came to believe that he was the Prophet of God. Alexander met Riehle in Hamburg when the old man was dying and nursed him through his last days. When Riehle died, Alexander announced to his wife that he had inherited the mantle of the Lorber Society leadership. Dagmar Alexander, equally possessed of her husband's single-minded beliefs, accepted him in his self-appointed role.

When their son Frank was born, Harald Alexander told his wife that their son was now the Prophet of God and that his every whim had to be observed and obeyed. As the boy grew up he was served by his family members—his older sister Marina, his younger twin sisters Sabine and Petra, and his parents—as if he were a potentate. They responded to his every whim, until Frank Alexander dictated their every movement. The boy, when reaching his teens, decided that he could never "pollute" himself with the bodies of women outside of their small sect. He informed his father that he would have sex with his mother and older sister and such incestuous relations became commonplace within the Alexander household, the father not only agreeing to such

practices but encouraging his son to have sex with his wife and daughters at any time, often joining with Frank as they both assaulted Dagmar Alexander or the older sister, Marina. The women accepted their roles as sex objects in

Religious zealots, Frank and Harald Alexander, at their mental hearing; they had slaughtered family members because they were "unclean."

the belief that they were serving the Prophet of God, Frank Alexander.

Such bizarre practices soon brought them to the attention of the Hamburg police, especially when the younger sisters began to talk about them to the few friends they had. To avoid police investigation into their activities, the Alexanders moved to a reclusive society, one far apart from the rest of the world—the Canary Islands—relocating to a small apartment at 37 Calle Jesus Nazareno in Santa Cruz, the capital of Tenerife.

Neighbors soon noted that the family remained aloof and its members seldom ventured out of the apartment. Harald Alexander was forever playing a small organ that had been left to him by George Riehle. For ten months the family occupied the small flat without incident, the girls and Frank supporting the family with low-paying jobs—the girls working as domestics and Frank as a shipping clerk, though he kept irregular hours.

Then, on Dec. 22, 1970, Harald and Frank Alexander appeared in the villa occupied by Dr. Walter Trenkler, asking to see 15-year-old Sabine Alexander. Trenkler found the girl in the kitchen preparing a meal for the family and told her that her father and brother were on the patio waiting to see her. She went to them and Trenkler, to his amazement and shock, heard Harald Alexander say to his daughter, "Sabine, dear, we wanted you to know at once that Frank and I have just finished killing your mother and your sisters."

The girl took her father's hand and put it to her cheek, saying, "I'm sure you've done what you thought necessary."

Dr. Trenkler stood in shock for a moment, staring at the Alexanders. Harald Alexander caught Trenkler's stare and said matter-of-factly, "Ah, you've overheard. We've killed my wife and other daughters. It was the hour of killing." The horrified physician then looked over the father and son carefully. What he originally thought was mud and dirt on their clothes, the result of laboring he imagined, was not what covered them from head to foot. It was human blood, gore that smeared their clothes and faces and hands, dried and caking in the hot sun of the courtyard where they stood.

Even more frightening was the conduct of the Alexanders. There was nothing secretive or sinister about them. They were calm and reported their gruesome acts as if nothing was amiss, that the killings they had just announced were perfectly acceptable. Trenkler asked the Alexanders to wait. He raced into the villa and called the police.

Officers quickly arrived and took the Alexanders into custody while Detective Inspector Juan Hernandez and Detective Sergeant Manuel Perera went to the Alexander flat, accompanied by a police physician, and forced open the door. They stepped into a place of carnage; all of the dishes, clothing, papers, including passports and family documents, had been torn to pieces. Everything was in shreds. The apartment was coated with blood—ceilings, walls, floors. In the middle of the living room floor were the mutilated bodies of the two daughters, 18-year-old Marina, and 15-year-old Petra. Their breasts and private parts had been hacked away and nailed to one of the walls. The older girl had been disemboweled. In the bedroom was found the remains of 39-year-old Dagmar Alexander, also horribly mutilated, her breasts and privates also hacked away. Her heart had been cut out, bound on a cord and this was nailed to the wall. The place was a grisly slaughterhouse running blood, a sight so overwhelming that even the hardened officers grew sick to their stomachs.

The Alexanders, at the local police station, freely admitted the gruesome murders. Frank Alexander, called "The Prophet" by his father, related how he was in the bedroom when Dagmar entered it. "I saw that Mother was looking at me and I had the feeling that it was not permitted for her to look at me in this manner. I therefore took the clotheshanger and struck her over the head. After I struck her several times she fell over and lost consciousness. Father had gone to the living room to play the organ and I also went there. First I struck Marina on the head with the hanger, and after she lost consciousness, I struck Petra. Father continued to play the organ and praise Jesus, but when I began to remove the offending parts, he came

to help me." Harald Alexander supported every heinous detail of his son's statements, saying that the sex organs of his wife and daughters were "offending parts," and had to be removed, adding that the women in the household had expected the "hour of killing" at any time, that the family had discussed this "holy time" and its eventuality and that the women accepted their role as human sacrifice for The Prophet, Frank Alexander. Both Frank and Harald Alexander then stated that they felt no guilt, that this was all part of their religious beliefs, that women were unclean and had to be purified by killing. They claimed that their victims had been released into heaven through their murders and they even celebrated their grisly acts by playing the organ, both taking turns, and singing hymns after slaughtering the females of their household.

Psychiatrists examined the father and son and concluded that they were both unfit to stand trial. Both were committed to an asylum for the criminally insane where they presently reside, neither, at last report, responding to any kind of treatment and both convinced, still, that the slaughter of their family members was a purification act in keeping with their religious beliefs. Both men still believe that they are being persecuted for their beliefs and neither has expressed one thought of guilt. Harald Alexander continues to address his son Frank as "The Prophet." Sabine Alexander, the surviving female member of the family, begged authorities to send her to the asylum with her brother and father but this was rejected. She was sent to a convent where she still resides, refusing to live in the outside world.

═══════════════════════════════════════

Allaway, Edward Charles, 1939- , U.S. Armed with a .22-caliber semiautomatic rifle purchased a week earlier at a K Mart, Edward Allaway entered the library building of California State University at Fullerton one day in July 1976. He searched the basement and ground floor, firing at co-workers whom he accused of "messing around with (his) wife," Bonnie, twenty-two. Allaway killed seven people and wounded two others before police subdued him.

Allaway who worked as a janitor at the library, was unable to cope with his wife's decision to end the marriage. He was arraigned on seven counts of murder at the Orange County Courthouse in Santa Ana.

The prosecutor asked for the death penalty, and in the subsequent trial Allaway was found Guilty of six counts of first-degree murder, one count of second-degree murder, and two counts of assault with a deadly weapon. However, the jury could not decide whether Edward Allaway was sane at the time of the shootings. Their deadlock threw the case into the hands of the judge, who declared him Not Guilty by reason of insanity. Allaway was committed to the Atascadero State Hospital, where he awaits further psychiatric review.

═══════════════════════════

Allen, Floyd, d.1913, U.S. The Allens of Carroll County, Va., had long been a potent force in local politics, a huge clan whose history stretched back to the American Revolution. Family members owned large tracts of land, and since the American Civil War the Allens were considered to be the leading citizens of the area. They possessed a fierce pride in their history and their place in the community, no more so than Floyd Allen, who became the patriarch of the clan by the turn of the century. A Democrat, Allen boasted that no Republican ever bested him at the ballot box or with fists. He had held a number of public offices and felt that his family prestige and his own self-inflated image put him above the law. Allen reveled in his political clout. On one occasion, in 1904, after he had been sentenced to jail for one hour after striking a lawman, Allen refused to enter a cell, sending a runner to the governor, who immediately issued a pardon. He was forever knocking down deputy sheriffs and other officials who disagreed with his blunt, brutal tactics, a violent habit that blossomed into mass murder in 1912.

It was Allen's intractable conviction that not only was *he* above the law but so too were all of his relatives. Two of his nephews, the fatherless Edwards boys, got into a bloody fight at school and, after seriously injuring several other students, fled. A small posse made up of Allen enemies tracked the boys to North Carolina and arrested them, bringing them back into Virginia. They were met by Floyd Allen and several of his more hardened back-county relatives, gun toters all, who ordered the posse members to release the Edwards boys, stating that the lawmen had no right to make arrests across the state line which was, in fact, the truth. The posse members hurled insults at the Allens and a battle ensued where guns were fired and punches were thrown. Although no one was killed, several men on both sides were badly injured. Floyd Allen was indicted for assault and battery and held for trial at the Carroll County Courthouse in Hillsville, Va.

There were three trials, the last ending on Mar. 13, 1912. In the last trial, since Allen's influence was so broad, jurors from faraway counties were brought in to judge the case. On Mar. 14, 1912, Floyd Allen was to hear the verdict of the jury. He took no chances. Allen summoned the most truculent of his clan members to pack the courtroom the following day and scores of Allens filed into the court, many with pistols hidden inside their coats and pants pockets.

Allen himself was not searched since he was thought too important a person to be treated as a common criminal. Inside of Allen's large sweater were two pistols. He sat grim-faced at the defendant's table with his attorney, Judge Bolen, a former local magistrate who had battled hard for Allen's vindication. On the bench was Judge Thornton L. Massie. At the prosecution table sat state's attorney Commonwealth Foster, an avowed enemy of the Allen clan, as was Sheriff Webb and most of his deputies who ringed the courtroom. The jury foreman, C.L. Howell, was asked for the verdict and Howell passed the written verdict to Judge Massie who read it aloud without emotion, "Guilty as charged in the indictment—one year in the penitentiary."

Allen stiffened in his chair, gripping the armrests so tightly that his knuckles showed white. His attorney, Judge Bolen, reached over to him and patted him on the shoulder, saying, "Take it easy, Floyd. There are better days ahead."

"I'm going to take it calm," Allen replied in a low voice as he stared at clerk Goad who handed the judge's order to the sheriff. "I just hate it on account of my two boys," the clan chief added.

"The sheriff will take charge of the prisoner," Judge Massie ordered. Sheriff Webb and several deputies began to approach Allen, who then stood up and fumbled with the buttons of his sweater.

"Gentlemen," Floyd Allen solemnly announced, "I don't aim to go." He then whipped out two pistols and the rest of the Allen clan produced guns. The firing commenced, filling the entire courtroom with clouds of black smoke. Panic seized the large crowd which bolted *en masse* for the doorway. The sheriff and his deputies returned fire, blasting away at Floyd Allen, Sidna Allen, and Floyd's son Claude, who fired their weapons resolutely at the deputies, the jury, and the judge. Allen took special aim at the prosecuting attorney, Commonwealth Foster, who had expected trouble and had armed himself. Foster, holding up a heavy law book in front of his face, traded shots with Floyd Allen as he retreated to a door leading to back rooms.

The crowd was in a frenzy to escape the bloody shootout. People knocked each other down and trampled upon one another. Chairs and benches crashed backward as the spectators scurried, scrambled, clawed their way toward the exits. Several fell, wounded in the murderous crossfire. Little Bettie Ayers, an Allen witness, ran screaming toward an exit, yelling, "Let me out of here!" A bullet slapped into her back, knocking her down. Judge Massie had watched in horror as his courtroom was turned into a bloody slaughter pen. He suddenly slumped forward on the bench, blood spreading out in front of him from a chest wound. Attorney Foster was struck several times by bullets as he emptied his guns in the direction of killer Floyd Allen, as did Deputy Queensberry who fired round after round from his .25-caliber pistol from the jury room doorway. Allen reeled backward, hit in the thigh, so that he crashed through the railing which broke and he fell on top of his lawyer, Judge Bolen. Cried Bolen, "For God's sake, get off me before they kill me shooting at you!" Allen got to his feet and then raced toward an exit. He turned to fire at clerk Goad who was shooting at him. Sidna and Claude Allen fired at the clerk who was hit by eleven bullets, one going into his open mouth, chipping a tooth and smashing out of the back of his neck. Goad, however, continued to fire back.

"I'm hit bad," Floyd Allen cried out to Sidna Allen, taking a gun from him since he was out of bullets and firing as he ran from the courtroom and down the steps to his horse which was tied up to a nearby railing. Before he could mount, however, Allen stepped on a rock and broke that part of his leg which had already been splintered by a bullet. The intense pain caused him to beg relatives to help him mount his horse. Once in the saddle, Floyd Allen briefly fainted and then, coming to, told relatives to bring a carriage. He was put into a carriage and taken down the street to Burnett's stable where he was removed and placed on the ground; his relatives believed Allen was dying. It began to rain. At the courthouse, clerk Goad, bleeding from his many wounds, hid behind one of the towering pillars of the building and traded shots with Sidna Allen who was hiding behind another.

Inside the courtroom, Judge Massie was dying. With his last breath he told juror Daniel Thomas, "Sidna Allen shot me...Give me a drink...Tell my wife..." By the time Judge Bolen reached him Massie was dead. Inside the juror's room, on a couch where he had collapsed, was Attorney Foster. He had been hit in the head and blood drenched the floor where he was lying. His wife rushed to the room just as he let the automatic in his hand fall to the floor. He was dead. When they lifted his large body to take it to the morgue, dozens of bullets spilled from his pockets. Commonwealth Foster had expected a battle with the Allens and he had gotten it. Sheriff Webb was also dead, his body riddled with bullets; in death he clenched between his teeth a toothpick. Little Bettie Ayers was mortally wounded. She died the next day, as did a juror named Fowler. Five were dead or dying in the courthouse and sixteen others were wounded, many of these just barely clinging to life until medical help was summoned and saved their lives.

The Allen clan fled as the courthouse was surrounded by scores of deputies who had been appointed for just this eventuality. A dozen deputies, guns drawn, then marched down the street to Burnett's stable where Floyd Allen lay in the rain, blood coating his pants. Staring down at his father was Victor Allen, who had taken no part in the shoot

out. "This thing hurts me," Victor told his father. "I've always tried to do right."

"I made my peace with my God about seven years gone," Floyd Allen said, looking up at his son, "and methinks I see him now."

Victor Allen shook his head and replied, "No—it's the devil that you see."

The Allens were rounded up and both Floyd Allen and his son Claude were convicted of murder and were executed in 1913, both going to the electric chair—first the father, then the son. Sidna Allen was convicted and sentenced to fifteen years but was pardoned in 1926 by Governor Harry Byrd. Victor Allen was acquitted.

Allen, John Edward, (AKA: **the Mad Parson**), 1912-   , Brit. Allen, twice committed to a mental institution by the time he was twenty-five, brutally murdered 17-month-old Kathleen Diana Lucy Woodward on Oct. 21, 1937. While employed as an assistant chef at the Lamb Hotel in Burford, Oxfordshire, he befriended the Woodward family and often played with the child, whom he had taken for a walk on the day she disappeared. When her body was later found lying beside a road, she had been strangled with a clothes-line. Her hand still clutched the two pennies Allen had given her. Two days later, Allen surrendered to authorities and was charged with murder.

On Nov. 6, 1937, Allen was convicted of the murder and remanded to psychiatric care at the Broadmoor Asylum where he joined an entertainment group—The Broadhumoorists—which performed comedy shows for the inmates. Ten years later, Allen escaped from Broadmoor dressed as a cleric—his Broadhumoorists costume. He was recaptured two years later, but while free he became known in the press as the Mad Parson. On Sept. 18, 1951, Allen, at the age of thirty-nine, was released from the asylum.

Allen, Kenneth, 1943-   , U.S. In December 1978, 24-year-old Allen engaged up to twenty-five Chicago police officers in a gunfight at his South Side apartment which eventually led to his slaying two undercover officers on a Chicago street three months later. Police arrived at Allen's apartment shortly after his girlfriend, Bianca Smith, reported a quarrel between herself and Allen, who would not allow her to remove property from their shared home. Allen held police at bay for nineteen hours with an arsenal of weapons—high-powered magnum revolvers, semiautomatic pistols, and a hand-held M-16 rifle—until his inevitable arrest that evening.

Three months later, on Mar. 3, 1979, Chicago plain-clothes narcotics officers William P. Bosak and Roger Van Schaik were gunned down in daylight after stopping a car suspected of carrying drugs. Heavily armed men in the car opened fire on the officers as Allen arrived and fired on them from the opposite direction. Witnesses claimed that one wounded officer, bleeding on the ground, pleaded for his life as Allen pumped three more shots into his body. Additional officers responded to the shooting and gave chase to Allen's automobile, which slammed into a Chicago Transit Authority bus and three police cars before coming to a halt. Allen fled and was captured seven blocks away.

Allen was charged with the murder of the officers and held in custody without bond. He later pleaded guilty, explaining in court that the murders were a case of mistaken identity. He was found Guilty and sentenced to death in the Illinois electric chair. In 1980, he filed a plea to the state supreme court requesting that any appeal of his conviction be denied and that he be put to death immediately. No reasons for the plea were given, but the court ruled that every death penalty conviction receives an automatic appeal.

Allen, Margaret, 1906-49, Brit. The murder of 68-year-old Nancy Ellen Chadwick by Margaret Allen in 1948 was a motiveless and mindless act which still baffles criminologists to this day. Allen, the product of an immense family—she was the twen-tieth child of twenty-two offspring—had always denied her own femininity. Everything about her was masculine and she preferred the company of burly male workers in Rawtenstall, Lancashire, England. At an early age, Allen took on jobs that were usually performed by men. She loaded coal, repaired houses, and even became a bus driver. She was fired from this last position for abusing passengers—shoving and cuffing them if they did not take their seats fast enough.

Margaret Allen murdered an old woman out of whim and went to the gallows.

Short and stocky, Allen, in 1935, checked into a hospital and had a "delicate" operation performed, one, she later confided to a friend, which changed her "from a woman to a man." Allen then made no pretense about her turnabout

sexual role, cutting her hair short, donning male clothes, drinking with roustabout workers in bars. She had no female friends, except for Mrs. Annie Cook, and this relationship evaporated when Allen, while on vacation with Mrs. Cook, proposed a sexual bout which was promptly rejected by the offended Mrs. Cook.

Allen next invested her savings in the purchase of a dilapidated building that once served as Rawtenstall's police headquarters, situated on the town's main street, Bacup Road. To this house Mrs. Nancy Ellen Chadwick, a drifter, came to knock on the door on Aug. 28, 1948, dragging all her earthly belongings in an old sack. Her body was found inside that sack the next day, her head crushed by what police later determined to be a coal hammer, the face coated with ashes.

Detectives had a relatively easy job tracing the victim to Allen since a bloodstained path led directly to Allen's home. Moreover, the suspect went out of her way to encourage Scotland Yard inspectors to arrest her. She dogged their footsteps and stood about, hands thrust into her trousers, staring at them as they inspected the area. At one point, she rushed up to a detective and pulled at his sleeve and pointed to the nearby river. "Look, there's something there!" The object floating in the river was Mrs. Chadwick's knitting bag which officers found empty of the money the victim was alleged to have carried in it.

But still she was not charged. Margaret Allen then barged into the local pub, swilled down several beers, wiped her chin, and bellowed, "I was the last person to see the old woman!" She, like many an arrogant criminal before her, was openly challenging the police to make a case against her. (A similar case where the killer's ego insisted he actually lead the police to his door to challenge the police to make a case against him, was that of the haughty Richard Loeb, of the notorious Leopold and Loeb of Chicago, who thought to commit the perfect murder as an intellectual exercise.)

By late August, however, Scotland Yard sleuths had already gathered enough evidence to convict Allen of the Chadwick murder, matching hairs from the head of the victim to Allen's clothing and discovering in Allen's house several effects of the victim. It only remained for Allen to confess her crime. This she did after inspectors came to her door on Sept. 1, 1948. When formally charged, Margaret Allen smiled and admitted killing the old woman. "I was in a funny mood," she said out of the corner of a crooked smile. "She seemed to insist on coming in (to the house). I just happened to look around and saw a hammer in the kitchen. On the spur of the moment I hit her. She gave me a shout and that seemed to start me off more and I hit her a few times, I don't know how many." She gave no other explanation. Margaret Allen had killed the elderly woman on a whim.

After a five-hour trial, Allen was found Guilty, despite her counsel's feeble attempt to prove her insane. She was sentenced to death. Her old friend, Mrs. Cook, got together a petition to ask for a commutation but only 162 people in the town of almost 30,000 signed the document. Margaret Allen didn't seem to care. She acted, in her last hours at Strangeways Prison, as if the whole matter was nothing more than an inconvenience. She complained about her cell's lack of creature comforts and when she was brought the last meal she had requested, a plate of scrambled eggs, she kicked it out of the jailer's hands, splattering the food onto the wall of the cell and sneering, "At least no one else will enjoy that meal!" Without a word, Margaret Allen stomped up the stairs of the scaffold on the morning of Jan. 12, 1949, and was hanged on schedule. See: **Leopold, Nathan.**

Allen, Peter Anthony, 1943-64, and **Evans, Gwynne Owen (John Robson Welby),** 1940-64, Brit. Both Allen and Evans were milkmen and thugs who committed small robberies in Liverpool and had, since their teens, been in trouble with police. On the night of Apr. 6-7, 1964, John Alan West, a 53-year-old laundry driver, was attacked by Allen and Evans as he interrupted their robbery of his small house. They stabbed West several times and struck him on the head many times, crushing his skull, before running outside and driving away with Allen's wife in the car. (She had gone along for the ride, not knowing, she later claimed, what the two men were planning.) Police, who had been summoned by a neighbor, found Evans' raincoat and a girl's phone number inside one of its pockets, along with other items that led them to pick up Evans forty-eight hours later.

West's watch was found on Evans, who immediately claimed that Allen had done all the hitting and stabbing and was responsible for West's death. He merely "took a few things." Allen put the blame for the murder on Evans, but admitted that the car the killers had used on the murder night had been stolen in another part of Liverpool. Both men were tried at Manchester Crown Court in June 1964 and little defense could be offered. The only question in the court's mind was who actually did the killing, Allen or Evans. A jury quickly decided that both men were Guilty and they were condemned. The distinction these two thugs held in the annals of crime was not the sordid murder they committed but the fact that they were the last two to hang in England before capital punishment was abolished by a bill originally introduced in Parliament in 1956, one finally passed ten years later when hanging was suspended. Both

men were executed on Aug. 13, 1964, but in separate prisons—Allen in Liverpool's Walton Prison, Evans at Strangeways Prison in Manchester.

Almarez, Stella Delores, 1951-   , U.S. On June 18, 1980, in despair over her failed marriage, Stella Almarez of Norfolk, Neb., brutally slashed the throats of her two infant daughters and then shot down her older girls, ages seven and ten. Failing in her suicide attempt, Mrs. Almarez was arrested the next day and arraigned on a murder charge. In November 1980 she was found Not Guilty by reason of insanity by a Madison County jury and was committed to the Lincoln Regional Center for hospitalization. The controversial verdict led to sweeping changes in state law. As a result, the burden of proof that a person was insane at the time they committed a murder shifted from the prosecution to the defense. It is now up to the defense counsel to prove that his or her client was insane at the time they murdered.

A second noteworthy change involved the disposition of defendants remanded over to the custody of mental health facilities, like the one in Lincoln. During Mrs. Almarez' five-year stay at the regional center, she was permitted to work outside the hospital. A revision of the legal codes, however, required that each inmate be reviewed annually to determine their mental fitness before being permitted to wander off the grounds. Also, an inmate could only be released after hospital officials received a written order from the judge.

Released in 1985, Stella Almarez was the first Nebraska patient to be affected by this new ruling. Judge Merritt Warren of the Madison County District Court, declaring Almarez no longer a danger to herself or society, ordered her unconditionally released on Oct. 2, 1985.

Almodovar, Anibal (AKA: **Terry**), 1916-43, U.S. Almodovar was a Puerto Rican sailor living in New York City, a ladies' man who did as he pleased with his girlfriends and his 23-year-old wife, Louise Petecca Almodovar, a waitress who met the handsome, dashing Almodovar, whom she called Terry, at the Rhumba Palace in Manhattan. After dancing with him, she fell in love and the two were married a short time later. Only a few weeks went by before Louise accused Terry Almodovar of seeing other women. He exploded and then moved out. A short time later, Louise called Terry and asked to meet with him, to see if they could patch up their differences. Almodovar arranged to meet his wife in Central Park. In Central Park, near 110th Street in the tall grass, is where police found Louise Almodovar's body on Nov. 2, 1942. She had been strangled. The waitress had apparently struggled with her killer; the sleeve of her jacket torn from the shoulder. Chief medical examiner, Dr. Thomas A. Gonzales, determined that the killer had murdered with expertise: "The killer did not throttle her by placing both hands around her neck. He did it with two fingers from each hand, placing them on the windpipe. The larynx was only slightly fractured."

Until the dead woman was identified, police thought she had been killed by park thugs, but then they received reports on Terry Almodovar's marriage to the girl, and their breakup over his womanizing and violent streaks of temper. He was arrested on suspicion. Almodovar's clothing was turned over to Dr. Alexander O. Gettler, chief toxicologist of the medical examiner's office. Dr. Gottler found seeds of various types of grass in Almodovar's trouser cuffs and these he passed on to Dr. Joseph J. Copeland, professor of botany and biology at City College. Meanwhile, Terry Almodovar confessed that he had met with his wife in Central Park, and when Louise began to accuse him of seeing other women, he lost control and strangled her to death. He later recanted this confession, saying that he had been coerced by authorities into making the admission. When Almodovar was brought to trial, however, the killer never for an instant thought he would be convicted by some seeds of grass.

Almodovar was placed on trial on Feb. 24, 1943, before Judge George L. Donnellan. The prosecution presented an impressive array of forensic evidence; the botanical evidence provided clearly placed Almodovar at the scene of the murder. Dr. Copeland testified he had examined the seeds of grass found in Almodovar's trouser cuffs and that he had determined these to be a rare species (*Plantago canceolata, Panicum dichotomiflorum, Eleusine indica*) which could be found only in the area of Central Park where Louise Almodovar had been strangled to death. No other spot in New York City had this uncommon form of grass, planted at the murder site for experimental reasons. Copeland, at the request of police to head off Almodovar's expected alibis, also emphatically stated that this type of grass could only be found in two spots in Long Island and three small areas of Westchester County. Copeland went on to add that the grass seeds in Almodovar's trouser cuffs had matured only within a week or so of the time of the murder, which clearly placed the killer at the murder site. Almodovar was convicted and sentenced to death, going to the electric chair in 1943. The case stands as a hallmark in scientific research dealing with a murder trial.

American Bluebeard, The, See: **Schmidt, Helmuth.**

Amerman, Max, 1923-   , U.S. Calling itself the "Sweetest Town on Earth," Medina, Ohio, proved to be anything but that on the night of Oct. 5, 1950, when Harold Mast was murdered on the back porch of his farmhouse. Mast was shot in the back with a bullet from a twelve-gauge shotgun just before entering the home Amerman was leasing to him. As no one saw his assailant, suspicion soon fell on Amerman who was in love with the dead man's wife, Randi Mast. Amerman had paid for the woman's parents to come to the United States from Germany, allowed the Masts to lease his luxurious farm very inexpensively, and often attempted to have sexual intercourse with Mrs. Mast.

At the time of the murder, however, Amerman was in New Jersey, giving him a solid alibi which was doubted only after questioning 17-year-old Jerry Killinger. Killinger and Amerman, ten years the teen's senior, had a very close friendship, so close that Killinger would not divulge what he knew about Mast's killing. When police confronted Amerman with knowledge of this friendship, he admitted to having arranged for Killinger to shoot Mast so that he could marry Mrs. Mast. Killinger then confessed to pulling the trigger. The day before Killinger turned eighteen, Nov. 16, 1950, the jury found him guilty of murder without recommendation for mercy. He was sentenced to be electrocuted at the Ohio State Penitentiary in Columbus, as was Amerman after he pled guilty to first degree murder in January 1951.

Anargeros, Sophie (AKA: **Sandra Peterson, Sophie Peterson, Mrs. Wally Hamilton**), 1931-   , U.S. For a girl whose own mother placed her in a juvenile delinquent school, and who was termed by a probation officer as "hell bent," Sophia Anargeros, by the age of fifteen, was already destined for a life of crime.

On her release from the school, Anargeros left her home town of Somerville, Mass., just outside Boston, changed her first name to Sandra, and headed west to Reno, Nev. She spent the next couple of years working for gambling establishments and similar businesses attracting customers. Anargeros was married briefly in Southern California, just long enough to gain another name, Sandra Peterson.

During the winter of 1950, Anargeros took up a new profession—stealing from Texas motorists whom she induced into offering her a ride. She soon teamed up with a 14-year-old girl, in whose house the hitchhiker-thief had been living. The two would lure a male driver into the car's back seat and rather than submit to sex, they would rob him at gunpoint, then order him to drive off or simply leave him on the roadside and drive off in his car. However, not all of their crimes were successful. One driver, Lewis Patterson, resisted being robbed, and for his efforts received two bullet wounds, one in his side and one in the chest, that killed him. Anargeros and her accomplice tried in vain to escape pursuit—buying bus tickets headed in the opposite direction from which they were traveling, though returning the tickets later, and even dyeing the color of their hair. The two were arrested in San Angelo, Texas, Anargeros confessing that she had killed the man, but only in self-defense after he had tried to rape her—a claim that the younger girl's statement repudiated, resulting in a charge of murder against Anargeros. After four days, a jury found her guilty of murder with malice on Jan. 20, 1951, for which she received a sentence of two life terms, serving just over ten years—under the name of Sophie Peterson—before she was pardoned on Dec. 19, 1961.

Anderson, Percy Charles, d.1935, Brit. Edith Drew-Bear's body was discovered floating in a water tank by Brighton police on Nov. 25, 1934, but neither drowning nor the five bullets in her back and head had caused death. She had been strangled with a silk scarf wound tightly under her chin, according to Sir Bernard Spilsbury, who conducted the postmortem two days later.

The attack on the 21-year-old movie theater usher was characterized during the trial of her murderer, Anderson, as maniacal, a point the defense tried to use in proving that Anderson was not guilty by reason of insanity. Spilsbury noted that the bullets were fired from a .22-caliber gun—presumably a Walden Safety Revolver which was never recovered—and thus had not seriously wounded the victim, but had likely induced unconsciousness before she was choked to death and then dumped in the water tank.

When arrested, Anderson was carrying poison, ammonia chloride, and zinc chloride, and possessed in his room bullets identical to those found in Drew-Bear's body. He admitted quarreling with Drew-Bear but beyond that remembered nothing. In March 1935 he pled insanity to the charge but was nevertheless convicted of murder and executed at Wandsworth.

Andrews, Lowell Lee (AKA: **The Nicest Boy in Wolcott**), c.1940-59, U.S. Referred to as "the nicest boy" in his hometown of Wolcott, Kan., by the local newspaper, Andrews did anything but live up to it when he attempted

to fulfill his secret dream of becoming a hired gun in Chicago. Andrews, at the age of eighteen, weighed 300 pounds, wore horn-rimmed glasses, never drank alcohol, never dated, regularly went to church, and was an honor student. But because he needed money for the trip to Chicago to see his dream through, Andrews decided to kill his sister and parents and sell the property owned by his well-off farming family.

While his family watched television, he entered the parlor carrying an automatic rifle and revolver and shot his sister between the eyes, his mother three times, and his father twice, before reloading, since the first round failed to kill his parents. He confessed the killings to his pastor a few days later. He was found Guilty of murder, despite being diagnosed as schizophrenic, sentenced, and hanged at Leavenworth Prison.

de Antiquis Murder, See: **Geraghty, Christopher James.**

Appelgate, Everett, See: **Creighton, Mary Frances.**

Appleton, John, c.1855, Brit. On Mar. 28, 1905, John Appleton, in a drunken stupor, confessed to police that he and Joseph Earnshaw had robbed and killed a man, later identified as William Ledger, near Newcastle in July 1882. Having no other evidence to go on—records showed the crime remained unsolved—the police believed Appleton and arrested him. Earnshaw, apparently, had since died.

Appleton was tried at the Durham Assizes in July 1905, where he recanted his confession, stating he had only read of the murder. He was convicted and sentenced to death, but the sentence was later commuted to life due to the peculiar circumstances of the case.

Appo, Quimby (Lee Ah Bow), 1814-1912, U.S. One of the most bizarre prisoners ever to be jailed in the New York Tombs was its first Chinese inmate, the berserk killer, Lee Ah Bow, known to the police as Quimby Appo. He was not, as some historians have claimed, the first Chinese in New York. The first Chinese settlers were those artisans stranded when their showboat, the junk *Ki Ying*, caught fire while docked in the East River. The newly-arrived Chinese took lodging on Mott Street between Pell and Chatham, and the area became New York's Chinatown. Appo, a murderer by temperament, arrived in New York from California as the personal slave of a landed gentleman. This was more than seven years after the Ki Ying group took up residence.

In no time at all, the unbalanced Appo attempted to kill a shopkeeper. He was booked for attempted murder in the summer of 1840. Female missionaries visited Appo in his cell, and he became their prime target for conversion to Christianity. With their help, Appo was released. In the next twenty years, the "Chinese Devilman" or "Devil Appo," as the press dubbed him, was arrested at least a dozen times for assaults and attempts to commit homicide. On Mar. 9, 1859, Appo attacked three women in his boarding house. One of these females was his mistress, who made the mistake of serving him a cold dinner. He stabbed her. When another woman rushed into the apartment, Appo drove a dirk into her heart.

Racing down a back stairs, Appo's escape route was blocked by the stout landlady. She turned her back on him and he promptly stabbed her in the buttock. Police arrived and carted the Devilman off to The Tombs, where he was scheduled to hang for murder. The persistent missionaries mounted a campaign to save their religious pet and convinced authorities to reduce his sentence to seven years, which he served in constant anger. He would bite the hands of jailers as they shoved his food through the bars. He screamed for hours on end. He spat at Warden Fallon and tried to claw anyone who recklessly got too close to his cell. Somehow, Appo's savage behavior only further endeared him to the missionaries.

Upon his release, the Devilman promptly stabbed his landlady, Lizzie Williams. Through a lawyer provided by the missionaries, Appo was again released. There was no end to the liberties Appo took with his fellow creatures. Drunk one day in 1872, the Devilman dug up a large cobblestone from the street and crashed it down upon the head of one John Linkowski. With one blow, the diminutive Chinese had dashed the man's brains out. Again, he was thrown into the Tombs, and again the religious zealots got him released. Appo was about to take up the cross, they doggedly insisted.

Instead, Appo took up another dirk and drove it into Cork Maggie, a Bowery whore. Since she survived the attack, the missionaries pointed out to police, there was no sense in prosecuting. The Devilman was not even taken into custody. A year later, on Oct. 21, 1876, this fierce little man jumped up from a card game and plunged a dagger several times into the chest of one John Kelly, whom he accused of cheating him. This time, authorities sent Appo to Matteawan, the state prison for the insane, the same prison which later housed the notorious train robber Oliver

Curtis Perry and millionaire murderer Harry K. Thaw.

The Devilman never left this prison. He would endlessly stare from his cell window and, upon seeing the searchlight of the Hudson River Nightboat, would scream: "Here comes my diamond!" Officials at the institute reported that Appo "believes that he has grand hotels, palaces, servants and horses outside the asylum; that he is King of the World and Omnipotent, the Second God; commands the wind and the sun; that Tom Sharkey and General Coxey are his military staff and that he must suffer for Ireland." The Devilman suffered for ninety-eight years before being buried on the grounds at Matteawan on June 23, 1912.

Archer-Gilligan, Amelia (AKA: **Sister Amy**), 1869-1928, U.S. Archer-Gilligan, or Sister Amy, as she was called by the charges of her nursing home in Windsor, Conn., was a marrying murderer who had the dubious distinction of being blessed by the unwitting relatives of her victims. Establishing a nursing home in Windsor in 1901, Archer-Gilligan began taking in old men whom she promptly married after their wills had been signed over to her. Five of these unsuspecting elderly gentlemen perished soon after the nuptials, all of them poisoned, it was later determined, over a period of fourteen years. In addition to these victims, Sister Amy also murdered at least a dozen other persons, elderly women who were entrusted to her nursing home, but only after each had drawn up new wills which made her the sole beneficiary. Relatives incredibly approved of such measures after listening to Sister Amy tell them that it was the only way in which she could be compensated for taking care of the old people since her monthly rates were bargain cheap. Of course, the patients did not live long enough to cause a severe drain on Sister Amy's coffers. Usually a new patient at Sister Amy's home lasted but a few short months before Archer-Gilligan helped them into eternity by poisoning their food. A few she suffocated with pillows and chalked up their deaths to heart failure, the death certificates signed by a senile doctor who merely wrote down the causes of death as Sister Amy described them.

This convenient murder factory became suspect when a relative learned that an elderly aunt had died only a few days after she had been placed in Sister Amy's home and only hours after the woman's will had been signed over to Sister Amy. The relative did some investigating and then went to officials to prove that the death rate at the Archer-Gilligan home was ten times higher than at other homes for the aged. Police placed an undercover agent in the home who witnessed the scheming Archer-Gilligan administering poison to some of the patients. Sister Amy was arrested by the policewoman and was tried and convicted of murder in 1914, sent to Weathersfield Prison to serve a life term. She began to have nervous fits and, after she tried to poison the warden and several turnkeys, Sister Amy Archer-Gilligan was sent to an insane asylum, kept in a padded, locked cell until 1928 when she died.

Armistead, Norma Jean, 1930- , U.S. In October 1974, Nurse Armistead of the Kaiser Hospital in Los Angeles quietly sneaked into the medical records section where she scribbled an entry into the ledger, a false pregnancy, her own. It was unusual but not impossible that a childless 44-year-old woman should suddenly become pregnant. There were more than a few sneering comments made by hospital personnel, but soon the matter was forgotten.

On May 15, 1975, Armistead paid a social call on 28-year-old Kathryn Viramontes in her Van Nuys apartment. The younger woman was completing her own term of pregnancy when she was suddenly accosted by knife-wielding Armistead, who was not interested in the family valuables or any cash hidden about the house. She slashed her victim in the throat and then performed a crude but successful caesarean section to extricate the living infant from the womb of the dead woman. Armistead checked herself into the hospital a few hours later and informed the doctors that she had given birth to the boy prematurely at home. It was not long afterward that the true facts of this bizarre murder came to light.

A jury later convicted Norma Jean of first-degree murder after declaring her to be legally sane when she took the knife to Viramontes.

Armstrong, Herbert Rowse, 1870-1922, Brit., Major Herbert Rowse Armstrong was a small, mousey-looking man whose wife Katherine Mary Armstrong henpecked him from morning to night. Armstrong had been a major during WWI and he insisted that he be addressed by the rank with which he retired. The only authority he really possessed was titular and his dominating wife stripped him of even that by ridiculing his military experiences. The couple lived comfortably with their three children in a cottage in Cusop Dingle closed to the border of Wales-England. The quiet and dignified Armstrong worked as a solicitor in the Welsh town of Hay-on-Wye. When Katherine Armstrong wasn't picking at her husband's habits, she was complaining about her constantly failing health as do most dedicated hypochondriacs. To neighbors

and friends Armstrong appeared to take the constant nagging and scolding with good-natured tolerance but he secretly seethed at the humiliation heaped upon him by his unbearable wife, so much so that he put into action a plan he was sure would allow him to get away with murder.

In the spring of 1920, Armstrong began spending all his extra time killing weeds about his cottage area, purchasing

Mr. and Mrs. Herbert Armstrong; the major fed his wife poison.

considerable quantities of arsenic to eliminate the unwanted growth. In July of that year, Mrs. Armstrong made out a will in which she left all her earthly possessions to her mild-mannered husband. Some weeks later, Katherine Armstrong was having so many delusions and visions that she was removed to an asylum where she was certified as insane. While his wife languished in the asylum, Armstrong began taking short vacation trips to London and, when at home, made a great show of practicing his hobby of weed-killing. At the turn of the year, Mrs. Armstrong made an amazing recovery which allowed her to return home but she soon grew ill and, on Feb. 22, 1921, she succumbed to illness. The cause of death was attributed to a combination of heart disease and gastritis. Major Armstrong grieved briefly, entering a terse comment in his diary, "K died."

Armstrong seemed to take his wife's death with relative calm. In fact, in the months that followed, his normally withdrawn personality seemed to grow more aggressive. He took many vacations to London and suddenly took a great interest in his lackluster business, going after clients with confirmed zeal. His chief rival in the town of Hay was a solicitor named Oswald Norman Martin who received in the mail a box of chocolates from an unknown person. Martin thought this to be a small favor from one of his clients who wished to remain anonymous and he later served the chocolates to a dinner guest who became violently ill only minutes later. The chocolates were turned over to a toxicologist who determined that they had been injected with arsenic. The solicitor was baffled as to who might send him such a lethal gift. Then on Oct. 26, 1921, in response to an invitation, Martin went to Armstrong's home to take tea. Armstrong chatted casually while the two men sipped their tea, then reached for a buttered scone on a nearby plate but instead of eating this himself, handed it to his guest, saying, "excuse my fingers." The crude manner of serving was overlooked by Martin who attributed such conduct as typical of an aging bachelor who had just been widowed. He ate the scone and later was taken violently ill.

Dr. Thomas Hincks, who had attended Armstrong's wife and had had reservations about the manner of her death, was summoned to Martin's home to treat the ailing solicitor. Hincks was concerned over Martin's erratic pulse which would not be the normal result of stomach disease. He sent a sample of the solicitor's urine to a clinic for analysis and received a report that it contained a substantial amount of arsenic. Police, now suspicious of Armstrong after reading reports from Dr. Hincks, encouraged the badly frightened Martin to continue his acquaintence with Armstrong. Martin was sent a barrage of invitations from Armstrong to have another tea with him but he nervously found one excuse after another to postpone the lethal appointment. When the solicitor could stand the game no more, he insisted that the police act. Investigators had been attempting to put a case together against the polite little major but were unsure of their case. They finally gave Martin relief by arresting Armstrong on Dec. 31, 1921, charging him with the attempted murder of Martin. A short time later, detectives obtained permission to exhume Mrs. Armstrong's body which was carefully examined by Scotland Yard's forensic bloodhound, Dr. Bernard Spilsbury, who found the remains of Katherine Armstrong filled with arsenic.

Armstrong was now charged with his wife's murder, in addition to his attempt on Martin's life, and placed on trial on Apr. 3, 1922, at the Hereford Assizes, appearing before Justice Darling and prosecuted by Attorney General Sir Ernest Pollock. Sir Henry Curtis-Bennett, one of the ablest criminal lawyers in England, defended Major Armstrong with the argument that Mrs. Armstrong had committed suicide by taking arsenic, such was her mental condition at the end. This claim was countered by Pollock when he produced a nurse who had been present at Katherine Armstrong's deathbed and quoted the victim in court as having said, "I have everything to live for—my husband and my children." This was not the comment of a suicidally bent woman. Further, Armstrong, who conducted himself with impressive ease while in the dock, seemed to incur the emnity of Justice Darling who personally questioned the diminutive major several times. The most damning evidence was a packet of arsenic which had been found on Armstrong by officers who arrested him and from whom

he appeared to be hiding the poison. He later claimed that this was but a small packet of poison he had put together, blending poison and other substances, to kill dandelions. Police found twenty packets of arsenic which Armstrong had put together which puzzled Lord Darling and he inquired why Major Armstrong would take the trouble to make separate doses of the poison instead of merely sprinkling the whole supply of arsenic throughout the weed-infested area.

"I really do not know," Armstrong replied to Justice Darling. "At the time it seemed the most convenient way of doing it." His indecisive response further damned the solicitor in the eyes of those who believed him guilty of killing his wife. Moreover, only nineteen dandelions were counted in the weed patch and Armstrong had prepared twenty packets of poison. It was assumed that the extra packet was to be used on Armstrong's rival, Oswald Martin. Also weighing heavily against the major was the testimony of a physician testifying for the prosecution who insisted that he had examined Armstrong and that the prim-and-proper major was suffering from advanced stages of a sexually-transmitted disease which he had apparently contracted following his wife's death. This evidence doomed the man in the dock perhaps more than anything else since he had postured himself as a man of high morals and great scruples. Major Herbert Rowse Armstrong was found Guilty of having poisoned to death his wife and sentenced to death. The poisoner was hanged on May 31, 1922.

The Armstrong case reminded the public of another sensational murder trial against another solicitor, Harold Greenwood, also from Wales, who was charged with poisoning his wife with arsenic in 1920, but who had been acquitted. It was speculated during Armstrong's trial that he had read about the Greenwood acquittal and believed that he could poison his own wife and, if charged, would be released as had Greenwood, convinced that his social position, his military rank, and his occupation as a solicitor would put him above suspicion and beyond conviction. Ironically, Greenwood wrote a series of articles for *John Bull* magazine during Armstrong's trial in which Greenwood described in bemoaning detail what it was like to be tried for murder. If indeed, Major Armstrong had been inspired by reading about the celebrated Greenwood case a year before he murdered his wife, he may have dug deeper into the history of murder and located the case of Cordelia Botkin, who mailed poisoned chocolates to one of her rivals twenty-some years earlier in America. Botkin's murder ploy may have also inspired Armstrong to dispose of his business rival, the hapless Oswald Martin.

Arrington, Marie Dean, 1935-   , U.S. In his capacity as the public defender of Leesburg, Fla., Robert Pierce was well acquainted with Arrington. He represented her teen-aged son and daughter when they stood trial for armed robbery and forgery in 1968. The outcome of these two separate trials did not please Arrington—herself an ex-convict who was free on bond while awaiting sentencing for the shooting death of her husband in 1964. The anger the black woman felt toward the public defender festered until Apr. 22, 1968, when she put on her best new outfit and took a cab down to Pierce's private office. To her dismay, the object of her vendetta was not in, just a 37-year-old secretary, Vivian Ritter. Later that afternoon Pierce returned to find Ritter gone. It was not like her to just walk out. Never once during her thirteen-year employment had the pretty brunette done such a thing. The police were immediately notified. Within hours several witnesses volunteered the information that Ritter and an unidentified black woman had been observed leaving the building together, but they were not walking side by side. It was quickly surmised that Ritter had been forcibly taken from the building, perhaps at gunpoint.

Six days later the shotgunned remains of Ritter were found. There was strong evidence that suggested she had been senselessly tortured before her death. Arrington was picked up shortly afterward by Florida police. She was convicted of first-degree murder in the slaying of Ritter and sentenced to die in the electric chair. A twenty-year prison sentence for the 1964 murder of her husband was tacked on by the courts.

Before her execution could be carried out, Arrington escaped from the women's prison in Lowell, Fla., on Mar. 1, 1969. Her name was added to the FBI's Most Wanted List and she remained a fugitive for nearly three years. There was some talk in Leesburg that a vigilante group located Marie Dean and had taken her into the swamps where Vivian Ritter was avenged. This was not the case, however. The murderer was captured in New Orleans in 1971 by FBI agents.

Atlanta Children Murders, See: **Williams, Wayne Bertram.**

Attebery, Ira (Attebury), 1915-79, U.S. For three years, Attebery regularly attended the annual Battle of the Flowers Parade in San Antonio, capping off a week-long fiesta celebration. The 64-year-old retired trucker lived in a small trailer park not far from the parade route, and

tended to keep to himself. "I thought it was strange that he went to parades since he had little to do with people," said Kate Copeland, the manager of the trailer park where Attebery lived until he went berserk on Apr. 27, 1979. "He was a loner," she added.

The self-styled parade aficionado lined up, by police estimate, six automatic rifles and enough bullet clips to supply a military arsenal. Near the intersection of Broadway and Grayson, Attebery began firing wildly into a crowd of 4,500 parade spectators through a window in his trailer home. "He would expose himself, fire, and then duck. The total gunfire lasted about thirty minutes, and it was another thirty minutes before we found him dead," said Captain Patrick Nichols of the San Antonio police. To the police officers standing in the middle of the parade route, Attebery yelled "Traitors! Traitors!"

Before he turned the gun on himself, Attebery killed two people and wounded fifty more. Blood samples taken from the dead man's body revealed the presence of the drug PCP, known in the streets as "angel dust," a deadly drug recently banned in Texas because of the unpredictable, occasionally suicidal behavior it brought on in addicts.

Attebery went berserk under the delusion that the police were chasing him because of a 1971 trucking accident he was involved in that killed two women. On at least one previous occasion he had contacted the police seeking psychiatric help. "I would have been very happy if police had brought the man here," said Robert Pugh, director of the county mental health department. "But unless the man was willing to come and was in violation of a law, the police could not have brought him in."

Aulisio, Joseph, 1966- , U.S. Aulisio liked to tinker with automobiles. His friends and schoolmates expected him to become a mechanic, like many other high school boys in the small town of Old Forge, Lackawanna County, Pa. By all accounts, he was a model student, loyal, obedient, and helpful, according to his principal Walter Ermolovich, who also knew the boy's father Robert, a biology teacher in the school.

Problems started when the Aulisios' youngest child died in its third month. Relations between family members became strained, ending in the parents' divorce. Joseph's school work declined, and he began cutting classes. He grew sullen and withdrawn, to the dismay of his parents, still engaged in the bitter divorce suit. His unhappiness finally culminated in murder on July 26, 1981, when the dark-haired youth abducted 8-year-old Cheryl Ziemba and her brother Christopher Ziemba, four, from their home on the outskirts of Scranton. Two days later their two bodies were found in an abandoned strip mine, shotgunned to death.

Aulisio was found guilty of first-degree murder and sentenced to die in the electric chair, which caused protest among opponents of capital punishment. "We're reading more and more about vicious crimes by younger and younger people," countered Judge James Walsh of the Lackawanna County Common Pleas Court. "Incidents like that are causing a lot of people to say that if they are guilty of adult criminal activity they should be subject to adult punishment." In 1982 Aulisio was the youngest offender to sit on death row in a U.S. prison. During the long appeals process he was transferred to the State Correctional Institution at Huntingdon where he currently resides.

Austin, Alice, and **Simmons, Ted,** and **Scott, Ira,** prom. 1930s, U.S. Alice and Earl Austin of Hardin County, Ill., were in the middle of a bitter divorce. Earl Austin was suing Alice for desertion; she had run away with a local swain, Ted Simmons. Alice countersued Earl, charging him with adultery, and named Lacene McDowell as the other woman. The divorce action raged on until Alice Austin decided that waiting for drawn-out divorce proceedings to bring her a proper financial settlement was a waste of time. She and her lover, Ted Simmons, thinking to cash in on a life insurance policy on Earl Austin's life (still signed over to Alice), planned to murder the estranged husband. They plotted his death in many schemes but finally went to Ira Scott, a farmer with a knack for putting mechanical things together—in this case a bomb—requested by his two eager clients. Scott fashioned an infernal machine and placed this in Earl Austin's car.

On Mar. 20, 1939, Earl Austin and Lacene McDowell got into Earl's car to go for a drive along the rural roads of Hardin County. An hour later a terrific explosion rocked the car as it sped along, blowing away the floorboards and sending the car careening off the road and into a ditch. Both Earl Austin and Lacene McDowell were blown skyward at the moment of the blast, flying more than twenty feet into the air. Austin was dead within seconds but Miss McDowell, with one leg blown off, managed to linger for an hour. She remained unconscious and could tell State's Attorney Clarence E. Soward nothing before she died. Soward, however, was aware of the violent divorce action between Austin and his wife Alice and knew that Alice's sweetheart, Simmons, had openly threatened Earl Austin. He interviewed both Alice and Ted Simmons. Both expressed their profound regrets at the deaths of Earl Austin and McDowell, adding that they were with a group of people when the car blew up. The matter rested in limbo for some weeks until police received a tip that a local

farmer, Ira Scott, had been acting nervously when going into town to buy some grain. Scott had purchased more items than his meager earnings would normally allow which also aroused suspicions.

When Scott was confronted by Soward, he broke down immediately, blurting, "I didn't mean to (kill them). I didn't know that there was going to be anybody in the car. Alice and Ted Simmons gave me fifty dollars to bomb it for the insurance. They didn't tell me that there would be anyone in it." He went on to say that he thought Alice and Ted wanted to collect insurance on the *car*, an implausible statement. Further, if no one was to be in the car, Scott failed to adequtely explain why he had set the timing device of the bomb on a delayed mechanism so that it would only go off after the car had been driven for about an hour after it had been started. His statements were downright idiotic in that his defense was built upon the car being driven by itself. By his own admission, Scott had run the fuse from the dynamite back into the exhaust manifold and this would have been impossible to ignite unless someone was indeed driving the auto. Simmons and Austin continued to deny their guilt when all three were later tried. All were found Guilty and each received a fourteen-year sentence.

Avril, Robert, 1911- , Fr. Avril, a common laborer with a miserable childhood, habitually attacked and raped women and, eventually, the attacks turned into murder. On Aug. 28, 1955, the body of a young woman was found in some tall grass off the roadway near the small village of Picquigny, between Amiens and Abbeville in northern France. The victim's clothes were in disarray and a band of white on her suntanned wrist showed police that the woman's wristwatch had been stolen. An English-made bicycle was found nearby along with some clothing that had been torn out of the bag fixed to the bicycle's rack. A check of the area disclosed that a 23-year-old school teacher named Janet Marshall from Nottingham, England, had registered in a nearby youth hostel the previous evening. The body was identified as Marshall and a search for her killer ensued. Police discovered that Marshall had stopped at a cafe in Picquigny on the morning of August 26 to have breakfast. Detectives, led by Inspector Henri Van Asche, concluded that the woman had been waylaid by one of the common laborers who worked in the area and they interrogated several men without charging anyone. Local residents described one particular laborer who had a brutal face and had been seen to watch Janet Marshall as she pedalled out of the village of Picquigny. A composite sketch was made of the suspect and this was circulated throughout the area. The circular also mentioned a rather unusual detail concerning this laborer; he was missing three fingers on his left hand.

Five months after the murder of Janet Marshall, Robert Avril, a 44-year-old laborer, was arrested, charged with stealing a bicycle. He was brought before Judge Jean DeTraux in Amiens. The judge took one look at Avril and then remembered the police composite that had been circulated in the Marshall slaying. He looked at the composite and realized that it bore an amazing resemblance to the man who stood before him. He asked Avril to hold up his left hand. Three fingers were missing. DeTraux asked Avril where he was on Aug. 26, 1955, and the laborer quickly, all too quickly for the judge, replied that he had been visiting his sister in Sucy-in-Brie. DeTraux also knew from police reports that Janet Marshall's German-made camera, along with her wristwatch, had been taken following her murder. When police visited Avril's sister she said that her brother had visited at the end of August and had left a camera with her. This proved to be Marshall's camera. Moreover, articles of clothing belonging to the victim were found in Avril's lodging. He was interrogated and confessed to having killed the school teacher, saying that he, at first, only thought to have sex with her but then he

French rapist and murderer, Robert Avril.

strangled her with a piece of string when she resisted. He insisted that he did not rape the woman but fled from the scene, stealing her watch, camera, and some small pieces of clothing.

At his trial in Amiens in May 1958, Avril recanted his original confession and was allowed play to the sympathy of the jury by relating in detail his sad childhood. He described how he had lost his fingers at age seven in an accident, how his mother died when he was still a child, and that his father committed suicide after it was revealed that he had had incestuous relations with Avril's older sister. In court, Avril also insisted that he had left Janet Marshall in an unconscious condition, that she was not dead and that someone else probably came along and murdered her after he fled. Against these self-defensive statements stood Avril's long history of attacks on women. In April 1944, Avril had stopped along a roadway to help 22-year-old Madeleine Thiery remove some dust from her eye. He had then dragged her into some woods, raped her, and stole

three pounds of butter from her. In June 1944 Avril attacked a 19-year-old girl and the following month he attacked and raped another 19-year-old girl and a 56-year-old woman, then another young girl some days later, this last victim escaping before Avril could drag her into a clump of bushes. In all these attacks, the victims had been on bicycles which Avril kicked out from under them as they pedaled past him, disabling them so that he could easily drag them off and compel them to have sex with him. He was arrested for these rapes in 1944 but not convicted until 1946 when Avril was sentenced to ten years of hard labor. He was released in 1951 and resumed his attacks on helpless women, culminating in his murder of Janet Marshall.

Every piece of evidence in the Avril case pointed to the man's guilt, and it was further claimed by the presiding judge, Jean Bourdon, that Avril had denounced members of the Resistance to the dreaded Gestapo during the Nazi occupation of France. This was vehemently denied by the accused. Inspector Van Asche testified that Avril, when first arrested, told police, "I killed her (Janet Marshall) without meaning to." Though the energetic Public Prosecutor Max Dussert argued long and hard for a death sentence, Avril escaped the guillotine. The jury deliberated his case for thirty-five minutes and then returned a verdict of Guilty "with extenuating circumstances," meaning that Avril's awful childhood had contributed mightily to his attitude toward women, and he was therefore not wholly responsible for his awful murder of young Janet Marshall. The killer was sentenced to life at hard labor with no chance of parole.

Baekeland, Antony, 1946-81, Brit. Barbara Baekeland's relationship with her son Antony bordered on obsession. On Nov. 17, 1972, Tony murdered his adoring mother at their lavish London penthouse.

Antony Baekeland, great grandson of the "father of modern plastics" and heir to the family fortune, was a troubled youth with homosexual tendencies. When he was twenty-one his parents separated. While living with his mother, Tony began experimenting with LSD. After he stabbed Barbara in the London penthouse, he placed an order for Chinese food just as the Chelsea detectives arrived. His trial began at the Old Bailey on June 6, 1973, and it was a sensational one, highlighted by rumors of incest between Barbara and her son. Witnesses told how the former movie star desired to "cure" her son of his homosexuality. Tony Baekeland, was convicted of manslaughter under the "diminished responsibility" statute in British law. He was sent to Broadmoor, where he remained for the next seven years. In July 1980, Tony was discharged from custody and flown to New York to live with his grandmother Nina Fraser Daly. A week later, Baekeland assaulted the elderly woman with a knife because she refused to "quit nagging him." Mrs. Daly survived the attack, but criminal charges were filed, and once again the young heir found himself behind bars, this time on Riker's Island. It was there that Tony Baekeland ended his life, on Mar. 21, 1981.

Bagg, Arthur Richard, 1914- , S. Afri. On Nov. 23, 1937, Arthur Richard Bagg, a 23-year-old South African, savagely stabbed his 17-year-old lover in a fit of jealousy and rage and later dumped her mutilated body under a viaduct on Oaklands Atholl Road outside Johannesburg. He was taken in for questioning several days after the partially-clothed body of Marjorie Patricia Rosebrook was found stabbed twice in the breast with a small knife.

Bagg became a prime suspect three days later when, during questioning, his accounts of his activities on the day of Rosebrook's murder did not correspond to those given by witnesses who had seen the two lovers together that day. After several attempts by Sub-Inspector U.R. Boberg to compel him to tell the truth, Bagg finally broke down and confessed to the murder. He later re-enacted the events of that day, taking detectives to the site of the crime and explaining his actions in detail.

Although Bagg had confessed, police were unable to locate the murder weapon and several articles of clothing missing from the dead girl's body. They repeatedly scoured the sites where Bagg claimed he disposed of them, but turned up nothing. After threatening to search his house,

Bagg agreed to lead police to the missing items.

Bagg, described as somewhat eccentric, was an artist interested in mysticism and the occult. Unknown to anyone was his special affinity for the legendary vampire, Count Dracula. Bagg worshipped him and frequently conducted ritualistic services in his honor. He led police to the site of these rituals—a secret earthen chamber located below the floor of his bedroom. A trapdoor hidden underneath the linoleum provided access to the chamber, where police discovered the murder weapon and the missing blood-stained clothing. In addition, they found a piece of leather with writing carved into it: "I hereby befile (sic) the living God and serve only the Dark One, Dracula; to serve him faithfully so I may become one of his faithful servants." It was signed by Bagg.

Bagg's trial began on Feb. 28, 1938. During his testimony, he changed his confession and claimed the girl had committed suicide and that he was covering up for her with his earlier confession. The jury failed to believe him, and, after slightly less than two hours of deliberation, they returned a verdict of Guilty. Justice Saul Solomon sentenced Bagg to death, the maximum punishment for his crime, but this was later reduced to life imprisonment based on psychiatric evaluations of his mental state. Bagg was released in 1947 after serving only nine years of his sentence.

Bailey, George Arthur, d.1921, Brit. The January 1921 murder trial of George Arthur Bailey was the first murder trial in England in which women served on a jury. After the four-day trial was over, the three women jurors helped convict Bailey for the poisoning murder of his wife. He was sentenced to death and executed on Mar. 2, 1921.

Bailey, Raymond (AKA: **Ray Carter**), d.1958, Aus. Raymond Bailey was driving a DeSoto sedan with his wife on the Alice Springs-Port Augusta Highway in South Australia on Dec. 6, 1957. In the middle of the night, Bailey left his caravan, carrying with him a Huntsman single-shot rifle. He used it on Thyra Bowman, her 15-year-old daughter Wendy, and their friend Tom Whelan, who had set up camp for the night in the wilderness.

The Bowmans were on their way to Adelaide when they were overtaken by Bailey. Their bodies were located by an aerial search party looking for their missing automobile. Near their campfire several .22-caliber shell casings were found which matched the rifle found in Bailey's possession. In Kulgera, several eyewitnesses reported seeing a DeSoto sedan. The car was spotted on Jan. 21, 1958, by Constable Glen Hallahan at Mount Isa in Queensland.

When questioned by police, Bailey said his name was Carter. He could not, however, explain a concealed .32-caliber handgun sewn under the front seat of his car. The suspect finally confessed to the shootings, but changed his story four times. Bailey was extradited to Adelaide and tried for murder. Deliberations opened on May 12, 1958, Sir Geoffrey Reed presiding. Less than eight days later the jury returned a verdict of Guilty. The death sentence was imposed within minutes, and Bailey was executed at the Adelaide Jail on June 24.

Ball, Edward, 1917-   , Ire. Though the body of 55-year-old Vera Ball was never found, her son Edward was tried and convicted of her murder. Mrs. Ball was the wife of a Dublin physician. Following their separation, she lived with her 19-year-old son in Boosterstown, a suburb of Dublin. On the morning of Feb. 18, 1936, a newspaper delivery man stopped to investigate an automobile parked on an odd angle in Shankill, County Dublin. He found traces of blood on the front seat.

Identifying the car as belonging to Mrs. Ball, police went to the Boosterstown home. Here they were greeted by Edward Ball, who said he had last seen his mother the previous evening. Police searched the house, turning up several items of bloody clothing and discovering a large stain on his mother's bedroom rug, none of which Ball could explain. When pressed further, he said his mother had suffered a recent bout of depression and had killed herself with a straight razor. Ball said he found her dead in her room, took the body to Shankill, and threw it into the sea.

His explanation did not convince the police, however, and Ball was charged with murdering his mother. Police believed he used a hatchet found in the garden, covered with blood. He was convicted of murder, but the jury also declared him insane. The judge ordered Ball detained at the discretion of the local governor-general.

Ball, Eli, prom. 1919, U.S. On Feb. 19, 1919, Ball murdered his sister Lilly Billings, and her husband Abe Billings, as they tried to remove furniture from the rural Kentucky home that had been willed to him by his sister, Nell Washam, when she died the previous year. Lilly Billings maintained that she was entitled to some of the farm's furnishings, as it had all been inherited from the family by Nell when her parents died. Ball served several

years in a state penitentiary for the murders, but was released to return to the homestead in Bear River Valley, Ky.

Ball, George (AKA: **George Sumner**), 1892-1914, Brit. The 22-year-old Ball worked as a clerk in the shop of John Bradfield in Liverpool. He was assisted by a dim-witted 18-year-old, Samuel Angeles Eltoft. The shop's manager was 40-year-old Christine Catherine Bradfield, a hard taskmaster who was known to neighbors as a kindly person. She tolerated no nonsense in the shop which sold tarpaulins manufactured by John, her brother, and she was forever prodding Ball, who was known as George Sumner by his employers. On the night of Dec. 10, 1913, Walter Musker Eaves, a ship's steward who was waiting for his girlfriend in Old Hall Street and who was standing directly in front of Bradfield's, suddenly had his new hat knocked off his head when one of the shop's shutters blew off. The shop appeared dark but within a few minutes Eltoft appeared and picked up the shutter. Eaves showed him his hat and demanded that he be paid for the damage done to his bowler by the shutter. Eltoft politely asked him to wait and soon emerged with Ball who courteously paid Eaves two shillings for the creases made in the hat.

Murderer George Ball.

Eaves was still in Old Hall Street when, a short time later, both Ball and Eltoft appeared, pushing a tarpaulin-covered cart with considerable effort up the street, and disappearing around the corner. The next day Eaves read a newspaper report about a woman's body being found in the Leeds-Liverpool canal by a bargeman who had fished the body, sewn into a sack, out of the canal. The steward went to the police who had just escorted John Bradfield from the morgue. Bradfield had also responded to the newspaper report when his sister had failed to return home from the shop and he had identified the body, telling officers that he had no idea who would want to murder his sister.

Detective Inspector Duckworth of the Criminal Investigation Department (CID), after interviewing neighbors and shop customers, realized that the only real suspects in the case were the two clerks, Ball and Eltoft. He decided to interview Eltoft first, realizing, when John Bradfield talked about the pair, that the younger clerk was impressionable and gullible. He waited until late on the night of Dec. 11, 1913, then forced his way into Eltoft's room, startling the youth and grilling him so intensely that Eltoft blurted out the fact that his superior, George Ball, had bludgeoned Christine Bradfield to death. Ball hated her constant nagging and, after she ordered him to do something, he had suddenly exploded and crushed the woman's head with an iron pipe, forcing Eltoft to help him dispose of the body. Duckworth, placing Eltoft under arrest, then raced to Bell's boarding house but the young man had fled. His landlady later stated that Ball had returned home the night

Christine Bradfield

before and she had noticed bloody scratches on his face. He told her that he had received the injuries at the shop where he worked, adding: "It's a rotten business."

The scratches, coupled with some of Eltoft's confusing statements later given in court, suggested that Ball had raped the spinster in a back room of the shop and she had scratched his face; in retaliation he had struck her on the head with the pipe.

The Liverpool police, despite a desperate search for Ball, were unable to locate him. Duckworth was struck with an inspiration. He was a movie fan who believed that the movie theaters springing up all over Liverpool could be of great service to the police in tracking down Ball. He had the fugitive's photograph shown on all the screens of the theaters between features, running beneath the photo a title card which read: "GEORGE BALL, WANTED FOR MURDER, REWARD." This was the first time that movies had been used in tracking down a wanted criminal, and the technique proved effective. Ball, who had moved and disguised himself, was identified by someone who had seen his photo in one of the theaters as he left a football match on Dec. 20, 1913. He was immediately arrested and tried in February 1914 at the Liverpool Assizes, Justice Atkin presiding. He was defended by Sir Alfred Tobin, who had been the lawyer for the notorious wife-killer, Dr. Hawley Harvey Crippen. Prosecuting the case was Sir Gordon Hewart.

The trial was one-sided with Hewart utterly destroying the testimony of the nervous Ball who rattled off a fantastic story about "a tall chap with a dark brown mustache" who sprang from behind a pile of tarpaulins in the shop just before closing and attacked Christine Bradfield, killing her, then held a revolver on Ball and Eltoft, telling them that if they did not dispose of the body for him, he would kill them both. Hewart shredded this tale quickly, asking Ball why, when he went to the street to pay Eaves for the destruction of his hat, he did not ask the burly steward for help since, according to Ball's own testimony, the killer was still in the shop at the time. Ball could only mutter: "I was afraid." Moreover, Hewart pointed out that the victim had been carefully sewn into a tarpaulin sack with a system of stitching that was peculiar to the method used by Ball.

The jury returned a Guilty verdict, and Ball, as he was being dragged away by four warders, cried out: "I am innocent! Innocent!" He was sentenced to death and his dull-minded accomplice Eltoft was given a four-year prison sentence. When realizing that there would be no appeals or commutations, Ball confessed the murder of Christine Bradfield to the Bishop of Liverpool only hours before he was hanged at Walton Prison on Feb. 26, 1914. See: **Crippen, Dr. Hawley Harvey.**

Ball, Joseph (Joe), 1894-1938, U.S. Joseph Ball was a serial killer who murdered perhaps as many as twenty-five women. All of his victims were young and beautiful. Though Ball took their possessions and whatever money they had when he murdered his victims, his motive was love. He killed one woman after another, including his second and third wives, so that he would be able to devote his time to his next paramour. To Joe Ball, these murders were not without a utilitarian end; he chopped up his victims and fed them piecemeal to the five pet alligators he kept in a foul-smelling pool behind his inappropriately named gin mill, The Sociable Inn, located near Elmendorf, Texas. This Lone Star native was educated at the University of Texas but he found legitimate pursuits uninteresting and, at the dawn of Prohibition in 1920, he became a bootlegger, amassing a considerable fortune.

The young bootlegger worked hard at his illegal profession which confused his friends who knew that his wealthy family had offered Ball any number of lucrative positions in its vast holdings in cattle and commerce. He had turned all this down to go his own way. He bought a house in Elmendorf and operated out of here during the 1920s, selling flavored alcohol at $5 a gallon. Though the house was modern, Ball lived without the benefit of a cleaning lady, and he was always in an unkempt condition.

He padded about in a dirty bathrobe when clients called to buy liquor and he spent most of his time in bed with beautiful young women, a bottle of booze, and a plate of fried chicken on the bed table at all times. His only greeting to customers was: "Got the cash?" When the client produced the necessary money, Ball whistled to his black handyman to bring forth the liquor shipment. Often as not the uncaring Ball returned to his bed and the arms of his lover, continuing his lovemaking, oblivious to the gaze of his caller.

Ball was a large, big-boned man, well over six feet, who was muscular but overweight, thanks to his ravenous eating habits. He was expert with a revolver and carried one with him at all times, on occasions whipping out this weapon and firing a practice shot or two to impress witnesses with his marksmanship. In the late 1920s, Ball opened his crudely appointed saloon, The Sociable Club, about fifty feet back from U.S. Highway 181. He developed a liking for alligators and bought five, placing them in a large cement pool behind his club. He would, after a night of drinking, take his best customers outside and amuse them by throwing large chunks of meat into the pool and hoot and holler as the roaring beasts jawed the food, their thrashing tails violently churning the murky water.

For the more sadistic of his friends, Ball arranged his own little horror shows. He kept stray dogs and cats in a pen near the pool and he would take these poor creatures out of the pen and hold them over the pool, teasing the always hungry reptiles and terrifying the animals. Tiring of the game, Ball would throw the strays into the pool where they would be torn apart by the alligators. As he brutalized these animals, he himself became more and more brutal. He shouted instead of talked and threatened anyone who disagreed with him. Yet Ball managed to keep employed a steady stream of beautiful barmaids, radiant young ladies he reportedly paid extremely well and all of whom, it was said, became his mistresses. These women came and went with alacrity which aroused the suspicions of a local constable and neighbor of Ball's, especially when such favorites as Hazel Brown and Minnie Mae Gotthardt disappeared.

When asked by the constable why the girls had suddenly vanished, Ball exploded and pulled his revolver, shoving this into the constable's face and threatening to kill him if he went on probing into his affairs. The constable, afraid for his life, did not report the incident. This was not the case with Texas Ranger Lee Miller. When relatives asked police to investigate the disappearance of Hazel Brown in the fall of 1938, Miller and several deputies went to Ball's roadhouse. They entered the Sociable Inn on Sept. 24, 1938. Ball greeted them affably and then asked if they wanted some beers. "No, Joe, we're here to have you answer some questions about Hazel Brown."

The saloon keeper shrugged and then walked behind the bar. "Then, I'll pour one for myself." Instead of pouring a beer, Ball went to the cash register and opened the bottom drawer. He pulled out a revolver and the officers, thinking he was about to fire at them, pulled out their own guns and aimed these at Ball. The saloon owner gave them a crooked grin, then put the revolver to his temple and squeezed the trigger, blowing off the top of his head. Later, the deputies found hunks of human flesh floating in a water barrel behind the house, and in the pool where the alligators swirled, there was a trace of blood. Clifford Wheeler, the terrified handyman who worked for Ball, admitted that his employer had murdered many young women and two of his own wives, that he had witnessed Ball shoot one of his wives and his subsequent chopping up of her body and the feeding of her remains to his alligators. Wheeler said he did not dare say a word to authorities about Ball since his employer said he would kill him. He was given a four-year prison sentence as an accessory to murder.

No clear number of Ball's victims was ever recorded but it was estimated that Joe Ball killed at least twenty women. Most of these young women had been impregnated by the killer and he murdered and dismembered them when they began to demand that he marry them. He did marry two of his victims, but he tired of these ladies and dispatched them to the alligator pool. "Joe, he weren't no marrying man," Wheeler told police.

Baniszewski, Gertrude Wright, 1929-   , U.S. A native of Indianapolis, Ind., Gertrude Baniszewski lived with her three children Stephanie, Paula, and Johnny, surviving on a meager income. To make ends meet Baniszewski took in children for the summer to earn extra money. In 1965, Baniszewski agreed to board Sylvia Likens, sixteen, and her sister Jennie, fifteen. Jennie Likens would be no problem, the housewife believed since she was crippled and could get about very little. The parents of the two sisters worked in a circus and paid Baniszewski $20 a week to take care of their children. During the first week of their stay, the two girls were fed little, receiving a few slices of toast in the morning and no lunch.

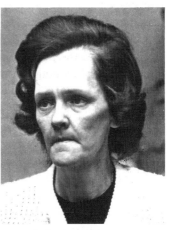

Gertrude Baniszewski

A bowl of soup was their only supper. At the end of the first week, Baniszewski dragged both girls to an upstairs room of the house and mercilessly beat them, screaming that she was boarding them "for nothin'!"

The hardened housewife, though receiving weekly payments from the Likens' parents, resented having the two girls in her home and cursed them whenever they were in her presence. A deep-seated streak of sadism began to manifest itself whenever she was near them; she struck out at them, hitting them so hard that her hands stung from the impact, she later admitted. She reserved her most sadistic treatment for the older girl, Sylvia, whom she beat regularly and then took to paddling on the bare buttocks with a board that left scars. Baniszewski then began encouraging neighborhood children and her own offspring to beat the poor girl, who begged them to stop without relief. The housewife then ordered the other children to put out burning cigarettes on the girl's arms and hands. One of Baniszewski's children, Paula, whipped into a frenzy of hatred by her mother, beat Sylvia so hard that she broke her hand which had to be put into a cast. The Baniszewski girl then used the cast to beat Sylvia on the head.

Baniszewski then decided that Sylvia Likens was a whore and tied her up in the basement, releasing her only to beat her and then force her to dance naked in front of other children. Directing a dim-witted neighborhood boy, Ricky Hobbs, needles were heated and used to brand the girl's stomach with the words: "I am a prostitute and proud of it." This horrible torture completed, Baniszewski then released the full fiendish fury of her nature, beating the girl, slamming her head against the basement wall with such force that Sylvia Likens died from the blow. The housewife panicked and called police, telling them that Sylvia had run off with a gang of boys, then returned and was mutilated and killed by them; she had found the poor girl in her basement. Her young children repeated this story to investigating officer Melvin Dixon. As Dixon was about to leave, Jennie Likens hobbled forward and whispered to him: "Get me out of here and I'll tell you the whole story."

The officer took the girl away and quickly learned the truth about the vicious Gertrude Baniszewski. She was charged with murder and convicted, given a life sentence. Baniszewski won a new trial on appeal but was again convicted and sent back to prison to serve out a life term. In all of the many interviews conducted with this murdering sadist, the housewife has but one excuse for her slaying of a defenseless girl left in her care: "I had to teach her a lesson."

Bankston, Clinton, Jr. (AKA: **Junebug**), 1971- , U.S. When it happened, everyone who knew him expressed the greatest surprise. "This all did shock me. He didn't seem the type," said Agnes Freeman, a neighbor in the Nellie B. Apartments of Athens, Ga., northeast of Atlanta. Clinton Bankston lived with his mother in this deteriorating section of Athens, an area of high unemployment and gang activity. Bankston was a high-school dropout who spent most of his time riveted to his television. His perceptions of the world were shaped by the images of violence on prime-time television.

On Aug. 15, 1987, Bankston committed a real-life crime so horrible and senseless that its barbarity eclipsed anything law enforcement officers of this small Georgia city had ever encountered.

Robbery was foremost in Bankston's mind when he entered the home of Sally Nathanson in the fashionable Carr's Hill section of Athens. Nathanson and her visiting sister, Ann Orr Morris, who lived in an adjacent house, were found dead. Her 22-year-old adopted daughter, Helen Nathanson, was later found lying dead in one of the bedrooms by police investigators. All three had been savagely butchered with a hatchet.

The mutilated bodies could be positively identified only through the efforts of the state crime lab in Atlanta. Athens Police Chief Everett Price conducted a thorough investigation and was able to link the murders of the three women to a similar crime committed against two elderly people the previous April. Items belonging to the earlier murder victims, Glenn and Rachel Sutton, had been found in the Bankston apartment. Bankston was arrested on Sunday morning near his grandmother's house on Moreland Avenue.

District Attorney Harry Gordon urged the courts to try the 16-year-old Bankston as an adult for the murders of five people. The Supreme Court of Georgia, however, ruled that underage offenders convicted of murder could not receive the death penalty. Bankston pleaded guilty, citing insanity as his defense. On his seventeenth birthday, the quiet boy who liked to ride around the neighborhood on his bicycle received five consecutive life sentences.

Bannon, Charles, 1909-31, U.S. In 1931, Bannon became only the eighth white man to be lynched in North Dakota following his slaying of a rural family of six. Bannon worked as a hired hand on the farm of A.E. Haven near Shafer, N.D. In February 1930, Bannon slaughtered the six-member Haven family and buried their bodies in the barn. He continued to live on the farm for nine months during which time the murdered family was not missed. Bannon was apprehended in November when he attempted to sell some of the Haven livestock at a local market. He was questioned in the family's disappearance and, after the bodies were found, charged with their murders. Bannon was lynched in February 1931.

Barber, Susan, prom. 1981, Brit. Barber was an Essex housewife engaged in a torrid love affair with her husband's best friend in May 1981. Her lover's name was Richard Collins, and the tryst had gone on for nearly eight months before the cuckolded husband came home unexpectedly one day to find them both in his bed. Michael Barber reacted violently. He beat his wife and threw Collins out of the house. But this did not cool his wife's ardor.

The next day Susan slipped a deadly weed poison known as Gramoxone into his steak and kidney pie. In small doses, Gramoxone is deadly to humans. Death is brought on by fibrosis of the lungs, which makes breathing all but impossible.

Michael Barber was admitted to Hammersmith Hospital in London where he was diagnosed as suffering from pneumonia and kidney failure. Upon further examination doctors concluded that Barber was afflicted with Goodpasture's Syndrome, a rare nervous disorder. After he died, a pathologist named David Evans conducted the postmortem. He was not convinced that the cause of death was natural. Blood samples were taken and sent over to the National Poisons Unit and to the company which had manufactured the weed killer. A trace of paraquat, a toxic herbicide, was found in each instance. Based on this chemical analysis, Mrs. Barber and Richard Collins were arrested in April 1982 and charged with murder. Collins received two years' imprisonment, and Susan Barber, who by this time was no longer interested in her former boyfriend, received a life sentence.

Bardlett, William, 1951-   , U.S. Without an apparent reason a 25-year-old elevator repair man named William Bardlett borrowed his sister's .22-caliber pistol and killed three family members on Nov. 25, 1976. The Thanksgiving Day tragedy on Chicago's West Side was a grim reminder of the random violence plaguing big city ghettos.

In this case Bardlett murdered two nephews, 9-year-old Dwayne, and 2-year-old Cecil Jr., and his brother-in-law Cecil White, Sr. White and the two boys had gone to the Bardlett home to share a Thanksgiving dinner, believing that William was at work. Bardlett burst into the Harding Avenue apartment and shot White and his son before fleeing. Police later found the revolver underneath the body of the 2-year-old and spent shell casings strewn around the apartment. Officers from the Shakespeare Avenue Police District arrested the suspect at his sister's residence when he stumbled in without warning during a routine interrogation.

Bardlett was brought before Judge William Cousins on Nov. 28, 1978, and charged with murder. He was declared unfit for trial, and the case continued. He appeared before Cousins again on May 29, 1979, and was remanded to the Department of Mental Health for a fitness hearing. On Nov. 6, Cousins ruled him Not Guilty by reason of insanity in a bench trial. However, in a separate ruling handed down on Dec. 17, the court found the defendant not in need of hospital treatment but decided that he should visit the Isaac Ray Center for periodic mental health checkups. William Bardlett was back on the streets.

Barlow, Kenneth, 1919-   , Brit. Elizabeth Barlow was pronounced dead in her bathroom on May 3, 1957, by a doctor called to her home at Thornbury Crescent, Bradford. He had been summoned by Kenneth Barlow, Elizabeth's husband, who told the physician that he discovered his wife in the bathtub, her head beneath the water. He had tried artificial respiration, he said, but it did no good. At first authorities believed that the dead woman, known to be ill and in a weakened condition, had suffered an accidental death, but the doctor who first examined the body took note that the dead woman's eyes were dilated. Also, at a later postmortem, several injection marks on the buttocks of the corpse were detected. Officials found hypodermic syringes in the Barlow residence, but this was not considered unusual since Barlow was a male nurse.

Police were suspicious from the beginning, noting that the pajamas Barlow had been wearing when the doctor arrived were not wet, in spite of his claim of seizing the dripping body and giving it artificial respiration. Also, detectives calculated, a drowning person would make some sort

Barlow and wife Elizabeth.

of splashing movement that would soak the floor about the bathtub, but the floor was dry when the doctor first arrived. Barlow was charged with murdering his wife, but he insisted that he loved her, saying that he did not have a reason in the world to kill her. (It was later learned that Barlow's first wife had died less than two years earlier at the young age of thirty-three, but her death had been attributed to natural causes; this death was never revealed in Barlow's trial.)

At Barlow's trial before Justice Diplock at the Leeds Assizes, the most damning statements came from Harry Stork, who had worked with Barlow two years earlier. He recalled how Barlow had boasted of discovering the perfect murder weapon, an injection of insulin which would quickly be dissolved in the bloodstream and be undetectable. Moreover, authorities at St. Luke's Hospital in Huddersfield where Barlow worked, reported that three ampoules of ergotamine had been discovered missing from the medical supplies. Involved statements from medical authorities then argued whether or not insulin was injected into the dead woman, although some traces were found in the body, according to one report. The defense, headed by Bernard Gillis, countered that Elizabeth Barlow, realizing that she was drowning, and in a state of utter panic, released a massive discharge of insulin into her own bloodstream. The prosecution made short work of this preposterous and obviously desperate claim by quickly proving that, for the dead woman to have done so, her pancreas would have had to produce in seconds more than 15,000 units, a physical impossibility.

It was Barlow's own darkly jocular talk with patients and nurses about the perfect murder that eventually brought him down. In addition to Stork, a nurse named Waterhouse at East Riding General Hospital, told the court how Barlow explained that insulin could kill a person without a trace. Barlow had also told a patient, Arthur Evans, then at Northfield Sanitorium in Driffield, Yorkshire, where Barlow was then working, that he could inject insulin into someone and that no one would ever know that this was the cause of death since it could not be traced. The jury stayed out for only a short while before returning to find Barlow Guilty. He was sent to prison for life.

Bartlett, Helen, prom. 1959, U.S. After her first husband died in 1940, Helen met Alfred Babin. They were married during the war and lived together until his death in 1956. Helen Babin discovered his body. She notified the police, explaining that she had found him in his bath lying face down. During the day, she said, Alfred had been drinking heavily. The coroner reported that Mrs. Babin's story was indeed true because a large quantity of whiskey had been found in his stomach. Husband number two left behind a $69,000 insurance policy.

During her short period of grief, Babin met 69-year-old Wright Bartlett, a veteran with an assured income of disability payments, who was recuperating from a long illness at the Veterans Hospital. They were married in 1959, and, at his wife's suggestion, Bartlett agreed to go on a long honeymoon to Texas and Florida. By this time insurance investigators became suspicious of Helen's motives—she had recently insured her husband's life in excess of $110,000.

Several months later the newlyweds returned to Buffalo, where Bartlett complained of poor health. He explained that his wife had fed him sandwiches instead of the hot meals to which he had been accustomed. By this time police had entered the case. Under heavy questioning Helen Bartlett admitted to murdering her second husband, Babin, by holding his head under water in the bathtub.

Battice, Earl Leo, 1903-   , U.S. A four-masted schooner named the *Kingsway* set sail from Perth Amboy, N.J., in 1926, bound for the Gold Coast of Africa where the skipper was to deliver a load of lumber. The *Kingsway*, a rusting, barnacle-infested hulk, was manned by a sullen, suspicious-looking crew and a captain named Lawry.

The ship dropped anchor in Puerto Rico. Lawry went ashore and recruited 23-year-old Earl Battice who signed on as a cook. Battice insisted on taking his wife Lucia on the long voyage, but Lawry said no, reasoning that one woman among a crew of men would cause trouble. Battice refused to compromise and at length the captain, with trepidation, agreed to hire them both.

What Lawry did not realize was that his cook never intended to bring his wife aboard. It was his mistress Emilia Zamot, a poor Creole girl from the streets of San Juan that he wanted to take with him. The jealous wife got wind of this scheme, however, and drove Zamot from the ship.

The *Kingsway* slipped out of the harbor of San Juan on Dec. 15. Battice proved to be an excellent cook and his wife a pleasing addition to the crew. But after several weeks, Lucia became enamored with the burly German engineer Waldemar Karl Badke, whom everyone feared. They began conducting an affair, flagrantly, and without regard for the cuckolded cook.

The situation became intolerable for Battice, but there was little he could do. His fellow crewmen held him in low regard, and the captain was powerless to intervene, for Badke was feared and respected, and any attempt to thwart him might end in mutiny. Both captain and cook were effectively emasculated by the time the ship approached Monrovia.

Battice finally took matters into his own hands. On Feb.

4, 1927, he seized a razor and assaulted his wife in the storeroom where she was with Badke. It was a surprising gesture from one as docile and timid as Battice. The other crew members now felt some grudging respect for their cook, who was placed in irons by Captain Lawry. Lucia lingered on for seven days before succumbing to her wounds, but during that time, she confided to the captain that Battice had planned her murder in Puerto Rico. When she finally died, her body was dropped over the side of the ship.

Lawry completed his business in Monrovia and headed back to the U.S. amidst growing fears among the crewmen that Battice had placed a deadly curse over them all. Four men became violently ill from the food prepared by the new cook, an African tribesman named Codgo.

Lawry removed Battice's leg irons and returned him to the kitchen. The *Kingsway* reached the coast of the U.S. in August 1927. The year-long voyage, filled with so many perils, had at last ended and Battice was arrested and tried for second-degree murder. He received a ten-year sentence at the Federal Penitentiary in Atlanta.

Bayly, William Alfred, 1906-34, N. Zea. Ever since William Bayly's father sold his farm in Ruawaro, N. Zea., to Samuel Pender Lakey, there had been bad feelings between the two. Then Bayly bought property next to the Lakey dairy farm and moved in. At first their petty disputes involved land boundaries and sheep-grazing rights, but over the years the problems took on more serious overtones. "You won't see the next season out, Lakey!" Bayly had threatened on one occasion.

The threat was not an idle one. On Oct. 16, 1933, Mrs. Christobel Lakey was found floating face-down in a duck pond. Her husband had disappeared, and Bayly volunteered a possible solution to the police. He said that the couple had been quarreling a lot lately, and that Samuel had probably murdered his wife and then run away. The police were suspicious. They searched William Bayly's property and uncovered evidence of a body. Bone fragments were scattered piecemeal on the farm. They also found Lakey's watch and cigarette lighter. Blood in Bayly's tool shed was clear evidence to investigating police officers of recent foul play.

Despite his denials, Bayly was found Guilty of murder after a month-long trial in Auckland. He was executed at the Mount Eden jail on July 30, 1934, just a few days after his twenty-eighth birthday.

Bean, Harold Walter, 1939- , U.S. Describing his scheme to get rid of a wealthy elderly widow, Harold Walter Bean told a cohort, "We've added another round to our bag of tricks...Murder."

Dorothy Polulach, an 81-year-old widow, lived quietly as a recluse in her expensive South West Side Chicago home, which was barricaded with locks and elaborate security systems to protect her costly antiques and jewelry. One afternoon in mid-February 1981, a man in priest's garb stopped to talk with her as she shoveled snow off her front walk, suggesting that a lady her age should have help, and offering to bring someone to assist her soon. On Feb. 17 the priest returned with a companion. Recognizing the one man, Polulach let them in. Bean, disguised as a priest, began to beat the elderly woman, who fought back. His accomplice, Robert Byron, also called "Spook," quickly filled his briefcase with jewelry and ransacked the house for other valuables, for the killing was intended to look like a robbery. Bean knocked Polulach down, then handcuffed her and dragged her upstairs, shackling her ankles and breaking her glasses before putting a .38-caliber pistol to her head and shooting her twice. Her body was discovered three days later by Phyllis Mahl and her husband. Mahl called Polulach's stepdaughter, Ann Polulach Walters, in Fort Lauderdale, Fla., to tell her of her stepmother's death. Though Walters appeared shocked, actually she had hired Bean to murder Polulach as she would inherit as much as $750,000 and the Polulach home when her father's second wife died.

Detectives Tom Ptak and Mike Duffin took over the case. Mahl told them that Walters was exhibiting strange behavior, like hiding pastries at the funeral services and finding mysterious messages in the wake register. Then a man named Jimmy Steele was heard to brag in a Cicero tavern about the slaying, saying the victim had been shot twice in the head—information only the killer could know. Ptak and Duffin questioned Steele, learning that he was the stepson of Harold Bean. Steele then confessed that he had rented the priest's outfit for Bean and had heard him talking to an attorney about Walter's potential inheritance. Bean, a master of disguise and a criminal since he was sixteen, had once hidden from the FBI for six years. With these leads, the detectives went to visit Walters, now enmeshed in witchcraft rituals to exorcise her murdered stepmother's spirit, and asked her to look at some mug shots, including one of Bean.

Walters' response was, "You know the whole thing, don't you?" She and her husband, Wayne Walters, confessed and were charged with murder and conspiracy on Apr. 5, 1981. Bean was arrested in a remote area of the Palos Hills Forest Preserve on Apr. 25, and Byron soon after, charged with helping Bean break into the Polulach home. Robert Danny Egan, who drove the getaway car, testified against

Byron and Bean and received a seven-year prison term for his part in the crime. In October 1981 Bean and Byron were convicted of murder and sentenced by Judge James M. Bailey to die in the electric chair. Walters pleaded guilty to plotting the murder and was sentenced to 25 years in prison. Wayne Walters received a seven-year prison sentence for conspiracy.

Beard, Arthur, prom. 1919, Brit. A notable criminal trial involved night watchman Arthur Beard, who raped and strangled 13-year-old Ivy Lydia Wood on July 25, 1919, in Hyde, Cheshire.

On Oct. 6, 1919, Justice Clement Meagher Bailhache sentenced Beard to death. An appeal was immediately filed, and the verdict in the first trial was overturned on the grounds that Beard was incapable of forming the intention to murder because of his severe state of drunkenness at the time of the assault. "Malice aforethought" was therefore absent, and the court ordered the charge reduced to manslaughter.

The Crown was displeased with the verdict, and Lord Hewart and Sir Charles Matthews brought the matter before the House of Lords. Lord Frederick Edwin Birkenhead, Lord Haldane, and Lord Reading reversed the judgment on Mar. 5, 1920. The judges argued that Beard had not been too drunk to rape the child. Lord Birkenhead re-established the original charge of murder but ruled that Beard could not be executed. The prisoner began serving a life sentence.

Beattie, Henry Clay, 1884-1911, U.S. In 1911, the city of Richmond, Va., was rocked with news of a bloody slaying five miles outside the city. Henry Clay Beattie, on the night of July 18, arrived at the home of Thomas E. Owen, which was off the Midlothian turnpike. Breathlessly, he pointed to his open auto. The Owens moved cautiously to the car. In the back seat they saw Mrs. Louise Beattie. The top of her head had been blown off.

Beattie told police that he and his wife had been stopped by a tall highwayman who waved a gun in their faces. The bearded man had shouted at them: "You had better run over me...You have got all the road!" or, at least, that's what Beattie claimed the man said. Beattie tried to drive around the tall highwayman, he said, but the man raised his weapon and fired just as the car passed him. Mrs. Beattie was killed instantly by the blast and the killer fled, howling through the nearby woods. Or had he been laughing? Beattie could not remember, he told police. The gun?

Beattie remembered stopping the car, running after the man, and wresting the weapon from him before the murderer escaped. He could not recall where he had thrown the gun.

Mrs. Beattie was buried before the coroner's jury could make up its mind about her demise. That was decided by Detective L.L. Scherer, who found the murder weapon alongside the C&O Railroad tracks. Tracing its sale, Scherer discovered that a Paul Beattie had purchased the gun for H.C. Beattie. The husband was quickly arrested and tried for the murder of his wife.

Beattie emphatically denied his guilt, although a staggering case had been built against him. Even after he was sentenced to die in the electric chair, the convicted man refused to admit to the slaying. The 27-year-old was led into the death room on Nov. 24, 1911, still mumbling about the tall, bewhiskered highwayman who had murdered his wife. (It was eventually learned that Beattie had been a student of the Old West and that he had described a photo of Jesse James which was kept in his album of gunslingers.)

Not until he was executed was the truth learned from Beattie himself. His religious advisors, the reverends J.J. Fix and Benjamin Dennis, provided newsmen with Beattie's handwritten confession which they had witnessed the day before his electrocution. It read:

"I, Henry Clay Beattie, Jr., desirous of standing right before God and man, do on this, the 23rd day of November, 1911, confess my guilt of the crime charged against me. Much that was published concerning the details was not true, but the awful fact, without the harrowing circumstances, remains. For this action I am truly sorry, and believing that I am at peace with God and am soon to pass into His presence, this statement is made."

Beck, Martha Julie (or **Jule**), 1921-51, and **Fernandez, Raymond Martinez** (AKA: **Charles Martin**), 1914-51, (AKA: **The Lonely Hearts Killers**), U.S. Fernandez, born in Hawaii of Spanish parents, was an adventurous youth who reportedly served with British Intelligence during WWII, winning commendations. He was wounded in the head in 1945, an injury that altered his personality from sanguine to phlegmatic, according to one report, and sent him on a criminal career in which he bilked well-to-do widows out of their savings after proposing marriage. He was tall and thin, covering his almost-bald head with a cheap black wig. But the love-desperate women who fell for his pedestrian pitch of woo, thought of him as an irresistible Latin lover. In the words of one newsman: "He was a rather seedy Charles Boyer." Fernandez found his victims in the then-popular lonely hearts clubs or through the lonely hearts columns of newspapers. He even married several women, having one family in Spain, another in the U.S., and according to some reports others still in Mexico and Canada.

One of the lovelorn ads Fernandez answered turned out to have been placed by Mrs. Martha Beck, a registered nurse who ran a home for crippled children in Pensacola, Fla. When the sleazy Lothario arrived on Mrs. Beck's front door in 1947, he was taken aback by the obese woman standing before him. She welcomed him with open arms and Fernandez the con man, for some inexplicable reason, fell in love with the unattractive Martha. Mrs. Beck, who had been divorced since 1944, lavished attention on Fernandez who confessed his swindling ways to her. To his surprise, she not only approved of his crooked pursuits but asked to be part of his widow-bilking schemes. The couple traveled northward, stopping in cities along the way to answer lonely hearts advertisements and mulct the lovesick widows.

Lonely hearts killers Martha Beck and Raymond Fernandez joke with guard.

Their usual procedure was for Fernandez to woo and win the lovelorn lady and, during the course of a brief courtship, introduce Beck as his sister. Then, following the wedding, Beck would move in with the newlyweds, and the looting of savings and jewelry quickly ensued. Most of the women, more than 100 of them, were in their late fifties or sixties, but Beck could not bear to be in the same house with Fernandez and a new wife, knowing he was making love to another woman. Her jealousy grew whenever the victim was young and attractive, such was the case with Mrs. Delphine Dowling of Grand Rapids, Mich. Mrs. Dowling, twenty-eight, had a 2-year-old daughter, Rainelle, and was apprehensive of Fernandez, allowing him and his "sister" to move into her home but delaying the nuptials with her newly found Latin lover until she was convinced her spouse-

to-be was sincere. Beck found it impossible to sleep in the next room while her own man was on the other side of the wall with a younger, more attractive woman. They would not wait for the wedding ceremonies, Beck told the docile Fernandez. Mrs. Dowling and her daughter had to go. Both disappeared in January 1949.

Neighbors, noticing the absence of Mrs. Dowling and her daughter, called police and when officers arrived at the Dowling residence, Beck and Fernandez calmly invited them inside, telling them they had no idea where Mrs. Dowling and her child had gone. Police thought the pair looked suspicious and insisted that the home be searched. Beck shrugged and Fernandez waved them into the parlor. Investigators found a fresh patch of cement on the floor of the basement. "It's the size of a grave," said one officer and they soon unearthed the bodies of mother and child. The Lonely Hearts Killers, as Beck and Fernandez were quickly dubbed by the press, collapsed immediately, freely admitting the murders and then bragging that there were as many as seventeen other victims they had killed. Beck, glorying in her publicity, explained that she dosed Mrs. Dowling with sleeping pills, but the young woman was strong enough to resist the drugs and Fernandez shot her in the head. They originally did not plan to murder the little girl. When she cried for her mother, Martha Beck said, as if displaying her humanity, they bought her a dog. But the child continued to whine so Martha dragged her into the bathroom, filled the tub, and held the girl beneath the water until she drowned.

Fernandez and Beck, of course, were well aware of the fact that the state of Michigan had no death penalty and undoubtedly reasoned that they would be imprisoned and later be paroled, in spite of their heinous crimes. (This was the same tactic earlier employed by Fred R. "Killer" Burke, one of the machine gunners at the 1929 St. Valentine's Day Massacre.) With that comforting thought in mind, the pair bragged about their other murders. "I'm no average killer," Fernandez boasted. "I only got five hundred off the Dowling woman," he said disappointedly, "but take Mrs. Jane Thompson, I took six thousand off of her." He explained how he married Thompson and took her to Spain where he murdered her, poisoning her with digitalis. He then returned to the U.S. to explain that he and his poor wife had been in a train wreck and she had been killed. The Thompson family did not bother to check if there had been such a wreck; they merely took his word for it. Fernandez was so convincing a liar that he moved in with Thompson's mother, Mrs. Wilson, wooed and bilked her and then murdered her, too.

Throughout the long confession, Beck was at Fernandez' side, chuckling perversely as he droned his litany of murder. She found it all too amusing but was solicitous of her lover.

When he began to sweat, he removed his cheap wig. Beck reached over to pat his bald pate dry with her handkerchief, thickly scented with cheap perfume. Then she urged him to continue, as if she were a child begging for a tale to be completed. Fernandez recalled a Mrs. Myrtle Young. He took her to Chicago in 1948 on their honeymoon. He laughed and said: "Poor woman, she died of over-exertion." Beck could no longer allow Fernandez to hog the limelight. She blurted out her own confessions rapidly, her heavy jowels jiggling as she rattled off murder after murder. One she vividly recalled—there were so many that taxed her memory—involved Mrs. Janet Fay of Manhattan. She and Fernandez had already taken the 66-year-old woman's last cent, but she was murdered anyway, only because Beck's jealousy exploded when the old woman cried out for Fernandez as the couple was leaving Fay's apartment.

Beck was incensed at Fay's display of affection for her man, and she grabbed a hammer and smashed it down on Fay's head, crushing her skull. Then Beck said in her best child's voice: "I turned to Raymond and said, 'look what I've done,' and then he strangled her with a scarf." Beck explained that although she had already murdered Fay, Fernandez, out of his deep love for Martha, insisted on taking part in the killing by strangling the lifeless corpse. Both killers were amazed when the state of Michigan abruptly allowed them to be extradited to New York to stand trial for their self-admitted slaying of Mrs. Fay—New York still had the death penalty. Both defendants were tried before Judge Ferdinand Pecora, pleading not guilty by reason of insanity. Psychiatrists examining both of them reported them sane and the trial went ahead. On one occasion, when Beck was being brought into court, she broke away from her female guards and lifted the startled Fernandez out of his chair, kissing him on the mouth and neck and cheeks. She had to be pried loose, screaming: "I love him! I do love him and I always will!"

A jury quickly convicted the pair and Judge Pecora sentenced them to death, their execution to be held on Aug. 22, 1949, at Sing Sing. While awaiting the electric chair, the couple exhanged love letters, sent between the male and female cellblocks. When Beck heard that Fernandez was regaling his fellow prisoners in death row with her eccentric behavior, she exploded, sending him the following message:

You are a double-crossing, two-timing skunk. I learn now that you have been doing quite a bit of talking to everyone. It's nice to learn what a terrible, murderous person I am, while you are such a misunderstood, white-haired boy, caught in the clutches of a female vampire. It is also nice to know that all the love letters you wrote 'from the heart' were written with a hand shaking with laughter at me for being such a

gullible fool as to believe them. Don't waste your time or energy trying to hide from view in church from now on, for I won't even look your way—the halo over your righteous head might blind me. May God have mercy on your soul.

M.J. Beck

Through appeals filed by their lawyers, Beck and Fernandez managed to postpone their date with the electric chair until Mar. 8, 1951. Fernandez ordered a large meal but, with his death only a few hours away, he could not eat it. He did smoke a long Havana cigar down to a small stub. Then he handed a note to one of the guards, saying that these words would be his last utterances on earth. The note, later widely published, read:

People want to know whether I still love Martha. But of course I do. I want to shout it out. I love Martha. What do the public know about love?

Martha Beck, who was tired of being portrayed as a flabby, fat woman, told a female guard that she would show the world what kind of woman she was; she would resist ordering a feast for her last meal. That said, she ordered fried chicken and fried potatoes and a salad—a double order of each. She announced that she still loved Raymond Fernandez. There existed at Sing Sing a tradition that when two persons were to be executed, the weakest was to be sent to the chair first. This was Fernandez. He was half-carried to the electric chair by several guards and was in a state of nervous collapse when the switch was thrown. Martha Beck followed, walking on her own, confident, smiling as she almost threw her great bulk into the chair.

Becker, Charles, 1870-1915, U.S. The image of the crooked cop without conscience, compassion, or remorse for his ruthless acts was devastatingly summed up in the character of Charles Becker, a lieutenant of the New York Police Department. Becker made a fortune by protecting New York City gamblers until he decided one of these sharpers should be killed, and he ordered the murder of Herman Rosenthal. This blatant slaying by hired killers under Becker's command eventually led Becker to the electric chair, but long before that, a decade before, Becker ruled the gambling empire of New York City. His word was law—to break *his* law was to face unendurable punishment, ruination, and early death. Becker, the corrupt cop, came into being not at his source environment, but in the heart of New York City, or, to be exact, in its Tenderloin, the most exciting, dramatic and vice-ridden area of America at the time. This land of payoff and kickback was far from the green, comfortable hills where Charles Becker was born on July 26, 1870. The sixth child of ten, Becker was born in Callicoon Center, N.Y., a hamlet in the foothills of the Catskills in Sullivan County. He was a large boy and did not shirk fights. At home he was truculent and slow to obey his parents. At school he was even slower to complete assignments. Yet his honesty was never questioned and he excelled in athletics and manual labor. By the time he was eighteen, he had developed a tall, powerful body with broad shoulders, massive arms, and enormous hands that, when doubled into fists, were like the flat sides of two stonemason hammers.

At this time Becker bid farewell to his family and rural life, and traveled to New York City to see a German baker who was a friend of his father's. The baker gave him a job and a room above the bakery, which was in the German section of the city in the old Seventh Ward. To the south was the Bowery and to the north was the wealth of Manhattan which beckoned like a beacon fire to the ambitious Becker. After a brief affair with the baker's daughter, which found Becker confronting the baker and being ordered from his establishment, the youth, then nineteen, went to work as a waiter at The Atlantic Gardens, a sprawling beer garden which had once been the pride of the German community, where free music and excellent nickel beer was offered to a generally middle-class patronage. With the ending of the Civil War, this great spa had declined so that by 1889, when Becker went to work there, the place was populated at night by gamblers, thugs from the Bowery, and prostitutes plying their trade. The well-built, no-nonsense Becker found himself knocking the heads of thugs who created disturbances. He soon built a reputation as a man who could best almost any plug-ugly with a mind to starting trouble.

The job of bouncer was offered to Becker, and the 21-year-old accepted, working in another beer garden. Here he became known as a brutal overseer no thug would think to anger. Even the most fierce of the early day New York gangsters such as Edward "Monk" Eastman gave Becker a wide berth. Eastman not only grew to respect the quick-fisted Becker but he befriended him, taking him to his political sponsor, Timothy "Big Tim" Sullivan, the powerful head of Tammany for the entire East Side of Manhattan. Sullivan used Eastman and his fearsome gang as strike-breakers and political strong-arm thugs who made sure that every election was a Tammany triumph. Tammany also dictated the politics for the entire city at that time and Sullivan lived like a czar, making appointments to political and police posts at will and whim. Sullivan sized up Becker as someone above the status of an ordinary thug, a young

man with intelligence and street savvy—one who not only would be loyal to Tammany but to Sullivan himself. The police force, Sullivan concluded, was the right spot for Charles Becker. In 1893 Becker paid a $250 fee to Tammany for his appointment to the police force. This was customary and was publicly known and excused, at least by the political sachems who ran things, as a way of assuring the fact that men known to the organization, who were screened as good candidates by Tammany and were not strangers with criminal records, were thus brought onto the force. The screening process cost Tammany money and the applicant was merely paying back the organization's investment. Such money was no small investment. At the time, $250 was one-third the yearly pay of an average cop on the NYPD. The force at that time had more than 5,000 men on the streets, all of them white and most of them, like Becker, Catholic.

The type of police officer the NYPD then hired and kept on the force was not very much different than the type of thug who worked for Monk Eastman, except that they wore uniforms and never openly committed theft. Patrolmen were burly, big men who used their long nightsticks to club anyone who got in their way, either innocent citizen or hooligan. Even to ask a question of the beat cop in those days was to risk being poked in the chest with his stick and hustled down the street for bothering an officer of the law. The man who established and maintained this hardboiled attitude was Inspector Alexander "Clubber" Williams, who was infamous for his brutality and ruthless manner. It was the grafting Williams who gave the wide-open vice district its name. He had been serving in a West Side precinct in the 1870s and when he was transferred to the choice area, he remarked to a newsman: "I've been living on chuck steak for a long time. Now I'm gonna get me some of the tenderloin." Williams supervised an area that stretched approximately between Twenty-third and Forty-fourth streets and between Third and Seventh avenues, this being the old Twenty-ninth Precinct. Here could be found the best hotels, the finest theaters and restaurants, as well as hundreds of posh gambling dens, bordellos, and vice dens of all sorts, a plum for grafting policemen such as Williams.

During the Lexow Committee Hearings, which began just about the time Becker joined the force, Inspector Williams was the focal point of the investigation into police graft. Prosecuting counsel John Goff, who, ironically, was to preside over Becker's own first murder trial almost twenty years later, revealed that Williams had more than $250,000 in the bank, owned a mansion and a yacht, and lived like a king. Williams boldly admitted that he took what he liked in the district he controlled and he was later dismissed from the force, though never prosecuted. His was the enduring image that etched itself into the mind of the ever ambitious Charles Becker. He, too, would someday preside over the Tenderloin and make his own fortune, this he vowed. Long before that time, however, Becker found himself in continuous trouble, so much trouble that he gleaned more press coverage in that day than any other common cop on the force. At first Becker was assigned to the Fulton Street area and later, due to the strings of his mentor, Inspector Williams, moved to the Tenderloin. It was here that he ran headlong into the famous writer, Stephen Crane, who had seen him years earlier on a dark street pounding the face of a helpless prostitute who had failed to pay him off that night.

Crane had established himself as one of America's finest authors the previous year, in 1895, with the publication of *The Red Badge of Courage,* and was the toast of New York at the age of twenty-four. He disdained the literary parties and salons, preferring the company of Bowery lowlifes, bums, and apprentice hoodlums and their women, mostly prostitutes. He had long taken the view that the beat cop in New York was nothing more than a thug in uniform and had been writing a series of articles exposing their grafting, brutal ways, communicating with the new police commissioner, Theodore Roosevelt. On the night of Sept. 15, 1896, Crane found himself at the Broadway Gardens, assigned by the editors of the New York *Journal* to write about the underworld types who crowded the tables there. With him were two streetwalkers of his acquaintance and they were joined by another whore named Dora Clark. At 3 a.m., Crane put one of the girls on a streetcar, and when he returned to the sidewalk, he found the large, lumbering Becker arresting his other two friends for soliciting. Crane stepped forth and said one woman was his wife. Becker, who was later described by Crane as "picturesque as a wolf," then reached out and grabbed the other girl, Dora Clark, arresting only her on charges of prostitution. As he dragged the girl off, Crane protested and Becker smirked, snarling: "You ain't married to both of 'em, are you?"

Rushing to the Tenderloin station house, Crane obtained Becker's name and badge number, then told newsmen that "whatever her character (that of Dora Clark), the arrest was an outrage. The policeman flatly lied!" Crane appeared as a witness for Clark later in court, where Becker insisted that he had seen the woman solicit two men within five minutes. Crane told the presiding magistrate that this was a boldfaced lie, that he had been with the woman for several hours and nothing of the kind happened. Dora Clark then testified that she had been persecuted for several months by Becker and other policemen in the area because she had resisted the advances of a cop named Rosenberg. This officer had solicited sex from Dora and she, thinking he was black because of his swarthy complexion, had replied: "How dare you speak to a decent white woman!"

Calling the officer black when he was not was thought by fellow officers to be the worst insult their ranks could receive and Dora Clark had been marked for vengeance.

After listening to the statements, the magistrate, who had recently received a favorable profile by Crane, shocked Becker and dozens of other officers who had lent him support by siding with Crane and accepting his version of the events. Dora Clark was released. Becker had received his first minor setback, but this incident was nothing compared to his next ill-fated news notice. Becker was working the graveyard shift on Sept. 20, 1896, with another officer named Carey when, close to dawn, the two patrolmen saw three men flee from a tobacco shop carrying sacks of loot. They gave chase, shouting for the burglars to halt. Though heavyset, Becker was fast on his feet and he caught up with one of the burglars, bringing him down with one blow from his nightstick. A second burglar outdistanced the pair. Then one of the officers, it was never determined who, shot the third from some distance. This escapade was played up in the press and Becker was hailed as a hero. The dead man, Becker insisted, was a notorious second-story man named John O'Brien. There was talk of giving Becker a commendation and an important promotion until, three days later, the relatives of the slain man identified him as 19-year-old John Fay, a plumber's assistant. Fay had accidentally stepped in the line of fire which both Becker and Carey knew, Fay's family claimed, but they assumed no one would inquire about a dead young man they were passing off as a notorious thief. John Fay's reputation had been tarnished, his relatives said, so that a pair of "gun-happy killers" could make the police force look good in the press. Becker and Carey were suspended for a month and were privately warned by their superiors to make sure of their targets in the future.

By the time Becker returned to his post in the Tenderloin, he was surprised to see Commissioner Roosevelt come into the precinct station to review the men there. He singled out Becker, shook his hand, and commended him for his considerable bravery in taking on thieves face to face but then he turned and told the entire group that they should all be more careful in their treatment of "unfortunate women," that even these fallen angels had the same rights as law-abiding citizens. In this way, without singling Becker out, Theodore Roosevelt had subtly upbraided him, warned him. But Becker was not a man of subtleties. He proved that when he sought out Dora Clark in October 1896 and beat her until he blackened both her eyes and broke her nose. He was stopped by fellow officers from choking her to death. He left her on the sidewalk, warning her that she would "wind up in the river" if she ever again accused a New York cop of anything. But Dora Clark was stubborn and brought charges against Becker. A police hearing was held,

The crooked NYPD Lt. Charles Becker.

Big Tim Sullivan

Herman "Beansie" Rosenthal

Bald Jack Rose

Harry Vallon

Becker henchman Bridgey Webber, front left.

Sam Schepps

Gambler Arnold Rothstein

Big Jack Zelig, gangster.

Herbert Bayard Swope

the longest on record up to that time, and Becker got off with a casual reprimand.

It appeared to Becker that his political influence through Big Tim Sullivan was not only intact but would protect him against any pesky citizen daring to challenge his authority. On one occasion Becker arrested a society woman whom he accused of soliciting. She turned out to be perfectly innocent, having said goodbye to one of her lawyers on the street after a meeting in his office. Becker, confronted with the testimony of the lawyer, gave the man his usual sneer, refusing to back down and stating: "I know a whore when I see one!" He was reprimanded and sent back to the street where, a short time later, he arrested another woman who approached him and asked directions to the subway. He mumbled something to her she did not understand and she questioned him again. Annoyed, Becker grabbed the poor woman and ran her into the station house, booking her as a common drunk. She turned out to be the wife of a New Jersey manufacturer. This incident caused Becker's superiors to slavishly apologize to both the woman and her influential husband, and even Becker's political sponsor, Big Tim Sullivan, had to step in and persuade the couple not to sue. Sullivan had a quiet talk with his protégé, telling him that he had to be more cautious in the future when arresting women. He had plans for Becker, Sullivan told him, big plans, so it was important that he maintain an unblemished record.

Some time later, however, the easy-to-anger Becker, while on a raid against a gambling house, was shoved by a gambler who boasted of his political influence. Becker, who was alone in the room with the man at the time, pulled a pistol and shot the gambler dead, later claiming that the man pulled a gun. No witnesses were present to contradict him but Becker's superiors again had a quiet talk with him, warning him severely to keep his hand off his gun unless it was absolutely necessary to use it. To make sure that he got the point, Becker was suspended for a month. The hamhock-fisted officer took this time to marry Vivian Atteridge. He had been married briefly in 1905 to a pretty young girl named Mary Mahoney, but she had died nine months later of tuberculosis. The marriage to Atteridge would last until 1905 when Becker would divorce her. Vivian would remarry in 1907, wedding Becker's brother John who was also a member of the NYPD.

In 1901, Becker came under the direct command of Captain Max Schmittberger, the very man who had exposed the corrupt practices of Inspector Alexander Williams. Though Clubber Williams was no longer on the force, he acted as an adviser to Becker, who had long ago embraced the Clubber's philosophy of brute force. Becker, by then a roundsman (one status above patrolman, similar to the rank of corporal), was known by Schmittberger to be a

Williams partisan and, as such, was treated coldly and suspiciously by his superior. Schmittberger was thought of as a squealer and a turncoat who had exposed his own people to the Lexow Committee and, as such, many high-rankers on the force wanted to see this man disgraced and deposed. It was with this in mind that Commissioner Bingham and later Commissioner Rhinelander Waldo, who had been told by angry police officials that Schmittberger was corrupt, secretly ordered Becker to dig up evidence that would expose Schmittberger. The police captain knew this, of course, and moved to get rid of Becker by having him transferred to another precinct. After meeting with Williams, Becker filed malfeasance charges against Schmittberger. The enraged captain filed countercharges, but all of these charges were dropped after Commissioner Bingham brought the aggrieved parties together and told them to forget their differences for the sake of the department.

For some time, little was heard of Charles Becker. He must have concluded that the ways of Clubber Williams could do little to advance his career and he maintained a low profile for several years, keeping his record clean. Then, in 1904, Becker suddenly received the department's highest award for heroism which put his name back into the headlines. He had seen a young man in the Hudson River struggling to stay afloat. Fully clothed and without a moment's hesitation, Becker jumped into the river and pulled the man to safety. He turned out to be an unemployed clerk named James Butler who blubbered his thanks to a grinning Becker before newsmen who had conveniently been called to the scene. Butler praised Becker to the newsmen as one of the bravest fellows he had ever seen, explaining that a plank he was walking on gave way and he fell into the River near 10th Street. But it was only a week later when Butler called up the same newsmen and complained that Becker had reneged on his promise. What promise was that, he was asked. Becker, Butler explained, had offered him $15 to jump into the Hudson so that he could jump in after him and appear to be the great hero. But Becker had never paid him the $15 and now Butler was angry at having ruined his only suit for nothing. Becker denied the whole story, laughing at the idea, which he called preposterous. By then he had his medal and a promotion to sergeant.

A short time later, through his Tammany contacts, Becker was promoted to lieutenant and he began to make his moves against the posh gambling and vice dens of the Tenderloin. One story has it that about 1907, Becker made the rounds of all the big time gambling dens and demanded $15 payment a week for himself even though the gamblers explained that they had already paid their "protection" money. After collecting $150, Becker was called into Schmittberger's office and the captain told him to put the money down on his desk, explaining that he knew exactly how much he had collected. Becker tossed the money on the desk and Schmittberger handed him back $15, telling him that that amount was his end, ten per cent, and from that day forward he would be Schmittberger's personal bagman and receive ten percent of everything he collected. Becker the bagman went to work with a vengeance, becoming rich in the course of the next few years. But in 1911, Police Commissioner Waldo decided to crack down on the Tenderloin gamblers after being goaded by scores of enraged reformers objecting to the blatant vice district. Waldo believed that Schmittberger was the core of the rotten apple in the Tenderloin. Years earlier he had, as a Deputy Police Commissioner, met with Becker secretly, ordering him to get evidence against Schmittberger, not knowing, of course, that Becker was Schmittberger's bagman and heir apparent to wholesale graft in the precinct. Becker, quite naturally, agreed to the secret investigation, sitting as he was in the catbird's seat, able to provide snippets of information on his captain without ever giving Waldo enough evidence to bring about Schmittberger's removal.

At the same time Becker made himself look good to downtown superiors by appearing to energetically attack the gambling and vice dens by conducting incessant raids against these places. Yet he went on making enormous illicit profits from the gamblers he was protecting, satisfying both Waldo and his protection-paying gambling dens. In 1911 Becker organized and led 203 raids into the Tenderloin where he and his men made 898 arrests which resulted in 103 convictions, a staggering record that outwardly made Becker look like a law enforcement crusader. But what the record also showed, if one dug deeper, were sentences that amounted to next to nothing. Most of the convictions ended in suspended sentences or small fines seldom exceeding $50. Waldo blamed the court system and corrupt judges for such leniency, and to some extent he was correct, since many judges were then, as before and after this golden age of kickbacks and payoffs, on the take. Becker, however, was the man who manipulated these judicial decisions. He simply ordered his men, when appearing in court, to have loss of memory as to the particulars of the raids they conducted. They conveniently misplaced or lost vital evidence that would have assured strong sentences. Faced with this type of shallow prosecution, judges were compelled to issue light sentences. The whole system worked both ways for Charles Becker.

By late 1910 Becker operated autonomously as the head of the gambling squad or, because of the violent manner in which the squad often tore apart gambling dens (those who had been slow to make payoffs), the group known as "the strong-arm squad." His word was law in the Tender-

loin by then and he paid nothing to Schmittberger who had been neutralized and later ousted by Big Tim Sullivan. Becker, after minor payoffs to his own officers, split his payoff take only with Big Tim and this further enriched his own coffers by tens of thousands of dollars. To keep the gamblers and vice lords in line, Becker, through Big Tim, employed the worst gang of thugs in New York to perform beatings and even murder, chores too messy for his own corrupt policemen. Monk Eastman had been sent to prison by then, abandoned by Tammany as uncontrollable and had been replaced by Jacob "Big Jack" Zelig (whose real name was William Alberts), a towering, fierce thug who had been Eastman's right-hand man, a gangster with much more cunning than Eastman, one who knew how to keep his organization in line. Zelig and his host of killers worked directly under Becker's orders, going on his payroll but being directed in their nefarious activities by gamblers who took their orders from Becker.

If any of these gangsters ever disobeyed Becker's dictates, he merely had them arrested for violating the Sullivan Law, a law ironically put on the books by none other than Big Tim when, in 1909, he decided to return to the state senate. A disloyal or disobedient gangster would be dragged into court and charged by Becker's minions with carrying concealed firearms, thus violating the Sullivan Law. This carried with it a mandatory eight-year sentence. Of course, when this law went into record, the gangsters never carried firearms unless on the job. Becker got around this by simply having his men provide "throw-away" guns or spare pistols and automatics which were supplied by police officers in quickly convicting a gangster who did not cooperate with the system. Herbert Bayard Swope, later the chief journalist covering the Becker-Rosenthal murder, would later write that "Becker *was* the System. Like Caesar all things were rendered unto Becker in the underworld. Like Briareus he had a hundred arms...and more power in the Department than the Commissioner."

But Becker was not without competition. A number of other lieutenants under his command lusted for his power position and they would do just about anything to come into the good graces of Big Tim Sullivan, the Tammany sachem and real czar of influence and power in New York. Big Tim was many times a millionaire with villas, mansions, yachts, and endless sources of cash; he had been on the take since Boss Croker abandoned his leadership at Tammany in 1901, retiring to the French Riviera with his own millions hustled from the city. Yet Big Tim had no ambitions to retire. He had to have more and more and knew that the Alexandrian philosophy of dividing and controlling his henchmen, Becker included, was the key to the flowing cornucopia of graft. Becker knew this also, that Big Tim would quickly replace him at any time if convenient. So

Becker shrewdly began to cultivate certain members of the press as early as 1910, giving crime reporters inside tips on raids and making sure that he and only he received glorification in print. He even went so far as to hire Charles Plitt as his press agent, making sure that the newspapers were informed of his daily activities, or those that made him look like a police hero to the public. Thus for two years leading up to the Rosenthal killing, he overshadowed almost every policeman in the department, except for the commissioner. This caused Becker to undoubtedly become the most disliked member of the department but he was also the most dangerous. As such, no officer dared to openly criticize or confront him. The specter of Big Tim cast a shadow across every precinct.

Becker's alliances with the press would later backfire on him, although he reaped numerous benefits for a short time from his liaisons with crime beat reporters. In late 1911 a reporter warned Becker that there was a conspiracy within the department to have him framed as a bagman, and Becker, fearing this report was real, went straight to Commissioner Waldo, asking that he be assigned to another position other than heading the "strong-arm" squad. Perhaps by then he had amassed what he considered to be the fortune that would take him comfortably through retirement. Perhaps his meeting with Waldo was nothing more than a fishing expedition. Waldo assured him that he was not being investigated, that he was doing an excellent job, and that he should keep up the good work. Becker went back to being the czar of the Tenderloin. But there was some truth to the reporter's tip. Waldo had been receiving letters from an informant using an alias. One of these letters, received in March 1912, stated: "I would like to have you investigate quietly Lieutenant Becker. He is now collecting more money than Devery (Big Bill Devery, New York's thoroughly corrupt chief of police during the 1890s), and it is well-known to everyone at Police Headquarters. Please do this and you will be surprised at the result."

This letter, incredibly, was sent by Waldo straight to Becker. It was the commissioner's policy, as sort of a naive procedure of fair play, to send such blind accusations to the officers being accused so that they could respond directly. In reality, the officer accused of misconduct was expected to investigate himself and dutifully report on his own wrongdoings. Of course, such officers never found credence in any of these accusations, all of them to the last letter being the work of cranks and malcontents. Becker shrewdly went one step further and returned this letter to Waldo, saying prudently that he was not in a position to react to such a document and that perhaps it would be better if the commissioner were to send this letter on to another person in the department. He knew that such a straightforward response would all the more readily confirm in Waldo's mind that he, Charles Becker, was beyond reproach and nothing more would come of the accusation, which is exactly what happened. Waldo's decision to simply file this and other letters concerning Becker's wholesale graft as crank mail later caused him much embarrassment.

Becker, unlike the high-living Sullivan and former police bigwigs who had taken payoffs with both hands for years, kept a low profile outside of his police duties. He was a conservative and cautious crook, secreting his illegal loot in so many banks that most of his fortune was never fully tracked down, even years after he was executed. He continued to live in a modest apartment at 159th and Edgecomb Avenue with his third wife, Helen, whom he had married in 1905 after his divorce from Vivian Atteridge. Helen was a schoolteacher, born in 1874 and a dedicated educator who went on teaching slow high school learners at P.S. 90 for $1,820 a year, even in 1912 when her husband had amassed a reported $1 to $2 million. As a couple, they enjoyed simple pleasures such as horseback riding and gardening. They planned to build a modest house in the near future. Helen would later defend her husband with a fierce loyalty that saw her pleading for his life right up to the last second, abandoning her pride to prostrate herself before Governor Whiteman, the very man who had convicted her husband. No matter what evidence was later put before her, Helen Becker refused to believe that her husband, whom she called Charlie-Lover (he called her My Queen), ever committed a single illegal act. Charles Becker was an honest man, Helen insisted, a simple man from a large family; she never tired of saying how she, like her husband, came from a family with ten children.

The one indulgence practiced by Becker was taking his grateful wife to the best restaurants in town. They dined with political dynamos and business tycoons who curried Becker's favor. They feasted upon sumptuous meals at Rector's, Sharkey's, Sherry's, Luchow's, and never picked up a check. When going to dinner or an occasional show, the Beckers rode in chauffeur-driven limousines owned by such people as millionaire broker Henry Sternberger. Although Helen Becker did not know them by profession, scores of other men would table-hop to sit with the Beckers and whisper in her husband's ear before then moving off, men glittering with diamonds and full of conspiracy. These were the top Tenderloin gamblers, not the least of whom were young sharpers who had come under the protective arms of Big Tim Sullivan, chiefly Arnold Rothstein and Herman "Beansie" Rosenthal. Sullivan had mentioned these two gamblers by name to Becker, telling him that he felt "paternal" toward both these two young Jewish sharpers and would like to see their careers blossom.

It was not surprising therefore that Becker went out of

his way to befriend the more social of the pair, Rosenthal, when meeting him at an Elks' Club Ball on New Year's Eve 1911. At the time, Becker sent Helen home and stayed to get drunk with the pudgy young gambler, or pretended to be drunk, displaying an inordinate amount of affection toward a man he had just met, throwing his bear-like arms around Rosenthal, kissing him on the cheeks several times and then lumbering onto a table and shouting to all his cronies: "Boys, Herman Rosenthal is my best friend and anything he wants, he gets!" He got down and hugged the gambler once more. "Anything in the world for you, Herman. I'll get up at three o'clock in the morning to do you a favor! You can have anything I've got!" Becker then called three of his top officers over and told them: "This is my best pal and you do anything he wants you to do." Becker continued to cultivate this strange new friendship by meeting with Rosenthal at the Lafayette Turkish baths, at the Elks Club, and various restaurants. In the Turkish baths the hulking Becker would sit, towel-wrapped, next to the chubby, flabby Rosenthal and pump him subtly about the strength of Big Tim's support. Rosenthal told him that Big Tim had authorized a new, posh club, which Rosenthal intended to call The Hester Club, that would be opened shortly. Becker not only promised him protection for this club but went on to tell the gambler that he was "getting hold of a lot of money" through the easy efforts of his strong-arm squad, and that he might be interested in investing in The Hesper Club. Of course, Becker was making a bid to short-cut Big Tim's own investment in the club so that he would be on an equal footing with Sullivan on the interest level of many clubs. Becker's ambition was still white-hot and he undoubtedly was thinking of somehow supplanting Big Tim as he had Schmittberger.

Thanks to Providence, Becker did exactly that. In the spring of 1912, Big Tim's dissolute lifestyle caught up with him. He was seized by paresis of the brain, generally caused by long-standing syphilis, and became bedridden, half-conscious most of the time. He was no longer an effective force in New York's system of graft. Becker, without waiting for approval from Tammany, took over Sullivan's role as soon as he heard his political mentor had fallen ill. Becker immediately leveled an enormous duty on all gambling dens and bordellos, sending his men around to obtain the weekly increase. Some of Becker's police goons arrived at the newly opened Hesper Club where the strong-arm cops were told: "No payoffs here. This is Big Tim's house." True, Sullivan had fronted a good deal of the money Rosenthal had used to establish this lavish gambling den in a three-story brownstone at 104 West 45th Street, just off Sixth Avenue. The place sported thick carpets and heavy, dark drapes, massive furniture, which was the vogue of the era, and the latest gambling wheels, tables, and

devices. But, ironically, Becker himself had also invested in the club, giving Rosenthal $1,500 for twenty percent of the profits, and holding a mortgage on all the furniture as well for his small investment. It was his thinking that, despite the profits Rosenthal paid him, he could still enjoy an additional $500-a-week payoff from The Hesper. Rosenthal, however, balked at this double payoff and refused to give Becker's boys a cent.

When Becker heard of this refusal, he met with Big Jack Zelig and ordered the thugmaster to see Rosenthal personally. Zelig went to Rosenthal and told him: "You better pay. Sullivan's out and Becker's the boss now." Rosenthal told Zelig that he was crazy and that he would see Sullivan about it. But Sullivan was dying in bed and Rosenthal found only the boss's politically inept brother Florrie, his nephew Jim, and Frank Farrell lounging in Big Tim's sumptuous office. They had no idea what he should do. They were trying to figure out Big Tim's secretly organized empire themselves and were getting nowhere. The obstinate Rosenthal left, later telling Zelig that he had no intention of giving Becker anything, including the twenty per cent on the investment.

When Becker heard this, he exploded. He roared at Zelig: "Make him pay!" Zelig and some of his goons, "Gyp the Blood" Horowitz, Whitey Lewis, Dago Frank and Lefty Louie, the four men who were to take Rosenthal's life in full view of dozens of stunned witnesses. They grabbed the gambler as he was stepping out of his club one night and beat him unconscious. Still the stubborn gambler refused to pay off. He went back to Big Tim's relatives who told him: "Make a deal with Becker, that's all we can tell you." Rosenthal was beaten. He called Becker and the two men met. Rosenthal complained that his club was new and not doing as well as he had hoped. He needed more time to pay the additional money Becker was demanding. Becker told him he had a month and to make sure he got his percentage, installed one of his cronies in Rosenthal's club. This man was Jack Rose, better known along the Main Stem as Billiard Ball Jack because he did not have a human hair on his shining bald head. Rosenthal had always hated the pugnacious Rose and he found the gambler's permanent presence in his club offensive. He brooded about this until his pent-up rage broke loose in diatribes against New York police lieutenant Charles Becker. He began to speak to anyone, everyone, about this "crooked cop," until his incessant carping was heard by the crusading district attorney, Charles Seymour Whitman.

Before Whitman acted on the Rosenthal rumors, Commissioner Waldo received another letter which complained about the blatant operations of a gambling den at 104 West 45th Street, Rosenthal's Hesper Club. This was in Becker's Tenderloin and Waldo called the lieutenant into his office.

Here he confronted Becker with the letter, his usual custom, informing him: "I can't understand how this could have escaped your attention." Waldo gave Becker a direct order to close The Hesper and keep it closed. This was one letter Becker did not return to the Commissioner. He had no alternative except to comply with orders. He informed Rosenthal that he had to "close you up for a while." Rosenthal protested but Becker was firm. Not only was the Hesper Club closed but, to make sure it remained closed, Becker placed a police guard around the clock in the front room on the main floor. The presence of these cops drove Rosenthal nearly crazy since he lived on the premises and he bitterly complained to any and all who would listen that it made him and his poor wife feel like prisoners. It was intolerable. He wouldn't stand for it. He would do *something* to show Becker that he could not treat Herman Rosenthal "like a dog."

The presence of the police in his home so enraged the beefy gambler that he began to war with the department. He announced that he would lock out these interlopers and, on one occasion, he slammed the doors and bolted them during a changing of shifts. He stood outside and dared the police to break into his place. The answer came in hours when a crew showed up on West 45th Street with a new hydraulic lift which could tear out the entire door frame. Before permanent damage was done Rosenthal capitulated, running across the street and unlocking the door. As the late spring brought hot weather, Rosenthal threatened to stoke up the furnaces in his building and "roast those cops out of there," but this proved to be an idle boast. Rosenthal's wife, Dora, a buxom and demonstrative woman, nagged her husband incessantly about policemen roaming her home, and every time the shift would change, she would lean out of her third-story bedroom window and shake her fist at the officers changing the guard, shouting that they were violating her home.

When Rosenthal could no longer bear this continuing indignity, he filed harrassment charges against several high-ranking policemen in the department but oddly never mentioned Becker. Although local judges scoffed at the complaints Rosenthal made, the gambler persistently filed new complaints. All of this got back to Becker. Now the crooked cop felt the kind of pressure he had only administered in the past. He became enraged. How dare this gambler create problems for the police and for him? He would not tolerate such defiance. He had Zelig's goons threaten Rosenthal again but the gambler refused to back down. Becker decided then and there that only one course of action was left to him. According to the sensational thirty-eight-page confession later made by Jack Rose, Becker came to him and ordered him to organize the death of Herman "Beansie" Rosenthal. Rose was to employ his

fellow gamblers, Harry Vallon (Harry Vallinsky) and Louis Bridgie Webber in organizing Rosenthal's death with Zelig's gunsels. Becker was specific in his command to Rose, telling him: "I want Rosenthal croaked! I want him murdered, shot, his throat cut, any way that will take him off the earth!" Rose told Becker that Zelig and his men might be hesitant to kill a man who was so much in the public eye, a man whose vendetta against the NYPD had put him on the front pages of the daily newspapers. "If those rats don't go along I will find out where they hang out and frame every one of them and send them up the river for carrying concealed weapons!" Becker emphasized that nothing would happen to anyone who killed the man he had marked for murder. "All that's necessary," Becker told Rose, "is to walk right up to where he is and blaze away at him and leave the rest to me. Nothing will happen to anybody that does it. Walk up to him and shoot him before a policeman if you want to and nothing will happen!"

Rose reluctantly set about organizing the murder of Rosenthal but he dragged his feet, as did Webber and Vallon. Becker pursued them like a terrier, at one point shouting that he would frame the gamblers unless they got the job done quickly. "Why isn't he croaked?" Becker would say in his daily phone call to Rose. "Why isn't that man dead yet? You're all a bunch of damned cowards!" He literally hounded the gamblers with threats up to the night when Rosenthal was finally murdered. Only hours before this happened, Becker was on the phone to Rose, saying: "If only that s.o.b. is croaked tonight, how happy I will be, how lovely it will be!" The problem in getting Becker's gruesome job done lay within the ranks of the gamblers who worked at cross-purposes. All of them owned interests in various gambling joints and competed with each other, distrusting each other's motives. All of them would have just as readily put each other on the spot if Becker had asked for *their* deaths. None of them, however, had any love for Rosenthal.

Only a few years earlier Rosenthal and Webber had fought Becker over gambling territories that brought out their respective gunmen in open warfare. Rosenthal had actually arranged for Webber's murder in 1909, hiring a notorious thug named Spanish Louie (or Louis) to beat Webber to death. Rosenthal had actually watched from a shadowy doorway while this goon nearly beat Webber to death but was interrupted by a patrolman who gave chase to the fleeing Louie. With that, Rosenthal sauntered across the street, pretending to be passing by, and helped Webber to his feet, wiping away the blood pouring from his broken nose with his own handkerchief and telling Webber how awful it was that the streets were no longer safe. The next year Spanish Louie was shot to death from a speeding auto by four gangsters in Webber's employ, these being Christian

"Boob" Walker, Harry "Gyp the Blood" Horowitz, Lefty Louie and Whitey Lewis. These were Zelig's boys but the same gunmen were for hire by anyone with money and they often free-lanced for Rosenthal. Still, the gamblers found dozens of excuses for not killing Rosenthal, hoping that Becker would change his mind. Rosenthal didn't aid his own cause by loudly accusing the police of wholesale graft. Not having any success with the local magistrates who refused to indict anyone on his accusations, Rosenthal went to the press, badgering newsmen to print his story of wholesale corruption in the police force. Everyone turned a deaf ear, except a reporter for the *World*, Herbert Bayard Swope. Swope had known Rosenthal for some years; a habitue of Tenderloin casinos, he and Rosenthal had been on more than speaking terms, the gambler steering the reporter to the best play in town, often enough feeding him tips on various horse races. Swope not only listened to Rosenthal but decided to print his affadavit in the *World*. The story that Rosenthal gave Swope was nothing like the tale he had brought to the city magistrates. To Swope the gambler described in detail his relationship with Police Lieutenant Charles Becker, from the very first moment they had met at the Elks Club on New Year's Eve to the massive payoffs he had made to the crooked cop, along with all the other payoffs Becker was receiving throughout the Tenderloin. Rosenthal named every gambler in on the payoffs, all the police collectors and bagmen, all the backup thugs who did the dirty work for the cops. After the Swope story ran, the most important of his life and the story that would make him into a newspaper magnate, the newsman went after Whitman to make sure the district attorney did his duty. He persuaded Whitman to take Rosenthal's direct statement and bring a grand jury indictment against Becker.

Before Whitman took Rosenthal's deposition, Becker heard of the affidavit in the *World* office and marched to the newspaper with his lawyer. He inspected the document and snarled: "This is a pack of lies!" He turned on his heels and went back to badgering Rose to have Rosenthal killed immediately. Rosenthal was oddly carefree about the lethal peril he had created for himself. "I know I'm a marked man," he told a newsman, "and I've probably signed my own death warrant but I don't care." Despite these words of bravado, Herman Rosenthal cared very much, and he took pains to stay out of his usual haunts, holing up on the third floor of his brownstone. He ventured forth to seek the advice of the rising young gambler, Arnold Rothstein, who offered him money to leave town. Rosenthal said he would never let himself be run out of New York but he later returned to Rothstein, asking for the money. Rothstein turned a cold shoulder to his one-time friend Rosenthal and told him it was "too late to do anything." This meeting with Rothstein occurred on the afternoon of July 15, 1912.

Rosenthal thought about Rothstein's remark and decided that there was something more to do. He had earlier stated that "this is a fight to the finish. I know that the whole police department will be against me and that all the gamblers, big and little, will fight me, too, because this means a big investigation that will clean up the city."

Late that day and into the evening, Herman Rosenthal talked for five hours to District Attorney Whitman and key staff members, reiterating everything he had revealed to Swope and promising to reveal even more when brought before a grand jury, if he lived that long. Whitman promised that if he stayed in his home, he would be all right. The district attorney was the only key official in New York who had no strings to Tammany, having gotten elected without that organization's help. He was the mortal foe of Tammany mayor William Jay Gaynor (who had disavowed his Tammany connection once in office) and especially eschewed the friendships of such sachems as Big Tim Sullivan. A crusader and a tireless reformer, Whitman vowed to use Rosenthal's accusations to clean up the city. Before leaving Whitman's offices that night, however, Rosenthal gave himself little chance of ever appearing before a Grand Jury, telling Whitman: "I may not live to do it. You may never see me again alive." His words, undoubtedly couched for dramatic effect, could not have been more prophetic.

That night, at about 10 p.m., Rosenthal received a phone call from someone he considered important enough to meet later. He told his wife that he would be going out to keep an important rendezvous but he refused to reveal the identity of the man who had called. Dora Rosenthal begged her husband not to go out, reminding him that he was in great danger but Herman Rosenthal somehow felt confident that no one would dare harm him; he had become too public, too well-known. Why, he was on every front page of every newspaper in New York. He had attacked the New York Police Department and the police of the city would never dare let anything happen to him now. His indictment against the NYPD was his insurance policy. He had not reckoned on the ruthless indifference Charles Becker had to such logic.

So confident was Rosenthal that he walked all the way to his meeting place, his favorite hangout, The Metropole Hotel, on 43rd Street, just east of Broadway. The hotel was owned by the Considine Brothers and Big Tim Sullivan, Rosenthal's mentor; nothing could happen to him there, the gambler reasoned. The place was a favorite after-hours haunt for actors, newsmen, gamblers, racetrack touts, and Broadway characters of every stripe. Its bar and restaurant teemed with the most colorful (and often dangerous) people in town, the kind of place Herman Rosenthal loved. As Rosenthal neared the hotel he ran into some gamblers he knew. One of them reached out and said: "Herman, it's not safe for you to be out tonight. Go home. Turn around and go home right now." Rosenthal laughed off the warning as he pulled away. He intended to keep his appointment at the Metropole. He turned into the hotel lobby shortly before 1 a.m., July 16, 1912, and as he passed the bustling, jam-packed bar, there was a moment of silence, a strange hush as the scores of drinkers paused for a moment as if to acknowledge the passing of a ghost.

Rosenthal sauntered into the dining room and sat down at his favorite table, and here, too, the crowd stared momentarily at him in a strange awe, not expecting him to be there in the flesh, to be alive at all. From the scores of statements made later and over the years it was evident that everyone in the Metropole, everyone "in the know" in Manhattan, knew that Herman "Beansie" Rosenthal was going to die that night, "go on the spot," as Damon Runyon later put it and he later intimated that he was present in the bar that night. The Metropole was teeming with Runyon characters, the very prototypes who would later people his *Guys and Dolls* and other Broadway tales. Oddly, Rosenthal sat down next to Christian "Boob" Walker, one of the goons who worked for his arch nemesis, Bridgie Webber. Other Webber cronies, Fat Moe Brown and Butch Kitte sat down for a while while Rosenthal ordered a steak and a horse's neck (ginger ale and a lemon twist). The Metropole had a number of unique drinks created by its gambler patrons. Billiard Ball Jack Rose, hated by Rosenthal, had created his own drink which was forever after known as a "Jack Rose," this being a cocktail containing a jigger of applejack, juice of half a lemon, and a half ounce of grenadine, which was all shaken with cracked ice and strained.

When the steak came, Rosenthal wolfed it down, keeping his eye on the door, as if expecting someone to come in at any moment. Boob Walker later stated that "Herman ate as if he could take it with him." Finishing his supper, the gambler excused himself, got up, and shuffled into the lobby where he bought the latest editions. He was on the front pages bigger than ever. He bought a copy of the *World* which blared the headline: "GAMBLER CHARGES POLICE LIEUTENANT WAS HIS PARTNER." He tucked this under his arm and ambled back to his table in the restaurant which was near one of the large windows that faced the street and still gave Rosenthal a clear view of the front door. He spread the newspaper out in front of him and the other gamblers at his table took one look at the headline and quickly excused themselves. A group of gamblers at the next table stared at him incredulously.

Rosenthal shot his French cuffs blazoned with huge gold links, shoved his chair back so that his stomach bloated forward over a huge gold belt buckle which featured his initials in large letters reading HR, and smirked at his friends sitting at the next table. "What do you think of the papers lately?" he said in a conspiratorial voice. "You boys aren't sore at me, are you?" Rosenthal asked this question without really expecting an answer. One of the gamblers shook his head and said: "Herman, you're a damned fool." Ignoring this remark, Rosenthal ordered a cup of coffee and began to read the newspaper, dwelling on every word that dealt with his accusations. Some of the gamblers sitting nearby who had been whispering among themselves looked up at the entranceway to the dining room and suddenly fell silent. At the doorway was a police detective named William J. File. He glanced about the room and then disappeared into the crowded lobby which, instead of emptying out at that time of the morning, was actually filling up so that standing room was getting scarce. It seemed as if everyone in the know on the Main Stem wanted to be there at the kill, or, at least, that was the image of the thronged Metropole that many writers later created. Other plainclothes NYPD detectives were also on hand that night, and out on the street, no less than six—some said more than a dozen—patrolmen strolled the sidewalk on both sides of the street on the block where the Metropole was located, its bright marquee lights flooding light up and down the street. The public killing of Herman Rosenthal was undoubtedly an event no one wanted to miss. Someone in front of the Metropole, a man in a dark suit and a straw boater, his voice full of authority, began to order the taxicabs parked there to move on and he continued to have the cabs pull away from the entranceway for twenty minutes, until the front of the hotel was completely clear of parked vehicles right up to the moment Herman Rosenthal stepped outside to meet his terrible fate.

Oblivious to his own impending execution, only a half hour away, Rosenthal went on bathing in his press glory. He was the talk of the town and he knew it, reveled in it, glorified in the danger he had brought to his own door. He feared nothing, his expression told everyone; he alone would clean up New York. Even when his arch enemy Bridgie Webber sauntered into the hotel dining room a little after 1:30 a.m., Rosenthal gave him a slight smile. Webber walked casually up to Rosenthal and placed his hand on the pudgy gambler's shoulder, saying affably: "Hello, Herman, how's everything?" Rosenthal nodded and said: "Fine, everything is just fine. How is it by you?" Webber did not reply, merely stood there for a moment, then he patted Rosenthal's shoulder several times, turned around, and walked quickly out of the hotel. This was the signal to waiting gangsters outside who could see through the dining room window which of the diners was to be their victim. Months later, at Becker's prolonged trial, Webber sat calmly in the witness stand and was asked: "When you went to the

The public murder of Rosenthal as depicted in New York's newspapers of the day.

Left: Four killers at a picnic: (top, left to right) Gyp the Blood, Lefty Louie, Dago Frank, and (bottom, seated at right) Whitey Lewis. Top: Gyp the Blood and Lefty Louie at trial; they were condemned to the electric chair.

Judge John W. Goff   D.A. Charles Seymour Whitman   Mrs. Helen Becker   Charles Becker, executed.

Metropole, for what purpose did you look for him (Rosenthal)? Was it for the purpose of having him murdered?" The answer was a quiet, unperturbed "Yes, sir." Webber's pat on the shoulder was his kiss of death. After making sure that Rosenthal was at the Metropole, Webber went outside to inform the eight men waiting there, four of them gangsters with guns bulging in their pockets, that their victim was almost ready for the slaughter.

It was almost 2 a.m. when a waiter carrying a tray of dishes stopped at Rosenthal's table and told him that "there is a man in the lobby who wants to see you," Rosenthal looked through the dining room door to see Harry Vallon, a gambling henchman of Webber's—a man with the face of a bloody hatchet. Vallon stood staring at him, impassive, his hands jammed into his coat pockets. Rosenthal got up and slowly walked up to Vallon in the lobby. "Can you come outside for a minute, Herman? There's someone outside who wants to see you," Vallon told him. The utterly unsuspecting Rosenthal shrugged and followed Vallon outside into the sultry, steaming night. The heavyset gambler followed Vallon outside to the sidewalk, standing under the bright lights of the Metropole, a perfect target. Vallon suddenly stepped back, out of the light and into the shadows. Several gamblers Rosenthal knew stood nearby, including Dave Mendelsohn, Sigmund Rosenfeld, and Chick Beebe. They stood off in the distance and in the shadows, twenty feet or so from the hotel entrance. Also standing in the shadows talking with cronies was Billiard Ball Jack Rose, talking with another gambling intimate, Sam Schepps. Down the block several uniformed policemen could be seen milling about. The street was crowded but no one seemed to take any notice of a huge 1909 Packard that was idling almost in the middle of the street. A dark, swarthy man sat at the wheel. Four other dark, swarthy men (some reports said five men), all described later as short in stature and dressed in dark suits and wearing soft felt hats, stood in front of the car, forming an arc before the hotel entrance.

One of the men shouted: "Over here, Herman!" Rosenthal, who had lit a cigar when crossing the lobby, squinted into the darkness, unable to identify the man who called out to him with an unfamiliar voice. Rosenthal took a hesitant step forward, saying: "Who's that?" The killers closed in on him, just barely entering the glaring arc lights from the marquee, and five shots rang out, striking Rosenthal at close range (powder burns were to blacken his face). The bullets struck him in the neck, the nose and two in the head. One wild shot struck the door frame of the hotel. Rosenthal, spouting blood, fell dead in the street, the newspapers he had been carrying flying upward and then settling over his crumpled, prostrate body.

Eyewitnesses later claimed that the chief killer, the fierce Gyp the Blood Horowitz, had stepped forward before the

fusillade erupted and hailed his victim with the words "Hello, Herman." After Rosenthal collapsed from his lethal wounds, Horowitz leaned over to make sure the gambler was dead, then stood up, and said, "Goodbye, Herman." He then casually stepped over the body and joined his fellow gangsters, getting into the Packard which quickly roared down the street. (One witness swore that Gyp the Blood had sneered at his fallen victim and snorted the word "Gotcha!") Rosenthal lay in the street for some minutes, the many witnesses on the sidewalks frozen in a murder scene motif. In a doorway down the street, some later insisted, mob leader Jack Zelig lit a cigar and walked away from the scene. Then the street exploded with shouts and panic. Police came running from everywhere and witnesses raced to patrolmen to give varied descriptions of the killers and several versions of the license plate on the Packard.

One unlikely witness to this gory murder was none other than the esteemed drama critic for the New York *Times*, Alexander Woollcott, who would later become a best-selling author and remembered for his radio appearances as the Town Crier. Recalling the Rosenthal murder twenty-two years later when writing *While Rome Burns,* Woollcott summed up the livid scene: "I shall always remember the picture of that soft, fat body wilting on the sidewalk with a beer-stained tablecloth serving as its pall. I shall always remember the fish-belly faces of the sibilant crowd which sprung in a twinkling from nowhere, formed like a clout around those clamorous wounds. Just behind me an old timer whispered a comment which I have had more than one occasion to repeat. 'From where I stand,' he said, 'I can see eight murderers.'"

As evidence and the testimony of several gamblers scrambling to save their necks would later prove, there were four murderers, plus the man who ordered the killing, all of whom would later sit down in the electric chair for their blatant display of firearms. The killers and their driver fled down 43rd Street in the large Packard sedan. As the car turned onto Broadway with a squeal of tires, Detective File raced from the hotel, his .38-caliber revolver in his hand. He took a look at Rosenthal's body, the left side of the face blown away, and ordered two patrolmen nearby to follow him. They ran down the street to Broadway where Police Lieutenant Edward Frye met them. The four officers jumped into a cab and order the taxi driver to follow the Packard which was fast disappearing down Broadway. It soon outdistanced the taxi and disappeared. Fortunately, a young, unemployed cabaret singer, Charles Gallagher, had been walking toward the Metropole when the shooting occurred and had the presence of mind to write down the license plate of the car as it sped past him. He later had to argue with policemen to give them the number "NY-41313."

District Attorney Whitman was awakened at home by the indefatigable Swope who told him that his star witness had just been murdered. Whitman climbed out of his pajamas and into street clothes, going immediately to the 47th Street Precinct Station where the body of Rosenthal lay on a slab in the back room. Some minutes after the bleary-eyed Whitman arrived at the station, he turned to see Charles Becker enter. Becker later claimed that he too had been awakened by a newsman giving him the news of the killing and rushed to his own precinct station to verify the slaying. He took one look at the body and then he met the eyes of Charles Whitman glaring at him. For a moment the hardboiled crooked cop tried to stare down the district attorney but Whitman's eyes narrowed to slits of contempt and Becker, without a word, lowered his eyes and turned around, leaving the station quickly. He later met with Rose, Webber, and Vallon to congratulate them on the killing, telling the gamblers that he had just gone to the station house and how "it was a pleasing sight to me to see the squealing Jew lying there, and, if it had not been for the presence of Whitman, I would have cut out his tongue and hung it on the Times Building as a warning to future squealers."

An hour later, Whitman returned home, beside himself with anger over the killing of Rosenthal, telling his wife that "I'm going to get Becker if it's the only thing I ever do. New York is supposed to be the greatest city in the world...But as long as Becker and all those like him are allowed to defy and corrupt every law by which decent people live, New York will never be anything but a human sewer!" He vowed to send the killers, including Becker, to the electric chair. Whitman was greatly aided in his goal by soon receiving word that the license plate of the murder car had been traced to a rental garage. The killers could not have selected a more conspicuous auto to use in New York's most sensational murder of the decade. It had once belonged to the great fighter, John L. Sullivan, and was easily traced. It had been rented by a number of gamblers and these—Vallon, Rose, and Webber—were soon under arrest. They were housed in the Tombs but refused to admit to anything until it appeared quite obvious to them that they, not the actual triggermen, would be charged with the killings.

Rose was the first to crack, giving Whitman his famous thirty-eight-page statement in which he liberally quoted Becker's "Croak Rosenthal" decree. Realizing that Rose was saving his own skin, Webber and Vallon soon joined the chorus, corroborating every damning word Rose said, all, of course, with the promise of immunity extended to them. Through the cooperation of the gamblers, the killers, Harry Gyp the Blood Horowitz, Lefty Louie (Louis Rosenberg), Whitey Lewis (Jacob Seidenschmer) and Dago Frank

Cirofici, were all convicted by a jury that took twenty minutes to make up its collective mind on Nov. 19, 1912. All four young killers were electrocuted in Sing Sing on Apr. 14, 1913, a Monday. The previous day, the three Jewish men, Horowitz, Rosenberg, and Seidenschmer, were fed a Passover Dinner prepared in an Ossining hotel, which consisted of stuffed Hudson River bass, chicken soup and macaroons, roast chicken, mashed turnips, matzos, hard-boiled eggs, and peaches. All claimed to be innocent, saying that Vallon was the real killer. Dago Frank Cirofici called for a Catholic priest, then later "confessed" to warders, saying that Vallon and Gyp the Blood had done the killing. He was innocent, he claimed, being at home that night. The men swaggered to their deaths, heroes to the underworld in their own weird code, dying without begging for mercy. Their end came long before that of the man who had ordered them on their murderous mission. It took three years for the law to run Charles Becker to ground.

Once the gamblers made their confession, District Attorney Whitman allowed them their freedom, provided they would testify against Becker at his trial which was scheduled for Oct. 7, 1912. Whitman took no chances. Knowing that he must have corroboration for all the damning statements made chiefly by Rose, he brought another gambler named Sam Schepps into the picture. Schepps was assured immunity and confessed his part in the Rosenthal killing which he too claimed was ordered by Lieutenant Becker. The once-powerful Becker was by then suspended from the NYPD and had been locked in the Tombs to await trial. His attorney, John F. McIntye, was able and quick-witted, but he was up against an almost predetermined case since the shocking, brutal statements by Rose, which revealed Becker to be nothing more than a bestial and inhuman creature, had been broadly printed in the press. Moreover, Whitman was an eloquent and formidable opponent who was by now imbued with a messianic crusade to rid the world of police corruption and that particular venality was personified by Charles Becker. To Whitman, Becker was evil incarnate and he had taken it upon himself to eradicate this scourge personally. He was no less inspired in seeking this legal goal than was the mythical Sir Perceval who had hunted through the bogs of hell to find the Grail.

For his part, Becker exuded confidence from his prison cell. It was all a frameup, the gamblers had lied to save their own skins, Whitman was using him as a scapegoat in winning the governorship. He told his wife the trial would come to nothing and he would be back on the job before Christmas. What reasonable jury would take the word of such Broadway trash as Vallon, Rose, Webber, and Schepps over that of an upstanding police officer who had received his department's highest commendation for valor? He expected aid from Mayor Gaynor and, of course, his gentle superior, Commissioner Waldo. Yet, curiously, support from these totemic government officials was absent. Also, no one in the department, other than Becker's brother John, by then a lieutenant on the force, had come forward to lend strong support. There was a silence that befell Becker, ominous and knowing. And all but Becker, his blindly loyal wife, and some close relatives, accepted this man's doom.

A quicker death awaited Becker's gangster chieftain Big Jack Zelig. One day before Becker's trial began, Zelig, the most feared thug in New York, was murdered by an obscure goon whose motives were as absurd as the manner he chose to rid the city of a crime czar. Zelig was to testify at Becker's trial; he was listed as a defense witness, but Whitman, as he later stated, intended to have the gangster speak on behalf of the prosecution. If this was known by members of the underworld at the time, the presence of Zelig's killer was not a lone act of an unthinking thug, but a planned killing ordained by the leaders of the system.

Zelig acted in the last moments of his life as if he hadn't a care in the world. On the night of Oct. 5, 1912, Zelig had dropped into Siegel's Coffee House on Second Avenue and there enjoyed the company of a half dozen gangsters under his command. He drank heavily, downing several glasses of gin. He decided to get some air and stepped outside, lit a cigar, and looked about for the two detectives whom he knew had been assigned to watch him—since he was now an important witness in the Becker trial—and also to gather information on his on-going illegal activities. Zelig had been off-handedly grateful for this police surveillance since he knew he had been marked for death by a fierce new rival for his underworld territory, Jack Sirocco.

Although he had been expected to return to his men at Siegel's, Zelig inexplicably strolled a block or so and then, seeing a streetcar going uptown, jumped on board, walked to the back of the car, and squeezed his large frame between an old man and a young woman. As the car moved away from the Fifth Street stop, Zelig noticed from his bench seat a young, tall man racing after the car. He took the cigar out of his mouth and encouraged the passenger to catch up with the car, saying, "C'mon, you can make it, old boy!" The young man reached out, caught the outside handle bar, and swung himself onto the running board of the streetcar. Instead of entering the car, the slightly breathless passenger worked himself behind the last bench on the outside of the car so that he hung from the rear, standing behind Zelig. He reached into his pocket and withdrew a .38-caliber revolver. Zelig and the others in the car were facing the other direction and no one saw the killer place the muzzle of the gun behind Zelig's left ear. He fired one shot. Zelig leaped forward with the impact,

his face a mask of blood, crashing to the streetcar floor where his dying body gave one shuddering spasm and went limp. Screaming women and shouting men in the car pointed frantically to the sour-faced killer hanging at the end of the trolley.

The killer wasted no time, leaping from the car as it moved on. His jump was ill-chosen for he landed almost at the foot of a startled patrolman, banging into him, his revolver still in hand. The cop raised his nightstick and instinctively began clubbing the killer until he lay senseless on the sidewalk. He was identified a short time later as 30-year-old Philip "Red Phil" Davidson, who had occasionally worked as a fruit peddler but had a long criminal record as a narcotics pusher, gambler, and white slaver. He laconically told police that he had killed Zelig because the gangster had stolen $400 from him earlier that day. Later Davidson changed his story, saying that he had misstated the amount. Zelig had cheated him out of $18 and that is the reason why he felt compelled to murder the man. Of course, it was all nonsense. Zelig was a wealthy man who gave $20 to bootblacks for a mere shine and would not have spent a second bruising his knuckles over such a paltry amount. Davidson, after a brief trial, was given twenty years in prison and was released in twelve.

Whitman made much of Zelig's killing, claiming that the gangster would prove that Rose and the other gamblers had been telling the truth and that Becker was guilty. McIntyre, for the defense, said that such statements were ridiculous, that Zelig would have proved that Rose, Vallon, and Webber, all sworn enemies of Zelig's, had planned the killing of their worst competitor on their own and had used Zelig's best killers to do it and that Becker had no connection with the Rosenthal murder. It was, however, with Big Jack dead on a morgue slab, a moot issue. Becker's trial went ahead as planned and was over in twelve days.

Judge John Goff, a no-nonsense law-and-order magistrate, argued throughout the trial with defense counsel McIntyre and seemed to show a decided interest in having Becker found guilty. He allowed Whitman every opportunity, and made McIntyre battle himself into illness to make the meagerest point. Goff had long been a conservative foe of political graft and police corruption in New York, challenging the powers of Tammany as early as the 1890s during the Lexow and Mazet hearings. (Goff, during this trial, as was his habit with any other, took his lunch inside his chambers; this consisted exclusively of milk and crackers which he always washed down with a long swig of Irish whiskey.) His conduct was much in question and it drove Becker, outwardly calm during the entire course of the trial, to near rage when talking with his attorney in his Tombs cell. At one conference with McIntyre, Becker shouted at his beleaguered attorney: "Between that judge and your inability to stop the DA, I'm going to fry! I could have done better by myself." He insisted on taking the witness stand to clear himself but McIntyre persuaded him against this, assuring Becker that Goff's high-handed ways would prejudice the case and assure a victory for the defense in the Appeals Court. "It doesn't matter what the jury does," McIntyre told his client. "No conviction will ever survive an appeal."

Becker came to believe that the prosecution's case would not hold up, that the jury would reason that a bunch of murderous gamblers were obviously trying to frame a police officer who had persecuted them. He became so confident that he would be acquitted that he told his wife to wear her best dress on the last day of the trial. They would go to one of the best restaurants in town to celebrate his release. No one was more shocked when he was found Guilty and later sentenced by Goff to reside in Sing Sing where he would later be executed. McIntyre, however, was proved correct. The Appeals Court overruled the conviction, citing Goff's conduct and other discrepancies in the trial. Becker was tried again, and brought back from Death Row to the Tombs.

Judge Samuel Seabury who was as famous as Goff in combating New York corruption, presided over Becker's second trial which began on May 2, 1914, Whitman's choice in that he was more even-handed and careful in his supervision of the trial. Whitman did not want another reversal. Becker had to die in the electric chair and that meant that the second trial must end in a conviction that would be upheld at any judicial level. W. Bourke Cochran, an ex-judge, served as Becker's attorney, but he was no match for Whitman who once more paraded his gamblers before the jury with their inflammatory but utterly memorable testimony. Seabury avoided the pitfalls of Judge Goff and was extremely cautious in his instructions to the jury. On May 22, 1914, the jury took one hour and fifty minutes to convict Charles Becker of the murder of Herman Rosenthal. Becker was later sentenced to die in Sing Sing's electric chair on July 6, 1914. But one appeal after another postponed that date with death.

While Becker and his lawyers fought for his life, Whitman ran for the governor's office and, with the Becker conviction as the single most important achievement in his career to bolster support, he was swept into the Albany mansion with a tremendous Republican landslide on Nov. 3, 1914. Now Becker and his attorneys were faced with seeking Whitman's mercy after all other appeals failed. This Becker found intolerable, saying: "My life has been sacrificed on the altar of Whitman." But, as Becker's final date for execution approached, July 30, 1915, the condemned man found himself writing a pleading letter to the very man who convicted him, begging Whitman to commute

his sentence. Whitman, through an aide, stated: "The Governor cannot pardon a man he convicted." Whitman himself, just before the execution, after denying Becker's plea for clemency, said: "As far as Becker's conviction is concerned, there was never a criminal case more perfectly proven in the annals of crime. I have never had any doubt about Becker's guilt. If I had any now I would pardon him."

In a dramatic last minute effort, Mrs. Helen Becker went personally to Governor Whitman and begged for an interview. Whitman, through an aide, agreed to see her but when she appeared at the Governor's mansion in Albany only twelve hours before her husband was to die, she found the governor gone. She learned he was in Peekskill reviewing a military event. She trailed him there only to learn he had gone to Poughkeepsie. She found him at the Nelson House. Here the governor, cornered, as it were, by the desperate wife who had never given up on her husband or lost a second of belief in his innocence, was forced to face Helen Becker who implored him to consider her husband's last plea for a review of his case. Whitman only stood in the center of the Governor's suite, arms clasped behind his back, saying nothing. Mrs. Becker, understanding his silence to be a final refusal, broke down.

Nothing stopped Becker's execution on July 30, 1915. He entered the death room at Sing Sing and stoically, some reporters later stated "arrogantly," approached the electric chair, sitting down while staring ahead, his chin up, his eyes glaring at the twenty-odd witnesses. He repeated the litany being said by the prison chaplain, Father James Curry. The convicted killer looked massive and powerful as he sat in the chair, thick, muscular legs that were exposed at the calf where the trousers had been slit for the electrodes, an expanding chest that breathed evenly. Charles Becker insisted upon his innocence to the end and decided to show himself unafraid. He held a crucifix and when the first jolt of electricity was thrown into him, 1,850 volts of current, his large body of 215 pounds lurched against the straps with such force that the leather creaked and groaned, almost bursting their anchors. In ten seconds the current was shut off but an examining physician, Dr. Charles Farr, reported that Becker was still alive. Another ten-second jolt was thrown into him. Again his body strained against the straps. The doctor listened again to Becker's heart with his stethoscope and announced that the man was still alive. For a third time the body was given another jolt and this time Dr. Farr, after listening closely for a heartbeat, turned and said: "I pronounce this man dead."

By then the witnesses were exhausted with the shock of Becker's awful death, one that had taken nine minutes and was later considered one of the most "botched" executions in Sing Sing history. The nine minutes had seemed like an eternity to the witnesses, one of whom was a *World* reporter who later wrote: "To those who had sat in the gray-walled room and watched and listened to the rasping sound of the wooden switch lever being thrown backward and forward and had seen the greenish-blue blaze at the victim's head and feet, and the grayish smoke curling away from the scorched flesh, it had seemed an hour." The Crookedest Cop in the World was dead.

Becker, Marie Alexander, b.1877, Belg. A native of Liege, Marie Becker, fifty-three, was a bored housewife, married to a cabinetmaker. While buying vegetables at a street stall in 1932 she was approached by Lambert Beyer, a middle-aged lothario who propositioned her. She accepted without qualification and was soon involved in a deep love affair, convinced that the only way to recapture her youth was to murder her husband and go on with her girlish affairs. Becker poisoned her spouse with digitalis and, after tiring of Beyer, poisoned him with the same lethal drug. The once proper Becker, much to the shock of neighbors, became a nightlife creature, haunting dance halls and nightclubs, wildly dancing with men half her age. She paid these gigolos to accompany her to her bed and was soon out of money. Becker had opened a dress shop some months earlier from the proceeds of her husband's insurance and, to obtain money for her expensive affairs, she began to poison her female patrons with digitalis, dropping this in a cup of tea in the back of her shop while discussing a new order with a customer. She would steal whatever money her patrons possessed and then, while the customer was in a drugged condition, manage to get them home where they shortly died of "unknown causes."

Mass poisoner Marie Becker.

The number of murders committed by the homely housewife totaled ten known homicides, but there may have been twice that before Becker was arrested. She brought suspicion to herself when a woman friend casually remarked that her husband was aggravating her so much that she wished he were dead. "If you really mean that," responded the poisoner, "I can supply you with a powder that will leave no trace." The friend went to the police who had long suspected Becker because of the number of her clients who had mysteriously perished after visiting her shop. She

was arrested and, while in detention, the bodies of her husband, Beyer, and some of her customers were exhumed and traces of the poison were found.

Witnesses at Becker's trial told how they had seen the killer attend the funerals of her victims, kneeling at gravesides and weeping hysterically. She would later be seen that night doing erotic dances in Liege nightclubs, spending the very money that she had pilfered from her hapless victims. Becker held back nothing at her trial, gloating over the murders and describing with arch disdain the way her victims died. One of her victims, she said, "looked like an angel choked with sauerkraut." Another she described as "dying beautifully, lying flat on her back." Convicted, Marie Becker was sent to prison for life, there being no death penalty in Belgium at that time. She died in prison sometime during WWII.

Belachheb, Abdelkrim, 1945-   , U.S. When a woman in a Texas bar refused the sexual advances of the man she was dancing with, he went out to his car and returned to shoot her, killing six other people at the same time.

Abdelkrim Belachheb, a 39-year-old from Morocco, was at Ianni's Restaurant and Club in North Dallas in the early morning of June 29, 1984. When a woman he was dancing with admonished him for his aggressive behavior by pushing him away, he blew her a kiss, then went to his car and loaded a Smith and Wesson .459 automatic pistol. Returning to the club, he walked over to the woman who was now seated on a barstool and shot her to death. Belachheb again returned to his car, reloaded the gun, walked a second time into the bar, and randomly shot patrons off their barstools, killing five more and critically wounding another, who died at Parkland Memorial Hospital shortly after. According to Sergeant Bill Parker, he then fled in his station wagon, abandoned it after a traffic accident, and walked to the home of Mohammed Benali, about ten miles from the restaurant. The two men spoke in Arabic, according to Benali's friend, Anne Avis, then went to a back room of the house where they sat for about an hour of fasting, honoring the last day of Ramadan, a religious holiday during which Muslims keep a strict fast from sunrise to sunset and refrain from even thoughts of violence. Three hours after the shootings, they called the police, who arrested the killer.

Victims included Marcelle Ford, thirty-two, Frank Parker, forty-nine, Joseph Minasi, thirty-six, Linda Lowe, forty-three, and Janice Smith, forty-six. The police withheld the name of the sixth victim, a woman. Belachheb was put on trial in the Dallas District County Court of Judge Meier, and convicted on multiple charges of murder and attempted murder. On Nov. 15, 1984, he was sentenced to life imprisonment, and is currently serving his term at the Texas Department of Corrections Prison in Huntsville, Texas. Police spokesman Bob Shaw called the case "the worst multiple killing in the city's history in modern times."

Bell, James E., 1901-29, U.S. A man with a persecution delusion terrorized the streets of Newark, N.J., during a morning rush hour, killing two people and wounding three others before he committed suicide.

At 9 a.m. on Apr. 2, 1929, Julius Rabinowitz, thirty-eight, a jewelry salesman, was directed to the third floor apartment of James E. Bell by Louise Hooper, a neighbor in the tenement building. Intending to drop off some laundry work for Bell's wife, he knocked on the door. Bell flung it open and fired four shots from an automatic pistol into Rabinowitz's body, then shot him in the head with a shotgun. As he raced down the stairs with a weapon in each hand, Bell called back to Hooper, "Please tell my wife I've killed a man." On the street, Bell fired at a passing car, attracting the attention of 45-year-old William H. Bahrs, a post office clerk who was at home reading. As Bahrs looked out his window, Bell fired, hitting the man in the face and killing a caged canary inside the house. Bahrs stumbled to the phone and called the police. Charles Ramsperger, a 51-year-old cashier on his way to work, was Bell's next victim. The crazed killer also wounded Louis Pollack, a 43-year-old store owner, with a random shot.

Patrolman Thomas J. Hackett of the Newark police arrived and Bell shot him as he tried to draw his gun. Hackett then commandeered a taxicab to drive him around the block in an effort to catch Bell from behind. Joined by officer Samuel Cobb, Hackett found Bell dead in the alley, shot through the head with one of his own bullets. The wounded were rushed to City Hospital, Ramsberger dying on the way. Police found an arsenal of weapons in Bell's apartment, including two swords, a long curved knife, two blackjacks, 100 shotgun cartridges, sixty bullets, and a bag of buckshot.

One of Bell's neighbors, the Reverend Mr. Douglas, told of going to the man's apartment a few days earlier, jokingly calling to him, "I've got a warrant for you." When the excited Bell saw who it was he begged the minister never to do anything like that again, explaining, "I've been persecuted something awful and I'm liable to kill somebody anytime." An autopsy revealed that Bell was suffering from a blood disease.

Bell, Mary Flora, 1957-   , Brit. Mary Bell was only eleven years old when she killed two small boys in Newcastle, England. Children in the Scotswood district of the city began to have serious accidents in the spring of 1968. On May 11, a 3-year-old boy fell from the roof of an air-

Child killer Mary Bell.

raid shelter where he had been playing with Mary Bell and another girl named Norma Bell (not related). The boy survived the fall but was seriously injured. The following day, the mothers of three small children went to police to complain that Mary Bell had been choking their boys and girls, all about age six. A constable visited Mary Bell and gave her a lecture about keeping her hands off other children.

On May 25, 1968, the night before Mary Bell turned eleven, some boys playing in an abandoned house found the body of 4-year-old Martin George Brown. No cause of death was apparent and it was concluded he had swallowed some pills he found in a bottle. Later that day Norma Bell's father stopped Mary Bell from choking his 11-year-old daughter; the father had to slap the girl to get her to stop.

On the following day, May 26, a nursery school was broken into and damage was done. Investigating officers discovered a crudely written note laced with misspelled obscenities and a line that read "We did murder Martin Brown." Some days later, Mary Bell went to the Brown house and asked if she could see Martin. The distraught mother told her: "No, dear, Martin is dead." Replied Mary Flora Bell: "I know. I wanted to see him in his coffin." On May 31, police responded to a recently installed alarm in the nursery which had recently been vandalized and found Mary Bell and Norma Bell inside. Both girls swore they had never been in the school before and were sent home with a stern lecture. Mary Bell then began telling people that her friend Norma had killed the Brown child. When she heard that Norma's parents had become incensed over these remarks, Mary Bell ran to her friend's house and pantingly apologized.

On July 31, 1968, 3-year-old Brian Howe disappeared in the Scotswoord area and when a search ensued, Mary Bell told Howe's older sister that she saw the boy playing on concrete blocks in a deserted lot. Searchers found the boy's body near the blocks. The boy had been strangled to death and there were cuts on his stomach and legs. A pathologist reported that the killer could have been a child since little force had been employed in the murder. All the children in the area were then questioned as to their whereabouts on the night of Howe's death. Mary Bell stated that she had been playing near the area where the boy was killed and that she had seen an 8-year-old boy beating Brian and that the older boy was carrying a pair of broken scissors. The boy was interviewed and found to have been somewhere else on the night of the murder. Suspicion was directed toward Mary Bell since no one knew that a pair of broken scissors had been found at the murder site. Norma Bell was then interviewed and she said that she and Mary Bell had walked through the murder area and that Mary Bell had stumbled over the body of the Howe child and then admitted to her that she had killed him.

When Mary Bell was brought into police headquarters for further questioning, she assumed a very adult posture, insisting that she be allowed to contact a solicitor while accusing the police of "brainwashing" her. Norma then informed police that she had been with Mary when Mary Bell killed the boy, but that she had run away when Mary had "gone all funny" and began strangling the child. She returned to see Mary Bell mutilating the corpse with the scissors and with a razor she used to cut the stomach. Norma Bell correctly told police that the razor could be found beneath a rock. Mary retaliated by accusing Norma Bell of the murder. Chief Inspector James Dobson of the CID had for some time suspected Mary Bell of murdering the Brown and Howe boys. He had been watching her for some days and witnessed her strange actions on the day that the body of the Howe boy was removed from his home in a small coffin. "That was when I knew I couldn't risk another day," Dobson later stated. "She stood there laughing, laughing and rubbing her hands. I thought, My God, I've got to bring her in or she'll do another one."

Both Mary Bell and Norma Bell were placed on trial on Dec. 5, 1968, but it was clear early on that Norma Bell was completely under the domination of Mary Bell and that she was innocent of the murders. Mary Bell, who had told a police woman that she wanted to be a nurse so she could stick needles in people and that she "liked hurting people," was found Guilty of manslaughter in both the Brown and Howe cases due to "diminished responsibility." She was sent to Moor Court, an open prison, to serve a life sentence, since no asylum would accept her. She escaped with another inmate for three days in September 1977 but was recaptured within three days. Mary Bell proudly announced that she and the other girl had picked up some boys and that she had lost her virginity. She added that she felt that if she were left at large she could quickly become a useful citizen, a claim that found no support with officials.

Mary Bell's childhood in the impoverished Scotswood area certainly played a key role in creating her murderous personality. Her mother was only seventeen and unmarried when she gave birth. When she did marry, the mother, whose personality was volatile, left Mary alone a great deal of the time and often vanished for days on end. Her father was also gone a great deal of the time, and the Bell home was described as "poorly furnished and dirty." In school, Mary was known to be a habitual liar and an exhibitionist, one who liked punishing others. After Mary Bell's imprisonment, her father was sent to prison for robbery.

Belvin, Paul Augustus, 1943- , Ber. Appealing to a killer's vanity, two Scotland Yard detectives invited him to be an amateur detective and help solve his own crime.

On July 4, 1971, at 4:30 a.m., the partly clothed body of Jean Burrows, a 24-year-old British journalist vacationing with her husband in Bermuda, was discovered floating in three feet of water in Hamilton Harbour, a yacht basin for millionaires. The night before, Burrows, her husband, and two other journalists had ridden mopeds home after a dinner date at the popular Hoppin' John's restaurant, but she did not arrive with the others. A post-mortem by Dr. Wenwyon, the local pathologist, revealed that she had been raped, knocked unconscious by a heavy blow to the head, and then drowned by being held under water. Bruises indicated an attempt at strangulation before the drowning. Her moped was hidden three hundred yards from the body in a tall patch of grass. Recruited from Scotland Yard in London to investigate the crime were detectives William Wright and Basil Haddrell. After sending slides and photographs assembled by Wenwyon for analysis in London, the detectives set up house-to-house inquiries and came up with the name of Paul Augustus Belvin, a 28-year-old local man frequently seen in the basin where the body was found. Two witnesses recalled him as the winner of a competition the year before in which he had found a hidden key and won a cash prize, gaining some publicity.

When the detectives called Belvin in for questioning they found him to be clever, with a great deal of information concerning local gossip and the area. Wright surprised Haddrell, his superior, by asking Belvin if he would like to be an amateur detective and assist them in the investigation. Belvin eagerly agreed, and then proceeded to act out the entire crime in accurate and precise detail, even leading the detectives to the murder weapon, an iron pipe he had thrown into the sea. Tests on Belvin's clothing proved conclusively that he was the murderer. On Sept. 1, 1971, he confessed. Belvin was found Guilty and sentenced to death, a sentence later commuted to life in prison.

Bembenek, Lawrencia (**Laurie Bembenek**), 1959-
, U.S. A former policewoman and ex-Playboy bunny was
convicted of murdering her husband's former wife because
the ex-wife received substantial alimony.

On May 28, 1981, Christine Schultz was shot dead in her
home in Milwaukee, Wis. In June, Laurie Bembenek,
married to Elfred Schultz, Christine's ex-husband and a
former police detective, was charged with the murder.
Bembenek had been fired from the police force in September 1980, and Elfred Schultz resigned as a detective in
December 1981. Witnesses at the March 1982 trial, said
Bembenek, a former Playboy bunny in Lake Geneva, Wis.,
had talked about having Christine Schultz killed, complaining that her alimony payments were too large. Prosecution witnesses included Schultz's two sons: Shannon
Schultz, eight, who testified that the person who came into
his room seconds after shooting his mother wore a green
jogging suit, and 12-year-old Sean Schultz who remembered
the murderer in a loose green army jacket. Four witnesses
testified that Bembenek owned a jogging outfit like that
described. Hairs from a wig found hidden in Bembenek's
apartment matched hairs found near the slain woman's
body. Robert Kraemer, assistant district attorney, headed
the prosecution's case, portraying Bembenek as a woman
addicted to "the fast life," while defense attorney Donald
Eisenberg said his client was framed, quoting the Bible and
Pope Paul VI in his four hours of closing arguments.
Bembenek was found Guilty of first-degree murder and
sentenced by Judge Michael Skwierawski to life imprisonment. A large crowd of spectators followed the
fifteen-day trial.

Benitez, Martin Rivera (**AKA: Big Soul**), prom.
1970s, Mex. A killer for hire, Benitez was a native of
Hildago who would murder anyone if the price was right.
Between 1969 and 1972, it is estimated by Mexican police
that he killed at least fifty persons. Twelve headless bodies
were found in his "morgue," in a woods near his Jazatipan
house. Benitez, serving life, explained later that he was so
much in demand that lines formed around his house and
that to prove that the victims were indeed killed by him, he
would cut off the heads and show these to his employers.
"I saw nothing wrong in killing for money," the mass
murderer said without a bit of remorse. "If I had not done
it, someone else would."

Benson, Steven, 1951- , U.S. Threatened with being
cut out of his wealthy mother's will, a 34-year-old would-
be entrepreneur planted two pipe bombs in her car,
murdering two people and severely injuring a third.

Steven Benson was born into money, the son of tobacco
tycoon Edward Benson and Margaret, his heiress wife.
Gifted at electronics, Steven Benson, at an early age, built
a television set, an achievement his mother spoke of
proudly. By the time he reached adulthood, however, he
had become greedy, unsuccessful at his many business
adventures, and twice divorced. Benson spent copious
amounts of the family money on small businesses that
repeatedly fell apart. After his father died in 1980,
Margaret Benson continued to give her eldest son money
for his ventures, but when she learned he was lifting funds
from the businesses into his own pocket, she threatened to
write him out of her will. On July 9, 1985, Benson, then
living with his mother and his nephew, Scott, twenty-one,
in Naples, Fla., planted two twenty-seven pound bombs in
his mother's car. Set off by an electronic device, they killed
Scott, Margaret Benson, and severely injured Carol Lynn
Kendall, Scott's mother and Steven's sister.

Kendall served as the state's main witness, testifying
against her brother. One year after the bombs exploded,
Benson was found Guilty of murder and condemned to
serve two consecutive life sentences, along with thirty-
seven years for attempted murder and arson.

Berkowitz, David (**AKA: Son of Sam**), 1953- , U.S.
David Berkowitz, an unbalanced slayer who terrorized New
York for more than a year as the "Son of Sam," was born
June 1, 1953, the bastard son of a woman who gave him up
for adoption. Throughout his miserable life, he had a deep
sense of rejection. He grew up shy and terrorized by
women. His stepfather, Nat Berkowitz, ran a hardware
store in the Bronx and later retired to Florida. His stepson
David remained in New York, living on Pine Street in
Yonkers. He worked at odd jobs and his room was always
littered with garbage. He could not sleep, he complained
in letters to his stepfather, because the sound of trucks on
the street and a neighbor's barking dog kept him up every
night. He became paranoid, insisting that strangers on the
street displayed hatred for him and spat at him as he
walked past. "The girls call me ugly and they bother me the
most," he wrote his stepfather. On Christmas Eve 1975,
Berkowitz attacked two girls with a knife at separate sites.
The first girl frightened him off with her wild shrieking, but
he plunged the blade into the lung of the second girl, a 15-
year-old schoolgirl and left her for dead. She survived.
Berkowitz waited seven months before striking again, this
time on the night of July 29, 1976. He found two girls,
Donna Lauria and Jody Valenti talking in the front seat of

a car parked on Buhre Avenue. Calmly taking a gun from a brown paper bag, he fired five shots into them, killing Lauria and wounding Valenti in the leg. Police were baffled—the killer was a person without motive and was thought to be one who killed for thrills. Berkowitz shot and wounded Carl Denaro on the night of Oct. 23, firing through the rear window of his car as Denaro sat with his girlfriend, Rosemary Keenan, in front of a Flushing bar. On Nov. 26, two more girls, Joanne Lomino and Donna DeMasi, sitting on the stoop of a house in the Floral Park section of Queens, were approached by Berkowitz, who began to ask them directions, but stopped in mid-sentence. He pulled his gun from the brown bag and fired blindly, wounding both of them before fleeing. Lomino was paralyzed by a bullet that lodged next to her spine. Other bullets dug out of the wooden stairs of the stoop matched those in the Lauria-Valenti shooting.

Police still had no clue as to the identity of the killer, despite efforts to trace the gun. Then, on Jan. 30, 1977, Berkowitz spotted a young couple necking in a car in Ridgewood. He crept up on the car, took the gun out of the brown paper bag, and fired through the window, one of his bullets striking the head of Christine Freund, who collapsed into the arms of her boyfriend, John Diel. She was pronounced dead a few hours later. On Mar. 8, 1977, Berkowitz walked up to Virginia Voskerichian, an Armenian student he had never met, pulled out his gun, and fired point-blank into the girl's face, killing her as she walked down a Forest Hills street. Witnesses described Berkowitz as about five feet, ten inches tall, with black hair combed straight back. He was described by authorities as "a savage killer" and women were warned not to travel alone at night in the city. On Apr. 17, 1977, Berkowitz came upon Valentina Suriani and Alexander Esau, sitting in a parked car in the Bronx, only a short distance from where he had shot Lauria and Valenti. He shot both of them at close range. Suriani was killed instantly and Esau, with three bullets in his head, died in the hospital some time later.

Mass murderer David Berkowitz.

Following this shooting, a note was found addressed to Police Captain Joseph Borrelli, who had made several statements about the killer to the press. To Borrelli, Berkowitz wrote: "I am deeply hurt by your calling me a weman-hater (sic). I am not. But I am a monster. I am the Son of Sam. I am a little brat...I love to hunt, prowling the streets, looking for fair game...tasty meat...The weman of Queens are prettyist of all." In this letter, Berkowitz, seeming to emulate the letters Jack the Ripper sent to authorities almost a century earlier when prowling the streets of London, claimed that he had been brutalized by his father when he was a child and that he was later ordered by his father to go into the streets and murder. Berkowitz sent a similar letter to New York columnist Jimmy Breslin, who had been writing extensively about the slayer.

Berkowitz struck again on June 26, 1977, shooting Judy Placido and Salvatore Lupo as they sat in a car in a street in Queens. This time Berkowitz had fired quickly and his aim was poor; his victims were only slightly wounded. Berkowitz roamed the streets of the Bronx and Queens looking for victims but police seemed to be everywhere. He went to Brooklyn and, on July 31, 1977, found Stacy Moskowitz and Robert Violante sitting in a car. He fired four shots through the window, killing Moskowitz and blinding Violante. A woman walking her dog saw Berkowitz run to his car and leap in, speeding away. She told police that the car had a parking violation ticket in its windshield. Police checked to find that only four parking tickets had been issued that morning and the carbon copy of one of these bore the registration number of David Berkowitz of Yonkers. Police Inspector Tim Dowd and others found the car parked near Berkowitz's apartment and waited for him to appear on Aug. 2, 1977. Berkowitz walked toward the car at 10:15 p.m. Dowd stepped forward and said: "Hello, David."

Berkowitz stood still for a moment, then his pudgy face crinkled with his peculiar beamish smile. "Inspector Dowd!" he said, recognizing the officer from his newspaper photos. "You finally got me." He surrendered meekly and later tried to mount a defense of insanity, but psychiatrists testified at Berkowitz's trial that he was faking. The sinister Son of Sam name was an invention of Berkowitz's, taken from his neighbor, Sam Carr. It was Carr's dog who had kept him up nights. He had shot the dog but the animal recovered and it was later claimed by Berkowitz that the dog spoke to him as one of the voices that told him to go out and murder. Berkowitz pleaded guilty to murder charges when he was arraigned on Aug. 23, 1977, and was never tried. He was sentenced to 365 years in prison with no hope of parole. His apartment was later looted by souvenir hunters.

Bernardy, Sigoyer de (**Marquis de Bernardy**), d.1947, Fr. Though placed in an insane asylum during the 1930s—once for claiming to have eaten a missing man whose identification papers were found in his home—Sigoyer de Bernardy managed to obtain his release and became quite wealthy during WWII by opening a restaurant selling wholesale liquor to German soldiers.

De Bernardy, who called himself a marquis, married Janine Kergot and they had two children. He also had one child by the nursemaid of his children, Irene Lebeau, for which his wife left him in 1944. The court ordered de Bernardy to pay 10,000 francs a month, but an attempt to collect this alimony one month proved to be fatal for Kergot, who disappeared without a trace after going to his home to inquire about the money.

Her disappearance would have remained a mystery if not for letters written by de Bernardy to Lebeau while he was imprisoned after the war for collaborating with the enemy. One letter alluded to a cask which held clothing and jewelry belonging to the missing woman, while another spoke of a red armchair which Lebeau said was the chair Kergot was sitting on when de Bernardy strangled her. De Bernardy claimed he was innocent, stating he had only helped Lebeau conceal the body after she had shot Kergot.

The missing woman's body was discovered in the wine cellar of de Bernardy's warehouse in the Rue de Nuits, but no bullet wound was found. At the joint trial of de Bernardy and Lebeau on Dec. 23, 1946, Lebeau was acquitted but de Bernardy was sentenced to death and guillotined in June 1947.

Bertucci, Clarence V., 1921- , U.S. The war was over. For the German prisoners still confined in the POW camp at Salina, Utah, in July 1945, all that remained was the long trip home to begin their lives anew. Located 150 miles south of Salt Lake City, Camp Salina received hundreds of Nazi prisoners during the war without incident. By day the buses transported the men to Sevier and Sanpete counties where they picked beets under the direction of U.S. Army personnel. It was a quiet, if not dull, existence for both POWs and GIs during the closing months of WWII.

All this changed on July 8, when in a moment of mental duress 23-year-old army private Clarence Bertucci seized a .30-caliber air-cooled machine gun perched atop a guard tower and began strafing the tents of the sleeping German prisoners.

Bertucci, who had been confined to the stockade on three occasions for insubordination and desertion, was scheduled to report for duty at Tower One at midnight. At 11 p.m. he shared a few beers in town with some local Salina girls before grabbing a quick cup of coffee at an all-night diner near the camp.

It was a cool, cloudless night as Bertucci climbed the guard tower and took over the gun. He looked out across the tent city where 250 Germans slept. He loaded 250 rounds into the weapon. Then, for the next fifteen seconds, he riddled forty-three tents from left to right as frantic prisoners scurried for cover. Wakened abruptly, Lieutenant Albert Cornell ran to the tower and ordered Bertucci to cease firing. He did, because all the ammo in the machine gun had been discharged. Corporal Delmire Butts charged up the ladder to bring him down from his post.

When all the tents were checked, eight Germans had been killed and twenty more wounded. The victims were laid to rest at Fort Douglas and accorded a proper military funeral. For the rest of the prison-camp population unhurt in the hail of bullets, there were more beets to pick. Colonel Arthur Ericsson, commanding officer of the Army Services Forces POW camp at Ogden, refused their request for a two-day layoff. "We declined the request on the grounds that it would be better for them to work than to stay idle," he said.

When questioned by an investigating board, Bertucci showed no remorse for what he had done. He said he hated Germans, and he wanted to kill them. The tedium of a noncombat assignment had apparently been too much for this young soldier. "Something must have happened to him," explained his mystified mother upon hearing the news.

On Aug. 18, a panel of medical officers and psychiatrists at Bushnell General Hospital concluded that Bertucci was "mentally unbalanced." Five days later he was granted a discharge from the Army and sent to Mason General Hospital, Brentwood, Long Island, N.Y., for further tests and evaluation.

Back home in New Orleans, his thirteen brothers and sisters recalled that shy, withdrawn Clarence had acted strangely when he returned on a furlough from England in 1944. After he left for his tour of duty in the Utah desert, they discovered a cryptic message penciled on a doorsill. It read: "Live and let live."

Best, Alton Alonzo, 1956- , U.S. When Alton Best was led away to prison to begin serving an 18-year sentence for the murder of 20-year-old nursing aid Janice Elaine Morton, defense attorney Neal Kravitz noted with a tinge of sadness, "Mr. Best is a really nice, thoughtful, nonviolent man who did something horrible because of his drug use. It is sad. It really is a tragedy." But many others would not agree.

What the baffled Washington, D.C., detectives do not know is just how many more deaths the "nice, thoughtful" drug user may have been responsible for. Between Dec. 13, 1986, and Jan. 12, 1987, five badly mangled bodies were found in a remote wooded area near the Bradbury Recreation Center in Suitland, in Prince George's County, Md. Janice Morton's body was found on Jan. 15, 1987, a couple of miles away. All six of the victims were poor, young, black women and they had all been sodomized.

Alonzo Best, a groundskeeper for the National Park Service on winter furlough, had a record of violent crime dating back to December 1981 when he kidnapped and robbed two young women, but the charges were later dropped. In 1983 he was arrested and convicted for possessing PCP and two years later was convicted of mail fraud. At the time of his arrest for murder, he had several arrests for drug possession.

On Jan. 15, 1987, Best drove a black van belonging to his nephew, Washington, D.C., policeman William Armah, into an alley near 414 Eastern Avenue, in the northeast section of the city. There he deposited the severely lacerated body of Janice Morton, who was twelve weeks pregnant when she died. Her body was found a few hours later by a witness who identified Best as the man who had left a large item in the alley. The hunt for the black van started. Later that afternoon, Best returned the van to his nephew, who discovered bloodstains in the rear. Best told him that the blood was from an injured friend he had taken to a hospital.

Janice Morton's mother had reported her disappearance to police, though she had not seen her daughter for nearly eighteen days. The body was not identified for another twelve days, when Morton's employer recognized the sketch in the newspaper. A search of the Morton residence turned up an address book and the name of an acquaintance who was able to link the killer to the victim.

Strangely enough, two days before Best was apprehended, the now-famous black van was pulled over by Prince George's County police, but the officer neglected to search the vehicle because the driver showed police credentials. Best, beside his nephew, must have thought he was safe, but he was finally arrested on Jan. 30 1987. The van was located in a repair shop, and the bloodstains were found. The police soon learned that Armah and Best had shared an apartment near Suitland prior to the murders of the five women. They also found that Best had tenous links to at least three of the women found at Suitland. But the evidence connecting Best to those murders stopped there.

Prosecutors presented the court with a seemingly airtight case against Best for the murder of Janice Morton. Best pleaded guilty to second-degree murder in exchange for the government's agreement to drop first-degree and rape charges. There was no chance of securing a death sentence against Best because capital punishment had long been abolished in Washington, D.C. Judge Reggie Walton of the D.C. Superior Court sentenced Best to fifteen years to life,

with an additional forty months to five years for sodomy. If Best had chosen to dump the body a few hundred feet away, he would have been in Maryland, where capital punishment exists.

Beto, Joseph Anthony, 1945-   , and **Zamp, Jerome,** 1947- , U.S. It took three months and a search as far away as New Orleans, La., before the killers of Dr. Hans Wachtel were caught.

Wachtel was shot twice in the head on Feb. 2, 1977, while sitting in his car parked outside his South Side Chicago apartment. The 67-year-old doctor was the chairman of the obstetrics-gynecology department at Woodlawn Hospital. His assailants were Joseph Anthony Beto, who was arrested May 13, and Jerome Zamp, arrested in New Orleans two days later.

Both were found Guilty of murder and sentenced by Judge Barbaro to spend from 200 to 300 years in prison. Others were sought and arrested for the crime but no other convictions were made.

Bianchi, Kenneth (AKA: **The Hillside Strangler; Steve Walker; Anthony D'Amato; Nicholas Fontana; Billy**), 1952- , and **Buono, Angelo, Jr.,** 1935- , U.S. These two bestial killers slew ten young women and girls who were

Kenneth Bianchi   Angelo Buono

mostly part-time prostitutes, murdering them from 1977 to 1979 in Angelo Buono, Jr.'s home in Glendale, Calif., committing the slayings attributed to the Hillside Strangler. Kenneth Bianchi, who had been born in Rochester, N.Y., and had been raised by foster parents, arrived in Los Angeles in 1977 to stay with his cousin Buono, who was a street-tough sub-normal creature always trying to prove his manhood and authority. He reveled in being Italian and flew the Italian flag 24 hours a day from a flagpole on the grounds of his house. He ran an upholstery business out of his garage and was already continually parading prostitutes through his home by the time Bianchi arrived. One night, as the cousins sat about getting drunk on beer, they speculated as to what it might be like to actually murder someone.

They started their mass murder spree by killing Elissa Teresa Kastin, twenty-one, on Oct. 6, 1977, dumping her naked body near Chevy Chase Drive in Glendale. Their next victim was 19-year-old Yolanda Washington; her body was found on the slopes of the distinguished Forest Lawn Cemetery, the resting place of movie stars, on the night of Oct. 18, 1977. The body was naked, cleaned by the killers so as to leave no clues, and posed in a lascivious position. Bianchi and Buono went on to murder eight more women. On Oct. 31, 1977, the naked body of 15-year-old Judith Lynn Miller was found on a hillside next to the road in Glendale. She had been raped, sodomized, and strangled to death. Her wrists, ankles, and neck bore the marks of the ropes that had bound her, as was the case with the Washington woman and those victims to come. Bianchi and Buono, to show their contempt for lawmen looking for them, made sure that this body and the others had been cleaned, leaving no clues whatsoever, but placed the corpses in spots where they could easily be found and usually close to police stations, as if to thumb their noses at police.

On Nov. 20, 1977, the killers slew three more, Kristina Weckler, twenty; Dolores Cepeda, twelve; and Sonja Johnson, fourteen, dumping the nude body of Weckler on a slope in Highland Park and the corpses of Cepeda and Johnson in Elysian Park. They killed Jane Evelyn King, twenty-eight, on Nov. 23, 1977, dumping her body at the off-ramp of the southbound Golden State Freeway. On Nov. 29, 1977, Bianchi and Buono murdered Lauren Rae Wagner, eighteen, placing her naked body on Cliff Drive in Glassell Park. Next, on Dec. 14, 1977, police found the naked body of Kimberly Diane Martin, eighteen. The intensity of the murders slackened but, on Feb. 17, 1978, Cindy Lee Hudspeth's naked body was found in the trunk of a car. The killings had all been committed in Buono's home and the bodies dumped in a rough circle around that house.

Police announced regularly that they were closing in on the Hillside Strangler and that several "good" suspects had been pulled in for questioning, but when the killings stopped, police had little to say and less to investigate, their special team of investigators reassigned to other chores. Los Angeles detectives were perplexed when the killings suddenly ended. The reason for this was hygiene. Bianchi left Buono's home because of the filthy conditions there,

going to Bellingham, Wash., where, in January 1979, he raped and strangled to death with a cord two college women, Karen Mandic and Diane Wilder, packing the bodies into the trunk of Mandic's car. Following a missing persons report, these bodies were found and Bianchi came under suspicion as having been seen with one of the women shortly before her disappearance.

Ironically, Bianchi was working as a security guard and had applied for a job with the Bellingham police department. (He had also applied for a job with the Los Angeles Police Department and, in fact, had gone along on a few rides with officers in Los Angeles while the Hillside Strangler was being sought.) Bianchi, who had steeped himself in psychiatric studies, played a game with doctors examining him, pretending, it was later reported, to have a split personality, or many personalities, one of which being the killer of the women. He claimed that he had blackouts and could not remember his actions. He presented all the symptoms of someone unbalanced, out of control, legally insane. His act, however, did not work, and he was charged with the murder of the two Bellingham women. Then Bianchi offered prosecutors a deal; he would turn over his cousin Buono, the real Hillside Strangler, he said, if he were removed to California and did not have to face the death penalty in Washington, that of hanging. Washington authorities agreed to the deal, as long as Bianchi pleaded guilty. He did and received a life sentence, then was shipped to California to testify against his brutal cousin, Buono, after which he would serve his time in a California prison, one less austere and rigid than Washington's Walla Walla Prison.

On Bianchi's statements, Buono was charged with murder but Bianchi, who had fooled six Washington state psychiatrists into labeling him legally insane, now could not testify against Buono since he was a lunatic. Yet it was shown that he had planned his "insanity" position years earlier, reading endless studies on psychiatry and particularly studying the novels *Sybil* and *The Three Faces of Eve,* preparing for his own positioning of multiple personalities, a psychological profile he assumed when confronted with the Washington murders. Bianchi had gone so far as to claim he had a degree in psychiatry and was about to actually open up a practice in Los Angeles before going off to Washington. Bianchi also had faked being hypnotized, according to most reports, when being examined in Washington, and then released his other "identities," claiming that these personalities had done the horrible murders with his beast-like cousin Buono.

Bianchi nevertheless gave a complete profile of the murders he committed with Buono once back in Los Angeles, describing how he and Buono drove about in Buono's car, using phony badges to identify themselves to young women as policemen, ordering them into Buono's auto, which they passed off as an unmarked police car. Once the women were in the car, they were taken to Buono's home, tortured, forced to have sex with both of them, and then tied up and murdered, usually strangled, although the killers experimented with injections and other murder methods that proved unsuccessful. Then the murderers fastidiously washed their victims and dumped their naked bodies at remote spots.

Buono was arrested in 1979 after Bianchi's Washington conviction, and he was eventually tried on Nov. 16, 1981. A grueling two years passed during which more than 400 witnesses were heard, 55,000 pages of trial transcript were compiled, and millions of dollars were spent to convict Buono. A jury, more than two years later, convicted him of nine counts of murder on Nov. 14, 1983. The trial was aptly labeled a "judicial extravaganza" by the press, one in which Buono insisted, in court and out, that he was innocent of the murders his cousin claimed he had performed. (He had been extremely thorough in cleaning up his home after Bianchi left, not one fingerprint of the victims, not even his own, could be found by police, although a single eyelash belonging to one of the victims was unearthed and a few strands of fiber from one of Buono's chairs was found on one of the bodies.) A surprise prosecution witness was 27-year-old Catherine Lorre who identified both Bianchi and Buono as the two men who had stopped her on a Holly-wood street in 1977, saying they were detectives and demanding her identification. She had shown her driver's license and next to it, Bianchi saw a photo of her as a little girl sitting on her father's lap, her father being the famous character actor of films, Peter Lorre. Bianchi later ad-mitted that he had let Lorre go because he feared that murdering the child of a celebrity would bring more police heat down upon him and Buono.

Judge Ronald George, who had refused to drop charges against Buono "for lack of evidence," as asked by the prosecution during the initial stages of his trial when it felt it would lose the case altogether, had conducted a fair and impartial trial for more than two years. He pronounced sentence on Angelo Buono, Jr., on Jan. 9, 1984, giving him life imprisonment without possibility of parole. Bianchi, against his clever designs, was ordered sent back to Walla Walla Prison in Washington to serve out a life sentence without possibility of parole until the year 2005. Stated Judge George after sentencing: "I'm sure Mr. Buono and Mr. Bianchi, that you will only get your thrills by reliving over and over the tortures and murders of your victims, being incapable as I believe you to be, of ever feeling any remorse."

Biegenwald, Richard F., 1941- , U.S. There is no honor among thieves. Richard Biegenwald, a sadistic killer from Asbury Park, N.J., realized this too late in the game. He also learned a valuable lesson in human nature: what you say in an unguarded moment can return to haunt you. While serving time in prison for killing during a holdup, Biegenwald made the acquaintance of Dherran Fitzgerald. Later, when both men were released, they decided to share an apartment together with Biegenwald's wife in Point Pleasant, N.J. Biegenwald took Fitzgerald into his confidence and revealed the sordid details of five different murders he had committed between 1981 and 1983.

Biegenwald had a long record of violent crime dating back to 1958, when he murdered New Jersey municipal prosecutor Stephen Sladowski during a grocery store holdup. The victim's wife urged the courts to spare the life of the young killer, with the tearful explanation that there had been too much bloodshed already. In 1959 the 19-year-old was sentenced to life in prison. He was twice denied parole and had been disciplined on several occasions before gaining release in 1975.

His next brush with the law occurred in 1980 when he violated his parole by moving to Teaneck, N.J. That same year he was implicated in a Staten Island rape case. The charges were dropped, but Biegenwald found himself behind bars at Rahway State Prison until his discharge was granted in February 1981. There he met Dherran Fitzgerald.

Acting on a tip from Fitzgerald, investigators searched a lonely spot off Route 35 in Ocean Township where the remains of 18-year-old Camden resident Anna M. Olesiewicz were found. The girl had been missing since Aug. 28, 1982, when she was lured into Biegenwald's car to share a marijuana cigarette. After driving aimlessly through Asbury Park, he shot her four times in the head with a small-caliber handgun.

Fitzgerald and Biegenwald were arrested in their Asbury Park apartment on Jan. 22, 1983, eight days after the body was discovered. An arsenal of handguns, grenades, shot-guns, and silencers were found along with a cache of illegal drugs. Monmouth County Prosecutor Alexander D. Lehrer followed up on Fitzgerald's tip and other pieces of evidence that led him to two unmarked graves in the quiet Charleston section of Staten Island where Biegenwald had disposed of the bodies of 17-year-old Maria Ciallella of Brick Township, N.J., and William J. Ward, a 34-year-old hoodlum who had tried to hire Biegenwald to perform a contract hit. The Ciallella woman was found in the back-yard of a frame house belonging to Biegenwald's mother. She had been abducted on Halloween night, 1981, while walking home on Route 88. Biegenwald had blasted two fatal shots into her head, then disposed of the remains in his mother's backyard.

The bodies of two other teenaged girls, 17-year-old Betsy Bacon and 17-year-old Deborah Osborne, were uncovered in two Jersey sites. Forensic experts identified the remains through dental charts. Deborah Osborne had been abducted at the Idle Hour Tavern in Point Pleasant, near a motel where she had been working as a chambermaid. Police theorized that she had left the tavern and hitched a ride with Biegenwald.

A sixth victim, 57-year-old convict John P. Petrone, was linked to Biegenwald when it was learned that the two men had become friends in prison. Petrone was silenced when Biegenwald suspected him of being a police informer.

Staten Island District Attorney Richard D. Murphy raised the possibility that the full extent of Biegenwald's crimes might never be known. Investigators continued to comb the areas adjacent to the grave sites but found only a few animal bones.

On Dec. 7, 1983, Biegenwald was convicted of murdering Anna M. Olesiewicz. He became the second New Jersey man to be sentenced to die by lethal injection under the newly reinstated death penalty, which took effect three weeks before he fired the first fatal shots. He sat on Death Row for more than three years, until Mar. 5, 1987, when the New Jersey Supreme Court ruled in a 6-1 decision that the law was constitutional, but that in Biegenwald's case the death sentence should be overturned because of grave errors in the sentencing hearing. The court upheld his conviction but ordered that a new sentencing hearing be scheduled to determine if he should be executed or sentenced to prison for life.

On Jan. 23, 1989, a jury in Freehold, N.J. deliberated for six hours before deciding that Biegenwald should be executed. The defense attorneys urged leniency, on the grounds that the defendant's sociopathic behavior should be carefully analyzed. The jury rejected this argument, and Judge Patrick McGann set Mar. 15 as Biegenwald's date of execution. The date was automatically postponed pending a mandatory Supreme Court review.

====

Bird, Jake, 1901-49, U.S., mur. Jake Bird was convicted of a double ax murder in Tacoma, Wash., and confessed to several other murders while awaiting his execution in prison. Bird was born on Dec. 14, 1901, in Louisiana. He spent his adult years wandering around the country, staying briefly in New York, Maine, Boston, Philadelphia, Chicago, and St. Louis. Though he worked several temporary jobs and found frequent employment with the railroad, he was a professional criminal who burglarized homes wherever he found himself. He spent a total of thirty-one years in prison in Utah, Iowa, and Michigan, all on burglary charges. While in prison, he read law books and learned the strategies and tactics of the legal system. Those investigators who worked on his case remembered Bird as a man who thought little of committing violent acts. A black man, Bird hated both whites and women, and especially loathed white women. He was described by many as sophisticated, calculating, witty, an able conversationalist, and extremely dangerous.

In the early morning hours of Oct. 30, 1947, two police officers, Patrolmen Evan "Skip" Davies and Andres "Tiny" Sabutis, responded to a report of a woman screaming in a neighborhood on South J Street in Tacoma. Approaching the house where the screams originated, Davis saw a man running from the back of the house. He pursued the man and cornered him in an alley. The man was not wearing shoes, and his clothes were spattered with blood. The man charged Davis, who drew his gun and repeatedly struck him over the head. The man drew a knife and slashed the officer's hand. Sabutis arrived and found Davis clubbing the man with his gun. But when he attempted to handcuff him, the knife wielder slashed Sabutis across the back. Enraged by the violence, Davis beat the man around the face until he lay panting on the ground. The officers brought the man back to the home, where they discovered the bodies of Mrs. Bertha Kludt, fifty-two, and Beverly June Kludt, her 17-year-old daughter. The daughter was lying between the bedrooms and the kitchen and her mother lay in one of the bedrooms. Both were beaten and slashed with the blunt end and the blade of an ax. They were dressed in their nightgowns and covered with blood. Police identified the suspect in custody as Jake Bird.

Within a few hours of his arrest, Bird signed a confession to the murders of the Kludt women. He said he had been in Washington only three days when he walked through a residential district seeking a home to burglarize. He found an ax in a nearby shed and took it with him for protection. Finding the back door of the home on South J Street unlocked, he entered the house, took off his shoes, went into one of the bedrooms, and took the purse he found there. As he tried to open the purse in the kitchen, he was startled by Mrs. Kludt, who approached him from behind. Bird threatened her, but told her he only wanted to rob the house. The commotion woke Beverly, who entered the kitchen and jumped on Bird's back. Mrs. Kludt likewise grabbed Bird and began screaming. Bird grabbed his ax and began swinging, knocking the two women down. He could not remember how many times he hit them after that.

Bird's prosecution, however, was not cut and dried. He withdrew his confession shortly after signing it, and claimed he signed it because the police beat him and he feared for his life. Bird claimed that the officers had cracked his ribs, whipped him around the legs until he had no skin left, and beat him around the face until four of his teeth were knocked out and he required several stitches in his head and face. The police neglected to mark evidence from the scene of the crime, and later had difficulty identifying it. Furthermore, there were no fingerprints, and Bird could be placed only within the vicinity of the crime. Yet, within hours of his arrest, several cities, including Los Angeles, Louisville, Ky., Orlando, Fla., Evanston, Ill., and Kansas City, Kan., indicated that Jake Bird might be involved in one of their unsolved murder cases. According to Bird's later confessions, he participated in more than ten murders throughout the U.S. Police retained the services of Dr. Charles P. Larson, a well-known criminal pathologist. Dr. Larson found brain matter and two blood types in Bird's pants. With this evidence, the prosecution secured Bird's conviction.

At his trial, the jury found Jake Bird Guilty of two counts of first-degree murder after only thirty-five minutes of deliberation. Sentenced on Dec. 6, 1947, Bird addressed the court for the first time when Judge E.D. Hodge asked him if he wished to say anything. Bird pronounced his own ominous sentence. "All of you who have had anything to do with my case will be punished," Bird claimed. "I am putting the Jake Bird hex on you. Mark my words, you will die before I do." With that, Judge Hodge sentenced Bird to be hanged by the neck until dead and scheduled the execution for Jan. 16, 1948. The convicted man began a campaign of legal manipulation and bargain making in order to stay his sentence. His first appeal went unacknowledged by Judge Hodge. Bird then informed Walla Walla Prison officials that he would help them solve ten murders if Governor Mon C. Wallgren granted a stay of execution. The governor agreed to listen to Bird and grant a stay only if he helped clean up unsolved murder cases.

In the presence of undersheriff Joe Karpach, governor's representative Pat Steele, a court reporter, and Warden Smith, Jake confessed for three days. As he was very clever and well read, he tricked his audience on several occasions, divulging only half-truths. He never claimed ignorance in any area, and twisted sentences and questions to his own ends. Bird was also well versed in law and understood how to make the most of the little he knew. His stories of two murder cases contained details that secured him one reprieve. One case, from Evanston, Ill., involved the burglary and murder of Lillian Galvin and Edna Sibilski, her maid, on Oct. 22, 1942, in which $31,000 in jewelry and fur coats was stolen. Because of the details Bird knew about this killing, he was granted a sixty-day reprieve on Jan. 16, 1948, only hours before the scheduled hanging. Bird also claimed to have committed several murders in Cleveland which had been attributed to the "Mad Killer."

He told in detail how he and an accomplice robbed a man, stabbed him to death, cut off his head, and dumped his body—cut in sections—into Bull Run Creek. They killed several others, making them look like victims of the Mad Killer, who turned out to be a 45-year-old man named Frank Carter. Bird won an appeal on May 20, but the court upheld the previous conviction and sentence. On the day of his second scheduled hanging, Bird won a hearing for a new trial "on order to show cause in the matter of the application for a Writ of Habeas Corpus." Appearing before Judge Sam M. Driver, Bird took the stand for the first time and acted as his own counsel. He claimed he was tortured to obtain a confession, that he was inadequately represented by counsel in his first trial, that his counsel, attorney J.W. Selden, encouraged the jury to find him guilty, and that the trial judge ignored his appeal. Judge Driver refused to grant a new trial. Twelve hours before his third scheduled hanging, Bird produced a "Certificate of probable cause for appeal to the Court of Appeals in San Francisco." This won him a thirty-day stay of execution, but did not ultimately save him. Chief Judge William Denman denied his appeal. When told of the decision, Bird said "Well, that's too bad." Bird returned to the court where he was originally convicted so that his execution could be rescheduled. On the trip to Tacoma, a guard asked Bird if he had any regrets about the murders he committed. Bird said he regretted only one—a little boy he killed with a rock in Omaha, because the boy called him a nigger. He said it was an accident and that he should not have done it.

Perhaps the strangest aspect of Bird's trial was the hex he placed on those who played an active role in convicting him. The condemned man claimed they would die before him. One month after sentencing Bird, Judge Hodge, who was in excellent health, died of a heart attack. One of Bird's attorneys, J.W. Selden, died on the anniversary of Bird's sentencing. Joe Karpach, who took Bird's three-day confession at Walla Walla, died in January 1948, followed soon after by chief court clerk Ray Scott. One of the officers who took Bird's confession after his arrest, Sherman Lyons, died of a heart attack. The last to die was Arthur A. Stoward, one of Bird's guards at Walla Walla. The strange coincidence of these deaths, however, left Dr. Larson nonplused. "Those six men who did die didn't die of Jake Bird, they died of coronary occlusions," he said.

Jake Bird was hanged on July 15, 1948, twenty months after his conviction. The prison physician pronounced him dead after fourteen minutes. See: **Carter, Frank.**

Bishop, Arthur Gary (AKA: **Roger W. Downs; Lynn E. Jones**), 1951-88, U.S. Arthur Bishop was born in 1951 in Hinckley, Utah. An honor student and popular teenager, he was also devoutly religious, and later served as a missionary in the Philippines for the Church of Jesus Christ of Latter-day Saints (the Mormons). Circumstances began to go wrong for Bishop in 1974, when the church excommunicated him. He went to work at a Ford dealership in Murray, Utah, but was arrested for embezzling $9,000 by forging the owner's signature on a check. In 1981, Bishop decided to disappear. He ended all contact with his family, and changed his name to Lynn E. Jones, and later, Roger W. Downs. By this time, two small boys had vanished from their homes without a trace.

Alonzo Daniels, four, was playing in the front yard of his Salt Lake City home on Oct. 16, 1979, when he disappeared. His abduction was the first of five that would puzzle police in the next four years. Kim Peterson, eleven, was taken on Nov. 27, 1980, followed by Danny Davis, four, on Oct. 20, 1981; Troy Ward, six, on June 22, 1983; and Graeme Cunningham, thirteen, on July 14, 1983. In the case of Danny Davis, eyewitnesses said they saw a man and a woman leading the boy out of a grocery store. Davis' grandfather was shopping at the time. Kim Peterson had told his parents that he was going to meet a man who wanted to buy his roller skates on a corner near his home. Police found his body in a shallow grave in Cedar

Sex killer Arthur Bishop.

Fort, Utah County. The bodies of Danny Davis and Alonzo Daniels were found nearby.

Police wanted Bishop for embezzling $10,000 from Ski Utah, one of his many employers. He was arrested on July 25, 1983, after police questioned him about the disappearance of Graeme Cunningham. They learned that Bishop had been planning a trip to Southern California with the boy the week after he had disappeared. The county sheriff revealed that Bishop had been living in the immediate vicinity at the time of the five murders. Bishop confessed to police, then led investigators to the shallow graves near Cedar Fort, and to a secluded area in Big Cottonwood Canyon where the remains of Troy Ward and Graeme Cunningham were found. There was evidence of sexual assault, and police found explicit sexual photographs at Bishop's residence.

Arthur Gary Bishop was convicted after a six-week trial in 1984 of five counts of first-degree murder, five counts of aggravated kidnapping, two counts of forcible sexual assault, and one count of sexual abuse of a minor. Under Utah law, he could choose death by firing squad or lethal injection. Bishop chose to take the injection on June 10, 1988. He spent his last moments studying the Book of Mormon, and expressing regret for his crimes.

═══════════════════════════════════

Bishop, Arthur Henry, 1907-26, Brit. Arthur Henry Bishop, angry at being fired from his position as hall-boy at the residence of Sir Charles Lloyd, murdered the sleeping Frank Edward Rix on the night of June 7, 1925. Bishop was tried for murder, although his lawyers attempted to have the charge reduced to manslaughter, arguing that Bishop was drunk at the time. Justice Swift sentenced him to death at the Old Bailey after the jury found him Guilty. He was hanged on Aug. 14, 1926.

═══════════════════════════════════

Bishop, Oliver, prom. 1939, U.S. Only his advanced age saved Oliver Bishop from the Florida electric chair. His crime was murder, and the victims were his son George and his son's fiancee Louise.

In the eyes of the old man, his son was about to commit a mortal sin by marrying a woman to whom he was distantly related. But George and Louise were in love, and they planned to drive from Oliver Bishop's Tampa Bay home to a place where they might procure a license legally. The night before they were scheduled to depart, Bishop went to his woodshed and found a heavy sash weight. He crept into his son's bedroom and crashed the piece of iron down on his skull, killing the young man instantly. Louise was still awake, and when she saw what Bishop had done, she tried to flee through the yard. Bishop caught up with her near the fence and bludgeoned her to death. He buried the bodies in the marshy sand of McKay Bay. Weeks later, on May 28, 1939, a crab fisherman scouring the beach found the remains of the young couple. Police checked the missing persons reports and interviewed the estranged wife of Oliver Bishop at her home in Palmetto Beach. She reported that George and Louise had set out on a trip on Easter weekend and had not sent word of their whereabouts.

The trail led to Oliver Bishop's home in Tampa. Assistant Chief of Detectives Malcolm Beasley connected Bishop to the crime by comparing the mud on his shoes to the sand and silt of McKay Bay. They were the same. Confronted with this evidence, Bishop confessed to killing both victims. He was indicted for first-degree murder, found Guilty, and sentenced to life in prison.

━━━━━━━━━━━━━━━━━━━━━━━━━━━━

Bishop, William Bradford, Jr., 1937- , U.S. A total mental breakdown was blamed for the slaughter of William Bishop's family on Mar. 1, 1976. Bishop, a rising foreign service officer in the State Department in Washington, D.C., had been a brilliant student, graduating from Yale and serving in Army Intelligence in the early 1960s. He married his childhood sweetheart, Annette Kathryn Weis, the couple producing three sons. In 1965 Bishop joined the State Department and he was quickly promoted with assignments as a foreign service officer in Addis Ababa, Ethiopia; Milan, Italy; and Gaborone, Botswana. Upon his return to Washington, Bishop bought a fashionable home in Bethesda, Md., and settled into Washington assignments at the State Department. By 1976 he was an incurable insomniac, constantly worried over not having had a promotion in five years. He suffered long periods of depression and began seeing a psychiatrist, taking sleeping pills, and even consulting a hypnotist in a desperate attempt to be able to sleep.

Living by the book became a credo to Bishop. He established a weird, unswerving regimen, allowing himself just so many hours in the week to do everything he felt he had to do, so many hours for work, so many hours for watching TV, so many hours to exercise by walking and playing tennis, so many hours with his family, and with his wife. Bishop even allocated exact hours each week in which he would allow himself to get drunk. All of this he entered in a diary, keeping precise notes on his every waking moment. Bishop spent so much time chronicling his every move that, in his own words, he developed an "enormous new capacity for love of self...a whole new confidence and style, an intellectual and moral integrity...the real self." Then the "real self" of Bishop's personality, according to psychiatrists later charting his lethal course, emerged on Mar. 1, 1976. Bishop was last seen at a Texaco service station filling a five-gallon drum of gasoline, chatting happily with attendants. He went home and beat to death his wife, Annette, thirty-seven, three children, William Bradford III, fourteen, Brenton, ten, Geoffrey, five, and mother, Lobelia Bishop, sixty-eight, piling the bodies into his station wagon. He drove to a lonely spot outside of Columbia, N.C., dumped the bodies into a ditch, soaked them with the gasoline from the five-gallon drum, and set them afire—or, that is the way police later reconstructed the mass murder of the Bishop family.

Smoke from the smouldering bodies was seen by some drivers on the road and the bodies were discovered a short time later. But Bishop had disappeared. Two weeks later his abandoned station wagon was found near Gatlinburg, Tenn., in the Great Smoky Mountain range. FBI agents investigating Bishop's disappearance were convinced, and still are to this day, that Bishop, indeed, murdered his family and then vanished. Agents proved that he had used one of his credit cards on Mar. 2, 1976, the day after the murder of his family, in Jacksonville, N.C. On that day the killer bought considerable sporting equipment, as if he intended to spend some time in the wilds. He was believed to have entered the Great Smoky Mountain range where he, an experienced camper, could lose anyone following him. Some speculation was made about Bishop going into these wilds to commit suicide but it was reported in July 1978 that Bishop may have been spotted in Sweden and that he could have reached that country through his contacts in the foreign service. Since Bishop was indicted as a federal fugitive, the FBI has not closed its books on this case and agents are still searching for the killer.

The profile of Bishop as a mental case, some officials claim, was one which the murderer invented for himself long before killing his family, a mass murder he had planned long in advance of the so-called breakdown symptoms he later openly manifested, symptoms and actions that were designed to convince psychiatrists that, coupled to his murderous acts, he had become insane. His blind, suicidal trek into the Great Smokies was also made to appear as the unbalanced act of a man who had lost all control and would later die in the wilderness of starvation. All of this was an act, officials state, to persuade police that William Bradford Bishop, Jr., was dead. Some claim that he had met a foreign woman, fallen in love with her, and killed his family to be with her, that he escaped the wilds of the Great Smokies and left the U.S. and is now residing somewhere in a Scandinavian country. Such a devilishly clever plan was not beyond the intellectual scope of Bishop, who prided himself on his mental agility and whose every act was directed by a bloated ego that told him he was capable of achieving any goal in life, even the perfect murder.

━━━━━━━━━━━━━━━━━━━━━━━━━━━━

Bittaker, Lawrence Sigmond, 1941- , U.S. The man who raped, tortured, and murdered five teenage girls between June and October 1979, in the suburbs of Los Angeles was captured five months after his last attack.

On Apr. 28, 1980, Lawrence Sigmond Bittaker was charged with five counts of murder, ten counts of rape, five counts of kidnapping, three counts for other sex crimes, and one count for conspiracy to commit murder, rape, and kidnapping. The killer was also charged with illegal possession of tear gas, and for allegedly soliciting two other inmates at the county jail to kill 29-year-old Jan Malin, the victim and a witness of his tear gas attack at Manhattan Beach.

After a month of testimony and almost a week of deliberation, Bittaker was convicted on Feb. 17, 1981, after California's first televised trial. Roy Lewis Norris agreed to plead guilty for his involvement in the slayings in order to

Mass killer Lawrence Bittaker.

avoid the death penalty. He received forty-five years to life imprisonment. Bittaker was sentenced to death by Torrance (Calif.) Superior Court Judge Thomas W. Fredericks on Mar. 24, 1981, with the stipulation that should the killer's sentence ever be reduced to life in prison, he would have to serve 199 years and four months.

This verdict was challenged in an appeal, but the California Supreme Court upheld Bittaker's death sentence on June 22, 1989. Lawrence Bittaker is currently awaiting execution in the gas chamber at California State Prison in San Quentin.

Bittaker's victims included 13-year-old Jacqueline Leah Lamp and 15-year-old Jackie Gilliam, both from Redondo Beach; 16-year-old Shirley Ledford of Sun Valley; 16-year-old Lucinda Schaefer of Torrance; and 18-year-old Andrea Hall of Tujunga.

Bjorkland, Rosemarie Diane (Penny), 1941- , U.S.

A resident of Daly City, Calif., Rosemarie Bjorkland awoke on the morning of Feb. 1, 1959, and told herself, as she related in court: "This is the day I will kill someone. If I meet anyone, that will be it." The 18-year-old girl was obviously in a deranged frame of mind when she took a .38-caliber pistol from her parents' home that day and began wandering through the hills of San Francisco, looking for a person to murder. She found a gardener, August Norry, emptying refuse from his pickup truck on a lonely road. He apparently thought she was stranded and asked if she wanted a lift into town. Penny Bjorkland smiled and thanked him. Then she drew the pistol and emptied it into the hapless father of two children, killing him. She reloaded the weapon and fired another clip of bullets into the dead body, twelve shots in all. Then the young killer climbed into the victim's truck and took it for a thrill ride through the hills.

Police, examining the bullets that killed Norry, noticed they were unusual "wadcutters" used mostly for target practice. They traced the bullets to a gun shop, and its proprietor, Lawrence Schultz, reported that the bullets had been purchased by Penny Bjorkland. She was quickly arrested at her parents' home and confessed almost immediately, explaining that all she did was follow a "sudden

Killer Penny Bjorkland.   Victim August Norry.

urge." Bjorkland was tried and convicted. Before she was led away to begin serving a life sentence, Bjorkland shook her head at reporters and said: "This is not what I expected."

Black, Edward Ernest, 1886-1922, Brit.

Ed Black, an insurance agent, was married to a woman eighteen years his senior who owned a candy shop in Tregonissey, near St. Austell, Cornwall, at the time of her death on Nov. 11, 1921. Badly in debt and no longer in love with his wife, Black purchased two ounces of rat poison from Timothy White's store in St. Austell, explaining that he planned to kill some pesky rodents.

He added the deadly substance to his wife's breakfast on Oct. 31, 1921. Three days before she died he fled Cornwall to take up residence at Cashin's Temperance Hotel in Liverpool. Mrs. Black died from what physicians believed was gastro-enteritis, an affliction she had suffered from for some time, and for which she received regular medication from her druggist. However, a post-mortem examination carried out by a second doctor dissatisfied with the original diagnosis showed arsenic in her tissues.

Meanwhile, police arrested her estranged husband in the hotel after he failed in an attempt at suicide by cutting his throat. In court, Black called his signature on the poison register at the apothecary a forgery. This defense failed him, and he was convicted and hanged at Exeter on Mar. 24, 1922. See: **DeMelker, Daisy Louisa.**

Black, Robert, 1947- , and **Hearn, John Wayne**, 1945- , U.S. Robert Black, of Bryan, Texas, decided to murder his wife Sandra in order to collect $175,000 from a life insurance policy—money that he planned to use to leave Bryan and run off with his cousin. With this plan in mind, Black responded to a classified advertisement placed in *Soldier of Fortune* Magazine in 1985. The advertisement read:

> Ex-Marines, 67-69 Nam Vets. Ex-DI, weapons specialist—jungle warfare. Pilot. ME. High risk assignments. U.S. or overseas...

John Wayne Hearn, a self-styled "Rambo" and an ex-Marine had placed the ad. Black contacted Hearn and offered him the job of killing his wife for $10,000. Soon thereafter, Sandra Black lay dead, shot twice in the head as she carried groceries into her home. She died instantly.

Robert Black was convicted of first-degree murder on Feb. 26, 1986, in the 85th District Court of Texas and sentenced to die in the electric chair. His conviction is under appeal. That same day, Hearn pleaded guilty and was sentenced to life in prison, with an affirmative finding—meaning that he must serve a minimum of twenty years before being granted a parole hearing. He was then returned to Florida and convicted for an earlier murder.

Meanwhile, attorneys for the family of Sandra Black filed a $22.5 million civil lawsuit against the publishers of *Soldier of Fortune,* charging them with criminal negligence for running a gun-for-hire ad. Defense attorney Larry Thompson defended the magazine's right to publish such material, and pointed out that it did not mention any illegal activity. "It's a very innocuous ad," he said. In March 1988, a federal court in Houston awarded $9.4 million in damages to the victim's family. *Soldier of Fortune* is appealing the award.

Blake, Robert, d.1929, U.S. Robert Blake was a condemned prisoner in Texas who was executed in 1929 for murder. Before going to the electric chair, Blake kept a curious chronicle of activities and dialog between other condemned prisoners on Death Row. His remarks, which detail the anxiety of nine condemned men waiting to be put to death, appeared in the July 1929 edition of *The American Mercury* and were later used in the grim prison drama, *The Last Mile.* The prisoners mostly concern themselves with the possibility of a reprieve. When a telegram does arrive for one of the prisoners, he is incensed that it is not from the governor ordering a stay of execution, but from a sheriff asking if he can bring some additional visitors to see the man electrocuted. The prisoners share their last cigars and fruit and endlessly discuss their impending deaths, one stating in forced doggerel:

> Why do they pull a black cap over your face
> And let it remain until you're dead?
> Because the high voltage of electricity
> Will make your eyes pop out of your head!

The Death Row area described by Blake in his grim narrative was immediately adjacent to the room housing the electric chair. At the end of his chronicle, Blake states: "These lines are written while Six (referring to the condemned prisoner taken from cell number six) is being strapped into the chair. The door between the death chamber and Death Row is open." He quotes the words of the condemned man which he and the others can hear as Six awaits the current of electricity which will end his life: "I hope that I am the last one who ever sits in this chair. Tell my mother that my last words were of her." Then Blake adds: "The lights go dim as we hear the whine of the motor when the switch is turned on...The lights go dim twice more." One of the prisoners shouts from Death Row: "They're giving him the juice again. Wonder what they're trying to do, cook him?" One of the condemned men says, "I won't be able to sleep for a week." Another replies from his cell: "I'm going to sleep now. You'll be able to sleep all right. Forget about it."

One week after writing the above report, Robert Blake himself walked into the dreaded room and sat down in the electric chair to face his own end.

Blazek, Frank, 1906-40, U.S. Born in Austria, Frank Blazek moved to New York City and went to work in the city water works department. He was a brooding intellectual, fond of poetry and classical Viennese music, all of which impressed 16-year-old Virginia Bender. Blazek, twenty-eight, was sophisticated and worldly. They became engaged in 1936 but her parents wanted Virginia to finish her schooling before she married.

During their two-year engagement Blazek's jealousy and possessiveness finally got the best of her. Virginia called off the engagement and moved away. A year later Blazek read in the newspaper about her impending engagement and called her on June 5, 1939, to wish her luck. "Do you mean that?" she asked. "You bet I do," he said. "You're going to need luck."

On June 19 Blazek purchased a hunting knife at an Army-Navy surplus store on 125th Street. He proceeded to her apartment on 137th Street in the Bronx where he stabbed and killed her. Then he covered her with a blanket, because, as he later explained, the sight of blood repulsed him.

Bender's fiance appeared in the vestibule a short time later and Blazek, peering through a crack in the door, told him to go away. Detective Captain Glen Armstrong of the Bronx Police was summoned and not long afterwards the Viennese killer was arrested. He confessed to Assistant District Attorney Martin Klaus and was tried, condemned, and executed in the electric chair on Sept. 11, 1940.

Bokassa, Jean Bedel, 1919-   , Bangui. In 1960 France recognized the independence of its former colonial possession Bangui, located in the Central African Republic. At the time, the arid wasteland was a drain on the French economy and many politicians were happy to see the government let it go.

The Republican government established by France in Bangui was deposed in a bloody coup headed by a tyrannical madman named Jean Bokassa, whose penchant for pomp and royal splendor was exceeded only by his reputation for lunacy. In December 1977 Bokassa crowned himself emperor of the new Central African Republic and invited a score of dignitaries from Europe and all across Africa to witness his coronation, which cost an estimated £10 million.

The forty-eight hour gala was patterned after his great hero, Emperor Napoleon's coronation, which flattered the government of France which generously established a £1 million credit line for Bokassa to purchase a fleet of Mercedes limousines for the royal procession. This took place in a country where only ten percent of the two million population could read or write. Bangui, despite an impressive uranium reserve, was an impoverished country.

Many Western nations refused to send envoys to attend the event as a sign of protest. The U.S. cut off all economic aid to express its displeasure over the policies of the new Napoleon. Those who attended feasted at a lavish table, not knowing that some of their appetizers were human entrails from the bodies of recently executed prisoners.

Two years after Bokassa's coronation the embarrassed French engineered a palace revolt after learning of Bokassa's genocide of Bangui school children. Two hun-

dred youngsters were rounded up by the Imperial Guard after their parents refused a direct order to outfit them in school uniforms they could not afford. Taken to a prison, Bokassa's guards systematically beat the children to death and their remains were fed to the emperor's pet crocodiles.

The deposed African statesman David Dacko was placed in charge of the government by his French protectors when Bokassa visited his ally Colonel Muammar Gaddafi in Libya. The power-mad emperor was exiled to Paris where he opened a boutique that supplied safari suits to African tourists.

Bolles, Don, See: **Adamson, John Harvey**.

Bolton, Mildred Mary, 1886-1943, U.S. From the very beginning, Charles W. Bolton, Jr., realized that he had made a mistake when he asked for Mildred's hand in marriage in 1922. The docile insurance broker from Chicago proved to be no match for the jealous, high-strung woman from Kalamazoo, Mich. The couple moved to Hyde Park, on Chicago's South Side. Charles Bolton commuted to his downtown office every day, and returned at night to

Charles Bolton, victim.   Mildred Bolton, killer.

face the stern admonitions of his jealous wife. Mildred believed that her dowdy, middle-aged husband was carrying on affairs with the women at the office.

Mildred beat her husband senselessly. When Charles refused to divorce her, his employers delicately suggested that he might want to go into business for himself. He did not and one night Mildred slashed him with a razor. Chicago Police later questioned Mildred at home. Smoking a cigar, her feet up on a table, she casually explained that his "accident" was the result of careless shaving. It was three in the morning.

Charles Bolton finally had enough. He filed for divorce on Jan. 20, 1936. Mildred, however, refused to give up so easily. On June 11, she purchased a revolver and four days later turned up in her husband's downtown office. She rode the elevator to the tenth floor and coolly discharged six bullets into her husband. As he lay in agony on the floor, Mildred said, "Why don't you get up and stop faking?" Charles Bolton died shortly thereafter. Mildred was originally sentenced to death in the electric chair, but Governor Henry Horner commuted her sentence to 199 years at the women's penitentiary in Dwight, Ill. There she died on Aug. 29, 1943, having slashed her wrists with a stolen pair of scissors.

―――――――――――――――――――――

Bonin, William (AKA: **The Freeway Strangler**), 1947-   , and **Butts, Vernon**, prom. 1980, U.S. Bonin was shuttled in and out of detention homes following his first criminal conviction at the age of ten. His father was a drunk and a gambler, and his doting mother more often

Bonin, "The Freeway Strangler."   Bonin's partner, Vernon Butts.

than not became the servile victim of her husband's murderous rage. In 1969, the young truck driver from Downey, Calif., was convicted of his first sex crime, charged with molesting five boys. Bonin was sent to Atascadero State Hospital but after two years physicians concluded he was not receptive to treatment. For the next five years William Bonin darted in and out of prison on a variety of sexual offenses. A psychiatrist's report concluded that his homosexual problems were related to his mother's domination during childhood.

By his own estimate, Bonin killed at least twenty-one teen-aged boys between 1978 and 1980. With the help of several willing accomplices including Vernon Butts, Bonin cruised the highways of Los Angeles and Orange counties

targeting young homosexuals for death. Butts, who was at first shocked, quickly became a more than willing participant in the killing orgy, which always accompanied "rough sex." "After the first one, I couldn't do anything about it," Butts explained. "He (Bonin) had a hypnotic way about him."

The naked and battered bodies were deposited near the on-off ramps of the Los Angeles freeways. The press quickly dubbed the unknown assailant the "Freeway Strangler." Police from four counties assisted in the investigation which yielded no new clues. Butts grew tired of the game and temporarily dropped out of sight, but this did not deter Bonin who recruited younger, more willing henchmen to help him locate victims. Two of these men, Greg Miley and James Monro, were drifters who wandered into Hollywood where they met Bonin.

Police finally were tipped off to the identity of the "Freeway Strangler" by a 17-year-old youth Bonin tried to enlist as an accomplice. Bonin was arrested in Hollywood after parking his van at a closed gas station.

Charged with fourteen counts of murder, he was arraigned in Los Angeles Superior Court along with Butts who confessed to helping in five of the killings. However, the prosecution lost its star witness when Butts hanged himself in his jail cell. On Mar. 12, 1982, Judge William Keene sentenced the serial killer to death. After the trial ended Bonin admitted that even if he were freed he would continue to kill. "I couldn't stop killing," he said. "It got easier each time."

―――――――――――――――――――――

Booher, Vernon, d.1929, Can. On July 9, 1928, four murders took place at the Booher farm at Mannville, near Edmonton, Alberta. Police found the bodies of field hands Gabriel Cromby and Bill Rosyk in the bunkhouse, and those of Mrs. Booher and her son Fred inside the house. Booher's son, Vernon Booher, had reported the multiple shootings, but could shed no light on the identity of the likely killer.

The police determined that the four victims had been shot with a .303 rifle belonging to a neighbor, Charles Stephenson, who said the weapon had been stolen from his home the previous Sunday. In desperation, police turned to a Viennese psychic, Dr. Maximilien Langsner, who was credited with solving a recent burglary case in Vancouver through ESP. At the inquest, he stared thoughtfully at Booher. When it was over, he declared with a degree of certainty that Vernon had killed his family, but was unsure of the motive. Langsner then led police to a patch of prairie grass where the murder weapon was buried.

Booher was arrested on July 17, and held as a material

witness in the Edmonton Jail. Langsner visited him and ascertained his motive for the murders. Booher had been denied permission to marry the daughter of a local farmer. In anger, he murdered his family. A diminutive woman, Erma Higgins, had witnessed Vernon sneaking out of church that Sunday to steal the rifle from Stephenson. When confronted by Higgins, Vernon broke down and confessed to the killings. The first of Booher's two murder trials began on Sept. 24 at the Supreme Criminal Court of Alberta. He was convicted of murder and sentenced to be hanged. However, the appellate division of the supreme court granted Booher a new trial because additional evidence had been produced by the defense. The second trial ended on Jan. 23, 1929, with another Guilty verdict. Booher was hanged in the Alberta Jail at Fort Saskatchewan on Apr. 29, 1929.

Boost, Werner (AKA: **The Dusseldorf Doubles Killer**), 1928-   , Ger. In the years following WWII, Werner Boost earned his living transporting refugees across the East German border. He then moved to Dusseldorf in 1950. On Jan. 7, 1953, Boost and a companion shot a lawyer named Dr. Serve, who sat in a parked car with his male lover. Serve's lover was beaten and robbed.

Two years later, on Oct. 31, 1955, Boost and his accomplice, Franz Lorbach, apparently struck again, this time allegedly taking the lives of a young couple who had just left a Dusseldorf restaurant. The battered remains of Thea Kurmann and Friedhelm Behre were found in a water-filled gravel pit. Their skulls had been crushed. The press dubbed the unknown murderer the "Doubles Killer."

On Feb. 7, 1956, a gardener employed in Lank-Ilverich, a village outside Dusseldorf, reported his discovery of two charred bodies in a burnt haystack. The night before, someone

German mass killer Werner Boost.

driving a stolen black Mercedes had raced through the neighborhood minutes before a fire of mysterious origin broke out. Boost allegedly set the fire and committed the murders of Peter Falkenberg and Hildegard Wassing.

Police captured Boost on June 10, 1956, as he crept up on a parked Volkswagen in the woods outside Dusseldorf. Lorbach, who had been taken into custody earlier said that

he had been "hypnotized" by Boost into carrying out the "Doubles Murders." Lorbach also said Boost would inject the couples with a sedative and rape the women before killing them. Lorbach received six years in prison. Werner Boost eventually was found Guilty of the murder of Dr. Serve. The evidence in the other murders proved inconclusive. He was sentenced to life imprisonment on Dec. 14, 1959.

Born, Ronald Joseph, 1935-76, U.S. Wanted for driving a stolen car, a fugitive killed three policemen, then shot himself rather than be captured.

On Apr. 2, 1976, Ronald Joseph Born, a fugitive believed to have been from Blue Island, Ill., was staying at the Beach Motel in Miami, Fla. Wanted for failing to show up in the U.S. District Court of Miami on charges of interstate auto theft, he had been registered at the motel for almost a month under the name Joseph Moulood. According to officials, three policemen, acting on a hunch, went to Born's room to ask about a stolen Lincoln sedan he had been driving. When they approached him Born fired on them with a shotgun. Fatally wounded were Thomas Hodges, thirty-two, Clark Curlette, twenty-eight, and Frank Dazevedo, thirty-one. Born then fired a pistol into his own head, apparently when he realized he was trapped by other policemen. A police spokesman explained, "U.S. marshals told me this morning that he had vowed he would never be taken alive."

Boston Strangler, The, See: **DeSalvo, Albert Henry**.

Bougrat, Dr. Pierre, prom. 1927, Fr. A Marseilles bank cashier, Jacques Rumebe, was reported missing by his wife on Mar. 15, 1925. Nearly 85,000 francs were also missing, causing police to conclude that the motive for the crime was robbery. Two months later, police searched the office of Dr. Pierre Bougrat, one of the last places the cashier was seen. In a large cupboard in the physician's operating room, the police discovered the decomposing remains of Rumebe. Dr. Bougrat explained that Rumebe had dropped by for his daily injection on the afternoon of Mar. 15. This time, Rumebe said that he was in dire financial difficulty. He needed to raise the equivalent of £800 or face ruin. Bougrat agreed to go into the city to try to locate the money, and when he returned he discovered

Rumebe dead on the floor and his poison cabinet broken into. It was a suicide to be sure, but given the incriminating circumstances, he had no other choice but to conceal the body, he said.

Bougrat was arrested on a charge of murder. His trial opened in Marseilles in March 1927, two years after the murder of Rumebe. The prosecution contended that Bougrat, and not the murder victim, was in serious debt. Various witnesses testified to Bougrat's numerous attempts to raise money, usually through highly illegal means. It was intimated at the trial that Rumebe was not the first victim of the physician. A Greek heiress named Odette Lepocal, who had been under Bougrat's care, vanished from her nursing home. She was found by the police bound and gagged. The story of her abduction, and Bougrat's subsequent ransom demand, led to his arrest.

Bougrat was found Guilty and was transported to Devil's Island in French Guiana for the remainder of his life. But he escaped to Venezuela in October 1928, one of only a handful of men to accomplish this feat in the long history of the penal colony.

Boulogne, Henri, prom. 1929, Fr. Clement Pascal fancied himself a master swindler and enjoyed the nickname given him by the editors of Paris' *Le Matin:* the "Napoleon of Crooks." Pascal was released from the Loos Prison in late August 1929, but his vanity got the best of him. He decided to write his memoirs, but in order to arouse interest in such a project he needed publicity.

Clement Pascal invented a French version of the Ku Klux Klan, a secret society known as the Knights of Themis. This organization sent a series of letters to *Le Matin* describing their abduction and ritualistic torture of Clement Pascal, each one more lurid in content than the last.

The Knights of Themis letters drew considerable attention. In his last correspondence, shortly before Oct. 1, Pascal said he was going to be buried alive. He actually went through with it, recruiting an ex-convict named Henri Boulogne to help him dig the grave near the Bois de la Justice. Detailed instructions were given to Boulogne. He was to mail a last letter to the newspaper announcing that Pascal had been buried alive. An oilskin package containing copies of the letters, newspaper clippings, and other paraphernalia was buried next to the grave. In twelve hours, Henri Boulogne was to return to make sure everything was alright.

There was only one problem. The breathing pipe connecting the coffin to the surface did not work. Pascal had tested the device in his cottage by placing himself inside the box and breathing through the pipe. The cracks in the

wood provided the necessary suction to draw the air into the coffin. But under the weight of the earth the suction disappeared, and it was impossible to extract air from ground level. Pascal perished within hours.

The unwitting Boulogne told this fantastic story to the police who charged him with "murder by imprudence." He was found Guilty and was sentenced to prison for eight months.

Bouvier, Leone, 1930- , Fr. Leone Bouvier was born into a peasant family in the village of Saint-Macaire-en-Mauges. She was the victim of drunken, abusive parents who imbibed "gniole," a locally produced cider whose properties were known to induce madness if consumed in excess.

In 1951, Emile Clenet, a 22-year-old garage mechanic, seduced Bouvier with false words of love and a vague promise of marriage. They met regularly for sex on Sundays, but after Leone became pregnant, Clenet soon lost interest and ordered her to get an abortion. She agreed to his demand, but contracted an illness from the operation which prevented her from working. Bouvier was dismissed from her factory job, and when she heard no further word from Clenet, she found him at his place of employment in Nantes.

Emile Clenet told his one-time girlfriend not to bother him at the garage again. Penniless, she spent the month engaged in prostitution. With the few dollars she earned, Leone purchased a cheap .22-caliber pistol from a Nantes gunsmith. Then in February 1952, at a local dance, Clenet told her of his decision to move to North Africa to start all over. As for marriage, it was never in the cards for them, Clenet said. During a farewell embrace, Leone fired a shot into the back of his head.

The young woman was charged with murder and

French murderess Leone Bouvier.

placed on trial at the Assizes of Maine-et-Loire, at Angers, on Dec. 10, 1953. Defense lawyer Claude Fournier pointed to the sorrowful homelife endured by his client. Her drunken father was brought forward into the witness box for everyone to see. But Leone's mother stated that her other daughter was a nun. Judge Diousidon then rebuked the defendant. "You see! There was no need for you to go wrong!" he cried. "I loved him," she replied meekly. Leone was sentenced to life imprisonment, the maximum penalty under French law.

Bowden, John, 1956- , Brit. In 1981 John Bowden, along with Michael Ward, a Camberwell gravedigger, and David Begley, a porter from Walworth, two other alcoholics, murdered Donald Ryan, a former amateur boxer. Bowden, who at twenty-four had already spent five years in jail, for crimes that included robbery, blackmail, burglary, assault, and carrying weapons, had taken to preying on derelict South Londoners. When he, Ward, and Begley met Ryan they lured him to a south London apartment, then struck him on the head, leaving him semiconscious. The sadistic killers then immersed Ryan in a tub of scalding water where he fainted. Taking him to another room, they cut off his arms and legs with an electric carving knife, beheaded him with a machete and a saw, disposed of his trunk and limbs in empty lots, and stored his head in the refrigerator for a time, later dumping it in the garbage.

Bowden was said to have joined and laughed as he held the decapitated head aloft. All three murderers went out to drink at a nearby pub before returning to the apartment to sleep near the grisly remains.

John Bowden, murderer.

Justice Mars-Jones who tried the case at the Old Bailey, said, "Bowden is a man who obviously enjoyed inflicting pain and even killing." Sentenced to life imprisonment, Bowden yelled at the judge, "You old bastard, I hope you die screaming of cancer." Evidence at the trial was so dreadful that court was adjourned when four members of the jury became ill after viewing photographs. Afterward, Bowden's parents said their son had been a "good boy, gentle and kind," until kept in solitary confinement for escaping when jailed on an earlier charge. A year after he began serving his sentence at the Isle of Wight maximum security prison, Bowden and another inmate, James McCaig took the assistant governor of the jail hostage, holding him at knifepoint while they called a Fleet Street newspaper to air their grievances, releasing the official after the British Home Office promised to look into their case.

Bowen, Nancy, prom. 1930, U.S. In March 1930, Nancy Bowen walked into the Buffalo, N.Y., home of artist Henri Marchand and confronted his wife, Clothilde Marchand, asking her if she was a witch. When Mrs. Marchand facetiously replied, "Yes," Bowen beat the woman to the ground with a hammer, stuffed chloroform-soaked paper down her throat, and left her dead. Lila Jimerson, a Seneca Indian woman who had posed for Marchand's pictures, commissioned by the Buffalo Natural History Museum, was charged with instigating the killing. Also known as "Red Lilac," Jimerson had fallen in love with Mr. Marchand after he seduced her, and believed that eliminating his wife would free her lover to marry her. Jimerson had told Bowen on the reservation where they both lived that Mrs. Marchand was a witch who had caused the recent death of Bowen's husband, Charley Bowen. Initially tried for first-degree murder, the consumptive Jimerson collapsed in the Buffalo courtroom. Judge F. Bret Thorn dismissed the jury and declared a mistrial. The prosecution's main witness at the first trial was Henri Marchand, who admitted his intimacy with Jimerson but insisted it had been a matter of "professional necessity" done to get her to pose as his model.

From her Buffalo City Hospital bed Jimerson pleaded guilty to reduced charges of murder in the second degree, answering all the questions posed to her by Judge Thorn by nodding her head. Not once did she speak. She was expected to be formally sentenced when released from the hospital but instead she hired new attorneys who refused to withdraw her initial plea of guilt to second degree murder, arguing that the improvised sickbed courtroom had been illegal and that their client was still on trial for first-degree murder. At Jimerson's retrial, late in 1930, she contended that the artist had plotted the murder of his wife and used her to carry it out. She was acquitted by a supreme court jury on Feb. 28, 1931. On Mar. 13, 1931, Nancy Bowen, who had pleaded guilty to reduced charges of first-degree manslaughter, was sentenced by Judge Thorn to a one- to ten-year prison term. But because she had already been detained in jail for longer than the amount of her minimum sentence, she was immediately freed.

Bowers, Martha, prom. 1903, U.S. Born Martha Byers, the daughter of a respectable mother in Portland, Ore., the fickle Martha had been married and divorced twice when she met and married a bridge builder, Martin L. Bowers, in San Francisco in 1902. On June 5, 1903, Mrs. Bowers called a Dr. Carl Von Tiedemann to prescribe medicine for her husband who was, she explained, ill as a result of ptomaine poisoning caused by eating ham. Von

Tiedemann treated Mr. Bowers, later dropping treatment after a financial misunderstanding with Mrs. Bowers. A second physician, Dr. J.F. Dillon, prescribed for the patient and then stopped visiting him when improvement was shown after a short time. When Martin Bowers suffered a relapse, his wife called in Dr. A. McLaughlin who concurred with the diagnosis of the previous doctors but insisted that the patient be taken to the Waldeck Sanitarium for observation. Though puzzled by some of the sick man's symptoms, McLaughlin was not suspicious. After a month's stay the convalescent was returned, at his spouse's entreaty, to his home, with a doctor's instructions for the wife to give her husband a daily massage. One week later, McLaughlin made a house call and discovered that his instructions had not been followed and that the patient's condition had deteriorated. He ordered that the sick man be taken to the German Hospital, where Bowers died on Aug. 25, 1903. The widow, present at the death, flung herself on the corpse and wept copiously.

Harry Bowers, the deceased's brother, was suspicious of his sister-in-law and demanded an investigation. Four grains of undissolved arsenic were found in the dead man's stomach, and two investigating chemists determined that it was impossible for Bowers to have died from ptomaine poisoning through eating ham, since the salt and creosote found in that meat would most likely have destroyed the arsenic. The report was highly publicized and brought forth a druggist, J.C. Peterson, who recalled a woman coming to him on Aug. 20 with a prescription, written on a blank sheet of paper and signed by a Dr. McLaughlin, that called for an unspecified amount of arsenic. The description of the woman fit that of Martha Bowers' sister, Zylpha Sutton, who was positively identified by Peterson.

Found in the Bowers' home was a composition school book with a page torn out that matched that on which the fraudulent prescription was written. A handwriting expert testified that songs in the book matched the handwriting on the prescription, and that both were the work of Martha Bowers. It was also proved that the grieving widow had been in the company of her lover, Patrick Leary, within two hours of her husband's death.

The prosecution contended that Bowers murdered her husband so that she would be free of his strong objections to her involvement with Leary. Mrs. Sutton was released for lack of evidence, but Bowers was charged with murder, tried on Jan. 14, 1904, and found guilty on Jan. 20. Appropriately, the woman undone by romance was sentenced to life imprisonment on Valentine's Day 1904.

Bowers, Sam H., Jr., prom. 1964-68, U.S. On June 21, 1964, members of the Ku Klux Klan murdered three civil rights activists on a deserted road in Neshoba County, Miss. The slain activists, Andrew Goodman, twenty, James Chaney, twenty-one, and Michael Schwerner, twenty-four, became a media sensation, and the ensuing trial evolved into the decade's most closely followed criminal proceeding. Schwerner, a veteran field worker for the Congress of Racial Equality, had moved to the town of Meridian, Miss., six months earlier to organize voter registration within the black community. The local white racist population hated Schwerner, not only because he was Jewish, but because he represented the civil rights movement. Goodman, also Jewish, was a college student who arrived in Philadelphia, Miss., June 20. Chaney worked with Schwerner as a co-organizer in voter registration drives and was the group's link to the black community. The three were driving back to Meridian after visiting a burned-out black church near Philadelphia, Miss., when Neshoba County deputy sheriff Cecil R. Price, a secret Klan member, arrested them on trumped-up charges of speeding. He released the three around 10 p.m. that evening. Price stopped them again, after a high-speed chase through the backroads of Neshoba County, and turned them over to a lynch mob formed by the Ku Klux Klan and led by the 43-year-old Klan Imperial Wizard, Sam H. Bowers, Jr. The lynch mob shot each of the victims individually and buried them in open graves, then created an earthen dam over them the following week. Just before he was killed, Schwerner reportedly turned to his executioner and said: "Sir, I know just how you feel."

The summer of 1964 was a time of optimism and hope for the civil rights movement. It was the year of the historic "Freedom Summer," during which more than 1,000 college students came to Mississippi to aid a grass-roots movement to register black voters. They hoped their work would focus national attention on the evils of segregation. At that time, only five percent of the 500,000 blacks eligible to vote in Mississippi were registered. Mississippi was an effectively segregated state. The Ku Klux Klan, with its law enforcement connections, intimidated the black community. Fear of Klan terrorism, bombings of homes and churches, and cross-burnings kept blacks from seeking basic voting rights. Occasionally, blacks who attempted to register simply disappeared.

The FBI involved itself in the case when state authorities grew lethargic. The FBI code named the investigation "Miburn" because the case began with the burning of the black church. For five months, 150 agents worked on the case, piecing together evidence of the plans that culminated with the lynch mob on June 21. Spurred by the grieving families and enraged civil rights workers from around the country, the investigations became one of the most extensive in FBI history. Forty-four days after the execution, and after days of wading through swampy land, volunteers unearthed the badly decomposed bodies of the civil rights workers. With the help of an informant and one confession, the FBI learned that the Ku Klux Klan ordered and executed the lynching. Twenty-one men were initially charged with murder and conspiracy to murder, but their prosecution was thwarted when the state court refused to allow the Justice Department to introduce the testimony of Horace D. Barnette, one of the accused who confessed to his part in the crime. The case was dismissed, and the department was forced to seek a grand jury indictment. Aided by the testimony of Barnette, the FBI's star witness James E. Jordan, and Philadelphia resident Florence Mars, the grand jury indicted eighteen men on an old federal law prohibiting conspiracy against the rights of another citizen. Each of those convicted faced a ten-year maximum sentence and $5,000 in fines.

The trial, which lasted two weeks and received national coverage, was presided over by U.S. District Court judge W. Harold Cox. Cox was decidedly unsympathetic to civil rights, and once publicly referred to several blacks registering to vote as "a bunch of chimpanzees." The all-white jury initially deadlocked when they could not convict all the defendants. Yet when Judge Cox further instructed them that they could find individual defendants guilty, they returned a verdict the following day, Oct. 20. Seven men were found Guilty of conspiracy to murder: Sam H. Bowers, Jr., Cecil R. Price, Horace Barnette, Jimmy Arledge, a 30-year-old truck driver, Billy Wayne Posey, a 30-year-old gas station operator, Jimmie Snowden, a 34-year-old laundry truck driver, and Alton W. Roberts, a 29-year-old sales representative. The jury, however, acquitted eight men, including the Neshoba County sheriff Lawrence Rainey, and came to no judgment on three of the defendants.

When the verdict was read, Judge Cox said, "I very heartily enter into this jury's verdict." The judge then denounced Roberts and Price and ordered their immediate incarceration because of the threats they made before the jury returned its verdict. On Dec. 29, the judge sentenced Bowers and Roberts to ten years' imprisonment, Price and Posey to six years, and Barnette, Arledge, and Snowden to three years' imprisonment. None of those convicted were fined. Jordan, the federal witness, received a four-year prison sentence on Jan. 13, after a separate trial.

The lynching and the trial had an enormous impact on Mississippi and on the civil rights movement. Blacks increasingly dominated the movement and abandoned nonviolence for militant action. Yet the voter registration campaigns that summer brought into the political process tens of thousands of blacks who had never attempted to register. And the town of Philadelphia, Miss., changed. The public schools eventually desegregated, and an effort was made to broaden job opportunities for blacks. Despite the tragedy, many civil rights workers echoed the sentiment of Freedom Summer volunteer Haywood Burns, who claimed, "...it was one of our finest hours."

Bowles, Frank, prom. 1902, U.S. Frank Bowles, a Kentucky youth, had been spending time with one of the girls in the Christie family against the will of her father, Isham Christie. These two families in the Honey Creek area of Kentucky had been at odds for some time, and tensions increased when Christie found two of his steers dead in the pasture and ordered young Bowles not to carry a gun on his land. According to Christie's daughter, several hogs belonging to the nearby Boyer family were discovered missing about a week after the Christie family's dead steers were found. Rumor had it that the notorious Bowles family had once again stolen hogs from their neighbors, had salted them, and hidden the meat away in a cave.

The girl's uncle, Carl Boyer, went to Magistrate Tom Washam and obtained a warrant to search the Bowles farm. Two of the Christie boys were deputized to go with him. Nearing the house, they saw Frank Bowles sitting on the side of the road, a shotgun in his lap. Isham Christie and Bowles began to argue and when Christie called Bowles "a damned sheep-eyed devil," Bowles shot and killed his visitor, then ran away. He was arrested a few days later, taken to Shelltown to appear before Magistrate Dale Rigney, and released, supposedly bartering for his freedom at the cost of ten dollars and a gallon of whiskey. Learning of the payoff, the dead man's youngest son went to the grand jury and obtained an indictment against the accused, who fled to Alabama to hide out at his parents' home. Sheriff George Crutchfield and his sons went to Alabama to arrest Bowles, bringing him back to Kentucky to stand trial, where he was convicted and sentenced to a ten-year term in the state penitentiary.

Bowles, Homer, prom. 1913, U.S. On May 13, 1913, Cindy Curtis, a landowning black woman who had recently lost her husband, went to Ben Emory's store to collect some money for laundering work she had done for Emory's wife. After collecting, she sat on the porch of the store to rest. Also on the porch were Homer Bowles, Bess Talbot, and Lura Lee Talbot, Homer's girlfriend. According to Emory's nephew, who witnessed the slaying, "All of them was barefooted...and Bowles kept pointing his gun at the girl's feet. This old colored woman was there, and he turned the gun on her and let it go off. On purpose." Curtis' head was blown off by the force of the blast. Though Bowles maintained that the killing was an accident, it was generally believed that he had been hired to murder the woman by her nephew, who lived with Curtis and would inherit the property at her death. Bowles was convicted and sentenced to serve time in the state penitentiary at Nashville, Tenn.

Boyce, Arthur Robert (AKA: **The Trousseau Murderer**), d.1946, Brit. In Summer 1946, an English woman, Elizabeth McLindon, was hired by King George II of Greece to refurbish his wartime home in Chester Square, Belgravia, London. She accepted, and moved in with her fiance, one Arthur Robert Boyce, a painter and decorator from Brighton. McLindon did not know that her man was already married and had, in fact, served a prison sentence on a bigamy charge.

The king dropped by to inspect his summer house on June 9, but was perturbed by his housekeeper's absence. Three days later, Papanikolaou, the king's private secretary paid a second visit, and still there was no sign of the 41-year-old McLindon. Police were called to investigate on June 14 and found the body of the housekeeper in a locked room. She had been shot once through the back of the head. A letter signed, "Your loving and true hubby, Arthur" was found next to the body.

A search of Arthur Boyce's lodgings in Brighton turned up a luggage label bearing the name of John Rowland, the owner of the .32-caliber Browning automatic pistol used to kill McLindon. Rowland told police that the gun had been taken from him, and he strongly suspected Boyce. A ballistics test conducted by Robert Churchill showed that the bullets extracted from the body were fired from the same gun. Boyce was put on trial in September 1946. No motive was clearly established; however, it was known that McLindon was increasingly suspicious of Boyce's background, and fearing possible scandal, he decided to murder the woman. Boyce claimed the gun was given to McLindon for her own protection, but the jury, discounting his claim, returned a Guilty verdict. Boyce was sentenced to die by Justice Morris. He was executed on Nov. 1, 1946.

Boyle, William Anthony (Tony), 1904-85, U.S. Tony Boyle and Joseph Albert Yablonski were longtime members of the American United Mine Workers Union. Boyle had served a term as president and Yablonski, suspecting him of embezzlement and of publicly lying about safety vio-

lations that led to a November 1968 mine explosion in West Virginia, decided to run against Boyle in an effort to clean up the union, which had been rife with strongarm and terrorist tactics for more than a decade. Suspected in the coal mining intimidation was Albert Pass, treasurer of the East Kentucky branch of the union. William Prater, a union representative who had been one of the strong-arm members, spoke to Silous Huddleston to set in action the plan for Yablonski's murder. Huddleston contacted his son-in-law, Paul Gilly, who hired two young burglars, James Phillips and Claude Vealey, to do the job. When Phillips got drunk the night they stole guns for the killing, Aubrey Wayne (Buddy) Martin, another young burglar, replaced him for the slaying. Yablonski lost the election. Convinced that Boyle had won dishonestly, he was prepared to challenge the election results in court.

On Dec. 30, 1969, Vealey, Martin, and Gilly drove from Cleveland, Ohio, to Clarksville, Pa., breaking into Yablonski's home just after midnight and brutally slaying him along with his wife, Margaret, and daughter, Charlotte. The three men then drove back to Cleveland, throwing their guns into a river along the way. The bodies were discovered six days later when the Yablonskis' son became alarmed at getting no response to phone calls. The police had one clue: the killers had visited Yablonski two weeks before the slayings, pretending to be miners looking for work. When Yablonski did not invite them in they decided not to kill him then. Suspicious, Yablonski had written down the license plate number of their car, and police traced it to Huddleston's daughter, Annette Gilly.

Police rounded up the three killers, along with Huddleston and the daughter. Vealey was the first to talk, bargaining for his life. Martin and Gilly were tried separately and both sentenced to death, Martin's sentence later being reduced to three consecutive life terms. Prater and Pass were each convicted of participating in the killings and sentenced to life in prison. William Turnblazer, another union executive, implicated Boyle when he admitted overhearing Boyle order Yablonski's murder. Before he could be arrested, however, Boyle, already sentenced to five years in jail for embezzlement of union funds and having lost the presidency, attempted suicide. When revived, he was tried and, in April 1974, found Guilty of the murders. Sentenced to life imprisonment for his part in the crimes, he was released on Mar. 17, 1977, for a retrial when the Pennsylvania Supreme Court ruled that the trial judge had improperly refused to admit testimony that might have aided the defense. Boyle, then seventy-five, was convicted a second time in 1978, and sent back to prison. He died on May 31, 1985.

Bozzeli, Peter, prom. 1953, U.S. Gloria Bozelli's nude, beaten body was found floating in a duffel bag in Iron Ore Creek, N.J. Known to be Peter Bozelli's favorite child among his eight offspring, Gloria, twenty-four, had been the surrogate mother for the family in the three years since her mother's death. An over-protective father, Bozelli was described by one of Gloria's boyfriends as "like one of those Spanish duennas...a chaperone." The father claimed that he and his daughter had eaten out together the night of her disappearance, but the restaurant where he said they had been at around 9:30 p.m. had closed at 7:30 p.m. When police examined Bozelli's home they found numerous traces of blood. Breaking down, Bozelli confessed to murdering his daughter, jealous of her possible marriage. "I loved my daughter...I didn't want her to leave," he said. He was sentenced to life imprisonment, dying in 1954 after a prison hunger strike.

Bradford, Priscilla, 1944-   , and **Cummings, Joyce Lisa**, 1962-   , and **Gould, Janice Irene**, 1946-   , U.S. John Young Bradford, Jr., a wealthy optometrist from Melbourne, Fla., suspected that his wife was trying to kill him. The 53-year-old doctor had even quickly prepared a new will. On Mar. 30, 1980, Dr. John Bradford, Jr. was found dead in the kitchen of his Melbourne, Fla., home. Bradford had been beaten by his 36-year-old wife Priscilla Ann Hadley Smith, who explained that she was fighting for her life. Police Chief C.W. "Jake " Miller was at first sympathetic to the wife, who bore the visible marks of violence. And so too, were Priscilla's companions: Joyce Lisa Cummings, eighteen, and Janice Irene Gould, thirty-four. Both worked in Bradford's optical lab.

Bradford left an estate worth $300,000 and a lucrative eyewear business that brought in $12,000 a month. Now it all belonged to Priscilla, Bradford's second wife. When police questioned the first wife Deenie, she said that in twenty-eight years of marriage, John had never struck her once. Tracy Smith and John Lockhart, two of Bradford's lab employees, told police about Priscilla's determination to push her husband out of the way to wrest control of the business.

This was mere conjecture though, until Priscilla's teenage daughter, Eden Elaine, came forward to provide substantive weight to the allegations. She told of a fiendish murder plot hatched by Priscilla Bradford with the connivance of Gould and Cummings. After failing in an attempt to poison him, they decided to ambush him as he sat down to what he thought was going to be a "reconciliation" dinner with his wife. "It's going to be his last supper," Priscilla joked. On Mar. 28, they carried out the plan, and Eden was ordered to keep the shower in the bathroom running, so that the three murderesses could wash off the blood traces. Gould and Cummings selected their murder weapons from the kitchen—Priscilla chose a frying pan. The three women beat him senseless, and then ordered Eden to "keep hitting him...everywhere!" Finally, after repeated blows to the head and face, he died.

Eden was granted immunity in the murder trial that began Apr. 10, 1980. While in jail Priscilla approached a prostitute named Ursula Mattox in hopes of finding someone to murder Tracy Smith and John Lockhart. Priscilla even brought her own mother into the plan. She was to "drop" the $2,000 down payment for the hired killer at a pizzeria. Mattox pretended to go along with the scheme but instead informed prison authorities, who notified the police. With the help of Mattox, police allowed the plan to continue, intervening when the money was actually dropped off to an undercover officer. The evidence gathered was then used to tack on additional charges of conspiracy to commit murder to the original murder indictment. Cummings, Gould, and Bradford were convicted of murder and sentenced to life imprisonment. Said Joyce Cummings at the conclusion of her trial: "All we wanted was an all-female lab."

Brady, Ian, See: **Moors Murders, The**.

Braeseke, Barry, 1957- , U.S. At twenty-five, Barry Braeseke was serving a life sentence for the 1976 killings of his mother, father, and grandfather, when, in 1982, the California Supreme Court upset the 1977 conviction, ruling that Braeseke confessed before police properly advised him of his rights. As part of the hearings for the retrial, Judge Stanley Golde of Alameda County ordered the CBS News Program "60 Minutes" to bring twenty-eight minutes of unused material from an interview it had aired with Braeseke. Golde had declared a 1980 California state law permitting reporters to withhold their sources unconstitutional on Jan. 18, 1982, calling the shield law a First Amendment privilege that must give way to the Sixth Amendment, which guarantees the right to a fair trial for the accused. The two minutes of "60 Minutes" that had been broadcast in 1977 showed Braeseke saying he was under the influence of the drug PCP when he murdered his relatives. On Jan. 26, 1982, when CBS News delivered the tape to Judge Golde, he responded by vacating his earlier ruling that called the shield law unconstitutional. CBS lawyer Edwin Heafey, Jr., said the network had "attempted to reach an accommodation to protect the rights the court was worried about." The tape was admitted as evidence for the defense in Braeseke's second trial and viewed by the jury. In February 1982, he was convicted of the murders a second time and resentenced to life in prison.

Brain, George, 1911-38, Brit. Twenty-seven-year-old George Brain drove a van for a shoe repair business on Pancras Street, Tottenham Court Road, London. Occasionally his employer would let him take the company van home for the night. On July 13, 1938, Brain used the van to pay a social call on his bride-to-be in Kingston. However, he missed his connection. Undaunted, he drove about the city in search of something else to do. Near Wimbledon Common he recognized a familiar face: 30-year-old Rose Muriel Atkins, a street walker known as "Irish Rose."

Brain offered her a lift, but she pan-handled him for money. He refused, and Atkins threatened to tell his employer that he had been driving the van around the city for pleasure. Furious with her demands, Brain struck her repeatedly with the starting handle until she died. To cover his tracks and alleviate suspicion he placed the body curbside and drove over it, hoping to give the impression that Atkins had been the victim of a hit-and-run driver.

Witnesses reported seeing Irish Rose enter a green van, possibly an Austin Seven or Morris Minor. These were the only two vehicles that matched the tire tracks found on the dead woman. The abandoned van was found on July 16. It was eventually traced back to Brain. Police sent his photograph to the papers and requested from the public any information regarding his whereabouts. A Richmond school boy recognized Brain near the Minister Cliffs at Sheerness on July 25. The following September he was placed on trial at the Old Bailey. It took the jury only fifteen minutes to debate his fate. A Guilty verdict was returned, and Justice Wrottesley passed sentence. The sentence was carried out at Wandsworth Prison on Nov. 1, 1938.

Branch, Mark, 1969-88, U.S. The celluloid delusions of teenage videophile Mark Branch became an inescapable horror for 18-year-old Sharon Gregory, found stabbed and mutilated in her Greenfield, Mass., home on Oct. 24, 1988. Branch's fascination with horror movies may have been a contributing factor in the brutal death of Gregory, because, as he once explained, "I want to know what it's like to murder someone." His alter ego was Jason, the fictional psychopath in the 1979 film *Friday the 13th*. When Branch cut firewood in back of his parents' house at 112 Meadow Lane in Greenfield, he would sometimes don a leather mask like the one worn by the maniacal killer in *Texas Chainsaw Massacre II*. Branch was a frequent customer at Greenfield's Video Expo One, where, according to owner Bob Quesnel, he rented everything on the shelf that promised blood and gore by the minute. "I could have seen this coming," Quesnel said. "I don't think he would watch a regular movie."

But Branch attended therapy sessions and had begun working in a store. By all accounts, he seemed to be putting his life back in order. Then Sharon Gregory was killed, and Branch, who quickly became a prime suspect, was missing. Quesnel recalled a statement Branch had made nearly four years earlier. "He said that if anything really bloody ever happened around here, people would automatically think he did it because they know he's into it."

Gregory's body was found by her sister in the bathroom of the family home on South Shelburne Road, Greenfield. A medical examiner from the coroner's office concluded that the girl had suffered multiple stab wounds. Police told reporters only that witnesses had observed Branch entering the Gregory home early that day. Based on the identification of Branch's gray Chevette near the murder scene, police issued an all-points bulletin for the young man. Later that day the vehicle was found on Avery Road in Buckland, a secluded spot west of Greenfield in Franklin County. The driver of the car was gone.

Police concentrated their search in the woods near Hog Mountain, but were unable to find a trace of the suspected killer. Michael Duquette, Branch's brother-in-law, conducted his own search of the area but came up with nothing. A full month passed without any new leads, until Nov. 29 when Kevin Purinton found Branch's body while tracking deer in the woods. It was hanging from a tree on Hog Mountain, two miles from where the car had first been found. Purinton had made it his own private mission to locate the remains. "I had told my mother I was going to find him," he said to reporters. "I just had that gut feeling."

Branch was hanging by his boot laces, an apparent suicide. "He's been there awhile," Greenfield Police Chief Joseph LaChance said, adding that police search parties had come within a hundred yards of the body when searching the densely wooded area. A final identification of the decaying corpse was made at the state police crime lab, closing the book on the "Jason" case.

Brandon, Mark, d.1944, Brit. On an October evening in 1942 Beatrice Swanson put her three children to bed and walked over to snuggle with her husband, Samuel Swanson. Outside the window of their home a shot shattered the glass and Samuel Swanson slumped forward. His frantic spouse tried to drag him out to their car in an effort to reach Meadville, the nearest town, for help. As she appeared in the doorway, a man jumped her, knocking her unconscious. When she revived and staggered toward the car again, he fired two shots at her and she dropped to the ground. At 5 a.m. Morton Brown, a friend who drove Swanson to work every day, came to pick him up and saw Samuel's body sprawled in the doorway. The Swanson children were still sleeping. Finding Beatrice Swanson unconscious and wounded, Brown carried her back into the house, put her to bed, then went for the police. Officers discovered threads of heavy blue serge cloth on the ground near the house. Later, as Mrs. Swanson lay dying, she said that their hired man, Mark Brandon, had made advances to her. Her description of Brandon was similar to that of the suspect in a Meadville case that the sheriff and undersheriff were working on. Calling Meadville to report the resemblance, they were told that the murder was known to officers there, for it had been related in great detail by a young man in a cafe to an officer having breakfast there. The description of the young man matched that of Brandon again.

Around midnight officers picked up a pedestrian who claimed he was Ted Harris from Phoenix, Ariz. But relatives of Brandon's quickly identified him. When confronted with the evidence of the threads that matched those torn from clothes he had been seen wearing the day before, Brandon confessed. The trial began on Dec. 10 and Brandon was found "Guilty of murder, with the recommendation of the death penalty," on Dec. 24. Later, the case went to higher courts, and Brandon obtained one stay of execution but lost an insanity plea. He was hanged for the double murder on Aug. 10, 1944.

Brannan, Joshua, prom. 1925, U.S. The Kentucky sawmill camp where Joshua Brannan and Boris Beary both worked was notorious for weekends of excessive drinking and aggressive behavior. Beary was married, but had been spending a great deal of time with Brannan's eight-months pregnant wife. The level of hostility had gotten so intense that Brannan had recently purchased a new pistol. On Saturday, May 2, 1925, Beary got drunk enough to follow Brannan home, presumably after again flirting with his co-worker's wife. When Beary forced his way into their house, Brannan shot and killed him. A man who surveyed the scene of the crime just after the shooting said Brannan's wife was temporarily trapped inside the logging camp house when Beary's corpse lay in the doorway, and a plank had

to be taken off the back of the lodging so she could exit, as she refused to step over the dead body.

Sentenced to life in the state penitentiary, Brannan was paroled early. His spouse divorced him not long after the murder and soon remarried, dying in 1970. Brannan also married again, dying in the late seventies.

Branson, William, prom. 1916-20, U.S. Convicted in 1916 of murdering, on Oct. 8, 1915, William Booth, a rancher in Yamhill county and the husband of Anna Booth, with whom Branson apparently was involved, the young man was tried, convicted of second-degree murder in 1916, and sentenced to life in prison. The decision was later appealed and reversed on the basis of improper jury instructions. In 1917 Branson again was tried, convicted, and given a life sentence. He was sent to the state penitentiary in Salem, Ore., on Mar. 3, 1917. The state parole board became so convinced of his innocence—one of the central questions in the trial apparently had been whether he or Anna Booth had actually pulled the trigger—that they wrote to Governor Olcott asking his release, explaining, "We...are satisfied after a full and complete investigation of this case that the accused was not guilty of the crime with which he was charged." Both the warden of the penitentiary, Louis Compton, and the state hospital superintendent, Dr. R. Lee Steiner, added their names to the parole board's recommendation for pardon. According to Olcott's statement when he paroled Branson, the accused had been (twice) convicted on "the sheerest kind of circumstantial evidence," and another man had confessed to committing the crime and was held afterwards in the insane asylum for life.

Anna Booth was paroled on Jan. 31, 1920. Branson received his unconditional pardon in September of the same year.

Braun, Thomas Eugene (AKA: **Mike Ford**), 1948- , and **Maine, Leonard**, 1948- , U.S. Thomas Braun was born in the state of Washington. When barely into his adolescence, he was forced to shoot the family dog because his drunken father thought the dog was "a chicken killer." On Aug. 17, 1967, Braun left his job as a gas station attendant in Ritzville, Wash., to ride off with Lenny Maine. They took with them a .22-caliber Luger and a Frontier Colt single-action .22-caliber pistol.

Heading for Seattle, they overtook a late-model Skylark driven by 22-year-old Deanna Buse on Route 72 outside Richmond. They motioned her over to the side of the road on the pretense that her tires were going flat. When she stepped out of the car, Braun pointed a gun at her head and told her to get into their car. Maine hopped in the Skylark and followed Braun to a secluded spot near Echo Lake. There Braun shot and killed Buse, with five bullets from his pistol. The two left her body and then continued on to Seattle, where they abandoned their car and took the Skylark.

The next day, Braun and Maine crossed into Oregon and tried to register at a resort motel. The owner was suspicious of the unkempt strangers, and asked to see their vehicle registration. They drove off, but had a flat tire a few miles away. Samuel Ledgerwood, who had just come from his favorite fishing spot, offered to help. Braun pumped two shots into Ledgerwood's head, and then set fire to the Skylark. The two killers drove off in Ledgerwood's shiny new Buick. They continued south to Northern California. On Route 120, Braun stopped to pick up two 17-year-old hitchhikers, Susan Bartolomei and Timothy Luce. Early the next morning, the Mease family stopped their car on the same highway to investigate what they be-

Killer Thomas Braun, left front, with co-murderer Leonard Maine behind him.

lieved was an accident. They found Susan Bartolomei lying on the side of the road, barely conscious. She said that two men named Mike and John from Oklahoma had shot them, killing Timothy. Meanwhile, searchers found the body of Deanna Buse. Oregon police reported the murder of Samuel Ledgerwood, and soon the manhunt had begun as three states pooled their resources. Several days later, Maine and Braun were captured at a motel in Jamestown, Calif., after Constable Ed Chafin noticed the green Buick Skylark with Oregon plates. The boys were barely awake in their rooms when the police broke in. Braun reached for a gun but was subdued. After being shown still photos and movies of the victims, they soon confessed to their

vicious crime spree.

On Dec. 2, 1968, Superior Court Judge Joseph Kelly of San Jose, Calif., sentenced Braun to die in the San Quentin gas chamber. However, the sentence was later commuted to life imprisonment. Leonard Maine also received a life sentence.

Brazier, Nicola, c.1950-70, Brit. On Sept. 17, 1970, Nicola Brazier was found dead, shot in the back of the head, and her body bound with wire, in the woods near Broxbourne, Hertfordshire. Brazier had last been seen driving from her High Street, Whitechurch, Buckinghamshire, home to go to work at her job as a company representative in the Broxbourne area. A few days after the murder, police found several of her belongings, along with a checkbook and a pistol engraved with the number 40084, in a locker at the Euston train station. Around that same time, a young man committed suicide by throwing himself under a train near Hoddesdon, Hertfordshire, not far from where Brazier was murdered. Following routine procedure, police fingerprinted the man's corpse. There was no reason to connect the suicide with Brazier's murder.

Toward the end of December, with the Brazier case still unsolved, police rechecked all the evidence and this time found that the dead man's fingerprints matched those on the weapon that killed Brazier. Checking into the suicide's background, they realized they had found the killer. The pistol was traced to Canada and to South Africa, where it had once been owned by a merchant seaman who had sold it to the murderer.

Brazilian Carnival Murders, prom. 1980s, Braz. Each year at least a dozen murders occur during the frenetic Brazilian Carnival held in Rio de Janeiro. Amidst the round-the-clock drunken revels, wild street dancing, constant parties, and fetes, hundreds of deaths, mostly accidental, occur. It is also a time when murder victims are most public and vulnerable to their enemies. In 1982, officials recorded 282 violent deaths in Rio during the festivities. In the following year, 110 persons died during the revelry. In 1984, 171 people were killed one way or another and nineteen of these deaths, according to authorities, were murders, this number considered average by police who find it impossible to cope with killings while the entire population is in the streets and most are wearing costumes—the perfect method by which killers disguise their identities. One recent murder victim was killed while dressed in lingerie and a blonde wig. He was reportedly killed by another man dressed similarly in female clothing.

Brekke, Carstein, prom. 1949, Nor. Odvar Eiken and Anders Muren had been the best of friends since they had served together in the Norwegian Air Force in the final days of WWII. Following their return to civilian life, they enrolled at the same medical college in Lund, Sweden, and became roommates. In the summer of 1948, Eiken visited Muren's family home in Norway, where he met and fell in love with Randi Muren, Anders' 22-year-old sister. The couple courted for nearly a year, and looked forward to announcing their engagement on Easter of 1949 when Eiken received an anonymous letter, telling him of Randi's alleged infidelities, and a newspaper clipping that announced Randi's engagement to Carstein Brekke, a fellow student and old-time friend of hers who also attended her teachers' college in Kristiansand. Randi also received several anonymous letters telling her about Eiken's affairs in Sweden. In February, Randi received a letter from a Signe Lundgren, who claimed to be Eiken's mistress and pregnant with his child. The lovers discussed these strange letters, deciding that they were practical jokes played on them by friends.

Shortly before Easter, Eiken received a parcel containing a small bottle of liquor in an old cigar box, mailed from a Kari Straume, with an indecipherable address. Both wondered vaguely who Kari Straume might be. He raised a toast to his upcoming engagement with his brother-in-law to be, and though both became mildly sick, they did not attribute it to the alcohol. One week later Eiken received another parcel, containing four matchboxes with chocolates inside, and a note from Randi, sending her love and asking him to eat them all. On Mar. 12, Eiken shared the candy with Muren, and with his landlady's 8-year-old daughter, Marianne Svendson, who in turn shared the sweets with her friend, Barbro Jakobson. That night all four were rushed to the hospital in Lund, where Marianne Svendson died in agony.

In the small town of Malmo, near Lund, Superintendent Alf Eliasson took over the investigation. Autopsy tests on Svendson revealed traces of arsenic. Randi Muren was questioned and told of the anonymous letters. Faint scribbles on the newsprint in which the lethal treats had been wrapped revealed the name Flemming Rosborg, a Dane who had met Randi Muren at a Vraadal hotel the year before and had been strongly attracted to the coed. But it was proved that he had no connection to the parcels or letters. Investigations in Oslo and Copenhagen revealed that neither Signe Lundgren nor Kari Straume had anything to do with the case—police suspected their names had been taken from telephone directories.

Police had little to go on until Carstein Brekke came into headquarters to announce that somebody had also sent him a box of poisoned chocolates, with the name S. Kihle on the wrapping. After eating one, he had been sick for three days and had come to the police because he was scared after hearing about Svendson's death. A model student from a good family, Brekke was courteous and cooperative. But when Randi mentioned that he had been in Oslo on both days when the parcels were postmarked, he quickly became a suspect. When Randi was also shown the cigar box in which the doctored liquor had been mailed she identified it as the same box in which Brekke once brought her fresh eggs from his family home. Detectives then found an old school notebook in the training college trash, with examples of Randi Muren's signature and practiced forgeries of her handwriting.

Five hours after his arrest Brekke admitted to poisoning the chocolates, refusing to be further cross-examined and insisting on writing out his confession in the intellectual form it required. His statement on a long, formal paper explained how unrequited love for Muren had driven him to create an elaborate scheme of revenge.

Brekke had happened to be visiting Randi at her house when she received a letter from Eiken thanking her for the liquor. She wrote him back, explaining she had not sent it. Addressing her lover, "My dear husband," she gave the missive to Brekke to mail on his way home. When Brekke opened the letter instead and read it, he later confessed to police, "Something snapped inside of me." It was then he decided to implicate Randi with the poisoned candy. Brekke was charged with two counts of attempted, premeditated murder, and with the manslaughter of Svendson. Found Guilty, he was sentenced to twelve years in prison and, according to Norwegian law, a ten-year loss of his rights as a citizen. When he appealed, a supreme court found him Guilty again. Judge Carl Kruse Jensen remarked to the jury that "the condemned's extremely serious actions disclosed an emphatic criminal disposition." In the May 1951 sentencing, an additional three years were added to Brekke's term.

Brennan, William Theodore, b.c.1898, Brit. On the Rowlands farm, at Model Farm, Penyffordd, near Mold, on Mar. 5, 1925, a farm laborer named Evans noticed a man he presumed to be a poacher and told his employer, John Rowlands, about it. When Rowlands went to check into the matter, Evans heard a gunshot and ran out into the field to see a man in a light coat fleeing. Chasing after him, Evans saw the man turn around and point his gun at him, and the farm worker retreated.

Under suspicion was William Brennan, a 27-year-old Irishman who had recently returned to Penyffordd to live with his parents. With a history of fits of rage, and a strain of insanity in his family, Brennan had frequently been in trouble since leaving school, and his parents decided it would be best for him to live with them in the relative quiet of the country.

Brennan claimed to have been home all day when Rowlands was shot, and no weapon was found in his house. His coat had been recently cleaned. A few days after his arrest, Brennan admitted to the killing, explaining that Rowlands had approached him and attempted to take his gun. Brennan had offered to pay for the rabbits he had stolen, but would not release his shotgun. The two men struggled, the gun went off once harmlessly, and then an enraged Brennan had reloaded and murdered the farmer, later hiding the gun in a drain. A jury at Mold Assizes found Brennan Guilty but Insane, and he was sent to the Broadmoor Criminal Lunatic Asylum.

Bretagna, Santo, and **Rosenberg, Willie**, prom. 1948, U.S. On New York's East Side on Jan. 13, 1948, a policeman heard shots in his own First Street building and rushed to the apartment of Benjamin (Chippy) Weiner, a minor hoodlum, who lay dying on his kitchen floor. When the officer asked Weiner who shot him, the man just shook his head, following the underworld code of refusing to give information to the law. He died moments later. Neighborhood residents had heard the shots but no one could, or would, tell the police who had done it. A month later, Edward Fennessey, arrested for a holdup in Brooklyn, told the King's County District Attorney's office that Weiner's killers were Santo Bretagna and Willie Rosenberg. Although Rosenberg was captured, Bretagna disappeared.

Police questioned Bretagna's East Side acquaintances for two months until one of them, a young tough on parole, confessed that he had been sending money to Bretagna. On Mar. 13, 1948, police arrested Bretagna in Boston.

He told them he went to Weiner's apartment with Rosenberg, who wanted to collect his share of the profits from a recent hijacking. On the way up to the apartment, Rosenberg casually asked Bretagna to kill Weiner for him as a favor. Weiner invited the two in, and when he went to the kitchen to make drinks, Bretagna followed and shot him. Faced with Bretagna's confession, Rosenberg admitted his part in the murder. Both men were later executed in the electric chair.

Brewer, Morris Sutton Ramsden, 1926- , Aus. Morris Brewer was a religious and dutiful son, raised in the Plymouth Brethren religion which forbade films, plays, and dancing. The overwhelming intensity of his moral fanaticism more than likely contributed to a nervous breakdown for he had been in a mental hospital. He had been seeing a psychiatrist, Dr. Alexander John Maum Sinclair, for more than a year when in 1949 he met 18-year-old Carmen Walters when they both took a course in herd-testing at Burnley Agricultural College in Melbourne, Aust. Walters' demure and reserved demeanor belied her spirit of adventure—in the short time since she left school she had studied to be a missionary, worked as a trainee nurse and as a tax department employee, and had run away to the Northern Territory, some 2,000 miles from her home, to work as a secretary.

This unlikely couple courted, fell in love, and became engaged in February 1950, planning to marry later that year. Brewer went into herd-testing for a while in the nearby dairy district of Gippsland, and Carmen, switching work again, became a dental nurse. But Brewer began to doubt his bride-to-be, remembering discrepancies in things she had told him, finally confronting her with, "Why did you lie to me?" Walters tried to explain that she had merely fibbed about the length of her stay in the Northern Territory because she had not known how much they would come to mean to each other.

When Brewer approached retired RAAF Squadron Leader Roy Walters to ask for his daughter's hand, the father, concerned about Brewer's rigid behavior, gave his prospective son-in-law three conditions: that his daughter be allowed to visit her family after marriage, that she be free to continue seeing movies with her relatives, and that the couple not get tied down with a family right away. Brewer agreed to the first, but was vague about the other two. Although wedding plans continued, Carmen Walters began getting moody, talking more about her traveling plans rather than about the upcoming nuptials and eventually admitting to Brewer that she had been close with another man when she lived in the Northern Territory. Brewer was shocked and repulsed, and a doctor advised the distraught young man to leave his betrothed.

On Mar. 10, 1950, Brewer met Walters at a railway station and ended their affair. According to his father, Robert Charles Brewer, his son did not sleep for five weeks after that day. The couple made several tentative and unsuccessful efforts to get back together. On May 13, they had dinner in suburban Mordialloc and were walking toward Walters' home when she told Brewer his parents had been a partial cause of their breakup, adding: "I have caused my parents a lot of worry and trouble in the past, and you'll do the same." Brewer then punched Walters in the face and strangled her to death.

When her body was found the next morning by a neighbor, Richard Hall, he did not recognize his longtime acquaintance. The police search for Brewer ended on May 17 in a State Electricity Camp, where he had gone to plead for food. The night of the murder, he had hitchhiked 100 miles into the bush, borrowing a razor at a workers' camp and unsuccessfully trying to cut his wrist. Confessing to Detective Cyril Currer, Brewer said: "She told me lies...she told me I would cause my parents a lot of trouble." Edward Francis Campbell, the Royal Melbourne Hospital psychologist who examined the killer, finding him to be a repressed personality with traits of schizophrenia, said Brewer had "hidden symptoms that could break out into aggressive insanity under emotional strain." A jury found Brewer Not Guilty on the grounds of insanity, and Mr. Justice Barry ordered that he be sent to an asylum for the criminally insane.

Brewer, Rudolph, d.1927, U.S. In September 1927, 70-year-old Charles Gundlacht, a native of Germany who continued making home brew in his adopted country after it went dry, offered a glass of beer to Rudolph Brewer, who had stopped for directions, as he did to every visitor to his small Leonardtown, Md., farm. Brewer returned later that same day, when Gundlacht was out, showed Mrs. Gundlacht his credentials from the Prohibition Bureau, and then broke every bottle he could find. When he returned on Sept. 16, with three other agents, Gundlacht held a shotgun on them, saying as they flashed their badges, "I know who you are and I don't give a damn." Warning them to stay where they were, he fired as they advanced, wounding one agent in the knee. They returned fire and Gundlacht fell to the ground, wounded in the foot by their bullets. As he lay prone, begging for mercy, Brewer stood over the old man and shot him through the head. Charges against the other agents were dropped, and a federal jury accepted Brewer's plea of self-defense. Gundlacht was one of the hundreds of liquor law violators or suspects killed by agents during Prohibition.

Brighton Trunk Murder, The, See: **Mancini, Tony**.

Brinkley, Richard, d.1907, Brit. At the death of 77-year-old Johanna Maria Louisa Blume, Richard Brinkley,

one of her lodgers, presented her will, claiming possession of Blume's money and Fulham, England, home. Blume's granddaughter contested the will, and Brinkley realized the people he had procured to witness the false will would quickly tell the truth in court. Thus, he set out to kill his witnesses, beginning with Reginald Parker.

Brinkley acquired some prussic acid—in order to kill a dog, he claimed—placing it in some stout he took to Parker's home on Apr. 20, 1907. He left the bottle of stout in the kitchen, not realizing that the beer might attract others. As it happened, Parker's landlords, Richard and Elizabeth Ann Beck, and their daughter drank the poisoned stout. It killed the elder Becks and left the daughter very ill. Police quickly discovered who provided the stout and Brinkley didn't help matters when he claimed to know nothing of it being poisoned before the police even brought up the subject. Even though Brinkley's intent was to kill Parker, there still was a willful act committed in the deaths of the Becks, so he was tried at the Guildford Assizes and convicted of murder. The trial was noteworthy because of the use of scientific evidence to determine the different kinds of ink used. It was shown that three different pens had been used in the will. Exhumation and examination of Blume's body showed that she had not been murdered. Brinkley was hanged on Aug. 13, 1907, at Wandsworth Prison.

Brique, Micheline, 1954-   , and **Chamand, Jocelyne**, 1956-   , Fr. It is more than likely that Jean-Michel Ray had believed himself lucky when he picked up two young, attractive, and scantily-clad female hitchhikers. Micheline Brique, eighteen, and Jocelyne Chamand, sixteen, had spent most of their adolescence in and out of trouble, finally being transferred from a juvenile delinquent home to the tighter security of a hospital. Two days after escaping from the hospital, on July 13, 1972, Brique and Chamand spent the last of their money on two butcher knives at a hardware store in Macon, Fr. The next day, Bastille Day, they began hitchhiking along Route Nationale 6, intent upon killing a driver for his money.

Ray was the fourth driver to pick up Brique and Chamand that day, the first three not being suitable victims. The women enticed him to pull off the road into a secluded glade where they savagely attacked him, stabbing him eleven times. They watched for more than half an hour as he bled to death. Brique and Chamand then caught another ride into Lyons. They were later apprehended carrying the bloodstained knives. Both women admitted their guilt and were sentenced to thirty years in prison.

Brisbon, Henry, Jr. (AKA: **The I-57 Killer**), 1956- , U.S. On the night of June 3, 1973, a car carrying four men forced a woman's car off Interstate 57, just south of Chicago. One of the men forced her from the car at gunpoint, then ordered her to strip naked and climb through a barbed-wire fence. He then shot her between the legs with a 12-gauge pump-action shotgun, leaving her in agony for several minutes before killing her with a shot to the throat. The four killers, returning to the road to seek out more victims, ran the car of a young couple off the road near Country Club Hills less than an hour later.

Dorothy Cerny and James Schmidt, both 25-years-old, were engaged to be married in six months. The couple, ordered to lie on the roadside, pleaded for mercy, but their killer shot them in the back after telling Cerny and Schmidt to "kiss your last kiss."

Henry Brisbon, Jr. was found Guilty of both conspiracy to commit murder and the murder of Cerny and Schmidt and was sentenced in November 1977 to 1,000 to 3,000 years in prison. His youth at the time of the killing—he was seventeen—and the law, which then prohibited capital punishment, prevented the judge from imposing the death penalty. At Brisbon's sentencing, Assistant State's Attorney Michael Ficaro said, "He is a wild, savage beast that should be caged...he would gladly kill again if he got the chance." Amazingly, Ficaro proved to be quite prophetic.

On Oct. 19, 1978, the I-57 killer struck again, but this time behind bars. While serving his sentence at the State-ville Penitentiary near Joliet, Ill., Brisbon used a sharpened soup ladle to murder fellow inmate Richard E. Morgan. Brisbon was convicted of this murder on Jan. 22, 1982, and it took an all-male jury less than an hour and a half on Feb. 24 to sentence Brisbon to death in the courtroom of Herman Haase. The I-57 killer, who had instigated a prison riot and taken part in fifteen attacks on guards and inmates, declared as he was led away from the trial, "You'll never get me. I'll kill again. Then you'll have another long trial. And I'll do it again."

Indeed, another murder attempt by Brisbon took place when he broke away from his armed escort at the Menard Correctional Center's death row unit on Feb. 15, 1983. He managed to arm himself with a piece of metal wire which he used to stab two other condemned inmates, including mass murderer John Wayne Gacy. Neither of the prisoners was seriously wounded.

Will County State's Attorney Edward Petka remarked that Brisbon was "a very, very terrible human being, a walking testimonial for the death penalty." The Illinois Supreme Court disagreed, overturning the death sentence on Apr. 19, 1985, claiming that the state had prejudiced the jury by introducing inflammatory evidence concerning the highway murders. Once again Brisbon appeared in court

for sentencing, and once again, on Oct. 7, 1986, he was sentenced to death.

Brisbon continues to cause trouble in prison, even in maximum security where he is currently being held at Menard awaiting further appeal of his sentence. On Aug. 3, 1987, he threw a dumbbell at another prisoner, fracturing the skull of 34-year-old convicted murderer John Phillips. See: **Gacy, John Wayne.**

Briscoe, Ricky, 1972-88, U.S. Linette West was only sixteen years old when she died on Mar. 25, 1988, in her home at 1200 Nova Avenue in the Capitol Heights district of Washington, D.C. She lived with her family and her 3-month-old child born out of wedlock. Linette's killer was Ricky Briscoe, a former boyfriend whom she had broken up with after her baby was born.

On Mar. 25, 1988, Briscoe turned up at the West residence. When Linette and Juanita, her sister, tried to send him away, Briscoe threatened Linette. "Don't go to sleep 'cause I'm going to kill you," he told her.

About 4 a.m., Juanita was awakened by the screams of her sister in the living room. Briscoe had her pinned to the floor. There was a distinct aroma of kerosene. "Help me!" cried Linette. "He's going to burn me!"

Pregnant herself, Juanita ran next door for help, but there was no answer. She ran down the street knocking on doors but there was no response. Returning to her home, she met the unspeakable horror of seeing her sister engulfed in flames. Linette fled the house and ran nearly a hundred yards to her uncle's house. She was rushed to Washington Hospital Center, where she was found to be burned over 90 per cent of her body. She died shortly before 9 a.m. on Mar. 28.

After setting Linette on fire, Briscoe was unable to escape the flames and died, after becoming entangled in some drapes. His body was found near the front door. Shocked and grief-stricken neighbors complied with the family's request and asked a local man to sing *I'm Climbing on the Rough Side of the Mountain* at Linette's funeral, the song echoing the life of one black family.

Brittle, William, prom. 1964-65, Brit. Peter Thomas had lent William Brittle £2,000. Coincidentally, Thomas was found dead the month the loan was due to be repaid. The discovery of Peter Thomas' body in Bracknell Woods on June 28, 1964, and its state of decomposition caused by bluebottle fly larvae led pathologist Dr. Keith Simpson to conclude that Thomas had been dead for at least ten days.

This estimation matched the information known to Detective Superintendent Horace Faber that Thomas had been missing from his home in Lydney since June 16 or 17. Dennis Roberts, however, claimed to have seen Thomas alive on June 20. Brittle claimed he repaid Thomas the day he disappeared. Even with a strong witness supporting his story, a coroner's jury still named Brittle as murderer, and he was tried at the spring assize of 1965, in Gloucester.

At the trial, Queen's Counsel Quintin Hogg represented Brittle. He had two more witnesses, Jane Charles and Gwendoline Padwick, who swore they saw Thomas alive on June 21—a minimum of three days after he was dead, according to Simpson. The prosecution, led by Ralph Cusack, could not refute the testimony of the defense witnesses, and the testimony of one defense witness, Professor McKenny-Hughes, unexpectedly corroborated Simpson's theory as to time of death. The jury decided that Thomas could not possibly have been alive when the witnesses stated and found Brittle Guilty of murder, for which he received a life sentence.

Brogile, Prince Jean de, 1921-76, Fr. Prince Jean de Brogile, a prominent politician and supporter of French president Valery Giscard d'Estaing, was shot in the neck and chest while walking along a Paris street on Dec. 24, 1976. His death was believed to have been politically motivated after a message—later proven bogus—was received from the extreme rightist Charles Martel Club. Within five days of the murder, however, police had arrested six people in connection with a plot involving two restaurateurs who planned to repay their debts with the proceeds of an $800,000 life insurance policy on Brogile. The six arrested were: the prince's business partners Patrick Allenet de Ribemont and Pierre de Varga; police detective Guy Simonet, who arranged the murder for the partners; a pimp named Gerard Frech, who had pulled the trigger; and Simon Kelkewitcz and Serge Tessedre, who assisted Frech.

The sudden arrests and solution to the case quickly erupted into a scandal concerning a possible coverup of the murder by Interior Minister Michel Poniatowski. Although the possibility of a coverup did affect the elections in France, no official misconduct was ever proved. Four men were found Guilty in the murder conspiracy; three were sentenced on Dec. 23, 1981, to ten years in prison and the fourth to five years.

Brook, John, c.1943-   , and **Johnson, Nicholas de Clare**, prom. 1970s, Brit. Knowing he was suspected of murder, George Ince turned himself into police but maintained his innocence. Police were seeking him for the murder of Muriel Patience, who was shot and killed on Nov. 5, 1972. It took two trials before Ince was proven innocent and a third before the true murderer was convicted.

When Bob Patience, the owner of the Barn Restaurant in Braintree, Essex, refused to open the safe for robbers, they shot him and his daughter Beverly and killed his wife Muriel. Then they got into the safe and stole £900. Ince testified that he was with his fiancee Dolly Gray that night. At Ince's first trial in May 1973, at Chelmsford, no verdict was reached, while at the second trial he was found Not Guilty. Not long after his acquittal, on June 15, the murder weapon was located.

The gun that killed Patience was discovered sewn into the mattress of John Brook's bed, and after his accomplice Nicholas de Clare Johnson admitted to the robbery and accused Brook of the shootings, the two were brought to trial. At the trial in January 1974, Brook was found Guilty of murder and attempted murder and sentenced to life in prison, while Johnson received ten years for manslaughter.

Brookins, Louis Dwight, 1925-46, U.S. The killer was as cold as ice as he recounted the exact moments leading up to the murder of a 32-year-old department store manicurist named Helen Caputo. Veteran police officers were shocked by Louis Brookins' laconic, unfeeling attitude. When he finished his story, he asked Deputy Elmer Wood of the Rochester (N.Y.) Police Department, "What do you think they will give me?" Wood's reply was unprintable.

The 20-year-old ex-soldier met his victim at a downtown Rochester restaurant on July 9, 1945. The charming young man dressed as a Marine flattered Helen Caputo, an older woman, and suggested that they go to Ontario Beach Park for a late-night swim. The suggestion appealed to the lonely woman who had been an orphan since childhood. Caputo, who was unmarried, had just been stood up by a girlfriend. She took Brookins to her rooming house at 5:15 p.m. The couple remained in the building until 8:30 p.m., when they were last seen walking near James Street.

Brookins had already decided to attack and rob Caputo, who did not know that she was being lured to the identical spot where a first victim had been assaulted twenty-four hours before. At a desolate spot near Cherry Road in the Lakedale subdivision, Brookins told his date to walk ahead. Puzzled, she complied with his request.

Knocking Helen to the ground, Brookins sexually assaulted her. A broken street light left the scene in darkness, unnoticed by passersby. She screamed, but neighbors paid no attention. He stuffed a handkerchief she had given him several hours earlier into her mouth. An autopsy later revealed that she had died of strangulation.

"Lots of people come up from the lake at night, laughing and screaming," Mrs. V.E. Lacy, who lived on Leander Road, explained later.

To conceal his crime Brookins dragged Caputo's body into a thicket next to the road. Before he fled, he removed $450 from his victim's purse, a wristwatch, and two expensive rings. The watch was later smashed. The body was found the next day by Mrs. Russell McFarland, who was taking a shortcut through the brush when she noticed a face partially covered by a bloody handkerchief.

Satisfied with himself, Brookins walked up to Lake Avenue where he hitched a ride with three young women and their male escort. They stopped for a sandwich at Ontario Beach Park before driving back downtown. With his pocket full of cash, Brookins picked up a young prostitute on Main Street and took her to a motel where he paid her with some of the jewelry lifted from Caputo.

The next day the pair took a bus to Brookins' hometown of Syracuse where they registered in a hotel as husband and wife. In a military surplus store, he purchased a new Marine uniform and enough campaign ribbons to make a person believe that he single-handedly won the battle of Corregidor. They returned to Rochester the next day, registering in a hotel with a second man.

Based on a tip supplied by room clerk Charles Hartel, a squad of detectives led by John Rowan and Victor Raycroft burst into the hotel room where they found Brookins, the 19-year-old prostitute, and the second man. Hartel had been supplied with a physical description of the suspect several hours earlier by city detectives. His suspicions were aroused when Brookins registered under his own name, though he claimed that the girl was his wife. Brookins and the prostitute were arraigned on vagrancy charges pending a hearing. It was one of the fastest arrests of a murder suspect made by the Rochester Police in many years, because they were on his trail before he even met up with Caputo. Brookins had been linked to three other recent assaults in the city, and was identified by a woman he had accosted near the Lake Avenue bus stop. She successfully fended off her attacker by pummeling him in the face. As she ran away, she heard Brookins mutter an angry curse, adding, "You'd make a good corpse."

Brookins accompanied the detectives to the murder site, where he reconstructed the events of that night. The police also learned that their suspect had been taken into custody by the Navy Shore Patrol in Rochester a few days earlier, when he was "unable to give a good account of himself." He claimed that he had been discharged from the Marine Corps in 1944, classified as unfit for service. When they checked out his story they found out he had been dis-

charged from the Army, not the Marines.

Brookins was convicted of first-degree murder and sentenced to die. He was on death row at Sing Sing for fourteen months before being executed in the electric chair at 11:06 p.m. on Sept. 12, 1946.

Brooks, Charles, 1942-82, U.S. In 1976, used-car sales-man David Gregory took Charlie Brooks and Woody Lourdes for a trial drive. The result was a trial for the murder of Gregory—for which each man was found Guilty and sentenced to death—and notoriety for Brooks as the first convicted killer to be executed by a lethal injection.

Lourdes was able to successfully appeal his conviction on the grounds that the jury had been improperly selected, and he received a commuted sentence of forty years in prison. Just minutes before his scheduled execution, Brooks was denied a stay of execution by the U.S. Supreme Court. Brooks' death at 12:16 a.m. on Dec. 7, 1982, also made history because he was the first man executed in Texas in eighteen years and the first black man put to death since the death penalty was reinstated by the Supreme Court in 1976. The lethal injection administered to Brooks by a medical technician—and not a physician, because the American Medical Association strongly opposed the taking of a life by a doctor—was a solution of pancurionum bromide, potassium chloride, and sodium thipental, also known as the truth drug, sodium pentothal.

Brooks, Donald (AKA: **Frank Whitney**), prom. 1944, U.S. Mary Finn was killed on her wedding day, July 1, 1944. The pretty young bride-to-be from Baltimore left her home the night before the wedding with $600. The money was the nest egg that Mary and her fiance Charles Rommell had been saving for their honeymoon.

When Rommell left for the graveyard shift at a nearby defense plant at 10:30 p.m., he told Mary to wait for him at her home. She was nervous about carrying the money back home again, but agreed. The next day at about 9 a.m., Rommell returned home to prepare for his wedding. He found his bride-to-be dead on the floor. There was blood everywhere. Dazed, he called a policeman.

The police questioned many friends and relatives who were on the guest list. All of them except Irene Ayres had airtight alibis. Ayres worked as a riveter at the bomber plant, and she had a boyfriend named Don Brooks who was well known to Rommell. When police talked to Irene, they discovered she had disappeared, along with her boyfriend.

A rented Buick coupe was traced to Brooks, who used

the name Frank Whitney. Inside, a blood-spattered newspaper section dated June 30 was found. It was part of the same paper found in the Rommell apartment. Under direct questioning, Irene Ayres denied that Brooks had killed Mary. But when threatened with a charge of accessory to murder, she broke down and admitted that her boyfriend killed Mary Finn for the $600, which they used to pay for a weekend in New York. Brooks was convicted of first degree murder on Oct. 6, 1944.

Broome, William (William Brooks), prom. 1910, Brit. Following on the heels of the sensational murder trial of Dr. Hawley Crippen, the British police had another notorious killer to contend with—William Broome, an army veteran whose father owned a shop on High Street, Slough.

When an elderly woman named Mrs. Wilson was found dead in the building next door, local gossip directed Elias Bower of Scotland Yard to young William Broome, who used the name William Brooks. One Sunday morning Bower took the man in for questioning just as he was leaving the local church. Bower discovered a facial scratch running from Broome's cheek to his nose. It was the kind of wound that would be sustained during a scuffle. In coming days, three different people told three different stories about the origins of the scratch, which at the very least proved that Broome was a bad liar.

When Broome's room near Regent's Park was searched, an envelope containing £20 in gold was found. This was the precise amount that had been taken from the old lady. Dr. William Wilcox of the Home Office conducted an exhaustive examination of a slip of brown paper found in Broome's possession that connected him to the victim.

William Broome protested that on the day of the murder he had been in London applying for a job as a taxi driver. No evidence could be found to back up this assertion, so Broome was tried and duly convicted at Reading. On the day of his scheduled execution, a stiff dose of brandy helped Broome overcome a severe case of the jitters. A second before he was dropped he screamed, "I am innocent!" But it was too late.

Brown, Arthur Ross, 1925-56, U.S. On Aug. 4, 1955, Mrs. Wilma Frances Allen, a prominent Kansas City, Mo., wife and mother, left a beauty parlor at 12:30 p.m. on a rainy day and hurried to her convertible. Five hours later, concerned about not finding his wife at home, Mr. Allen, a car dealer, sent his salesman to search for her car; a few hours later, he notified the police. At 2:10 a.m. patrolman

Ronald Erhardt found Mrs. Allen's locked Chevrolet under a dark viaduct. There were bloodstains on the rear seat and floor, and in the trunk were her torn and bloodstained clothing. Finger and palm prints found by police inside the auto were too blurred to be clues. From the Allen's mileage logs, police estimated that the Chevrolet had been driven sixty to seventy miles. They blocked out an area covering parts of Missouri and Kansas, and police nationally were notified to question any violent sexual deviants in their records. Leads poured into Kansas City, but none of them yielded any clues.

On Aug. 7, a Kansas farmer, Richard A. Taylor, noticed a blue handbag in a ditch on Highway 69. When he read about the Allen case in the paper, he notified police. On Aug. 7, Clifford Erhart and his son Milton were searching for a stray cow and calf about six miles from where the handbag had been found. They discovered an open pasture gate and then saw the nude corpse of Wilma Allen. She had been shot twice in the back of the head, her hands were tied behind her back, and all her jewelry was missing. With proof that the victim had been carried across state lines, Midwestern FBI agents poured into Kansas City. But rains had washed away any footprints or other evidence, and for weeks the case dragged on with no further clues.

On Aug. 31, Arthur Ross Brown, a parole violator from California, critically wounded a sheriff in Wyoming and escaped when the officer tried to arrest him. Brown's criminal record of assaults, robberies, and attempted abductions reached back sixteen years. Soon after the Wyoming incident, Brown stole a car in Sheridan, Wyo., then robbed a liquor store in Rapid City, S.D. A man matching Brown's description stole several cars as he made his way through Florida, Texas, and Indiana, holding up liquor stores, preferring those with women clerks working alone. The FBI, still connecting him only with the charges in the shooting of the Wyoming sheriff, kept surveillance on the homes of Brown's relatives.

On Nov. 9, a Kansas City caller reported to police that his neighbor, Mrs. Arthur Ross Brown, had just been abducted at gunpoint by her estranged husband. Four hours later, the incoherent woman returned home; her spouse had disappeared. Anticipating that Brown would return to California, FBI agents interviewed his mother in San Jose. The anxious woman said that she believed her son was mad, and asked the police to stop him before he did further harm. On Nov. 13 Brown called his mother, saying he had tried to visit her, but fearing a trap, had fled. He added that he was going to kill himself. That night, he was picked up by officers outside his aunt's house in San Francisco, asleep in his car.

Initially denying his guilt, Brown soon broke down and confessed to shooting the sheriff in Wyoming, adding: "But where I'm really wanted is Kansas City." In a full confession to the murder of Wilma Allen, Brown said his motive was robbery, explaining: "I was looking for someone to rob. She looked wealthy." He had climbed in beside Allen as she got into her car in the beauty-shop parking lot, and forced her to drive at gunpoint. Finding the open pasture gate was, he told police, "just...lucky." He had shot her as she begged for mercy, then stripped the body to prevent identification before dumping her in the field. He tried to clean the car before driving it back into town. Court-appointed psychiatrists found Brown sane, and the jury found him Guilty. He was executed in the gas chamber at the Missouri State Prison on Feb. 24, 1956.

Brown, Barry Austin, prom. 1974, U.S. In a San Mateo, Calif., Superior Court, Barry Austin Brown pleaded guilty to three first-degree murder charges. He admitted killing Lois McNamara, the mother of a high school friend; a hitchhiking, discharged sailor whom he had picked up; and Richard Pipes, a grocery store employee whom Brown murdered when he held up the Santa Cruz store. Robbery was the motive in all three slayings, and the killer had netted about $1,500 and a car from McNamara, but only a backpack from the sailor. The thoughtful slayer told a probation officer, "I don't believe murder is part of my character. I believe I can, if given the chance, offer a lot to the people around me. I want to discover why I committed those acts. I don't want to be put in prison to rot away." Brown received three concurrent life sentences.

Brown, Conrad, 1935- , U.S. On Mar. 23, 1977, two men came into Conrad's Food & Liquors on Chicago's South Side. They were Thomas Patzke, twenty-six, a loan specialist, and Robert Fender, fifty-two, an auctioneer; both worked for the U.S. Small Business Association. Patzke had been friendly with owner Conrad Brown for some time, and was trying to help him out with his many financial problems. Reportedly $500,000 in debt, Brown had lost his liquor license, begun bankruptcy proceedings, and was about to be evicted for non-payment of rent. When Patzke and Fender came into the store, they told the employees to leave, intending to take an inventory and padlock the place as a preliminary step in foreclosing on the SBA loan. Brown beat both men with a metal pipe, then set fire to the store. When their bodies were found in the smoldering ruins by firemen the next day, Fender's hands had been tied behind his back.

Brown was charged with murder, felony murder, and

arson. Tried before Judge Frank J. Wilson, Brown admitted that he had beaten both men and started the fire. Three psychiatrists testified that Brown had lost touch with reality and was legally insane when he committed the murders, but Assistant State's Attorney Robert Quinlivan declared that the killings were premeditated because Brown was "all washed up in business." Defense Attorney Frederick Cohn said that his client "went berserk" when Patzke and Fender tried to padlock his store. On Aug. 31, 1978, Brown was found Guilty on two counts of involuntary manslaughter and one of arson. He was sentenced to two fourteen-year prison terms on each of the three counts, to be served concurrently.

Brown, Ernest, 1898-1934, Brit. Ernest Brown murdered his employer, Frederick Ellison Morton on Sept. 5, 1933. Morton was a well-to-do cattle farmer in Yorkshire, England. Brown was having an affair with Morton's wife, Dorothy. When Mrs. Morton tried to end the liaison, Brown intimidated her into continuing it. On Sept. 5, while Frederick was away, Brown and Mrs. Morton quarreled because she had been swimming with another man. Brown knocked her down. While she hid in the house waiting for her husband to return, Mrs. Morton heard a gunshot. Brown appeared shortly and explained that he had been shooting at a rat in the barn. Around 3:00 a.m., there was an explosion and Mrs. Morton looked out to see the garage ablaze. She escaped with her baby and her companion, Ann Houseman, and reported the fire to the police.

When the fire was extinguished, both of Frederick Morton's cars and his badly burned body were found in the garage. The body, the cars, and garage had been doused in gasoline. Morton had been shot in the stomach before his body was set on fire. Brown was charged with murder and tried at the Leeds Assizes. He was convicted and hanged at Armley Prison on Feb. 6, 1934.

Brown, Leslie, 1944- , U.S. Leslie Brown, twenty-eight, a secretary for the Environmental Protection Agency in Chicago, Ill., was apparently tired of her husband, Clarence Brown, fifty-four. She would later tell police that her spouse forbade her to spend money and beat her. Leslie Brown hired Hubert Lewis, twenty-two, on Dec. 29, 1982, to kill Clarence, asking that the job be done during a New Year's Eve party and offering Lewis $500 on completion of the killing, with another $1,000 promised later. Obtaining a sawed-off shotgun from Emmitt Neal, eighteen, Lewis purchased gun shells from Todd Allen, twenty-seven, before coming to the party. At the celebration, Lewis asked Leslie Brown if she was sure she wanted to go through with the murder, and she said yes. She gave her husband $10 and handed Lewis her car keys so the two could buy more liquor. Brown was shot about 1:40 a.m. in an alley on his way back to the party with Lewis. The killing was Chicago's first of the New Year. Lewis returned to the New Year's event, and Mrs. Brown gave him $300, which was later found in his sock.

Indicted on charges of murder and conspiracy to murder were Brown, Lewis, Neal, and Allen. Lewis pleaded guilty to murder charges on Oct. 26, 1982, before Criminal Court Judge Earl E. Strayhorn, and was sentenced to twenty-five years in prison. Allen pled guilty to conspiracy charges and was sentenced to three years in prison, and Neal also pleaded guilty to conspiracy and was sentenced to four months of a work-release program and thirty months in jail. Brown, who was also charged with murder, was judged to be psychologically unfit to stand trial and was sent to the Mental Health Center in Elgin, Ill.

Brown, Thomas Mathieson, prom. 1906, Brit. In the winter of 1906, Thomas Mathieson Brown, a retired coal mine manager, mailed an iced shortcake as a gift to his wife's aged uncle, William Lennox, of Old Cumnock, Ayrshire. The card enclosed read, "Hearty greetings to an old friend." Lennox and Grace McKerrow, his housekeeper, ate some of the shortcake and both became ill. Lennox recovered but McKerrow died. When the dessert was analyzed, it was found to contain large amounts of strychnine, as did the dead woman's body. Brown, who had called at Lennox's house to offer his condolences, was arrested and tried at the High Court of Justiciary in Edinburgh. Medical evidence revealed that Brown suffered from chronic epileptic insanity; he had been an epileptic for more than forty years and was affected with the mental deterioration that may result from extensive, severe epilepsy. Brown was found Guilty but insane, and was detained in strict custody.

Browne, Frederick Guy (AKA: **Leo Brown; Sydney Rhodes; Harris**), 1881-1928, and **Kennedy, William** (AKA: **William Henry Kennedy; Ginger**), 1891-1928, Brit. Both Frederick Guy Browne and William Kennedy were small-time British gangsters who had criminal records dating back to their early teens. Browne had been a bicycle thief at the turn of the century, leading a gang of thugs at Oxford. He received several prison sentences for burglary

and housebreaking, and when released from Dartmoor Prison in 1927, Browne vowed he would never again be taken alive to spend another moment behind bars. Kennedy, who also had a long police record, albeit one less

Guy Browne and William Kennedy, killers of George Gutteridge.

serious than Browne's, operated a garage in Clapham. Browne joined him after leaving prison, and the two embarked on a series of car thefts, bringing autos to the Clapham garage where they were altered and later sold.

On the night of Sept. 27, 1927, the pair stole a Morris Cowley car in Billericay, Essex, from the garage of a Dr. Lovell and drove back to Clapham, going through the back roads to avoid constables they knew to be on duty in Brentwood. Between Romford and Ongar, Browne and Kennedy were flagged down by Constable George W. Gutteridge, who waved his flashlight at them. Browne ignored the signal and kept driving, but Gutteridge blew his whistle and Browne brought the car to a stop. Constable Gutteridge walked to the driver's side of the car where Browne was seated and began to question him, writing his report in a notebook. Browne drew his Webley and shot Gutteridge twice. Then he got out of the car and looked down at the constable who was either dead or dying, but whose eyes stared back up at the killer. "What are you looking at me like that for?" Browne demanded. Then, at close range, he shot out the officer's eyes. (It was later claimed that Browne believed in the old canard that a dead man's eyes photograph his murderer, and wished to eliminate the possibility of later being detected in this way. It is more likely that he performed this sadistic act through his own intense hatred for the police.)

Hurrying from the murder scene, Browne recklessly smashed into a tree and damaged the car's front bumper. He and Kennedy later abandoned the car on Foxley Road in Brixton. The killers then caught a train for Clapham. Gutteridge's body was found the next morning, along with the abandoned car. A thorough examination of the stolen car revealed not one fingerprint. Blood was found on the driver's side of the car, but this was assumed to be that of the slain officer. A single cartridge was found at the scene of the killing. The murder rested there, unsolved, and Scotland Yard officials believed that there was scant chance of locating the murderer. Then Browne stole another car and, while driving wildly through the streets of Sheffield, he forced a van into a wall. The irate driver wrote down the license plate number of the car Browne was driving and notified police. Detectives from Scotland Yard tracked down the car to a Clapham garage and arrested Browne, holding him for trial.

A search of the Clapham garage unearthed the Webley Browne had used to murder Constable George Gutteridge. A routine check of this weapon led to a comparison of the cartridge found after the Gutteridge murder; a ballistics expert matched the cartridge to the Webley, and Browne was charged with the policeman's murder. Kennedy, arrested in Liverpool on Jan. 25, 1928, quickly confessed to wholesale car robberies and detailed Browne's murder of Gutteridge. Both men were tried at the Old Bailey before Justice Avory on Apr. 23, 1928, with Browne represented by E.F. Lever and Kennedy defended by F.J. Powell. Solicitor General Sir Boyd Merriman prosecuted for the Crown. The defense had a doubly hard time with Browne who was offensive and bullying in court and surly in the dock. Kennedy, who tried to blame the murder of Gutteridge on Browne and therefore avoid the expected death penalty, was proved to have the same murderous temperment as his friend Browne. When he was about to be arrested in Liverpool, officers testified, Kennedy pulled a gun and aimed it at a detective, squeezing the trigger several times, but the safety catch was on and the weapon did not go off. Officers arresting Browne told how the killer had snarled that he would have shot six of them had he been in his car and had his weapon, adding: "What I can see of it, I shall have to get a machine gun for you bastards next time!"

Ballistics expert Robert Churchill testified at great length during the Browne-Kennedy trial, demonstrating in exacting detail how Browne's Webley was matched to the cartridge and the bullets which killed Constable Gutteridge. It was this newly developed forensic science, coupled to Kennedy's testimony, that convicted both men of the murder. Churchill presented graphics in court that showed how the markings of the weapon and the bullets matched. He also pointed out how the ammunition used for the Webley revolver was an obsolete brand that had not been available since WWI; the same kind of bullets were removed from Gutteridge's corpse. The skin of the murder victim had been discolored by black powder burns which could only result from the type of ammunition employed by Browne,

according to expert Churchill.

The evidence provided by Churchill was a triumph for forensic ballistics and, because of this case, established this form of police science in England as readily as it was accepted in the U.S. in the recent Sacco and Vanzetti case. Both men were quickly convicted and sentenced to death, Browne being hanged at Pentonville Prison and Kennedy at Wandsworth on May 31, 1928.

Bruhne, Vera, 1910-   , and **Ferbach, Johann**, prom. 1960, Ger. Each time Dr. Otto Praun of Munich found himself a new lover, he would set her up in his sprawling pleasure estate on Spain's Costa Brava. Then, after his ardor had cooled, Praun would reclaim the $250,000 villa and give it to his next girlfriend. Praun, who was rumored to have earned his fortune through rum-running, dope peddling, and by performing illegal abortions, finally met his match with Vera Bruhne, an elegant 50-year-old blonde.

When the time came for her to lease the premises in 1960, she devised a little scheme. She informed Dr. Praun that she had arranged a sale of the villa to one Dr. Schmitz, who wanted to finalize the transaction at the mansion. Praun, who wanted to sell the estate, agreed to meet Schmitz. The next day, police found Otto Praun and his housekeeper dead. They concluded that Dr. Praun had suffered a nervous breakdown, killed the housekeeper, and then took his own life.

The Munich police began receiving reports that Praun and the housekeeper were murdered. Their remains were exhumed. He had been shot twice in the head, ending the suicide theory. Vera's 14-year-old daughter supplied the missing details. She said that the killer was Johann Ferbach, a German army deserter who fled from his regiment in 1944. He became Vera Bruhne's devoted love slave through her previous marriages and numerous affairs. When ordered to pose as Dr. Schmitz, the ex-Nazi readily agreed. Ferbach murdered Praun, killed the housekeeper, and then tried to make it appear that the doctor had gone berserk. But he made one mistake. Ferbach left behind the letter of introduction that Vera had written.

Handwriting samples were compared, which revealed Vera Bruhne's duplicity. The twosome was found Guilty of murder and given life sentences.

Bryant, Charlotte, 1904-36, Brit. Charlotte Bryant married a British soldier who was part of a regiment sent into Ireland to maintain peace and order in the early 1920s.

Frederick Bryant took his bride back to England where they set up housekeeping in Dorset. Though Charlotte bore her husband five children, she also engaged in many sexual liaisons with men she met in the Dorset ale houses. Charlotte often brought her lovers home to share the bed she slept in with her husband. Frederick did not seem to care about his wife's activities.

One young man in particular seemed to catch Charlotte's fancy. His name was Leonard Parsons, an itinerant gypsy who had his own wife, and several children. Yet, he moved in with the Bryants in 1933. The affair lasted until 1935, at which time Charlotte forsook the formalities of a divorce, and decided instead to poison her husband with arsenic. Bryant died on Dec. 22, 1935. Charlotte stood trial for murder the following year, but Parsons was totally unconcerned about her fate. The gypsy was drinking and cavorting in a local pub when he heard the news that Charlotte had been hanged on July 15, 1936. While awaiting her execution, the condemned woman's hair had turned white. See: **DeMelker, Daisy Louisa.**

Bullock, David, 1960-   , U.S. Openly defiant and lacking all concern for the six people he murdered, street hustler, part-time male prostitute, and armed robber David Bullock told Justice Burton Roberts of the New York State Supreme Court that killing was "fun." Bullock told of murdering Herberto Morales on Dec. 22, 1981, because he had started "messing with the Christmas tree." So he decided to shoot him. "It was in the Christmas spirit," Bullock said. "It makes me happy."

Two weeks earlier, the remorseless killer took the life of James Weber, a 42-year-old actor who was appearing in a production of Victor Herbert's "Babes in Toyland" at the 74th Street Playhouse. The body was left in Central Park.

Bullock was a criminal sociopath who derived an emotional high from the murders he committed. He used a .38-caliber pistol to extinguish the lives of five of his victims.

A special task force under the command of Lieutenant Thomas Power arrested Bullock in his apartment on Jan. 14. He confessed in a ninety-minute videotape to committing over 100 armed robberies and the murders of the six Manhattanites. It was later played back during the trial.

David Bullock pleaded guilty before Justice Roberts on Oct. 26. On Nov. 29, the defendant received six consecutive sentences of twenty-five years to life. In a lengthy prepared statement, Justice Roberts angrily denounced the defendant as "a small-time street punk, a petty thief, a shoplifter, a male prostitute." He warned the cold-hearted killer, "You are going to die in prison and then go before the Supreme Judge of us all and let Him impose whatever additional sentence He feels you so rightfully deserve."

Bundy, Theodore (Ted, AKA: Chris Hagen), 1947-89, U.S. The public personality of Ted Bundy suggested nothing of the serial killer he truly was. Handsome, apparently well educated, and a glib talker, Bundy struck those who met him for the first time, if they were to think ill of him, as someone who might be guilty of practicing smooth confidence games, but never one capable of violent crime. Everything in his posture and conversation smacked of culture, and his sense of humor was instant and infectious, one that won over new friends quickly and established trust on the part of the women who found him attractive. This was a fatal attraction for perhaps as many as forty young females, all of them brutally murdered. A number of pretty, young women began to suffer violent attacks from a strange intruder and others disappeared in western states in early 1974. The first of these was Sharon Clarke of Seattle, who was attacked in her bedroom while she slept, her head brutally smashed with a metal rod. She suffered skull fractures but survived and the rod was found in her room. There was no explanation for the attack and Clarke could not identify her attacker, even as to whether or not the attack was made by a male or female.

While authorities pondered this strange attack, Lynda Ann Healy, a student at the University of Washington in Seattle, who lived only a few blocks from Clarke, disappeared from her rented room on Jan. 31, 1974. Then, over the next seven months, young women began to disappear with dreadful regularity. Donna Gail Manson, a student at Evergreen State College in Olympia, Wash., went to a concert on Mar. 12, 1974, and vanished. Susan Rancourt, a Central Washington State student, disappeared in Ellensburg while going to see a foreign film on Apr. 17, 1974. Out for a late night walk on May 6, 1974, Roberta Kathleen Parks, an Oregon State University student living in Corvallis, disappeared. Brenda Ball left the Flame Tavern near the Seattle Airport with an unknown man at 2 a.m. on June 1, 1974, and vanished. On the evening of June 11, 1974, Georgann Hawkins left her boyfriend and began walking back to her sorority house at the University of Washington and she, too, disappeared.

At Lake Sammanish, Wash., on July 14, 1974, a number of attractive, young women were approached by a good-looking, dark-haired young man who called himself Ted. He had an arm in a sling and asked a number of women to help him load a sailboat on top of his car, a Volkswagen. One woman agreed and accompanied Ted to a parking lot but when he told her that they had to drive to a house on a hill to load the boat, she refused. Others did the same. Blonde-haired Janice Ott agreed to help Bundy and disappeared. Some hours later Denise Naslund was seen walking toward the public washrooms at the lake and was not seen again. Other women were seen talking to the handsome young man with the arm sling and many were seen to accompany him to the parking lot that day. On Sept. 7, 1974, two hunters near the lake found the decomposed bodies of Denise Naslund and Janice Ott, along with that of another unidentified female. The remains found were in bits and pieces, scattered by wild animals, officials later concluded.

Detectives began an extensive investigation, learning from a young woman in Ellensburg that a young man wearing a sling had tried to pick her up on the night Susan Rancourt vanished. Another Seattle woman recalled a young man wearing a sling and driving a Volkswagen who tried to pick her up. When she refused to get into his car, he shrugged and blithely took his uninjured arm out of the sling and drove off, using both hands on the wheel. Another woman reported that a man wearing an arm sling drove onto a sidewalk, attempting to block her path, in an effort to get her into his Volkswagen, but she managed to avoid him. During these investigations, the remains of two young women were found, one in northern Washington who was identified as Carol Valenzuela of Vancouver, Wash., who had vanished some months earlier. The second body, or what was left of it, was found in southern Washington State near the Oregon border. She remained unidentified. Both women had been apparently murdered. Police by then had many suspects they thought capable of having committed the abduction-murders.

One strong suspect was a depraved young man named Warren Forrest, a park employee who had picked up a Portland, Ore., woman, convincing her to pose for him. In a secluded area of the park, he tied her up, taped her mouth, stripped her naked, and fired darts at her naked breasts. Forrest sexually attacked her before strangling her and leaving her for dead. She survived, however, and identified her attacker. Another strong suspect was ex-convict Gary Taylor, who was accused of abducting Seattle females under various pretexts. Then an anonymous female caller phoned police to tell them that she believed that Ted Bundy was the man who had been abducting and killing young women in Seattle. Officers duly noted the report and filed it with the thousands of other leads they had collected. But the women continued to disappear. On Oct. 2, 1974, Nancy Wilcox vanished and, on Oct. 18, after leaving an all-night party in Midvale, Utah, Melissa Smith, daughter of the local police chief, disappeared. Her raped and strangled body was found on Oct. 27, 1974, in the Wassatch Mountains, east of Salt Lake City. In Orem, Utah, Laura

Aimee went to a Halloween party after midnight on Oct. 31, and vanished.

Then, on Nov. 8, 1974, a young man pretending to be a police detective approached Carol DaRonch in a Salt Lake City shopping mall, demanding the license plate number of her car, explaining that someone had tried to break into it. She accompanied him to her car but found that it was undisturbed. The fake detective persuaded her to accompany him to police headquarters to view a suspect. She got into his Volkswagen but once they were on a quiet street, the imposter stopped the car and produced a set of handcuffs, snapping one end onto DaRonch's wrist. She let out a scream and he pulled a gun, placing this next to her head and ordering her to keep quiet. DaRonch was not the typically submissive type of woman the abductor-killer had dealt with in the past. She forced the door open and jumped out, he went after her with a crowbar in his hand. He tried to smash her skull with this but she caught the bar in mid-air and struggled with him. Then DaRonch saw a car coming down the street and leaped in front of it, forcing it to come to a stop. She leaped into the auto which drove away.

The gall of the killer knew no bounds. Even with a potential victim escaping and now able to identify him, the young man tried to pick up a pretty, young French teacher outside Viewmont High School but she turned him down. A short time later Debbie Kent vanished when she went off to meet a brother at an ice-skating rink. Police searching for Kent found a key to a set of handcuffs in the school playground where she disappeared. Salt Lake City police received the name of Ted Bundy from Seattle detectives, who stated that they had received an anonymous tip that Bundy had been kidnapping and killing young females. Bundy's photograph was also sent along to the Salt Lake officials and shown to Carol DaRonch, who said that Bundy was not the man who tried to abduct her. Laura Aimee, who had vanished in Orem, Utah, on Oct. 31, was found dead, her naked body having been tossed into a canyon.

The killings went on. In Snowmass Village, a Colorado ski resort, on Jan. 12, 1975, Dr. Raymond Gadowsky, staying at the Wildwood Inn, went to the room of his fiancee, Caryn Campbell, only to find her gone. Her remains were not found until Feb. 17, the naked corpse hidden in some thick underbrush. She had been raped and her skull had been crushed. In another resort town, Vail, Colo., Julie Cunningham vanished on Mar. 15, 1975, after going to meet a girlfriend in a bar. A short time later the remains of two missing women, Susan Rancourt and Brenda Ball, were found on Taylor Mountain, Wash. Then Melanie Cooley of Nederland, Colo., disappeared on Apr. 15, 1975, her body found on Apr. 23, only a dozen miles from her home. Unlike the other victims, she was fully clothed but

SOME OF TED BUNDY'S MURDER VICTIMS

Lynda Healy

Donna Manson

Susan Rancourt

Roberta Parks

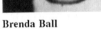
Brenda Ball

Georgann Hawkins

Denise Naslund

Janice Ott

Melissa Smith

Laura Aimee

Debbie Kent

Caryn Campbell

Lisa Levy

Margaret Bowman

Kimberley Leach

her jeans had been slipped from her waist, showing that sex was the motive for the attack that killed her. Her head had been battered with a rock found nearby. Shelley Robertson disappeared on July 1 from her Golden, Colo., home. Three days later, Nancy Baird, a gas station attendant in Golden, Colo., vanished from her workplace. On Aug. 23, Shelley Robertson's naked body was found in a mine shaft outside of Berthoud Pass, Colo.

Then police, on Aug. 16, 1975, arrested Ted Bundy. He was stopped by a Salt Lake City patrolman who thought he was acting suspiciously, driving his Volkswagen down a street slowly as if inspecting homes for possible break-ins; the area had suffered a rash of recent burglaries. Bundy did not stop when ordered to by the patrol car and a chase ensued. His car was finally brought to the curb and Bundy was placed under arrest. His room was searched but nothing incriminating could be found, only a pile of maps and brochures of Colorado. At the station, Bundy explained that he was a psychology student who lived in Seattle. He said that he had also worked on the governor's campaign there and was presently in Salt Lake City studying law. The Colorado brochures reminded detectives that a number of girls had recently been abducted and murdered in that state, and they took particular notice of brochures about Golden, Colo., which Bundy had in his possession. The detectives knew that Shelley Robertson had been killed in that town. Forensic experts went over Bundy's car and found a hair on one of the seats that matched that of Midvale, Utah, victim, Melissa Smith. Then a witness insisted he saw Bundy at the Snowmass retreat in Colorado on the night Caryn Campbell disappeared.

Bundy was charged with murder and taken to Aspen, Colo., to stand trial. Here he charmed his wardens and prosecutors, affably cooperating with them, or seeming to, and giving an impression of an intelligent young man who was anything but a berserk sex slayer. He was shown every courtesy, given special health foods to eat and allowed to attend court without being manacled. Bundy insisted that he defend himself and received whatever law books he requested. Witnesses, however, showed Bundy for what he was, an inveterate liar, a cunning, crafty character who would go to any impossible lengths to get his way. Carol DaRonch, who had at first failed to recognize Bundy from a photo as the man who tried to abduct her in Salt Lake City, then came forward and identified Bundy as the man who had attacked her. As the pretrial hearings dragged on, Bundy was allowed to roam about the law library in Aspen. Even though he was under guard, Bundy managed to open a window of the library and drop twenty feet to the ground, escaping. He was tracked down eight days later at a deserted shack on Smuggler's Mountain and brought back to Aspen, where he was now kept under heavy guard.

Bundy insisted that he was a victim of circumstance, that he merely *happened* to have been in the same places where all these women disappeared and that there were many young men who bore a resemblance to him. He was also adept in using the law to create one legal motion after another to delay the case. While implementing this systematic legal stall, the insidious Bundy slowly took off weight in preparation for his next escape attempt. He somehow obtained a hacksaw and carved a hole around the light fixture of his cell; removing the fixture on Dec. 30, 1977, and squeezing through the one-foot opening (by then he had lost enough weight) Bundy made his escape. He moved to Chicago, then Ann Arbor, Mich., then on to Atlanta, and finally, he settled in Tallahassee, Fla., living only a few blocks from the sorority houses of Florida State University.

On the night of Jan. 15, 1978, Nita Neary saw a man holding a log and lurking about the front door of her sorority house. As she thought about calling the police, a student named Karen Chandler, blood flowing from wounds, staggered from her room. A madman had entered her room and had savagely beaten her on the head. Her roommate, Kathy Kleiner, had also been attacked in the same room, her jaw being broken. In another room of the sorority house police later found two other students Lisa Levy and Margaret Bowman. Both had been sexually abused. Bowman was dead, strangled with her own pantyhose. Lisa Levy had been brutally battered about the head and died en route to the hospital. Only a few hours later another female student, Cheryl Thomas, was brutally attacked in her room at another sorority house and was severely injured, but she survived the attack.

Though police began a widespread manhunt for the sorority house killer, they could find no one answering the sketchy description of the attacker. On Feb. 9, 1979, 12-year-old Kimberley Leach left her classroom in Jacksonville and disappeared. Some days later Bundy, who had been living in Tallahassee under the name of Chris Hagen and using stolen credit cards to purchase essentials, sneaked out of his Tallahassee apartment when his rent was long overdue. He stole an orange Volkswagen and drove to Pensacola, where a policeman stopped him and checked the license plates. Discovering the car was stolen, the officer arrested Bundy. Bundy bolted and the officer tackled him, struggling with him. When the officer fired a shot, Bundy meekly surrendered. He first identified himself as Chris Hagen, then admitted he was the fugitive, Theodore Bundy, wanted by Colorado authorities on charges of murder. He was held on charges of using stolen credit cards and stolen autos while detectives worked hard to tie Bundy-Hagen to the Tallahassee sorority house slayings. Meanwhile, the body of Kimberley Leach was found in the Suwannee River

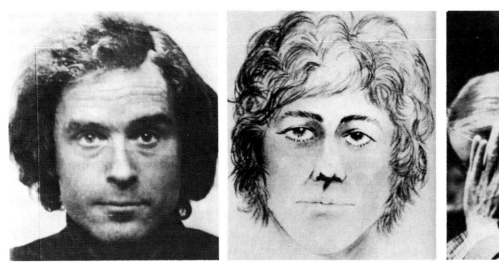

Ted Bundy's first police photo and 1974 police sketch.

The mass killer in court.

Bundy, a prisoner in Florida and his FBI poster.

Bundy as his own lawyer, acting.

Bundy in custody, Salt Lake City, left; Florida, center and right, before his 1989 execution.

Park, her privates violated and mutilated; she had been strangled to death.

Still, the vain and strutting Bundy refused to admit to any murders. He claimed he was innocent. The police had made a terrible mistake. Detectives then came for Bundy on Apr. 27, 1979, and took him to an examining room. When he learned that they intended to take a wax impression of his teeth, Bundy went berserk, struggling violently so that a half-dozen men had to pin him down and hold his mouth open for the impression to be made. Bundy knew what they were after. The impressions of his teeth were later perfectly matched to the bite marks found on the buttocks of the murdered student, Lisa Levy, and it was this bizarre piece of evidence that would later, more than anything else, convict Ted Bundy of the many serial murders he had so ruthlessly committed.

Charged with the Levy and Bowman murders, Bundy was taken to Miami and placed on trial. He pled innocent, again acting as his own lawyer. He smiled at jurors, swaggering before the judge as he spouted law and precedent-setting cases of the past. He exuded confidence that he would never be convicted. His demeanor changed as he was compelled to sit quietly and listen to arresting officers tell the court how he had admitted having sexual problems, that he had begun his sexual offenses in Seattle as a voyeur and quoting Bundy as having said: "Sometimes I feel like a vampire." Dental experts then came forward to positively identify Bundy's teeth impressions with the bite marks on the body of Lisa Levy, and this convinced the jury of Bundy's guilt. He was found Guilty and sentenced to death by Judge Edward D. Cowart, who expressed regret that Bundy had gone "the wrong way" and that "you'd have made a good lawyer...I'd have loved to have you practice in front of me." Bundy was also found Guilty of the murder of the Leach girl and sentenced again to death.

Oddly, all of those around this vile and utterly cunning killer, his guards, arresting officers, the judges who heard his cases and ordered him executed, as well as most of those who later devoted tedious books to his rather unimaginative murders, especially Ann Rule, and Michaud and Aynesworth, who warmed too brightly to the man, showered him with the kind of attention given to Hollywood celebrities. The writers complained about the limelight Bundy bathed in and then flooded him with it. The killer was an actor as well as an unrepentant criminal and the portrait he drew of himself caused all about him to empathize about a future he never had, as if he deserved a future. Though various crime scribes tried to point out his talents, there was nothing redeeming about Ted Bundy and nothing to learn from him, except to recognize his pattern of serial murder as an alarmingly increasing *modus operandi* among modern killers. Like the vicious killer Jack

Henry Abbott, Theodore Bundy was undeservedly a *cause célèbre,* and he played his part to the hilt, acting the pundit and even the criminologist as he waited to be executed, issuing cautionary statements to the young on how not to go wrong, to avoid pornography, to stay in school, to follow the legitimate road through life.

For a decade, this vile murderer kept himself alive with one appeal after another, reaping millions of words from the nation's press about his so-called "intellectual thought process," and his "psychological makeup," but his act finally closed when all appeals, stays, and last-minute delays were exhausted. In a last ditch stand to save his miserable life, Bundy began a recital of all the murders he committed, twenty-three in all. (At least fifteen more murders were attributed to Bundy by authorities.) The killer finally went to the electric chair at Florida's State Prison on Jan. 24, 1989. His last nervous words were: "Give my love to my family and friends." He was led to the execution chamber, his head and right calf shaved so that the electrical conduits would work properly. He sat down in the chair and was strapped in.

Bundy gripped the arms of the chair and his head, strapped to a stationary position, could not move, but his eyes darted about wildly and, according to witnesses: "He was totally white, very scared." His eyes rolled frantically before the twenty-four witnesses gathered to observe the awful killer's end. Then, promptly at 7:07 a.m., 2,000 volts went through his body, and he was pronounced dead four minutes later. Outside the prison, more than 100 reporters moved through a huge crowd that had assembled, trying to milk one more story out of Theodore Bundy. But none in the crowd protested this execution. Signs were held high that read "Buckle up, Bundy, it's the law," and "Roast in Peace!" When the black flag went up to signal the serial killer's death, the throng cheered wildly and firecrackers and other fireworks were set off in celebration. One Florida resident, hoarse from cheering the execution, told a reporter: "I waited eleven years to see that creep fry."

Buono, Angelo, See: **Bianchi, Kenneth.**

Burch, Ronald (William George Arthur), d.1968, S. Afri. A South African schoolteacher first discovered the remains of a human torso on Oct. 27, 1964, during an early morning jog around a lake at Boksburg in the Transvaal region. In the next few weeks, more body parts were found floating in the lake. Someone had cut up the victim, carefully placing the remains in suitcases, which were then deposited in the lake. But the cases had torn open and the body pieces rose to the surface. The Johannesburg police surmised that the victim was a female who had been gruesomely decapitated while still alive. The unpleasant task of identifying the body still remained.

Four years passed and still the police were unable to provide positive ID to the Boksburg torso, until the daughter of Catharina Louisa Burch came forward to identify her mother based on forensic photos supplied by the District CID. A young girl at the time of Mrs. Burch's disappearance, she had been unable to offer any viable clues at the time of the disappearance. But now her testimony began to make sense. The composite drawing of the victim matched the description and photos provided by the daughter.

Suspicion fell on Mrs. Burch's second husband, Ronald William Burch, who had informed his wife's employer that she was leaving the company the same day she turned up missing. But now Ronald Burch was missing as well. Efforts to glean information from his 77-year-old mother proved fruitless. The trail led to Cape Town where Burch had moved after his wife's disappearance. He was reported to have been seen in various brothels and vice dens catering to prurient sexual tastes.

The investigation gradually shifted back to Johannesburg and the house where the elderly Mrs. Burch lived. There, on Nov. 28, 1968, police found the killer hiding in a wooden shed on the back of the property. When they burst in on Ronald Burch, he threw a light switch that activated an electric current that flowed into a pair of metal handcuffs attached to his wrist. He was dead within seconds. The aged and infirm mother went to her grave in 1974, still refusing to share any additional information with the police. Finally, after 30,000 statements had been taken and over 500 missing-person reports thoroughly investigated, the case was officially closed.

Burke, Charles, d.1933, U.S. It was St. Patrick's Day 1933. The flood waters of the Ohio River had risen to a dangerous level. Officer Harry Levey of the Covington, Ky., police had strict orders to control the flow of traffic in his river town just outside of Cincinnati by whatever means necessary.

As he observed the slowly moving traffic, Levey could not help but notice a car with expired 1932 license plates. He pulled the vehicle over and questioned the driver, Charles Burke of New York. The man was nervous and fidgety, and his face bore three unmistakable cut marks. Curious, Levey examined a tarpaulin sack lying on the back seat. Reaching inside, he discovered the severed remains of a human body!

Suddenly Burke pulled a straight razor and sliced his throat and wrists. He was dead before the ambulance could arrive. In his clothing police found a court order from the Hudson County Circuit Court directing Burke to pay $50 a month, beginning Mar. 15, to Ella Burke pending a divorce trial. The Covington Police later determined that Charles Burke had killed his wife on Mar. 16, 1932, after deciding not to pay alimony. He was about to begin a new life with a younger girlfriend. After cutting up his ex-wife's body into small parts, he drove to Kentucky with the package in the back seat. He never expected the flood waters of the Ohio River to be his undoing.

Burkley, Bluitt, 1914-34, and **Burkley, Thurman**, 1915-34, U.S. The stillness of a warm summer night in Texas was punctured by loud blasts of gunfire. The murder of a young couple was an ugly crime, made uglier by its racial overtones. When the farmers of Pleasant Mound, Texas, learned that the killers were two black men who tended crops nearby, the lobby of the tiny jail at Main and Houston Streets was filled to overcrowding. Deputy sheriffs milled through the crowd reminding people that matters were well in hand. It was Labor Day weekend, 1933. Sentiments against blacks ran deep in the South at this time, and the word "lynch" was now on everyone's lips.

Bluitt Burkley, nineteen, and his brother Thurman, eighteen, were arrested on Aug. 31, 1933, for the murder of Katheryn Prince, a 21-year-old woman, and her escort, 27-year-old Mace Carver. The pair were last seen alive as they walked home from the Oak Cliff Baptist Church. The Burkley brothers, approaching them from behind, fired into the back of their heads. Death was instantaneous for Prince. Carver was removed to Parkland Hospital in Dallas where he lingered until the next day.

The wheels of justice turned quickly. Within twenty-four hours, the two men were arrested by Deputy Sheriff Ted Hinton and brought to the home of William McCutcheon, where they were transferred under heavy guard to the Dallas city jail. Their signed confessions were taken by Captain E.V. Bunch and Lieutenant Will Fritz.

Before another day had passed, an indictment was returned by the grand jury charging the brothers with murder and assault. The case came before Judge Grover Adams of the Criminal District Court. Five months later, on Feb. 9, 1934, the Burkley brothers were executed.

Burnett, Melvin, 1955- , and **Martin, Billy**, 1959- , U.S. Carl Stohn had just finished working as an extra during the filming of the movie *Thief,* when he was overtaken by four youths near his home on Chicago's Gold Coast. The 58-year-old theatrical executive who had previously worked as a producer and director at the suburban Drury Lane Theatre and Pheasant Run Playhouse, had taken a bus back to his car at 1:45 a.m., Aug. 21, 1980,when he was heldup at gunpoint. Stohn grabbed one of the assailants, later identified as 20-year-old Billy Martin, by the lapels in a vain attempt to thwart the robbery. When Stohn refused to release Martin, Melvin Burnett shot and killed him. Afterwards, he made off with his cash and jewelry.

Burnett and Martin were arrested on Nov. 15, when Clay Steen and Wayne Griffin of the Chicago Police Department Gang Crimes Unit received a tip from a suspect in custody. The two killers were named as members of a South Side street gang known as the Disciples. Carl Stohn had been randomly selected, police learned. "This is just awful," said Michael Mann, director of *Thief.* "You should be able to get off a bus and get in your car and drive away without being killed."

Appearing before Judge Earl Strayhorn in a bench trial that began at the Criminal Court in December 1981, Burnett claimed that he was nervous and that the gun went off accidentally. Judge Strayhorn convicted both men of conspiracy, attempted armed robbery, and murder. Melvin Burnett received a sentence of twenty years' imprisonment, followed by ninety years' imprisonment, and accomplice Billy Martin received a seventy-five-year sentence.

Burns, Alfred, and **Devlin, Edward Francis,** prom. 1951, Brit. Alfred Burns and Edward Devlin cut open a kitchen window pane and entered the home of Beatrice Rimmer of Cranborne Road, Liverpool, the night of Aug. 20, 1951. The two house burglars then battered the 54-year-old widow to death.

When they were arrested two months later and charged with murder, Burns told police that they were breaking into Messrs. Sunblinds Limited on Great Jackson Street, Manchester, at the time of the widow's death. There had been a robbery committed that night in Manchester, but Devlin and Burns were both convicted of murdering Rimmer even though it could not be positively proved that bloodstains found on their clothing matched those of the victim.

Based on the testimony of 17-year-old Marie Milne, who was acquainted with the suspects, Burns and Devlin were sentenced to die by Justice Finnemore that same year.

Burrows, Albert Edward, 1861-1923, Brit. In 1918, Albert Burrows, a 57-year-old farmer from Glossop, Derbyshire, began seeing a pretty young woman named Hannah Calladine. The 28-year-old mother of two bore him an illegitimate child.

Determined to make things right, the aging lothario married Calladine without bothering to divorce his wife. He received a six-month prison sentence for bigamy and was required to pay Hannah Calladine seven shillings a week. Balking at the payment, he was sent to prison in November 1919 for defaulting on a court order. Meanwhile Calladine moved into his house in Glossop, and the first Mrs. Burrows angrily walked out. The offended woman filed a maintenance suit against her husband. As Burrows languished in jail, he realized that he was hopelessly obligated to two women regardless of which one he chose to live with.

Recovering his wits and his freedom, Burrows resolved to do something about his problem. On Jan. 11, 1920, he took his new wife and her bastard son Albert Edward to Symondley Moor where he murdered them both. He tossed the bodies down a 105-foot air shaft into an abandoned coal mine where they remained undetected for nearly three years. To avoid any slip-up, he added a third victim the next day, Hannah Calladine's 3-year-old daughter.

On Mar. 4, 1923, a small boy named Thomas Wood disappeared from his Glossop home. Burrows became a suspect when several townspeople reported having seen him with the 4-year-old. Under steady questioning by the police, he admitted to sexually molesting the boy and dropping him down the mine shaft. A search of the area uncovered the remains of young Thomas as well as Hannah Calladine and her children.

Brought before the Derby Assizes, Burrows was pronounced Guilty by a jury that deliberated for only eleven minutes. He was hanged at Nottingham on Aug. 8, 1923.

Burrows, Erskine Durrant (AKA: **Buck**), and **Tacklyn, Larry Winfield,** prom. 1973, Ber. A frantic call to Scotland Yard in London brought detectives Bill Wright and Basil Haddrell racing to Bermuda in September 1972, to investigate the mysterious shooting death of colonial police commissioner George Duckett at his suburban home.

It was the first of many politically motivated assassinations on the island that soon had the local police baffled. Duckett had been killed by a bullet from a .22-caliber revolver fired from his backyard at close range. On Mar. 10, 1973, Sir Richard Sharples, royal governor and commander in chief of Bermuda, was shot with Captain Hugh

Sayers of the Welsh Guards on the terrace of the Government House by two unidentified black men.

On Apr. 6, before any viable leads could be established, two shopkeepers named Victor Rego and Mark Doe on Victoria Street, Hamilton, were killed execution style, which was apparent by the prone position of the bodies.

There were now five victims and no new clues to these puzzling, yet seemingly related crimes. The colonial government posted a reward of $3 million for the apprehension of the killers. Eyewitness discriptions of the shopkeepers' murder led police to Larry Tacklyn. His accomplice was Erskine Burrows, who came to the attention of the police after he robbed the Bank of Bermuda on Sept. 25, 1973.

Burrows remained a fugitive for nearly a month. He was finally ambushed and captured on Oct. 18, after being knocked off his motorbike under cover of darkness by Detective John Donald of the Bermuda police. Guns belonging to the pair were found cached at various locations around the island. With the two bandits in custody, nervous residents came forward to supply evidence against them.

Tacklyn and Burrows were career criminals whose motive was robbery. They killed Sir Richard, Captain Sayers, and the police commissioner in sympathy with the aims of the Black Power movement which sought autonomy from the Crown. Erskine Burrows was convicted of killing George Duckett. Tacklyn admitted to murdering the shopowners and was found Guilty on two counts. Both men were hanged later that year.

Burton, Walter William, 1884-1913, Brit. In the little town of Gussage St. Michael, there lived a 29-year-old man named Walter Burton who was employed as a rabbit catcher at the Manor Farm. He lived above the local post office with his wife who taught school and cared for their only child. His wife was quite a bit older than Burton, and he no longer found her interesting. So he gadded about town with various women and created quite a scandal.

In October 1912, Burton made the acquaintance of Winifred Mary Mitchell, a cook at the farm. She had a sophisticated beauty but was innocent in her ways. Walter Burton spent the next two months trying to seduce her. He promised her many things, including a new life in Canada. By March 1913, he had won her over, but when he suspected she was pregnant, he quickly lost his enthusiasm for the girl.

Promising to elope with her on the 29th, Burton made plans for her early death instead. He borrowed a gun to "kill a cat," and then lured Mitchell to an isolated spot near Sovel Plantation where he shot her. The body was not discovered until May 2, when the shallow grave was opened.

Fragments of torn letters written by Burton were found at the Manor Farm. These hastily scrawled notes were enough to implicate him in the murder. Tried before Justice Ridley, Walter Burton was condemned to death at Dorchester Prison. He was the last man to be hanged there.

Butler, William, prom. 1938, Brit. William Butler was identified as the assailant who had bludgeoned Ernest Percival Key to death in his jeweler's shop in Surbiton on Dec. 24, 1938.

The shopkeeper's body was examined by Sir Bernard Spilsbury and Dr. Eric Gardner, the county pathologist for Surrey. The killer left behind a black bowler hat, which was enough evidence from which the two examiners could gauge its owner's physical characteristics. Stories were planted in London and Berlin newspapers, and it was not long before the killer was flushed out. Butler was tried, condemned, and hanged for the crime. Scotland Yard received a letter from the Reichkriminal-Polizeiamt in Berlin asking for additional information about the amazing powers of the "clairvoyant" Eric Gardner.

Butterfield, Neale Allen (AKA: **Butterfingers**), 1933- , U.S. Explaining later that he just wanted to "see someone die," 16-year-old Neale Butterfield decided to cut his classes on Nov. 16, 1949, so that he could conduct his own experiment in murder.

Frank Watson, principal of Heyburn High School in Burley, Ida., recalled how Butterfield freely joined in the murder gossip the day after the body of 7-year-old Glenda Joyce Brisbois was found in an irrigation canal outside town. "He showed no signs of worry or even of knowledge of the affair," Watson said. "He came into my psychology class and asked me calmly, 'Did you know, Mr. Watson, that they found that girl's body?'"

"Butterfingers" Butterfield was a member of the high school football team and a student leader, popular with both boys and girls. It seemed inconceivable at the time that he could wantonly take the life of a little girl. As a matter of habit, Butterfield had provided taxi service to a number of small children attending the local grammar school. He picked them up and drove them home, and none of the parents seemed to notice the peculiarity of it, or to even comprehend that the pleasant-looking high school boy was a dangerous pedophile.

The killing took place in Cassia County. The murder weapon was a tire jack, and Butterfield's motive was purely sexual. When he went home after murdering Glenda, Butterfield ate a full meal, popped some corn, and went to bed.

Arresting officers held Butterfield in the Twin Falls county jail, a distance of forty-one miles from Burley, where emotion was running high. Judge Hugh A. Baker advised Twin Falls law enforcement personnel "not to take Butterfield to Burley, or he might not be alive in the morning." Because Idaho law required that a criminal must be charged in the county where the deed was committed, Butterfield was arraigned just inside the Cassia County line in an open field.

In jail Butterfield remained dispassionate. He ate heartily and slept well. The only emotion he showed was when the sheriff denied him a package of cigarettes.

Prosecutors believed that Idaho law would permit them to seek the death penalty, though Butterfield was a minor. They cited the case of a 15-year-old boy from Idaho County who was tried as an adult and sentenced to death. However, that boy's sentence was commuted to life imprisonment by the state pardons board. In regard to Butterfield, Dr. Paul De River, in his case study *Crime and the Sexual Psychopath,* concluded that the defendant was "medically and legally sane at the time he committed the crime."

Butterfield was convicted of first-degree murder but was spared the death penalty. The prison doors slammed shut on Feb. 14, 1950. He served twelve years before receiving a parole on Nov. 14, 1962. He was granted a final discharge on Nov. 30, 1967, after meeting all of the board's requirements. At last report, Butterfield was married and had become a father.

Button and Badge Murder, See: **Greenwood, David**.

Butts, Vernon, See: **Bonin, William**.

Byrne, Patrick Joseph, 1932- , Brit. Patrick Joseph Byrne's blustering swagger around the boys could not disguise his anxieties toward women. The few he managed to date in Birmingham would later recall his painful shyness. Byrne, an Irish construction worker fond of strong drink and the companionship of his pub mates, was too shy to ask his dates for a goodnight kiss. Byrne's gnawing feelings of sexual inadequacy drove him to commit a heinous murder at Edgbaston YWCA hostel on Dec. 23, 1959.

He selected his victim, 29-year-old Sidney Stephanie Baird, at random. She worked as a shorthand-typist in the city. After watching Baird undress from outside her room, Byrne summoned the necessary courage to rap on her door. "I watched her for a long time, and stood close to the window...the urge to kill her was tremendously strong. Before she could say no, I kissed her," he said. "She tried to shove me away but couldn't, and for a second I got her around the waist." Byrne stifled her screams with his hands and kissed the struggling woman until she fell over backwards, fracturing her skull. Baird was dead, but Byrne stripped to his shorts, sexually abused the corpse, then cut off its head. Byrne left behind no fingerprints, just a hastily scrawled note that read: "This was the thing I thought would never come." The police discovered Baird's remains when they investigated a complaint filed by a second female assault victim who lived in the hostel, Margaret Brown, whose loud screams saved her life when Byrne attacked her in the hostel laundry rooms.

Detective Chief Superintendent Jim Haughton, head of the Birmingham CID, conducted a relentless investigation.

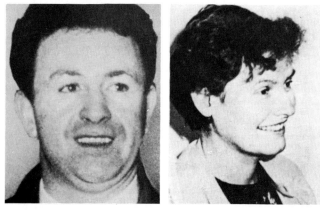

Killer Patrick Byrne.   **Victim Sidney Baird.**

Over 20,000 men were interviewed, before the identity of Byrne was established. Detectives were put on Byrne's trail after questioning a bus driver who had picked up a passenger near the YWCA. Drops of blood found on the seat of the bus were found to be the same type as Baird's. Byrne was traced to Warrington, and was brought in for questioning on Feb. 10, 1960. After some verbal sparring between the suspect and the detective, Byrne suddenly blurted out his confession.

Byrne was placed on trial at the Birmingham Assizes the next month before Justice Stable. He was found Guilty of murder and sentenced to life imprisonment. Following an appeal, the charge was reduced to manslaughter on the grounds of the defendant's probable insanity. The penalty however, remained unchanged.

Bywaters, Frederick, See: **Thompson, Edith Jesse**.

Calbeck, Lorene, 1922-89, U.S. Thirty years after Lorene Calbeck shot and killed her three toddlers outside a trailer park in Polk County, Fla., she shot herself.

The tragedy occurred on May 24, 1956, when the 34-year-old housewife took her three children for a ride in the family car. For reasons known only to herself, she shot each of them four times in the left side of the chest, and then carried them back to the trailer. Lorene placed them side by side: Shirley, five; Pamela, three; and Jane, aged fifteen months. She wrapped them in cellophane and then called the family doctor and asked him to come to her house in half an hour. After she hung up the phone, she fired two shots into her chest.

She left behind a suicide note explaining how to water the gardenias and giving various other instructions to her husband Mark, who was away in Michigan at the time. However, doctors were able to save Lorene Calbeck's life. She was pronounced mentally incompetent by medical investigators. A Polk County grand jury refused to return an indictment, but remanded Lorene to the care of the state mental hospital at Chattahoochee, Fla. Seemingly on the road to recovery, she was released from the doctor's care and returned to her husband Mark. On Jan. 3, 1989, Lorene Calbeck staged an eerie re-enactment of the events of that long-ago night. Armed with a .32-caliber pistol, Calbeck sat down in her lawn chair near the family plot at Lake Wales Cemetery. Despondent over the death of her husband and the direction her life had taken in the last few years, she fired a bullet into the left side of her chest, and then, in pain, drove back to her mobile home off U.S. Highway 27.

Calbeck phoned the 911 number to report the shooting. The emergency team arrived quickly, but was unable to get her to the hospital in time. She died in the ambulance. A search of her trailer turned up several notes explaining how to operate various mechanical devices, including her television and the car. The boxes on the utility shelves had been pre-arranged according to size, and her funeral had been paid in advance. In her last set of detailed instructions, Calbeck explained that she wanted to be buried beside her husband and children.

Caldwell, Roger, 1933- , U.S. Marjorie Caldwell and her husband Roger stood to inherit $8.2 million dollars upon the death of her adoptive mother, 83-year-old Elisabeth Congdon, inheritor of a Duluth, Minn., mining fortune, who lived at the thirty-nine-room family mansion on the shores of Lake Superior.

Marjorie's financial recklessness disappointed Elisabeth, and she and Roger Caldwell were always short of money.

For a time they used a credit card bearing Congdon's name. In May 1977, Caldwell traveled from his home in Golden, Colo., to Duluth to ask for a $750,000 loan from the family trustees to buy a ranch. The family twice refused.

A month later, on June 27, 1977, an intruder broke into the Congdon mansion in the early daylight hours and climbed the stairs leading to Congdon's bedroom. But he was accosted by the night nurse, 65-year-old Velma Pietila. He seized a brass candlestick holder and bludgeoned the nurse to death, then smothered Elisabeth Congdon with a satin pillow. He fled from the residence and drove off in the family's 1976 Ford, which was later found at the Twin Cities Airport.

The Caldwells emerged as prime suspects in the murders. On July 5, police found a suede travel bag purchased at the Twin Cities Airport and jewelry and personal effects from the mansion in Roger Caldwell's hotel room in Bloomington. Caldwell had checked himself into a hospital in St. Louis Park, where he was arrested on July 6 and charged with murder.

The case went before a Crow Wing County jury on Apr. 10, 1978. Defense attorney Doug Thomson tried unsuccessfully to show that the Caldwells were framed by Marjorie's cousin Thomas Congdon and private detective William Furman. Strangely, Caldwell did not take the stand in his own defense.

On July 8, after eight weeks of testimony, Roger Caldwell was convicted of murdering Mrs. Congdon and her nurse. He was sentenced to two consecutive life terms in prison. Three days later, Marjorie Caldwell was charged with conspiring to murder her mother. Her trial began in March and became the longest in Minnesota history, ending on July 21, 1979, with a Not Guilty verdict.

Around the time of Roger Caldwell's 1977 arrest, a 1972 murder mystery filmed on the Congdon estate was re-released, entitled, appropriately enough, *You'll Like My Mother*.

Camb, James, 1916- , Brit. A ship's steward on board the ocean liner *Durban Castle*, Camb was considered a shipboard Lothario and attempted to seduce many a young woman sailing the high seas. Attractive, 21-year-old Gay Gibson was no exception. She was a wide-eyed actress who had been acting in a number of plays as part of her duties with the Women's Auxiliary Territorial Service. Her full name was Eileen Isabella Ronnie Gibson. Gay Gibson was her stage name. She sailed for England from Cape Town, S. Afr., on Oct. 10, 1947, occupying Cabin 126 on B deck, a first-class berth aboard the *Durban Castle*. On the following morning, when the liner was about 150 miles off the West Coast of Africa, the actress was reported missing. Captain Arthur Patey ordered the vessel turned about and a desperate search of the shark-infested waters

James Camb, ship's steward, and actress Gay Gibson.

was made. No trace of the woman was found.

Captain Patey conducted an investigation aboard ship as it continued to steam toward Southampton. Watchman Frederick Steer reported that the service bell of Cabin 126 had been pushed several times, as if frantically, at 2:58 on the morning of Oct. 18, 1947, and he had responded to the call. He stood outside the cabin and knocked. Steer noticed that both lights, a red and a green one, positioned outside the cabin, were on, indicating that the occupant had called for *both* the steward and the stewardess. Usually passengers rang on only one or the other. The door opened a crack, and the watchman caught a brief glimpse of a man in uniform, the steward Camb, who quickly closed the door and said through the grille of the door, "It's all right." Steer went back to his duties, assuming that Camb, a steward, had answered the call. Camb, however, denied having been in Gay Gibson's cabin, insisting that Steer was mistaken. He drew suspicion, however, during the rest of the voyage by wearing a long sleeve jacket when short sleeve uniforms were commonly worn in that tropical zone. When asked to bear his arms, Camb revealed scratches on his arm which he claimed resulted from a tropical heat rash. Meanwhile, Patey had informed authorities of the Union Castle Line in London about the actress' disappearance to which he received a cable from the Criminal Investigating Department of Scotland Yard instructing him to "padlock and seal the cabin—disturb nothing—CID officers will come aboard at Cowes Roads."

When the ship docked in Cowes Roads, Southampton, officers came aboard and quickly put together background on Gay Gibson and James Camb. The actress had not had a happy experience in her most recent play, enacting the role of Lorna, the prizefight manager's trampy girlfriend in *Golden Boy*, a South African production that paid very little

in salary. Witnesses were later to state that Gay Gibson was, in real life, close to the role she was playing in *Golden Boy*. She had proved to be an emotional actress subject to fits of hysteria and fainting. She also told someone before leaving South Africa that she was pregnant. One account had it that she had accepted the fare of £350 for the trip home from a less-than-reputable nightclub owner. Passengers attended a dance on the first night at sea and Gay Gibson was present, dancing with several male passengers. She caught the eye of steward Camb who remarked to another steward: "I have half a mind to take a drink to her cabin tonight."

This kind of remark was typical of the 31-year-old Camb who wore his black hair slicked back like some Latin lover from the 1920s. He thought of himself as irresistible to young women who found his Lancashire accent amusing. To his shipmates, Camb was known as "Don Jimmy," a notorious womanizer who, though married, boasted about having an affair with a female passenger on each voyage he made. Two women had accused him of rape in the past, but this did not lessen the ardor and efforts of Camb in approaching female passengers, taking great pride in attracting the prettiest women on each trip. Said one of his fellow stewards: "Jimmy was always saying that we were jealous of him."

Camb was brought before Sergeant Quinlan who interrogated him slowly, telling him that if he had any explanation for Gay Gibson's disappearance, this was the time to volunteer such information. The handsome steward seized upon this idea, volunteering the following remarks: "You mean that Miss Gibson might have died from a cause other than being murdered, she might have had a heart attack or something?" He then said that Gay Gibson had invited him to her cabin that night and he had brought her a drink. She was wearing a nightgown with nothing on beneath it and that when she removed this, he climbed into bed with her. During sexual intercourse, Camb said, her body suddenly stiffened, then went limp. He climbed out of the bed and described how he saw that she was foaming brownish froth at the mouth and that only one eye appeared to be slightly open.

"I tried artificial respiration on her," Camb claimed. "While doing this, the night watchman knocked at the door and attempted to open it. I shut the door...I panicked. I did not want to be found in such a compromising position." He related how he went to the door of the cabin and told Steer that everything was "all right." When Steer went away, Camb returned to the actress on the bed, saying that he "could not find any sign of life...After a struggle with the limp body, I managed to lift her to the porthole and push her through." In another police interrogation, Camb was quoted as saying that the body, upon hitting the water surface "made a helluva splash," thus revealing his cruel, indifferent attitude toward Gibson. In the first police interview aboard the *Durban Castle,* Camb expressed wonder at the service bells having been pushed. "I cannot offer any explanation as to how the bells came to be rung as I most definitely did not touch them myself." He admitted lying to the captain about being in the actress' cabin, stating he had decided to tell the truth later. "I realized," Camb admitted, "that I was definitely incriminated by the witness Steer."

On Mar. 29, 1948, Camb was tried for murdering Gay Gibson before Justice Hilbery at the Winchester Asizzes, prosecuted by G.D. Roberts and defended by J.D. Casswell. His defense was a feeble one. He had already admitted shoving the body of Gay Gibson through a porthole for a lonely burial at sea. Camb undoubtedly and mistakenly thought that by getting rid of the body, he would be getting rid of the evidence of his crime, and that conviction was not possible without the presence of a body. (This, of course, was not the case; the previous murder-without-a-body case in England was that of Thomas Joseph Davidson who was convicted of drowning his 8-year-old son in 1934 and who had been sent to prison for life for the murder.)

But there was evidence. The scratchmarks on Camb's arms had been examined by the ship's physician, Dr. Griffiths, after Captain Patey had ordered the steward to submit to a medical examination. Griffiths testified that he found these marks on Camb's shoulders and wrists and these scratches, in his opinion, had been made by a woman defending herself, not by someone undergoing some sort of seizure. Stains on the pillow in the cabin were examined by Dr. Donald Teare, a well-known pathologist and he testified that these were bloodstains. The blood was Type O. Since Camb's blood was Type A, it could be assumed that this was blood from Gay Gibson's body, not Camb's. Dr. Teare stated that these stains, along with emissions of urine could be expected from one who had been strangled to death, emissions that would not stem from someone having a heart attack. Ironically, Dr. Frederick Hocking, a defense witness, reported that, indeed, urine stains had been found on the sheets of Gay Gibson's bed.

Camb was caught in a number of untruths. He insisted that the actress had been wearing only a flimsy yellow nightgown with no undergarments when she lured him into her room. Yet Gay Gibson's black pajamas which she was known to have packed and taken with her on the sea voyage, were missing and it was concluded that she had been wearing these when Camb pushed her through the porthole which further suggested that she had not invited the steward to have sex with her. The prosecution insisted that Camb had invented the story of being invited into the cabin, that he arrived at the actress' door under the pretext of delivering a drink to her and once she opened her door he forced his way inside, and tried to rape her. She fought furiously, scratching his arms and wrists and he strangled her. Somehow, during the struggle, Gibson had managed to press the service buttons and this brought Steer to Cabin 126. By the time he arrived Camb had just finished murdering the actress and pretended that nothing was amiss when he sent away the watchman. (The watchman Steer, it can be assumed, though he knew that Camb was in the cabin, did not ask to see Gibson, the legitimate occupant, since he was accustomed, as it were, to the numerous "shipboard romances" occurring regularly on such voyages.)

The steward's own admission that he had callously shoved the victim's body through a porthole worked against him, along with the impressive forensic evidence provided by the prosecution. After four days of trial and following a forty-five-minute deliberation, the jury found Camb Guilty of murdering Gay Gibson. The steward, who had posed like a peacock in the dock, was stunned at the decision. Before sentence was passed by Justice Hilbery, he was asked if he had anything to say. He replied in a quavering voice: "My Lord, at the beginning of this case...I pleaded not guilty. I repeat that statement now. That is all." He was then sentenced to death. His attorneys filed an appeal and while this was being considered, the House of Commons added an amendment to the new Criminal Justice Bill then before Parliament, one which would abolish capital punishment. The Home Secretary, while this bill was still being debated in the House of Lords (which later rejected it), decided to commute all capital sentences still pending to life terms and Camb was one of those who benefited from this decision.

It was after this commutation that several women came forward to tell how Camb had sexually attacked them on previous voyages of the *Durban Castle,* two of them claiming they had been raped. Another woman said that she had been attacked on deck by Camb who dragged her into a tool room where she fought desperately as he tried to strip her clothes away. He had lost patience and strangled her. She passed out, she claimed, and when she regained consciousness, she said that Camb was standing over her, grinning. Camb was paroled in 1959, changed his name to Clarke and was working as a head waiter in May 1967 when he was convicted of sexually attacking a 13-year-old girl. He was, incredibly, placed on a two-year probation. He later went to Scotland where he worked once more as a head waiter in a restaurant. A short time later he was charged with sexual misconduct with three schoolgirls and this time Camb's parole was revoked and he was returned to prison to serve out a life term.

Campbell, Cecil, prom. 1928, U.S. On the morning of Feb. 6, 1928, the New York City police were notified that a murder had taken place at the Grand Hotel on Thirty-first Street. A young woman in her mid-thirties had been bludgeoned to death with a cheap dimestore hammer. A timetable listing the trains running in and out of Grand Central Station was found on the nightstand. The desk clerk informed the police that a man had signed the registry cards as Mr. T.J. James of Troy, N.Y., and that he had rented the room in the company of a woman, apparently his wife.

Using as evidence a timetable found in the hotel room and the maid's description of Mr. James, police focused their search in the vicinity of New Rochelle in Westchester County. In the sleepy little hamlet of Mamaroneck, police learned the identity of the mysterious Mr. James from an apartment-house owner. He was Cecil Campbell, reputed to be a globe-trotting soldier-of-fortune who had taught military tactics at several academies before he settled down as the headmaster of a school in New Jersey.

In 1922, Campbell had married Mary Lyle McLean while he was still wedded to a telephone operator from South Wyndham, Mass. The bigamous marriage continued until his first wife filed for divorce in 1925. When Campbell was arrested by the police, he claimed that he and his wife had grown tired of life and of poverty and had agreed on a suicide pact. They discussed various methods of killing themselves, including drowning. Campbell and McLean boarded the Hudson River Ferry but lost their nerve in the presence of a deckload of passengers. Campbell bought the ten-cent hammer at his wife's urging. He hit her over the head and prepared to jump out of the window. Campbell said that, looking down at the people in the street, he decided against it, fearing that he might injure an innocent passerby.

Against his protestations that he wanted to die, Cecil Campbell was convicted of second-degree murder and was sentenced to twenty years to life.

Campbell, Gary Lee, 1958-   , and **Glasder, James**, c.1958-   , and **Craig, Daniel**, 1957-   , and **Shine, Joseph**, 1959-   , and **Shine, John**, 1957-   , U.S. A deadly prank resulted in a murder conviction for a 19-year-old Algonquin, Ill., youth named Gary Campbell. Campbell and four of his friends were attending a marijuana and beer party on Oct. 20, 1977, when they hit upon the idea of turning U.S. Highway 14 into a rock-throwing range.

Campbell, Glasder, Craig, and the two Shine brothers removed thirteen white-washed rocks weighing twenty to twenty-five pounds apiece from the nearby Stone Lake apartments in Woodstock. They dropped boulders into the oncoming lane of traffic, resulting in the decapitation death of David Klawes, 26, who was driving down U.S. 14 in McHenry County. A second victim, Arthur Engle of Sharon, Wis., was severely injured in the incident.

On Feb. 11, 1977, Joseph and John Shine, Daniel Craig, and James Glasder pleaded guilty to a reduced charge of manslaughter and were sentenced to six years in prison by Circuit Court judge James H. Cooney. Gary Campbell was tried separately, and was convicted of murder on Apr. 1. The Campbell youth received fourteen to twenty-one years in prison for his part in the crime.

Campbell, Dr. Henry Colin, c.1870-1930, U.S. By all appearances, Dr. Henry Colin Campbell was a temperate, unassuming physician possessing all the desirable middle-class virtues. He resided with his lawful wife and two daughters in the pleasant neighborhood of Westfield, N.J. Then the police found the body of Mildred Mowry, a Pennsylvania woman, dumped on the side of a road outside Cranford, N.J., and the facade began to come apart.

Friends and neighbors of Mrs. Mowry explained to the police and members of the Pinkerton National Detective Agency that she had left her home in February 1928 to marry a man named Campbell, whom she had met through a Detroit matrimonial agency. Mrs. Mowry was a wealthy widow who had been persuaded by Campbell to deposit several thousand dollars in cash into a joint bank account. They were then married at Elkton, Md. Puzzled by her new husband's long absences from home, Mrs. Campbell traced his movements to New York City, where she confronted him and demanded some answers. The bigamist decided to kill his second wife.

Soon he did. Police who discovered Mary's corpse beheld a gruesome scene. There was a gunshot wound in her head, and her body had been doused with gasoline and burned. The crime closely paralleled a similar murder a year before, that of Margaret Brown, a New York governess.

Detectives quickly located the marriage certificate, which listed Campbell's address as 3707 Yosemite Street in Baltimore. That was not enough to disguise the address, which was actually 3705 Yosemite Avenue. The murderer was soon located and taken into custody. It was discovered that the fast-living doctor had maintained a number of mistresses over the years, and had previously been convicted of forgery and embezzlement. No definite link was established with the widowed Margaret Brown, who had been involved with a Dr. Ross and was murdered. But with

Campbell, Peter, prom. 1967, Scot. Peter Campbell was an incorrigible young offender who bludgeoned a woman to death when he was only sixteen. In 1967, while serving his sentence, Campbell stabbed and killed a fellow inmate. He was sentenced to life imprisonment and transferred to a penal institution at Dumfries, which was specifically reserved for youthful criminals of Scotland.

Cantero, Jonathan Eric, 1969- , U.S. "The devil made me do it!" was a favorite gag-line of 1960s comics. It was always good for a laugh or two in those times. Twenty years later, however, it was no longer a laughing matter, for teenagers across the country were embracing Satanism, and its accompanying violence.

For Jonathan Cantero, a 19-year-old nursing student and short-order cook at a Tampa, Fla., Pizza Hut, it was the devil *and* the Geraldo Rivera television program that drove him to murder. On Oct. 6, 1988, Cantero watched a syndicated hour-long Geraldo Rivera program about Satanism and its practice by street gangs. Rivera interviewed teenagers who had, among other things, ritualistically killed animals. Cantero sat transfixed. Here were real-life stories about other youths like him from average American homes, young people who worshipped the devil.

Jonathan had been interested in devil worship for years. In recent weeks he had spent long hours in the public library, poring over every book he could find about demonic possession, the occult, and devil worship. In his bedroom he studied from a satanic bible, wrote letters of allegiance to the devil, and scrawled demonic symbols on his body, all of which terrified his mother, Patricia Cantero. She was a 38-year-old woman who worked nights as a waitress at the Toddle House Restaurant in Tampa. She also wrote religious verse in her spare time under the name "The Purple Rose," and her son's blasphemy broke her heart.

But Jonathan hated his mother and after watching the Geraldo Rivera program he summoned the courage to kill her. On Oct. 12, 1988, he drove to his mother's apartment on West Hillsborough Avenue to "just say hello," an unusual occurrence, given the strained relations between the two. This strain was brought on by Patricia Cantero's despair at her inability to change her son and it led to her suicide attempt in 1986. According to a note written at the time, Jonathan had placed a spell on her.

When her son knocked on the door in 1988, however, she did what a mother would do. She let him in. Newly inspired by his demonic fantasy, Jonathan followed her into the kitchen and stabbed her forty times. He read a poem over the lifeless body and tip-toed out of the apartment, locking the door behind him.

He had completed the last item on his daily list of things to do. "Go to school. Pull up at mom's house. Enter/greet mom. Go to bathroom. Prepare knife and handkerchief. Go directly to mom. When her back is turned stab until dead. Cut off her hand." He buried the gruesome note, his bloody clothes, and a satanic poem in his grandfather's back yard, where they remained until police investigators dug them up nearly two weeks later.

David Cantero, Jonathan's 16-year-old brother, found his mother in the hallway of the apartment. Jonathan was brought to the police station for questioning, his hand heavily bandaged. He claimed the wound was caused by glass in his school parking lot, not as the attending physician at St. Joseph's Hospital later told detectives, by a knife. When confronted with the doctor's testimony, Cantero confessed. He was charged with first-degree murder, and locked up at the Hillsborough County Jail. According to the police report, Cantero said he "couldn't take it anymore because his mother got on him for not coming to see her enough." He also said he hated her for forcing Christianity on him and that demonic voices in the night ordered him to kill her.

To avoid a trial and the possibility of the death penalty, Jonathan Cantero agreed to serve a life sentence with no chance of parole for twenty-five years. He was led off to jail on Mar. 18, 1989, after embracing his aunt, the sister of Patricia Cantero. It was her wish that the boy be spared the electric chair.

Carey, Mary, and **Carey, Howard**, and **Carey, James**, prom. 1927-34, U.S. A mother and her two sons thought they had committed the perfect crime. And for seven years it certainly seemed that way.

Mary Carey and her boys lived in the small town of Omar, Del. Shortly before the local elections were held in November 1927, Carey decided to murder her brother Robert Hitchens. He was a reserved bachelor who was content to sit back and listen to the opinions of others. Hitchens was well-liked, and it seemed inconceivable that anyone wanted to murder him. Carey's motive, though, was simple: she wanted to collect on his sizeable life insurance policy. To enlist the cooperation of her sons, she promised them a new car.

On Nov. 5, Hitchens told Mrs. Daisey, the grocery store owner's wife, that he felt ill. It was the perfect opportunity for his sister to carry out her plans. The next day when Robert did not show up at the store as he usually did, Mrs. Daisey was concerned and notified Mary Carey. They went over to his place and rapped on the door, but there was no answer. A neighbor man jimmied open a window and climbed in to see what the trouble was. He found Hitchens on the living room rug. He had been beaten and shot.

The presence of a whiskey bottle near the corpse led the police to the conclusion that perhaps it might have been the work of a gang of bootleggers. The case was later entered into the records as "unsolved."

In fact, the case was forgotten, until Dec. 5, 1934, when Mrs. Irving Powell returned to her darkened house and was accosted by an intruder. She dropped in her tracks after being winged by his errant bullet, but she had obtained a good look at the assailant before passing out. It was Mary Carey's youngest boy Lawrence. The police took him into custody and questioned him about the Powell shooting and the murder of his Uncle Robert. "I know plenty," he said, recalling the conversations he had overheard between his mother and two older brothers. As a result, Mrs. Carey, Howard Carey, and James Carey were tried and convicted of murder. Mary and Howard were hanged, and James was given life. Lawrence Carey received seven years for breaking and entering into the Powell residence.

Carey, Walter Burton, III, 1949- , U.S. The question of when a victim is legally dead became the central issue during the murder trial of Walter Burton Carey III, accused of killing 17-year-old Karen Ann Pomroy on the grounds of Long Island's Islip High School, Nov. 29, 1976.

The girl was on her way to a tutoring job when Carey assaulted her with a heavy railroad spike. He stole $1 from her purse and left her for dead. However, she did not lose her vital signs. Taken to the Southside Hospital in Bay Shore, Karen Ann was placed on a respirator. She was pronounced neurologically dead on Dec. 2 by Dr. William Bloom. With the consent of her parents, Pomroy was disconnected from her life-support system. Contrasting her condition to that of Karen Ann Quinlan, Bloom pointed out that Quinlan "never had a loss of electrical activity in the brain. She never had a loss of movement. She never had loss of response to painful stimuli."

District Attorney Henry O'Brien pressed for a murder indictment ment against Carey. Defense attorneys argued that Pomroy died when the respirator was cut off, not from the beating administered by the defendant. New York penal laws did not adequately define the condition of death at the time. "A court will be obligated to charge the jury...at least giving them a criterion that they can use to determine for them the question of fact, that is, when did death occur?" O'Brien said.

The case was tried before Justice George F.X. McInerney of the State Supreme Court, in Riverhead, Long Island. During deliberations, the judge sent the jury back to reconsider the matter after they reported that they were hopelessly deadlocked and unable to reach a verdict. Then, on May 27, 1977, the jury found Carey Guilty of murder. On June 20, Carey was sentenced to twenty-four years to life in prison. In passing sentence, Judge McInerney said, "If the assailant's conduct is proven to be a sufficiently direct contributing cause of death, he may be held criminally responsible for the death and his criminal responsibility is not lessened or excused by the existence of another contributing cause or factor."

Caritativo, Bart, 1906-58, U.S. Many wealthy Californians employed male servants from the Philippines. Bart Caritativo, one such houseboy, worked in a large home in Stinson Beach, a suburb north of San Francisco. He became friendly with the housekeeper at the house next door, who had the good luck to marry her employer. The homeowner soon died and left her his fortune. Caritativo continued his friendship with this lady, Camille Malmgren.

Murderer Bart Caritativo.

Malmgren was soon remarried to an Englishman named Joseph Banks, an alcoholic. During the next several years she committed him to an institution for treatment a number of times. She ultimately divorced Banks, though he continued to live in her Stinson Beach house. In September 1954, Camille Banks decided to leave the country for a while. A neighbor came by to see her just before she left on her trip and found her dead in her bedroom, her skull split open. Banks lay dead in the living room, surrounded by empty liquor bottles. In his hand was the handle of a large knife which was stuck in his stomach.

Among the papers police located in the house was a suicide note signed by Banks which read, "I am responsible to what you see and find." Another was Camille Banks's will, leaving everything to Caritativo. It, too, contained grammatical errors and awkward misspellings. Don Midyett of the San Rafael sheriff's department compared Caritativo's handwriting with that on the documents and, when experts found them the same, arrested Caritativo for murder.

Caritativo's trial began in January 1955. The major evidence against him were the handwritten documents and the testimony of a pathologist that Banks, thoroughly drunk, could not have killed his wife or himself. When Caritativo saw things going against him, he fired his lawyer, telling the court, "I have lost the trust to my attorneys," misusing the word "to" as it had been misused in Banks's so-called suicide note. The jury found Caritativo Guilty of murder in the first degree. He was executed at San Quentin on Oct. 24, 1958.

Carney, John, prom. 1930s, Can. The murder of James Agnew, a farmer from Lindsay, Ontario, was a relatively simple matter for Canadian detectives. Agnew had been shot behind his barn during the middle of a blinding snowstorm. The unknown assailant ran off with a gold watch and a few dollars from the victim's pocket. The shots were not heard by Agnew's wife inside the farmhouse, and the killer slipped away undetected.

Detective Murray was called in to examine the evidence. The snow had covered the footprints by this time. But Murray dug deep in the snowdrifts and found impressions of a buckle and strap. The trail led to the door of Henry Logie, a neighbor who employed an 18-year-old youth named John Carney. Carney wore a pair of boots that matched the impressions in the snow near the Agnew farm. A search of Logie's wash house turned up the stolen items.

Carney was convicted on a charge of murder and sentenced to life imprisonment. He avoided the death penalty because of his age.

Carpenter, Richard, 1929-56, U.S. Richard Carpenter entered neighborhood bars and small grocery stores in Chicago as they were preparing to close, held two Western-style guns on the clerk, and demanded whatever money was in the cash register. In this way, he made a steady though precarious living for two years.

In August 1955, Police Detective Bill Murphy, who had been briefed on Carpenter, spotted the 26-year-old thief on a subway train, and immediately arrested him. When they got off the train, Murphy tried to pull an identification poster from his pocket, giving Carpenter a chance to pull his gun. Carpenter fired once, directly into the policeman's chest, killing him. Carpenter ran out of the station and hijacked a waiting limousine, telling the driver, "I've just

killed a man, and I'll kill you, too, unless you drive on and keep quiet!" Carpenter got out in the Loop business district.

Carpenter could not go to any of his familiar haunts, so he slept where and when he could. He was asleep in the

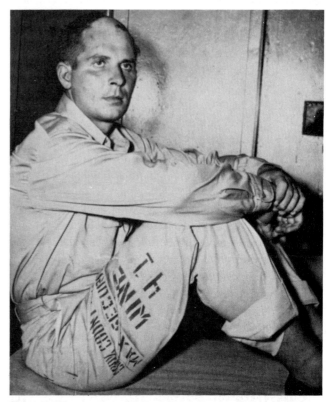

Chicago robber-murderer Richard Carpenter, executed in 1956.

back row of a downtown movie theater when he was spotted by another policeman, Clarence Kerr, who was spending an evening out with his wife. Kerr sent her out of the way, then woke the sleeping Carpenter to take him into the lobby. Carpenter pretended to trip, pulled out his gun as he rose, and shot Kerr in the chest.

As Carpenter rushed from the theater, a passing policeman shot him in the leg. Later that evening Carpenter knocked on the back door of the home of Leonard Powell, a truckdriver, and demanded to be let in. Powell and his wife calmly went about their business, held at gunpoint by the frantic murderer for more than a day. They kept their son and daughter ignorant of who Carpenter was, and Powell even went to work the next day, knowing that his family was held hostage. That evening, probably having no idea how he was going to get out of the situation, Carpenter said to the Powells, "It was a lousy life I led—but it's too late now. Either the cops will kill me or I'll go to the chair, but I hope I can see my mother before I die." Powell told Carpenter that his wife's mother would be expecting them to visit that evening, as they did every evening. Carpenter let them go, and the Powells ran for help. Within minutes, police surrounded the building. Carpenter ran to another apartment, but soon gave himself up. Found Guilty of murder, Carpenter, after a brief visit from his mother, was sent to the electric chair at Joliet State Prison.

Carroll, Janet Faye, 1940- , U.S. After murdering her second husband, a North Carolina woman drove with her four children and her new lover to bury her spouse's corpse.

On June 13, 1969, Donald Carroll, recently discharged from the U.S. Army, fought with his wife, Janet, over the attention she had been paying to Jimmy D. Goins. Janet soon telephoned Goins from the Carroll's Greensboro, S.C., trailer home, saying, "I've shot my husband. Come right over and help me. I don't know what to do." At the Carroll's house Goins found Donald's body on a blood-stained mattress; Janet Carroll had killed her husband with a .22-caliber rifle while he slept. The couple put the body in the car trunk, then placed Carroll's children in the car and drove to nearby Sanford to leave them with Janet's parents. Carroll and Goins took the corpse to Moore County, where they buried it and threw the rifle in the Deep River.

Within a month of the murder Carroll took out a warrant charging Donald with nonsupport, claiming that he had deserted her to seek work somewhere in Tennessee, and reporting him as missing. A year later, after she and Goins had moved to New York and then back to Greensboro, Carroll divorced her husband on grounds of desertion and married Goins. All went well until they quarrelled, and an angry Goins went to the sheriff's office to complain about his wife's behavior. But Sheriff D.F. Holder of Lee County knew he had more on his mind than marital woes, "So we just kept pouring him coffee, and he just kept a-talkin'." By midnight, Goins confessed all, taking deputies to the scene of the crime and leading them to the decomposing corpse.

Condemning evidence at the trial included the blood-stained mattress on which Donald Carroll had been killed, still being used by the trailer's new tenants. Goins, convicted as an accomplice after the fact, regretted that his wife would have to do time, saying, "I wish I could do time for her." When arrested, Carroll was driving with a loaded .22-caliber rifle under the seat. At first calling the killing an accident, she later confessed to committing the murder in a fit of anger. The judge sentenced Carroll to four to six years in the state penitentiary. Goins later received the same term.

Carroll, Mario, and **Johnston, James**, prom. c.1972, U.S. A slow-witted boy became convinced that an elderly, crippled man had money and jewels hidden in his mattress and enlisted the help of his mother's lover to kill the old man.

Twelve-year-old Mario Carroll lived in a home with his crippled, divorced mother and admired Nazi uniforms, knives, and guns. From classmates he heard the rumor that Harry Lillywhite, also called Pops, an 82-year-old hunchback in the neighborhood, had a fortune hidden in his home. When he failed to persuade a schoolmate to help attack the old man, Carroll suggested the scheme to James Johnston, a 23-year-old laborer who was his mother's lover. When Carroll rang the doorbell Lillywhite told the pair to go away, but they forced their way in, and Johnston smashed a heavy wrench down on the elderly man's head. As Lillywhite screamed for help, Johnston bashed his skull. Searching the house, the killers found that Lillywhite had no hidden valuables, but instead lived in poverty on a small pension.

Within hours, police traced and questioned Carroll, who admitted his guilt. Carroll and Johnston were charged with murder and conspiring to rob Lillywhite. At the trial it was determined that Carroll had a low intelligence, with the reading skills of a 6-year-old. The judge, explaining that he did not want to punish the boy, but "to insure that he will receive the education and training that he has been so lacking in life," sentenced Carroll to six years in a state school for boys. James Johnston, Carroll's accomplice, was sentenced to life imprisonment.

Carter, George, 1931- , Brit. Apparently because he resented the financial burden of a family, a British laborer murdered his wife and caused permanent brain damage to his 6-year-old son. On Jan. 2, 1960, when 29-year-old George Carter came home from work for lunch, his pregnant wife, Ruby, thirty-three, lay dead in their bed, her skull fractured by three heavy blows. Carter's 6-year-old son, Alun, was severely wounded in a similar way, and would suffer permanent brain damage. Carter claimed he had gone to pick up his wife at the Cowbridge High School for Girls, where she worked, and became concerned when she didn't come out. A bureau in the Carter home was clumsily smashed, and according to Carter, £35 was missing. The wife had been dead for about six hours, so the murder had occurred at around 5:15 a.m., the time Carter left for work. The grieving but composed husband appeared on television to ask for assistance in finding his wife's slayer.

On Jan. 3 a heavy metal object was discovered in a field near the Carters' house. It was established as the murder weapon, and found to be from the factory where George Carter worked. On Jan. 16, he was charged with killing his wife. Although he maintained his innocence during his trial, Carter talked a great deal, presumably trying to deflect suspicion, and once claimed, "I have had to say I did not do it. But they can prove I did."

Carter was tried at Glamorgan Assizes, Cardiff, on Mar. 21 in front of Justice Barry, with W.L. Mars-Jones, Queen's Counsel as prosecuting attorney, and Norman Richards, Queen's Counsel for the defense. Evidence against him included twenty-three tiny spots of blood on his right jacket sleeve and testimony from his coworkers that he had flashed a number of banknotes at work on the morning of the murder, presumably hiding them later to give credence to his claim of burglary and a mysterious intruder. Carter's coworker, Paul Galton, testified that Carter, heavily in debt, had asked him for advice on how to end a pregnancy. Carter had been very proud of his recent purchase of a new car but was having difficulty making the monthly payments of £16, and apparently resented the financial strain of a growing family. Though all evidence was circumstantial, the jury found Carter Guilty as charged in just thirty-five minutes. He was sentenced to life imprisonment.

Carter, Polk, 1906- , U.S. The death of an elderly farmer in a small town in Georgia provoked so many rumors that, within a year, three of his relatives were accused of poisoning the old man. On Aug. 6, 1969, James Clark, a 77-year-old grocery store operator and farmer, died after a brief illness. He had married Effie Bell Clark less than three months earlier, and rumors that his marriage had hastened his death began to spread. Gossip also focused on Fannie Pearl Carter, Effie's 34-year-old daughter, and Fannie's husband, Polk Carter, fifty-three, who inherited most of Clark's estate. The illiterate farmer had died of a stomach ailment, and an autopsy generated whisperings that poisoning was suspected. Local law officials investigated the case for a year before they issued indictments against Effie Bell Clark Bennett, who had since remarried, and Fannie Pearl Carter and Polk Carter, charging them with poisoning Clark with arsenic from July 27 until his death.

At the trial, less than a month after the three were charged, Georgia State Crime Laboratory toxicologist Dr. June Jones testified that Clark's liver contained an arsenic concentration more than three times higher than normal, and said that he had suffered "massive liver and kidney damage." Jones also stated that all products with substantial amounts of arsenic in them were colored pink in accordance with the law. Effie Bennett, granted immunity in exchange for her cooperation, testified that she had seen her daughter

and her son-in-law lace her late husband's food with "pink powder" several times.

Polk Carter, testifying in his own defense, denied preparing any food for his father-in-law and showed credit card receipts to prove he had been out of town during Clark's alleged poisoning. Despite this alibi and his claims that Clark had died of lead poisoning from tainted moonshine, the jury found Polk Carter Guilty of murder after a two-hour deliberation and sentenced him to life imprisonment.

Carter, Rubin (AKA: **Hurricane**), 1937- , U.S. In a highly publicized and controversial case that spanned more than a decade, former leading middleweight boxing contender Rubin Carter became a *cause célèbre* of civil rights fund-raising efforts. On June 17, 1966, at 2:30 a.m., three people were killed by shotgun blasts at the Lafayette Grill, a tavern in Paterson, N.J., during a period of racial tension in that city. The victims were James Oliver, the 52-year-old bartender and part-owner of the tavern, Fred Nauykas, a patron, and Hazel Tanis, fifty-one, who died from bullet wounds a month later. Separately arrested and charged with the crime on Oct. 14 and 15, 1966, were John Artis and Rubin Carter, who claimed he barely knew Artis. The motive was said to be revenge for the killing of a black tavern owner in the same area earlier that evening; all three of the victims at the Lafayette Grill were white.

The policeman who apprehended Carter and Artis later testified that neither man had acted nervous or guilty, and that both had followed him to the scene of the crime with no reservations. A key witness at the initial trial, Alfred P. Bello, said he saw the defendants flee the tavern with guns and escape in a white car; Bello allegedly had been robbing a factory nearby when he was drawn to the scene of the murders after hearing shots. He admitted stealing money from the cash register of the Lafayette Grill soon after the shootings, and was present when police brought Carter and Artis in about half an hour after the attack. Both Bello and Arthur D. Bradley identified Carter and Artis four months after the shootings. Bello, who had served prison terms for burglary and robbery, recanted his testimony in 1974, claiming that detectives had coerced him into identifying Carter and Artis. He later disavowed his testimony a second time, offering two different versions of what he had seen. Another witness, Patricia Graham Valentine, who lived above the tavern, identified the two men although she had seen them only from the back, but she also described their escape car. And Emil DiRobbio, a homicide detective, testified that he had turned in shotgun shells found at the scene to the police property clerk's office.

In May 1967, Artis and Carter were convicted, found

Guilty on three counts of first-degree murder and sentenced to life imprisonment. The case became a liberal cause, with Carter receiving support from the black community and from sports and entertainment figures. In December 1975 a "Night of the Hurricane" benefit held at New York City's Madison Square Garden helped raise money for an appeal. By March 1976, the New Jersey State Court overturned both convictions, ruling that important evidence had been withheld from the defense. Carter was freed on $20,000 bail, and Artis on $15,000 bail.

Because of prejudicial publicity against the defendants in Passaic County, the second trial was moved from Patterson to Jersey City. It began on Oct. 12, 1976, and was presided over by Judge William J. Marchese, who disqualified himself on Oct. 19 when defense lawyers protested that he might become a witness at the trial since he had sentenced Bello in an unrelated 1974 case.

Marchese was replaced by Judge Bruno L. Leopizzi. Patricia Valentine added to her testimony of ten years earlier that police had shown her a cartridge and shotgun shell they said they had found in the car Carter and Artis were driving when they were arrested. In the 1966 trial, detective Emil DiRobbio never mentioned showing the shell or cartridge to anyone but the police. The question of whether they had been found the day of the killings was a key issue in the 1966 trial. An investigation by New York *Times* reporter Selwyn Raab led to the reopening of the case.

Bello, the key prosecution witness, recanted earlier testimony which claimed that he had been "brainwashed" by police into identifying Artis and Carter as the murderers. Bello then renounced his recantation and declared in court on Nov. 15 that he had lied consistently throughout the trial and during the 1975 grand jury hearings. Asked about statements he had made in an affidavit to Assemblyman Eldridge Hawkins in 1975, Bello replied, "It's true that I said it, but it's not true." He later added, "Most of the things I said were complete lies to avoid the issue." Bello would later claim that both a television producer and an investigator from the State Public Defender's Office had offered him bribes to change his testimony.

On Nov. 22, Detective Donald LaConte corroborated Patricia Valentine's testimony when he said he, too, had seen the bullet and shell when he brought her to police headquarters so she could identify the car driven by Artis and Carter. The defense contended that the bullet and shell were planted by police to frame their clients. LaConte, the officer to whom Bello had first identified Carter and Artis as the men he had seen at the murder scene, said Bello told him later that he was "scared" because friends of Carter's had threatened him. LaConte said Bello told him, "You guys had the right men and you let 'em go," referring to Artis and Carter.

On Nov. 18, Judge Leopizzi prohibited anyone from contacting the jurors or their families about the case. The defense emphasized that the descriptions of the killers did not match either defendant, except that they were black, and that there was no strong case against the defendants until they were identified by Bello and Bradley four months after the crime. Vincent DeSimone, Jr., who had headed the initial investigation into the shootings, told a 1966 grand jury twelve days after the triple murders that the clothing worn by Carter and Artis did not fit descriptions from witnesses. DeSimone had said, "With the time element, we feel it is almost impossible that these men could have changed clothes." In the four-month interim between the incident and the arrest of Carter and Artis, DeSimone secured a positive identification of the defendants from Bello. In the 1976 trial, DeSimone, referring to a deal he made with Bello to drop charges on Bello's robbery attempt on the night of the killings, said, "If I could solve a murder by not taking action on a lesser crime, I'd do it every day of the week. I'd do it again tomorrow." William Hardney and Welton Deary, two former friends of Carter's, testified on Nov. 27 that they had been asked, prior to the 1967 trial, by Carter and his attorney at the time, Raymond Brown, to say that they had been with the former boxer at the time of the slayings. Hardney did not testify at the first trial. Deary had testified, and now admitted giving false testimony when he said he had been with Carter at the time of the murders.

Artis testified on Dec. 15, again telling the jury that he was not guilty. Carter declined to testify, just as he had in 1967. In final summations on Dec. 20, Passaic County Prosecutor Burrell I. Humphreys said the evidence built a "rope strong enough to bring two murderers to justice," while defense lawyers Myron Beldock and Lewis Steel, attorneys for Carter and Artis, respectively, challenged the credibility of most of the state's witnesses and focused on the uncertainty of the identifications of the defendants. On Dec. 26, 1976, Carter and Artis were found Guilty for the second time on three counts of first-degree murder. On Feb. 9, 1977, Carter was sentenced to two consecutive life terms and one concurrent life term and will not be eligible for parole until 1996. When Chicago novelist Nelson Algren died in 1981, he was working on a novel about Rubin Carter.

Carter, Theodore H., 1932-   , U.S. A mildly retarded youth was discovered to be the murderer of a young woman in a small town after police spent several weeks following false leads.

On May 13, 1950, Alice Huen discovered the body of Lorraine Hess, a 17-year-old high school student, when she went to collect her son's socks from the clothesline in the backyard of her Millville, N.J. home. The socks, along with a green belt from Hess' coat, were wrapped around the neck of the strangled woman.

Heading the investigation were Public Safety Commissioner David Reid and Police Chief Samuel Fithian, later joined by State Police Lieutenant Jules Westphalen and detectives from nearby Bridgeton, the county seat. The investigators discovered that Hess had seen a play with friends the night of the murder, May 12, and had been dropped off by them about two blocks from the house of an uncle, John J. Sherman, where she planned to spend the night. Two men who had been out that evening, Charles Whilden, a college student returning from a date, and Edward Keen, a factory worker driving home, both had seen Hess with a man on the street corner about a block from the murder scene, at around 12:30 a.m. Whilden's parents and a neighbor had heard screams, but had dismissed them.

After following several false leads, including the arrest and questioning of a local millhand and a traveling chemist with previous arrests as a Peeping Tom, police picked up Theodore Carter, an 18-year-old stockboy from Millville, who had left town shortly after the killing. Arrested in Bridgeport, Conn., where he had gone to stay with an uncle, Carter had been charged with disorderly conduct and was serving a ten-day jail sentence when turned over to New Jersey police for questioning.

On June 15, District Attorney Stanger stated that Carter had made a full confession to the slaying, saying, "I'm awfully glad to get these things off my mind. I'm full of shame." Though his mother denied that Carter had left town right after the murder, claiming her son had not gone to Connecticut until late May, Carter made five separate confessions to the crime. Since he could neither read nor write, he signed his name with an X and later declared in court that he made the confessions voluntarily. He was tried in late October 1950, in Bridgeton, N.J., in a trial that lasted two weeks and involved more than 100 witnesses. Carter's defense attorney pleaded for acquittal, saying that Carter had the mentality of an eight-year-old and that the police had dictated his statements and confessions. After several hours of deliberation the jury found Carter Guilty of first degree murder, recommending mercy based on his mental condition. On Nov. 10, 1950, Carter was sentenced to life in prison.

Cartier, Andre, prom. 1936, Brit. On Jan. 25, 1936, the body of a 55-year-old man was found on a quiet road on the outskirts of London, in St. Albans, Hertfordshire. The victim had been thrown out of a moving car after being shot six times. Scotland Yard detectives sent in the cleaning tag from the man's expensive coat and learned that the murdered man was Emil Haye, a jewelry salesman from Canada who lived in the Soho district of London. Sending Haye's fingerprints to the Yard, investigators discovered through American police and the French Surete investigations that "Haye" was actually Bull Jaw Donohue, a notorious American racketeer. When police Constable Howard Barber, walking his regular beat in Little Newport Street, found three large glass splinters, he disposed of them by pushing them into the curb, and reported the incident to his sergeant. An inspector called Barber a few days later, showing him the photograph of Hayes, which Barber recognized from newspaper reports on the killing.

The two police officers went to the house in front of which the glass splinters were found and checked out the apartments there, discovering one, formerly occupied by a couple named Taylor, that had been abandoned in obvious haste. Sending the charwoman and the landlady to Scotland Yard, the police learned that the "Taylors" were really Yvette Constantine, who had previously operated an illegal racket in Paris, and Andre Cartier, a notorious gangster once sentenced to Devil's Island. In the apartment inspectors found a broken window, a half-burned slip of paper bearing the name Yvonne Ducre, with a list of wages paid for her services as a maid. Under questioning Ducre said Donohue had come to France from America to set up organized racketeering, and Cartier, his partner, had killed him in a fight over money. When Donohue was shot in Constantine's apartment, he staggered to a window, breaking the glass before falling dead. Cartier and Constantine were arrested soon after in Paris, and both were tried for Donohue's murder. Constantine was acquitted, and Cartier got a twenty-year jail term.

Case, William, 1855-1939, U.S. An elderly man who had raised evergreen trees on his Ohio farm since early childhood committed murder when thieves stole more than 200 trees after a local magazine publicized him.

William Case, eighty-four, of Strogsville, Ohio, was known as "Santa Claus" for his generosity in donating an evergreen tree annually to decorate Cleveland's public square and for his tradition of handing out nickels to children at Christmastime. Since boyhood, Case had tended the trees on his farm. In December 1939, he was written up by *The American Magazine* for his charitable nature. Following the article, people came to his farm to steal trees by the truckload. On Christmas Eve Day, Case heard the sounds of yet another tree being chopped down. He picked up his shotgun, slipped up on two people tying a tree to their car, and fired twice, killing William Rousseau, thirty-seven, an unemployed man, and wounding his wife, Minnie Rousseau, twenty-nine. Case calmly explained his actions, saying: "The tree was theirs for the asking...But when people steal them it's different." After being told his arraignment was a formality, Case pleaded innocent to manslaughter and was released on bail. Later, at the request of Mrs. Rousseau, a grand jury refused to indict Case for manslaughter. He died in June 1939; his demise was withheld by relatives to avoid further publicity.

Casella, Louis, prom. 1910s, U.S. A hit-and-run driver was tracked down through the painstaking detective work of a police sergeant who trained officers how to identify cars in the early days of the automobile.

In New York City, prior to WWI, streets held a combination of the motor car and the horse and buggy. One June evening, around Sixty-ninth Street between Park and Lexington Avenues, a speeding car hit the horse and buggy of John McHugh, a city street cleaning foreman, as he began his night inspection tour. McHugh was found by Patrolman John G. Dwyer and taken to the hospital where he died a few hours later. Dwyer assembled twenty-one broken pieces of glass from the scene of the hit-and-run and reported the incident. The next morning a street cleaner found a fragment of rubber, about three inches long, that apparently had come from a tire of the car.

Assigned to investigate the case was Sergeant John F. Brennan, instructor in the new field of car identification at the police training school. Carefully reconstructing the glass fragments, Brennan discovered that they were parts of lenses from gas and oil lights, and he uncovered patent dates showing the lenses had not been manufactured since 1912. Discerning minute fragments of gray paint on splintered wood shards the officer narrowed the make down to a gray 1909 Packard, Model 18, and surmised that it was probably in a garage for repairs that had resulted from the accident. Police checked all cars of that type, finding in a Long Island City garage a Packard of that make that belonged to Louis Casella which had been stored in the Long Island shop but had disappeared two days earlier. Brennan went to Casella's home address, found him missing, and traced his mail to Allenhurst, N.J., fifty miles north of New York City. When he finally located Casella in Allenhurst the suspect had an airtight alibi, but Brennan managed to detach a small piece of rubber when he examined Casella's car and sent it to a chemist for analysis, where it was matched with the piece found at the scene of the crime.

Brennan, with the assistance of detective Edward J. Cousins, tracked down receipts for repairs to Casella's car, the evidence was assembled, and an indictment of first-degree murder was made. Casella, however, had disappeared. Brennan, presuming that the suspect would contact a lawyer, found the name of Casella's attorney and hid in a phone booth outside the law office, with the doors arranged to reflect the sun and keep him out of sight, until Casella finally appeared and was arrested.

Castalas, Louis, prom. 1980, Fr. A decorated and patriotic Frenchman killed his wife's lover when he realized that his 7-year-old son was sired by another man.

Louis Castalas had been a leader in the French Resistance in 1941. He was captured by the Gestapo and sent to Buchenwald and though experimented on by Nazi doctors, refused to reveal the names of his comrades. Awarded the Croix de Guerre and the Legion of Honor, Castalas continued to fight for his country against the Viet Cong in Indochina. He was again decorated with the Military Medal for gallantry. Married twice, Castalas did not tell his first two spouses that the Nazi operations left him sterile, hoping the diagnosis would prove wrong. Working as a police inspector at the age of forty-three, Castalas married a third time to Josiane, a woman seventeen years his junior. When his wife announced her pregnancy, Castalas was thrilled and became a devoted father to his son, Herve.

When Herve was seven, Castalas came home one night and learned that his wife, visiting a nearby village, was stranded by a snowstorm, and would spend the night with her friends, the Tardes. Castalas went to pick her up the next day and found her talking with Pierre Laurent. Noticing the marked resemblance between Laurent and Herve, Castalas immediately confronted Josiane, who angrily confessed, "Yes, he is my lover and the true father of Herve!" Castalas shot Laurent, drove his wife home, then turned himself over to the police. He was tried and sentenced to a seven-year prison term by the judge who described him as "a Frenchman of great courage and a glorious soldier of France." Castalas refused to see his wife or the boy he once called "son" again.

Cawley, Brian, prom. 1929-60, Brit. An unemployed radio technician has the dubious distinction of having the shortest murder trial on record in England.

Brian Cawley, thirty, lived with his wife and their three

children in a New Road, Basingstoke, house owned by Rupert Steed, a retired bachelor who had befriended the Cawley family. The Cawleys lived rent free with Steed, who enjoyed giving them gifts and being their benefactor. Cawley began to drink and his wife left him, taking the children. One night, Cawley returned home and beat Steed to death for no apparent reason. Cawley was tried on Dec. 14, 1959, at Winchester Assizes. He pleaded guilty and was sentenced to life imprisonment, with the entire proceedings taking only thirty seconds.

Cayson, Jesse, and **Cayson, Doyle**, prom. 1958, U.S. When his father was murdered by local thugs, a 12-year-old boy vowed he would find the killers. Eighteen years later he did. On Mar. 15, 1940, Les Wilson, father of six and candidate for sheriff in the Okaloosa County race, was in his Crestview, Fla., home with his wife and children, listening to the radio, when a shotgun blast through the porch window killed him. Ray Wilson, his 12-year-old son, told himself that night that he would track down whoever had murdered his father, and help clean up Okaloosa County, where gambling proliferated and illegal whiskey was sold openly, and where murders and unusual disappearances were regular occurrences. Les Wilson's life had been threatened before; as police chief of Crestview, criminals despised him, and his candidacy for sheriff threatened the gangsters' free rein.

An investigation into his murder was ordered in October 1940 by Governor Fred P. Cone and closed by Governor Fuller Warren in 1949 after there had been no results. Ray Wilson graduated from high school, served in the U.S. Army and returned to Crestview around 1950, determined to run for sheriff. With no initial support, he garnered the confidence of the public on a platform of impartial law and order and won the post in 1956, becoming, at twenty-eight, Florida's youngest sheriff and embarking on a successful campaign to clean up Crestview.

With Walter R. Steinsiek, Jr., Pensacola police superintendent of identification, Wilson began the search for his father's killer. He looked through old police files and eventually came up with Jesse and Doyle Cayson as possible suspects. The brothers had become unaccountably prosperous after Wilson's murder, and connections with organized crime were thought to be the cause. A woman who had twice changed her name was tracked to San Antonio, Texas, and interviewed by Wilson. She refused to testify but admitted that she had heard the Caysons leave with shotguns the night of the murder and had later been beaten by them and told to keep her mouth shut. She and her husband had been shot at sometime after that, and they

moved from Crestview in fear for their lives. When Wilson promised her protection, "Jane" agreed to testify, saying, "I'm scared, but I've been waiting all these years to clear my mind of what happened that night."

Another witness who had overheard Jesse Cayson tell several people he had murdered Les Wilson was found, and a switchboard operator who had listened to one of the suspects call to find out if Wilson was driving a taxi that night also came forth. In June 1958, after eighteen months of intensive investigation, having questioned more than 200 people, Ray Wilson went before a grand jury to present evidence in his father's murder. The Caysons were brought to trial soon after and in November of that year, were found Guilty of the first-degree murder of Les Wilson. The killers were sentenced to life in prison.

Cerny, Wenzel, prom. 1936, Czech. When a prominent judge's bride took a contract out on her husband's life, the killer she hired agreed to do the job, saying the judge had sent him to jail two years earlier because he "didn't like my looks."

An upstairs neighbor called the police at about 10:20 p.m., Mar. 16, 1936, to report a commotion in the apartment of Czechoslovakian Court Judge Jan Velgo. Police officers broke in to find a man groaning on the living-room floor, shot in the forehead, after his attempt to kill himself. In the bathroom the body of Judge Jan Velgo lay submerged in the bathtub, a deep gash in his head. A medical examiner announced that he had been dead for fifteen minutes, and pronounced the cause as drowning. In the closet of one room police found Marie Havlick Velgo slumped on the floor and unconscious. The 21-year-old woman opened her eyes and asked after her husband of six weeks, saying she had been forced into the closet where she had fainted. The wounded man was identified as Wenzel Cerny, a petty criminal with a record of arson, assault and battery, robbery, and fraud dating back ten years.

Questioning the Velgo's maid and several other people, police learned that the couple had just recently married for convenience only, and that Velgo had planned to divorce his wife when he learned of a vacancy in the supreme court. Hoping to be appointed, he decided a divorce scandal would disqualify him. The distressed bride confided to her maid that she would like to get rid of Velgo and the maid procured Cerny's name. When Cerny was questioned, he was more than willing to talk, with no idea of "shielding that she-devil."

He had met with Marie Velgo in a cafe and agreed to murder her husband for a fee of $200. They had even drawn up a promissory note, which he told police to look for in the lining of his coat. The official-sounding document was dated Feb. 16, 1936, one month before Velgo's death. Tricking Marie Velgo into signing her name, police found that her signature matched that on the promissory note. Confronted with this evidence, she dropped her story of a burglary and confessed to arranging the murder, but said she had had a change of heart later and unsuccessfully begged Cerny not to go through with it. According to her testimony, the killer had brushed her off, then locked her in the closet when he heard Velgo's key in the door.

Cerny and Velgo were tried on Feb. 11, 1937. A jury took twelve minutes to find Cerny Guilty as charged and the less than bereaved widow Not Guilty "in view of irresistible force exercised upon her" by Cerny. The state's attorney called for a new trial based on improper evidence brought in by the defense. Velgo was retried in October 1937, found Guilty, and sent to jail for a twelve-year term.

Chapin, Charles (AKA: **Rose Man of Sing Sing**), 1858-1930, U.S. As the editor of Pulitzer's New York *Evening World,* Charles Chapin made numerous enemies among the reporters for the way he used his power. Chapin invested every penny he earned for many years in speculative stocks, which provided him with a yacht, servants, and multiple homes.

When the bottom fell out of the sugar market, only a loan from a friend kept Chapin from going to jail for misusing a trust fund for which he was guardian. He swore never to speculate again, but could not keep the promise. In 1914, he lost $100,000 overnight when Germany declared war. For the next four years, Chapin was continually hounded by creditors and frequently contemplated suicide. As bankruptcy neared, he decided that he could not ask his wife to live in the poverty he foresaw. He purchased a gun and, on Sept. 16, 1918, as his wife slept, Chapin shot her in the chest, planning to kill himself immediately. However, she did not die at once, and by the time she did, he had lost the nerve to take his own life. Chapin turned himself in to the police and asked that he be electrocuted. The newsman refused to defend himself, but a volunteer lawyer managed to get the charge reduced to second-degree murder. The 60-year-old Chapin was sentenced to serve twenty years at Sing Sing.

Warden Lewis Lawes got Chapin interested in publishing a prison newspaper. When that was suspended, Chapin asked to be allowed to create a garden out of the prison yard, and was so successful that he earned the nickname "Rose Man of Sing Sing." His gardening skills became known throughout the area, but, again, the men who were required to work for him found Chapin an arrogant and intolerable slavedriver. Chapin died at the age of seventy-two on Dec. 13, 1930.

Chapin, Kenneth R., 1936- , U.S. Bernard Goldberg and his wife were out for the evening when their 4-year-old son Stephen, and his babysitter Lynn Ann Smith were brutally murdered in the family home in Springfield, Mass. The murderer later served as one of the pall bearers at the funeral.

Lynn Ann Smith was reading *Gone With the Wind* when 18-year-old Kenneth Chapin, the brother of her best friend, rapped at the window the night of Sept. 25, 1954. The teenage babysitter had been warned about admitting strangers in the house. But Kenneth was no stranger. He was active in Boy Scouts and was a regular church-goer. Once inside the house, Chapin attempted to force himself on Lynn. When she resisted, he killed her with a knife. Fearing that Stephen would tell his parents what he had witnessed, Chapin bludgeoned the boy to death in his bedroom.

The police found a length of crocheting yarn near the Goldberg residence. Chapin had used it to tie a piece of paper around the handle of the knife. A house-to-house search revealed that the Chapin family had the only matching ball of yarn. On Oct. 8, Kenneth confessed to the double murder. In March 1955, he was convicted of first-degree murder and was sentenced to die. A day before his scheduled execution, Chapin's sentence was commuted to life imprisonment, after Dr. Frederic Wertham pronounced the young man a schizophrenic and therefore not responsible for his actions.

Chapman, Mark David, 1955- , U.S. "We're going to live, or we're going to die. If we're dead, we're going to have to deal with that; if we're alive, we're going to have to deal with being alive." A few hours after he said those words, rock star and former Beatle John Lennon was shot to death by Mark David Chapman, a deranged fan who thought that he was Lennon.

Chapman, born in Texas and raised in Georgia, ran away from home when he was fourteen. He was away only a few weeks, but remained part of the drug scene for another two years. Becoming a Beatles fan as a teenager, he tried to emulate them with his own band. However, after Chapman became a born-again Christian, he was offended by Lennon's remark, "We're more popular than Jesus now." Thus, Chapman gave up the Beatles, as he had given up drugs, and used his spare time to work with children at the YMCA. Chapman's friends watched him become increasingly preoccupied with internal struggles concerning the sinfulness of the "Bad Mark." He moved around the country, working at various jobs and studying religions in his free time. He was arrested for armed robbery, kidnapping, and possession of drugs. He tried to commit suicide in 1977, and received psychological care. In 1979, he married a travel agent and moved to Hawaii, where he insisted that she never watch television or read newspapers. He frequently stood outside a Church of Scientology and shouted abuse, and month by month he became more irrational, although he kept that side of him hidden from most people. In 1980, he changed the name tag on his security guard's uniform to read "John Lennon," and on Oct. 23 he quit his job, signing out as John Lennon.

From that time, it became necessary for Chapman to get rid of the other Lennon. That other Lennon had dropped from the public eye and turned introspective. Chapman wanted the brash Lennon from the old days back again, so he became that Lennon. Chapman first bought a .38-caliber pistol. Then he borrowed $2,500 from a credit union

and flew to New York City on Dec. 6, 1980. He began to spend long hours stationed outside the Dakota, the apartment building where Lennon lived with his wife Yoko Ono and their son. On Dec. 8, Lennon emerged to go to a recording studio, and Chapman had him autograph his most recent album, *Double Fantasy*. Chapman stayed where he was as Lennon and Ono drove off, then turned to

John Lennon's killer, Mark David Chapman.

continue reading a copy of J. D. Salinger's *The Catcher in the Rye*. At 11 p.m. that night, Lennon and Ono returned to the Dakota. Chapman called out, "Mr. Lennon." Lennon looked up and Chapman shot him five times in the chest. Lennon died in a squad car as a patrolman tried to get him to a hospital.

After killing Lennon, Chapman sat down and returned to reading the Salinger novel. He was arrested and charged with second-degree murder. He told the police, "I have a small part in me that cannot understand the world and what goes on in it. I did not want to kill anybody, and I really don't know why I did..." His lawyer, Jonathan Marks, wanted him to plead not guilty by reason of insanity, but Chapman told the court that God had told him to confess to murder. He was sentenced on July 24, 1981, to twenty years to life in prison, with a recommendation that he be

treated psychiatrically. Even his own attorney asked the judge not to sentence him too lightly. "All reports came to the conclusion that he is not a sane man. It was not a sane crime. It was...a monstrously irrational killing." Chapman's only response to the sentencing was to read aloud a passage from *The Catcher in the Rye*. He was sent to Attica State Prison in upstate New York, where he was put to work as a janitor.

Charing Cross Trunk Murder, The, See: **Robinson, John.**

Charlton, Porter, b.1889, Italy. Porter Charlton was the son of Paul Charlton, who served as judge of the territorial court of Puerto Rico. A shy, withdrawn type who suffered from epileptic seizures, Charlton married a divorced woman named Mary Crittenden Scott Castle, the wealthy daughter of a San Francisco coal merchant who was also a minor star of the theater. The fiery Mrs. Castle was considerably older than Porter Charlton, and from the very beginning of their marriage there were quarrels and angry outbursts between them.

On June 10, 1910, a cable reached the U.S. with the news that Charlton had bludgeoned to death his wife with a crowbar while on a European tour, and the remains were found floating in a trunk on Lake Como, near the village of Moltrasio, Italy. The 21-year-old husband readily confessed, explaining that his wife's uncontrollable temper finally got the best of him. He seized a wooden mallet and had struck her over the head repeatedly. Two weeks later, police detectives arrested Charlton in Hoboken, N.J., as he disembarked from the German liner and onto U.S. shores. He was taken to the Hudson County Jail in Jersey City, where he languished for the next three years, while Italian authorities and the U.S. State Department attempted to resolve the delicate matter of extradition.

The case went before the U.S. Supreme Court which ruled that Charlton had to be returned to Italy to stand trial. In August 1913, the prisoner was transported to the jail at Como, Italy, but given the numerous court delays, and the outbreak of WWI, Charlton did not go to trial until Oct. 18, 1915, when he was found Guilty of murder and was sentenced to six years and eight months imprisonment. Given his epileptic conditions, and some lingering doubts about his sanity, Charlton served just twenty-nine days before earning a final release from custody.

Charriere, Henri-Antoine (AKA: **Papillon**), 1907-73, Fr. On the morning of Mar. 26, 1930, 24-year-old Roland Legrand was shot dead on the Boulevard de Clichy in Montmartre, Paris. Legrand was a pork-butcher by trade, who doubled as a pimp. His assailant was Henri Charriere, commonly known as Papillon, because of a bow tie he always wore and a butterfly tattooed on his chest.

Papillon lived off the earnings of Georgette Fourel, a 19-year-old prostitute he lived with in Montmartre. He supplemented his income by receiving and selling stolen goods, and trafficking in drugs. Legrand discussed Charriere's underworld activities with the police, and so was killed. George S. Goldstein identified Papillon as the murderer. The killer was tried, and on Oct. 28 was sentenced to penal servitude for life. On Dec. 22, 1931, he married Georgette Fourel as part of a strategy to avoid deportment to French Guiana. But the plan failed. Authorities detained him for a year in prison in Caen, then shipped him to Cayenne.

He spent three years in the penitentiary there before he escaped. He hid in a leper colony, then made his way by boat to Venezuela, where he lived among the natives near Maracaibo Bay. When French authorities recaptured Papillon, they sent him to the notorious and supposedly inescapable penal colony on Devil's Island and kept him in solitary confinement for two years. On his eighth attempt, Papillon escaped from Devil's Island and paddled his raft made of dried coconuts through shark-infested waters to Venezuela. He settled there, married, and became a restaurateur and Venezuelan citizen.

In 1969, 62-year-old Charriere published *Papillon,* his memoir of his adventures and escapes. The book became a best-seller, and in 1973 the movie of the same title premiered, starring Steve McQueen as Papillon.

Chase, Richard Trenton, 1950-80, U.S. A man who was once found with the blood of a cow covering his naked body confessed during his trial that he had drunk the blood of one of his six murder victims.

Richard Trenton Chase admitted not only to drinking blood, but also to killing six people, five by shooting them to death and then butchering them. The killing rampage occurred between Jan. 23 and 27, 1978, and Chase's five-month trial began in January 1979. It was in Palo Alto, Calif., after the venue had to be changed from Sacramento because of the widespread publicity. Farris Salamy, the public defender representing Chase, pleaded that Chase was not guilty by reason of insanity, but the jury, finding Chase sane, returned a verdict of Guilty on May 8, 1979, after deliberating for six hours over two days. He was sentenced

to life imprisonment and died in prison on Dec. 26, 1980.

Chenault, Marcus Wayne (AKA: **Servant Jacob**), 1951- , U.S. Just over six years after his son, Dr. Martin Luther King, Jr., was shot to death outside a Memphis, Tenn., motel, the Reverend Martin Luther King, Sr., watched, along with 400 others, as his wife, 69-year-old Alberta Williams King, was shot and killed at Ebenezer Baptist Church in Atlanta, Ga., by Marcus Wayne Chenault.

Chenault, a 23-year-old black Ohio State University dropout from Columbus, Ohio, had traveled by Greyhound bus from Dayton, Ohio, to shoot Reverend Martin Luther King, Sr., on June 30, 1974. Instead, Chenault shot Mrs. King, daughter of the church's founder Reverend A.D. Williams, in the face as she was playing the church organ. He then shot in the neck 69-year-old deacon Edward Boykin, who died later at Grady Hospital, and wounded 65-year-old Mrs. Jimmy Mitchell. The gunman yelled, "I'm taking over, I'm taking over," before church members managed to wrestle Chenault to the floor. He had fired all the bullets in the two handguns he carried. With the shooting spree ended, it was learned that Chenault's intended victim was only the second target on a list of ten assassinations he had hoped to commit.

In March 1973, Chenault met 70-year-old Hananiah E. Israel, who preached that only by killing all black ministers could black people be free. A month later, Chenault told the Reverend Billy Robinson that he planned to kill the Reverend Howard B. Washington in Akron, but he did not act on the threat. Two weeks prior to his rampage in Atlanta, Chenault had planned to kill the Reverend Jesse L. Jackson, whom investigators learned was number one on the gunman's hit list. A bus ticket to Chicago, where Jackson lives, was found in Chenault's apartment with the message, "Father's Day massacre canceled," written on it. Chenault, who called himself "Servant Jacob," informed the police that he was on a mission from his god to kill the Reverend King. These statements and the killer's actions led police to investigate Chenault's possible connection with the shooting deaths of Dayton, Ohio, ministers 56-year-old William Wright on May 12, 1974, and 29-year-old Eugene Johnson, Sr., on June 3, 1974. His lawyer, Randy Bacote, attempted to enter a plea of no contest, but Judge E.T. Brock entered Not Guilty pleas and Chenault stood trial.

At Chenault's trial, the defense tried to prove that the killer was insane at the time of the shooting, a contention that prosecutor Lewis Slaton was able to disprove by the testimony of two psychiatrists who stated that Chenault knew the difference between right and wrong. On Sept. 12,

1974, the jury in the court of Judge Luther Alverson took one hour and fifteen minutes to decide that Chenault was Guilty and sentence him to die in the electric chair. Upon hearing the jury's recommendation for capital punishment, Chenault blew kisses to the jurors and pointed his finger like a gun at Alverson and Slaton.

Chigango, Chief, prom. 1923, Rhodesia. In order to appease the Rain Goddess and bring an end to the drought that began in 1922, Chief Chigango ordered that his own son Mandusa be offered as a sacrifice to the great spirit Mwari. The sacrifice may or may not have ended the drought—the day after Mandusa was killed, it began to rain profusely—but it did bring an end to Chigango's reign as tribal chief.

Like his ancestors, Chigango, the chief of a Mtwara tribe village, believed in and followed the traditions concerning the Rain Goddess. Legend has it that the Mtwara god, Mwari, had given an earlier tribal chief a wife who was to remain a virgin throughout her lifetime. This woman became known as the Rain Goddess, and it was through her that the tribe would ask Mwari to send them rain. If no rain came even after offerings were made to Mwari, then it was a sign that someone had seduced the Rain Goddess, and that person must be sacrificed to Mwari. When the drought continued into January 1923, it was believed that Chigango's son was the man who had defiled the Rain Goddess, who was personified by a young girl chosen at birth. Instead of trusting members of his own village to carry out the human sacrifice, Chigango called upon another chief, Chiswiti, to handle the affair. The following night Mandusa was taken in his sleep to be burned alive.

Police in Mount Darwin learned of the murder from Mandusa's younger brother, who feared for his own life in the event that rains did not come. Seven tribesmen were arrested and tried for the murder, including Chigango, Chiswiti, and Chiriseri, a tribal leader. All were found Guilty of murder except Chiswiti, who was acquitted. Because of the circumstances of the crime, the death sentences were commuted.

Childers, Jimmy, 1961- , U.S. On July 9, 1978, 17-year-old Jimmy Childers of Pekin, Ill., arrived home late from a date. An argument ensued with his parents that escalated when mention was made of the boy's intention to marry the girl that winter. The fight ended with three dead at the hands of young Childers.

In a taped confession, Childers admitted killing his stepfather, 42-year-old Robert Rotramel, when the gun he was waving about went off. He then chased after his mother, 37-year-old Nora Rotramel, stabbing her to death with a knife in the kitchen, and finally using the knife to kill his 15-year-old brother, Warren Childers, as he tried to run out the front door. The confession, taken twenty-four hours after the killings, was played in court and convinced the jury to return a verdict of Guilty on Feb. 3, 1979.

Defense attorney Joseph Napoli had argued that Childers was temporarily insane, which was corroborated by two psychiatrists for the defense. However, two prosecution psychiatrists determined the boy to be perfectly capable of distinguishing right from wrong. Although tried as an adult, Childers was too young to receive the death penalty, but Judge James Heiple sentenced the youth to three terms of life imprisonment on Mar. 8, 1979. Childers burst into tears at hearing the sentence, just as he did upon hearing the jury's verdict.

Choi, David Puilum (AKA: **Choi; Tsoi Pui**), c.1952- , U.S. After allegedly stabbing a person to death in California, David Puilum Choi escaped capture and has since eluded the FBI. The one-time Chinese waiter is known for wearing flashy and trendy clothing as well as prescription glasses. Choi was last seen in San Jose, Calif., where a federal arrest warrant was issued on Nov. 18, 1985. At this writing, Choi is still at large.

Christie, Balm, prom. 1973, U.S. Balm Christie, a criminal with a long list of offenses beginning in the 1960s, shot and murdered his wife on Jan. 1, 1973. Earlier charges lodged against Christie included theft, assault and battery, and breaking and entering. Reputedly, Christie's past criminal activities and the strong objections of his wife's relatives were partially responsible for the friction within the household. Christie stood trial and was sentenced to prison. Balm Christie lived in the Kentucky-Tennessee mountains.

Christie, John Reginald Halliday (AKA: **Waddingham**), 1898-1953, Brit. One of the most horrific killers in modern British history, Christie was half monster, half human, although in appearance he seemed to be nothing more than a meek-mannered middle-class citizen. Christie lived in a grimy, grubby little house at 10 Rillington Place in Notting Hill Gate, North Kensington, London. In 1948,

Timothy John Evans, his wife Beryl, and baby daughter Geraldine rented the top floor of the Christie house (the Christies lived on the ground floor). On Nov. 5, 1949, Mrs. Evans' father visited with her and this was the last time she was seen alive. Police conducted a search and, on Dec. 2, 1949, the bodies of Mrs. Evans and her infant were found in a wash house in Rillington Place, both strangled to death. Evans, a 24-year-old, dim-witted truck driver, had walked into the small police station at Merthyr Tydfil, South Wales, to inform officers that he had found his wife dead in his apartment and he had placed her body down a drain. After the bodies were found, Evans was returned to London under guard and there he confessed to murdering his wife and child.

Evans was charged with murdering his child, but before he was brought to trial at the Old Bailey, he withdrew his confession. He insisted that Christie had performed the killings. Christie emphatically denied having anything to do with the deaths of Mrs. Evans and her child. Moreover, he and his wife appeared as witnesses for the prosecution and gave evidence that helped to convict Evans. He was sentenced to death and hanged at Pentonville Prison on Mar. 9, 1950. Mrs. Christie then disappeared. She was last seen alive on Dec. 12, 1952, and Christie gave nervous explanations for her absence, claiming she was visiting relatives or that she had gone on a vacation. He then left his apartment in early 1953, subletting the place to a couple named Reilly. These people were quickly evicted by the owner of the building, a Jamaican named Beresford Brown, who moved into the Christie residence.

On Mar. 24, 1953, Brown went into the kitchen of the Christie apartment and began looking for a beam behind the wall into which he could screw a bracket for a wall-mounted radio. He tore away a loose piece of wallpaper and discovered an opening in the wall, a sort of large closet that had been covered by a thin sheet of posterboard and then covered with wallpaper. Taking out the board, Brown saw that three bodies had been stuffed inside the hollow area. He immediately called the police. Another body was discovered beneath the floorboards, and officers unearthed the skeletal remains of two more corpses found in the garden. These were easy to detect when an officer noticed that a human bone was propping up a fence and the police merely dug at this spot to find the rest of the remains. All of the bodies and remains were that of women. The corpses found in the closet and the one beneath the floorboards in the front room were for the most part naked, and three had been wrapped in blankets. Contrary to most later reports, there was very little odor from the bodies and there was no "overpowering stench" which led to their discovery. All were dehydrated and the atmospheric conditions in the apartment kept the smell of the dead bodies to a minimum.

The body beneath the floorboards was Mrs. Ethel Christie, whose husband had left 10 Rillington Place three days earlier. Those in the cupboard area were all known prostitutes, Hectorina McLennan, twenty-six; Kathleen Maloney, twenty-six; and Rita Nelson, twenty-five. The remains found in the garden were subsequently identified as those of Ruth Fuerst, an Austrian girl who had been murdered by Christie in 1943, and Muriel Eady, a girl who had worked with Christie at the Ultra Radio Factory in Park Royal in 1944. The shocking story of the mild-mannered mass murderer broke just at the time when police were conducting a nationwide search for Christie. He was found on Mar. 31, 1953, by Constable Ledger as he stood near Putney Bridge, watching a group of children at play. Christie, bald, wearing horn-rimmed glasses over weak eyes, with a flabby, middle-aged body, offered no resistance. He quickly confessed to the murders of the six women, saying that his first victim had been the Fuerst girl, followed by Muriel Eady. Christie stated that he strangled the Fuerst girl while he was having sex with her. He had not murdered for nine years but he suddenly went on a murder spree in late 1952, luring the prostitutes to his apartment when his wife was away and, after killing them, raping the corpses. He detailed his necrophiliac acts, which made him appear to be all the more inhuman. He had murdered his wife on Dec. 14, 1952, Christie said, as an "act of mercy." He could no longer bear to witness her "convulsive attacks"—she suffered from some sort of undefined malady—and so, when she went into one of her fits while they were still in bed, Christie grabbed one of her stockings, rolled over, and strangled her with it.

Sir Francis Camps, one of England's most brilliant pathologists, examined Christie and his murders in minute detail. He learned that when Christie had brought his prostitute victims to his flat, he would ply the women with liquor. When they were drunk, he'd get them to sit in a chair with a canopy, under which he had affixed a gas pipe. He would then turn on the gas, and, when they were unconscious, strangle the women, then rape them. The trick with the gas explained the carbon monoxide Camps found in the blood of the three women hidden in the kitchen enclosure. But there were strange sexual undertones to this case which puzzled Camps. He found that all three prostitutes were naked, but were wearing what amounted to handmade diapers. Semen had been found in them, as well as in an old pair of Christie's shoes, indicating that he had ejaculated following the murder-rapes. A tin can was found in the kitchen enclosure, and inside of this was found four separate tufts of pubic hair which Christie had plucked from his victims and preserved, but for what purpose Camps could not determine.

Left, John Reginald Halliday Christie, British mass murderer. Right, Timothy John Evans, hanged in 1950 for murders Christie may have committed.
Below, 10 Rillingon Place, Christie's house of murder; bodies were hidden behind walls, under the floorboards, in the garden.

Left, Christie with his wife Ethel, whom he also murdered, putting her body beneath the floorboards; right, Christie in wax at Madame Tussaud's.

Camps probed deeper into the sexual mysteries of John Reginald Halliday Christie, discovering that the myopic, always frail Christie had had psychological problems rooted in childhood. Born in Boothstown, Yorkshire, in April 1898, the son of carpet designer Ernest Christie, and one of seven children, Christie was treated with unloving harshness by his martinet father. He was disciplined often for the slightest infractions. Introverted, weak, the boy was labeled a "sissy" by his classmates who made fun of his poor eyesight. He took to stealing small things which caused him to be returned home by constables. His father, at these times, responded with the typical Victorian action, a beating. At the age of fifteen in 1913, Christie quit school and took a job clerking for the Halifax Borough Police, but he was fired when he was suspected of stealing small items. About this time, Christie was seduced by an older girl who later made fun of him when he could not finish the sex act. The girl spread the story and Christie was the butt of sex jokes among his peers who called him "Can't Do It Christie." He was confined at home for a time, ill again. Christie's confession was punctuated repeatedly by statements claiming his lifelong illnesses, and it was apparent to Camps that he was a confirmed hypochondriac.

Following a severe bout with pneumonia, Christie claimed, he went to France in 1915, serving in the trenches until he was blown out of a trench and inhaled mustard gas, which caused him to go blind for several months and lose his voice for three years. This was attributed to hysteria and not physical damage received when the artillery shell blew him out of a trench. Whenever Christie was excited after that, he would lose his voice or it would rise to a high whine. In 1920, Christie met and married his wife Ethel, a union which produced no children. Christie claimed that he did not have sex with his wife for two years following the marriage and continued to have a pervasive feeling of inadequacy. Following a quarrel with his wife in 1923, the couple separated and Christie lost his voice completely, he claimed.

Bad luck followed Christie wherever he went, he said in his confession. In 1934, a hit-and-run driver knocked him down, injuring his head, knee, and collar bone. Worse luck, most brought about by Christie himself, dogged his work life. He seldom kept a steady job, the longest being five years while working as a clerk for a transport company. He was a postal employee at one time, but it was proved that he stole money orders and he was sent to prison for seven months. During his 1923 separation from his wife, Christie was imprisoned briefly for false pretense; he had falsified documents which claimed that he was a rich man at one time but had lost his money. He went to Brixton and Battersea and there put on the air of a once-wealthy man who was down on his luck. When a woman rebuffed

his advances, Christie hit her on the head with a cricket bat and was arrested and sent to prison once more.

During WWII, Christie was a member of the War Reserve Police, a blackout warden who marched about his neighborhood pumped up with authority. He delighted in turning in those who ignored blackout rules. In 1943, his wife went to visit relatives in Sheffield, and it was at this time that Christie committed his first murder, bringing Ruth Fuerst home with him and murdering her, burying her corpse in the back yard. Although Christie admitted to murdering the six women, he was contradictory about Mrs. Evans and her child. He claimed that he found Mrs. Evans unconscious in her flat after she had quarreled with her husband about "a blonde woman." She had tried to commit suicide by turning on the gas, Christie said. He gave her a cup of tea and told her to calm down.

Mrs. Evans tried to kill herself once more, Christie said, and he again came to her rescue. Then she said she was pregnant and Christie, who had no medical knowledge, offered to perform the abortion she desired. She panicked when he was applying the gas to make her unconscious prior to the operation and thus died. He varied this tale by saying that Mrs. Evans, despondent over her husband's sexual escapades, asked Christie if he would kill her since she had botched two other suicide attempts. She said he could have sexual intercourse with her, Christie claimed, if he would but help her die. He strangled her, Christie said at one point, and *then* had sexual intercourse with her corpse. When Evans returned home, Christie told him that she had gassed herself and that he had best flee since authorities would think Evans murdered his wife. Evans then reportedly murdered his child and sold off the household furniture before fleeing. His confusing statements throughout his trial concerning the death of the Evans child and his wife are impossible to decipher at this time.

Following the deaths of the three prostitutes, Christie said he sold his wife's wedding ring and the household furniture, and wandered about London with a total loss of memory. When he was arrested, he said, he had been sleeping in a cheap hotel. At the time he looked like a common tramp with dirty clothes, unshaven beard, and empty pockets. Christie was tried at the Old Bailey for three days, June 22-25, 1953, before Justice Fennemore. The killer was prosecuted by Sir Lionel Heald, then attorney general, and defended by Derek Curtis Bennett. Little defense could be offered on Christie's behalf, so Bennett opted to plead his client insane. Several medical experts examined Christie and testified that he was sane. The jury returned a verdict of Guilty and Christie was sentenced to death. He was hanged at Pentonville Prison on July 15, 1953.

The conviction and execution of the monster Christie left

many believing that Timothy Evans' conviction and hanging was a gross miscarriage of justice, that he had been executed for a crime that Christie himself had committed, the murder of Mrs. Beryl Evans, although considerable doubt exists that Christie killed the Evans child. This is the one murder that he said he did not commit, and the one murder that Evans admitted committing. The Evans case remains a baffling mystery, which is exactly the way Christie wanted it, for he in no way cleared up the Evans murders but, through his whining statements, seemed to add even more confusion as to who was the real killer of Mrs. Evans and her child. Such were Christie's strange perversions that he would be content to go to the hangman knowing that he had created a lingering doubt in the minds of those who sent Timothy Evans to his death. From the grave, Christie would nag the consciences of good men, whereas he was without conscience altogether.

Christofi, Styllou, 1900-54, Brit. A Greek Cypriot peasant woman was charged in 1924 with murdering her mother-in-law by jamming a burning stick down her throat, but a jury acquitted her. The woman, Mrs. Styllou Christofi, continued to live with her husband and to raise her son, Stavros Christofi, in the island's matriarchal tradition.

In 1937, Stavros went to England, where he soon married a German refugee named Hella Bleicher. They had three children, and by July 1953, Mrs. Christofi had saved enough money to visit them in England. She moved into Stavros' Hampstead apartment and tried to take charge of his life. She was particularly scathing about Hella and the way she spent money. Within days, Hella, who was to take the children to visit her parents in Germany, told her husband that if his mother was there on her return, she would leave him.

That evening, July 29, 1954, as Hella prepared to take a bath in the basement apartment, Mrs. Christofi grabbed a heavy ash plate from the stove and rushed into the bathroom, where she slammed it down on her daughter-in-law's head. She then dragged her unconscious into the kitchen, where she strangled her to death with a scarf. To hide the crime, she poured kerosene over the corpse and tried to set fire to it. A neighbor, a John Young, happened to look down through the glass doors into the basement entrance to the kitchen. He saw the woman working with the fire but, assuming that the waxy-looking figure on the floor was a mannequin, he went on his way. Soon thereafter, Mrs. Christofi began to fear that the flames were getting out of control. She ran out into the street and stopped a car, begging, "Please come! Fire burning, children sleeping!" Mr. and Mrs. Burstoff ran into the

kitchen, saw blood on the floor, the smoldering figure, and called the police.

Mrs. Christofi tried to tell the constable that she had been wakened in the night and found Hella burning, but her bed had not been slept in and she inadvertently added, "My

Mrs. Styllou Christofi, strangler.

son married Germany girl he like, plenty clothes, plenty shoes, babies going to Germany." Mrs. Christofi was charged with murder. Her attorney tried to persuade her to plead insanity, especially in light of the earlier death of her mother-in-law, but she would not. She was convicted of murder and executed on Dec. 13, 1954.

Chung Yi Miao, 1900-28, Brit. Chung Yi Miao, a 28-year-old Chinese-American, married Wai Sheung Siu, the daughter of a wealthy merchant from Hong Kong, in New York in May 1928. Their whirlwind courtship and subsequent marriage ended in murder during a two-month honeymoon trip abroad in June. After a brief stop in Edinburgh, the couple continued on to England where they desired to tour the English Lake District. They arrived at the Grange-In-Borrowdale Gates Hotel, Cumberland on June 18, 1928.

The next day the couple went out for a walk, but the husband returned to his hotel alone with the explanation that Wai Sheung had gone on toward Keswick to do some shopping. When she did not return that night he made inquiries with the police. By this time a local farmer had notified constables from the Southport Borough station that he had found a young woman lying dead under a tree. She was clad in a very expensive fur coat.

When questioned by police at his hotel room, Chung revealed more information than what he would have otherwise known if he had not been mixed up in her death. A search of his suitcase turned up two rolls of undeveloped film. When the contents were emptied out, Wai Sheung's diamond wedding ring and a diamond solitaire tumbled out. It was the same jewelry she had been wearing when she left the hotel. The young law student was charged with murder and placed on trial at the Carlisle Assizes on Nov. 22, 1928. The trial lasted just three days, after which a Guilty verdict was returned. Chung Miao was hanged at the Strangeways Jail in Manchester on Dec. 6, 1928. The motive for the murder, according to a published article in the *Sunday Express* of Mar. 24, 1929, was Wai Sheung's inability to bear her husband children.

Church, Harvey, 1898-1922, U.S. Guards carried Harvey Church to the gallows in a kitchen chair. He could neither move nor speak, and in his last days was force-fed through a tube. Church, according to psychiatrists, became paralyzed with fear, when, on Dec. 21, 1921, Judge John R. Caverly had pronounced the death sentence. If he was trying to cheat the hangman, it did not work.

Known as the "Twin-Six" murderer, Church, at 135 pounds, seemed incapable of killing—least of all the two burly car salesmen he murdered on Sept. 9, 1921. Church lived on the West Side with his aging mother, working as a brakeman for the Chicago and Northwestern Railway.

At 4 a.m. on the morning of Sept. 10, a black Packard sedan stopped on the Lake Street bridge over the Des Plaines River between west suburban Maywood and River Forest. The driver of the car was observed dropping a large weighted object over the stone railing and into the river. Thinking it was just a prank, the pedestrians who witnessed it continued on. Later that morning, 10-year-old William Baker of nearby Melrose Park identified the mysterious object as a man. With a grappling hook, the body was fished out by suburban police.

They found a cord wrapped around the victim's neck and severe cuts on the skull. The victim's hands were shackled. Chicago police were contacted and an effort was made to identify the large-boned man. The mystery was solved when the Chicago sales office of the Packard Automobile Company reported that two salesmen—Bernard J. Daugherty and Carl Ausmus—were missing after selling a car to Harvey Church of West Fulton Street. A company employee, Edward Skelba, was sent to locate the salesmen, but all he found was a note tied to the steering wheel of a roadster. It read: "Ed, go back to office. Will come in later."

Church had just purchased a twin-six Packard for $5,400, explaining that the car was for his father in Adams, Wis. He asked the two salesmen to accompany him to the Madison-Kedzie State Bank where he would withdraw the money, but first he had to get his passbook at home.

Daugherty, a former football star and war hero, followed Church into the basement while Ausmus waited outside. In the basement, Church pulled a gun on the salesman, handcuffed him, and strangled him with a rope. He then beat him with a baseball bat.

He followed the same procedure with Ausmus, who entered the house to see about the delay. Church then buried Ausmus in a shallow grave in the garage, beneath the broken-down Harroun automobile he wanted to replace, and, early next morning, dropped the mangled body of Daugherty into the river.

When police detectives entered the Fulton Street house, Church was out joyriding with his mother. The baseball bat, a hatchet, and a trail of blood led the police to where Ausmus' body had been buried hours earlier. The salesmen's hats were found on the floor. Police worked through the night excavating the yard.

Mother and son were located in Adams, Wis. When presented with the evidence, the old woman fainted, but she would later stand by her son's alibi. "My mother was with me at the time. She saw the payment," Church said.

How such a small man alone could easily overpower two men, one a former athlete, baffled police. They were convinced Church had help in committing the crime, but he neither named accomplices nor confessed.

Back in Chicago, Church was interrogated but he refused to bend. The police, in frustration, took him back to the scene of the crime, forced him to his hands and knees, and pressed his face into the empty gravesite. Only later, upon seeing the corpse, did Church finally crack. He claimed that Leon Parks and Clarence Wilder had helped him. The two men, it turned out, were clearly not involved.

Church then said he killed the men out of fear, that a mysterious telephone caller threatened to kill his father unless he produced a new car before Sept. 10. Nonetheless, despite expert testimony that he was deranged, Harvey Church was convicted of the "twin-six" murders. During the trial, he slipped into a stupor, impervious to all efforts to rouse him—even being jabbed with needles and touched on the nose with a lighted cigar evoked no response.

Defense attorneys argued for a new trial, but Judge Kickham Scanlan sustained the death sentence. At the last minute, attorneys Frank Tyrrell and J.C. McGloon ran from court to court frantically trying to procure a written order. They found Judge Caverly and pleaded for a little more time, but the judge declined, at the moment when guards were carrying Church from his cell in a kitchen chair.

Cibuku, Gazi, 1947-   , U.S. Numerous plastic bags

strewn about a field in Detroit, Mich., led to the arrest of a 23-year-old cook from Albania. Inside the bags were the remains of 25-year-old Sandra Sue Snell, whose body was identified from fingerprints in police files taken from a check she had bounced in December 1969, the year before her death.

The cook, Gazi Cibuku, was arrested along with his roommate and fellow countryman, 21-year-old Accra Khan. Khan was arrested in New York. Cibuku admitted that he shot Snell to death after she had attacked him with a knife during a fight over money. He denied dismembering the woman's body, which he said he had placed in a closet, accusing Khan of doing so. Khan, in turn, testified that he had returned from work one evening to find Snell's body in the closet, and two nights later noticed that her body had been cut up and placed into four bags. First-degree murder charges against Khan were dismissed by the judge, but Cibuku was sentenced to forty years in prison.

Ciucci, Vincent, 1925-62, U.S. Thinking to rid himself of a burdensome family, Vincent Ciucci, on the night of Dec. 4, 1953, chloroformed his wife Anne and three children, then shot each one in the head. He then set fire to his Chicago, Ill., apartment, a three-room affair which was behind his grocery store. He intended to collect the

Vincent Ciucci, left, who murdered his family, is shown with lawyer at his 1954 trial.

insurance money and marry another woman. Ciucci remained in the burning apartment until the firemen arrived. He then stumbled outside, pretending to be overcome with smoke, feigning surprise that his entire family was dead. The murder plan was idiotic. Ciucci had ignored the basic routine of medical examiners, who soon reported that the Ciucci family members had been shot in

the head. He believed that the burned flesh of his victims would hide the bullet wounds.

Detectives confronted Ciucci, but he denied having anything to do with the killings. "I admit that I am a gambler," he blurted at police headquarters, "and I like to fool around with women, but I wouldn't do a thing like that. How could a man kill his own children? He would kill himself instead!" He refused to admit his guilt, even stating at his trial that unknown killers had framed him by sneaking into his apartment, shooting his wife and children to death and then setting the house on fire. When asked how he could not have heard four shots being fired, Ciucci mumbled something about being a "heavy sleeper." Ciucci was convicted and given a death sentence. After a number of appeals, Ciucci was sent to the electric chair in 1962.

Clark, David Scott, 1954- , U.S. Believing that his roommate was trying to steal his tree-trimming business from him, David Scott Clark murdered the man on Christmas Day 1978. The next day all but the torso of 27-year-old Lynn Allen Lizer was recovered from three trash containers in Lake Worth, Fla.

Clark confessed to dismembering Lizer, whose blood was discovered in the apartment and in Clark's car, under a plea-bargain agreement with prosecutors, whereby he was convicted in March 1981, of second-degree, rather than first-degree, murder. Clark was sentenced to life

David Scott Clark

imprisonment, and had served more than seven and one-half years as a model prisoner before he escaped on Dec. 27, 1988. Because of Clark's prison record, he had been transferred to the Brooksville Road Prison, designed for inmates unlikely to escape or pose a threat of danger. His escape came while he and four other prisoners, watched by an unarmed guard, were mowing the grass alongside the road. Clark ignored the guard's commands to come back and fled into the woods.

Clark, Douglas Daniel (AKA: **The Sunset Slayer**), 1959- , and **Bundy, Carol**, 1943- , U.S. Carol Mary Bundy was anxious to please the depraved sexual fantasies of her young lover, Daniel Clark. In 1980, Clark and Bundy committed a series of grisly sex murders in Los Angeles. Bundy would cruise the Sunset Strip in search of blonde prostitutes for Clark to allegedly shoot and then engage in sexual acts with the corpse.

By his own estimate, Clark, a former factory worker, killed fifty women. According to Bundy, he hoped to double that figure before his arrest on Aug. 11, 1980. No one could say with absolute certainty just how many women he killed, but Clark was officially charged with six murders when his trial opened in Los Angeles in January 1983. On Feb. 15 the jury sentenced him to die in the gas chamber. He remains on Death Row. Bundy, a former Burbank nurse and the mother of two children, was sentenced to fifty-two years in prison for murdering her former lover John Robert Murray in 1980, and then decapitating him.

Clark, Joseph Reginald Victor (AKA: **Kennedy**), c.1907-29, Brit. Upon his return to England in 1927, after living with relatives in the U.S., Joseph Reginald Victor Clark became a parasite on women. He had a number of intimate relations with women who willingly gave him money. Clark persuaded one to give him money so that she could have a well-dressed escort; another, in Nova Scotia, regularly sent him cash; and at one point, he dated four sisters in Liverpool, England, without any of them knowing about the others until he tried to marry the youngest girl by using the birth certificate of the eldest sister. In fury at the failure of his plan, Clark tried to strangle the youngest sister with a pajama belt. No charges were brought for the assault.

Clark was using the last name of Kennedy when he met Alice Fontaine and became a lodger at her mother's home in Liverpool, living rent-free and constantly borrowing money. But when Fontaine discovered a letter from one of Clark's former girlfriends, she told him to leave. He returned, however, in October 1928, and strangled Alice Fontaine's mother, and again tried to use a pajama belt to murder his former sweetheart. At the Liverpool Assizes Court on Feb. 3, 1929, Clark was tried for murder. His lawyer, Basil Nield, pleaded insanity for Clark, but the defendant chose to plead guilty and the trial was over. Only four-and-one-half minutes had elapsed from the opening of the trial till the close when Clark was sentenced to death—one of the quickest murder trials on record.

Clark, Lorraine, 1926- , U.S. Lorraine and Melvin Clark began to draw apart after ten years of marriage. The night of Apr. 10, 1954, Melvin came home early and found his wife in bed with another man. Lorraine had been active in a new pastime in Amesbury, Mass.—wife swapping. A group would get together, throw their house keys in a bowl, and then each choose a key and go with its owner for the evening. When Melvin found his wife with her lover, the couple quarreled. Lorraine Clark ended by stabbing her husband with a knitting needle. That gave her time to grab the gun she kept at their lakeside home, and she shot Melvin twice.

When Lorraine realized that she had killed her husband, she set about methodically disposing of the body. She trussed it in chicken wire to make a small parcel. After transporting it by car to the Merrimack River, she tied weights to it and dumped it from a bridge. Assuming that the motion of the tidal river would carry the corpse out to sea, Lorraine pretended to friends and neighbors that her husband had left after a major quarrel. She backed up this story by suing Melvin for divorce on grounds of cruelty. But on June 2, Melvin's badly decomposed body was found in the marshlands by a birdwatcher, and it was identified by its fingerprints.

When the police asked Lorraine for an expla-

U.S. murderer Lorraine Clark.

nation of the bullet holes in her husband's body, she confessed to killing him. Although she was indicted for first-degree murder, she was found Guilty of second-degree murder and sentenced to life in prison.

Clark, Michael, 1949-65, U.S. A 16-year-old boy decided to play "king of the hill" overlooking a California freeway north of Los Angeles, where Mexican bandit Solomon Pico had fired at stagecoaches more than a century ago. Clark's "game," however, played in Spring 1965, involved his father's powerful Swedish Mauser deer rifle and armor-piercing bullets aimed at unsuspecting drivers.

Michael Clark stole his family's Cadillac and drove about 150 miles north along the California coastline to just outside Santa Maria, where he rammed the car into a guard rail on Route 101. From a vantage point on top of a nearby hill, Clark opened fire at 6 a.m. the next morning on the freeway below. He missed the first driver but shot the second, William Reida, through the neck, seriously wounding him.

Another shot hit Reida's 5-year-old son, Kevin Reida, in the head and killed him. Reida's wife managed to flag down two passing cars, but Clark shot and killed each driver before they could help the woman. While Mrs. Reida, who did not know how to drive, steered the car down the road, Clark continued to shoot at passing motorists. No one else was killed, but three others, including a police officer, were wounded by bullets, and six others were struck by flying glass. At 8:30 a.m., the siege came to an end as police and civilians closed in on Clark. Clark yelled, "Come and get me," then pointed the rifle at his forehead and fired. It was never determined why a seemingly normal and happy youth had gone berserk.

Clark, Dr. Ronald E., c.1913- , U.S. Dr. Ronald Clark was granted a license to practice medicine in the state of Michigan in 1954. Four years later, his wife committed him to the state mental hospital following a series of incidents that endangered the lives of several of his female patients. The same year that Dr. Clark opened his practice, he was accused of raping two women after giving them an anesthetic. A third woman complained to the police that Clark had performed an unauthorized abortion on her.

After two and a half months in the state hospital, Clark was permitted to return to his practice in Farmington Township near Detroit, but the complaints continued. By the time of his arrest on Nov. 16, 1967, Ronald Clark had had his license revoked four times, once for what officials called "gross moral conduct," twice for "moral turpitude," and a fourth time for unspecified charges. Three patients died in Clark's office from drug overdoses, and two girls, aged eleven and fifteen, were molested. Yet the Michigan State Board of Registration had reinstated Clark in each instance.

On Nov. 3, 1967, a policeman found the body of Mrs. Grace Neil, forty-three, in Dr. Clark's office after he noticed an illegally parked hearse outside. Neil had worked for Clark as a part-time office assistant. Her death was the result of a lethal dose of sodium pentothal that Dr. Clark administered. It was the second time in less than a year that one of Clark's female employees died under mysterious circumstances. On Mar. 20, 63-year-old Hannah Bowerbank of Detroit also died from a drug overdose.

Dr. Clark was arrested on Nov. 16, 1967, outside Port Austin, Mich., 125 miles from Detroit. He was captured in deep snow after a bloodhound was put on his trail. Oakland County prosecutor S. Jerome Bronson announced that his office would investigate six other deaths that might have been linked to "therapeutic misadventure" on the part of Dr. Clark.

Clark was charged with manslaughter and held on a $50,000 bond, but after considering the evidence in the case of Mrs. Bowerbank, the judge ordered the defendant arraigned on first-degree murder charges. In a plea-bargaining arrangement engineered by defense attorney Philip E. Rowston, Dr. Clark offered to plead guilty to manslaughter to reduce the severity of sentence. He received three to fifteen years at the state prison in Southern Michigan.

Clarke, Philmore, 1918- , U.S. A rejected lover murdered his ex-girlfriend and dumped the body in the Anacostia River where it was laden with black silica slag.

Philmore Clarke, a 40-year-old carpenter, was dating a divorcee, Ruth Reeves, a 38-year-old elevator operator who worked in Washington, D.C., at the time she cut off her relationship with him and began seeing another man. Enraged, Clarke strangled Reeves on Sept. 7, 1958, left the body in her house, and then visited another girlfriend, who provided his alibi that night. Slipping out of her house, he then picked up the body, attached concrete weights to it, and dumped it in the river.

A building engineer where Reeves worked noticed a newspaper article about an unidentified body found on Sept. 8 in the Anacostia River. When she failed to show up for work, he notified police. Police found Clarke's picture at Reeves's home, and, in a search of his residence, they discovered baling wire and holes where slabs of concrete had been removed from the front of the house, materials identical to the concrete slab and wire fastened to the dead woman's leg. On Sept. 9, Clarke was arrested, but he refused to confess. However, the police case against Clarke grew stronger after black silica slag, a residue from industrial furnaces, was found on Clarke's shoes, in the car he drove, and on Reeves's clothing. Police also learned that a power company's refuse containing slag had been put on the road near where the body was found.

Clarke was tried on Dec. 9, and convicted of second-degree murder. He received a five- to twenty-five-year sentence.

Clements, Dr. Robert George, 1890-1947, Brit. At first, the examining physicians at the Astley Nursing Home in Southport, Lancashire concluded that the fourth Mrs. Clements died from myeloid leukemia. But Dr. Andrew Brown, the Staff Surgeon, noticed the "pin-point" positioning of the pupils of her eye—an indication of morphine poisoning. Thus, the death of wealthy heiress Amy

Victoria Burnett Clements on May 27, 1947 ended the murder spree of husband George, a Belfast doctor who belonged to the Royal College of Surgeons.

During a thirty-five-year span, Dr. Clements married and killed four wives, three of whom were quite wealthy. In 1912 he joined hands with Edyth Anna Mercier, who expired in 1920, about the same time as her fortune. A year later, he married Mary McLeery, who lasted until 1925 when her death was occasioned by what Dr. Clements described as endocarditis. Katherine Burke, his third wife, was the only poor woman in the group. The third Mrs. Clements died in 1939 from cancer, arousing suspicion of the police. Before an autopsy could be conducted, the body was cremated.

Wife murderer Robert Clements.

The police concluded that Clements had turned his fourth wife into a morphine addict. A second postmortem examination was ordered, and the examiners concluded that she had been poisoned. When the police arrived at his Southport home, they found Clements dead. He had poisoned himself with cyanide, leaving behind a note which read in part: "To whom it may concern...I can no longer tolerate the diabolical insults to which I have been recently exposed."

Clutter Family Killings, See: Hickock, Richard Eugene.

Codarre, Edwin, 1930- , U.S. When 13-year-old Edwin Codarre of New York City was led from the courtroom to begin his sentence at Sing Sing Prison, he wore long pants for the first time since the trial began.

Codarre murdered 10-year-old Elizabeth Voigt on a road near Fishkill, N.Y. Her body was found the next day partially concealed under a pile of brush. She had been sexually assaulted and bludgeoned to death.

Elizabeth's parents owned a dairy farm near a Kiwanis Boys Farm Camp where their son Arno was spending the summer, along with boys from the city, including Edwin Codarre. John Horton, a 70-year-old neighbor, saw Edwin walking along the road where the corpse was found. He led detectives to the camp.

Codarre was arrested on Aug. 14, 1943, after breaking down under questioning. He admitted that he sexually assaulted Elizabeth as they walked through a secluded area. A blow to the larynx with a large stone caused her death. Codarre said they were looking for Arno at the time.

When the case went to trial in November 1943, Edwin Codarre pleaded not guilty, but later changed his plea to guilty in hopes of a reduced sentence. Judge J. Gordon Flannery of Dutchess County sentenced him to thirty years, of which he served nearly twenty-three before his parole on July 26, 1966.

Coetzee, Jacobus Hendrik, prom. 1935, S. Afri. A police officer with a bright career was sent to investigate the murder of a pregnant girl, a murder he himself had committed on Jan. 31, 1935.

The victim, Gertrina Petrusina Opperman, worked as a nurse at a farm 126 miles from Pretoria. She met Jacobus Hendrik Coetzee, a detective sergeant with the Railway Police, at a local dance in Summer 1934. One night two weeks later, on July 17, her employer discovered them together in bed. Opperman became pregnant, and Coetzee wrote her a letter two days before her death which said, "...Everything is still arranged. We will then talk."

The girl's body was found, bruised and with a bullet wound to the head, nineteen miles from Pretoria. The baby, which had been due in February, was born just before she died, but it did not survive. Alerted to the murder, Coetzee and another officer went to investigate. When Opperman's employer heard about the murder, he called the police, thinking it might be the nurse. He identified the body and turned over the damning letter. Coetzee was arrested on Feb. 3, and tried on murder charges in May 1935. During the trial, he said that although he was not the baby's father, he had offered to support it. The jury found Coetzee Guilty but recommended mercy because the girl had falsely tried to pin him with paternity. Coetzee was sentenced to imprisonment with hard labor for life. He was released on Feb. 25, 1947.

Coffelt, Elijah, prom. 1947, U.S. Elijah Coffelt shot his 21-year-old nephew, killing him, because they both liked the same woman. Both men were allegedly drinking at the time. Coffelt then turned himself in to police in Washington, Ky. In November 1947, he was convicted on murder charges and sentenced to life imprisonment.

Cohen, Ronald John Vivian, 1929- , S. Afri. Ronald Cohen was a self-made man. The 41-year-old millionaire owned and operated a lucrative finance company that bankrolled various South African building projects. In 1963, he married for the second time. His wife Susan Cohen was considerably younger, but she ran the affairs of the Cohen household in a competent manner. Seven years later, in a moment of insanity, Ronald killed his young bride.

The murder occurred on Apr. 5, 1970. Cohen roused his housekeeper from a deep sleep to tell her that a home invader had assaulted them, and that Susan was dead. The police found no signs of upheaval that bore out the presence of an intruder. Further, there were scratches on Cohen's arms which indicated that he was the assailant Susan had unsuccessfully tried to fend off.

There was no evidence of rape or robbery, therefore police concluded that Cohen's motive was purely rage. Arrested and tried in Cape Town, Cohen pleaded loss of memory and an anguished mental state for his actions. He was sentenced to twelve years in prison under the terms of the "diminished responsibility" statutes.

Colby, Robert A., 1922- , Ger. In June 1945, Robert Colby, twenty-three, of Geetingsville, Ind., was stationed in Germany with the U.S. Army. On June 10, he went AWOL and was found near Wiesbaden, Germany, outside his unit's restricted area. His company commander, Captain Richard J. Brown, directed that he be punished with four days at hard labor after training hours. That evening, Colby worked until 10 p.m., and then went to his tent and got a rifle. Going to the officer's area, he shot Captain Brown and First Lieutenant Donald H. Wade, firing four times at the men. Both men died within an hour. Colby then turned over his rifle to a sergeant, saying, "I shot the old man, but didn't want to shoot the lieutenant."

Colby was tried by a general court-martial on June 23 and sentenced to death. The sentence was approved by a divisional commander and by General Dwight D. Eisenhower on Aug. 29. In December 1945, Colby's sentence was commuted to life at hard labor by General Joseph T. McNarney, commander of the U.S. forces in Europe.

Collins, James Thomas, 1900- , Brit. On June 13, 1926, 69-year-old grandmother Janie Tremayne Swift, her 35-year-old daughter Janie Stemp, and her 13-year-old granddaughter Peggy Stemp were picnicking in King's Woods near Ashford when a serviceman approached them with a rifle and shot all three to death. The 26-year-old army private, James Thomas Collins, picked up the body of Peggy Stemp, carried it to their car parked nearby, and dumped the corpse in a ditch several miles down the highway.

London police later received an anonymous telephone call from a man who told them they could find three badly injured bodies near the road between Ashford and Chatham. The unknown caller was James Thomas Collins. When police arrived at the picnic site, Swift still held in her hand the sandwich she had been eating the moment she died.

Collins was taken into custody in London after he pulled his gun on a policeman and engaged others in a chase and shootout. Filled with remorse, he later confessed to shooting the three women.

Collins was convicted but determined insane. Presiding Justice John Anthony Hawke sentenced him to Broadmoor hospital for the mentally insane.

Collins, John Norman (AKA: **The Ypsilanti Ripper**), 1947- , U.S. Between July 1967 and July 1969, seven young women were found raped and murdered near the campus of the University of Michigan. The communities of Ann Arbor and Ypsilanti recoiled in horror. Before the identity of the killer was learned, police officials desperate for information brought in European psychic Peter Hurkos to lend his talents to the investigation.

The killing rampage began on July 10, 1967, when Mary Fleszar, a student at Eastern Michigan University (EMU), disappeared. Her mutilated body was found on Aug. 7 by two teenagers in Superior Township. The killer struck again on July 1, 1968, when 20-year-old Joan Schell disappeared after accepting a ride from a stranger driving a red car. Her body was found five days later by construction workers in Ann Arbor. It, too, bore evidence of sexual assault. In 1969, the unknown killer, no doubt encouraged by the lack of progress in the police investigation, stepped up his attacks. Between March and June, four more women were killed: Jane Mixer, a student at EMU; Maralynn Skelton, who was reputed to be a drug abuser; Dawn Basom, thirteen; and Alice Elizabeth Kalom, a recent college graduate. Peter Hurkos entered the investigation at this point. While he could not positively identify the killer, he guessed that the man was about twenty-five, heavily built, and would strike again.

He did, one more time. On July 26, the body of Karen Sue Beineman, an 18-year-old freshman at EMU, was found near a wooded gully. Eyewitnesses reported that Beineman had accepted a ride from a man on a motorcycle three days earlier. The police checked the available leads and identified 22-year-old John Norman Collins of Center Line, Mich., who attended classes at EMU. His aberrant behavior was well known. An average student, Collins was preoccupied with women. One of his girlfriends said he was oversexed. He was positively identified as the "Ripper" when police found hair clippings that matched those found in the briefs of the last victim, Karen Beineman. The suspect had recently cut the hair of the children of State Police Sergeant David Leik. Collins was the nephew of Officer Leik's wife. He was arrested on July 31, 1969.

Described as a "bondage freak" who had fantasized about torturing women for years, Collins was convicted of murder in Ann Arbor on Aug. 19, 1970, and was sentenced to life imprisonment by Judge John W. Conlin. "I know my son didn't do it," sobbed Mrs. Loretta Collins, who had mortgaged her home to pay for her boy's defense.

Collins, Melvin (AKA: **Bad Boy**), 1910-48, U.S. Melvin Collins had already stabbed his brother and served two terms in a Virginia state penitentiary for two shooting incidents when, in November 1948, he went on a shooting spree that wounded three people and left seven dead, including one police officer.

Collins had recently moved to Chester, Pa., where he rented a room in a downtown boarding house. One morning, he leaned out the window of his second-story room and began firing his rifle at the pedestrians below. One man was dead before police Detective Elery Purnsley returned fire from across the street. Collins gunned down Detective Purnsley as pedestrians scattered, running for cover. When curiosity seekers ran to windows to see what the commotion was about, Collins picked off additional victims from open windows and balconies.

Over seventy-five officers arrived on the scene soon after the shooting began. Collins barricaded himself in the apartment and continued firing at the officers. They responded by riddling Collins' building with heavy gunfire and lobbing some twenty canisters of tear gas through his open window. When Collins ceased firing, police entered the building. As they forced his door open, he shot himself through the roof of the mouth.

Columbo, Patricia, 1957- , and **DeLuca, Frank**, 1938- , U.S. At eighteen, Patty Columbo went to work for an Elk Grove Village, Ill., pharmacy. She and the pharmacist, 38-year-old Frank DeLuca, quickly fell in love and were soon sharing an apartment, despite the fact that DeLuca had a wife and five children. But Patty wanted her parents to approve of the relationship, which they refused to do. Frank Columbo, forty-three, was so angered by the situation that he accosted DeLuca in front of his pharmacy, jammed the butt of a rifle into his mouth, and broke his teeth. Patty began to worry that perhaps her angry parents would disinherit her.

In October 1975, Patty Columbo met Lanyon Mitchell, an employee of the Cook County sheriff's office. Within days, she convinced him and his friend, Roman Sobcynski, former deputy sheriff, to kill her parents in return for sexual favors. She joined in orgies with them for several months as they continued to bring up reasons why they could not keep their part of the bargain. First they demanded photos of the would-be victims, then floor plans of the Columbos' house, then money that they knew she could not provide. Finally, on May 4, 1976, Patty and DeLuca went to her parents' house and did the deed themselves. Three days later, neighbors called the police, who found Frank Columbo shot four times and with his head crushed; Mary Columbo, shot between the eyes; and Patty's younger brother, Michael Columbo, stabbed eighty-four times.

The day after the murder, Frank DeLuca went to work and proudly told his employees about the deed as he washed his bloodstained clothing, but he threatened their lives and their children's lives if they told anyone. Patty told anyone who would listen that she was certain that the murders had been done by wild kids high on drugs. But the police found on the steering wheel of Frank Columbo's car the print of a three-fingered hand. Frank DeLuca had only three fingers on one hand, the result of a skydiving accident. A friend of Patty's told the police about Lanyon Mitchell, who told them the whole story. Patty Columbo and Frank DeLuca were arrested for murder. Their 1977 trial lasted six weeks, during which Patty tried to distract the jury with her attractive body. On July 1, 1977, the jury found the couple Guilty of three counts of murder. They were each sentenced to two hundred to three hundred years in prison. At the Dwight (Ill.) Correctional Center, two years later, Patty Columbo was accused of arranging sexual orgies for inmates and prison officials.

Combe, Michael, 1960- , U.S. Military recruits from around the country filled the U.S. Navy's Rescue Swimming Pool at the Naval Air Station in Pensacola, Fla., on Mar. 2, 1988, for a routine course on naval lifesaving techniques taught by several instructors, including 28-year-old Michael Combe. Nineteen-year-old Airman Recruit Lee Mirecki had a diagnosed phobia of submersion in water. He feared this segment of his military training, but cooperated with instructors until the training became violent.

Combe attempted to teach Mirecki a lifesaving technique in which he grabbed him from behind and held him in a headlock underwater. Mirecki had been taught to break such a hold, but was afraid of the water and so resisted Combe's encouragement to try.

Students in the class later testified that Combe forced Mirecki back into the pool, though Mirecki repeatedly shouted requests for permission to drop the class. Witnesses said Mirecki was pried from the equipment rack he clung to and thrown back into the pool where Combe once again practiced the stranglehold on him. The private struggled to break the hold.

When Combe received the cease command from Petty Officer Richard Blevins, who stood outside the pool, he released Mirecki, who had turned pale. When Mirecki was pulled to the side of the pool, he was dead. He died in Combe's arms after suffering a heart attack caused by panic.

Combe faced a court martial on charges of manslaughter and battery. He testified that he did nothing incorrect or against Navy regulations. On Nov. 25, 1988, Combe was found Guilty of negligent homicide and conspiracy to commit battery. He was demoted a rank, reprimanded, and sentenced to ninety days in a military prison.

Coneys, Theodore Edward (AKA: Matthew Cornish; Spiderman), 1882-1967, U.S. After twenty-nine years, Theodore Edward Coneys returned to Denver to haunt and inadvertently kill one of the few friends he had as a child.

Born in Petersburg, Ill., Coneys was a sickly, overprotected child. His mother, who had lost her husband when Coneys was an infant, feared a second loss and so sheltered the boy, diverting him from sports into music. At seventeen, after years of mandolin lessons, Coneys and his mother moved to Denver, where he performed for the West Moncrieff Mandolin Club.

It was there that he first met Phil Peters and his wife, Helen—regular concert-goers who admired the young Coneys and listened, often over dinner at their bungalow, to the story of his troubled young life. The relationship continued until the death of Coneys' mother in 1912.

Coneys then left Denver, and would not return for twenty-nine years. By then, Phil Peters, now seventy-three, was preoccupied with the recovery of his wife, then in the hospital. His neighbors were looking after him, inviting him for meals, but one evening he never showed up. Checking the house, and finding all the doors and windows locked, they pried open a screen and crawled inside.

Furniture was overturned, things were strewn about, blood was splattered on the walls, and Phil Peters lay dead on the bedroom floor—beaten about the head with the handle of a gun and an iron shaker, used to stoke the flames in the wood-burning stove.

Led by Captain Jim Childers, the Denver Police Department could find no clues. But had their investigation been as thorough as they thought it was, had they discovered the false plyboard ceiling in the closet, they would have turned up the only clue they needed—the murderer himself.

One year later and still no leads. Helen Peters, after learning of her husband's October 1941 murder, had since abandoned the house. It stood empty, except for the ghosts: images in the windows that could be described in no other way were sighted first by children, then by adults—sightings dismissed as superstition until Helen moved back in 1942.

Needing round-the-clock care, Mrs. Peters hired a live-in nurse. But the nurse and later her replacement both quit within weeks after seeing sights and hearing sounds they could not explain. Helen Peters moved out again soon after, having fallen and broken her hip. She said she had been startled but would not say by what.

Captain Childers began a twenty-four-hour stakeout of the now locked and vacant home. One morning, Childers and his partner saw a shadow pass behind the front window. They bolted to the porch and kicked in the front door. Hearing footsteps on the floor above, they ran upstairs just in time to glimpse a figure climbing through a tiny hole in the ceiling of the bedroom closet.

Theodore Coneys told police he had been living in the bungalow's attic since his return to Denver in September 1941. Broke and homeless, he went to the Peters for a loan. They were not at home, but he went in anyway, eventually coming upon the hole in the closet leading to the attic.

For one month Coneys lived above the Peters, lying still, when they were home, on a makeshift bed—an ironing board laid across suitcases—and stealing food downstairs when they were gone.

In time Coneys grew brazen, climbing down from his attic hideout while Peters was home. (By then his wife was in the hospital.) He told police he would often shadow the man as he walked through the house, hiding behind doorways to avoid detection. Coneys maintained he meant no harm to Peters, that he stalked him for entertainment.

One evening in October 1941, Coneys crept down to the kitchen, thinking Peters was out. Standing at the icebox, however, he soon found himself face to face with Phil Peters, who had been asleep on the couch. Startled, Coneys grabbed a gun from a kitchen drawer and beat Peters on the head, hitting him with the iron shaker when he tried to escape.

Never actually knowing if Peters recognized him as the 17-year-old mandolin player he had last seen thirty years before, Coneys was nonetheless convicted for murdering him and was sentenced to life in prison at Colorado's Canon City Penitentiary, near Colorado Springs.

Conroy, Thomas, 1903-42, U.S. When 10-year-old Genevieve Connolly disappeared from her Bronx tenement house on Nov. 6, 1940, her parents suspected anyone but soft-spoken Tom Conroy, their friend from the old country.

The thin-faced Irishman worked as a janitor in an apartment building on East 138th Street. The Connollys lived nearby, on Brook Avenue in the South Bronx. From time to time they fed and entertained Conroy and his 10-year-old son, taking pity on the motherless child.

At 7:30 p.m. on Nov. 6, Genevieve left home to visit her girlfriend, who lived next door to where Conroy worked as a maintenance man. When she didn't return by 11:30, Genevieve's father, Robert Connolly, telephoned Conroy to find out if he had seen her in the neighborhood. The janitor explained that yes, she had stopped by, and he had asked the girl to run over to Frank Moran's candy shop to buy him a package of cigarettes.

That much of the story was true. Moran told police he sold the girl cigarettes and she left the store, seemingly carefree. Over 140 Bronx detectives and sanitation workers combed the neighborhood. The police had no leads so they returned to question Conroy. This time, they noticed he wore his shirt inside out. Detectives ordered him to remove it only to find blood stains on the inside.

"Tommy, if you know anything about Jan, I ask you for God's sake and from a mother's heart to speak up," Mary Connolly pleaded in the Alexander Street police station. When the parents left the room, Conroy confessed. He said that after Genevieve left her friend Eileen O'Brien, she made a second trip to the candy store to buy some penny chocolates. At 9 p.m., as she walked to her tenement building, Conroy called her. He fondled her. Then, afraid the girl would tell her parents, he carried her into the cellar of his building. "I threw her on the coal pile," he explained. "She made gurgling sounds. I pressed her throat and she stopped." He disposed of the corpse in the furnace. At 1 a.m., shortly after the detectives visited him for the first time, he removed the ashes and placed them in a trash barrel for pick-up.

When the case went to trial Conroy repudiated his confession on the grounds that it had been obtained under duress. On Apr. 4, 1941, the jury convicted him of strangling Genevieve Connolly. He was put to death in the electric chair at Sing Sing Prison on Jan. 29, 1942.

Coo, Eva, d.1935, U.S. Canadian-born "Little Eva" Coo set up a combination brothel, roadhouse, and gas station outside Cooperstown, N.Y. But when the end of Prohibition caused the demise of many such houses, Eva Coo took in Harry Wright, the crippled alcoholic son of an old friend. He stayed with her for four years, until June 15, 1934, when his battered body was found in a ditch about 300 feet from her place. Police first thought he was the victim of a hit-and-run driver, but then an insurance policy on Wright's life, with Eva Coo as the beneficiary, turned up. She and her best friend, Martha Clift, were arrested as material witnesses, then interrogated by the police and insurance investigators until they incriminated each other.

Martha Clift and the prosecution held that Eva Coo had taken Harry to an empty "haunted" farm nearby and hit him over the head with a mallet. Then she had Martha Clift run over the body with her car, after which she moved it to the highway where it was found. They showed that Coo had taken an interest in the terms of Wright's life insurance, double checking that accidents were covered. Harry Nabinger, Coo's live-in lover, testified that he had written to insurance companies for her, comparing policies and helping her determine which one to buy. Martha Clift, who said she had been promised immunity from a charge of first-degree murder, then reported that Eva had discussed ways of killing Harry Wright with her several times, and she described the murder in detail. Eva Coo was found Guilty and sentenced to die in the electric chair. She was executed on June 28, 1935.

Cooney, Terence George, 1939-   , Brit. On the night of Feb. 24, 1958, Terence George Cooney stabbed to death Alan Godfrey Johnson at a dance hall in Barking, in the county of Essex.

A fight broke out when a group of men who had been at a nearby billiard hall arrived at the dance looking for men who were from Canning Town. Only one of the attackers reportedly carried a knife. The others were unarmed. When Johnson was approached and admitted he was from Canning Town, he was attacked and wounded fatally in the stomach. The fight spilled into the street and escalated into a small riot.

When apprehended, Cooney, a 19-year-old laborer, admitted stabbing Johnson, eighteen, but swore that he did not kill him. He claimed that he arrived after the fight began, and that Johnson had attacked him and made a move to his pocket as if fishing for a knife. Cooney said it was then that he pulled his own knife and stabbed Johnson in self-defense. Cooney admitted that Johnson did not have a knife, but said he had no way of knowing that at the time.

Four days of testimony and a twenty-minute deliberation brought the jury to a verdict of Guilty. Terence Cooney was sentenced to life imprisonment.

Cooper, Herbert, d.1911, Brit. A coroner's jury found Herbert Cooper Guilty of the Nov. 28, 1911, murder of 85-year-old Lord George Sanger on Sanger's farm in East Finchley. Cooper, an emotionally unstable man, was the son of the manager of Sanger's farm. He apparently felt that the lord was not lavishing enough attention on him, and, therefore, killed him with several blows of a hatchet. Soon after, Cooper committed suicide by lying on the railroad tracks between Crouch End and Highgate. He was decapitated.

Forty-five years later, the victim's grandson published a very different account of the events that took place on Nov. 28, 1911. According to the book, *The Sanger Story,* Sanger was accidentally struck on the head with a brass candlestick during a fray with Cooper. Sanger, still conscious, then went to bed and died while asleep.

Cooper, Ralph, and **English, Collis**, prom. 1940s, U.S. Known in the media as members of the "Trenton Six," Cooper and English were originally convicted and sentenced to death along with four other black men for the murder of Fred Horner, a 72-year-old junk dealer, in Trenton, N.J. Their trial and conviction set off a flurry of legal controversy that consumed the interests of the American Civil Liberties Union, The National Association for the Advancement of Colored People, and the Communist Party.

The Trenton police force and judicial system were under intense pressure to convict someone for this crime. The year was 1948. The mayor of Trenton had recently been indicted for bribery. That, plus the failure of his administration to solve a number of other crimes had both the public and press screaming for law enforcement reform. The six men who became known as the "Trenton Six"—Ralph Cooper, Collis English, Forrest McKinlay, John McKenzie, James Thorpe, and Horace Wilson—were rounded up and arrested for the crime. They all had strong alibis, but after days of brutal police interrogation that included sleep deprivation and the refusal to grant them access to attorneys, five of the six signed vague, confusing confessions to the murder. In June 1948, on the strength of these confessions all six black men were convicted of murder by an all-white jury and sentenced to death.

The Communist Party, ACLU, and NAACP all became involved in an appeal process that eventually won the "Trenton Six" a new trial when the New Jersey Supreme Court overturned their conviction in June 1949. The defense of five of the six men was assumed by the NAACP and members of Princeton University and Princeton Theological Seminary. The second trial began on Mar. 5, 1951, and lasted for more than fifteen weeks. The result: four were acquitted; English and Cooper were once again convicted of murder and sentenced to life.

The decision was peculiar because the widow of the victim, Elizabeth Maguire, said with certainty in her first recorded statements that the men she had seen enter the store on the day of her husband's murder were light-skinned blacks. Of the six, Cooper and English were the darkest.

During the second trial, Dr. J. Minor Sullivan III, who testified at the first trial that all the suspects had signed their confessions of their own free will, admitted that four of the six appeared to have been either drugged or bribed to sign their confessions. Sullivan was later convicted on seven counts of perjury for giving this contradictory testimony.

Another appeal was made, this time on behalf of English and Cooper. English died in prison before the appeal was heard, and Cooper eventually pleaded *non vult,* a plea equivalent to "no contest," and was released.

Cooper, Ronald Frank, 1950-78, S. Afri. "I have decided that I think I should become a homosexual murderer and shall get hold of young boys...and I shall rape them and then kill them...My first few victims shall each be killed in a different way, which shall be as follows: Victim No. 1: Strangled by hands..."

This Mar. 17, 1976, entry in the diary of Ronald Frank Cooper made it easy for the prosecution when Cooper was tried for murdering a child in Johannesburg, S. Afri.

A 26-year-old, unemployed laborer, Cooper had described at length in his diary how he would murder thirty boys and six women and possibly use human sacrifice or rape. He had, in fact, already tried to fulfill his written promises a month before by pulling a gun on Tresslin Pohl, ten, and forcing him into a park. After a few minutes, however, he lost his nerve and released the boy.

Cooper botched two more attempts but finally succeeded on the fourth try. On May 16, 1976, he trapped Mark John Garnet, twelve, in a Parktown area apartment building elevator and strangled him until the boy was unconscious. Tying a rope around Mark's neck, Cooper tried unsuccessfully to rape him. Failing at this, he loosened the rope, hoping the boy might survive. "To murder someone is not a nice thing to do, as I have now found out," he later confided to his diary. "I really am a monster."

When Tressin Pohl, Cooper's first attempted victim, found out that his friend Mark had been murdered, he went to the authorities. He told them that in April, during a Saturday matinee, he had noticed Cooper sitting in a theater filled with children. When the movie was over, Tressin had shadowed him home to the St. Kilda Hotel.

With this information, Cooper was easily apprehended. His diary did the rest. On Jan. 16, 1978, Ronald Frank Cooper was hanged.

Cooper, Ronald John, 1938- , Brit. On the evening of July 23, 1964, Ronald Cooper shot and killed Joseph Hayes, sixty-seven, the managing director of a ship repairing company at his home in Barking, Essex. Cooper snatched £1,878 in payroll checks from the kitchen table and then fled through the hallway, shooting Mrs. Elsie May Hayes in the back. Cooper fled to New York the next day, and then continued on to the Bahamas where he went to work as a gambling casino croupier. Meanwhile, British police established the suspect's identity through fingerprints left behind on a newspaper and on a chromium stair railing.

Cooper was arrested in the Bahamas and extradited back to England where he went on trial in the Central Criminal Court on Dec. 3, 1964. Two weeks later, on Dec. 14, a Guilty verdict was returned against Cooper and the death sentence was passed. He became the first man to be convicted of a capital offense after Sydney Silverman's bill to abolish hanging was introduced into the House of Commons. Four days before the scheduled execution at Pentonville Prison on Jan. 27, 1965, Cooper was given a reprieve by the Home Office.

Copeland, Michael, 1934- , Brit. Before Michael Copeland was arrested for the murders of William Elliott and George Stobbs, the police referred to these murders as the Carbon Copy Murders. Both victims frequented a tavern called the Spread Eagle, both were found dead near Chesterfield, England and both of their automobiles had been abandoned on Park Road in Chesterfield.

Elliott and Stobbs were homosexual, which Copeland later told police was "something I hated." Elliott's body was found on June 13, 1960, on Clod Hill Lane in Baslow. On Mar. 29, 1961, Stobbs's body was discovered beside a road near Wingerworth.

The trail eventually led to Copeland, a 26-year-old former soldier, whose home was near the location of the abandoned cars. He was also accused of the November 1960 murder of Guenther Helmbrecht, a young soldier, in Verden, Ger. At his trial, Copeland retracted his original confession to the murders of Stobbs and Elliott, but the evidence was overwhelming. He was found Guilty of all three murders and sentenced to death. The sentence was later commuted to life in prison when it was proven that Copeland was under mental stress at the time of the murders.

Coppolino, Dr. Carl, 1933- , U.S. Dr. Carl Coppolino, a Brooklyn-born anesthesiologist, was accused of murdering his first wife with a relaxant called succinylcholine, a drug commonly used during surgery. Used to excess, the drug was capable of paralyzing the muscles of the lungs, bringing on death. Once in the body, the drug broke down into its component parts making it difficult, if not impossible, to trace its presence.

After suffering heart problems, Dr. Coppolino abandoned his practice in New Jersey and moved to Sarasota, Fla., with his wife, the former Carmela Musetto. Although the insurance company suspected that Coppolino was faking his illness, they paid him a yearly benefit of $22,000. The couple lived comfortably in Florida from the insurance money, and the income derived from Carmela's own medical practice. Shortly before Carmela Coppolino died in 1965, her husband insured her life for $65,000. The cause of death was listed as heart failure, and the matter was pursued no further until Carl Coppolino's jilted lover Marjorie Farber informed the police and a Florida physician that she had watched him kill her husband in 1963.

Motivated by jealousy when Coppolino married a 38-year-old divorcée named Mary Gibson, Farber told Dr. Juliette Karow that she had carried on a love affair with Coppolino back in New Jersey. Coppolino became jealous of her new husband, a retired army colonel, and injected him with a chemical substance, and then smothered him with a pillow. The cause of Colonel Farber's death was listed as coronary thrombosis. Coppolino was subsequently indicted for murder in both New Jersey and Florida. Confused by conflicting medical evidence, the jury found Coppolino Not Guilty in Farber's case. When Carmela's body was exhumed and re-examined it was found that the victim had been in good health and had not suffered a heart attack, as Coppolino had alleged.

Dr. Joseph Umberger, a noted toxicologist, conducted six months of intensive research before locating traces of succinic acid in the system of the corpse. On the witness stand, Dr. Umberger testified that while succinic acid is naturally present in the human brain, it is in "bound" form.

The evidence showed that the acid found in the victim was "unbound." This evidence and the fact that Carmella was injected immediately prior to death tended to confirm the view that she had been murdered.

Despite the efforts of defense attorney F. Lee Bailey, Dr. Coppolino was convicted in 1967, of second-degree murder, and was sentenced to life imprisonment at the Avon Park Correctional Institution. At the conclusion of the trial, Bailey publicly assailed the prosecution and the battery of witnesses, behavior for which he received a one-year suspension from practicing in New Jersey. In 1977, Mary Gibson Coppolino began a fight to win her husband's freedom. She gathered reports from scientists claiming the New York City medical examiners were "out to get" Coppolino at the time. Although these statements had little effect on the parole board, Coppolino was released on Oct. 16, 1979, for exemplary behavior at the prison facility.

Corens, Henry, prom. 1945, U.S. When Henry Corens reported to the Bethesda, Md., police that his wife had vanished, it seemed like another routine missing-persons case—until police received two cryptic notes in the mail. "Pearl gone for good. Not returning," the first one said. It was postmarked Norfolk, Va. A few days later, a second letter arrived from Miami, Fla., that said: "Don't bother to look for Pearl."

Police ascertained that the couple had had marital problems for years. Henry Corens' affairs led Pearl's brother, Grover Walker, to surmise that she had finally run off with someone else.

The police investigation was stymied until two farmers who were fishing in the Potomac River noticed a human head in a wooded area adjacent to the bank. Dental charts confirmed that it belonged to Pearl Corens.

A young sailor who had shown an interest in Pearl was located and questioned, but it was impossible to establish a direct link to the murder. A search of the Corens' house produced a hacksaw and washtub cover with traces of human blood . A pathologist claimed that the blood was Pearl's, but it was pointed out that Henry Corens shared his wife's blood type.

A young girl that Corens had an affair with supplied the motive when she told the court that Corens had begged her to marry him. Circumstantial evidence and a batch of love letters written to his sweetheart helped convict Corens of second-degree murder. He was sentenced to eighteen years at hard labor. No clues were ever found as to who had sent the letters from Miami and Norfolk.

Corll, Dean Allen, 1939-73, and **Henley, Elmer Wayne**, 1956- , and **Brooks, David Owen**, 1955- , U.S. On Aug. 8, 1973, 17-year-old Elmer Wayne Henley called the Pasadena (Texas) Police Department and said he had just shot his friend Dean Corll. The police found Dean Corll lying face down with six slugs in his shoulder and back, and then the whole story began to come out. Henley and his friend David Brooks were accomplices to twenty-seven murders in the previous three years as Corll indulged his sado-masochistic sexual fantasies by murdering teenaged boys.

Corll was punished harshly as a child, and when his parents divorced, he and his brother Stanley were shuttled between nursery schools and baby sitters. In 1964, Corll

Service photo of Dean Allen Corll, left, and his partner in mass murder, Elmer Wayne Henley, right. They killed at least twenty-seven.

was drafted into the army, and by 1969 his disturbing personality disorders came to concern his friends and relatives. After the army, Corll returned to Houston and went to work for the Lighting and Power Company. He began to associate with teenaged boys, and sniffed glue with two of them, Elmer Wayne Henley and David Owen Brooks.

The killing began in 1970 when Corll lured hitchhiking University of Texas student Jeffrey Konen to his house in Pasadena. But Corll usually relied on Henley, a high school dropout, to find victims from the depressed Heights section of Houston. Corll promised to pay $200 for each victim lured into the trap, but he usually reneged. Brooks, Corll's first willing recruit, said he met the man in the schoolyard and Corll gave him some candy, after which they lived together for a time. In 1970, Brooks came home and found Corll engaged in sexual acts with two young men who had been bound and gagged. Brooks was given a car to keep silent.

Brooks and Henley soon became willing participants in murder. In the next two years, the three murdered twenty-seven young boys. Victims were lured to Corll's home for drug and alcohol parties. After the victims fell unconscious, Corll tied them up, sexually molested them, and killed them. He disposed of the bodies in either a remote spot near the Sam Rayburn Reservoir or a boat shed in southwest Houston rented for the purpose.

On Aug. 8, 1973, Henley violated the "trust" by bringing 15-year-old Rhonda Williams to the apartment. "You weren't supposed to bring any girl!" Corll bellowed. The girl had run away from home and needed a place to stay for the night, and Henley said his friend Dean wouldn't mind. Varnish sniffing began, and Henley, Williams, and Timothy Kerley, sixteen, passed out. When he awoke and discovered that Corll had tied them up, Henley pleaded for his life. Corll released him when he promised to rape and kill Williams while Corll did the same to Kerley. But Henley was too upset to perform a sexual act with the girl. He seized a .22-caliber pistol and pointed it at Corll, who taunted him. Henley fired six shots, and then called the local police. Later that day he took police to shed number eleven at the Southwest Boat Storage and the excavation began. After the twenty-seventh body was removed from the shallow graves at the boathouse and near the lake, the search stopped. A "record" had been established, eclipsing the slayings of twenty-five migrant workers in California in 1971. But Mary West, Corll's divorced mother, thought there might be more victims. The Houston police were unwilling to continue, despite hundreds of parents' requests for information about their missing children.

On Aug. 11, 1973, the Houston district attorney filed murder charges against Brooks and Henley. Judge Preston Dial barred the press during jury selection. The trial opened in San Antonio in July 1974. Henley and Brooks were convicted of the murders of six of the twenty-seven victims, and were each sentenced to life imprisonment.

Jack Olsen's 1974 book about the case, *The Man With the Candy,* referred to Mary West's confectionery business, which she had operated with the help of her son in Vidor, Texas.

Corona, Juan Vallejo, 1933-   , U.S. Few mass murderers match the ruthlessness and systematic slaughter demonstrated by Juan Corona, a killer who murdered at least twenty-five migrant workers in the space of six weeks during 1971. Corona, a Mexican migrant worker himself, had arrived in Yuba City, Calif., in the 1950s. By the early 1970s, he was a labor contractor, hiring migrant workers to pick the various fruit crops in the Yuba City area. He was also, by that time, a man who suffered from several forms of mental illness. He had been diagnosed as suffering

from schizophrenia. He was also a homosexual and a brutal sadist. As early as 1970, the Corona family was involved in violent sex. Corona's half-brother, Natividad, was charged with sexually attacking a young Mexican worker who was found bleeding in the washroom of the half-brother's Guadalajara Cafe located in Marysville, close to Yuba City. When the youth sued the half-brother and won a $250,000 settlement, Natividad fled back to Mexico.

The odd thing about Corona's murder spree which was umbilically connected to homosexual attacks was the fact that he was a married man with children. Heterosexual or not, Corona also craved sex with his own gender, an uncommon but not unheard of tendency on the part of some sex killers. As a labor contractor, Corona hired migrant workers, and housed these single men in a barracks-like building on the Sullivan ranch. These men were, for the most part, elderly alcoholics, social dropouts, and misfits. They began disappearing in early May 1971. On May 19, a Japanese fruit farmer noticed a large hole seven feet long and three and a half feet deep that had been scooped out of his land in a peach orchard. The next night he went to the same spot and saw that the earth had been packed back into the hole. He called the police who dug into what was a fresh grave. Inside of it was Kenneth Whitacre, a hobo who had homosexual literature in his back pocket. He had been sexually assaulted and then stabbed to death, his head chopped with a machete.

Another farmer noticed what appeared to be a freshly dug grave on his land and police began digging again, this time finding an elderly man. More graves in this area yielded more men, all of them sodomized, stabbed—one was shot—and chopped viciously about the head with a machete. In one grave police found a meat market receipt made out to "Juan V. Corona." The bodies kept turning up including that of John Henry Jackson, an elderly worker who had been seen some weeks earlier riding in the back of Corona's pickup truck. The police kept digging until June 4, 1971, unearthing twenty-five bodies, along with more receipts that had the name of Juan Corona on them. Corona was arrested and charged with murder. He pleaded not guilty, but his defense lawyers, who maintained that another person had done the murders, had an uphill battle against the overpowering evidence of bodies, receipts, and eyewitnesses who had seen the murdered workers with Corona shortly before they disappeared.

There was speculation that Corona and another man had committed the murders, but no other suspect was ever found, let alone arrested. Psychiatrists ventured many theories about Corona, one claiming that as the spring deepened and the fruit ripened, Corona's madness increased until the climate drove him into a frenzy of murder and mutilation so that he was compelled to kill someone each day to satisfy his blood lust. The availability of victims increased as warmer weather set in and scores of migrant workers drifted into the Marysville-Yuba City area. Corona simply had to stop his truck at any roadside and pick up the lonely workers, social pariahs no one would ever miss. He would work these men a few days and, when it came time to pay them, the burly, 200-pound Corona would sexually

Mass killer Juan Corona, waving to friends, en route to prison.

molest them, murder them, and bury the bodies. These included Kenneth Whitacre, Charles Fleming, Melford Sample, Donald Smith, John J. Haluka, Warren Kelley, Sigurd Beierman, William Emery Kamp, Clarence Hocking, James W. Howard, Jonah R. Smallwood, Elbert T. Riley, Paul B. Allen, Edward Martin Cupp, Albert Hayes, Raymond Muchache, John H. Jackson, Lloyd Wallace Wenzel, Mark Beverly Shields, Sam Bonafide—also known as Joe Carriveau—Joseph Maczak, and four men who remained unidentified.

In several instances, the prosecution at Corona's trial proved that Corona had planned his murders in advance, digging graves days before he had any victims to put into them. Added to this were the damning bloodstained knives, machete, pistol, and Corona's blood-caked clothes found in his home, along with an equally damning ledger in which Corona had officiously listed the names of his victims and the dates of their murders. The jury in the Corona case deliberated for forty-five hours and then brought in a verdict of Guilty in the case of each of the twenty-five murdered men. In January 1973, Judge Richard E. Patton sentenced Corona to twenty-five life terms to run consecutively with no hope of parole. Corona was attacked in prison, stabbed thirty-two times, losing sight in one eye. He later won an appeal that claimed he had not received adequate defense, that he should have pleaded insane. He was placed in an asylum for the criminally insane.

Cossentino, Armando, c.1942- , U.S. A 19-year-old man used a hammer to rid his lover of her domineering husband. New York police felt they had found a crime of passion when they examined the body of Dr. Joseph DiFede, thirty-eight, who had been hit with a hammer and stabbed repeatedly on the night of Dec. 7, 1961. An investigation of the doctor's patients led police to the stylish apartment of unemployed Armando Cossentino and his jobless roommate.

They soon learned that Cossentino's rent was paid by the doctor's wife, Jean DiFede, thirty-five, with whom he was having an affair, and interrogated the roommates. Cossentino revealed nothing, but his roommate confessed that he and Cossentino killed the doctor, who also was involved in affairs. Cossentino was convicted of murder and received the death sentence, later commuted to life imprisonment. DiFede was found guilty of manslaughter and sentenced to life in prison.

Costa, Antone C., c.1945- , U.S. An admitted drug addict failed to prove insanity in his trial for the murders of two 23-year-old women from Providence, R.I.

The dismembered bodies of Patricia H. Walsh, a second-grade teacher, and Mary Ann Wysocki, a college senior, were found in shallow graves in Truro, Mass., on Mar. 5, 1969, about six weeks after they disappeared. They were last seen, with Costa, on Jan. 25, 1969, in Walsh's car in Provincetown, Mass., en route to Truro, where Costa invited them to use drugs he had hidden in the small town. Costa was suspected of taking part in the women's disappearance because he was seen driving Walsh's Volkswagen, which he claimed she had sold him.

When the women's graves were discovered, the Provincetown resident was immediately arrested. In his room police discovered a .22-caliber revolver with bullets that matched the bullets found in the victims' bodies, bloodstains, fingerprints linking Costa to the women, and some possessions the women brought for their weekend visit in Provincetown. With so much evidence against his client, defense attorney Maurice Goldman claimed the defendant's extensive drug use—he had been taking mind-altering drugs such as LSD since 1965—had caused him to lose the ability to distinguish right from wrong. The prosecution, however, pointed to Costa's deliberate efforts to conceal his crime, such as forging a note and telegram in the dead women's names. After six-and-a-half hours of deliberation, Costa was found Guilty of both murders and sentenced to life imprisonment with no possibility of parole.

Cowan, Frederick W. (AKA: **Second Hitler**), 1944-77, U.S. Frederick Cowan's pleasures in life were Nazi memorabilia, his weapons collection, and weightlifting. He bore tattoos of Nazi symbols on his arms, and expressed his hatred of Jews and blacks to anyone who would listen. He attributed his hatred of blacks to a time during the Vietnam War when a black man refused to help him. But Cowan was never in Vietnam. Then his neighbor in New Rochelle, N.Y., Theresa Schmidt, started dating a black man. On Aug. 2, 1975, when Schmidt walked by Cowan's house, he pointed her out to a nearby kid as a "nigger lover." Schmidt, overhearing, turned on him and demanded to know what he had said. Cowan went to the trunk of his car, grabbed a rifle, and said, "Get out of there before I blow your brains out!" Schmidt ran to call the police, but the officer who answered the call expressed no interest in pursuing the matter when Cowan was not in sight on his arrival. Months later, when Schmidt passed Cowan's house again, he pointed a rifle at her and pulled the trigger, but the weapon was not loaded.

Mass killer Frederick Cowan.

In January 1977, 33-year-old Cowan's opinions got him in trouble at his job. He was suspended after refusing to work for a man he thought was Jewish. The superior who suspended him, Norman Bing, was himself Jewish, and later said, "The guys figured he was a lot of talk. He had no history of violence. Everybody said he was a pussycat." But on Valentine's Day 1977, his first day back at work, Cowan drove to work at the Neptune Moving Company, stood in the parking lot, and armed himself as if for battle with pistols, hand grenades, bandoliers of ammunition, and a semi-automatic rifle. He walked into the main entrance searching for Bing, and immediately shot and killed two black men passing through the office. Cowan told another employee, "Go home and tell my mother not to come down to Neptune." He continued into the company cafeteria, up the stairs, killing two more people on the way. When a squad car arrived, Cowan saw it from a window and killed one policeman as he emerged from the car. Within minutes, the Neptune building was under siege, a New York City Police Department armored personnel carrier on hand to help.

The killer, moving back and forth from the offices to the roof, would not answer loudspeaker calls for several hours, even when his mother arrived and spoke to him. Once he shouted that he had "plenty of grenades and other guns to last me all day." Another time he answered a phone and said, "I'm sorry for your trouble. Tell the mayor that I'm sorry to be causing the city so much trouble." At 2:40 p.m., a single shot sounded. As the police cleared the building, they found that Fred Cowan, killer of five, had killed himself with a gunshot to the head.

Cox, Frederick William, c.1897-1924, S. Afri. A young man failed to fulfill his part in a suicide pact with his paramour, resulting in his death by execution for murder.

Frederick William Cox, who was unemployed at the time, attempted to defraud a neighbor, borrowing £15 to supposedly establish a partnership between the two. When the man threatened to press charges of theft against him, Cox denied the ruse, agreeing to meet the disgruntled partner and a detective at a bank the next day. On Feb. 21, 1924, Cox met the men, then excused himself briefly to pick up his secret girlfriend, his cousin Annie Cox, whom he called Dolly. Aghast at the thought of being separated because of Frederick's crime, and already forced to hide their feelings because of Annie's disapproving father, the couple decided they would rather die together than be apart, according to Frederick Cox's testimony at his sentencing.

As arranged, Frederick led his lover into an office where he stabbed her, surprising Annie who probably expected a quicker death, according to witnesses who observed her fight to live. Cox, apparently devastated that Annie suffered and that he had no time to kill himself, confessed.

Cox's trial started on May 19, 1924, with examining doctors calling him sane. Cox, protesting any efforts by his lawyer to help him avoid the death penalty, was found Guilty after twenty-five minutes of jury deliberation. Sentenced to die at the gallows he lost some of the composure he showed during sentencing and was hanged on July 1, 1924.

Craig, Christopher, 1936- , Brit. Christopher Craig grew up in comfortable surroundings in the suburb of Croydon. His father was a bank executive, and by all accounts Christopher and his brother were never in want. Despite his obvious advantages Craig turned to a life of crime, and together with his partner Burney were trafficking in stolen furs and clothing. Both men were living in Kensington where they were cornered by police on Sept. 14, 1952. After a violent struggle, the pair were arrested and charged with armed robbery. Craig and Burney were convicted and sentenced to twelve years and nineteen years in prison, respectively. The matter did not end there. On the night of Nov. 2, two men broke loose from prison and holed up inside a London warehouse. The Croydon police arrived on the scene minutes later, attempting to reason with the felons. "If you want us, well come and get us!" shouted Craig. Shots rang out. Two unarmed policemen were felled by bullets: Officer P.C. Miles who was killed instantly, and Detective Constable Fairfax who sustained a shoulder wound but nevertheless managed to subdue the second man, Derek Bentley.

Bentley was convicted of murder, and summarily executed at Wandsworth Prison after the Home Secretary turned down his request for a pardon. Craig, who was only sixteen years old at the time, was ordered detained at the Queen's pleasure.

═══════════════════════════

Crane, Cheryl, 1944-   , U.S. The only child of Hollywood actress Lana Turner, Cheryl Crane was born to Turner and Stephen Crane, the actress' second husband, a marriage that lasted only a few months. Turner had already been married to Artie Shaw and, after her annulment from Crane, went on to marry Henry J. "Bob" Topping, Lex Barker, Fred May, Robert Eaton, and Ronald Dante. The marriage to Barker, it was claimed, had been broken up by Cheryl, who continued to live with her mother through her host of husbands. The girl was surrounded by her mother's enormous wealth—a mansion, servants, jewels, expensive cars, and mostly fame. Teenage jealousy of her mother prompted Cheryl, some claimed, to whisper nasty gossip to her mother about her husbands and those she dated between marriages. One of these was the handsome, smooth-talking gangster, John Stompanato, one-time chauffeur and bagman for Los Angeles gambler and gangster Mickey Cohen.

Stompanato, born in Woodstock, Ill., in 1925, had served as a Marine during WWII. He had attended an exclusive military school and then Notre Dame briefly before enlisting in the Marines in 1944, serving three years. The rugged Stompanato had married and divorced twice by 1948 when he went to work for Cohen in Los Angeles as Cohen's bodyguard, driver, and later as bagman, collecting the profits from Cohen's gambling and extortion rackets. He then struck out on his own, operating as a Hollywood lounge lizard, picking up lonely but wealthy women who were married, then making love to them in a room where hidden motion picture cameras recorded every move. Stompanato would then sell the film to the compromised women at staggering extortion prices.

When Lana Turner's marriage to Lex Barker ended, she received a call from Stompanato, asking her for a date. He first used the name John Steele when introducing himself to Turner and her daughter Cheryl. The lonely 38-year-old Turner accepted and their tempestuous affair began. The gangster was nothing like Turner's husbands or previous lovers. He was loud, crude, gauche, a braggart and a bully, who wore shiny shirts open almost to his navel to reveal his chest. He oozed Latin charm and earthiness, but at the same time his passions were violent and menacing. Cheryl Crane was enamored by her mother's new lover; she and Stompanato spent hours horseback riding or swimming together in her mother's Olympic-sized pool. Stompanato played the older brother to her, writing her long letters when she was traveling with her mother. Turner, meanwhile, lavished Stompanato with expensive gifts, clothes, and then loaned him $10,000—money that was never repaid. When he joined her and Cheryl in London while Turner was filming *Another Time, Another Place*, Stompanato moved into the luxurious townhouse Turner and Cheryl were sharing. The gangster then asked the actress for another loan, $50,000, to secure the rights to a film script for a movie in which, he, Johnny Stompanato, would star. The gangster had long nurtured the secret ambition to become a film star.

The actress turned him down, saying that she did not have that kind of cash and that her financial advisers had ordered her not to give him any more money. Her refusal caused Stompanato to go berserk. He threatened the star, who walked out on him, going to the set of *Another Time, Another Place* where she began to rehearse with co-star Sean Connery. Stompanato suddenly appeared on the set, raging, ordering Connery to "stay away from Lana!" Connery turned his back on Stompanato, who grabbed the burly actor and swung him about, waving a gun in Connery's face. The actor's response was to land a powerful punch to the gangster's jaw, sending him to the floor in a half-conscious state. Stompanato got up and walked away, swearing revenge. Back at the townhouse, the gangster cornered Turner and shrieked: "When I say hop, you'll hop! When I say jump, you'll jump!"

The actress ordered Stompanato out of the townhouse. He yelled: "I'll mutilate you! I'll hurt you so that you'll be so repulsive you'll have to hide forever!" With that he leaped forward, grabbed the actress around the throat and began to choke her. He then threw her down to the floor and threatened her with a razor, saying that he could cut her "just a little" but he could "do worse." She pleaded with Stompanato, who then relented, but he warned her: "That's just to let you know that I'm not kidding. Don't think that you can ever get away!" Cheryl Crane had heard the commotion and expressed fears for her mother's life. The director of the film Turner was working on called Scotland

Lana Turner with Johnny Stompanato.

Return from Mexico; Lana is interviewed, Stompanato chats with Cheryl Crane.

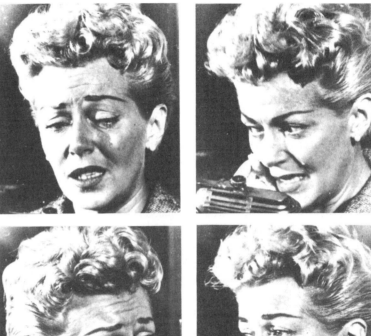

Stompanato was an accomplished blackmailer.

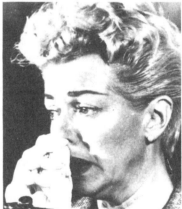

Lana Turner, on stage, testifying at her daughter's trial.

Actress Lana Turner after her daughter received a verdict of "justifiable homicide"; her lawyer, Jerry Giesler, is at right.

Yard, and Stompanato was politely escorted to the airport and put on the next plane to the U.S. Lana Turner had successfully gotten rid of the menacing thug.

Once the film in England was completed, however, Turner and Cheryl returned to Los Angeles and the actress made the mistake of calling Stompanato, showing herself to be much more dependent upon him than she had previously admitted. Stompanato now moved into her mansion to fully enjoy Lana Turner's luxurious lifestyle, swimming in her pool, lounging in the sunray and massage rooms, watching the latest Hollywood films in her private screening room. The couple took a seven-week vacation to Acapulco, renting a suite at the Via Vera Hotel. When they returned to Los Angeles, Cheryl Crane, now a tall girl who towered over her mother, was present to welcome the pair home. The arguments began all over again, beginning with the Academy Awards. Turner had been nominated for an Oscar for her performance in *Peyton Place* (she did not win) and had decided to attend the ceremonies without Stompanato. When he learned that he was not invited, the gangster went into a raging tirade, accusing the actress of being ashamed of him, that she did not want to be seen in public with him.

More importantly, Stompanato had been gambling heavily in gambling spas owned by his former employer Mickey Cohen, and Cohen held several IOUs Stompanato had signed. On the evening of Apr. 4, 1958, Stompanato demanded that Turner pay these debts. He confronted her in her lavish bedroom and she, in turn, utterly refused to give him any more money. Again the gangster lost control and began screaming that he would use a razor to disfigure her for life. Cheryl Crane, downstairs, could hear the gangster yelling: "If a man makes a living with his hands, I would destroy his hands. You make your living with your face, so I will destroy your face. I'll get you where it hurts the most! I'll cut you up and I'll get your mother and your daughter, too...That's my business!"

Stompanato grabbed the actress by the arm and she broke away. She opened the bedroom door to see her daughter standing there. "Please, Cheryl, please don't listen to any of this," the actress told her, and closed the door. She then ordered Stompanato to return to his own room. He picked up a hanger with a jacket on it and approached her, poised it seemed, to attack her with it. The actress then told the gangster that she was finished with him and that he was to get out of her house. She again opened the door and Stompanato came rushing toward her, holding the jacket and the hanger. Cheryl Crane was there, moving past her mother into the bedroom, holding a butcher knife with a nine-inch blade which she had gotten in the down-stairs kitchen. The actress was later to testify: "I swear it was so fast, I—I truthfully thought she had hit him in the

stomach. The best that I can remember is that they came together and they parted. I still never saw the blade."

The gangster, holding his stomach, fell backward on the thick carpet. Lana Turner went to him and pulled back his shirt to see the deep knife wound. Stompanato tried to speak but only a gurgle came out of his throat. She grabbed a towel from the bathroom and tried to staunch the flow of blood but it was useless, her lover was dead. Her daughter stood sobbing nearby as Turner called her mother and then her lawyer, the famed Jerry Giesler. She said to Giesler: "This is Lana Turner. Could you please come to my house. Something terrible has happened." Within minutes, Giesler was driving toward the Turner mansion. Cheryl Crane then called her father and asked him to come to the house. Crane asked a patron in his restaurant to drive him to Turner's Beverly Hills home and was the first to arrive there. Cheryl met him at the door. Crane looked at Stompanato's stiffening body in the upstairs bedroom while his sobbing daughter blurted: "I did it, Daddy, but I didn't mean to. He was going to hurt Mommy. I didn't mean to, I didn't mean to."

Giesler showed up, meeting the actress for the first time, but promising her that his office would do all to protect her and her child. Clinton Anderson, Beverly Hills police chief, then arrived with several officers. Reporter Jim Bacon quickly appeared, gaining access to the house by telling uniformed officers stationed outside that he was from the coroner's office. Lana Turner was by then pleading with Anderson to put the blame on her, that her child only meant to protect her. "I don't want her involved, poor baby," Turner said through tears. "Please say that I did it." Stompanato was by this time examined and pronounced dead.

Giesler immediately introduced his defense by putting his arm around Turner and saying: "Your daughter has done a courageous thing. It's too bad that a man's life is gone but under the circumstances the child did the only thing she could do to protect her mother from harm." Giesler looked at Chief Anderson and spoke to Turner but kept his eyes on the police officer: "I understand your concern for the child's welfare. But you won't get anyplace by hiding the truth, will she, Chief?"

Lana Turner then gushed the whole sordid affair between herself and Stompanato while Bacon and other reporters took notes. Anderson sympathetically listened to her and then to Cheryl's description of how she plunged the knife into the gangster who was about to attack her mother. The chief reluctantly informed the actress that he would have to lock up her 14-year-old daughter. "Can't you arrest me instead?" Turner pleaded with him. "Poor baby's not to blame for all this mess."

Cheryl Crane was arrested and locked up in the Juvenile

Section of the city jail, charged with murder. The newspapers blared the killing from coast to coast and most of the gossip columnists used the Stompanato death to parade Turner's torrid love affairs in print. She was pilloried for subjecting her daughter to a series of reckless marriages and love affairs, and some even wildly speculated that Turner herself had murdered Stompanato after finding her daughter in bed with him. Only Walter Winchell came to the defense of the movie queen, asking that fans understand the tragedy and give their hearts "to the girl with a broken heart."

Few of Turner's peers had anything to say about the killing. The outspoken Gloria Swanson, sex goddess of the silent era, did voice a scathing opinion, attacking Winchell for defending Turner, saying that his defense of the actress was "disgusting...You are trying to whitewash Lana...She is not even an actress...she is only a trollop." Gangster Mickey Cohen then suddenly appeared in the editorial offices of the Los Angeles *Herald Examiner,* dumping Lana Turner's love letters to Stompanato into the editor's hands. He had ordered his goons to go to Stompanato's apartment after hearing about the killing and obtain these gushing *billet doux,* after being stuck with the bill for Stompanato's funeral, costs he expected the actress to bear. He released the letters out of spite.

By the time Cheryl Crane appeared in court, the charge against her had been reduced to manslaughter. Giesler brilliantly placed Lana Turner on the stand and softly talked her through the nightmare killing. The actress detailed everything that occurred that evening, weeping, wiping away perspiration with her handkerchief, her face distorted in anguish, a mother's pain. Some say it was the greatest performance of her career. Then Cheryl Crane testified, repeating almost word for word the story her mother had given. The coroner's jury, relying exclusively on the testimony of the two females, ruled that Cheryl Crane had committed justifiable homicide. She was made a ward of the state and placed in her grandmother's custody. The press photographers had a field day with Lana Turner on the stand that day and reveled in taking photos of her kneeling at her mother's feet, a penitent pose that was no doubt meant to elicit sympathy.

Cheryl Crane did not adjust well. Her grandmother, Mildred Turner, could not control her. The girl ran away several times and was later placed by court order in the El Retiro School for Girls in the San Fernando Valley. She later worked for her father as a hostess in his restaurant. The American public favored Lana Turner and her daughter in this sensational killing, and the actress' next few films were box office hits. She and her daughter survived the scandal, emerging as heroines. Cheryl Crane later became a success as a San Francisco real estate broker and wrote a book about her life, detailing the Stompanato murder in terms that repeated her original statements, a book in which she revealed she was a lesbian. Only the publicity-seeking gangster Mickey Cohen angrily spoke up on behalf of Johnny Stompanato, declaring to the world: "Look, this was a great guy!"

Crane, James, 1947- , Brit. Fifteen-year-old James Crane could not stand to see his mother abused by his father. In Fall 1962, Mrs. Crane told her husband of her plans to end the marriage and take her three children away. The 42-year-old dock-worker was furious, and vowed to kill her if she did so. But James promised to protect her, and to kill his father.

As his father slept in the daybed on the first floor of their home, James fired a shotgun at him from a distance of three feet. When Mrs. Crane heard the shot, she ran downstairs and found her husband dead. The police were summoned and took the boy into custody. James Crane was later found Not Guilty of murder, but Guilty of manslaughter. He was ordered confined to a mental institution on the grounds of diminished responsibility.

Crawford, George, prom. 1932, U.S. The murder of prominent socialite Agnes Boeing Ilsley at her estate in Loudoun County, Va., on Jan 12, 1932, was apparently motivated by revenge. Police investigators found no evidence of theft, just the mangled bodies of Mrs. Ilsley and her elderly maid, Mina Buckner, in their beds. The likely culprit was George Crawford, a young black chauffeur recently dismissed for pilfering liquor from the Ilsley wine closet. The men of the nearby village organized a posse to track down Crawford.

But Crawford had fled to Boston, where he was arrested for larceny one year later. The controversy over his extradition pitted New England liberalism against the entrenched racial attitudes of the South. U.S. District Court Judge James Lowell, a descendant of famous abolitionists, granted a writ of *habeas corpus* to Crawford in April 1933. As grounds, he cited the exclusion of blacks from Virginia juries, and ruled that any conviction returned there would be voided by the U.S. Supreme Court.

The ruling incensed Southern legislators. U.S. Representative Howard Smith of Virginia introduced impeachment proceedings against Lowell on the floor of the House, charging him with high crimes and misdemeanors. The U.S. Circuit Court of Appeals later overturned Lowell's controversial ruling.

While the House Judiciary Committee was investigating his conduct, Judge Lowell died at his home in Boston. In October, the U.S. Supreme Court refused to review the decision of the Court of Appeals. Crawford was returned under heavy guard to Leesburg, Va., where his trial began on Dec. 11.

After a five-day trial the jury returned a Guilty verdict, and Crawford was sentenced to life imprisonment. He narrowly escaped the death penalty because, as defense attorneys argued, he would eventually be needed to testify against his accomplice, Charles Johnson, who was still at large. On Feb. 12, 1934, Crawford received a second life sentence for the murder of the housemaid Mina Buckner.

═══════════════════════════════

Crawford, James (AKA: **Harry Kirby**), prom. 1922, U.S. Facial reconstruction so expert it made the victim's sister faint led to the arrest and eventual suicide of the woman's killer.

On Apr. 13, 1922, a skeleton found in a shallow grave on Cheesecock Mountain in New York caused a scandal in nearby wealthy Tuxedo Park. Commissioner Richard Enright of the New York City police department, seeing an opportunity to climb the social ladder, gladly accepted the case although it was outside his force's jurisdiction. Enright relied on retired police captain Grant Williams, a skeletal expert, to identify the corpse. Williams, inspired enough by the challenge to suspend retirement, instantly set about his investigation, soon identifying the body as belonging to a woman who had suffered from curvature of the spine. Three small fractures on the left side of the woman's head were caused by blows from a hammer, Williams revealed, most likely struck by a left-handed attacker.

After treating the skull with a formaldehyde solution and covering it with a thin layer of sculptors' clay, Williams embarked on a two-day project to reconstruct the victim's face. The shape of the jaw and nose convinced him that the victim was of Irish descent, and, when a policeman gave Williams the woman's scalp, complete with hair, he added blue eyes that typically belong to the Irish. Armed with photographs of Williams' work, police stormed the area adjacent to the mountain, most notably Letchworth Village, an institution for the mentally ill, where the victim was identified as Lillian White, a waitress who quit Sept. 15, seven months before the body was found. White was Irish and had curvature of the spine. She also had a dislocated jaw, as Williams had foretold.

Mary Hamilton, the first woman to serve in the New York City police department, took over the investigation, apparently to protect the residents of Tuxedo Park from interrogations by a brusque male. Hamilton quickly learned that White had a roommate named Mabel, who gave a box of White's love letters to the policewoman. Inside were slightly illiterate notes from a man named John, who, according to handwriting experts, was right-handed. Instead of losing faith in Captain Williams' theories, Hamilton concentrated on a Robert Browning verse found in the box, written by someone other than John or White.

Letchworth Village staff members revealed that Ruby Miller, a nurse who had quit the previous September to get married, was an avid fan of Browning. Officer Hamilton found a marriage certificate linking Miller to James Crawford, an attendant at Letchworth, who had quit the same day as White. He and Miller were married on Sept. 17, but the minister who performed the service remembered the groom had an infection on his right hand, which explained the location of White's head wounds. Williams, upset that his work in reconstructing the woman's face had not led to any arrests, again sidestepped retirement to search for Crawford. He gathered fingerprints at Crawford's home in Maine, but the suspect had fled. Three years later, New York Police found the fingerprints matched those of Harry Kirby, who had fled Maine after shooting to death Aida Hayward. Crawford, or Kirby, was captured shortly thereafter and jailed in Winthrop, Maine. He killed himself after admitting he murdered White with a hammer as Williams had deduced.

═══════════════════════════════

Creighton, Mary Frances, d.1936, and **Appelgate, Everett**, 1899-1936, U.S. Everett Appelgate worked as an investigator for the Veterans Unemployment Bureau of Nassau County, N.Y., and lived with his wife Ada and their 12-year-old daughter Agnes at the home of Mrs. Appelgate's parents. It was an unpleasant arrangement, and Appelgate asked his friend John Creighton if the family could live in his house until things began to turn around. In November 1934, the Creightons welcomed the Appelgates into their home.

The Creightons had two children, 15-year-old Ruth, and a 12-year-old son named Jackie. Their mother, Mary Frances Creighton, also had a skeleton in her closet. In 1923, she had been tried for murder in connection with the poisoning of her brother Raymond Avery, who left her his insurance money. There was evidence that she administered arsenic to her brother, but since there were no witnesses, she was acquitted. Mrs. Creighton was also indicted for murdering her mother-in-law, but the jury decided that the small quantity of arsenic found in the body was not enough to cause death. The Creightons left New Jersey in disgrace and settled on Long Island.

The rather small Creighton house was inadequate for the

two families. The girls slept in a cramped, dirty attic, while the Creightons were consigned to a small back bedroom. This overcrowding led to some peculiar sleeping arrangements. The Appelgates invited Ruth Creighton to share their bed on occasion, which led to sexual intimacy between Everett and Ruth. Mrs. Appelgate, in whom Everett had lost all interest, apparently approved. Mrs. Creighton found out about it, but kept quiet after Appelgate threatened to expose her as a poisoner. On Sept. 25, 1935, Appelgate gave Mrs. Creighton some arsenic to place in his wife's eggnog, intending after her death to marry Ruth Creighton. At the same time, he was having an affair with Mrs. Creighton behind her husband's back.

Mrs. Appelgate became sick and eventually died in the hospital. Newspaper clippings describing the circumstances of Raymond Avery's death reached the district attorney, who, ordered an autopsy. The world-famous toxicologist Dr. Alexander Gettler was brought in to examine Mrs. Appelgate's internal organs in which traces of arsenic trioxide were found. Dr. Richard Hoffman questioned Ruth on behalf of the district attorney's office, and she admitted having sexual relations with "Uncle Everett."

Only then did Mrs. Creighton confess her involvement in the murder. She and Appelgate were indicted for murder and placed on trial side by side on Jan. 13, 1936. The murder trial became national news. The jury returned a Guilty verdict on Jan. 30. On July 19, 1936, the two poisoners were executed in the electric chair. Mary Frances Creighton, prostrate with fear, had to be wheeled to the chair unconscious.

Crimmins, Alice, 1941- , U.S. The attractive, 26-year-old Alice Crimmins lived in Queens, N.Y., with her two children, Eddie, age five, and Alice Marie, called Missy, who was four. She had been separated from her husband Edmund, who visited regularly with the children. On the morning of July 14, 1965, Edmund Crimmins visited his children only to find them missing from their room in the ground-floor Crimmins apartment. A desperate search took place and Alice Marie was found later that day in a vacant lot, strangled to death with her pajamas. Eddie Crimmins was found a week later about a mile from the Crimmins home and he, too, had been strangled, although forensic experts were uncertain if this was truly the case because the little boy's body had rapidly decomposed. Mrs. Crimmins explained to suspicious investigators that a hook-and-eye fastener on the door leading to her children's room was missing, that she always fastened this apparatus to prevent them from leaving their room to raid the refrigerator.

Mrs. Crimmins seemed rather unemotional at the time

of her children's death. When she was taken to the barren

Alice Crimmins and her two children, Alice Marie and Eddie, Christmas, 1964.

lot at 162nd Street where her daughter's body was discovered, Crimmins appeared to go into a faint but recovered within moments. She shed not a single tear, nor was any trace of emotion present in the woman. Later, Mrs. Crimmins explained precisely what happened on the night her children left their room. She said that she had fed both her children manicotti and string beans at 7:30 p.m. She said she looked in on them at midnight and they were sleeping peacefully in their beds. Mrs. Crimmins added that she was awake until 4 a.m., and that her children must have left their room after that time or were kidnapped and later killed for inexplicable reasons after that time. Questioned repeatedly about these time periods, Alice Crimmins insisted that the times she had provided were correct, that she had checked several clocks in the house. These statements led to the conviction of Crimmins later in one of the most sensational murder trials of the 1960s.

The police suspected Mrs. Crimmins from the start, but they cautiously built their case against her. Twenty-three months later, she was charged with murdering her children, and in May 1968, placed on trial for the murder of her daughter Missy. The prosecution demonstrated how Mrs. Crimmins had led a promiscuous life and even her own lawyer described his client as "amoral." It was for this reason that her husband was suing for divorce at the time of the children's deaths. The custody battle was intense and full of vicious charges from both sides. Mrs. Crimmins, the prosecution contended, had murdered her children rather than let her husband take custody of them; an act, she felt, that would label her as an unfit mother.

Dr. Milton Helpern, one of the leading pathologists in the country, testified that he had examined the contents of the Crimmins daughter and that the child had, indeed, been fed manicotti and string beans. But the girl had not digested this food, Helpern said, at the time Mrs. Crimmins insisted she had fed her children, the little girl having died about two hours after eating the meal. Helpern stated that the girl had eaten the food only a short time before her murder and that Mrs. Crimmins' statements were "impossible—just impossible. If she said she saw them alive before midnight, how could the stomach of Missy show that she must have died within two hours of taking a meal at 7:30...It is patently absurd to think that death might have occurred in the predawn hours after her mother had gone to bed."

A neighbor, Mrs. Earomirski, then testified that she looked out her second-story window about 2 a.m. on the morning of the deaths, and recognized Alice Crimmins with a man, going toward a car. The man was carrying a blanket bundle and Alice Crimmins was leading a small boy by the hand. The man threw the bundle into the back seat of the car and Crimmins said to him: "My God, don't throw her like that!" Mrs. Earomirski said she then began to close the window which squeaked and caused Crimmins to look toward the window and say to the man: "Somebody's seen us!"

The guilt of Alice Crimmins was firm in the minds of the jury, who convicted her of first-degree manslaughter. She was sentenced to twenty years in the New York State Prison for women. Her lawyers, however, managed to win an appeal and the appellate court quashed the sentence, ordering a new trial which occurred in March 1971. This trial proved to be more devastating to Crimmins than the first one. One of her lovers, Joseph Rorech, a building contractor, testified that Crimmins was with him in a motel room following the deaths of her children and that she confessed that she had murdered both the little boy and girl so that their father would not get custody of them. This drew Crimmins' only emotional outburst in her long fight for freedom. She called Rorech a liar and then lapsed into silence. Crimmins was found Guilty of first-degree murder in the death of her son Eddie and of first-degree manslaughter in the death of her daugher Missy. She was sentenced to life imprisonment. After two more appeals, Crimmins was released on bail in 1975. The New York Court of Appeals dismissed the murder conviction of her son but upheld the conviction of manslaughter in the case of her daughter. Crimmins was transferred in 1976 to a release institution in Harlem where she finally took work as a secretary.

Crimmins, Craig (**Phantom of the Opera Case**), 1959-   , U.S. A husky, baby-faced, young man with extraordinarily large hands, Craig Crimmins grew up in the North Bronx, N.Y. As a child he was a slow learner, and was afraid to appear stupid in front of his teachers. Withdrawn and oversized for his age, Crimmins was the favored child of three offspring. At the age of three, he began to sleepwalk, which was often a problem for his parents. One night his mother followed him out of the apartment building and through a snowswept street to return him to his bedroom; he had no recall of the event. After managing to squeak through high school, Crimmins followed his father, brother, and stepfather into stagehand work. He was employed by the Metropolitan Opera House in Manhattan, and there he was attracted to pretty Helen Hagnes Mintiks, a 30-year-old violinist who worked in the orchestra pit during regular performances. On the night of July 23, 1980, Crimmins was in a sub-level elevator when Mintiks entered. Impulsively, Crimmins leaned next to her and suggested they have sexual intercourse. Mintiks turned crimson and slapped his face. Then, realizing she was alone in the elevator with the hulking Crimmins, the violinist panicked and hit several buttons on the elevator control board. The elevator stopped at a lower level and she got out. Crimmins followed her.

The violinist realized that the area was deserted and tried to strike up a friendly conversation with Crimmins, according to his later confession. He grabbed a hammer and ordered her to undress. She obediently disrobed. When she was naked, the stagehand attempted to rape the woman but was unsuccessful. In frustration, he marched Mintiks up the backstairs of the Met to the roof and there tied her to a pipe. He claimed later that he had no real intention of hurting her and that he told her he would "call someone" and let them know where she was. As he went to a rooftop door, Mintiks broke free of the rope which Crimmins had used to tie her up. He raced back to the pipe, caught the woman, and tied her up again with rags he found in a nearby bucket.

Again, according to his later statement, Crimmins started to leave the roof, but he turned around to see the violinist about to once more break free. "I heard her pouncing up and down," Crimmins was later quoted, "and that's when it happened. I went back and kicked her off." Crimmins, at that point, walked up to the bound woman and kicked her through an opening in an air conditioner fan shaft. Her naked, bound body was found the next day. New York police conducted an exhaustive search for the killer, combing the maze-like dressing rooms, backstairs, elevators, basements, and sub-basements for clues. More than 200 suspects were interviewed; their backgrounds examined in detail. On Aug. 14, 1980, the two chief detectives assigned to the case, Michael Struk and Jerry Giorgio, began to systematically photograph and fingerprint every Met employee. They noticed that one of them, Craig Crimmins, was extremely nervous when it came his turn to have mug shots taken and his fingerprints and palms printed. Both officers noticed that Crimmins was hyperventilating while the printing process went on. Shortly thereafter, the detectives matched Crimmins' palm print to a perfect print found on the pipe of the roof of the Met where the victim had been tied.

The two officers played a cat-and-mouse game with Crimmins, interviewing him several times but not charging him with the murder, running him about the Met as if seeking information from him. In a final marathon and exhausting interrogation on Aug. 29-30, Craig blurted his confession to Giorgio. He was charged with the murder and tried before Judge Richard G. Denzer the following spring. Crimmins' attorney argued that the stagehand's confession had been manipulated out of the slow-witted youth and obliquely referred to the case of George Whitmore, Jr., another dim-witted youth who had been manipulated into confessing the murder of Janice Wylie in 1963—a celebrated Manhattan slaying. (Whitmore was later released when pharmacist Richard Robles admitted killing Janice, the daughter of writer Max Wylie, and her roommate Emily Hoffert.)

Both Giorgio and Struk underwent grueling courtroom examinations but remained unruffled. Their testimony reflected proper police procedure during their investigation of the killing and their conduct concerning Crimmins. The jury believed the detectives and that the confession was legitimate. On June 4, 1981, the jury, after deliberating five-and-a-half hours, found Crimmins Not Guilty of intentional murder but Guilty of felony murder. Judge Denzer later sentenced the killer to twenty years to life, which meant that Crimmins would not be eligible for parole until serving the entire twenty-year sentence. At the turn of the next century, Craig Crimmins will be forty-one, in the prime of life, and will begin petitioning the parole board for his freedom.

Crippen, Dr. Hawley Harvey (AKA: **John Philo Robinson**), 1862-1910, Brit. Dr. Hawley Harvey Crippen was a meek, inoffensive man and the last person anyone would select as a brutal murderer. For that very reason, and because of his sensational escape and capture, Crippen has found a permanent place in the annals of murder as a celebrated slayer. Born in Coldwater, Mich., Crippen attended the University of Michigan and received his medical degree from the Homeopathic Hospital College in Cleveland, Ohio, in 1885. He then served his internship at Hahnemann Hospital in Manhattan where he met and married a student nurse, Charlotte Jane Bell, who was born in Ireland and brought up in the strict manners and morals of a convent. The first Mrs. Crippen was a moody, young woman who had to get a special dispensation to wed the doctor—he being Protestant, she having been baptized a Catholic. After making love, Crippen later complained, she would hurry to a local priest to confess her "sin." Charlotte nevertheless bore the doctor a son, Otto Hawley Crippen, and was about to give birth to another child in January 1892 when she died of apoplexy. Crippen left his son to be raised by his parents in California while he looked about for another wife in New York.

The woman who became the second Mrs. Crippen was a bosomy teenager, the daughter of a Polish grocer, named Kunigunde Mackamotzki who was then appearing on the stage under the name Belle Turner. She was being kept by a wealthy Brooklyn stove manufacturer named Lincoln, and had apparently suffered a miscarriage for which she was treated by Dr. Jeffrey who was assisted by Crippen. Young Crippen was impressed by the sensual, ambitious Belle, but he was quick to see her dominant personality. "She would never give in to anything," he later lamented from the dock when tried for her murder. Belle Turner took a liking to Crippen, and the couple married on Sept. 1, 1892. Belle had told Crippen the lie that her father had been a Polish nobleman whose vast estates she was still trying to regain. The mild-mannered Crippen soon learned that his second wife was just the opposite of the first, so sexually demanding that she "fairly exhausted" him. Moreover, she never stopped talking about how she would some day be a great opera star like the celebrated Adelina Patti who received $5,000 a performance.

There would be no children in the marriage as Belle had had an operation which prevented her from giving birth. The couple settled down to a hum-drum life, and Belle soon began complaining that Crippen's meager salary did not cover the cost of her singing lessons—an expense that her lover Lincoln had absorbed. Economic depression and the public's declining patronage of homeopathic medicine, one which relied heavily on drugs, caused Crippen to field about for a way to make the kind of money his wife thought due their station. He and his wife opened up a patent medicine shop on East 14th Street and Sixth Avenue and they began to make considerable money selling quack drugs and cure-alls, most of which were nothing more than alcohol and opiates colored and sweetened with sugar. Crippen then came under the wing of Professor Munyon, king of the patent medicines. He was soon promoted to general manager of Munyon's widespread U.S. operations.

Though the couple saved no money from Crippen's considerable income, they began to live luxuriously, and Belle hired the best singing coaches in New York. They spent most of their money on diamonds for Belle and she would, each night, take these out and "babble to her diamonds and kiss them," according to one report. Belle also flirted with almost every man she met, and Crippen suspected her of having brief affairs when he was out of the city on business for Munyon. Crippen was sent to England in 1897 by Munyon to open a London branch of Munyon's operations with a $10,000 salary, a hefty sum for that time. When the Crippens arrived in London, they took up residence in a comfortable flat, but Belle insisted that she launch her singing career, and Crippen spent most of his money arranging for her to appear at the Old Marleybone Music Hall. She appeared as Cora Motzki in an operetta which left the audience sitting on their hands. She was cancelled after a week and thereafter appeared occasionally in the cheaper music halls.

Belle, however, felt that her failure was due to Crippen who had meekly opposed her music hall career and that he had somehow sabotaged her future on the stage. She was forever criticizing him and his lack of vision in her talent. To vex him further and to enhance her own vanity, Belle took several lovers, including an actor named Bruce Miller, flaunting these affairs in front of her cuckolded husband. The five-foot-four-inch Crippen took these humiliations in silence. Meanwhile, he lost his job with Munyon's and began selling his own quack remedies. He muddled along year after year, abused and ignored by his wife, trying to make ends meet, especially struggling to pay for the new Crippen residence, a sprawling house at 39 Hildrop Crescent, Camden Town, in North London.

Crippen's prospects improved, however, when in 1903 he hired a new assistant, a pretty, young girl named Ethel Clara LeNeve who had large grey eyes and a sensual mouth. Her father had been a drunken brute, and she craved any type of affection. The gentle, kind-hearted Crippen provided that, and by 1905, a deep relationship had developed between the two. Crippen promised that he would rid himself of his now overweight, vain wife and marry Ethel, but he kept putting this off, making no move to finish his second marriage. His wife intimidated him so much that he feared she might resort to violence. Her lover, Bruce Miller, had returned to Chicago where he had a wife and child, and Belle, who was now using the stage name Belle Elmore, finally had enough of her do-nothing husband, informing him in December 1909 that she intended to leave him and would be drawing their life savings from the bank.

On Jan. 17, 1910, Crippen ordered five grains of hydrobromide of hyocine, a deadly drug he knew was fatal if only a few grains were ingested. On Jan. 25, 1910, Ethel LeNeve arrived at her boarding house in a state of near hysteria,

and her landlady later reported that she was ill and trembling all through the night. Whether or not she was aware of Crippen's recent decision to murder his wife was never learned, but Ethel did tell her landlady that Crippen's accounts were very low and that she worried about the future. Six days later, on Jan. 21, 1910, Crippen and Belle held a small dinner party for Belle's music hall friends, Mr. and Mrs. Paul Martinetti. Following dinner, Belle "entertained" her guests for several hours, as was her usual custom, by babbling about her stage career—a career that her friends, and silent husband, knew was practically nonexistent. The guests did not leave until 1:30 a.m. Belle saw them to the door and was about to step outside as they walked down the steps of her house. Mrs. Martinetti turned and called back to her: "Don't come out, Belle, you'll catch a cold!" Belle waved goodbye and closed the door, never to be seen alive again.

Two days following the dinner with the Martinetti's, a letter from Belle was received by the Music Hall Ladies' Guild, of which Belle was a staunch member, informing the Guild that she was resigning her position and was hurrying to the U.S. to visit a dying relative. The letter was written by Crippen who informed the Guild that his wife left in such a hurry that she had no time to write the note herself. Some days later, Crippen pawned some of Belle's jewelry, receiving £80. Neighbors were then shocked to see Crippen's petite secretary, Ethel LeNeve, move into the Crippen house at 39 Hildrop Crescent. She appeared in local restaurants with Crippen, wearing Belle's furs and jewelry, and Crippen introduced Ethel as his new housekeeper. Then Crippen placed an advertisement in *Era* Magazine, informing its readers that his wife had died. The ad informed Belle's fans that "she passed on of pneumonia up in the high mountains of California." Crippen next appeared at the grand ball given by the Music Hall Ladies' Guild with Ethel LeNeve on his arm. Ethel was wearing a diamond brooch which had been Belle's favorite piece of jewelry. In fact, the Martinetti's had last seen the brooch on the bosom of Belle when they dined with the Crippens on Jan. 31, 1910. Then the doctor and the housekeeper packed their bags and took a vacation to Dieppe together, a trip Crippen made no pains to hide. Such scandalous conduct on the part of the otherwise proper Crippen raised more than a few eyebrows with neighbors who promptly notified Scotland Yard about their suspicions.

In response, Inspector Walter Dew, accompanied by Sergeant Arthur Mitchell, began looking into the disappearance of Mrs. Crippen. Dew, who was the intrepid Chief Inspector of Scotland Yard's Criminal Investigation Department (CID), was anything but a severe detective. He was kind-hearted, understanding, and always gave the benefit of a doubt to any suspect. Dew visited Crippen's

Dr. Hawley Harvey Crippen, and in disguise with beard.

Above, the ambitious Belle Elmore Crippen, part-time music hall singer, full-time cuckolder who moved the mild-mannered doctor to a slaughter-house murder. There was nothing left of her except a few gruesome pieces. Left, Dr. Crippen's pretty mistress, the long-suffering Ethel LeNeve, shown here disguised in men's clothing as Crippen tried to pass her off as his son during a dramatic attempt to escape Scotland Yard in a sea chase.

Dr. Crippen, at right, hat pulled down, scarf on face, is escorted off ship by Inspector Walter Dew.

Captain Kendall's famous telegram, the first used to catch a criminal.

offices while the doctor was periodically treating some patients, asking a few polite questions concerning Belle's whereabouts. Crippen was most affable and cooperative, finally telling Dew with considerable embarrassment: "It's extremely humiliating, sir, to inform you that my wife is not visiting any ailing relative in America, nor did she die in California. I've tried to protect her reputation and my own humiliation and failure. The truth is, sir, that my wife has left me for another man, a man better able to support her than myself." Crippen then told Dew that the man was none other than the actor, Bruce Miller, who had returned to the U.S. Belle had simply followed him.

Dew's suspicions were further put to rest when Crippen suggested they have lunch the next day, which they did. Crippen then suggested that Dew inspect his home at 39 Hildrop Crescent. Dew, accompanied by the extremely cooperative Crippen, walked through every room of the house while the detective looked about rather sheepishly. Dew even inspected the cellar and garden and concluded that, aside from the absence of Belle, nothing was amiss. The matter seemed to be one of a domestic nature and Scotland Yard washed its hands of Belle Elmore Crippen and her cuckolded husband. The woman Dew was seeking was, at one point during his search of the Crippen house, directly beneath the detective's feet, buried in the cellar. Crippen had poisoned Belle with hyocine, then dragged her heavy body to the cellar where he decapitated the body, the limbs, and filleted the rest of the corpse, burning the bones in a cellar grate, a job that took several days and nights. Crippen, on hands and knees, cleaned the blood and bone chips from the grate for hours. The rest of the remains he buried in small hole in the cellar floor, wrapped in men's pajamas which were packed with quicklime.

The visit from Inspector Dew alarmed Crippen to the point that he felt he would be arrested at any moment. He and Ethel packed their bags and left for the Continent, arriving in Rotterdam. Ethel was dressed as a boy, wearing some of Crippen's clothing, and pretending to be his son to avoid detection as a couple traveling together. On July 11, Dew returned to 39 Hildrop Crescent to check the exact date Belle had left for America, but he found that the doctor and his housekeeper had left three days earlier. Dew acted immediately, ordering his men to thoroughly search the house and surrounding area. For several days, investigators tore apart cupboards, peeled back wallpaper, dug up the garden and, finally, dug up the cellar where the bundle of flesh wrapped in a man's pajama top was unearthed. There was not much to go on. The sexless remains consisted of pieces of skin, a human buttock, chest and stomach organs, and bits of muscle. One hunk of flesh revealed a scar which appeared to have been the result of an abdominal operation. This scar was checked against

Belle's medical records and it was identified as an old incision made during one of Belle's many operations.

Dew swore out a warrant for Crippen and LeNeve on July 16, 1910, and a nationwide manhunt ensued. Unaware of the search being conducted for them, Crippen and Ethel boarded the S.S. *Montrose* at Antwerp on July 20, traveling as father and son. The *Montrose* was en route to Canada. Once in Canada, Crippen hoped to begin a new life with Ethel. No sooner was the 5,431-ton *Montrose* out of Antwerp harbor than its captain, Henry Kendall, looked through a porthole of his cabin to see two men on deck, standing behind a lifeboat and holding hands in what for that day was a shocking display of homosexual affection. Said Captain Kendall later in triumphant retrospect: "The younger one squeezed the other's hand immoderately. It seemed to me unnatural for two males, so I suspected them at once." Kendall did not explain exactly what it was that he suspected. Kendall encountered the pair when the *Montrose* reached the open sea and invited the two to have lunch with him at his table.

Crippen introduced himself as John Philo Robinson, a merchant who was taking his 16-year-old son to California for his health. At this point, Ethel, her hair pulled back and tucked beneath a cap, dutifully coughed and looked ill. (Crippen's alias was plucked from his family tree; his uncle was named Harvey Robinson and he had a cousin in Michigan named Philo Robinson.) Crippen was not wearing a beard as a disguise as later artists would draw him but was clean-shaven for the voyage. He had discarded, however, his glasses, although the tell-tale marks from his spectacles remained at the bridge of his nose. He seemed to talk incesssantly, making remarks about the weather, the speed of the ship, other passengers, the scenery. In contrast, the boy appeared to be a mute, saying little or nothing. The youth appeared to Kendall to be dressed awkwardly; some of the clothes Ethel wore drooped and sagged on her. Other garb seemed too tight, and the youth appeared to be bursting at the seams.

Captain Kendall noticed also that the youth had curves instead of angles, and that Robinson's "son" had a face that was decidedly feminine. All of these observations by Kendall were later made, some said, to enhance his image as an amateur sleuth, when, in reality, he had read about the murder of Belle Elmore before sailing and immediately identified Crippen and Ethel in their ineffective disguises. Kendall had taken pride years earlier when he exposed a number of card sharps who were traveling on board the *Empress of India,* for which he was then first mate. Ever since that day, Kendall had suspiciously eyed every passenger traveling on the vessels he commanded, ferreting out culprits and malefactors.

Captain Kendall did admit later that he thought about

wiring Scotland Yard about his two suspicious passengers almost from the time of his first conversation with the Robinsons, but he was uncertain as to their true identities and that he would be risking his reputation, as well as that of the Canadian Pacific Line if he was proven wrong. He conducted an experiment, he later pointed out, by going to his cabin and leafing through the latest Continental editions of the London *Daily Mail,* finding one dated July 14 which bannered the murder of Mrs. Crippen and offered a photograph of Dr. Crippen. Kendall took a piece of chalk and whited out the glasses and mustache on the Crippen photo and was satisfied that the merchant Robinson was one in the same. Before the *Montrose* was 150 miles from land, the longest distance where its wireless messages would be picked up, Kendall sent the following message to the directors of the ship line: "Have strong suspicions that Crippen, London cellar murderer, and accomplice are among saloon passengers. Mustache taken off, growing beard. Accomplice dressed as boy. Voice, manner and build undoubtedly a girl. Both traveling as Mr. and Master Robinson. Kendall."

The message was to electrify the world. It was forwarded by the ship owners to Scotland Yard and Chief Inspector Walter Dew. The policeman took a copy of Kendall's telegram to his superior, Sir Melville Macnaghten, asking for permission to chase Crippen across the Atlantic, saying: "I want to go after them in a fast steamer. The White Star liner *Laurentic* sails from Liverpool tomorrow. I believe it is possible for her to overtake the *Montrose* and reach Canada first."

Smiling at the thought of this daring plan, Macnaghten authorized Dew to begin the chase. Dew had already learned that the *Laurentic's* sailing time was only seven days but the *Montrose,* a much older cargo ship which also carried passengers, had a sailing time to Canada of eleven days. The code name given to Dew's assignment was Operation Handcuffs, and the chief inspector was so secretive about his mission that he told his wife only that he had "to go abroad for a few days on a matter of some urgency." Like Crippen and Ethel LeNeve, Dew chose to disguise himself, boarding the *Laurentic* as a simple passenger and using the alias "Dewhurst." The newspapers by this time had gotten hold of Kendall's telegram—the first time any criminal was identified and hunted down through an electronic device. They also learned that Dew was in pursuit on a faster ship and readers clamored for each day's editions to learn whether or not the chief inspector would reach Canada before the fleeing Crippen. The drama was intense, and readers on both sides of the Atlantic were held in suspense while the chase went on. There was a grim irony to it all. While Crippen and Ethel were sitting at the captain's table deciding what to order from the menu, the

rest of the world, unknown to them, was reading about their flight to Canada and the dedicated detective from Scotland Yard who had vowed to apprehend them.

On board the *Montrose,* Crippen let his beard grow but shaved his upper lip. He strolled along the deck with Ethel, stoking his beard. He sat in deck chairs with her, holding her hand and cracking nuts for her. He was solicitious and attentive to her at all times, giving her half his salad at dinner. Kendall, playing his role of detective to the hilt, began to keep a diary, and whenever possible, sent off more wires to authorities, saying that he had spotted a revolver in Crippen's pocket. Here he was mistaken; the mild-mannered murderer was unarmed. Kendall also stated that he had crew members collect all newspapers that carried the story of the Crippen murder which were on board when the *Montrose* sailed so as not to alert the disguised couple to the fact that they were suspected by the captain and crew. Kendall, who had been commended for his actions by his superiors, now heightened the tension by sending out wireless messages, no matter how trivial, that dealt with the Robinsons, whom he openly identified as Crippen and Ethel. His wireless message on July 29, 1910, read: "Ethel's trousers are very tight about the hips and split a bit down the back and secured with large safety pins. Kendall."

When this was published in the next editions, the tense drama changed to comedy. That very night in a London music hall, a singer sauntered to the footlights and sang:

> Oh, Miss LeNeve, Oh, Miss LeNeve,
> Is it true that you are sittin'
> On the lap of Dr. Crippen
> In your boy's clothes
> On the *Montrose*
> Miss, LeNeve?

Captain Kendall enjoyed the cat-and-mouse game he played with Crippen, often joining him and Ethel in their walks about the deck. On several occasions, he would approach the pair from behind, calling after Crippin, using the alias the murderer had assumed. Crippen did not respond to the name Robinson, called out three times by Kendall, until Ethel tugged at his sleeve. Crippen turned about and said: "Excuse me, I didn't hear you. The cold air of the sea has made me a bit deaf." On another occasion, Crippen looked up at the wire stretching from the mast to the wireless shack and said to Kendall, not realizing that he was talking about the instrument that had spelled his own doom: "What a marvelous invention it is! How privileged we are to be alive in an age of such scientific miracles!"

On July 27, the *Laurentic* passed the slow-moving *Montrose.* At one point, the ships were reportedly in sight of each other. Inspector Dew wired from the *Laurentic* to the *Montrose* the following message for Kendall: "Will board you Father Point. Please keep any information till I arrive there strictly confidential. Walter Dew, Chief Inspector, Scotland Yard." Kendall testily wired back: "What the devil do you think I have been doing?"

Crippen, as the voyage neared its end, became more and more nervous, asking questions about their arrival in Canada and checking the boat chart showing the *Montrose's* progress. He and Ethel no longer attended the ship concerts and sing alongs. They kept more and more to their cabin, and when Crippen was seen on a deck chair he was absorbed by an Edgar Wallace thriller, *The Four Just Men*. He later went to Ethel and gave her all his money, telling her that she might have to go on alone without him, a statement that perplexed and troubled her. He assured her that she would like Quebec, their ultimate destination, and that she could always find work with her typing and millinery skills.

It was later believed that Crippen had planned to fake a suicide attempt, leaving a note and hiding out with a bribed ship's quartermaster who would later smuggle him ashore. In his memoirs, Dew stated that he believed Crippen honestly meant to kill himself before the ship docked, by that time believing that he was identified and would be captured. He did not want his fate to befall the woman he loved. Most British criminolgists at that time, and even the celebrated detective writer Raymond Chandler in later years, agreed that Crippen could have escaped had he not brought along his lover, Ethel LeNeve. It was her easily detected disguise which gave him away. But love ruled the passions of Crippen, and for this reason he became one of Britian's most memorable murderers. He would not give up the woman he loved to escape the hangman.

In the early hours of July 31, 1910, a Sunday, with the *Montrose* off Father Point, Inspector Dew, along with members of the Quebec Police Department, boarded the vessel from a small tugboat. Still in disguise, wearing a pea jacket and the visored cap of the pilot service, Inspector Dew and the other officers went straight to the bridge where Captain Kendall met them. Kendall pointed out a small man in a frock coat who was emerging from behind a funnel on deck. Dew went to the man, followed by the Quebec officers and Kendall. As Dew was later to write: "Presently only a few feet separated us. A pair of bulgy eyes were raised to mine. I would have recognized them anywhere." Then, in a statement certainly equal to the "Doctor Livingston, I presume" salutation of H.M. Stanley, Dew said to the fugitive: "Good morning, Dr. Crippen. I am Chief Inspector Dew of Scotland Yard. I believe you know me."

Crippen blinked his large eyes up at the tall Inspector Dew. His adam's apple worked up and down and then he replied in a low voice: "Good morning, Mr. Dew."

The chief inspector informed Crippen that he was being arrested for the murder of his wife and the doctor was taken to the stairs leading to the decks and cabins below. Crippen suddenly turned and said to Chief Constable McCarthy of the Quebec Police: "Do you have a warrant? What is the charge?"

McCarthy produced the warrant and Crippen grabbed this out of the constable's hand, reading for himself: "Murder and mutilation! Oh, God!" Crippen threw the warrant to the deck and he was moved into a cabin under arrest. Some minutes later, passengers heard Ethel LeNeve shriek as Inspector Dew burst into her cabin and he placed her under arrest. With the fugitives safely under guard, Kendall, by prearranged signal, ordered a crewman to give three blasts on the *Montrose's* siren.

The tugboat *Eureka,* which had been waiting off some distance, then came alongside and swarms of reporters poured from the tugboat onto the *Montrose,* running wildly about the deck, molesting passengers who spoke no English, to see if they might be Crippen and Ethel LeNeve. Mayhem ruled the decks of the *Montrose* as Captain Kendall gave quick interviews to dozens of reporters who jammed their scribbled stories into bottles and frantically threw these overboard to be picked up by little boats waiting to take these "scoops" to the Quebec newspapers. The *Montrose* then leisurely made its way up the St. Lawrence River to Quebec where Crippen and Ethel were taken ashore and locked up. The historic chase was over. Crippen and Ethel sailed back to England under guard, and his trial took place at the Old Bailey on Oct. 18, 1910. From the beginning, Crippen's only thought was to protect Ethel. He insisted that she had nothing to do with the killing of his wife. Crippen alone was convicted after a four-day trial, and sentenced to death.

Crippen awaited the hangman in Pentonville Prison where he pleaded with authorities to spare his lover who was being tried at the time as an accessory after the fact. One of Crippen's imploring letters to authorities read: "In this farewell letter to the world, as I face eternity, I say that Ethel LeNeve has loved me as few women love men, and that her innocence of any crime, save that of yielding to the dictates of her heart, is absolute. My last prayer will be that God will protect her and keep her safe from harm and allow her to join me in eternity." A few days later, Ethel was found Not Guilty which allowed Crippen to go to his death with some satisfaction. His last request, before being hanged on Nov. 23, 1910, was that a photo of Ethel LeNeve be placed in his coffin. This was done.

At the hour appointed for Dr. Crippen's execution, Ethel

The Crippen case, particularly the wild sea chase to catch the murderer, caught the attention of readers on both sides of the Atlantic.

Inspector Dew's terse telegram announcing the capture of Crippen.   Dr. Crippen with Ethel LeNeve in the dock, on trial for murder.

LeNeve boarded the White Star liner, *Majestic,* which was sailing for New York. She was dressed in black and a heavy black veil covered her face. Using the alias "Miss Allen," Ethel sailed to a new life and oblivion in America. Captain Kendall later went on to become the skipper of the *Empress of Ireland* which was rammed and sunk by the collier *Storstad* on May 29, 1914, while the two ships were trying to navigate the St. Lawrence in a dense fog. The *Empress of Ireland* suffered the loss of 1,024 passengers and Kendall, once the hero of the Crippen chase, was digraced by the disaster.

The fate of the Crippen residence, 39 Hildrop Crescent, was worse. Following Crippen's hanging, the owner tried repeatedly to rent or sell the property, but no one wanted to live in a house everyone said was haunted. An entrepreneur named Sandy McNab then purchased the property. First he tried to run the place as a boarding house for elderly musical hall entertainers, but none cared to live in the place. Next, McNab turned the place into a Crippen museum of sorts, displaying press clippings of the murder and the chase, along with clothing and family artifacts. Only handfuls of the curious paid to see the place, and soon the house was again empty, except for, of course, the ghost of Belle Elmore, according to local residents who swore for years that they heard her piercing screams from the basement. Gone to ruin, the boarded up house remained empty until WWII when well-placed Luftwaffe bombs hit it squarely and demolished the landmark of murder.

Croft, William James, d.1943, Brit. The accused said his girlfriend had killed herself and that he had tried, but failed, to take his own life. The jury said he was lying, but they gave him what he said he had wanted anyway: death.

It was against the backdrop of early winter in war-torn England, 1943, that a young soldier, William James Croft, claimed that he and his beloved, Joan Lewis, had decided to make a commitment. Theirs was to be a commitment to death. Each would sit beside the other in the summer home at Camborne, in Cornwall, sharing a revolver between them, until one of them decided to make the first move. "Don't let us do it in the News of the World way. We will each shoot ourself," Lewis supposedly said.

Lewis, Croft said, made the first move, putting the revolver to her heart and pulling the trigger. The blast wasn't enough to kill the girl so Croft went running for help, when, he said, he heard a second shot. He returned to find his girlfriend lying on the floor with a fatal bullet wound to her head. Croft said it was then that he tried to shoot himself in the temple, but the gun wouldn't fire.

Neither of Lewis' wounds could have been self-inflicted, pathologist Dr. Hocking testified. Croft was subsequently found Guilty of murder at the Winchester Assizes and was sentenced to die.

The jury didn't believe Croft's story, but in England at that time, the survivor of a suicide pact was guilty of a double crime. Even if the trial's outcome had been different, the sentence would have been the same. Croft was destined to die from the moment he said he wanted to die.

Crosby, Henry Grew (Harry), 1898-1929, U.S. Following WWI, wealthy Americans, many of them young and purposeless, went to Europe, specifically Paris, where they embraced the expatriate life. It was a manner of living wherein that which was labelled as vice-ridden at home was an expression of art in Europe. One of the leaders of these youthful, effete dilettantes was a young man who lived only to dwell upon self, Harry Crosby. He was a sensualist and a part-time poet, a publisher for the sake of literary image and excuse for excesses, one who made a career of glorious disillusionment, and one whose fatalism was his only confidence. He was the saint of sophisticated sin, this heir to one of America's great fortunes. He was Harry Grew Crosby, nephew and godson of billionaire J. Pierpont Morgan, and his premature death would be marked by murder.

Crosby, born into great wealth on June 4, 1898, in Boston's Back Bay, could boast of a lineage (though he expressed hatred for all that was ancestral in America) that ran to the marrow of the founding fathers. He was related to Alexander Hamilton, William Floyd, and other luminaries of the American Revolution. Riches had flowed into the Crosby coffers since the early seventeenth century when another relative, General Stephen Van Rensselaer, established a fiefdom on his land (through a Dutch grant) that ran for twenty lucrative miles along the Hudson River.

Harry's father, Stephen Van Rensselaer Crosby, a pillar of Harvard and Back Bay society, was the eternal club man who became a partner in the banking investment firm of F.S. Mosely. Harry's family ties knotted tightly about the vast fortunes of the richest man in America, if not the world at that time, J. Pierpont Morgan. It was as natural as sunrise that Harry would attend the exclusive St. Mark's Preparatory School and then go on to Harvard. WWI interrupted the schedule with Harry sailing to France to become an ambulance driver just after taking his entrance examinations to Harvard in 1917.

For Crosby and his schoolmates, the war in Europe was high adventure—not much more, at the beginning, than a tour similar to those European junkets taken by offspring of the rich before entering college. The difference became sharply apparent when the youthful Crosby encountered horrible, mutilating death. The shock of recognition changed his life forever, especially after his close friends, Oliver Ames, Jr., Richard Fairchild, and Aaron Davis Weld, were killed in battle.

Worse still, on Nov. 22, 1917, the 19-year-old Harry Crosby was hemmed in by a barrage as he attempted to rush his ambulance to a field hospital near Verdun with a friend bleeding to death inside. It was a brutalizing incident he was never to forget, writing ten years later in his diary (absent of almost all punctuation, a writing quirk): "The hills of Verdun and the red sun setting back of the hills and the charred skeletons of trees and the river Meuse and the black shells spouting up in columns along the road to Bras and the thunder of the barrage and the wounded and the ride through red explosions and the violent metamorphose from boy into man."

Crosby's abrupt loss of innocence was replaced by anger and resentment. He blamed God for the war and, in justifying his own slim survival, he concluded that there was a bit of the Superman about him; that he had been forged into a special human being who was, by birth and station, already special in his own mind.

He returned home with a chestful of medals, including the Croix de Guerre, which he coveted and likened to achieving an "H" grade in college. Crosby, impatient to get out of the service at war's end, begged his parents to prevail upon his omnipotent uncle, J. Pierpont Morgan, to "try and get me a discharge," according to Crosby's *War Letters*. "Anything can be done by means of graft." Whether or not Crosby meant for Morgan to use his considerable influence or merely buy off authorities to get him released early is not known. But there certainly was a venal streak in Crosby, among myriad eccentricities and vices, all of which, in his short life, he would tax to exhaustion.

When he was mustered out, Crosby arrived in New York and immediately went to the Morgan mansion where, in the absence of his uncle, he ordered a feast which he devoured alone while servants did his bidding. (He called them "lackeys" and "menials.") Then he began to down goblet after goblet of ancient, priceless wine until he was drunk. In that state, he later arrived by train in Boston, staggering into the arms of his waiting family.

Harry's intoxication did not alarm Mr. and Mrs. Crosby; he was their only son and his ordeal in France was excuse enough for his unpredictable behavior. Crosby was quick to take up the same rationale, using his war experience for the rest of his short life as an excuse to wallow in the libertine life.

At first Crosby seemed to adjust, entering Harvard where his grades were less than spectacular. He studied literature and language, excelling in French in which, by virtue of his war experience, he was fluent. Crosby, like many other veterans of that day, was allowed to earn a "War Degree" at Harvard, which granted a shorter time of study in achieving a degree as compensation for serving overseas. He graduated in 1921.

A year earlier, Crosby had met and fallen in love with a married woman; he was to develop a habit—approaching mania—of trysting with married women for the rest of his days. The buxom, attractive female, six years older than Crosby, was Mrs. Richard Rogers Peabody (maiden name Mary Phelps Jacob), whom everybody called Polly. They met at a beach outing and both were smitten. Crosby told his parents that he intended to marry Polly, no matter what the consequences.

The Crosbys recoiled in shock. Polly would have to divorce her husband, another scion of a Back Bay fortune, to marry their son, and divorce, at that time, was inconceivable. Yet Harry persisted, telling his father that he would kill himself if he failed to have Polly as his bride. Polly reciprocated Harry's dedication. Her husband, the youthful Mr. Peabody, was a gentleman about it all. He told his wife to think it over during a trial separation. Polly did exactly that, going to New York with Crosby. At the end of six months, she still asked for a divorce and Peabody, who had taken to heavy drinking (he would later write about his alcoholism in *The Common Sense of Drinking*), agreed to let his wife go.

Harry and Polly married seven months after she received her divorce. Before that time, Crosby took to drink. He had accepted a desk job, arranged by his father, in the Shawmut National Bank in Boston, and hated it. He told his parents that he found Boston stifling, that the environment strangled his will to write great works. He promptly went on a six-day binge and quit his job. Next he begged uncle Jack (Morgan) to get him a job in Paris, something that would allow him and Polly to live in the "City of Light" where he could follow his artistic urges. Morgan arranged for Crosby to work in the Paris offices of Morgan, Harjes & Co. Delighted, Harry asked Polly to marry him and they were wed on Sept. 9, 1922, in New York City. Two days later, they sailed to France on the *Aquitania*. It was all idyllic, a fantasy come true; but then again, Harry Crosby had been born into fantasy and he always got what he wanted.

After living in expensive Paris hotels and running up staggering bills paid for by Crosby's relatives, Harry and Polly took a series of apartments, finally renting the huge flat once occupied by Princess Marthe Bibesco in St. Germain. For a year, Crosby halfheartedly worked at his uncle's banking concern, but he spent more time during each workday strolling the boulevards, drinking in bistros, and chasing women, than he did in his office.

Another rich relative, an older cousin, Walter Van Rensselaer Berry, who had been living in European luxury for more than a decade, learned of Harry's writing ambitions and suggested that he quit his job with Morgan. Crosby, using his older cousin as a sanction of the literary life, quit, and wrote his parents that he was, from that point on, dedicating his life to the muse, so would they please sell off a few thousand shares of the great amount of stock he held and forward spending money? They did—they always did.

By 1923, the Crosbys set the style of the young rich expatriates in Paris, or, at least, the mode of morality, a sort of glossy, intellectual hedonism. Harry was an artist and his temperament demanded that he seek release with women other than his wife. Among the many affairs he openly conducted was a torrid interlude with Constance Coolidge who was the niece of Frank Crowinshield, editor of *Vanity Fair*. The darkly attractive and willful Constance, divorced from diplomat Ray Atherton, had once been the scandal of China where here husband had been stationed. There she had raced horses and carried on in such a manner as to earn herself the sobriquet of "The Queen of Peking." Crosby, who met her at a racetrack in Paris, called her "The Lady of the Golden Horse." He was forever dubbing his mistresses with romantic names—Helen of Troy, The Tigress, The Lady of the White Polo Coat, The Sorceress, Nubile, The Youngest Princess, The Fire Princess. These were the names he used in his diaries in referring to his many sexual escapades.

Polly, whose name the Crosbys later changed to Caresse for alliterative, arcane reasons, seemed not to care about her husband's sexual adventures. She knew these "other" women well; they were social acquaintances and many of these ladies were introduced to her womanizing husband by none other than herself.

Yet Harry was inexplicably loyal to Caresse. Constance Coolidge insisted Harry leave Caresse for her. When he refused, she went off to marry the Comte de Jumilhac, thereby becoming a rich and landed countess. Harry continued to see her periodically, considering her part of his stable.

There were others, many of them, including petite, dark Polia Chentoff, a Russian painter who excited the Crosbys with her weird, bizarre tales of famine in Russia. On one occasion, she said that the people in her village were so hungry that they ate an American missionary who had brought them a little food.

While Harry's harem increased in numbers, Caresse was not idle. She, too, took on a series of lovers, boldly mentioned by Crosby in a letter to his over-indulgent mother. "Caresse's boy friends are," wrote Crosby casually, "the

Comte Civry, the Tartar Prince, Ortiz, Frans de Geetere (the husband of a couple who had been living on a barge docked on the Seine), Lord Lymington..."

As early as 1923, Crosby had gotten the reputation of a crazy millionaire American who gave vent to any sensual urge and wrote poetry on the side. One of Harry's passions was attending the raucous Four Arts Balls which heralded the closing of the art academies in Paris each summer. These were nothing more than costume orgies into which Crosby hurled himself with glee. In 1923, Crosby attended the ball wearing a Roman toga. He returned to his apartment stripped of this garment, his underpants, and all his money. Emerging completely drunk and stark naked, he staggered down the street and into his lodgings, to the amazement of his bug-eyed neighbors. Had this been the conduct of a resident Frenchman, the police would certainly have been summoned, but Crosby was too rich to arrest. Two years later, he found a monkey at the ball and got it drunk.

In 1926, Harry and Caresse shocked even the wild students attending the ball. Crosby went as an Incan chieftain, donning a loin cloth and coating his almost naked body with red ocher. Around his neck he wore a necklace of dead pigeons. Caresse matched Harry's abandon by appearing with a turquoise wig and was naked from the waist up, displaying her large breasts to hundreds of hooting students. (Caresse Crosby consistently complained that no female undergarments served as a proper halter for her mammae and, so she later claimed, she invented the brassiere.) The ball culminated with Caresse, breasts flopping wildly, being carried about the ballroom in the mouth of a papier-mache dragon made up of dozens of students.

These balls were held in enormous halls, where as many as three to five thousand people jammed inside. Half of the guests were whores plying their trade. The police looked the other way on these occasions, tolerating any and all excesses, except assault and battery. It was not an uncommon sight, following the closing of the ball, to see hundreds of naked men and women dancing in the streets and atop cabs, and scores more fornicating in doorways and near the hall.

Before the balls, the Crosbys invariably gave a party which became *the* pre-ball party. Hundreds flocked into their spacious apartment to guzzle their gin-laced punch and fall to the floor in amorous embrace. In 1927, Crosby threw a party that alarmed even his own sense of expansive tolerance. Males in attendance mobbed his maid and almost raped her. Ushering out most of the guests, Harry retired to the bathroom with Caresse and other close friends, and all stripped down and sank into the hot water held by an enormous, specially built bathtub. Then Harry

THE ELEGANT PLAYBOY WORLD OF HARRY CROSBY, 1920S ILIAD WHICH ENDED IN MURDER & SUICIDE

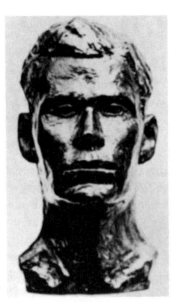

Harry Crosby in bronze.

Crosby, left, at his French estate with friends, Caresse on donkey.

Harry behind the wheel of his Bugatti, 1926.

Crosby with unidentified woman, Four Arts Ball, Paris, 1928.

Left to right, Caresse, Harry, and Crosby's sister, Kitsa, Deauville, France.

painted himself green, grabbed a bag of snakes, and headed for the ball, where he distributed the reptiles as necklaces to horrified guests.

When bored with Paris, Harry would suddenly hustle Caresse off to Athens or Africa to see the sights and sample the perversions. In 1925, Harry and Caresse traveled to Tunisia, where they both made love to an 11-year-old girl named Zara. In Constantinople, on a later trip, Harry scouted the city to find just the right kind of entertainment and one night took Caresse to an enormous whorehouse, where they paid exorbitant prices to watch couples fornicate.

In Egypt, they visited a huge brothel, one of Harry's favorite visiting spots; the Crosbys sank into utter sexual perversion, seeking out young girls with which to sleep. It was here that they (especially Harry) developed a great taste for opium and hashish, buying the drugs in great quantities. Crosby consumed so much opium on one occasion that he almost died from an overdose (he developed the habit of swallowing opium pills and mixing this with champagne).

The ancient land held a deep and morose fascination for the American millionaire. He collected strange artifacts from its crypts and tombs. On one occasion, he paid a large sum for three mummified hands of young girls, each having a blue ring on the forefinger. Another time he bought the skeleton of a young girl, which he pridefully hung in the library of his Paris apartment at 19 Rue de Lille. What cabalistic rites attended these purchases was never learned. Yet the mysteries of Egypt continued to hold Crosby in a trance throughout his short life.

His uncle, Walter Van Rensselaer Berry, had an abiding interest in all things Egyptian, and his influence upon Harry to seek the answers to that land's mystical secrets was permanent. It was in Egypt that Harry Crosby became enamored with sun worship, following the ancient Egyptian rites to the sun god, Ra. He thought of the sun as God, and at every opportunity stripped naked and baked beneath its rays, absorbing its heat, its fire, until, toward the end of his life, the normally pale-skinned young man from Boston appeared to friends as a "red Indian."

Walter Berry further enriched Crosby's life when he died on Oct. 12, 1927, leaving to Harry most of his estate and his collection of rare books, almost eight thousand tomes. This behest infuriated author Edith Wharton, who expected not only Berry's fortune, or part of it, but also Berry's library of priceless volumes. (The two had been lovers and Berry, an aristocratic, knowledgeable intellectual, had served as Mrs. Wharton's mentor.) For weeks—after Harry supervised the cremation of his cousin and sneeringly greeted distinguished mourners at the funeral in Paris—Crosby and Wharton vied for the library. Crosby feared that Mrs. Wharton, who, under the Berry will could

choose whatever books she wanted, would swallow the entire library. Harry thought of her as "a bad sort," and Mrs. Wharton, according to Geoffrey Wolf, writing in *Black Sun*, told a friend that "Walter's young cousin Crosby turns out to be a sort of half-crazy cad." In the end, Mrs. Wharton selected only a few books and Harry received the bulk of the library.

That he read any of these rare volumes is debatable. What he did do with many of the books would have caused Mrs. Wharton, had she known, to collapse with apoplexy. The Berry library caused the normally spacious Crosby apartment to overflow with books; they were everywhere—on the walls and piled high on the floors of many rooms, so that the Crosbys had to move about the place through narrow paths. Harry solved the problem by giving hundreds of books away to complete strangers, cab drivers, prostitutes, bartenders, those whose interest in ancient literature was considerably less than ravenous. Crosby then amused himself by donning disguises, a rag peddler, say, and slinking through the open-air book stalls lining the Seine where cheap books were sold. He would slip from a bag slung about his shoulders many of his cousin's priceless books and secretly bury them among the tawdry novels. It amused him to think that uneducated book buyers would casually pick up one of Berry's cherished volumes for a few francs, not knowing the book's true value, which would also be the case with the unschooled book dealers along the Seine.

Crosby's own literary aspirations were grossly inflated by himself, his wife, and his friends. He and Caresse started the Black Sun Press to publish their own awkward poetry and then expanded to include the most well-known writers of the day—Hemingway, Joyce, Pound, and others, but these writers merely tolerated the Crosbys, giving them fragmentary works that were expensively published and for which the authors received handsome pay. D. H. Lawrence, for instance, demanded that the millionaire playboy pay him for a short work in gold pieces, and Harry dutifully complied.

Literary figures Crosby admired repeatedly told him he was a talented poet. They should have known better, but perhaps they were merely stroking the golden goose. As a result of such boulevard flattery, Crosby began to submit his material to other publications, but not before he made substantial financial contributions to such struggling expatriate periodicals as *Transition*. In this fashion, Crosby's neurotic, erotic poetry found a wider audience than the Black Sun Press could provide. To the literary set, he quickly became known as a weird playboy poet whose work screamed out doom and death wish.

To Ernest Hemingway, Crosby was certainly nothing more than a rich social acquaintance who paid the way at the restaurant and racetrack during the author's lean years. It amused the author, once he learned of Crosby's fanatical sun-worshipping, to jibe him about it. From Cuba in 1929, Hemingway sent Harry a newspaper clipping that ridiculed sun-worshippers, but it did not daunt Crosby's belief in the ancient rite. By 1929, Harry Crosby had become hopelessly involved in himself. He lived only for pleasure. More and more, he escaped the real world to indulge in his fantasies, not unlike the time when he was on the way to a Paris bank to place Caresse's expensive jewelry in a safe deposit box. He spotted an attractive female relative, a distant cousin, and drank with her, attempting to seduce her. When Crosby departed the cafe, he left Caresse's jewels behind; they were never found. More and more, Harry sank into prolonged stupors from drugs and great quantities of absinthe (wormwood alcohol, banned even in Paris where the deadly drink had driven poet Paul Verlaine insane and killed others).

In 1928, Caresse and Harry moved into an old mill in the Ermenonville forest, near Paris, on the 9,000 acre estate of Armand de la Rochefoucauld, renting it by the year. Renovating the place to a posh spa-like quarters, the Crosbys invited phalanxes of artists, writers, and bon vivants to spend weeks with them, drinking and cavorting. Hart Crane, the distinguished poet published by Crosby, came to marvel at the luxury and flaunt his insatiable homosexuality—he seduced Crosby's chauffeur. (Crane would commit suicide in 1932 by jumping from a ship while returning from Mexico, swimming directly into the propellers.) Guests were encouraged to drink themselves blind night and day, and when not blind with booze, to amuse themselves in the gleaming, enormous pool (into which they consistently jumped fully-clothed), or participate in donkey races which Harry religiously conducted. Some of the guests stayed but briefly at Harry's wild retreat.

Writers Robert McAlmon and Kay Boyle, as recalled in *Being Geniuses Together,* left one of the wild parties late at night, going from the main building to the guest cottages after a riot erupted. "It's too damned depressing," McAlmon groaned to Boyle, "so depressing that I can't even get drunk. They're wraiths, all of them. They aren't people. God knows what they've done with their realities."

Reality had long run out on Harry Crosby. He shielded himself from it with money and the rays of the sun. Crosby was forever adorning his body with pagan symbols; in Africa he had crosses tattooed on the soles of his feet. In 1928, he paid a Hindu to tattoo a huge sun on his back in the dead of night as he lay face down in a boat wallowing on the Nile. It was also in 1928 that Harry Grew Crosby began planning his suicide and that of his wife. Caresse agreed with her husband to end their lives on Oct. 31, 1942, a date Harry had arrived at through crazy-quilt theories of his own

mad invention.

The year 1928 was momentous for Crosby. It was also in that year, on July 9, that he met at the Lido 21-year-old Josephine Noyes Rotch, a darkly attractive Boston socialite. He fell madly in love with her, calling her his "Fire Princess." For three weeks they carried on a torrid affair, but when Harry refused to leave Caresse for her, Miss Rotch sailed for the U.S. The following year, on June 21, she married Albert Bigelow, a wealthy member of a distinguished East Coast family.

Harry brooded over the loss of another mistress. His extravagances increased as did his erratic behavior. He leaped into a cab one night to drive down the Champs Élysées in Paris, hurling gold coins to startled passersby. He bought racehorses he never raced, and lost fortunes through reckless, stupid gambling, paying for his debts by selling off huge blocks of stock. (In 1929, Crosby wired his father: PLEASE SELL TEN THOUSAND DOLLARS WORTH OF STOCK. WE HAVE DECIDED TO LEAD A MAD AND EXTRAVAGANT LIFE. This wire came as no surprise; the Crosbys had led nothing but the life of wastrels to that time.)

Desperate to occupy his hours with something, anything, that would provide stimulation, Crosby suddenly became obsessed with flying. His mania led him to take many commercial flights between Paris and England (at a time when only a handful of passengers, at great expense, could cram aboard the small planes available, traveling at about 100 mph and at an altitude of no more than 1000 feet). Looking down from a plane on one flight, it occurred to Harry Crosby that it would "be fun to drop bombs" on the peaceful French countryside below.

Crosby took flying lessons and, in his gnawing vanity, saw himself as another Lindbergh, to whom he bore a striking resemblance. He saw himself a hero, a pathfinder, but he never went beyond student status as a pilot. Next came racing cars. Crosby raced for weeks, but soon exhausted his zest for dirt tracks, sputtering engines and oil-smeared hands. For a while, the would-be literary giant decided to become the world's greatest photographer and purchased almost every known camera. He tired of this, too.

Caresse tolerated her husband's excesses and went her own way, becoming engrossed with the duties of a publisher at Black Sun Press. Harry thought only of Josephine, his fire princess, and corresponded with her. His thoughts also, more and more, turned to suicide, about which he wrote reams of poetry and talked incessantly. He had apparently little regard for his own poetry. Early in March 1929, while staying at the old mill, he dragged out eighty-some copies of his self-published book, *Red Skeletons,* and blew them to pieces with a shotgun. He then burned the remains.

On Nov. 18, 1929, Crosby received a trans-Atlantic wire

from Mrs. Josephine Rotch Bigelow, urging him to come to her in America. Harry was at first reluctant to return to his native land. His last visit in 1928 produced in him a hatred for his hometown. In one poem, he called Boston a "City of Dead Semen." Worse, on that trip Harry had barraged Boston's literary bastion, *The Atlantic Monthly*, with more than fifty poems, all of which were rejected.

But Harry did return with Caresse. Keeping him company on the boat trip was an other old flame, Constance, the Comtesse de Jumilhac. After going to Boston, Harry met with Mrs. Bigelow on Nov. 28, 1929. Caresse went to New York and registered at the Savoy-Plaza Hotel on Nov. 25. Her husband showed up three days later but stayed only a week. Harry then took a train to Detroit, where he had arranged to meet Mrs. Bigelow. He and Josephine registered under the name of Mr. and Mrs. Harry Crane, using the name of Crosby's poet friend, Hart Crane. The love tryst lasted for two days before both returned to New York and their spouses.

Crosby began drinking heavily in early December as he and his wife prepared to return to Paris. Hart Crane gave them a party, but Harry seemed disinterested, even when Crane let in a horde of drunken sailors whom he, Crane, attempted to seduce on the spot. Unknown to Caresse, her husband had broken more than his marriage vows; it was already settled in his mind that he would not live up to their suicide pact scheduled for 1942. He intended to end it in 1929 "with a bang, not a whimper," (Harry's convolution of T. S. Eliot's premise) and with another woman, the fire princess.

Dec. 10, 1929, was an auspicious day for the Crosbys. They were to dine in the august presence of J. Pierpont Morgan, Harry's uncle. That morning, Harry and Caresse attended an exhibition by a sculptor who had done a bronze of their dog, Narcisse Noir. Then Harry left his wife, kissing her and telling her he would see her and his mother at "uncle Jack's." From there, they would join Hart Crane for dinner and the theater.

Following a quick lunch, Crosby took a cab to 1 West 67th Street, getting out at Hotel des Artistes and going to the duplex studio occupied by his friend, Stanley Mortimer, a portrait painter. Here, he met Mrs. Josephine Bigelow. They had met several times at Mortimer's and the artist, an obliging friend, had given Harry a key to his ninth-floor abode. They arrived together at noon to be greeted by Mortimer. They had a few drinks and then Crosby led Josephine to an upstairs bedroom with an overhanging balcony. Mortimer continued painting, but the couple leaned over the balcony and "kidded me," according to Mortimer later. "Crosby gave me a signal and I got on my street clothes and went out."

While Crosby spent unknown hours in Mortimer's place

with Mrs. Bigelow—described as a "strange wild girl who delighted in saying things to shock people" and who was extremely possessive of Harry—Crosby's wife and mother spent an uncomfortable tea-time with uncle Jack Morgan in the financier's behemoth mansion, trying to explain the absence of the errant Harry. Caresse and Mrs. Crosby finally left the Morgan house without waiting for Harry, returning to the Savoy, where they dressed for dinner. Still, Harry did not arrive. They went to the Caviar Restaurant and met Hart Crane. Halfway through the meal, Caresse later claimed, she had a terrible premonition, and left the table to phone Stanley Mortimer at his mother's house (this, of course, made it obvious that Caresse knew all along that her husband was not only meeting with Mrs. Bigelow, but was using Mortimer's apartment as a love nest). Mortimer told Caresse that he would check on Harry.

The artist reached his studio at 9:30 p.m. and found it bolted from inside. No one answered his calls. He raced to the superintendent of the building and demanded he break down the door. The man wielded an ax to batter down the door. Inside, Mortimer found Harry Grew Crosby and Josephine Rotch Bigelow—he was then thirty-one, she twenty-two—both dead on his bed. A bullet hole was in Josephine's left temple, another in Harry's right temple. Both were fully clothed, according to later newspaper reports. Their left hands were entwined and Harry's free arm was wrapped loosely about her neck, the right hand clutching a .25-caliber Belgian automatic pistol.

Police arrived to find more than $500 in cash stuffed in Harry's pockets, along with the steamship tickets which Harry and Caresse were to use on their return voyage to France. Crosby had removed a gold ring, one he called his "sun ring," which he had promised his wife he would never take off. It had been flattened, as if he had stomped on it.

Caresse learned of the suicide-murder, as it was later termed by police, late that night. She did not go to the scene of the crime, nor did the Crosbys utter a word of the disgrace their son had brought down upon the family name. It became their practice for decades that none of the Crosby relatives ever mention the name of Harry Crosby again.

The bizarre end of Harry Crosby and his Bryn Mawr-trained mistress captured the nation's headlines. The Chicago *Tribune*, which bannered the deaths with the headlines, CROSBY DIED FOR A THRILL, stated that: "As a writer and publisher and a wealthy, amusing fellow besides, Crosby just about set the pace for the whole crowd of expatriates, who credit him with having 'lived more fully than any man of his generation.' None of his fast-moving crowd believe Crosby committed suicide for love, and are sure he sought death just to see what it was like..."

But for Josephine, according to Deputy Chief Medical Examiner Thomas Gonzalez of New York City, there was

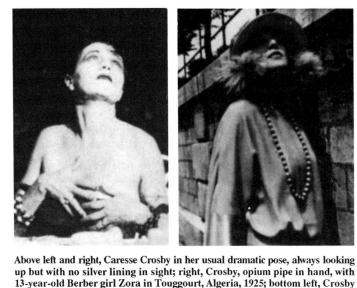

Above left and right, Caresse Crosby in her usual dramatic pose, always looking up but with no silver lining in sight; right, Crosby, opium pipe in hand, with 13-year-old Berber girl Zora in Touggourt, Algeria, 1925; bottom left, Crosby in his most famous pose, baking in the sun he worshipped, a self-styled religion that obsessed him and drove him to the brink of madness; bottom right, Josephine Rotch Bigelow, a Crosby mistress whom he called "The Fire Princess," the woman he loved and murdered before taking his own life in a Manhattan studio apartment in December 1929, ending his Roaring Twenties with a bang.

no such intention. Gonzalez, along with Inspector Mulrooney, stated that, from the position of the bodies and the varying states of rigor mortis, Crosby had murdered Josephine, then spent several hours alone in the apartment before killing himself. Gonzalez was quoted as saying that homicide was obvious, along with "the expression of smiling expectancy on the dead face of the beautiful young wife, indicating that she had gone to her rendezvous expecting a caress, not deadly bullets."

Albert Bigelow arrived in New York from Boston the following day, while his wife and Harry were taken to separate mortuaries to await burial. The outraged husband, a Harvard man, told a reporter from the *Daily News:* "This man lured her to his apartment and murdered her. I don't believe in any suicide pact no matter what the police or anybody else says, and I believe my wife to be the victim of a mad poet who turned murderer because he could not have the woman he wanted—and who was true to me."

Bigelow proved his loyalty to Josephine by having her remains buried in the family plot at Old Lyme, Conn. Harry's body was cremated two days later, and the remains were given to Caresse in an expensive urn which she took with her to Paris. (She would die on Jan. 24, 1970, still promoting Harry Crosby to the world as an offbeat, misunderstood rebel poet who simply happened to be rich.) Critic Malcolm Cowley further eulogized Crosby in his 1920s literary memoirs, *Exile's Return,* remarking about this supremely self-indulgent young man: "Harry Crosby, dead, had...become a symbol of change...In spite of himself he had died at the right time." It was Cowley's thought that the death of Harry Crosby signaled the close of the Roaring Twenties, the age of excess, only moments before a great night of depression and war blanketed the world.

Poet E.E. Cummings dealt with the murder-suicide as would a deadline-hounded newspaper editor, captioning the strange deaths with:

> 2 Boston
> Dolls found
> with
> Holes in each other
> 's lullaby

Crossman, George Albert (AKA: **Charles Seymour**), 1871-1904, Brit. The honeymoon at Kensal Rise in England ended too soon for Mrs. Ellen Sampson when George Crossman murdered his bride the day after the wedding.

Because Crossman couldn't settle on just one woman, he "married," under various names, at least seven. The first three marriages were legitimate, the last four were polyga-

mous. The fifth "Mrs. Crossman" turned out to be the unluckiest of all. Crossman, under the name Charles Seymour, took Ellen Sampson, nurse and widow, as his wife in January 1903. The two moved to Ladysmith Road to live, as Sampson no doubt believed, in wedded bliss. But the pressures of married life got to Crossman and the morning after the wedding night, he killed her by hitting her over the head. He hid the body in a room upstairs, so as not to disturb the fourth Mrs. Crossman, Edith Thompson, who was to return from a visit with friends in Peckham that day.

For more than a year, the two lived happily together. Thompson remained ignorant of the facts that downstairs, the remains of her husband's fifth "wife" were decaying in a tin box, and that her husband was, in fact, not her legal husband, and that during that year he married "wives" six and seven during occasional trips to London.

But Crossman and Thompson didn't live happily ever after. Crossman's lodger, William Dell, started to complain about smells seeping from a closet under the stairs. He continued to complain until, in March 1904, Crossman made arrangements to have the 15-month-old corpse removed. Meanwhile, the suspicious Dell had arranged to have the police come and check the house. The police found the body, and in the ensuing confusion, fearing retribution, Crossman took off at a run. Three quarters of a mile away, he pulled out a razor and slit his throat, ear to ear.

Crump, Michael Tyrone, 1961- , U.S. Between October 1985 and February 1986, the bodies of six Tampa, Fla., prostitutes were found in empty fields near cemeteries. The county police could not identify the killer, but they suspected Michael Crump, a former construction worker with a criminal record for aggravated assault dating back to 1981. Crump was arrested and indicted for the Oct. 9, 1986, murder of Areba Jean Smith, a 34-year-old prostitute. When the woman became "impatient" with Crump, she pulled a knife. According to his own testimony, Crump strangled her during the fight. Following Crump's conviction in July 1987, Circuit Court Judge Donald C. Evans sentenced him to life imprisonment. On Mar. 31, 1989, Crump was found Guilty of murdering a second prostitute, Louvinia Palmore Clark, whose body was found near the Shady Grove Cemetery on Dec. 12, 1985. Citing Crump's violent history, Judge M. William Graybill imposed the death sentence. Michael Crump accepted the verdict impassively.

Crump, Paul, 1930- , U.S. It was a question of life

and death, and it took nine years and fourteen reprieves to answer. For nine years in post-slavery/pre-civil rights America, convicted murderer Paul Crump, waited while the state of Illinois decided his fate. At the very last minute, even as he watched officials test his electric chair twenty steps away, the 32-year-old black man was granted his final sentence: He would live—all of his days in prison—but he would live.

At twenty-three Crump was found Guilty of killing a guard in a March 1953 robbery of payroll clerks at Libby, McNeill & Libby's Chicago plant. Originally called "savage" and "animalistic," he had become, under the guidance of Warden Jack Johnson, thoughtful, insightful, a convert to Catholicism, and truly sorry for what he had done. His attorney, Donald P. Moore, based an appeal to the state parole board on an argument rarely attempted: that Crump had been rehabilitated. The convict read Socrates, Nietzsche, William Blake, and the *Bible*. To give his own life some meaning in the face of death, he had written a novel, *Burn, Killer, Burn*. "One ought to be ashamed to die," he said, "until he has contributed something in justification of his living." Through all those years of learning, Crump was scheduled fourteen different times to die. Finally, clergymen, newspaper columnists, penologists, politicians, and convinced citizens called for a permanent stay of execution for the young man.

Crump's salvation became a massive public cause. Even opposing Assistant State's Attorney James Thompson was moved by the eloquence of trial lawyer Louis Nizer's testimony that Crump was "a rehabilitated man, a newborn man, a transformed personality." Nizer read from fifty-seven affidavits attesting to this change of character. In the end there was no end. Illinois Governor Otto Kerner changed Crump's sentence to life in prison without parole.

Crumpley, Ronald K., 1942- , U.S. A minister's son, former New York City transit police officer, husband, and father of two, stalked and killed homosexuals for the good of the nation and himself.

Ronald K. Crumpley, thirty-eight, faced his aversion to homosexuality with two automatic pistols, a magnum handgun, a machine gun, and the will to kill. He entered Greenwich Village, known for its gay nightclubs, in a black Cadillac he stole from his father, let go of all inhibition and began shooting at random. In seconds, two lay dead, four injured.

Crumpley believed that "demons in the guise of homosexuals" were after him and that he "was merely protecting the nation and himself." He was found Not Guilty on two counts of murder by reason of mental disease or defect and

sentenced to a battery of psychiatric tests. In September 1981, Judge James J. Leff committed Crumpley to the Mid-Hudson Psychiatric Center in New Hampton, N.H.

Cullins, Eddie, c.1903-31, Ire. A native of Crete, Eddie Cullins, twenty-eight, and a Turk, Achmet Musa, twenty-six, formed a partnership to profit from a human oddity. They charged people money to see Zara Agha, said to be a 156-year-old native of the Asia Minor region.

On Sept. 4, 1931, Musa's body was found near Belfast, Ire. He had been shot in the head twice. His bloodied clothes were found in the Belfast town center, and in Britain, police recovered a suitcase containing a pistol that was linked to the murder by Scotland Yard detective Frederick Churchill. Eddie Cullins was arrested, tried, convicted, and hanged. No motive was established, but after Cullins was executed, a girlfriend alleged that the two associates were gunrunners and that Musa had threatened to reveal the scheme.

Cummins, Gordon Frederick (AKA: **The Count; The Duke**), 1914-42, Brit. The British press believed they were onto a second "Jack the Ripper." Within four days in March 1942, four women were savagely murdered in London air raid shelters during the blackout.

Gordon Frederick Cummins was the illegitimate son of a member of the House of Lords. Cummins' friends called him the "Duke," or the "Count," because of his social pretensions. When the war came, he enlisted in the RAF. On Feb. 9, 1942, the mutilated body of Evelyn Hamilton, a 42-year-old

Gordon Frederick Cummins, hanged in 1942 for killing four women.

schoolteacher, was found in the central district of London known as Marylebone. The killer placed the body in an air raid shelter. The next day, Mrs. Evelyn Oatley was found dead in her Soho apartment. Police also discovered a blood-stained can opener nearby which the killer had used to rip open the lower portion of the victim's body. Oatley, under the name of Nita Wood, had turned to prostitution to support herself. Cummins attacked again, murdering his latest victim, 42-year-old Margaret Lowe, on Feb. 11, but the body was not discovered until three days later. The mutilation convinced police that the same killer was responsible. Like Oatley, Lowe was a prostitute.

The body of the fourth murder victim, 40-year-old Doris Jouannet, was found just hours later in Paddington. Another prostitute, she was in the custom of picking up servicemen in Leicester Square. Cummins assaulted two other women, Greta Heywood and Catherine Mulcahy who were fortunate to escape with their lives. Cummins left one clue near the shelter where he accosted Heywood: a gas mask bearing an easily traceable serial number. The police arrested him near St. John's Wood. Fingerprints found at the murder locations matched Cummins'. It took a jury at the Old Bailey in London only thirty-five minutes to find Cummins Guilty of murder. Lord Chief Justice Humphreys dismissed his appeal, and Cummins was taken to Wandsworth Jail, where he was hanged on June 25, 1942.

Curtis, Charles, 1960- , U.S. Before Charles Curtis, a drifter from Martinsburg, W. Va., confessed to the murder, the disappearance of Judith Lynne DeMaria of Sterling, Va., baffled Loudoun County Deputy Sheriff Robert Turner. After two years, everyone else had given up hope. But Turner kept the case alive and made it his own personal crusade. He even carried DeMaria's driver's license in his pocket.

Turner painstakingly reconstructed the events of the afternoon of Aug. 2, 1985, when the 27-year-old jogger disappeared from the Washington & Old Dominion bike path in rural Loudoun County. Witnesses later told police that Judith DeMaria was last seen crossing the bridge over Broad Run Creek. Blood was found in a field nearby, but there was no trace of a body.

The case might have gone unsolved if not for the killer's desire to confess to someone he trusted. Charles Curtis admired Captain John Sealock, who had befriended him in 1975. "Chuckie and I go back a long way," Sealock said.

On Sept. 9, 1987, a man called the Loudoun County Sheriff's Police to talk about the DeMaria case. He would speak only to John Sealock. In the company of Police Investigator Jay Merchant, Robert Turner, and Captain Sealock, Curtis pointed out a shallow grave near Dulles International Airport. The remains were identified as those of Judith DeMaria.

Charles Curtis told Jay Merchant that in his drug-induced state he had intended to rape DeMaria but she put up a struggle. Her death was caused by repeated slashes from a carpet razor. Curtis said that he had been on his way to a marijuana growing area where he was "going to rip off a couple of pot patches" in order to buy more PCP.

Charles Curtis claimed to have experienced visions, and to have spoken with "the Lord." "I am absolutely certain that his reason for coming forth when he did was the result of the torture he had been going through," explained his attorney Blair Howard.

Indicted on a charge of first-degree murder, Curtis pleaded guilty on Feb. 22, 1988. On May 5, 1988, Curtis was sentenced to the maximum two life terms plus twelve years, which were to be served consecutively.

Cvek, George, 1918-42, U.S. George Cvek hitchhiked along U.S. Highway 1 in New Jersey and told whoever picked him up that he was the "Mayor of Boy's Town," and that he was on his way to his sister's home. Cvek panhandled for money, which the drivers were often willing to give after hearing his sad tales. Cvek asked for each driver's address so that he could send a check.

Cvek would then turn up at his benefactor's door a few days later and introduce himself to the wife as a business associate or "close friend" of the husband. After providing just enough details to be convincing, Cvek would be admitted. Once inside, he would ransack the house and often sexually assault the woman. He repeated this crime fifteen times between July 1940 and January 1941.

On the night of Feb. 4, 1941, Cvek entered a Bronx apartment house in search of a victim. He rang the doorbell of the first apartment he passed and was greeted by a middle-aged Greek woman, Mrs. Catherine Pappas. Cvek pretended to know her husband, who was away. The woman even put out a plate of cookies and some brandy for her guest. Cvek wrapped his arm around her neck and choked her. She lapsed into unconsciousness as Cvek bound her hands with his necktie and placed a cloth around her ankles. He made off with a small amount of cash, and some jewelry items that were later pawned. The police, who by this time were familiar with Cvek's technique, questioned the other robbery victims at length. They traced him to the Mills Hotel on Seventh Avenue at 36th Street. The next night Cvek was arrested. He was taken to the Bronx Police Headquarters and interrogated around the clock. The next morning Cvek broke down and confessed. The "Mayor," as the press referred to him, went on trial for his life two months later. But a mistrial was declared on Apr. 28 because adverse newspaper publicity prejudiced the jury. A second trial was held in the Bronx County Court in May, which resulted in Cvek's conviction. He was sentenced to die at Sing Sing, and was executed on Feb. 26, 1942, after Cvek's appeals were exhausted.

D

Dacey, Edwin, prom. 1947, Brit. Edwin Dacey lived with his wife Iris Dacey and her parents in the town of Doncaster, England. A veteran of WWII, Dacey was training to become a miner so that he could save enough money to buy a home. However, things did not go according to plan. He drank heavily, and became violent toward his wife.

In July 1947, Iris's father had had enough of Dacey's outbursts. He ordered his son-in-law out of the house, forcing Dacey to find lodging in Edlington, six miles south of Doncaster. Early in the morning of Aug. 25, Dacey accosted his wife in the streets and seized his infant son, Alan, from her arms. Four days later, the little boy was found dead near the banks of the River Don. He had been repeatedly stabbed and hit over the head.

When confronted by the police, Dacey explained that he had given Alan to a pair of strangers who were going to take him to his own parents. He then confessed, whereupon he was convicted of murder and sentenced to die. But on the day of his execution, Dacey was stricken with a case of appendicitis. He recuperated, and was later pardoned.

Daguebert, Achille, prom. 1920, Fr. Achille Daguebert was court martialed and dishonorably discharged from the French army in 1918 for impersonating an officer.

In November 1920, while managing a garage outside Boulogne, he met two Englishmen named William Gourlay and Mr. Norman who wanted to sell their Vauxhall automobile. Daguebert agreed to buy the car for £600 and to take delivery on Nov. 30. Gourlay and Norman flipped a coin to see who would deliver the car.

Gourlay lost the toss and was driven by a chauffeur to Daguebert's shop. After drinks and lunch, the two men went to the mechanic's private office to complete the transaction. As Gourlay signed the receipt, Daguebert pulled out a Browning pistol and shot him in the back. He then told the waiting driver that Gourlay had gone to Boulogne alone. That night, Daguebert buried the body in his backyard. When police questioned him about Gourlay's disappearance, Daguebert told them that Gourlay drove off with three other Englishmen in a gray automobile.

Six months later, while Daguebert was in custody for auto theft in Calais, a local man told detectives that the prisoner had approached him months before with a proposition to murder a Paris garage owner. Detectives dug up Daguebert's yard on June 21, 1921, and found Gourlay's remains.

Daguebert was tried at the St. Omer Assizes on June 23, 1922. Despite his claims that the shooting was not premeditated and that he was drunk when it happened, he was sentenced to die on the guillotine. But French president Alexandre Millerand commuted the sentence to life imprisonment. Daguebert served twenty years in prison, and in 1941, was exiled to French Guiana, where he was ordered to remain until 1961.

Daniels, Murl, 1924-49, and **West, John Coulter**, d.1948, U.S. While incarcerated in the Mansfield, Ohio, Reformatory, Murl Daniels and John Coulter West swore that if they were ever free they would return to kill a guard named Harris who had treated them badly. Daniels was serving a twenty-five-year sentence for robbery, and West was in prison for stealing the tires off a truck. When Daniels and West were paroled, they committed a series of armed robberies throughout the Midwest, and killed a tavern owner. The two then returned to Mansfield, but were unable to find Harris. They decided to get his address from John Elmer Niebel, Harris's immediate superior. Daniels and West roused Niebel one night and led him into a cornfield along with his wife and daughter. The robbers planned to tie them to a post and force Niebel to reveal the whereabouts of Harris, but they forgot to bring any rope, so they simply shot the family and drove to Cleveland.

One of the most intensive manhunts in Ohio history began. Daniels and West drove around the state, avoiding one roadblock after another. They commandeered a car and a truck and killed both drivers before they were finally tracked down. The killers climbed aboard a haulaway carrying new Studebakers. The police became suspicious when they realized the vehicle was driving back toward the plant rather than away from it. When the truck stopped, West began firing, wounding a policeman before being shot to death. After the death of his cohort, Daniels was forced to surrender. He was executed in the electric chair on Jan. 3, 1949.

Dann, Laurie Wasserman, 1957-88, U.S. The question most often asked about child murderer Laurie Dann after the shooting tragedy that left an 8-year-old boy dead and five other youngsters wounded, was how could a woman with a long history of mental illness obtain a permit to carry a .357 magnum?

On the morning of May 20, 1988, Dann, a 30-year-old divorcée, drove to several area homes where she had worked as a baby-sitter leaving packages of food laced with arsenic on the doorsteps. She soon arrived at the home of Padraig and Marian Rushe in Winnetka, Ill., a suburb on

Chicago's fashionable North Shore. The couple had employed Dann as a baby-sitter for their two sons, aged four and six. Dann was to drive the boys to a carnival, but instead went to the Ravinia Elementary School, where she set fire to a plastic bag filled with incendiary liquid. The fire was quickly extinguished. Dann then drove to a daycare center in Highland Park and after lurking around the grounds with a gasoline can, returned to the Rushe home. She locked the two Rushe children in the basement where their mother was doing laundry, and set fire to the stairwell. But, Mrs. Rushe shattered a window to escape with her children.

Meanwhile, Dann drove to the Hubbard Woods Elementary School. She casually walked into the building carrying three handguns, slipped into the boys' rest room, and fired on 6-year-old Robert Trossman with the .357 magnum. The boy crawled into the hallway, where a teacher found him and notified the principal. By then Dann had entered the second grade classroom of Amy Moses, thirty, who had divided the children into six study groups. Brandishing the second gun, Dann ordered the teacher to line up the children at one end of the room. Moses tried to disarm Laurie Dann, whose shots hit six children. Eight-year-old Nicholas Corwin was fatally wounded. The other five youngsters, Lindsay Fisher, eight, Kathryn Miller, seven, Mark Tebourek, eight, Peter Munro, eight, and the Trossman boy were removed to area hospitals after Dann fled the building. The school was in chaos when the police arrived a few minutes later.

Dann drove her white Toyota into a tree a few blocks from the school. She abandoned the car and entered the home of Ruth Ann Andrew and her son Philip, a 20-year-old University of Illinois college student. She told them she had been raped and had shot the rapist, but now the police were after her for the killing. When Philip Andrew tried to wrest the gun from Dann, she shot him. After a harried phone call to her mother, Dann holed up in the second floor washroom while police officers from nine adjoining suburbs surrounded the house. Dann's father, Norman Wasserman, with whom she had lived following her divorce from Russell Dann, pleaded with his daughter to surrender to authorities. A police commando squad from the Northern Illinois Police Alarm System stormed the house, but Laurie Dann had already shot herself to death.

Laurie Dann attended the University of Arizona in the late 1970s, but never earned a degree. A former boyfriend remembered her as dangerous and unstable. He had received a series of threatening phone calls from Dann after the relationship ended. In 1982, she married Russell Dann, whom she met while working as a waitress at a North Shore country club. The marriage ended four years later, and while the divorce was pending, Russell Dann told police that

an assailant had entered his room one night and stabbed him with an ice pick. He believed the intruder was his estranged wife, but could not be certain. The case was dropped due to insufficient evidence. Laurie Dann later accused her ex-husband of raping her and bought the first of three handguns.

Shortly after Russell Dann reported the ice pick incident, Laurie Dann's former boyfriend in Tucson, Ariz., began receiving more threatening calls and letters, which prompted an FBI investigation. Agents traced Dann to the University of Wisconsin, where she was sporadically attending classes as a "guest" student and had a reputation as a dangerous eccentric after several acquaintances reported their property vandalized. Neighbors at the student housing complex recalled that Dann had ridden the elevators up and down for no apparent reason. Dann moved back to her parents in Glencoe, where she had a police record for shoplifting and had allegedly vandalized homes where she worked as a baby-sitter. "The parents had a responsibility and a duty to act," said attorney Robert Patterson, who filed a lawsuit against the Danns on behalf of Philip Andrew. The Illinois Mental Health and Developmental Disabilities Code mandates the involuntary commitment of individuals who are deemed a threat to themselves and members of the community.

Lawsuits against the Danns accumulated. Meanwhile, the five wounded children returned to school after receiving medical and psychological treatment. A few months later, Police Chief Herbert Timm told a gathering of 280 police investigators and school officials, "If it can happen in an idyllic community like Winnetka, which really does believe it's Camelot, then it can happen anywhere."

D'Arcy, Patrick, d.1967, Ire. Patrick D'Arcy was a lady-killer involved with a mother and her daughter at the same time. He murdered them both in 1967.

The battered body of 28-year-old Maria Domenech was found at the bottom of a steep cliff on the west coast of Ireland. The dark-haired young social worker from New York had joined D'Arcy at Orly Airport in Paris just two days before. They had flown to Ireland the same day, and chartered a car in Dublin to drive across the country. When they arrived at Moher two days later, D'Arcy threw her over the side and rifled her handbag of traveler's checks.

At the same time, Maria's 51-year-old mother Virginia Domenech was reported missing from her home in New York. Her body was never found, though investigators surmised that D'Arcy panicked and killed them both when he was no longer able to carry on the multiple affair. The answers to the puzzle were never supplied by the killer, who committed suicide in a Florida motel room several weeks after Maria's body was found.

Darden, Willie Jasper, 1933-88, U.S. On a rainy day in September 1973, Helen Turman was tending to her furniture store in Lakeland, Fla., when a black man entered. He examined some items on display, then left. He returned a few minutes later, and pressed a gun to Mrs. Turman's back. At that moment, her husband, James Turman, returned from feeding their two poodles. The gunman whirled around and fired a shot into the unsuspecting man's head. He then ordered Mrs. Turman to perform oral sex in the presence of her dying husband.

A 16-year-old named Phillip Arnold ran in to see what the commotion was all about. The killer fired a shot at Arnold, hitting him in the jaw. Two more bullets further wounded the teenager, who stumbled out the door calling for help. The same day, two other whites were killed in unrelated shooting incidents. Hostility was running at a fever pitch.

The next morning Willie Darden was arrested in Tampa, thirty miles away. Eyewitnesses told police that he was the man who had crashed his car into a telephone pole a little before 6:00 p.m. the night before. A detective located a .38-caliber Smith & Wesson pistol buried in a ditch about forty feet from the pole. Police were not sure at what time Mr. Turman had been shot, but estimates placed the time of the shooting between 5:15 and 6:00 p.m. It would have been difficult for Darden to drive through Lakeland and crash his car into the telephone pole at 6:00 if he had committed the murder. This puzzling factor helped keep Darden alive for fourteen years as his court-imposed death sentence went through an exhausting series of appeals.

Darden, who had a previous record of seven felony convictions for robbery and forgery, became a national celebrity. His case was publicized by Amnesty International, and a flock of show-business people, including actress Margot Kidder and rock star Peter Gabriel, filed protests with Florida prison officials and Governor Bob Martinez. A Darden defense committee was even organized in the Netherlands.

In published interviews from his jail cell in Starke, Fla., Darden accused the courts of overt racism. "It was close to election time," he said. "They needed a suspect. I was available." Darden denied carrying a gun, and produced eight witnesses who verified his whereabouts at the time of the shooting. But the positive identification given by Mrs. Turman and Arnold helped convict Darden. In March 1988, his appeals exhausted, Willie Darden died in the electric chair.

Davidson, Thomas Joseph, 1900- , Brit. Thomas Davidson, a poultry farmer in Stockley, Middlesex, England, was separated from his wife. She lived with their 8-year-old son, John Desmond, in Hanwell at the home of a Mrs. Clack.

In December 1933, Davidson went to his wife's house to pick up his son. After a brief argument with Mrs. Clack, Davidson left with Johnny. The boy was never seen again. The police were summoned, but all Davidson would say was that his son had died in the canal and a funeral was about to take place.

Six months later, Davidson confessed to murdering his son. He explained that he no longer wanted to go on living after his wife refused to come home. Taking his son's hand, Davidson jumped into the canal, but recovered on the opposite shore. His son did not survive.

Davidson said he buried the boy in a shallow grave near a garbage dump in Yiewsley, but neither he nor the police could find the body. During the trial, Davidson retracted his earlier confession, saying he had found the boy in the canal. However, the jury did not believe the killer and found Davidson Guilty of murder. His sentence of death was later commuted to life in prison.

Davies, Gerald, 1942- , Brit. A young schoolboy on his lunch break in a suburb of London discovered the body of 52-year-old Mrs. Stephenson, near a cemetery. She was found 100 yards from her home. A three-foot-long metal pipe lay across her corpse. Stephenson was the third woman in several weeks to be attacked in that area. Within twenty-four hours, 15-year-old Gerald Davies was arrested. When he was tried three months later, it was revealed that he had owed £3 to a schoolmate and had decided to rob to get the money. Carrying the metal tube and wearing gloves, he murdered Stephenson with a fatal blow to the back of her neck. Her purse contained only two bus tickets. The defense psychiatrist contended that Davies was maladjusted, but prosecution witnesses, including a psychiatrist and the principal medical officer of Brixton Prison, maintained that Davies was not abnormal. Found Guilty of capital murder, and sentenced to an indefinite detention, Davies was the first youth under sixteen to be indicted for murder in Wales or England under the 1957 Homicide Act, enacted on Mar. 21, 1957.

Davies, John Michael, 1933- , Brit. John Davies was a member of a ferocious South London gang known as the Teddy Boys. In the summer of 1953, he was indicted for a murder that drew attention to the problem of juvenile delinquency in London. The victims were two young men who inadvertently made disparaging remarks to the gang members near the bandstand of Clapham Common.

On July 2, 17-year-old John Ernest Beckley and his friend Frederick Chandler were walking on the north side of the common when they were set upon by gang members who had taken exception to their comments. The assailants wore the traditional tight-fitting stovepipe trousers and "zoot suits." Beckley and Chandler boarded a bus and were on their way to safety when the "Teddy Boys" dragged them off at the next stop. Chandler got back on the bus, but Beckley ran in the other direction, pursued by the gang, who cornered him. "Go on, stab me! Stab me!" he cried. The murder was witnessed by seven commuters who were either on the bus or waiting on the platform. The police identified five other gang members in addition to Davies: 15-year-old Ronald Coleman; Terence Power, a 12-year-old carpenter; Allan Albert Lawson, an 18-year-old carpenter; Terence David Woodman, sixteen; and the oldest of the gang, 21-year-old John Frederick Allan. All were known to the police, having committed a number of petty offenses.

The murder trial of Davies and Coleman began at the Old Bailey in September 1953. The other four boys were tried on lesser charges. The question before the courts was whether Coleman knew that Davies had a knife when he ordered the attack on Beckley. The defendants entered a plea of not guilty through their attorneys, Derek Curtis-Bennett and David Weitzman. The jury was unable to agree on a verdict, and the Crown dropped its case against Coleman. Davies was retried on Oct. 19, 1953. He had one stock

Murderer John Michael Davies.

answer for his accusers. He said that he never had a knife and never used a knife. Because of the eyewitness testimony given by bus passenger Mary Frayling, Davies was found Guilty and sentenced to die. The Court of Criminal Appeal and the House of Lords both turned down his request for a reprieve, but the home secretary commuted the death penalty to life in prison on Jan. 22, 1954.

Davis, Lolita, d.1940, U.S. Eleven-year-old Chloe Davis of Los Angeles awoke on the morning of Apr. 4, 1940, to strange sounds. She found her mother, Lolita Davis, beating her two sisters, Daphne, ten, Deborah Ann, seven, and her 3-year-old brother Marquis to death with a hammer. Chloe managed to get the hammer away from her mother. When Lolita tried to set fire to Chloe's hair, it did not ignite, so she turned the flame to her own, and succeeded only in making her nightgown flare off her, leaving her naked. She then lay down on a mattress, slit her wrists with a razor blade, and told her daughter to "Hit me until I quit talking." When Chloe asked why, her mother replied that the demons were after her. The child did as she was asked, stopping occasionally to get water for her mother and, once, at her mother's urging, to finish killing her brother, who was moaning. "I always did what mother told me to do," she said. Even though the claw head came off the hammer, the girl continued "conking" her mother until she was silent. Then she got dressed and went to a neighbor's house to telephone her father, saying he'd better come home right away.

Los Angeles authorities and psychiatrists first believed that Chloe herself killed her siblings and her mother. A police psychiatrist, Dr. Paul de River, said of Chloe, "She is cool, has no depth of feeling, has great powers of imagination for fantasy and is distinctly capable of planning and committing the murders. But so far, I believe her story more than I disbelieve it." It was not until the next day that Chloe remembered to tell the police about her mother slitting her wrists. Then she learned that her mother had, in fact, bled to death, and did not die of bludgeoning. Chloe's father, Barton Davis, said that his wife Lolita had been mentally ill and had frequently threatened suicide to escape the "demons" that pursued her. When the family doctor verified his story, Chloe was released. She was later made a ward of the state.

Davis, Ralph Orin, 1918- , U.S. Ralph Davis, sixty-nine, had served in WWII and had been held prisoner by the Japanese for two-and-a-half years. In 1981, Davis moved from California to Mt. Pleasant, Iowa. His new neighbors in Iowa did not know that Davis had been acquitted of a murder charge on Jan. 16, 1980. He had been charged with the shooting of a neighbor in Bell Gardens, Calif., after a dispute in which Davis accused the neighbor's children of throwing rocks at his truck.

But Davis' new neighbors knew he was eccentric. Unemployed, he rode a motorcycle around town with his dog riding behind him in a milk crate. He reportedly shot birds in a neighbor's yard because they ate cherries from his tree. On Dec. 10, 1986, Davis stormed into a city council meeting, furious that his backed up sewer had not been fixed. He shot Mayor Edward M. King, fifty-three, and wounded Joann Sankey, thirty-nine, and Ronald Dupree, forty-four. Davis was tried and found Guilty of two counts of attempted murder and one count of first-degree murder, which carried a mandatory sentence of life imprisonment.

Dawson, Sie, c.1910-64, U.S. On Apr. 14, 1960, Maggie Clayton, thirty-six, and her 2-year-old son, Roger, were found beaten to death in Gasden County, Fla. Their bodies were found by her husband, Alva Clayton, and two other men. Sie Dawson, a black man who had worked for the Claytons for ten years as a babysitter and handyman, was accused by his employer and arrested. For seven days, Dawson was denied counsel and driven continuously from jail to jail, interrogated at each stop. Dawson finally confessed after County Deputy Sheriff Robert Martin threatened to hand him over to a mob if he didn't confess.

During the trial, Dawson testified that Clayton had become angry when he smelled whiskey on his wife's breath and had beaten her to death with a hammer. However, an all-white male jury convicted Dawson of murdering the child. He received the death sentence, but was never tried for the murder of Mrs. Clayton. Two years later, the 54-year-old Dawson died in the electric chair.

Day, Jack, d.1961, Brit. Jack Day suspected his wife of having an affair, and allegedly said he would shoot anyone he found with her. On Aug. 23, 1960, Keith Arthur visited Day's wife. Arthur was married with two children, but was said to brag about his success with other women. According to a babysitter, Day came home with a gun in his hand and, after arguing, shot Arthur. Day then hid the man's body at a farm outside of town.

Police later found an unlicensed .38-caliber revolver in the garage where Day worked as a car salesman. They also found blood, soil, fertilizer, and straw on Day's clothing and shoes. Day contended that the gun had accidentally discharged, but he was convicted of murder and executed.

Dean, Dayton, prom. 1936, U.S. The investigation of a murder in Detroit, Mich., uncovered the existence of the Black Legion, a group of 200,000 Michigan citizens dedicated to fighting—and sometimes murdering—blacks, Jews,

Catholics, communists, and anarchists.

On May 13, 1936, the body of Charles Poole was found in a pasture on Detroit's West Side. A neighbor, Frank Shettlehelm, said he heard several shots just before midnight on May 12. A number of cigarette butts and several empty shells from a .38 revolver were found near the corpse. Ralph Hyatt, Poole's co-worker, told Inspector Navarre that he had been with Poole the night of his death, drinking with several friends, including a man named Eugene Sherman, at some West Side bars. When Sherman was brought in for questioning he told police that he had gone to Poole's home that night, and that a man came over to invite Poole to join the Timken Axle Company baseball team later that night. Poole left for the meeting, and was never seen again.

The detectives told Becky Poole her husband was dead at the hospital; she had just given birth to a daughter. Detectives Meehan and Havrill worked on the investigation, when a call came in from Poole's friend Sherman, who had just seen one of the men who had been looking for Poole the night of his death. The detectives rushed to the Fort Street location and picked up Harvey Davis, and brought him in for questioning. Davis admitted knowing Marcia Rushing, Becky Poole's sister, and her husband, Owen Rushing. Havrill interviewed the couple again, and Marcia Rushing began sobbing uncontrollably, saying, "We can't tell you! You don't know those people! They kill people that talk. They carry guns, and there are thousands and thousands of them—like the Ku Klux Klan—only bigger and more awful." Owen's brother, Lowell Rushing, was one of them. Havrill and Meehan brought Lowell to Davis, who claimed never to have seen him before. But when Meehan asked Davis, "What about your organization?," Davis fell for the trap and said, "I can't tell you." With a list of names, the detectives began to round up members, including Erwin Lee and John Bannerman, discovering blackjacks, .38 revolvers, and robes of black satin trimmed with skull and crossbones in their homes.

The most crucial suspect they turned up was Dayton Dean, who was the only one who brave enough to talk. He told the story of the Black Legionnaires, a secret "patriotic" organization of white, native-born, Protestant Americans, sworn to defending the laws, according to their interpretation of decency, especially regarding womanhood. At a meeting of the Wolverine Republican League (a pseudonym for the Black Legion) at Finlander Hall, the organization charged Charlie Poole with mistreating his wife. After wearing down uninitiated members who left after endless hours of speeches and business meetings, the Black Legionnaires locked the doors and swore to kill the man they said had not only beat his wife, but killed his own unborn child in the process. Several men were dispatched to find their prey, while others put together rope, ceremonial gear, and instruments to punish Poole. Facing a group of seven men with ropes and guns, Poole professed his innocence, but was shot down. Learning that Poole was actually an upright family man, Dean regretted his mistake, adding, "But I was just following orders from my superiors."

The Black Legion case remained in the press for some time as reports of vicious vigilante killings and beatings continued to grow. Dean unveiled a twisted conspiracy of a group similar to the Klan, to which he had belonged in 1922, rising to the station of captain. He joined the Black Legionnaires in 1933, attending his first meeting in a small town north of Detroit. With secret rites of "Black Knights" signing death's head agreements in blood, vowing to use extra-legal methods to preserve the white race and keep it strong, members received .38-caliber cartridges with the warning that they would be killed if they ever broke their oaths. Davis testified to a plot to take over the government which involved planting typhoid germs in milk supplies to create a national emergency during which the Black Legionnaires would seize government arsenals, power plants, and buildings. Dean explained how, as death squad leader, he had been assigned to assassinate Mayor William Voisine of Encorse, Mich. Voisine was charged by the organization for hiring blacks for civic jobs. When an attempt to bomb Voisine's home failed, the frustrated Legionnaires murdered Silas Coleman "to see what it was like," Davis explained. Coleman was picked up by Davis, who promised him that he would be taken to a contractor's to collect some back wages owed to him. Davis instead took the black man to a swamp, ordering him out of the car with the words, "Okay, nigger, start running," while a hunting party chased him through the swamps and murdered him.

At least fifty deaths were attributed to the Black Legion, including that of John Bielak, a union organizer; Paul Avery, a prison guard who was a former member of the group but had been excommunicated; and Paul Piddock, a steelworker. Dean's testimony helped convict twelve killers. He was sentenced to a term of life in prison, and the Black Legion disappeared.

Dean, Dovie, prom. 1954, U.S. Dovie Dean, a grandmother of eight from Ohio, was arrested, tried, and convicted for murdering her husband by feeding him rat poison. Sentenced to die in the electric chair, she was executed in 1954. The press, amazed by the fact that the woman never wept during her trial, called her "the Murderess Without Tears."

Dean, Laurence Michael, prom. 1964, Brit. In December 1963, Laurence Michael Dean, eighteen, brought the dead body of Susan Moon, his four-month-old daughter, to a doctor. Dean explained he had found her dead in her crib; when the examining doctor noticed bruises on the child's body, Dean said she had hit her head a few days earlier. The coroner performing the autopsy, Dr. Francis Camps, found several fractured ribs, a ruptured liver, fractured skull, and several recent bruises on the child's abdomen, jaw, and scalp. Dean said that when he had found his daughter not breathing, he gave her artificial resuscitation, probably causing the damage in the process. Incredibly, this excuse was accepted and an "open verdict" was returned by the coroner. Dean moved to Wadhurst, in Sussex, with his wife, who soon gave birth to their second child, Michael. Five weeks later, Dean brought Michael to see a doctor; the infant died in the doctor's arms. Dean claimed that after being fed, the child began whimpering and breathing laboriously.

The autopsy of Dean's second child, by coroner Dr. Keith Simpson, revealed nineteen bruises in six different parts of the body, and a ruptured liver. Dean explained that when the child began to roll off his lap, Dean tried to save him, but his "knee came up and hit him in the abdomen." His story was rejected. Both deaths were reported to the director of public prosecutions, and Dean was tried for the murders of both children on Jan. 19, 1965, at the Old Bailey. Dean's conviction for murder was the first in England for such a case. He was sentenced to death, but later reprieved and imprisoned for life.

Dean, Dr. Sarah Ruth, prom. 1933, U.S. On Aug. 8, 1933, District Attorney Arthur Jordan charged Dr. Sarah Ruth Dean, a 33-year-old eminent Greenwood, Miss., pediatrician, with killing her lover, Dr. Preston Kennedy. Dean and Kennedy had worked together for several years and had been lovers for some time; their romance began while Kennedy was still married. On July 27, 1933, they had a midnight tryst at the Kennedy Medical Building in Greenwood; Kennedy became ill after drinking what he later said was a poisoned whiskey highball that Dean gave him. On Aug. 1, he was then sent to Jackson Hospital for treatment. Five days later, Kennedy died after allegedly telling his brothers that he had been slain. Dean was arrested on murder charges, and on Feb. 3, 1934, she was tried in the Leflore County Circuit Court in Greenwood, Miss., in front of Judge S.F. Davis.

At the trial, Henry Kennedy, Preston's brother, explained that Preston had told him that Dean had poisoned his whiskey and that his drink had "a strong metallic taste—an astringent taste." Henry Kennedy contended that his brother was planning to remarry his first wife, and that Dean had previously destroyed that family. On Feb. 7, defense attorney Dick Kenman turned over 145 love letters that Dean had written to Kennedy. District Attorney Arthur Jordan handed out copies of one of the letters to members of the press, noting: "That's the last letter she sent. He never got it." The letter said: "I want to turn over something to you."

On Feb. 9, defense attorney J.J. Breland contended, in questioning Dr. Barney Kennedy, the other brother, that the dying man had been "unconscious or in a stupor" at his deathbed. There was additional controversy about the medicines that the dying doctor had been treated with at Jackson Hospital, and no explanation as to why the autopsy had been performed after both the embalming and the burial. State chemist Dr. W.F. Hand gave his expert testimony regarding the amount of mercury found in the body of the deceased, admitting that the amount was "minute."

On Feb. 27, Dr. Sarah Ruth Dean took the stand to say that Dr. Kennedy had divorced his wife in order to marry her, had given her a diamond ring that she had worn for almost two years, and had threatened to "kill them both" when Dean broke off their engagement with the intention of marrying another man, Franklin C. Maul. She denied putting mercury in Kennedy's drink. On Mar. 3, 1934, after almost five weeks of testimony, the jury returned a verdict of Guilty. Judge Davis sentenced Dean to life at hard labor in the state penitentiary. The case was then taken to the State Supreme Court where the judgment was upheld by a tie decision. Dean then appealed to the state governor for a pardon. On July 8, 1935, Mississippi governor Martin Sennett Conner granted Dean a full pardon, based on "the benefit of information not available to the courts either in the original trial or on appeal," and Dean was freed.

Dearnley, Albert Edward, prom. 1923, Brit. On May 24, 1923, James Frederick Ellis, a drum bugler with the Leichester Regiment at Aldershot, England, disappeared. Of all of his comrades questioned, only Lance-Corporal Albert Edward Dearnley had any suggestions as to his whereabouts. Dearnley said that Ellis, his close friend, had recently suggested that they desert together and return to their hometown. On this evidence, it was presumed that Ellis had abandoned his post. Authorities in his hometown were told to watch out for Ellis.

On Sept. 26, a man gathering berries discovered Ellis' decomposing body. The corpse was bound up in a military raincoat that covered the head, with the arms wrapped around the body, the hands and feet tied behind the back, and the knees and ankles pulled together in a position that would have caused great pain. Ellis had been gagged, and had obviously suffocated quickly. Questioned a second time, Dearnley said he and Ellis had played a game of Cowboys and Indians, and that when he last saw Ellis, the soldier was trying to free himself. Dearnley also admitted that he had quarreled with Ellis over a girl, and that they often argued and made up later. Two days after his arrest, Dearnley withdrew his earlier statements, saying that he had gone for a walk with Ellis, who had suggested they take turns testing their skills using a rope as a lasso, and that he had left Ellis tied up "as a bit of punishment for his having insulted my sweetheart."

Pathologist Sir Bernard Spilsbury testified at Dearnley's trial, held before Mr. Justice Avory in November at the Winchester Assizes, with Rayner Goddard for the prosecution, and attorney R.E. Dummett for the defense. Spilsbury said that the way Ellis was trussed had almost immediately started to suffocate him, that there would be no way that he could have moved or made a sound, and that he had died within ten minutes at the most. Dearnley testified that he had no idea that Ellis would die as a result of the trussing, saying that he had intended to leave him there until early the next morning. Dearnley had later been detained, and had assumed that Ellis had worked himself free of the rope and had deserted. Evidence was given that Dearnley had told his girlfriend, "You have no need to worry any more about Ellis. He is dead, and he is not a mile from here."

Dummett asked for reduced charges of manslaughter, but the jury found Dearnley Guilty of murder, and he was condemned to die. The convicted man's appeal was denied, as was a last-minute petition for a reprieve. The evening before he was scheduled to die, when the coffin and grave had already been prepared, additional facts were brought before the House of Commons and the Home Secretary. Dearnley was retried, and Spilsbury's opinion that Ellis was masochistic and had asked to be tied up was important. Dearnley's sentence was commuted to penal servitude for life.

---

de Beer, Petrus Cornelius, c.1891-1926, S. Afri. Petrus De Beer, an agent of the South African Railway Administration, hired a governess and nurse to care for his four children. Soon after she arrived, she claimed that de Beer began to make unwanted advances. On Jan. 11, 1926, the family, the governess, and her sister were traveling by train from Fort Beaufort to Cookhouse, South Africa. Just before they went to sleep, de Beer got two glasses of ginger ale from the bar car and gave one to his wife and the other to the governess and her sister. The governess later said she saw her employer put some powder into one of the glasses. His wife began having convulsions, and died at 1 a.m.

Police found a bottle of strychnine in a cabinet at de Beer's home, and an autopsy revealed one-seventh of a grain of strychnine in his wife's body. Both de Beer and the governess were arrested and tried in Grahamstown. The young woman was acquitted, but de Beer was convicted of murder and hanged in East London, South Africa, on July 30, 1926.

de Deurwaerder, Louis, prom. 1940, Belg. Louis de Deurwaerder cheated on his wife Alexandrine, first having an affair with a family friend, and then with a young typist. He met the typist in 1947, and asked his wife, a devout Catholic, for a divorce, which she refused. Shortly after, her husband became interested in pharmacopoeia, the study of drugs, and he informed his wife that he would begin giving her various poisons as experiments. She uncomplainingly took the poisons, which were given in unusually high doses, and she meticulously recorded the effects in a diary. In March 1949, he gave his wife five injections of morphine. Soon after, thunderstruck friends and neighbors urged her to leave him, but she replied, "My husband may do what he wishes with me." On Apr. 7, 1949, de Deurwaeder gave his wife, who was suffering from colic, an enema of soapy water and sublimate of mercury. He left the house and when she screamed in pain, neighbors called her father.

Alexandrine died, and her father gave police the diary. During his trial, de Deurwaerder said, "I only hoped to weaken her a little so that she would agree to a divorce or a separation." He was convicted and sentenced to death. However, at that time in Belgium those condemned to death were not executed, but continued to live in solitary confinement with no legal or civil rights, even though a notice of execution was posted.

DeFeo, Ronald Joseph, Jr., 1951- , U.S. On Nov. 13, 1974, Deborah Cosentino was driving home from her job as a barmaid in Amityville, N.Y., at about 3:45 a.m., when she noticed that the house of the DeFeo family was blazing with light. Around 3:00 a.m., John Nemeth, a teenage neighbor, had been awakened when he heard the DeFeo family's sheepdog howling. At 6:35 p.m. a call came in to the Suffolk County Police Department to report a

shooting. Joey Yeswit reported that the entire DeFeo family, except for the eldest son, had been slain. Officer Kenneth Greguski of the Amityville Village Police arrived at the home to find the bodies of Ronald DeFeo, Sr., his wife, Louise DeFeo, and four of their children, Dawn, eighteen, Allison, thirteen, Mark, eleven, and John, nine. All were lying face down, shot with .35-caliber bullets. Ronald Joseph DeFeo, Jr., the only surviving member of the family, sat at the kitchen table crying and mumbling incoherently, though just after shooting the victims he had calmly showered and then gone to visit his girlfriend, telling her "something strange" was going on at his house, and later getting a heroin fix. DeFeo told another friend at a bar that he was going to "break a window to get in" to his home. At about 6:30 p.m. DeFeo returned to the bar, shouting for help, and brought several friends back to the Ocean Street house. One of them, Yeswit, called the police. When police arrived, they found DeFeo at the kitchen table sobbing.

Detective Gaspar Randazzo was the first officer to question DeFeo, who suggested the name of an alleged Mafia hit man with a grudge against his family as the possible killer. Describing his activities the day of the killings, DeFeo explained that when he had broken into the house, all the lights were out except for one in the living room. DeFeo told homicide detective George Harrison, "I hope you find out who did it." Then, detectives discovered empty boxes for rifles in DeFeo's room. Within a short time, they were reading him his rights.

The case was tried in October 1975 before Judge Thomas M. Stark, with Gerard Sullivan, prosecuting attorney, and Bill Weber for the defense. On Nov. 19, the jury found DeFeo Guilty on six counts of second-degree murder, and he was sentenced to twenty-five years to life in prison, which he is now serving at the New York State Correctional Facility in Dannemora, N.Y. Jewelry and $200,000 that DeFeo stole from his family home, have never been recovered. A non-fiction account of the case, *High Hopes, The Amityville Murders,* published in 1981, was written by prosecutor Sullivan.

DeGroot, Robert, 1951-82, U.S. On Nov. 9, 1982, Robert DeGroot, thirty-one, owner of the Bobill Music Store in Waukegan, Ill., called a priest to discuss his upcoming divorce from his 27-year-old wife of two years, Anne. The priest then notified police in Park City, Ill., that he thought DeGroot might commit suicide. Police found no one at DeGroot's Park City home. According to Lake County Coroner Barbara Richardson, DeGroot had left for the home of Anne DeGroot's parents, where his estranged wife was staying with her three children: Maureen Mahar, nine, from a former marriage; Robert DeGroot, eighteen months, and Ian DeGroot, three months. When her husband arrived, brandishing a .30-caliber carbine, he told Anne's brother-in-law, Mark Boarini, that he had "better get out before he gets his." Boarini rushed from the house to notify police. About ten minutes later, DeGroot fired seven shots, killing Anne, Robert, and Maureen, and seriously wounding Ian, who was found still in his mother's arms. DeGroot then shot himself. According to Richardson, DeGroot "was under extreme depression and did not want the divorce."

---

de Kaplany, Dr. Geza (AKA: The Acid Doctor), 1926- , U.S.

In the annals of medical murderers it is difficult to find one as cruel and inhuman as the monstrous Dr. Geza de Kaplany, convicted of the torture-murder of his beautiful wife in 1963.

De Kaplany was a Hungarian refugee who, in 1962, was working for a San Jose, Calif., hospital as a well-paid anesthesiologist. He was arrogant, vain, and wholly self-centered, a man few called friend. He was attracted to a stunning model and beauty queen in the Hungarian community of San Jose and avidly pursued the 25-year-old woman, finally marrying her in August 1962. Hajna de Kaplany, however, found her new husband to be a strange and unpredictable man. After only a few days of marriage, according to later statements made by de Kaplany, the doctor found himself impotent, unable to make love to his ravishingly

A beautiful model, Mrs. Geza de Kaplany, was tortured to death by her physician husband.

beautiful wife. He acted in a paranoid manner, convincing himself that all the bachelors in the apartment complex where they lived were having affairs with his wife. He vowed to "ruin" her beauty, "to fix her."

On the morning of Aug. 28, 1962, neighbors heard loud music blaring from the de Kaplany apartment and through this, piercing screams. After repeatedly pounding on walls, windows, and the front door to the de Kaplany apartment without getting a response, the neighbors called police. Officers arrived and banged on the front door until the music inside suddenly stopped. The door slowly opened. Grinning madly and sweating, dressed only in his underwear, his hands covered with rubber gloves, Dr. de Kaplany stood before the officers, telling them that he had been at work. The officers stepped inside and went to a nearby bedroom where they reeled back in shock. On the bed, naked, was his wife, horribly mutilated but alive. It was learned how de Kaplany had spent several days preparing to perform this "work." He had decided to "operate" on his wife, to disfigure her to the point where no other man would look at her, let alone covet her once alluring body.

De Kaplany had purchased stereo equipment some days earlier and installed several speakers in the apartment. He had also gotten a manicure so that he would not puncture the rubber gloves he would wear when handling the many bottles of sulfuric, nitric, and hydrochloric acids he brought from the hospital to his apartment and carefully arranged on the bedroom bureau while his wife slept. He then leaped upon his wife, stripping her, and tying her hands and legs to the bedposts. He then walked into the other room and turned on the stereo to its maximum volume. When he returned to the bedroom he held up a note for her to read, one which de Kaplany had written the night before on his own prescription forms. It read, "If you want to live—do not shout; do what I tell you or else you will die."

Then de Kaplany began making small incisions all over his wife's body, pouring various acids into the open cuts which caused the poor woman to scream in agony. The "Acid Doctor" ignored her pleas and screams as he systematically obliterated her face, slashing and cutting, savagely mutilating her genitals and breasts. After an hour of this barbarous torture, the police arrived to stop the monster. By then his wife was fatally injured with third-degree corrosive burns. She was removed by hospital attendants who, attempting to cover her body with ointments, burned their hands on her acid-coated body. The brave young woman lived for twenty-one days while her mother, unable to bear her child's cries of anguish, prayed at Hajna's bedside for her daughter to die.

Following his wife's death, de Kaplany was jailed and charged with murder. He claimed that he had not intended to kill his wife, only spoil her good looks. He explained his horrendous torture of Hajna as being "my one-hour crackup." The doctor went to trial for murder before Judge Raymond G. Callahan on Jan. 7, 1963, a little more than a month after his wife's death. He pled not guilty and not guilty by reason of insanity. On the witness stand de Kaplany appeared calm and composed, patiently explaining that he never intended to kill his wife, only destroy her beauty so she would not be attractive to other men, so that he believed he could have her all to himself. It was the only way he believed he could regain his peace of mind, which had been wracked with jealousy, and restore his ability to make love.

When the prosecution displayed photos of the victim as

The de Kaplanys on their wedding day; a few weeks later the barbaric de Kaplany butchered his wife.

police had found her, de Kaplany lost all composure, viewing the photos with hysterical outbursts, shouting to the court: "I am a doctor! I loved her! If I did this and I must have done this—then I am guilty!" The trial dragged on for thirty-five days, at the end of which de Kaplany was found Guilty. He was sentenced to prison for life but he was, for

Dr. de Kaplany at his murder trial, reacting violently to exhibits of his wife's carved-up corpse.

reasons never explained, classified as a "special interest prisoner." This was made clear to some extent when de Kaplany was prematurely released in 1975, six full months

before his first official parole date would have gone into effect. When news reporters probed the reason for this, they were told that de Kaplany was released since his expertise as a "cardiac specialist" was vital to a Taiwan missionary hospital.

This was far from reality since de Kaplany was never a heart specialist. Ray Procunier, who headed the parole board reviewing de Kaplany's case, resigned his position before he could be interviewed by news reporters, stating that he had quit his position for "personal reasons." De Kaplany by then was long gone, departed for Taiwan, to assume his unspecified medical duties, having literally been smuggled out of the country before his release and departure was made public. This was one of the most flagrant abuses of the parole system in California history, releasing a maniac to continue administering medical treatments to those unaware of the torture-murder of his wife. At last report, de Kaplany still resides in Taiwan, working and enjoying his freedom.

de la Mare, Gertrude, 1908- , Brit. Gertrude de la Mare, a slow-witted woman who was estranged from her husband, worked as a housekeeper for the elderly Alfred Brouard. She and her 3-year-old daughter lived with the old man at his home on Guernsey, one of the Channel Islands. On Feb. 6, 1935, at 9 a.m., de la Mare told her next door neighbor, "The old man is dead. He had cut his throat." Police officers found Brouard lying in his bed, with his throat cut from left to right. A letter left for the police said there was "no blame attaching to Mrs. de la Mare," and left the funeral arrangements to the housekeeper. A will, supposedly left by Brouard, was written by a semi-literate and purported to leave everything—possessions that amounted to only around £60—to de la Mare. The attorney general, Ambrose Sherwill, contended that both documents were forgeries by de la Mare, who had murdered her employer in a "predetermined plan to make herself rich." De la Mare, when first questioned, instructed her daughter to tell the police what Brouard used to say when he saw the bread knife, which had been the murder weapon. When the child did not speak, the mother explained, "She wants to say that Mr. Brouard said, when he sharpened it, that we would be able to butcher ourselves with it."

Following the prosecutor's opening remarks, the entire court piled into cars and drove to the farmhouse where Brouard died. A policeman re-enacted the death, showing how it would have been impossible for the farmer to cut his own throat from left to right with his right hand. De la Mare's mother gave testimony that her daughter had told her three days before the employer's demise that Brouard had committed suicide, and corroborated this premature announcement. The housekeeper had also gone to a real estate agent to inquire about buying a large house, later admitting that she had no money. The most damning evidence of all was the dress of her small child. It was flecked with bloodstains, which the prosecutor contended had gotten on the garment when the mother dressed her child right after murdering the old man. The question of de la Mare's sanity was debated by doctors. Found Guilty of murder by the jury, which brought in a divided six-to-five vote regarding her sanity, de la Mare was sentenced to die by hanging. An appeal to the king reprieved de la Mare on May 14, 1935. Weeks after her release, she left Guernsey and vanished.

de Lara, Enrique, b.1891, U.S. In September 1908, a wounded Santo Domingo clergyman, Father Arturo Ascencio, was found in New York City's Central Park, with a revolver nearby. He died later in the hospital, and the death was initially deemed a suicide. Captain Carey and Detective Jimenez learned that one of the priest's frequent visitors at his Upper West Side hotel was Enrique de Lara, a 17-year-old student from Santo Domingo who had recently come to New York and renewed an old acquaintance with Ascencio. The two men had taken a walk together in Central Park the day of Ascencio's death, as they often did, according to a woman who knew them both. When the officers questioned de Lara on Sept. 22, he admitted stealing a watch and $15 from the priest after shooting him because he had talked in a way that made de Lara angry. "He was about twenty paces in front of me before I could get my revolver out of my pocket. Then I fired," de Lara said. After admitting his guilt, de Lara tried to kill himself by taking morphine which he had hidden in his shoe. He pleaded guilty to second-degree murder and was sentenced to a twenty year term in a state prison. He was released twelve years later.

De La Roche, Harry, Jr., c.1958- , U.S. In 1976, Harry De La Roche, Jr., enrolled in the Citadel, a military academy in Charleston, S.C., at the urging of his father, Harry De La Roche, Sr., who wanted his son to pursue a military career. Harry, Jr., disliked the college intensely. He had arguments with his company sergeant, and upperclassmen often tormented him. For Thanksgiving, the freshman returned home to Montvale, N.J.

On Nov. 28, 1976, he shot his father Harry, forty-four, his mother, Mary Jane, fifty, and his two brothers, Ronald,

fifteen, and Eric, twelve. He initially claimed that his brother Ronald had committed the murders after a fight over marijuana, and that he then killed Ronald while temporarily insane. His lawyer suggested that the "private hell" Harry suffered at military school led to the slayings. In De La Roche's confession, obtained at the time of his arrest, he said that he shot his parents as they slept and then shot his brothers in their bedroom. He was convicted of all four murders and sent to Trenton State Prison to serve a life sentence.

Del Petrarca, Robert, 1948- , U.S. On May 14, 1973, the bodies of two women were found strangled to death in the basement of a home in Montclair, N.J. Both women, 45-year-old Renee Cali and her daughter, 24-year-old Leslie Grant, wore bathing suits and were situated in a way that suggested a double suicide. At first organized crime was suspected because Renee Cali's husband John Cali and his brother had been brought before a New Jersey State commission to testify about municipal corruption in Somerset and Middlesex counties. Both denied any knowledge of such corruption. On Aug. 4, 1973, while in custody for the attempted strangling of an 83-year-old South Orange woman, 26-year-old Robert Del Petrarca was charged with the murders of Cali and Grant. Del Petrarca, who had been a window washer for the Calis, had been paroled from the Bordentown Reformatory two months before the double slaying. He was formally indicted on Sept. 28, 1973, and brought to trial on Mar. 12, 1974, in the Essex County Superior Court of Judge Ralph L. Fusco. On Mar. 25, Petrarca was convicted of first-degree murder, and on May 16, 1974, he was sentenced to two consecutive life terms for the double murder.

DeLuca, Frank, See: Columbo, Patricia.

DeMelker, Daisy Louisa Cowle Sproat, d.1932, S. Afri. Daisy Cowle was married to William Cowle for fourteen years, and they had one son, Rhodes. In 1923, the South African nurse killed her husband with strychnine and collected £1,700 from his life insurance policy. She then married Robert Sproat. This time she waited only four years before killing him for £4000 in savings. In 1931, she married Clarence DeMelker, a famous rugby player. But her son, Rhodes Cowle, now aged twenty, wanted the money that he thought should have come to him from his father. Rather than give him what she had, Daisy De-Melker purchased arsenic and killed him.

The pharmacist from whom she purchased the arsenic, after hearing of young Rhodes' strange death, went to the police and reported the purchase. When arsenic was found in Rhodes' body, the bodies of Daisy's two late husbands were also exhumed and found to contain strychnine. Daisy de Melker was found Guilty of the murders by a Johannesburg court and was hanged on Dec. 30, 1932.

Denke, Carl, d.1924, Ger. In post-WWI Germany, economic conditions left many people unemployed and starving. A famine in 1918, the year the Armistice was signed claimed thousands of lives. Carl Denke, the landlord of a public house in Munsterberg, Silesia, was unaffected by the economic turmoil all around him. In fact, Denke often provided free shelter for an army of homeless tramps who passed through the city. By all appearances, he was a God-fearing, law-abiding man who played the organ in the local church on Sundays. Denke was also a cannibal.

Denke was accused of murdering at least thirty people between 1921 and 1924, and devouring parts of the corpses. Denke preserved some of the remains in a tub of brine, and kept a ledger of names and the dates the vagrants checked into his resort. The ghastly nature of his crimes was discovered on Dec. 21, 1924, when a coachman who lived one floor above heard pitiful cries. He rushed downstairs and found a robust young man bleeding profusely from the scalp. The man, one of Denke's boarders, had been struck with a hatchet. Before he lapsed into unconsciousness, he gasped that Denke had assaulted him from behind. Police were summoned and during a search of the premises the vats of bones and pickled flesh were discovered. Denke was taken to the jail where he used his suspenders to hang himself.

DeSalvo, Albert Henry (AKA: **The Boston Strangler; The Green Man; The Measuring Man**), 1931-73, U.S. Between June 1962 and January 1964, thirteen Boston-area women were sexually assaulted and then strangled to death by a fiend the press dubbed the "Boston Strangler." This man proved to be Albert Henry DeSalvo. Born in Chelsea, Mass., in 1931, DeSalvo was one of six children. His father was a severe taskmaster who beat him and the other children over the smallest infraction. He did not spare his wife either, using his fists on the poor, overworked woman whenever he was displeased. DeSalvo's father was also criminally bent and served two prison terms

for theft before his wife divorced him in 1944. Like his father, DeSalvo began stealing when he was in his teens, and was charged with breaking and entering numerous times before joining the army at age seventeen. He served in the occupation forces in Germany, where he began boxing on a U.S. army team. Small, but squat and tough, DeSalvo became the U.S. Army welterweight and, while stationed in Frankfurt, met and married a petite German girl.

Returning to the U.S. with his new wife, DeSalvo was stationed at Fort Dix, N.J., where, in January 1955, he was charged with molesting a 9-year-old girl, his first sex offense. The child's mother, fearing publicity would affect her daughter, refused to prosecute. The Army, therefore, had no case against DeSalvo and released him. He received an honorable discharge a short time later and moved back to Boston with his wife. DeSalvo worked as a handyman and he and his wife had two small children. DeSalvo's sex drive was almost overwhelming. He exhausted his wife Irmgard, who told him to control himself. DeSalvo demanded sex from her on an almost non-stop basis. "Five or six times a day don't mean much to me," he later stated. Finally, Irmgard told her husband, "Al, you can learn by yourself to control yourself. It is just a matter of self-control."

When it came to sex, however, DeSalvo had no control. He thought about sex night and day, according to his later admissions, and he found little release. He was arrested for breaking and entering and given a suspended sentence in 1958 and a short time later he embarked on a sexual game whereby he became known to the police as "Measuring Man." DeSalvo approached young, attractive women in their apartments, telling them he represented a modeling agency and that they had been selected as possible candidates for modeling in television commercials. If chosen, they could make considerable money and would become famous, and they might even be offered a movie contract. Hundreds of young women opened their apartment doors to him after hearing this pitch and DeSalvo, clipboard and tape measure in hand, would then measure the woman's vital statistics. At these times DeSalvo would not make overt sexual approaches, but he did seduce a number of these gullible females. He later claimed that many of the would-be models, however, seduced *him* and invited him back.

On Mar. 17, 1960, Cambridge, Mass., police responded to an alarm of a break-in and they chased and caught DeSalvo. He had thrown away a screwdriver which he had been using to force apartment door locks, but this was recovered. On his person was found a pair of gloves and a tailor's measuring tape. He admitted that he was the "Measuring Man" about whom police had received several

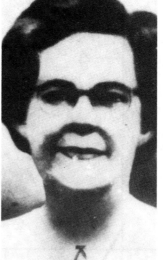

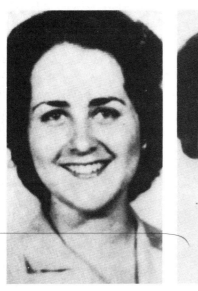

Top row, left to right, Albert DeSalvo, the infamous Boston Strangler, 1967; DeSalvo victims Helen E. Blake and Ida Irga. Middle row, left to right, Joann Graff, Patricia Bissette, Sophie Clark, and Mary A. Sullivan. Bottom right, DeSalvo under arrest in Boston.

complaints. DeSalvo received a two-year sentence for breaking and entering and was released in ten months. The police did not list him as a sexual deviant, but put him on their list of potential burglars. When DeSalvo was released from prison, he returned to his family, but he now became more aggressive, breaking into apartments and tying up and raping females. He was described by his victims as the "Green Man" since he wore green work pants and shirt. DeSalvo later bragged that he tied up and raped six women in one morning. Moreover, he ranged throughout New England, assaulting, according to police in Massachusetts and Connecticut, hundreds of women. DeSalvo put the number at more than 1,000.

In the summer of 1962, DeSalvo began to add murder to his sexual attacks, raping and strangling his victims, the first of whom was 55-year-old Anna Slesers, found in her apartment on Gainsborough Street in Boston, her body placed in a lascivious position. DeSalvo had used a cord to strangle his victim and had tied the ends in a bow beneath her chin, a technique he would continue to employ, as if it were his trademark. Within two weeks, DeSalvo attacked and killed 85-year-old Mary Mullen, a victim he later reluctantly talked about since she reminded him of his grandmother. On June 30, 1962, DeSalvo raped and strangled Helen Blake, a 65-year-old nurse. Next was Nina Nichols, a woman in her sixties. She fought her attacker, digging her nails into his arms as he strangled her from behind.

On Aug. 19, 1962, DeSalvo raped and strangled 75-year-old Ida Irga. Jane Sullivan, sixty-seven, died at DeSalvo's hands the next day. Boston police were inundated with demands to solve the rash of horrible rape-murders. Though scores of sexual deviants were arrested and questioned, DeSalvo escaped attention. DeSalvo refrained from making more attacks until Dec. 5, 1962, his wedding anniversary. He later claimed that then, as on former attacks, he became obsessed with the image of violent sex, that the top of his head "was so hot that I thought it would explode." He spotted an attractive girl entering an apartment and followed her. DeSalvo knocked on her door and employed the usual technique that invariably gained him access to an apartment, saying through the door that he was a repair man sent by the landlord to check the pipes and toilet. The girl, however, refused to let him inside. He went to another apartment and knocked on the door. Inside was 25-year-old Sophie Clark, a tall, attractive black woman. She opened the door a crack and DeSalvo persuaded her to open the door, saying that he was from a modeling company, using his old Measuring Man technique. As he walked inside the apartment, Clark turned her back on DeSalvo, who later reported that he was stunned by her curvacious body. He leaped on her from behind,

subduing her, raping her and strangling her, leaving her as he had the others, her naked body propped upward, legs spread, the bow tied beneath the cord he had used to strangle her.

His next victim was Patricia Bissette, a 23-year-old secretary he had visited years earlier as Measuring Man. On Dec. 8, 1962, she invited him inside, gave him a cup of coffee and, when she turned her back, he placed his arm around her throat and then raped her, strangling her with her own nylons. On Feb. 16, 1963, DeSalvo gained entrance to the apartment of a woman who was home sick. He attacked her, but she fought so desperately, scratching him and biting him while screaming out for help, that DeSalvo fled. (This woman, whose identity is withheld, proved that by ignoring quiet submission to the rapist, as is often counseled, she had saved her life.) On Mar. 9, 1963, 69-year-old Mary Brown allowed DeSalvo into her apartment, thinking him a workman sent by the landlord to fix her stove.

This time DeSalvo's violence was unchecked. He had brought along a lead pipe, which he used to crush his victim's head. He raped Brown *after* killing her. He then drove a fork into her breast several times, leaving it embedded in the flesh. He also strangled her, although, by that time, she was dead. On May 6, 1963, instead of driving to work, DeSalvo drove to Cambridge, "on an impulse" he later said, and there spotted pretty Beverly Samans, a 23-year-old undergraduate living on University Road. He gained entrance to her apartment, tying her to bedposts. He then blindfolded and gagged her and then repeatedly raped her. DeSalvo used the girl's nylon stockings to strangle her. Before leaving his victim, DeSalvo got out his jackknife and began stabbing the girl. The autopsy reported twenty-two stab wounds. DeSalvo later stated, "Once I stabbed her, I couldn't stop. I kept hitting her and hitting her with that knife...She kept bleeding from the throat...I hit her and hit her and hit her..." His savage bloodlust exhausted, DeSalvo walked into the kitchen, wiped off the handle of the knife and dropped it into the sink. When found by police, this knife offered no fingerprints.

DeSalvo's eleventh victim was 58-year-old Evelyn Corbin, whom he strangled and raped on Sept. 8, 1963. When Corbin failed to make an appointment, police were summoned and they found the woman as they had the others, except that she had been manually strangled. The killer had left his trademark, a nylon with a bow, tied about her ankle. Boston police seemed helpless to catch the killer. The city was in a near panic with thousands of husbands constantly calling their wives or staying home from work to protect them against a fiend who seemed to come and go at will. Not a single person reported seeing this mass killer and police were admittedly stymied.

A special "Strangler Bureau" was set up and a dedicated detective force began running down the slimmest clues around the clock. Dozens of sex offenders, muggers, and even peeping toms were rounded up, questioned, and subsequently released. At one point, the brilliant medium, Peter Hurkos, was brought into the case. He examined a number of personal items belonging to suspects and gave a startling and somewhat accurate description of the killer, although he never pinpointed DeSalvo or any other person as the Boston Strangler. A number of good suspects were kept under surveillance, but proved innocent. On Nov. 23, 1963, a day following President John F. Kennedy's assassination in Dallas, Texas, DeSalvo struck again, gaining entrance to the apartment of Joann Graff, a 23-year-old dress designer. He raped and strangled her with her own black leotards, tying these in a bow about her neck. Following the killing, DeSalvo went home, helped his wife clean up their apartment, played with his children, watched a television news report, and then sat down to dinner. DeSalvo had watched a television report on the death of Joann Graff. He later stated, "I knew it was me who did it but why I did it and everything else, I don't know...I wasn't excited. I didn't think about it. I sat down to dinner and didn't think about it at all."

On Jan. 4, 1964, DeSalvo struck for the last time, claiming his thirteenth victim, 19-year-old Mary Sullivan. Once inside her apartment, he flourished a knife, tied up the girl, and raped her. He then strangled her with his hands. He left her naked and, as a bizarre afterthought, inserted a broom into her and placed a card he found in the apartment between her toes which read, "Happy New Year." In Fall 1964, a young woman reported being sexually assaulted in her apartment, describing a man police identified as DeSalvo, using the same technique as DeSalvo had when labeled the Measuring Man. DeSalvo was arrested for breaking and entering, held on a $100,000 bond, and sent to the mental institution at Bridgewater. Amazingly, police never coupled DeSalvo with the crimes of the Boston Strangler. Officials later stated that DeSalvo's police rap sheet listed him only as a felon guilty of breaking and entering. Police records revealed nothing of his sexual offenses.

At Bridgewater, DeSalvo claimed that he was hearing voices and he was diagnosed by psychiatrists as "schizophrenic." On Feb. 4, 1965, he was ordered to be detained indeterminately by Judge Edward A. Pecce. Another inmate at Bridgewater, George Nassar, who had killed a garage attendant and who was himself a suspect in the Strangler killings, met DeSalvo and, after listening to him talk for some time, mostly about sex and violence, came to believe DeSalvo was the Boston Strangler. He informed his young lawyer, F. Lee Bailey, and Bailey interviewed

DeSalvo, recording his conversations. DeSalvo admitted being the Strangler and even added two killings to the known murder count of thirteen. More importantly, DeSalvo related facts about the murders which the police had kept secret, the positioning of the naked bodies, the tying of bows in the strangling cords, nylons, and pantyhose, the wounds inflicted, all the sordid details that only the killer would have known.

Police were still puzzled since they had no eyewitness who could positively identify DeSalvo. Bailey was convinced that DeSalvo was the killer and said so, but officials were disinclined to officially prosecute DeSalvo as a mental patient. DeSalvo was kept in confinement and the strangulation murders stopped. Most reliable authorities considered DeSalvo the Boston Strangler, including court authorities who transferred DeSalvo to the Walpole State Prison where, in his cell, on Nov. 26, 1973, he was found dead, stabbed to death in his heart.

Desha, Isaac B., prom. 1825, U.S. Isaac B. Desha was the arrogant, spoiled son of the governor of Kentucky, a thoroughly disreputable and amoral young man who impulsively insulted his elders and peers, beat slaves at a whim, and made life generally impossible for all who encountered him. A wealthy landowner, Francis Baker, who was traveling through Kentucky en route to his home in Natchez, Miss., met Desha on the road. Baker told Desha he was lost and Desha said that he knew a comfortable place to sleep for the night, and in the morning he could resume his journey with the proper guides. Baker followed Desha down a lonely road where the youth turned on him, beating him unconscious with a club, and then cutting his throat. Desha was later found with some of Baker's goods, and he was arrested and twice tried, condemned each time. Before Desha was hanged, his father intervened and pardoned him in one of the most flagrant abuses of governmental authority.

Desnoyers, Guy, prom. 1956, Fr. To avoid a scandal, Father Guy Desnoyers decided it would be best to kill the girl he had impregnated and her unborn child.

As the priest of the small town of Uruffe, France, in the province of Lorraine, Desnoyers was still rather young and greatly attracted to the village's young women. Such was the case of 19-year-old Regine Fay, who was noticeably pregnant in the fall of 1956. Fay decided against leaving home to have the baby or having an abortion—a decision which greatly concerned the priest, who feared the child-to-be might have features similar to his and thus tarnish his name. On Dec. 2, 1956, Desnoyers told his parishioners that he would be out of town for a few days. However, he returned two nights later to keep an appointment he had made with Fay. Desnoyers claims he attempted to absolve Fay of her sins. But upon her refusal, he killed her. The priest shot her through the back of the neck, and then proceeded with a grotesque mutilation which he declared was in keeping with his religious faith. He took a pocket-knife and slit open the girl's abdomen, and then after further slashing her, Desnoyers baptized the child he had ripped from Fay and proceeded to destroy any likeness to him the baby might have had. Later that evening, Desnoyers conducted the search for the missing girl and was the leader of the party which discovered her body.

Police soon discovered that the bullet that killed Fay was of the same caliber as the 6.35-mm gun owned by Desnoyers, and with the discovery of a blood-stained handkerchief, the priest confessed his guilt. Although the prosecution sought the death penalty, the jury found him Guilty with extenuating circumstances, and the President of the Nancy Court, Judge Louis Facq, sentenced Desnoyers to life in prison.

Diaz, Robert R., 1938-   , U.S. Robert R. Diaz finished nursing school at the age of forty and moved from Gary, Ind., to Apple Valley, Calif. He was arrested on Nov. 23, 1981, following the investigation into the unexplained deaths of sixty hospital patients in Los Angeles, Riverside, and San Bernadino counties in California. Officials were able to link Diaz to twelve deaths from overdoses of lidocaine. Eleven patients died between Mar. 30 and Apr. 22, 1981, at the Community Hospital of the Valley in Perris where Diaz worked, and one died at San Gorgonio Pass Memorial Hospital on Apr. 25, the one night that the temporary nurse worked there.

Diaz, who waived his right to a jury trial, appeared before Riverside Superior Court Judge John H. Barnard on Oct. 31, 1981. Deputy District Attorney Patrick F. Magers produced seventy-one witnesses, including several co-workers who stated that Diaz had predicted patients in stable conditions would soon become ill—they later died. Three syringes were also displayed in court as those used in the murders. The defense, conducted by Public Defender Michael B. Lewis and Deputy Public Defender John J. Lee, provided experts who claimed that the large amount of lidocaine in the corpses may have accumulated over time, but their testimony was far outweighed by the prosecution's case. Barnard found Diaz Guilty on Mar. 29, 1984, and on June 15 sentenced him to die in the gas chamber. See:

Jones, Genene.

Dickman, John Alexander, 1865-1910, Brit. Wages clerk John Innes Nesbit regularly made the brief train trip from a bank in Newcastle back to Alnmouth, in Northumberland, carrying a leather satchel containing the money to pay his coal mine's wages. But his journey of Mar. 18, 1910, ended in death. His body was found stuffed beneath the train seat, and the satchel containing £370 was missing. In Nesbit's head were bullets of two different calibers. On the floor was a small wad of paper. Plenty of witnesses along the way had seen him with another man identified as John Dickman, a 43-year-old bookie. Even Nesbit's wife, who usually came down to the train for a brief chat as it passed through Nesbit's hometown, had seen him with Dickman. Dickman left the train at a station two miles from where Nesbit was last seen alive.

Dickman had an answer for everything the police asked, but his story did not add up, especially when it was found that he was badly in debt and that he had purchased a gun through the mail. A line-up was held, at which Percival Hall, a co-worker of Nesbit's who had seen him board the train with a man, picked out Dickman. But, it was learned later that Hall had caught a glimpse of Dickman before he was placed among eight other men. The money satchel was found down a pit near where Dickman left the train.

Dickman's trial began on July 4 at Newcastle Assizes. Mrs. Nesbit identified Dickman as the man she saw with her husband. Nine employees testified that Dickman had taken pains to learn about the wages transport method and schedule. But the defense claimed that the two kinds of bullets proved that the murder had been committed by two different people and, therefore, Dickman, never seen with anyone else, was not the murderer. However, when the ticket collector testified that Dickman had had the exact fare in one hand while his other hand was held completely out of sight (the inference being that the satchel was in it), the jury found Dickman Guilty and sentenced him to death. An appeal based on Hall's premature sighting of Dickman was turned down. Dickman was hanged on Aug. 10, 1910. Later, it was learned that Dickman had wrapped paper around the slightly smaller bullets to make them fit his gun. They did not fire very well, but the proper bullets did their job. The paper from the smaller bullets was found on the carriage floor, but not recognized.

Dietl, Marilyn, prom. 1978, U.S. Rather than allow her 18-year-old daughter to enter a world of prostitution,

Marilyn Dietl shot her to death.

Judy Dietl graduated from Colchester (Vt.) High School where she was voted the prettiest girl in the class of 1977. She moved to Boston, Mass., with her friend Diane Brochu, and enrolled at Bay State Junior College. The girls lived at the nearby YWCA to save on expenses. They began dating two men who turned out to be pimps. Judy's mother learned of the situation when Brochu dropped out of school. Judy did not know she was dating a pimp, but agreed to return home with her mother in the spring of 1978. Judy eventually decided to return to her boyfriend in Boston. Her mother, convinced she would end up a prostitute, decided to stop her. On May 5, 1978, Judy and her mother went for a ride. They got out of the car in the parking lot behind the Ohavi Zedik Synagog in Burlington, Vt., where Dietl emptied a .38-caliber revolver into her daughter's chest, arms, and legs. Dietl then had someone call the police. She was found Guilty of second-degree murder and sentenced to five to fifteen years in the Chittenden County Correctional Center.

D'Iorio, Ernest, prom. 1933-35, U.S. On Dec. 6, 1933, the Detroit, Mich., home of Jennie Zablocki, her parents, and five siblings was found in a shambles. Jennie's body was found with a lamp cord wound tightly around her neck and tied to a door knob. Her body showed ten bloody wounds. Witnesses told police that a car believed to be her boyfriend's was parked in the driveway at the approximate time of death. Her boyfriend, Anton Cebelak, was arrested for Zablocki's murder, which he denied committing. George Moitke later informed police that it was his car, not Cebelak's, that was in the Zablocki driveway. Moitke finally told police that the killer was Ernest D'Iorio, the boyfriend of Sonia Marzek, Zablocki's best friend. D'Iorio admitted killing Zablocki because she threatened to tell Marzek that he was on parole. D'Iorio pleaded guilty to second-degree murder and was sentenced to twenty to forty years in prison by Judge Arthur J. Gordon on Jan. 11, 1935.

Dobkin, Harry, c.1893-1943, Brit. Three days after he married the former Rachel Dubinski in 1920, Harry Dobkin, a Russian-born laborer living in London, walked out on her. The couple's brief union produced a child nine months later. Although the courts ordered him to pay child support to Rachel, Dobkin was regularly imprisoned over a twenty-year period for failing to pay the court-ordered compensation.

In April 1941, Dobkin went to work as a fire spotter for a paper storage building behind a bombed out church in St. Oswald's Place, Kennington. On Apr. 15, he reported a fire in the vestry of the destroyed chapel. The authorities extinguished the blaze, but as such fires were common during the London Blitz, they made no effort to determine the cause. However, a team of workmen clearing debris from the area on July 17, 1942, pulled up a loose paving stone and unearthed a badly burned human skeleton.

Home Office pathologist Dr. Keith Simpson conducted an autopsy and found that someone had severed the limbs from the body in a crude attempt to disguise a murder. When the missing persons ledger was checked, it was found that 49-year-old Rachel Dobkin was reported missing by her sister just three days before the cellar fire on Apr. 12, 1941. The body was eventually identified as that of Rachel Dobkin.

Harry Dobkin immediately became the prime suspect in the investigation and was eventually arrested and charged with Rachel's murder. Dobkin's trial began at the Old Bailey on Nov. 17, 1942. The evidence of guilt was conclusive, especially after the victim's dentist took the stand and testified that the top jaw and the teeth and gums were those of Rachel Dobkin. Dobkin had strangled his wife in a dispute over maintenance payments. The fire had apparently been started in order to conceal the remains. Harry Dobkin was convicted and hanged at Wandsworth Prison on Jan. 27, 1943.

Doelitzsch, Fritz, b.c.1893, Egypt. Fritz Doelitzsch and his accomplice, Herman Klaus, both German, risked their lives to rob wealthy Syrian merchant Max Karam in his luxurious villa on the coast near Alexandria. The two performed an expert job of breaking in but panicked when Karam fought to save his fortune. Robbery turned into murder and Doelitzsch and Klaus ran away without touching the safe.

Police were impressed with the professional way the intruders had entered the home without detection, attempted to commit their deed, and left without leaving a clue. But when the two robust Germans had one too many beers and started bragging about their dubious accomplishment, police were on them in seconds.

Katina awoke early on the morning of Jan. 15, 1923, and went about her duties as the Karam villa maid. But her daily routine took a jag when she discovered her friend and employer motionless, slumped beside his bed entangled in the mosquito net that had hung over his bed, and an overturned commode stained with blood and buckshot lying on the body.

The initial investigation seemed to indicate an inside job.

An entry hole carved on a ground floor wall opened into the exact spot which would allow a person to reach in and unlock the door. Police thought it unlikely that strangers would have been able to position their entry so perfectly. Further, it appeared the assassins knew the layout of the house well.

But interviews with the widow Karam, with Katina, and other staff members, and with Karam's brother and sister-in-law who also lived in the house, cleared all as suspects. The Medico-Legal Department in Cairo eventually took over the investigation and concluded that the robbery had been committed by professional or semi-professional burglars, for the intruders had entered the home through a lower door, crossed the hall, and climbed the marble staircase to the first floor to avoid the nightwatchman. The burglars then cut the bell and telephone wires in both Karams' suites.

An autopsy on Karam revealed that the 40- or 50-year-old man was exceptionally strong and able to take care of himself. Regardless, the assassins had overcome him by striking him with an iron crowbar three or four times from the front to the back of the vertex. It appeared that Karam then jumped out of bed and became entangled in the mosquito netting. He may have shouted for help loudly enough to scare off the intruders, but only until one shot him in the back of the head. The intruders then ran off in a panic and no attempt was made to open the safe. Wounds inflicted by the crowbar and gun originated from different directions, proving conclusively that there were, indeed, two assailants in the crime.

Police were baffled until a French woman named Henriette stepped forward requesting the £2,000 reward in exchange for incriminating evidence she could provide. The killer was her lover's best friend, she said. She overheard him one night, after he drank too much, bragging about a burglary he and a cohort had committed. The names she gave were Fritz Doelitzsch and Herman Klaus. The police then found everything they needed in Doelitzsch's unkempt Alexandria room. Inside the pockets of a jacket they found wood and plaster fragments identical to fragments from Karam's house. Hairs on the collar of a suit proved to be those of Karam.

Tracked down, the pair were brought into the German Embassy in Alexandria and subjected to a strict German court trial. The evidence had Klaus and Doelitzsch down cold. The two soon confessed to being the men sought in the murder but, because German law requires determination of who actually killed the victim, both men denied firing the fatal shot. Separate recollections by Klaus and Doelitzsch each implicated the other. But Doelitzsch's story was better than his partner's for Klaus had made the grave error of trying to pin both the crowbar and pistol

attacks on Doelitzsch. Police already knew that two persons had been involved in the brutality waged against Karam. Klaus had to be lying. The attorney-general charged Klaus with murder and deemed the act premeditated because, he said, if it had not been, both men would have fled immediately after Karam awoke.

The defense counsel did not lose the case for the accused. They lost it for themselves. In light of a preponderance of evidence the court departed from precedent, found both men Guilty of murder, and handed down life sentences for both.

Doetsch, Gunter, 1926-82, U.S. Gunter Doetsch, fifty-six, pleaded for help when he told friends he planned to kill himself and his two young children. Nobody took him seriously, and so, on June 29, 1982, the middle-aged executive from the fashionable Chicago suburb of Lake Forest drove his son Gunter Alexander Doetsch II, five, and daughter Catherine Doetsch, two, along a rural highway near scenic Lake Geneva, Wis., and shot them both. He immediately turned the gun on himself.

Doetsch's neighbors were incredulous. Not one had any inkling things were wrong in the Doetsch household. To them the family was a privileged group with a lovely $200,000 ranch-style home with an indoor swimming pool on a one-and-a-half-acre lot. Doetsch owned Scientificom, a firm that produces audio-visual aids for the medical industry.

But Joyce Doetsch, thirty-five, Gunter's second wife, knew the truth. The couple had been having marital problems for some time and Joyce had filed for divorce, saying her husband was of a "violent and uncertain temper who occasionally displayed his temper by striking objects within his reach and by beating his head against the wall." She was scheduled to leave for Martha's Vineyard, Mass., with the children the day after the murders. Joyce also knew of Doetsch's financial troubles. The Lake Forest National Bank had filed a lawsuit in April to foreclose on a $95,000 mortgage on the family's home.

Neighbors still could not believe it. One said, "He certainly didn't seem like anyone who was going to die." Except that he had told friends that was his plan.

Dominici, Gaston, 1877-1965, Fr. Elderly Gaston Dominici, the patriarch of a large French farm family living near Lurs, Provence, became the hub of one of the most sensational murder cases in modern French history. Sir Jack Drummond, a brilliant 61-year-old British biochemist, his wife Ann, forty-six, and their daughter Elizabeth, ten, were vacationing in France, driving through the Durance Valley. They decided to camp on the night of Aug. 4, 1952, and pulled their car off the road outside the town of Lurs, near a farmhouse. The Drummonds pitched a tent and began to dress for bed. Someone hiding in nearby bushes and watching them was discovered by Drummond, who berated the Peeping Tom, who, in turn, shot Drummond and his wife to death and chased the terrified Elizabeth Drummond through the tall grass and crushed her head with the butt of a carbine.

The bodies of the Drummond family were found the next morning by railway workers. Police also received a report from 33-year-old Gustave Dominici that he had also discovered the bodies on a large, sprawling farm called La Grande Terre, belonging to his father, Gaston Dominici. The deaths of the prominent Drummond and his family members made headlines in Paris, London, and New York, and Edmond Sebeille, the superintendent of police in Marseilles, personally directed the investigation. Sebeille was convinced that the killer or killers were part of the Dominici family at La Grande Terre. The family included Gaston Dominici, seventy-five, his reticent wife Marie, his son Gustave, Gustave's wife, Yvette, and their child. Another son, 49-year-old Clovis Dominici, lived on a nearby farm. Supt. Sebeille methodically conducted dozens of interviews with residents and workers in the area. One of the railway workers who had discovered the bodies told the superintendent that Gustave Dominici had stated that Elizabeth Drummond was alive when he found her, although she was apparently dying of head wounds. Sebeille confronted Gustave Dominici, who admitted this was the case, but he was quick to say that he had nothing to do with the murders.

Sebeille ordered Dominici's arrest for failing to come to the aid of a dying person. He was tried at Digne on Nov. 13, 1952, convicted, and sentenced to two months in prison. The sentence was appealed and Dominici was released. Sebeille, however, persisted in visiting the Dominici family, questioning members over and over throughout 1953. Finally, with Gustave and Clovis Dominici present in the farmhouse alone with the superintendent, Sebeille openly accused Gustave of murdering the Drummonds. Gustave's nerves were frayed by the prolonged police investigation and he shouted: "It was my father!" Sebeille looked at Clovis and the older brother nodded. Gustave then stated that he heard two shots at about 1 a.m. on the night of the murders and he ran to the field where he saw his father with an American carbine. He had just shot the Drummonds after being caught spying on them and had bludgeoned the little girl. Gustave, terrified that his father might turn on him, fled and returned at 5:30 to find Elizabeth Drummond in

a dying condition. He left her to be found later, still fearing that his father would kill him if he knew Gustave had witnessed the murders.

The fierce old man, with a head of white hair, a droopy

Sir Jack Drummond, murder victim.

Ann Drummond, murder victim.

Elizabeth Drummond, murder victim.

Gaston Dominici, mass murderer.

mustache, and dark, beady eyes, was arrested and taken to jail. He cursed his sons when he learned that they had informed on him and he later confessed to police that he had indeed slaughtered the Drummond family because Jack Drummond had accused him of gaping at his half-dressed wife and making lewd advances to her. The proud old man felt it was his right to do as he pleased on his own land, even to commit sexual assault and murder. The old man made several confessions but these were later retracted and denied when Gaston Dominici was placed on trial at the Digne Assize Court in November 1954. Before that time, Dominici accompanied police to the scene of the murders which were re-enacted before him, so unnerving the hoary old killer that he tried to commit suicide by jumping off a railroad bridge.

At the end of the eleven-day trial, Gaston Dominici was found Guilty and sentenced to death. As the old man was led from the dock and back to his cell, he turned to the court and hissed: "My sons—what swine!" Dominici's death sentence was commuted to life in prison. Meanwhile more developments and revelations in the case left considerable doubt about who had killed the Drummonds. One story had it that the old man killed the adults but someone else

La Grande Terre, the Dominici farm in Provence, France.

in the Dominici family murdered the child. Another account insisted that Gaston Dominici was a senile old man who confessed out of ignorance and confusion and that his sons had done the killings. The old man was released in 1960 and returned to La Grand Terre where he lived until 1965, inside a household that held nothing but hostility and hatred.

Dominiquez, Orin, 1950-82, U.S. Orin Dominiquez, thirty-two, and Forest Park, Ill., police officer Michael Caulfield, twenty-two, are both dead because Dominiquez was erroneously found to be mentally fit. This supposedly stable man had been arrested more than forty times in fifteen years, serving two prison terms in Joliet for robbery and arrested four times in the year he died, 1982.

On Sept. 30, 1982, three weeks after Caulfield had graduated from the police academy, he and another officer brought Dominiquez in when they saw him loitering and learned there were outstanding traffic warrants against him. The day before, a Chicago officer had taken Dominiquez to a mental health clinic for evaluation because family members urged him to seek aid. Doctors advised he voluntarily admit himself but could not force him to stay because he did not meet the requirements for involuntary admission.

When police brought Dominiquez in and freed his hands for fingerprinting and booking, he grabbed Officer James Sebastian's gun and started shooting. He was shot and killed by Officer James McNally, but not until he had killed Caulfield.

Donahue, John Xavier, 1933-53, U.S. Police officers lay their lives on the line even on routine patrols. State trooper Ernest J. Morse lost his life on Connecticut's Merritt Parkway in February 1953 attempting to hand out an ordinary speeding ticket.

The speeder, young, dark-haired John Donahue, was described by Dr. Harry Hemmendinger, defense psychologist at Donahue's murder trial, as a man without a conscience who would kill again if it suited his purposes. He had killed Morse the minute the officer stepped out of his car to hand the ticket.

The jury considered the evidence for little over an hour and returned a verdict of Guilty of murder in the first degree, which automatically carried the death sentence. Judge Thomas E. Troland scheduled an emotionless Donahue to die on Dec. 5, 1953.

Donald, Jeannie Ewen, b.1896, Scot. In 1934, the Donalds and the Priestlys of Aberdeen, Scot., lived in close quarters in an apartment building on Urquhart Road. Alexander and Jeannie Donald did not care for the Priestly family. The disagreement between Mrs. Donald and Mrs. Priestly dated back to 1929, and the two women did not speak. Eight-year-old Helen Priestly picked up on the tension and taunted Jeannie Donald, calling her "coconut," a nickname the older woman deeply resented.

On Apr. 20, 1934, Helen's mother sent her to the store to buy a loaf of bread. Helen paid for the bread and ran off down the street, never to be seen alive again. A search for the child in the city parks, hospitals, and schools produced no trace of her. The next morning, a neighbor at 61 Urquhart Road, near the Donald residence, found a brown sack in the hallway. The sack contained the body of Helen Priestly. Since the search party had already checked the building, the murderer was thought to have left the body there the previous evening.

The body bore marks of strangulation, but not of sexual assault. A maintenance man later said that he heard two screams from inside the building. Suspicion fell on the Donalds, who had refused to join the search for the girl. Alexander Donald proved that he was at work when the child disappeared. But Jeannie Donald did not have an alibi, and blood stains were found in her kitchen cupboard. She was arrested and charged with murder. Her trial began in the High Court of the Justiciary in Edinburgh on July 16, 1934. Pathologists proved the bacteria in the girl's body were similar to those in the Donald house, and the receipt for the bread that Helen bought was found in the Donalds' fireplace.

Mrs. Donald was found Guilty of murder and was sentenced to death. Her sentence was later commuted to life imprisonment, but she served less than ten years and was released on June 26, 1944.

Donnell, Richard, prom. 1970, U.S. In October 1978, Richard Donnell was doing time in a federal prison for transporting stolen goods, when the State pressured him to testify about a homicide he had committed years earlier. With the help of Leslie Eugene Dale, a member of the Johnston Gang, Donnell had beaten and drowned dishwasher John "Jackie" Baen, after they learned that Baen would inform on Donnell and Dale. Eight years after the murder, Chester County, Pa., investigators exhumed Baen's body from the Glenwood Memorial Garden Center, determined to find a cause of death other than drowning. The frightened Donnell admitted to his participation in the murder, and agreed to testify against Dale, in exchange for a reduced charge of voluntary manslaughter, and a prison sentence of not more than three years. Since he was already doing that much time, Donnell never served any additional time for murdering Baen.

Donovan, Conrad (AKA: **Rotten Conrad**), 1870-1904, and **Wade, Charles**, 1882-1904, Brit. The general criterion for conviction in a criminal case is "beyond a reasonable doubt," and that is why the jury sent Conrad Donovan, thirty-four, and his half-brother Charles Wade, twenty-two, to the gallows following the Oct. 12, 1904, murder in Stepney, England. Not until Donovan said on his way to his death that he had not meant to kill Emily Farmer could the townspeople rest assured that they had convicted the right men.

It was hard to believe, however, that Donovan and Wade had not meant to kill Farmer who was found, hands bound and face down, choked by a gag placed in her mouth. Her home had been ransacked, obviously in a robbery attempt.

An easy target, Farmer lived alone and owned a small newspaper and tobacco shop in what was deemed a bad neighborhood. When alone, she enjoyed adorning herself with fine jewelry. She had been attacked once before and luckily escaped because passing police heard her scream.

It finally took two sturdy men to take her on. They were apprehended due to a tipoff provided by a fish curer named Rae who had seen the two men, whom he knew to be gang members, emerge from the shop the morning of the murder. Rae led detectives to the men's hideout and identified them.

The testimony of a Sunday school teacher convicted the

pair. The night before the murder, he had gone to see that the chapel was safely locked up and saw Wade talking to another man not far from Farmer's shop. The next morning the teacher passed the same men near to the shop. At Brixton Prison, he identified Donovan as the second man.

After three days of deliberation, jury members found both men Guilty of murder. There was little evidence, but it was enough. The two men were hanged the next day.

Doss, Nannie (AKA: **Arsenic Annie**), 1905-65, U.S. Nannie Doss of Tulsa, Okla., murdered eleven people because, she said, "I was searching for the perfect mate, the

Nannie Doss with husband Samuel.

real romance of life," which left everyone wondering why it was necessary for her to do away with her mother, two sisters, and the nephew of one of her deceased husbands. The crimes of Nannie Doss came to the attention of the police in October 1954 when Dr. N.Z. Schwelbein decided to conduct an autopsy on Mrs. Doss' fifth husband, Samuel. Dr. Schwelbein had been the first to examine Mr. Doss after he was admitted to the local hospital. The stomach pains Doss complained of seemed highly suspicious to Schwelbein. "Whatever he had might kill somebody else," Nannie said. "It's best to find out."

The results of the autopsy startled even the most trained medical observers. There was enough arsenic in Samuel Doss to kill twenty strong men. The police took Nannie Doss into custody. She expressed bewilderment. Samuel had eaten his stewed prunes and there was certainly no arsenic to be found there. The police were relentless. Before the Miranda Supreme Court decision, a suspect could be questioned for hours without an attorney present. It was known as the third degree, and for the next several days Mrs. Doss sat under the hot light. Police asked her about her fourth husband, Richard Morton, who had perished under similar circumstances. "I never heard of any Richard Morton," she demurred. The police pressed further. "What? You don't remember your previous husband?" "Oh, that Richard Morton!" Suddenly it was all clear to her. "Yes, I was married to him."

Finally, Doss broke down and told an incredible story. She had poisoned four of her five husbands, and two infant children. Her first husband survived, but two of their three children died at an early age. The symptoms were always the same: horrible stomach pain followed by sudden death.

Nannie Doss at her trial in Tulsa, Okla., with daughter Melvina and grandchildren.

Nannie gave husband Arlie Lanning rat poison for breakfast one morning. Mystified investigators went tracking through graveyards in search of other victims. By the time the bodies of the victims had been exhumed the death toll stood at eleven. Large quantities of arsenic were found in the remains. At least four of the victims had perished in great pain. At her trial, Nannie Doss ticked off the names of the victims and circumstances of the murders. She said that she had collected small insurance premiums on each of her husbands, but financial gain was never the real motive. Nannie Doss had ended the lives of her husbands, she explained, because they were "dullards."

Marriage was unlike anything Doss had read about in *True Romance*, her favorite publication. Convicted of murder, Mrs. Doss was sent to prison for life. She died there of leukemia in 1965. Copies of romance magazines were found strewn about her cell.

Dotson, Clint, d.1904, and **Fleming, Jim**, d.1902, U.S. While serving a life sentence for murdering a prospector, Clint Dotson of Montana devised a way to get himself absolved of all charges. He summoned a good friend, Jim Fleming, and offered him a share of $50,000 he had made in a Union Pacific robbery if Fleming would kill

Dotson's father, staging the scene to make it look as though Oliver Dotson had killed himself in remorse for being the one truly guilty in the murder of Gene Cullinane.

The plan almost worked but clever undersheriff John Robinson was able to get Fleming to admit that he had killed Oliver Dotson and staged the scene to look like suicide. The two men were sentenced to death. Fleming was hanged on Sept. 6, 1902, and Dotson in April 1904.

Double S Murder, See: **Morrison, Steinie**.

Downs, Elizabeth Diane, 1956- , U.S. In 1983 a brutal attack on a divorced mother and her three children shocked the town of Springfield, Ore., just east of Eugene. Elizabeth Diane Downs informed police officers that an unidentified "shaggy haired man" flagged down her car outside Springfield, pulled a gun and shot dead her 7-year-old daughter Cheryl, then critically wounded 3-year-old Danny and 8-year-old Christie, and shot Downs in the arm before he fled.

In February 1984 police arrested Downs and charged her with murder in the death of daughter Cheryl and the attempted murder of her two other children. Downs, a 27-year-old divorcee, was believed to have attacked her own children because they apparently were coming between her and her new boyfriend, who insisted he did not want children.

Downs maintained her innocence during a lengthy trial. When a tape recording of the hit song *Hungry Like the Wolf* by the popular music group Duran Duran, which had been playing during the attack, was played in court, Downs was observed to be tapping her foot and singing along with the song.

Elizabeth Diane Downs was convicted of murder, two counts of attempted murder, and two counts of first-degree assault. She was sentenced to five concurrent terms, including life plus five years minimum for murder with a firearm, two terms of thirty years each for attempted murder, and two terms of twenty years for assault. In closing, presiding Judge Gregory Foote told Downs: "The Court hopes the defendant will never again be free. I've come as close to that as possible." The leading prosecutor in the case, Lane County Assistant District Attorney Fred Hugi, adopted Downs' two surviving children.

Three years later, in July 1987, Downs escaped from the prison in Salem, Ore., where she had been confined since July 1984. She was recaptured just ten days later at a nearby house she was sharing with 36-year-old Wayne Seifer, estranged husband of a fellow inmate.

Downs was later transferred to a New Jersey penitentiary. She has written a 318-page book chronicling her struggle to clear herself of the crimes for which she has been convicted. Over 50,000 copies of *Diane Downs: Best Kept Secrets* were printed by May of 1989.

Dowry Murders, prom. 1980s, India. The tradition of dowries was established thousands of years ago in India. As the practice became increasingly corrupt during the 1960s, the marriage incentive was outlawed. But it still flourishes today, as shown by the alarming increase in "kitchen accidents" in India over the past decade. Marriage has become a means of acquiring material wealth, and wives have become a disposable commodity to be eliminated as seen fit.

During the 1980s, husbands have been murdering their wives in increasingly large numbers after first extorting as many valuables from their in-laws as possible. Once the in-laws stop providing additional dowry items, the wives are disposed of in what has become known as a "kitchen accident." Most of the "kitchen accidents" reported since 1980 are murders in which a husband ties his wife to a kitchen chair and sets her afire. The husband is then free to remarry and receive yet another dowry. A typical dowry could include video recorders, stereos, refrigerators, automobiles, motorcycles, and money.

Newly formed women's rights organizations have been tracking the "kitchen accidents" since 999 deaths were reported in 1985. That number rose to 1,319 in 1986 and to 1,786 in 1987. The Ahmedabad Women's Action Group in the state of Gujarat claims that the numbers are much higher since most domestic quarrels in India go unreported. Research conducted by the organization has shown that more than 1,000 women are executed annually in Gujarat alone.

Drabing, Michael Edward, 1955-   , U.S. Three members of the Schneider family were out for the evening in nearby Lincoln, Ill. Only 17-year-old Terri Schneider was home with her 19-year-old boyfriend Jeffrey Richardson, at 11 p.m. on Aug. 19, 1976, when the doorbell rang. Terri opened the door and found 21-year-old Michael Drabing, a Lincoln housepainter, standing on the porch with a hunting knife in his hand. Drabing burst into the house and forced Schneider and Richardson into a bedroom, where he bound their hands and feet. He then hid in the house to await the arrival of the rest of the Schneider family.

Shortly afterwards, 44-year-old hog farmer Lloyd Schneider, his 45-year-old wife Phyllis, and another daughter, 16-year-old Cheryl, arrived home. They entered the house and found the two teenagers tied up in the bedroom. They slammed the bedroom door in the intruder's face as they raced to free Terri and Jeffrey, but Drabing knocked the door off its hinges. Richardson and Cheryl Schneider jumped out the window as Drabing burst into the room and ran to where Lloyd and Phyllis were working to free Terri. He began stabbing the three of them with his hunting knife. Outside, Cheryl ran to a neighbor's house to call for help and Jeffrey hailed a passing car on a nearby highway.

By the time police arrived at the home, Drabing was gone. He left behind the mutilated bodies of Phyllis Schneider, Lloyd Schneider, and their daughter Terri. Drabing was arrested the following day at Abraham Lincoln Hospital where he sought treatment for cuts on his leg. He recounted his story in great detail to local police. Charged with three counts of murder, Drabing was scheduled for trial three months later.

The bench trial lasted eight days in December, during which time Drabing's defense attorney, Walter Kasten, attempted to portray Drabing as a schizophrenic and psychotic who should not be held accountable for his actions. But Drabing himself said, "I know exactly what I was doing at the time of the murders, and it was right... Nothing could stop me from murdering them."

Drabing testified that the triple murder was sparked by the book *Helter Skelter* and its television adaptation chronicling the activities of Charles Manson and his "family" of murderers in California. Drabing, like the Manson family, believed that the mass murder of the nation's rich citizens would start a revolt that would end in the overthrow of the capitalist society. Drabing was beginning with the Schneider family. He provided a long list of targets, including the governor of Illinois.

On Dec. 16, 1976, more than 250 curious people crammed the courtroom to hear Judge James D. Heiple's verdict. The irreverent Drabing, who had twice fallen asleep during the proceedings, rocked slowly in his chair as Heiple explained that Drabing's own testimony had convinced him that he was mentally stable on the night of the murders. After Heiple read his verdict of Guilty and adjourned the trial, those in attendance applauded. The unremorseful Drabing said only that he regretted that Cheryl Schneider and Jeffrey Richardson had escaped the fate of the other three victims. Heiple sentenced Drabing to three concurrent terms of 75 to 100 years on Jan. 21, 1977. See: **Manson, Charles.**

Drachman, Louis, d.1913, Fr. Background concerning Louis Drachman is sketchy, but it is known that he was born and raised in rural Provence and later moved to Marseilles where he was arrested in 1911 for burglaries and sexual attacks on prostitutes along the city's docks. He was judged insane and confined to a local asylum, from which he escaped in late 1912. Using the alias Nordeau, Drachman went to work as a janitor for several Marseilles boarding houses. On the night of July 18, 1913, Drachman waylaid a priest, Father Josef Marochel, who had been visiting the sick in one of his buildings, and killed him. Donning the priest's cassock, Drachman went to a small church, St. Michel of the Angels, and boldly took a position in a confessional. When Pierre Wrangel went into the confessional, Drachman reached through the screen and strangled Wrangel to death. Then Drachman burst from the confessional, screaming "Vengeance is the Lord's." He ran from the church, and when police found Wrangel's body, a chase ensued which led to a wharf where Drachman ran into the water and drowned.

Draw, Derrick, prom. 1971, U.S. Detroit police stumbled on the frozen body of 16-year-old Gary Frandle in a downtown alley. The youth had been beaten, stabbed, and his ears had been amputated.

Frandle had disappeared the previous day after telephoning his mother to explain that he was on his way home from his girlfriend's house and would be hitchhiking back to suburban Warren, Mich. When Frandle had not arrived by 11 p.m., his mother notified authorities.

Police searched for Frandle. One witness saw him climb into a 1966 Plymouth driven by two black men near the intersection of Twelve Mile and Van Dyke roads. With the description of the driver, 21-year-old rookie police officer William Tullock led police to the home of Derrick Draw, an employee of General Motors Tech Center. Tullock had once worked with Draw at General Motors. Draw denied all knowledge of the crime until his Plymouth was discovered to contain evidence implicating him in the boy's death.

Lionel M. Alexander, Draw's 19-year-old companion and fellow General Motors employee, told police that he and Draw had picked up Frandle as they drove home from work. He explained that Draw beat the boy in the back seat of the car and, disregarding Alexander's pleas that he stop, stabbed Frandle and sliced off his ears in response to instructions from a United Urban League speaker known only as Enoch. Alexander told authorities that Enoch, speaking at a gathering of black ghetto residents, said, "To prove yourself as a black warrior, bring in the ear of a dead

white man." The man called Enoch denied that he made any such statement. He soon resigned from the Urban League to avoid further embarrassing the organization.

On the testimony of Alexander, Draw was convicted of second-degree murder and sentenced to life at Michigan's Jackson State Prison.

Dreamer, Robert, 1898-1937, U.S. Bloodhounds were used on Dec. 30, 1927, in an attempt to track down the brutal murderer of Thelma Young, seventeen. The murder occurred the night before, in Washington, Pa. Police later complained that thousands of curiosity seekers gathering at the murder site obliterated the killer's scent.

For the next eight years, that trail remained cold. The murderer not only escaped detection, but as later revealed, he passed the victim's house twice each day, on his way to and from work, often greeting members of her family.

The long-sought break in the case came when two young women were attacked, in separate episodes, near the scene of Thelma's murder. Both women managed to free themselves from the attacker. The attacker had fired three shots at one of the women as she fled. It was the other woman, however, who proved dangerous to the attacker. She recognized the man as neighborhood resident Robert Dreamer, a 38-year-old railroad worker. He was quickly arrested for the two bungled attacks. Officer Clark Miller, one of the arresting officers, pointed out the similarities between the recent attacks and the murder of Thelma Young more than eight years before. At first, Dreamer denied any knowledge of the Young murder.

He was arrested on Jan. 21, 1936. Eight officers from the state, county, and Washington Police operated around the clock in questioning the suspect, a non-stop interrogation that went on for five days. On the fifth day, he was shown a button found near Thelma's body. "Did you ever see this before?" one of the officers asked.

"Yes," the suspect admitted, "It's off of a raincoat I used to have."

"When did you lose it?"

"I guess the night of the murder."

"What murder?" one of the officers asked.

"The night Thelma was killed," Dreamer answered. Then he calmly confessed to killing Thelma Young, the sister of one of his best friends and a schoolmate of the woman who was now his wife.

Dreamer's wife, the former Mary Caldwell was also questioned by police. When asked if her husband had ever mentioned killing Thelma, Mary Dreamer replied, "Only once. We were out one night with another girl, and he quarrelled with her. He grabbed her by the throat, half in fun. 'I'll fix you like I did Thelma,' he told her." Dreamer's wife said her husband had been joking. When asked later if she would stand by her husband, she answered, "No. If he did what they say he confessed, then he had better stay right where he is now."

Clyde Young, one of Thelma Young's brothers (there were fifteen children in the Young family), and a boyhood friend of Dreamer's said, "Of course, none of us ever suspected him. But I often wondered why, right after the killing, he quit going around with me."

"Who would have thought that a neighbor had killed our girl?" said Iva Young, the mother of the murdered girl.

Dreamer was convicted of the murder and sentenced to death. He was also a suspect in the brutal murder of Elizabeth Louden, sixteen, who was found beaten to death near her home in Walker Mills, three days before Dreamer's arrest on Jan. 21, 1936. Dreamer never confessed to the crime, but Walker Mills police put together a strong circumstantial case against him. He worked in a railroad yard only two miles away, fit the description of the man that Elizabeth had told friends was following her, and had admitted to police that he had attacked young girls for over ten years. Although he was never tried for this second murder, the Louden murder case was closed on Feb. 1, 1937, one half hour after Dreamer was executed. Robert Elliott, the executioner at Sing Sing who some called the loneliest man in the world, pulled the switch at the Pennsylvania state prison in Rockview that sent Robert Dreamer to his death. Elliott, who traveled between prisons in New York, New Jersey, and Pennsylvania, plying his grim trade, had executed nearly a thousand men.

Dreher, Dr. Thomas, 1875-1929, and **Le Boeuf, Ada**, d.1929, and **Beadle, James**, prom. 1929, U.S. Ada Le Boeuf, a resident of the Louisiana bayou country, began seeing Dr. Thomas Dreher about her headaches in December 1926. In the next few months, Dr. Dreher visited the Le Boeuf residence frequently. Ada Le Boeuf's husband, Jim Le Boeuf, preoccupied with sport fishing in the swampy bayous in and around Lake Palourde, paid no particular attention to the visits.

Le Boeuf was oblivious to the local gossip about a possible affair between his wife and Dreher. One evening, however, when Le Boeuf failed to return his boat on time, James Beadle, the boat's owner, made the comment, "Just because you are careless with your property, you can't be free with mine!" Pressed by Le Boeuf to explain his statement, Beadle told him the gossip. Although Le Boeuf confronted his wife about the affair, Ada claimed that the sole purpose of Dr. Dreher's visits had been to bring her

headache medicine.

On July 1, 1927, the Le Boeufs set out across Lake Palourde to visit relatives. They left for home at midnight. Five days later Jim Le Boeuf's body was fished out of the water. There were bullet holes in the head and evidence that the corpse had been weighted down with heavy irons. When questioned about her husband's murder, Ada Le Boeuf claimed he had been seeing another woman. Although Dr. Dreher admitted conspiring to murder Le Boeuf, he accused James Beadle of firing the shots.

Beadle likewise admitted to a part in the murder but claimed Dreher had actually shot Le Boeuf. When Ada Le Boeuf, Dreher and Beadle came up for trial the next year, all three were convicted of first-degree murder. Despite the fact that no woman had ever been executed in Louisiana, Ada Le Boeuf was sentenced to hang alongside Dr. Dreher. Amidst protest, Governor Huey Long decided that this case should break precedent, saying that a reprieve would be a "mockery against decency and order." The couple were hanged together on Feb. 1, 1929.

Dubuisson, Pauline, 1929-   , Fr. During the German occupation of France, Pauline Dubuisson openly conducted an affair with 55-year-old Colonel Von Domnick, who commanded the German Hospital in Dunkirk. Only sixteen at the time, her indiscretions doomed her after the liberation. Like many other Frenchwomen who had consorted with Nazis, Dubuisson was publicly humiliated in the square of Dunkirk by having her head shaved.

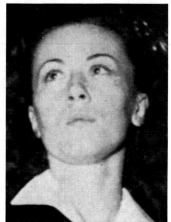
French killer Pauline Dubuisson.

In 1946, she took up the study of medicine at Lille University, where she met and fell in love with Felix Bailly, also a student. During her two-year affair with him, she had many lovers, and recorded their names and sexual preferences on a secret list. In 1949, Bailly moved to Paris and planned to marry Monique Lombard. For eighteen months, Felix Bailly heard nothing from Dubuisson.

Pauline suddenly appeared in Paris in March 1951 to try to win back Bailly's affections. On Mar. 10, Dubuisson purchased a .25-caliber handgun, explaining to the registrar that she needed it for self-protection. Dubuisson left her rooming house on Mar. 15 after leaving a note for the landlady stating that she intended to shoot first herself, then Bailly. The astute landlady sent wires with this information to Bailly and his parents. When Bailly heard about this, he acquired several bodyguards, but Dubuisson slipped past the sentries and shot Bailly in his apartment. His body was found a short time later by a friend. Dubuisson was lying unconscious nearby. She had tried to asphyxiate herself with gas.

She recovered from her suicide attempt to stand trial at the Assizes of the Seine on Nov. 18, 1953. Pauline's diffidence earned her the nickname "Mask of Pride." Bailly had cast her out, she explained, and life no longer meant anything. Pauline Dubuisson was found Guilty of murder and was sentenced to life imprisonment.

Duchess, The, See: **Spinelli, Evelita Juanita.**

Duff-Smith, Markham, 1945- , and **Janecka, Allen Wayne,** prom. 1979, U.S. When the Houston, Texas, medical examiner's office finished the investigation of the deaths of Diana Wanstrath, thirty-six, John Wanstrath, thirty-five, and their son, 14-month-old Kevin Wanstrath, the ruling was that on July 6, 1979, Mrs. Wanstrath had shot her husband and son and then herself.

Detective Johnny Bonds found it strange that a gun was never found at the scene. Though the case was closed, Bonds did not stop his investigation.

The Wanstraths left a large inheritance, so the search focused on family heirs. The family was gathered and told that they would be subjected to polygraph tests. Markham Duff-Smith, a 34-year-old investor and the adopted brother of Mrs. Wanstrath, brought his attorney with him to the test, which he failed.

Detective Bonds discovered that Duff-Smith's mother, Trudy Zabolio, had also died under suspicious circumstances. Her case had been ruled a suicide by strangulation. Bonds believed that both cases were murders, but he needed proof.

An anonymous caller told him that Duff-Smith had arranged his mother's death through a middleman who hired a hit man. The middleman was identified only as a "realtor and coin collector." Interviews with Duff-Smith's business associates turned up one coin collector: Walter Waldhauser, Jr. Detective Bonds dug through Duff-Smith's trash and found correspondence from Allen Wayne Janecka, a prison inmate.

Janecka confessed to the murders of Zabolio and the Wanstraths. Waldhauser had hired Janecka, but he agreed to testify against Duff-Smith in exchange for exoneration from charges. Both Duff-Smith and Janecka were found Guilty of murder in April 1981 and sentenced to death.

Duffy, Renee, 1928- , Brit. Renee Duffy asked of the courts an extended definition of self-defense. She had been severely and repeatedly beaten by her husband, George Duffy, to whom she had been married for a year and with whom she had a son. Her mother saw the results of these beatings, and on several occasions threw Mr. Duffy out of the house until he pleaded to come back. Mrs. Duffy, nineteen, never complained. She told others that the numerous bruises, black eyes, and scratches were accidental. She told no one of her 23-year-old husband's cruelty.

Finally, on Dec. 7, 1948, her submissiveness turned to fury. After another beating, she decided to leave her husband. As she prepared to go, he attacked her again, but she pushed him away and ran to the kitchen to find a hammer with which to defend herself. He told her she could not take the baby. She remembered only that she hit her husband twice with the hammer.

From the looks of the bedroom where Mr. Duffy's unconscious body was discovered, she hit him more than twice. The police found Mrs. Duffy and her child at her sister's home. She was charged with attempted murder on Dec. 8, and when Mr. Duffy died later that day, the charge was changed to murder.

The trial began in March 1949 at the Manchester Assizes. Justice Devlin, in a summation later called classic by higher courts, explained to the jury that the husband's history of violence could not be considered, except in relation to its contribution to his murder. "What matters is whether this girl had time to say, 'Whatever I have suffered, whatever I have endured, I know that: Thou shalt not kill.'"

The jury, consisting of ten men and two women, took an hour-and-a-half to come to a verdict of Guilty, with a strong recommendation for mercy. Justice Devlin sentenced Rene Duffy to death. On Apr. 4, her appeal was heard and denied, but a few hours later the governor of Strangeways Prison notified her that she had been given a reprieve.

Dugan, Eva, 1878-1930, U.S. The first woman to be executed in the state of Arizona, Eva Dugan was convicted of the murder of the Tucson rancher for whom she worked. She murdered the rancher with the misguided hope of inheriting the man's property, but fled in his car soon after she had buried his body. After serving a one-year sentence in New York for stealing the car, Dugan was charged with the murder.

Dugan was tried in Arizona and found Guilty of the murder and sentenced to be hanged until dead. Cheerful to the end, Dugan faced the hangman on Feb. 21, 1930. Dugan shook the warden's hand, kissed each of the prison guards she had grown close to and fond of during her stay at the State Prison in Florence, Ariz., and ascended the steps to the gallows.

Mrs. Eva Dugan, first woman hanged in Arizona.

Duncan, Elizabeth, c.1904-62, and **Baldonado, Augustine**, c.1934-62, and **Moya, Luis, Jr.**, c.1937-62, U.S. "There is nothing good that can be said about Elizabeth Duncan," said her own attorney. When seen in court, the respectable-looking middle-aged woman had a lifetime behind her of getting what she wanted: a new husband while still married to an old one; a new house when she did not have the money for a mortgage payment, let alone the down payment; and an annulment of her son's marriage, acquired by having another man pretend to be her son. When she went on trial in Santa Barbara, Calif., for engineering the murder of her son's wife, a college friend of her son, Stephen Gillis, who was also one of her many husbands, said, "She had a tremendous spell on everybody that she came in contact with, and no matter what lie she told, no matter how fantastic, it was believable."

The investigation of "Mother Duncan" revealed an amazingly chaotic life. Born Hazel Sinclara Nigh in Kansas City in 1904 (or 1906, or 1913, or possibly 1900), she first married, at fourteen, a man named Dewey Tessier. She had three children, but sent them to an orphanage. In the following years, she married at least eleven, and possibly as many as twenty men. Only rarely was she actually free to do so, but that did not bother her. Many of the marriages were annulled on the basis of nonconsummation, although she sometimes managed to blackmail her husbands into support payments. She ran beauty shops, cafes, massage parlors (was arrested for prostitution), and a real estate business.

Perhaps because she never kept a husband, she was fiercely determined to hang on to her son, Frank, whom she had by Frank Low in 1928. She later changed Frank's last name to Duncan, because that particular husband had a better credit rating than most of her husbands. Frank

managed to get through college and obtain his law degree. His mother delighted in attending his court cases and cheering her son on, always identifying herself as the attorney's mother. There is some evidence that they had an incestuous relationship. Gradually Mrs. Duncan became obsessed with the idea that one day her son would marry and leave her.

In November 1957, Frank and his mother quarreled about buying a beauty parlor, and the son ordered his mother out of his apartment. She responded by taking sleeping pills, ostensibly to commit suicide. In the hospital, one of her nurses was Olga Kupcyzk, a 29-year-old Canadian. Olga and Frank fell in love, and his mother began the maneuverings that would end in murder. Olga became pregnant, and as she and Frank talked of marriage, Elizabeth Duncan began harassing her over the phone, even threatening to kill her. Duncan began discussing murder with her best friend, Mrs. Emma Short. Frank and Olga married secretly, but Frank went home to his mother on the wedding night so she would not suspect it. But his mother found out, and intensified her campaign against her daughter-in-law.

She began by inserting an ad in the paper, signed by Frank, saying he would not be responsible for any debts except those of his mother. She and Emma Short planned to kidnap Frank and force him to divorce his wife. But Frank did not act as anticipated and the plot failed. Next, she posed as Olga and hired an ex-con, Ralph Winterstein, to pose as her son and get an annulment. Winterstein was later convicted of perjury. The harassment proved ineffective, so Duncan began to search for a hired killer.

Working with Mrs. Short's help, Duncan found Luis Moya, Jr., a 21-year-old parolee, and his friend, Gus Baldonado, twenty-six. They agreed on a price of $6,000 for the murder of the seven-months-pregnant Olga Duncan. Elizabeth Duncan did not have that kind of money, but she managed to keep the killers interested with a cash "advance" of a couple hundred. On Nov. 17, 1958, they knocked on Olga's apartment door and told her that her drunk husband was in the car. She went to the car and, once there, they knocked her out and drove off. When they reached a culvert in the mountains south of Santa Barbara, they strangled her (having to "take turns" to finish the job, Moya later testified) and buried her body.

As Olga's friends and husband were searching for her, Moya and Baldonado were demanding their $6,000 from Elizabeth Duncan. She put them off again and again. Then, when she was questioned by the police about her relationship with Olga, Duncan, hoping to scare the killers into leaving town, told the police that she was being blackmailed by two Mexicans and described Moya and Baldonado. The police found and arrested Moya, but Duncan refused to identify him. Emma Short, however, told them the whole story. Baldonado, under arrest, finally told where the body of Mrs. Duncan's daughter-in-law could be found.

Elizabeth Duncan, Luis Moya, and Gus Baldonado went to trial in Mar. 1959, and all three were found Guilty of murder and sentenced to death. The jury left it to Judge Charles F. Blackstock to determine whether Duncan should be sent to a mental hospital, but he rejected that option. The trio were executed in the gas chamber at San Quentin on the same day, Aug. 8, 1962.

Dunn, John M. (AKA: **Cockeye**), 1911-49, and **Sheridan, Andrew** (AKA: **Squint**), 1900-49, and **Gentile, Daniel** (AKA: **Danny Brooks**), 1907- , U.S. When Andrew Hintz was fatally shot in the doorway of his New York City apartment by three men on Jan. 8, 1947, it was clearly the outcome of rivalry struggles on the city's crime-ridden waterfront. Hintz was in charge of hiring longshoremen on Pier 51 on the Hudson River, a position eagerly sought by others wanting to receive kickbacks from grateful employees. He lived for three weeks after the shooting, and was able to identify the gunman, John M. Dunn, from his hospital bed. Dunn had served time for extortion and had been arrested nine times since 1926. He worked for the American Federation of Labor, as did Hintz. Andrew Sheridan, another AFL worker and an accomplice to the crime, was apprehended by the FBI in Hollywood, Fla., on Mar. 17. Daniel Gentile, the second accomplice, turned himself in to the district attorney's office thirteen days later. Both men worked for Dunn.

In January 1948 all three were convicted of murder and sent to Sing Sing to await the electric chair. Gentile's sentence was commuted to life imprisonment on July 6, 1949, because he was unarmed at the time of the slaying and had cooperated with District Attorney Frank S. Hogan's investigation into waterfront crime. Dunn and Gentile were electrocuted the next day.

Durand, Earl, 1913-39, U.S. The son of a respected rancher, Earl Durand had admired backwoods heroes since his earliest childhood and modeled himself after the character of Daniel Boone. Jailed for shooting game out of season, Durand, according to his father, "went nearly crazy thinking about having to give up his outdoor life," and killed two officers as he made his escape. Another three men would die before Durand himself was slain.

Durand was well known around Powell, Wyo., where he grew up. An inveterate woodsman, he left school after the

eighth grade to hunt and camp in the Beartooth Mountains east of Yellowstone National Park. Sleeping in shelters and caves which he called "forts," Durand grew a beard to his chest and hair to his shoulders. In mid-March 1939, when game wardens came to arrest the 26-year-old woodsman for killing an elk out of season, they found him eating raw meat from a cow he had recently killed, also illegally. Sentenced to six months in jail for shooting the elk, and facing a possible additional ten years for slaughtering the cow, Durand was held in the Cody County jail. According to a later statement by his rancher father, he seemed "to have gone insane." He took the keys from Deputy Sheriff Noah Riley and then forced him to drive to the Durand ranch. When Under-Sheriff D.M. Baker and Marshal Charles E. Lewis followed, Durand killed them with three shots from his gun. He then clubbed Riley unconscious, and forced his father to give him provisions before heading for the mountains, where he was soon followed by a posse of eighty Montana and Wyoming law officers, headed by Sheriff Frank Blackburn.

About thirty miles northwest of Cody, near Clark's Fork Canyon, in a fortress of boulders and timber, Durand lay in wait for his pursuers. The letter Durand left for Blackburn bore the return address of "Undertaker's Office, Powell, Wyo.," and said: "Of course I know I am done for and when you kill me I suggest you have my head mounted and hang it up in the courthouse for the sake of law and order." It was signed, "Your beloved enemy, Earl Durand." After the posse had circled Durand's hideout, riflemen Orville Linabary and Arthur Argento started directly toward him. He killed them both with shots to the abdomen. That night, Durand looted the corpses, smashing their rifles, and taking boots from one body and bootlaces from the other. Making a false trail, Durand escaped his fortress and, while the posse searched for him with bloodhounds, Durand held up a car on the road. He soon went striding into Powell's First National Bank with a rifle and a six-shooter, where he grabbed $3,000 in cash and started shooting randomly through the bank's walls and windows while Bank President Bob Nelson, three employees, and five customers looked on. Telling his terrified captives, "They'll plug me anyway," Durand fired forty or fifty shots, then tied Nelson and employees Maurice Knutson and John Gawthorp together at the wrists with twine, and pushed them in front of him into the street.

Although no one was visible on the streets, bullets began whizzing around Durand and he began shooting. Gawthorp was hit, and fell to the pavement, dead. Otis Gillette, owner of a nearby gas station, loaded his rifle and handed it to a 17-year-old school boy, Tipton Cox, who, like many local boys, knew and admired the outlaw Durand. Cox fired at his hero, then watched him crumple to the ground. After crawling back into the bank, Durand put a gun to his temple and fired. The bank president shot the dead man one additional time through the head.

Dusseldorf Doubles Killer, The, See: Boost, Werner.

Dwe, San, prom. 1928, Brit. In 1927 San Dwe came from Burma to the Zoological Society in London to be in charge of a white elephant, which was returned to Burma within the year because it could not adjust to the climate. Dwe stayed on to look after two zoo elephants that gave children rides when his co-worker, Mohammad Sayed Ali, returned to Calcutta. On Ali's return to London in June 1928, Dwe was relegated to more menial jobs, giving up both his post and the extra pay to Ali. The two men shared rooms above the zoo's tapir house. On Aug. 24, 1928, two policemen heard groans as they passed by. Investigating, they found Dwe scantily dressed, hysterical, and with an injured foot. In the rooms above the tapir house they found the body of Ali, brutally murdered. In broken English, Dwe explained that four men had broken into the tapir house and killed Ali, and that they had managed to escape. The murder weapons, a sledge hammer and pick axe, were found on the premises.

Dwe was tried for Ali's murder at the Old Bailey in November before Justice Swift. Curtis Bennett, for the defense, brought no evidence, asserting that the prosecution had not proven its case. The jury found Dwe Guilty, discounting his story of intruders as a fabrication. The death sentence Dwe received was later commuted to life imprisonment. In 1932, a special board released Dwe and sent him back to Burma.

Dworecki, Reverend **Walter** (AKA: **Iron Mike**), c.1891-1940, and **Schewchuk, Peter**, 1918-   , U.S. On the night of Aug. 7, 1939, when Reverend Dworecki of Camden, N.J., reported his 18-year-old daughter missing to the local police, he, in fact, knew where the girl was. Not until the next day was the body of Wanda Dworecki found, beaten and strangled, lying in some weeds near a cemetery on the outskirts of town. The pastor of the Polish Baptist Church appeared shocked by the grisly death, as did his parishioners. Three weeks later, the parishioners were shocked again, as was the nation, when the minister was arrested and charged with first-degree murder. Dworecki

was accused of hiring a local youth to kill his own daughter in a murder-for-profit scheme.

Dworecki had promised to pay Peter Schewchuk, 21-year-old carnival roustabout, $100 for killing the girl; he arranged his own daughter's date with death by instructing her to meet the youth, a former boarder in the minister's home, on a Camden street corner. Schewchuk met the girl on the evening of Aug. 7, bought her a soft drink, and then took her to a secluded lover's lane, where he strangled and beat Wanda Dworecki to death.

This was the second time the minister had paid to have his daughter killed. In April that same year, he had paid two local youths, Alexander Franklin and John Popolo, $50 but they had botched the job. They abducted Wanda, beat and choked her, and then had thrown the unconscious girl from their speeding car on a rural road twenty-five miles outside of Camden. But Wanda had survived. Her avaricious father, who had once been charged with arson-for-profit, continued with his scheme until finding the money-hungry Schewchuk to perform the murder for a mere $100. His daughter was insured for $5,000 with a double-indemnity clause making the girl's death by accident or murder worth $6,000 to Dworecki, who would never see a dime of the money.

In August, the minister hired Schewchuk, but, learning a lesson from his previous murder attempt, only gave the youth a 50-cent advance on his $100 fee. It was all the money Schewchuk would ever receive for his role in the killing, and 10 cents of that money he'd spent on the soda which was Wanda Dworecki's last drink, leaving the killer a profit of 40 cents for the killing.

Schewchuk surrendered on Aug. 26, 1939, describing the entire scheme to police; the minister's arrest soon followed. The two were arraigned on Aug. 29, and both attempted to plead guilty. But Judge Gene Mariano refused to accept the plea, which, under New Jersey law, would have made them ineligible for the death penalty, and ordered a plea of not guilty instead.

On Oct. 5, 1939, a jury of seven men and five women returned a verdict of Guilty against Dworecki. Judge Clifford A. Baldwin instructed the defendant to stand and approach the bench. "You have been convicted by a jury of your peers and must be sentenced to death in the electric chair," the judge intoned and then asked the minister if he had anything to say.

"Well, I'm not guilty of that," Dworecki stammered.

"May God have mercy on your soul," the judge said.

On Mar. 28, 1940, after spending an hour in prayer with prison chaplain Reverend John B. Oman, Dworecki walked to the death chamber of the New Jersey State Prison at Trenton and was strapped into the electric chair a few minutes after 8 p.m. The two ministers prayed together before the electric current shot through Dworecki's body. On May 2, 1940, Peter Schewchuk was sentenced to life imprisonment by Judge Baldwin.

E

Eaton, Helen Spence, 1912-34, U.S. On July 11, 1934, Helen Eaton, twenty-two, escaped from the Arkansas state prison farm for women for the fourth and final time. She was on a work detail at a farm near Jacksonville, Ark., when she asked permission to return to the prison to take some medicine. When she did not return the prison was searched. In Eaton's locker, prison officials found a note stating: "I'll never be taken alive." It was also discovered that Eaton had stolen a pistol before making her escape. Authorities knew they faced a dangerous chore in recapturing Eaton, who was known as "the toughest woman in Arkansas."

Eaton had been serving a term for the murder of Jack Worls whom she shot to death in a DeWitt, Ark., courtroom in 1930. Worls had been standing trial for the murder of Eaton's father, Cicero Spence, a riverman. The jury was about to begin deliberations when Eaton, who decided Worls would be found not guilty, rose from her front row seat and executed Worls herself. She was sentenced to five years but the state supreme court later reduced her sentence to two years. She was paroled in 1933, moved to Little Rock, Ark., and worked as a waitress, but her conscience was bothering her. Soon after her 1933 release Eaton went to Little Rock Police and confessed to the murder of Jim Bohots, a restaurant operator Eaton had worked for in DeWitt while her conviction for the previous murder was under appeal. According to Eaton, Bohots had made unwelcome advances towards her. In July 1933, she was sentenced to ten years for the second murder.

Eaton had been an incorrigible prisoner, escaping from the prison three times earlier. She had been returned each time, twice tracked down by bloodhounds. A few hours after her final escape she accosted a farmer's wife in a farm house seven miles northeast of the prison. Eaton demanded that the woman drive her out of the area. Instead, the wife ran into the fields where her husband was working. Eaton fled into the woods, and the farmer called the police. An hour and a half later, she was spotted by police and, as her note had warned, she elected to shoot it out. Helen Eaton died in a hail of bullets, the toughest girl in Arkansas to the very end.

Edel, Frederick W. (AKA: **The Man With Five Hundred Names**), prom. 1928, U.S. The door to Emeline Harrington's New York apartment was open for five days before a neighbor discovered her body on the bathroom floor. The 39-year-old actress had been beaten to death and robbed.

Less than one month later, in January 1928, Connecticut police were alerted to a suspicious guest who left a New Haven hotel without paying his bill. The man's room contained a suitcase filled with bills made out to Mrs. Harrington and letters addressed to Frederick W. Edel. The police were familiar with Edel because he had been acquitted of murder in 1925 and was currently in violation of parole.

Murderer Frederick Edel used more than 500 aliases.

In March 1928, a postal clerk in Hopkins, Minn., recognized Edel from a wanted poster when the suspect tried to buy a money order. As the clerk moved to alert police, Edel ran out of the post office but was captured a mile away. He was returned to New York and charged with the murder of Emeline Harrington. Edel confessed that he had used more than 500 aliases, but refused to admit that he killed Harrington. Edel was convicted of murder and sentenced to death in 1928. Less than two years later, New York governor Franklin D. Roosevelt commuted Edel's sentence to life in prison. New evidence was uncovered following the original trial, which prompted several of the jurors who convicted Edel to inform the governor that the new information created a reasonable doubt in their minds. While Roosevelt said he did not believe the evidence proved Edel innocent, it did warrant a reduced sentence.

Edghill, Carlos Antonio, 1953- , U.S. When New York State Supreme Court Justice Hyman Barshay sentenced Carlos Antonio Edghill to two concurrent twenty-year prison terms for shooting two police officers, he said his hands were tied by a recent court ruling outlawing the death penalty. Officer Robert W. Mandel was killed and officer Peter J. Christ wounded when Edghill shot the policemen during a narcotics investigation in Brooklyn on Apr. 19, 1977. Edghill, an illegal alien from Panama, had been released from jail on a gun charge, less than eight hours before the shooting incident.

Police Commissioner Michael J. Codd called for Edghill to be executed and accused the courts of leniency in releasing the prisoner on $500 bail. Edghill confessed to the shootings and was given the maximum allowable sentence by Barshay in March 1978.

Edmunds, William Charles, 1935- , Brit. Blanche Mary Matthews, who lived with six cats in Monmouthshire, England, was so fearful of being burglarized that she had the downstairs windows of her house sealed shut. On Nov. 19, 1955, the spinster's worst nightmare was realized; an intruder broke a window and attacked the 70-year-old woman. Matthews suffered nine broken ribs, numerous cuts and bruises, and a wound to the throat. A neighbor, Alice Knight, called the police, but when Constable Norman Ellis arrived, Matthews lay barely breathing on her bloodstained bed. She died in a hospital two days later.

During his rounds earlier on the evening of the murder, Ellis had encountered a blood-spattered William Charles Edmunds, who told the officer he had been in a fight. The policeman had let Edmunds go at the time of the incident, but visited the 21-year-old laborer when the murder was discovered. Officials discovered Edmunds' bloodstained clothing in his apartment, and found two rings that had been stolen from Matthews. Edmunds was charged with murder and he subsequently confessed, but tried to prove he was insane at the time. Despite testimony from family and friends that he was mentally unstable, the jury wasted little time in returning a murder conviction. Because of a recent ruling in the House of Commons, Edmunds was spared the death penalty.

Edwards, Edgar (AKA: **Edwin Owen**), d.1903, Brit. In 1902, Edgar Edwards, recently released from prison, told an acquaintance he intended to buy a grocer's shop and hire someone to run it for him. Edwards hired a man named Goodwin to run the shop. He also asked Goodwin to obtain a heavy sash weight for the door. On Dec. 1, 1902, Edwards arrived at the shop in Camberwell, England, while owner William John Darby was talking to a customer. In the next hour, Edwards, using the sash weight, killed Darby, his wife, and their small daughter in the living quarters over the shop. He pawned Darby's gold watch and chain, then returned to the shop in time to meet Goodwin and his wife. Two days later, Edwards rented a house in Leyton, and on Dec. 5 began moving furniture from Darby's apartment.

On Dec. 10, Edwards instructed Goodwin to close the shop as he was going to sell it. He dug a very deep hole in the back garden of the Leyton house on Dec. 16 and buried six sacks containing the cut-up bodies of the Darby family. A neighbor saw him digging the hole but not burying the sacks.

On Dec. 23, Victoria Park grocer John Garland met Edwards at his Leyton home to discuss arrangements for selling his business. When Edwards went after the elderly Garland with a new sash weight, Garland broke some glass in the front door and screamed for help. Edwards was arrested for the attack. During their investigation, police found business stationery in the Leyton house with the name of William Darby of Camberwell, whom police knew to be missing. When the neighbor saw the police at the Leyton house, he told them about Edwards digging a hole, and the bodies were found. The murder weapon was found in the empty, blood-stained, second-floor apartment above the Camberwell shop.

Edwards was arrested for murder and was tried before Justice Wright. Although he refused to plead, the jury found Edwards Guilty and he was hanged.

Edwards, Joseph Sinnott (AKA: **Jose Sinnott; Joseph Wickham**), 1964-   , U.S. A native of Chicago, Joseph Edwards is wanted by the FBI for the murder of his adoptive parents. The victims were shot at close range with a .9-mm handgun. Edwards has been missing since the murders in the early 1980s. At this writing, Edwards is still at large.

Edwards, Paul, and **Shaw, Jill**, prom. 1975, U.S. Paul Edwards and his wife Clover managed an apartment complex in Stone Mountain, a popular vacation resort in Georgia. Jill Shaw was a tall, muscular brunette who was staying with the couple in 1974 until Mrs. Edwards discovered the woman was also sleeping with her husband. Even after Shaw left the resort, the affair continued. The lovers then devised a plot in which they planned to kill Mrs. Edwards and live happily ever after.

On Jan. 30, 1975, Edwards gave Shaw his revolver. Early the next morning as he sought to establish an alibi by talking to a teller at a local bank, Shaw drove to Edwards' apartment, seemingly to talk with his wife. During the conversation, Shaw shot Edwards' wife in the face twice, killing her almost instantly. As prearranged, Paul returned home to find his wife dead and called for an ambulance. When police arrived, Edwards claimed robbery as the motive, but authorities abandoned that theory when they found $50 in the victim's purse.

Meanwhile, Shaw waited for Edwards at an Atlanta airport. She had left a message for him with a security guard and said that it was for someone whose wife had been shot in the face. The lovers were soon arrested and charged with murder. Edwards and Shaw were sentenced to life in prison for killing Mrs. Edwards.

Edwards, Robert Allan, 1913-35, U.S. Two days before Edwards planned to elope with Freda McKechnie, police discovered the young woman's body in Harvey's Lake, outside of Wilkes-Barre, Pa. She had been clubbed over the head and drowned on July 30, 1934. When first questioned by the police, Edwards admitted that he had been with his pregnant girlfriend on the evening of the murder, but said he had dropped her off and gone home. When told police found tire tracks that matched his car in the sand at the beach, Edwards concocted a story about McKechnie fainting. He said he clubbed her over the head so people would think McKechnie had bumped her head. Edwards' third story was a confession, in which he admitted smashing McKechnie over the head with a blackjack and leaving her in the lake.

On trial for first-degree murder, the prosecution introduced evidence that linked Edwards romantically with an East Aurora, N.Y., woman and said he killed McKechnie because he wanted to marry Margaret Crain. The 21-year-old man took the stand in his own defense and said he was innocent. While he admitted his attraction to Crain, he told the jury he planned to marry McKechnie. Following eight hours of deliberation, Edwards was convicted of murder and sentenced to death. He died in the electric chair on May 6, 1935.

Edwards, Vernon David, Jr., 1937- , U.S. When Edwards turned himself into police in Decatur, Ga., in July 1972, and confessed to two Florida slayings, he said his conscience had finally caught up with him. Thirteen years earlier, after getting drunk and being spurned by an older woman at an office party, Edwards stopped at a cottage on the Miami block where he lived. Edwards admitted that he had watched 55-year-old Ethel Ione Little undress a number of times, but his intent that evening was to rob the spinster so he could continue his drinking binge.

Little's landlord found his tenant early on the afternoon of Dec. 15, 1959. She was naked and her body had been tied to the four bedposts. The killer had sliced off Little's left breast in addition to stabbing, strangling, and sexually assaulting the woman. Despite the efforts of Miami detective Mike Gonzalez the Little slaying had remained unsolved for thirteen years.

Edwards also confessed to the 1961 murder of cocktail waitress Johanna Block. The 33-year-old victim was stabbed repeatedly with a pair of scissors, strangled, and beaten about the face. Mary Alice Bratt, who had known Block quite well, aided police in the initial investigation, but the case remained unsolved until 1972, when Mary Alice Edwards convinced her guilt-ridden husband Vernon to turn

himself in to police. Dade County Court Judge Paul Baker accepted Edwards' guilty plea and sentenced the house painter to life imprisonment.

Edwardson, Derrick, 1926- , Brit. Five days after the disappearance of 4-year-old Edwina Taylor, British police discovered the girl's body in the basement of a house on Aubyn's Road in Upper Norwood. Taylor's skull had been fractured and she had been strangled. Police directed their attention towards Derrick Edwardson, the building's ground-floor tenant, who had a lengthy criminal record, including an arrest for the assault of a 5-year-old.

The police found a note in Edwardson's locker at work; he admitted killing the girl, but said he had not raped her. He would turn himself in, he wrote, because "I cannot get the smell of her decaying body out of my system." On Sept. 9, 1957, Edwardson surrendered to police. He pleaded guilty to charges of murder and was sentenced to life in prison.

Egan, Frank J., and **Tinnin, Albert**, and **Doran, Verne**, prom. 1932, U.S. Frank J. Egan was a well-known, well-liked public defender in San Francisco during the 1930s. In trying to maintain a classy, generous image, he went severely into debt. Looking around for a way to solve his problems, his glance fell on Mrs. Jessie Scott Hughes, an elderly client who had made him her executor and heir. When the police had previously warned her that Egan had fantasized about her death, the woman had scoffed and insisted that he was like her own son.

Egan's chauffeur and another man were both "in debt" to Egan because of his assistance in getting and keeping them out of prison. When he asked for their help, they did not feel they could say no. On Aug. 29, 1932, Egan and Dr. Housman went to the fights and made sure they were seen there. That night, Albert Tinnin and Verne Doran drove Egan's car into Mrs. Hughes's garage. When Mrs. Hughes came out to chat for a few minutes, Tinnin knocked her unconscious and placed her on the floor and Doran ran her over with the car. Then they drove out to a highway, and dumped her body as if it had been struck by a hit-and-run driver.

Captain of Inspectors Charles W. Dullea who had eavesdropped on Dr. Housman's office and heard Egan wishing Mrs. Hughes dead, located the car that neighbors had seen at the old woman's garage and found gray hairs on it that matched hers. He also, just on the chance that it might pay off, had Tinnin and Doran brought in. They readily told the whole story and Egan was brought in, his contrived alibi useless. All three were tried and found Guilty of murder. Each man was sentenced to life in prison.

Egyptian Dragons, prom. 1957, U.S. Looking for a cool spot on a stifling New York City night in July 1957, 14-year-old Michael Farmer and 16-year-old Roger McShane thought the pool at High Bridge Park in Washington Heights might be the answer. At the same time, eighteen armed members of a Manhattan street gang called the Egyptian Dragons were headed towards the park to confront The Jesters, a rival gang. When the Jesters failed to show for the rumble, the Dragons remained in the mood for mayhem. Farmer and McShane were preparing to enter the pool when they were attacked by the Dragons. The handicapped Farmer was beaten and stabbed to death, and McShane was seriously injured with knife wounds in his back and stomach. Police arrested eighteen suspects in the case, and seven gang members went on trial for murder in February 1958. The other eleven boys, all juveniles, were sentenced to the state reformatory for their part in the slaying.

Assistant District Attorney Robert R. Reynolds alleged that Dragon leaders Louis Alvarez, seventeen, and Charles "Big Man" Horton, eighteen, had led the attack. The prosecution charged that Farmer had been beaten, kicked, and punched prior to being stabbed. The trial took ten weeks, engaged twenty-seven defense lawyers, and cost the state nearly $250,000. After a day of deliberation, the jury convicted Alvarez and Horton on charges of second-degree murder on Apr. 15, and the pair were sentenced to twenty years to life in prison. Leroy "Magician" Birch, nineteen, and Leoncio "Jello" DeLeon, seventeen, were convicted of second-degree manslaughter and sentenced to five to fifteen years. Three gang members, Richard Hills, seventeen, George Melendez, sixteen, and John McCarthy, fifteen, were acquitted of all charges.

Ekai, Paul Wakwaro, prom. 1980, Kenya. Joy Adamson arrived in Kenya in 1937. She was the wealthy daughter of a prominent Austrian family, and in 1960 her account of her years spent training an orphaned lion cub named Elsa was published as *Born Free*. It became a best seller and drew worldwide attention to the wildlife preservation activities of Adamson and her husband George, a former game warden.

Joy Adamson lived in a remote game reserve 170 miles north of Nairobi. Each evening before the sun went down, she took a walk around the perimeter of the Shaba Game Reserve. On the night of Jan. 3, 1980, she did not return and a search party led by Pieter Mawson went out to look for her. Not far from the camp, they found Adamson with multiple stab wounds. There was evidence that she had been clawed by a wild animal, but a physician in Isiolo determined that the attacker was human. Death was caused by a simi, a double-edged knife used by the natives. The president of Kenya ordered an immediate inquiry. Three suspects were arrested, including Paul Wakwaro Ekai, a herdsman who had once worked for Adamson. Local magistrate Toweet Arap Aswani charged Ekai with murder on July 12, 1980, after two and a half months of hearings.

Ekai, who claimed that he was eighteen, though published reports had him as old as twenty-three, was found Guilty of murder on Aug. 28, 1981, and was ordered detained at the president's pleasure. He narrowly escaped Kenya's mandatory death penalty after convincing the courts that he was not yet eighteen at the time he committed the murder. Ekai may have killed Adamson because of a personality conflict with his former employer. According to Joy Adamson's former secretary, Kathy Porter, the famed naturalist had retreated into a world of her own, and had little patience with her employees.

Elbert, John, 1920- , and **Ferdinand, Phil**, prom. 1942, and **Humphrey, Josephine**, 1924- , U.S. The cantankerous Giovanni Leonidas lived in a shack just outside of Beverly Hills and eked out a living selling goat's milk. Leonidas had few friends, but most of the people in the Sigismundo Valley had heard rumors that the hermit kept a stash of gold in his tiny house.

On Sept. 6, 1942, John Elbert and Paul Ferdinand, with Josephine Humphrey as a lookout, rented a car and went to Leonidas' shack. After forcing their way into the house, Elbert and Ferdinand tied up the old man and tried to get him to reveal the whereabouts of the gold. Torturing him, the pair burned the soles of the old man's feet with matches, but Leonidas refused to talk. When police found the goat-herder he was barely alive. Before his death, Leonidas told authorities, "They wanted my gold...they could not make me tell."

After two weeks of investigating the case, police discovered that a car was seen in front of Leonidas' house on the day of the murder and had been rented by Elbert. He and Ferdinand were soon arrested and charged with murder. Humphrey was arrested later and served as chief prosecution witness against Elbert and Ferdinand, who were found Guilty and sentenced to life imprisonment. Humphrey pleaded guilty to the charge of manslaughter and was given a ten-year suspended sentence. Fortune-hunters scoured Leonidas' hillside home for months following the murder, but no gold was ever discovered.

Elder, Ronald, prom. 1943, U.S. Ronald Elder was in love with June Reinman. Although the girl was a few years older than he was, she was pretty and popular with most of the boys in Pendleton, Ore., in 1943. After nursing his crush on Reinman for a considerable length of time, Elder decided to confront her. One afternoon in October he met the 16-year-old girl in a field as she was out hunting rabbits. Elder offered to teach her how to shoot fish, and the girl let him carry her gun. When Elder told her that he loved her, Reinman failed to take the youngster seriously. Elder was enraged and shot the girl as she walked away from him. He smashed her in the head with the gun butt and tossed the gun in the creek.

Several hours later, Elder joined in the search for Reinman, whose body was later discovered by her father. Although he was questioned about the murder, Elder was not suspected during the initial investigation. It was only after a number of leads fizzled that police again questioned Reinman's friends. Elder was taken to the scene of the crime and asked to recall what had happened the afternoon he and Reinman were together. After being presented with incriminating evidence, Elder confessed to the killing and was sentenced to life in prison.

Ellis, Blaine, 1920-52, U.S. When Blaine Ellis went to visit his boss, George Mensinger, at midnight during the first week of April 1952, he shot and killed the rancher with a shotgun. Ellis then gunned down Mensinger's wife as she tried to call for help, wounding the baby held in her arms. A neighbor, Clifford McDonnell, tried to stop Ellis as he drove off the Mensinger property, but Ellis shot him in the neck. While trying to make his way out of Merriman, Neb., Ellis' car stalled and another of Mensinger's neighbors, Deo Gardner, pulled up to offer help. Ellis shot Gardner, then drove off down the dark, deserted farm road.

In the morning, Ellis arrived at the farm of Andy Andersen and decided to hide out in the rancher's barn. While more than 100 men surrounded the barn, Ellis set the structure on fire and retreated to a tool shed. After several hundred rounds of ammunition were pumped into the shed, Ellis called for the ranchers to come and get him. When the wounded murderer was dragged into Andersen's yard and asked why he killed Mensinger, he said: "He bawled me out a few times. I don't know. Just the meanness in me.

I've been a bad boy." The killer died in an airplane en route to a hospital.

Ellis, Charles, prom. 1935, U.S. Charles Ellis, a butcher, and Frank Cohen, a druggist, operated businesses across the street from each other in the Jamaica section of New York City. The two men were good friends going in opposite directions. Ellis had exhausted his credit with wholesalers and was being pressured by his landlord for rent money. Cohen's pharmacy business was prospering. He and his wife had a 6-month-old baby and Cohen was known throughout the community for his generosity. One of the chief beneficiaries of the druggist's kindness was Ellis.

It was just past noon on May 24, 1935, when police found Cohen's body slumped behind his store counter. His skull had been smashed and the cash drawer had been emptied. As police scoured the neighborhood for witnesses, Ellis was in and out of the pharmacy offering suggestions and trying to assist police in their investigation. Authorities located a young girl who said she was in the drug store the morning of the murder, but never saw Cohen. She did see, however, a man wearing a white apron leave the store. As evidence pointed toward Ellis, police discovered he had paid off an overdue loan the night of the murder and placed, and paid for, a large order with a meat distributor.

Ellis soon confessed to the murder of his friend. He said that Cohen had caught him going through the cash drawer and so he bashed the druggist over the head with a pestle. After being judged "sane" by psychiatrists, Ellis pleaded guilty to second-degree murder and on Feb. 25, 1936, was sentenced to twenty-five years to life imprisonment.

Ellis, Ruth (Ruth Neilson), 1926-55, Brit. In 1944, when Ruth Neilson of Manchester, England, was seventeen, she took up with an American flyer who was soon killed. Shortly after his death, she gave birth to a child. In 1950, she married George Ellis, a dentist, but was divorced within a year. Three years later she got a job at London's Carrolls Club, where she met the love of her life, sports car driver David Blakely.

In 1954, Ruth Ellis met a friend of Blakely's named Desmond Edward Cussen and became infatuated with him. For nearly a year she saw both men. Blakely at first accepted the situation, but there were frequent quarrels between him and Ellis which often resulted in violence. Blakely began seeing younger women, and Ruth retaliated by drawing closer to Cussen, which angered Blakely. On Christmas Eve 1954, Blakely caught Ellis and Cussen together in Cussen's apartment. During the argument that followed, Ellis swore she would never see Blakely again.

But the tortuous relationship continued for a few more months until Blakely announced, on Apr. 6, 1955, that he was going to Hampstead, a suburb of London, to see a mechanic about a race car. Suspecting him of meeting someone else, Ellis went to his apartment and knocked. There was no answer, but Ellis would later swear she heard a woman's laughter through the door. The next day she saw Blakely and a woman together. "I had a peculiar idea that I wanted to kill him," she admitted. Ellis took a taxi to the Magdala Pub in Hampstead on the evening of Apr. 10. As she left the cab, Blakely emerged from the pub with his friend Bertram Clive Gunnell, a car salesman.

Ruth Ellis, hanged in 1955.

Blakely darted to the other side of the car in an apparent attempt to hide. Ellis produced a pistol and shot him. Staring at Gunnell, she coolly said, "Now call the police." At the station Ruth freely confessed her guilt. Her trial began at the Old Bailey on June 20, 1955. Christmas Humphreys, representing the Crown, asked Ellis directly, "When you fired that revolver at close range into the body of David Blakely, what did you intend to do?" Without a moment's hesitation, she replied, "It was obvious that when I shot him I intended to kill him." A jury of ten men and two women deliberated for fourteen minutes before returning a verdict of Guilty. Justice Havers passed the death sentence. Ruth Ellis was to hang on July 13, 1955, at the Holloway Women's Prison in North London.

In the days before the execution, opponents of capital punishment collected some 50,000 signatures on appeals for clemency to the Home Office, but all were turned down. She was the last woman hanged in England.

Elmore, Belle, See: **Crippen,** Dr. **Hawley Harvey.**

Elwell, Robert, prom. 1950, U.S. Before he reached the age of ten, Robert Elwell had already had his first sexual encounter. He later had intercourse with his two sisters and was present on a number of occasions when his father threatened to have sexual relations with his sisters. At eleven, Elwell fell down a set of stairs and suffered a head injury. The fall marked a tragic turning point in Elwell's life. He resumed wetting the bed, could not adjust to school, and began to suffer epileptic fits.

After a year and a half in the U.S. Marines, Elwell was discharged for medical reasons. He had suffered numerous blackouts and required extensive medical observation. What the Marines characterized in Elwell as an "immature personality" turned into ugly, aggressive behavior after his discharge. He was accused of assaulting two girls. In May 1950, Elwell killed his aunt, Mrs. Tully, in her Melrose, Mass., home. When questioned by the police, he first denied any knowledge of the crime, and then told a tale in which two men had murdered his aunt and forced him to drive them to Portland, Maine, with the body in the trunk.

Upon further questioning, Elwell admitted to killing his aunt and dumping her brutalized body in a ditch in Maine. At a preliminary hearing, Elwell wanted to plead guilty, but because of his mental instability a formal plea of not guilty was entered. On trial for murder, Elwell's attorneys pleaded their client guilty but insane. The defense argued that Elwell's history of epilepsy and troubled childhood combined to form an uncontrollable personality. Elwell said that he recalled striking his aunt, but his next memory of the evening was buying gasoline in Maine. A jury found Elwell Guilty and he was sentenced to death. His sentence was later reduced to life in prison.

Emmeloth, David, 1956-78, U.S. It was a despondent David Emmeloth who returned from a fishing trip in Kankakee, Ill., on the evening of July 28, 1978. As he and a friend were driving home, Emmeloth was reminded of how he and his deceased father used to fish nearby. The two fishermen had been drinking much of the day and Emmeloth's partner was forced to stop the car twice as his distraught passenger attempted to jump from the moving vehicle. When Emmeloth finally returned to his Blue Island home, on Chicago's far South Side, he told his mother, "I feel like I've got the devil in me and it's got to come out."

Marge Emmeloth was scared by her son's behavior and ran across the street to enlist the aid of Timothy Gee and his stepbrother David Gee, two of her son's longtime friends. As the Gee brothers tried to calm Emmeloth, he grabbed a knife and inflicted a superficial wound on his mother's throat. Mrs. Emmeloth and her 14-year-old son fled the house. At the same time, David Emmeloth grabbed a 12-gauge shotgun from his upstairs bedroom and returned to kill the Gee brothers.

When police arrived, Emmeloth walked out the front door clothed in a bathrobe carrying the shotgun. The officers ordered him to drop the gun, but Emmeloth just smiled and walked towards the squad car. By the time a backup unit arrived, Emmeloth was seated in the patrol car. Once again, the police told him to surrender the shotgun, but Emmeloth fired and wounded one of the officers. The Blue Island police then opened fire on Emmeloth. The murderer tumbled out of the car with nine bullets in him.

Emmett-Dunne, Frederick, c.1923- , Ger. Sergeant-Major Frederick Emmett-Dunne of the Royal Electrical and Mechanical Engineers became infatuated with the German-born wife of fellow soldier Reginald Watters toward the end of 1952. The two men were stationed in Duisburg, Ger., at the time. Emmett-Dunne lived in the Fourth Infantry barracks, and Watters lived with his wife Mia near the grounds of the technical training school. He was a popular, easy-going man apparently unaware of his wife's relationship with Emmett-Dunne.

In the early morning hours of Dec. 1, 1953, Sergeant Watters was found hanging from the banister of Block Two in the Glamorgan Barracks, apparently a suicide. Later that day, Emmett-Dunne issued a statement saying that he had driven Watters back to quarters at 7 p.m. the night before. No one else had seen Watters until he was found the next morning. Dr. Alan Womack conducted the post-mortem, and concluded that death was the result of shock brought on by strangulation. Womack, young and inexperienced, concluded that Watters' death was a suicide.

The matter was forgotten until June 3, 1954, when Mia Watters hastily married Emmett-Dunne in England, fueling old rumors. A former army special investigator communicated his growing suspicions to Scotland Yard, which prompted a re-opening of the case. Watters' remains were exhumed in February 1955 and given to pathologist Dr. Francis Camps, who startled the press by announcing "that this man never died from hanging, but that he died as a result of a severe blow across the front of the throat." It was the kind of blow that a military man trained in self-defense might inflict during

Murderer Frederick Emmett-Dunne.

intense hand-to-hand combat. Frederick Emmett-Dunne, now living quietly with his wife in Taunton, Somerset, was charged with murder on Apr. 15, 1955. His trial began in Dusseldorf on June 27. The prosecution was led by Mervyn Griffith-Jones. The defendant was represented by Derek Curtis-Bennett, who claimed that Emmett-Dunne killed Watters in self-defense, and staged the suicide because of a growing fear that he would be drummed out of the service.

Emmett-Dunne said he met Watters outside the barracks. The young sergeant accused Emmett-Dunne of carrying on with his wife while he had been away on an army exercise in Cologne two months earlier. Emmett-Dunne said Watters produced a pistol, and that in an effort to disarm him, he struck him a glancing blow to the throat. He had not meant to kill Watters, only to disable him. On July 7, the jury retired and after an hour and a half, they returned with a Guilty verdict. Sergeant-Major Emmett-Dunne was to die on the gallows. The verdict was confirmed on July 19, with one amendment. Emmett-Dunne was spared the death penalty in light of an accord signed in Bonn on May 26, 1952, by the British government, which outlawed capital punishment on federal lands by military authorities. The sentence was commuted to life imprisonment. The convicted murderer served ten years and was then released.

Engleman, Dr. Glennon E., 1927- , U.S. Glennon E. Engleman, a dentist from south St. Louis, Mo., who would sometimes treat people for free, was a killer who murdered for money and power. Respected in a blue-collar community of St. Louis, Glennon encouraged women to marry future victims, and take out insurance on their new spouses' lives. After killing them, Engleman and the wives would share the profits. The murders of seven people were linked to Engleman; over twenty-two years, he was alleged to have killed five men and two women. The first death, on Dec. 17, 1958, was the shooting of James Bullock near the Art Museum in Forest Park. Bullock had been married for six months to Engleman's former wife, Ruth Ball Engleman Bullock, who collected $64,500 in life insurance when her husband died. She later invested $15,000 in a dragstrip, in which Engleman was both director and shareholder. Although police interviewed Engleman and Bullock, there was not enough evidence for a case against them. The widow later remarried.

The next death connected to Engleman was that of Eric Frey, a partner with the dentist in the dragstrip operation. Frey was the victim of a dynamite explosion at the dragstrip on Sept. 26, 1963. Engleman was the first person to reach

Frey, and pronounced him dead. Based on the dentist's statement, the Franklin County coroner ruled the death an accident. Frey's widow, Saundra Frey, was a niece by marriage to Engleman, and gained $37,000 in insurance benefits when her husband died. She later invested $16,000 in the dragstrip. At one of Engleman's trials years later two witnesses said that Engleman had bragged about murdering his partner. Peter Halm was shot in the back with a rifle in a wooded area near Pacific, Mo., on Sept. 5, 1976. He was lured there by his wife, Carmen Miranda Halm. Mrs. Halm had known Engleman since childhood and had once worked for him as a dental assistant. She would later testify that her marriage had been planned by Engleman so that Halm could be killed for insurance money. Carmen Miranda Halm shared her $60,000 in life insurance benefits with her brother, Nicholas Miranda. She was granted immunity when she testified against her former employer. The prosecutor in the Halm case, Gorden Ankney, remarked on the peculiar "hold" Engleman had over Miranda. Ankney said, "I'll never forget the sadness of Carmen Halm. She wasn't a killer, but he got her involved through manipulation."

The next three murders, to which Engleman would later confess, were those of the Guswelle family. On Nov. 3. 1977, Arthur Guswelle and his wife, Vernita Guswelle, were slain on their farm outside Edwardsville. Their son, Ron Guswelle, was murdered on Mar. 31, 1979, in his garage; his body was later dumped in East St. Louis, Ill. The killings were alleged to be a conspiracy between Barbara Guswelle, who was married to Ron, and Engleman, who she had met in 1960 when they lived in the same St. Louis apartment building. Guswelle stood to inherit more than $500,000 from the combined insurance of the Guswelles and her husband. Guswelle was cleared on all charges of murdering her in-laws but was convicted in April 1985 of murdering her husband. She was sentenced to fifty years in prison.

The car bombing murder of Sophie Marie Barrera on Jan. 14, 1980, was different from the previous killings in that there was no conspiracy involving insurance benefits. Barrera, who ran a dental lab, was suing Engleman for $14,500 in unpaid bills. After this slaying, Ruth Bullock began to fear that Engleman would destroy her if she became angry. She went to the police, and agreed to be wired, taping conversations that helped convict Engleman. On June 19, 1985, Engleman pleaded guilty to three counts of murder, for slaying Barrera and the Guswelle couple. All three killings were committed in Madison County. He was sentenced to two fifty-year jail terms. Richard B. Dempsey, Engleman's former defense attorney, described his client: "I think probably his desire to control individuals was his driving force—to make all the little dummies walk in line and sing at the same time."

========

Enkhardt, Max, 1910-1979, Aus. On the afternoon of Nov. 3, 1969, Enkhardt, fifty-nine, kissed his sleeping wife Anna Enkhardt and then shot her dead. In 1970, in Melbourne's Criminal Court, Enkhardt pleaded not guilty, claiming the death was a mercy killing. "My wife was badly mangled in a car accident in 1968," he told the court. "She was very ill. She needed my help...My wife was convinced she had incurable cancer. In 1968 she was in great pain and losing weight...In 1969 we got behind in our rent and my wife was getting sicker and sicker.

"I felt helpless. I worked at many things but they offered no success. I was marked for failure. I drank sometimes but I could not control my drinking. We talked a lot. The weekend before she died I picked her up, carried her to the bathroom and put her on the scales. She weighed six stone (eighty-four pounds). She was very ill. She had some sort of convulsive fit. I thought she was going to die on the Monday night. She was certain she had cancer." On Monday morning the real estate agent called to tell Max they would have to vacate the house that same day. "I couldn't tell her."

When the doctor arrived, Enkhardt went to get a bottle of brandy. When he returned he gave his wife some medicine. "She was very ill...she said it was the end. I drank the rest of the brandy. I couldn't stand it. I went outside and got the pistol which had been in a trunk since we were married. I kissed her before I shot and she didn't show any response to my kiss. I loved her. I only did it for her. Believe me. I didn't come here to grovel for anything. She was my love...my only love for thirty-five years...she didn't nag me, she loved me. I couldn't bear to see her suffer."

Enkhardt testified that he then tried to kill himself but the gun jammed. The dead woman's sister testified that she had gone to visit Anna Enkhardt at 4 p.m. on the day of the killing. "I leaned over to talk to her and could see the blood all over her. I shouted out several times but could get no answer. I called outside a few times. Suddenly Max approached from the garage. I said, 'What have you done to Anna?' and he said, 'Nothing.'

"I went into the kitchen and he followed and I said again. 'What have you done to Anna?' and he replied, 'I killed her.'" According to the sister, Max had never mentioned trying to kill himself.

An all-male jury found Enkhardt Guilty of murder and Justice McInerney sentenced him to death. The sentence was later commuted to twenty years and in August 1978, after serving almost nine years Enkhardt, who had been a model prisoner, was released. He said he felt like a man out of place and time. "I have got no one, no family, nothing...where do I go?"

Enkhardt continued to insist upon his innocence. "All that's left to say is, my conscience is clear. I can face my maker. He knows." A few months later in September 1979, after a year of freedom, he was hit by a car in Elsternwick. He had better luck than his wife who had lingered on in pain for sixteen months after being hit by a car. Enkhardt died soon afterwards.

Epton, George Cyril, 1907-   , Brit. When police finally found Winifred Virginia Mulholland, the 26-year-old woman had been dead for three days. Mulholland's body was discovered under a balcony in Brixton. After determining that her death was not an accident, police questioned George Cyril Epton, who lived in an apartment above where the body was discovered. The 41-year-old engineer said he did not know the woman. On the following day, Epton was charged with murder. Police had discovered blood stains and what they believed to be the murder weapons in Epton's apartment.

After pleading not guilty, Epton proceeded to tell the courtroom how he met Mulholland at Piccadilly and invited her home to supper. After they had supper, Epton accused the woman of stealing money from him. He said Mulholland denied taking £9 and he struck her, sending her headfirst into the fireplace mantelpiece. Epton said he saw his money by her feet as she lay unconscious and proceeded to beat her about the face with one of her shoes. For three days he left the corpse lying beside his bed, and then dumped her body over the balcony. Epton was found Guilty of murder and sentenced to life in prison.

Erler, Robert John, prom. 1968, U.S. Robert Erler, a Vietnam veteran who joined the Hollywood, Fla., police department, almost had psychic powers in perceiving where, under a respectable facade, crime might be taking place. He was known for finding stolen cars that had not yet been listed as stolen, and seeing an apparently deserted house and knowing that it was occupied by crooks on the run.

All that changed on Aug. 12, 1968, when Erler, walking along the beach at night, found a woman and her daughter sleeping on the sand. He told Mrs. Dorothy Clark and her 12-year-old daughter Merilyn Clark to go along to his trailer to sleep, that his wife and son were there. But he and his wife were divorced, and no one was there but Erler. He raped Mrs. Clark, then took Merilyn outside and shot her

five times, killing her. He then shot Mrs. Clark five times, but the older woman survived. Erler called his police station and said he had killed two people but did not identify himself. Instead, he appealed for them to stop him

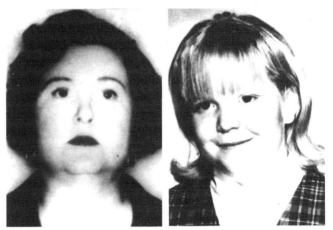

Left, Mrs. Dorothy Clark and daughter Merilyn, murdered by Erler.

and hung up. He reported for duty the next morning and, of course, had no trouble leading his colleagues to the body of the girl and Mrs. Clark.

Before Mrs. Clark could recover, Erler resigned from the force, citing as his reason that his mother was dying of cancer in Arizona. However-er, Erler's phone call to the police had been recorded, and when Mrs. Clark re-covered, she and the police were able to identify him. Erler allowed himself to be returned to Florida and stand trial. He was found Guilty and sentenced to ninety-nine years in prison plus six months at hard labor. After four years in the penitentiary, he was transferred to a minimum-

Killer cop Robert Erler.

security prison. He later escaped through an alligator-filled moat. Erler was eventually apprehended in Missis-sippi—an escapade in which he had been captured, then broke free, and finally stopped by gunshot blasts.

Essex, Mark James Robert, 1949-73, U.S. Mark James Robert Essex, a black man, grew up with religious parents in the small town of Emporia, Kan. Joining the Navy in 1969, he encountered discrimination and developed an intense hatred for whites. After receiving a general discharge after two years service for "character and behavior disorders," he became involved in militant black politics. When he returned home from the service, he could not hold down a job because, a former friend explained, "he couldn't stand taking orders from white people. After spending time in New York with black radicals and becoming increasingly bitter and militantly opposed to white society, Essex, twenty-three, moved to New Orleans. He lived in four apartments during his five months in the city, making few friends. Just before Christmas he wrote to his mother, declaring that "the white man is my enemy," and "I will fight to gain my manhood or die trying." He gave away a few prized possessions to friends, and completed his plans for a sniper attack.

On Jan. 7, 1973, Essex, armed with a .44-caliber rifle and several thousand rounds of ammunition, positioned himself in a concrete bunker on the roof of a seventeen-floor Howard Johnson's Motor Lodge, about five blocks from New Orleans' French Quarter. He began firing from the motor lodge at about 10:15 a.m., after setting fires in several empty rooms to draw out people to shoot. By the time he finished his twelve-hour, guerrilla warfare rampage, nine persons would be killed and nine more wounded. Essex fired on guests as they fled from their rooms after the fire alarm was sounded. Five people killed were hotel guests, four were policemen; one of them was Deputy Police Chief Louis Sirgo. Hundreds of policemen surrounded the hotel as a crowd of thousands watched. Firemen used their trucks for protection against the sniper as they attempted to fight the hotel fire. Police sharpshooters fired hundreds of bullets into the concrete bunker. At night, with a borrowed Marine helicopter, police moved in on Essex, killing him with about thirty red tracer bullets. A newsman who observed the scene from the building next door said the officers in the helicopter fired at the dead body for three or four minutes. The .44-caliber Magnum rifle, smashed into four pieces from the bullets shot into it, was the only weapon found on the roof, lying near Essex's corpse. Ballistics tests confirmed that the rifle was the same weapon used in the New Year's Eve 1972, attack on New Orleans police, in which a 19-year-old cadet was killed.

Evans, Chester, 1945-   , U.S. Chester Evans, a member of Chicago's Black P. Stone Nation gang, was convicted of murdering two men in 1973 and sentenced to thirty to ninety years in prison. Throughout the trial, Evans maintained his innocence. He spent the evening of Nov. 29, 1969, in Milwaukee with friends, Evans said, and was nowhere near the 1000 block of East 46th Street in Chicago, where the shootings took place. He was convicted solely on the testimony of 16-year-old Robert Lee Johnson, who

saw the murders from across the alley. After being interrogated by Chicago police for eleven days, Johnson signed a statement naming Evans as the murderer. Johnson also implicated Lawrence Griffin in the shootings.

In prison, Evans studied painting and religion. In 1978, he was credited with saving a female prison guard from almost certain death during a prison riot. Despite the help of his godfather, the Reverend George Clements, an influential leader in Chicago, Evans' 1981 request for parole was denied.

Evans, Haydn Evan, prom. 1947, Brit. When the battered corpse of Rachel Allan, a 76-year-old washer-woman, was found outside her house in Hillside Terrace on Oct. 12, 1947, police had no clues as to her killer other than that she had spent the evening at the Butcher Arms public house. The key to her front door was still in her hand, and walls and doors nearby were bloodstained from the vicious assault.

Glamorgan County police notified Scotland Yard, and Detective chief superintendent John Capstick was put in charge of the investigation. Asking local police constable Stephen Henton to supply a list of any possible murder suspects, Henton submitted a list that included the name Haydn Evan Evans. Evans had been seen at the pub earlier that night wearing a brown suit and had quarreled with Allan when she teased him about his new clothes. Questioned in the home he shared with his parents and sister, the 22-year-old coal miner said he had been at the Butcher Arms the Saturday night of the slaying, but was wearing a blue suit and did not own a brown one.

Taken to the police station for further questioning, Evans confessed to killing Allan, but still denied owning a brown suit. Capstick returned to Evans' home, and asked the mother to check her son's room once more for the missing suit. While she was out of the room, Capstick pulled up the upholstery on the couch where she had been sitting and discovered the blood-stained clothing. More traces of blood and fragments of skin tissue and bone were found on Evans' socks and trouser cuff. Tried in the Cardiff Assizes Court before Justice Byrne, Evans was found Guilty of murder and was executed on Feb. 3, 1948.

Eyler, Larry W., 1953-   , U.S. Convicted mass-murderer Larry Eyler first emerged as a suspect on Sept. 30, 1983, when an Indiana state trooper driving south along I-65 noticed two men climbing out of a roadside ditch. One of the men, later identified as Larry Eyler, was carrying a bag that contained sections of rope. The second man told the police officer that his name was Darrell Hayward, and that he had been offered $100 to engage in roadside sex with Eyler.

A quick search of the police records revealed that Eyler, originally from Indianapolis, was a suspect in a series of Indiana sex murders. After spending the next twelve hours in custody, Eyler was released by the Indiana police. When he returned to his Chicago apartment on Oct. 3, detectives from Lake County, Ill., were waiting for him. Eyler was suspected in the Aug. 31 murder of 28-year-old Ralph Calise, whose remains were found in suburban Lake Forest.

Eyler was released a second time, but was placed under police surveillance. The police had reason to believe that Eyler was the man responsible for the deaths of at least twenty young men in four states. The 30-year-old house painter lived in Chicago during the week, but commuted to his other residence in Terre Haute, Ind., on weekends.

Indignant over what he called police harassment, Eyler filed a lawsuit against Lake County and the Indiana State Police. While the case was being prepared by his attorneys, Eyler was arrested on Oct. 30 and charged with the murder of Calise, based on evidence found in the back of his truck. A piece of rope which Eyler used to tie his victims up was located in the cab.

However, the judge declared that the evidence had been obtained illegally, and Eyler was ordered released. Free to kill again, the house painter from Indiana wasted little time. On Aug. 21, 1984, the body of Daniel Bridges was found in a garbage dumpster on Chicago's North Side. Eyler pleaded not guilty to charges of aggravated kidnapping, armed violence, unlawful restraint, and murder. Held without bond in the Cook County Jail, Larry Eyler was convicted and sentenced to die by Judge Joseph Urso on Oct. 3, 1986. "You are an evil person," the judge said. "You truly deserve to die for your acts."

The case was air-tight after Assistant State's Attorneys Richard Stock and Mark Rakoczy brought into court several men who testified to having been handcuffed and beaten by the defendant. Frustrated in their earlier attempts to bring the felon to justice, police and the families of the twenty victims who were slain between 1982 and 1984 were at last satisfied that justice had been served. "One of the most dangerous people that ever stepped in this building is now behind bars for good," Rakoczy said.

F

Fairris, Hurbie Franklin, Jr., 1933-56, U.S. When Hurbie Fairris, Jr., was sent to the electric chair in January 1956 for murdering Detective Bennie Cravatt during a robbery, he was repeating family history.

The Oklahoma boy had an interesting, but sordid past. When he was sixteen months old his uncle Ray Hamilton was electrocuted in Texas for killing a prison guard. Hamilton was an early associate of Clyde Barrow and Bonnie Parker. Another uncle, Iwana Fairris was serving a life sentence for various crimes. His mother, separated from Hurbie's father when her son was a tyke, had shot and killed two husbands. The first shooting was ruled committed in self-defense, but when Mrs. Fairris shot her third husband, she drew a five-year prison sentence.

Fairris had a girlfriend named Peggy Ann Fry who was serving time in a West Virginia prison for transporting a stolen car across state lines, and his brother Bethel Fairris was in jail for burglary. It had come as no surprise that Hurbie Fairris, Jr., had resorted to a life of crime. His stint on Death Row at the Oklahoma State Prison was "longer than I've ever stayed in one place before," he explained. He had no final words for the executioner other than to say "let's get on with it."

Falleni, Eugene (AKA: **Harry Leo Crawford; Jean Ford**), 1876-1938, Aus. Born in Florence, Italy, Eugene Falleni, whose real name might have been "Eugenie" Falleni, since she was a girl, moved with her parents to New Zealand at an early age. She was a strong, compactly built young woman who yearned to be a man. At the age of sixteen she passed herself off as a cabin boy and signed on with a Norwegian barque engaged in commercial trading along the Pacific rim.

Falleni worked hard and acquired enough of the masculine affectations to fool her shipmates. An Italian named Martello was the only one to see through her ruse. A relationship developed between them, and by the time the vessel moored in New South Wales in 1899, Falleni was pregnant. The child she bore was named Josephine, but seeing no easy way out of her predicament, Falleni continued to pass herself off as a man to secure higher wages and better employment.

Josephine was placed in the care of an Italian couple named De Anglis who resided at Double Bay. Falleni identified herself as Harry Crawford, and paid the De Anglises a small stipend to care for Josephine. At the same time she began to court a widowed cook and housemaid, Annie Birkett, who worked for a prominent physician, Dr. Clarke. Birkett was easily deceived, and quickly fell under the influence of Crawford. She pooled her life savings together and bought a small candy store in Balmain, a suburb outside of Sydney, Aus. Birkett's teenaged son, Harry, tried desperately to dissuade his mother from foolishly marrying Crawford.

Nevertheless, this is just what Annie Birkett did in 1914, and for the next three years they lived together as "man and wife." When Mrs. De Anglis died a year later, Josephine came to live with the Crawfords. She kept her rightful mother's dark secret from Harry, but the widow Birkett finally understood what had taken place. Falleni-Crawford decided to kill Birkett, lest she reveal her true identity and foil her ambitions and future plans. On Sept. 28, 1917, while the two were picnicking near Chatswood, Falleni bludgeoned Birkett to death and then incinerated the body under a heap of logs. The crime had been cleverly disguised, and it wasn't until two years later, in 1919, that Crawford was arrested and charged with murder. Harry Birkett had gone to live with his aunt during this time, and Falleni quickly found himself a second "wife."

Convinced that his mother had been murdered by Falleni, Harry and his aunt went to the police. An examination of dental charts established it was the body of Annie Birkett. Confronted by the police with an arrest warrant and the probability of confinement in the men's section of the prison, there was little else to do but confess to her identity. Crawford admitted that she was a woman and was forced to appear in female clothing on Oct. 5, 1920, for the first time since her daughter was born.

She was found Guilty and given the death sentence, which was commuted to life imprisonment. Falleni-Crawford remained at the Long Bay Jail for ten years, before earning her release in February 1931. Following her discharge from custody, she assumed a woman's identity. Under the name of Jean Ford, she opened a lodging house in Paddington, which she maintained until 1938, when the place was sold. Several months later, on Oct. 6, 1938, Falleni was struck by a car and was killed instantly.

Fallon, Mickey, and **McDonald, Eddie,** prom. 1934, U.S. Before dawn on the morning of Mar. 3, 1934, Joe Arbona was gunned down in his car on New York's fashionable upper West Side at 183rd and Riverside Drive. The hysterical screams of his fiancee Lillian Dawson awakened residents to the tragedy. When police arrived, Arbona was dead. A gun shot had torn away most of his jaw. Three men and one woman held them up at gunpoint, Dawson said, but she was unable to provide a positive identification.

Three weeks passed before the New York police could identify the killers. Officers alerted Assistant District Attorney P.F. Marro that a missing girl had returned home after living it up in Manhattan in the company of her boyfriends. Detective John Bunschrow questioned a waitress at the restaurant where the girl once worked. She could not remember their last names, but provided enough salient facts so that Bunschrow felt compelled to write a full report to his superior, Lieutenant Thomas Neilson. He, in turn, notified Lieutenant James Donnelly.

Marro and Donnelly entered the case, and extracted the first names of the other girl's boyfriends: Harry, Eddie, and Mickey. The waitress was driven around the vicinity of 125th Street and the Hudson River where one of the young men had recently bragged about holding up a shopkeeper. The store owner said that he had been robbed of a .45-caliber Colt revolver, which was the same weapon that had killed Arbona.

Confronted with this evidence, the ex-witness confessed to the police. She identified Mickey Fallon as the trigger man the night of the murder, and Eddie McDonald as the one who supplied the car. According to her, the selection of Arbona as their victim was purely haphazard. A third man, Harry Hood, moved into the front seat with the girl to act as decoys in case a police car drove by.

The four were indicted on charges of second-degree murder on Mar. 22, 1934. McDonald received thirty years to life at Sing Sing Penitentiary, and Fallon was sentenced to thirty-five years to life. Harry Hood was acquitted in a jury trial, and the ex-waitress who was in it for a good time was dismissed after a motion was filed by Assistant District Attorney Marro.

Faria, Albert, and **Simmons, William**, and **Chadwick, William**, prom. 1930s, U.S. On a rainy day in East Orange, N.J., two sullen strangers entered the Hi-Hat Lunchroom. When the counterman emerged they ordered him to open the cash drawer. At that moment, Patrolman Thomas Ennis, a WWI veteran, entered the diner. The gunmen shot him in the stomach and fled. With the cooperation of the Newark Police Department, the killers of the East Orange policeman were quickly identified and captured. Playing a hunch, Lieutenant Joseph Cocozza investigated the Hi-Hat employees. He learned that an ex-convict named William Chadwick had recently been employed at the Newark branch.

His accomplice Albert Faria was seized at a hospital in Hoboken where he was being treated for a gunshot wound. Faria was a notorious stickup man who had been arrested six years earlier. In the office of Joseph Linarducci, captain of the Essex County homicide squad, a third man, William Simmons, confessed to the crime and identified Chadwick as the "finger man" of the operation. He picked the time and the place based on the layout of the lunchroom. Faria and Chadwick broke down and admitted their roles in the robbery. The three men were quickly brought to trial. Faria and Simmons, who had carried out the robbery, were held responsible for the death of the police officer. They were sentenced to death. Chadwick received fifteen years in prison.

Farley, John, 1943- , U.S. A 26-year-old paper hanger from Brooklyn, John Farley was accused of raping and murdering Margaret Burke, forty-nine, in an alley after following her out of a Queens, N.Y., bar on Aug. 21, 1968. Because Farley had an extra set of Y chromosomes, his defense attorney, Marvin Kornberg, contended that his client had characteristics of a "supermale," and was predisposed to violence as a result. Based on research done in European prisons, a theory developed that a disproportionate number of criminals convicted of violent crimes possessed the extra Y chromosome. The prisoners found to have the extra chromosome were also tall and mentally dull and had facial acne. During the trial in the Queens Supreme Court, Justice Peter T. Farrell dismissed the original rape charge against the six-foot-three-inch, 240-pound defendant. Lawyer Kornberg asked the jury to find Farley not guilty by reason of insanity, but on Apr. 30, 1969, after ten hours of deliberation, the jury found the defendant Guilty of first-degree murder. On July 10, 1969, Farley was sentenced to a prison term of twenty-five years to life.

Faysom, David, 1959- , U.S. On Oct. 6, 1981, David Faysom, twenty-two, befriended 13-year-old Nicole Lee, who had run away from her home in Chicago. He bought her a meal and persuaded her to work for him as a prostitute. Nicole was reluctant and pretended to be sick to avoid appointments that Faysom arranged, according to Karen Brandon, eighteen, who formerly worked for Faysom. On Oct. 9, the pimp drove Lee and Brandon into an alley and ordered Lee to take off her clothes. He scolded her for not making enough money. He then told her to "Show me your heart," and shot her with a handgun. When she promised to make more money, he shot her again.

In January 1983, Faysom was convicted of murder, pandering, armed violence, and unlawful restraint. On Feb. 16, Judge R. Eugene Pincham sentenced Faysom to life in prison with no chance for parole. The judge later commuted the sentence to seventy years in prison. Brandon, who was originally charged with murder, pleaded guilty to concealing a homicide and was sentenced to a thirty-month probation.

Fazekas, Suzanne, d.1929, Hung. The women of Nagyrev, Hung., an isolated village southeast of Budapest, while their husbands were away during WWI, took lovers from among the prisoners of war in nearby camps. After several years of such promiscuity, the war ended and the husbands returned. But domesticity no longer satisfied the women of Nagyrev, and with the help of local midwife Suzanne Fazekas, they began poisoning their husbands. Once the murders had begun, anyone considered inconvenient was in danger. Fazekas sold arsenic to the women, which she obtained by boiling the flypaper she purchased in bulk. Officials later learned that, for several years, Nagyrev and a neighboring village bought more flypaper than the rest of Hungary combined.

The first murder occurred as early as 1911, the beginning of a spree that lasted nearly twenty years and involved perhaps fifty women. Returning husbands, relatives who owned land, mothers-in-law, even recalcitrant children—few were exempt from Fazekas' poison. Added to the ease of perpetration was the fact that the official who approved death certificates was Fazekas' cousin, so when outsiders noted the region's high death rate, a routine check of the death certificates showed nothing amiss. Further, the village of Nagyrev and its neighbor, Tiszakurt, were so isolated that no one paid much attention—until 1929, when two potential victims of Mrs. Ladislaus Szabo claimed that she had tried

Suzanne Fazekas sold poison to women who wished to eliminate their husbands.

to poison them. Once she was arrested, she implicated another woman, Mrs. Bukenoveski, who confessed to having obtained arsenic from Fazekas five years earlier to kill her mother. The mother's body was exhumed and found to contain arsenic.

Fazekas was arrested, held only briefly when she refused to talk, and then released—free to run from house to house in Nagyrev, letting the women know what was happening, and telling the police whom to arrest. When they came for Fazekas again, she admitted them to her house, drank her own poison and died before their eyes. Thirty-eight women were arrested, chief among them Susanna Olah, the "White Witch of Nagyrev," who also sold arsenic and was believed to possess the power to protect the women from the law.

Each woman had her own victims and reasons: Rosalie Sebestyen's husband bored her; Maria Szendi was tired of her husband always having "his own way"; Maria Varga could no longer put up with her husband, who had returned from the war blind—she preferred her young lover, but after five years disposed of him and his grandfather; Mrs. Kardos had an invalid son who was a burden to her—she found it easy to kill him because she had already eliminated a lover and her husband; Juliane Lipka killed, not for love but for real estate—in seven to eight years she disposed of seven relatives, gradually becoming the richest woman in the region. Eventually, twenty-six women were tried for murder. Eight were sentenced to death and seven to life in prison. The rest received varying prison terms. Three of the women committed suicide. The bodies of those hanged were displayed as a warning to others.

Fein, Mark, prom. 1963-64, U.S. Wealthy up-and-coming New York businessman Mark Fein settled a $7,200 bet by murdering the bookie instead of paying him. "We had words and I shot him," Fein said of the murder of Rubin Markowitz on Oct. 10, 1963. And that was the explanation Fein gave when he called his girlfriend, prostitute Carmela Lazarus. He asked her to help dispose of the bookie's body. When Lazarus came to his Manhattan apartment, Fein had already acquired a trunk in Spanish Harlem and deposited Markowitz's body in it.

Lazarus called a couple of male friends who carried the heavy trunk to a rented station wagon. Leaving Fein behind, they drove to the Harlem River and pushed the trunk into the water. When the trunk was found, the police discovered a list of Markowitz's "clients" on his body. The name "Gloria Kendall", an alias used by Lazarus, was on the list. When the police located Lazarus, she promptly told what had happened. Fein was arrested and tried. Although his defense attorney tried to get the jury to question whether a prostitute with thirty aliases could be relied on to tell the truth, Mark Fein was convicted and sentenced to thirty years to life in prison.

Fentress, Albert, 1941-   , U.S. On Aug. 18, 1979, Albert Fentress, thirty-nine, a history teacher at Poughkeepsie Middle School in New York, wrote two scripts concerning murder and sexual mutilation. Two days later, he invited Paul Masters, eighteen, into his house for a drink. Fentress then assaulted, mutilated, and shot the boy. Afterward, he cut the body into pieces and cooked and ate them. Fentress, who had no previous record, was committed to a mental institution indefinitely.

Ferguson, Paul Robert, 1946- , and **Ferguson, Thomas Scott**, 1951- , U.S. The Ferguson brothers were just two in a long line of homosexual boyfriends that actor Ramon Novarro, the "Latin Lover," invited to party at his home in Hollywood. The famed sultry-looking star

Silent film star Ramon Novarro, murdered in 1968.

of the silent screen who made women swoon had stopped making movies in the 1930s. He had built up his fortune in real estate and was still living very well thirty years later. On the night of Oct. 30, 1968, he invited 22-year-old Paul Ferguson and 17-year-old Tom Ferguson to his home. The brothers had heard a rumor that Novarro kept at least $5,000 in

cash in his house, and they began demanding to know where it was. While Paul tortured and beat Novarro so he would tell where the money was hidden, Tom looked around the house, tearing hundreds of valuable paintings from the walls, shredding couches, ripping out drawers. He took time out to telephone a friend in Chicago, Brenda Lee Metcalf, and they talked for almost an hour, while Metcalf heard Novarro's screams in the background. Eventually they found only the money that Novarro had in his pockets, but when they left the mansion, the great screen actor was dead, suffocated by a sexual device.

The next day, Novarro's secretary, Edward J. Weber, found the destruction and the dead body. The police, carrying out their regular routine, checked Novarro's long-distance telephone calls for the previous month and located Brenda Lee Metcalf. She told about the call she had received from the Fergusons, old friends who had lived in Chicago until Paul went to Hollywood and Tom ran away from home to join him.

Paul tried to place the blame for the gruesome murder on Tom. At first Tom believed his older brother when he said that Tom, as a juvenile, would only get six months in jail. But Julius Libow of the Juvenile Court said that Tom would be tried as an adult, and at the trial in August 1969,

each brother tried to convince the court that the other had committed the murder. District Attorney James Ideman held that Paul had committed the crime. "It was...done cruelly by a man who has no respect for himself or others...who has no remorse, no compassion, no regrets...and who got his brother to perjure himself," Ideman said. Both

Two hustling killer brothers, Tom, left, and Paul Ferguson, right, at their trial with lawyers.

men were found Guilty of murder and sentenced by Superior Court judge Mark Brandler to life in prison, with a recommendation that they never be paroled.

Ferguson, Walter, 1894-1939, U.S. Walter Ferguson's tirades often disturbed his neighbors in a Manhattan tenement. Only Elizabeth Schneider, fifty-five, a midget and his upstairs neighbor, could calm him. In July 1939, the 45-year-old Ferguson started raving again, and when Schneider went down to quiet him, he grabbed her and pulled her into his room. Insurance collector Sam Fox saw the incident and ran for police. When they returned, Ferguson yelled, "Nobody can come in here but Jesus Christ!"

The two men forced open Ferguson's door and found him standing naked over the bathtub, holding the midget under water. The policeman grappled with Ferguson, but the maniac managed to drown Schneider. Fox then called three more policemen to the scene, where Ferguson fended them off, using a table and chairs as weapons, until he suddenly fell dead of a heart attack.

Fernandez, Raymond Martinez, See: **Beck, Martha Julie.**

Ferrara, Florence, 1913- , U.S. On Nov. 28, 1942, a woman under a strange delusion went to Missouri Baptist Hospital in St. Louis. She calmly walked into the office of

Dr. Marion Klinefelter, a nationally-known bone surgeon. She greeted the physician by saying, "Well, Mister Mad Man, how are you?" The woman suddenly pulled a gun from her coat and shot the doctor in the head. As Klinefelter slumped over in his chair, the woman shouted, "Now, Mister Wilder, you're exposed." She then fled from the scene.

The 69-year-old physician, known to colleagues as a "poor man's doctor" because of the volume of work he did without fees, died before reaching the emergency room. An hour later, the police arrested 29-year-old Florence Ferrara in the parking lot where she left her automobile. She confessed to the killing and gave this unusual account: "Dr. Klinefelter is not the man I shot. The man shot is named Meldrum Wilder and he is the one who killed Dr. Klinefelter in 1904. He has been posing as Dr. Klinefelter ever since and has been chloroforming and crippling people for years. In 1936, I had an infected finger and he treated me for that, but he didn't get me and he's been trying to get me ever since. So last summer I went over to East St. Louis and bought a pistol for my own protection, and this morning I decided to go out and see him face to face.

"I said, 'Mister Wilder, here I am,' and he grabbed the telephone. He wanted to get somebody to use ether on me, so I shot him in self-defense. He had been having me followed, watched, and the men who were following me were trying to place a cloth filled with chloroform on my face so they could take me to the doctor and he could break my bones."

After being evaluated by psychiatrists, Ferrara was diagnosed as insane and was institutionalized for life.

Fiedler, Paulette, 1949- , U.S. Paulette Fiedler, a 38-year-old employee of the Illinois Department of Children and Family Services, shot and killed her supervisor, Dale Rowell, thirty-nine, as he sat at his desk in the Lombard, Ill., office. Another worker, Robert Heft, thirty-nine, heard the shot and when he went to check, Fiedler shot him as well.

Prior to the killing, the state had tried to discharge Fiedler, but a psychiatrist determined that she was fit to work. Fiedler's sex discrimination suit against her union was dismissed on the morning of the crime. She had also filed several complaints accusing her supervisor and others of treating her unfairly.

When Fiedler's trial began, she first claimed she was mentally unfit and pleaded guilty by reason of insanity. However, in September 1988, a jury found her competent to stand trial. She was convicted in November of murder and attempted murder. Fiedler was sentenced on Dec. 1,

1988, to life in prison.

Field, Frederick Herbert Charles, 1899-1936, Brit. The body of prostitute Norah Upchurch, twenty, was found inside an abandoned London shop on Oct. 2, 1931. The discovery was made by a sign fitter and his assistant, Frederick Field. Field told police that the day before he had given the shop keys to a man he thought was a prospective buyer of the property. The man, Field explained to coroner Ingleby Oddie, had prominent gold fillings in his teeth. Coroner Oddie brought the suspect before the jury at the inquest, and as he had no gold fillings, an open verdict was returned.

After nearly two years, on July 25, 1933, Field informed the editor of the *Daily Sketch* that he murdered Upchurch. Field recounted in detail how he had brought the girl into the shop and then strangled her. He claimed he emptied her handbag of money and dropped it into a ditch at Rose Hill, Sutton. Field repeated the story to police and was arraigned on a charge of willful murder. At his trial at the Old Bailey in September, Field retracted his confession, saying that it was his intent all along to clear his name. His

Killer Frederick Field.   Upchurch, murder victim, 1931.

confession contained so many factual errors that it was impossible to link Field conclusively with the murder. Justice Rigby Philip Swift directed the jury to return a verdict of Not Guilty. Field apparently wanted publicity and the reward money offered by the newspaper.

Following Field's acquittal, he joined the Royal Air Force, but soon deserted his squadron. He avoided the law until Apr. 4, 1936, when middle-aged Beatrice Vilna Sutton was found suffocated in her apartment at Elmhurst Mansions, Clapham. That same night, Field advised a girlfriend to look for an interesting item in the newspapers. The girl's mother grew suspicious and notified police, who booked Field on suspicion. At the station, he confessed to killing Sutton, but again gave incorrect details. Before Justice Charles, Field repudiated his earlier statements. When asked how he had been able to describe accurately the victim's injuries, Field claimed it was supposition. After fifteen minutes of deliberation, the jury convicted Field, and on June 30, 1936, Field was hanged.

Field, George Morton, d.1926, U.S. A dynamite blast powerful enough to level a church and kill an intended victim, failed to destroy a single sheet of paper, which implicated George Morton Field. Field, in 1915, was the wealthiest man and the religious leader in rural Mustoch, Kan., where he often delivered vitriolic sermons from the pulpit.

Field also had a girlfriend, Gertie Day, a church choir member, who was more than twenty years his junior. When Gertie Day informed him she was pregnant, he agreed to pay her $2,000 to leave the area, but soon worried of possible blackmail. He planted a dynamite bomb beneath the church, and when Gertie Day arrived to pick up the money, she was killed in an explosion which leveled the church. However, the paper the dynamite was wrapped in, a sermon soon to be delivered by George Field, was found untouched in the rubble. Clerks in Kansas City confirmed that Field had purchased the dynamite and he was arrested by Sheriff James R. Carter. Field was convicted of the murder of Gertie Day and sentenced to life imprisonment. He died while incarcerated, in 1926.

Field, Jack Alfred, 1901-21, and **Gray, William Thomas**, 1892-1921, Brit. William Gray, born in South Africa, sailed to England during WWI where he married an Eastbourne girl who supported him while he kept company with Jack Field. Field was well-known to the police as a petty hoodlum, and after leaving the Navy in April 1920, wandered aimlessly about Eastbourne. On Aug. 19, 1920, the two men met typist Irene Violet Munro, seventeen, and the trio was observed by William Putland and Frederick Wells, who followed them through town. Munro and her companions walked toward the Crumbles, a two-mile stretch of wasteland outside Seaside, Eastbourne. Putland and Wells followed the party just to the outskirts of Pevensey. The next day, a 13-year-old boy picnicking at the Crumbles stumbled upon Munro's battered body. Wells identified Field and Gray on Aug. 24, as Munro's companions, and police learned that the suspects had tried to enlist in the military within an hour of Munro's disappearance. They were charged with murder and brought to trial at the Lewes Assizes on Dec. 13, 1920. The prosecution contended that Munro had refused them sex, and Field and Gray had knocked her to the ground, then hit her with a heavy stone. The jury found them Guilty, appeals were dismissed, and the two were hanged at Wandsworth Prison on Feb. 4, 1921. Before they died, each accused the other of the murder.

Fielding, Charles, prom. 1924, U.S. Lottie Freeman of Cumberland County, Maine, first married William Sanborn. He disappeared in the summer of 1910, leaving his wife alone on the farm with three children. Next, two farmhands disappeared. In 1915, Freeman married Alphonse Cote and had one more child. But in November 1924, Cote, too, vanished. Freeman had plotted his death with Charles Fielding, a plumber who was married to her half-sister. Fielding killed Cote with a gunshot in the back and then he, Freeman, and her second son, Ralph, buried the body in the field.

When Freeman reported the disappearance of her second husband, saying he had taken money from her purse and Ralph's bank account, Deputy Sheriff Norton became suspicious and checked her history. He and two other officials visited her farm where they talked with Freeman, her son, and Fielding, and also discovered a pile of ashes. When the three were brought in for questioning, Ralph confessed, as did Fielding, who was infatuated with Freeman. Freeman admitted nothing. Charges against Freeman's son were eventually dropped, and Freeman died before Fielding's trial. Fielding was convicted of murder and sentenced to life. He was later transferred to a state hospital for the insane.

Finch, Dr. Raymond Bernard, 1918- , and **Tregoff, Carole**, prom. 1959-71, U.S. Dr. Raymond Bernard Finch, a prominent physician in Los Angeles, and his wife Francis agreed to divorce so that they could marry other people. Following the divorce, Francis married Forrest Daugherty, and Raymond married Barbara Daugherty, a couple who had also divorced so that these new marital arrangements could be made. The second Mrs. Finch, Barbara, was shocked when she discovered that the man she had married was a wife-beater. In the spring of 1959, she was convinced that her husband was trying to kill her, and therefore immediately informed her lawyer of her suspicions.

In the meantime, Raymond Finch's latest mistress, Carole Tregoff, left her job as his secretary and moved to

Las Vegas, Nev. Finch met her there whenever possible, and it was there, the prosecution would later hold, that they planned to murder his wife.

On July 18, 1959, the adulterous pair went to Finch's home in West Covina, Calif., and waited for Barbara to return home in the evening. When she saw Finch and Tregoff waiting, Barbara drew a gun, threatening to shoot the pair unless they left immediately. Barbara Finch was shot in the back, the

Dr. Bernard Finch, convicted wife-slayer.

sound of gunfire bringing forth the maid, who saw Dr. Finch standing over his slain wife. The maid called the police, and the two conspirators were arrested.

The police found on the lawn of the house an attache case that they called a "do-it-yourself murder kit." It included, among other items, a gun, a butcher knife, and two hypodermic needles. They also located John Patrick Cody, whom Finch had hired to follow his wife and whom Carole had tried to hire to kill Mrs. Finch. The jury was brought to tears by Dr. Finch's testimony of how his dying wife had taken the blame for their problems and, saying that she loved him, had died. That jury was not able to reach a verdict. Neither was a second jury. It was only on the third try that the prosecution was able to obtain a verdict of

Finch's mistress Carole Tregoff, convicted with her lover of killing Barbara Finch in 1959.

Guilty against the pair. They were both sentenced to prison for life. Carole Tregoff was released in 1971.

Fine, Louis (AKA: **Henry Miller**) prom. 1932, U.S. When the owner of a boarding house noticed an unpleasant odor coming from a new tenant's room, he called police to investigate. Inside a double trunk they found the strangled corpse of an elderly woman.

Julius Hoffman, proprietor of the Philadelphia rooming house, was pleased to receive three weeks of rent in advance from his new boarder, Henry Miller. But on Mar.

7, 1932, Hoffman called the Atlantic County, N.J., police to report a repulsive smell in Miller's room, and Police Captain Frank J. Harrold discovered the body of a white-haired woman in the double trunk.

Hoffman explained that Miller, about forty years old, had the quirk of always wearing a dark felt hat pulled down over his face. The trunk, Harrold found out, had been delivered at night by two local truckers, and was sent from Atlantic City at 4:00 p.m. on Mar. 4 via the Pennsylvania Railroad. Investigating leads on elderly women in the area who were listed as missing, police discovered that Mamie Schaff, a wealthy widow, recently had disappeared. According to her maid, who positively identified the body, one of Schaff's boarders, Louis Fine, had left town the day after his landlady, leaving a note asking the maid to keep his room clean until he returned, and telling her to let Mrs. Schaff know he would be back. In Fine's possessions police found a locked strongbox; inside were several letters, one of them addressed to "H. Miller" in Atlantic City, N.J.

Waiting for Fine's return, police hid in his room and surprised him on the night of Mar. 7. Accused of murder by Harrold, Fine claimed he knew nothing and had just returned from a business trip to New York City. Fine also had a heart attack, though only a mild one, and was taken to an Atlantic City hospital. Assured by doctors that Fine was not seriously ill, police brought Hoffman in as the first witness; he positively identified Fine as the man he had known as Henry Miller, as did several other witnesses. Police had found Mrs. Schaff's will, naming Fine as her beneficiary, and when it was learned he was also wanted in New York for murdering an older woman, he was indicted.

While in prison awaiting trial, Fine continued to deny his guilt, but was overheard by guard Harold Johnson as he exclaimed, "The old fool! I wanted her to give me some money. It was the only way I could get it." On June 6 Fine's trial began, and on June 10 the jury deliberated for two hours to return a verdict of Guilty of first-degree murder, with no recommendation of leniency. Fine was sentenced to die in the electric chair, the first time in thirty years that the death penalty had been imposed in an Atlantic County courtroom.

Finlay, Edwin, 1934-52, Brit. Edwin Finlay, whose childhood was spent in the shadow of the massive bombings of England during WWII, grew up to become a killer. Finlay was eight years old in 1942, at the height of the bomb attacks on England. He later became a bank clerk at a Glasgow bank and, at age eighteen, successfully stole £900 from the institution where he worked. Although he was under no suspicion, Finlay decided to purchase three revolvers "in case of trouble." On July 18, 1952, when two plainclothes policemen came to question the clerk, he shot them both, wounding one and murdering Constable John MacLeod, then turned the gun on himself, committing suicide.

Curiously, the six boys with whom Finlay had gone through childhood wartime experiences all met unhappy ends: two were hanged, one was killed in a battle with police officers, one was sentenced to life in prison, and one was jailed.

Fish, Hamilton Albert Howard (AKA: **The Cannibal; Robert Hayden; Frank Howard; John W. Pell; Thomas A. Sprague**), 1870-1936, U.S. Raised in a Washington, D.C., orphanage, Albert Fish blamed his later heinous crimes on his years in the orphanage where sadistic cruelty was inflicted upon children. "Misery leads to crime," Fish later stated. "I saw so many boys whipped it ruined my mind." Fish later claimed to have molested more than 400 children in a span of twenty years. He was a sneaky child killer who, according to a psychiatrist examining him before his execution, "lived a life of unparalleled perversity. There was no known perversion that he did not practice and practice frequently."

Fish married in 1898 and the union produced three children. For a good many years he lived a normal life, making a living as a house decorator and painter. But Fish's mental state seemed to collapse in 1917 when his wife ran away with a half-witted lover, John Straube. Fish had taken his children to a movie and, upon returning home, he found the place stripped of all its furniture and his wife gone.

The brazen Mrs. Fish returned with Straube in tow some time later, asking to stay with Fish. He told her she could return to the family but Straube had to depart. Mrs. Fish ordered her bumbling lover to leave but Fish later found Straube hiding in the attic of the Fish house. Mrs. Fish smuggled him into the attic during the night. Straube stayed in the attic for weeks while Mrs. Fish smuggled him food and visited him nocturnally for sexual bouts. When Fish discovered Straube in the attic he ordered his wife and her dim-witted lover from the house.

The family never saw Mrs. Fish again. Fish himself began to act strangely a short time later. He took his family to a small cottage in Westchester County, N.Y., and there practiced bizarre rites, climbing to the top of a hill at night and baying at the moon: "I am Christ! I am Christ!" He made meals that consisted of raw meat, serving this to his children and saying: "That's the way I like my meat and you'll have to eat it that way, too." He ran around at night naked and howled at the moon, antics that later earned him the press sobriquet, "The Moon Maniac."

Fish took to beating himself and then encouraged his own children and their friends to paddle his bare buttocks until his flesh bled. Fish made a paddle studded with inch-and-a-half nails. His perplexed son, Albert Fish, Jr., discovered this device and asked his father why he had constructed such an instrument. "I use them on myself," Fish blurted to the boy. "I get certain feelings over me. When I do, I've got to torture myself." He burned himself with white hot pokers, needles, and irons. For many years he collected articles on cannibalism and became obsessed with flesh-eating, carrying these rare journalistic writings with him until the clippings yellowed and finally crumbled to dust.

Fish was involved in several postal swindles and spent three months in jail for practicing a con game in the mails. He was examined by psychiatrists but released as a "harmless" old man suffering from a "severe guilt conscience." Fish was later examined at Bellevue Asylum in New York but was again released as a non-violent masochist. He was known by authorities to practice self-flagellation, burning of his flesh, coprophilia, and other self-punishing acts such as inserting small needles beneath his flesh.

An avid reader of the lovelorn columns, Fish answered scores of ads from lonely widows. Forty-six of these letters were later recovered and submitted as evidence at Fish's murder trial but the prosecution refused to read from them, so filled with vile obscenities were they. Fish informed these lonely women that he was not at all interested in marriage. He merely wanted these lonely women to paddle and punish him. Fish received no replies. It is not certain when Albert Fish embarked on murder as a way of satisfying his dark inner longings. He later confessed to murdering a man in Wilmington, Del., in 1910. He also said that he had murdered and mutilated a boy in New York in 1919 and that same year noted he had murdered another boy on a houseboat in the Georgetown area of Washington, D.C.

By the late 1920s, Fish avidly sought children to attack and, by his own later admission, he molested and murdered 4-year-old William Gaffney on Feb. 11, 1927. On Mar. 3, 1928, Fish abducted and murdered 12-year-old Grace Budd, the crime for which he paid with his life in Sing Sing's electric chair. Using the name Frank Howard, the killer ingratiated himself to the Budd family. After several visits to the Budds in Manhattan, Fish convinced the naive Budd family members that he was a kindly old gentleman who merely dropped by to see their children. Fish brought them presents and when he suggested he take 12-year-old Grace to a children's party, Mrs. Budd allowed Fish to take her daughter. It was the last time the Budds saw Grace alive.

Albert Fish, murderer and cannibal, who, according to psychiatrists, "lived a life of unparalleled perversity. There was no known perversion he did not practice and practice often."

Mrs. Budd and her children; Grace Budd stands at right; she went away with Fish on June 3, 1928, and never returned.

Fish's murder retreat, Wisteria Cottage in White Plains, N.Y., where the cannibal killed and dismembered little Grace Budd.

Police and newsmen crowding about the burial site of Grace Budd's remains outside of Fish's blood-stained Wisteria Cottage, 1934.

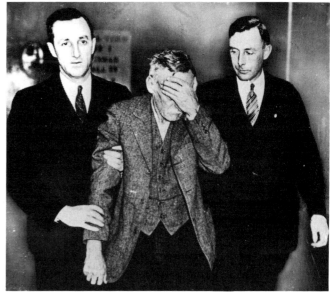

Albert Fish, under arrest, after signing his horrific confession in which he admitted to decades of murder and cannibalism.

Fish examining his confession in preparation for a trial he expected to lose; he spent his time reveling in his terrible past.

Albert Fish, second from left, handcuffed to another prisoner, entering Sing Sing Prison; he looked forward to his execution.

The trusting Grace Budd left her home with Fish on June 3, 1928, taking a train with him to White Plains, N.Y. Between them on the seat was a box in which Fish kept what he later described as his "instruments of hell." The box contained a butcher knife, a cleaver, and a saw. The old man and Grace got off the train but Grace quickly went back aboard and then returned with the box which Fish had forgotten. The pair walked the long distance to the Fish cottage where Fish took all his clothes off. The girl screamed: "I'll tell Mama!" Fish jumped forward and strangled Grace. He then decapitated her and sawed her body in half. In a later confession, so grisly and gruesome in detail that it caused listeners to retch, Fish happily recounted how he carved up the girl's body and made a stew out of it which he lived on for several days.

The Budds reported their daughter's disappearance but continued to believe that Grace had somehow survived and was alive. Then, in 1934, for inexplicable reasons, Fish sat down and wrote a letter to the Budds, telling them that he had murdered their daughter. He took great pains to point out that he had not sexually molested her before killing her. It was about this time that Fish, walking down a street in Fort Richmond, Long Island, spotted 5-year-old France McDonel playing outside his home. He picked up the boy and carried him away, taking him to Wisteria Cottage in White Plains where he strangled the boy.

By then detectives had traced the letter Fish had sent to the Budd family finding the old man shortly after he had killed the McDonel boy. One puzzled detective asked Fish why he had risked revealing himself by writing the letter. The killer became defensive. He told detectives that he had kept track of police activity on "the case in the papers. If they had accused someone else I would have come forward. My best days are over." Fish was brought before the Budds and they identified him as the Frank Howard who took their daughter away with him. The area around Fish's Wisteria Cottage was dug up and Grace Budd's remains were found.

Placed on trial, Fish's attorneys pled the cannibal killer not guilty by reason of insanity but the prosecution provided a small army of psychiatrists who testified that he was sane. After a prolonged trial, Fish was found Guilty and sentenced to death. Fish was sent to Sing Sing, handcuffed to another killer named Stone. Ironically, both Fish and Stone had had forefathers who had fought in the American Revolution. While awaiting execution, Fish delightedly told newsmen and prison officials that he was ecstatic at the prospect of being electrocuted in Sing Sing's electric chair. "What a thrill that will be if I have to die in the electric chair," Fish said with a broad smile. "It will be the supreme thrill. The only one I haven't tried."

On Jan. 16, 1936, Fish walked without help into Sing Sing's execution room and sat down almost eagerly in the electric chair. He helped the executioner affix the electrodes on his legs. The enthusiasm Fish displayed toward his own painful death shocked reporters who were present to witness his execution. Fish, the oldest prisoner ever to be electrocuted in Sing Sing, smiled happily as the electrodes were applied to his head. When the switch was pulled, a jolt of 3,000 volts coursed through his body. A blue cloud of smoke rose from Fish's head as he let out a guttural laugh. He did not die. Thanks to the hundreds of tiny needles he had inserted in his body over the years, the old man's abused body actually short-circuited the electric chair. Another prolonged charge of electricity was sent through his body before Albert Fish was pronounced dead.

The cannibal's last statement had been given to one of his defense attorneys only an hour before Albert Fish encountered his "supreme thrill." Reporters begged the attorney to release the statement but the lawyer grimly shook his head, saying: "I shall never show it to anyone. It was the most filthy string of obscenities that I have ever read."

Fisher, Dennis, prom. 1975, U.S. When a young, healthy farmer suddenly and inexplicably disappeared, his wife and a farmhand came under suspicion, and soon confessed to murder. In Delaware County, Iowa, the sheriff's office received a missing person's report from 19-year-old Myra Miller, mother of three, telling how she and her husband, Howard Miller, had an argument two weeks earlier, after which he had gone to Dubuque, driven there by the Millers' farmhand Dennis Fisher. The sheriff found no reason for the prosperous farmer to have left the home which he valued and cherished. Nor had the farmer contacted any of his Dubuque relatives.

In the next two months, Fisher and Myra Miller auctioned off most of the farm machinery and cattle. Arrested on Apr. 23, they were discovered to be in the process of moving to a new home in West Plains, Mo. According to police, both admitted their guilt the night they were arrested, with Fisher admitting that he shot his employer when Miller threatened to kill his wife because of her liaison with the farmhand. Digging up the dirt floor of the calf shed at the Miller farm, police found the corpse with bullet holes in the right shoulder and the head. Fisher was sentenced to life in prison with the help of Myra Miller's testimony against him, while the widow, originally charged with murder, was allowed to plead guilty to reduced charges of conspiracy to obstruct justice, in exchange for her evidence against Fisher.

Fisher, Julius, 1912-46, U.S. Catherine Cooper Reardon, 37-year-old librarian at the Washington, D.C., Cathedral, went home for lunch on Mar. 1, 1944. She shared a small three-room apartment with her invalid widowed mother. After lunch, Catherine returned to work. When she did not return home by nine that night, a friend reported her as a missing person to the police.

The following morning the Washington police received an anonymous call. "A young woman has been murdered at the Washington Cathedral," a male voice said, "You fellows had better get busy." At the same time John Bayliss, the curator of the library, and Helen Abbey Young, an archivist, had just reported to work. They noticed blood-stains on the basement floor and began a search of the library. In the attic they found Catherine Reardon's coat, gloves, hat, and purse. In the sub-basement they found Reardon's battered body. Only moments after the anonymous call the police were notified of the murder.

The victim had been beaten on the head and neck. Her clothes were bunched around her head and her panties were missing. At first police believed the woman had been sexually assaulted. Within the hour, the police had a suspect in the case. He was Julius Fisher, thirty-two, a workman at the library. In his home they found blood-stained clothes. Fisher, who was in a restaurant when police arrived, pulled a .32-caliber revolver but was quickly subdued by detectives E.E. Scott and Richard Felber. Fisher confessed that he killed Reardon when she complained about his work. The murder weapon was a piece of firewood. The killer had not raped the woman but removed her panties to "sop up the blood." The autopsy confirmed this.

On Dec. 20, 1946, Fisher went to the electric chair at the District of Columbia Jail. That same day two other men were executed in the same jail for the murder of women. Joseph Dunbar Medley was executed for the murder of Nancy Boyer, and William Copeland was executed for the murder of his sister-in-law.

Fitzgerald, Thomas Richard, 1880-1919, U.S. On July 22, 1919, 6-year-old Janet "Dollie" Wilkinson failed to come home for dinner. Around midnight, her parents, who operated a grocery store on Chicago's Rush Street, around the corner from their Superior Street home, reported to police that she was missing. They mentioned to police a neighbor, Thomas Fitzgerald, who worked as an elevator operator in a Rush Street hotel, as a possible suspect because he had shown unusual interest in the little girl. Police brought Fitzgerald to the station for questioning, beginning a six day interrogation that newspapers dubbed

"the fourth degree."

Fitzgerald, whom police described as "a moron," admitted during questioning that he knew the Wilkinson girl, but denied any knowledge of her whereabouts. One of his fellow employees, however, told police that he had seen the two together, the girl sitting on Fitzgerald's lap in the basement of the hotel only a week before.

Given this, police and reporters grilled the suspect for more than eight hours, during which time he was not allowed to use his eyeglasses. At one point a reporter dressed as a priest entered the room, and the police left the two alone. "As a priest of the church it is my duty to visit my brethren in distress," the reporter said.

"Yes, father," Fitzgerald answered.

"I want you to tell me the truth. If the girl is alive, tell me where she is and I'll have her sent back, so they will never know you had her..."

"But..."

"Now wait, my friend, if she is dead I'll have the body located and...

"If I knew I'd tell you, Father. I know you are bound by the vows of the church not to repeat what I tell you in confession, but I don't know. I really don't. So help me God, I don't."

Sometime later another reporter came in and posed as a relative of the dead girl. "If you loved your mother, tell us the truth," he pleaded with Fitzgerald. "The girl's mother is nearly dead from grief and suspense. She cannot live another eight hours unless she knows where Janet's body is. Tell us! Tell us! Tell us!"

Fitzgerald was unmoved by the plea: "Why, if I knew I'd tell you."

Through hours and hours of relentless questioning, Fitzgerald continued to deny his guilt. "I wish to sleep," he told his interrogators. "Please let me alone."

But he wasn't allowed to sleep. The police and reporters worked in shifts; a few would slip away for breakfast or a catnap as another crew took their place. Their prisoner was forced to stay awake. When his head would nod, somebody would slap him lightly until he was fully awake. "Tell us the truth," they would demand.

At last, Fitzgerald looked up, "Send down Mr. Howe," he said quietly.

A few minutes later Lieutenant Howe was at his cell. "You have been the only friend I have had. I wouldn't tell anyone else. But I think I'll tell you. I'm afraid you'll think me a horrible man," Fitzgerald said.

"No, I won't," the police officer said. "What I'll think is what I have thought all the way through this case: that you have a diseased brain. Tell me the truth, my man."

"I did it," Fitzgerald said with his head bowed, "I killed her."

"How did you do it?"

"Just the way you have described it twenty-five times, Mr. Howe. Just as you told me. Every time you described the killing in detail I shivered."

"I know you did, Fitzgerald, I saw you tremble."

"It was just the way you pictured it, even to the taking of Dollie's body down to the coal pile...I'll show you the spot. I want you to stick by me and be a friend. I need friends. And say, Mr. Howe, you won't hang me now, will you? I've confessed, haven't I? They won't string me up if I'm crazy, will they? Tell me, Mr. Howe."

"I don't know," Howe said.

"I didn't mean to kill her," Fitzgerald explained later. "When I married fourteen years ago I found I was not fit for marriage. I lured Janet into the apartment with candy. While I held her in my arms she screamed, and in my excitement I choked her. She was unconscious. I hurried down to the basement with her and covered her with coal." When police examined the body they found cuts on her head and broken teeth. It was later determined that the girl was probably still alive when Fitzgerald buried her in the coal.

Assistant Cook County State's Attorney James C. O'Brien was assigned to the case. O'Brien was known in the argot of the underworld as a "rope man" for the many death sentences his prosecutions had achieved. He was also known as "Red Necktie" O'Brien for the color of the tie he was known to wear to sentencing hearings, to remind the judge and jury of the victim's blood. In the Fitzgerald case he was successful again. On Oct. 17, 1919, Thomas Richard Fitzgerald was hanged for the murder of Janet Wilkinson.

Flanagan, Sean Patrick, 1961-89, U.S. In 1987 in Las Vegas, Sean Patrick Flanagan, twenty-six, met James Lewandowski, a 45-year-old chef who bought the younger man clothes and rented a room for him. Not long after accepting Lewandowski's assistance, Flanagan strangled and then dismembered the older man, leaving body parts in plastic bags in a trash bin near the motel where he stayed. Four days after murdering Lewandowski, Flanagan took a ride with pianist Albert Duggins, fifty-nine, before he killed him. Arrested for jaywalking in Orange County, Calif., soon after Duggins' murder, Flanagan voluntarily returned to Las Vegas to show police the vacant lot where he had left Duggins' corpse.

Refusing to seek appeals of his death penalty, Flanagan explained, "Every man who has committed a crime of murder knows deep down inside he should die for taking another man's life." The confessed killer gave a seven-page statement in which he said he hated his homosexuality,

and thought he might have been motivated to kill other homosexual men with "the thought that I would be doing some good for our society."

Before his death by lethal injection on June 23, 1989, Flanagan told Deputy County District Attorney Dan Seaton, "You are a just man." Strapped to a gurney at the Nevada State Prison in preparation for the execution, Flanagan lifted his head to tell Seaton, "I love you." Since the 1976 U.S. Supreme Court ruling allowing states to resume using the death penalty, Flanagan was the fourth person to be executed in Nevada, and the 114th person to be put to death nationally.

Flavell, Joseph Edward, 1902-   , Brit. A slow-witted crane driver, 24-year-old Joseph Edward Flavell was violently jealous of his half-brother, James Thomas Bayliss, an intelligent and promising 14-year-old art student. In March 1926, at the home they shared in Dudley, Flavell killed the sleeping Bayliss with an ax. Flavell confessed to Birmingham police, explaining his sibling had not felt any pain because, "I did it while he was asleep." At the trial at the Worcester Assizes, he was defended by attorney Marshall Hall. Evidence showed that there was a history of Bright's disease and epilepsy in Flavell's family, and some of his relatives had been confined to or had died in asylums. It was also determined that Flavell, who was known as "the village idiot," had a history of cruelty to animals. Hall's plea for a guilty but insane verdict was rejected. Flavell was found Guilty of murder, and Justice Avory sentenced him to death. On appeal, the sentence was commuted to penal servitude for life.

Folkes, Robert E. Lee, 1922-45, U.S. One of the most gruesome train murders on record occurred at the height of WWII when U.S. railroads were packed with servicemen. Some were transferring between bases, others going home on their final leave before shipping overseas, still others were returning to their duty stations. Ensign Richard F. James was traveling south from Seattle, Wash., with a contingent of other Navy personnel being transferred to a new base in California. The ensign's wife of four months, Martha James, twenty-one, from Virginia, was traveling with her husband aboard the Southern Pacific's *Oregonian*. When the train reached Portland, Ore., on Jan. 23, 1943, the newlyweds were separated. Mrs. James lost her reservation to some California-bound servicemen. Twenty-five minutes later, she boarded the next southbound train the Southern Pacific Railroad's *West Coast Limited,* making its 1800 mile run between Seattle and Los Angeles. Mrs. James was assigned the lower sleeping compartment in berth number 13.

At 4 a.m., as the train neared Tangent, Ore., halfway between Salem and Eugene, a woman's piercing scream broke the stillness of the sleeping car. "My God, he's killing me!" the voiced cried out. Private Harold R. Wilson, twenty-two, of the U.S. Marines, was jerked from a sound sleep. After a moment of fumbling, he snapped back the curtain on the upper compartment of berth 13 and looked into the darkened aisle, still half-asleep. A dark man was moving rapidly down the aisle toward the rear of the train. Wilson later described the man as being about five feet, ten inches, with a heavy build, smooth-shaven, with curly hair combed straight back and wearing a brown pin-striped suit. He thought the man was black, but he was not sure. As other faces peeked out from behind slightly parted curtains, the body of Martha James slipped almost silently from the lower berth into the aisle.

The nightgown-clad woman was covered with blood, her throat slashed. Wilson looked toward the end of the car, but the dark figure had disappeared. He jumped from the berth and headed toward the back of the train, but a quick search proved fruitless. On his way back to the murder car he stopped in the galley of the dining car where he found a black cook at work, wearing a white uniform. He asked the man if he had seen anyone run by and the man said no. Told that a murder had been committed in one of the sleeping cars, the man grinned and asked Wilson if he had been drinking. When Wilson returned to the sleeping car, the body of Martha James still lay in the aisle, but someone had draped a sheet over her.

Police boarded the train when it pulled into Eugene, Ore. Crew members told them that a man fitting the description supplied by Wilson had been aboard the train but could no longer be found. A trail of blood spots led from the murder berth all the way to the back of the train. The door leading to the small observation platform of the last car was open. Police believed that the man could have leaped from the train soon after the murder. Sheriff Herbert Shelfon found footprints in the Tangent railroad yard and surmised that the man could have leaped off the southbound train and boarded one heading north. Police and posses of private citizens searched for the killer in the area but found nothing.

On board the train, police searched the victim's possessions, which seemed intact, and this included over $100 in cash. Robbery was ruled out as the motive. The body was removed at Eugene, but police stayed aboard the train, questioning passengers and crew, as it made its way toward California.

When the *Limited* reached Los Angeles on Jan. 25,

Robert E. Lee Folkes, twenty, the black cook that Private Wilson had found in the train's galley, shortly after the murder, was arrested. According to police, he first denied but then confessed to the murder. He then recanted the confession saying he did not commit the crime but he knew who did. Police had originally suspected Folkes after finding he had a police record for, among other charges, assaulting a woman and attempting to rip rings off her fingers, and for attempting to break into a house where three women lived.

After a second confession, police put together this story of the murder: On the night of the killing Folkes had attended a party with other members of the dining crew and had consumed a great deal of liquor. During the party some of the crew discussed the various attractive women aboard the train, and the striking blond in berth 13 had been prominently mentioned. After the party, Folkes put an overcoat over his white uniform and entered the Pullman sleeping car. He opened the curtain on Martha James's berth and slipped next to the woman. As he was closing the curtain, the woman suddenly awakened. "She wanted to know who I was and told me to get out," Folkes told police. He placed a knife to her chin. "I told her to keep still. She hollered and tried to throw me out. So I cut her."

Folkes, who later recanted both confessions, was convicted and on Apr. 26, 1943, Judge L.G. Lewelling sentenced him to the Oregon gas chamber. Almost two years of appeals followed. On Jan. 4, 1945, Oregon Governor Earl Snell refused to commute the death sentence and told reporters: "I have before me evidence, information, and confessions that convince me beyond a doubt of Folkes's guilt. He was tried in the circuit court, appealed to the state supreme court and then to the U.S. Supreme Court. Other appeals for habeas corpus writs were filed in the state supreme court, U.S. District Court, and the Marion County Circuit Court. In view of all circumstances, I do not see how I could possibly interfere."

The next day, Jan. 5, 1945, Folkes proclaimed his innocence for the last time, then said: "So long, everybody." With a smile on his face, he walked into the gas chamber in the state prison at Salem, Ore., without a blindfold. About 100 witnesses watched as the poison pellets were dropped at 9:07 a.m. Six minutes later, Folkes was pronounced dead.

Forsyth, Francis Robert George, and **Harris, Norman James**, and **Darby, Christopher Louis**, and **Lutt, Terrence**, prom. 1960, Brit. Four broke, young men prowled the streets late at night on June 25, 1960, and met up with 23-year-old Alan Jee who had taken a shortcut down an alley. Francis Forsyth, Norman Harris, Christopher Darby, and Terrence Lutt found him alone and vulnerable. Lutt, only seventeen, knocked Jee down, then the others tried to take his money. When Jee resisted, 18-year-old Forsyth kicked him in the head with his pointed Italian shoes. The shoes still showed traces of blood when he was arrested.

Alan Jee died two days later. When 23-year-old Harris bragged about the killing in public, the police found the foursome. Forsyth admitted the crime in his mother's presence, saying, "I'm sorry, Mum, but I did it, and that is all there is to it." The four were tried for murder. Lutt, as a juvenile, was sent to reform school. Darby, a 23-year-old coalman who did not, according to all four, play a role in beating Jee, was sentenced to life in prison. Forsyth and Harris were hanged on Nov. 10, 1960.

Fortner, Clifford, 1944- , U.S. When 12-year-old Lorna Lax left her parents' home near San Francisco on Nov. 14, 1959, she left a note stating she was "mad at the world" and would return the next morning. Her parents were not alarmed, explaining later that Lorna was "an unfortunate child, physically retarded and emotionally troubled." When she had not returned by Monday morning, they grew concerned. That afternoon Norman Fortner, thirteen, found Lorna's body in a wooded area about two hundred yards from her home. Fortner told how Lax had often used the thicket as a "sex club," charging "initiation fees" of thirty-five cents to a dollar to local boys. Visitors to the sex club were questioned. Clifford Fortner, fifteen, told police he had gone to the thicket with Lorna early that night. Eventually, Fortner admitted that he had had sex with Lorna and then "something came over him." He first battered her head with a torch, then strangled her with a rope from a swing nearby, and finally stabbed her in the stomach several times. Fortner was sentenced to be detained for an indefinite time.

Fowler, George E., and **Leatherberry, J.C.**, prom. 1943, Brit. Two American soldiers stationed in Colchester, England, during WWII were charged and convicted of murder.

An abandoned taxi was discovered with its lights still on at 11:30 a.m. on Dec. 8, 1943, between Birch and Colchester. There was evidence of a struggle inside the car, including a bloodstained raincoat and a blue jacket with a sleeve inside out, identified as that of driver Claude Hailstone. Hailstone was last heard from the previous night between 11:00 and 11:10, when he told his landlady he would not be stopping for dinner because he had a job. Hailstone's body was later discovered lying in the bushes, scratched and bruised. He had been struck repeatedly and killed by strangulation. Blood from Hailstone's coat was of the rare AB type.

A raincoat found along the road was traced to Captain J.J. Weber of the 18th Canadian General Hospital, Colchester, who led police to Private George Fowler. Apparently Weber and Fowler had met and had drinks together. When Weber left the room, Fowler grabbed the overcoat and ran out.

Fowler denied any knowledge of Weber or the December killing, but a search of his belongings turned up a sergeant's tunic with type AB bloodstains, and a Dec. 6 pawn ticket for a Rolex Victory watch, which Weber had already told police was in the overcoat pocket. Fowler testified that he found the pawn ticket on Dec. 3 or 4, but the watch was not pawned until Dec. 6. Fowler frequently changed his testimony, and contradicted concrete evidence. He fit Weber's description of the man who took his coat. Fowler tried to absolve himself by implicating Private J.C. Leatherberry. According to Fowler, the two men had been riding in Hailstone's cab, Leatherberry with the expressed purpose of robbing the driver. Fowler said that when the cab stopped in Colchester, he got out and Leatherberry attacked Hailstone. By the time Fowler climbed back in the cab, Leatherberry had killed the driver.

Leatherberry's story was entirely different. He said he and Fowler were not together the night of the murder. But a search of his belongings revealed a bloodstained shirt, pants, and vest. Investigators found human blood under the nail of the third finger on Fowler's left hand and under all of Leatherberry's nails. The woman Leatherberry claimed to have been with on the night of Dec. 7 swore she was not with him then.

Both men were convicted of murder. Fowler was sentenced to life imprisonment with forfeiture of all civil rights, and dishonorably discharged. Leatherberry was sentenced to death by hanging. Just prior to his execution at Shepton Mallet, he confessed to his role in the crime, but said Fowler had actually killed Hailstone.

Fraden, Harlow, c.1930- , and **Wepman, Dennis**, c.1929- , U.S. Harlow Fraden had always been an awkward misfit from his Bronx, N.Y., upbringing onward. His mother's treatment of him alternated between abuse and overindulgence. In the morning, his mother would tell him he was a sissy whom nobody would ever befriend, and in the evening he slept by an air conditioner while his parents sweltered in the next room. His mother protected him from a fire marshal after he set fire to the apartment one night. His father remained passive.

Fraden's mother had been nagging him to use his chemistry degree from New York University to get a job "like other boys." When Fraden immersed himself in poetry instead, she called him a fairy and eventually kicked him out of the house. With a generous allowance from his parents and the financial help of roommate Dennis Wepman, Fraden was managing. But when he still failed to get a job, the allowance was cut off and real problems in the Fraden family began. Aware that he would get $96,000 in insurance at his parents' death, Fraden and Wepman made plans.

In August 1953 Harlow told his parents he had finally found an appropriate job, and the family gathered for a celebration. The son poured three glasses of champagne, but added cyanide to his mother's and father's drinks. After one toast, the two were on the floor. Shortly thereafter, they were dead. Fraden staged it to look like a suicide, but followed the funeral with a series of extravagant purchases and a string of parties. Detectives became suspicious. Fraden and Wepman had a falling out, and in the end Wepman confessed everything.

Fraden was committed to the Matteawan State Hospital for the criminally insane. Wepman was diagnosed as being mentally ill, but not insane, and was sentenced to twenty years to life in Sing Sing.

═══════════

Franc, Max Bernard, 1930- , U.S. On Aug. 25, 1987, a California rancher found a human head and torso alongside a rural highway twenty miles north of Fresno. The head was that of a teenage boy who had dyed black hair which was cut in the current punk fashion, according to the Madeira County coroner. The boy had been shot in the head and had been dead about two days.

Two days later, more body parts were found wrapped in a sheet alongside a guardrail on the Golden State Freeway near Valencia in north Los Angeles County. "Both the torso in Fresno and the body parts in Valencia were mutilated with the same type of instrument, like a chainsaw," reported Sergeant John Andrews of the Los Angeles County sheriff's office. "The way the remains were hacked, it appears to be the work of the same person." At the same time a Los Angeles equipment rental company had reported to local police that one of their chainsaws had been returned with what appeared to be blood and skin tissue on it. On Aug. 29, 1987, Los Angeles police arrested the renter, a California State University professor, Max Bernard Franc, fifty-seven, at his weekend apartment in West Hollywood, and charged him with the murder of the boy whose identity had not yet been discovered.

The arrest shocked the Cal State campus at Fresno where Franc, who was single, had taught political science since 1969. "I find it rather incredible that he has been accused of this," said David Provost, who had once been Franc's department head. "He's a very low-key kind of individual....He was one who was always seeking compromise when faculty disputes arose. He was...a very gentle type of individual."

Another professor at the university reported that "I saw him about ten days ago on campus. He had finished his summer school course and was upbeat, friendly, chatty. He looked as positive and as constructive as I had seen him in years. Nothing seemed amiss....None of this fits the psychology of the person I know....He's not the kind to blow up. He's more the kind who tries to avoid a sticky situation."

But police investigating the man, who was known as a conservative professor in Fresno, found that Franc lived a double life. In West Hollywood, they had learned that he was a known homosexual voyeur who paid young men to allow themselves to be photographed in sexual poses. A search of his house in Fresno uncovered a large collection of homosexual pornography as well as the ongoing construction of what police believed was intended to be a sound-proof room. In Franc's desk at the university, police found a handgun which was later, through ballistics analysis, identified as the murder weapon.

The victim was identified as Tracy Leroy Nute, eighteen, who had followed countless others when he had run away from his Kansas City home in hopes of becoming a Hollywood actor. Instead, Nute ended up on the streets of West Hollywood where he supported himself by working as a homosexual prostitute.

The youth had visited the Gay and Lesbian Community Services Center shortly before his murder, reported Youth Services director Gabe Kruks. "He came in on a Saturday, tired of it all. He was seventeen and he wanted help....Underneath Nute's tough street punk image was a sweet kid, but confused. He had not been happy in Kansas City, but he was not happy here." Kruks said he had seen many runaways drift into a life of prostitution. "He was like a kid in a candy store, very naive. He was prostituting for survival, both material and emotional. He needed love and a little security." Instead Nute found Max Bernard Franc, death, and mutilation.

Franc refused to confess to the killing. He told police he had rented the chainsaw to cut up a dead dog that he had hit with his car. Later he admitted that the chainsaw had been used to dismember Nute's body, but he blamed the killing on an acquaintance named Terry Adams. But Adams was never found and, according to Deputy District

Attorney Sterling E. Norris, who prosecuted Franc in front of Judge John H. Reid, "Adams is a figment of the defendant's imagination." On June 28, 1988, a jury in Los Angeles Superior Court found Franc Guilty of first-degree murder. On July 29, 1988, Judge Reid sentenced Franc to twenty-five years to life in prison, the maximum allowed by California law, which will leave Franc eligible for parole in 2005 at the age of seventy-five. The judge then told the defendant, "You're two different people," and he urged Franc to use his education to help prepare his fellow inmates for life on the outside.

Franklin, Timothy, 1928- , Brit. In 1971, Timothy Franklin smashed in his lover's face, wrapped a rope around her throat, and when she was finally dead, buried her six feet under the wind shelter in his flower garden in an effort to give her a Christian burial.

Franklin, a 43-year-old business consultant from North Otterington, England, met sophisticated Tina Strauss while on a business trip in Jamaica. They soon fell in love and moved in together back in England. But the whirlwind affair was over as quickly as it began. She was tired of life in the small village and he grew weary of her constant complaints and vicious temper; one more threat by her to move back to Jamaica proved more than he could stand. The final fight left Strauss mangled beyond recognition.

Franklin attempted to hide his vicious crime by telling friends Strauss had left him for another man, and once flew to Jamaica to send telegrams in her name to her mother and lawyer saying all was fine on her splendid vacation.

Eventually rumors concerning Strauss' real fate reached Scotland Yard Detective Arthur Harrison. Harrison contacted Franklin for questioning and knew immediately from his sweaty glance that Franklin had committed murder. All the evidence he needed to convict the killer was the date on Franklin's passport and corresponding dates on the telegrams Strauss supposedly sent from Jamaica.

In a tearful hearing, Franklin swore he killed his beloved out of self-defense. He was "devoted to her, loved her, cared for her and cherished her." But he had been overpowered by her and was fearfully forced to crush her skull, nose, cheekbone, jaw, and voice box. The jury convicted him, and he was sentenced to life in prison at York Assizes.

Franks, Robert (Bobby), See: **Leopold, Nathan F., Jr.**

Fratson, George, b.1899, Brit. Despite two attempts at appeal, widespread public doubt of his guilt, and the outright confession by another man, George Fratson remained incarcerated for murder.

Fratson, thirty, was originally sentenced to die at Manchester Assizes, England, on July 9, 1929, for the murder of George Armstrong, 65-year-old manager of a men's clothing store. Armstrong was in the habit of entertaining young men in his shop after hours. One night he entertained the wrong man, and the next day, May 4, 1929, his body was found on the floor, badly beaten. Fratson was found in a brothel in Preston and immediately arrested. Taken aback, he made fifteen different statements to the police. The first fourteen were contradictory, inconclusive, and incoherent. The fifteenth statement was a confession. At his trial he recanted his confession, claiming he was despondent and wanted to die. However, Fratson was sentenced to die.

After the sentencing, Fratson's attorney revealed a key fact that the jury had not heard. Fratson was granted a new trial so the jury could learn of a cardboard collar-box that had been found in Armstrong's shop after the murder. It was stained with blood and marked by a fingerprint that matched neither the victim nor the accused. The new testimony was enough to cast doubt about Fratson's involvement, but not enough to acquit him of the murder.

On Aug. 9, Fratson was reprieved and given still another chance at the Court of Criminal Appeal. He sat before five King's Bench judges, instead of the usual three, and all evidence was methodically re-examined. Fratson's conviction was upheld and he was again given a life sentence. Years later, Fratson went insane and had to be admitted to Broadmoor Criminal Lunatic Asylum (now Broadmoor Institution).

Later still, a man named Walter Prince was found Guilty of murdering a young woman named Harriet Shaw. Faced with the death penalty, he confessed to also having killed George Armstrong. This confession carried little weight, however, when Prince was found to be insane. He was committed to Broadmoor, where both men lived out the remainder of their lives.

Frazier, John Linley, 1946- , U.S. The coastal village of Santa Cruz, about forty miles south of San Francisco, Calif., was the setting for a reenactment of the 1969 Manson killings. On Oct. 19, 1970, the home of wealthy eye surgeon Dr. Victor Ohta went up in flames. After firemen brought the blaze under control, they found the bodies of Ohta, his wife, Virginia, their two children, Taggart, eleven, and Derrick, twelve, and the doctor's secretary, Dorothy Cadwallader. A note attached to the family's Rolls Royce read, "Halloween 1970. Today WWIII will begin, as brought to you by the people of the Free Universe. From this day forward, anyone and/or company of persons who misuses the natural environment or destroys same will suffer the penalty of death by the people of the Free Universe. I and my comrades from this day forth will fight until death or freedom against anyone who does not support natural life on this planet. Materialism must die or mankind will stop." The note was signed "Knight of Wands—Knight of Pentacles—Knight of Cups—Knight of Swords."

The ritualistic nature of the murders indicated that a cultist familiar with tarot cards was responsible. The groups of hippies camped in the adjacent woods suggested another Manson cult. Police came to suspect 24-year-old John Linley Frazier, a local car mechanic who experimented with hallucinogenic drugs. Frazier was separated from his wife and lived near a hippie commune in Felton. He was known to be a militant ecologist and tarot card practitioner. He had a criminal record at the time of his arrest, and had been seen driving Virginia Ohta's station wagon the day after the murders.

Mass murderer John Linley Frazier, left.

Frazier refused to confirm or deny his guilt, but his fingerprints were found on the Rolls Royce. He was ruled legally sane, tried, and convicted on five counts of murder. Frazier was sentenced to die in San Quentin's gas chamber, but California abolished the death penalty in 1971, automatically commuting his sentence to life imprisonment.

Freedman, Maurice, 1896-1932, Brit. An ex-policeman, Maurice Freedman, thirty-six, professed to be in love with Annete Friedson. Although he was already married, Freedman courted the young woman and constantly promoted the idea that his wife was going to divorce him. Finally, the dissatisfied Friedson decided to end the relationship and told her brother of her decision. On Jan. 26, 1932, just after this decision, Friedson went to her job in London. At about 9:30 a.m., she was found with her throat cut on the stairwell leading up to her office. Freedman was arrested the next morning as he went out for coffee with a friend. Three days after his arrest, a passenger on a bus discovered a blood-spattered safety razor behind the cushion of his seat, and took it to the Snow Street Police station. The bus conductor remembered picking up Freedman at about 10:50 a.m. the morning of the killing. Freedman was tried at the Old Bailey before Justice Hawke on Mar. 8, with prosecutor Sir Percival Clarke bringing out that the unusual blood type found on the razor matched Friedson's own. Freedman claimed that he had gone to see the woman to change her mind about leaving him, and had brought an old fashioned straight razor along to frighten her into believing he was going to kill himself if she did not change her mind. After pleading his case with her on the stairs, he had taken the razor out and laid it against his throat, they had struggled, and she had been accidentally slashed. The safety razor blade, which was obviously the murder weapon, and which the accused said he had never seen before, would not have been able to deliver a fatal cut or cuts under those circumstances. Freedman was found Guilty of murder and was executed at Pentonville Prison on May 4, 1932.

Freeman, Jeannace, 1940- , and **Jackson, Gertrude**, 1928- , U.S. Jeannace Freeman and Gertrude Jackson took Jackson's two children for a walk in Oregon's Peter Skene Ogden Park. Freeman and Jackson had been lovers ever since Jackson's husband left her and the children. Freeman, who dominated Jackson, had been raped at the age of four by her male baby sitter.

In the park, Freeman stripped the 6-year-old boy and strangled him to death. Once he was dead, Freeman castrated the boy with a knife and threw his body over a cliff. Jackson then

Murderess Jeannace Freeman.

joined her in the murder of the girl. The women tossed her into the canyon to land near her brother.

The naked bodies of the two children were discovered by a park visitor who told rangers she had seen two children's dolls lying at the bottom of Crooked River Canyon. Rangers identified the children as those of Gertrude Jackson, who had left her Eugene, Ore., home two days before with Freeman.

The two women were captured in Oakland, Calif., after a description of their car led investigators to a used car lot where Jackson had sold the automobile. They were arrested at their home and charged with the murders. Jackson immediately confessed to the crimes and explained that Freeman was the dominant partner in their relationship and had engineered the children's deaths.

Both were convicted of murder and sentenced to death. The sentences were commuted to life in 1964.

Freeman, John Gilbert, 1930- , U.S. Described as "a danger to society," John Gilbert Freeman was to be released from the Arizona State Mental Hospital in 1975 after four years of confinement. A 1971 diagnosis of mental incompetence kept Freeman from standing trial for the murder of seven people. By 1975, it was technically illegal to indict him.

The Arizona prosecutor's office was outraged, and a legal battle ensued between the state's attorney and defense counselors. The state supreme court reviewed Freeman's case, and ruled that he could indeed be indicted because the 1971 diagnosis prevented the state from indicting within the specified 120 days. In early 1975, Freeman stood trial for the murder of seven people in Phoenix on the evening of Sept. 3, 1971.

In May 1970, Freeman's wife, complaining of her husband's behavior, left their Phoenix home with their two children. Freeman searched for a way to explain his wife's actions. A former co-worker had recently told him of his extramarital affair. Freeman became obsessed with the idea that the unfaithful man had seduced his wife and caused the abrupt end of his marriage. He flew to destinations around the country looking for the adulterous couple. He frequently visited Novella Bentley, his former friend's wife, and questioned her about her estranged husband's activities. Bentley was never able to give him any information.

On the night of Sept. 3, 1971, Freeman purchased two .38-caliber revolvers and ammunition before visiting Novella Bentley. When Freeman arrived, Bentley was entertaining relatives in her Phoenix home. Freeman burst into the house and shot Bentley, her daughter, and her daughter's husband. Four children slept through the attack in a back bedroom. Freeman reloaded the guns, and shot each of the children in the head. Police apprehended him as he walked from the house. Shortly thereafter he was found insane and transferred to a mental hospital.

In 1975, the jury found Freeman Guilty and the judge sentenced him to seven consecutive life terms. Following sentencing, Freeman was ordered back into treatment at the mental facility that had previously certified him sane.

Freeway Strangler, The, See: **Bonin, William.**

French, Harry, 1907- , U.S. "Tonight about 6:30 Harry French shot Claude L. McCracken, editor of the Modoc *Mail,* with an automatic pistol. Condition of McCracken serious," was the message received by wire services on the evening of Mar. 25, 1937. The story was sent by McCracken as he died in his Alturas, Calif., office after being shot five times by French, the son of a rival newspaper publisher.

McCracken, forty-six, editor and publisher of the Modoc County *Daily Mail* and Associated Press correspondent, was eating dinner at his home with two newspaper employees when the drunken French burst into the house and shot him five times. French was the son of R.A. and G.P. French, who had been involved in a professional rivalry since McCracken began publishing the Modoc *Mail* three years earlier.

The resentment started in 1934 when McCracken moved to Alturas and began printing his daily Modoc *Mail* in direct competition to the French family's established weekly, the *Plaindealer & Modoc County Times.* For years, the two publishers had playfully insulted each other often printing practical jokes and insinuations about the other in their respective newspapers. The Frenches' response to a McCracken letter ridiculing the *Plaindealer* was to print a falsified story on the McCrackens' arrest for narcotics. McCracken then ran several stories in the Modoc *Mail* listing individuals named French who had been arrested for various crimes. On the day of his death, the Modoc *Mail* ran a story about a Montana man named French who was hanged for stealing horses.

Upon surrendering to police, immediately after the shooting, Harry French confessed and said, "I have stood all of the insults my family can stand." He was convicted by an Alturas court on July 2.

Friend, Wilbert Felix, 1910- , U.S. On the early morning of Sept. 1, 1936, a woman out for an oceanside walk in La Jolla, Calif., found the badly beaten body of Ruth Muir, forty-eight, a YWCA executive secretary, near a bluff overlooking the Pacific Ocean. Following his examination, Dr. F.E. Toomey, the San Diego County coroner's surgeon reported that the woman had been beaten with a club and raped the night before. San Diego Police concluded the killer crept up behind the vacationing woman as she sat on a bench enjoying the ocean breeze.

Police Chief George Sears ordered a roundup of all persons arrested on morals charges in recent years and by evening more than twenty suspects had been questioned. Two of them, E. Carl Eckdohl, forty-one, and Leon Russell were held for further investigation. Eckdohl had been arrested at his hotel just as he was packing to leave town. Police also issued an all-points-bulletin for a bright yellow roadster which had been driven back and forth in front of Muir's cottage on the night she was killed. The roadster was never found and neither Eckdohl or Russell was ever charged with the murder. Unknown to police at the time, detectives had actually interviewed the murderer in their initial roundup of suspects. Not until May 1955, almost nineteen years after the murder was the case finally solved.

At that time, Wilbert Friend, forty-four, an unemployed gardener, went to place flowers on his mother's grave over the Memorial Day weekend. In the fit of remorse that followed, he called the San Diego *Union* and told a reporter that he had killed Ruth Muir. Friend had been a 25-year-old caddie at the La Jolla Country Club at the time. Friend admitted robbery had been his original motive but when he discovered Muir had no money, he dragged her into the weeds, raped her, then killed her.

The killer's remorse evaporated by the time Friend came to trial in August 1955; he pleaded not guilty. After examining the details of Friend's confession a jury found him Guilty of murder and on Aug. 17 Superior Court Judge John A. Hewicker sentenced him to death. The verdict was upheld on appeal, but the California Supreme Court ordered a new sentencing trial. On June 20, 1957, Friend was once again sentenced to die. As the verdict was read, Friend bolted for the back door of the San Diego courtroom. He was tackled by two deputies who dragged him back to the defense table.

There was confusion as to how Friend would be executed. California's gas chamber law had gone into effect in 1937, a year after the murder, and a provision of that law was that murderers condemned before that date should be hanged. But in August 1958, twenty-two years after the murder, a judge ruled that because Friend had been sentenced to die, the execution could take place in the pea-green gas chamber at San Quentin Prison. Execution was then scheduled for Oct. 10, 1958. On Oct. 8, Governor Goodwin J. Knight commuted the sentence to life in prison. Friend was paroled on Sept. 23, 1974. On Oct. 23, 1978, he was released from parole and, at the age of sixty-eight, Wilbert Friend once again became a free man.

Fugate, Caril Ann, See: **Starkweather, Charles.**

Fugmann, Michael, 1884-1937, U.S. During the Easter season in 1936, in the midst of labor strife in the coal-mining region near Wilkes-Barre, Pa., six men received what appeared to be gift boxes of cigars. On Good Friday, Tom Maloney, a former anthracite coal miner's union leader who had recently defected to the United Mine Workers of America and his 4-year-old son were blown up by a bomb when he opened his box. Shortly thereafter, 70-year-old Mike Gallagher became the victim of a second bomb. Luther Kniffen, a former county sheriff, received a similar parcel, but escaped injury when he inadvertently opened the bottom of the box and saw the deadly contents. Police broadcast warnings and the remaining cigar boxes were returned undetonated.

Michael Fugmann, a fervent opponent of the United Mine Workers, was apprehended and charged in the bombing attacks. Arthur Koehler, who was instrumental in tying Bruno Richard Hauptmann to the murder of Charles Lindbergh, Jr. through the physical evidence of wooden fragments from a ladder rung, was brought to Wilkes-Barre. Koehler determined that the wood used in the bombs matched wood found in the home of Fugmann. Fugmann was subsequently convicted of the murders and executed in the electric chair in June 1937.

Fullam, Augusta Fairfield, 1876-1914, India. While stationed with her husband Edward in Agra, India, Augusta Fairfield Fullam began a love affair with Dr. Henry Lovell William Clark, a Eurasian assigned to the Indian Subordinate Medical Service. The couple met at a military ball in 1911. Clark told Fullam that he found his wife and four children no longer desirable, and Fullam responded by saying that she had had about enough of her husband, an accounts examiner. Fullam and Clark began to see each other regularly and started a correspondence that was to be their undoing. Clark wrote several notes to his wife, one of which read: "I am fed up with your low disgusting ways, for I am quite sure you don't care a damn what becomes of me. With fond love and kisses to self and the rest at home, I remain, Your affectionate husband, H.L. Clark."

By the autumn of 1911, both marriages had deteriorated badly. Mrs. Fullam resolved to kill her husband, and enlisted Dr. Clark, whose medical skills helped him select a suitable poison for the job. It was decided that sprinkling arsenic in Edward's soup would simulate heatstroke. But after Augusta applied inordinate quantities of the poison to the food with no visible effect, Clark injected Fullam with a powerful dose of an alkaloid poison known as gelsemine. Fullam died on Oct. 19, 1911, from what Clark recorded as "heatstroke."

On Nov. 17, 1912, four Indians with swords crept into Mrs. Clark's bedroom and slashed her to ribbons. The killers took the sum of 100 rupees, or about $5 per man. When questioned by police about his movements on the night of the murder, Clark said he was dining with Mrs. Fullam. Investigators searched her residence and found a large tin box under the bed. An officer who attempted to pry the lid open was sharply reprimanded by the murderess. "That's Dr. Clark's dispatch box—you dare not touch it!" Inside the box was a stack of carefully preserved letters. The correspondence told of the unfolding murder plot, and it proved to be enough evidence to convict the pair before the judges of the high court in Allahabad. Clark was executed on Mar. 26, 1913, after his lover turned king's evidence.

Augusta Fullam bore Clark's baby in prison. A year later, on May 29, 1914, she died in prison from what doctors diagnosed as heatstroke.

Furnace, Samuel James, 1890-1933, Brit. Samuel Furnace, a builder who served in the Black and Tans

Murderer Samuel Furnace.

Regiment during the Irish uprising of 1921, tried to fake his death to hide a murder. On the night of Jan. 3, 1933, in a dilapidated wooden shed in Kentish Town, he murdered his friend, Walter Spatchett, from whom he had borrowed £60. Furnace had rented the building, allegedly for business purposes, and it was destroyed by a fire of mysterious origin. Firemen pulled from smoldering rubble a man at first believed to be Furnace. The victim apparently left a suicide note that read, "Goodbye to all. No work. No money. Sam J. Furnace." It was known that Furnace was only £90 in debt. He was happily married and had a child, which made coroner Bentley Purchase doubly suspicious. After examining the body, he concluded that the deceased had been shot in the back of the head, and had not died in the fire. The teeth were those of a much younger man than Furnace. Purchase's conclusions were

confirmed by the discovery of an overcoat found hanging in the shed. It contained a passbook listing the name of the rent collector, Spatchett. Police surmised that Furnace murdered Spatchett for the money he was carrying, and then tried to make it look like suicide.

An intensive manhunt involved nearly every law enforcement agency in Britain. On Jan. 14, Furnace wrote a letter to his brother-in-law, Charles Tuckfield, revealing his whereabouts in Southend. Tuckfield gave the letter to the police, who arrested Furnace. He told police he had shot Spatchett by accident, and not knowing what do, he decided to burn the body beyond recognition and then fake his own death. He threw the murder weapon into Regent's Canal. In his cell, Furnace consumed hydrochloric acid and died at St. Pancras Hospital the next day. The coroner's jury found Furnace Guilty of murder.

G

Gacy, John Wayne, Jr., 1942- , U.S. John Wayne Gacy had a long record of homosexual abuse, sodomy and other acts of perversion. In 1968, at the age of twenty-six, while he was married and operating a fast food operation in Waterloo, Iowa, Gacy lured a youth into a back room after closing time and handcuffed him. He tried to pay the youth to perform oral sex on him and when this was refused, Gacy attempted to sodomize the youth; he escaped and reported Gacy. Before going to trial, Gacy paid some thugs to terrorize the youth into not testifying against him but this only strengthened the youth's resolve and he did testify.

Mass killer John Wayne Gacy.

Gacy drew a ten-year sentence but, because his past indicated no serious crime and because he proved to be a model prisoner, he was released in eighteen months.

Moving to Chicago in 1971, Gacy went into the construction business and soon developed his own contracting company. He also continued his sexual abuses. In the year he arrived in Chicago, Gacy picked up a teenage boy and attempted to force the youth to have sex with him. He was arrested but was released when the boy failed to appear in court to testify against him. A young man later insisted that Gacy, in 1977, had held a gun on him in his Norwood Park home when he arrived to apply for work as a construction worker. Gacy attempted to force the man to have sex with him. He flourished the gun and snarled through full lips: "I killed a guy before." The construction worker did not believe Gacy, thinking he was only acting out a fantasy and nothing came of the incident. Gacy, however, had, indeed, killed several persons by this time but not until years later would the secret of this vile mass murderer be revealed.

With each sexual offense and murder that went unpunished, Gacy became more bold, daring to abduct boys from the street and force them to participate in unspeakable sexual perversions while holding them captive in his modest Norwood Park home. He then murdered them and buried their bodies. In 1977 Gacy was arrested and charged with sexually abusing a youth at gunpoint. Gacy admitted to the sexual attack and brutality but said the youth was a willing participant and was blackmailing him. He was released with a warning.

By 1978, Gacy was operating with abandon. He earned considerable money from his contracting business and he was a small but important precinct captain for the Democratic Party in Norwood Park Township's 21st Precinct. He felt that he was insulated against detection. He would drive about in his sleek, black Oldsmobile, cruising near notorious homosexual hangouts in Chicago, such as "Bughouse Square" across from the Newberry Library, and, particularly, along North Broadway in the New Town section. On Mar. 21, 1978, Gacy picked up 27-year-old Chicagoan Jeffrey Rignall on North Broadway in New Town.

Gacy, by then grown fat with a triple chin and bulging eyes, suggested that Rignall join him in the car to smoke some marijuana and take a drive. Rignall accepted. Gacy pulled the car over to a curb and suddenly whirled about, forcing a chloroform-soaked rag over Rignall's face. Rignall passed out and vaguely remembered later traveling at high speed and then seeing an expressway exit. He awoke in the basement of Gacy's home, his body naked and pressed into a pillory-like rack which held his arms and head. Gacy, a powerful, heavyset man, was also naked, his fat, hairy belly sticking out obscenely. Gacy showed Rignall various whips, and instruments of torture, along with a number of strange-looking sexual devices, explaining lasciviously how he intended to use these implements on his victim, Rignall.

The assaults and torture went on for hours. Gacy periodically applied the chloroform and waited sadistically until his victim regained consciousness to renew his attacks. He bragged that he was a policeman, and said to his terrorized victim: "I'd just as soon shoot you as look at you." The sexual attacks became so acutely painful that Rignall wanted to die, he later said. He begged Gacy to release him, saying he would leave town and say nothing about the incident. Rignall finally blacked out with another dose of chloroform and woke up later beneath a statue in Chicago's Lincoln Park. He was fully clothed and his wallet and money were in his pockets, although his driver's license was missing. He discovered that he was bleeding from the rectum and medical tests showed that his liver had been permanently damaged by the heavy doses of chloroform that had been administered by Gacy. Rignall's face had been burned by the chloroform.

Going to the police with his story, Rignall was told that there was little hope of locating his attacker since he had no name, address or license number for the man's car. Rignall was determined to bring to justice the hulking sadist who had attacked him. He rented a car and drove the route he vaguely remembered while being abducted. He sat at the expressway exit he remembered clearly, patiently waiting in his car for hours, watching for the big black Oldsmobile. Finally, his perseverance was rewarded. The car turned off the expressway and passed Rignall's parked car. He wrote down the license number, then followed the car. It turned into a driveway at 8213 West Summerdale Avenue in Norwood Park, an unincorporated area bordering on Des Plaines.

Having worked for a law firm which dealt with real estate, Rignall was able to check real estate records and unearth the name of his attacker: John Wayne Gacy, Jr. He went to police with this information, having performed some excellent amateur detective work. The Chicago police took his information and then told Rignall that Gacy had served time in Iowa for sodomy. Rignall had difficulty in getting the Chicago Police Department to act but finally managed to have a warrant for Gacy's arrest issued. He met CPD officers at Gacy's home, only to be told that since the subject lived in Norwood Park, he was beyond the jurisdiction of the Chicago Police. Rignall, through his attorney, finally had Gacy arrested on a misdemeanor charge of battery on July 15, 1978, but police refused to charge Gacy with a felony, despite the protests from Rignall and his attorney, Fred Richman. Some time later, Gacy agreed to settle $3,000 on Rignall for the medical bills incurred from this sexual attack.

Everything seemed to be closing in on John Wayne Gacy in 1978. He mentioned to his neighbors that he was running out of space in his home where he lived alone after his wife had left him. Gacy spoke of adding more floors to his house which perplexed residents in the area. One told him that if he needed more space it was easier to sell his home and buy a new and larger house. He agreed and made plans to sell his Norwood Park house.

At 11:30 p.m. on Dec. 11, 1978, Mrs. Elizabeth Piest appeared in the Des Plaines Police Department, asking them to check on her son Robert, age fifteen, who had been missing since 9:05 that night. She and her son had been in the Nisson Pharmacy in Des Plaines at that time. Robert, who had been looking for a job for the following summer, told his mother that he had to see a "contractor" who lived nearby. "I'll be right back," he told her but he did not return. Mrs. Piest talked to the druggist who told her that her son might be seeing Gacy, a contractor who had given the druggist an estimate for remodeling the drugstore.

Mrs. Piest and her husband Harold, her son Ken, and daughter Kerry had searched for Robert but could find no trace of him. Des Plaines police captain Joseph Kozenczak heard Mrs. Piest's story and believed her son had met with foul play, especially since he had left her in the pharmacy with the words "I'll be right back," and he knew he was to accompany her home to celebrate her birthday that night. Nothing in Robert Piest's background suggested he might be a runaway. Kozenczak asked Des Plaines youth officer Ron Adams to follow up. Adams interviewed the pharmacist, Phil Terf, and again talked with the Piest family

members. The following morning, Adams called the contractor, Gacy, a definite suspect at that time.

Gacy picked up the phone on Dec. 12, 1978, at 9:30 a.m. He was terse with Adams, telling him: "I don't talk to any

Gacy dressed as a clown for one of his children's parties.

kids. I can't help you. I don't know anything about it." Gacy had already murdered the Piest boy and the body was lying in Gacy's bedroom as he made his denials to Adam on the phone. The Des Plaines police, however, were dogged. They checked Gacy's background and found his conviction for sodomy in Iowa. Kozenczak and several officers visited Gacy that night and questioned him further. Gacy admitted nothing, merely staring back at the officers as they described the Piest boy. He then mumbled something about talking "to one of the boys about some shelves" that were discarded in the remodeling of the Nisson Pharmacy. "I don't remember who it was."

Kozensczak asked Gacy to go to the police station and make an official statement about the Piest boy. Gacy then received a call from a relative about an uncle who had just died. He stretched out his long distance phone conversation but the policemen remained in his home. After hanging up the phone Gacy started to get his coat. Two more officers then burst through the door and Gacy suddenly became obstinate, saying loudly: "Hey, I got a lot of important work to do. I can't be going down to the police station. I know this kid is missing but that's not important to me."

"Well, it's important to the parents," Kozenczak replied, angrily impatient. Yet, without evidence, he realized he was powerless to make a formal arrest, and left after giving Gacy his card and asking him to come to the station and make a voluntary statement. Police now put Gacy under close surveillance. On one occasion, Gacy, realizing he was being watched, jumped into his car and roared off at high speed, losing his pursuers. Meanwhile, Gacy managed to remove the body of the Piest boy from his home. He put the corpse into his trunk and then drove to the Des Plaines River at Interstate Highway 55, and dumping the body into the swirling waters. This undoubtedly unnerved the mass killer since, upon his return trip home, his car inexplicably went out of control and wound up in a ditch, requiring a tow.

In the afternoon of Dec. 13, 1978, Gacy appeared at the Des Plaines police station. His clothes were disheveled and his trousers and shoes were coated with mud. His glassy-eyed appearance caused one officer on duty to describe Gacy as "spaced out on some kind of drug." He asked for Kozenczak but the police captain was not in at the time. Gacy left. Later, Assistant State's Attorney Terry Sullivan helped Kozenczak obtain a search warrant for Gacy's house

Rosalynn Carter shaking hands with Gacy, thanking him for his work with the Democratic Party.

from Judge Marvin Peters, a considerable feat because such warrants were nearly impossible to obtain without substantial evidence.

The police searched Gacy's home but found little. Kozenczak spotted a receipt from the Nisson Pharmacy and took it along. As it turned out, this was the most important piece of evidence in the case. The receipt was made out to the Piest boy, indicating Gacy had had contact with the boy, possibly inside Gacy's house. The killer later admitted that he had emptied his victim's pockets, thrown the receipt into a garbage can, and forgotten about it.

The police returned to the Gacy residence to take up a round-the-clock surveillance. Gacy watched the police sitting outside of his home for days. On Dec. 19, 1978, he

boldly invited two of the officers into his house to have breakfast with him. As they sat down to eat, the policemen noticed a peculiar smell. Gacy explained that he had unplugged his sump pump. The resulting water flowing beneath the building had softened the dirt of the crawl space and disturbed the twenty-nine bodies Gacy had buried there over the years.

Another warrant was quickly obtained and the bodies were dug out of the crawl space. Four more bodies found in nearby rivers over the next four months, including that of the Piest boy, were linked to Gacy. The victims ranged from a 9-year-old boy to grown men such as John Butkovich, reportedly murdered by Gacy as early as 1976. Others included Greg Godzik, John Szyc, Billy Carrol, Randall Reffett, Samuel Stapleton, Michael Bonnin, Rich Johnston and Piest, the last victim of the thirty-four sexually abused and murdered by Gacy. The mass killer was tried in 1980 and sentenced to death.

Garcia, Inez, prom. 1974, U.S. Inez Garcia, a Cuban-Puerto Rican woman barely fluent in English, was brutally raped in a back alley of Soledad, Calif., on Mar. 19, 1974. Her assailant was 17-year-old Louis Castillo. A large, oafish bully named Jiminez kept a sharp lookout for police.

Normally a soft-spoken woman, Inez returned to her home and loaded a .22-caliber rifle, which she then turned on Jiminez. After dropping Jiminez in the street with a single shot, the gun jammed and Castillo escaped.

Despite having been a patient of a local mental hospital, Inez was arraigned on a murder charge. She was defended by the well-known attorney Charles Garry, who sought an acquittal on a diminished capacity plea. Complicating the proceedings were various radical feminist groups, who interrupted the deliberations with catcalls, inflammatory signs, and insults which may have adversely influenced the jury. Inez Garcia was convicted of second-degree murder. One of the jurors later expressed the opinion that a "rapist is not trying to kill her. He's just trying to give her a good time." With this sentiment prevailing, a conviction was virtually inevitable.

A court of appeals later overturned the conviction. But Louis Castillo was never charged or tried for rape.

Garcia, Joe, Jr., 1967-   , U.S. Pointing to Joe Garcia's checkered driving record, Guy Chipparoni of the Illinois Secretary of State's office told reporters: "This guy had no business being on the road." Garcia, a 21-year-old Chicago resident, was driving the city's South Side on a revoked license on Aug. 23, 1988, when he crashed into a bus and ran up the sidewalk, striking two sisters.

Ester Estrada, twenty-nine, and her sister Sandra were standing near the corner of Ashland and Archer Avenues when they were hit by Garcia's vehicle, which was traveling over eighty miles an hour. The driver, under the influence of alcohol, had sideswiped a Chicago Transit bus and ran a stop sign before striking the two sisters. Ester Estrada was killed, and her sister seriously injured.

Garcia abandoned his car and fled on foot. Police arrested him eight blocks away. He was charged with reckless homicide and driving under the influence. Twice in the previous two years Garcia's license had been suspended: once for failing to carry insurance, and a second time for leaving the scene of an accident.

On Jan. 30, 1989, Joe Garcia was sentenced to four-and-a-half years in prison after pleading guilty in the Cook County Criminal Court. He admitted to the judge that he had consumed a dozen cans of beer and had smoked marijuana before embarking on his fatal ride.

Gardner, Margery, See: Heath, Neville George Clevely.

Garlick, Edward Donald, 1937- , Brit. Edward Garlick and his first wife made a suicide pact and she died from gas poisoning. Garlick was tried for her murder and acquitted.

Sometime later, on Oct. 11, 1962, he spotted 16-year-old Carol Ann White standing by a telephone booth. When he talked with the girl, she kidded him about his lack of sexual experience. The two went for a walk in a nearby field in West Drayton, near the London Airport, where he sexually molested and stabbed the girl. The next evening, Garlick, his second wife, two children, and their dog were walking to his mother's home. During their walk, the dog ran into the field where White's body lay. Garlick ran after the dog and "accidentally" stumbled over her body. He reported the find to police, but after questioning, Garlick confessed and led police to where he had buried the knife used in the attack.

Garlick was convicted of murder and sentenced to life in prison in February 1963.

Garner, Vance, and **Johnson, Will**, and **Hunter, Jack**, and **Richardson, Bunk**, prom. 1905., U.S. One evening in the spring of 1905, Sarah Jane Smith, a white widow who lived near Gadsden, Ala., attended a show in Gadsden with her two sons. Unable to find them later, she started home alone and was attacked along the road less than a mile from the town. She reportedly called for help and when Vance Garner heard her cries, he investigated and found a man standing over her body. Garner said he was told to leave. Later he was held along with Will Johnson, Jack Hunter, and Bunk Richardson on murder charges in the Gadsden jail. Outside, a mob gathered and screamed for vengeance. Only the arrival of military reinforcements prevented a lynching.

Garner, Johnson, and Hunter were convicted of murder charges and given the death penalty. On Dec. 29, 1905, as Garner and Hunter stood at the scaffold, Hunter said he was guilty and the others were innocent. Hunter and Garner, nevertheless, were hanged, and Johnson was given a temporary reprieve. Meanwhile, Richardson, who had testified against the others, was held in Gadsden to await a hearing by a grand jury. When the locals learned of Johnson's reprieve, they were furious. On Feb. 11, 1906, twenty-five armed and masked men broke into the jail and took him three blocks away to the Nashville and Louisville bridge, where they lynched him.

Garrow, Robert, 1940-78, U.S. In 1973, the body of 18-year-old Philip Domblewski of Schenectady, N.Y., was discovered tied to a tree in the Adirondack Mountains with a knife in his chest. When Robert Garrow was apprehended for the murder eleven days later, he was shot and his injuries caused a partial paralysis. During his trial a year later, Garrow confessed to seven rapes and to the murders of two more, 22-year-old Daniel Porter of Concord, Mass., and 21-year-old Susan Petz of Skokie, Ill. He also admitted strangling 16-year-old Alicia Hauck of Syracuse, N.Y. He was convicted for the Domblewski murder and sentenced to twenty-five years to life imprisonment.

In September 1978, Garrow was serving his time in Fishkill Correctional Facility in Beacon, N.Y., in a building for disabled and elderly prisoners. There, he was confined to a wheelchair, but the 38-year-old managed to escape the medium-security facility. He was located several days later on Sept. 11. Guards saw him lying near an interstate highway and ordered him to stay where he was. Garrow ignored the command, shooting at the guards and wounding 25-year-old Dominic Arena in the leg. Guards then shot and killed the escapee.

Gartside, John Edward, c.1923-c.47, Brit. On about May 20, 1947, a well-to-do 44-year-old businessman and his wife were shot after apparently startling a burglar. Percy Baker, a representative for a shoe manufacturing firm, and his wife, Alice, lived in a secluded area of the Pennine Mountains. Their naked bodies were found buried not far from their home.

On May 22, John Edward Gartside, claiming to be Percy Baker, contracted with a furniture dealer in Yorkshire to sell a load of furniture for £300. While the dealer was at the Bakers' house loading the furniture, one of the Bakers' friends dropped by to visit. The dealer told her the Bakers' were separating and selling the furniture. Suspicious, the friend went to the police. Police discovered that eight of the Bakers' suitcases had been delivered to a store rented by Gartside.

After questioning, he finally admitted that he had buried the bodies and showed police where they were located. Gartside maintained that the Bakers were having a fight when he arrived, that Baker accused his wife of seeing another man, and that she grabbed a poker. Gartside said Baker shot his wife and then, when he struggled with Baker for the gun, it accidentally fired, hitting Baker. Gartside said he then shot the dying Baker twice more to end his pain. When Gartside went to trial at the Leeds Assizes in July, however, the jury did not believe his tale, which was not substantiated by the evidence. He was convicted on murder charges and hanged.

Gaskins, Donald Henry (AKA: **Pee Wee**), prom. 1970s, U.S. Described by South Carolina law enforcement officials as the "meanest man in America," Donald "Pee Wee" Gaskins was remembered in different terms by his bemused neighbors in Prospect, a town of 500 located in rural South Carolina. Local residents chuckled at the mention of his name. As his nickname, Pee Wee, suggested, Gaskins was "comic," five foot, three inches tall with a foul temper. There was nothing amusing about Gaskins, however, especially after the police began digging up bodies in his own "personal graveyard."

Prior to the disappearance of a Florence County teenager in October 1975, Pee Wee drove around town in a hearse. No one paid much attention when he said he had started a graveyard in the woods in back of a wheat field near his home. Then police began investigating and found human bones buried a few feet below the surface. Gaskins had murdered at least nine people. The victims were locals who had angered him for one reason or another. Johnny Sellers, for example, was shot in the back because he owed some friends of Gaskins a small sum of money. Jesse Judy, who

was with Sellers, was also killed.

Gaskins confessed to the murders of the nine people, including Avery Leroy Howard, Dennis Bellamy, Doreen Dempsey, and her child. Placed on trial for the stabbing death of 45-year-old farmer Silas Barnwell Yates, he was sentenced to life in prison on Apr. 27, 1977, by Circuit Court Judge Dan F. Laney, and began serving his sentence at the Central Correctional Institute in Columbia, S.C.

But not even criminals were safe from Gaskins. Convicted murderer Rudolph Tyner occupied a cell a few yards away. Tyner was serving time for the murder of an elderly couple. The stepson of the victims was not satisfied with the court-imposed sentence, however, and decided to have Tyner murdered in prison with the help of Gaskins who would be paid $400. After failing to poison Tyner, Gaskins obtained a plastic explosive known as C-4. From cell 19, he ran a wire through the air vent, telling Tyner he was installing a cell-to-cell phone system. The explosive, attached to Tyner's coffee cup, went off the instant he picked up the "phone," and killed him instantly.

"He is a back-stabbing, baby killing, mangy cur," said Jim Anders, who prosecuted Gaskins for murder the second time around. "If he were out he would kill again." Gaskins was sentenced to die in South Carolina's electric chair. At present he remains an inmate on Death Row.

Gbrurek, Tillie, b.1865, U.S. An unattractive woman, Tillie Gbrurek, decided that a matchmaker was the surest means of finding a husband. Her marriage broker found John Mitkiewitz, who married Gbrurek because she was known to be a great cook. Gbrurek kept her job in a dark, dreary factory; her lazy, unemployed husband took her money for beer. In 1911, Gbrurek, finally fed up with Mitkiewitz after twenty-six years, punched her husband, knocked him out, and forced him to go to work.

Gbrurek soon gained a reputation in her neighborhood as a fortune teller. First she predicted the death of a dog—"ancient powers" told her it would happen. The dog died within one week, as predicted. Later, she accurately predicted her husband's death. Using the proceeds from his life insurance policy, she visited the marriage broker again. This time, the matchmaker produced John Ruskowski, a railway employee. Some months later, Gbrurek predicted his death, and he too died.

Joseph Guszkowski married Gbrurek in 1914 and died soon after. She spent four years with Frank Kupczyk before he died in 1920. An additional death occurred when neighbor Rose Chudzinski died after questioning Gbrurek about the likelihood of so many natural deaths. In October 1921, the Chicago police, hearing rumors about Gbrurek, called upon Anton Klimek, Gbrurek's latest husband, who was sick in bed. Gbrurek was urging him to get better by eating her stew. The police took him to the hospital and had his stomach pumped. The contents were laden with arsenic. Gbrurek was tried for the murders of her three previous husbands. She was found Guilty and sentenced to life in prison.

Geary, Charles Russell, 1892-1935, U.S. Charles Russell Geary had driven from Pennsylvania to Newark, N.J., on Sept. 18, 1935, to participate in final arrangements for Kathryn Le Van's burial, who had died three weeks earlier while visiting relatives in Easton, Pa. Her husband, Orlando Le Van, fifty-five, employed by the Pennsylvania Railroad, wanted his wife buried in a grave already occupied by Geary's mother, who had died fourteen years earlier. Geary vehemently opposed the disinterment of his mother's body for this burial. The relatives, including Benjamin Le Van, forty, an unemployed brother of the widower, and John S. Geary, forty-one, a nephew who worked for an interior decorating firm, had stopped at a local beer garden to continue their discussion, and were apparently, according to witnesses, on good terms at that time, until a heated discussion of the burial site arrangements ensued.

At around 12:30 a.m., Newark police captain Thomas Rowe received a call at headquarters; a man informed him, "I've just murdered three men and I am going to kill myself." The man gave his address and then hung up. Police crashed through the door at the South Twentieth Street address to find the lights on in the apartment, and the bodies of John Geary and the two Le Vans sprawled on the kitchen floor, two shot in the back and one through the abdomen. In the living room was the body of Charles Geary, shot through the heart with a shotgun that lay close to the corpse. The kitchen chairs were overturned, and on the table were several bank books, indicating a discussion of finances that preceded the slaughter. Further investigation into the case indicated that Geary was angry that his aunt, Kathryn Le Van, had left him out of her will.

Gein, Edward, 1906-84, U.S. One of the most horrendous killer-cannibals in U.S. history was Edward Gein, a strange little man who lived in a remote farmhouse in central Wisconsin and was the grisly role model for Alfred Hitchcock's horror movie *Psycho*. Gein and his brother Henry had been dominated at an early age by a strong-willed mother who did her utmost to warn her sons against the wiles and ways of scheming women. When Mrs.

Gein died of a stroke, the 160-acre family farm outside of Plainfield, Wis., was left to her two sons. Henry Gein died in a forest fire and Ed was left alone.

Gein's mind began to take strange twists. He sealed off his mother's bedroom and the parlor and confined himself to a bedroom and the kitchen on the main floor of the farmhouse. He never used the five small rooms upstairs. He got books and periodicals dealing with human anatomy and studied these for hours when not performing his chores. There was little work to do on the farm anyway since Gein lived off the considerable funds he received through the federal soil conservation program. Gein picked up extra cash doing odd jobs for neighboring farmers and residents in tiny Plainfield, population 700.

Then Gein began secretly digging up corpses in remote graveyards. He paid a cretinous farmer named Gus to help him, explaining to this dim-witted fellow that he needed the bodies for his "experiments." Through later confessions, Ed Gein revealed that at this time he wanted to study the female organs of bodies since he had recently read about the sex change made by Christine Jorgensen and had long harbored the secret desire to be a woman. The bodies Gein and Gus dug up were taken to a shed behind Gein's farmhouse and stored there. Gus never knew what Gein did with these corpses, or so he later said, though he probably did not care to ask.

Gein periodically removed the bodies from the shed and studied them for hours, then dissected them. These crude operations led to wild aberrant behavior where Gein would skin the corpses and wear the skins about as though they were shawls or scarves. He fondled female organs for hours and later admitted that wearing and caressing these gruesome human remains gave him inexplicable thrills. The little farmer butchered his cadavers with care, keeping several of his victim's heads, sex organs, livers, hearts, and intestines, and discarding the parts that held no interest for him.

When Gus was removed to a retirement home, Gein decided that it was too laborious to dig up bodies alone. It was easier, he concluded, to murder women and bring their bodies to his farmhouse for more "experiments." His first victim was 51-year-old Mary Hogan, operator of a Pine Grove, Wis., saloon. One winter night in 1954, Gein waited until all of Hogan's patrons left the remote bar. Then he walked calmly inside. Mary Hogan recognized him and told him she was closing. Gein said nothing as he walked around the bar to Hogan's side. He took a .22-caliber pistol from his pocket, placed this close to Hogan's head, and fired a single bullet into her skull, killing her. He then dragged her body from the bar to a sled he had placed outdoors. It took the diminutive Gein several hours to drag the corpse back to his farm, his way made more difficult by a blinding snowstorm.

Gein's next known victim was Bernice Worden, who operated a hardware store in Plainfield. In November 1957

Wisconsin cannibal-murderer Ed Gein.

he began frequenting this store more than usual. He hung about talking to Mrs. Worden and her son, Frank Worden, who was the town's deputy sheriff. When Worden told Gein he would be going hunting on Saturday, Gein realized that Mrs. Worden would be left alone in the store. He arrived at the store and found the middle-aged woman alone. Gein went to a gun rack and took a .22-caliber rifle from the wall. He inserted a single bullet into the chamber, one he had brought with him, then turned on the startled woman and fired a shot which struck her in the head, killing her. Gein locked the front door of the store, dragged Mrs. Worden's corpse out the back, and took it to his farmhouse. He carried along the store cash register which contained about $41. Both Mary Hogan and Mrs. Worden resembled, to some extent, Ed Gein's long departed mother.

When Frank Worden returned home he had to break into the store. He found his mother and the cash register missing, and he spotted a small pool of blood on the floor behind the counter. A sales slip, half written out in his mother's handwriting, was on the counter. It was for antifreeze. Worden remembered that Gein said he would be stopping by the store to buy this item. Worden told the sheriff that Ed Gein was probably behind his mother's disappearance. The sheriff drove to Gein's farmhouse but Worden went to a West Plainfield store where he knew Gein was probably visiting friends. He found the meek little farmer just finishing dinner.

Worden confronted Gein concerning his mother's disappearance. "I didn't have anything to do with it," Gein replied in an even voice. Worden nevertheless placed Gein

in custody, taking him to the local jail. The sheriff returned from the Gein farm a short time later, in shock and for some time unable to describe what he had seen there. Then he began to make a verbal inventory of the gruesome "trophies" he had found: Four human noses in a cup on the kitchen table, bracelets made of human skin, a crude tom-tom made from a coffee can with human skin stretched over the top and bottom, a pair of human lips on a string which hung from a window sill. Bracing four chairs were strips of human skin and two human shin bones propped up a table. Skin from female bodies had been made into a crude vest, leggings, and purse handles.

On the walls the sheriff had found nine death masks, the skinned faces or skulls of women. There were ten heads from female corpses, all sawed off just above the eyebrows. One skull had been made into a soup bowl. The refrigerator contained human organs, all frozen. In a pan on the stove lay a human heart. The basement looked like a slaughterhouse, with pieces of human bodies hung from hooks along the walls and the floor coated with dried human gore. From what the sheriff was able to determine, the remains found in Gein's horror house were of about fifteen women.

Gein did not deny anything. He admitted his ghoulish grave robbing and the two murders of Mary Hogan and Mrs. Worden. There might have been more but he could not remember. He also talked freely about eating the dead flesh of the bodies taken from graves and those he had killed. He even talked about how he adorned himself in the crude garments made of skin and how, if the mood suited him, he would dance naked around his kitchen and bedroom, playing fitfully with his gruesome trophies. Gein talked matter-of-factly about these nightmares, as if such conduct was normal. He had been at such devilish work

Ed Gein, seated at right, at his 1974 parole hearing; parole was denied.

for a number of years and had grown used to his abnormal practices.

What did bother Gein was that he stood accused of robbing the Worden cash register. "I'm no robber," Ed Gein said indignantly as he was led away to a cell. "I took the money and the cash register because I wanted to see how it worked." Ed Gein was sentenced to life in prison for the Worden murder. He applied for parole many times over the years but was consistently denied freedom. He died in the psychiatric ward at Mendota on July 26, 1984, of respiratory failure.

The Gein farmhouse had died many years earlier. It became the symbol of everything horrible and disgusting. Local youths broke its windows and hurled rocks and snowballs at it whenever passing the place. One night several residents went to the farm and reportedly set it afire in an attempt to blot out the sinister presence of this evil place. It remained for years a blackened, gutted ruin. The remains of Edward Gein, the monstrous Wisconsin cannibal, went beneath the earth without the possibility of being disturbed, as Gein had disturbed others. He was buried secretly in an unmarked plot in a Plainfield cemetery, right next to the woman whom he loved and feared most, his mother.

Genovese, Catherine (Kitty), See: Moseley, Winston.

Geraghty, Christopher James, 1927-47, and **Jenkins, Charles Harry**, 1924-47, and **Rolt, Terence**, 1930- , Brit. Christopher James Geraghty, twenty-one, had twice escaped from Borstal Prison when in 1947 he joined several other hardened young criminals in South London. Geraghty, who said of the prison system in Borstal that "the idea of going straight is laughed at," explained that he learned to be vicious and take pride in terrifying others while serving time. At lunchtime on Apr. 29, 1947, Geraghty, along with Charles Harry Jenkins, who had two previous convictions for assaulting police officers, and Terence Rolt, robbed a jewelry store off Tottenham Court, on Charlotte Street. The three beat two old men and fired at one of them. When assistants chased the thieves out, the robbers' stolen car was hemmed in by a truck which had backed out in front of it during the robbery attempt. The thieves attempted to flee, and a passing motorcyclist, Alec de Antiquis, bravely decided to stop them, and used his cycle to block their path. Geraghty shot de Antiquis through the head. Another passerby, George Grimshaw, also tried to stop the young criminals, and was severely beaten and kicked by them.

Police superintendent Robert Fabian was put in charge of the case. He had little to go on—two revolver bullets from different weapons, contradictory descriptions of the criminals, and no fingerprints or other clues in the abandoned get away car. Fabian and his investigators were able to get information from a cab driver which led them to an abandoned office. There they found a hat and gloves, and a raincoat with a tailor's mark that led them to the Jenkins family home. Harry Jenkins refused to talk, but Geraghty betrayed Rolt. Then, Rolt gave the details of the robbery and murder to the police when he was captured. When two revolvers were found in the mud of the Thames River at Wapping, charges of murder were brought against the criminals on May 19. Tried at the Old Bailey in July, Geraghty and Jenkins, who both had carried guns during the crime, were sentenced to die. Rolt, because of his age, was given a lighter sentence of detainment for not less than five years. On Sept. 19, 1947, Harry Jenkins and Geraghty were hanged at Pentonville Prison. Jenkins was twenty-three, and Geraghty, twenty-one. Their victim, Alec de Antiquis, who was a naval hero, was posthumously awarded a medal for bravery a year later.

Gibbs, Edward Lester, 1925- , , U.S. In the early afternoon of Jan. 10, 1950, Marian Louise Baker, a secretary in the treasurer's office of Franklin and Marshall College in Lancaster, Pa., went to make a daily bank deposit for the school and never returned. A search for the missing woman proved fruitless.

On Jan. 14, Mrs. Frances Harnish visited her summer cottage at Mill Creek and discovered Baker's body in a hole under the house that had been made for a water heater, covered with sheets of corrugated metal. The fresh footprint of a man was visible in soft dirt near the excavation. Lancaster police commissioner Fred McCarney arrived on the scene, accompanied by detectives Captain Kirchner and Frank Matt, along with state trooper Captain Frank Gleason and several plainclothes sergeants. Dr. Charles Stahr, deputy coroner, examined the body and determined that the cause of death had been several shattering blows to the skull. Baker's rings and purse were missing, and there was no indication of sexual assault. Her wristwatch had been smashed, the time stopped at 2:36, indicating that, if this was the actual time of death, Baker had probably been slain by someone she knew, possibly a student from the college. Two carpenters who had been working near the Harnish cottage corroborated this theory when they said they had heard high-pitched screams at about 2:30 p.m., and presumed it was a child being spanked.

Intensive and rigorous questioning of hundreds of people,

many of them students or workers at the college who had been absent when Baker was murdered, began, headed by Captain Kirchner. On Jan. 17, the son of a local undertaker told the police that a college senior had asked him questions about how long it took a body to decompose. The queries were made just after Baker's death by Edward Lester Gibbs.

Gibbs, a 25-year-old married student attending school on a GI Bill, was a popular, well-liked student of good social and academic standing. With the increasingly tense atmosphere created by the murder investigation at the school, police kept Gibbs under careful observation, and waited until the next day to call him in to Dean Breiden-stine's office for questioning. After a brief exchange with the dean, the shaken Gibbs left, only to rush over to the college president's office and announce, "I'm the man you're looking for. I did this terrible thing. I have brought disgrace on the college." Gibbs then began to cry, asking why the police had questioned everyone else and left him to "sweat it out." He confessed he had given Baker a ride in the early afternoon, parked the car at a scenic view, and had a sudden impulse to strangle the woman. He had grabbed her, she struggled, and he then choked her some more, pulled a lug wrench from his car trunk, and bludgeoned her to death. After signing his confession Gibbs told District Attorney Ranck, "I'm an intelligent man. I didn't think you'd catch me."

Tried in mid-March 1950, a jury found Gibbs Guilty of first-degree murder and recommended death after deliberating for almost five hours. After a state Supreme Court turned down his appeal for a new trial, Gibbs was electrocuted in April 1951.

Gibbs, Janie Lou, prom. 1967-76, U.S. Young "Granny" Gibbs—she was only thirty-four when she became a grandmother—poisoned her eldest son and worked as a Sunday School teacher that same day. By that time, she had already killed four family members over a two-year period, each time contributing a tithe from the insurance money to her church. Janie Lou Gibbs began by killing her husband and insisted that no autopsy be performed. Three sons died over a period of some months, and Gibbs again refused autopsies. She was not able to quell suspicions when her grandson died, apparently in the same way.

When the infant and his father were found to have died from poison, other family members were exhumed and all were found to have been poisoned with arsenic. Gibbs was arrested on Dec. 24, 1967. She admitted guilt, but because of her questionable sanity, the state of Georgia took more than eight years to find Janie Lou Gibbs ready to stand

trial. She was found Guilty of all five murders and sentenced to five life sentences. See: **DeMelker, Daisy Louisa.**

Giberson, Ivy, prom. 1922, U.S. At around 3 a.m. on Aug. 13, 1922, two railroad workers in Lakehurst, N.J., heard a woman's screams coming from an apartment. Rushing over and trying to get in, they heard a woman begging for help, and broke in the door, finding Ivy Giberson bound hand and foot with a napkin gag clinging to her chin. In the bedroom lay the body of William Giberson, the middle-aged owner of a taxi company: he had a bullet through the base of his skull.

Ivy Giberson explained to local police that she had been awakened at a few minutes after 3 a.m. and come into the kitchen, finding two men. One had bound and gagged her while the other went into the bedroom and shot her husband when he woke up. The robbers got away with $700 in cash, which Mr. Giberson had recently withdrawn to buy a new cab.

Called in to investigate the case was Burlington County, N.J., Chief of Detectives, Ellis Parker, whose promising career would later be shattered by his involvement in the infamous Hauptmann-Lindbergh kidnapping case. At the Gibersons' apartment, Parker asked the widow to tell him again what had happened. In recalling the robbers' exact words, Ivy Giberson explained how they had not started talking until after they had shot her husband, when the man who was tying her up in the kitchen shouted to his partner in the bedroom, "Why the hell did you shoot him?" and the thief in the bedroom replied, "I had to; he was waking up." Parker then accused Giberson of murdering her husband, basing his deduction on the fact that no robber would have made such remarks. There would be no way a robber could have seen what occurred in the bedroom shooting, and would have gone to investigate the possibility that Giberson had his own gun and had shot their accomplice. Additional evidence, including the murder weapon and the facts that Giberson was interested in another man, and had purchased a widow's outfit more than a week before the murder, was brought in and Ivy Giberson confessed. She was tried and convicted, and sentenced to twenty years in the state penitentiary at Trenton.

Gibons, Jacqueline, 1962- , and **St. Pierre, Robert,** 1963- , and **Wilson, Barry Alan,** 1959- , U.S. Jacqueline Gibons was an adopted child with a history of stealing, truancy, and lying. She once reportedly attacked other children with a pair of scissors. As a teenager, the girl was admitted to hospitals for emotionally disturbed children and to group care homes. Her parents, Benjamin and Sybil Gibons, made the girl seek counseling, and placed her on restrictive diets for her obesity. When she was charged with writing bad checks, her parents signed over custody to the state. Gibons returned to her adoptive parents permanently after dropping out of college.

On July 27, 1982, someone smashed Jacqueline Gibons' bedroom window and stole a pair of gold earrings. Her mother called police, though Jacqueline later reported that her boyfriend, Barry Alan Wilson, had been looking through her window and fell through the pane. Mr. and Mrs. Gibons were considering filing a complaint against Wilson, but their daughter objected. On July 29, 19-year-old ex-convict Robert St. Pierre was with the 20-year-old Gibons and her 23-year-old boyfriend at her parents' Skokie, Ill., home. Gibons' 62-year-old father was bludgeoned to death with a claw hammer in the kitchen. Gibons then picked her 60-year-old mother up at a train station and returned home, where Mrs. Gibons met a similar fate. Gibons, St. Pierre, and Wilson concealed the bodies in plastic bags in the trunk of the family car. They drove to Albuquerque, New Mexico and dumped the corpses on a side road.

Wilson was arrested in Phoenix, Ariz., on Aug. 4, 1982. Earlier, Gibons and St. Pierre had been arrested, and both had accused Wilson of committing the actual murders. At the trial of the three, however, Gibons claimed St. Pierre was the murderer. The prosecution argued that Wilson had killed Mr. and Mrs. Gibons because of the possibility they would file a complaint against him. Each attorney tried to blame the other's client. Gibons, who stood to inherit her parents' estate, was also accused. The defense argued that St. Pierre, after getting drunk, was persuaded to kill the couple. On Oct. 11, 1983, all three were convicted of murder. Gibons and her boyfriend Wilson waived their right to allow the jury to determine sentencing, and were sentenced to life in prison by Judge Leonard Grazian on Nov. 4. St. Pierre chose to have the jury decide his fate and was sentenced to death.

Giffard, Miles, 1926-53, Brit. Miles Giffard, twenty-seven, angry at his father for trying to break up his romance, killed him and his mother. Giffard beat his parents over their heads with an iron bar and dumped them off the cliff on which their house was perched in Cornwall, England, into the sea below.

As a boy, Giffard had been unwilling to learn and expelled from school. He indulged in petty theft, and, finally, lived off his parents. Moving to London in August 1952, Giffard met Gabriel Vallance, nineteen, and fell in love.

The following November, needing a fresh supply of clothing, he returned to his parents' home. His father denounced his lifestyle and forbade him to return to London, cutting

Miles Giffard, who killed his mother and father.

off his allowance. On the maid's evening out, Giffard killed his parents, and then drove his father's car back to London. Arriving the next morning, Nov. 8, he promptly sold some of his mother's jewelry, and then cleaned up at Vallance's apartment. That evening he took his girlfriend and her mother to the movies, telling Vallance what he had done when they were alone. She thought he was joking. As he dropped her off late that evening, the police were waiting, as his parents' bodies had been found. Giffard was arrested for car theft, and the next day he confessed to the murders.

At the Bodmin Assizes in February, the defense, led by John Maude, attempted to demonstrate that Giffard was insane, based on a psychiatrist's warning to his parents that Giffard was unstable. In addition, Giffard claimed to have been regularly locked in a dark closet by a cruel nursemaid, but the jury was not moved. Miles Giffard was found Guilty and hanged on Feb. 24, 1953.

Gillette, Chester (AKA: **Carl Graham**), 1884-1908, U.S. In 1906, in upstate New York, 22-year-old factory foreman Chester Gillette murdered his pregnant girlfriend, who stood in the way of his social ambitions. Novelist Theodore Dreiser sat through much of the ensuing trial, recording the testimony of the witnesses. The material he gathered formed the basis of *An American Tragedy*, published in 1925.

As a boy, Chester had helped his parents preach for the Salvation Army in seamy red-light districts. At fourteen, Gillette was orphaned, and he began traveling the country, taking odd jobs. He worked for a time as a railroad brakeman, but this job did not interest him. Remembering that he had a prosperous uncle in Courtland, N.Y., Gillette wrote him a letter asking for a job in his skirt factory. The uncle agreed, but told Gillette he would have to start on the bottom.

Chester Gillette accepted the offer in 1904, and soon proved worthy of his uncle's confidence. He advanced to shop foreman, and soon entered local society. During one of the numerous parties and balls he attended, Gillette met a beautiful young socialite and fell in love with her. He was readily accepted as a social equal by the younger members of Courtland society, and there was talk of marriage.

But Gillette harbored a secret. While working at the factory, he began seeing Grace "Billie" Brown, a farm girl

who had come to Courtland to work as a $6-a-week secretary. Just as Gillette's prospects were improving, Grace Brown announced she was pregnant with his child. Gillette sent her back to her father's farm with the assurance he would make things right. When Gillette failed to come for her, Brown wrote him a series of letters, each more desperate than the last. She threatened to expose him to his uncle. In July 1906, Gillette asked his uncle for

Murderer Chester Gillette, who sold this photo of himself to buy catered meals while in prison.

some time off and traveled by train to Utica, N.Y., to meet Brown. They spent the night in a rented cottage before going on to Herkimer County in the Adirondacks. Billie naively believed he had at last come to her rescue.

Gillette took her to Tupper Lake, where they rented a room at a resort lodge, but the area was too crowded with vacationers for what he had in mind. They left for Big Moose Lake and the Glenmore Hotel, renting separate rooms. The next morning, July 11, Gillette hired a rowboat, packed a suitcase with a picnic lunch, and rowed out into the lake with Brown around noon.

That night, Gillette was seen walking through the woods carrying his suitcase. His clothes were dripping

Gillette's victim, Grace "Billie" Brown.

wet. At 9 p.m., he registered at the Arrowhead Inn on Eagle Bay, then walked down to the beach and sat by a bonfire. He joined a group of tourists in a round of songs before returning to the cabin. "Has there been a drowning reported at Big Moose Lake?" he asked the clerk, who

said there had not. The battered body of Grace Brown surfaced later that day. The coroner ruled she had been killed, not accidentally drowned. Suspicion fell on Gillette, who was traveling under the name of Carl Graham.

The police quickly caught up with Gillette, who was wearing a jaunty straw boater and seemed to be in an ebullient mood. When questioned about his connection with the deceased, Gillette became nervous and his replies were

The Glenmore Hotel on Big Moose Lake, N.Y., where Grace Brown stayed with Gillette before he killed her.

evasive. The murder weapon was soon found buried in the sand along the shore of Big Moose Lake. Gillette had apparently used a tennis racket to knock Brown into the water. At his trial, he claimed Brown had attempted suicide by throwing herself into the lake. He then changed his story and said that the boat had accidentally capsized, and that Brown had struck her head against the hull and lost consciousness. "But can you swim?" the prosecutor demanded. "Yes," Gillette answered. "And yet you made no effort to save her?" the prosecutor continued. For twenty-two days, the prosecution and defense sparred. A hundred witnesses gave testimony, and a rowboat was brought to court so the defendant could re-enact the crime. Meanwhile, Gillette sold autographed pictures of himself for $5 a piece. He decorated his cells with photos of various women. The evangelist's son had become quite a celebrity.

On Dec. 4, 1906, the jury found Gillette Guilty of murder. The judge sentenced him to die in the electric chair at Auburn Prison, but to the very last Gillette continued to deny his guilt. He marched into the death house on Mar. 30, 1908, after the last of his appeals had been exhausted. Years later, when Dreiser was researching *An American Tragedy,* he rented a boat at Moose Lake and rowed to the very spot where Gillette had killed Grace Brown.

Gilmore, Gary, 1940-77, U.S. The execution of Gary Gilmore on the morning of Jan. 17, 1977, for the murder of a Utah gas station attendant and a motel clerk, was the first execution in the U.S. in ten years. The case became a national *cause celebre* and was treated at monumental length by Norman Mailer in his *Executioner's Song,* which was later made into a television movie.

On July 19, 1976, only three months after his release from an eleven-year prison term for armed robbery, Gilmore killed 24-year-old service station attendant Max Jensen in Orem, Utah. The following night, in the same

The chair in which killer Gary Gilmore was shot to death.

vicinity, he murdered 25-year-old Bennie Bushnell, a motel manager. Both victims were young married men with children, as well as students at Brigham Young University. They were murdered in cold blood with gunshots to the head after being ordered to lie down. Gilmore had been distraught over the breakup with his girlfriend, Nicole Baker, the mother of two, who had already been married three times. Baker had co-sponsored Gilmore's parole, and after the two murders, it was her testimony which led to his conviction.

In October 1976, Gilmore was convicted of the slaying of Bushnell, but on Nov. 8, the Utah Supreme Court stayed his execution. Gilmore had spent eighteen of his thirty-seven years behind bars. He refused to fight the execution order, even encouraging it, demanding a death by firing squad. He garnered further attention by attempting suicide twice, and underwent a twenty-five day hunger strike during his two-and-a-half-month death watch. He refused aid from the American Civil Liberties Union, and waived his right to appeal to the U.S. Supreme Court. At the end he had to resist the efforts of a federal judge who had granted a

stay of execution at the insistence of a group of lawyers.

Shortly after 8 a.m. on Jan. 17, 1977, Gilmore was strapped into a wooden chair in front of an embankment of mattresses, plywood, and sandbags, and blinded by a hood. In his last words, Gilmore implored, "Let's do it." Five marksmen, standing thirty feet away, fired at a target placed over Gilmore's heart. Four guns contained bullets, and the fifth a blank, so that the unidentified sharpshooters would not know who fired the fatal shot. All four bullets hit the mark, and within two minutes Gilmore was dead.

Giordano, Gregorio, d.1914, U.S. On Aug. 12, 1913, the body of a young woman was found in the woods of Inwood Park in Manhattan. The woman's throat had been slit, her skull fractured, and her chest repeatedly stabbed. A brown-handled, seven-inch-long knife, and a shoemaker's iron last, both heavily bloodstained, were found near the body. Identification of the woman was not possible, and the body was placed on display at the morgue to be viewed by those who might recognize her.

Giordano, as killers often do, returned to see his victim, and though he claimed that the woman was his wife, Salvatrice Giordano, he immediately retracted the statement. Acting Captain William Herlihy was curious as to how Giordano could have confused the body with his wife's, who he claimed was twenty pounds lighter than the deceased and had black hair and not brown. Giordano said his wife had been missing since Aug. 11, but had not reported this to authorities. Herlihy asked neighbors about the Giordano's, and from them learned that Giordano told people his wife had gone to the country and that her description matched that of the body and not the picture Giordano had painted. The captain arrested the suspicious character and upon searching his bedroom discovered a bloodstained shirt and a pair of pants, another shoemaker's last, and a picture of Salvatrice, who seemed to resemble the dead woman. Giordano soon pleaded guilty, and gave as the motive his fear that his wife was going to leave him. A jury in the Court of General Sessions took thirty-five minutes to find Giordano Guilty before Judge Forster on Oct. 23, 1913. He was executed in the electric chair at Sing Sing Prison in April 1914.

Girard, Henri, 1875-1921, Fr. After being cashiered out of the French Hussars in 1897, Henri Girard, a petty swindler and amateur scientist, turned to crime. But even the many financial swindles he perpetrated between 1897 and 1910 did not provide him with a comfortable lifestyle, nor did they keep him out of the clutches of the law. In 1909, Girard's bogus insurance company, Credit General de France, was fined 1,000 francs for deceptive practices. However, in the process he met Louis Pernotte, who seemed willing to go along with Girard's schemes.

Pernotte, an insurance broker, gave Girard power of attorney. Then Girard insured Pernotte's life for 316,000 francs, which evidently didn't strike Pernotte as unusual. Meanwhile, Girard began to experiment with poison in his Paris laboratory. He realized that it was nearly impossible to come up with an untraceable poison, so he prepared a typhoid germ culture, which he planned to test on Pernotte. In August 1912, Girard poured a vial of deadly bacilli into a pitcher of water on Pernotte's dining table. Shortly afterward, the Pernotte family left for Royan where they became ill.

They returned to Paris, but Pernotte did not recover. Shortly before Pernotte's death on Dec. 1, Girard administered an injection of camphorated chamomile. "Notice, madame," he said to Mrs. Pernotte, "that it is quite definitely your own syringe. You observe that I have nothing in my hands." It was a curious remark, but was quickly forgotten when Pernotte expired from what the family doctor diagnosed as embolism resulting from typhus. Upon Pernotte's death, Girard informed the widow that her husband had owed him 200,000 francs.

Pleased with the results of this first "experiment," Girard insured the life of Mimiche Duroux and then fed him the poisonous germs. For the next three days, Girard recorded

Frenchman Henri Girard, the "experimental" murderer.

in a journal the progress of the disease. However, Duroux was strong and healthy, and he did not die. Girard had to select another victim, with the help of one of his many mistresses, Jeanne Droubin. Together they chose a widow named Madame Monin, and then took out a policy on her life with the Phenix Insurance Company. Fifteen minutes after ingesting one of Girard's mushrooms in the Metro station, Madame Monin died. The insurance company began an investigation which culminated in Girard's arrest on Aug. 21, 1918. He was taken to the Fresnes Prison, where he told the guards, "Yes, I have always been unhappy, no one has ever tried to understand me. I will always be misunderstood—abnormal, as I have been called—and for all

that I am good, with a very warm heart." Before the case could go to trial, Girard swallowed a germ culture and died in his cell in May 1921.

Glabe, Karen, 1942- , U.S. Karen Glabe considered divorcing her husband, Kenneth Glabe, to marry pharmacist Mitchell Link of Arlington Heights, Ill. Instead, she and Link hired an ex-policeman, Preston Haig, to kill Kenneth Glabe for a fee of $5,000. Haig stabbed Glabe to death on June 21, 1971. The crime remained on the unsolved list for eight years. Then, in May 1979, Haig and his wife, living in Roswell, N.M., had an argument, and his wife told police that he was a murderer.

Haig agreed to testify against the Links, who went on trial in July 1980. They were both found Guilty of murder, and Circuit Court judge Robert K. McQueen sentenced them each to thirty-five to forty-five years in prison.

Glass, Jimmy, 1962-87, U.S. On June 12, 1987, 25-year-old Jimmy Glass became the third person in five days sent to the electric chair in Louisiana, following a period of twenty-eight months without an execution in the state.

Preceding Glass were murderers Benjamin Berry, on June 7, and Alvin Moore, Jr., on June 9. Glass was convicted in the shooting deaths of a rural Louisiana couple. His accomplice, 35-year-old Jimmy Wingo, followed Glass to the chair just five days later. The last words Glass spoke were, "I'd just as soon be fishing."

All four men had appealed their sentences because it was claimed that the death penalty was meted out disproportionately to those who killed white people. The U.S. Supreme Court denied the appeal in April 1987.

Gohl, Billy, d.1928, U.S. In 1903, Billy Gohl was assigned to Aberdeen, Wash., as a delegate of the Sailors' Union of the Pacific to handle payrolls, mail, and the storage of valuables. His office was built on stilts at the edge of the Wishkah River near Gray's Harbor, and had a trap door which led directly to the water. Gohl began murdering sailors who had entrusted him with their valuables. He would shoot the victim in the head as he sat across from him at his desk, methodically check the corpse for identification, and dispose of the body through the trap door. Forty-one bodies were taken from the water during a three-year period. Gohl was finally apprehended when he mistakenly thought an engraved watch found on one of his victims bore the name of the man and left it on the body, afraid that keeping it would incriminate him. The name was actually that of the watchmaker, who identified the seaman, who was traced to Gohl's office. In 1913, Gohl was convicted of two murders and sentenced to life imprisonment. The state of Washington had repealed the death penalty only one year before his trial, and lawmakers used his case to argue for restoring capital punishment, which they accomplished in 1914. In 1928, Gohl died in prison.

Goldenberg, Jack (Abraham), 1902-24, Brit. On Apr. 3, 1924, 28-year-old William Hall, the manager of a small bank near Bordon Camp, England, was shot to death at close range in the neck and head from a .455-caliber Webley revolver—a third bullet missed the victim and struck a window. The robber-turned-murderer escaped with more than £500 in bank notes and silver. Suspicion fell on soldiers at the camp and an officer's gun was reported missing after the murder. Private Abraham Goldenberg, twenty-two, of the East Lancashire Regiment, informed police that prior to the shooting he had seen two men outside the bank in a car—an allegation that proved to be fatal for Goldenberg.

Goldenberg boasted to the local press that "my evidence will be very important, and that it will be through me that the murderer or murderers will eventually be arrested." The soldier was correct; his evidence did convict the murderer. A sergeant-major at Bordon Camp discovered a parcel containing £500 in stolen bank notes that Goldenberg had hidden on Apr. 8, 1924, in the rafters of a latrine roof. Goldenberg, on whose person was found an additional £37 which he claimed was his own, confessed to the killing after he was arrested, but before his trial retracted the statement and told of how another man had pulled the trigger, and that he was only an accomplice. Nevertheless, the crime was still murder—the other man was never found, or ever likely existed—and Goldenberg was tried before Justice Bailhache at the June 1924 Winchester Assizes. His defense noted that the young Jewish man had been disowned by his family when he told them of his plans to marry a Christian girl, and was in need of money, hence the robbery. Neither jury nor judge found this reason for murder—nor was his plea of insanity accepted—and Goldenberg was found Guilty and hanged. Ironically, Goldenberg asked the judge after pronouncement of his sentence, "Can I be assured that the thirty-seven pounds found upon me will be declared to be my property?"

Goldsborough, Fitzhugh Coyle, 1880-1911, U.S. Fitzhugh Goldsborough was born into a wealthy family and had two interests in life: reading popular sentimental novels and doting on his socially ambitious sister. If Goldsborough ever heard his father chastise his sister for some slight offense, Fitzhugh would rush to her defense, threatening his father with physical harm if he so much as laid a hand on the girl.

Deranged killer Fitzhugh Goldsborough.

In 1911, author David Graham Phillips' *The Fashionable Adventures of Joshua Craig,* captured Goldsborough's overactive imagination. The story concerned a selfish, egocentric young woman of the leisure class, a character with whom Goldsborough and his sister both believed to be the sister, though they had no reason to believe that Phillips knew her.

Phillips was a rising star in the New York literary world. Born in Indiana, he had attended Princeton before becoming a reporter for the New York *World.* Phillips once said that, given the choice, he would "rather be a reporter than president." He attained success with such best-sellers as *The Great God Success,* and had completed another book, *Susan Lenox: Her Fall and Rise,* when he encountered Goldsborough in Gramercy Park in New York on Jan. 23, 1911.

David Graham Phillips, murder victim.

Phillips had stepped out of his apartment to mail a new short story to the *Saturday Evening Post* when Goldsborough approached him. The withered, poorly-dressed young Goldsborough could have been mistaken for a tramp, and Phillips reached into his pocket for a few pennies to give to Goldsborough. "Here you go!" Goldsborough shouted as he drew a pistol from his vest pocket. He fired several shots at close range into Phillips, killing the young writer. Seconds later, Goldsborough turned the gun on himself. "Here I go!" he shouted and fired. Goldsborough died in the hospital a few days later.

Police learned the motive for the murder when Goldsborough's parents came forward to explain their son's peculiar obsession with *The Fashionable Adventures of Joshua Craig.*

Golkowski, Johann (AKA: **Raschad Hussein Golkowski; Johann Leonhard**), prom. 1958, Turk. Johann Golkowski met Gerhard Moritz on Mar. 5, 1958, at a Turkish border checkpoint where officials were denying Moritz, a known black market car dealer, entry into Iran. Golkowski offered to interpret the argument and even persuaded Moritz to drive with him toward Istanbul, where the phony physician was sure he could obtain a visa for his fellow German in Ankara. The two were unable to procure a visa in the country's capital and journeyed on to Istanbul. There they checked into the Yayla Palas Hotel on Mar. 10. Three days later Golkowski purchased an Italian Beretta automatic gun from a pawnshop. The next day he used it on Moritz, whose body was discovered with a bullet in his skull, several knife wounds, and a badly beaten face. That same day Golkowski returned the gun he had allegedly bought for a friend, laughingly explaining that "my friend didn't like the gun." Leaving Istanbul, Golkowski drove Moritz's car to the Mediterranean town of Mersin, where he abandoned the vehicle. The police, meanwhile, were piecing together the mystery.

Beside the corpse, found off a dusty road two hours from Istanbul, was a key to a German car with the initials G.M. imprinted on it. The initials soon led police to the hotel registry at the Yayla Palas, which further led to the pawnbroker's shop—as no murder weapon was found at the scene, a search of shops was conducted—and finally a broadcast of the killer's identity. Golkowski read of the search in a newspaper at a railway station in Adana, and decided to return to Istanbul until he could escape. He arrived in the city on Mar. 18, and had the misfortune of checking into a hotel where the clerk recognized him as the wanted man and called police. Confronted with the evidence against him, Golkowski admitted the murder, and how he had placed the body in the trunk of the car and dumped it near Gebze. He claimed that the crime was committed in self-defense when Moritz attacked him—a futile claim considering that he had purchased the gun well in advance. The court in Istanbul found Golkowski Guilty in October 1959, and sentenced him to twenty-four years in prison.

Goluneff, Paul, b.1899, Bul. Bad teeth and a half-eaten apple led police in Bulgaria to apprehend the murderer of 41-year-old Elena Milanoff, who was killed on Oct. 5, 1936, while taking the forty-five minute train ride from Vakarel to Sofia.

In the second-class compartment beside Milanoff's dead body, which had been stabbed in the heart, police found a shattered goldfish bowl and a dead goldfish. A half-eaten apple was discovered under a seat in third class. The apple indicated that whoever ate it only used the left side of his mouth. The eater had obviously rinsed his mouth with silver nitrate, a common solution for bad gums, as traces of the chemical were found on the fruit. Police soon learned that Milanoff's bungalow in Vakarel was in great disorder, and that an empty bottle, which had once contained silver nitrate, was found in the garden there. Commissar Kilko Dubesseneff, who was in charge of the case, became suspicious of the fiancé of Milanoff's daughter, 37-year-old Paul Goluneff, who had identified the body when the daughter, 23-year-old Steffy Milanoff, had refused. Dubesseneff learned from Goluneff's dentist that the man had a prescription for silver nitrate, and when the commissar confronted Goluneff with this information, he confessed to the crime.

Goluneff admitted that he had had past relations with Milanoff, and that she had objected to his marriage to her daughter. He had left behind the bottle of nitrate after a failed attempt to persuade Milanoff against informing Steffy of the love the two once shared. He claimed he had to kill Milanoff because "she threatened to tell Steffy the truth rather than see me marry her." At the trial in February 1937, Goluneff was sentenced to life in prison.

Goode, Arthur Frederick, III, 1954-84, U.S. The man who said his last request would be to have sexual intercourse with a "sexy little boy" died in the electric chair in Florida State Prison on Apr. 5, 1984. Goode apologized to his parents, expressed remorse for what he had done, and then was killed. He was thirty years old.

Arthur Frederick Goode III met 9-year-old Jason VerDow of Fort Myers, Fla., on Mar. 5, 1976, while the boy waited for his school bus. Goode persuaded the boy to come with him, saying he needed help in finding something in a nearby wooded area. "I told him he was going to die and described how I would kill him," Goode said. I asked him if he had any last words, and he said, 'I love you,' and then I strangled him." Cape Coral police questioned Goode twice concerning the incident and let him go. A week later Goode abducted 10-year-old Billy Arthes, and took him to Virginia, where Goode raped and strangled 11-year-old Kenny Dawson.

A Maryland woman saw Billy and Goode and, recognizing the boy's face from a television announcement "Missing-believed kidnapped," alerted police. It took her three calls to three different police departments around her area before she found an officer who had heard of Goode and was willing to do something about it.

Police apprehended Goode and a jury tried him. He pleaded not guilty by reason of insanity, but the Virginia court gave him life imprisonment for killing Kenny Dawson. Goode later was extradited to Florida and tried, convicted, and executed for killing Jason VerDow.

Goode had seemed to look upon his slayings almost with pride since his arrest, taunting the victims' parents with graphic descriptions of their sons' deaths, conducting his own defense for the Florida killing, and harassing his parents. But a new side of Goode was shown on the evening of his execution. Visibly shaking and verbally remorseful, Goode was led, almost dragged, to the electric throne, knowing now the terror he had inflicted on others.

Goodmacher, Marks, 1863-1920, Brit. Fellow Jews of murderer Marks Goodmacher in Whitechapel, England, believed that if the man and his daughter had only sought reconciliation on the Day of Atonement as ancient custom prescribes, the two would not have died.

Instead, 57-year-old Goodmacher and his daughter Fanny Zeitoun had been quarreling so furiously that Zeitoun and her husband had moved out of the home they shared with Goodmacher. On Sept. 23, 1920, the young woman was found lying on her bed with her throat cut. At her side lay her father, also with a sliced throat. Goodmacher recovered only to be put on trial for the murder of his daughter. He was found Guilty and on Dec. 30, 1920, hanged at Pentonville Prison.

Goozee, Albert, prom. 1956, Brit. When Goozee murdered a woman in June 1956 because of her possessiveness and the woman's 14-year-old daughter because he desired her, the court found him Guilty of murder and sentenced him to life in prison.

Albert Goozee was Mr. and Mrs. Leakey's tenant in a Parkstone lodge when he and the landlady became involved. Together with her 14-year-old daughter Norma Leakey, they formed a ménage à trois.

During a camping trip in Bignell Wood near Cadnam, about four miles west of Southampton, Goozee was found on the road suffering from a knife wound. In the wood, beside campsite preparations lay the bodies of Mrs. Leakey and her daughter. Though Goozee insisted that all three had gone mad and began attacking each other at random, authorities soon deduced that the woman and girl had been attacked first by Mrs. Leakey's former tenant and lover, who then had inflicted the knife wound on himself to make things look better. A letter found in Goozee's car told the whole grisly tale. "...Mrs. Leakey still comes after me so I have come to the only possible way out before I go after another young girl."

Gordon, Harry W. (Wilhelm Johannsen), 1905-41, U.S. "It got so I couldn't get the sight (of dead bodies) out of my mind. Ever since, I'd get blue flashes when I'd been drinking, and would have to kill." Thus did Harry W. Gordon explain why he murdered Florence Johannsen in 1933, Betty Lena Coffin in 1935, and Irene McCarthy in 1940. It had all started with his job as a janitor at New York's Mount Sinai Hospital morgue, where he saw all those dead bodies.

On the evening of Oct. 19, 1933, Wilhelm Johannsen showed up on the doorstep of his estranged wife, Florence, wanting to talk. He had been drinking, and she knew it, but she let him in. This talk, like most, turned into an argument, and then became violent. Florence heaved a flower pot at Wilhelm, so Wilhelm strangled Florence with his hands. Then, laying her body across the bed, he mutilated her with a boning knife, imitating what he'd seen at Mount Sinai's morgue.

Johannsen fled to Brooklyn, changed his name to Harry W. Gordon, and met Lydia, who would eventually become his second wife. Harry and Lydia were married in New York but soon after moved to southern California. Lydia opened a flower shop in Long Beach and Harry became a merchant seaman. Although he worked out of the docks at Los Angeles, his work often took him out of town for several days at a time. One such trip took him to San Francisco.

On the evening of Apr. 5, 1935, a man and a woman checked into a hotel on San Francisco's waterfront as Mr. and Mrs. H. Meyers. The next morning, Mrs. Meyers, later identified as Betty Lena Coffin, was found dead in the hotel room. Coffin, whose long police record included arrests for narcotics and prostitution, was discovered nude, having been severely beaten, strangled, and mutilated with a razor.

On Mar. 10, 1936, Jerome von Braun Selz, being held in connection with the stabbing murder of another woman, was linked to the Coffin murder. The hotel night clerk had identified him as the man who had checked in with Coffin.

In 1940, Gordon lost his job as a seaman. Unable to find work on the Los Angeles docks, he drove north to San Francisco in June of that year, hoping for better luck. On June 25, 1940, the body of Irene McCarthy was found in a Fourth Street hotel. Having met Gordon on the evening before in a waterfront bar, she checked into a hotel with him as Mr. and Mrs. J. Wilkins of Los Angeles. The next morning, a hotel maid found McCarthy's nude body wedged between the bed and the wall. McCarthy had been slashed with a sharp weapon and strangled with a belt, still tied around her neck.

Unable to find work in San Francisco, Gordon returned home to Long Beach. On July 8, three weeks after the McCarthy murder, Gordon was apprehended and held on suspicion of killing the woman. His wife, Lydia, shocked at the charges, refused to believe them. The next day, however, Gordon confessed to the McCarthy murder and to the murder of his first wife, Florence Gordon, seven years earlier. Twenty-four hours later, having been extradited to San Francisco, Gordon revealed yet another crime, confessing to yet a third murder—that of Betty Lena Coffin in 1935.

Three months later, Gordon stood before Superior Court Judge Alfred Fritz and explained that he knew he was a menace to society and that he did not care what happened to him. "I've killed three women, and I'd probably do it again unless they get me out of the way," he said. On Oct. 16, 1940, Gordon received two death sentences for the murders of Coffin and McCarthy, and Fritz scheduled him for a date with the San Quentin gas chamber on Dec. 20. The day the decision was handed down, Lydia Gordon decided not to support her husband any longer. She filed for divorce.

After more than a year of appeals, and a plea for a stay of execution based on religious beliefs, Gordon was executed at San Quentin. The cyanide gas took only ten minutes to work, and at 10:11 a.m. on Sept. 4, 1941, Gordon was pronounced dead.

========

Gordon, Iain Hay, 1932-   , Ire. In the village of White Abbey outside Belfast, N. Ire., in the late evening hours of Nov. 12, 1952, Patricia Curran, a 19-year-old student at Queen's University and the daughter of a prominent local judge, was stabbed thirty-seven times and left for dead in a wooded glade on the outskirts of town. Her brother, Desmond Curran, found her later that night after he became worried and went out to search for her.

Patricia died a short time later. Chief Superintendent John Capstick of Scotland Yard was called into the case by the Royal Ulster Constabulary. Capstick concluded from the careful arrangement of Patricia's clothes near the body that she had known her assailant. Two months passed before the arrest of 21-year-old aircraftsman Iain Hay Gordon, which followed extensive questioning of the military personnel stationed at the Royal Air Force camp

at Edenmore. Gordon's black eye first aroused Capstick's suspicions. The soldier explained that the injury resulted

Right, murderer Iain Hay Gordon.

from a "playful scrap" in the barracks. Desmond Curran, who had frequently received Gordon at his home, told of the airman's strange obsession with violent crime and of his amazement that Curran's murderer had inflicted so many knife wounds when only four were needed.

The police interrogated Gordon at length. They were not satisfied with his alibi or his far-fetched stories. Finally, after three days of questioning, Gordon broke down and confessed to killing Curran in a fit of passion. He explained that he had met her at the bus stop the night of the murder and wished to walk her home. As they approached the girl's home, he suddenly grabbed her and began showering heated kisses on her. Afterward, he stabbed her with a service knife which he threw in the sea. The wood-handled knife was found during a search of the beach on Jan. 8.

Gordon was tried at the Belfast Assize Court on Mar. 2, 1953. He pleaded guilty but insane to the charge of murder. Dr. Arthur Lewis, a London psychiatrist, theorized that Gordon was suffering from schizophrenia and hypoglycemia, and said that the defendant probably did not know he was doing wrong. On Mar. 7, the jury found Gordon Guilty, but also insane.

========

Gorringe, Jack, prom. 1948, Brit. Gorringe could have avoided a murder conviction if only he had kept his mouth shut. The 1948 murder conviction of Gorringe represents one the earliest examples of casts being made of teeth marks to be used successfully as courtroom evidence.

Newlyweds Jack Gorringe and Phyllis Gorringe were having a hard time adjusting to married life as their interests varied widely and they fought often. Their last fight began on Christmas Day 1947 with a disagreement on whether they would attend an upcoming dance and ended on New Year's Day 1948 with the young bride's murder. Because the two had decided to continue their fighting at a New Year's celebration and had been anything but discreet, Gorringe was immediately suspect. His alibi was weak and the detectives were clever.

Among other hideous marks of violence on the victim's body were severe bite marks on her right breast. With no other evidence, detectives made impressions, and from those, positive casts of Gorringe's teeth. Next, impressions were made of the dead woman's breast to determine the location and direction of bite marks, using the Moulage method of casting, considered then to be the best way to obtain an accurate model. Then the plaster impressions of the man's jaw were fastened into a dental tool known as an articulator, thus giving the two models the exact movement of the jaw when biting. A simulated bite with the plaster molds was made into the wax impression of the breast. This bite mark then was photographed and the negative placed over the actual bite injury for comparison. In this case, it was a perfect match. Every cusp mark of the simulated bite fitted every cusp mark of the injury.

In a short time the jury turned in its verdict of Guilty of murder. Gorringe went to prison for life and the models of teeth and breast were sent to the Gordon Museum at Guy's Hospital in England, where they will forever serve as a permanent illustration of progress made in police detective work.

Goslett, Arthur Andrew Clement (AKA: **Captain Arthur Godfrey; Captain Goslett**), d.1920, Brit. Arthur Goslett was a man with two wives and two aliases. Calling himself "Captain" Goslett, he shared an apartment with his wife Evelyn Goslett, in Golders Green. He also shared a small cottage in Kew, with his wife Daisy. With her, he was known as Captain Arthur Godfrey. In fact, he had committed bigamy before, being convicted of it in Dover during WWI. He had also been convicted of diamond smuggling in West Africa, for which he served time in a German prison. In August 1919, Daisy became very ill while pregnant and had to go into a nursing home. When she returned to Kew, she found that the cottage had been returned to the owner and that Goslett had confessed to being a bigamist. However, he offered to let her and the new baby live with him and Evelyn in Golders Green as his brother's widow. Since he gave her no alternative, Daisy agreed, although she refused to let him sleep with her in his house.

When a woman who had known Daisy as Mrs. Godfrey heard her addressed as Mrs. Goslett, she went to Evelyn Goslett and told her about it. Evelyn demanded that they move to another part of London where people did not know the truth. But by then Goslett had another marriage in the works, with a wife living at Richmond, who became pregnant. On May 1, 1920, Goslett returned home about ten, and the servant saw him, most unusually, remove his shirt and jacket in the dining room and go to bed, not at all concerned about his wife not being there.

The next day, Evelyn Goslett's body was found in the river Brent at Hendon with four deep wounds on her head, though she had actually drowned. Blood was found on the river bank. She was identified through a shop bill, and Goslett was arrested within one day because the handbag she had with her at Hendon was found in the house. "I am going to have the rope," he said, though he tried to place the blame for the murder on Daisy, saying that she had driven him to it. Superintendent Neil of Scotland Yard testified that there was no substance to Goslett's story. Goslett was tried and found Guilty. The last person to visit him before he was hanged on July 27, 1920, was the wife from Richmond, who forgave him.

Goucher, Allen (AKA: **"Kid" Goucher; Roy Williams**), prom. 1902, U.S. On the night of Jan. 20, 1902, Goucher and his gang of hoodlums scoured San Francisco looking for trouble. That same night, police officer Eugene C. Robinson walked his beat looking for criminals. The chance meeting of the thugs and Robinson left the young lawman dead. Goucher and cronies Frank Woods, William Kaufman, William Kennedy, John Courtney and Henderson ran off, but on their tail was officer Charles Taylor. Taylor's arrest of Henderson proved to be all he needed. Henderson readily confessed to the crime and gave the names of his accomplices. One crook at a time, they were brought in.

Goucher made it from San Francisco to St. Paul, Minn., before being arrested on a burglary charge. He was put up in the Stillwater Penitentiary as "Roy Williams" the burglar, instead of in San Quentin Prison as Allen Goucher. But at the end of his term he was returned to San Francisco, and there he was sentenced to twenty-five years for his part in the Robinson murder. Goucher would have been hanged had it not been for influential family ties. His father, respected California state senator Goucher, made a heartfelt plea to the jury that left his son alive and ungrateful, and the rest of the courtroom in tears.

The other thugs were not quite as lucky. Woods was executed on Oct. 6, 1905, convicted of firing the fatal shot. Kaufman was sentenced to twenty-five years in San Quentin on Jan. 31, 1903. The charge against Kennedy was dropped because of insufficient evidence but the following year, arrested for burglary at Woodland, Yolo County, he was sentenced to forty-five years at Folsom Prison on Mar. 22, 1905.

Goulter, Sidney Bernard, 1903-28, Brit. Sidney Bernard Goulter, twenty-four, frightened even his own mother, but when Constance Oliver, twenty-one, introduced the young man to her parents in 1927, she described him as "a delightful young man." Then her missing body turned up a few days later, brutally tortured, strangled, and burned.

Detectives were convinced that her burned clothing and scorched skin indicated an attempt by Oliver's assailant to burn the body. This strongly suggested the workings of an irrational mind, and Goulter was the obvious suspect. In December 1927, he stood trial for Oliver's death and after just one day of testimony and less than ten minutes of deliberation, the jury found him Guilty of murder. He was executed early in 1928.

Grabowski, Klaus, c.1946-1981, Ger. The mother of a 7-year-old murder victim shot and killed the accused man in front of judge and jury after he testified that he killed the girl only after she tried to blackmail him. Klaus Grabowski, thirty-four, had a long history of molesting young girls. His early offenses involved removing children's underclothes and tickling their genitals. When his infractions escalated to choking a girl until she passed out and then sending her home in tears, Grabowski was voluntarily castrated.

Even so, his interest in young females did not diminish, and a girlfriend of his would later testify that he had been taking hormone injections and was virile. On the morning of May 5, 1980, Marie Anne Bachmeier went to work, leaving her 7-year-old, Anna Bachmeier, at home to play. The girl ventured outside and never returned. Neighbors later testified that they had seen a man fitting Grabowski's description coaxing her into his house. He later confessed that he strangled Anna with her tights and buried her body at the east end of town. In his defense, however, he insisted he had no sexual feelings for the child and had only resorted to murder when she demanded money.

The first person to rise at the hearing the following day was mother Bachmeier. She stood up, crossed the courtroom and emptied a 5.6-mm Beretta pistol into Grabowski, killing him instantly.

A defense fund for Bachmeier reached thousands of pounds when details of her life became well-known. The daughter of a former Nazi SS officer, born in a refugee camp near Hanover, she was sexually assaulted at age nine by a man who gave her money and sweets. At sixteen, her parents disowned her for being pregnant. At eighteen, while pregnant again by a different man, she was raped. When Anna was born she swore never to give her up. The father, a local restaurant owner, persuaded her to marry his Pakistani chef so the man would not be deported.

The defense fund dried up, however, when women in prison with Bachmeier described her as arrogant and haughty and said she enjoyed playing the role of a sorrowing mother and that she had not genuinely cared for Anna. In March 1982, Bachmeier was sentenced to six years for manslaughter but was free on bail pending appeal.

Graham, Barbara (Barbara Elaine Wood), 1923-55, U.S. Barbara Graham was born in 1923 in Oakland, Calif. When she was two, her mother, Hortense, was sent to a reformatory as a "wayward girl." As a result, Barbara was raised by neighbors and received only a superficial education. As a teenager, she was picked up for vagrancy and sent to the same reformatory where her mother had spent time. Barbara was released in 1939.

Graham enrolled in a business college to study for an office job. She also married and had a child. However, by 1941, she was divorced and traveled aimlessly around California for the next few years. Arrested twice in San Diego for vagrancy and "aggravated lewd and disorderly conduct," she served two months in jail before going to San Francisco, where she was arrested for prostitution in 1944. Also in San Francisco, she married a second time, but the marriage lasted only a few months. By 1946, Graham associated solely with criminals, many of whom had ties to organized crime.

For a time, Graham worked as a cocktail waitress in Chicago, but she moved back to San Francisco in 1947 to work as a call girl for the infamous madam, Sally Stanford. After an incident in which she perjured herself to defend small-time criminals Marck C. Monroe and Thomas M. Sittler, Graham tried again to straighten out her life.

She became a nurses' aide in a hospital in Tonopah, Nev., in 1948, and married for the third time. She soon left her husband and moved to Seattle where, in 1951, she met and married Henry Graham. She stayed with Graham until 1953 and gave birth to her third child.

Graham introduced Barbara to drugs and to a crook named Emmett Perkins. Barbara soon left her husband and went to Los Angeles with Perkins, who introduced her to three other criminals, Baster Shorter, John L. True, and Jack Santos, members of a vicious robbers gang.

On Mar. 9, 1953, Barbara Graham and the four men tried to enter the Burbank home of an elderly widow, Mrs. Monohan, who they believed had large amounts of expensive jewelry. Graham led the way and, when the elderly woman resisted, beat her with the butt end of her pistol. In the attack, the woman's skull was cracked and she died.

Condemned killer Barbara Graham.

Graham was arrested and brought to trial. Despite John True's testimony that she had committed the murder, Graham insisted that she was innocent. The prosecution finally planted in her cell a police officer posing as a mob figure, who offered to provide Graham with an alibi for $25,000. Graham accepted his terms and the prosecution made the deal public, forcing Graham to admit her guilt. She was convicted and sentenced to die in the gas chamber at San Quentin. After a number of appeals failed, Graham was executed at San Quentin on June 3, 1955.

Graham, Eric Stanley George, d.1941, New Zealand. Eric Graham tried repeatedly and unsuccessfully to breed pedigree Ayrshire cattle on his Koiterangi farm. Each time he failed, he grew increasingly angry and lost more money. He began arguing with neighbors, blaming them for his troubles. The neighbors finally lost their patience, when, on Oct. 7, 1941, Graham threatened one with his rifle. Police were called, and when they arrived Graham gunned down three and mortally wounded a fourth. Hearing this, two more men approached and Graham responded once again with his rifle, killing one of the men. He then ran off into the bush, later returning home to find Home Guardsmen there.

Upon returning to the scene of the crime, Graham killed two guards and ran off. On Oct. 20, police finally found Graham in a remote farm building and fatally shot him. At the inquest for the six victims, the coroner commended the policeman who had shot Graham, stating he had "removed a great danger before there had been any further loss of life."

Graham, Harrison (AKA: **Marty**), 1959- , U.S. In 1987, "Marty" Graham, a 28-year-old self-employed handyman, was closest to Cookie Monster, a furry blue hand puppet. Graham and his best friend, Cookie Monster, strolled together through the North Philadelphia neighborhood where Graham lived in a $90-a-month apartment.

Although his best friend was a puppet, Graham did not lack girlfriends. However, the women he entertained in his apartment did find him and his surroundings odd. In particular, they questioned the odor coming from the back room behind a door which was nailed shut. When asked, Graham explained that the smell came from a bucket he had used as a toilet and kept in that room. If they knew what was best, he would add, they would not ask any more questions because the back room was "too much for them to handle." His visitors stopped asking questions, conceding that what they already knew of Graham and his relationship with Cookie Monster was enough.

In August 1987, Graham was evicted from his apartment after neighbors complained about the foul smell coming from his unit, and the woman living directly below found what looked like blood dripping down her wall. On Aug. 9 and 10, police found six human bodies decomposing in the back room, either stacked in a corner or covered by dirty mattresses and garbage. Part of a seventh body was found in a closet.

After police searched for him for a week, Graham turned himself in at his mother's urging. At first he told police that the bodies had been in the room when he rented it, but on Aug. 17, 1987, he confessed. He had strangled the women during intercourse, under the influence of drugs and alcohol.

Joel Moldovsky, Graham's court-appointed attorney, maintaining that the defendant was "incompetent, illiterate, and incoherent," recommended that he be confined to a mental-health care facility until he was fit to stand trial. A panel of psychiatrists disagreed, however, and a trial date was set for the spring of 1988. Graham and his attorney waived a jury trial, and on May 3, 1988, after a seven-week session, Judge Robert A. Latrone found Graham Guilty of seven counts of first-degree murder and sentenced him to one life sentence without the chance of parole and six death sentences—a lenient sentence, given that Graham could not be executed unless his life sentence was commuted.

Graham is now serving his life sentence for the murders of 30-year-old Robin DeShazor, 36-year-old Mary Mathis, 33-year-old Sandra Garvin, 22-year-old Barbara Mahoney, 26-year-old Valerie Jamison, 24-year-old Patricia Franklin, and 26-year-old Cynthia Brooks.

Graham, John Gilbert (Jack), 1932-57, U.S. John Gilbert Graham, called Jack by family and friends, was a clean-cut young man—tall, well-mannered, his hair cropped close to his head. A stranger might guess that he had played center for the local high school basketball team; his politeness and quiet voice suggested years as a Boy Scout. He would be the kid down the block selling cool drinks at a cardboard stand outside his house in the summer, the boy next door who shoveled the walk in winter, cut the grass in spring. But he was none of these things, as his neighbors in Denver, Colo., would slowly discover, along with the FBI. He was a killer, moreover a mass murderer who plotted not only the death of an overindulgent mother but would be responsible for the first in-flight plane bombing in U.S. history.

Mrs. Daisie King, Jack's mother, doted on her only son. She had led a roller-coaster life, marrying in and out of poverty three times. Her second marriage produced her only child, Jack, who was born in Denver in 1932. When Jack was five, his father, William Graham, died, and Daisie Graham was left without a dime, forced to place her son in an orphanage. In 1943, Daisie met and married a wealthy Colorado rancher, John Earl King, and she immediately recovered her son, bringing him to an upper middle-class home where comfort and convenience replaced spartan discipline.

Yet the disparity of the two lifestyles young Jack had lived seemingly affected him little. He was bright, some said highly imaginative; he was an above-average student through his first year of high school. Then, at sixteen, he ran away to join the Coast Guard, lying about his age. Graham served only nine months, being AWOL for sixty-three days which caused his detention. Officers learned that he was underage and dismissed him from the service. His mother took him back into her home and, when he said he did not want to complete school, nodded patient understanding.

Jack Graham went to work, taking odd jobs. To his neighbors he appeared the same easygoing boy, but close friends noticed that he would become restless when talking about his mother and then sink into brooding silence. Mrs. King urged her son to return to school so that he could qualify for a white-collar job. By 1951, Graham had accumulated enough night school credits to earn himself a job as a payroll clerk for a Denver manufacturer.

Graham's tastes were rich; he wanted fast, new cars and a handsome wardrobe. He insisted upon taking his girlfriends to better restaurants. He could afford little of this lifestyle on his $200-a-month salary, so Jack Graham did what had become a habit at home—he merely helped himself, in this case forging the name of his company's vice president to checks he had stolen from his firm and cashing these to collect $4,200. He bought a convertible and drove away from Denver to see the sights. For several months, Graham went on a crime spree, but when he took up bootlegging in Texas, the Rangers and other lawmen closed in on him. Outside of Lubbock, police set up a roadblock on a tip that a bootlegger would be taking a certain route, his car loaded with moonshine. Graham approached the barrier at high speed, ignoring police warnings to stop. When he drove through the roadblock, officers riddled his new convertible, which Graham crashed into a house. Miraculously he was uninjured when police took him into custody.

After serving sixty days in the county jail, Graham was turned over to Denver officials who intended to prosecute him for forgery. But Daisie Graham King wouldn't hear of it. She couldn't bear to see Jack behind bars and begged authorities to be lenient toward her errant son, a good boy really, who had made a mistake for which he was sorry. Mrs. King offered her son's former employer $2,500, saying that Jack would work off the balance of the stolen $4,200. Authorities agreed, placing the apprentice forger on probation. For a time, it seemed as if Mrs. King's unswerving belief in her son was vindicated. Graham did get a job and did make regular payments to the firm he had looted.

In 1953, Graham married Gloria Elson in Denver and settled down, working hard as a mechanic, righting his wrong. Like many another citizen, Jack Graham had his "brush with the law" and had been spared prison. It appeared that, like any other citizen having made one mistake, he was on his way to becoming a respected member of his community. His friends found him hardworking, conscientious, and faithful. Graham's relatives marvelled at the consideration and affection he showered upon his mother, especially after her third husband died in 1954.

Following King's death (he had been a successful rancher), a large sum of money was left to Mrs. Daisie Graham King. Thrice widowed, Mrs. King turned to her son for consolation and, to occupy her time, a business partnership. She invested $35,000 of her husband's money in a drive-in restaurant in West Denver; Jack became her partner, managing the restaurant. Graham labored to make the restaurant business a success, and he continued working nights at a Hertz Drive-Ur-Self garage to further reduce the money owed against his forgery theft, until the balance remaining was no more than $106. He had learned his lesson, his mother was fond of saying; Jack was a good boy, a solid citizen.

Then, on Nov. 1, 1955, an earth-shattering event took place that would slowly strip away that upstanding image of John Gilbert Graham, penitent lawbreaker, hardworking married man, and dutiful son. At 7:03 p.m. on that day, United Airlines flight number 629, only eleven minutes from Denver's Stapleton Airport and en route to Portland, Ore., with forty-four passengers and crew members aboard, passed directly over a Colorado beet farm near Longmont. The farmer stood near his barn, looked up, and saw a terrific explosion that sent to earth the shattered remains of the silver plane, burning wreckage that littered his fields and sent him scampering for help when help was useless.

Within an hour, nearby citizens and National Guardsmen arrived to recover the mutilated bodies. These were

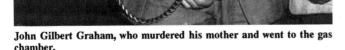

John Gilbert Graham, who murdered his mother and went to the gas chamber.

taken to the National Guard Armory at Greeley, Colo. Responding to one of the worst air disasters in American aviation, the FBI routinely offered the aid of its Identification Division in an effort to help authorities pinpoint the identities of the victims. Two of the Bureau's fingerprint experts arrived in Greeley the following day. Of the forty-

four aboard Flight 629, including one infant and five crew members, nine had already been identified by grieving relatives and friends; the FBI experts fingerprinted the remaining thirty-five bodies, or what was left of the bodies, and twenty-one of these were identified from prints which were in the Bureau's files. The reason why so many sets of prints were on file was explained by FBI officials: a Canadian couple had had their fingerprints taken in 1954 when applying for citizenship, another for personal identification, and many had been government workers during WWII, holding jobs requiring fingerprinting.

FBI experts joined with investigators from United Airlines, the Douglas Aircraft Company, and the Civil Aeronautics Board to help in determining the cause of the crash. Mechanical failure and human error were likely probabilities; sabotage was an almost unthinkable possibility. At the same time, other investigators looked into the unthinkable by examining the backgrounds of every passenger and crew member. They were shocked to learn that $752,000 in flight insurance had been taken out by eighteen of the passengers, almost as if these travelers had had a collective premonition of disaster, making Flight 629 one of the most heavily insured flights in the history of commercial aviation up to that time. The policies were put through thorough examination.

Other experts collected jagged pieces of the plane, from tail to nose, which, when falling to earth had spread over a mile-and-a-half of cropland. The pieces were carefully moved to a Denver hangar and pieced together meticulously, until the ill-fated DC-6B's fuselage was completely reassembled except for a section near the tail from Number 4 Cargo Pit. Not a fragment remained of this section of the plane. The metal shell of the fuselage surrounding the area that had once been Number 4 Cargo Pit, engineers discovered, was bent outward in jagged pieces. This could only mean that a force more powerful than any crash had torn out that part of the plane. Moreover, bits of steel from the fuselage had been driven through the soles of some of the shoes worn by passengers sitting near the cargo section of the plane. Even the brass fittings of one suitcase had been driven through a stainless steel container known to have been in the hold. An explosion had occurred in the cargo hold and, since no gas lines or tanks were located near this section, experts investigating the crash concluded that *something* in the hold had exploded by accident, perhaps an illegal dynamite shipment or—and this was the last possibility any of the experts wanted to include—someone had deliberately sabotaged the plane, planting some sort of bomb on board.

The tragedy of Flight 629 was quickly known to many of those who had friends and relatives on board. One of them was John Gilbert Graham, whose mother, Mrs. Daisie Graham King, had been en route to Portland, then Seattle, and finally to Alaska, to visit her daughter. Graham and his wife Gloria, accompanied by their 2-year-old son, Allen, had driven Mrs. King to Stapleton Airport and walked her to the gate, kissing her goodbye. After Mrs. King boarded, the Grahams went to a nearby coffee shop to have a snack. Jack got sick, rushed to the rest room, and threw up. When he returned he told his wife: "It must be this airport food." As they were leaving the airport, they heard rumors that a plane had crashed. When they returned home, Jack turned on the radio to listen for news about the supposed air crash. Said his wife later: "We finally heard his mother's name on the radio and Jack just collapsed completely."

Graham appeared to be in shock for days after learning of his mother's death. Said one neighbor: "He was really broken up about it—they were very close." While Graham was recovering from the loss of his mother, FBI lab technicians were sifting through the smallest remains of the crash found in the sections of the plane and at the crash site. One technician finally emptied the contents of an envelope onto the desk of Roy Moore, assistant special agent in charge in the Denver FBI office, saying: "These fragments were found among the wreckage but they are the only pieces of debris that we have been unable to identify in any way with parts of the airplane or with known contents of the cargo." Before Agent Moore were five tiny pieces of sheet metal. The technician went on to say that the pieces of metal contained foreign deposits of white and dark-gray colors which consisted mainly of sodium carbonate and traces of nitrate and sulphur compounds. That added up to dynamite, and that meant a bomb had been placed in the luggage of one of the passengers on Flight 629; the cargo hold carried nothing that day but passengers' luggage.

The tedious job of checking every piece of luggage carried by the forty-four persons on board the flight began. The only person for whom no luggage, except tiny fragments, could be found was Mrs. Daisie King. Airport authorities then informed the FBI that Mrs. King had taken out $62,500 in flight insurance—very heavy for those days and far in excess of the amounts taken out by other passengers. The beneficiary was her son, Jack. Although Mrs. King's luggage had vanished in the explosion, the handbag she carried was found intact, and inside, tucked into a small purse, yellowed and folded into a wad, was a newspaper clipping which Mrs. King had been careful to keep with her. The clipping reported her son's forgery of stolen checks and his subsequent arrest. Why a mother so devoted to her son would carry about such an item, as one might carry about a keepsake, remains imponderable. Perhaps, some later theorized, she kept the clipping as a reminder of what her son was capable of doing, or, it was

also later said, she kept the clipping *to remind him* of his errant ways. No one ever knew for sure, but it was this very clipping—which Mrs. King may have wanted authorities to find should she ever meet with foul play—that led FBI agents to the door of Jack Gilbert Graham.

Before interviewing Graham, agents learned that he was not the penitent wrongdoer attempting to set things right. He and his mother had been arguing constantly about Jack's management of the drive-in restaurant, particularly about a strange fire from an even stranger gas explosion that had caused more than $1,200 in damages. The explosion had occurred only a few months before Flight 629 exploded in the clear skies of Colorado. Graham had tried to collect insurance on the restaurant after the fire but had failed. Insurance must have been much on Graham's mind, agents thought, when they discovered that on another recent occasion, the 23-year-old had apparently stalled his pick-up truck in front of a speeding railroad train to collect insurance. Then a neighbor told agents that Jack had boasted of his demolition work while serving in the Coast Guard.

On Nov. 10, 1955, agents went to the home of John Gilbert Graham. Jack was cordial, offering the agents coffee and telling them the story of his life, detailing his days in the orphanage, his mother's three marriages, even his forgery of stolen checks, being careful to point out that he had just about made complete restitution. He told them that his mother was going to Alaska to visit his half sister and hunt caribou. He added that she was carrying in her luggage a large amount of shotgun shells and other ammunition for hunting purposes. The agents nodded, already knowing that Mrs. King was an outdoorswoman, a woman who loved to fish and hunt.

Then one of the agents inquired: "Exactly what did she have in her luggage and did you help her pack it?"

"I can describe her luggage," replied Graham in an even voice, "but I can't tell you what was in it. Mother would never allow anyone to help her pack. She always insisted upon doing it herself."

Jack's wife, Gloria, stepped forward to support her husband's statements, saying that Mrs. King, who had recently been living with them, was always particular about her things. Jack excused himself, telling the agents he was going to make some more coffee. Gloria Graham then remembered a small item about Mrs. King's luggage: "Just before Mrs. King left for the airport Jack gave her a present, or, I presume he did."

"A present?" asked one of the agents. "What kind of present?"

"Oh, I think it was a small set of tools, like drills and files. My mother-in-law used these things to make art gifts out of sea shells. Jack had talked of buying her a set for

Christmas. On the day she was to leave, he came home with a package and took it to the basement where his mother was packing. I just assumed that this contained the tool set and that he gave it to her to take along."

When the agents left the house, they immediately interviewed Graham's next-door neighbors. One woman stated that she remembered the gift Jack had bought for his mother, that "he had wrapped it in Christmas paper and I was told that he put it in his mother's luggage before he left."

"What else were you told?" asked an agent.

"Nothing important...only someone told me later that Jack became suddenly ill only a short time after the plane had taken off, and was very pale. I remember also having been told that when the Grahams were informed of the crash, Jack remarked: 'That's it.' I guess he was too stunned to know what he was talking about. It was really a great blow to him...Why, the poor fellow has been unable to eat or sleep since. All he does is walk up and down the house."

On Nov. 16, agents requested that the Grahams come to headquarters to identify, if possible, some fragments of luggage which might have belonged to Mrs. King. Both appeared on time and agreed that,

Graham's mother, Mrs. Daisie King.

yes, the pieces looked like parts from a small suitcase Mrs. King had taken with her. Agents then asked Graham to stay behind for some more routine questions, while sending his wife home.

The young man stretched out his six-foot-one-inch, 190-pound frame in an office chair and smilingly agreed to answer any questions. Agent Moore conducted the interrogation, beginning slowly, detailing all the facts the agents had gathered, then stating that Jack's wife had told them about the Christmas gift he had slipped into his mother's suitcase, a package approximately eighteen inches long, fourteen inches wide, and three inches deep, as described by Gloria Graham.

Graham's attitude was cool and cooperative. Calmly, and with a smile, he replied: "Oh, you've got your facts all mixed up. I had intended buying her a tool set but I couldn't find the right kind so I didn't buy any."

"But your wife told us you did and that you brought it home with you."

"She's wrong about that. I'd been talking a lot about the

tools and I guess she just supposed I bought them. That's reasonable, isn't it?"

Moore did not respond but asked about Graham's conduct at the airport restaurant. "You did get sick, didn't you, Jack?"

"We had a snack to eat out there," he responded quickly, "but the food was miserable and it turned my stomach."

Then Moore took the hard line, saying: "I want you to know that you have certain rights. The door there is open. You can walk out any time you wish. There is a telephone. You can call your wife or an attorney if you wish. You don't have to tell us anything—and if you do, it can be used in a court of law. There will be no threats and no promises made while we talk with you." Moore stared at John Gilbert Graham for some moments, then said firmly to the smiling young man: "Jack, we have gone over what you told us. You blew up that plane to kill your mother, didn't you?"

"No, I didn't," Graham answered in a calm voice.

"Then you don't mind making any statements?"

"Of course I'll make a statement," Graham said. His voice was full of confidence. "Why shouldn't I? And I'll do a lot more. I'll take a lie detector test if you wish. What's more you have my permission to search my house, my car or anything else. I haven't done anything wrong."

To prove his claim, Graham signed a waiver giving the agents the right to search his home, eliminating a court-ordered search warrant. Agents went immediately to Graham's house. Within minutes one of them called to inform Moore that "Mrs. Graham says Jack told her not to tell about the Christmas present. She signed a statement." Moore immediately confronted Graham with his wife's contradiction of his statements.

Graham thought for a moment, then said: "Oh yeah, I remember now. I did get her that present." He related that he had bought an X-Acto tool set from "some guy" whose name he did not know, paying him $10 for it. Yes, he had slipped the present into his mother's luggage. It now came back to him, all of it, he said.

Agents busy searching the Graham home kept calling with more information. A small roll of copper wiring, a type used for detonating dynamite, had been found in a pocket of one of Graham's shirts. An hour later agents found the insurance policies his mother had signed at the airport, all of them making her son the beneficiary. These had been hidden in a cedar chest in Graham's bedroom. Then they found the shotgun shells and ammunition Mrs. King was supposed to have taken with her. Also left behind by Mrs. King were presents she intended to give to her daughter in Alaska.

Agent Moore outlined the discoveries to Graham, one by one, then summed up the evidence, mounting every minute, surrounding the suspect with his guilt. "Why didn't your mother take these things (the ammunition and gifts) with her?"

Graham grew solemn, then said: "I told her not to take them because her baggage was overweight."

Moore threw a report in front of Graham. "This is from our lab and it proves that the crash was caused by a dynamite explosion." The agent looked at his watch. It was past midnight. They had been at it for almost six hours.

Then Graham sat stiffly in his chair. "May I have a glass of water, please?" he said. He was given a glass of water, which he drank slowly with long gulps. He put down the glass and, in a hard voice, said: "Okay, where do you want me to start?"

"Wherever you want to," replied Moore.

"Well, it all started about six months ago. Mother was raising hell because the drive-in wasn't making any money." He then explained how he had caused the explosion that wrecked the kitchen of the restaurant.

"And what about the truck you left on the railroad tracks so that you could collect the insurance after the train had wrecked it?"

"I did that, too—for the insurance." Graham's confidence had vanished. He squirmed in the chair. Sweat welled up on his forehead and ran down his cheeks. When he wiped it away with his handkerchief, his hand visibly trembled.

Moore leaned close to Graham. "What about the plane crash? You did that, too, didn't you?"

Graham wet his lips and looked at the ceiling nervously.

"What about the plane crash, Jack?"

Graham drank some more water, spilling some on his shirt-front, but said nothing.

"Come on, Jack," Moore persisted. "The truth. You blew up that plane for your mother's insurance. We know it. Let's have the truth from you."

Graham's bloodless face greeted the question. Slowly, he nodded, as if unable to speak the words. He then asked for more water. This was brought to him and he drank slowly, then said: "I might as well tell you everything." With that, Jack Graham became calm and in a deliberate, seemingly indifferent tone, he told in exacting detail how he had made his bomb from twenty-five sticks of dynamite, two electric primer caps, a six-volt battery and a timer (the fragments of sheet metal found by the technicians were from the battery). He seemed proud to announce the fact that he had worked in an electric shop for more than a week to learn how to connect and activate the timer before buying the dynamite. Yes, he had taken the ammunition and the gifts for his half sister from the suitcase and replaced them with the bomb. After twenty minutes, Graham fell silent. A stenographer was then called into the office and he repeated the entire story, and then signed the confession.

John Gilbert Graham was arrested for sabotage and later turned over to Colorado authorities. The stores where he had purchased the dynamite and timer were checked and Graham was identified as the buyer. Graham's half sister arrived from Alaska and told how Jack had once grimly joked about the possibility of his mother's hunting ammunition exploding during one of her plane trips. She quoted him as saying: "Can't you just see those shotgun shells going off in the plane every which way? Can't you just imagine the pilots and the passengers and Mother jumping around?" She thought he was insane.

Graham was placed in the Denver jail to await trial. He refused to see his wife, to whom he had transferred all his assets, and told a guard: "You can send my mail to Canon City (Prison) until next month. After that, you can send it to hell."

Graham claimed that he was without funds on Dec. 9, 1955, when being arraigned for murder. Three lawyers were assigned to defend him. He was then charged with murder in the first degree, but Graham, ignoring his confession, entered a plea of "innocent and innocent by reason of insanity before, during, and after the commission of the crime."

The State then sent Graham to the Colorado Psychopathic Hospital where four psychiatrists examined him. As a way of repudiating his confession, Graham told a weird, wholly unbelievable tale. He said to the doctors sitting before him: "While the FBI men were interviewing me in Denver, I saw a photograph on the wall and it fascinated me. It showed the capture of Nazi saboteurs on the coast of Florida during World War II and FBI men were digging up dynamite. Somehow, that gave me the idea of confessing that I'd used dynamite to blow up the plane but, really, I didn't do it."

Graham's ridiculous tale failed to convince the doctors that he was insane, and he was returned to jail to await trial. On Feb. 10, 1956, Graham was found by guards in his cell almost dead, after trying to strangle himself with a pair of socks. He was revived and made his confession all over again, almost word-for-word with the statement he had given the FBI. Night and day in his cell, he professed his deep sorrow for the murdering of his mother and forty-three other helpless human beings, but he would often recant his confession and turn brutally callous, telling guards that the people on Flight 629 were no more than strangers to him, saying the number of dead was unimportant, that "...it could have been a thousand. When their time comes there is nothing they can do about it."

Graham's trial took place on Apr. 16, 1956, at which time the confessed killer admitted signing his confession but said that the confession was not true. Graham chewed gum incessantly and shrugged indifference at the testimony of the eighty witnesses and 174 exhibits brought against him. Though he had bragged that he would take the witness stand and demolish the State's case, Graham never sat in the box. He was convicted of first-degree murder on May 5, 1956, by a jury of five women and seven men after they deliberated only seventy-two minutes.

The Colorado Supreme Court heard Graham's appeal on Aug. 8, upholding the decision of the lower court. Graham unexpectedly did take the stand this time, but only to inform one and all that his appeal had been made by his lawyers against his wishes. He was promptly sentenced to death. His lawyers went on appealing for many months, until the state supreme court ordered that the bomber's execution take place on Jan. 11, 1957.

On that Friday morning, Jack Gilbert Graham stepped coldly into the gas chamber at the Colorado Penitentiary where he would be pronounced dead within eight minutes after the lethal gas was let loose. Only a few moments before gingerly stepping into the death chamber, Graham turned to a few reporters standing nearby. One newsman who had incurred Graham's ire because of the criticism he had heaped on the bomber, asked the condemned man if he had any last words.

"Yeah," snapped Jack Graham, ending his life with a wisecrack: "I'd like you to sit on my lap as they close the door in there."

Grant, Thomas, 1905- , Can. Thomas Grant, a 45-year-old bus driver in Moose Jaw, Saskatchewan, killed his old friend Wenzel Wilhelm Hartel in a rural area of the province by first burning the man alive, then shooting him three times in the neck for good measure. No motive was ever determined.

Constable Art Zimmerman of the Royal Canadian Mounted Police was called into the investigation after two motorists discovered Hartel's partially nude body near a dirt road six miles south of Moose Jaw. Hartel had been shot and his body badly burned. Tire tracks matching those of Hartel's car led from the scene, and a partially full can of gasoline lay hidden behind a nearby fence.

At Hartel's funeral, Grant inadvertently exposed himself by suggesting to Zimmerman that he investigate Hartel's half-brother Eddie Miller, who Grant said had been quarreling with Hartel because Miller had recently broken off a relationship with his girlfriend, Lorraine Mitchell. This line of investigation led him directly back to Grant, who was taken into custody for questioning. After several days of incarceration and several futile attempts to secure an alibi, Grant admitted that he accidentally murdered Hartel and intentionally covered up the crime to protect himself.

Grant appeared before Justice Adrian Doiron in a King's Bench courtroom on Sept. 26, 1950, and was found Guilty of murder and sentenced to death. Grant immediately appealed the decision and his request was granted by the Saskatchewan Court of Appeals. A second jury once again found him Guilty, but only of manslaughter as the prosecution had failed to prove that he had premeditated the crime. Following the decision, Justice Harold F. Thomson sentenced Grant to nineteen years at a Canadian prison camp.

Gray, Henry Judd, See: **Snyder, Ruth May Brown.**

Gray, William John, 1910- , Brit. Sentenced to hang for the murder of his wife, William John Gray was saved from the noose because medical examiners determined that hanging would have put him in "extreme physical agony."

On Mar. 16, 1948, Gray was convicted of murdering his estranged wife Una Gray, while she and three friends walked down an Andover sidewalk. Gray shot Una and later turned the gun on himself, fracturing his jaw. He pleaded guilty to the crime and within five minutes was sentenced to death.

On Apr. 3, Gray was reprieved after medical examiners ruled that hanging would cause him too much pain. Their conclusion was based on the extent of his injuries, and they explained that if hung, the rope noose would not dislocate his neck and that he would either die of strangulation or he would be decapitated altogether as his injured jawbone was too weak to hold the rope around his neck. They ruled that death by either of these methods would be inhumane and they could not condone his prescribed punishment.

Green, Winona, c.1920- , U.S. The metal buckle off a shoe was found near a woman's footprint in the mud next to the bullet-ridden body of Robert Green, a railway employee in Arkansas. Detective Pitcock interviewed Green's son, LeRoy Green, and his wife, Winona, who lived some distance from the older Greens, at their own home. While there, he smelled something burning. Pitcock gave orders that all garbage from the Green home was to be collected. In it he found the remains of a pair of woman's shoes—only one had a buckle.

Going back to the Greens' home, Pitcock found that Winona Green and her mother-in-law, who had collected a considerable amount of life insurance on the death of her husband, had disappeared together. Pitcock started a search for the two and found only Winona, after she had cashed a large check, with her mother-in-law's signature forged. Under arrest, Winona tried to maintain her alibi, but eventually was forced to confess to killing Robert Green as well as his wife. After Green's death, Winona had loaned money to Mrs. Green, on condition that it be repaid out of the insurance money. Later, Mrs. Green refused to pay, holding some knowledge of the murder against Winona. Neither felt safe out of the other's sight, and so her mother-in-law willingly went along when Winona suggested that they go for a drive. Winona shot Mrs. Green in the head and buried her in deep woods, then went to cash the forged check. Pitcock arrested her when she returned to her husband. Tried and found Guilty, Winona Green was sentenced to life in prison.

Greenwood, David, b.1897, Brit. David Greenwood, a 21-year-old employee of a London manufacturing firm, left work on a Saturday in February 1918 wearing an overcoat with a fake military badge fastened to it. When he returned to work on Monday, his co-workers noticed that the badge was missing. Over the weekend, 16-year-old Nellie Trew had been raped and murdered on Eltham Common. A fake military badge shaped like a tiger and a coat button made of bone with wire in it were found near the body. Pictures of the items appeared in the Sunday newspapers. A colleague questioned Greenwood about the objects, and persuaded him to go to the police. The detective interviewing him observed that Greenwood's overcoat had no buttons at all, and that the bottom one had clearly been torn off. Greenwood gave a variety of excuses as to why they were missing. He said he had used two of them to repair his lathe, which his boss said was impossible. Greenwood claimed to have sold the badge over the weekend.

Nellie Trew had gone to the library on Saturday evening and started home across the Common. Greenwood's mother's house was adjacent to the Common, and he had been there that evening. Greenwood was tried for murder on Apr. 26, 1918, and found Guilty. The jury recommended however, that he not be executed because he had suffered shell shock as a soldier during WWI. He was sent to prison for life for what was called "the Button and Badge Murder," but sympathy for him grew. In response to petitions, authorities released Greenwood after he had served fifteen years in prison.

Greenwood, Vaughn Orrin (AKA: **Los Angeles Slasher; Skid Row Slasher**), 1944- , U.S. For two months beginning in early December 1974, the bodies of Skid Row derelicts were found with their throats slit in alleys and doorways in Los Angeles. The murderer sought out alcoholic bums and slit their throats with a precision and regularity that amounted to a signature. The slayings were performed ritualistically: the murderer scattered salt around the corpses, removed the shoes, and pointed them at the victims' feet—details that police kept secret in order to prevent copycat murders. Seven bodies were found in Los Angeles, and in late January 1975, two more were found in transient hotels in Hollywood. The first eight victims were all between the ages of forty-two and sixty-seven, of small stature, and either lived alone or were homeless. Police developed a psychological profile of the killer as a sexually weak individual who killed in a psychotic or homosexual frenzy.

In the largest manhunt since the search for Charles Manson, police searched for a young, powerfully built white man with long blond hair, a composite description derived from dozens of interviews with Skid Row residents. On Feb. 3, 1975, however, three days after the ninth victim was found, a black man, 31-year-old Vaughn Greenwood, was arrested for attacking two men with a hatchet in a Hollywood home. A month later, police announced that they expected to charge Greenwood in the "slasher" murders. On Mar. 18, Greenwood's attorney obtained a court-imposed gag order preventing police from discussing the case publicly.

Ten months later, on Jan. 23, 1976, Vaughn Greenwood was formally indicted for eleven murders, including the nine slasher slayings and two murders committed in 1964. On Dec. 29, 1976, Greenwood was convicted on nine counts of murder and one count of assault with intent to commit murder. A mistrial was declared on the two remaining murder charges. On Jan. 19, 1977, Judge Earl C. Broady, sentenced Greenwood to life imprisonment.

Gretzler, Douglas, c.1950- , and **Steelman, William**, c.1945- , U.S. Douglas Gretzler, from the Bronx, N.Y., met Willie Steelman, a former mental patient and convict from the San Joaquin Valley in California, and the two became a team of mass murderers. They met in Denver, Colo., and traveled to Arizona where they randomly robbed homes and blithely killed anyone who got in their way. Arizona police attributed seven deaths to them, two of which were their partners in an alleged drug deal. The pair drove to just south of Sacramento, Calif., with Michael Adshade and Ken Unrein of Phoenix held captive in their van. There they killed and buried them by a small creek. They returned to Arizona where they offered two hitch-hikers a ride, then killed them. In Tucson, they broke into the apartment of Michael and Patricia Sandberg, killed them, took their car, and drove to the little farming community of Victor, Calif.

On the evening of Nov. 6, 1973, Walter and Joanne Parkin, who owned a successful grocery store in Victor, went bowling with their friends, Dick and Wanda Earl. They left their two children with the Earls' teenage daughter, Debbie, her brother Rick, and her boyfriend, Mark Lang. When the two couples returned, they were confronted by Gretzler and Steelman who were holding the children at gunpoint. One of the men took Parkin to his store and forced him to take $4,000 from the safe. They then returned to the Parkin's home, tied up all nine hostages and shot them one by one.

The next morning, Laura Carlson, a house guest who had returned late the night before and gone straight to bed, found the victims. First she saw the two children dead in their parents' bed. Then, she found the three older children and four adults all crammed into a bedroom closet. When the police arrived it was noticed that the ropes binding the victims were tied with unusual knots. A bulletin was put out and word was sent from Arizona that killers using similar knots there had been identified as Gretzler and Steelman. Photos of the two were immediately published

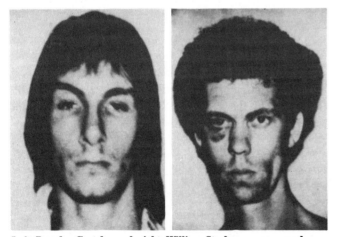

Left, Douglas Gretzler and, right, William Steelman, mass murderers.

in the newspapers. A hotel clerk in Sacramento recognized the pair as they were checking in and called the police. Gretzler was easily seized, but Steelman escaped and was not captured until a SWAT team had sent tear gas into the room where he had holed up.

Gretzler confessed to the killings and pleaded guilty. Steelman did not plead before the California judge, letting his grand jury testimony speak for him. They were both found Guilty of the nine murders in Victor. California had outlawed capital punishment, so the men were sentenced

to life in prison, which would make them eligible for parole in seven years. California willingly sent the men to Arizona, where the death penalty was still in use. They were sentenced to death in the gas chamber for the killing of the Sandberg couple. It is believed that Gretzler and Steelman are responsible for at least eleven other murders for which they have yet to be tried, and as of this writing, they remain on Death Row.

Grills, Caroline, b.c.1888, Aus. In a case that could be considered a tribute to Joseph Kesselring's 1940s Broadway comedy, *Arsenic and Old Lace,* 65-year-old Caroline Grills was convicted of murdering four relatives and attempting to murder three others with rat poison.

Her motive for the murders was never fully explained, though the Crown Prosecutor, Mr. C. Rooney, Q.C., ventured that Mrs. Grills had killed Adelaide Mickelson, eighty-seven, her stepmother, so that she could have the victim's cottage, and then continued poisoning her family because "she got a psychological lift and sense of power from watching the effect of poison."

For whatever reason, after Mrs. Mickelson died in 1947, Angelina Thomas, eighty-four, a close friend of Mrs. Grill's husband, Richard, also died. Soon after, John Lundberg, a 60-year-old sailor and brother-in-law to Mrs. Grills, began losing his hair and finally died in October 1948. In February 1953, Mary Ann Mickelson, Mrs. Grill's sister-in-law, also died after a long period of illness and hair loss.

Detective-Sergeant Donald Fergusson was starting to notice that all these deaths were related—literally. He began to quietly investigate, though he had no idea who in the family might be responsible. It wasn't until John Downey, a cousin of Mrs. Grills, brought Sergeant Fergusson a cup of tea that he had a clear suspect in the deaths. Mr. Downey told the detective that he, his wife, and his mother-in-law had all started to show signs of having the afflictions their late relatives had had. Mrs. Grills had been making numerous visits to their house, and had often offered to make tea or other drinks. On two occasions, Mr. Downey had noticed the woman's hand come out of an apron pocket and hover over a cup that was about to be handed to his mother-in-law. On the second occasion, he took the cup away before his mother drank it and gave it to the detective.

When the lab results on the liquid showed significant amounts of rat poison, Mrs. Grills was arrested for the attempted murder of John and Chrissie Downey, and Chrissie's mother, Eveline Lundberg, who eventually went blind from the poisoning. Soon after, the deaths of the other four relatives were also added to the charges.

The only thing in Mrs. Grills' favor at her trial was the fact that she had absolutely no motive to kill her relatives. The prosecutor, however, was able to place in the jury's collective mind the thought that there were sick people in this world "who poison for sport, for fun, for the kick of it, for the hell of it...." The jury found Caroline Grills Guilty, and in return for all of the lethal beverages and cakes she prepared for her kin, served her a life sentence.

Groesbeek, Maria, 1937-70, S. Afri. Maria and Christiaan Buys married quickly and spent the next fifteen years quarrelling over Maria's inability to stop flirting with other men. In 1968, she met 20-year-old Gerhard Groesbeek. When Buys refused to divorce her so that she could marry young Gerhard, she began to feed him an arsenic-based ant poison. He was admitted to the hospital on Feb. 14, 1969, and died six weeks later. An autopsy showed the presence of arsenic, and Maria was arrested. She and Gerhard, now man and wife, were tried together. She said that she had poisoned Buys to make him sick enough to let her divorce him. Gerhard Groesbeek was acquitted, but Maria was found Guilty and hanged on Nov. 13, 1970.

Grondkowski, Marian, and **Malinowski, Henry K.,** d.1946, Brit. Marian Grondkowski and Henry K. Malinowski, two Poles involved in the London black market immediately after WWII, planned to rob Reuben Martirosoff (alias Russian Robert), an international criminal known to police all over Europe. Late on Oct. 31, 1945, Martirosoff met the pair at a subway station, then drove them to a pub, where they held a conference on their common business. When they left the pub, they found the car stalled. While Martirosoff sat at the wheel, the other two pushed until the engine turned over. And as they did, one of them suggested killing Russian Robert. One got into the front seat beside him. The other, in the back, shot him in the head. They pushed the body into the back seat, and took the cash he was carrying. They covered him with a blanket, then left the car in Notting Hill Gate.

The dead man was found early the next morning and quickly identified. Police noticed that Frank Everitt, a cab driver popularly called "the Duke," had been killed in a similar way two weeks before. Within a short time, the police learned that Martirosoff had received a phone call the previous evening from a Polish friend. From there, they soon determined that he had been friends with a Pole named Marian and a Polish naval officer. The Polish community identified the 33-year-old Grondkowski, and

he was soon arrested. He was carrying a cigarette lighter and a wallet belonging to Russian Robert. He promptly blamed the 25-year-old Malinowski for the murder. Malinowski, when arrested, blamed Grondkowski. They were both found Guilty and hanged. The police tried for a long time to link the murderers to Everitt. Even as they were about to be hanged, an investigator subtly questioned them, hoping that they would confess at the last moment.

Gross, Reginald R., 1961- , U.S. A former heavyweight boxer who once fought Mike Tyson was convicted on three murder charges in mid-1989. Reginald R. "Reggie" Gross, twenty-eight, was involved with a west Baltimore, Md., drug gang led by Warren Boardley. Gross admitted to the shooting of Andre J. Coxson on Sept. 12, 1986, as well as Zachary Roach, a narcotics dealer, and Rodney Young on Sept. 23, 1986, on Boardley's directive. Gross was paid between $2,000 and $3,000 for the murders. On June 5, 1989, Gross pleaded guilty and on July 27, 1989, he received three life sentences, two consecutive and one concurrent. Boardley, twenty-seven, had been sentenced to a forty-seven-year term a month earlier.

Grossmann, George, d.1921, Ger. The years between WWI and WWII in Germany were fraught with poverty and rates of inflation so high that a wheelbarrow of banknotes bought barely a loaf of bread. But meat, when it was available, sold well nonetheless. In 1921, tenants in a Berlin rooming house heard sounds of a struggle coming from one of the rooms, and upon investigation found George Grossmann with the body of a plump young woman. Grossman confessed to having picked up many a young woman, preferably plump, at Berlin's railroad station. Then he killed them, cut them into pleasing-looking cuts of meat, and sold them to the citizens of Berlin. Arrested and tried, Grossman was sentenced to death, but he killed himself in his cell before the execution. See: **Haarmann, Fritz.**

Grzechowiak, Stephen, 1895-1930, and **Bogdanoff, Alexander,** 1895-1930, and **Rybarczyk, Max,** 1899-1930, U.S. In the space of twenty minutes on the evening of July 17, 1930, three men were put to death in the electric chair at Sing Sing Prison in Ossining, N.Y. As the third man, Alexander Bogdanoff, entered the chamber, he asked to make a final statement. He turned to the witnesses and said: "Gentlemen, the state of New York has just killed two innocent men. I tried to save them but my word was no good."

Bogdanoff had asserted this for weeks. He had been convicted along with Stephen Grzechowiak and Max Rybarczyk of the murder of Ferdinand Fechter, a restaurant owner, during an armed robbery in Buffalo, N.Y. After receiving a death sentence, Bogdanoff accepted his own fate but vehemently denied that the two other men had anything to do with the crime. His accomplices, he maintained, were two Chicago gunmen who were still at large.

Saving Rybarczyk and Grzechowiak, who also asserted their innocence with the same fervor, from the electric chair should have been easy. All Bogdanoff had to do was give the names of the real gunmen. But he refused, asserting that the state would have to believe him when he said that the other two convicts were blameless.

Without those names, there was nothing the state could do. New York's governor gave all three men a two-week reprieve on July 3, perhaps hoping that Bogdanoff would disclose the names of the real killers, or that new evidence would come to light. When that time passed and nothing more was revealed, the three men went to their deaths.

Guay, Albert, 1919-51, and **Pitre, Marguerite**, and **Ruest, Genereaux**, prom. 1949, Can. On Sept. 9, 1949, Canadian Pacific Airlines Flight 108 from Quebec to Baie Comeau exploded in flight forty miles from Quebec. All twenty-three passengers and crew members were killed in the crash, which was initially considered an accident. But investigators found evidence of a dry battery cell and dynamite in the wreckage, indicating that a bomb had been planted on the plane.

Albert Guay, who planned the 1949 explosion of a Canadian airliner.

The cargo manifest listed a package being sent to a nonexistent address. Airport freight handlers recalled that a woman dressed in black had left the package. Ten days after the crash, a taxi driver came forward to say that he remembered driving a woman in black carrying a package to the airport on the day of the crash. He gave police an address that turned out to be that of Marguerite Pitre. When police arrived to question Pitre, however, they were informed that she was in the hospital recovering from a suicide attempt.

Pitre admitted taking the package to the airport, and told police that she had done so at the request of a friend and former lover, Albert Guay, a Quebec jeweler. She explained that it was all part of a plot to kill Guay's wife, Rita Morel Guay. Albert Guay had become involved with 19-year-old waitress Marie-Ange Robitaille and wanted to get rid of his wife so he could marry her. He got help from Pitre, who in turn convinced her brother, Genereaux Ruest, to build the bomb. Guay asked his wife to go to Baie Comeau to pick up two suitcases of jewelry for him.

Guay, Pitre, and Ruest were arrested and charged with murder. All three were convicted and hanged.

Guenzel, Guel Sultan, 1956- , Turk. In about 1968, an Adana, Turk., woman died of tuberculosis, leaving her husband and three daughters. Not long after the wife died, her husband, Kadir Karayigit, about thirty-seven, began sexually abusing his oldest daughter. He would give 13-year-old Guel Sultan strong, sweet wine after dinner, and after she passed out, he sexually assaulted her. When her two younger sisters also reached thirteen, the father treated them similarly. The oldest daughter's suspicion that she might not be a virgin was confirmed on her wedding night in June 1974. Six days later, on June 22, Guel Sultan Guenzel, eighteen, went to her father's restaurant at 3:30 p.m. She found him resting on a couch in his office and shot him once in the head and seven times in the groin. Then she wiped her fingerprints from the gun and tossed the weapon on the couch. A waiter, Omar Demir, found Karayigit and immediately ran out to the street, to call for help. Police first suspected Demir, but he was released. One of the constables remembered that the eldest daughter was sitting inside the restaurant drinking wine after the murder. The young woman was questioned and she confessed, telling the story of abuse, which was confirmed by her two sisters. She was tried in September 1974 on a charge of premeditated murder. Guenzel was convicted and received a five-year suspended sentence.

Guerin, Joseph, prom. 1971, U.S. On Nov. 29, 1971, Albany, N.Y., police Sergeant Mike McNeil was fatally shot by a driver he had stopped because his license did not conform to his car's registration number. McNeil had frisked Joseph Guerin, who it was later discovered was wanted for grand larceny and robbery, but failed to find the pistol in his pocket. Guerin fled after the shooting, but a man and woman who were in Guerin's car stayed behind and gave police information that led to his arrest. He was convicted and sentenced to life in prison.

Gufler, Max, 1910- , Aust. Max Gufler became a confidence man and "bluebeard" murderer after the police closed down the stand from which he had sold pornographic photos. Gufler was an illegitimate child who had moods of unpredictable violence after he was struck on the head with a stone at age nine. He drove an ambulance for the Wehrmacht in WWII and suffered a second head wound. After the war, he sold books for seven years. When he met Herta Jonn, the woman who became his mistress, he began working in her father's tobacco shop, extending the inventory to include pornography. Gufler's sales of pornographic photos led to prison terms for Gufler, his mistress, and her father. The tobacco stand was permanently closed.

Upon his release from prison, Gufler began his career as confidence artist and bluebeard. His method was to read matrimonial advertisements, write letters to lonely widows, and propose marriage. As a test of the woman's love, he would ask her to withdraw all her savings. On the way to the marriage ceremony, he drugged the victim, disposing of the body so that the death looked like suicide.

Gufler is suspected of eighteen murders, the earliest in 1946, but was convicted of only eight. He confessed to bludgeoning to death 50-year-old prostitute Emilie Meystrzik in her room in Vienna in 1952, and to giving an overdose of barbiturates to 45-year-old Josefine Kemmleitner, whose body was found in the Danube on June 3, 1958. Gufler also confessed to killing Maria Robas three months later, and 50-year-old Juliana Nass, found in the Danube on Oct. 15, 1958. Gufler was arrested following the Robas killing because he sent her father a letter eventually traced to Gufler saying he witnessed her death in a car accident.

Austrian bluebeard Max Gufler.

The police also found sufficient evidence to prosecute Gufler for murdering Augusta Lindebner, Theresa Wesely, Juliana Emsenhuber, and Josephine Dangl, and suspected him of murdering ten other women. They also found intended victim Marlene Buchner in tears at the registry office. Gufler's arrest had prevented him from keeping their appointment. Gufler was sentenced to life imprison-ment in May 1961.

Guillen, Jose, and **Guillen, Antonio Arias**, prom. 1974, U.S. On June 16, 1974, Chicago police officer Robert J. Strugala was shot to death by two gunmen in Chicago's Rio Grande Lounge on West 26th Street. Strugala's partner, officer John A. Wasco sustained injuries to his right elbow, lower right side and right leg. The officers were stopped at a traffic light in their patrol car when they heard gunshots from inside the bar. They stormed inside only to face Jose Guillen, who had just fired four shots at the bartender with a .38-caliber automatic pistol. Guillen's cousin, Antonio Arias Guillen, sprayed about three dozen rounds from two pistols at the policemen. Wasco was hit, and fell back through the side door. Strugala, meanwhile, was reloading his pistol behind the bar when Antonio Guillen shot him from behind. Jose Guillen also shot the fallen officer. He was captured outside the bar by police officers Joseph Mucharski and Edward Kodatt, who had found their colleague's empty patrol car. For the murder of Strugala, Jose Guillen was sentenced to fifty to one hundred years at Stateville Correctional Center, and given concurrent terms of ten to thirty years for attempting to murder officer Wasco and the bartender. Antonio Guillen escaped to Mexico, according to police.

Gunderman, Stacey, prom. 1937, U.S. On Sept. 12, 1936, 64-year-old Frank C. Monaghan was arrested for drunk driving. But before he could be taken to the Fayette County jail in Uniontown, Pa., he stabbed the arresting officer. The next day, Monaghan was dead; the coroner's report read, "Heart disease superinduced by acute alcoholism." But Monaghan's two sons were not satisfied. A second, more thorough autopsy detected a fractured jaw and nose, eleven broken ribs, and hemorrhages in the brain, throat, and internal organs. A three-day investigation led Pennsylvania Attorney General Charles J. Margiotti to conclude that Monaghan had been savagely tortured in order to obtain a confession.

On Feb. 25, 1937, a jury found Stacey Gunderman, a burly, six-foot state trooper, Guilty of second-degree murder. He confessed to throwing Monaghan on a concrete floor and jumping on him, though he claimed to do this in self-defense when the old man attacked him. In his instructions to the jury, State Supreme Court Justice George W. Maxey condemned a third-degree verdict and asked for the jury to return one of three verdicts: second-degree murder, voluntary manslaughter, or acquittal. "The practice of torturing prisoners or suspects in order to force them to confess crimes is a practice which belongs only in the barbaric ages of the world," stated Justice Maxey, who sentenced Gunderman to ten to twenty years in prison. But after only ten months in jail, the same justice paroled the former law officer, saying, "You have conducted yourself with candor, courage, and dignity. There is no malice in your make-up. I have complete confidence you will be a law-abiding citizen."

Gunness, Belle (AKA: **Bella Poulsdatter Sorensen Gunness; Belle Brynhilde Paulsetter Sorenson Gunness; Female Bluebeard**), 1859-1908?, U.S. A stonemason's daughter who was born near Lake Selbe, Trondheim, Nor., Belle migrated to the U.S. in 1883, following her sister to America. (Another report has it that Belle was born Belle Paulson in Christiana, Nor., and that her father was a traveling magician who taught Belle all sorts of magic and had her walk a tightrope as a child outside his tent to lure customers into his magic show.) She married Mads Albert Sorenson in 1884 in Chicago, a union that produced no children. Sorenson died in 1900, heavily insured, the cause of death listed as heart failure.

Belle immediately put in for the insurance money, $8,500, the day following her husband's funeral, a suspicious act, according to her in-laws. Sorenson's relatives claimed that Belle had poisoned her husband to collect the insurance money and an inquest was ordered, according to records. It is unclear, however, whether or not the inquest ever took place or whether Sorenson's body was exhumed to check for arsenic as his relatives had demanded. Belle used the insurance money to open a confectionery store at Grand Avenue and Elizabeth Street, but this store mysteriously burned down just after Belle had the place heavily insured. The insurance company at first resisted paying off, but it finally relented after the outspoken Belle threatened to take the matter into court and to the newspapers.

With her insurance money, Belle moved in 1902 to La Porte, Ind., where she purchased a large farm, six miles outside of town. She had, while married to Sorenson, adopted three children, all girls, Jennie, Myrtle and Lucy. Just after moving into a large farmhouse, Belle met a local man, Peter Gunness, a fellow Norwegian, and they were married a short time later. This union produced a son, Philip, in 1903. Gunness did not last long. He met with a "tragic accident," according to Belle's sobbing story, in 1904. While working in a shed on the farm, a meat chopper fell from a high shelf and struck Gunness square in the head, splitting his skull and killing him on the spot.

Belle, still a great believer in insurance, had, of course, insured her husband Peter for just such an unforseen event. She collected another $4,000.

Local authorities refused to believe that Gunness, who ran the hog farm and butchering shop on the property, could be so clumsy. He was an experienced butcher and the local coroner reviewed the case and announced: "This was murder!" He convened a coroner's jury to look into the matter. Meanwhile, Jennie Olson, age fourteen, the oldest of Belle's adopted children, was overheard confessing to a classmate: "My momma killed my poppa. She hit him with a cleaver." Jennie was brought before the coroner's jury but denied having made this remark. While she testified, Belle sat nearby at a witness table, silently glowering at her adopted daughter. Then Belle took the stand and, weeping, told her tale. She managed to convince the coroner's jury that she was innocent of any wrongdoing and that she now bore the responsibility of raising her children without the help of a strong man. She was released and the matter was dropped.

In September 1906, Jennie Olson suddenly vanished. When neighbors inquired about her, Belle told them that she had sent Jennie to finishing school in Los Angeles. A short time later, Belle hired a somber little man with a drooping mustache, Ray Lamphere, to perform the chores on her farm. Next, in late 1906, she inserted the following advertisement in matrimonial columns of all the Chicago daily newspapers and those of other large midwestern cities:

Personal—comely widow who owns a large farm in one of the finest districts in La Porte County, Indiana, desires to make the acquaintance of a gentleman equally well provided, with view of joining fortunes. No replies by letter considered unless sender is willing to follow answer with personal visit. Triflers need not apply.

Several middle-aged men with comfortable bank accounts and property responded to Belle's lovelorn column ads. They traveled to Belle's La Porte farm, fat wallets in their pockets and deeds to their farms, all proving that they were men of substance and worthy of Belle's attentions. One of these was John Moo, who arrived from Elbow Lake, Wis. He was a husky man of fifty and brought along with him more than $1,000 to pay off Belle's mortgage, or so he told neighbors who were introduced to him by Belle as her cousin. He disappeared from Belle's farm within a week of his arrival. Next came George Anderson who, like Peter Gunness and John Moo, was a migrant from Norway. Anderson, from Tarkio, Mo., was also a farmer with ready cash and a lovesick heart.

Anderson, however, did not bring all his money with him. He was persuaded to make the long trip to see Belle in La

Porte because her eloquent letters intrigued him. Once there, he realized that Belle, in her mid-forties and gone portly, was not the beauty he expected. Her face was hard, and she had a severe manner about her, but she made Anderson feel at home and provided good dinners for him while he occupied a guest room in her large farmhouse. One night at dinner Belle raised the issue of her mortgage. Anderson agreed that he would pay this off if they decided to wed. He was almost convinced to return to Takio and retrieve his money, then go back to Belle and eternal bliss.

But late that night, Anderson awoke "all in a cold sweat," and he looked up to see Belle standing over him, peering down with a strange look in her eyes. She held a guttering candle in her hand and the expression on her face was so foreboding and sinister that Anderson let out a loud yell. Belle, without a word, ran from the room. Anderson jumped out of bed, dove into his clothes, and fled the dark farmhouse, running up the road and all the way into La Porte, peering over his shoulder down the moonlit road, expecting Belle to come chasing after him at any moment, wildly driving her carriage. Anderson reached the train station and waited for the next train to take him back to Missouri.

The suitors kept coming, but none, except for the apprehensive Anderson, ever left the Gunness farm. At this time, Belle began ordering huge trunks to be delivered to her home. Hack driver Clyde Sturgis delivered many such trunks to Belle from La Porte and later remarked how the heavyset woman would lift these enormous trunks "like boxes of marshmallows," tossing them onto her wide shoulders and carrying them into the house. She kept the shutters of her house closed day and night, and farmers traveling past her house at night saw Belle working in the hog pen area, digging. Her handyman, Lamphere, also spent a good deal of time digging in the hog pen and all about the house and barn.

Meanwhile, the suitors kept coming, all responding to Belle's enticing ads. Ole B. Budsburg, an elderly widower from Iolo, Wis., next appeared. He was last seen alive at the La Porte Savings Bank on Apr. 6, 1907, when he mortgaged his Wisconsin land there, signing over a deed and obtaining several thousand dollars in cash. His sons, Oscar and Mathew Budsburg, it seems, had no idea that their father had gone off to visit the widow Belle. They finally discovered his destination and wrote to Mrs. Gunness who promptly wrote back, saying she had never seen Mr. Budsburg.

Several other middle-aged men appeared and disappeared in brief visits to the Gunness farm throughout 1907. Then, in December 1907, Andrew Hegelein, a bachelor farmer from Aberdeen, S.D., wrote to Belle and was warmly received. The pair exchanged many letters, until Belle unleashed her most amorous masterpiece yet, a letter that overwhelmed the simple Hegelein, written in Belle's own careful handwriting and dated Jan. 13, 1908. (This letter was later found at the Hegelein farm in South Dakota.) It read:

To the Dearest Friend in the World: No woman in the world is happier than I am. I know that you are now to come to me and be my own. I can tell from your letters that you are the man I want. It does not take one long to tell when to like a person, and you I like better than anyone in the world, I know.

Think how we will enjoy each other's company. You, the sweetest man in the whole world. We will be all alone with each other. Can you conceive of anything nicer? I think of you constantly. When I hear your name mentioned, and this is when one of the dear children speaks of you, or I hear myself humming it with the words of an old love song, it is beautiful music to my ears.

My heart beats in wild rapture for you, My Andrew, I love you. Come prepared to stay forever.

That, of course, is exactly what the hapless Hegelein did. In response to her love-gushing letter, the farmer flew to her side in January 1908. He brought with him a check for $2,900, his savings, which he had drawn from his local bank. A few days after Hegelein arrived, he and Belle appeared at the Savings Bank in La Porte and deposited the check for cashing. Hegelein vanished a few days later but Belle appeared at the Savings Bank to make a $500 deposit and another deposit of $700 in the State Bank.

At this time, Belle started to have trouble with her hired hand, Ray Lamphere. The hired hand was deeply in love with Belle and was an apparent slave to her ambitions, performing any chore for her, no matter how gruesome. He became jealous of the many men who arrived to pitch woo at his employer and began making scenes. Belle fired him on Feb. 3, 1908, and then appeared at the La Porte courthouse and declared to authorities that Lamphere was not in his right mind and was a menace to the public. She somehow convinced local authorities to hold a sanity hearing and the grim little Lamphere was examined. He was pronounced sane and sent on his way. Belle was back a few days later to complain to the sheriff that Lamphere had arrived at her farm, despite the fact that she had fired him, and argued with her. She felt that he posed a threat to her family and had Lamphere arrested for trespassing.

The little handyman was persistent. He returned again and again to see Belle but she drove him away. Lamphere made thinly disguised threats about Belle and, on one occasion, said to farmer William Slater that "Hegelein won't

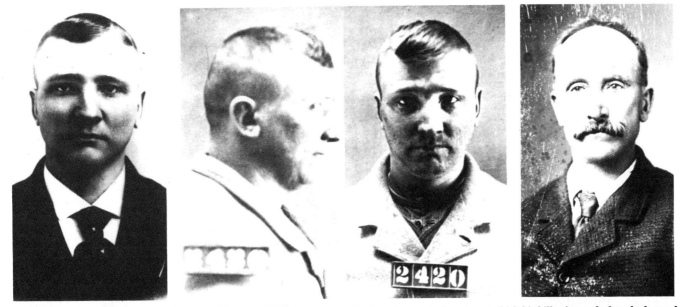

Above left, Belle Gunness as a young woman; middle top, Belle and her three children; middle bottom, Jennie Olson, who disappeared with Belle and may have been the headless corpse the murderess left behind hoping pursuers and gravediggers would believe the body to be her own; right, the cover of a lurid pamphlet of 1908 which depicted Belle approaching one of her victims while he slept—she chloroformed her male suitors in their slumbers.

Left and center (police photos), Andrew Hegelein, one of Belle Gunness' last suitors, had a checkered past which his killer ignored after she learned that he possessed considerable property and a fat bank account; at far right, Asle Hegelein, Andrew's brother, who began investigating his brother's mysterious disappearance, and his snooping caused Belle to panic and quickly arrange her own horrible end, a faked death that included more grisly murder.

bother me no more. We fixed him for keeps." Hegelein had long since disappeared from the precincts of La Porte, or so it was believed. His brother, Asle Hegelein, however, was disturbed when Andrew failed to return home and he wrote to Belle in Indiana, asking her about his brother's whereabouts.

Belle boldly wrote back, telling Asle Hegelein that his brother was not at her farm and probably went to Norway to visit relatives. Hegelein wrote back saying that he did not believe his brother would do that and, moreover, he believed that his brother was still in the La Porte area, the last place he was seen or heard from. Belle Gunness brazened it out, telling Hegelein that if he wanted to come to La Porte and look for his brother, she would help conduct a search for him, but she cautioned Hegelein that searching for missing persons was an expensive proposition, and if she was to be involved in such a manhunt, Asle Hegelein should be prepared to pay her well for her efforts.

Obviously worried about the turn of events, Belle went to a La Porte lawyer, M.E. Leliter, telling him that she feared for her life and that of her children. Ray Lamphere, she said, had threatened to kill her and burn her house down. She wanted to make out a will, in case Lamphere went through with his threats. Leliter complied, drawing up Belle's will. She left her entire estate to her children and then departed Leliter's offices. She went to one of the La Porte banks holding the mortgage for her property and paid this off. Oddly, she did not go to the police to tell them about Lamphere's life-threatening conduct. The reason for this, most later concluded, was that there had been no threats, but that Belle was merely setting the stage for her own arson.

Joe Maxon, who had been hired to replace Lamphere in February 1908, awoke on the night of April 28, 1908, smelling smoke in his room which was on the second floor of the Gunness house. He opened the hall door to a sheet of flames. Maxon screamed Belle's name and those of her children but got no response. He slammed the door and then, in his underwear, leaped from the second-story window of his room, barely surviving the fire that was closing in about him. He raced to town to get help, but by the time the old-fashioned hook and ladder arrived at the farm at early dawn, the farmhouse was a gutted heap of smoking ruins.

The floors had collapsed and four bodies were found in the cellar. The grand piano, Belle's pride and joy, was on top of the bodies. One of the bodies was that of a woman who could not be identified as Belle since she had no head. The head was never found. Nearby, officials found Belle's false teeth. The pathetic little bodies of her children were found next to the corpse. Sheriff Albert H. Smutzer took one look at this carnage and quickly arrested Ray Lamphere

who he knew had made threats about Belle. Lawyer Leliter came forward to recount his tale about Belle's will and how she feared Lamphere would kill her and her family, and burn her house down.

Lamphere did not help his cause much. At the moment Sheriff Smutzer confronted him and before a word was uttered by the lawman, Lamphere blurted: "Did Widow Gunness and the kids get out all right?" He was then told about the fire, but he denied having anything to do with it, claiming that he was not near the farm when the blaze occurred. A youth, John Solyem, was brought forward. He said that he had been watching the Gunness place (he gave no reasons for this) and that he saw Lamphere running down the road from the Gunness house just before the structure erupted in flames.

Lamphere snorted to the boy: "You wouldn't look me in the eye and say that!"

"Yes, I will," replied Solyem bravely. "You found me hiding behind the bushes and you told me you'd kill me if I didn't get out of there."

Lamphere was arrested and charged with murder and arson. Then scores of investigators, sheriff's deputies, coroner's men and many volunteers began to search the ruins for evidence. The body of the headless woman was of deep concern to La Porte residents. C. Christofferson, a neighboring farmer, took one look at the charred remains of this body and said that it was not the remains of Belle Gunness. So did another farmer, L. Nicholson, and so did Mrs. Austin Cutler, an old friend of Mrs. Gunness. More of Belle's old friends, Mrs. Nellie Olander and Mrs. Sigurd Olson, arrived from Chicago. They had known Mrs. Gunness for years. They examined the remains of the headless woman and said it was not that of Belle.

Doctors then measured the remains, and making allowances for the missing neck and head, stated the corpse was that of a woman who stood five feet three inches tall and weighed no more than 150 pounds. Belle, according to her friends and neighbors, as well as the La Porte clothiers who made her dresses and other garments, swore Belle was more than five feet eight inches tall and weighed between 180 and 200 pounds. Detailed measurements of the body were compared with those on file with several La Porte stores where Belle purchased her apparel.

	Victim (inches)	Mrs. Gunness (inches)
Biceps	9	17
Bust	36	46
Waist	26	37
Thigh	25	30
Hips	40	54
Calf	12½	14
Wrist	6	9

Top left, the burned and smoking remains of the Gunness farmhouse outside La Porte, Ind., Apr. 29, 1908, a fire that the infamous Belle set herself; top right, Henry Gurholdt, another Gunness victim whose body was dug up in the pigpen of Belle's farm; bottom right, Ray Lamphere, Belle's ghoulish handyman who helped dig the many graves of her victims and went to prison for life; bottom left, the lonely roads near Belle's house choked with the curious and, middle left, searchers sifting the Gunness house ruins through sluices, looking for human remains.

When the two sets of measurements were placed side by side, the authorities reeled back in bewildered amazement. The headless woman could not possibly have been Belle Gunness, even when the ravages of the fire on the body were taken into account. (The flesh was badly burned but intact.) Moreover, Dr. J. Meyers examined the internal organs of the dead woman. He reported that the woman died of strychnine poisoning. Asle Hegelein then arrived in La Porte and told Sheriff Smutzer that he believed that his brother had met with foul play at Mrs. Gunness' hands. Smutzer seemed disinterested in searching the blackened grounds of the Gunness farm once again, but Hegelein persisted. Then Joe Maxon came forward to tell the sheriff that Mrs. Gunness had had him bring loads of dirt by wheelbarrow to a large area surrounded by a high wire fence where the hogs were fed. Maxon stated that there were many deep depressions in the ground that had been covered by dirt. These filled-in holes, Belle had told Maxon, contained rubbish. She wanted the ground made level, so Maxon filled in the depressions.

Smutzer took a dozen men back to farm and began to dig. On May 3, 1908, the diggers unearthed the body of Jennie Olson. Then they found two more small bodies, that of unidentified children. Then the body of Andrew Hegelein was unearthed. As days progressed and the gruesome work continued, one body after another was discovered in Belle's hog pen: Ole B. Budsburg; Thomas Lindboe of Chicago, who had left Chicago and had gone to work as a hired man for Belle three years earlier; Henry Gurholdt of Scandinavia, Wis., who had gone to wed Belle a year earlier, taking $1,500 to her; Olaf Svenherud, from Chicago; John Moo (or Moe) of Elbow Lake, Wis.; Olaf Lindbloom from Iowa. There were many others who could not be identified. There were the remains of more than forty men and children buried in shallow graves throughout Belle's property.

Ray Lamphere was arrested and tried for murder and arson on May 22, 1908. He pleaded guilty to arson, but denied having murdered Belle and her three children. He was sentenced to twenty years in prison. The little handyman grew ill in prison and died of consumption on Dec. 30, 1909. On Jan. 14, 1910, the Rev. E.A. Schell came forward with a confession that Lamphere had made to him while the clergyman was comforting the dying man. In it, Lamphere revealed the true nature of Belle Gunness, a human monster who killed for profit and who survived her own reported death.

Lamphere had stated to the Reverend Schell and to a fellow convict, Harry Meyers, before his death, that he had not murdered anyone, but that he had helped Belle bury many of her victims. She had her lethal system down to precise procedures. When a victim arrived, Belle made him comfortable, charming him and cooking a large meal. She then drugged his coffee and when the man was in a stupor, she split his head with a meat chopper. Sometimes she would simply wait for the suitor to go to bed and then enter the bedroom by candlelight and chloroform her sleeping victim. A powerful woman, Belle would then carry the body to the basement, place it on a table, and dissect the body. She then bundled the remains and buried these in the hog pen and the grounds about the house. Belle had become an expert at dissection, thanks to instruction she had received from her second husband, the butcher Peter Gunness. To save time, she sometimes poisoned her victims' coffee with strychnine. She also varied her disposal methods, sometimes dumping the corpse into the hog-scalding vat and covering the remains with quicklime. Lamphere even stated that if Belle was overly tired after murdering one of her victims, she merely chopped up the remains and, in the middle of the night, stepped into her hog pen and fed the remains to the hogs.

The handyman also cleared up the mysterious question of the headless female corpse found in the smoking ruins of Belle's home. This woman had been lured from Chicago by Belle on the pretense of serving her as a housekeeper only days before Belle decided to make her permanent escape from La Porte. Belle, according to Lamphere, had drugged the woman, then bashed in her head and decapitated the body, taking the head, which had weights tied to it, to a swamp where she threw it into deep water. Then she chloroformed her very own children, smothered them to death, and dragged their small bodies, along with the headless corpse, to the basement.

She dressed the female corpse in her old clothing, and removed her false teeth, placing these beside the headless corpse to assure it being identified as Belle Gunness. She then torched the house and fled. Lamphere had helped her, he admitted, but Belle had not left by the road where he waited for her after the fire had been set. Belle had betrayed her one-time partner in crime in the end by cutting across open fields and then disappearing into the woods. Lamphere said that Belle was a rich woman, that she had murdered forty-two men by his count, perhaps more, and had taken amounts from them ranging from $1,000 to $32,000. She had accumulated more than $250,000 through her lovelorn murder schemes over the years, a great fortune for those days. She had also left a small amount in one of her savings accounts, but local banks later admitted that Belle had indeed withdrawn most of her funds shortly before the fire.

Belle Gunness was, for several decades, allegedly seen or sighted in cities and towns throughout the U.S. Friends and acquaintances had apparently spotted the wretched woman on the streets of Chicago, San Francisco, New York, and Los Angeles. As late as 1931, Belle was reported alive and living in a Mississippi town where she owned a great deal of property and lived the life of a grande dame. Sheriff Smutzer, for more than twenty years, received an average of two reports a month. She became part of U.S. criminal folklore, a female Bluebeard. A bit of doggerel later emerged which captured the character of the horrific Belle Gunness:

> Belle Gunness lived in In-di-an;
> She always, always had a man;
> Ten, at least, went in her door—
> And were never, never seen no more.
>
> Now, all these men were Norska folk
> Who came to Belle from Minn-e-sote;
> They liked their coffee and their gin:
> They got it—plus a mickey finn.
>
> And now with cleaver poised so sure
> Belle neatly cut their jug-u-lar
> She put them in a bath of lime,
> And left them there for quite some time.
>
> There's red upon the Hoosier moon
> For Belle was strong and full of doom;
> And think of all them Norska men
> Who'll never see St. Paul again.

====

Gurga, Jeffrey, 1947- , U.S. Attorney Jeffrey Gurga tried to commit the perfect murder. In his Chicago apartment, he sketched diagrams and made notes relating to his plans, and in the early hours of Aug. 9, 1982, he broke into a northwest Chicago apartment and stabbed 19-year-old Jeannine Pearson and fatally stabbed her mother, 39-year-old Kathleen Pearson. Gurga, who had worked as a McLean County prosecutor and a defense lawyer, was captured in the apartment where police later found his notes.

During his trial, prosecutors argued that the 36-year-old, who was not acquainted with the women, had attempted to commit a perfect crime by murdering a person without getting caught. During his trial, Gurga, who in 1966 had spent four months in a mental institution, pleaded not guilty by reason of insanity. He was found Guilty, and on Aug. 24, 1983, Judge Thomas Maloney sentenced him to forty years in prison. The Illinois Appellate Court later decided that Gurga should have been found guilty but mentally ill and ordered Maloney to resentence the prisoner. The judge tacked mentally ill on to the ruling but resentenced the lawyer to forty years imprisonment on Oct.

9, 1987, saying, "the court finds no reason whatsoever to change the sentence."

====

Guyon, Melvin Bay (AKA: **Tyrone Little**), 1959- , U.S. In October 1978, officials issued a federal warrant for the arrest of Melvin Bay Guyon, who, with his brother Michael, was wanted on rape, kidnapping, and aggravated robbery charges. About 10:15 a.m. on Aug. 9, 1979, six FBI agents followed Preston Mathis to the apartment of his former girlfriend, Catherine Little, who lived in the Carver Park public housing project in Cleveland with her boyfriend, Guyon, and their two children. When Mathis knocked on the door, Guyon apparently told Little to let Mathis in and went into the bedroom with his son. One FBI agent entered, pushing Mathis and Little aside while 35-year-old Special Agent Johnnie L. Oliver, trailed by another agent, walked down a hallway, shouting that they were FBI officials. When Oliver entered the bedroom, Guyon fatally shot him in the chest with a pistol and then crashed through a small window as the second agent fired at him. Oliver was the third FBI casualty on a day when an unprecedented three agents were shot to death; two FBI agents were shot and killed in an unrelated incident elsewhere. This proved to be the largest single day loss of life in the history of the federal agency.

A few hours after the shooting, Guyon was placed on the FBI's Ten Most Wanted list and the U.S. Justice Department offered a $10,000 reward for information leading to his capture. Five days later, the Cuyahoga County Police Chiefs Association offered an additional $10,000 reward and put the incident in its Silent Tip Observer Program. The search for Melvin Guyon became the most intensive and largest in Cleveland's history. Just after the shooting, 325 officials joined the hunt. Police received about 2,000 tips within a week after the shooting.

Meanwhile, Guyon escaped to Akron, Ohio, and then hitchhiked to Youngstown, where police tracked him through a wiretap on a Cleveland home. On Aug. 16, agents spotted Guyon in a phone booth about 9:30 p.m. and tried to pin him in it with a car, but Guyon escaped. After tumbling down a twelve-foot bank, he ran to the home of Paul Flint. Bleeding, Guyon identified himself and said he was tired of running. Flint drove the fugitive to a hospital where Guyon turned himself over to a security guard. The guard notified Youngstown police who arrived at the hospital and arrested Guyon about 10:25 p.m. Guyon, pleading self-defense, was tried in Cleveland for murder. He said he had mistaken Oliver for a hit man hired by Mathis, Little's rejected boyfriend. On Nov. 1, 1979, he was found Guilty of first-degree murder and sentenced the same day to life imprisonment. Later, Guyon was convicted on a robbery charge, and on Dec. 1, 1979, he received a sentence of six to twenty-five years in prison. See: **Maloney, James.**

H

Haarmann, Fritz (AKA: Ogre of Hanover; Vampire of Hanover), 1879-1925, Ger. Fritz Haarmann was born in Hanover, Ger., on Oct. 25, 1879. As a child he eschewed active games in favor of playing with dolls and dressing in his sisters' clothing. He spent some time as a teenager at a military school but was discharged when he showed signs of epilepsy. After a brief stint working in his father's cigar factory, Haarmann was arrested for sexually assaulting small children and was sent to a mental institution. He escaped from the institution and joined the army but was eventually released as an undesirable.

German mass murderer and cannibal Fritz Haarmann.

Back in Hanover, Haarmann secured a position as a police informer, a job which gave him a small salary and a police badge. At the end of WWI large numbers of young boys poured into Hanover, hunting for work. They slept wherever they could, many camping out in the train station. It was here that Haarmann found most of his victims. Beginning in 1918, Haarmann, often with the help of his homosexual lover, Hans Grans, started the chain of rapes, cannibalism, and murder that earned him the title of the "Ogre of Hanover" or "Vampire of Hanover." Often using his police badge to intimidate the young men, he took them

The Hanover apartment (arrow) where Fritz Haarmann murdered his victims by biting their throats.

to his apartment in Hanover's Jewish ghetto where he sexually assaulted and then killed them, as he later testified at his trial, by biting their throats.

Haarmann's atrocities did not stop with the rapes and murders. When he had killed a victim, he took the body to an attic room where he butchered it. Any clothing or belongings of the victim were sold. Bones, skulls, and other unusable portions were thrown into the nearby river Leine. Haarmann then transported the "edible" portions of the butchered flesh in buckets to the open market in Hanover where he sold it as horse meat to Hanover's starving citizens.

In May 1924, some boys fishing in the river found several human skulls and police investigated. The next month, a homeless boy who had been sleeping at the train station told police that Haarmann had taken indecent liberties with him. As Haarmann was being questioned, police searched his apartment and found incontrovertible evidence of his guilt. Haarmann confessed to the murders and implicated his lover, Hans Grans, as his accomplice.

The skeletal remains dredged from the river and surrounding area accounted for twenty-seven victims. When asked how many boys he had killed, Haarmann cavalierly responded, "It might have been thirty. It might have been forty. I don't remember." Estimates ranged as high as one hundred. Haarmann and Grans were tried at the Hanover Assizes beginning on Dec. 4, 1924. While Grans remained quiet and withdrawn throughout the proceedings, Haarmann smoked cigars, complained that too many women were in the courtroom, and acted bored. Of the twenty-seven murders with which he was charged, Haarmann denied only three, in one case disdainfully claiming that one of the boys was not sufficiently attractive to have merited his interest. Haarmann was finally convicted of the murders of twenty-four young men ranging in age from thirteen to twenty, and he was sentenced to death by decapitation. Grans was convicted also and sentenced to life imprisonment, a sentence later reduced to twelve years. Haarmann was beheaded in Hanover Prison on Apr. 15, 1925.

Haerm, Teet, 1954- , and **Thomas, Allgen Lars**, 1949- , Swed. Beginning in 1984, a number of Swedish prostitutes were murdered and their bodies dissected. On July 19, 1984, the carefully dissected body of 28-year-old Catrine da Costa was found in a plastic garbage bag on a sports field used by the police department. The department's leading expert in forensic medicine, Dr. Teet Haerm, reconstructed the body and determined the identity through fingerprints. A week later, the body of another prostitute, 26-year-old Annika Mors, was found in a public park. Dr. Haerm determined that the victim was savagely murdered and then strangled, and that the same person committed both murders. On Aug. 1, the body of 27-year-old Kristine

Cravache was found naked and strangled near Stockholm's red-light district. Lena Grans, Cats Falk, Lena Bofors, Lena Manson, and Lota Svenson subsequently disappeared and were assumed to have suffered the same fate. Police interviewed other prostitutes, who described a dark-haired boyish man who drove a white Volkswagen. One remembered the license plate number, which was traced and found to belong to Dr. Haerm.

Haerm was arrested as he was performing an autopsy, but he vigorously denied involvement. He was a widower whose wife, Ann-Catrine Haerm, was thought to have committed suicide on Jan. 7, 1982. But after his arrest, police found in Haerm's house pictures of Ann-Catrine with a cord around her neck. Haerm also had published articles in medical journals describing suicide by strangulation and methods of sexual psychopaths. Because of lack of evidence, Haerm was not indicted, but he was released from his medical position, after which time no other prostitute was attacked. In March 1985, the bodies of two of the previous victims, Lena Grans and Cats Falk, were found in a car submerged in the sea near Hamarby. And on Jan. 7, 1986, the body of 22-year-old Tazuga Toyonaga, a Japanese student, was found in Copenhagen, strangled and mutilated in similar fashion.

An interview with a four-year-old girl cracked the case. The social welfare department suspected that she had been sexually molested. The perpetrator was found to be her father, 38-year-old Dr. Allgen Lars Thomas, a colleague of Haerm. Thomas confessed to the molestation, saying that Haerm had been a witness. Then, he confessed to helping Haerm murder the prostitutes. He believed Haerm to be the head of a secret sect dedicated to the extermination of prostitutes, and to cannibalism and necrophilia. On Oct. 28, 1987, Haerm was arrested for the second time and charged with the murders of da Costa, Mors, Cravache, Grans, Falk, Svenson, Manson, Toyonaga, and his wife, Ann-Catrine. Thomas was charged with the rape and murder of Catrine da Costa, and incest with his daughter. Thomas pleaded guilty, while Haerm pleaded not guilty. On Sept. 16, 1988, both Haerm and Thomas were convicted and sentenced to life imprisonment.

Haga, Eric L., 1943- , U.S. Five years after the Sheriff's Department of Kent, Wash., determined that there was not sufficient evidence to continue the investigation into the murder of Mrs. Judith Haga and her daughter Peri Lynn Haga, Prosecutor Christopher Bayley reopened the case and charged the woman's husband Eric L. Haga with first-degree murder on Aug. 30, 1971.

The case presented more than the usual amount of contradiction and innuendo, involving an unfaithful wife, a jealous husband, and a mysterious prowler no one could identify. On the night of July 6, 1966, Haga's wife and daughter were strangled in their suburban home. The next morning, Haga awoke to find them both dead. It was alleged that a prowler had broken into the family's home in the middle of the night.

It was widely known that domestic relations between the Hagas had deteriorated ever since Judith began an extra-marital affair with Dennis Harman of Oregon. The case was reopened in 1971 after Mr. and Mrs. James Matuska of Bothell provided secret testimony to a grand jury concerning the murders. Matuska, who employed Haga as a race car driver, appeared for the prosecution when the case went to trial in December 1971. It was brought out during the trial that Haga doubted Peri Lynn was his daughter, and that he was driven to murder by revenge and desire. Mrs. Haga had a large insurance policy on herself and her daughter, the prosecution argued, which was to be used to finance the purchase of a new sports car. As to the identity of the killer, defense attorneys theorized that Harman, who had a record of mental illness, may have been the prowler who entered the Haga home that night. The argument did not sway the jury.

On Dec. 24, 1971, a Superior Court jury convicted Haga of first-degree murder. The jurors recommended against the death penalty, and Haga was instead sentenced to life in prison.

Hagan, Michael, 1964- , U.S. Vowing to return to the streets with a vengeance, Los Angeles gang member Michael Hagan was sentenced to twenty-seven years to life in September 1987 for the rifle murder of 17-year-old Kellie Mosier, who was in the wrong place at the wrong time.

Claiming that he was high on the drug PCP at the time of the girl's death, Hagan promised that: "One day I'll be back on the streets, and I'm gonna be hard, hard, hard..."

Judge Robert Altman described the defendant as "one of the most remorseless and dangerous individuals" he had encountered during his career on the bench.

Haggart, Robert Lee, 1951- , U.S. Robert Haggart was a drifter. When he worked it was usually as a livestock auctioneer. At least this is what he was doing at the time he married Garnetta Post of Farwell, Mich., in February 1982. Haggart was an ex-convict who was wanted by the police for passing bad checks.

After less than six months of marriage, Garnetta realized

she had made a mistake, and left her husband. She went to live in Florida, but returned to Michigan on Feb. 16 to finalize her divorce and to visit her parents and family members at their secluded frame house in Farwell, 150 miles north of Grand Rapids. It was to be a family reunion for George and Vaudrey Post, who were looking forward to seeing their grown children and grandchildren. Instead, it ended in wholesale slaughter.

Armed with a shotgun, the vengeful Haggart advanced on the Posts' home, which was tucked into the snow-covered backwoods. He shot and killed Garnetta, her parents George and Vaudrey, their other daughter, Helen Gaffney, and three of her children: Angela, ten, Tom, six, and Amy, four. A fourth child, one-year-old Mandy, narrowly escaped death only because her mother had thrown her body over her siblings when the shooting started. It was the first of two grisly Michigan mass murders in thirty days. A month later, five members of an Allendale family were found shot to death in their home. A deranged co-worker of one of the victims was charged in that shooting.

A seven-count murder warrant was issued for Haggart. He was arrested near Jasper, Tenn., on Feb. 18 after George Post's stolen automobile was recognized by a restaurant patron at a roadside diner not far from the Alabama state line. Extradition proceedings were filed with Tennessee authorities, and within a week the murderer was back in Michigan. Haggart was convicted of first-degree murder on Oct. 8, and sentenced to life in prison without parole two weeks later.

Hagger, Harold (AKA: **Sydney Sinclair**), prom. 1946, Brit. On Halloween, 1946, the strangled corpse of a middle-aged woman was found in a clump of bushes on Labour-in-Vain Hill beside the A20 highway outside Wrotham, England. The dead woman was soon identified as Dagmar Petrzywalski, better known as Dagmar Peters, forty-eight, a spinster who traveled weekly to London to visit her brother. Peters' 80-year-old mother explained that her daughter would leave at 5 a.m. to hitchhike into the city, and always carried with her a briefcase and a yellow crocheted bag, a gift from her sister-in-law. Scotland Yard's Chief Inspector Robert Fabian asked Peters' sister-in-law to crochet a duplicate, and then published its photograph in the newspapers. A 15-year-old farm boy, Peter Nash, recognized the bag as one he pulled from Clare Park Lake three days after Peters' body was found. Fabian learned from a local Girl Guide leader that objects tossed into the lake by the mill stream at East Malling floated to Clare Park Lake in a few hours, via an underground stream.

Fabian visited the old mill, which had been turned into a cider factory, and tried the experiment with the crocheted purse.

Pieces of Peters' briefcase were found strewn for a mile along the highway. Fabian found at the cider works a pile of bricks delivered by truck on Oct. 31 by a Cambridge contractor. The driver, Sydney Sinclair, was questioned and soon admitted that his real name was Harold Hagger. An ex-convict with a record of sixteen convictions, including one for assaulting a woman, Hagger confessed that he had given Peters a ride. He claimed that she had tried to steal his wallet from a jacket pocket, they had struggled, and he had accidentally pulled her wool scarf too tight around her neck. Fabian abruptly asked Hagger, "Where was your jacket?" The accused said that it had been "hung on a peg inside the cab." When Hagger was tried at Maidstone Assizes, this ill-considered response (it was a bitterly cold morning when Peters left for London) helped convict him. Hagger was hanged for the murder.

Haggerty, John F., prom. 1917, U.S. Harry Lorenzo Chapin of Cleveland was a physician, poet, and a noted world explorer. His book of verse, *Twilight and Death,* in some ways foreshadowed his own untimely demise. What the poetry-reading public did not know was that Chapin was also a desperate cocaine addict, falling into debt with his supplier John Haggerty, former owner of a Cleveland drug store. In November 1917, Haggerty murdered Dr. Chapin in a room at the Colonial Hotel, off Public Square in downtown Cleveland. Impatient to receive the money that was due him from previous drug transactions, Haggerty tricked his client into meeting him at the hotel with the promise of receiving a new shipment of cocaine. Haggerty had sent the package of worthless junk from Chicago, and had claimed it at the express office.

The pusher and the junkie quarreled briefly; Chapin accused Haggerty of deceit. There was a brief struggle in which Chapin supposedly reached for his gun, according to the testimony later given by the accused murderer. Haggerty crashed a weight down on Dr. Chapin's head and fled the building. Cleveland detectives, working closely with police officials in Chicago, traced Haggerty to Kansas City where he was arrested at the Washington Hotel. Extradited back to Ohio, Haggerty was indicted for first-degree murder at the Common Pleas Court on June 4, 1918. In a plea-bargaining arrangement Haggerty pleaded Guilty to a reduced charge of second-degree murder. Judge Manuel Levine sentenced him to life in prison in the Ohio Penitentiary. Eleven years later he was granted parole, but shortly after he was arrested in Illinois on a robbery charge. When

Haggerty completed his sentence at the Joliet Penitentiary on Oct. 1, 1937, he was returned to Columbus to serve out his original term.

Hahn, Anna Marie, 1906-38, U.S. German-born Anna Marie Hahn moved to Cincinnati, Ohio, with her husband, Phillip Hahn, and their young son, Oscar, in 1929. With her rich contralto voice and her plump, blonde good looks, Hahn delighted the elderly German men in the immigrant community and soon became an unofficial nurse, a self-described "angel of mercy." Many of those under her care died, but grateful relatives left her thousands of dollars from the estates anyway. Ernest Kohler died while under Hahn's care, in 1933, and left her a large house. Dr. Arthur Vos, the second-floor resident of that house, soon found several blank prescription forms missing from his offices and complained to the new owner who shrugged and suggested "maybe one of your patients took them." On June 1, 1937, Jacob Wagner became Hahn's patient. He died on June 2. Days later, George Opendorfer, seventy, died under Hahn's care. The fact that both men had died after acute stomach pains and vomiting was brought to Cincinnati police chief Patrick Hayes' attention. Hayes ordered an autopsy of Wagner's body, and discovered four types of poison in the corpse. Subsequent autopsies of Hahn's other patients, including a man named Palmer and George Gsellman, sixty-seven, revealed more evidence of arsenic and croton oil. Hahn denied killing anyone and asked Hayes, "Why pick on me, chief?" Hayes explained to her that the search of her home had turned up "enough poison to kill half of Cincinnati."

At the trial, Hahn's history of theft, adultery, and forgery was brought out by her own defense lawyers, including Hiram Bolsinger, in an attempt to establish robbery, not murder, as her motive for her dealings with the old men. Dubbed "the beautiful blonde killer" by the press, Hahn was convicted and sentenced to die in the electric chair. The night before her execution, on Dec. 7, 1938, Hahn refused to see her husband or son, but threw a farewell party for the newsmen who had covered her trial, treating them to punch and cakes in her cell. None of these reporters came to her execution early the next morning.

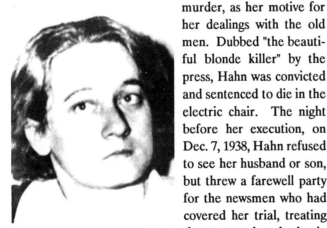
The poisoning nurse, Anna Marie Hahn.

Hahn was the first woman to die in the electric chair in Ohio. She was thirty-two.

Haigh, John George (AKA: **The Acid-Bath Murderer; The Vampire Killer**), 1909-49, Brit. In 1949, John George Haigh burst into the headlines of the British press as an inhuman monster who had been killing for profit for many years. Worse, according to his own statements, the mass murderer had dissolved his victims in acid after drinking their blood. Born in Stamford, Lincolnshire, England, on July 24, 1909, Haigh was raised with strict religious discipline. His parents were ardent members of the Plymouth Brethren, a severe religious sect for whom all manner of casual entertainment, movies, carnivals, musical shows, even the reading of magazines and newspapers, was sinful. A bright child, Haigh received a scholarship to the Wakefield Grammar School and then won another scholarship as a choirboy at Wakefield Cathedral. His life was governed by strict routines and he was allowed no freedom to enjoy the small entertainments shared by his peers.

Acid bath killer John George Haigh.

Haigh scratched for a living in his early twenties, usually working as a salesman. He was glib and somewhat flashy in his appearance, preferring loud ties and tight-fitting suits. He married Beatrice Hamer in 1934 but this marriage quickly collapsed after Haigh was arrested in November of that year for fraud. After serving a brief prison sentence, Haigh was released, and continued his illegal schemes, living hand to mouth through the 1930s and the war years. In 1937, Haigh was convicted of his second serious crime, attempting to obtain money by false pretenses and was given a four-year prison term. He was released in 1940. In 1943, Haigh managed to make enough money through his small-time schemes to take up residence at a highly reputable address, the Onslow Court Hotel in South Kensington where he occupied Room 404. The residents here were professional people and retired persons of some wealth. The other residents regarded Haigh as a congenial entrepreneurial businessman. However, he made few friends because he was a bit too gregarious and showy for the other residents' tastes.

In 1944, Haigh renewed his acquaintance with the Mc-

Swan family. In 1936, he had worked for W.D. McSwan as a secretary and chauffeur. The McSwans owned an arcade in an amusement center and had considerable means. At the time Haigh rented a small basement work-room at 79 Gloucester Road in Kensington where he devoted some time to his "inventions." He took the Mc-Swan's one by one—first the son, Donald McSwan, on Sept. 9, 1944, then Mr. and Mrs. W.D. McSwan the following year. When the McSwan couple expressed concern over their son's disappearance in 1944, Haigh was ready with a glib answer, explaining that their son had gone into hiding to avoid being drafted into the army, a not uncommon occurrence during the war. Haigh's murder system was simple; he invited the McSwan family members to see the place and there bludgeoned them to death. He destroyed their bodies by placing them in vats of acid and disposing of the remains by simply pouring the gooey residue onto the dirt surface of an open yard behind his workshop.

By forging McSwan's name on transfer deeds, Haigh was able to obtain the McSwan properties in Raynes Park, Wimbledon Park, and Beckenham, Kent, as well as £4,000 in cash. Endowed with considerable funds, Haigh tried to make a fortune through a betting system he had devised which he believed could predict regular winners at the dog track. When he lost, he turned again to murder for profit. This time his victims were Dr. Archibald Henderson and his wife Rosalie, well-to-do middle-aged retirees, who, in August 1947, were advertising a house for sale. Haigh, though he had no money, answered the ad and began negotiating for the purchase of the Henderson house in Ladbroke Grove. He later explained that one of his business deals had fallen through, preventing him from purchasing the house immediately.

The amiable Hendersons struck up a friendship with the scheming Haigh. On Feb. 12, 1948, he drove Dr. Hender-son to his workshop where he shot him in the head and disposed of the body by dumping it into a vat of sulfuric acid. He then returned to Mrs. Rosalie Henderson and told her that her husband had taken sick and needed her. She accompanied Haigh to his workshop where he killed and disposed of her body in the same manner. In both the McSwan and Henderson murders, Haigh duplicated his victims' handwriting and sent notes to their servants, relatives, and friends explaining that they had moved to Australia or some other distant place, mentioning that "Mr. Haigh" would settle their affairs. The profits from this double murder exceeded those in the McSwan killings. Haigh, through clever forgeries, sold off the Henderson house and car, and obtained more than £10,000 from their bank accounts. But, within a year, Haigh had gone through most of this money, losing heavily to an army of bookies.

By early 1949, Haigh was running out of money. He was overdrawn at the bank and the manager of the Onslow Court Hotel was pressing him for back rent. Desperate for money, Haigh was looking about for more victims when his needs were answered in the dining room of the Onslow Court Hotel. Sitting opposite Haigh in the hotel dining room was a wealthy, retired matron, Mrs. Henrietta Helen Olivia Robarts Durand-Deacon. The 69-year-old widow knew that Haigh was then in the business of leasing and renting expensive cars to rich patrons and be-lieved that, as a salesman, he might be interested in promoting an idea she had about manufacturing plastic fingernails.

Haigh as a choir boy.

Haigh responded favora-bly to the idea and im-mediately suggested that Mrs. Durand-Deacon dis-cuss the proposition further in his workshop. On Feb. 18, 1949, Mrs. Durand-Deacon accompanied Haigh to the Gloucester address. As soon as she entered the basement workshop, Haigh shot the woman in the back of the head, killing her instantly. He stripped her and then dumped her body into a 40-gallon vat of sulfuric acid. Haigh drained the vat through a basement sewer and then scraped the sludge from the vat and dumped this onto the dirt of the back yard. This was hard work and Haigh, according to his later statements, paused to go to the nearby Ye Olde Ancient Prior's Restaurant where he ate an egg on toast. He then returned to his workshop to "tidy up."

This killing produced little profit for the money-desperate Haigh. He sold Mrs. Durand-Deacon's Persian lamb coat and pawned her jewelry, obtaining only a few hundred pounds. He used this money to pay off his hotel bill and some other pressing expenses and then looked about for more victims. But Haigh had struck too close to home by killing the wealthy widow. To avoid being asked about the widow's disappearance, Haigh thought it clever that *he* make some inquiries about the missing woman. Haigh approached Mrs. Durand-Deacon's good friend, Mrs. Constance Lane, another retired lady living at Onslow Court, plying her with questions: "Do you know anything about Mrs. Durand-Deacon? Is she ill? Do you know where she is?"

Mrs. Lane shocked Haigh with her response: "Don't *you* know where she is? I understood from her that you wanted to take her to your factory."

Haigh said that he had not taken the widow with him to his factory, that he was not yet ready to show her his operation. "Well, I must do something about that," Mrs. Lane said.

The following morning, Haigh again asked Mrs. Lane if she had heard anything about Mrs. Durand-Deacon and she said that she had not, adding that she intended to report the matter to the police that day. In an attempt to avoid suspicion, Haigh then offered to go to the Chelsea Police Station and report the matter with her. But when Mrs. Lane and Haigh appeared in the police station, an officer recognized Haigh and had his background checked. His criminal record made the police suspicious and Haigh was brought in for questioning on Feb. 28, 1949. At first, he denied having had anything to do with the missing Mrs. Durand-Deacon but the police kept grilling him and finally Haigh blurted: "Mrs. Durand-Deacon no longer exists! I've destroyed her with acid...You can't prove murder without a body."

But Haigh was wrong. Police searching his workshop uncovered enough gruesome remains of Mrs. Durand-Deacon to make an identification. Though most of her remains had been reduced to hardened sludge that coated the back yard behind Haigh's workshop, forensic investigators unearthed twenty-eight pounds of body fat, false teeth which were identified as Mrs. Durand-Deacon's, a pelvis, an ankle, gallstones, and a red handbag found in the workshop beneath the acid vat. Haigh had been sloppy in his workshop, as well as in his room at Onslow Court. Here investigators found his diary in which he had kept abbreviated details of his previous murders. Some personal effects from the McSwan and Henderson families were also unearthed.

Haigh was charged with murdering Mrs. Durand-Deacon and placed on trial on July 18, 1949. Prior to this, while being held, Haigh had asked his jailors how hard it was to escape from Broadmoor, the prison where criminally insane persons were sent. Haigh then tried to convince everyone that he was insane. He stated that "in each case I had my glass of blood after I killed them." He then went on to describe in detail all sorts of ghoulish acts performed on his victims, before giving their bodies acid baths. The press, when learning of Haigh's statements, had a field day. No newspaper gave the story more sensational coverage than the London *Daily Mirror,* which, on Mar. 4, 1949, bleated to its fifteen million readers that "the Vampire killer will never strike again. He is safely behind bars, powerless to lure his victims to a hideous death." Above this front-page story, the tabloid emblazoned the headline: "Vampire—A Man Held."

The British courts were appalled at this coverage, so much so that the *Daily Mirror* was fined £10,000 and its editor, Silvester Bolam, was given a three-month jail term for contempt of court, the paper having been previously warned by Scotland Yard not to publish details of the case before Haigh's trial. Bolam, ironically, was placed in the same prison that held Haigh. The mass killer continued to feign insanity while in prison, purposely drinking his own urine in front of guards and performing other irrational acts to convince them that he was a lunatic.

Haigh was tried before Justice Travers Humphreys with Sir Henry Shawcross prosecuting. Sir David Maxwell defended, but he could do little more than plead his client insane. He brought Dr. Henry Yellowlees, a noted psychiatrist, to the stand to testify that he had examined Haigh and believed him to be a "paranoic," because of his early childhood and that he was "pretty certain" that Haigh drank the blood of his victims.

None of this impressed the jury. It took only fifteen minutes for the jury to render a verdict of Guilty. He was sentenced to death. While awaiting execution, Haigh penned his brief, nightmare-filled memoirs, recounting how all his boyhood pleasures had been suppressed by his father, a religious fanatic. His father, an electrician, had had an accident which caused him to bear a blue scar down the middle of his forehead. Haigh quoted his father as telling him when he was a boy: "I have sinned and Satan has punished me. If you ever sin, Satan will mark you with a blue pencil likewise." For years, Haigh, as a child, nervously ran his fingers over his forehead, frantically looking into mirrors each morning to see if a blue scar had appeared while he had slept.

Haigh also related a recurring nightmare he had following a 1944 car accident in which he was injured and blood ran down his forehead and into his mouth, the year in which the killer began his murders: "I saw before me a forest of

Crowd outside Wandsworth Prison, waiting to read Haigh's death notice, Aug. 6, 1949.

crucifixes which gradually turned into trees. At first there appeared to be dew or rain dripping from the branches, but as I approached I realized it was blood...A man went to each tree catching the blood. When the cup was full he approached me. 'Drink,' he said, but I was unable to move."

These horrifying words were penned by a man who undoubtedly still thought he might be reprieved and sent to Broadmoor as criminally insane. Haigh was highly intelligent and able to contrive such lunatic images for his own ends, just as he very probably researched the methods he used in disposing of his victims' bodies, most likely reading about the exploits of Georges Sarret of France who used remarkably similar methods in 1925 to eliminate the bodies of his victims. John George Haigh's horror stories did him no good in the end. The Acid-Bath Murderer was hanged at Wandsworth Prison on Aug. 6, 1949. See: **Sarret, Georges.**

Halberstam, Dr. **Michael**, See: **Welch, Bernard Charles, Jr.**

Hall, George Albert, 1906-54, Brit. A little girl named Mary Hackett disappeared from her home in Halifax, Yorkshire, on Aug. 12, 1953. Scotland Yard was brought into the case when the local authorities had exhausted all their leads.

The girl's parents told officials that their daughter had gone to play just a few hundred feet from her home. Mary had simply vanished; but the detectives were reasonably certain that her murderer was in the immediate area. Across the road from the family home stood the Congregational church, with a maze of crypts and tunnels that had been constructed to protect the townspeople from air raids during WWII. The caretaker of the property, George Albert Hall, aroused the suspicion of Scotland Yard when he claimed to have heard voices emanating from the region of the crypt. After another day had passed, Hall explained that he had observed a stranger lurking on the grounds the day Mary Hackett disappeared.

Superintendent John Ball ordered a detail of police and firemen to dig out the church crypt. It was there, on Sept. 21, 1953, that Mary's body was found. She had been bludgeoned to death, and though Hall denied killing the girl, his testimony showed he knew that she had been battered before the police made this information public.

Hall was tried and found Guilty of murder. He was hanged at Leeds Prison in April 1954, protesting his innocence to the end.

Hall, James W., 1921-46, U.S. "I guess I'll get the electric chair for this, but it don't matter. That would be better than life imprisonment," said James W. Hall, ruminating on his punishment for the murder of six people, five of them during a four-month period.

Not much mattered to the 24-year-old taxi driver from Enola, Ark., who laughed as he confessed to five of the murders, including that of his 19-year-old wife. When a detective asked if he had committed any other murders, Hall at first said no, but then, laughing again, said, "I killed a Negro woman in Salina, Kansas, when I was seventeen. That was seven years ago."

Described by his Little Rock landlady as "a nice, clean boy who never smoked or drank or swore and who always paid his rent on time," Hall killed six people: Faye Clements Hall, his second wife; J.D. Newcomb, Jr., a state boiler inspector; Doyle Mulherin, a meat truck driver; E.C. Adams, a war plant worker; and an unidentified man and woman.

The son of a preacher farmer, Hall was drafted into the navy at nineteen, but discharged after six weeks for indifference. "I don't know what that means," Hall later complained to police when he was arrested. Asked to explain himself, Hall spoke of the past, his ten brothers and sisters. "My early life was far from happy...My father was very strict," he said. By way of explaining the murders, he tapped his head. "Something seemed to snap up here a long time ago," he said.

Hall found most of his victims hitchhiking. Hall would thumb a lift, ride for a bit, and then, after forcing the driver off the road, shoot him or her in the face or the back of the head and take what they had. During four months in which he committed five murders, Hall collected a grand total of less than $200, some cigarettes, electric clocks, watches, and a suitcase. "I always looked in the newspapers the next day to see who they were," he later said.

Hall's most brutal crime was the murder of his second wife. He decided to kill her because she was "wasting our money," he told detectives. "I took her out...near the Riverside golf course," he continued, "led her into a ravine on the riverbank and beat her to death with my hands. I must have hit her more than twenty times over the head." After demonstrating his technique on a police sergeant, Hall led police to the scene of the crime. There he identified his wife's skull. "There's the tooth that used to hurt me when I kissed her," he said.

Hall's mother-in-law, who called him "Red," said, "He...had a wonderful personality until you knew him and found the devil way back in him."

After a three-day trial, Hall was convicted of first-degree murder for killing his wife, a verdict that carried an automatic death penalty. On Jan. 4, 1946, Hall was executed.

Hall, Leo (AKA: **Stewart**), 1902-c.1935, U.S. On a March day in 1934, a gruesome tragedy was uncovered at the Flieder cottage in Erland Point, Wash. The battered and bullet-riddled bodies of six people were found: Mr. and Mrs. Flieder, Mr. and Mrs. Chenovert, Mr. Jordan, and Bert Balcom. The motive was robbery, evidenced by the empty purses and wallets strewn about the house.

It took many months and a new county sheriff before headway was finally made on the case. In January 1935, Sheriff William Severyns assigned Chief Criminal Deputy O.K. Bodia to the case. Bodia had a tough assignment ahead, but he identified Leo Hall, who had been convicted of auto theft several years earlier, as a prime suspect. Loose barroom talk, and the desire for revenge on the part of one of his former associates who had lost his wife to Hall, further convinced Bodia that this was the man responsible for the tragedy.

Hall's wife told of her husband's desperate plan to rob the Flieders of their cash and valuables. Hall was arrested in Portland, Ore., when a complaint was filed with the local police about a man named Stewart who had professed interest in investing in a carburetor business. The individual registering the complaint had invented a carburetor and had discussed the possibility with Mr. Stewart, who had become threatening during the course of the interview. Escaping unhurt, the man tipped the police off about Hall, who was arrested shortly after.

On Dec. 9, 1935, Hall and his girlfriend went on trial. The woman who was a passive witness to the murders was acquitted. Hall was convicted and later hanged.

Hammond, Geoffrey, prom. 1969, Brit. Considered a perfect student, Geoffrey Hammond of Wimbledon had won the Duke of Edinburgh's Award and had demonstrated life-saving techniques on British television. Together with his friends, Hammond selectively harassed homosexuals, on what the boys commonly referred to as "queer bashing" missions.

The boys mostly confined their activities to the vicinity of the Queensmere subway, where they indulged in petty acts of vandalism. One night in 1969, Hammond and his gang pounced on 28-year-old clerk Michael de Gruchy. It was not known if de Gruchy was homosexual, but this did

not matter to Hammond, who was eventually given a life sentence for the murder. Four other boys, ranging in age from fifteen to eighteen, were remanded over to the state. Hammond's father actually defended his son's actions, comparing him to the mountain climber who "scales a mountain just because it is there."

Hampton, Melvin, 1941- , U.S. The controversial insanity plea came under sharp criticism in Cook County, Ill., when the Chicago Read Mental Health Center released murderer Melvin Hampton after determining that he was cured. Twenty months after his discharge on Oct. 24, 1974, Hampton strangled 59-year-old Ruth Thieben to death in her North Side Chicago apartment. The widow had taken pity on the homeless drifter and had provided him with food and lodging before he killed her on July 17, 1976. Police officials expressed amazement at Hampton's release after reviewing his lengthy criminal record.

He had been arrested thirty-seven times in California, Florida, Alabama, Georgia, and Illinois on charges of auto theft, theft of property, assault, and armed robbery. He was convicted only once for prowling. Melvin Hampton was first implicated in a murder in 1968. Three years later, he killed his 39-year-old girlfriend Martha Knight, but was ruled incompetent to stand trial on the grounds of insanity by Judge Louis Garippo. Hampton was sent to a mental health center in downstate Chester, Ill.

He was transferred to the Read Center on Aug. 28, 1974, where he remained until officials pronounced him cured. "The process is beginning to become like a revolving door," said Dr. Edward Kelleher of the County Circuit Court's Psychiatric Institute, echoing the concerns of court watchers. "Basically the law as it's written makes it impossible to keep a fellow like this confined."

Then, on July 27, 1976, Hampton was again found incompetent to stand trial. He was sent back to the Chester facility by Judge James Strunk of the Cook County Criminal Court. "Good Lord in heaven. It's appalling," commented Joseph DiLeonardi, the citywide homicide commander of the Chicago Police Department. "This is his third murder charge and he's beaten all three. That makes him a killer. It's the responsibility of the courts to review his record and put him away. I can see once maybe, but this is the third time. Let's lock him up and keep him there. If they (hospital officials) take into consideration his record, I don't see how they can let him go."

Hanson, William P., 1949- , U.S. A killer who apparently struck at random turned out to be a young man with a divided personality who believed he was avenging the rape of a former girlfriend. William P. Hanson confessed to his crimes, explaining, "I know at least four times I've tried to kill him."

On Oct. 16, 1973, Lorenzo Carniglia was gunned down by a slight blond man who ran up behind him on a San Francisco sidewalk, and shot him with a pistol he had concealed in a brown paper bag. A parking lot attendant watched the man flee, and another witness who had heard the shots looked out his window to see the assailant change shirts, get into a white van, and pull into traffic. Carniglia, who died later that day, was a middle-aged man with a slight limp. The killer became known to police and citizens as the Paper Bag Killer, because he concealed his weapon in a bag.

Detectives Frank Flazon and Jack Cleary investigated the murder, and culled a composite description of a white male, eighteen to twenty years old, with long, blond hair and a "baby face." Crime laboratory reports identified the murder weapon as a .22-caliber pistol. On Dec. 20, 1973, a man in an overcoat stood waiting for the free breakfast at the Life Line Mission at about 8:50 a.m. when a slight, young, blond man approached him. With a pump action shotgun partially hidden by a supermarket shopping bag, the youth fired on the heavy-set, middle-aged man, then sped off in a white Econoline van. Ara Kuznezow, the Paper Bag Killer's second victim, had, like Carniglia, been older and heavy-set, with an apparent limp.

Checking out vans, detectives Flazon and Cleary were contacted on Jan. 25 by a nervous young man who had information, but insisted on anonymity. Meeting with the caller, the detectives learned he was a friend of Hanson. Hanson had shown the youth several guns, and told him he was trying to kill a man who was raping young girls. Hanson explained to his friend that he had in fact killed the man several times, but he kept coming back. Tracking Hanson down to the Redco Delivery Service where he worked, Flazon and Cleary realized that he fit the description of the killer. At the records bureau, Hanson's name came up in connection with the February 1973 attempted knifing of a businessman. When the case was brought to trial, the businessman was traveling and was not present to testify, so charges were dropped. A similar case had occurred in December 1972 when a heavy-set, older man was stabbed at the Greyhound bus depot near Market Street; the man, who survived, had a limp.

On Jan. 26, 1974, Cleary and Flazon went to the upper-middle-class home where Hanson lived with his parents. Making no attempt to resist, Hanson directed them to the closet where they found the loaded shotgun that had killed Kuznezow. A new pistol, also loaded, was under Hanson's

mattress; he had, he later explained, thrown the gun he had killed Carniglia with into San Francisco Bay. Clothing that linked him to both deaths was found in the closet.

Arrested and taken to the Hall of Justice, Hanson confessed. With murder indictments against him in both cases, he was transferred to county prison and held without bond. Attorney Patrick Hallinan told the court that Hanson had a longtime girlfriend who had been raped in late 1972, and believed he was somehow responsible for the occurrence, subsequently murdering in the twisted belief that he was killing her rapist. On May 16, Judge Morton Convin found Hanson Not Guilty by reason of insanity. He was sent to the Atascadero State Hospital for the Criminally Insane.

Hardaker, Betty, 1915- , U.S. "I didn't want her to endure what I had gone through," Betty Hardaker said by way of explaining why she had killed her 5-year-old daughter, Geraldine, a child her mother thought "too good to live."

On the afternoon of Feb. 19, 1940, Hardaker, twenty-five, of Montebello City, Calif., took Geraldine, her eldest and favorite child, for a walk in Montebello City Park. They rode the seesaw, looked at the fish, and then went to the rest room. "I hadn't decided on anything," she told Chief of Police Harry Bispham. "But suddenly I had a strange impulse to end it all...for both of us."

Hardaker then "raised Geraldine up real quick above me, and then pulled her down and hit her head as hard as I could on the washbowl so she wouldn't feel anything." After that, everything went black. Hardaker could not recall leaving the park but did find her way home, where she considered sticking her head in the stove. She decided against it, however, because "the others would be home soon."

Hardaker then put on a sweater and hitchhiked to a nearby Indian reservation, where she spent the night hiding in a shack. Picked up just after noon the next day, she said her name was "Betty Rice," and that she was married and had a small child.

Hardaker's estranged husband, 29-year-old Charles Hardaker, told police that Betty had recently joined a cult that believed in human sacrifices. "She thinks God tells them to kill people."

"Betty started acting strange just a few months ago after she began attending this church," said Betty's mother, Etta Karnes, concurring with her son-in-law. Betty's father, Samuel Karnes, in turn revealed that his daughter had suffered a nervous breakdown three months earlier. And Hardaker herself told Palm Springs physician Dr. Russell

Gray that her breakdown had been precipitated by the birth of her two youngest children, Charles, Jr., five months, and Dixie Ann, fifteen months.

Hardaker said that during the last year she had thought often of killing herself by gassing and had once tried to throw herself in front of a truck. "I heard the voice of God every morning," she told Dr. Gray. "I can't understand what the voice tells me, but it wakes me up." Of her murdered child, Hardaker said, "I can't explain the reason for it. I didn't hate her. I loved her." Hardaker was judged insane.

Hardin, Andrew, 1956- , and **Payne, Clyde**, 1955- , U.S. In the popular 1975 film *Cooley High,* about a high school near Chicago's Cabrini-Green housing project, the part of Robert, a street-tough, inner-city black man, was played by Norman Gibson. A year after the film's release, on Sept. 29, 1976, the 26-year-old Gibson was shot and killed near the same street corner where Hollywood talent agents had discovered him. Two men who jumped out of a car killed him with a shotgun blast to the middle of his back, followed by a shot to the head with a small-caliber handgun. Eyewitnesses were able to identify the attackers. The attack was in apparent retaliation for Gibson's assault of the sister of one of the attackers. Gibson had a long criminal record for robbery and narcotics, and had been released from the Cook County House of Corrections two days before his murder. The two assailants were subsequently arrested. On Jan. 31, 1978, before Judge R. Eugene Pincham, 22-year-old Andrew Hardin and 23-year-old Clyde Payne pleaded guilty to Gibson's murder and were each sentenced to between eighteen and ninety years in prison.

Harper, Calvin, prom. 1920s, U.S. In a Midwestern city during Prohibition, August Greving gave a home brew party and angrily told one of his guests, Calvin Harper, to leave when Harper made overtures to Greving's wife. Threatening revenge as he left, Harper returned several hours later, rang the doorbell, and shot Greving dead when he answered the door. Witnesses to the slaying included Greving's wife and two other female guests. Harper fled, taking a train to a nearby town. Still drunk, his gun fell to the train floor, discharging, and wounding a passenger.

When Harper was arrested at the next stop, police recognized him as Greving's murderer. In the long delay between the arrest and the trial, two of the eyewitnesses were killed in a car accident, and the other vanished. Because there were no ballistics services or medical examiners in the place where the slaying occurred, no autopsy

was performed. The anxious prosecutor ordered the corpse exhumed, and was able to prove that the bullets in the body matched those in Harper's gun. The district attorney, concerned about getting a conviction, made a deal with Harper. Pleading guilty to second-degree murder, the killer was given a ten-year sentence.

Harrelson, Charles, prom. 1979, U.S. On May 29, 1979, U.S. District Judge John Wood, about to preside over a drug conspiracy trial, was shot to death outside his home in San Antonio. A local drug kingpin, Jimmy Chagra, was about to appear before Wood—known as "Maximum John" for the severity of his drug case sentencing. Chagra, a former carpet salesmen, had been smuggling marijuana into the U.S. since the 1960s and had built a drug empire that stretched to both coasts. Local prosecutors and the FBI viewed the murder as an attack on the judicial system and spent three years and $11 million to conduct 30,000 interviews and collect over 500,000 bits of information in an attempt to apprehend the killer. Chagra's brother Joe told investigators that his brother had offered Charles Harrelson $250,000 to kill Wood. In 1983, Chagra was acquitted of murder and of conspiracy to commit murder. He did however, admit to another conspiracy and was sentenced to life imprisonment. To avert his sentence, he became a government witness, and is currently residing in prison under a new identity established by the Federal Witness Protection Program.

Joe Chagra, allowed to plea bargain, was given a six-year sentence for his involvement, but was paroled in March 1988. Charles Harrelson, although denying any involvement, was convicted of Wood's murder, and sentenced to two consecutive life sentences, as well as another five years for obstructing justice. Harrelson had previously served time for a 1968 murder-for-hire. His wife Jo Ann Starr Harrelson, accused of buying the murder weapon, was convicted of perjury and obstructing justice, and was sentenced to twenty-five years. Elizabeth Chagra, Jimmy's wife, was convicted of conspiracy and obstruction of justice, as well as tax fraud, and was sentenced to forty years.

Harries, Thomas Ronald Lewis, 1931-54, Brit. John and Phoebe Harries owned a farm in Llanginning, Wales, and their 24-year-old nephew, Thomas Harries, lived with them. The Harries were last seen on Oct. 16, 1953, at a church service. Thomas Harries told Chief Constable T. Hubert Lewis of Carmarthenshire he had driven them to the Carmarthen railway station where they were to board a train to London for a "secret holiday." But it seemed uncharacteristic of 63-year-old John Harries and his wife to leave the farm in disarray and the animals unfed. Three weeks later, Lewis notified Scotland Yard.

Chief Superintendent John Capstick soon learned from 15-year-old Brian Powell that Thomas Harries had made some peculiar remarks about his aunt and uncle. Summoned to help with the farm work, Powell heard Harries say, "They won't miss this one," as he slipped a paintbrush in his pocket. Capstick also noticed an uncooked piece of meat in the stove. Thomas Harries had recently cashed a check made out to his father on which £9 was overwritten to read £909.

Thomas Harries, British killer.

Capstick strung reels of thread around the farm and every exit from it to the surrounding fields, believing that sooner or later Harries would visit the grave site where he had buried the bodies. On Nov. 16, police found the shallow graves of the victims, whose heads had been smashed in. "I am sorry to hear uncle and auntie are dead. I was their favorite," Harries said. Further investigation revealed that Harries had murdered the couple with a borrowed hammer. Harries was convicted on Mar. 16, 1954, and later hanged at Swansea Prison.

Harris, Jean Struven, 1923- , U.S. Dr. Herman Tarnower, known as "Hi," grossed more than $11 million from his best-selling *Scarsdale Diet,* published in 1979. Tarnower met Jean Harris, a divorced mother of two, at a Manhattan dinner party in 1966. She had graduated *magna cum laude* from Smith College in 1945, and by 1972, was the headmistress of the exclusive Madeira School for girls in McLean, Va. Her students called her "Integrity Jean" because of her numerous lectures about self-control, commitment to excellence, and propriety.

Following their meeting at the home of Leslie Jacobson, Tarnower and Harris began their lengthy courtship. There was talk of marriage, but it never got past the discussion stage. Tarnower, fifty-eight at the time of his "engagement" to Harris in 1967, entertained a variety of women at his estate in Purchase, N.Y. One of these several women, Lynne Tryforos, a 38-year-old medical assistant, replaced Harris as the doctor's favorite. In 1977, Jean Harris first became aware of Tarnower's philandering. On New Year's Day, Harris was with Tarnower at a Palm Beach resort when she saw a personal advertisement in the New York *Times* that read "Happy New Year, Hi T. Love Always, Lynne."

A long struggle followed between the two rivals for the doctor's affections. Harris and Tryforos cut up each other's clothes, and Harris accused Tryforos of placing obscene phone calls. It was clear that Tarnower favored the younger Tryforos, but he continued to rely on Harris to help him prepare his diet book. The situation soon became intolerable to Harris, who drove directly from McLean to the Tarnower estate on Mar. 10, 1980. In her purse was a .32-caliber handgun and the amphetamines she needed for courage. At eleven that night, after Tarnower's dinner guests had left, Harris drove up in her blue 1973 Chrysler. She climbed the darkened staircase, entered the doctor's bedroom, and fired four shots. Tarnower slumped over dead and Harris fled the grounds. Rushing to the window, the startled housekeeper saw Harris getting into her car.

Before Jean Harris could make her getaway, Scarsdale police intercepted her. "He wanted to live. I wanted to die," she told them. Harris' intention had been to persuade Tarnower to shoot her. A long, rambling letter describing her physical and mental subjugation to Tarnower corroborated her story and established a motive. Jean Harris was charged with second degree murder. Her trial, sensationalized in tabloids, began in the White Plains, N.Y., courtroom of Judge Russell R. Leggett in November 1980. On Feb. 4, 1981, the infamous "Scarsdale Letter," mailed from Virginia the day of the murder, was introduced into evidence. "Going through the hell of the past few years has

Jean Struven Harris, rejected lover and killer; her victim, millionaire doctor Herman Tarnower.

been bearable only because you were still there and I could be with you," it read in part. The letter failed to sway the jury. On Feb. 24, they returned a verdict of Guilty. Harris was sentenced on Mar. 20 to a term of life in prison at the Bedford Hills Correctional Facility. She remains an inmate there and is involved in prison reform. Her book about her

Dr. Tarnower's Scarsdale, N.Y., estate, the murder site.

prison experience, *They Always Call Us Ladies,* was published in 1988.

Harris, Pleasant, prom. 1923-28, U.S. In New Orleans on May 20, 1923, just after midnight, a woman's screams were heard. Dashing toward the nearby police headquarters was Katherine Wilson, pursued by a man with a gun, who, overtaking the woman, beat her with the butt of his gun and then shot her. As scores of detectives and officers poured from headquarters, the killer simply vanished. The trail of blood followed by Captain Archie Rennyson, warden of the prison, and detective sergeant Joseph Hadley led to a boarding house, where they questioned Wilson's friend, Edith Wright. Wright told them she had met some friends of Wilson's, including Pleasant Harris, Wilson's sometime boyfriend. Harris had apparently followed Katherine Wilson when she went downstairs to answer the doorbell and pursued her into the street, where he murdered her.

Tipped off about a fight in a bar the night prior to the killing, police learned that Harris had assaulted a friend of Wilson's. Superintendent of police Thomas Healy tracked down Harris' brother's house; there he found a stained, pink silk shirt on a clothesline, and a matching collar flecked with blood. Further investigation showed that Harris was wanted in several other cities, including Detroit, Mich. In July 1926, more than three years after the crime, Detroit chief of detectives Fox tracked Harris through baggage checks to Atlantic City, N.J. Extradited to New Orleans, Harris was tried on May 27, 1927, before Judge J. Arthur Charbonnet; District Attorney Stanley and assistant J. Bernard Cooks prosecuted. The state's surprise witness, a woman who overheard Wilson and Harris fighting, testified that Harris had fired on Wilson another time before the murder.

This, combined with the evidence of Cassius L. Clay, the city chemist, who proved that the silk shirt and collar were stained with human blood, convicted Harris after a four-day trial. Found Guilty of first-degree murder, Harris was sentenced by Judge Charbonnet to be hanged, but the sentence was later commuted by Governor Huey P. Long to a term of life in prison at Baton Rouge Penitentiary.

Harris, Robert Alton, 1953- , U.S. On the morning of July 5, 1978, two 16-year-old boys from Mira Mesa High School in San Diego, Calif., sat in their car in the parking lot of a fast food restaurant. As the youths, John Mayeski and Michael Baker, prepared to eat the hamburgers they had just bought, two brothers, Robert Alton Harris and Danny Harris, approached the car. Robert Harris showed the boys the 9-mm Luger he carried, told them he wanted their car for a bank robbery, and falsely assured them that they would not be harmed. The gunman then forced the boys to drive the car to a deserted area near the Miramar Reservoir.

Once at the reservoir, Harris had the boys get out of the car and shot both boys execution style, forcing them to beg for their lives, pleas which the vicious murderer had no intention of granting. Robert and Danny Harris fled the scene with the stolen auto. Apparently unaffected by the slayings, Robert Harris had the impunity to consume the half-eaten hamburgers the two boys had left in the car. Later that same day Robert Harris was arrested by San Diego police officer Steve Baker, who, at the time of the arrest, did not know that his own son had been one of Harris' victims.

Harris was brought to trial in 1979. He took the witness stand twice during the trial and claimed that his brother, Danny, had killed the boys. Danny Harris testified later in the trial against his brother. Robert Harris was convicted of the murders and during the sentencing phase of the trial confessed to the killings and said he was sorry. He was sentenced to die in the gas chamber at San Quentin prison and has been on Death Row ever since. If carried out the sentence would be the first execution in California since 1962. Harris and his lawyers have engaged in continual appeals since his conviction and sentencing. Four different execution dates have been set, but all have thus far been stayed.

Harrison, Daniel Paul (Paul), 1903- , U.S. "I feel the overpowering urge to kill. I must conquer this impulse or it will drive me to take someone's life," wrote

Daniel Paul Harrison in his diary. He could control the impulse only so long, however, before it began to control him. By the time he was apprehended, he had murdered five people, three of them friends.

Born in North Carolina to a genteel Southern family, Harrison spent the leisure hours of his childhood painting, writing poetry, making music, and reading Shakespeare. In his early twenties he moved to Chicago, found work as a clerk, and married. Life seemed to be on his side, but slowly he began to change. Observing himself with alarm, Harrison considered seeing a psychiatrist. "But I'm afraid to do so," he wrote in his diary, "for he may confine me to an institution."

One night, Harrison's wife, Marie, woke to find her husband leaning over her, a heavy clock in his hand. "I'm going to kill you! Kill you!" he cried. Marie escaped and locked herself in the bathroom, and when she emerged thirty minutes later, Harrison was asleep. The next time she saw him, at her lawyer's office, he said he must have been having a nightmare and pleaded with her to return. Marie refused and soon filed for divorce.

Harrison remarried soon after, in an afternoon ceremony, but that very night his second wife, Margaret, walked out. Ostensibly having left for work that evening, Harrison returned to their rooming house at midnight to find his wife gone. (She had gone out for food.) "I'm going to kill her! Kill, kill, kill!" he shouted, brandishing a hammer at the landlady. Margaret returned to find Harrison gone. After listening to the landlady's alarming story, Margaret fled to her mother's and soon after filed for divorce.

Harrison was losing control. Fired from his clerking job, he found work as an auto mechanic but not for long. In December 1930, sent by his garage to repair a car that had broken down in a funeral procession, Harrison joined the mourners. Upon seeing the face of the deceased—a young woman—he felt an intense pleasure. So began his visits to wakes and the morgue. "Soon the satisfaction of looking at corpses probably will pass away and then I will kill! Oh, why was I born?" he wrote.

Fired from the garage and low on funds, Harrison moved into a dollar-a-week hotel on West Van Buren Street. One by one he sold off his mechanic's tools until only his hammer remained. Then one night he awoke from a dream of murder to find that he had smashed a fellow derelict in the head with his hammer.

On Mar. 1, 1931, Harrison met Joseph Hardy, a 26-year-old Kentucky mountaineer who was selling moonshine for twenty cents a pint to homeless men on West Madison Street. The two decided to go south together, and Hardy handed Harrison a revolver, "just in case." Hours later, in Elmwood Park, they forced Frank J. Murray and Norma Newby to drive them to the Elmwood Park Forest Preserve.

There, in an isolated grove, Harrison, provoked when Newby called him "crazy," beat Newby to death with his gun and Murray into unconsciousness.

En route to Virginia, Hardy and Harrison robbed at least six businesses. One night, however, Hardy fled when he heard Harrison moan in his sleep of his need to kill. Harrison returned to Chicago and on Jan. 9, 1932, crushed the skull of his friend Charles Pagel, an itinerant laborer, with five hammer blows. Some days later he killed acquaintance Charles Tyrell with the same hammer.

On Jan. 23, Harrison visited Dr. James Shaffer, a 56-year-old dentist. Occupied by a crossword puzzle, Shaffer asked Harrison if he knew a five-letter word for "insane." "Crazy," murmured the dentist, answering his own question. Harrison killed him with the hammer. Then, on Jan. 31, Harrison visited acquaintance Gene Davis, twenty-two, at the garage where he worked. When Harrison asked Davis to loan him a car, Davis laughed and said, "You must be crazy." Harrison crushed his skull.

Finding a bottle of sleeping pills near Davis' body, police were able to track Harrison to his home. He confessed, and the next day was pronounced a homicidal maniac by two psychiatrists. On Feb. 25, 1932, Harrison entered the State Hospital for the Criminal Insane at Chester, Ill., where he would often request solitary confinement. "I feel it coming on," he explained to the guards. "If you leave me with the others, I'll have to kill."

On Feb. 12, 1938, Harrison and fellow inmate Peter Florek, escaped from the hospital, only to be recaptured several days later. Harrison often vowed to escape, once telling a guard: "I'm not mad. You're mad to think you can keep me in here. I'll get loose again some day and then I'll kill. Do you understand? Kill!"

Harsh, George S., 1907-80, U.S. In 1929, in Atlanta, George Harsh and Richard Gallory were sentenced to death by electrocution following their conviction for the murder of a drugstore clerk. The two men, both from wealthy, socially prominent families, were also accused of seven other crimes, including a second murder. Harsh's family sought to save his life and enlisted a dozen psychiatrists to explain his social inadequacies. Harsh and Gallory later had their sentences commuted to life imprisonment on a Georgia chain gang. In 1940, Harsh was paroled after saving a fellow prisoner's life by performing an appendectomy.

After his release, Harsh joined the Royal Canadian Air Force and was shot down by the Germans during WWII. Harsh was held in a Nazi prison camp and was instrumental in aiding more than 100 Allied prisoners to escape, an effort which was documented in the film *The Great Escape*. After the war, Harsh began a crusade against capital punishment, recounting his moral redemption and experiences in an autobiography entitled *A Lonesome Road*. He brought attention to the fact that he had been saved only because he was a member of a wealthy and white class, and that a poor, underprivileged person might never have had the opportunity for redemption. Harsh lived in Toronto until his death on Jan. 25, 1980.

Hart, Michael George, 1947-   , Brit. A thorough and painstaking investigation by Scotland Yard turned up a murderous bank robber, who was arrested within a year of his crime.

On Nov. 10, 1976, Michael George Hart walked into the Barclays Bank in Richmond, Surrey, England, on Upper Ham Road, and shoved a sawed-off shotgun at teller Angela Woolliscroft, twenty, ordering her to give him money and to hurry up. When Woolliscroft turned over £2,500 in notes of different denominations, the robber fired, hitting her in the chest and hand; she died on the way to the hospital.

Through the bank staff, Scotland Yard detectives James Sewell, Alan Wadsworth, and Bob Hancock put together a description of a slim man of about twenty-five, wearing large-framed sunglasses. When the killer fled, he had left behind a woman's yellow raincoat with two pieces of crumpled paper in the pocket, and an orange plastic bag that had once contained chemical fertilizer. The papers proved to be an entry to a wine-making contest, signed by "Grahame," and a shopping list. Grahame James Marshall heard this information on the radio and went to the police to identify his 1974 paper, explaining that the list was written by his sister. On Nov. 10, the sister had parked her car in a ramp space, and noticed that it was in a slightly different position when she returned. Her raincoat and sunglasses were also missing from the back seat; she did not bother to report it. Detectives pieced together the theory that the killer had parked his own car nearby, used Marshall's to commit the crime, then drove back to the ramp after the robbery, taking off with his original car.

When ballistics experts at the Scotland Yard laboratory determined that a twelve-gauge shotgun had been used in the slaying, they soon after received news from an informant that Hart had been observed transferring what appeared to be a shotgun from one car to another the day of the crime. Hart was interviewed, but, because he had a good alibi, and there was no evidence to connect him with the Barclays robbery, he was released, remaining just one of many suspects.

Twelve days after the killing, police answered a call about a car accident in Basingstoke; Hart had abandoned his car at the scene and fled. In the trunk of the auto police found a Hendal .22 automatic pistol and seventy-two rounds of ammunition. Police then went to Hart's home address, where they found a box containing cartridges that matched those found in Woolliscroft's corpse.

A self-employed builder before the slaying, Hart had worked at a gas station. On Jan. 20, 1977, he went to pick up some back wages from the Station Supreme Ltd. in Middlesex, and was arrested by officer Ronald Hines. Held for questioning, he unsuccessfully attempted to hang himself, then later confessed all, calling the death "an accident," and showing detectives where he had thrown the gun into the river. In the time following the murder, Hart had lived by burglary, fraud, theft, and receiving stolen property—some thirty-nine offenses, often assisted by his chauffeur, Sharon Stacey. Stacey was sentenced at the Old Bailey to three years in prison for passing £777 in worthless checks while with Hart. Justice Melford Stevenson sentenced Hart to life in prison.

Hartson, Dorothy, prom. 1978, S. Afri. On Aug. 13, 1978, Wilford Cahill, thirty-six, a strong, vital farmer in Cape Province, S. Afri., was discovered dead in his bed by his wife, Laura Cahill. When the family physician, Dr. Ian Barton, examined the corpse, he told the widow he could not issue a death certificate until he had a second opinion. Dr. Peter Drysdale, the Cape Town coroner, confirmed Barton's suspicion that the rich farmer had been poisoned. Police discovered an empty beer bottle in the kitchen garbage that contained traces of strychnine. They also found a bundle of love letters in Laura Cahill's bedroom, and soon discovered through servants Buster Diggens, a 44-year-old mechanic on the farm, and Melanie N'Gomo, a 16-year-old maid, that Mrs. Cahill and the farm manager, Denis Hartson, had been carrying on an affair for almost a year. Hartson, who had come to the farm in May 1974, and married Dorothy Ekquist soon after, had been involved with his employer's wife since September 1977.

Both Cahill, the sole heir to her husband's estate, and Hartson were arrested and taken to Cape Town police headquarters for questioning. Both admitted to their liaison, and both denied killing Cahill. Suspicious that the couple could not maintain their stories independently, and unable to believe that they would have chosen such an obvious and detectable method, police questioned both N'Gomo and Diggens. Although he had been discharged twice before for violence against an employer, Diggens had an air-tight alibi. N'Gomo, who had accused Diggens of committing the crime, had thrown out the lethal beer bottle, but had not noticed anything unusual.

Laura Cahill and Denis Hartson were turned over to the prosecutors office and were about to be charged with murder and conspiracy to commit murder when, on Sept. 1, Dorothy Hartson went to Inspector Brian Harrison to tell him that she had killed Cahill, poisoning him, with the hope that his wife would be hanged for the murder, after she had discovered her husband's affair. "It didn't occur to me that Denis would be suspected," she explained, adding that she loved him even though he had cheated on her. In February 1979, Dorothy Hartson was tried and found Guilty, but given the relatively light sentence of twenty years in prison because of extenuating circumstances.

Harvey-Bugg, William Benjamin, c.1931- , Aus. William Harvey-Bugg was raised primarily by his grandmother, and as a young boy was constantly in trouble with police. By the time he left school at age fifteen, he had been charged twice with theft and five times with burglary.

When Harvey-Bugg was seventeen, he decided to leave Sydney, Aus., to take a job as a farm hand in the Blue Mountains of New South Wales. On Sept. 26, 1948, his employer, 50-year-old James Lyon Walker Barton, and Barton's 45-year-old sister, Luie Loveday Walker Barton, drove to church, leaving the teenager to amuse himself. He practiced shooting a .22-gauge rifle and then read a crime paperback. When he heard the Bartons returning, he hid in the garage with the loaded gun, listening as Barton stopped the car to let his sister out. Barton drove into the garage, got out of the car, and the teenager shot him in the head. When the man dropped to the ground, Harvey-Bugg shot him in the head again. Then the youth shot at Barton's sister through the window of her upstairs bedroom. When she came out the front door, she saw the farm hand pointing the rifle at her. As she turned, he shot her twice in the back. After putting Barton's body in the grain shed and taking Luie Barton's body into the pantry, the young man stole about twenty-five war savings certificates worth one pound face value each. He then packed and drove the Bartons' car to Sydney where he stayed with his friend, Charles Ivan le Gallien. He told le Gallien that he had killed his boss for the car, but le Gallien did not take him seriously.

Harvey-Bugg then traveled to Brisbane and checked into a Salvation Army hostel on Sept. 29. The next day he was arrested by New South Wales investigators and taken to Sydney for trial. About the same time, another murder was splashed across the newspapers. Charles Louis Havelock le Gallien had been killed by his son, Charles Ivan le Gallien.

At Harvey-Bugg's trial, his defense lawyer entered the first plea of insanity in Australia's history. The teenager was, however, found Guilty of murder and sentenced to life in prison.

Hauptfleisch, Petrus Stephanus Francois, c.1885-1926, S. Afri. Petrus Hauptfleisch served in WWI for four years before he returned in 1919 to Richmond, in Cape Province, with a wife and child. After losing his wife and child because of his drunken rages, Hauptfleisch lived with his 67-year-old widowed mother, Barbara Gertrude Hauptfleisch, in Richmond. He eventually took a job in a slaughterhouse and his drinking binges became more frequent. His mother discussed his temper with a neighbor and soon the town blacklisted him, preventing anyone from selling alcohol to him. Sober, his conduct improved and on Dec. 7, 1924, he was taken off the town's blacklist.

He stumbled home three days later, drunk and threatening to stone his mother to death. She was so frightened that she went to a neighbor's house and a constable was called. Hauptfleisch was jailed for the night to sober up, and two days later he was blacklisted again.

Hauptfleisch blamed his mother for cutting off his alcohol supply and on Jan. 13, 1925, he suffocated the old woman as she napped. Dragging her body to the kitchen, he poured gas on her and set her body on fire. Then he ran to a neighbor's house, yelling that his mother had died in a kitchen fire.

Hauptfleisch was arrested and tried for murder in September 1926. The residents of Richmond were so infuriated that the trial was moved to Cape Town. His mother was found to have been suffocated but no soot was found in her lungs, indicating that she did not die while cleaning a chimney with gas, as her son had claimed. He was convicted of murder, and on Dec. 23, 1926, he was hanged.

Hawk, Ralph, prom. 1937, U.S. Ralph Hawk made plans to marry 20-year-old Catharine Gelwix on Jan. 1, 1937, but in the meantime found a new love in a nearby town. On Dec. 31, Hawk and Gelwix sat up late discussing their upcoming wedding. Then Hawk left, saying he might return. He later went back to the Gelwix house where he doused a sleeping Mrs. Gelwix and her daughter, 15-year-old Helen Louise, in Marion, Pa., with kerosene. Setting them ablaze, he found his fiancée and struck her on the head with a flashlight. He then soaked her with kerosene and set her on fire. A couple sitting outside in a car saw the fire and the young man rushed into the house, pulling Catharine to safety.

Police had little to connect Hawk with the crime until they discovered that Mrs. Gelwix had written a letter to Hawk, accusing him of dating another girl. After questioning the girl, they arrested Hawk and he confessed to the crime. He was tried, convicted, and sentenced to death.

Hay, Gordon, 1940- , Scot. On Aug. 5, 1957, Gordon Hay met 15-year-old Linda Peacock at a fair in Scotland, and talked with her for less than a minute. The next night, at about 10:20, the 17-year-old struck Linda on the head and strangled her in a cemetery in Biggar, a town between Glasgow and Edinburgh. The graveyard was not far from Hay's boarding school. When detectives found her body the next day there was a bite mark on her right breast.

Hay was arrested after police investigations and forensic odontology linked him to the murder, the first murder suspect in Scotland to be identified by teeth marks. Hay was convicted of murder, but because he was a minor at the time of the crime, was sentenced to be held in custody.

Hays, Henry Francis, 1952- , and **Knowles, James Llewellyn** (AKA: **Tiger**), 1964- , U.S. In 1981, a racially charged trial became the catalyst for a murder of an innocent teenager in Alabama. The trial, in which a black man was charged with the murder of a white Birmingham police officer, was originally scheduled to be held in Birmingham, but received a change of venue to Mobile at the last moment. Ku Klux Klan members in the town became incensed when jurors were unable to come to a decision, and a mistrial was declared on Mar. 30, 1981.

To retaliate, that evening two Klan members, 29-year-old Henry Francis Hays and 17-year-old James Llewellyn Knowles, went out searching for a black man to murder. They spotted 19-year-old Michael Donald, asked him for directions, and abducted him at gunpoint, forcing him into their car. The Klansmen drove to the next county where Donald attempted to flee his captors. Once recaptured, the two assailants beat him more than a hundred times with branches from a tree before slitting his throat. They put his body into their car and drove to a party at the house of Klansman Bennie Jack Hays. There, they hung Donald's body from a tree.

Hays and Knowles were tried for murder and on Dec. 10, 1983, a jury of one black and eleven whites found 29-year-old Hays Guilty and recommended life imprisonment. On Feb. 2, 1984, Circuit Judge Braxton Kittrell, Jr., in-

creased the penalty, and sentenced the killer to be electrocuted. Knowles pleaded guilty to a federal civil rights charge, was convicted, and sentenced to life in prison.

Later, Michael Donald's mother, Beulah Mae Donald, and the National Association for the Advancement of Colored People sued the Ku Klux Klan. On Feb. 12, 1987, an all-white jury awarded them $7 million in damages.

Hearn, John Wayne, See: **Black, Robert**.

Heath, Neville George Clevely (AKA: **Lord Dudley; Group Commander Rupert Brooke; Lt. Col. Armstrong; Blyth; Denvers**), 1917-46, Brit. On the night of June 20, 1946, Neville George Clevely Heath met Margery Gardner at the Panama Club in the South Kensington section of London. The rakish, handsome Heath was a recent veteran of the South African Air Force but was discharged in August 1945 for wearing military decorations he had not earned. Earlier in his career Heath joined the Royal Air Force, but was court-martialed in August 1937 for being absent without leave. Heath had been in trouble with the law before joining the military. In July 1938 he was sentenced to Borstal for housebreaking and stealing jewelry. But until he picked up Gardner, he had never murdered.

Gardner was separated from her husband, and lived a bohemian life, frequenting London pubs while earning her living as a part-time film extra. At the Panama Club she was known as "Ocelot Margie" for the imitation animal skin coat she often wore. Gardner and Heath left the Panama Club together. They took a taxi to the Pembridge Court Hotel in Notting Hill. The next morning the badly beaten corpse of Gardner was found in the hotel room. The body bore evidence of a sadistic sexual assault. Gardner had been tied to the bedpost and whipped. The police quickly identified Heath as the probable murder. Photographs of Heath were taken from his residence in Wimbledon, but the photos were withheld from the newspapers to avoid compromising the case against Heath. However, his name and description were released.

Heath then traveled down the south coast to the Sussex resort of Worthington. There he wined and dined Yvonne Symonds, a girl he had met at a public dance in Chelsea. Though she had known Heath for only a few hours, she found him fascinating. When she saw his name in the papers as a suspect in the Gardner murder, she confronted him, asking, "What sort of person could commit a brutal crime like that?" "A sex maniac, I suppose," Heath replied. He assured Symonds that he planned to return to London to clear himself of the accusation, but instead proceeded to Bournemouth. Heath registered at the Tollard Royal Hotel using the name Captain Rupert Brooke, the British poet who was killed in Greece during WWI. Heath sent a letter to Police Superintendent Thomas Barratt disclaiming any responsibility for Gardner's murder. He did admit however, renting the room in which Gardner was found murdered. "She had met an acquaintance with whom she felt obliged to sleep," Heath went on to say. Heath said when he returned to the room later and found the body he realized he "was in an invidious position. I have the instrument with which Mrs. Gardner was beaten and am forwarding this to you today. You will find my fingerprints on it, but you should find others as well."

On July 3, Heath invited 21-year-old Doreen Marshall to tea. The young woman was recovering from influenza at the Norfolk Hotel, and appeared to be pale and distressed while in Heath's company. Two days later the hotel

manager notified police of her disappearance. On July 8, a search party found the woman horribly mutilated and lying dead in a patch of rhododendron bushes in Branksome Chine. She had been slashed with a knife and a string of artificial pearls were found strewn about the body. They matched a single pearl found in Heath's pocket. Authorities also found in his

Lady killer Neville Heath.

pocket a cloakroom ticket, which led them to a suitcase in a locker; the suitcase contained a riding whip.

Heath was charged with murdering both women, but when the trial opened at the Old Bailey on Sept. 24, the court concerned itself only with the murder of Margery Gardner. Defense attorney J.D. Casswell attempted to show that his client was certifiably insane at the time the murders were committed. He called Dr. William Henry De Bargue Hubert to the stand. Hubert testified that Heath was "morally insane." But the jury was not satisfied that the lady killer was deranged when he committed his crimes. A verdict of Guilty was returned, and the defendant was sentenced to die by hanging on Sept. 26. The sentence was carried out at Pentonville Prison on Oct. 26. Neville George Clevely Heath's last request was for a shot of whisky. He said, "In the circumstances, you might make that a double!"

Heldenberg, Raymonde, 1916- , and **Heldenberg, Isoline**, 1943- , and **Heldenberg, Martine**, 1954- , Fr. Robert Heldenberg, a 56-year-old Parisian trumpet player who drank heavily and chased women, frequently beat his 53-year-old wife, Raymonde. In early 1966, Raymonde Heldenberg sought and obtained a legal separation, which allowed cohabitation until the end of September. On Sept. 26, 1966, Raymonde and her two daughters, 26-year-old Isoline and 15-year-old Martine, murdered Robert Heldenberg by giving him barbiturates and strangling him with a scarf. They overturned furniture and gave bruises to one another to support a defense of justifiable homicide. After three years, on Sept. 23, 1969, Raymonde Heldenberg was found Guilty of the murder of her husband and sentenced to five years in prison. The two daughters received suspended sentences.

Henderson, Clem (Clemmie), 1947-88, U.S. The shooting rampage that Clem Henderson began on Sept. 22, 1988, might have lasted a good deal longer than it did, and cost many more lives than the five who died, if not for two Chicago police officers who happened to be on hand. Although both officers were shot by Henderson, 38-year-old patrolman Gregory Jaglowski shot the gunman to death with his last bullet, as he lay at the side of his dead partner.

Almost three years before the shooting, on Oct. 6, 1985, Henderson was alleged to have been shot in the head by youthful attackers; an incident believed to have led to the murder spree. No police record of the shooting was on file however, and the autopsy of Henderson revealed no evidence of the earlier shooting—though the Cook County Hospital did have a record of Henderson shooting himself in the head. Henderson also had been arrested twelve times between 1973 and 1984, spending more than six years in jail and one-and-a-half years on probation for mostly battery and disorderly conduct charges.

The 1988 shooting began at the Comet Auto Parts store on Chicago's Near West Side. In the store, Henderson fired his .38-caliber revolver three times, killing the store's 41-year-old owner John Van Dyke, and 27-year-old manager Robert J. Quinn, and missing 24-year-old employee Christopher Ferguson, who pretended he was shot as Henderson left the building. Outside the store Henderson wounded city street and sanitation worker Chestnut Ladose, with a gunshot to his hand, and then ran toward the Moses Montefiore Public School—a school for problem youths in need of discipline—where he shot 34-year-old school custodian Arthur Baker in the chest. Baker staggered to the principal's office and gasped, "Please call the police," before he fell to the floor and died. The police, however, were already on the premises, answering a call about a student who had pushed a teacher. By the time Jaglowski and his 40-year-old partner, Irma Ruiz arrived, the student had fled, but on their way out they encountered the killer.

Jaglowski reached the front entrance ahead of Ruiz, and a bullet barely missed his face before he dove to the ground where Henderson shot him in the leg. Henderson left Jaglowski lying on the sidewalk and ran into the school where he shot Ruiz in the chest. The mother of four became only the second female officer in Chicago to be killed in the line of duty. (Dorelle C. Brandon was accidentally killed by her partner on Jan. 25, 1984, as the two struggled with a suspect for control of her service revolver.) While Henderson was reloading his gun down a corridor, Jaglowski went to Ruiz's aid, and was calling for help on her radio when Henderson returned. During an exchange of gunfire, Jaglowski was shot in the other leg before he fatally shot Henderson. For his heroics, Jaglowski received the Blue Star Award on Sept. 28, 1988, for being wounded while in the line of duty. Jaglowski was also promoted to detective by police superintendent LeRoy Martin, in lieu of a $500 check presented to the department by an appreciative citizen. Officers are not allowed to accept monetary gifts for performing their duty. Jaglowski did not see himself as a hero, but claimed that Ruiz was the true hero.

⸻

Hendricks, David, 1954- , U.S. Between the hours of 8:30 p.m. on Nov. 8, 1983, and 2 a.m. the following morning, 30-year-old Susan Hendricks and her three children, aged five to nine, were stabbed and bludgeoned to death with an ax and butcher knife in their Bloomington, Ill., home. Her husband, David Hendricks, claimed that he had left on a business trip to Wisconsin at 11 p.m. on the night of the killings. Evidence later showed that Hendricks had left much later.

The prosecution case sought to demonstrate that Hendricks had changed from a member of a fundamentalist religious organization, called the Plymouth Brethren, into a man who craved extramarital affairs. He was accused of committing the brutal murders because his wife and children stood in the way of his social life, which had changed considerably since 1980 when he shaved his mustache, got a new hairstyle, and began to dress more fashionably. Aside from the change in his appearance and character, prosecutors noted that the murder weapons belonged to Hendricks, no forced entry into the home was used, and the alleged business trip was probably a poorly planned alibi.

After a ten-week trial, Hendricks was found Guilty in 1984 following a change of venue to Rockford, Ill., where Judge Richard Baner refused to invoke the death penalty because he was not without a reasonable doubt that Hendricks was guilty. Instead, he sentenced Hendricks to four consecutive terms of life in prison.

Hendricks appealed his conviction to the Illinois Supreme Court which upheld the jury's decision on Dec. 21, 1988. Justice William Clark, who wrote the dissenting opinion for the court, argued that the prosecution's case was based solely on the defendant's character, and that a man's past did not point to a motive and thus was no basis for conviction of murder. In writing the majority opinion, Justice Joseph Cunningham agreed with Clark, but in the case of Hendricks he felt that "the relationship between the two key aspects of the motive theory is not tenuous but convincing."

⸻

Henley, Elmer Wayne, See: **Corll, Dean Allen.**

⸻

Henriot, Michel, 1910-45, Fr. Silver fox breeder Michel Henriot of Kerbennec, Fr., needed money to raise his foxes, and to remedy this predicament, he decided to marry—with his eye on the dowry a wife would bring him. The 24-year-old bachelor met Georgette Deglave, nineteen, through a matrimonial journal, and the two were married on Oct. 10, 1933; Deglave brought 160,000 francs with her. That amount proved insufficient for his needs, so Henriot set about to insure the life of his new bride.

Deglave was an unhealthy girl, having sustained a head injury early in life which left her partially paralyzed, and she did not enjoy physical or sexual contact. In addition to Henriot's ugly appearance, he had sadistic tendencies—it was well known in Brittany that he would shoot animals just to watch them die, rather than kill them outright—to which he soon subjected Deglave. Before the wedding, her family did not heed her reservations about marrying Henriot, but her younger sister retained all the letters Deglave wrote telling of the horrors her husband perpetrated.

While the two lived at the isolated home on the dunes of Kerbennec, Henriot arranged for he and his wife to be insured. The policy he finally settled on would bring him 800,000 francs in the event of Deglave's death due to "accidents, murder and cyclones." The policy, Henriot later noted, also covered his untimely death; a clause which proved highly unnecessary.

On May 8, Deglave refused her husband's sexual advances. Enraged by her refusal, Henriot grabbed a fireplace poker and beat her over the head. She managed to free herself and staggered up the stairs to the telephone where she called for help. She had contacted the operator when five shots from Henriot's Lebel 5.55mm gun interrupted the call. Deglave fell dead with wounds to her head and chest, and the operator, not understanding the importance of the gunshots and screams he heard, disconnected the line. Blood stains indicated that Henriot then dragged his wife's body into the bedroom, before running out to inform his neighbors of the mysterious intruder who had shot her. Understandably, they saw no stranger enter or leave the home.

Before making a statement to the police, amid tears and spells of faintness, Henriot instructed someone to contact his insurance company in Paris. At first the police did not suspect the husband—mainly because his father was the local prosecutor—but Henriot was soon the suspect when police learned that an intruder would not likely know how to use Henriot's foreign shotgun with its complicated mechanism. The discovery of Deglave's incriminating diary, along with the letters to her sister, heaped suspicion on Henriot. The last entry, five days before the killing, noted, "Michel told me he would kill me." Henriot confessed and stated that "the argument began over a sexual matter...but there was also the desire in me to see blood flowing." He later added, "I wanted the pleasure of shooting something new." Henriot was found Guilty but insane at his trial in Vannes.

Henry, Toni Jo (AKA: **Annie Beatrice McQuiston; Annie Beatrice Henry**), 1916-42, U.S. Toni Jo Henry had spent the better part of her life in and out of trouble. This reformed drug addict became a prostitute in her early teens; was arrested six times between seventeen and twenty-one; once for beating a man with a bottle and snipping his ears.

Claude D. "Cowboy" Henry was a customer of his wife-to-be in the Fall of 1939; they married in November. Claude Henry had been convicted of killing a former San Antonio, Texas, police officer after a barroom fight, and was out on bail awaiting a retrial when the two met and married. On Jan. 27, 1940, a second jury in Hondo, Texas—after a change of venue was ordered—found him Guilty and he was sentenced to fifty years in prison. Within two weeks, Toni Henry decided to break her husband out of prison with the help of Harold Finnon "Arkansas" Burks, also known as Lloyd Adams, a former prisoner held at the same prison in Huntsville. She paid two youths to steal sixteen guns, mostly .32-caliber and .38-caliber revolvers, and ammunition from a Beaumont, Texas, hardware store. Henry and Burks then hitchhiked along a Louisiana highway looking for a fast getaway car.

Unfortunately for Joseph Calloway, he picked up the rain-drenched hitchhikers en route to Jennings from Houston. After passing through Lake Charles, La., Henry pulled a gun on Calloway, and then Burks drove the car toward the Gulf of Mexico. Burks pulled the car over and Henry forced Calloway to walk a short distance from the car. Out of Burks' view, she told Calloway to strip and say his prayers. He did as he was told, and Henry shot him directly between the eyes with her .32-caliber revolver. She grabbed his clothes so her husband could change out of his prison gray's after his escape, and returned to the car. At that point, Burks became scared of his partner and soon ditched her in Camden. He was later arrested in Warren, Ark., and Henry turned herself in.

The police did not at first believe Henry's story of murder when she surrendered to authorities in her hometown of Shreveport, La. Nor did the story seem plausible as the search, led by Henry herself, failed to turn up a dead body. The "haystack," where the body was supposed to be hidden, proved to be a rice-chaff stack, and when police finally believed her story, she remembered she still carried the man's wallet and license.

Henry became quite unruly after the body was found, attacking newspaper photographers, and refusing to identify Burks until convinced to do so by her husband. She then retracted her confession and blamed Burks for the killing, but her detailed account of the murder scene proved to be too knowledgeable for the innocent man. Burks, in his turn, claimed he never intended to break her husband out of jail.

Defense lawyers for Mrs. Henry managed to have separate trials for the murderers. Each was found Guilty and sentenced to die in the electric chair. Henry appealed the conviction, but a second jury also found her Guilty. She again appealed, and a third jury convicted her on Jan. 24, 1942. This conviction was upheld by the Louisiana State Supreme Court. With the governor, Sam H. Jones, stating no pardon would be granted, her death was scheduled for Nov. 28, 1942. Mrs. Henry then admitted she alone had murdered Calloway, but Burks was executed anyway in March 1943.

Announcement of Henry's impending execution prompted her husband to escape from a prison farm on Nov. 22, with the hope of freeing her. Rumors spread throughout the area that he planned to kidnap or kill the judges, John T. Hood at the first trial, and Mark Pickrel of the last two, and security around the men as well as the prison holding Henry was extremely tight. Claude Henry made it as far as Beaumont before a number of heavily armed officers apprehended the escaped convict in a hotel. Husband and wife were not allowed to see each other, but a long-distance phone call was granted and the condemned woman told her husband to give up crime.

Henson, Tom, prom. 1943-44, U.S. On June 6, 1943, the bodies of Milt and Clyde Clayton were found on Lookout Mountain, near Gadsden, Ala. Their throats had been cut and their pockets emptied, indicating a possible robbery. Milt's car was discovered abandoned two-and-one-half miles from the bodies. The front seat was soaked with blood—apparently the site of the murder. A complaint to the police earlier that morning by Tom Henson provided the first lead in the case. Henson notified Gadsden's Chief of Detectives, Fay Boman, that the night before a man named Jed Johnson had forced him at gunpoint to jump off Noccalula Falls. Henson claimed that Johnson had threatened to kill him after he had beaten up a friend of Johnson's, Harry Paxton, and that Milt had intervened on his behalf. According to Henson, Johnson decided not to kill him, but still ordered him to jump over the falls. Henson claimed that before he jumped, he heard Johnson threaten the Claytons. It was true that Henson had beaten up Paxton, but the rest of his story was false.

Police questioned Johnson, and though he knew of Henson and Clyde, he claimed he did not even know who Milt was. His alibi of drunkenness the night before was corroborated by the operator of a bootleg joint. Johnson was even wearing the same clothes he wore the previous evening, which should have been blood-stained if he had killed the Claytons. Boman decided to question Henson once again. The chief realized that Henson knew too much and was probably lying. He believed that Henson had dressed like Johnson—accounting for witnesses who saw a man wearing similar clothes—and killed the Claytons for the $800 that Milt was reported to have been carrying. Boman's hunch was correct; after cleverly bluffing, Henson confessed. Two trials were needed before the jury was convinced of Henson's Guilt, and on Feb. 17, 1944, he was sentenced to life in prison at the Alabama State Penitentiary.

Henwood, Frank Harold, 1879-1929, U.S. On May 24, 1911, a dispute between 31-year-old Frank Harold Henwood and 32-year-old Sylvester Louis "Tony" Von Phul over the affections of Isabelle Patterson Springer ended in the shooting death of Von Phul and an innocent bystander, who died one week later.

In the spring of 1911, Von Phul, a St. Louis wine salesman, had come to Denver, where Mrs. Springer and her wealthy banker husband John W. Springer lived. He soon became involved in an intimate relationship with Mrs. Springer, as letters the two wrote one another clearly showed. The wine salesman returned to St. Louis, and in his absence, Henwood arrived in April and replaced him

as Mrs. Springer's lover. On May 18, the two were observed in compromising situations at the Springer's ranch by the maid, the housekeeper, Cora Carpenter, and the chauffeur, Thomas Lepper. Mrs. Springer told Henwood of some letters Von Phul was threatening to reveal to her husband, unless she continued as his mistress. On May 23, Von Phul returned to Denver, and Henwood met him at the Brown Palace Hotel, where Springer rented a suite for his wife. The two agreed to discuss matters that evening.

Before their arranged encounter, Henwood caught Von Phul meeting with Mrs. Springer and her mother at a department store. An argument ensued which the two men agreed to settle later at the hotel. Once inside the hotel room, Von Phul locked the door, and after Henwood pleaded with him to return the letters in question, he slapped him and then struck him over the head with a wooden shoe rack. Von Phul then threatened Henwood with a gun that he carried in his hip pocket, and ordered him to leave. Von Phul returned to Mrs. Springer's suite and warned her to stay away from Henwood. He mutilated her photographs of the man, and later mailed them to his rival.

Meanwhile, Henwood notified Police Chief Armstrong of the fight, but Armstrong could do nothing unless Henwood filed a complaint, which he refused to do. That night Von Phul exchanged his hotel room for one next door to Mrs. Springer's. During the change his gun was placed in the hotel safe, where it remained for the fatal confrontation the following night.

On the morning of May 24, Von Phul again warned Mrs. Springer not to go near Henwood. She in turn warned Henwood, who after purchasing a .38-caliber revolver tried to persuade her to speak to Armstrong. Springer refused. Later that night in the hotel bar, Von Phul walked up to Henwood and stuck his finger in Henwood's glass of wine and made a comment that caused an angry reply from Henwood. Von Phul then punched Henwood in the face, knocking him to the floor. Henwood drew his gun and fired all six shots. The first bullet hit Von Phul in the shoulder, the second in the wrist, and the third in the groin. Henwood's remaining shots were fired at random, one struck J.W. Atkins and two hit G.E. Copeland; both men were shot in the leg. Henwood surrendered to police in the lobby. Von Phul was taken to the hospital by taxi—refusing an ambulance. He died the next morning without revealing the reason for the fight. On May 31, District Attorney Willis Elliot officially charged Henwood with murder and repeated the charge on June 2, the day after Copeland died from gangrene. Mrs. Springer, meanwhile had fled Denver, but returned to the city on June 12, the day Henwood's trial for the murder of Copeland began.

For Henwood to be found Guilty of murdering Copeland,

the prosecutor would have to prove he murdered Von Phul first, but for reasons unknown the case before Judge Greely W. Whitford was for the murder of Copeland. John T. Bottom represented Henwood, but to no avail, especially after Mrs. Springer testified that Henwood was an "unwanted meddler" in the affair. The jury found him Guilty of second-degree murder on June 28, 1911. Before sentencing, Bottom informed the judge and prosecutor that if the Von Phul case was tried and his client found Not Guilty, he would demand Henwood's release with a writ of habeas corpus. The Von Phul charge was not pressed. On July 26, Bottom called for a new trial, complaining of Judge Whitford's charge to the jury—he had informed them that "there is no manslaughter in this case"—and of collusion on the part of the district attorney. Henwood then made a statement in which he harangued Whitford for holding prejudicial proceedings and of cavorting with the prosecution. Whitford sentenced him to life imprisonment.

The Colorado Supreme Court agreed to look into the matter, allowing Henwood to remain in the city jail under a writ of supersedeas. Because of Whitford's charge to the jury, a new trial was granted and began on May 28. In February, Bottom was granted a dismissal of the Von Phul murder charge, but was unable to have the Copeland murder charge dismissed. Judge Charles C. Butler presided over the retrial, allowing testimony from the first trial to be read, since Carpenter, Lepper, and Mrs. Springer no longer lived in Denver. On June 17, Bottom introduced Springer on Henwood's behalf. Henwood thought he would be acquitted after Springer said only good things about Henwood. The jury felt otherwise and found Henwood Guilty of first-degree murder. He was sentenced to death, and after numerous appeals by Bottom were denied, the lawyer finally convinced Governor Elias M. Ammons to commute the sentence to life in prison on Oct. 16, 1914, a week before his scheduled execution. Ten years later Henwood was paroled, but was returned to prison after a waitress filed a complaint against him.

Hetenyi, George Paul, c.1909- , U.S. The body of 25-year-old Jean G.R. Gareis Hetenyi was found in the Genesee River near West Brighton, N.Y., on Apr. 23, 1949. Her death resulted from two .25-caliber bullets that lodged in her torso after entering her body at each shoulder and following a downward path. Two days later, after more than 600 people had paraded through the morgue, fingerprints taken during a job application were matched to those of the victim, an Amherst, N.Y., mother of two. Suspicion fell upon her husband, the Reverend George Paul Hetenyi, who had not yet reported his wife missing. He first refused

to identify the body, but finally consented. Prior to returning to Rochester with Sheriff Albert W. Skinner to view his wife's corpse, Hetenyi was taken to breakfast where he remarked, "I prefer to pay for my breakfast. I only will let you pay for my funeral."

Though at first held only as a material witness, Hetenyi was officially charged with murder on Apr. 27. Police discovered that a slug found in the Hetenyi car matched the slugs found in Mrs. Hetenyi's body. The car also displayed signs of a careless attempt to remove blood stains from the upholstery, and bloodstained rags were found behind the driver's seat. It was also determined that the woman's death had occurred in Monroe County, where the trial would be held, and not in Erie or Genesee county as earlier believed. Witnesses noted that the Hetenyis fought constantly since their marriage on Aug. 16, 1945. William B. Gareis claimed that Hetenyi had threatened his daughter's life. The defense argued that Hetenyi was insane. He had displayed fits of rage, including breaking a window with his hand, before being charged with the murder. But on June 4, 1949, he was found fit to stand trial.

A jury deliberated for seven hours before finding Hetenyi Guilty of second-degree murder on Dec. 16, eleven days after the trial began. One month later, Monroe County Judge Daniel J. O'Mara sentenced the Hungarian-born pastor to fifty years in prison. Defense counsel George J. Skivington, who argued that no motive had been proved, successfully appealed the decision, which was reversed on July 13, 1950. The success was short-lived, however, for a second jury took six hours on May 12, 1951, to find Hetenyi Guilty of first-degree murder. Judge James P. O'Connor sentenced him to death in the electric chair on May 29. This verdict was also appealed, and, as before, a new trial was granted. Hetenyi was found Guilty for a third time on Mar. 6, 1953, again for second-degree murder. He was sentenced to forty years in prison on Mar. 30. He remained imprisoned until his parole on June 6, 1966.

Hewett, Jack, 1907- , Brit. Sarah Ann Blake, the 55-year-old widow who owned the Crown and Anchor Inn between Pangbourne and Henley, England, was found dead on the morning of Mar. 4, 1922, the victim of a brutal attack the previous night. More than sixty bruises and wounds covered her body, according to pathologist Sir Bernard Spilsbury, who conducted the autopsy. Blake's skull had been fractured four times, and it was apparent that many of the blows and stab wounds had been inflicted after the fatal four-inch-long gash to the back of the neck. No weapon was found on the premises, though there was evidence of a violent struggle, and bloodstained beer mugs indicated that the murderer might have been a guest. The last guest to see the woman alive was 15-year-old Jack Hewett, but no one suspected the boy, who was eager to help police.

On Mar. 14, the knife that killed Blake was found in a hedge thirty-three yards from the inn. Three days later Robert Alfred Shepperd, who had just been released from jail for a petty offense, confessed to the crime, but it was proved he could not have committed the murder. It was not until almost a month later that a photo of the knife was recognized by Joseph Haynes, foreman of the Paddocks Farm where Jack Hewett worked. Haynes identified the knife as Hewett's. Jack was questioned on Apr. 4, 1922, by local Police Superintendent Wastie, Scotland Yard Chief Inspector Helden, and Detective Sergeant Ryan. He confessed to the murder and signed the statement. Following his arrest, Jack stated, "I wish I had never seen the pictures. They are the cause of all this." Two days later he made a second confession to Caversham police constable Buswell, identifying his beer mug from a picture of the crime scene. Jack's trial took place on June 2 and 3 before Justice Shearman at the Oxford Assizes.

At his trial Jack recanted his confessions, claiming that he had not known what he was signing. The evidence against the youth, however, was overwhelming. The murder weapon had been identified as his and he was placed at the scene of the crime. Two officers had observed him searching through the hedge where the knife was later found. No one had seen him outside the grocery store during the time of the murder, when Jack claimed he was there. Grocer Samuel Smith did not remember seeing Jack at all that night. Human blood stains were found on the jacket he wore that day. Jack asserted his innocence, stating he had sold the knife long ago, though to whom he could not remember. The only evidence in his favor was that the iron bar used to bludgeon Blake was never found, nor was the mysterious bicyclist witnesses claimed to have seen on Mar. 2. The jury found Jack Guilty, but spared him the hangman's noose. He was sentenced to be detained indefinitely.

Hickock, Richard Eugene, 1932-65, and **Smith, Perry**, 1929-65, U.S. Richard Hickock and Perry Smith were habitual criminals, professional burglars, and thieves. Neither man was mentally sound, according to reports. Hickock had suffered headaches since a car crash in 1950 and Smith was diagnosed a paranoid long before both men became infamous for their slaughter of the Clutter family. While serving time in the Kansas State Penitentiary at Lansing, Hickock learned from his cellmate, Floyd Wells,

of a wealthy farmer in Holcomb, Kan., Herbert W. Clutter. Wells, who used to work for Clutter, told Hickock that the farmer often kept as much as $10,000 in a safe in his home.

Upon his release, Hickock teamed up with Smith. Both men planned to rob the Clutter family and then retire to South America where they would while away their lives diving for treasure from a boat they would buy from the spoils of the Clutter robbery. The two thieves entered the home of the Clutter family on the night of Nov. 15, 1959. Both men held their victims at bay with guns and knives, deciding what to do with them. They tied them up and then systematically searched the house. Failing to find anything other than about $50, Hickock and Smith turned in a rage upon the helpless Clutter family, which included Herbert Clutter, forty-eight; Bonnie Clutter, forty-five; daughter Nancy, sixteen; and son Kenyon, fifteen. They stabbed and shot the four members of the family and then fled the Holcomb, Kan., farmhouse.

Wells, who was still an inmate of the Kansas State Prison, heard the news of the Clutter deaths on the radio in his cell and he asked to see the warden, telling him about

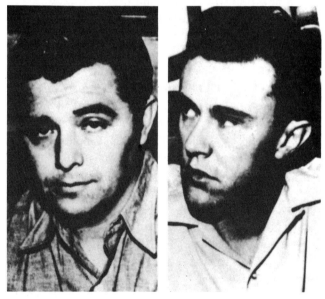

Richard Hickock and Perry Smith, killers of the Clutter family.

Hickock's talk with him earlier concerning the Clutters. Detective Al Dewey then led an exhaustive hunt for Hickock and Smith, finally running both men down in Las Vegas, N.M., where they were arrested. The murderous thieves immediately turned on each other. Hickock told authorities that "Perry Smith killed the Clutters. I couldn't stop him. He killed them all!"

Smith denied killing anyone. Then he said of Herbert Clutter: "He was a nice gentleman. I thought so right up to the time I cut his throat." He later said he killed only the wife, Bonnie Clutter, and that Hickock murdered the rest. Smith added, as if to make himself appear noble, that

Hickock insisted upon raping the 16-year-old daughter Nancy but he had kept Hickock from sexually abusing the girl. Only Herbert Clutter was knifed, his throat cut from ear to ear and his body then thrown into the basement of the house. The others were murdered as they sat tied to chairs, Hickock and Smith taking turns blowing off their heads with a shotgun.

Both Hickock and Smith were tried in March 1960 in Kansas City. The prosecutor in the case aggressively pilloried the two men, aptly describing them as inhuman beasts and reminding the jury that "chicken-hearted jurors" before them had allowed ruthless murderers to go free. The jury found Hickock and Smith Guilty on four counts of murder and both men were sentenced to death. Appeals were denied and each man, quaking and screaming for mercy, were half-dragged to the gallows inside the Kansas State Prison at Lansing on Apr. 14, 1965, and promptly hanged.

Hicswa, Joseph, prom. 1946, U.S. Private First-Class Joseph Hicswa was found Guilty of murder for the killing of two Japanese civilians during a drunken fight. For the crime the U.S. Army sentenced Hicswa to death, but in May 1946, President Harry S. Truman used his power as chief executive to reduce the sentence to thirty years at hard labor. The president's decision was based on the advocate general's review of the case, which claimed there was no premeditation, Hicswa was mentally incapacitated at the time, and the death penalty was excessive punishment. Truman's decision also overturned what would have been a case involving the first serviceman executed for killing or raping a German or Japanese citizen.

Hilaire, Marcel, 1906- , Fr. Hard-working Marcel Hilaire put in long hours at the mill he owned and ran in the Loire Valley, in the small town of Mer, Fr. He thought that a man working this hard deserved a little pleasure, and he found his in a tryst with Christiane Page, the 20-year-old daughter of one of Hilaire's investors. Odette Hilaire, Marcel's wife, hoped that his interest in the woman half his age would eventually wane.

Hilaire's relationship with Page had started in January 1948, and had never been very discreet. She worked as his secretary in his new business—importing and selling agricultural machinery. This business required frequent trips to Paris, and Page always accompanied Hilaire. As time passed, she began pressuring him to get an apartment in Paris. In December 1948, he finally relented, though he was not happy about how much it cost to keep his mistress.

Soon after Page moved into her new home in Sceaux, the couple began to have frequent and often brutal fights. Hilaire was apparently having second thoughts about sacrificing a prosperous career to support both a family and an affair. He tried to break off the relationship, but Page would not let him go. She claimed she wanted to become a nun and got all the way to the gate of the Convent of Salbris before losing her nerve and begging Hilaire to take her back.

He did, but only until another plan could be formulated. That plan was carried out on Feb. 20, 1949, when Hilaire and the foreman of his Mer mill, Roland Petit, picked Page up for a drink at the airport in Orly. They stopped off at Saint-Ay, where they picked up another friend, Robert Bouguereau. With Hilaire driving, the four were riding along the busy highway when Hilaire suddenly killed the headlights, claiming there was something wrong with the car. When they pulled over, Page got out to stretch. Hilaire walked up behind her and shot her twice in the back of the head.

With the help of Petit and Bouguereau, Hilaire dumped the body in the well on the Hilaire property in Mer. The killer promptly terminated his lease on the home in Sceaux, and returned to his wife and three daughters. Two weeks later, when a rotten smell was wafting up from the well, Hilaire ordered Bouguereau and Petit to fill the well with sand. Mrs. Hilaire, relieved that her husband had reappeared, asked no questions.

The police asked questions, but not for almost ten months. The landlord of Page's Sceaux apartment was suspicious of her disappearance, and of Hilaire's story that she had run off after a fight. Pressed by police, Hilaire lost his confidence and his story became shaky. Eventually, he admitted to the killing.

A confession might seem enough to convict a man of premeditated murder, which in France is known as assassination. But Marcel Hilaire hired the most able defense attorney in France, Rene Floriot, who managed to convince the jury that the murderer made too many mistakes to have planned it. Killing Page on a busy highway in front of two witnesses proved that Hilaire had acted on the spur of the moment, Floriot argued.

The argument worked, and Hilaire was found Guilty of murder, not assassination. He was sentenced to life in prison, but eventually had his sentence reduced due to good behavior and because, while serving as chief accountant for the Melun Penitentiary, he devised an accounting system that was to be accepted by the entire French penal system. Roland Petit was found Guilty of complicity and sentenced to two years. Robert Bouguereau was found Guilty of illegally receiving and disposing of a human body, and was given a two-year suspended sentence.

in prison pending further legal action.

Hileman, Doyle, 1939-71, U.S. In 1971, Doyle Hileman approached his step-daughter Diane Linn McConnell, sixteen, on a Des Moines, Iowa, street, and attempted to pull her into his car. When she broke free and ran, Hileman took a .22-caliber pistol and fired twice into her back. He walked up to her and fired once more into her stomach, then returned to his car and drove away.

Diane died in an ambulance on the way to the hospital. The police later found Hileman's car in a bean field near Des Moines, with a hose hooked to the exhaust pipe and leading into the car. Hileman's body was in the back seat. It was revealed through the step-father's diaries that he had been in love with his step-daughter and had attempted in the past to seduce her, but she had spurned his advances.

Hill, James Douglas, 1959- , U.S. Eight years after he murdered a 12-year-old girl, James Douglas Hill was in plea negotiations to reduce his death sentence to a twenty-five-year prison term.

Hill, a mildly retarded 29-year-old, was convicted and sentenced to death for the 1980 murder of Rosa Lee Parker. The girl's partially clad body was found in a water-filled ditch on Tampa, Florida's eastern side, an area referred to by residents as "The Pits." The key witness, Daniel Munson, testified that on the night Parker was killed, Hill told him that he had thrown the girl in the water to make sure she was dead. Police later wired Munson, and the subsequent recording of another conversation between Munson and Hill was the deciding evidence in the trial. Hill was on death row for more than five years until Florida state rulings reopened the case for a possible reduction of sentence.

The Florida Supreme Court ruled that Hill's trial judge should have held a hearing to determine whether the defendant, who had an IQ of between sixty-six and seventy-nine, was competent to stand trial. Although Hill was found competent, another judge ruled that Munson's taped conversation was illegally obtained by police and could not be used as evidence in a new trial.

Hill could no longer be convicted of first-degree murder, and could not be returned to death row or given a life sentence. Assistant State's Attorney Stephen Crawford complained that he could no longer find witnesses. Hill's lawyer, Sarasota defense attorney Dan Danheisser, asked for a conviction of second-degree murder for a maximum sentence of twenty-five years. At this writing, Hill remains

Hill, Joe (Joel Emmanuel Hagglund; Joseph Hillstrom), 1879-1915, U.S. Joe Hill, best known for his songs and poems created in the infant days of the American labor movement, was convicted and executed for murdering a one-time Salt Lake City policeman and his son in revenge for previous oppressions against striking workers. Hill became a martyr to the union movement but he was unmistakably a killer who deserved his grim fate. Born on Oct. 7, 1879, in Gavle, Swed., as Joel Emmanuel Hagglund, Hill was one of nine children. His father, Olaf, was a railroad conductor who was killed in a railway accident in 1886, leaving 8-year-old Joe to go to work to help support the family. He went to sea, sending most of his earnings back to his mother. When she died in 1902, and his brothers and sisters were grown to adulthood, Hill immigrated to the U.S. and immediately became involved in the labor movement. He was unschooled, rough mannered, and believed that the way to labor reform was through violence. After spending a year in New York City, Hill moved to Chicago where he worked as a machinist, but was fired from his job when he tried to organize the workers of his plant.

To avoid the traditional blacklisting, Hill then changed his name to Hillstrom but he was known far and wide as Joe Hill, the name under which he wrote stirring union songs, such as the memorable "Casey Jones, The Union Scab." His most popular work was entitled "The Preacher and the Slave," which contained a line that later became a permanent part of American idiom: "You'll get pie in the sky when you die." Hill's rhymes and lyrics were packed with irony, expressing hopeless resignation for a doomed American work force that would never rise to the good things of life until capitalism was completely destroyed—a paradoxical credo in that if such a thing were to happen, there would be no jobs at all. Of course, Hill was really advocating early-day communism, or primitive Marxism, without providing a constructive course for workers to follow.

In 1910, Hill joined the Industrial Workers of the World (the IWW), or the Wobblies as they were popularly known, a radical union sect that was headed by such bombastic personalities as William D. "Big Bill" Haywood, who was, along with others, later tried for union violence, destruction and murder. His chief executioner, Harry Orchard, was sent to jail for terrorist bombings that took the lives of workers, government figures—just about anyone who got in the way of the IWW. From Chicago, Hill next went to Los Angeles where he worked with IWW radicals who later blew up the Los Angeles *Times* building, killing many non-union workers, a crime for which the McNamara Brothers were later convicted, despite a vigorous defense of their case by Clarence Darrow. Hill may well have helped plan the *Times* explosion in 1910 but was never charged.

In 1913, Hill left Los Angeles, intending to return to Chicago to organize machinists, but he stopped in Salt Lake City and took a job there as a miner. He grew ill and was fired after having been absent from his job for two weeks. Penniless, Hill moved to Murray, Utah, and stayed with the Eselius Brothers, IWW organizers. The IWW in Salt Lake City was a hotbed of union terrorists who busied themselves with the blowing up of mines and the killing of all those who opposed their movement. IWW organizers were issued guns and bombs, along with lists of those to be executed. One of these was John Morrison, a prosperous storeowner in Salt Lake City. Morrison had been a police officer who had helped to break many strikes, had uncovered many IWW plots to bomb mines in the Salt Lake City area, had made countless arrests, and had survived shootouts with union thugs, killing and wounding a number of Wobblies. He left the Salt Lake City police force and established a store in the city but lived in constant apprehension of retaliation from the fierce IWW goons. Twice he had survived attempts on his life. He and his two sons, Arling and Merlin, kept revolvers behind the counters of their store and never went anywhere without their weapons.

On the night of Jan. 10, 1914, Hill and another Wobbly thug, Otto Applequist, left Murray for an unknown destination. About two hours later, at approximately 10 p.m., two men wearing masks and brandishing pistols barged into Morrison's grocery store just as Morrison and his sons were closing the place. One of the men shouted: "We've got you now!" The intruders opened fire just as Morrison and his boys went for their revolvers. Within minutes Morrison and his son Arling were dead and the killers had fled. Inside the store, filled with gunsmoke, Merlin Morrison rose from the floor to find Arling's revolver, which his brother had apparently used to fire off a single shot.

At 11:30 p.m., Joe Hill appeared at the home of Dr. Frank M. McHugh, showing him a gunshot wound and saying: "Doctor, I've been shot. I got into a stew with a friend of mine who thought I had insulted his wife." He would not give the name of the "friend." Dr. McHugh noted that the bullet had passed through Hill's body, grazing the left lung, but that the patient would easily recover. He dressed and bandaged the wound and Hill returned to the home of the Eselius Brothers to recuperate. When McHugh heard of the Morrison killings, he notified police about Hill's wound. Police arrived at the Eselius house in Murray and ordered Hill to come with them. He reached quickly for something on a table and an officer fired a shot

at him, shattering his hand. The object Hill was reaching for, it was later proved, turned out to be a handkerchief. Four other suspects had been arrested and charged with the Morrison murder, but they were released when Hill was brought in. Applequist, the man who had accompanied Hill on the night of the killing, was never seen again.

Hill's reputation as an IWW terrorist convicted him out of hand, and his whereabouts on the night of the murder,

his mysterious bullet wound and his earlier statements about "getting even" with Morrison all stood in evidence against him. When tried, Hill proved to be a recalcitrant client. He argued with his attorneys and then fired them. Other defenders were appointed by the court but had little success in getting their client to cooperate. Hill adamantly refused to reveal how he had been wounded. The circumstantial evidence against Hill appeared overwhelming to the court and

Murderer Joe Hill, whose songs and poems made him a legend in the U.S. labor movement.

Hill was convicted and sentenced to die on July 18, 1914. Big Bill Haywood, head of the IWW, then organized a massive campaign to save Hill's life, and he was profiled as a sacrificial lamb to be slaughtered on the altar of capitalism. The campaign to save Hill caused several appeals and stays of execution. Many notable citizens sent pleas for clemency to Utah authorities and these included Helen Keller, President Woodrow Wilson, and Swedish Foreign Minister W.A. F. Ekengren. In the end, Hill's execution was firmly fixed and he accepted his fate, sending a wire to Haywood: "Don't waste any time mourning—organize!"

The state of Utah offered condemned prisoners (and still does today) a selection of one of two methods of execution; they could elect to be hanged or shot. Joe Hill chose a firing squad, saying: "I'll take shooting. I'm used to that. I have been shot a few times in the past, and I guess I can stand it again." But Hill thought to cheat the firing squad. At 5 a.m. on the day he was scheduled to die, Nov. 19, 1915, Hill broke a broom and used the jagged handle to tear apart his blankets in his cell, using the strips to tie the cell door together. He then barricaded himself behind his mattress. Wardens broke into the cell a half hour later and it took several guards to subdue the violently struggling Hill who was dragged outside to the courtyard and strapped to a wooden chair. "Well," said Hill, "I'm through. You can't blame a man for fighting for his life." A paper target was pinned over his heart and he stared at a canvas twenty feet away. Five holes had been cut in the canvas and rifle barrels projected through them. As is the custom, one of the marksmen in the execution squad had a blank in his rifle. None of the squad would know who had the blank so that all would aim to kill and none would know who had done the actual killing. A warden then shouted: "Ready...aim..." Hill himself then shouted: "Fire! Go on and fire!" The five rifles barked and jumped behind the canvas and three bullets ploughed into the heart of Joe Hill, instantly killing him. From that moment on he became a martyr to the cause of unionism and, as late as the radical 1960s, a coffeehouse hero where his songs were wailed by folk singers who had, for the most part, never heard of the IWW, Wobblies, Big Bill Haywood, or, specifically, John and Arling Morrison, who were murdered in cold blood and for whom no poignant, rabble-rousing tunes had ever been written.

Hilton, Paul Emanuel, d.1927, U.S. Henry Groh, known to his fans as "Heinie," spent the best years of his baseball career playing third base for the New York Giants. He retired after the 1927 season with a batting average of .292, almost 1,300 games at third base, and one assist in the apprehension of a murderer.

Paul Hilton was stubborn: if he could not play third base for the prison baseball team, he simply would not play. He always stood or sat near third base when watching a game. And, in the words of a friend, Hilton held Heinie Groh in high esteem. "He thinks Heinie oughta be President of the United States," the man told investigators. It would be the clue they needed to catch Hilton.

In February and March 1926, a total of four Queens, N.Y., policemen had been shot in the line of duty. All of them had been shot after approaching a man in a light overcoat, gray cap, and scarlet muffler. Upon being questioned, the man would go to his inside overcoat pocket, presumably to reveal some identification. Instead, his hand came out holding a pistol. Four officers had been shot in the side of the neck. Detective Arthur Kenny had died.

One of the survivors, Detective George McCarthy, had managed to get a good look at his assailant before being shot, and was able to pick out Hilton's photo. Once detectives James A. Pyke and William Jackson knew that Hilton was their prime suspect, they began to compile information on him. From prison guards they learned of Hilton's penchant for baseball. They hung out in a bar that they knew Hilton used to frequent and talked baseball, until eventually someone mentioned Hilton and his love for the

New York Giants, especially their third baseman.

By this time it was April, and the Giants' home opener was imminent. Pyke and Jackson had a hunch that if Hilton's baseball hero was playing in that game, he could probably be found sitting in a seat on the third-base side of the Polo Grounds. The detectives' suspicion paid off: Heinie Groh was slated to start at third base that day. They positioned themselves outside the entrance to the park that was nearest third base and waited. It was not long before Paul Hilton strolled into their trap. He attempted to pull a gun on the detectives, but they disarmed him and he was placed under arrest. Hilton was charged with first-degree murder. He was eventually convicted and executed in the electric chair on Feb. 17, 1927.

Hindley, Myra, See: **Moors Murders, The.**

Hinks, Reginald Ivor, d.1934, Brit. A petty thief and fast talker, Reginald Ivor Hinks was a vacuum cleaner salesman in Bath, England, when he met Constance Anne Pullen, a divorced woman with one child who lived with her 85-year-old, senile father, James Pullen. Interested in her inheritance of about £2,000, Hinks courted Pullen, and married her in March 1933. He soon got rid of Mr. Pullen's full-time male nurse, and put the old man on a strict diet in the hope of further enfeebling him. With £900 of his father-in-law's money, Hinks moved the family from their large house to a smaller one in Bath. When Hinks tried to use more of the money, Pullen's lawyer stopped him. Despite his anger, Hinks could not get at the cash. He began to take the elderly Pullen on long walks, hoping to exhaust him, and even sent him out by himself. When no fortuitous accidents occurred, Hinks took matters into his own hands.

On Dec. 1, 1933, Hinks called the Bath fire department to report that he had found Pullen dead in the kitchen with his head in the gas oven. Voluble as always, Hinks explained he had found his father-in-law, turned off the gas, and tried to revive him before summoning the police, the fire department, and a doctor. He helpfully explained, "If you find a bruise on the back of his head, that happened when I pulled him out of the gas oven." It was proved however, that the bruise had been caused before death. Tried before Justice George Branson at the Old Bailey in London, Hicks was found Guilty, sentenced to death, and hanged on May 4, 1934.

Hoch, Johann Otto (John Schmidt, AKA: **Jacob Huff; Martin Dotz; Henry Bartels**), 1862-1906, U.S. Johann Hoch was bald and sported a handlebar mustache. He was a bigamist, who, in the 1890s, passed on six rules for success with women in an article appearing in the Chicago *Sun* in 1906, shortly before he was hanged for murder. "The average man can fool the average woman if he will only let her have her own way at the start," was one of them.

Hoch was born in Horweiler, Ger. In 1887, he left his wife, Christine Ramb, and their three children. After arriving in Wheeling, W.Va., in 1895 under the name Jacob Huff, he opened a saloon in a German area and began to look for monied widows and divorcees to marry. In April he married Caroline Hoch (Johann adopted the last names of his wives) in a small ceremony. Reverend Hermann C.A. Haas, who performed the nuptials, recalled seeing Hoch give his wife some white powder, which he thought to be a poison. The woman died in agony a few days later and was buried with great haste. Hock sold the house, withdrew his wife's savings, and cashed a $2,500 life insurance policy. After apparently pretending to commit suicide, he was not seen in Wheeling again.

In 1898, Inspector George Shippy of the Chicago Police Department investigated Hoch for cheating a furniture dealer. Not knowing that this man was responsible for perhaps a dozen murders from coast to coast, Shippy was surprised to receive a letter from Reverend Haas who saw a newspaper photograph of the bigamist in a Chicago journal. Hoch, who was using the name of Martin Dotz, admitted his identity when confronted by Shippy. Hoch was convicted of swindling and sent to the Cook County Jail for a year, but authorities did not have evidence substantial enough to charge him with murder.

Reverend Haas theorized that Hoch may have

Wife-killer Johann Otto Hoch.

feigned suicide by leaving personal belongings on the banks of the Ohio River, and had waded out to a moored boat and sailed away to his freedom. Shippy investigated Hoch's progress after he was released from jail. From New York to San Francisco he found reports of dozens of abandoned women who had been murdered for their money, perhaps fifty of them, Shippy surmised. He contacted the police in Wheeling and asked them to exhume the remains of Caroline Hoch to be tested for arsenic poisoning. Local officials discovered that the vital organs had been removed,

leaving no tell-tale clues. He made one mistake, however. Hoch lingered too long in Chicago.

On Dec. 5, 1904, he married Marie Walcker and then poisoned her shortly after their marriage. Before she died, Hoch hugged his sister-in-law, Amelia. "I cannot be alone in the world. Marry me when she goes," he pleaded. "The dead are for the dead," he told the shocked woman. "The living are for the living." Days after Marie died, Amelia married Hoch and turned $750 over to him. Then he vanished. Inspector Shippy then had Walcker's body exhumed and he mailed the suspect's photograph to newspapers nationwide. The photo was recognized by Katherine Kimmerle in New York, who had taken Hoch in as a new boarder. He had proposed to her twenty minutes after renting the lodging. He was immediately arrested and returned to Chicago.

Hoch was convicted of murdering Marie Walcker and was hanged on Feb. 23, 1906, still maintaining his innocence.

Hoffman, Victor Ernest, 1946-   , Can. At 5 a.m. on Aug. 15, 1967, Victor Ernest Hoffman went for a drive to stave off his urge to kill. But at a farm just outside Spiritwood, Saskatchewan, he could no longer resist.

By 3 p.m., an inquest was being held at the farm of James Hodgson Peterson and his wife, Evelyn May Peterson. A neighbor had found both of them dead of gunshot wounds. Seven of their eight children, ranging in age from one to seventeen years old, were also dead. The uninjured survivor was three-year-old Phyllis Peterson. Except for James Peterson, who had been shot several times in the stomach, all of the victims had been shot once in the head with a .22-caliber rifle bullet. The only evidence was five shotgun shells and three bloody footprints.

Three days later, a tip from a farmer led police to the Hoffman home, and Victor Hoffman was questioned about the night of the murder. Hoffman, who had earlier been convicted of breaking and entering three times and was under medication for a psychiatric disorder, said that he had been home the night of Aug. 14. He said he had a .22-caliber rifle and a pair of rubber boots, and would not mind having the police examine them. Subsequent examination proved that Hoffman's Browning rifle was the gun used in the murders and that his boots matched the footprints found at the Peterson home. On Aug. 19, Hoffman was arrested for the murder of James Hodgson Peterson.

Hoffman confessed soon after he was arrested. "I don't know what made me do it," he said. He explained that he had tried to collect all the cartridges after the shooting and thought he had them all. He planned to change the firing pin and the rifling on the gun so that no one could identify it as the weapon. The devil had led him to do this, he said.

Hoffman, according to doctors, was a schizophrenic, and had been off his medication for about a week. According to his family, he had been acting strangely the past few weeks, shooting his gun at the sky and saying he was shooting at the devil. He often talked gibberish and was withdrawn. At Hoffman's trial in January 1968, a jury found him Not Guilty by reason of insanity, and he was committed to the Correctional Institute at Prince Albert, Saskatchewan.

Hofmann, Kuno, 1931- , Ger. Between April 1971 and May 1972, sections of northern West Germany were besieged by a series of sick crimes. Corpses were removed from their resting places and defiled in various ways—decapitated, mutilated, or partially eaten. There were also instances of attempted sexual intercourse. Finally, on May 6, 1972, in the village of Lindelburg, when a teenage couple was shot dead in their car, a witness saw a man with a leather hat and glasses dash away on a red motorbike. There was evidence that the murderer had drunk some of the dead young woman's blood and had been examining her genitals before he fled. He became the prime suspect.

On May 10, a transport company worker told authorities that the man they wanted was quitting his job at the company, and that they had better apprehend him quickly. The police drove quickly to the company and arrested Kuno Hofmann, forty-one. Hofmann and his brother had been brutally beaten by a sadistic father as they grew up, beatings that had left Hofmann a dwarfish deaf-mute with an IQ of seventy. Hofmann, who had served nine years for theft, confessed to all the crimes against the corpses and several others as well. In addition to killing the teenagers, he had shot and wounded mortuary attendant George Warmuth, who discovered him kissing a corpse. Doctors explained that he could not separate reality from the fantasy crimes he committed in his head.

Searching Hofmann's house, which he shared with his brother and sister, police found books on satanism and witchcraft. Hofmann had garnered from these books the idea that he could be strong and handsome if he performed rituals on dead bodies. When that had not worked, he had switched to live victims, killing the teenagers. He was never brought to trial but was committed for life to an institution for the criminally insane.

Hofmann, Mark W., 1955- , U.S. A self-described "eighth generation Mormon," Mark Hofmann was a native of Salt Lake City, Utah. He was fascinated with Joseph Smith, the founder of the Church of Jesus Christ of Latter-Day Saints, describing him as a man who understood how to "create history." Hofmann's father insisted on absolute adherence to the Mormon doctrine. Apparently, Hofmann became disillusioned with his religion as a teenager, and, unable to express his doubts, channelled them into an elaborate plan.

By his mid-twenties, Hofmann was a celebrated and respected member of the Mormon community. He had sold scores of historical documents, earning more than $2 million for his "discoveries." The early documents justified the church's position, and were sold to the Mormon church as well as to collectors. But then Hofmann began to "find" papers that cast serious doubt on the origins and truth of the church's history. They included the infamous "White Salamander Letter" which linked church founder Joseph Smith with early nineteenth century folk magic, including such superstitious practices as digging for money, spell casting, and divining the future with "seer stones." The letter said that a spirit in the form of a white salamander, not an angel, had told Smith to found the church. Hofmann sold the letter in 1984 to Steven F. Christensen, a Mormon bishop, for $40,000. Another forgery suggested that Joseph Smith's sacred *Book of Mormon* was a fictional story about American Indians. Concerned Mormon officials bought Hofmann's papers at exorbitant prices and hid them in vaults to keep them from critics and curious historians.

Hofmann began to deal in other historical materials, including a document supposedly prepared by seventeenth century members of the Massachusetts Bay Colony. The Library of Congress confirmed the paper's authenticity through the Federal Bureau of Investigation, and planned to buy it. But it later decided it could not afford the $1 million price.

Hofmann came increasingly under suspicion. He bounced checks, and was unable to deliver a forged "McLellin Collection" that he had promised the church. A Mormon leader had already arranged a $185,000 bank loan to make the purchase.

Facing angry investors and obligations he could not possibly meet, Hofmann looked to murder as a way out. He planted pipe bombs that killed Steven Christensen, thirty-one, his associate in the document trade, and Kathleen Sheets, fifty, the wife of James Gary Sheets, Christensen's business partner. Christensen had recently been hired as a consultant in a deal Hofmann was working on and would have known Hofmann's articles were counterfeit. Both murders occurred on Oct. 15, 1985. On Oct. 16, Hofmann himself was badly injured when a third bomb exploded in his car in downtown Salt Lake City, just minutes away from the Mormon Temple. Although Hofmann later claimed that he had tried to kill himself, authorities believe the third explosive was meant for another Mormon document collector.

Hofmann was initially charged with first-degree murder, which, in Salt Lake City, carries a mandatory death penalty. A plea bargain reduced the charges to two counts of second-degree murder, though Hofmann's father encouraged Hofmann to accept death according to the Mormon doctrine of "blood atonement." On Jan. 23, 1987, Hofmann pleaded guilty to two counts of second-degree murder and multiple counts of fraud in the forgery of historical documents. He was sentenced to five years to life in prison. In September 1988 he overdosed on an antidepressant drug and was found comatose by his cell mate at Utah State Prison, but survived.

There are several books about Hofmann's exploits, a film is in development, and a four-hour miniseries, *The Mormon Murders,* was cancelled indefinitely for "script rewrites and revisions," possibly due to the influence of the Mormon Church.

Hofrichter, Adolph (AKA: **Dr. Haller**), b.1879, Aust. On Nov. 18, 1909, Captain Richard Mader of Austria's High Command received a package containing "potency pills" and a letter describing their wonderful effects. He eagerly ripped open the pill packet, according to an aide, and was dead by the time the aide returned thirty minutes later. Dr. Stuckart, chief of the criminal investigation department of Vienna, soon learned that eleven other officers received the same packages but had not taken the enclosed wonder drugs. The pills were analyzed, and identified as potassium cyanide. Austrian Emperor Franz Josef I, concerned that a conspiracy was afloat to dismantle his army, assigned Colonel Freiherr von Kutschera and Captain-Auditor Kunz to investigate. They searched for someone within their ranks who could benefit from the deaths of General Staff officers. Kunz discovered that all of the package recipients graduated from the Military Academy in 1905. A search of records revealed that 1905 graduate Lieutenant Adolph Hofrichter had been rejected for a permanent General Staff post after a temporary, unsuccessful appointment to the staff. His handwriting matched that on the letters sent with the packages.

On Nov. 27, Hofrichter, serving with the 14th Infantry Regiment in Linz, was arrested. Two cardboard boxes identical to the packages, a mimeograph machine, and capsules were found in his home. As an amateur photographer, he had access to potassium cyanide. The War Ministry issued a statement that they suspected Hofrichter "with a probability bordering on certainty." He was taken to the military prison in Vienna, where he was held for seven months before his court-martial began. Hofrichter was denied visitors after trying to escape and attempting to smuggle a letter to his wife requesting atropine or hyoscyamine with which to kill himself. Lieutenant Hofrichter signed a confession after his wife was arrested for being an accessory to murder. He retracted the confession three days later, after the charge against his wife was dropped.

Hofrichter was tried before a military tribunal on June 8, 1910. As he was not allowed to have his own attorney, Captain Kunz served as prosecutor and defense lawyer in the case. Trying to give more impact to circumstantial evidence, Kunz explained that one of the letters was addressed with a misspelling—an identical misspelling occurred on a list of army officers in the Linz garrison that Hofrichter had apparently copied. The capsules found at Hofrichter's home, however, were dog medicine, Kunz said in Hofrichter's defense.

Hofrichter's case was particularly damaged by witnesses who verified rumors that the officer had committed crimes under the alias Dr. Haller. One young woman stated that Hofrichter, using his Haller identity, tried to assault her when she answered an advertisement for a babysitter. The cases for and against Hofrichter were presented in one day, and on June 9, the lieutenant was ordered dishonorably discharged and sentenced to twenty years at Mollersdorf Jail.

Holle, Edward, prom. 1938, U.S. On Apr. 17, 1938, the body of 23-year-old Sophie Kujat was discovered in the Passaic River by two men working a small skiff near the derricks and oil tanks of Newark, N.J. The corpse had been submerged for one week with forty-foot-long automobile chains that weighed more than sixty pounds. A medical examination by Essex County coroner Harrison Martland determined that Kujat was dead before her killer dumped her body in the river. Police detectives learned that she had once been engaged to Edward Holle, who had married another woman ten months earlier, and that she had been seen with Holle on the night she disappeared. Officers apprehended Holle in East Orange, N.J., and took him into custody for questioning.

For two days, Holle insisted he was innocent. Visiting an oil refinery near where the body had been found, detectives discovered that chains used on the company's trucks were identical to those in which Kujat's dead body had been wrapped. In addition, a set of chains were missing from the storehouse. A night watchman said he had seen Holle on the docks several weeks earlier, and that Holle had borrowed a hand truck from him. Accompanying police to headquarters, the watchman was brought into the room where Sergeant of Detectives Luke Conlon, and officers John Staats, John Haller, and Thomas Bolan were questioning Holle. Taking one look at the watchman, Holle turned pale, cursed, shook his fist, and then confessed. He explained that he had been trying to break off his relationship with Kujat after he married, and had been having an argument with her when he choked her. Not knowing if she was dead or merely unconscious, he strangled her with a clothesline, stuffed her body in the trunk of his car, drove to the garage, and wrapped her in chains before borrowing the truck and discarding her in the river. The day after his confession, Holle reenacted the killing in front of a police camera, marking the first time film had been used to present a case before a New Jersey jury. Arraigned on May 16 before Police Judge Klein, Holle was tried for murder and sentenced in July to a twenty-year to life term.

Hollis, David Lee, 1961- , U.S. On Feb. 27, 1982, police in Hammond, Ind., found the bodies of 18-year-old Debbie Hollis, 18-year-old Kim Mezei, and Mezei's 2-year-old son, Craig Mezei, stabbed to death with a butcher knife in an apartment complex. The following day, 21-year-old David Lee Hollis, the estranged husband of Debbie, was arrested in neighboring Griffith, Ind., after he broke into the apartment of his friends William Davidson and Donald White and held them hostage with a 12-gauge shotgun. He bound the men with electrical cord, but when Hollis fell asleep they escaped. Police using tear gas stormed the apartment, but found it empty. They searched the complex and eventually found Hollis hiding in a clothes dryer.

On Oct. 13, 1982, in the Lake County Criminal Court of Judge James Clements, Hollis surprised even his own defense attorney by pleading Guilty to the murders. On Nov. 12, 1982, Hollis was sentenced to die in the electric chair. He remains on Death Row.

Holmes, Leonard, d.1945, Brit. In October 1944, after returning home to New Ollerton, Nottinghamshire, England, at the end of WWII, Leonard Holmes suspected that his wife, Peggy Agnes Holmes, had been unfaithful to him. After coming home from an evening of drinking in a local pub, the couple began to fight. Peggy Holmes responded to her husband's accusations by saying, "If it will ease your mind, I have been untrue to you." Holmes hit her in the head with a hammer and then strangled her. Tried for murder before Justice Charles in February 1945 at the

Nottingham Assizes, Holmes was found Guilty and sentenced to death.

Holmes appealed to the Court of Criminal Appeals claiming the trial judge did not offer the jury the option to consider a verdict of manslaughter rather than murder. Justice Wrottesley explained in the appeal judgement that a person who has been absent and returns, suspecting that his wife has been unfaithful, may not use lethal weapons on his spouse, and may not "...claim to have suffered such provocation as would reduce the crime from murder to manslaughter." Previous to this judgment, the discovery of a wife or husband in the act of adultery had long been held to be adequate provocation to justify a manslaughter verdict. Holmes was executed on May 28, 1945.

Holt, Emory, d.1949, U.S. When Emory Holt married Norma Bew in 1943, they seemed an odd match. He liked classical music and chess and she had a penchant for good times and flirting. An engineer officer in the Merchant Marines, Holt returned from a tour of duty to find his wife acting strangely. With methodical, professional care he recorded her actions in his log, noting her drunkenness, her smeared lipstick, and meticulously keeping nautical-time for his facts. He hired a private detective who confirmed his suspicion that she had taken a lover. Holt wrote a note to his mother in North Carolina, which said: "I expect to be dead in a few hours...All my love." He then left, carrying a gun, to find Norma Holt at her lover's apartment. It was a March night in 1949 when Mrs. Elsie Thomas in Hollywood, Calif., received a phone call from her daughter, Norma, who pleaded, "Emory is going to kill us. Please talk him out of this awful thing."

Thomas begged her son-in-law, "Please be a good boy," and heard him respond, "It's too late, Mama, it's too late." She passed out as she heard shots and screams from the Manhattan apartment of David Whittaker, and telephoned the New York police when she recovered. Manhattan officers discovered Holt's body sprawled over a chair, with his 9-mm Luger still clutched in his hand. The corpses of his wife and her lover were on the couch.

Holt, Frederick Rothwell (AKA: Eric), d.1920, Brit. Frederick Holt was drafted into the British army at the onset of WWI. In 1918, after suffering amnesia and depression, Holt was discharged. He returned home to Lancashire where he met Harriet Elsie "Kitty" Breaks, an attractive woman whose marriage had fallen apart. For the next eighteen months they lived together.

On the morning of Dec. 24, 1919, the body of Kitty Breaks was discovered partially buried in the St. Anne's sand hills close to Blackpool. She had been shot with three bullets. A revolver and a set of footprints matching Holt's were discovered and he was arrested and charged with murder.

The trial was conducted at the Manchester Assizes in February 1920, where defense counsel Marshall Hall attempted to show that his client carried out the crime as a result of uncontrollable passion while in a state of shell shock and mental illness. Holt had been badly jarred by the Festubert bombing. The jurors and even the judge wept when love letters written by Holt to Breaks were read aloud in court. But the appeal to sentiment was squelched by Sir Gordon Hewart who accused Holt of murdering for profit. Holt had taken out a £5,000 insurance policy on Breaks's life and was also named in Breaks's will. The jury found the defendant Guilty of murder. The Home Secretary ruled that Holt was sane, thereby paving the way for his execution, which took place at Strangeways Prison on Apr. 13, 1920.

Holy Child Orphanage Case, 1951, China.

Five French-Canadian Catholic nuns were charged with murder following the deaths of 2,116 infants brought to the Holy Infant Orphanage in Canton for medical treatment. Arrested on Mar. 19, 1951, Antoinette Couvrette, Germaine Gravel, Elizabeth Lemire, Germaine Tanguay, and Imelda Lapierre worked at the orphanage, where abandoned babies were brought. Of all the infants brought to the orphanage from October 1950 to February 1951, 135 survived. The nuns were also charged with mistreating, enslaving, and illegally selling the babies that lived. On Dec. 2, 1951, the women were formally tried at Sun Yat-sen Memorial Hall, which was packed with more than 6,000 people, many bearing signs and shouting for revenge. Listeners to the Canton radio station broadcasting the two-hour session could hear Chief Justice Wen Szehsien warn the crowd not to "beat the nuns" or swarm too closely by the platform on which they were placed. The five were paraded and spat upon after the hearing. Couvrette and Gravel were sentenced to five years imprisonment each, and the others were ordered deported from the country. Father Thomas J. Bauer and Sister St. Joseph, Mother Superior of the Order of the Immaculate Conception from where the nuns originated, said the five had committed no crimes, and that little could be done for the infants, who were dying when they were brought to the orphanage.

Holzaptel, Floyd Albert, See: Peel, Joseph Jr.

Honka, Fritz (AKA: Fiete Honka), 1936-   , Ger.

While battling a fire at an apartment building in Hamburg, Germany's St. Pauli district on the morning of June 17, 1975, fire fighters uncovered the secret of the missing women of the Golden Glove. In the attic apartment, where the building's caretaker lived, they found the charred remains of dismembered human bodies and a plastic bag filled with the decayed and liquified body parts of four elderly prostitutes who had disappeared from a seedy neighborhood bar over the last four years.

The Golden Glove was a St. Pauli district saloon frequented by many of the neighborhood's prostitutes and its customers. Beginning in 1971, prostitutes began disappearing from the bar; all of whom were elderly, shorter than five foot, five inches, and toothless. No one seemed to notice their disappearance until the decapitated head of 42-year-old Gertraude Braeuer was discovered by two children playing in a vacant lot three blocks from the bar. Upon investigation, the Hamburg police department found all of the remaining pieces of the woman's body, except her torso, which was rotting in the storage area hidden in the walls of Fritz Honka's upstairs apartment.

Honka was the caretaker of a neighborhood apartment building where he worked in exchange for a rent-free attic apartment. Honka, an alcoholic, spent many evenings at the Golden Glove. After a heavy bout of drinking, Honka would return home drunk, oblivious to the stench that had begun to circulate through the building. Although unaware himself, two of his live-in lovers had noticed, and many of the building's tenants complained. Some moved out, including Honka's former girlfriends.

When fire fighters burst into his apartment in 1975, they ripped through the walls in an attempt to extinguish remaining embers. They were shocked when they tore the wooden panels from the walls. Hidden within was Braeuer's torso, and the mutilated bodies of 54-year-old Anna Beuschel, 57-year-old Frieda Roblick, and 52-year-old Ruth Schult.

After police took Honka into custody, he confessed to the crimes and explained that he had strangled the women only after they had refused to comply to his demands to perform oral sex. He later disposed of the corpses by cutting them up with a knife and a handsaw in the kitchen sink, and hiding the remains in the attic. When the stench from the decaying bodies, which were hidden in the walls, became too overpowering he would bathe the room in deodorant spray. Police also learned that at least on two occasions, Honka had sexual intercourse with the corpses.

Honka, who had previously been charged with assaulting two other St. Pauli women, was found Guilty and sentenced to life in prison.

Hooded Man, The, See: **McKay, George**.

Hook, The, See: **Molina del Rio, Francisco**.

Hoolhouse, Robert, 1917-38, Brit. Margaret Jane Dobson and her husband had a farm at High Grange near Wolviston, England. A dispute with a tenant laborer in 1933 resulted in the Dobsons' evicting the family, the Hoolhouses, who moved to a village four miles away. Five years later, on Jan. 18, 1938, Margaret Dobson's body was found on a farm track. The 67-year-old woman had been stabbed and sexually assaulted. Among those questioned was Robert Hoolhouse, twenty-one, the son of the family ousted from their home. Within thirty-six hours, Hoolhouse was arrested on considerable circumstantial evidence. He had a motive to kill Dobson, he approximately matched the description of a man seen near the farm, and there were scratches on his face as well as blood and hair on his clothes. At his trial at Leeds Assizes in March 1938, his defense declared that the prosecution had no case, but did not offer any evidence. Although the prosecutors acknowledged that a footprint near the body was not that of Hoolhouse, and an acquittal was expected, the jury found the accused Guilty. An appeal was dismissed, and a 14,000-signature petition for a reprieve was rejected. Hoolhouse was hanged on May 26, 1938, at the Durham Jail.

Hope, Edgar, 1960- , U.S. Chicago police officers Robert Mantia and James E. Doyle were patrolling on the city's South Side on the evening of Feb. 5, 1982. Mantia, a fourteen-year veteran of the force, was training the rookie Doyle when 22-year-old Charles Harris flagged them down. Harris told the officers that he had seen a man who had recently robbed him riding the 79th Street Chicago Transit Authority (CTA) bus. The officers stopped and boarded the bus.

As officer Doyle was removing the suspect from the bus, the man reached under his coat, pulled out two handguns, and shot Doyle to death. He fled the vehicle firing wildly and injured two passengers, 17-year-old Cynthia Houston and 23-year-old Kevin Page, before Officer Mantia brought him down with one of seven bullets he fired into the dark.

At police headquarters, the gunman was identified as 22-year-old Edgar Hope, an ex-convict paroled in June 1981 after serving a two-and-a-half-year sentence for armed robbery. Police found two revolvers in his possession, one of which was registered to off-duty sheriff's policeman Lloyd Wickliffe, who had been murdered during an attempted burglary at a South Side McDonald's on January 11. Wickliffe had been working at the fast food chain as a security guard when two men entered the restaurant and opened fire, killing him and wounding his partner, Alvin Thompson.

Hope was charged with the murder of Officer Doyle and the attempted murder of his partner Mantia, and in a police lineup, Thompson identified him as one of the two men involved in the January shooting. Shortly after Hope's arrest, police apprehended his partner in the restaurant shooting, Alton L. Logan, and both were charged with murder.

Hope's trial for the murder of Doyle began on Oct. 20, 1982. Hope was found Guilty, and presiding Judge James M. Bailey sentenced him to be executed in the electric chair. Already sentenced to death for the CTA murder, Hope and Logan were found Guilty on Feb. 16, 1983, of the shooting death of Lloyd Wickliffe, and for the attempted murder of his partner.

Hopwood, Edward, 1867-1912, Brit. Edward Hopwood fell in love when he saw actress Florence Dudley perform in a play at London's Tivoli Theater. His fatal love led to murder less than four months later.

Dudley, whose real name was Florence Alice Bernadette Silles, was murdered in a taxi on Sept. 28, 1912. In the back of the car, Hopwood shot her to death and then turned the gun on himself. Distraught that Dudley had broken off their relationship after discovering that he was married and was wanted by police for passing bad checks, Hopwood developed this scheme to murder the woman and kill himself. Although she was dead, his suicide attempt had failed. He succeeded in injuring himself, but was nursed back to health to stand trial at the Old Bailey.

The three-day trial ended after the jury deliberated only twelve minutes and returned with a conviction for Hopwood, who had maintained that he intended only to kill himself and not Dudley. Justice Avory, in what was believed to be his first murder trial, sentenced Hopwood to death. He was hanged in December 1912.

Horry, George Cecil (AKA: **George Arthur Turner;
Charles Anderson**), 1907- , N. Zea. In August 1951,
George Cecil Horry was convicted of murder for the death
of a woman whose body was never found. Mary Eileen
Spargo was last seen in Auckland, N. Zea., on July 12, 1942,
while she honeymooned in Titirangi with her new husband,
George Arthur Turner, a British Secret Service agent.
Turner and Spargo were married the previous day—the day
after Spargo had sold her house for £676 in preparation for
a move to Europe with her new husband.

Later that day, Horry drove his fiancee, Eunice Mercel
Geale, to her parents' home in the Auckland suburb of Mt.
Eden. When the couple arrived, Geale's parents noticed
that Horry had two suitcases and a hat box in his car. It
appeared that he was either planning, or had just returned
from, a trip, but neither questioned the items. Horry and
Geale were married on Dec. 12.

The week after the wedding, George Turner appeared
at the home of his in-laws, Mr. and Mrs. William Spargo.
Turner, visibly upset, explained that their daughter had been
killed after a German U-boat sunk the cruise liner *Empress
of India* as they sailed to England. The Spargos were
shattered. They believed their son-in-law until several
months later, when they learned that no ship named the
Empress of India had sailed since WWI. Mr. Spargo then
went to police with this information, and took with him a
letter mysteriously delivered to him several months before
while Turner and his daughter were honeymooning.

Police detectives, with assistance from the Auckland post
office, captured the man who had been passing himself off
as George Arthur Turner. In reality, Turner was George
Cecil Horry, a man who during a 19-year span received
forty-seven separate convictions. Horry was immediately
suspected in the disappearance of his wife, whom he said
he married at her request as she had been involved with a
married man and wanted to move with him to the U.S.
Even though his story was weak, police were unable to link
him to her death until nine years later, when legal limita-
tions on missing persons had expired and Spargo was legally
pronounced dead. Police immediately arrived at his home
and took him into custody on murder charges.

Horry's trial began on Aug. 5, 1951. Based on testimony
from the dead woman's friends and relatives, letters Horry
mailed to Spargo's parents during their "honeymoon," the
jury found him Guilty and sentenced him to prison. The
most damaging evidence came when Horry's wife asked why
police were arresting him.

With police officers at the door, she asked, "What's the
matter?"

"It's that Turner business," answered Horry.

"Why? Has she turned up?"

"That's impossible. She couldn't have."

The body of Mary Elaine Spargo Jones has never been
found.

Horseface, See: Moreira, Manuel.

Horton, Floyd, b.1896, and **Johnston, Anna**, prom.
1936, U.S. Lovers Floyd Horton and Anna Johnston were
sentenced to life in prison for poisoning Horton's wife Elta,
who died on their farm near Bedford, Iowa, on Feb. 15,
1936.

Horton and Johnston had been involved in an affair for
some time before they plotted to kill Elta Horton with
strychnine. On the evening of Feb. 14, Horton administered
the fatal dose to his wife. Johnston had purchased the
poison several weeks before, telling the local pharmacist it
was to kill rats in her basement.

An autopsy of Elta Horton's body revealed strychnine
poisoning. Floyd Horton and Anna Johnston were charged
with murder. Prosecutors coerced a confession from
Johnston by convincing her that Horton had turned state's
evidence against her. She provided investigators with a full
confession. Both Johnston and Horton were convicted of
first-degree murder, and sentenced to life in prison. Horton
was sent to the state prison in Fort Madison, Iowa, and
Johnston served her life sentence at the State Women's
Reformatory.

Horton, Kenneth, 1923- , Brit. In March 1939, 16-
year-old Kenneth Horton murdered his employer, who had
threatened to fire him from his job as a clerk at a London
paper mill. Horton had worked at the mill for two months,
but was warned in February that he faced termination if his
performance did not improve.

On Mar. 2, Horton's employer worked late. That
evening, Horton beat him over the head more than thirty-
four times with a ruler, hammer, and chisel, fracturing his
skull twenty-two times. The man's disfigured body was
found by the building's janitor later in the evening.

Horton was apprehended two days later at a hotel in a
seaside resort. Upon being taken into custody, he confessed
to the murder and explained that he had also stolen money
from the man. Horton was tried at the Old Bailey, where
he was convicted and sentenced to spend an indeterminate
time in prison.

Horton, William Robert (AKA: **Willie**), 1951- , U.S. On Oct. 26, 1974, William Robert Horton robbed a Lawrence, Mass., gas station and killed the station's 17-year-old attendant Joseph Fournier by stabbing him nineteen times. Horton stole more than $100 from the cash register, but left $57 in Fournier's pocket. On Nov. 8, the 23-year-old Horton and two other men, 37-year-old Roosevelt Pickett and 30-year-old Alvin L. Wideman, were arrested in their Lawrence homes in connection with the robbery and murder. Horton, eventually convicted of the murder, was sentenced to life and incarcerated in the Northeast Correctional Center.

Horton remained behind bars for twelve years until he escaped in 1987. He was one of the Massachusetts convicts approved for the state's prison furlough program, which allowed inmates short leaves and temporarily eased overcrowding in prison. Though Governor Michael Dukakis did not enact the program, he supported it, believing furloughs an integral part of the state's prison program. In June, Horton failed to return to prison following his scheduled furlough period, and Massachusetts law enforcement authorities began a statewide search for him. Ten months later, officers shot Horton as he fled the Oxon Hill, Md., home of Mr. and Mrs. Clifford Barnes. Horton had forced his way into the home, tied Barnes up, and raped his wife as the man watched.

At the time of this attack, Governor Dukakis was running for president in the 1988 election. As the race continued, nationwide polls showed Dukakis, the Democratic nominee, gaining on incumbent Vice-President George Bush. In an attempt to sway public opinion, the Bush campaign launched an extremely successful negative advertising blitz designed to portray Dukakis as a "liberal" who was "soft on crime." In their most effective television spot, they used the Willie Horton case to illustrate how Dukakis dealt with criminals in his own state. Advertisements included appeals from the victimized Barnes couple, who were shown pleading with voters to elect Bush. The ads also accused the Massachusetts penal system of having an open-door policy for convicted criminals. Although the ads were repeatedly denounced for exploiting racial prejudice (Horton was black and Mrs. Barnes white), they were probably the single most important issue in the campaign that won Bush the presidency.

After his capture in 1988, Horton was convicted of the Barnes attack and sentenced to double life plus eighty-five years. He is currently serving his sentences in the Maryland Penitentiary. Governor Dukakis has since signed legislation prohibiting furloughs for inmates convicted of murder.

Houghton, Charles, d.1929, Brit. Elinor Drinkwater Woodhouse and her sister Martha Gordon Woodhouse lived on their 300-acre estate near Hereford, England. On Sept. 6, 1929, they notified Charles Houghton that he was to be released as their butler because his alcoholism was beginning to affect his work. They gave him a twenty-four-hour notice and two months' wages. The next morning, after serving the two women breakfast, he shot them dead. He was apprehended in his room where he had attempted suicide by cutting his throat with a razor.

Houghton was charged with murder and tried at Hereford Assizes. In his defense, his attorneys cited a history of epileptic seizures that often resulted in uncontrollable actions. The judge failed to see their case, and sentenced Houghton to be executed. He was hanged on Dec. 6, 1929.

Housden, Nina, 1916- , U.S. Nina Housden imagined that her husband, Charles, a bus driver, was engaged in an endless string of affairs. The couple lived in a modest apartment in Highland Park, Mich., a suburb of Detroit. Despite his protests to the contrary, Charles Housden was unable to convince his wife of his fidelity. When he visited the local bowling alley, Nina would go there and embarrass him in front of his friends. Finally Charles had enough. He filed for divorce and moved out. But on Dec. 18, 1947, Housden phoned her husband and told him to come over. That night she plied him with a plenty of liquor. Charles accepted his wife's hospitality and soon passed out.

Seeing her chance, Housden wrapped a clothesline around his neck and strangled him. She rolled back the carpets, got a meat cleaver, and mutilated his body. Afterward she wrapped the body parts in Christmas paper and piled them into the back seat of her car. The next day she left Michigan for her family home in Kentucky where she planned to bury the remains. In Toledo, Ohio, Housden had car trouble. She left the vehicle with a local mechanic who said it would take at least two days to fix the car. "It's okay, I'll live in the front seat until you're done. I'm low on cash and can't afford a motel," she replied.

The mechanic agreed to let Housden sleep in the garage. On the second day he noticed a powerful odor wafting from the back of the car. Housden explained that this was venison intended for her family. Later that night the mechanic decided to have a look for himself. He found the remains of a human leg protruding from the package. Housden was extradited to Michigan, judged sane by the courts, and tried for murder. She was found Guilty and sentenced to life in prison.

Huberty, James Oliver, 1943-84, U.S. On July 18, 1984, James Oliver Huberty of San Diego, Calif., told his wife he was "going hunting for humans." Despondent over a recent job loss, the 41-year-old Huberty took a rifle, shotgun, pistol and hundreds of rounds of ammunition to a local McDonald's restaurant and started shooting. By the time the SWAT team arrived and shot Hubert, twenty-one people, mostly children, lay dead beside him. Nineteen others were wounded in California's largest single mass shooting to date.

Hufnagel, Thomas E., 1903-79, U.S. Thomas E. Hufnagel, the 76-year-old custodian of a four-unit house in San Francisco, was fussy about its appearance. He had warned tenant Joel Blackman, a young lawyer from Madison, Wis., not to park his car on the sidewalk in front of the house, but Blackman ignored the elderly man. Hufnagel's wife Isabel also ignored Hufnagel when he began drinking heavily and told her he would kill Blackman, her, and himself.

On Friday, Jan. 19, 1979, Hufnagel shot Blackman and his 28-year-old companion, Mimi Rosenblatt, with a .38-caliber revolver and a 12-gauge shotgun. The two were seriously injured in what would turn into Hufnagel's six-and-a-half-hour siege against his tenants. Another tenant, Catherine Henry, forty-five, was shot as she stood in the hallway and Mark Johnson, who left his twenty-fourth birthday party to help Blackman, was shot and killed. Blackman and the two women were rushed to San Francisco General Hospital.

Hufnagel went on to exchange fire with police officers before barricading himself in his apartment. After waiting five hours and emptying six tear gas canisters, police entered the apartment to find that Hufnagel had killed himself. Hufnagel's wife escaped unharmed.

Hughes, Susan Piasecny, prom. 1977, and **Piasecny, Henry**, d.1977, U.S. The Piasecny family of Manchester, N.H., had a troubled history of violence and emotional problems, culminating in the murders of two family members. Hank Piasecny returned from WWII to open a small grocery store in Manchester. Fifteen years later, with an attractive wife and two children, he was proprietor of a thriving sporting goods store. But Hank drank a great deal and was ferociously jealous. His wife Doris, a Manchester secretary, pushed him to buy material possessions. Police were called repeatedly to quell threats of domestic violence, until 1963, when Doris Piasecny was

granted a divorce.

In December 1963, Doris and John Betley, a Manchester architect, were alone in her house following a Christmas party, when Hank Piasecny emerged from a hiding place and stabbed both of them to death with a kitchen knife. Hank was found drunk a short time later at his store after having smashed his truck on a highway guardrail. During his arraignment, Hank was examined by a Boston psychiatrist who determined him to be legally insane. The state committed him to the New Hampshire hospital at Concord. Two years later, Piasecny's lawyer, claiming Hank was no longer a threat to himself or others, petitioned for his release. On Aug. 6, 1966, Piasecny was released and went to work in a Manchester boat store. But as he sought to return to a peaceful existence, his relationship with his daughter Susan deteriorated.

Susan Piasecny was a talented and intelligent girl who had recurring emotional problems before and after her mother's brutal murder. At age fourteen, she falsely claimed to have been abducted while returning from a babysitting job. Two years later, she was hospitalized, temporarily unable to speak. After her mother's death she spent several weeks in a Massachusetts mental hospital. She finished college, married, and in 1967, entered medical school at the University of Vermont. Shortly afterward, her marriage broke up, and one day she was found unconscious on the side of a road, having been beaten or tossed from a car. She claimed that her former husband had ordered her beating, but police were suspicious, given her emotional past. In 1970, she entered the same New Hampshire hospital where her father had been incarcerated, and remained there for three years. After her release, she married a fellow patient, Edward Hughes, but the union ended quickly when Hughes slit his throat with a razor blade and died in the presence of his wife. Susan began working various jobs in nursing homes and had petty legal problems from passing bad checks. Finally she moved in with her father.

In June 1977, Hank and Susan had a violent argument and Hank said he never wanted to see her again. In late August, Susan pleaded no contest to two charges of forgery. The following week she phoned police asking them to check up on her father because he had sounded so distraught. They found him dead, half his head blown off, from an apparent shotgun blast. It seemed to be suicide. However, his daughter suspected murder because the body was found ten feet from the pool of blood, and an autopsy revealed the presence of a second bullet, a .22-caliber slug, in Hank's chest. A month later, Susan confessed to the murder, saying she had shot him in the chest with the handgun stolen from a cousin, and then in the head with his own shotgun. Susan Hughes became the second family member to be found Not Guilty by reason of insanity and was again sent to the New Hampshire Hospital "for life until or unless earlier discharged, released or transferred by due process of the law."

Hugon, Daniel, c.1936-   , Fr. The trial of Daniel Hugon, later found Guilty of murdering an elderly French prostitute in 1965, represented one of the earliest cases where a person's abnormal genetic makeup was considered in determining a verdict.

Hugon, described as tall, myopic, moon-faced, and balding, possessed a chromosome structure of XYY, instead of the normal male XY. Court physician Lejeune suggested this may have accounted for diminished responsibility on the part of the accused, but did not directly cause the murder. Hugon was sentenced to seven years in prison.

Hulme, Juliet Marion, 1939-   , and **Parker, Pauline Yvonne**, 1938-   , N. Zea. So that they could remain together, a teenage girl and her best friend killed her mother. Juliet Hulme and Pauline Parker were very close. When possible they would bathe together, sleep in the same bed, and discuss sex at length. Pauline's mother, Honora Mary Parker, forty-five, grew anxious about their relationship and at one point voiced her concerns to Juliet's father. When Juliet's father decided to move from Christchurch, N. Zea., to South Africa and take Juliet with him, the two girls decided they were "...sticking to one thing. We sink or swim together." Pauline decided she would move to South Africa with her friend, but when her mother would not allow it, the two girls plotted to kill her.

On June 22, 1954, while the girls and Mrs. Parker walked along a path in a park, Pauline and her mother began to argue. Pauline swung a brick stuffed inside a stocking at her mother, hitting her repeatedly, and then Juliet took the brick and continued to hit her. Their clothes were stained with blood. After pulverizing Mrs. Parker, the two girls ran to a tea house, hysterical, and gasped, "Please help us. Mummy's been hurt. She's hurt, covered with blood." They claimed Mary had slipped on a board, fell, and bumped her head on a brick while her head "kept bumping and banging."

The pathologist's examination revealing forty-five distinct injuries proved the girls were lying. Arrested, Pauline confessed and took the blame for the murder stating that Juliet had been walking ahead and witnessed nothing. But when Pauline was caught trying to burn a note saying she was "taking the blame for everything," Juliet confessed to the murder as well.

At their trial they pleaded not guilty by reason of insanity, a plea impossible to maintain when Pauline claimed, "I knew it was wrong to murder and I knew at the time I was murdering somebody. You would have to be an absolute moron not to know murder was against the law." The jury found the two girls Guilty of murder and sentenced them to prison until the queen chose to release them. Hulme and Parker were released four years later, in 1958.

Hulten, Karl Gustav, 1923-45, and **Jones, Elizabeth Maud** (AKA: **Georgie Grayson**), 1926-   , Brit. Born in Stockholm, Swed., Karl Hulten was taken to the U.S. as an infant and raised as an American citizen by his parents. He worked as a clerk and a mechanic shortly before his induction into the U.S. Army in 1943. Hulten was assigned to the 501st Parachute Infantry Regiment and stationed outside of London at the time he deserted his outfit in September 1944.

On Oct. 3, Hulten met a "party girl" named Elizabeth Jones, who was employed as a strip-tease dancer in a local night club. In the next few days the fast-living Jones dared

Killers Karl Hulten and Elizabeth Jones.

him to "do something dangerous," like steal a U.S. Army vehicle from the base. According to her version of the events, Hulten passed himself off as a Chicago gangster who controlled a mob in London. The thrill-seeking couple went out for a walk the night of Oct. 7. As they made their way along the Hammersmith Road, they spotted a car driving slowly toward them. Hulten stepped into the shadow, while Jones flagged down the car. The driver of the vehicle, George Edward Heath, thirty-four, was not a licensed taxi driver but was operating the car as such in defiance of local statutes.

Hulten and Jones got in and directed the driver to proceed to Great West Road. According to Jones' sworn testimony, Hulten fired two shots into Heath. Afterward, the woman rifled through the pockets to remove whatever valuables she could find. The body was dumped alongside the road. Hulten was arrested two days later in a house outside Fulham Palace Road, and soon he was dubbed the "Cleft Chin Murderer" by the press for the hollow in his chin. Jones was captured later that day after casually remarking to a war reserve policeman that "if you had seen someone do what I have seen done you wouldn't be able to sleep at night." The remark was reported to Inspector Tansill at the Hammersmith Police Station, culminating in her arrest.

The U.S. Government agreed to waive its rights under the terms of the Visiting Forces Acts. Hulten was tried at the Old Bailey on Jan. 16, 1945. Both were found Guilty, but the jury recommended mercy in the case of Jones. Hulten was hanged on Mar. 8. Elizabeth Jones served nine years of her sentence before being released in May 1954.

Hume, Brian Donald, c.1919-   , Brit. Murderer Brian Hume of England had not counted on the ocean currents washing his bloody parcels ashore, but in the end the swift flowing tides revealed the diabolical nature of his crimes.

Hume was a former RAF pilot turned gangster. He frequented the shady hotels and bistros of London's West End where his boyish charm won him many female admirers. His business associate, Stanley Setty, a 46-year-old car dealer born in Baghdad, was both black marketer and fence, and in 1949 entered an arrangement whereby he would procure stolen cars which Hume later would sell.

Hume and his partner had a falling out which resulted in the Oct. 5, 1949, murder of Setty. Believing that the only way to ensure that he did not get caught was to dispose of the body properly, Hume rented a private plane from the United Services Flying Club at Elstree. Over the next two days, Hume flew his craft over the English Channel and dropped three large bundles out the side door. Returning to the airfield, Hume thought he had committed the perfect crime. But the tides had washed one of the parcels to the Essex flats at Tillingham where it was recovered by a farm laborer named Sidney Tiffen. Inside, he found the severed limbs of a man. An autopsy was conducted, and through old criminal records it was learned that the deceased was Stanley Setty, who had been born Sulman Seti. Fingerprints on record with Scotland Yard confirmed the identity of the victim. From the manager of the Flying Club, detectives were able to trace the murder of Setty to the civilian pilot Hume.

Arrested on Oct. 27, Hume stoically denied complicity in the crime. After further questioning he admitted that three underworld figures, identified only as Greeny, Mac, and "The Boy," had hired him to dispose of three hot properties—believed to be printing plates used to manufacture forged gasoline coupons. These men were never found and Hume was bound over for trial at the Old Bailey on Jan. 18, 1950. However, the jury failed to arrive at a verdict.

Justice Lewis ordered that another jury be sworn in and then directed the jury members to return a verdict of Not Guilty on the murder charge. Hume

Murderer Brian Hume.

pleaded guilty to the lesser charge of being an accessory, and was sentenced to twelve years at Dartmoor prison. He served only eight years, and was back on the streets Feb. 1, 1958. In May, he disparaged the British judicial system by brazenly confessing to the *Sunday Pictorial* newspaper that he had killed Setty in his London apartment in 1949, knowing full well that he could not be tried again for the same crime. Mac, Greeny, and "The Boy" were all literary inventions designed to cover the murder, he said.

Just as this story made front page news for the second time, Hume was already planning a new caper: the robbery of the Midland Bank on Boston Manor Road. On Aug. 2, 1958, he shot and wounded a cashier at the bank and then made off with £1,500. He hit this bank a second time on Nov. 12, seriously wounding a branch manager, and tucked the money away in Zurich, Switz., but was arrested there on Jan. 30, 1959, after holding up the Gewerbe Bank. While attempting to escape Hume shot and killed a taxi driver named Arthur Maag. Since there was no capital punishment in Switzerland, Hume was spared the death penalty but he did his utmost to feign insanity. Said Chief Investigator Hans Stotz, "I think he is a very good actor." Brian Hume was tried at Winterthur, found Guilty, and sentenced to prison for life.

Humphrey, Geneva M., b.1899, U.S. Mrs. Geneva Humphrey, forty-seven, suspected her husband of having an affair. On the night of Dec. 7, 1945, after drinking at a local bar in Little Falls, N.J., she chased 43-year-old Hugh Edward Humphrey with her car into an alley and smashed him between a cellar door and the car bumper.

At her trial, Humphrey consistently denied premeditated murder and claimed she could not see her husband as the windshield was steamed over and the wipers did not work. She further denied saying, after running him over, "Well, I got that so and so." On Jan. 30, 1946, Humphrey was convicted by a jury of men and women of manslaughter and sentenced by Judge Joseph A. Delaney to eight to ten years in New Jersey State Prison, the state's maximum sentence for manslaughter.

Humud, Mohammed, d.c.1955, Zanzibar. Although a British colony until 1963, Zanzibar was dominated by an Arab elite. In 1955, the British decided to allot legislative seats on a racial basis, in an attempt to usurp Arab power. Racial tensions between Africans and Arabs led to violence when in November 1955, an unidentified Arab stabbed retired police inspector Ahmed el-Mugheiry as he walked down the street. Seriously wounded and hospitalized, he was attacked again, fatally, by Mohammed Humud. Humud was convicted and sentenced to death, but received a reprieve when the sultan commuted his sentence.

Hunt, Joe, 1960- , U.S. Joe Hunt, wealthy and supposedly charismatic, was the founder and leader of an investment group called BBC Consolidated, commonly referred to as the "Billionaire Boys Club." Its membership consisted of friends from Harvard Business School whose sole purpose was to make a fortune. Ronald G. Levin, a 42-year-old journalist and con artist, set up an account with BBC that supposedly contained $5 million. Through their efforts BBC turned the initial investment into $13 million; however, in actuality the initial $5 million never existed. While Hunt and his cohorts thought they had earned $8 million, in fact no money had been made.

Hunt learned of Levin's trick and retaliated. According to Dean Karny, a BBC member granted immunity for his testimony, Hunt and the BBC security officer Jim Pittman, confronted Levin in his Beverly Hills, Calif., duplex on June 6, 1984. Hunt forced Levin to write a check for $1.5 million (which bounced), then bound and gagged Levin, killed his dog, shot Levin in the face with a shotgun, and dumped his body in Soledad Canyon. The body was never found. Later, Hunt bragged to his BBC brothers of committing the perfect crime and warned them not to tell anyone or they would be dealt with "severely."

Police charged Hunt with the murder of Levin after obtaining seven sheets of paper from Levin's duplex containing Hunt's fingerprints and handwriting. On the pages were lists, the top page headed "At Levin's TO DO," delineating such tasks as "close blinds, scan for tape recorder, tape mouth, handcuff, put gloves on, explain situation, kill dog."

At the trial, Brooke Roberts, Hunt's close friend, testified she and Hunt were elsewhere at the time of the murder. Defense attorney Arthur Barens claimed that Levin vanished to escape creditors and is, in fact, alive, having pulled off the ultimate con. To support this theory, the defense produced two witnesses who claimed they saw Levin near Tucson, Ariz., in a car with another man. The prosecutor, Fred Wapner, son of *The People's Court* judge, claimed that Hunt killed Levin for "profit and revenge" and produced the pages of lists as well as a Billionaire Boys Club member, Dean Karny, who testified to the details of the murder.

The jury found the prosection's case more convincing and, on Apr. 22, 1987, found Joe Hunt Guilty of first-degree murder. Though Hunt was eligible for the death penalty, Judge Laurence J. Rittenband of the California Superior Court sentenced him to life in prison without the possibility of parole.

When convicted of the crime, Hunt told reporters, "It's just astonishing...I think it's a tragedy because Ron Levin's alive."

Hyde, Dr. Bennett Clarke, b.1869, U.S. Dr. Bennett Clarke Hyde was an opportunistic physician who reportedly tried to wipe out an entire family through systematic poisoning. At age forty, the tall, good-looking Hyde was married to the niece of Thomas Swope, the richest man in Kansas City, Mo. Hyde was the medical adviser to the Swope family and lived in Swope's huge mansion. Swope, in 1909, was eighty-two and in ill health. He appointed James Hunton, an old family friend, as executor of his will and estate. Hyde realized that to control the Swope millions he would have to position himself in Hunton's role. When Hunton fell ill in September 1909, Hyde treated him, or, more specifically, mistreated him by using an ancient cure-all of doctors. He bled Hunton to "purify" his blood. In truth, Hyde simply bled the old man to death and then attributed the cause of his death to apoplexy, signing Hun-

Dr. Bennett Clarke Hyde, who tried to kill off the Swope family.

ton's death certificate himself.

Swope was so overwhelmed by the death of his good friend that he himself grew ill and Dr. Hyde tended to him. A nurse attending to Swope later reported that Dr. Hyde took her aside one day and said to her: "Now that Hunton is dead, Mr. Swope will require a new administrator for his estate. I think it would be a good idea if you suggested to Mr. Swope that I take over those duties." The nurse refused, telling Hyde that it was not her place to make such suggestions. Hyde then went into Swope's bedroom and gave him a number of pills. In a few minutes, Swope's pallor turned a marked blue and his skin was cold to the touch, according to the nurse.

"I wish I hadn't taken those pills!" Swope cried out to the nurse.

Hyde told the nurse to leave the millionaire's room, ordering her to boil some water. When she returned with the water about ten minutes later, she saw Hyde covering Swope's face with a bed sheet. "He's gone, poor soul," the doctor told her.

"What? Already?" The nurse checked Swope's pulse. There was none. He was dead and the nurse found it hard to believe that the patient could have died in such a short amount of time, especially from the symptoms he had manifested.

"At that age, they can go quickly," Dr. Hyde told her. He then added that the cause of death was apoplexy, which had also claimed Hunton. Swope's millions were then distributed to several nephews and nieces. Mrs. Frances Hyde received more than $250,000, of which her husband immediately took control. Though that was a great fortune for the day, Dr. Hyde meant to obtain the rest of the money. Four of the five nephews and nieces were quickly stricken by what their doctor diagnosed as attacks of typhoid. Christian Swope, one of the nephews, died in November 1909, while being tended by Hyde in the old Swope mansion, but the others recovered. Hyde reported the death as a result of typhoid. The family nurse went to Frances Hyde and told her: "People are being murdered in this house."

Instead of becoming suspicious, the devoted spouse angrily fired the nurse and then reported the nurse's statements to the family lawyer, which brought suspicion upon Hyde himself. The lawyer cautioned Mrs. Hyde to employ another doctor to tend to the still-living nieces and nephews. Another doctor was brought in and he consulted with a bacteriologist, who reported that there were no typhoid germs in the family's water supply system. Hyde no longer tended to the sick Swope relatives and they improved greatly.

While under suspicion, Hyde began taking long walks at night and was followed on one of these nocturnal sojourns.

He was seen taking something from his pocket, which he crushed into a mound of snow. The object, a capsule, was retrieved by the person following the doctor; it proved to contain grains of potassium cyanide, a deadly poison. Family members went to the police and a full-scale investigation ensued. The bodies of Hunton and Swope were exhumed and were found to contain strychnine and cyanide. Hyde had cleverly poisoned both men with the two poisons, knowing that each poison would disguise the symptoms of the other. The physician was charged with murdering Swope and Hunton on Feb. 9, 1910. The resulting trial made headlines coast to coast. Shocked readers learned how Hyde intended to murder off the entire Swope family to gain the family millions. Only Frances Hyde believed her husband innocent and she put up the money to cover the $100,000 bond to free her husband until the conclusion of his trial.

A pharmacist testified that Hyde had purchased both strychnine and cyanide from him. At the time, said the pharmacist, Hyde said he needed these deadly poisons to get rid of wild dogs who had been "howling near my house and causing me no end of sleepless nights." Then Dr. L. Stewart, a bacteriologist, testified that Hyde had come to him, stating that he intended to take up the study of bacteriology and, for that purpose, he needed typhoid germs. Stewart gave these cultures to Hyde but, a short time later, he

Mrs. Frances Hyde, who believed her husband innocent of murdering her relatives.

grew nervous about releasing such dangerous germs to Hyde and went to Hyde's home, asking that the cultures be returned. Hyde told him that, unfortunately, he had dropped the glass slides containing these cultures and that he had thrown them out for fear of contamination. This was only a few days before Christian Swope died of typhoid.

Such damning testimony brought a verdict of Guilty after a month-long trial. Dr. Hyde was given a life term but, before leaving for prison, the physician turned to reporters and used his greatest weapon, his wife, who was convinced of his innocence. "This case is not closed," Hyde told members of the press with a smug smile. "My wife Frances will not forsake me. She knows that this is a plot by certain members of the Swope family to get rid of me. They have hated me from the start—thought of me as an interloper. Yes, Frances will know what to do."

Frances Swope Hyde remained loyal to her murderous

husband, as he knew she would. She hired the most expensive and talented lawyers available and they bombarded the courts with every known appeal. Mrs. Hyde went so far as to hire a publicist who spread the news that the Swope family had formed a conspiracy to defame her husband. By that time, Mrs. Hyde had denounced her entire family and had vowed her undying loyalty to her imprisoned husband. Mrs. Hyde's lawyers found some technical errors in her husband's trial and convinced the Supreme Court of Kansas to order a new trial in 1911. At the end of this trial, one juror grew ill and the proceedings were declared a mistrial. This juror's ailments were never disclosed and it was claimed that he was bribed to feign sickness. A third trial ended in a hung jury. It was again claimed that Mrs. Hyde's money was used to bribe several members of this jury to bring about a hung jury.

Hyde was sent to trial a fourth time in 1917, and this trial, like the two before it, had been the systematic plan of Hyde's clever lawyers. As soon as this trial commenced they moved to have their client released, pointing out a rule of law that stated that their client had gone to trial three times and, according to existing laws, could not be tried a fourth time. Dr. Bennett Clarke Hyde was released and went to live with his wife. He no longer practiced medicine. Almost a decade later, Mrs. Hyde separated from her husband. She had complained to him one day of a stomachache and he told her that he would prepare a special medicine for her. At that juncture, Mrs. Hyde thought it was time she left her husband, preferring the treatment of another doctor and, apparently, the preservation of her own life.

I

I-57 Killer, The, See: Brisbon, Henry, Jr.

Iggulden, George William, prom. 1923, Brit. "Lonely bachelor desires marriage with homely person (spinster or widow)," read the advertisement that George William Iggulden placed in a London newspaper. Ethel Eliza Howard, a divorcee with two children, responded to the ad. Within a short time, Iggulden, a portrait painter, had proposed marriage to Howard. On Nov. 15, 1923, as the couple rode in a taxi, Iggulden reached into his pocket and pulled out a razor. After slashing Howard's throat, he told the driver to take him to the nearest police station.

While admitting he was responsible for the murder of his fiancee, Iggulden said he did it because Howard was always talking about suicide, and he wanted to end her pain and suffering. Judged fit to stand trial, Iggulden was found Guilty of murder. Despite the jury's recommendation for mercy, the judge sentenced Iggulden to death. His penalty was later reduced and the convicted murderer was removed to the Broadmoor Criminal Lunatic Asylum.

Illingworth, Monty, prom. 1932-42, U.S. On a summer morning in 1939, two fishermen hooked an inanimate object in Crescent Lake, Wash. As they pulled the heavy bundle to the surface they discovered what looked like a foot projecting out from the blanket wrapped around the object. The two men were not sure whether it was the body of a woman or a mannequin. There was no odor, the facial area was obscured, and the whole bundle weighed less than fifty pounds.

In examining the fishermen's catch authorities determined that it was the body of woman in her early thirties, the body remarkably well preserved underneath the covering. In fact it had turned almost entirely to soap due to process called saponification. The victim became known as the "Lady of the Lake."

Not until 1942 did police positively identify the body as that of Hallie Illingworth, a waitress from nearby Port Angeles. During the investigation, evidence surfaced that Illingworth's jealous husband often beat her. Through exhaustive research the city coroner from Olympia, Dr. Charles P. Larson, estimated 1932 as the year of death, the same year in which Monty Illingworth had told friends and neighbors that his 36-year-old wife had run off to Alaska with a sailor. Now remarried and living in California, Monty was extradited to Washington and charged with murdering his wife. With little evidence to support his story

of desertion, Illingworth was found Guilty of murder in the second degree and sentenced to life imprisonment.

Ily, Nicole, 1932- , Fr. A web of childhood fantasies involving secret agents, hidden fortunes, and dangerous underworld figures spun by 16-year-old Nicole Ily of Paris, encouraged two of her classmates to shoot and kill Alain Guyader, the son of a French writer and public official in December 1948. The senseless killing took the French police more than two years to solve. Eventually two schoolboys, Claude Panconi and Bernard Petit, were convicted of the killing and received ten-year and three-year prison sentences, respectively. Petit, the son of a police inspector in Paris, had stolen his father's shotgun to protect the "honor" of Nicole, who was sent to prison for three years.

Ingenito, Ernest, 1924- , U.S. Ernie Ingenito was a violent youth from the time his parents separated in 1937. Mrs. Ingenito found it impossible to control him during his childhood, and by the time he was fifteen he was known to police in Gloucester County, Pa., as an incorrigible thug. Before another year had passed, Ingenito was serving a term in the Pennsylvania State Reformatory, convicted of attempted burglary. After his release, he returned to his mother's home. Her death in 1941 created an emotional scar the young man found difficult to overcome.

Ingenito married at seventeen, but his angry tirades proved to be too much for his young bride and she left him while she was pregnant with their child. He then enlisted in

Ernie Ingenito, who murdered his family in 1950.

the army where his habit of sleeping late did not endear him to his sergeant or the officers on the base. In 1943, during a heated argument, Ingenito beat up a sergeant and an officer. He was sentenced to spend two years in the stockade, and he was dishonorably discharged in 1946. The next year he met Theresa Mazzoli, a dark-haired Italian beauty whose parents owned and operated a prosperous truck farm in Gloucester County, and though her mother objected loudly to the couple's relationship, they soon married.

The impoverished young couple went to live with the Mazzolis in their home and from the start there was trouble. Pearl Mazzoli, the mother, did not care for her son-in-law and daily made a point of expressing her disapproval of him. At first Mike Mazzoli, the father, took Ernie's side. But when he learned that Ingenito had cheated on his daughter, he immediately evicted Ingenito from the home.

Ingenito moved to a residence a short distance away, to be closer to his two sons. When Theresa refused him visitation rights, Ernie consulted a lawyer, Fred Gravino, of Woodbury, N.J., who told Ernie to get a court order to see his children. Ernie rejected the advice because it would take too long, he said. A second lawyer told him the same thing. Agitated, Ingenito selected two pistols and a carbine rifle from his extensive weapons collection and, on Nov. 17, 1950, banged on the Mazzoli's front door armed with his guns.

Theresa fled. When Mike Mazzoli appeared, Ernie leveled a German-made Luger and fired two times, then stepped into the house and fired on his estranged wife, wounding her. Next, he went after Pearl Mazzoli but was unable to locate her in the house for she had run screaming to the home of Armando and Theresa Pioppi who lived down the block. "It's Ernie!" she cried, running upstairs to hide in a bedroom closet. "He's shooting everybody!"

Before Gino Pioppi, Pearl's brother, could call police, Ernie burst through the door with his guns blazing. He fired on Mrs. Pioppi and Gino's wife Marion, killing them. Ernie fired repeatedly at Pearl Mazzoli and then fired on his 9-year-old daughter before exiting the Pioppi home.

As he left, Gino's brother John grabbed a knife lying on the kitchen table and chased the gun-toting madman across the lawn until Ernie turned and fired, killing Pioppi instantly. Ingenito next drove to the home of Frank Mazzoli in Minatola, N.J. Screaming a torrent of curses he shot Hilda and Frank Mazzoli and then tried to escape.

The killing spree had begun at 9 p.m., and ended shortly after midnight when a patrol car flagged Ingenito down. As the police officers approached, Ernie tried to kill himself with the jagged edges of a tin can but failed. Speaking from her hospital bed, Theresa told a reporter: "I wish they would hang Ernie." In January 1951, Ingenito was tried for the murder of his mother-in-law. His severe psychological problems led to a sentence of life imprisonment at the New Jersey Hospital for the Insane, in Trenton. In 1956 he was brought to trial for four additional murders committed that same night, and received a sentence of life for each killing.

Irwin, Robert (AKA: Fenelon Arroyo Seco Irwin), prom. 1937, U.S. Robert Irwin was born in Los Angeles during a religious convention, a portent of things to come; the notion of original sin plagued him for much of his adult life. While still a child, Irwin was abandoned by his father, and as a result, became increasingly withdrawn and attached to his mother, a woman obsessed with religion. At an early age he developed an interest in art, particularly soap sculpting. In 1930, Irwin drifted to New York, where he began consulting psychiatrists. At one point he requested someone to castrate him to conserve his sexual energy for "higher purposes." In October 1932, he severely injured himself in an attempt at self-emasculation and was placed in an asylum.

Religious delusions and increasing paranoia drove Irwin to commit one of New York's most heinous murders of the 1930s. In June 1934, he rented a room from a family of Hungarian immigrants named Gedeon in midtown Manhattan. Joseph Gedeon, an upholsterer, his wife Mary and their two grown daughters, Ethel and Veronica, shared living quarters. Ethel Gedeon was a pragmatic woman who did not share her sister Veronica's "wild" compulsions—Veronica worked as an artist's model and dreamed of being a movie star.

Irwin had known Ethel for some time and was secretly in love with her. When Ethel married and left home, Veronica showed an interest in Irwin. When he rebuffed her attempt at seduction, she spread rumors that he was homosexual. Meanwhile, domestic relations between the elder Gedeon and his wife deteriorated after frequent quarrels about Veronica's promiscuous lifestyle, and Joseph Gedeon moved out of the house.

Irwin had left the Gedeon's home and had begun studies at a theological seminary. However, he fought with a fellow student, and was expelled from the institution. In despair, he vowed to end his life, but only after he had taken care of Ethel. On Mar. 27, 1937, the day before Easter, Irwin went to the Gedeon home. He entered the apartment but Ethel was not there. After strangling Mrs. Gedeon, and stabbing to death lodger Frank Byrnes, Irwin waited in Veronica's room. When she returned from a date some time later, he strangled her. The three bodies were found the next day, but the police were stymied. There were no fingerprints, and the motive did not appear to be robbery or sex. Joseph Gedeon was taken into custody and grilled about the triple murder which became a sensation.

The first break in the case came a few days later when a suitcase was found in Grand Central Station. Among its contents were a pair of trousers from the Rockland State Hospital—Irwin's last known address. A check of the serial number printed on the pants established his identity. After learning that Irwin was a sculptor by trade, things began to add up. A sculptor's tool had been used to kill Byrnes; strong, powerful hands had strangled the two women—a sculptor's hands.

Irwin fled to Chicago where he contacted the *Herald-Examiner*, offering to sell his story to the newspaper. The Hearst paper ran a blazing front page extra on June 25 and the sculptor seemed to enjoy his moment in the limelight, laughing and joking with reporters at the Morrison Hotel. By prior arrangement, Irwin surrendered to the Cook County sheriff and was extradited to New York where he was arraigned on murder charges. Famed defense attorney Samuel Leibowitz represented him when the case went to trial in November 1938. Leibowitz maintained his record of never losing a client to the electric chair by securing for Irwin a sentence of 139 years in prison.

Ivory, Henry, and **Perry, William**, and **Stirling, Amos**, prom. 1900, U.S. When police discovered the brutalized body of Professor Roy Wilson White on a side street near Powelton Avenue Station in Philadelphia, the University of Pennsylvania community was shocked. The popular law professor had distinguished himself with students and colleagues and had yet to turn thirty. White had been beaten over the head with an iron bar and robbed of some of his possessions. Within an hour of the May 19, 1900, murder, Ralph Hartman, a messenger at the train station, reported to police he had seen two black men near the murder scene at around 10 p.m. and had even engaged in a brief conversation with one of them.

From Hartman's description, police rounded up 135 suspects, narrowing these down to sixteen. In a lineup Henry Ivory was identified by Hartman as the man with whom he had spoken. The suspect admitted conversing with the messenger at the train station but denied knowledge of the crime. After intense questioning he confessed to being party to the murder but swore he did not kill the victim. The police traced White's stolen watch to William Perry, and a city employee, John Leary, helped identify a third suspect in the murder. When police apprehended Amos Stirling in New Jersey, the man's clothes were covered with blood. Stirling said his nose had been bleeding and that he was innocent of any crime. A few weeks later Ivory finally told police the complete story. He said Stirling had pounded the victim with the iron bar and then they had robbed the professor. All three men were tried and convicted on murder charges. Ivory, Perry, and Stirling were then hanged.

J

Jackson, Calvin, 1948- , U.S. A Manhattan police detective admitted that "depersonalization" and a "lack of interest" on the part of the homicide squad was partly to blame for the murder of nine elderly women at the seedy Park Plaza Hotel between April 1973 and September 1974. Even after the first victims had been found dead in their shabby, ill-equipped apartments, "no immediate police action was taken on any of them." The shoddy detective work and casual disregard for the lives of these elderly women led to a general shakeup in the New York City Police Department's Fourth Homicide Zone. Lieutenant James Gallagher, who failed to consider that the murders might have been the work of one man, was transferred to internal affairs. The long overdue reorganization had unfortunately come at the expense of at least nine lives.

The Park Plaza was located on West 77th Street in Manhattan. Despite the rather elegant name, most of its elderly residents lived barely above the poverty level in tiny, cramped rooms. The corridors were poorly lit and many residents dead bolted their doors at night to keep out muggers, thieves, and rapists. The eleven-story hotel was a seedbed of crime on the West Side. Beginning on Apr. 10, 1973, when 39-year-old Theresa Jordan was found suffocated in her apartment, the Park Plaza took on an even more sinister character. A homicidal maniac was loose in the building, but the police were hard pressed to provide answers to the anxious residents.

The killer struck again on July 19. Kate Lewisohn, sixty-five, was strangled to death and her skull crushed by the unknown assailant. For the next few months no more bodies were found, until on Apr. 24, 1974, 60-year-old Mabel Hartmeyer was found dead in her room. The Medical Examiner's Office attributed her death to "occlusive coronary arteriosclerosis." Although the police accepted this verdict without question, it was subsequently shown that the woman had been strangled and raped. Four days later 79-year-old Yetta Vishnefsky, a retired sewing machine operator, was stabbed to death with a butcher knife. She had been bound, gagged, and

Mass killer Calvin Jackson.

raped before she was murdered. A television set, some jewelry, and a few items of clothing had been stolen. Following the Vishnefsky murder the body count rose steadily. Forty-seven-year-old Winifred Miller, an accomplished pianist and singer, was the victim on June 8; followed by Blanche Vincent, seventy-one, on June 19; Martha Carpenter, sixty-nine on July 1; and 64-year-old sculptor Eleanor Platt, on Aug. 30. At first the medical examiner ruled out homicide in the cases of Vincent and Platt. Their deaths were blamed on chronic alcoholism and heart failure. Detectives from the Fourth Homicide Zone classified their files as "pending," an acknowledgment that murder could not be ruled out entirely.

On the morning of Sept. 12, 1974, the police received a frantic call from Dorothy May, the maid of Mrs. Pauline Spanierman, a 59-year-old widow living in an apartment building adjoining the Plaza. She said that her employer had been murdered. The medical examiner affixed the time of death at shortly after 3 a.m. It was the first time the killer had selected a victim outside the residential hotel. Police detectives questioned the residents of Spanierman's building and learned that a suspicious-looking man had crawled down a fire escape clutching a small TV set under his arm. Later that afternoon police detectives arrested 26-year-old Calvin Jackson at the intersection of 77th Street and Columbus Avenue and charged him with murder and possession of stolen property. Jackson was a former inmate at the Elmira, N.Y., State Correctional Facility, with a long record of robbery and drug convictions. He had been living at the Park Plaza Hotel since 1972 and had been arrested on Nov. 7, 1973, for pilfering a television and stereo set from one of his neighbors——a crime for which he plea-bargained his way to a thirty-day sentence rather than the fifteen years it normally carried. Jackson returned to the Plaza where he earned his living working as a porter.

Born in Buffalo, Jackson's career up to the time he moved into the Park Plaza with his girlfriend Valerie Coleman was a road map of crime. He had drifted aimlessly from one flophouse to another, committing petty robberies and dealing drugs. He was described by Coleman as a soft-spoken, "caring" individual. "Jack was the kind of person if you needed something and he had it, he'd give it to you," she said. Jackson was taken to the Manhattan Criminal Court for arraignment the day after his arrest. Under direct questioning from Assistant District Attorney Kenneth D. Klein and a battery of detectives, Jackson confessed in hushed tones to killing Spanierman and the other elderly women. He was kept under close watch at the Manhattan House of Detention for Men to prevent a suicide attempt.

On Nov. 3, 1974, State Supreme Court justice Joseph A. Martinis ruled that Jackson was mentally competent to stand trial, against the strongly vociferous objections of defense attorneys Donald Tucker and Robert Blossner. "If Calvin Jackson is not legally insane, who is legally insane?

He raped women, some in their seventies and eighties. He raped some of them after death. Is this a legally sane man?" Tucker wanted to know. "He went to the refrigerator in nearly every apartment. He prepared a meal and ate it as he watched the body. Sometimes he stayed for an hour. Is this a legally sane man?" The jury agreed with the judge, returning a verdict of Guilty against Jackson on nine counts of murder on May 25, 1976. Jackson's five-hour taped confession that had been played inside the jury room was a major factor in their decision. Justice Aloysius J. Melia of the State Supreme Court sentenced the defendant to two life terms for each victim. Jackson will not be eligible for parole until the year 2030.

Jackson, Louie (AKA: **Louise; Louisa Gomersal; Louie Calvert**), b.1897, Brit. When Arthur "Arty" Calvert hired Louie Jackson as housekeeper for his Hunslet, England, home in 1925, he knew only that she was a widow with two small children. As the weeks went by, the watchman grew intimate with Jackson. Soon she informed Calvert she was pregnant with his child and they were married. With the baby due soon, Louie told her husband that she was going to stay with her sister until the baby was born. Three weeks later she returned with a baby girl. A suitcase arrived at the house, which Louie Calvert said contained baby clothes. Later that day, the police came to the house and arrested her.

Louie was better known to English officials as Louisa Gomersal, a thief and prostitute, and now she was wanted on charges of murder. Gomersal had lied to Calvert about the pregnancy and left to find a baby. She took a room in a boarding house run by Lily Waterhouse, and found a 17-year-old girl willing to give up her baby. While she waited for the baby to be born, Gomersal stole from Waterhouse. The 40-year-old spiritualist, who had already confronted the hot-tempered Louisa, went to the police with her complaint. Waterhouse was found dead the next day. A letter in the rooming house led authorities to Calvert's home. Police found cutlery in the bag which supposedly contained baby clothes. Gomersal was found Guilty of murder and her plea of pregnancy was disregarded. Before her execution, Louie Calvert admitted also killing John Frobisher and dumping his body in a canal in 1922.

Jackson, R.E., prom. 1962, and **Jackson, Clemmie,** 1943- , U.S. At sixty-one years of age, Samuel L. Resnick suffered from incurable cancer, heart trouble, and diabetes. The jeweler from Albany, N.Y., had retired to Phoenix,

Ariz., and now he wanted to die there. He scanned the job-wanted ads in the newspapers each day for someone to end his pain. At least five men turned Resnick down when he asked them to kill him. Resnick finally contacted Clemmie Jackson, a Texas farmhand who had arrived in Arizona with dreams of owning a car wash.

Jackson first refused to have any part of the murder plot, but when Resnick promised the 19-year-old enough money to open his own business, Jackson agreed. Jackson recruited his brother, R.E. Jackson, and three other youths to help. Resnick promised the young men cash and jewelry and drove with four of them into the desert just north of Phoenix. By this time, Clemmie Jackson had backed out. When the youths tried to strangle Resnick to death, the rope broke. Resnick then assisted the amateur murderers in completing their task. The killers ended up with $3,000 worth of jewelry, but no cash. Three days later the body was discovered and the youths had left so many clues that they were quickly apprehended. The four conspirators were all tried, convicted and sentenced to life imprisonment. Clemmie Jackson was acquitted.

Jacobson, Howard (AKA: **Buddy**), 1930-89, U.S. At the age of seventeen, Melanie Cain arrived in New York in 1972 with dreams of becoming an actress. Within months, the Naperville, Ill., native signed with one of New York's top modeling agencies and began a relationship with her landlord, Howard "Buddy" Jacobson. Formerly one of the country's top trainers of thoroughbred race horses, following a dispute with the New York Racing Association Jacobson was forced to turn to real estate, a field in which he became successful. When Cain was fired from Eileen Ford's modeling agency, she and Jacobson started their own agency. Christened My Fair Lady after Cain's favorite musical, the agency prospered with Melanie as its star attraction.

Jacobson, who had told Cain he was twenty-nine, was really forty-two. The two men he introduced as his brothers were really the divorced man's sons. For nearly five years, Cain tolerated rumors that her boyfriend slept with a number of women at the agency. In 1978, Cain met handsome young restaurateur Jack Tupper while jogging, and within weeks she left Jacobson and moved in with her new boyfriend, who also lived in Jacobson's building.

Jacobson harassed Cain and Tupper with phone calls and noise. He turned off the hot water in their apartment and offered the 34-year-old Tupper and some of his friends $100,000 if Cain would return to him. On the morning of Aug. 6, 1978, Cain left the apartment building at 155 E. 84th St. to sign the lease for a new apartment, so she and

Tupper could escape their tormentor.

When Cain returned early that afternoon, Tupper was not home and she went to Jacobson's apartment. No one answered the door and Cain returned to her apartment to wait for Jack. Upon hearing noise in the hallway, she peeked out to see Jacobson and one of his sons tearing up the rug in the hallway. After the men left, Cain stepped out in the hall and discovered reddish, moist stains on the padding which had been covered by white paint. She also found a tuft of hair, a smeared palm print on the elevator, and other spots in the hall that had been freshly painted. Cain returned to Jacobson's apartment and asked him where Tupper was, but he said he hadn't seen him all morning. Cain called police.

The next day, Estella Carattini identified a car belonging to Jacobson. She said that Jacobson and one of his employees, Salvatore Prainito, dragged a crate from the trunk of the 1974 Cadillac into a vacant lot, set fire to the crate and then fled the scene. When police found Jack Tupper's body, it was barely identifiable. He had been beaten, stabbed repeatedly, and then set afire. Police arrested Jacobson and charged him with murder. In a 1980 trial, Jacobson was found Guilty of second-degree murder. But only three days before he was scheduled to receive his prison sentence, he escaped from jail on May 31 by calling in a debt. An old friend, Anthony DeRosa, posing as a lawyer, brought a razor and a change of clothes into the Brooklyn House of Detention and Jacobson walked out minus his bushy moustache. Jacobson's latest girlfriend, Audrey Barrett, was waiting in the parking lot and the two fled the state. The court sentenced Jacobson in absentia to twenty-five years in prison.

On June 29, Barrett surrendered to authorities and was charged with criminal facilitation, first-degree escape, and possession of legal stationery. Ten days later, in the Los Angeles suburb of Manhattan Beach, local police arrested Jacobson. He was on a restaurant pay-phone calling the district attorney's office in Brooklyn to make arrangements to turn himself in. Jacobson died of cancer in Buffalo, N.Y., in May 1989.

Jacoby, Henry Julius (AKA: **Harry**), 1904-22, Brit. Henry Jacoby, eighteen, who worked at Spencer's Hotel on Portman Street, London, had planned for weeks to rob one of the wealthy guests at the hotel. His opportunity came on the night of Mar. 14, 1922, when he crept into the room of Lady Alice White, believing that the 60-year-old dowager was not in. In precarious health since the previous December, she was asleep in her room.

Alice White, the widow of Sir Edward White, a former London County Council chairman, was startled by Jacoby's invasion, and he struck her with a hammer. The elderly woman died the next morning. Jacoby was arrested and charged with murder a few days later. He casually remarked to a police officer, "Isn't it funny how much strength a man's got?" referring to the brutal blow he had given White.

The trial began at the Old Bailey on Apr. 28, 1922. Jacoby said he had "heard voices" and had gone to the guests' rooms to investigate. The door of room Number 14, belonging to White, stood open. "I thought I heard murmurings inside," Jacoby said, "I rushed in and seeing a form, lashed out. I did not know it was Lady White." Jacoby was found Guilty of murder, but the jury recommended mercy, given his age. The plea was rejected by the home secretary and Jacoby was hanged at Pentonville Prison on June 5 over a storm of protest. Ronald True, a member of a titled family, had recently murdered a London prostitute, but had been reprieved on the grounds of insanity.

Lady killer Henry Jacoby.

Jagusch, August, prom. 1951, U.S. At twelve, August Jagusch's father stabbed him in the arm with a bread knife when Jagusch refused to eat unpeeled potatoes. He then ran away from home, and when he was returned home by police his father suggested he should be locked up. For sixteen months, Jagusch endured a series of sexual liaisons at Children's Village in Dobbs Ferry, N.Y. He was constantly assaulted by male counselors, and slept with several female teachers and fellow inmates, all before turning fifteen.

Upon his release from the children's home, Jagusch continued to be sexually promiscuous. Although he later married and had a daughter, the relationship ended in divorce. In June 1951, Jagusch strangled to death a young Staten Island striptease dancer named Mildred Fogarty. His ex-wife turned Jagusch in to the police when he contacted her after the murder. He told police that Fogarty had enraged him during a sex act and that he went berserk and strangled the woman. Jagusch was found Guilty of second-degree murder and sentenced to twenty years in prison. He was released on Aug. 23, 1967, after serving sixteen and a half years in Auburn State Prison.

Jahnke, Richard J., 1967-   , U.S. The beatings began at age two for Richard J. Jahnke. His father, Richard C. Jahnke, also beat young Richard's sister, Deborah Jahnke, and his mother, Maria Jahnke. The IRS agent and his family lived in Cheyenne, Wyo. He collected guns, had few friends and rarely socialized with neighbors or co-workers. After years of unreported abuse, 16-year-old Richard confided in Major Robert Vegvary, his ROTC instructor at Central High School. In May 1982, Vegvary accompanied Jahnke to the sheriff's office to file a complaint. A perfunctory visit to the Jahnke household a few weeks later only enraged the father.

Richard C. Jahnke told his son that he would never forgive him for going to the authorities. On Nov. 16, Richard fought with his mother over cleaning the basement. Later, as the parents left to celebrate their twentieth anniversary, Jahnke told his son he did not want to see him there when he returned.

During the hour-and-a-half the couple were gone, Richard and his sister loaded a number of guns and placed them around the house. Deborah was stationed in the living room with a rifle, and her brother hid in the garage with a shotgun. The parents' car pulled in the driveway, and the elder Jahnke turned off the engine and got out of the car. As he approached the garage door entrance to the house, two shotgun blasts hit the 38-year-old man. The younger Jahnke fired four more times into his father who lay on the garage floor. Richard C. Jahnke died within minutes from chest wounds. His son was arrested and charged with murder.

In February 1983, a jury deliberated seven hours before declaring Jahnke Guilty of voluntary manslaughter in the death of his father. He was also found Not Guilty on one count of conspiracy. Although his murder conviction was upheld by the Wyoming Supreme Court, Jahnke's five- to fifteen-year sentence was reduced to three years by Governor Ed Herschler.

James, Robert (Raymond Lisemba), 1895-1942, U.S. Born Raymond Lisemba in rural Alabama in 1895, Robert James had done the back-breaking work of a cotton baler until he inherited $2,000 from each of two uncles who had named him beneficiary of their insurance policies. Receiving such a windfall without expending any effort made a lasting impression on the young man. He took his inheritance and traveled to Birmingham, Ala., where he attended a barbers' college and changed his name to James. It was also in Birmingham, in 1921, that he met and married Maud Duncan. This first marriage ended when James's wife could no longer tolerate his requirements of her for sadomasochistic sex. In the divorce suit, Duncan claimed that James frequently stuck hot curling irons under her nails.

James reportedly had also fathered several illegitimate children during his time in Birmingham and decided it would be healthier to move on. He then moved to Emporia, Kan., where he opened a small barber shop and married again. He suddenly left Emporia and his wife when the father of a girl he had gotten pregnant threatened his life. Only weeks after arriving in Fargo, N.D., his next stop, he opened another barber shop and married for a third time to Winona Wallace. The newlyweds' honeymoon trip to Colorado's Pike's Peak was marred when Winona was seriously injured in a car accident. When she recovered sufficiently to be released, James took her to a remote cabin in Canada. A few days after their arrival, James appeared at the police station to report that his wife, dizzy from the accident, had drowned in the bathtub. Shortly after the funeral, James collected $14,000 in life insurance—a policy he had taken out on her life a day before the wedding.

In Alabama, in 1934, James met a local girl, Helen Smith. The two were married and moved to Los Angeles. Helen Smith later told authorities that James was sexually impotent unless she whipped him. This fourth wife became suspicious when he told her he wanted her to have a medical examination for a life insurance policy. She refused saying that "people who have it (insurance) always die of something strange." James resented her obstinacy and the two were soon divorced. Next, James took out a $10,000 life insurance policy on a nephew, Cornelius Wright, then a sailor stationed at San Diego. Wright had a long history of being accident-prone—he had been hit several times by cars; some scaffolding had once collapsed on him; he had been knocked unconscious at a baseball game. James, playing the magnanimous uncle, loaned him his car to use while on leave and told him to go off and have a good time. Three days later, Wright drove the car off a cliff near Santa Rosa and died. Only later did the mechanic who towed the wrecked car away tell police that something was wrong with the steering wheel.

With the money he collected on his nephew's death, James opened a posh barber shop in Los Angeles and he began an affair with his manicurist, 25-year-old Mary Bush. When Bush became pregnant and insisted that James marry her, he did so. Not long after their marriage, however, James again took out another insurance policy. Then he persuaded one of his employees to find a couple of poisonous snakes, explaining that he had a friend whose wife was

Robert James under arrest.

Left, Mrs. Mary James, murder victim; center, Charles Hope (left) and Robert James (center) at the pool where Mrs. James drowned; right, a black widow that failed.

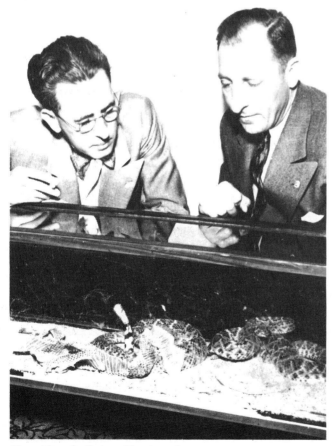

The rattlesnake that would not murder.

Hope tries the rattlesnake box in court.

Robert James on the witness stand; he was executed.

bothering him and he wanted the snakes to "take care of her." In July 1935, the employee, Charlie Hope, went to "Snake Joe" Houtenbrink, a reptile collector, and procured two Crotalus Atrox rattlers. James then brought Hope in on his plot to kill his wife and promised him part of the insurance money.

After working out the details, James took Hope home with him for dinner one evening, introducing him as a doctor. After Hope had been in their home for a brief period, he told the pregnant Mrs. James that she did not look well and probably should not go through with her pregnancy. The naive woman agreed to let this "eminent physician" perform an abortion on her that very night. In lieu of anesthetic, James encouraged her to drink whiskey until she passed out. Once she was incoherent, he brought the snakes into the house in a specially designed box constructed so that he could insert her leg into it without letting the snakes escape. He left her for several hours with her leg in the box, and she was bitten repeatedly. She did not die, however. When she revived and complained of terrible pain in her leg, James assured her it was nothing important. The leg, however, swelled to twice its normal size and became increasingly painful. Early in the morning, James suggested that she take a bath to soothe the pain. He ran the water into the bathtub for her and stood by to help her into the tub. As she got into the tub, James pushed her down, pulling her legs high enough so that her head was submerged and held her in this fashion until she drowned.

After dressing her, he and Hope carried her body to the yard, where they placed it face down in a small lily pond in such a way as to make it appear that she had become dizzy and collapsed, and accidentally drowned. After going over the alibi with Hope, James went on to work. He worked through the day as though nothing at all was wrong, and that evening returned home with two friends whom he had invited to dinner, ostensibly after clearing the impromptu dinner party with his wife. As planned, the three "discovered" his wife's body in the pond. The death was classified as accidental.

Three months later, however, a Los Angeles captain of detectives, Jack Southard, saw a report that James had been arrested for propositioning a woman and thought it peculiar that a man so recently widowed should be apprehended for such a crime.

Southard learned from neighbors that a green Buick sedan had been seen outside the James home and that Charles Hope had been phoning James constantly. Southard also discovered that Hope owned a green Buick sedan, so he searched Hope's apartment. There he found a receipt for two rattlesnakes. Southard collected enough evidence against Charlie Hope to arrest him on suspicion of murder. Once arrested, Hope confessed, implicating James. James

was arrested in May 1936 and after a quick trial, was sentenced to death. Hope received a life sentence. James remained in the Los Angeles County Jail for the next four years while appealing his case. In 1940, he was finally moved to San Quentin. As it became evident that commutation of his sentence was unlikely, James fought to die in the gas chamber instead of by hanging because the law changing the manner of execution was enacted after his sentencing. On May 1, 1942, Robert James was hanged at San Quentin, the last man to be hanged in California.

Jeffs, Doreen, d.1965, Brit. In November 1960, in Eastborne, England, Doreen Jeffs killed her baby daughter and then fabricated a kidnapping. When the corpse was found, Jeffs's story was challenged and she soon confessed and pleaded guilty to murder. Her defense attorney successfully presented a case for duress based on the fact that the child, Linda Jeffs, was a month premature. Contending that Jeffs was "a woman who committed an offense while under the stress of childbirth," the lawyer got Jeffs sent to a mental institution. She was later put on probation. Jeffs attempted suicide by taking gas, but was interrupted. Over four years later, in January 1965, she neatly folded her clothes by a cliff overlooking the English Channel near Beachy Head and dove into the ocean. Her body surfaced near the shore several days later.

Jenkin, William Thomas Francis, 1934- , Brit. On Apr. 13, 1959, the body of 12-year-old Janice Anne Holmes was found in Binbrook, Lincolnshire, England. Four days later, a 24-year-old truck driver, William Thomas Francis Jenkin, of Hall Farm Estate, was arrested for the murder. The prosecution charged that Jenkin lured the little girl into the woods, where he assaulted and strangled her. He denied the charge, and his wife claimed that he had spent the evening searching for the missing child. The first trial ended with a hung jury, but at the retrial on July 16, 1959, Jenkin was found Guilty of the murder and sentenced to life imprisonment.

Jenkins, Allison, 1960- , U.S. For Chicago police officers Jay Brunkella and Fred Hattenberger, Sept. 22, 1986, was a routine day in the war on drugs. The officers, part of an eight-man unit assigned to patrol the neighborhoods north of Howard Street, near Evanston, were staked out on the third floor of an aging elementary school. The officers observed small-time dope peddlers in operation, and radioed the license plate numbers of buyers to an arrest car waiting a few blocks away. Allison Jenkins was a familiar face to Brunkella. The 28-year-old native of Belize had been arrested on a number of minor charges, most recently for selling cocaine to an undercover police officer. When the policemen observed what they thought was a drug transaction, they left the building to arrest Jenkins.

During the attempted arrest of the pusher, Hattenberger's gun discharged and hit Brunkella in the chest. There were no ambulances immediately available to transport Brunkella to the hospital, so his fellow officers placed him in the back of the squad car. After eleven days in intensive care, Brunkella died on Oct. 4, 1986. Jenkins, who had originally been charged with selling marijuana and aggravated battery, was now charged with the murder of a police officer. In January 1987, a jury convicted Jenkins of delivering a controlled substance, and Criminal Court Judge Joseph Urso sentenced him to six years in prison.

Urso also presided over Jenkins' murder trial, which began in September. The defendant's lawyer, Craig Katz, argued that his client was framed by a trigger-happy cop who had taken unnecessary risks with his weapon. The prosecution contended that Jenkins, on parole, had tried to flee from the officers. State's Attorney Dennis Dernbach argued that Jenkins and Hattenberger struggled, and that the defendant caused the policeman's gun to fire. A jury found Jenkins Guilty of murder, but within days one juror called the judge and said that she had been pressured into rendering a Guilty verdict. Katz then petitioned the court to set aside the jury's verdict because he had new evidence in the case.

Police officer James Crooks then testified that he had seen Hattenberger use unnecessary force on one occasion. It was also revealed that Hattenberger had once before wounded a fellow officer in the line of duty. On Nov. 13, 1988, Urso denied the motion for a new trial. Jenkins was sentenced to twenty years in prison for murder.

Jennings, James Brandon (AKA: **Kid Carter**), b.1880, U.S. On New Year's Day 1913, James Brandon Jennings, better known to his boxing fans as "Kid Carter," shot and killed Bill MacPherson after a fight began in Garrity and Prendergast's Saloon in Boston's South End. Although there were many witnesses to the crime, no one was able to give a reason for the slaying. Jennings was taken into custody immediately and tried for the murder beginning on Mar. 24, 1913. On Mar. 28, the jury returned a verdict of Guilty of murder in the second degree. On Apr. 18, 1913, just after his sentencing to life in prison,

Jennings blurted out to a crowded courtroom that he had also murdered his girlfriend, Mildred Donovan, as well as "many others." No further legal action was taken against "Kid Carter," although he was found unfit to serve time in the state penitentiary and was committed instead to the Bridgewater State Hospital for the criminally insane.

Jesse, Frederick William Maximilian, 1897-1923, Brit. Frederick William Maximilian Jesse strangled and dismembered his aunt, Mabel Jennings Edmunds on July 21, 1923. A week later when Jesse confessed, police found Mrs. Edmunds' legs on the table on the top floor, and her trunk on the bed wrapped and tied with rope. According to Jesse, he and his aunt quarrelled and when he went to his room to get away from her, she followed and continued to hit him and throw a liquid on him. By Jesse's account the next thing he remembered was finding his hands around his dead aunt's neck. He told police that he had intended to dispose of the body but became afraid. Jesse was tried at the Old Bailey in September 1923. He was found Guilty, sentenced, and, on Nov. 1, hanged.

Jobin, Marie, prom. 1920, Fr. In 1920, Gaston and Marie Jobin were married and living in Paris. Marie consorted with other men and Gaston led a life of petty thievery.

On Mar. 23, 1920, Gaston Jobin was seen for the last time. Marie claimed that he had fled to Spain to avoid military conscription. On Apr. 8, 1920, however, a man's torso, minus head and limbs, was dragged from the Seine. Then, eighteen months later, a postal official examining a stack of undeliverable mail discovered an underlined paragraph about the body's discovery in a letter addressed to Paul Jobin, Gaston's brother. The letter had been sent by their sister in Switzerland, who was convinced that their brother was murdered.

The police again visited Marie Jobin, who was living in a Toul hotel with a man named Burger. Although Marie repeated her original story, she asked her lawyer a curious question: Legally, when would she be free to marry again? This querry from a woman who claimed her husband was alive and well. Mr. Warrain, the interrogator, kept at them until the two confessed to having murdered Gaston Jobin on Mar. 23, 1920. Burger was sentenced to death, and Marie Jobin to hard labor for life. She died a few years later.

Johnson, Milton, 1950- , and **Lego, Donald**, 1933- , U.S. In the summer of 1983, five multiple murders in Will County, Ill., resulted in seventeen deaths. A small, citizen-financed crime fighting organization, Crime Stoppers of Will County, helped apprehend two suspects, Milton Johnson and Donald Lego. Lego was convicted in the stabbing and bludgeoning murder of an 82-year-old widow, the last of the seventeen victims, on Mar, 16, 1984. On the same day, Johnson pleaded not guilty to charges of the murder of an 18-year-old man and the rape of his 17-year-old female companion. In August, he was convicted of the attacks and when given the choice of being sentenced by Judge Michael Orenic, or by the jury, he opted for the judge. On Sept. 19, 1984, Judge Orenic, who was on record as opposing the death penalty, sentenced Milton Johnson to die by lethal injection. On Jan. 28, 1986, Johnson was convicted of four more deaths in the same murder spree.

Johnson, Robert, 1924- , U.S. Robert Johnson, of Wilmington, N.C., clubbed four of his children to death within twenty-four hours of his wife's abandoning the family in September 1971. A fifth child survived the brutal beatings. His wife Bonnie Louise Johnson had recently threatened to leave him, saying that she felt trapped in her marriage and that she had too many children to care for.

Before clubbing his children, Johnson had contacted a Wilmington television station, hoping to broadcast an appeal for his wife's return. Two hours later, he contacted police and led them to the murder site. He was charged with the murders of the four children and the attempted murder of one daughter, the only survivor. He was sent to Cherry Hospital in Goldsboro, N.C., for a sixty-day mental observation period, and later to prison at Southport, N.C.

Johnson had a troubled past. He received a dishonorable discharge during WWII, after serving time for desertion. He also had a civilian record for forgery and the interstate transportation of a stolen airplane. But he had stayed clear of trouble for twelve years until September 1971.

Johnson, Terry Lee, 1949- , U.S. Johnson, an ex-Marine from rural Alabama, turned to a life of crime after being released from the service. Dealing in narcotics replaced the occupations of carpet installing, landscaping, logging, welding, and construction work. Through his Marine experience, Johnson was adept at living in the wilderness and with handling a wide array of firearms. He was charged with murder and found Guilty of killing an un-armed farmer.

Johnson subsequently escaped from prison and was last seen in Alabama, carrying a high-powered rifle. At this time he is still a fugitive.

Johnson, Vateness, 1951- , and **Johnson, Frank**, c.1947- , U.S. Vateness Johnson and her husband, Frank Johnson, were convicted of the Mar. 12, 1985, murder of 5-year-old Judy Moses, who was in their foster care. The child, along with her three-year-old sister, were put in the Johnson's care after the Illinois Department of Children and Family Services deemed their real father incapable of properly caring for them. The children were repeatedly beaten and on the last day of her life, 5-year-old Judy was tied to a chair in the Johnson's unheated garage.

In 1985, Vateness Johnson was convicted and sentenced to sixty years in prison while her husband was sentenced to twenty-two years. The Illinois Court of Appeals ordered a new trial, saying that the couple should have been tried separately. Frank Johnson denied the actual beatings, and was allowed to plea-bargain a lesser sentence of involuntary manslaughter. His sentence was reduced to eight years. On Nov. 24, 1988, a Will County, Ill., jury was shown pictures of the brutally-beaten children, listened to a medical examiner's report, and upheld the earlier conviction of Vateness Johnson.

Johnston, Bruce, Sr., 1939- , and **Johnston, David**, 1948- , and **Johnston, Norman**, 1951- , U.S. In two separate trials in eastern Pennsylvania in 1978, the Johnston brothers were convicted of murdering six people, including a family member, and of attempting to kill one other person.

Two generations of the Johnston clan formed a theft ring that was accused of stealing well over $1 million in cars, jewelry, and farm equipment. When family member Bruce Johnston, Jr., suspected his father of having raped his friend Robin Miller, however, he went to authorities, unaware that his betrayal would result in five murders.

On July 17, 1977, Bruce Johnston, Sr., murdered Gary Wayne Crouch, thirty-one. Then on Aug. 16, 1978, David and Norman Johnston murdered James Johnston, eighteen, Bruce, Jr.,'s half-brother, Wayne Sampson, eighteen, and Duane Lincoln, seventeen, near Chadds Ford, Pa. On Aug. 20, Wayne's brother, James Sampson, twenty-four, became the fourth victim. And on Aug. 30, Bruce, Jr., and his fiancee Robin Miller, fifteen, were ambushed; Miller died.

On Mar. 18, 1980, in Edensberg, Pa., David and Norman

Johnston were convicted of four murders and were each sentenced to four life sentences. On Nov. 15, 1980, in the West Chester courtroom of Judge Leonard Sugarman, Bruce Johnston, Sr., after testimony by 126 witnesses, including his son, was found Guilty of all six murders and sentenced to life in prison.

Jon, Gee, d.1924, U.S. After he was found Guilty of murder and sentenced to death, Gee Jon was held in the Carson City (Nev.) Courthouse and became the center of a controversy. In an effort to clean up Nevada's image as a comparatively lawless frontier state, Governor Emmet Boyle signed a new capital punishment bill from the state legislature in 1921. There had been debate over whether to abolish the death penalty entirely or to substitute some improved form of execution. The bill rejected electrocution, and instead mandated introducing a lethal gas into the convict's cell while he slept. When it proved too complicated for the public executioner to introduce lethal gas into an ordinary cell, Jon was temporarily saved from execution. When the Nevada Supreme Court declared the gas execution bill valid and ordered the sentence to be carried out, an improvised structure was constructed and made air tight. On Feb. 8, 1924, Jon died from inhaling cyanide gas.

Jones, Genene, 1951- , U.S. In September 1982, a 15-month-old baby girl mysteriously died in Kerrville, Texas, after a routine examination by a local pediatrician. A powerful muscle relaxer, Anectine, which had not been prescribed, was later found to be the cause of death. Six other children at the clinic had suffered similar attacks in a six-week period, with nurse Genene Jones always nearby. Aiding healthy babies did not offer a great enough challenge, so Jones created "life-and-death" situations. She became euphoric when administering CPR and other life-saving techniques to her victims.

A subsequent investigation in San Antonio uncovered more horrors. When Jones worked the night shift at a local hospital, more than twelve inexplicable deaths had occurred, earning her the name of the "Death Nurse." On Feb. 15, 1984, she was convicted of murder and sentenced to ninety-nine years in prison.

Jones, James Warren (Jim), 1931-78, Guyana. Boyhood friends of the Reverend James Jones would recall the times when he held mock funeral services for dead animals in the Indiana town of Lynn, whose cottage industry was casketmaking. "Some of the neighbors would have cats missing and we always thought he was using them for sacrifices," recalled Tootie Morton. Jones, whose father was a drunken Klansman unable to hold a job, became obsessed with religion. At fourteen, the Bible-toting boy delivered his first sermon. In 1949, Jones married Marceline Baldwin, his high school sweetheart.

After dropping out of Indiana University, the couple moved to Indianapolis where they started a Methodist Mission, but the church fathers found his religious pretensions objectionable and he was expelled in 1954. Jones then raised money by importing monkeys and selling them for $29 each. He accumulated $50,000, which was used to purchase a rundown synagogue in a black neighborhood of Indianapolis. During this time he and his wife adopted eight Korean and black children.

The mayor of Indianapolis, impressed with Jones' community work in the impoverished neighborhoods of the city, appointed him director of the Human Rights Commission. But

The psychopathic religious fanatic James Warren Jones.

when Jones found Indianapolis too provincial in its racial attitudes, he moved to Belo Horizonte, Braz., after reading that this was the safest spot in the world to survive a nuclear holocaust. The family later relocated to Rio de Janeiro where Jones taught in an American school. Hearing that the People's Temple in Indianapolis, which he had founded in 1957, was in the midst of a leadership crisis, Jones returned home. In 1964, he affiliated his group with the Disciples of Christ and was ordained a minister.

Influenced by the Reverend Ross Case, and half-believing that the world was about to end, Jones led a migration of 100 followers from Indiana to Redwood Valley, in Mendocino County, Calif. The minister purchased a synagogue in the deteriorating Fillmore district of San Francisco. He provided a day-care center and food kitchens for the black inner-city residents, who accounted for 80 percent of the congregation of the People's Temple and won the enthusiastic support of politicians. Governor Jerry Brown was a visitor to the People's Temple. Mayor George Moscone appointed Jones to serve on the city's housing authority as a reward for his political support in the 1975 election. After hearing of the Jonestown horror, Moscone would say, "I proceeded to vomit and cry."

Money began to roll in. Jim Jones purchased Greyhound buses and began traveling around the country accompanied by bodyguards and press aides. At the same time he preached sexual abstinence to his congregation, he surrounded himself with female followers. In 1974, he purchased 27,000 acres of rain forest in Guyana on the northern coast of South America, which he hoped to turn into a socialist utopia for himself and his followers. Despite warm endorsements from top Democratic leaders like Henry "Scoop" Jackson, Walter Mondale, and Jimmy Carter, whom Jones supported for president in 1976, he became obsessed with the notion of mass suicide as a way of escaping governmental persecution, a fascination with suicide dating to 1953 when Ethel and Julius Rosenberg were executed in the U.S. as spies. By 1976, Jones was indoctrinating his followers in the concept of a "White Night," a mass suicide ritual that was being "rehearsed" at his People's Temple.

The first clue the public had about Jones' hidden agenda and the secret cult activities occurred at an anti-suicide rally held at the Golden Gate Bridge on Memorial Day 1977. Speaking before hundreds of spectators, Jones called for the construction of an anti-suicide barrier to be constructed on the bridge. Dr. Richard Seiden, professor of behavioral science at the University of California, later recalled how the direction of Jones's speech changed. His condemnation of suicide became almost a blanket endorsement for it. "He saw himself as the victim, persecuted and attacked, and from there proceeded to the concept of suicide as an appropriate response. We were not aware of the nuances and implications," Dr. Seiden said.

Membership in the People's Temple swelled to nearly 20,000, and his services became increasingly bizarre. He claimed to have the power of faith healing, and would draw out the "cancer" from the sufferer during ceremonies—the cancer actually a bloody chicken gizzard. No longer content to be the reincarnation of Jesus, Jones began calling himself God. With the help of local authorities in Guyana and private contributions from his followers, he began clearing large sections of jungle in 1977. That year, the religious colony of Jonestown was founded and about 1,000 members made their exodus from San Francisco to the jungle retreat.

Jones enforced his will through physical and mental coercion. The San Francisco *Examiner* reported in August 1977 that members were publicly flogged for minor infractions like smoking and falling asleep during religious sermons. Electrodes were attached to children who were ordered to smile at the mention of the leader's name. These reports began filtering back to California congressman Leo Ryan, fifty-three, who pressured the U.S. State Department to investigate. A delegation from the U.S. embassy in Georgetown interviewed seventy-five members of the cult, but none indicated a desire to leave. Ryan was not convinced. His friend, Robert Houston of the Associated Press, had lost a son to the cult. The young man had been murdered in San Francisco after attempting to quit the People's Temple. Ryan embarked on a fact-finding mission on Nov. 14, 1978, accompanied by eight journalists and several relatives of Jonestown cultists.

They were greeted by the congenial Jones, who led a guided tour through the compound, proudly showing off the spacious library, hospital, and living quarters. That night Congressman Ryan and his party were entertained at the pavilion. Even Ryan was impressed. He arose from his chair and said, "From what I have seen, there are a lot of people here who think this is the best thing that has happened in their whole lives." Jones led the thunderous applause.

The next day NBC reporter Don Harris asked Jones about his military arsenal and if it were true that the compound was under heavy guard. Jones exploded in rage. "A bold-faced lie!" he screamed. One of the cultists slipped a note to Ryan which read "Four of us want to leave." There were other similar requests. While Ryan spoke with Jones about moving these people out, a cultist named Don Sly attacked him with a knife but was subdued by attorney Charles Garry. Ryan and his entourage departed for the airfield at Port Kaituma and an awaiting Cessna. As they deliberated about the best way to squeeze the extra passengers into the tiny craft, a flatbed truck rumbled by. Three armed men standing in the trailer suddenly opened fire. From inside the plane, Larry Layton produced a gun and began shooting. The crossfire left five persons dead—Congressman Ryan, photographer Greg Robinson, NBC cameraman Bob Brown, Don Harris, and one of the departing cultists, Patricia Park.

While Ryan and his entourage were being fired upon, Jones was preparing to order his followers to carry out "revolutionary suicide" at the compound. The brainwashed followers, who had rehearsed this scenario dozens of times, were herded into the main pavilion where they received purple Kool-Aid laced with cyanide. Mothers gave cyanide voluntarily to their children. Infants received the substance with a syringe squirting it into their mouths. Next came the older children who received it in paper cups, and finally the adults who accepted the poison as a loudspeaker intoned, "We're going to meet again in another place!" Those who refused to accept this fate were prodded by heavily armed guards. Within five minutes, most of the 913 victims were dead. Not since the Japanese citizens of Saipan hurled themselves from the rocky cliffs of the island in WWII had the world witnessed anything like this.

Jones, like Adolf Hitler years earlier, killed himself with a bullet to the head. No witnesses survived. Investigators found rows of bodies, most of them lying face down. The U.S. Air Force sent planes to retrieve the remains of the victims while experts in human behavior and sociology grappled with larger issues. "Most members have little or no sense of inner value," theorized Stefan Pasternack, associate clinical professor of psychiatry at Georgetown University. "In joining (Jones) they regress and relax their

The bodies of Jones' deluded parishioners in Guyana, after being forced into mass suicide, 1978.

personal judgments to the point that they are supplanted by the group's often primitive feelings. With a sick leader these primitive feelings are intensified and get worse."

One person went to trial for complicity in the Jonestown Massacre. Thirty-five-year-old former Quaker Layton, a member of Jones's death squad, was charged with injuring U.S. diplomat Richard Dwyer and conspiracy to kill Congressman Ryan. The jury in the San Francisco courtroom was unable to agree on a verdict. The courtroom was packed with relatives of the victims when, on Sept. 23, 1981, a mistrial was declared by Judge Robert Peckham.

Jones, Jeremiah, 1913-   , Brit. As a youngster, Jeremiah Jones, the son of a London chambermaid, had a violent and unpredictable nature. At only six years old, he

was a truant, a delinquent, and a thief. In June 1920, at age seven, he was playing with two younger boys when one refused to give him a toy. He pushed the child into a canal, stoned him, and stepped on his fingers until he drowned. When accused, he testified that the boy had fallen, and the death was ruled accidental.

He soon began to have wild outbursts. When interviewed by child psychiatrist Cyril Burt, Jones admitted to the murder. The other boy agreed, saying that he had remained silent because Jones threatened him. Jones was sent to a series of homes, where his temper remained violent and he developed an intense fear of water. At age nine, he began to show signs of stability. It is unknown what happened to him in his adult life.

Jones, Reginal, d.1982, U.S. A sniper in River Rouge, Mich., killed two people and wounded four on July 18, 1982. The gunman, Reginal Jones, was killed by police when they returned fire. He had begun shooting randomly with a .30-caliber rife from the porch of his second-story apartment. He killed Desiree Burton, a 15-year-old girl, and Mabel Arrington, an elderly woman who was sitting on her porch. Four others, including a River Rouge policeman, were wounded.

Jones, Rex Harvey, prom. 1950s, Brit. Rex Harvey Jones, a miner in the Rhondda Valley of rural Wales, was a man of exemplary character. But after drinking seven pints of beer with his 20-year-old girlfriend, he strangled her. He then called the police and led them to her body. During his trial, the judge told the jury, "You have to steel your hearts against good character and steel your hearts in order to see that justice is done." Despite this admonishment, the jury made a strong recommendation for mercy. But the judge was adamant, and Jones was hanged.

Jordan, Chester, d.1912, U.S. Chester Jordan and his wife Honora Jordan were actors in Boston in 1908. One day in September, he bought a pair of shears, a hacksaw, and a knife. A few days later, he was seen around town carrying a trunk that was unusually heavy for its size. A hackman reported this to police officers Irving Peabody and Michael Crowley. Two officers went to the Jordan home to investigate. Jordan showed the men the trunk, which held a few light articles of clothing. However, it also emitted a powerful stench, and when asked what was at the bottom,

Jordan confessed that it was the torso of his wife. He had struck and pushed her down a flight of stairs. After she died he dissected her, and tried to burn her head and legs. He was arraigned on murder charges on Sept. 3, 1908.

With the help of his brother-in-law, famous stock-market plunger Jesse Livermore, Jordan raised money for his defense. The trial began Apr. 20, 1909, in the Superior Court of Middlesex County in East Cambridge, before Justices William B. Stevens and Charles U. Bell. The prosecution paraded witnesses, including police officers, medical experts, neighbors, a cab driver, and Jordan's landlady. Particularly gruesome was the exhibition of the late Mrs. Jordan's skull, tongue, and larynx, all carefully preserved in formaldehyde. The defense countered that Jordan was not mentally fit due to suffering from cerebro-spinal syphilis during early manhood. His family agreed, adding their versions of various emotional traumas. The jury was not dissuaded and handed down a Guilty verdict on May 4, 1909.

However, four days later, the jury foreman, Willis A. White, was committed to an insane asylum. The defense appealed the conviction, but the motion was rejected by Justices Stevens and Bell. A further appeal to the Massachusetts Supreme Court was also rejected. On Mar. 12, 1911, with appeal attempts exhausted, Jordan was sentenced to death by execution. The appeal was taken to the U.S. Supreme Court, where it was denied on May 27, 1912. On Sept. 24, 1912, Jordan was electrocuted in Massachusetts.

Jordan, Clayton, 1970- , U.S. On Jan. 9, 1988, Taneka Jones, an 11-year-old girl, was sexually molested and murdered in her home in unincorporated Du Page County, Ill. Her mother found her in a basement storage room the following afternoon. A 10-year-old upstairs neighbor provided testimony which implicated three men: Clayton Jordan, John Kines, and Saul Berry. Jordan was prosecuted in Du Page County Circuit Court before Judge John Bowman.

Jordan had been sentenced earlier to five years on battery charges and was free on bail. He was convicted of the murder and assault of Taneka Jones, and sentenced to serve eighty years for murder, and to serve concurrent terms of thirty years for aggravated criminal sexual assault, five years for intimidation of a witness, and five years for concealment of a homicide. Jordan was ordered to serve out the earlier battery sentence before beginning the murder sentence. Berry received a 70-year sentence and Kines fifty years.

Jordan, Thomas, 1860-1909, U.S. Anton Nolting was a well-educated and popular patrol sergeant when he reported for duty on Jan. 8, 1909, in San Francisco. Shortly after 1 a.m., he heard a shot, and ran to see a soldier with a drawn pistol forcing two other soldiers down the street. When Nolting confronted them, the two hostages were able to flee, leaving the officer to grapple with the assailant. A shot was fired, wounding the officer, and three more were fired, killing him as he lay on the ground. The assailant, Thomas Jordan, was quickly apprehended.

Jordan testified that he was a member of the Coastal Artillery at Fort Baker, but that his mind was a complete blank regarding the shooting of Sergeant Nolting. Hiram Johnson was hired as special prosecutor, and on Mar. 12, 1909, Jordan was found Guilty of murder and sentenced to life imprisonment. He died later that year.

Joubert, John J., 1963- , U.S. A native of Portland, Maine, John J. Joubert joined the Air Force after flunking out of Norwich University in Vermont. Stationed at Offutt Air Force Base near Omaha, Neb., the 21-year-old Joubert was fascinated by detective magazines and their glossy reenactments of sex and violence. In 1983, the fantasy world of Joubert exploded.

Danny Jo Eberle, thirteen, was abducted Sept. 18, 1983,

Murderer John Joubert.

on his way to school. His bound body was found three days later south of Bellevue, Neb. He had been stabbed repeatedly. Three months later, on Dec. 5, the brutalized body of Christopher Walden, twelve, was found north-west of Papillion, Neb. The autopsy reported that Joubert had first tried to strangle the boy and then stabbed him five times. While there was no evidence of sexual assault, both boys were forced to strip down to their underwear before being killed. On Jan. 11, 1984, Joubert was arrested for the murders of Eberle and Walden.

During his trial, psychiatric evidence showed that Joubert had been fantasizing about bizarre acts with women and young boys since he was six years old. Police found twenty-four detective magazines in his room, and Joubert admitted to having sexual fantasies about the captives depicted in them. On July 3, 1984, Joubert confessed to the murders of Danny Jo Eberle and Christopher Walden.

Three months later, a three-judge panel sentenced him to death. The parents of both victims had implored the court to give Joubert the death sentence, while Beverly A. Joubert had asked that her son be spared so that he might help other prisoners. John J. Joubert awaits execution at the Nebraska State Penitentiary in Lincoln.

Judd, Winnie Ruth (Winnie Ruth McKinnell), 1906-

, U.S. Born and raised in a well-to-do Illinois family, Winnie Ruth Judd moved to California to study nursing and there met and married an elderly, wealthy physician, Dr. William J. Judd. She contracted tuberculosis and was sent to the desert community of Phoenix where it was hoped the dry air would cure her condition. In 1931, Judd moved in with two of her best friends, Agnes Ann LeRoi, thirty, and Helwig Samuelson, twenty-three. The three women shared a trim bungalow and all went well for some months. But then Judd, according to later statements, began to harbor deep resentment toward LeRoi and Samuelson who, she claimed, were stealing her male friends.

Judd was then twenty-five, had a curvaceous figure, copper hair, and large blue eyes. She confronted her two friends on the night of Oct. 16, 1931, and asked them why they were interfering with her love life. Both women laughed at her, she later claimed. With that, Judd pulled

One of the trunks containing one of Winnie Ruth Judd's victims.

a small revolver and shot both women dead. She crammed their bodies into a trunk and booked a reservation on the Golden State Limited, intending to return to California. For some strange reason, she intended to take the bodies

of her friends with her. A train porter arrived at the bungalow and told Judd that the trunk was too heavy to be shipped as personal luggage. Winnie told him that it contained important medical books belonging to her husband. The porter suggested that she rearrange the books into two trunks, and she agreed. She had the porter take the large trunk to an apartment she had rented and there she removed Samuelson's body, and sawed it into pieces so that it would fit into a smaller trunk and a suitcase. She then shipped these three pieces of baggage to Los Angeles and climbed aboard the Golden State Limited.

Winnie Ruth Judd with bandaged hand during her murder trial.

Once she arrived in Los Angeles, Judd took a taxi to the University of Southern California, going to the political science building to see her 26-year-old brother, Burton J. McKinnell. When he arrived, Winnie implored McKinnell to accompany her to Union Station to retrieve her trunks. "You must help me get them right away!" she told him. "We must take them to the beach and throw them into the ocean!" She was frantic and her hand was bandaged. (Judd had fired a bullet into her own hand at the time of the LeRoi and Samuelson killings so that she could later claim she had been shot by LeRoi and had killed the two women in self-defense.) McKinnell, so as not to agitate his sister further, agreed to help her. They went to Union Station and, at the baggage counter, claimed the two trunks and large suitcase. Baggage clerk Andrew Anderson, however, suspected that Judd and her brother, who had no idea that his sister was a murderer, were meat smugglers. Hunters had recently shot deer illegally in Arizona and had been secretly shipping venison to Los Angeles in trunks.

One of the trunks smelled like a dead animal, Anderson believed, and the other trunk was seeping a dark, gluey substance. He told Judd and her brother that he had to inspect the baggage she was claiming before he could turn it over to her. Judd quickly answered that only her husband had the keys to the baggage and she would have to get them first. She turned on her heel and walked quickly away, her puzzled brother following. Anderson trailed the pair to the parking lot and there spotted the couple getting into a car. He wrote down the license plate and then called the police. Two detectives arrived at the station and broke open one of the trunks. They stepped back in shock. Some spectators standing nearby became ill at the sight of Samuelson's dismembered corpse. A woman fainted.

Police traced the license number Anderson had written down to McKinnell, who was then meeting with Dr. Judd. He told detectives that his sister had told him as they drove away from Union Station that there were "two bodies in those trunks and the less you know about it, the better off you are." She had borrowed a few dollars from him and then gotten out of his car at Sixth and Broadway in downtown Los Angeles, disappearing into a crowd. A police dragnet for Winnie Ruth Judd ensued but she was nowhere to be found. Judd was, at the time, hiding in an unused building on the grounds of the La Vina Sanitarium in Altadena where she had once been a tuberculosis patient. She remained in the empty building for three days, sneaking into the sanitarium's kitchen at night to steal food. Meanwhile, her hand, which bore a gunshot wound, became infected. After three days, Judd picked up a newspaper and read an ad which her husband had placed, in which he begged her to surrender herself.

Winnie contacted her husband, who took her to a clinic where her hand was treated. Police then arrived to arrest her. She was extradited by the state of Arizona and tried for the murders of LeRoi and Samuelson. Winnie at first claimed that she had killed her two friends in self-defense. She held up her hand and said that Samuelson had shot her in the hand and that she had struggled with her, grabbing the gun and shooting first Samuelson, then LeRoi when the other woman also attacked her. The jury, believing that Judd had shot herself in the hand to support her claim of self-defense, convicted her and sentenced her to death. While awaiting execution, prison doctors became convinced that Judd was insane and a mental hearing was held. Winnie's mother and other relatives stepped forward to state that the McKinnell family had, for generations, been afflicted by insanity.

Winnie made a great show of being deranged. She pulled at her hair, constantly ripped away at her clothes, mumbled to herself and, at one point, leaped up and pointed to the jury and shouted: "They're all gangsters!" She later called her husband to her side and said, loud enough for the courtroom to hear: "Let me throw myself out that window!" Guards finally had to be called in to remove Winnie, who had become hysterical. It was agreed that she was hopelessly insane. Her death sentence was commuted to a life sentence in the Arizona State Mental Asylum. She escaped many times. Once she made a "sleeping dummy" of herself and fled into the wilderness, walking many miles before she was picked up by a motorist who returned her to the institution. "When she looked at you with those great big eyes brimming with tears you

would believe anything she told you," stated a nurse.

In 1952, Judd escaped again but was recaptured. She was brought before a committee looking into conditions in mental hospitals. Before she could testify, guards found a

Winnie Ruth Judd at her sanity hearing.

passkey hidden in her hair and a razor secreted under her tongue. She escaped again in 1962 and managed to reach Concord, Calif. There she became a live-in housekeeper for John and Ethel Blemer, earning additional money as a baby sitter for neighbors. She was recognized on a street in 1969 and arrested. She managed to fight extradition back to Arizona for some time, defended by Melvin Belli, but the governor of California, Ronald Reagan, returned Judd to Arizona.

On Dec. 22, 1971, the Arizona Parole Board commuted Judd's life sentence to time served and she was released on the provision that she live out her life in California. She returned to the Blemer home to resume housekeeping duties. Ethel Blemer died in 1983 and Winnie sued for a goodly portion of the Blemer estate, claiming that the Blemers, since her 1971 parole, had kept her a virtual "indentured servant," and that she had been "thrown out" of the Blemer home after Ethel's death by other Blemer relatives. She was eventually awarded a $225,000 settlement, plus $1,250 a month for life.

Juenemann, Charlotte, 1911-35, Ger. Charlotte Juenemann kept her three children locked in a basement room until they died in 1935. The woman, whose husband was in an insane asylum, had been given welfare money but refused to apply it to the children. Instead, she became enamored with a musician and spent the money on nightlife. At the time of her arrest, she was pregnant.

On Mar. 30, 1935, Juenemann was sentenced to death by beheading. Nazi Germany's new justice also determined that her unborn baby would be a debit to the race. The sentence was carried out on Aug. 27, 1935, at Plotzenee Prison.

K

Kaber, Eva Catherine, d.1931, and **Calla, Salvatore**, and **Piselli, Vittorio**, and **Colavito, Erminia** (AKA: **Big Emma**), prom. 1919, U.S. Publisher Daniel D. Kaber of Cleveland, Ohio, thought someone, his wife perhaps, was trying to kill him. For months he lay motionless in his bed at the family home in plush Lakewood after suffering a stroke. Paralysis set in, despite the constant attention of physicians, who were convinced that he had a rare stomach disorder.

On July 18, 1919, a hideously penetrating scream was heard from Kaber's room. F.W. Utterbach, a male nurse on duty in the house, rushed into the room to find Kaber lying in a pool of blood on the floor, slashed repeatedly by

Daniel Kaber, murder victim.

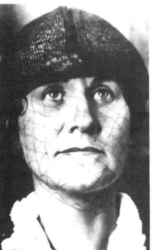
Mrs. Eva Kaber

a knife-wielding assailant. An ambulance carried him to the Lakewood Hospital where he died a few hours later, his last words fueling speculation that the murderer had been hired by a family member. "The man in the cap did it," he gasped. "That woman had me killed." Moses Kaber, the dead man's 75-year-old father, was convinced that his daughter-in-law Eva was responsible because during her husband's illness she had shown little concern, and on the night of the murder was vacationing at a popular lake front resort, leaving her flapper-daughter Marian McArdle and Mary Brickel, Kaber's mother-in-law, to attend to Daniel.

Eva's first two marriages had ended in divorce. She had lived an impoverished life. When she married Kaber in 1911 her driving ambition was to attain a degree of wealth for herself and Marian. At the coroner's inquest, Eva Kaber denied the charges brought against her by her father-in-law and Prosecutor Samuel Doerfler. Since her alibi was unshakable the case was dismissed. Eva collected the insurance money due her, sold the house, and moved to New York to open a millinery shop. Daughter Marian followed her east and became a chorus girl in *Pretty Baby.*

Back in Ohio, Moses Kaber continued the investigation. He hired Pinkerton agents to follow Eva Kaber and also posted a $2,000 reward. Two women came forward, Mrs. Ethel Berman, a former acquaintance of Eva, and Mrs. M.A. Deering. In New York, Berman had renewed her friendship with Eva and went to work in the millinery shop as a secretary. Meanwhile, Deering got to know Mrs. Brickel who freely admitted that her daughter "did it for the money."

Erminia "Big Emma" Colavito

Nearly two years passed before the Cuyahoga County district attorney wired New York police to arrest the widow Kaber and her daughter on suspicion of murder. They were brought in for questioning on June 2, 1921, after Mrs. Berman had pieced together an incredible story. She had found out that Eva had consulted with a number of psychics to determine the time when her invalid husband would die. Dissatisfied with what they told her, she resorted to more direct methods. A $5,000 "bounty" was placed on her husband's head, but her chauffeur, Frank DiCarpo, was not interested in collecting. Next, she went to a pair of mediums who refused to conjure up "evil spirits" to carry out a murder.

Salvatore Calla, killer for hire.

Finally, Eva found a soul mate in Mrs. Ermina "Big Emma" Colavito of Sandusky, who promised to deliver a special medicine to hasten Kaber's demise. What she had in mind were two hired thugs whose names were Vittorio Piselli and Salvatore Calla. The murder-for-hire scheme was given its final blessing by Mrs. Brickel, who had given the conspirators the "all-clear" signal. Calla was arrested in Buffalo. Piselli had fled to

Italy after the murder, but was picked up there and jailed. Eva confessed to her role in the plot but refused to implicate her daughter Marian.

The charges against Mrs. Brickel were dismissed, and Marian, the dupe in the scheme, was acquitted. But the other defendants received life sentences. Eva Kaber, often described as the "meanest prisoner in Ohio," died in the Women's Prison in Marysville in 1931.

Kadlecek, Joseph (AKA: **Joe Cadillac**), prom. 1938, U.S. In 1938, Joseph Kadlecek, known to many as Joe Cadillac, lived in a rooming house on the West Side of Chicago and worked in a Fulton Street box factory. His neighbors rarely saw him, but they were familiar with his late night escapades which always involved alcohol and sometimes women.

On the morning of Nov. 17, a maid found the naked body of Ella Pehrson, twenty-eight, in Kadlecek's closet. The smell of death mixed with the overpowering scent of perfume in the tiny room. Pehrson, who sold beauty supplies, had been stabbed repeatedly and sexually assaulted after her death. Chris Stavard, the landlord of the rooming house on Warren Avenue, told police that Cadillac kept to himself, paid his rent on time, and was missing a finger on his right hand from a recent industrial accident. The victim had lived just blocks away at the West Manor Hotel on South Ashland Avenue.

Kadlecek was arrested outside the Lawndale National Bank on 26th Street when he tried to withdraw money from a bank account he shared with his brother. He admitted he was a regular business customer of the murder victim, but said he didn't kill her. Hours later, Kadlecek claimed he found Pehrson's body in his room and stuffed her in the closet in panic. Still later, he admitted that he murdered her and assaulted her after she resisted his sexual advances. He said he soaked the room in perfume to cover up the stench of the bloody corpse. On Jan. 9, 1939, Judge Walter Stanton sentenced Kadlecek to sixty years in prison. "I had it coming—and more," Joe Cadillac said. "I couldn't have beefed if the judge had given me the hot seat."

Kagebien, Joey Newton, 1956- , U.S. When Joey Kagebien of De Witt, Ark., was sentenced to die in the electric chair for the 1971 murder of 27-year-old Jimmy Wayne Wampler, he became the youngest person to sit on Death Row.

Wampler, a prosperous rice farmer from Wynne, Ark., had purchased three six-packs of beer at a small general store in Gillet for his 15-year-old friend Kagebien, who was going on a hunting trip with three friends: Teddy Kittler, sixteen, Larry Mannis, seventeen, and Benny West, sixteen. According to Kagebien, Wampler approached them for sex, and when his request was denied Wampler became abusive. Kittler shot Wampler after Kagebien struck him over the head with a rifle butt. His naked body was found late that night after the boys reported the crime to De Witt police chief, James Mason.

The youths claimed it was an act of self defense. But the jury in the first of two sensational murder trials disagreed. Kagebien was found Guilty and sentenced to die in the electric chair. Because of Kagebian's youth, Governor Dale Bumpers was flooded with petitions to commute the sentence. Responding to public pressure, the governor stayed Kagebien's execution in September 1971, a month before he was scheduled to die.

In January 1974, the Arkansas youth was granted a second trial by the state supreme court. It was held before Judge Andrew Ponder, who found the defendant Guilty of second-degree murder. Under Arkansas law, anyone who aids and abets a murderer is as guilty as the person who actually committed the crime. Joey Kagebien was sentenced to twenty-one years in prison, with twelve years suspended. Teddy Kittler, who pulled the trigger, received a life term. The two accomplices, Benny West and Larry Mannis, were given sentences of twenty-one years and twenty years, respectively.

Kantarian, Nancy Lee, 1954- , U.S. In a moment of unexplained frenzy, the 30-year-old daughter of media tycoon John Heselden, deputy chairman of Gannett Corp., publishers of the *USA Today* newspaper, murdered her two young children and set fire to her spacious home in the Great Falls section of Fairfax County, outside Washington, D.C. The tragedy occurred the night of May 23, 1984. Nancy Lee Kantarian was alone in the house with her children, preparing them for bed. Her husband Harry, a Washington-based attorney, was in Denver on business.

Police and fire officials puzzled over just what transpired inside the $400,000 suburban house before they arrived. When they appeared the residence was ablaze and Kantarian was at her neighbor's home sobbing incoherently. Inside the burning house they found 5-year-old Jamie Lee Kantarian and her 6-year-old sister, Talia, lying unconscious. The younger girl was pronounced dead at the scene, killed by the fire. Talia Kantarian died as a result of thirty-two stab wounds inflicted by her mother. At first Mrs. Kantarian told police the children were responsible for the fire, but later amended this story. "Jamie was angry...She built ...she wouldn't sleep...she piled blankets to make a house when she should have been sleeping," Kantarian sobbed. "I got mad... Harry was gone...I get so frightened."

Nancy Kantarian pleaded guilty to murdering her two children in an emotionally charged hearing before Judge Bernard Jennings in the Fairfax County Circuit Court on Oct. 2, 1984. "There is no question that the killings are the result of some form of mental or emotional sickness," said Prosecutor Robert Horan, who supported a recommendation to hospitalize the woman rather than send her to jail. Judge Jennings agreed. On Oct. 6, he sentenced Kantarian to the maximum of ten years in prison on two counts of manslaughter, but suspended it on the condition that she enter a private facility to be paid for at the family's expense. "There is no need to incarcerate you as a deterrent to others," Jennings stated. "And I don't think we really need to protect society from you."

Kaplan, Joel David, 1927- , U.S. Thirty-four-year-old Joel David Kaplan entered Mexico in 1961 as president of the American Sucrose Company, a U.S. firm owned by Kaplan's uncle, J.M. Kaplan. In November of that year, the treasurer of American Sucrose, Luis Melchior Vidal, was reportedly shot to death and a body initially thought to be his was found on the road to Cuernavaca. Kaplan and two other men, Harry Kopelsohn and Evsle S. Petrushansky were arrested and charged in the murder. Kaplan fled Mexico but was arrested in Spain by Interpol and returned to Mexico City. He was convicted of Vidal's murder in late 1962 and sentenced to serve twenty-eight years in prison.

Kaplan's uncle was also the founder of the Kaplan Foundation in New York, which has been identified in Congressional testimony as one of the otherwise philanthropic agencies used for channeling CIA funds to labor and student organizations. Joel Kaplan had a long-standing interest in the politics of Third World countries and was rumored to have acted as a mercenary in various Caribbean and Central American locations. Kaplan, once in prison in Mexico City, hinted broadly at having served in the CIA. Furthermore, it was rumored that Vidal had been a supplier of arms to Third World countries. Additionally, Kaplan's attorney claimed that the body purported to be that of Vidal was actually that of a man twice Vidal's age, bearing little or no physical resemblance to Vidal.

On Aug. 18, 1971, Joel Kaplan, who had already made several attempts to escape from prison, finally succeeded. While the guards at Santa Maria Acatitla prison watched a movie, Kaplan and another inmate, Carlos Antonio Contreras Castro, dashed across a courtyard to a waiting helicopter and flew away. The escape was reportedly arranged and paid for by Kaplan's relatives.

The helicopter flew to Actopan, Mex., where a small plane piloted by Victor E. Stadter waited to take them to La Pesca, Mex. There, Castro, a pilot who was serving a prison sentence for swindling, left for a destination in Mexico while Kaplan and his pilot headed for the U.S. When the plane reached the border at Brownsville, Texas, shortly before midnight, Stadter notified U.S. Customs of their approach, giving his own name and Kaplan's as the plane's passengers. It was later surmised that this identification was necessary because Kaplan had to be in the U.S. legally in order to claim an inheritance that awaited him. Stadter flew Kaplan, who was reported to be ill, to an unknown destination where he went into hiding. Neither the U.S. nor the Mexican governments appeared very interested in tracking Kaplan down. Due to a loophole in Mexican law which makes prison escape illegal only if violence is used, Kaplan had committed no further crime.

Kashney, Roland, 1937- , U.S. The 1970 armed robbery and slaying of 65-year-old Margaret Riggins and the 1974 armed robbery and slaying of 55-year-old Benjamin Peck in Chicago, Ill., remained unsolved until a former girlfriend of Roland Kashney informed police that he had committed the crimes. In 1974 when police arrested Kashney, a self-proclaimed evangelist, he confessed to both murders and armed robberies, but claimed that he had been forced by the devil to do it. Kashney was found unfit to stand trial and was committed to a state mental hospital.

Kashney spent five years in the hospital before he was found sane in October 1979 and ordered to stand trial. During the May 1981 trial, 43-year-old Kashney denied committing the crimes, claiming that he had confessed to them earlier only because the police officers questioning him were possessed by the devil. Kashney claimed that he could see the devil squeezing the heads of the officers and confessed because he was afraid of the demons. In spite of testimony from two "demonologists," the jury found Kashney Guilty of Peck's murder but Innocent of both armed robberies and the Riggins murder. He was sentenced to thirty to sixty years in prison.

Kasper, Karl, 1933- , Ger. Karl Kasper of Rotzel, Ger., summoned the local physician to come at once to his home on Nov. 5, 1972. The 39-year-old farmer had come home from the fields and found his wife dead in her bedroom.

Dr. Harald Nussbaum concluded that Ingrid Kasper's death was neither accidental or natural. A coroner from Waldshut concluded she had been electrocuted while in a state of extreme sexual agitation. The Kaspers had been married for fourteen years, and had three children. At first it seemed unlikely that Kasper would kill his wife.

But the facade of marital bliss was soon ripped away by investigators. Kasper was heavily in debt, partly because of the money he had borrowed to purchase the farm. He had a mistress, Erika Jung, whom he met through an ad in a local newspaper, and was fond of aberrant sexual activities. Mrs. Kasper died from a massive electrical shock from a pair of medical tongs intended to provide sexual stimulation.

Kasper claimed the murderer was Luigi Antoninni, an Italian who allegedly had intercourse with Ingrid. The Italian had left the country, and it was unlikely that he was involved. The electrical cords used to kill Ingrid were later found in her husband's car. Confronted by this evidence, he made his confession. It was an accident during sex, he explained. But he also had taken out a life insurance policy on his wife six months before her death. On Oct. 5. 1973, Kasper was found Guilty of murder and sentenced to twelve years in prison.

Katz, Arthur, 1934-87, U.S. The stock market crash of October 1987 exacted a heavy toll, not only financial, but in human lives as well. Across the nation there were reports of distraught financial speculators committing acts of violence. Arthur Katz of Miami walked into a Merrill Lynch brokerage office on Oct. 26, 1987, and asked to speak with the manager. Katz was well known to the office workers as major investor who apparently did not understand the dangers of buying stocks on margin. Katz casually opened a briefcase and pulled out a gun, which he turned on himself after killing Jose Argilagos, fifty-one, and his broker Lloyd Kolokoff, thirty-eight, both Merrill Lynch vice presidents.

Katz had suffered serious financial reversals since moving to Florida in the 1970s under the witness protection program. He had been involved in a stock manipulation scheme and had started over in Miami as a Social Security claims examiner. His passion, however, was the world of high finance. When his creditors called in his accounts after the crash, Katz became desperate. He vented his anger against the system with a gun.

Kauffman, Paul, prom. 1930, U.S. The newspaper want ad asked for a girl to care for a small child for $10 a week. To Avis Wooley, a 17-year-old girl from Webb City, Mo., it seemed like the ideal job. She agreed to meet the man who identified himself as Paul Kauffman, a young widower with one child.

She left home on Aug. 17, 1930, and was never seen again. The only indication that her mother received that her daughter was still alive was a telegram, dated Aug. 17, which read: "Like job very much. Will write later. Love Avis."

On Oct. 12, Alfred Erickson was walking through Swope Park in Kansas City when he stumbled over a skull which forensic experts identified as that of a young woman. The remains were Avis Wooley's. When the police investigated the ad placement in the Kansas City newspapers, they learned that Paul Kauffman was a fictitious name. The man who used this alias had been arrested before for imprisoning a teen-age girl in his room.

When Kauffman was arrested and taken into custody he told the Kansas City police chief that after picking up Avis at the train station, they had walked through Swope Park. When he offered her a drink, she refused. A quarrel ensued when the girl insisted on going home. It was then that Kauffman strangled Avis with her nylon stockings. He then robbed her of seventy cents. For killing Avis, Kauffman was found Guilty of murder in the first degree and was executed at the gallows.

Kawananakoa, David Kalakaua (AKA: **Prince Koke**), 1904-   , U.S. David Kawananakoa was the last surviving male member of the Hawaiian Royal family. His grand-uncle, David Kalakaua, earned a reputation as a lustful, fun-loving playboy known to play poker for hours on end.

Like his uncle, Kawananakoa had a yen for the fast life, and could frequently be found cavorting with the island girls on the Flapper's Fast Acre, Honolulu's night club district and sin-strip. Prince Koke got into trouble for the first time in 1932 when Felicity Connors of California was killed in an automobile crash. He was given a five-year probation, but violated the terms of the sentence when he openly lived with Arvilla Kinslea, a 22-year-old Hawaiian-American.

In October 1937, Kawananakoa was arrested a second time when he assaulted his live-in lover with a crockery shard during a beach party held in his cottage, adjacent to the "strip." When the police arrived they found Kinslea's body wrapped in a sheet and bleeding from the neck. The prince, Major Bernard Tooher of the U.S. Army, and two other guests stood by as police surveyed the ransacked cottage.

Prince Koke pleaded guilty to manslaughter and was sentenced to ten years in the Oahu Penitentiary by Judge H.E. Stafford.

Kearney, Frank, d.1925, U.S. When a thief tried to rob tailor Harry Hamburg, the tailor testified against the man, who, convicted and sentenced to a jail term, swore he would get revenge. Months later Hamburg was shot and killed on New Year's Eve.

A phone call on Dec. 31, 1924, brought police to Hamburg's shop in Boston's South End. A hard-working, courageous man, Hamburg had battled it out with thieves before. This time he lost his life. Owners of the fruit store next to Hamburg's shop had called in when they heard sounds of a struggle and then a gunshot, and saw two men in overcoats running away.

Police investigators Louis DiSessa, Captain Driscoll, and Sergeant Gale discovered that Joe Colanso, convicted for attempting to rob the tailor months earlier, was serving a prison term at the Reformatory in Concord, Mass. Though Colanso had sworn revenge, he could not be connected to Hamburg's murder. Soon after questioning him, a police officer discovered an overcoat in an alley and a .32-caliber pistol in a garbage can, both near the scene of the killing. The slugs matched those found in Hamburg's skull, and the coat was identified by the fruit sellers as one worn by one of the fleeing men. The pistol, tracked to sailor John Moran, had been lent by him to a woman he had picked up at a Fraternity Hall dance. She wanted to borrow it for her husband who, she explained, needed to kill a rat. Through the manager of the dance hall police eventually learned the husband's name was Frank Kearney, and picked up his accomplice, young Harry Alexander. Alexander insisted that Kearney had committed the crime. When Kearney's wife was brought in, she said her husband had disappeared after talking about traveling around the world as a sailor. Alexander was tried and given a thirty-year jail term on charges that included armed robbery. False leads on Kearney's whereabouts went on for years, and his wife eventually divorced him in absentia.

In July 1941 the FBI in Washington wired the Boston police that a man answering Kearney's description had been picked up at the Arizona-Mexico border. A virtual derelict, Kearney had spent seventeen and a half years fruitlessly trying to escape the haunting images of his past and of the murder as he traveled the world as a sailor. He kept his identity a secret for some time by using the passport of a Spaniard who died of natural causes and he later fought for the Loyalist army in Spain. Kearney also worked in France and Mexico, and finally was picked up by a border patrol.

Tried on Nov. 17, 1941, Kearney pleaded guilty to reduced charges of manslaughter and was sentenced to nineteen years in prison. In 1945, sick and listless, he was transferred to the penal colony in Norfolk where he became violently ill and died a few days later, the cause of his death a mystery. One theory said he had died from a tropical disease picked up during his travels and another claimed that he had taken poison.

Kearney, Patrick Wayne, 1940- , U.S. On July 13, 1977, an electronics engineer for the Los Angeles Hughes Aircraft Co. was indicted on three counts of murder by a Riverside, Calif., grand jury. Charges against his roommate and best friend, David D. Hill, thirty-four, were dropped because of lack of evidence. Patrick Kearney was being investigated in connection with at least twenty-eight murders of homosexual men.

Hill and Kearney, roommates for fifteen years, turned themselves in to authorities on July 1, pointing to a wanted poster with their pictures and announcing: "We're them."

Most of the information about the killings came from Kearney's statements to police. Bodies of many of the victims were found in plastic garbage bags along highways from south Los Angeles to the border of Mexico and several of the corpses had been dismembered after being shot. Kearney was indicted for the slayings of Albert Rivera, twenty-one, Arturo Marquez, twenty-four, and

Murderer Patrick Kearney.

John Le May, seventeen. The first victim, Rivera, was found in April 1975, with five more bodies turning up by the end of 1976. All the victims were nude, shot in the head with a small-caliber gun, and dumped alongside the highway. Almost all were transient young men who frequented the homosexual cruising areas and hangouts in and around Los Angeles and Hollywood.

At Hill and Kearney's Redondo Beach home investigators found a hacksaw which proved to be stained with Le May's blood, as well as hair and carpet samples which matched those on tape found on the victims' bodies. Kearney and Hill had fled to Mexico, but surrendered when persuaded by relatives to turn themselves in.

On Dec. 21, 1977, Kearney pleaded guilty to three murders and was sentenced to life imprisonment by Superior

Court Judge John Hews. On Feb. 21, 1978, Kearney pleaded guilty before Judge Dickran Tevrizzian, Jr., to eighteen slayings of young men and boys in exchange for a promise from the prosecution that he would not be given the death penalty. Kearney also provided details of the related killings of another eleven homosexual men, bringing the probable total to thirty-two victims.

Keeling, Frederick, 1868-1922, Brit. Frederick Keeling returned to his career as a plasterer following his time in the army, and became landlord of a boarding house in St. George's Road, Tottenham. The muscular 53-year-old was a blunt and aggressive man who did not drink but had a penchant for romance. For years, one of his boarders, Emily Dewberry, stayed in his room so often that she came to be known locally as "Mrs. Keeling."

At the end of 1921, Dewberry and Keeling broke up. Keeling soon became involved with Mrs. Haynes, a melancholy alcoholic, a relationship that galled Dewberry and influenced Keeling to drink as heavily as Haynes, whom he often beat up, as he had Dewberry and others.

When an inspector from the Ministry of Pensions came for a routine inquiry about Keeling's "wife," a deceit the landlord had practiced for years to increase his pension, the angry Dewberry overheard their talk from another room in the house. She called out to the inspector as he was leaving and told him all about Keeling's domestic status. Arrested a few days later, Keeling was brought before a magistrate, charged with fraud, and informed that he would be tried with Dewberry as a witness against him. Released on bail, Keeling drank excessively, beat up Haynes, leaving her unconscious, and disappeared. When the case came up the following day, Keeling had vanished and Dewberry was found murdered in her room, brutally beaten with a plasterer's hammer. Police searched for ten days, capturing Keeling when a charwoman, aware of the reward, followed him and had him arrested.

Tried in front of Mr. Justice Darling on Mar. 6, 1922, Keeling was found Guilty and sentenced to death. Haynes, called as a witness for the prosecution, was morose at the trial and, when the judge made a facetious remark, cried out bitterly, "Laughter in court. I suppose they'll put that in the paper." Keeling was hanged on Apr. 11, 1922.

Keeton, Ouida, prom. 1935, U.S. In January 1935, in Laurel, Miss., a hunting dog led its master to two mysterious-looking parcels. The parcels contained parts of a human body. The police found evidence of a car having

been stuck in the soft ground near where the packages were found. Local garage employees said that a popular young local woman, Ouida Keeton, had gotten her car stuck in this spot recently and had been towed out by garage employees.

When she gave police an obviously fabricated and easily disproved story about her mother being away on a visit to New Orleans, the police pressed her for more information. Then Keeton said that her mother and she had been kidnapped and the mother held for ransom. The police did not believe this story, and Keeton concocted yet another in which she had been seduced by a former employer, an older man, who had murdered her mother to give them greater freedom. The man had assigned her the task of disposing of the body parts which she had attempted to do. Parts of the mother's body were never recovered but evidence in the home indicated that the murder had most likely taken place there, and the murderer had burned a portion of the remains in the fireplace. On Mar. 13, 1935, a jury found Ouida Keeton Guilty of murder and sentenced her to life in prison. Despite Keeton's conviction, police expected to bring murder charges against her former employer, 67-year-old W.M. Carter. Keeton had accurately predicted Carter's alibi, causing police to suspect his collusion in the crime.

Kehoe, Andrew, 1882-1927, U.S. Andrew Kehoe was a fastidious farmer, an electrician, and the treasurer of the Bath, Mich., school board. The 45-year-old's tubercular wife had been in and out of hospitals for the past year and the medical bills were mounting. He was on the verge of losing the farm he had tended so meticulously for the past eight years. Kehoe was also stealing money from the school treasury to make ends meet.

Two years earlier, the childless Kehoe had vehemently opposed a tax increase to build a new school in Bath, a farming town twelve miles northeast of Lansing. He said it would bankrupt local taxpayers. But Kehoe was alone in his opposition, and the new Bath Community Consolidated School was built. The three-story brick structure housed nearly 300 students and teachers from across the county while Bath itself had only 250 residents.

Kehoe, a depressed and bitter man, did not plant a spring crop in 1927. When Sheriff Fox served him with the foreclosure notice, Kehoe reportedly told him: "If it hadn't been for that $300 school tax, I might have paid off this mortgage."

Early on the morning of May 18, Kehoe set in motion a plan he had been working on for months. First, he killed all the fruit trees on his farm. Then he crushed his wife's skull and tied her to a cart. He then set off the dynamite charges that he had placed near his farm buildings. Next, he drove to town and cut the wires to the central telephone office. Kehoe's last stop was the school.

Andrew Kehoe was sitting in his car shortly before 10 a.m. when he triggered the dynamite blast that buckled the floors, blew out the walls, and lifted the roof off the north wing of the school building. The force of the explosion sent bodies flying into the schoolyard. A second, more powerful explosion collapsed the building inwards, burying many fourth-, fifth-, and sixth-graders, and their teachers. When Superintendent Emery E. Huyck sprinted toward the car, Kehoe fired a shot into the back seat, which was loaded with explosives. Huyck and Kehoe were killed instantly, their bodies thrown thirty feet in the air.

Authorities removed three bushels of dynamite that Kehoe had rigged to destroy the rest of the school. If a janitor had not shut off a light switch to make some repairs, the entire school would have been leveled. Thirty-seven children and seven adults died in the explosions and more than fifty others were injured.

Wired to the fence in front of Andrew Kehoe's charred farmhouse was a crude sign that read: "Criminals are made, not born."

Kelbach, Walter, 1938- , and Lance, Myron, 1941- , U.S.

Eight days before Christmas 1966, Walter Kelbach, twenty-eight, and his friend Myron Lance, twenty-five, went on a killing spree that left six people dead. A 1972 television NBC documentary titled "Thou Shalt Not Kill" profiled these two killers from Salt Lake City, Utah. The two ex-convicts were also lovers and had consumed large amounts of drugs the night of Dec. 17, 1966. Kelbach drove to a Salt Lake City gas station where the two robbed an attendant of $147 and forced him into the back seat of their station wagon. They drove into the desert

Mass killer Walter Kelbach.

where, after forcing their victim to engage in sex, Kelbach stabbed him repeatedly and threw the body into a roadside ditch. Victim number two was Michael Holtz, who also worked in a filling station. He was abducted and murdered in the same fashion, this time by both Kelbach and Lance. Police issued a citywide order that all gas stations be closed at nightfall.

Four days before Christmas, Kelbach and Lance got into

the back seat of a taxi belonging to Grant Creed Strong.

Myron Lance, who with his lover and murderous partner Kelbach, killed six people.

Suspicious about the two grinning men who wanted to go to the airport, Strong radioed the dispatcher. He said that if he encountered problems, he would click his microphone twice. As the taxi pulled over to the curb, Lance thrust a gun at Strong's head and demanded all his money. Strong handed over $9, which angered Lance, and he shot Strong through the head.

The two men proceeded to Lolly's Tavern, near the airport. Announcing to the stunned patrons that this was a stickup, Lance casually shot 47-year-old James Sizemore through the head. The killers took $300 from the till and sprayed the bar with gunfire, killing Beverly Mace, thirty-four, and Fred William Lillie, twenty. Kelbach and Lance fled, but were soon captured at a police roadblock. They were charged with first-degree murder, convicted, and quickly sentenced to death. But when the Supreme Court outlawed capital punishment, the pair were spared. Neither killer ever expressed remorse. "I haven't any feelings towards the victims," Lance said. "I don't mind people getting hurt because I just like to watch it," Kelbach added. Both men are being held at the Utah State Penitentiary.

Keller, Eva, prom. 1947-50, U.S.

On Jan. 25, 1947, Max Keller's neighbors forced open a kitchen window of his suburban Los Angeles home when they had not seen him for several days. They found his body in the den. Police investigators Edgar Kortan and Newt La Fever discovered that Keller had been shot and killed with two .38-caliber bullets. There was no sign of a struggle, indicating that he knew his assailant. Though he still wore an expensive gold watch, his wallet was missing. Neighbors and relatives recalled that he had recently changed the locks of his home because small valuables were disappearing. Also, a suspicious gas explosion occurred at his home on New Year's Eve, not long after he and his wife of twenty-two years, Eva Keller, had separated. Keller had recently changed his insurance policy, naming his stepdaughter, Elsie Keller Petrichella, beneficiary instead of his estranged wife. Hearing of her husband's death, Eva Keller burst into tears, saying he must have been slain by "a jealous husband or a boyfriend of one of those women," referring to girlfriends she insisted he had been seeing. Police learned that Eva had been seen climbing in a window of her husband's home just before the New Year's Eve explosion. The gas meter showed signs of tampering, and the ensuing fire was reported and filed under "Suspicion of Arson." His attorney confirmed that Keller feared his wife was trying to hurt him.

As an alibi, Eva claimed that she had been at the movies. But the feature she named was shown only in the daytime. Without sufficient evidence to bring charges, police kept tabs on Eva. In May, she brought to the sheriff's office two handwritten pages she said she found at Keller's Wilmar bungalow. The first was a will in which Keller revoked his earlier changes and left everything to Eva. The second was a note in which Keller complained that an unnamed business enemy had threatened to kill him. A handwriting expert identified the note and the will as Eva Keller's work.

Marrying sixteen months after the killing, Keller mortgaged her home furnishings and her car. She returned from a trip on Oct. 24, 1948, to find her home burned to the ground. When underwriters became suspicious of her insurance claim, an investigation by an arson specialist led officers to the insured goods, carefully stashed in another cabin. They also found a .38 Smith and Wesson which ballistics experts proved was the murder weapon. But the only witness who could identify the gun had been killed in an airline accident.

Tried for arson and found Guilty on May 3, 1949, Eva Keller was sentenced to twenty-two years at the Tehachapi Women's Prison. In 1950, three years after Max Keller's death, a woman who had spent a weekend with the Kellers positively identified the weapon as Eva Keller's. Indicted for murder at last, Keller was found Guilty of first-degree murder in a non-jury trial by Judge Thomas L. Ambrose on Aug. 7, 1950, and sentenced to life in prison.

Kelley, William H., 1942- , U.S. On Oct. 3, 1966, Charles Von Maxcy was stabbed and shot to death in his home in Sebring, Fla. The 42-year-old citrus and cattle millionaire was purported to have been involved in a love triangle with his 43-year-old wife, Irene, and 48-year-old John Sweet. Irene Maxcy and Sweet were accused of hiring two men to kill Charles Maxcy. On Nov. 8, 1968, in Bartow, Fla., Sweet was found Guilty of first-degree murder, largely on the testimony of Mrs. Maxcy, who was given immunity from prosecution. She said she had given Sweet $36,000 to arrange Maxcy's murder. Sweet was sentenced to life imprisonment, but the verdict was overturned three years later by an appellate court, and the prosecuting attorneys decided to drop the case.

Following Sweet's release, Irene Maxcy was arraigned on

a charge of perjury, and on Nov. 11, 1971, she was sentenced to life by Criminal Court Judge Alfonso C. Sepe in Miami. Mrs. Maxcy served four-and-a-half years of her sentence until she was paroled in 1978.

In June 1983, almost seventeen years after Maxcy's murder, police arrested William H. Kelley in Tampa, Fla., and charged him with first-degree murder. He had been indicted by a grand jury two years earlier after prosecutors procured new evidence. John Sweet, given immunity from prosecution, said he paid a Boston bookmaker named Bennett, who in turn hired Kelley and Andrew Von Etter to commit the murder. The two were given $20,000 to divide, but Von Etter was found bludgeoned to death in a car in 1967, and Bennett mysteriously disappeared at the same time.

Kelley was defended by noted attorney William Kunstler. After a January 1984 mistrial, Kelley was found Guilty of first-degree murder on Mar. 30, 1984, in the Sebring, Fla., Circuit Courtroom of Judge Randolph Bentley. On Apr. 2, 1984, he was sentenced to death, and is currently on Death Row.

Kelly, Leo E., Jr., 1959- , U.S. In the early morning hours of Apr. 17, 1981, a 22-year-old University of Michigan student set off a firebomb in the dormitory where he lived, and then shot two fellow residents as they fled from the smoke and fire. Police went to the room of Leo E. Kelly, Jr., and arrested him. In Kelly's room, they found the sawed-off shotgun used in the shootings, additional ammunition, a "zip gun," and a list of students' names with the name of one of the slain students highlighted. Both students, 19-year-old Edward R. Siwik and 21-year-old Douglas C. McGreaham died of their wounds shortly after the attack.

Kelly, a psychology student, claimed to have been under the influence of pills prescribed for an emotional problem at the time of the shooting, and he denied having any recollection of the shootings. Kelly was brought to trial on two counts of first-degree murder and was convicted on June 21, 1982. His crimes carried a mandatory life sentence. Kelly tried to appeal the conviction on the grounds of racial bias (Kelly is black; the men he killed were white, as was the jury that convicted him), but the attempts have been unsuccessful.

Kemmler, William Francis, 1861-90, U.S. The first man to die in the electric chair, William Kemmler was convicted of murdering his mistress, Tillie Zeigler, of Buffalo on Mar. 29, 1889, with a hatchet. The recently built electric chair was still experimental at the time. At the appointed hour on Aug. 6, 1890, Warden Charles F. Durston led the condemned man into the room. Kemmler was strapped into the chair and electrodes were fastened to his back and head. A portion of his shirt had been torn away in the rear to accommodate the lower electrode. "Don't get

The first electrocution in America, that of murderer William Kemmler, Aug. 6, 1890.

excited Joe, I want you to make a good job of this," Kemmler cautioned the deputy sheriff, Joseph Veiling.

A mask was placed over his head and 1,000 volts of electricity were activated by an executioner in an adjoining room. The switch stayed on for a full seventeen seconds, but it was not enough to kill Kemmler: he exhibited definite signs of life. The executioner threw the lever a second time, and this proved effective. Most of the press called the invention inhuman torture. Only the New York *Times* disagreed, saying it "would be absurd to talk of abandoning the law and going back to the barbarism of hanging."

Kemper, Edmund Emil III (AKA: Big Ed; The Coed Killer), 1948- , U.S.

Edmund Kemper's sadism manifested itself at an early age. Soon after mutilating his sister's doll, he tortured and killed the family cat. The oversized youngster caused his divorced mother so much trouble she sent him at fifteen to live with his grandparents. The next year, on Aug. 27, 1964, Kemper shot his grandmother in the back of the head with a .22-caliber rifle and then fired two more shots into her as she lay on the floor. Kemper shot and killed his grandfather when he returned, and locked his body in the garage. Kemper then called his mother and told her what he had done, explaining, "I just wondered how it would feel to shoot Grandma." His mother told him to call the police, which he did, and waited

for them on his grandparents' porch. Kemper was committed to the Atascadero State Hospital. The California Youth Authority's file on Kemper contained a psychiatric recommendation that he never be released into his mother's custody, but in 1969 the Authority did exactly that. Kemper was not twenty years old, but already was six feet, nine inches tall, and weighed 280 pounds.

Clarnell Kemper worked as a secretary at the University of California in Santa Cruz. When Edmund moved in with her, she got him a university parking sticker so he could park on campus. This would later prove a valuable tool with which to lure coeds into his car. Kemper learned every back road of the local highway system and rigged his car so that the door on the passenger side could not be opened from inside. In 1971, he left his mother's home and moved to San Francisco, where he began "practicing" getting victims into his car.

Edmund Kemper, mass killer and cannibal.

On May 7, 1972, he picked up two young hitchhikers from Fresno State College: Anita Luchese and Mary Anne Pesce. He assaulted them with a knife, but was surprised to discover that real killing was different from the television or movie version. He panicked and found himself standing outside the locked car. Incredibly, Pesce let him back inside. After Kemper had killed them, he disposed of the torsos in the Santa Cruz Mountains, but kept their heads in his room as a souvenir. He methodically searched for new victims, and found Aiko Koo, who was hitchhiking to her dance class in San Francisco.

The act of decapitation excited Kemper sexually. Sometimes he had sex with the headless bodies he brought back to his apartment, but soon disposed of the torsos, often after eating part of the flesh. He kept the heads of his victims, however, and even buried one in his yard, facing his bedroom, so he could talk to it at night. From the television show *Police Story*, Kemper picked up useful tips on how to avoid detection. Sometimes he met and chatted with homicide detectives at their favorite haunts to check on the progress of the investigation. The so-called "Coed Killer" killed six women in all, and police were stumped.

Kemper began to fear he would commit a murder so blatant that he would be caught. On Easter Sunday 1973, he entered his mother's bedroom as she slept and bludgeoned her to death with a hammer. He then decapitated her and removed her larynx, which he threw into a garbage disposal. He called his mother's best friend, Sara Hallet, and invited her for dinner. When she arrived, Kemper strangled her and, again, cut off the head of his victim. He then rented a car and drove to Pueblo, Colo., to await the massive manhunt he was sure would follow. When his crime was still undetected three days later, he called Santa Cruz police and confessed, having to repeat his story several times before he was believed. Kemper was arrested, returned to California and, in April 1973, arraigned on eight counts of first-degree murder. Though he asked for the death penalty, he was sentenced to life in Folsom Prison.

Kendall, Arthur James, 1910-   , Can. Arthur Kendall and his wife Helen lived with their five children in southern Ontario, Canada, in Elma Township. Kendall sharecropped, but on a trip near Tobermory in May 1952, he met a mill owner who offered him work.

On May 26, the 42-year-old Kendall began work at the mill, agreeing to remain until September, and stayed with three other workers in a cabin on the Bruce Peninsula on Lake Huron. During this time, he dated redheaded Beatrice Hogue, a waitress who lived in Wiarton with her seven children and whose husband was sailing on the Great Lakes. Kendall's 33-year-old wife and his children later joined the workers during the summer. The men described Helen Kendall as a good housekeeper and cook, pleasant, and devoted to her children. On July 26, the last two mill workers left the cabin for the season, riding with Kendall to Wiarton where he picked up Hogue and six of her children. After letting the two men out, he drove the Hogues to the Kendall farm.

The next week Kendall returned to the cabin where his wife and children had remained. In the early dawn of Aug. 2, three of the Kendall children heard their mother cry, "No, Art, please don't," and saw him get up from a lower bunk and lay a butcher knife on the table. They watched him as he carried her body across the room and out the door. When he came back about half an hour later he cleaned up the blood and called the children to get up. He told one of the girls what to say if anyone inquired about their mother, then, later in the day, took the children to live at the Kendall house with the Hogues, telling police and neighbors his wife had left him.

In the years following, Hogue divorced her husband and married Kendall. In 1953, his children were taken away from him but he regained custody. Afraid of their father, the children finally spoke up nearly ten years after the

murder. Kendall was arrested on Jan. 27, 1961. Police found blood stains still on the cabin floor and on pillows, and after a thorough search, police speculated that Kendall had put his wife's body in Lake Scugog, located near the mill. Kendall was tried, convicted, and given the death penalty. His sentence was later commuted to a life term in the Kingston Penitentiary.

Kennedy, William Henry, See: Browne, Frederick Guy.

Ketchel, Stanley, See: Kurtz, Walter A.

Kid McCoy, See: Selby, Norman.

Kilpatrick, Andrew Gordon, 1920 -   , and **Hill, Russell William**, 1931 -   , Aus. On Aug. 1, 1953, a diver recovered a decapitated body from the Barwon River near the Princes Bridge in Geelong, Aus. The torso was stuffed into two sacks and tied to a 126-pound boulder. The victim's head and hands, which had been severed with a hacksaw, were discovered an hour later underwater in a kerosene tin.

Colac, located 100 miles inland from Geelong, was hit hard by a series of robberies in Summer 1953 and Detective Sergeant Fred Adam, a member of Victoria's Homicide Squad, was dispatched to Colac. While investigating an assault case, Adam thought that suspects Andrew Gordon Kilpatrick and Russell William Hill might be connected to the crimes. Notifying the local authorities of his suspicions, Adam was told to take on the case himself. Adam finally caught up with Hill, who had skipped bail, in late July in Hamilton, where he had been arrested on a vagrancy charge.

On July 30, Hill broke down and told Adam where he could find the body of 22-year-old Donald Brooke Maxfield. The gruesome discovery of Hill's former accomplice was made in the Barwon River the next day. Hill informed police that Kilpatrick, a 33-year-old welder, had carried out the murder and dismemberment because Maxfield had talked too much about the trio's criminal activity. When Kilpatrick was finally arrested, he refused to talk, but when faced with Hill's accusation, he said the 22-year-old William Hill was as responsible for the crime as he was.

The trial began in October, with each man accusing the other of murder. Hill testified that only days after the slaying, Kilpatrick had stopped at the Princes Bridge on the way to Melbourne and forced him to help sink the body. Kilpatrick contended he was home in bed on the night of the murder. A key prosecution witness was taxi driver Maxwell George Benson. Benson told the Geelong courtroom that about three weeks after Maxfield's disappearance, he had driven Hill, Kilpatrick, and two other men to Melbourne. On the way to the capital, Benson said Kilpatrick told him to stop near the Princes Bridge, where the men went under the bridge for about ten minutes.

After three hours of deliberation, the jury found both Kilpatrick and Hill Guilty of murder and they were sentenced to death by Mr. Justice Martin. The sentences were never carried out; Will's sentence was commuted to twenty years in jail, and Kilpatrick's to life. He was later released from jail in August 1976.

═══════════════════════

King, Alvin Lee, III, 1934-82, U.S. Alvin Lee King III majored in education at North Texas State University where he met his wife Gretchen Gaines. The couple was married in 1956. Ten years later, King taught math at Dangerfield High School in Dangerfield, Texas, until 1972 when he resigned. King's legal troubles began in October 1979 with a warrant for his arrest following an allegation of incest by his 19-year-old daughter Cynthia King. After a change of venue to Sulphur Springs, the trial was set to begin on June 23, 1980. King never faced trial, because the day before he killed five people—he had already accidentally killed his father in 1966 when he dropped a loaded twelve-gauge shotgun in his parents' Corpus Christi home—and seriously wounded ten others in a crowded church.

At 9 a.m. on June 22, King tied up his wife, loaded his pickup truck with more than 240 rounds of ammunition, an M-1 automatic carbine with bayonet, an AR-15 automatic rifle with scope and bayonet, a .38-caliber and a .22-caliber revolver, two bullet-proof flak jackets, and a WWII combat helmet. He drove to the First Baptist Church in Dangerfield and carrying his small arsenal he walked into the church where more than 300 parishioners were attending Sunday service. King burst in the sanctuary doors, shouted, "This is war," and opened fire with the carbine, discharging five rounds in less than ten seconds. Killed by the first round were 7-year-old Gina Linam, whose skull was shattered as bullets riddled her head; 49-year-old Gene Gandy, whose wound just below the heart would keep her alive until late into the night, and 78-year-old Thelma Robinson.

Chris Hall, who helped operate the radio broadcast of each sermon, dove at King, who outweighed the younger man by some seventy pounds, and pushed him out into the lobby, knocking both automatic rifles from King's hands, the helmet from his head, and his glasses from his eyes. If those glasses, which King needed to see anything more than six feet away, had stayed on, Hall may not have been able to scramble down the steps to the church basement, evading two shots from the .38-caliber revolver.

James Y. "Red" McDaniel, fifty-three, and 49-year-old city councilman Kenneth Truitt were the next heroes. McDaniel wrapped his arms around King and charged him out the front door, which broke as the two fell onto the front steps. King fired his .38 at McDaniel until the older man rolled off the gunman dead. He then shot and killed Truitt who dove at him while he still lay on his back. Inside the church, Larry Cowan picked up the carbine and ran after King, who dropped the revolver and fled. At a nearby fire station, King shot himself in the head with the .22 but failed to take his own life.

On July 11, King was charged with five counts of murder and ten counts of assault with intent to kill. Seventeen days later, a jury judged him incompetent to stand trial and sent him to Rusk State Hospital for the criminally insane until he was determined to be of sound mind. Although less than a month after the shooting King's IQ was determined to be 151, Dr. James Hunter did not find him ready for trial until Nov. 24, 1981. King's trial before Judge B.D. Moye on Jan. 25, 1982, never took place. During the hearing for a change of venue request by defense attorney Dick DeGuerin, King was held in the Dangerfield jail. On Jan. 19, 1982, he tied together strips he had torn from a towel, fashioned the strips into a noose, and hanged himself from the jail cell crossbar.

═══════════════════════

Kinman, Donald, 1923-1958, U.S. Details in the deaths of Ferne Redd Wessel, forty-three, and Mary Louise Tardy, twenty-eight, were remarkably similar, leading California police in Los Angeles and Sylmar to combine evidence and forces. The result was a double murder conviction against 36-year-old Donald Kinman. Before sentencing, Kinman said to the judge, "I guess I should get the gas chamber. I think I have it coming, don't you?"

Wessel had been raped, and strangled, and found lying in a Los Angeles hotel bedroom the morning after Easter in 1958. She last had been seen on Easter, drunk, being helped to her room by a man she called "Don."

Late in the afternoon on Nov. 22, 1959, Tardy's body was found in a trailer in Sylmar, a trailer owned by Chester Baker but rented by Kinman. Several days before her body was discovered Tardy had been seen fighting with and then leaving her boyfriend. Later she was seen at a bar with a stocky, curly-haired man she called "Donald." That description fit Kinman. As in the Wessel murder, Tardy had been strangled and raped after being partly suffocated by a pillow, and her clothes had been dumped on top of her body. Fingerprints taken at both scenes were identical. On Dec. 2, Kinman turned himself in, confessing to the Tardy murder. "I don't know what came over me, but it just seemed like something I had to do," he said, adding that he had finally surrendered because "my conscience has been bothering me." When presented with overwhelming incriminating evidence, Kinman confessed to having killed Wessel as well.

Kinne, Sharon, 1941- , U.S.-Mex. On the night of Mar. 19, 1960, police arrived at the home of James A. Kinne, an electronics engineer who lived just outside Kansas City, Kan., to find the man dead on the floor, with his wife, Sharon, and their 2-year-old daughter nearby. Sharon Kinne explained that her daughter was playing with her husband's .22-caliber handgun when it accidentally discharged. Her story was accepted—friends testified that the child occasionally played with guns—and the shooting was ruled accidental.

With her insurance settlement, Kinne bought a new Thunderbird. She began spending time with the salesman who had sold her the car, but eventually aroused the suspicions of the salesman's wife, Patricia Jones. On May 26, 1960, friends of Jones told police that they had seen her climb into a Thunderbird with a dark-haired woman, who turned out to be Kinne. The next night Jones' bullet-riddled body was found in a lover's lane in Jackson County. Based on the many coincidences, a murder indictment was returned against Kinne in September 1960. When the bullets that killed Jones, however, were compared with shells known to have held bullets from James Kinne's .22-caliber handgun, it was revealed that his gun could not have been used to kill Jones. Kinne was acquitted.

Meanwhile, however, witnesses had since come forward to testify that Kinne had put a $1,000 contract out on her husband, and ballistics experts had declared it impossible that a 2-year-old had pulled the trigger on a heavy gun like a .22-caliber handgun. Kinne was found Guilty of killing her husband and sentenced to life in prison.

The verdict was challenged on a legal technicality, and a mistrial was declared. There was yet another mistrial before the case was heard again. This time Kinne was freed after the jury failed to agree on a verdict. Flushed with her success, she traveled to Mexico City, where she met radio announcer Francisco Paredes Ordonez in a bar on Sept. 18, 1964. He went with Kinne to her room. Soon, a motel

desk clerk heard shots ring out from the room. Upon investigation, he found Kinne on the floor struggling for control of a gun—finally shooting Ordonez. When the motel owner tried to intervene, she shot him too.

A Kansas City prosecutor arrived to examine the gun and determined that the gun that had been used to kill Ordonez was the same gun that had been used to shoot Jones. It did not matter though, as Kinne could not be tried for Jones' murder again. In October 1965, Kinne was sentenced to ten years in jail in Mexico for killing Ordonez. She appealed, and the courts added three more years to her sentence.

Kinney, David, prom. 1970, U.S. On June 1, 1970, in Temple Terrace, Fla., the Reverend Jerry C. Monroe, ostensibly out ministering to parishioners, instead picked up drug-crazed David Kinney across from a bus depot, took him to a bar where he bought beers, drove him to a dump, performed a homosexual act on him, and then was murdered by Kinney. Kinney, who said he was "high" at the time of the shooting and did not know why he did it, will spend the rest of his life in prison.

The news, revealed in court testimony after Monroe's death, of the priest's other life, shocked his widow and congregation at St. Catherine's Episcopal Church. The first inkling Monroe's wife had that there was something about her husband she knew nothing about came when police called two weeks after his disappearance, saying they had found her husband's decayed body under a refrigerator in the city dump. The pastor had died of two .38-caliber gunshot wounds in the lower chest and abdomen.

After hearing of his death, workers for a local roofing company reported that one of their co-workers had bragged that he had killed a man. Police soon tracked down Kinney, a young man who earlier claimed to have slept through the shooting incident. They found a .38-caliber Victor revolver in his room that matched ballistically with the bullets taken from the priest's body.

Kinney had no choice but to confess. He made one feeble attempt at a lighter sentence, saying he had been "high" that night on two "Purple Wedges," a form of LSD. The jury said that was no excuse for murder and sentenced Kinney to life in prison.

Kiss, Bela (AKA: Mr. Hoffmann), b.1872, Hung. When Bela Kiss of Czinkota, Hungary, learned that his 25-year-old wife, Maria, was having an affair with Paul Bihari, he immediately ordered several enormous metal drums—for gasoline storage he said. It was February 1912, and a war loomed. Gas would soon be in short supply. Bihari and Maria then mysteriously disappeared, and Kiss said they had run off together.

His housekeeper, Mrs. Kalman, noted with growing alarm the number of female visitors coming to his house. At the same time, more metal drums began arriving—for the war effort, Kiss reiterated. The Budapest police were alerted to the disappearance of two widows whose names were Schmeidak and Varga, who, at last report, had visited the Budapest apartment of Mr. Hoffmann. Their whereabouts were not accounted for until much later.

In November 1914 Kiss was drafted into the army and sent to the front in Serbia. Nearly two years later, in May 1916, Constable Trauber received word from the military that Kiss had died in a military hospital in Belgrade. Recalling his earlier words about the gasoline he had hoarded at his home, Trauber dispatched soldiers to Czinkota for the fuel. Seven drums were found, each containing the body of a woman who had been garrotted. Letters written to Kiss were found in his personal belongings. It was clear that he had lured the victims to his home

Hungarian mass murderer Bela Kiss, who killed at least nine people placing their corpses in steel drums he buried. Kiss was never brought to justice.

through advertisements placed in the newspaper under the name of Professor Hoffmann, Poste Restante, Vienna, who promised companionship and marriage. What these unfortunate women encountered instead was a madman interested only in acquiring their cash and jewels. A search of the countryside turned up seventeen more drums. Found

inside two of them were the unfaithful wife and her lover Paul Bihari.

In 1919, Kiss was seen in Hungary. It was learned that he switched tags with a fallen comrade on the battlefield and had assumed a new identity. A man matching the description of Kiss was seen in New York in 1932. The individual was observed exiting the Times Square Subway Station by Detective Henry Oswald of the homicide squad. He quickly disappeared into the crowd.

Knight, Virgil, 1961-87, U.S. When a newly divorced man learned he lost a custody battle and would not have the right to care for his two small children, he killed them, along with his ex-wife, two neighbors, and himself.

Virgil Knight, twenty-six, took six lives on Dec. 14, 1987, one week after his divorce was final. Using a small-caliber pistol, the Oklahoma man in a jealous rage gunned down his 26-year-old ex-wife, Deetta Knight, as she lay in her bed, his 6-year-old son, Curtis Knight, his 2-year-old son, Kevin Knight, his 23-year-old former sister-in-law, Carrie, and a next-door neighbor. He then turned the gun on himself. Twin 18-year-old brothers of Knight's former wife escaped from the duplex. They confirmed that Knight was the assailant. Knight's mother said he had been depressed for days.

Knighten, Greg, 1972-   , U.S. Greg Knighten, sixteen, was convicted of murder on Oct. 23, 1987, in the brutal slaying of undercover police officer George Raffield. The 21-year-old officer was posing as a Midlothian, Texas, High School student for an undercover investigation to identify drug users in the school. The officer's identity was revealed before any arrests were made. After a Friday night football game, Raffield failed to call in his daily report. Police found his body the next day and hours later arrested Richard Goeglein, seventeen, Jonathon Jobe, sixteen, and Knighten, the son of a Dallas police officer. Cynthia Fedrick, twenty-three, was charged with soliciting the murder. Raffield had been shot in the back of the head, allegedly by the .38-caliber revolver that belonged to Knighten's father.

If Knighten had been charged with capital murder he would have automatically received a life sentence. Because he was only sixteen the death sentence was not an option. Instead, the jury sentenced the youth to forty-five years in prison.

Knowles, Dr. Benjamin, prom. 1920s, W. Afri. Without a jury trial a husband was accused, convicted, and sentenced to die for murdering his wife, though before she died his wife emphatically told the police the incident was an accident.

Dr. Benjamin Knowles lived in Bekwail, in the colony of Ashanti, W. Afri., with his wife, the former Madge Clifton, and he was the medical officer of health for the area. The couple occasionally quarreled and Knowles frequently drank. Also, Knowles kept a revolver loaded and cocked beside his bed to protect his wife and himself from house-breakers.

On the evening of Oct. 20, 1928, Mrs. Knowles was preparing for bed after a dinner party. Dr. Knowles already was in bed when she accidentally sat down on the revolver lying on a chair beside the bed. When she stood up to move the gun somewhere else, the trigger caught in the lace of her nightgown, causing the gun to discharge. Mrs. Knowles was shot in the left buttock with the .45-caliber soft-nosed bullet which exited above her right hip. The wound was serious and demanded surgery yet Dr. Knowles simply sterilized, dressed, and plugged the wound and then gave them both sedatives.

District Commissioner Mangin was notified that a gun was fired inside the Knowles's bungalow and investigated that night. Dr. Knowles told him that while there had been a slight domestic quarrel, everything was under control. Mangin returned the next day with the surgeon Dr. Howard Gush who, upon examining Mrs. Knowles, took her immediately to the hospital. It was too late for surgery. Two hours before she died Mrs. Knowles told police and Mr. Mangin that the shooting had been an accident and even detailed the events. When she learned her husband was under suspicion, she was surprised and repeated as emphatically as she could in her weak condition that the shooting was an accident.

The police chose to believe otherwise and arrested Dr. Knowles who then was quickly tried in November without a jury. The commissioner of police prosecuted the case and Knowles defended himself. The prosecution was very shaky, being based on a theory the police developed on two bullet holes in the bedroom which they claimed were aligned. According to this theory, when Dr. Knowles shot his wife, the soft-nosed bullet passed through his wife, a tabletop, and a heavy wardrobe door. Aside from the implausibility of a .45-caliber soft-nosed bullet passing through three objects, a house servant had picked up a spent bullet next to the chair where Mrs. Knowles was shot, and a neighbor testified that the bullet hole in the wardrobe was old.

Nevertheless, Knowles was found Guilty and sentenced to die. Sir A.R. Slater, governor of the Gold Coast, commuted the sentence to life in prison and Knowles was transported to London where he appealed to the Judicial Committee of the Privy Council. There, his sentence was quashed because a ruling of manslaughter had not been considered in his initial trial. Dr. Knowles died in London three years later.

Knowles, Paul John, 1946-74, U.S. A petty thief went on a rape and murder spree, killing eighteen people in a four-month period before police caught him.

Paul Knowles, a small-time thief, spent half of every year between 1965 and 1972 behind bars. While serving a longer sentence in Raiford Penitentiary in Florida he corresponded with Angela Covic, who eventually agreed to marry him. After finding a lawyer, securing his parole, and flying him to San Francisco, Covic decided not to marry Knowles because he made her uneasy. She sent him back to Jacksonville, Fla., where he got in a bar fight and was locked up at the police station. He picked the lock on July 26, 1974, and escaped.

The night of his escape Knowles broke into the home of Alice Curtis, bound and gagged her, and stole her money and car. Curtis died that night from the gag stuffed too far down her throat. A few days later, Knowles abducted two friends of his family, Mylette Anderson, seven, and her sister Lillian, eleven, and killed them because they recognized him. He drove to Atlanta Beach where he strangled Marjorie Howe in her home and stole her television. A few days later, he picked up a female hitchhiker whom he raped and killed. The body was never identified. On Aug. 23, in Musella, he strangled Kathie Pierce in her home while her 3-year-old son watched. Less than two weeks later, Knowles met William Bates in Ohio whose nude and strangled body was found in the woods a month later. He then shot and killed an elderly couple in their camping trailer in Ely, Nev. On Sept. 21, he raped and throttled a woman he accosted beside the road.

Knowles met Ann Dawson two days later in Birmingham, Ala. They liked each other and traveled together for six days, spending her money. While her body was never found, Knowles later confessed to killing her. He then drove to Connecticut where he knocked on the door of a house in Marlborough. When teenager Dawn Wine answered, Knowles forced himself inside and ordered her to her bedroom where he raped her for an hour. When the mother, Karen Wine, came home, Knowles forced her to cook him a meal and then took her upstairs where he made mother and daughter strip, bound their hands, raped the mother, and strangled them both with a nylon stocking. On Oct. 19 at a house in Virginia, he demanded a gun from Doris Hovey and she gave him a .22-caliber rifle from her husband's gun cabinet which he loaded and used to shoot her in the head. He then wiped the gun clean and left it in the house without taking anything.

Knowles contacted his attorney in Miami, telling him he

Rapist and murderer Paul John Knowles, center, under arrest.

wanted to confess to fourteen murders. While his lawyer could not persuade him to turn himself in, Knowles did agree to tape a confession. His lawyer, Sheldon Yavitz, notified police, but by the time they responded Knowles had already left Miami.

He then stabbed Carswell Carr repeatedly and strangled his 15-year-old daughter. Carr, whom he met at a gay bar, had taken Knowles home to spend the night. On Nov. 8, Knowles met Sandy Fawkes, a journalist. Fawkes and Knowles became lovers and she later wrote of her few days with him in her book *Killing Time*. She thought him sexually inexperienced and said he often acted as a tender, protective husband. He did not harm Fawkes but did attempt to rape a friend of hers, Susan MacKenzie. She escaped and Knowles left town the same day. He drove to Key West, Fla., where he took Barbara Tucker hostage and left her tied up in a motel room while he drove off in her Volkswagen. Police were notified of the stolen Volkswagen and Patrolman Campbell spotted the car and pulled Knowles over. Knowles took him hostage at gunpoint and hijacked the patrol car. He then overtook businessman James Meyer, handcuffed him, and drove off in a new car with his two hostages. A few hours later he handcuffed the two men to a tree and shot each in the back of the head.

On Nov. 17, 1974, when Knowles attempted to break through a police roadblock his car skidded and crashed into a tree. On foot, with 200 police chasing him, Knowles was apprehended by Terry Clark, a young man who ran after Knowles with only a shotgun. The following day, Knowles was shot and killed by FBI agent Ron Angel as he was being transported to a jail when he picked his handcuffs and attempted to take a sheriff's revolver.

Kogut, William, d.1930, U.S. When William Kogut received the death sentence in 1930 for killing a woman with a pocketknife, he told the judge that no one would ever execute him. Therefore, prison officials were careful to keep all potential tools of suicide away from Kogut.

Yet, unknown to the guards, Kogut had removed the red spots from the hearts and diamonds of a deck of cards. The spots contained nitrate and cellulose—ingredients used in the manufacture of explosives. Putting the spots in a pipe and soaking it in water, Kogut made a bomb which, on Oct. 9, he placed on the hot oil heater in his cell at San Quentin Prison. He laid his head on top of the bomb and waited. The bomb worked. One story tells of the doctor who performed the autopsy picking the ace of hearts out of Kogut's skull.

Kopsch, Alfred Arthur, prom. 1925, Brit. Alfred Kopsch was a sensitive young boy who lived with his parents in Highbury, north London. When he was fourteen, his uncle, Arthur Walter Thornton, and his new wife moved in with the Kopsch family. Thornton's wife, Beryl Lilian Thornton was only a few years older than Alfred. Alfred was infatuated with Beryl and over the next four years they became lovers.

When Alfred was eighteen Beryl told him she was pregnant and he was the father. She asked Alfred to kill her. On Sept. 15, 1925, the two lovers went into Ken Wood. There, Beryl asked Alfred again to kill her. The next day Alfred turned himself into the police, stating: "We lay down by the side of a tree and she asked me to strangle her while she was asleep. At 2 a.m. I thought she was asleep. I put my thumb on her neck and tied my necktie round her neck. I then covered her with my overcoat."

At his trial in October with Justice Branson, the counsel for the defense based its case on "irresistible impulse," that Alfred's act was an unconscious one urged on by Beryl's insistence that he kill her. The jury found him Guilty and while it recommended mercy, Alfred was sentenced to death. A few weeks later he gained a reprieve.

Koslow, Jack, 1936- , U.S. Jack Koslow was the leader of a group of four youths (including himself) who engaged in what the press called "thrill" violence. In August 1954, they beat, horsewhipped, set on fire, and drowned a number of old men who lived on the Brooklyn streets. Eventually arrested by two police officers walking a beat, they were charged with the murder of an old man they dragged seven blocks and threw in the East River where he drowned. One youth turned state's evidence against his friends while the indictment was dismissed for another. The two remaining youths, Koslow, eighteen, and his 17-year-old cohort, were found Guilty of felony murder as the man died while being kidnapped. Both received life sentences.

Kroll, Joachim (AKA: **The Ruhr Hunter**), 1933- , Ger. West German murderer-rapist Joachim Kroll began acting out murderous sexual fantasies in 1955 although his crimes did not specifically distinguish themselves to police until 1959. When arrested in 1976, Kroll, called a mental defective by authorities, told police that he committed his first rape-murder in February 1955 near the village of Walstedde. He attacked 19-year-old Irmgard Strehl and raped her apparently after knocking her unconscious. In June 1955, Klara Tesmer's body was discovered in the woods near Rheinhausen, some distance from where Kroll's first victim had been found but still within the Ruhr area where all of his crimes were committed. She, too, had been raped while unconscious.

Kroll continued raping and killing girls and women. Beginning in 1959, however, he began adding another gruesome detail to his crimes. In July 1959, police found the body of 16-year-old Manuela Knodt, strangled and then raped. Her murderer—Kroll, as it turned out—had also taken slices from her buttocks and thighs, cuts made in such a way that police concluded they were intended to be eaten.

Kroll continued to rape, murder, and butcher. His victims included 13-year-old Petra Giese in the village of Rees on Apr. 23, 1962, and 13-year-old Monika Tafel in nearby Walsum on June 4, 1962. On Dec. 22, 1966, he strangled and raped 5-year-old Ilona Harke, cutting flesh from her shoulders and buttocks.

German cannibal-murderer Joachim Kroll.

Kroll was nearly caught on a number of occasions. In August 1965, he became sexually excited watching a young couple having sex in the front seat of a car. When he punctured the car's front tire with a knife, the man began to drive away, but when Kroll flagged him down, he stopped and got out of the car. Kroll stabbed him but was driven off when the woman tried to run him down with the car. The man died several days later of the stab wounds. On another occasion in 1967, Kroll lured a girl into a meadow and showed her a book of pornographic photographs. The child recoiled in horror and ran away before Kroll could strangle her. Nine years later when Kroll named her in his lengthy confessions, police located her and she confirmed the story although she had never reported it at the time.

In 1976, Kroll killed 4-year-old Marion Ketter. Police made door-to-door inquiries to find the child and were told by one resident of the area that his neighbor, a lavatory attendant, had just told him not to use a particular lavatory in their building because it was stopped up with "guts." The toilet was in fact blocked with the internal organs of a child. In Kroll's apartment, police found plastic bags of human flesh in the freezer and, cooking on the stove, a "stew" which contained a child's hand.

Once apprehended, Kroll readily confessed. His memory was poor, but he was able to recall fourteen victims over a twenty-two year span. He also talked freely to police about his sexual habits. As a young man he was too self-conscious to have sex with a conscious woman which explained his habit of rendering his victims either unconscious or dead before raping them. Kroll had strangled plastic dolls during sex before he graduated to living victims. Kroll claimed that he had taken flesh from the most tender-looking victims to save money on meat.

Kubiczek, Jose, d.1984, Fr. Jose Kubiczek, recently divorced from his wife, strangled her when she went to their Saint-Amand-les-Eaux home on Aug. 27, 1984, to take custody of their only son. Kubiczek dressed the corpse in a wedding gown, lay down on the bed next to her, and took his own life.

Kulak, Frank, 1928- , U.S. Frank Kulak, a WWII and Korean War veteran, and recipient of the Purple Heart, held more than 100 Chicago policemen at bay from his South Side apartment on Apr. 14, 1969, after officers questioned him about a series of bombings that had plagued the neighborhood for several weeks. To show the public what the Vietnam War was really like, Kulak embarked on a self-appointed mission of blowing up war toys in department stores, explaining to police that it was necessary to alert the public to the threat of Chinese Communism.

When Chicago bomb squad officers Sergeant James Schaffer and Detective Jerome A. Stubig arrived at Kulak's home, Kulak reached into an arsenal of weapons that included an M-1 rifle, automatic pistols, 2,000 rounds of ammunition, twenty-five pounds of explosives, and several homemade pipe bombs, and threw a grenade at the two men standing on his wooden back porch. The porch splintered in the explosion, and the officers were blown to the ground. Kulak then riddled their dying bodies with machine-gun fire. He began heaving bombs from his window to the street and started randomly firing at pedestrians who scrambled for cover. Soon afterward, more than 100 officers had assembled outside the building, and three hours later he surrendered.

Arrested on two counts of murder, Kulak confessed to the bombings. Found mentally unfit to stand trial, he was remanded into the custody of doctors at the psychiatric facility in the state prison at Chester, Ill. Kulak remained in the Chester prison until 1981. He was then brought back to Chicago to appear before Criminal Court Judge Frank B. Machala who was to decide whether to dismiss charges against him, in accordance with a new Illinois state law requiring the release of those prisoners incarcerated in a mental institution for a length of time equal to that which they would have been required to serve before becoming eligible for parole. Kulak had served eleven years at Chester, thus meeting the requirements of the law. Machala rendered his decision in January 1981 and sent Kulak back to jail, refusing to dismiss the charges against him.

Kummerlowe, Karl Kenneth, prom. 1970s, U.S.

Karl Kenneth Kummerlowe, a graduate of Yale University, worked as an engineer at AiResearch manufacturing in Phoenix, Ariz., where he developed many items, including a portable field hospital that contained specially designed incinerators for the cremation of body parts. If Karl Kummerlowe had used this invention when he brutally murdered his lover's husband, Harley Kimbro, he might never have been caught.

Kummerlowe was captured after Phoenix police officers, who were watching a parking lot for automobile burglars, noticed him dump the contents of his briefcase—a blood-stained shirt and towel, and ID cards belonging to Kimbro—into the dumpster. When police stopped him and searched his truck, they found several dismembered body parts and the tools that Kummerlowe had used to cut Kimbro up. Kummerlowe killed Kimbro in the bathtub of a Phoenix motel after he had conned the man into the city by pretending to be interested in the home that Kimbro was selling. After searching area dumpsters, officers located

almost half of Kimbro's body. The remaining body parts were never located.

Kummerlowe pleaded not guilty maintaining that he had no knowledge of the murder, but Kimbro's head found in the back of his pickup truck proved too damaging. Kummerlowe was sentenced to life in prison where two weeks later he attempted suicide by jumping over a second-story railing and crashing head first onto the concrete floor below. He severely injured his skull and paralyzed both an arm and a leg.

Kurten, Peter (AKA: The Vampire of Dusseldorf; the Monster of Dusseldorf), 1883-1931, Ger.

The courtroom appearance of the "Dusseldorf Vampire" surprised many Germans who expected to see a real-life incarnation of the Frankenstein monster. Far from being the hulking sadist of expectation, 48-year-old Peter Kurten more clearly resembled a shy businessman. He wore a conservative, well-tailored suit and smelled of Eau de Cologne. Although Kurten was officially charged with nine murders and seven other assaults with intent to kill, Kurten had confessed to sixty-eight other crimes during his interrogation by police.

Peter Kurten was one of thirteen children born to a sand molder and his wife in the village of Cologne-Mulheim. The father, an alcoholic, sexually abused the children and beat his wife. In 1897, he was sentenced to prison for attempted incest. Published reports indicate that young Peter exhibited criminal tendencies before his sixth birthday. While playing on a raft in the middle of the Rhine River, Kurten allegedly pushed one of his playmates over the side and held his head under water. His sadistic tendencies were encouraged by the local dog catcher, who taught the boy to torture animals. Kurten allegedly derived sexual pleasure from watching the blood flow from pigs and sheep. At the age of eight he ran away from home after quarreling with his mother. Peter slept in the woods at night and survived by stealing from the local stores before returning home. In 1894, his family moved to Dusseldorf, where he went to work as a molder's apprentice.

Kurten's sexual attacks commenced when he was fourteen. In the Grafenberger Woods outside Dusseldorf he assaulted and choked his young girlfriend to the point of death. The experience left him sexually drained, but firmly resolved to duplicate the crime. "I thought of myself causing accidents affecting thousands of people and invented a number of crazy fantasies such as smashing bridges and boring through bridge piers," he once explained. A two-year prison sentence at age seventeen for petty theft reinforced his growing sado-sexual compulsions. Kurten deliberately violated prison rules so that he would be put in solitary confinement where he passed the time daydreaming about fresh new tortures. With each new jail sentence for burglary or assault, Kurten's desire to lash out at society grew. Within a few years he became an arsonist. "The sight of the flames delighted me, but above all it was the excitement of the attempts to extinguish the fire and the agitation of those who saw their property being destroyed." Kurten traced his fire fixation back to 1904 when he started three fires. A year later he was arrested and jailed on thirty-four counts of theft and desertion. The day after Kurten began his military service, he ran away from the regiment. He would spend the next seven years in hard labor. In total, Peter Kurten spent twenty of his forty-seven years in prison.

Following his release from prison in 1913, Kurten decided to enact his murder fantasy. On May 25, he broke into the private rooms of the Klein family, owners of a public inn at Koln-Mulheim. Kurten discovered 13-year-old Christine Klein lying asleep near the window. He reached for her throat and choked her into unconsciousness

Two views of German mass murderer Peter Kürten.

before cutting her throat with a pocket knife. The next day, Kurten returned to the inn to share in the local gossip and speculation which accompanied the discovery of the body. "People were talking about it all around me," he recalled. "All this amount of indignation and horror did me good." The girl's father, Peter Klein was suspected by police after a bloody handkerchief bearing the initials "P.K." was found near the body.

Kurten was married in 1923. There was nothing irregular about his conduct, according to his wife and neighbors. By all accounts he was a conservative, soft-spoken man with few vices. Beginning in 1925, he sexually assaulted several women, none of whom reported him to the police. In 1929, the peak year of Kurten's blood lust, twenty-three people were set upon by the "vampire" who said that he enjoyed drinking the blood of his victims and often attained sexual

climax immediately afterward. On Feb. 2, he stabbed Apollonia Kuhn with a pair of scissors. Fortunately, her screams scared off Kurten and she was saved. Six days later he accosted 9-year-old Rosa Ohliger near the Vinzenz Church in Dusseldorf. Using the same pair of scissors, he stabbed the girl to death, and burned the body with kerosene several hours later.

On the night of Feb. 12, Kurten attacked a drunk named Rudolf Sheer. Kurten knocked Sheer to the ground and stabbed him repeatedly. As he lay dying, Kurten drank the blood that spurted from the open wound. Maria Hahn, a housemaid who was enamored with Kurten, became the next victim on Aug. 11, 1929. When the fiend could get no further than kissing and caressing, he took out his scissors and stabbed her in the throat, and then dumped the body in a ditch. Pleased with his work, Kurten went home whistling a tune.

Scarcely two weeks later, the "Vampire" claimed his next two victims in the suburb of Flehe, outside Dusseldorf. Gertrude Hamacher, fourteen, and her 5-year-old sister Louise Lenzen were on their way home from a country fair when a stranger approached. "Oh dear," the man said. "I've forgotten to buy cigarettes. Look, would you be very kind and go to one of the booths and get some for me? I'll look after the little girl." Louise ran off to fetch the man's cigarettes. When she returned a short time later, Kurten seized the girl and dragged her to the adjacent footpath. A dozen hours later, Kurten met up with Gertrude Schulte, a 26-year-old servant girl whom he stopped on the way to the fairgrounds in Neuss. She agreed to accompany him to the fair, with a side trip through the woods. When Schulte refused his sexual advances, he stabbed her repeatedly, but was unable to administer the fatal blow because a passerby heard her screams and scared Kurten off. These crimes awakened the city of Dusseldorf to the presence of a madman in their community. The newspapers were filled with lurid accounts of the sado-sexual murders amidst growing rumors that Satanism and vampirism—the common superstitions with many of the local peasants—were behind the murders. Berlin detectives discounting these notions attributed the crimes to a "club of sadists." With no viable leads except the vague descriptions of Gertrude Schulte, the police employed a new gambit.

Believing that their killer frequented one or more of the popular Dusseldorf beer halls, Berlin detectives enacted a grisly tableaux-vivant. A coffin containing the embalmed remains of Maria Hahn was paraded into the center of one of the pubs. The detective addressed the hushed crowd. "The clay must have stuck to the murderer's clothes," he said, describing the manner in which Hahn met her death. "But he got away! He got away!" The police detective threw back the lid of the coffin, and a spring mechanism enabled the corpse to sit bolt upright. "And here is Maria Hahn!" The police carefully studied the faces of the patrons, operating under the theory that if the killer were present he would likely reveal himself in his facial expressions. When this ploy failed, the detectives sent out the first of their "decoy victims" to entrap the killer. And still the killing continued.

After the blade of his scissors broke off inside one of his victims, Kurten decided the time was right to change weapons. On Sept. 29, 1929, he used his hammer for the first time on Ida Reuter, a servant girl, in the woods outside Dusseldorf. Two more hammer murders followed. Elizabeth Dorrier was out for a walk in the woods on Oct. 11 when she too was felled by hammer blows. The last victim was a 5-year-old child, Gertrude Albermann whom Kurten stabbed thirty-six times with a pair of scissors.

An uncharacteristic show of compassion for one of his intended victims finally led to Kurten's apprehension. Twenty-one-year-old Maria Budlick was preparing to board her train in Dusseldorf on May 14, 1930, when Kurten offered to lead her to the local youth hostel. Budlick had recently lost her position as a domestic servant and had come to Dusseldorf from Cologne to meet with a Frau Brugmann, who had promised her a job. The woman failed to keep the appointment and Maria was about to return home when Kurten appeared. She went with him through the city toward the Volksgarten Park, a secluded patch of woods. Recalling the stories about the "Vampire," Maria hesitated, but Kurten coaxed her and she agreed to accompany him to his flat on the Mettmannerstrasse for a warm meal. After feeding her, Kurten offered to take her to the hostel. They rode the tram to the edge of the city and then walked together into the Grafenburg Woods. Suddenly Kurten turned to her and said: "Do you know where you are? I can tell you! You are alone with me in the middle of the woods. Now you can scream as much as you like and nobody will hear you!" Kurten pressed her up against a tree and tried to rape her, but suddenly relaxed his grip. He asked if Maria remembered where he lived. When she cleverly said that she did not, Kurten turned and walked away.

Maria Budlick reported the incident to the police the next day and led detectives to his flat on the Mettmannerstrasse. Kurten saw the detectives in the foyer of the building talking to the landlady and fled. The next day, he met with his wife at a sidewalk cafe and confessed his crimes to her. Kurten convinced her to go to the police and report him so that she would receive the reward money. "It was not easy to convince her that this was not betraying me," he said. Frau Kurten eventually collected one-third of the reward and Kurten was arrested on the morning of May 24.

Kurten cooperated fully with police. He astounded the detectives and court-appointed psychiatrists with his ability to recall events dating back twenty years. The doctors learned about this extraordinary killer's childhood influences. At sixteen, he had visited the Chamber of Horrors exhibition at the Kolnerstrasse Waxworks. "I am going to be somebody famous like those men one of these days," Kurten remarked to a friend as he viewed the likenesses of some of history's greatest villains. The story of Jack the Ripper amused and delighted him. "When I came to think over what I had read, when I was in prison, I thought what pleasure it would give me to do things of that kind once I got out again," he said.

Kurten's trial began on Apr. 13, 1931. Spectators lined the hallways of the courtroom to catch a glimpse of the murderer and the collection of skulls, knives, scissors, and clothing items placed on public display. In court, Kurten assumed a defiant posture. "I did not kill either people I hated or people I loved. I killed whoever crossed my path at the moment my urge for murder took hold of me," he said. After nine days, the jury returned a verdict of Guilty in each of the nine murders he was charged with. Kurten was given the traditional last meal on July 1, 1931. The next day he was beheaded in the courtyard of the Klingelputz Prison in Cologne. Turning to the executioner seconds before the blade fell, Kurten asked: "After my head has been chopped off, will I still be able to hear at least for a moment the sound of my own blood gushing from the stump of my neck? That would be the pleasure to end all pleasures."

Kurtz, Walter A. (Walter Dipley), prom. 1910, U.S. Acting out of jealousy over a woman's affections, Walter Kurtz shot and killed possibly the greatest middleweight boxer in history. Stanley Ketchel, born Stanislaus Kaicel on Sept. 14, 1886, in Grand Rapids, Mich., earned the nickname of the "Michigan Assassin" early in his career. After running away from home at the age of sixteen, Ketchel worked his way west doing menial labor on the railroad and in mining camps. Before he could accomplish his dream of becoming a cowboy, he discovered a talent for fighting. Ketchel's temper frequently got him into fights which he won more often than not.

In Butte, Mont., in 1903, Ketchel got his big chance. The Big Casino saloon management offered a $50 purse to anyone who could defeat the local champion, Kid Tracey. Tracey's reputation was such that Ketchel was the only opponent. Although Tracey and everyone else discounted the slighter, teen-aged opponent, Ketchel knocked Tracey out in the first round.

After this first formal victory Ketchel traveled through-out Montana racking up victory after victory. He had a particularly vicious style in the ring which he achieved by imagining that his opponent had insulted his mother, for whom Ketchel bore a deep affection. His "maniacal" style, however, gained him fifty-nine wins in sixty-three fights in his professional career, forty-nine by knockouts.

In 1910 Ketchel fought what many thought was the greatest fight of his career. The only person whom Ketchel had not yet fought and beaten was heavyweight champion Jack Johnson. Ketchel agreed to fight Johnson even though Johnson out-weighed Ketchel by forty pounds. Johnson scoffed at the smaller man and refused to train for the fight, expecting to win easily. To his surprise, the fight went into the twelfth round before Stanley Ketchel finally succumbed to one of Johnson's powerful punches.

Boxing champion Stanley Ketchel, killed by Walter Kurtz over a woman's affections.

Although Ketchel went on to win a few more fights, the Johnson fight had ruined his health. In the fall of 1910, he traveled to Conway, Mo., to stay at a friend's ranch. Once there, Ketchel became in-volved with Goldie Smith, the ranch cook. Smith was also involved with one of the ranch hands, Walter Kurtz, actually a Navy deserter whose real name was Walter Dipley. Kurtz put up with seeing Ketchel and Smith together for a time. One morning, how-ever, he came into the din-ing room where Ketchel was sitting with his back to the door. He told Ketchel to put up his hands. When Ketchel refused, Kurtz shot him in the back, killing him. Kurtz was captured the following day. He was tried and found Guilty and sentenced to life imprisonment. He was paroled from prison in 1934.

L

Labbe, Denise, c.1926- , and **Algarron, Jacques**, c.1930- , Fr. Denise Labbe was the daughter of a postman in the village of Melesse, near Rennes, Fr. After the Germans invaded in 1940, Denise's father killed himself. She then diligently pursued her university studies at Rennes, and also worked as a secretary at the National Institute of Statistics there. She had numerous affairs and gave birth to a daughter named Catherine whom she left with her mother while she went to Paris to work for the Institute. There, she met 24-year-old Jacques Algarron, an officer cadet at the Saint-Cyr School and a devotee of Jean Paul Sartre and the Marquis de Sade. The intense, brooding Algarron had already fathered several illegitimate children

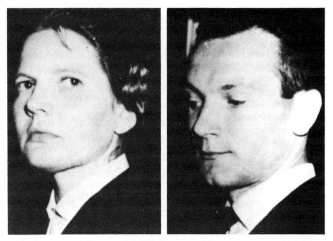

Denise Labbe, who murdered her child at the orders of her lover, right, Jacques Algarron.

of his own. "In the manner of Andre Gide," he would say, "I offer you fervor."

Algarron, who was himself born out of wedlock, compensated for his feelings of inadequacy by pretending to possess superhuman qualities. He tested Labbe's devotion by ordering her to pick up strange men in the streets, and then take them back to the apartment she shared with him. Labbe made love to these men while Algarron hid in the closet. He then forced her to seek his forgiveness. "To merit my love, you must go from suffering to suffering," he said. Algarron threatened to leave her unless she murdered two-and-a-half-year-old Catherine. He first broached the subject to her on Aug. 29, 1954.

Labbe obeyed. She tried to drop her daughter out a window, but a neighbor intervened. Then she threw Catherine into a canal, but a passerby rescued her in time. Then, on Nov. 8, 1954, Labbe drowned Catherine in a zinc washtub at her mother's home in Rennes. "It takes courage to kill your own daughter," beamed Algarron. Labbe confessed to the Rennes Police, describing her lover as a "cultist devil." "You promised to marry me if I killed Cathy, but you threatened to abandon me if I did not kill her,"

she sobbed. The pair were tried for murder at the Loir-et-Cher Assizes in Blois on May 30, 1955. The jury returned a Guilty verdict but pleaded for mercy for Labbe, whom they believed Algarron had placed under a "spell." She was sentenced to life imprisonment. Algarron received twenty years' hard labor.

Lacroix, Georges (AKA: **Roger Marcel Vernon; Mr. Georges**), and **Alexandre, Pierre Henri**, prom. 1936, Brit. In the 1930s, London mobster Max Kassel, was known in the streets of Soho as "Max the Red" for his flame-colored hair. He was said to have immigrated from Latvia on a forged passport, but some insisted he was French-Canadian. Kassel was a drug trafficker and pimp with connections throughout Europe. In 1935, the 56-year-old Kassel was in debt, and his creditors were growing anxious, especially one who called himself Roger Vernon, but who was actually an escapee from Devil's Island named Georges Lacroix. Lacroix, a pimp and a murderer, lived off his girlfriend Suzanne Bertron. Occasionally he arranged marriages for European women so they could stay in Britain. Bertron herself married an English seaman, William Naylor, to remain in the country and then abandoned him for Lacroix.

Lacroix had loaned Kassel £25 and was anxious to collect. Lacroix tried to collect at his apartment on Little Newport Street one night in January 1936. The two men quarrelled in Bertron's presence, and Lacroix, feeling himself insulted, was even more determined. On Jan. 23, Lacroix summoned Kassel to Newport Street. Bertron's maid, Marcelle Aubin, led Kassel upstairs, where Lacroix was waiting. The radio blared. From downstairs the maid strained to hear what was going on, but it was impossible. Suddenly she heard gunshots and a cry for help from Lacroix. Aubin ran upstairs, where she saw the two men struggling. Kassel had been shot, and was pleading for his life. He begged them to take him to the hospital, but they refused. "I'm going to die! Give me water," he pleaded. Kassel made one last bolt for freedom, but was immediately captured and locked in the bathroom, where he died a few minutes later. Lacroix swore Aubin to secrecy and then telephoned his friend, Pierre Henri Alexandre, to ask his help in disposing of the body. He arrived around 4 a.m., and decided they should wrap the body in a rug and drive out of the city. They drove Alexandre's Chrysler to the village of St. Albans and left the body by the side of the road. Henry Sayer, a local carpenter, discovered it five hours later.

Under Chief Inspector Frederick Dew Sharpe, Scotland

Yard quickly learned the identity of the killers and issued warrants for their arrest, but Lacroix and Alexandre had fled to France. A legal dispute between the French and British governments made extradition impossible. The home secretary maintained that Lacroix was a British subject because he was Canadian-born. The French, on the other hand, insisted that Lacroix had escaped from Devil's Island, and they maintained jurisdiction in the case. Lacroix and Bertron were tried for murder at the Assize de la Seine in April 1937. Bertron was acquitted by a sympathetic jury. Lacroix was found Guilty and sentenced to ten years at hard labor and twenty years exile from France. Alexandre received five years of penal servitude after trial in the British courts.

LaMarr, Harley, 1931-51, U.S. A mother's simple request to her son carried with it a death sentence for a socially prominent Buffalo woman and her own son.

Harley LaMarr lived in a run-down section of Buffalo, N.Y., in 1950. On Jan. 8, 1950, his mother killed her second husband John Palwodzinski with a kitchen knife during a domestic quarrel in their apartment.

The 50-year-old mother pleaded guilty to manslaughter and was sentenced to serve thirty years at the Bedford Hills Prison for Women. When LaMarr visited her in jail he asked if there was anything he could do. "Yes, bury Pa," she said. This he agreed to do, but being jobless it was hard for him to pay for the funeral. He decided that the only sure way to bury his stepfather was to find someone to rob.

On Feb. 11, he set out to find a victim in the fashionable part of town, with an ancient hunting rifle that had been collecting dust under the eaves. He took public transportation to his destination with the gun hidden under his trench coat.

Lurking behind trees and bushes, LaMarr spotted his victim, Mrs. Willard Frisbee, wife of the sales manager for the Queen City Pure Water Company. LaMarr was most attracted to the flashy automobile she drove and her obvious wealth. Beyond that he knew nothing about her. At a stoplight, LaMarr bounded into the unlocked passenger side of her car and ordered the woman to keep driving. Frisbee, thirty-six, attempted to talk him out of his course of action and a struggle ensued, the woman apparently not frightened or intimidated. As she grappled with her abductor the gun accidentally discharged and she was killed.

The body was tossed in a ditch and young Harley discovered to his dismay that she had only $6. He ignored the fur coat and jewels. Police traced the bullets to a hardware store, and the identity of Harley LaMarr was

established. He was arrested and confessed freely to the crime. On May 15, 1950, LaMarr was convicted of first degree murder and sentenced to death. He died in the electric chair at Sing Sing on Jan. 11, 1951, a little more than a year since his stepfather had been killed.

Lance, Myron, See: Kelbach, Walter.

Landru, Henri Desire (AKA: **Bluebeard; M. Diard; Georges Petit; M. Dupont; M. Cuchet; Lucien Guillet; M. Fremyet; M. Forest**), 1869-1922, Fr. Henri Landru was a mass murderer, a lady killer whose repetitious slayings, except for the manner of disposal, were uninspired and must have been wearisome for him, if, indeed, he slew the more than 300 women estimated by French police. The number of his victims positively known was ten women and a boy, but in all probability, this systematic killer murdered twenty to thirty people, almost all women. He, like Belle Gunness, his American counterpart, preyed upon lovelorn, middle-aged people. Those women with means who answered his enticing ads were charmed by Landru and readily succumbed to his magnetism and animal craving for sex, little realizing that this passionate, thickly-bearded, bald-headed lothario was planning their murders.

Little in Landru's childhood and early life foretold the monster to come. The Paris-born Landru was educated at Ecole des Freres and received good grades. He went on to study at the School of Mechanical Engineering and was then conscripted into the army, serving four years and reaching the rank of sergeant. In 1893, while still in the service, Landru began an affair with his cousin, Mlle. Remy. When she became pregnant with his child, Landru married the attractive young girl. Upon re-entering civilian life in 1894, he obtained a job where he had to provide a deposit against goods he was to sell. He never got the goods and his employer decamped to the U.S., taking Landru's deposit with him. This so embittered the 24-year-old Landru that he decided to turn crook himself. He opened a second-hand furniture store in Paris but concentrated on swindling schemes.

Landru was not a successful confidence man. He was arrested four times between 1900 and 1908, receiving prison terms that ranged between two years and eighteen months, all for various frauds. Shortly before the outbreak of WWI in 1914, Landru, using many aliases, began placing advertisements in newspapers, addressing them to lonely women reading the lovelorn columns. Though he remained married and had by then fathered another three children, Landru, unknown to his wife, advertised himself as a well-to-do bachelor looking for "proper" female companionship. Landru maintained a separate address for the assignations that resulted in this lovelorn scheme. He apparently enticed the women answering his ads to his bachelor's residence and, after promising marriage and obtaining their money from small savings accounts or deeds to parcels of land or buildings, he murdered them and disposed of their bodies. The first such victim was 40-year-old Mme. Izore, who vanished into Landru's arms in 1914, along with her dowry of 15,000 francs.

By this time police were looking for Landru for swindling an elderly couple out of their savings. Landru had disappeared, however, and with the coming of the war was able to assume other identities. What launched Landru into a career of murdering for profit is uncertain. The war, with its awful devastation and utter unconcern for human life, may have altered his otherwise reasonable perspectives. It was also suggested that he turned to this most atrocious form of making a living since his family ties had been severed by the deaths of his mother and father. It is also safe to assume that Landru, having failed miserably at lesser illicit schemes to make a dishonest franc, felt that he had nothing to lose in his lovelorn murder schemes.

In late 1914, Mme. Cuchet, a 39-year-old widow with a 16-year-old son, answered one of Landru's ads, thinking him to be M. Diard, a successful engineer. Falling in love with Landru, the woman informed her family that she intended to marry him and asked that her parents, sister, and brother-in-law visit the man of her dreams at a villa he kept in Chantilly. The family, unannounced, went to the villa but found Landru absent. The inquisitive brother-in-law looked through a chest and found it crammed with love letters from other women, who had been answering his dozens of lovelorn ads. The brother-in-law denounced Landru to Mme. Cuchet, but the woman would hear no criticism of him and she and her teenage son moved away from her family to a small villa in Vernouillet where Landru joined her. The woman and boy vanished a short time later, in January 1915, as did Diard-Landru.

Opening up new bank accounts, Landru deposited about 10,000 francs, claiming he had received an inheritance from his father. The bankers, had they checked, would have realized how unlikely this story was since Landru's father was a common laborer who had worked in the Vulcain Ironworks. In June 1915, Landru met through his ads Mme. Laborde-Line, a widow from Buenos Aires who moved out of her Paris apartment, telling the concierge that she was going to live in a villa at Vernouillet with a "wonderful man." She was seen picking flowers in Vernouillet on June 26, 1915, and was never seen again. Landru later sold her securities and moved Mme. Laborde-Line's

furniture to a ramshackle garage he kept at Neuilly which he called his used furniture store. From here he sold off his latest victim's household goods one by one.

Mme. Guillin, a 51-year-old widow who had just converted some insurance policies to 22,000 francs, answered one of Landru's ads on May 1, 1915, later visiting Landru at his villa in Vernouillet and then moving there to ostensibly become Landru's bride on Aug. 2, 1915. She too vanished and on Aug. 4, Landru moved all the furniture from the Vernouillet villa to his Neuilly garage and later cashed some of Mme. Guillin's securities. Late in 1915, Landru, using the alias George Petit, forged Mme. Guillin's signature to certain bank documents in order to withdraw 12,000 francs from her account in the Banque de France. When questioned about his actions at the bank, Landru coolly explained that he was Mme. Guillin's brother-in-law and that she could no longer conduct her own business affairs since she had suffered a stroke that left her paralyzed.

Apparently, after having murdered Cuchet, Laborde-Line, and Guillin—juggling his time tables closely in the cases of the last two—Landru felt it was dangerous to keep his villa at Vernouillet. He moved to the village of Gambais, renting the Villa Ermitage from M. Tric in December 1915. He said his name was Dupont and that he was an engineer from Rouen. This was to be his murder headquarters for several years to come. A few weeks later, Landru enticed 55-year-old Mme. Heon to the Gambais villa. She was a widow whose son had been killed in the war and whose daughter had just died. Landru consoled her and promised marriage. She went to Gambais with him; after Dec. 8, 1915, Mme. Heon was seen no more. Landru's neighbors noticed that the chimney at his villa belched black smoke at odd hours. He had purchased a new stove when he occupied the villa. This stove would be one of the chief exhibits at Landru's murder trial years later.

A short time later, Landru again inserted one of his lovelorn ads in the Paris newspapers. It read:

> Widower with two children, aged forty-three,
> with comfortable income, affectionate, serious
> and moving in good society, desires to meet
> widow with a view to matrimony.

This ad was answered by yet another widow, 45-year-old Mme. Collomb, a typist who was living with a man named Bernard who had refused to marry her. Mme. Collomb had saved more than 10,000 francs, a tidy sum Landru covetously eyed. But before this lovesick woman succumbed to Landru's persuasive ways, she insisted that he meet her family. He stalled but then reluctantly agreed to meet the woman's relatives. Landru at the time was using the alias of one of his victims, Cuchet. None of Mme. Collomb's relatives liked Landru and her sister, especially, found him odious and offensive. Mme. Collomb nevertheless went off with Landru to his Gambais villa and, after Dec. 24, 1916, was seen no more.

On Mar. 11, 1917, Landru's youngest victim, Andree Babelay, went to see her mother. The 19-year-old girl, who had lived in poverty all her life, told her mother that she had met a wonderful man in the Metro and that she intended to become his bride. Babelay accompanied Landru, who bought two tickets to Gambais and a single ticket returning to Paris. Andree Babelay was last seen alive on Apr. 12, 1917. The next victim was Mme. Buisson, who had been corresponding with Landru for more than two years. She was a 47-year-old widow with a nest egg of 10,000 francs. After announcing to her relatives her plans to wed Landru, she disappeared on Aug. 10, 1917. Her killer appeared in her Paris apartment with a forged note from Mme. Buisson, which demanded her furniture. This was taken to Landru's second-hand furniture store, the Neuilly garage.

His next victim was Mme. Jaume, who had separated from her husband and gone to a marital agent who introduced her to Landru. Using the name Guillet, Landru soon took Mme. Jaume off to Gambais and her doom. She was last seen leaving her house in Rue de Lyanes with Landru on Nov. 25, 1917. Landru appeared in Paris a few days later and withdrew Mme. Jaume's savings, 1,400 francs, from the Banque Allaume through forged documents. Mme. Pascal was next, a 36-year-old Landru had been seeing on and off since 1916. She had little money, but, like the young Babelay, she met his strong and almost incessant need for sex. Landru, using the alias of Forest, kept Mme. Pascal in a Paris apartment until he tired of her. He then took her to the Gambais villa on Apr. 5, 1918, where she, like her predecessors, went up in smoke.

In 1918, Mme. Marchadier began corresponding with Landru, who was using the alias of Guillet. Mme. Marchadier owned a large house on Rue St. Jacques, but she had little money. Landru promised to buy her house from her but had little cash himself. He proposed marriage and, on Jan. 13, 1919, Mme. Marchadier left with Landru to go to the villa at Gambais. She brought along her two small dogs and both she and the dogs were seen no more after a few days. Landru later appeared in Paris, selling off Mme. Marchadier's house and belongings.

Landru's many victims left considerable relatives searching for vanished women. This proved to be Landru's undoing. On Apr. 11, 1919, Mme. Lacoste, the sister of Mme. Buisson, one of Landru's early victims, spotted Landru strolling down the Rue de Rivoli with a young,

attractive woman on his arm. She followed Landru to a china shop where she pretended to examine items while overhearing Landru ordering some china and giving the name of Lucien Guillet and an address for the delivery of the china. Mme. Lacoste then went to police with this information and detectives returned to the shop and obtained Landru's address on the Rue de Rochechouart. Here, on Apr. 12, 1919, officers found Landru living under the alias of Guillet with a 27-year-old clerk, Fernande Segret, who was planning to go off with Landru to his villa in Gambais. The intervention of the police undoubtedly saved her life.

In Landru's pocket detectives found a black loose-leaf notebook which contained cryptic remarks about many of the women he had taken to Gambais. Landru was arrested and charged with murdering Mme. Buisson. He was then taken to the villa in Gambais where the gardens were dug up and the villa torn apart. Only the bodies of three dogs were found buried in the garden. The clothes and personal effects of all of Landru's known victims and those belonging to many more unknown women were found in the villa at Gambais, but the bodies of his victims were nowhere to be found. Landru challenged the police, as he later did the court, to "produce your bodies." He admitted to nothing and proved utterly uncooperative.

The stove in the villa was loaded with ashes and tiny bone fragments were found inside of it. The stove was removed to a Versailles court where, between Nov. 7-30, 1921, Henri Desire Landru was tried for murder. Police had found the voluminous correspondence Landru had maintained with 283 women and almost none of them could be located. Authorities were convinced that Landru murdered them all, but busy as he was in the murder-for-profit business, it would have been humanly impossible for him to have juggled that many romances and effected that many murders from 1914 to 1919, the known period of his killings. The press, of course, made much of this arrogant, strutting mass killer, aptly dubbing him "Bluebeard," a name that had once been attached with terror to France's all-time mass killer, Gilles de Rais.

The press obtained a copy of Landru's notes, wherein he had systematically classified all those writing to him in response to his lovelorn advertisements. He had labelled each group of marital applicants:

1. To be answered *poste restante*.
2. Without money.
3. Without furniture.
4. No reply.
5. To be answered to initials *poste restante*.
6. Possible fortune.
7. In reserve. For further investigation.

Lady killer Landru with his first victim, Mme. Izoré, 1914.

Landru's villa in Gambais.

Maitre Moro Giaffery.

Landru addressing the court: "Produce your bodies!"

Mme. Cuchet, murdered.

Mme. Laborde-Line, murdered.

Mme. Guillin, murdered.

Mme. Héon, murdered.

Other Landru murder victims: Mme. Jaume, Mme. Pascal, Mme. Collomb, Mlle. Babelay, Mme. Buisson.

It was believed that Landru drugged his victims into insensibility, then suffocated or strangled them. He then spent hours, even days, chopping the bodies into tiny pieces and exhaustively burning the remains, meticulously taking care not to leave any traceable remains. Landru's defense attorney was the brilliant Maitre Moro Giaffery who found that his client agitated the court and defied the prosecution to convict him without the presence of bodies. Landru claimed that the whereabouts of his female friends was his business, that these women had been his clients, and he had been in the furniture business with them at one time or another.

The court was filled up with bulky exhibits during Landru's lengthy and volatile trial. In addition to the stove, which sat ominously before the bench, a great deal of furniture was piled up in the courtroom, all items which Landru had filched from his victims. Meanwhile, Landru became a dark *cause célèbre*. Cartoons portrayed him in the newspapers and ribald songs about him and his lady killings were sung in Paris music halls. Reporters from around the world came to sit in court each day and write thousands of pages about the bald, bearded killer in the dock.

Moro Giaffery worked hard to develop a line of defense. The best he could offer was that his client was no murderer but a white slaver who had abducted the women in question and had shipped them to brothels in South America. The prosecution destroyed this theory with ridicule. Roared Prosecutor Robert Godefroy in derision: "What? Women who were all over fifty years of age? Women whose false hair, false teeth, false bosoms, as well as identity papers, you, Landru, have kept and we captured?"

"Produce your corpses!" shouted Landru, his usual refrain. He occasionally found time for jest. At one point, the presiding judge asked Landru if he were not an habitual liar. Replied Landru: "I am not a lawyer, monsieur." He was brazen and bold to the point of shocking the court. When his notebooks with their incriminating but cryptic data were presented to him, Landru merely shrugged and then sneered that he was not obligated to interpret his codes for the court. He mockingly added: "Perhaps the police would have preferred to find on page one an entry in these words: 'I, the undersigned, confess that I have murdered the women whose names are set out herein.'" It was then pointed out to Landru that his neighbors at Gambais had often complained about the putrid smell emanating from the smoke belching from the chimney of his villa. Landru ran a bony hand over his bald head, jerked his head upward and laughed menacingly, saying: "Is every smoking chimney and every bad smell proof that a body is being burned?"

The evidence that the prosecution did produce was

enough to convince a jury of Landru's guilt. He was convicted and sentenced to death. At that time, he smiled and bowed to the courtroom, which was packed with female spectators anxious to examine this strange little man. All were fascinated with the secret powers and persuasion he held over his female victims. Knowing this, Landru said, before leaving court for the last time: "I wonder if there is any lady present who would care to take my seat?"

France's modern Bluebeard was arrogant and distant to the end. On Feb. 25, 1922, a priest entered his cell to give him religious comfort on this, the last day of his life. He asked the mass killer if he wished to make a last confession. Landru waved him away and then pointed to the guards who had come to escort him to the waiting guillotine. "I am very sorry," he said, "but I must not keep these gentlemen waiting." He then walked between his guards into the courtyard of the Versailles prison and up the stairs of the scaffold. His hands were tied behind his back, his legs were tied together, and his shirt was ripped off. Landru was then placed upon a plank and his head was placed upon the block. In seconds the blade of the guillotine descended with terrifying suddenness, decapitating him.

Lang, Howard, 1935- , U.S. Howie Lang offered a cigarette to his 7-year-old playmate, Lonnie Fellick, and then casually informed him: "That will be the last one you ever smoke." In the presence of a third boy, 9-year-old Gerald Michalek, Lang threw Fellick to the ground and attacked him with a switchblade and a heavy stone in Thatcher Woods, northwest of Chicago. Satisfied that Lonnie was dead, Lang and his friend covered the body with leaves.

Howard Lang was only twelve years old when he murdered Fellick on Oct. 18, 1947. The young suspect attended classes at the Von Humboldt Grammar School on the city's far northwest side. Lang had a 17-year-old girlfriend named Anna Mae Evans, who hid his blood-stained clothes. His defiant air surprised and shocked police officials. Lang giggled as he reconstructed the murder for Police Sergeant Robert Fisher. The three boys took a streetcar to the forest preserve and walked to Thatcher Woods. "Lonnie asked me for a cigarette and I gave him one, and then he said he was going to tell my mother that I took $10 of her money." That's when Lang noticed the thirty-five-pound concrete boulder imbedded in the ground.

Howard knocked Lonnie to the ground, stabbed him, and then crushed him with the stone. Gerald Michalek told police what happened next. "Howie told me to hold his legs or else I'd get it the same way. I thought Lonnie was breathing when we left but I was sure he'd die. I covered him with the leaves."

The two boys went to the home of Anna Evans, who refused to believe the story. The next day, she and two older boys went to the forest to see for themselves. Anna took Lonnie's blood-soaked clothes with her and hid them in the woods.

When the state's attorney's office received the evidence of the crime from Chicago police, a decision was made to prosecute the boy to the fullest extent of the law, despite the long-standing policy of the Illinois courts that prohibited criminal prosecution of offenders under the age of fourteen. Serious questions were raised about a child's understanding of right and wrong. The police and the state's attorney believed that Lang knew what he was doing and they pressed for a murder indictment.

The boy was eventually convicted, but the decision was reversed by the Illinois Supreme Court on Apr. 27, 1949. The ruling was handed down by Judge John Sbarbaro who explained that Lang was too young to be able to distinguish between right and wrong. As a result he was acquitted of all charges.

La Satira, See: Spinelli, Evelita Juanita.

Latham, James Douglas, 1942-65, and **York, George Ronald**, 1943-65, U.S. James Latham, nineteen, and George York, eighteen, escaped from the guard house at Fort Hood, Texas, on May 24, 1961, to "wage war against the world." The two buck privates hated serving in the army under black officers. Latham and York were arrested by Utah state policemen on June 10 for the murders of seven people in five states.

Latham and York began their cross-country killing spree on May 26 in Baton Rouge when they assaulted Edward Guidroz, forty-three, of Mix, La. They left Guidroz in the road and made their escape in his pickup truck. Thinking the man was dead, the two soldiers continued east until they reached Jacksonville, Fla., where they strangled two vacationing Georgia women, 43-year-old Althea Ottavio and 25-year-old Patricia Anne Hewitt, who were playing a "lucky hunch" at the dog tracks on May 29. The two women were found near their abandoned car on June 7. They had been choked with their underclothing.

Racial hatred was their reason for killing 71-year-old John A. Whittaker of Shelbyville, Tenn., on June 7. After robbing the black man of his money, Latham and York shot him in cold blood. Whittaker's body was found near the abandoned pickup stolen from the recovering Guidroz.

They drove into Illinois on June 8 where they robbed and killed 35-year-old Albert Reed of Litchfield, and Martin Drenovac, fifty-nine, of Granite City. They explained that they would not have killed Drenovac had he not tried to wrestle their gun away.

On June 8, Otto Ziegler, a 62-year-old man from Sharon Springs, Kan., became their sixth victim. Ziegler, who worked as a road master for the Union Pacific Railroad, was found shot to death off U.S. 40, three miles east of Wallace, Kan. He had pulled off the road to help York and Latham, who pretended to have car trouble. They ordered Ziegler to drive his pickup to a remote spot off the side of the road. After Ziegler turned over $51, York and Latham shot him as he leaned over to retrieve his discarded wallet. The killers left the body in the ditch and stole Ziegler's red Dodge. "That was their fatal mistake," Kansas police later recalled, "Three boys who were driving farm equipment on the road saw them get out of the truck and back into the car." The pair drove through Cheyenne, Wyo., into Craig, Colo., where they stopped at a local carnival. There they met 18-year-old Rachel Marian Moyer, who worked as a maid at the Cosgriff Hotel.

York convinced Moyer to accompany them to California for the weekend, explaining they had to pick up a "prisoner." The two men, going by the names Ronnie and Jim, left the carnival with Moyer shortly before midnight on June 9. Before reaching the highway, Moyer stopped at the Cosgriff Hotel to inform the night clerk of her plans. The next day, Moyer's body was found on a deserted road south of Craig. She had been shot three times in the face and chest.

Sheriff Faye Gillette of Tooele County, Utah, issued an all-points bulletin for the arrest of the men driving the red Dodge, suspecting them of the Kansas murder. A road-block was set up on U.S. 40 near Grantsville. Their car was stopped and in the glove compartment police found two revolvers. One had eight notches carved into the handle. Latham said they would have shot it out with police, but did not want to endanger their passenger, 21-year-old soldier Vincent Olson, who was hitchhiking to San Francisco. Colorado and Florida both lost their battles to extradite the teenage killers back to their states to stand trial. The two men were returned to Sharon Springs by agents of the Kansas Bureau of Investigation on June 14.

George York and James Latham had only one request to make of their captors: that they be executed together in the electric chair. The courts were unable to accommodate the request. The glib, defiant pair were convicted of murdering Otto Ziegler. On June 23, 1965, Latham and York were taken to the gallows in Lansing, Kan., where they were hanged.

Latimer, Irving, 1866-1946, U.S. Irving Latimer, the son of wealthy parents, was born in 1866 in Jackson, Mich. At the age of twenty-three, Latimer, a handsome, well-educated young man, operated his own pharmacy. Since his father's death two years earlier, Latimer had lived with his widowed mother. Latimer soon incurred substantial debt through mismanagement of his business or, more likely, through bad habits. In addition to owing the tax collector and about sixty creditors, Latimer had also borrowed $3,000 from his mother which was due on Jan. 31, 1889.

On Jan. 24, Latimer made one of his frequent "buying" trips to Detroit. Although Latimer usually stayed in the more elegant Cadillac Hotel, on this occasion, he registered at the second-rate Griswold. Late in the morning of Jan. 25, authorities told Latimer that his mother had been murdered the night before. Her badly beaten body, which had two bullet wounds to the head, was found in her bedroom. Neighbors noted that she had not let her dog out in the morning, and called police. The police initially assumed the crime to be a bungled burglary. But investigation revealed that none of the murdered woman's valuables had been disturbed and no one had heard her dog barking in the night, though they did when they tried to rouse Mrs. Latimer the next morning.

While trying to locate Latimer, police chief John Boyle spoke to the boy Latimer had left minding the pharmacy. The boy claimed that Latimer had refused his request for the day off, saying that he had to be a pallbearer at a funeral in Detroit. Boyle finally located Latimer at the Griswold. When questioned about the funeral, Latimer explained that he had lied to his employee to avoid having to delay his trip. Finding Latimer's responses unsatisfactory, Boyle began searching for witnesses who might disprove his alibi. A railroad conductor on the Michigan Central Railroad said he had picked up a passenger in Jackson at 6:20 on the morning of Jan. 25. The man demanded a sleeper, which he immediately closed himself into, and he left the train in West Detroit, ten or fifteen minutes before reaching downtown. From photographs supplied by the police, the conductor identified the man as Latimer. In Detroit, the Griswold's night porter told police he had seen a man slipping out a side door of the hotel at about 10 p.m. on Jan. 24. The maid assigned to Latimer's room reported that she had found it empty and the bed unused the next morning. She also saw a man she identified as Latimer entering the room stealthily fifteen minutes after she had checked it.

The case against Latimer grew when a barber near the hotel identified Latimer as the nervous young man who had come in for a shave between nine and ten on the morning of Jan. 25. When the barber pointed out to Latimer that he had blood on his coat, Latimer replied that he had a nosebleed. Finally, with the testimony of two conductors who had seen Latimer on the train going toward Jackson on the night of Jan. 24, Chief Boyle concluded that he had enough evidence to arrest Latimer for his mother's murder.

Latimer hired two expensive lawyers with some of his inheritance from his mother's estate. During the trial, he changed his story and admitted having come back to Jackson on the night of the murder. He explained that he had followed a prostitute named Trixy, whom he thought had boarded the Jackson-bound train. Despite his alibi and his attorneys' efforts, Latimer was found Guilty. As there was no capital punishment in Michigan, Judge Erastus Peck sentenced Latimer to life imprisonment.

Four years later, Latimer, having proven an ideal prisoner, was serving a snack to prison guards on Mar. 26, 1893. He had prepared these snacks frequently, but this time he laced the food with prussic acid and opium. Although he claimed later that he had only intended to knock the guards out, one of them died. Latimer escaped but was captured and returned to prison three days later. Latimer once again became the ideal prisoner and gradually regained his privileges within the prison. In 1935, the governor of Michigan granted Latimer a release. Latimer was sixty-nine years old and had spent forty-six years in jail. He became a vagrant for five years until he was put into a state home for the elderly. Latimer died at the Eloise State Hospital in 1946 without ever confessing to his mother's murder.

Laubscher, Miemie, prom. 1957, and **van Jaarsveld, Jacobus Frederick**, 1935- , S. Afri. When she became involved with a younger man, a married woman and her new lover eventually conspired to murder her drunkard husband, later blaming each other for the crime at their trials.

Miemie Magdalena Josina de Jager married Marthinus Johannes Laubscher, nicknamed Spokies, a car mechanic, in Zastron, South Africa, in 1950. Her husband-to-be promised to stop drinking before they wed, but resumed drinking shortly after their marriage. Children had no effect on him, and the couple grew increasingly unhappy as he physically assaulted his wife, piled up debts, and engaged with her in constant fights.

In 1956, Laubscher brought home a friend, 21-year-old Jacobus Frederick van Jaarsveld, another car mechanic, who frequently visited and often stayed over at the couple's house on weekends. After about a year, Miemie Laubscher and van Jaarseveld began an affair, soon moving to nearby Senekal where they lived together. Laubscher went to the boarding house where his friend and wife lived and asked her to return to him. She refused and they decided to divorce, the husband insisting on having custody of their children. Various complicated negotiations followed, with van Jaarsfeld actually moving back in with the reconciled couple at the husband's invitation. As the trio continued to drink and play musical beds, the situation led to a quarrel at a party during which Miemie Laubscher apparently tried to strangle her husband. On July 10 the wife actually went to her mother-in-law and told her she intended to kill her husband so she could leave him and take the children. The mother-in-law, shocked, understandably advised her to take the offspring and leave the husband alone.

The not-surprising conclusion of this triangle occurred when the drunken Laubscher disappeared on Aug. 1. His body, strangled with a belt from his wife's raincoat, and his head bruised from a blunt instrument, was discovered by police on Aug. 9. Weighted with a heavy steel pulley, the corpse had been dumped into the Rusfontein Dam several miles from Bloemfontein.

Both van Jarsveld and Laubscher were charged with first-degree murder. Tried before Acting Judge-President of the Free State, Justice A.J. Smith on Oct. 14, 1957, at a Bloemfontein jury trial, van Jaarsveld was found Guilty of murder "with extenuating circumstances" and sentenced to a fifteen-year jail term, in part because of his age, 21 years. Two days later Laubscher was tried before a jury and Justice D.H. Botha. With the same verdict as her lover, Laubscher was given a twelve-year jail term.

Law, Walter W., 1905- , U.S. When 28-year-old New Haven *Journal-Courier* reporter Rose Brancato disappeared on July 5, 1943, authorities conducted a nationwide search believing her to be the victim of amnesia. The following January, however, they arrested 39-year-old Walter W. Law, the married father of three children, when he returned from his war production job in Sparrow Point, Md., for a weekend visit with his family. After forty-eight hours of questioning, Law broke down and admitted that he lured Brancato into the basement of the Woolworth Building and then strangled her during an ensuing struggle. Law, who had met Brancato in the Woolworth Building where she did

Rose Brancato, murdered by Walter Law.

volunteer work, then placed her body into the firebox of a boiler without knowing whether she was alive or dead.

Law signed a written confession of the crime and reenacted it for police. He pleaded guilty to second-degree murder and was sentenced to life in prison.

Le Boeuf, Ada Bonner, and **Dreher,** Dr. **Thomas E.**, d.1929, and **Beadle, James**, d.1929, U.S. In 1927, James Le Boeuf was a power plant superintendent in Morgan City, La. When Dr. Thomas Dreher began to pay Le Boeuf's wife unwanted attentions, Le Boeuf reportedly threatened to kill the doctor. However, Le Boeuf's wife and the doctor plotted to murder Le Boeuf. On July 1, 1927, Le Boeuf was shot to death. His body, though weighted at the neck and ankles with two railway irons, floated to the surface of Lake Palourde, where some boys spotted it. Police discovered that Le Boeuf and his wife had been seen together at the lake. Ada Le Boeuf and Dr. Dreher were arrested along with James Beadle, a handyman who worked for the doctor and who actually shot Le Boeuf. The three turned on each other, but they were all found Guilty. Beadle received a life sentence and Ada Le Boeuf and Dr. Dreher were sentenced to death. They were hanged at the St. Mary Parish prison on Feb. 1, 1929.

Ledbetter, Huddie (AKA: **Lead Belly**), 1889-1949, U.S. A Louisiana native, Huddie Ledbetter traveled the South, taking jobs as a laborer and a cotton picker. About 1918, he murdered a man in Texas during a fight over a woman, was convicted, and sent to prison. About 1925, after serving seven years of his term, Ledbetter sang his way free. Governor Pat Morris Neff pardoned Ledbetter after the prisoner sang his request. In 1930, Ledbetter was arrested again in Louisiana for stabbing six people in a dispute over some whiskey. He was convicted and sent to the Louisiana State Penitentiary. In 1933, U.S. folk song authority John A. Lomax was searching for folk ballads and he discovered Ledbetter. Lomax helped win another pardon for Ledbetter and took the singer to New York. There he thrilled audiences with black spirituals, ballads, and work songs, singing in concert halls, night clubs, and on the radio. But once again, in 1939, he landed in prison. He stabbed Henry Burgess at a party in a New York rooming house and was convicted and sentenced to one year. Upon his release, Ledbetter resumed his singing career and, in 1949, died of a bone disease.

LeDoux, Emma (AKA: **Emma Head; Emma Mc-Vicar**), 1871-1941, U.S. Emma Head of Amador County, Calif., first married Charlie Barrett, who died in Mexico. Then she married Mr. Williams, who died under mysterious circumstances, leaving Emma a large sum from an insurance policy. In September 1902, she married Albert N. McVicar, but they separated and she worked as a prostitute.

On Aug. 12, 1905, she became the bigamous wife of Eugene LeDoux and the two lived with her mother in California. On Mar. 11, 1906, Emma met her estranged husband, McVicar, in Stockton, Calif., where the couple ordered a load of furniture to be sent to Jamestown, Calif. Shortly afterward, Emma called the store and tried to delay the shipment, but the furniture had already been sent. A

Bigamist killer Emma Le-Doux.

few days later, she purchased morphine from a San Francisco doctor, and on Mar. 14 bought some cyanide from a pharmacy, saying she wanted to develop photographs. On Mar. 15, McVicar and his wife returned to Jamestown, where he worked as a timber man. But he quit his job on Mar. 21, saying he was going to work on a farm belonging to his wife's mother. On Mar. 23, the couple traveled to Stockton, Calif., and Emma selected more furniture, sending it to LeDoux's home. Sometime that night or the next day, she administered knockout drops and morphine to McVicar. On Mar. 24, she bought a trunk and ordered it delivered to her hotel. She also bought some rope and, at about 2 p.m., she had the trunk, which contained the body of her dying husband, delivered to the train station. The trunk was almost placed on a train bound for San Francisco, but since it bore no identification the trunk was sent back to the baggage room, where the baggage man and several others present noticed the peculiar odor eminating from within and called police.

Emma was arrested in Antioch, Calif., and her trial began Apr. 17. Convicted and sentenced to death, her hanging was delayed when the Supreme Court of California ordered a new trial in May 1909. Emma pleaded guilty, was sentenced to a life term in prison, and sent to San Quentin. She was paroled on July 20, 1920, but sent back to prison for parole violations on July 9, 1921. She was paroled a second time on Mar. 30, 1925, and married Mr. Crackbon, a rancher who died within two years. Her parole was yet again revoked, and in 1933 she was transferred to Tehachapi Women's Prison, where she died in July of 1941.

Lee, Barney, 1928- , U.S. On Apr. 29, 1942, Nickoli "Dick" Payne reprimanded his teenaged nephew, Barney Lee, because the boy had not finished his chores. The youngster was working on a ranch in the mountains of Monterey County, Calif. In retaliation, the 14-year-old Barney fatally shot his 36-year-old uncle. Barney was tried, convicted, and sentenced to life in prison in San Quentin where he was held in the prison hospital because officials believed that his integration with the prison population would deter his rehabilitation and, further, they had no legal right to transfer the boy to another institution.

Lee, John, 1945- , U.S. On Apr. 14, 1977, John Lee, an employee of a south suburban Chicago chemical plant, argued with another employee, 60-year-old Charles Kochenberg, after Kochenberg told Lee to finish some work. Following the dispute, 32-year-old Lee was suspended from the Stauffer Chemical Company. On Apr. 18, a disciplinary hearing was held at the plant, attended by the two employees, and management representatives John Kurzdorfer, William Good, and Thomas J. DeMarinis, and union representative Osborne Tinsley. After the meeting, Good told Lee that he would be notified of the outcome later. Lee got out of his seat and said, "You'll tell me now." He became more agitated, pulled out a .38-caliber revolver and shot Good in the head. Kochenberg and Tinsley escaped from the room before Lee fatally shot Kurzdorfer and wounded DeMarinis. Lee then fled in his car and, at about noon, turned himself in to Chicago police at the Englewood District Station. He was transferred to Chicago Heights and charged with murder and two counts of attempted murder. Lee pleaded guilty to the charges, was convicted, and sentenced to twenty to sixty years' imprisonment.

Lee, Ludwig Halvorsen, 1889-1928, U.S. While walking his beat in Battery Park, on the southern tip of Manhattan, N.Y., on the morning of July 10, 1927, a policeman found a neatly wrapped bundle on a subway air vent containing a severed human leg. The wrapping paper came from a grocery store and was covered with penciled notations. The next day a 16-year-old boy discovered a second package, wrapped much the same way, on the front lawn of a Brooklyn Catholic church. It contained the decomposing remains of a woman's torso.

Bundles were soon found all over Brooklyn—body parts without heads—making it nearly impossible to determine who the victims were. Police did know the two bodies were female, and that the wrapping paper had come from one of two grocery store chains: Bohack's or the A & P. But to visit every single A & P and Bohack's store in New York's five boroughs seemed an insurmountable task; one the homicide squad did not relish. Before their search for the grocery store clerk who might have penciled the figures on the brown paper had begun, however, Alfred Bennett of Lincoln Place, Brooklyn, came forward to report the disappearance of his wife, Selma. Last seen on July 9, 1927, by the Bennett's 19-year-old son, John, Selma Bennett disappeared after crossing her backyard to visit 76-year-old Sarah Elizabeth Brownell, who owned a rooming house on Prospect Place.

Detective Arthur Carey of the New York Police Department visited the rooming house that night. Met at the door by 38-year-old Ludwig Lee, a Norwegian immigrant who had lived there for two years, Carey immediately discerned the sickeningly

Murderer Ludwig Lee, right, in custody.

sweet smell of rotting flesh. "I think you're coming with us," Carey said. After Lee had been taken to precinct headquarters, a man named Christian Jensen was intercepted as he entered Brownell's rooming house. A long-time employee at a Brooklyn A & P, he had given wrapping paper to Lee.

A team of medical examiners found more body parts in the basement of the rooming house, including the head of Mrs. Bennett. By way of explanation, Lee said that Brownell had made repeated overtures to him, that he had finally consented to marry her, but then reneged, deciding instead to kill her and collect her $4,000 in savings. He was in the process of chopping Brownell's body up, Lee continued, when Mrs. Bennett walked in. He killed her, too, to prevent his arrest. "It was a lot of work doing all that running around," Lee said sardonically. After a short trial, he was convicted, and in 1928, electrocuted.

Lee, Maria Helena Gertruida Christina (AKA: **Maria Helena Gertruida Christina van Niekerk**), 1899-1948, S. Afri. Maria van Niekerk, the daughter of a South African family, was first married in 1915 at the age of

sixteen. After two divorces, she married her third husband, 24-year-old Jan de Klerk Lee who died in 1941, apparently from tuberculosis. Within the next few years, she met Alwyn Jacobus Nicolaas Smith, took a job with Lennon Ltd., in Cape Town, and married C.J.B. Olivier. In June 1945, she shared a room in Cape Town with her lover, Smith, but she married Olivier early the following year.

After her fourth marriage, she persuaded Smith to move to Durban, and he stayed there from May to October, 1946. On Dec. 5, Lee divorced Olivier. Meanwhile, she had been stealing jewelry from her employers, and both Lee and Smith had profited from the sale of the stolen goods. After she was fired in early 1947, Lee became angry because Smith had bought a car and registered it in his name. He also lied to Lee, telling her that her mother had died, and she became enraged when she learned her mother was still alive. She apparently began poisoning Smith with arsenic in October 1946, administering larger and larger doses. The solicitous Lee attended Smith as he grew ill. She called a doctor in March 1947 and Smith recovered in the hospital. However, back with Lee, he again became ill and eventually died on May 2. After an autopsy revealed arsenic poisoning, Lee was arrested. She was held at Pretoria Central Prison and later transferred to Cape Town for her trial, which began Apr. 6, 1948. Lee was found Guilty on May 10, and was hanged on Sept. 17, 1948.

Lefebre, Jean-Marie, 1916-   , Belg. On Jan. 9, 1956, the personal barber of General Emile Deisser visited his client in his Brussels home as usual. But instead of shaving the 87-year-old general, Jean-Marie Lefebre strangled him.

The general's sister-in-law, Louise Marcette, witnessed the murder and just had time to telephone police before Lefebre strangled her with telephone wire. The 39-year-old killer then bashed the head of the 60-year-old housekeeper, Marie Foulon. He proceeded to search through the rooms for valuables. Then he walked out the front door. The police never arrived because they took down the wrong house number.

During the police investigation, someone who knew the housekeeper mentioned Lefebre and he was questioned. Police grew more suspicious when they found his fingerprints in rooms of Deisser's house where a barber probably would not have gone. They also discovered that Lefebre had recently paid off his debts and sold several items. After further questioning, Lefebre confessed. To strengthen the highly publicized case, police reenacted the crime with the killer present, having driven him past angry and riotous mobs to the general's house. Lefebre, forty, was tried in

Brussels in November 1956. He was convicted on Nov. 28 and sentenced to death.

Lego, Donald R., 1933- , U.S. The last of seventeen victims killed in a string of murders, 82-year-old Mary Mae Johnson was stabbed and beaten to death in Joliet Township, Ill., on Aug. 26, 1983. A newspaper delivery man discovered her body later that day when he noticed she had not picked up her paper. He found her body in a living room chair. After receiving a tip from a tow-truck driver, police arrested Donald Lego. On Mar. 16, 1984, the 51-year-old Lego was convicted, and on Mar. 19 he was sentenced to death. Police said Lego was not a main suspect for the other murders in Will County.

Lehmann, Christa Ambros, 1922- , Ger. Christa Ambros was alone almost from the beginning. Her mother had been confined to Germany's Alzey mental hospital; her father, a cabinetmaker, had remarried and severed his ties to his daughter.

In 1944 she married Karl Franz Lehmann, a tile setter with a medical deferment from military service, but by 1949

German killer Christa Lehmann in custody.

Christa Lehmann was preoccupied by her affairs with American servicemen stationed in Germany, and the marriage began to fall apart. On Sept. 17, 1952, Karl Lehmann died from what physicians diagnosed as stomach convulsions brought on by an ulcer. Two years later, on Oct. 14, 1953, Mrs. Lehmann's father-in-law, Valentin Lehmann, died much the same way as his son.

Mrs. Lehmann inherited her father-in-law's exclusive apartment in Worms, Ger., where she often entertained her friend, Annie Hamann. A widow who lived with her 75-year-old mother, Eva Ruh, her brother Walter, and her 19-year-old daughter, Uschi, on the Grosse Fischerweide in the Old Town of Worms, Hamann associated with Mrs. Lehmann against her mother's wishes. On Feb. 14, 1954, Mrs. Lehmann purchased five truffles from a chocolate shop and delivered four of them to friends. The fifth, earmarked for Ruh, she laced with the chemical insecticide E-605. First developed at the Bayer Works in Leverkusen by Gerhard Schroeder before the end of WWII, E-605 is virtually impossible to detect in the system. Upon receipt of the truffle, Ruh left it in the kitchen cupboard as a treat for her daughter. On Feb. 15, Hamann took one bite and dropped it to the floor. "It's bitter," she said, and then collapsed, suddenly blinded. When the doctor arrived, Hamann was dead; so was her dog, who had also sampled the truffle.

In his autopsy report, Professor Kurt Wagner of the Institute of Forensic Medicine in Mainz, concluded that Hamann had been poisoned, but he was not sure what the poison was until he recalled reading about E-605. Even then, he had his doubts—there was no known use of E-605 as a poison—but then detectives did a background check on Mrs. Lehmann and had the remains of her husband and father-in-law exhumed.

Mrs. Lehmann was arrested on Feb. 19, as she left Hamann's funeral. On Feb. 23, she summoned her father and a clergyman to her jail cell and confessed to filling the cream truffle with E-605. Her intention, she said, was not to murder Ruh, but only to make her ill. "By the way," she added, "I also poisoned my father-in-law, and I killed my husband too."

On Sept. 20, 1954, Mrs. Lehmann was convicted of murder and sentenced to life in prison. As a consequence of her well-publicized trial, dozens of Germans—in some instances entire families—began ingesting E-605 to commit suicide and escape the bleakness of postwar Germany.

Lehnberg, Marlene, c.1955-   , and **Choegoe, Marthinus,** 1940-   , S. Afri. South African Marlene Lehnberg aspired to become a model and to marry Christopher van der Linde, a married man nearly twice her age. She began to harass the van der Lindes with telephone calls. In September 1974, she told Mrs. van der Linde that she was having an affair with her husband. Mrs. van der Linde knew this was not true, and dismissed the girl as a nuisance. Growing more desperate by the day, Lehnberg recruited 33-year-old disabled Marthinus Choegoe.

Lehnberg promised him her car, a radio, and sex if he would kill Susanna van der Linde. On the night of Nov. 4,

1974, Choegoe entered the van der Linde's Cape Town residence and stabbed Mrs. van der Linde to death with a pair of scissors. Witnesses in the neighborhood recognized the man with a noticeable limp and police soon picked up Choegoe. He implicated Lehnberg, who denied any connection with the crime. But Choegoe produced a note from her which read: "If you think it will be better or quicker, then use a knife, but the job must be done."

The letter convicted the killers. Tried in Cape Town in March 1975, the pair were found Guilty of premeditated murder. Lehnberg and Choegoe were both sentenced to die, but their sentences were later commuted to life imprisonment.

Lennon, John, See: **Chapman, Mark David.**

Leopold, Nathan F., Jr., 1906-71, and **Loeb, Richard A.,** 1907-36, U.S. Nathan Leopold and Richard Loeb were the products of immense wealth, two brilliant students who had been allowed to expand their personalities and intelligence at will without having to work or worry about money. They had, since early childhood, been given everything, and as a result, they indulged their fantasies as their parents had satisfied their childish cravings. These two University of Chicago students, brilliant by comparison to other youths their age, had proven themselves superior in all their pursuits. Leopold, with an estimated I.Q. of 200, had graduated from the University of Chicago at age eighteen, the youngest ever to do so. He spoke nine languages fluently and was an expert botanist and ornithologist. There was, however, little warmth in his home. Leopold lived in a loveless household. Money replaced affection. His father, Nathan Leopold, Sr., was a millionaire transport tycoon who assigned a governess to his son at an early age. Babe, as Leopold had been nicknamed, came under the supervision of a sexually disturbed woman who had the boy practice all sorts of sexual perversions with her, distorting his young mind.

The Leopolds noticed their son's reluctance to associate with girls and they unreasonably placed him in an all-girl's school to correct his attitude. The governess went with the boy, continuing to warp his sexual growth. Moreover, this strange situation caused Leopold to reject female companionship altogether. By the time Leopold graduated from college, his mother was dead and his father, as usual, compensated for the loss by showering his son with money. He gave his son $3,000 and sent him on a European tour. When Leopold returned he was given a new car and a $125-a-week allowance and then ignored. Leopold immersed himself in the works of Friedrich Nietzsche, advocate of the superman concept. But the youth was anything but the physical ideal. He was stoop-shouldered and undersized. He had an overactive thyroid gland and he was physically unattractive with huge, bulging eyes and a weak chin. He was a sexual deviate at age fourteen when he met Richard Loeb, another early-aged homosexual.

Loeb was later to fulfill Leopold's concept of the superman. He was also the son of a millionaire, and like Leopold, had been spoiled with gifts and money since childhood. At thirteen, Loeb became Leopold's sexual master and continued to dominate him until they sought what they considered the ultimate thrill, that of murder. Loeb was always the leader. He grew up a tall, handsome, and clever youth. He was a charming and captivating conversationalist. His father was a senior executive for Sears, Roebuck, and Co., and he bestowed a $250-a-week allowance on his son, a sum that amounted to twice that earned by most men during the early 1920s. Loeb also suffered from physical defects. He had a nervous tic, stuttered at times when nervous, and suffered fainting spells which had been interpreted as petit mal epilepsy. He often talked of suicide with Leopold, and his character, beneath the glossy charm he showed to others, was decidedly morose and fatalistic.

A graduate of the University of Michigan at age seventeen, Loeb believed himself to be an excellent detective, and his most passionate daydream was to commit the perfect crime. He often talked of this with Leopold, who encouraged his superman theories with such a crime. The two not only satisfied each other in their sexual liaison, but they fed upon each other's egos and together believed themselves to be perfect human beings. The youths had two driving obsessions. With Leopold it was abnormal sex, and with Loeb, crime. Both were later termed by their own defense attorneys as "moral imbeciles." It was Loeb who led the pair into active crime. At first Leopold resisted the idea, but Loeb perversely withheld his sexual participation until Leopold agreed to commit crimes with him. They signed a mutual pact in which both agreed that they would support the other's needs.

This agreement had been signed when Leopold was fourteen and Loeb was thirteen and the youths embarked on setting fires, touching off false fire alarms, committing petty thefts, and vandalizing the homes of their wealthy neighbors. They spent months creating an elaborate system in which they could expertly cheat while playing bridge, the game of the rich and socially esteemed. They constantly argued with each other, but neither formed friendships with other children. The arguments grew violent and Loeb beat up Leopold on several occasions. Both boys threatened to murder each other someday. Loeb laughed at this idea, saying he would kill himself before Leopold could murder him.

When Leopold told Loeb that he would be going on an extended tour of Europe, Loeb proposed that they commit a spectacular crime before Leopold's ship sailed. Leopold was reluctant but Loeb appealed to his lover by cleverly positing the idea as worthy of Friedrich Nietzsche, Leopold's intellectual idol. Loeb wrote Leopold a note which read: "The superman is not liable for anything he may do, except for the one crime that it is possible for him to commit—to make a mistake." This prompted Leopold to reconsider Loeb's proposition. The most dangerous crime, the most serious crime, was the only type of crime that Loeb would consider and that, of course, was murder.

They would kidnap and kill someone, and *then* send a ransom note and collect money for a victim who was already dead, mocking the awful crime they meticulously planned to commit. They were utterly unconcerned with the identity of the victim, as long as that person came from wealthy parents who could afford to pay the ransom. Loeb took Leopold to his room and showed him a typewriter that he had stolen in November 1923 from the University of Michigan when he graduated. Since this typewriter could not be traced to them, Loeb reasoned, the ransom note could be typed on it. The next step was to obtain a car that could be used for the kidnapping. Both boys knew, of course, that their own cars might be identified, so they established fake identities which would enable them to rent a car. This element of their plan was elaborate, but it provided the youths with some dramatic play-acting.

One spring morning in 1924, Leopold, using the alias of Morton D. Ballard, checked into Chicago's Morrison Hotel. He registered as a salesman from Peoria. He then went to the nearby Rent-A-Car agency and selected a sedan. The salesman asked for a reference and Leopold gave him the name of Louis Mason, along with a phone number. The salesman called Mason (who was really Loeb) who gave "Ballard" an excellent recommendation. Leopold then took the car around for about two hours and returned it to the agency, telling the salesman that he would pick it up later when he needed it. Loeb and Leopold had already used their aliases to open up bank accounts. They intended to deposit the ransom money in these accounts.

Several weeks before the crime, Leopold and Loeb had boarded the 3 p.m. train for Michigan City, Ind. Loeb brought along small parcels the size of those in which the ransom money would be paid and threw these parcels from the rear platform of the observation car at points selected by Leopold, open fields where Leopold had, months before, spent time studying birds. Returning to the car rental agency, Leopold obtained a car on May 20, 1924, and he and Loeb then drove to a hardware store on 43rd and Cottage Avenue. Here they purchased a chisel, a rope, and hydrochloric acid. All these were tools of murder. The rope was to be used to garrote their victim, the chisel to stab him in case he struggled too much, and the acid to obliterate their victim's identity. The murderous pair debated the use of sulfuric acid before opting to use hydrochloric.

On the morning of May 21, 1924, Loeb wrapped adhesive tape about the handle of the chisel to allow a firmer grip. This, along with the rope and acid, were placed in the rented car, along with strips of cloth to be used to bind their victim, and a lap robe to cover the body. A pair of hip boots were also put into the car to be used in burying the body in a swamp the killers had previously selected. Both Leopold and Loeb each pocketed a loaded revolver, and Loeb carried the ransom note typed the day before. This note demanded $10,000 for the return of the victim, who they had no intention of returning. Neither boy needed the ransom money, but they had to make it appear that the kidnappers were lowly, money-craving underworld types, motivated by cash, not the "supreme thrill" they both sought. This element of the plan Loeb thought to be the most ingenious. Police, he told Leopold, always pinned their investigations on motive and worked backward; with the false clue of cash-hungry kidnappers planted, the police would never look for two respectable, well-to-do students. Never, he said.

The most bizarre aspect of these dark procedures was the fact that on the very day they planned to commit the crime, May 21, 1924, the boys had not yet picked out a victim. This cold indifference was the root of their inhumanity, their utter lack of moral code. They did not care about the human life they were about to take. The identity of their victim was of total unconcern to their clinical minds. The person to be killed was merely another element of their test to prove their own superiority. The victim was a number, a thing. Leopold and Loeb sat down and wrote out a list of possible kidnap victims. First they thought to kidnap and murder Loeb's younger brother Tommy, but they dismissed the idea, only because both felt that it would be difficult to collect the ransom from Loeb's father and that Loeb might arouse suspicion.

Little William Deutsch was then discussed. He was the grandson of multimillionaire philanthropist Julius Rosenwald. He, too, was eliminated since Rosenwald was the president of Sears, Roebuck and Co., and thus, Loeb's superior. The Deutsch boy was simply "too close to home" for the murderous youths. Richard Rubel, one of their few friends, was also considered as a candidate for the kidnapping-murder. Rubel often had lunch with Leopold and Loeb, but he was dismissed after the killers concluded that his father was a tightwad and would probably refuse to pay

Dear Sir:

Proceed immediately to the back
platform of the train. Watch the east side
of the track. Have your package ready. Look
for the first LARGE, RED, BRICK factory situated immediately adjoining the tracks on the
east. On top of this factory is a large, black
watertower with the word CHAMPION written on
it. Wait until you have COMPLETELY passed the
south end of the factory - count five very ra-
idly and then IMMEDIATELY throw the package as
far east as you can.

Remember that this is your only
chance to recover your son.

Yours truly,

GEORGE JOHNSON

Left, Bobby Franks, the 14-year-old boy brutally slain by thrill killers Leopold and Loeb and, right, the ransom note written by the murderers to make it appear that kidnappers were the culprits; the real motive was to commit the so-called "perfect crime."

Leopold sitting in the driver's seat of his car, chatting with Richard Crowe, Cook County state's attorney, the man who trapped him in his lies.

The culvert where Leopold and Loeb buried the naked body of Bobby Franks. They poured acid on the remains to obliterate its features and prevent identification.

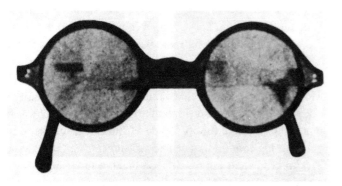

The glasses found at the burial site by police; they were of an unusual make and police traced them to Leopold through the manufacturer.

Nathan Leopold, Richard Crowe, and Richard Loeb, following the confessions of the killers; they were cleverly manipulated into their admissions.

a ransom for his son. What to do? The boys finally decided to pick a random victim in the neighborhood. They got into the rented car and cruised around a few blocks near Leopold's home, focusing upon the young boys coming and going from the Harvard Preparatory School. This was an exclusive school which was attended by children of very wealthy parents.

As they drove, the killers casually discussed their problem. They agreed that they should select a small child since neither of them was strong enough to subdue a child with any strength. They stopped next to the Harvard School yard, spotted little John Levinson, and decided then and there that he would be their victim. But since neither knew the address of the Levinson family, they drove to a nearby drugstore and looked it up in the phone directory. They wanted to make sure that they would have the correct address in order to send the ransom note. By the time the pair drove back to the schoolyard, the Levinson boy was leaving. Leopold, who had brought along binoculars for the purpose of selecting a victim at some distance, spotted Levinson across the field.

Loeb drove at considerable speed around the block in order to catch up with their prey, but the Levinson child went up an alley and vanished. Frustrated, the pair drove about aimlessly, searching for a victim. As they drove down Ellis Avenue they spotted some boys playing. One of them was Bobby Franks, a distant relative of Loeb's. "He's perfect," Loeb stated, telling Leopold that the Franks child came from great wealth, that the boy's father, Jacob Franks, was a multimillionaire box manufacturer, and could certainly afford to pay the ransom for his child, one he doted upon. After parking the car at a curb, Loeb called 14-year-old Bobby Franks to the car. Loeb asked Bobby if he wanted to go for a ride.

"No thanks," Bobby said. He looked at Leopold who gave him a long, hard stare. "I don't know this man," Franks said, pointing to Leopold. There was some apprehension in his voice. "Besides, I have to go home," he said. Loeb persisted, telling Bobby that they would drive him home. He recalled playing tennis with the Franks boy and knew the child had an avid interest in the sport. Loeb then told Bobby that he had a new tennis racket he wanted to show him. The Franks boy got in the back seat of the car. Leopold remained in the front seat behind the wheel, driving and Loeb got into the back seat with Bobby Franks. Leopold drove northward as Loeb fondled the rope he intended to use to strangle Franks. He quickly discarded this idea as being too clumsy. He grabbed the chisel and with four lightning moves, stabbed the startled child four times. The helpless child fell to the floor, gushing blood from savage wounds to the head.

Leopold turned briefly while driving to look in the back seat to see the dying boy. He saw the contemptuous sneer on Richard Loeb's face. Loeb had enjoyed killing the child and said so. Leopold winced at the sight of the blood and groaned: "Oh, God, I didn't know it would be like this!" Leopold continued driving through heavy traffic. Meanwhile, Loeb ruthlessly tied up the child, stuffed strips of cloth in his mouth, and then threw the lap robe over him. Bobby Franks lay on the floor of the back seat of the sedan slowly bleeding to death. Leopold kept driving about aimlessly until dusk. He then parked the car and the boys went to a restaurant to get sandwiches. They were waiting for the cover of darkness before hiding the body at a site selected earlier. Leopold called his father and told him he would not be home until late that night.

The boys then got back into the car and began driving south. They stopped at another restaurant and ate a heavy meal, finding themselves famished, even though they had just eaten sandwiches. Outside, parked at the curb, the windows of the car open, the lap robe and the body of the Franks boy beneath it was open to the view of all passersby. This was another element of the contempt the killers displayed for the ability of anyone to detect their crime. It was Loeb's belief that no one in the world cared about anyone else. He joked with the somber Leopold about the fact that anyone passing the car outside could lean through the windows and pick up the robe and discover the body. "But nobody will," he said in a low voice. Both were wholly insensitive to the murder they had committed. They ate their way through a five-course meal, concerned only with completing the routines they had established for themselves.

At nightfall, the killers got back into the car and drove to an area called Panhandle Tracks at 118th Street. Here a swamp drained into an open culvert and this was the spot they had selected as the burial site for their victim. Loeb got into the back seat of the car and checked the Franks boy. "He's dead," he announced proudly. He then stripped the boy of his clothes and poured the acid over the child's face to mar his features and prevent identification. While Loeb was performing this monstrous task, Leopold was slipping into his pair of hip boots. He then took the child, walked to the culvert, and stuffed the body into the pipe. It was difficult work and Leopold removed his coat. As he did so, he made the one mistake that would spoil the so-called "perfect crime" he and Richard Loeb had so carefully planned. His glasses fell from the pocket of his coat. Moreover, he believed that he had thoroughly hidden the body of their victim, but in the darkness he failed to notice that a small, naked foot protruded from the drainpipe. He grabbed his coat and went back to the car.

The boys then parked the car near a large apartment building. They noted that the back seat and the lap robe were stained with Bobby's blood. They abandoned the car and then burned the robe in a vacant lot. They went to Leopold's house and there burned all of Bobby's clothes, except the metal he had been wearing, his belt buckle and class pin. They typed the Franks's address on the envelope of the ransom note and then left, driving to Indiana where they mailed the note and buried the class pin, belt buckle, and shoes of Bobby Franks. They then drove back to Chicago and Leopold called Jacob Franks, who had been worried ever since his child failed to come home that afternoon. Leopold told Franks: "Your boy has been kidnapped. He is safe and unharmed. Tell the police and he will be killed at once. You will receive a ransom note with instructions tomorrow." Without allowing Franks to respond, Leopold hung up. The boys then made themselves drinks and played cards until past midnight in Leopold's room, working out the final details of their "perfect crime."

A ransom note signed "George Johnson" was delivered to Franks the next day. It demanded that Franks pay $10,000 for the return of his child, the payment to be made in twenty- and fifty-dollar bills. The bills were to be placed in a cigar box and this box was to be wrapped in white paper and then sealed with wax. Franks would receive more instructions at 1 p.m. that day, the note stated. Franks had by then notified the police through his lawyer of his son's kidnapping. The police were told that the Franks wanted no publicity in fear that the kidnappers would murder their child, as the anonymous caller had threatened.

Meanwhile Leopold and Loeb had second thoughts about the bloodstains in the rented car. They retrieved it, drove to the Leopold house, and parked it in the family garage. Sven Englund, the Leopold family chauffeur, noticed the boys scrubbing down the back seat of this car. When he asked them about it, they told him that they had been drinking wine in the back seat of the car, borrowed from a friend, and had spilled wine on the seat. They were merely trying to remove the stain before returning the car to their friend. Englund, who had been berated and humiliated by both Leopold and Loeb over the years, would later prove his lack of affection for Leopold by staunchly maintaining that Leopold's own car never left the family garage on the night of the Franks murder, rebuffing Leopold's claim that he and Loeb had been using Leopold's car that night, cruising for girls.

The typewriter on which the boys wrote the ransom note bothered Loeb. Even though it was an item stolen the previous year, he feared its discovery. Leopold drove through Jackson Park slowly while Loeb tore the keys from the typewriter and threw them into a lagoon. He threw the dismantled typewriter into another lagoon. By then it was time to contact Jacob Franks once more. Loeb boarded a train en route to Michigan City. He went to the observa-

tion car and, at the writing desk of this car, left a note addressed to Jacob Franks in the telegram slot of the desk, behind many forms. He wrote on the envelope: "Should anyone else find this note, please leave it alone. The letter is very important." Loeb got off the train at 63rd Street to be met by the waiting Leopold. Apparently, the boys intended to inform Franks that the note was on the train and have the victim's father personally retrieve it. However, Andy Russo, a train worker, rummaged through the forms in the telegram slot looking for a piece of paper to write on and found the letter addressed to Franks. Russo personally delivered the letter to Franks the next morning.

By this time, however, Jacob Franks knew that his little boy was dead. A member of a train crew working alongside the culvert where the body had been hidden spotted the boy's foot sticking from the drainpipe and the corpse was quickly removed and identified by one of the Franks family. The newspapers were given the full story and huge headlines announced the brutal murder. A massive, widely publicized manhunt for the ruthless killers ensued. Scores of suspects were picked up, hustled into police headquarters, and grilled. Leopold and Loeb quickly realized that no ransom would ever be paid and that their perfect crime had serious flaws. Leopold grew silent and morose. He kept to his room, staying out of the limelight. Richard Loeb, however, revelled in the manhunt and played amateur detective. He approached police officials searching through his neighborhood for clues and offered his sleuthing services.

Loeb babbled his crime theories into the ears of detectives and followed them about during their investigations. To one he remarked: "If I were going to pick out a boy to kidnap or murder, that's just the kind of cocky little son-of-a-bitch I would pick." The detective took a long, long look at Richard Loeb and then encouraged him to talk further, inviting the arrogant self-appointed sleuth to accompany officers on their quest for the killer. Such conduct on the part of killers was not uncommon. In this instance, Loeb's voluntary aid to the police was spawned by his desire to present himself as a suspect and *still* outwit them. It was all a game, a challenge to Loeb, who felt himself superior to the "dumb coppers" who bumbled about looking for a killer who was right beneath their noses, secretly jeering at them.

Then the "bumbling" police began to make discoveries that unnerved Loeb. Loeb's stolen typewriter was found in the shallow waters of the Jackson Park lagoon and the keys to it were found in another lagoon. Then the bloody, tape-wrapped chisel was found. The most startling discovery was that of Leopold's glasses. The police traced the horn-rimmed glasses to the manufacturer, Albert Coe and Co. Officials at the firm reported that the glasses were unusual, the frames being specially made for only three people. One pair belonged to a lawyer who had been visiting Europe for some time. The second pair was owned by a woman and she was wearing them when police arrived to interview her. The third pair had been sold to Nathan Leopold, Jr., dear friend of Richard Loeb, the boy who had been dogging the footsteps of investigating detectives, the self-appointed Sherlock Holmes of Chicago.

Richard Crowe, the shrewd, tough state's attorney for Cook County, had Leopold brought into his office for questioning. He showed him the glasses and asked him if they were his. Leopold said no, his were at home. Crowe sent Leopold back home with two detectives but thorough searching of the Leopold home failed to produce the glasses. Then Leopold was told that the glasses had been found near a culvert at 118th Street, and Leopold, thinking fast, told Crowe that he often went to that area for his bird-watching studies. Crowe was hesitant to charge Leopold, initially believing that he was a victim of circumstance. He came from incredible wealth and his social position was lofty. There was no reason Crowe had to believe that Leopold had anything to do with the killing of Bobby Franks. Yet he had Leopold interrogated by two detectives who kept questioning him about his glasses and his whereabouts on the night of the murder.

Leopold first stated that he could not recollect what he was doing on the night of May 21, 1924, but he later said that he and his friend Richard Loeb had been driving around looking for girls and picked up two attractive girls named Edna and Mae. He could not remember their last names. The four of them, Leopold insisted, had gone to a Chinese restaurant on the South Side and had dinner on the murder night. Leopold then said that he and Loeb had been drinking gin out of a flask and that he did not want to talk about his outing with Loeb and the girls because Loeb's father strongly disapproved of drinking and he did not want his friend Loeb to get into trouble.

He said he did not know the murdered boy, but was acquainted with his family. He admitted to reading "everything I could find" about the murder in the local papers. He also said that he had seen photos of the glasses found at the murder site but he never believed them to be his own, which he had lost near the spot some time earlier. Leopold stressed his ability to buy anything he wanted, implying he had no need to kidnap anyone to obtain ransom money. "My father is rich," he said. "Whenever I want money, all I have to do is ask for it. And I earn money myself teaching ornithology."

Crowe realized that, despite Leopold's high social position, he was a primary suspect in the killing of Bobby Franks. He ordered Leopold taken to a comfortable room in the LaSalle Hotel and questioned further. Crowe also

ordered Richard Loeb picked up and taken to another room in the same hotel. He was also to be questioned to see if his statements contradicted Leopold's. They did. Loeb insisted that on the murder night he was at home. He had not gone anywhere with Leopold. He said nothing of the two girls. No one but Crowe and a few high-ranking police officials really believed that either boy was guilty of the Franks murder. Newspaper reporters who knew the boys were allowed to interview them and felt they were innocent, caught in a web of circumstantial evidence.

Both boys remained calm and freely talked to reporters and the police. They were officially under arrest, but they were not formally charged. They were held as "guests" of the city while the lengthy interrogations went on. Their families did nothing to free them, believing that the youths would soon be released and that the questioning was merely a matter of routine. Crowe continued to play the fatherly host to the boys. He even took them to the posh Drake Hotel where they leisurely ate an expensive dinner for which the city paid $102, a lavish sum for those days. For Crowe it was money well spent. One reporter later claimed that he interviewed Leopold who modestly displayed "his superior education." The reporter was so impressed with the calm demeanor of Leopold that he asked a psychiatrist friend to interview Leopold, which he did. The psychiatrist later stated that "this boy certainly had no part in the murder." The psychiatrist later denied having made any such statement.

Leopold made himself look cooperative at every turn. He said to one reporter: "I don't blame the police for holding me. I was at the culvert the Saturday and Sunday before the glasses were found and it is quite possible that I lost my glasses there. I'm sorry this happened only because it will worry my family. But I'll certainly be glad to do what I can to help the police." It was apparent that Leopold was enjoying the limelight shed upon him by the press. He pontificated on art, literature, politics, sports, and especially philosophy, as if giving lectures, pointing out that he favored such writers as Oscar Wilde and Friedrich Nietzsche, but he added: "I won't add Socrates, for I never thought such a lot of him." Loeb adopted the same kind of superior air. For sheer arrogance and bluff, their equal had never been seen.

Their family members believed that the police were merely using the boys to see if they had information that might lead to the identification of the real killer. Nathan Leopold, Sr., said: "While it is a terrible ordeal both to my boy and myself to have him under suspicion our attitude will be one of helping the investigation, rather than retarding it...The suggestion that he had anything to do with this case is too absurd to merit comment." Loeb's father had been ill for several weeks and made no comment from his sick-

Famed criminal lawyer Clarence Darrow, center, flanked by Leopold, left, and Loeb; he realized that his case was hopeless and he sought only to save the youthful killers from the electric chair by pleading his case in a bench trial before Judge John R. Caverly.

Leopold and Loeb while waiting to enter court, 1924.

Leopold, released, 1958.

Left, Leopold and Loeb, laughing at their trial; center, James Day, Loeb's killer in prison; right, Leopold in 1961.

bed but Mrs. Loeb coolly told a reporter: "The affair will so easily straighten itself out."

While the police were politely interrogating the boys, two newspaper reporters, Al Goldstein and Jim Mulroy, of the Chicago *Daily News,* conducted their own dogged investigation, interviewing dozens of persons, chiefly the friends of Leopold and Loeb. One of them, Arnold Maremont, told Goldstein that he was a member of a legal study group to which Leopold belonged. The group met once a week to write "dope sheets" to prepare for examinations. Maremont stated that several of these meetings were held in the library of the Leopold mansion. He recalled that Leopold usually had a large Hammond typewriter which the group used to prepare the "dope sheets." But in one meeting Leopold produced a small portable typewriter that was used to type some "dope sheets."

Maremont had some of these sheets typed on the portable typewriter which Loeb had stolen in 1923. Goldstein and Mulroy took these pages to H.P. Sutton, an expert working for the Royal Typewriter Company. Sutton compared the "dope sheets" and the ransom letter and pronounced that they were one and the same. When confronted with this, Leopold still held onto his nerve, saying that the typewriter belonged to Maurice Shanberg, who had brought the typewriter to the study group. Shanberg denied this allegation angrily and then Leopold, thinking quickly, stated that another student friend, Leon Mandel, owned the typewriter. Mandel was in Europe. Then Leopold said that the typewriter was still somewhere in his house. Another thorough search in the Leopold home failed to unearth the typewriter. Of course, the typewriter was the one found in the Jackson Park lagoon.

More and more evidence mounted against the boys. Sven Englund, the Leopold chauffeur, was brought in for questioning. Englund told Crowe that Leopold, contrary to Leopold's claim, had not used his red Willys-Knight car on the night of the murder. Leopold had insisted that he had been driving this car around that night with Loeb and two girls in it. Crowe turned to one of his aides and exclaimed: "God damn it! I think we got them!" He then ordered Richard Loeb into his office and Loeb was confronted with this new evidence. When he heard that Englund had insisted that he had been working on Leopold's car on the murder night, trying to fix its noisy brakes, and that it never left the garage, Loeb's face went ashen. He slumped in his chair and found it difficult to speak. Finally, he said: "My God! He told you that?" He asked for a cigarette and then let out a brief, low-voiced curse.

Leopold, in another room, was faced with the same evidence given by Englund. He remained passive and silent. "There were no two girls in that car, were there, Nathan?" one of his interrogators said, "Just one little boy, Bobby

Franks. Why don't you come clean and get it off your conscience? Your alibi about driving around with Dickie Loeb and those girls is exposed as a lie by your family chauffeur." Leopold merely smiled, proving his superiority to such police tactics.

Loeb, on the other hand, had lost his composure as the questioning went on into the early morning hours of the day after the boys had been picked up. He trembled and was visibly shaken with each new question that pointed to his guilt. Crowe studied him for some time, realizing that though he was the leader of the pair he was the weaker of the two and his veneer of bravado and haughty airs had evaporated. He showed all the signs of a trapped animal. Crowe then decided to bluff with the more stoic Leopold. At 4 a.m., he walked into the room where Leopold sat calmly puffing on a cigarette and said: "Well, your pal has just confessed, told us the whole story."

A sneer passed Leopold's face: "Do you think I'm stupid. I'm not going to believe that. Anyhow, it's impossible. There's nothing to confess!"

Crowe had all the evidence and more. His men had tracked down the rented car used in the murder and then traced its user to the Morrison Hotel. The car rental agent and employees at the hotel identified a photo shown to them by detectives as that of Morton D. Ballard, the young man who had rented the car and had checked into the hotel. Crowe walked back and forth in front of Leopold, saying nothing. He then stopped and slowly removed his glasses, wiping the lenses meticulously as he stared down at Leopold, who stared back at him.

Crowe then slipped the glasses into the breast pocket of his coat, much in the manner Leopold claimed he had done before losing his glasses at the culvert area. Leopold smiled slightly at the ploy, but his smile faded when Crowe began to talk quietly. Said Crowe: "What about your getting the other automobile at the Rent-A-Car Company because your car was red and too conspicuous? What about the false identity at the Morrison Hotel? What about waiting in hiding on Ingleside Avenue for Johnny Levinson to appear? Your friend says you planned the kidnapping. He says you were the one who killed Bobby Franks." Leopold crushed a cigarette angrily into an ashtray and then nervously lit another. He realized that only Richard Loeb could have provided the information Crowe had related. He had not, but Crowe had pieced this information together from various statements the boys had made to their interrogators.

Leopold began to confess and Crowe had a court stenographer take down his statements. He then marched into the hotel room where Loeb sat and played the same game. Loeb nodded slowly and then he began to confess, detailing the murder of Bobby Franks. The killers' stories matched in every detail except one. Each said that they were driving the car when Bobby Franks was killed and that the other did the actual murder. Most authorities later determined that Loeb was the actual killer. Their conclusion was based upon Loeb's statements; he described in exact detail how *Leopold* killed the Franks child while Leopold could only offer slight information on how many times the boy was stabbed and how the rags had been stuffed down his throat to prevent his crying out. Both were nevertheless charged with murder. When the boys were first brought together after their confessions, Loeb said to Leopold: "We're both in for the same ride, Babe, so we might as well ride together." Leopold turned to a detective and repeated his claim that Loeb was the killer. Loeb, hearing himself denounced by his best friend, sneered and turned to Crowe, saying: "He's only a weakling after all."

The fathers of these merciless killers realized that their sons were headed straight for the electric chair. They also knew one man might save them from that fate, Clarence Darrow, the greatest criminal attorney of the day. Darrow knew immediately that he had no hope of freeing the boys. Their guilt was completely established. They were also so unsavory that he could not make appeals on behalf of their inhuman characters. He took on their defense for only one reason. It offered an opportunity for him to attack the concept of government-sanctioned execution. "While the State is trying Loeb and Leopold, I will try capital punishment," he declared. He wisely chose to abandon a jury trial and plead his clients Guilty before Judge John R. Caverly. Darrow knew Judge Caverly to be fair-minded and exceptionally conscientious and he played to Caverly's sensitivities regarding the taking of human life.

For thirty-three gruelling days, Clarence Darrow put on one of the greatest and most dramatic performances ever seen in a U.S. courtroom. His tireless assault on capital punishment remains a classic argument to this day. He fought with all his strength and intellectual powers. He also exhausted every ounce of his emotion to save two boys he himself had branded as guilty. Darrow's summation was stunning. He ended with: "I am pleading for the future...I am pleading for a time when hatred and cruelty will not control the hearts of men, when we can learn by reason and judgment and understanding and faith that all life is worth living and that mercy is the highest attribute of man...If I can succeed...I have done something for the tens of thousands of other boys, for the countless unfortunates who must tread the same road in blind childhood..."

Judge Caverly was deeply moved by Darrow's appeal. He also stated that Illinois had never executed boys of the age of Leopold and Loeb, and having that precedent, sentenced both youths to life imprisonment for the murder of Bobby Franks and ninety-nine years each on the charge

of kidnapping. Clarence Darrow had achieved the impossible. He had saved the lives of two youths who had, in everyone's mind, been destined for the electric chair.

Darrow's fee was reported to have been $1 million but he had difficulty in obtaining the one and only payment he did receive, $30,000 paid by Nathan Leopold, Sr. Loeb's father reportedly paid not a red cent. Jacob Loeb disowned his son, Richard, after the sentence and died a few months later. When Leopold finally paid Darrow, he handed him his check and then said to Darrow with the same kind of arrogance displayed by his son: "The world is full of eminent lawyers who would have paid a fortune for a chance to distinguish themselves in this case." With that he walked wordlessly from the offices of the man who had saved his son's decidedly worthless life.

Leopold and Loeb were sent to the Northern Illinois Penitentiary at Stateville, outside Joliet. Though Judge Caverly had stated in his deliberation that both boys were to be kept separate for the rest of their lives, this order was immediately ignored once the boys were put behind bars. They were placed in cells separated only by one other cell. The "Fun Killers," as the press had dubbed them, were allowed desks, filing cabinets, and their own private libraries. Their cells, which were on a special wing, were left open at night so they could visit each other.

Leopold and Loeb were separated from the rest of the prisoners and given special meals, often catered from restaurants, in the officers' mess. Both youths were permitted to walk freely outside the prison where Leopold kept a garden. They washed in the officers' shower and they were provided with bootleg liquor and even narcotics for which they were charged $1 a shot. Visitors were allowed to see the boys at all hours and at any time, in total disregard of prison rules. Leopold and Loeb could make phone calls at any time from a phone in the prison storeroom. They had plenty of money to bribe the guards and officials to continue living lives of relative comfort.

Richard Loeb was the worse offender of the two. While Leopold retreated into books and his garden, Loeb sauntered about the prison, selecting any young prisoner he admired and then foisting his homosexual attentions on them while guards ignored his vile sexual assaults. In 1936, Loeb was attracted to a young prisoner, James E. Day. Loeb accosted Day in the library on one occasion and said that he loved him and that Day should "be broad-minded and be nice to me." Day, disgusted at such behavior, pushed Loeb away. But Loeb insisted that Day respond to his affection. Day later stated: "I never had a peaceful day. He was always after me. I became desperate. I had to get him off my back. I was looking for the right day."

The day occurred on Jan. 28, 1936. Day was in the shower alone and Loeb entered, stripping and then trying to assault Day. Loeb brandished a razor and barked at Day: "Do as you're told! Keep your mouth shut and get your clothes off!" Day pretended to go along with the idea but then, when Loeb was off guard, Day kicked him in the groin and the two men struggled for the razor. In the fight Loeb slashed Day several times until Day wrenched the razor away from him and used it to slash Loeb fatally. Loeb staggered naked from the shower, walking down a corridor before falling into the arms of another convict.

Loeb had been slashed fifty-six times. He was rushed to the prison hospital where his mother visited him within hours. Leopold was brought to his bedside and held his hand. Loeb said to his partner in murder: "I think I'm going to make it." He died a few minutes later. When Clarence Darrow was informed of Loeb's passing, he remarked: "He is better off dead. For him death is an easier sentence." Nathan Leopold continued to be the star boarder at the penitentiary until his parole on Mar. 13, 1958. He said at a press conference: "I am a broken old man. I want a chance to find redemption for myself and to help others." To that end he traveled to Puerto Rico where he worked as a laboratory technician in a small church. He later met Tudi Feldman Garcia de Quevedo, a widow who owned a flower shop. The man who planned the "perfect crime" married her in 1961.

Leopold then wrote a book, *Life Plus 99 Years*. At a press conference connected with the book's release, Leopold was asked about the murder of Bobby Franks. He replied: "The crime is definitely still the central part of my consciousness. Very often it occupies the forefront of my attention, and I can think of nothing else. More often, it is not the center of my attention, but it always is present in the background." It was the same kind of mannered, cautious statement that Leopold had made when he was first confronted with his awful guilt by police in 1924. Bobby Franks, three decades after his death, was a *thought* in the mind of Nathan Leopold, where the victim had been an *idea* in Nathan Leopold's mind in 1924. Nothing really had changed. For all the posturing of remorse and rehabilitation, Leopold still observed his crime and his long-dead victim as a distant intellectual entity, not as a flesh-and-blood young boy whose life he and the equally perverted Richard Loeb had snuffed out in the exercise of their "perfect crime." Nathan Leopold, Jr., had gone on to live out a life. Bobby Franks had perished at age fourteen, slaughtered by two beasts who feared only the failure of their own mad schemes.

Levin, Seymour, 1932-   , U.S. Seymour Levin was a serious-minded youth whose interest in chemistry drove him to commit murder. The bespectacled 16-year-old attended the Oak Lane Country Day School in Philadelphia, and his father owned a dry goods store in nearby Toms River, N.J.

Levin met 12-year-old Ellis Simons on a street corner the night of Jan. 8, 1949. He struck up a conversation with the younger boy, and asked him whether he was interested in chemistry. According to Levin, "We walked to my home. I showed him my chemistry set in the bathroom. He said it was a cheap set and I got mad and told him to get out of the house."

Levin told police that Simons threatened him with a knife and there was a brief struggle. Levin reached for a pair of sharp scissors and repeatedly stabbed him until he was dead. "I went out and got a couple of aspirins, I returned and then I saw blood. After I saw the blood I drew a complete blackout," he said.

Investigators later surmised that the assault was sexually motivated. Simons' partially clad body was tied with rope and placed behind the family's garage in the Wynnefield section of Philadelphia. It was discovered the next day. The police arrested Levin on a murder charge after they retrieved the fatal weapon from the bathroom.

On Mar. 17, 1949, Seymour Levin was found Guilty of first-degree murder and sentenced to life imprisonment by Judges James Gay Gordon, Gerald F. Flood, and Eugene Allesandron, who issued a solemn warning against parole officers who might be inclined to free the boy at some future time. After examining Levin, psychiatrists determined that he was psychopathic, but not insane. The original sentence of life in prison was eventually commuted by the governor with the recommendation of the Pennsylvania Board of Prisons. Levin served a minimum sentence of twenty-eight years and five months before receiving his parole from the Pittsburgh Community Service Center on June 10, 1977.

Lewis, Al Junior, prom. 1976-77, U.S. On Nov. 10, 1976, Al Junior Lewis walked into a classroom at Burt Elementary School on Detroit's West Side and shot Bettye McCaster five times in the head in front of twenty-nine first- and second-graders. The 45-year-old school teacher, who had taught at the school less than three weeks, was Lewis' estranged wife. His trial for murder took place in May 1977. Ten students testified at the two-day trial, with three students identifying Lewis as the killer. He was found Guilty of second-degree murder and sentenced on June 27 by Judge Patricia Boyle to life in prison at hard labor. She recommended that Lewis not be paroled.

Lewis, Harry, c.1926-49, Brit. Needing money in the early morning of Dec. 26, 1948, Harry Lewis entered the Marylebone, England, apartment of Harry Saul Michaelson. Lewis searched about and found some loose change and a wallet before the 50-year-old commercial artist awoke and called out. To make a clean escape, Lewis grabbed a metal tubular chair and struck Michaelson over the head twice, then fled and caught a taxi. Michaelson staggered from his apartment and alerted the porter who called an ambulance. At the hospital, a complicated brain operation was performed, after which Michaelson died on Dec. 27.

The bloodstained chair was inspected by fingerprint expert Superintendent Frederick Cherrill of Scotland Yard. Prints from the chair matched those on file for Lewis, who already had a criminal record. On Jan. 19, 1949, Lewis was arrested and charged with murder. He confessed to the burglary that went awry, but protested that he had not meant to kill Michaelson. The one-day trial at the Old Bailey was before Lord Chief Justice Goddard on Mar. 9. Defense counsel for Lewis attempted to prove that it was the operation that killed Michaelson, not the defendant. A surgeon from St. Mary's Hospital, where Michaelson died, claimed that the victim would have died no matter what. This assertion was substantiated by pathologist Dr. Donald Teare. Goddard informed the jury that a verdict of murder, not manslaughter, was to be returned if they found Lewis guilty. The jury found Lewis Guilty, but recommended mercy. Lewis did not receive mercy from the judge or the Home Secretary, and was hanged on Apr. 21, 1949.

Ley, John (AKA: **Thomas John Ley**), 1879-1947, and **Smith, John Lawrence**, prom. 1946, Brit. John Ley's mental instability was evident long before he was arrested in connection with the notorious "Chalk-Pit Murder" of 1946. Ley served as minister of justice in New South Wales, Aus., until his career was ended by a bribery charge and the suspicious deaths of two business associates whose disappearances advanced his interests. Then, in 1929, Ley returned to England and was soon followed by Maggie Brook, a 47-year-old widow with whom he had been having an affair. Although the affair ceased being sexual sometime in the late 1930s, the couple remained close.

Ley, extremely jealous of Brook, accused her on June 12, 1946, of having an affair with her son-in-law, with whom she was staying during her daughter's hospitalization. Brook denied the accusation. Ley contacted Brook's son-in-law, inviting him to tea with Brook at Ley's home in Beaufort Gardens. The son-in-law declined when he learned Brook knew nothing about the invitation. Ley took out his jealousy

on 35-year old John McMain Mudie, a barman who had lodged in the same house as Brook. Ley tried tricking Mudie into revealing his supposed involvement with Brook by sending him checks requiring her countersignature. Mudie, who had moved to a new address and had no idea where Brook was, returned the checks to Ley.

In November 1946, Ley hired chauffeur John William Buckingham, Mrs. Bruce, and carpenter John Lawrence Smith to participate in what he described to them as the kidnapping of a blackmailer. Bruce, for her part in the plot, met Mudie, and posing as a wealthy woman, hired him to tend bar for a party in her home. On Nov. 28, Bruce and Buckingham's son drove Mudie to Ley's home, where Bruce let him in and then drove away. Once Mudie was inside, Buckingham and Smith seized him, threw a blanket over his head, and bound him with a rope. Buckingham was then paid and dismissed by Ley. At this point either Ley or Smith, or both, severely beat Mudie and then strangled him.

Mudie's body was taken to a nearby chalk pit, where Walter Coombs discovered it half-buried two days later. When the body was identified and the police searched Mudie's rooms, they found letters relating to his dealings with Ley. The police soon arrested Ley, Smith, and Buckingham, and charged Ley and Smith with murder. Buckingham, who had gone voluntarily to Scotland Yard two weeks after the discovery of Mudie's body, was not charged.

Ley and Smith stood trial together beginning on Mar. 19, 1947. The trial took place at the Old Bailey before Lord Goddard, chief justice. The prosecutors were Anthony Hawke and Henry Elam. Walter Monckton defended Ley and Derek Curtis Bennett defended Smith. Both men pleaded not guilty and Ley claimed to have never heard of Mudie. Ley and Smith were found Guilty and were sentenced to death. However, on May 5, after a psychiatric examination, Ley was found insane and sent to Broadmoor Criminal Lunatic Asylum. He died there on July 24, 1947, of a meningeal hemorrhage. Smith's sentence was subsequently commuted to life imprisonment.

Liao Chang-Shin, prom. 1945, China. Liao Chang-Shin, an innkeeper in Changshow, a small Yangtze River port, did not think it was strange that, between April and July 1945, so many people disappeared from the small town.

Confronted by police, Liao and his accomplice, Hsui Chang-shan, confessed to robbing and killing seventy-nine people, most of them guests at his inn. The men were given the death penalty after admitting that they had averaged about a murder a day.

Lincoln, Warren, d.1941, U.S. In the early 1900s, Warren Lincoln was a brilliant court attorney and a skilled gardener. His wife's domineering physique and personality overshadowed Lincoln, leaving the meek man with one retreat: his sweet pea garden. Then his brother-in-law Byron came for dinner, made himself at home in the Lincolns' Aurora, Ill., bungalow, and transformed Lincoln's beloved greenhouse into a gym. It was in 1922, when his tyrannical relatives bought themselves extravagant Christmas gifts with money from Lincoln's garden account, that the man cracked.

First, Lincoln typed phony letters from an imaginary lover to his wife, took them to town, and showed them to an understanding bartender. Lincoln counted on the bartender to be outraged and loose-lipped. Soon the whole town heard rumors of Mrs. Lincoln's sordid affair. Lincoln returned home, cried on his gardener's sleeve, and told him he planned to order the couple away. He marched into the house. From outside, the gardener heard screams of accusation and protest. The scene was staged so that the hired man could overhear. No one was surprised when the siblings were gone the next day.

Lincoln went too far when, six weeks later, he staged a fight from which he emerged bloodied and bruised, and which revealed a misplaced business card from Milo Durand, private detective, Chicago. Aurora police chief Frank Michels wanted answers. Lincoln said he wanted to be left alone.

So Michels investigated on his own. First, he tracked down the "love letters" from Mrs. Lincoln's alleged boyfriend, and found Lincoln's recently sold typewriter. A defective "e" on the typewriter was evident on Mrs. Lincoln's purported love notes. Next, Michels went to the Chicago shop that printed the business cards for Lincoln's private detective. Employees there described Lincoln, who ordered the cards supposedly to play a trick on a friend.

When Detective Michels confronted Lincoln with his evidence, the man confessed that the bodies of his wife and brother-in-law were buried in quicklime in his greenhouse. Lincoln mistakenly believed that quicklime would destroy his victims' remains, and that hearsay alone would not convict him. But the detective found two well-preserved heads in the flower boxes, easily identifiable as Byron and Mrs. Lincoln. What Lincoln thought was quicklime was actually slaked lime, which preserves rather than destroys. He was found Guilty of murder and sentenced to life in the Joliet Penitentiary. He died there in 1941.

Lippart, Joseph, prom. 1976, U.S. Joseph Lippart, a truck driver, and his 29-year-old wife Betty Lippart lived in Gaithersburg, Va., next door to the Childress family. At a pool party, Betty became attracted to 17-year-old Kenneth Childress. The two had an affair until Joseph found a love letter to Kenny in Betty's handwriting. Joseph confronted Kenny's parents and threatened to kill him if the affair continued. The Childresses attempted to stop the affair by grounding Kenny and taking away his car, but Kenny skipped school to see Betty.

One morning Joseph woke with stomach pains. He begged Betty to take him to the hospital but she refused and told Joseph she was going next door. Joseph grabbed a double-barreled shotgun from under the bed and fired both barrels into Betty's chest. He then called the police and told them what happened, saying "I'll be sitting in front of my house and I'll surrender peacefully." Lippart was tried in the Montgomery County Circuit Court and found Guilty of second-degree murder. Judge John Mitchell sentenced Lippart to twenty years in prison, but suspended all but eighteen months of the term, making him eligible for parole after only four-and-a-half months in prison.

Little Red, See: **Starkweather, Charles**.

Lock Ah Tam, 1872-1926, Brit. Lock Ah Tam was born in Canton, China, in 1872 and emigrated to England as a sailor in 1895 where he soon established himself as a leader of the Chinese community. His business prospered, and as leader of the Koch Mai Tong, a worldwide Chinese Republican society, he functioned as Sun Yat Sen's ambassador. Lock also represented a Hong Kong-based sailor's union, and established a sailor's club in Liverpool. He married a Welsh woman, Catherine Morgan, with whom he had three children, a son Lock Ling Tam and two daughters, Doris and Cecilia. Lock Ah Tam was known for his generosity and sweet temperament, and the English police often consulted him when there were problems involving the Chinese community.

Lock Ah Tam was playing billiards in his Liverpool club just before the Chinese New Year in 1918 when he was caught in a brawl involving several drunken Russian sailors. One of the sailors struck Lock Ah Tam on the head with a pool cue. He recovered from the injury, but those around him noticed a distinct change in his personality. He became despondent and unpredictable, and was prone to fits of violence, especially after he had been drinking. But Lock Ah Tam insisted that liquor did not affect him because he added salt to his whiskey. His business deteriorated, and after a particularly heavy loss in a shipping venture, he declared bankruptcy in 1924.

On Dec. 1, 1925, Lock Ah Tam hosted a party in honor of the twentieth birthday of his son, who had recently returned from his studies in China. The occasion seemed to bring out the best in Lock Ah Tam. He was loving to

his son and hospitable to his guests. But after the last guests had gone, he went into a rage, viciously berating his wife. When Lock Ling Tam realized the state his father was in, he left the house to get the police. Then, Lock Ah Tam loaded a shotgun and a revolver and, one at a time, shot to death his wife and daughters, 18-year-old Cecilia and 20-year-old Doris. Immediately afterward, Lock Ah Tam called the police and calmly told them what he had done.

Chinese killer Lock Ah Tam.

Lock Ah Tam's trial was held in February 1926 before Justice Mackinnon at the Chester Assizes. His defense attorney, the renowned Sir Edward Marshall Hall, never denied that his client had committed the murders, but insisted that he had done so while in a state of 'unconscious automatism' brought on by a fit of epilepsy. Hall said to the jury, "I do not suppose that if you were to search the tragedies of the Greek poets you would find anything more poignant than this tragedy....Some minute happening in the brain caused a change for which none of us can account. It turned a man—a mild, loveable, peaceable man—into a raving madman." Lock Ah Tam's hapless plea of insanity was found to be inconceivable by the fact that he called police moments after the murders and confessed in a totally rational manner. The jury took only twelve minutes to find Lock Ah Tam Guilty of murder. He was sentenced to death and he was hanged.

Loeb, Richard A., See: **Leopold, Nathan F., Jr.**

Lonelyhearts Killers, See: **Beck, Martha Julie.**

Lonergan, Wayne, 1918-   , U.S. Born in Toronto, Ontario, in 1918, Wayne Lonergan was incorrigible as a

child, spending time in and out of juvenile reformatories. He arrived in New York City in 1939, and worked as a bus driver at the World's Fair.

One night, as he lounged about the lobby of a hotel in Gramercy Park, Lonergan met William Burton, a member of the elite sophisticates known as the "International Set," who had inherited a fortune from his father, a German brewer. Burton and his teenage daughter, Patricia, had fled Europe to escape the impending war. They were living a life of ease in the sumptuous Ritz Towers when Lonergan entered the picture. Burton took a special interest in the handsome young Canadian, and set him up in his own apartment and provided him a generous expense account. There were rumors that Burton and Lonergan were engaged in a homosexual relationship.

Patricia fell hopelessly in love with Lonergan. In October 1940, William Burton died, and Lonergan, rather than return to the work-a-day world, decided to pursue Patricia. Mrs. Lucille Burton, Patricia's mother, who had stayed in France until December 1940, tried to keep Patricia away from Lonergan. But on July 30, 1941, Patricia eloped with Lonergan.

With her income of $25,000, Patricia supported the whims of her bisexual husband, who enjoyed their swanky apartment on 51st Street. When a son was born to the couple in April 1942, Patricia's desire to stay home and care for the child put a damper on Lonergan's extravagant lifestyle. A year later, the couple separated and Lonergan joined the Royal Canadian Air Force, but often visited Patricia and his son in New York.

On the night of Oct. 24, 1943, Elizabeth Black, the Lonergans' nursemaid, and Peter Elser, an old friend of Patricia's, concerned that Patricia had not come out of her room all day, broke into her room and found her naked body sprawled on the bed. She had been bludgeoned and strangled to death. Dr. Milton Helpern, deputy medical examiner, concluded that Patricia had been struck repeatedly with an onyx-inlaid brass candlestick, then choked. The night before, Patricia had gone out with a man named Mario Gabelline, but neither Gabelline nor Captain Elser emerged as prime suspects.

Wayne Lonergan was notified in Toronto of Patricia's death. He agreed to return to New York for questioning. He was the investigators' prime suspect, but it would have been difficult to extradite him without hard evidence. Back in New York, Lonergan's interrogation lasted eighty-four hours, after which he finally broke down and confessed to the murder.

As a New York psychiatrist explained at the trial, Lonergan was a psychopathic personality. The prosecution pointed out that Patricia had cut him out of her will after deciding to divorce him. The arraignment in February 1944 resulted in a mistrial. On Apr. 17, 1944, he was convicted of second-degree murder. Wayne Lonergan was sentenced to thirty years in prison, of which he served all but nine years before being paroled on Dec. 2, 1965, and subsequently deported to Canada.

Longhi, Luigi, 1954- , Den. "I never intended to kill her," claimed Luigi Longhi, the shampoo-and-strangle murderer from Padborg. "But suddenly she went limp and I realized she was dead." Longhi, a 29-year-old unemployed truck driver, was arrested for the strangulation murder of a German hitchhiker. Doctors who examined him determined he had never engaged in sexual intercourse with a woman and possessed a sexual obsession about shampooing women's hair. He claimed that more than a dozen women in the Padborg area allowed him to wash their hair. At the age of ten, Longhi frequently stole shampoo bottles and wigs. As he grew older, he persuaded and forced women to submit to his hair washing—though he never criminally assaulted his victims.

On May 30, 1981, Longhi picked up a German hitchhiker, Heike Freiheit, at the Danish-German border. He talked her into allowing him to shampoo her hair and they went to his apartment. After the first shampoo, they both fell asleep. When he woke, he felt the urge to shampoo her hair again. Longhi bound and gagged Freiheit so she could not resist him and proceeded to shampoo her hair. When he ran out of shampoo, he began using cottage cheese, honey, and salad dressing. He then ripped her clothes off "because I wanted to see how she looked naked." When Freiheit attempted to summon help by drumming the floor with her feet, he placed a noose around her neck and tightened it. She died of asphyxiation. Unsure of what to do, Longhi stuffed the body behind a wall in his apartment and threw some lime on it. Much later, while insulating the roof, a workman found the body and notified police. Longhi was arrested and charged with murder. At his trial he pleaded not guilty, but was sentenced on Mar. 11, 1983, to psychiatric confinement for an indefinite length of time.

Los Angeles Slasher, See: Greenwood, Vaughn Orrin.

Lowenstein, Allard, See: Sweeney, Denis.

Loy Yeung (Leung Hing), b.1896, U.S. Wong Gee, a prosperous Chinese rancher, lived six miles northwest of Fairfield, Calif., a small town between San Francisco and Sacramento. Hundreds of Chinese immigrants with little understanding of U.S. customs lived and worked on Wong's Bryan ranch. One of them, Loy Yeung, was a professional tong man believed to have been hired by Chinese gangs to kill Wong Gee.

The 32-year-old Loy lived in a squalid shack near Suisun Creek. He did odd jobs for the wealthy rancher, whose family lived more than a mile away from the decrepit Chinatown enclave. Loy Yeung used opium and was deeply resentful of Wong Gee and his children. In June 1928, he attacked Nellie Wong, the rancher's 16-year-old daughter. When the father learned of this, he discharged Loy Yeung, warning him never to show his face near the camp again.

Loy stayed away until Aug. 22, when he returned to Fairfield armed with a rifle, a hatchet, and a club. He ran through the complex assaulting and maiming other Chinese. He then visited the home of Wong Gee, where he killed the rancher's wife and three of his children, leaving Nellie near death. Two other daughters escaped the murderer by crouching inside a second floor closet.

After Loy left the house, he set out for the camp in search of Wong Gee. Along the way he killed two more Chinese who were working in an orchard. By this time the camp was in an uproar. Loy found Wong Gee in the main building of the colony. He chased him into the basement and shot him. By the time he was finished, Loy Yeung had killed ten people. He escaped in a car and avoided police barricades blocking the main roads to Sacramento.

After an all-night search by sheriff's deputies, Loy Yeung was captured the next morning in the loft of a chicken house in Grass Valley. Sheriff Jack Thornton found the suspect asleep. When asked the reason for his rampage, Loy shrugged his shoulders and said that his enemies were trying to poison him. Authorities suspected that his drug dependency or his connections to the Tong gangs of San Francisco led to the slaughter.

Lucas, Arthur, prom. 1961, Can. Police found Therland Crater shot to death in the front hall of a duplex on Kendall Avenue in Toronto on Nov. 17, 1961. Carolyn Ann Newman was lying dead, slashed in the throat, on a bed upstairs with a ring beside her. Two Detroit women who were brought to the Toronto police station under suspicion of prostitution identified the ring as belonging to Arthur Lucas, who was arrested in Detroit the day after the murders. The murder weapon—a revolver—was found lying on the Burlington Skyway bridge and was linked to Lucas via serial numbers and a description of the firearm. Lucas was convicted of the murders, and hanged in December 1962.

Lucas, Henry Lee, 1937-   , and **Toole, Ottis Elwood**, 1947-   , U.S. The child of Virginia prostitute Viola Lucas—a double amputee—Henry Lee Lucas never knew his father and was often forced to remain in the same room while his mother entertained her clients. By his early twenties, Lucas and his mother had moved to Michigan, where he met a 16-year-old girl he intended to marry. Viola Lucas, however, upon meeting the girl, so ridiculed her that Lucas stabbed his mother to death that night while she slept. For her murder, he began his first life sentence in 1960 in a Michigan prison.

Freed by the parole board in 1975, Lucas pleaded with officials not to release him. He knew he was going to kill again, and before leaving the city he did just that, beginning

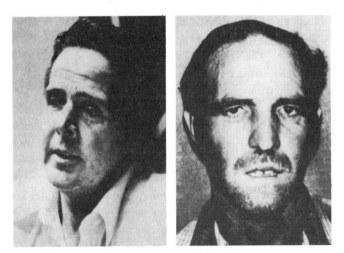

Mass killers Henry Lee Lucas and Ottis Toole.

a spree that would leave 300 people dead in seven years, a claim by the killer thought to be wildly exaggerated by police. Traveling west from Michigan, Lucas dumped his victims on secluded prairies, in deserts, and in mountain canyons. He later claimed to have strangled, stabbed, shot, bludgeoned, and suffocated them. When he had time, he dismembered his victims alive or filleted them in a style of torture first used by Native Americans.

While dining at a Florida soup kitchen, Lucas met Ottis Toole, a serial killer with a proclivity for homosexual slaughter and pyromania. Although both schemed to murder the other, they instead teamed up, realizing what they could accomplish together. Lucas and Toole soon became lovers and traveled cross-country, practicing their brand of ritualistic abduction and torture. Preying indiscriminately on both men and women, they blazed a trail

of terror across seventeen states.

The couple eventually enlisted the help of Toole's nephew and abducted his 9-year-old niece, Freida "Becky" Powell. The foursome traveled around the country for several months as a family and Lucas made Becky his common-law wife, although he vowed not to have sexual intercourse with the girl until she turned fifteen. Eventually the family broke up. Lucas and Becky continued their nomadic life while Toole and his nephew remained in Florida, where Toole would soon abduct from a shopping mall and kill 6-year-old Adam Walsh. Years later, Walsh was the subject of the made-for-television movie *Adam*.

Lucas and Becky settled in Stoneburg, Texas, where they lived with Pentecostal preacher Stanley Shane. Shane's next-door neighbor, 80-year-old Katherine Rich, would be Lucas' next victim, but afterward he thought better of further activities in so small a town. Instead he devoted more time to Becky. After having intercourse with her for the first time, Lucas stabbed her in the chest and didn't realize he had killed her until he found bloodstains on his shirt. Returning to the field where her body lay, he began talking to the corpse. That is where police found him on June 11, 1983, taking him into custody on an illegal weapons charge.

In the Montague County Jail, Lucas confessed to the murder of Rich and began reciting the long list of crimes he had committed since his release from prison in 1975. In return for a seventy-five-year sentence, he pleaded guilty to the murder of Rich. By the time he appeared in court for murdering Becky he had confessed to twelve other homicides. Found Guilty once again, Lucas continued his confessions, implicating Toole, who was currently serving a twenty-year sentence in Florida's Raiford penitentiary for arson.

"I started when I was fourteen," Lucas said of his first murder, the strangulation death of a woman who refused to have sex with him. During the next year he directed officers to more than 200 murder sites in thirty states. By 1984, he had confessed to 360 deaths. It is believed that Lucas himself was not responsible for more than a dozen or so murders. He attributed his ability to recount the deaths with such accuracy to God, who he had said recently appeared in his prison cell on a beam of sunlight.

By June 1984, Lucas had been convicted of five murders and sentenced to death for the slaying of a female hitch-hiker near San Angelo, Texas. Twenty-one murder charges were pending in Arkansas, Louisiana, New Mexico, Texas, and Washington, and an additional 113 slayings nationwide had been laid at his doorstep. Today, Lucas awaits execution on Death Row in Texas.

Ludke, Bruno, 1909-44, Ger. German mass-murderer Bruno Ludke had slipped through the hands of the Nazi police more than once. In fact, several innocent men had been executed for murders that he committed. When the truth was discovered, Ludke was quietly done away with and his file became "classified."

Born in 1909, Ludke was a murderer by the time he was eighteen. He confessed to strangling and knifing eighty-five women to death between 1928 and 1943, and then having sex with the corpses. The police had apprehended Ludke once before and, on orders from SS Chief Heinrich Himmler, he had been sterilized. Undeterred, Ludke kept killing until he was finally caught, on Jan. 29, 1943, having sex with the body of his latest victim in a wood outside Berlin. When brought before the magistrate by Kriminal Kommissar Franz, Ludke recounted a long list of past murders, but pointed out that, under Paragraph 51 of the Nazi criminal code, mental defectives could not be indicted for murder. The Nazis faced a political embarrassment and a legal dilemma. But they found a solution. Bruno Ludke was remanded to the custody of Viennese doctors, to be used as the subject of laboratory experiments. He died from a fatal injection on Apr. 8, 1944.

Luetgert, Adolph Louis, 1848-1911, U.S. The infamous sausage vat murder of 1897 disgusted the residents of Chicago's North Side for many years. For a time those who lived near the Luetgert factory at Hermitage and Diversey refused to eat its sausage, believing that it might contain bone fragments of its owner's deceased wife.

Adolph Louis Luetgert immigrated to the U.S. in the early 1870s. He was a powerfully built German who tried his hand at farming, then tanned animal hides for a living, before settling in Chicago to become a sausage maker. He was a thrifty, hard working entrepreneur whose business prospered in the North Side German neighborhood known as Lakeview. Luetgert's first wife died, leaving behind one child. In the 1880s he married his second wife Louisa Bicknese of Kankakee, Ill., who was unable to satisfy his seemingly insatiable sexual tastes. Luetgert had a variety of lovers during his marriage, including his wife's maid Mary Simering, a long-time mistress named Mrs. Christine Feldt, and a barkeeper, Mrs. Agathia Tosch, whose establishment was located near the sausage factory.

Whatever fascination this hulking, middle aged businessman held for these women can only be surmised. It is doubtful that any of them ever dreamed of the day they might become the third Mrs. Luetgert, for the sausage maker was on his way to bankruptcy by 1897. Though unable to meet his supplier's costs, Luetgert convinced his business partner William Charles to expand their operation, because someday Luetgert believed that he would become America's reigning sausage king. Before that could happen though, he had to reconcile his domestic relations, Louisa was about at the end of her rope with her husband's endless tomcatting. During one angry confrontation, Luetgert grabbed her throat and nearly choked her to death. At the last minute, fearing that the neighbors were watching, he let her go. But more heated quarrels and angry denunciations were to come.

Murderer Adolph Luetgert.

Luetgert's plot to murder his wife unfolded on Mar. 11, 1897, when he purchased 325 pounds of potash and fifty pounds of arsenic from the wholesale drug firm of Lor Owen & Company. On Apr. 24 Luetgert ordered an employee, Frank Odorowsky, to take a barrel of potash from the shipping room to the factory basement. "This is strong stuff, this potash," he warned Odorowsky. "Be careful not to burn yourself." Odorowsky ground up the potash into small pieces, then he and Luetgert placed it in the vat and turned up the steam until it boiled over. A week later Luetgert sent his night watchman, Frank Bialk, to a drugstore to purchase a bottle of celery compound. When he returned, Bialk found Luetgert standing near the door leading to the main factory. The door had been barricaded. Luetgert sent Bialk back to his post without further explanation. Later that evening he again sent the watchman on an errand, this time to purchase a bottle of Hunyadi water, while he tested the steam valves under the middle vat.

Nothing unusual happened until late that night, when a woman named Emma Schiemicke would later recall seeing Luetgert leading his wife by the arm down the alley in back of the factory. He would remain there until two the next morning grinding his wife into tiny pieces.

When Bialk came in the next day, he asked "Should I go out under the vat?"

"Bank the fires at fifty pounds of steam pressure," Luetgert replied.

Bialk did so, but he was puzzled by the sticky, unpleasant, glue-like substance that covered the floor. Bending down for a closer look, he could not help but notice what appeared to be bone flakes. It did not occur to him that it might be something other than animal offal, and he went on with his work.

Odorowsky was another who noticed the slime, bringing it to Luetgert's attention. "Don't say a word Frank, don't say anything about it and I'll see that you have a good job as long as you live," Luetgert told him.

The waste material was scraped off the floor and flushed down the sewer. Larger chunks were placed in a barrel and dumped by some railroad tracks. Next day, Louisa's brother Diedrich Bicknese came to Chicago for a visit, but the maid told him that Louisa never returned home for dinner the night before. When Bicknese asked Luetgert about this, he simply said that she had left on the first and not returned home yet.

"Why didn't you go to the police?" Bicknese demanded.

"I don't want a scandal," Luetgert replied. "I paid five dollars to two detectives to find her."

Bicknese went to Kankakee to look for his sister but found no trace of her. Returning to Chicago in a state of near panic, he contacted Captain Herman Schluetter of the Chicago Police Department.

Schluetter, one of the sharpest criminal investigators in the history of the department, called Luetgert in for questioning. "You made a vigorous appeal to me to find a lost dog for you not long ago," he said. "Why did you not report the absence of your wife?"

Luetgert replied that he believed she would come back soon, but in the interest of avoiding a scandal he was keeping matters quiet. Schluetter let him go, but ordered his men to drag the river. When nothing turned up the captain visited the factory on May 7 to question Bialk and Odorowsky. They sparked his interest with a description of the greasy slime and the running water leading into the middle vat. He returned on the fifteenth to conduct a thorough examination of the basement, where he made a shocking and gruesome discovery. The middle vat was half-filled with a brown liquid. Using a gunny sack as a filter, the detectives trapped all the solid matter. They found several pieces of bone, and a wedding band bearing the initials "L.L." established that Louisa was not off visiting her relatives in Kankakee. Luetgert maintained that the bones were those of an animal, which were very common in his line of work, but under analysis the bone matter was found to be human.

At Luetgert's subsequent trial, the prosecution was quick to point out that Luetgert had spent a considerable amount of money to purchase potash—what possible use could he have for this material, if he was making soap as he had earlier claimed? The most damning evidence against him came from the various women who had been lovers. Agatha Tosch recalled that on the day of Louisa's disappearance Luetgert was drinking beer in her saloon, proclaiming "I am as innocent as the southern skies!" between sips of beer. Luetgert's secret love letters to his favorite girlfriend, Christine Feldt, were read aloud in the courtroom. She said that Adolph had entrusted her with $4,000 for "safe-keeping" shortly before Louisa disappeared.

Luetgert was found Guilty and sentenced to life largely on circumstantial evidence. He went to prison steadfastly protesting his innocence. He swore that Louisa would return someday to prove that the courts and the police were wrong, but she never did, and he died in the Joliet State Penitentiary in 1911.

Lukens, Albert B., 1883-1956, U.S. In 1940, Albert Lukens was hired as a janitor at the North Hill Methodist Church in Akron, Ohio. Church officials forgave his criminal past, which included an indictment for first-degree murder in the 1899 slaying of Mrs. Julia Stiegler of Cincinnati, and gave the quiet, gray-haired man a chance.

Ruth Zwicker, a 24-year-old substitute music teacher in the Akron public school system, would occasionally stop by the church on weekends to practice the piano. Lukens sometimes watched her playing while he cleaned the third floor. He never said much to her until Apr. 12, 1941, when he cautiously walked over to the piano and asked her for a kiss. "I thought for a moment that she was going to kiss me but the next thing I knew she gave me a slap, which I probably deserved," Lukens later said, not knowing exactly what possessed him to make such a request. Ruth Zwicker stepped back from the piano and, according to Lukens, came at him in a rage. He grabbed her wrist, and in the ensuing struggle she fell backwards, hitting her head on the piano.

Albert Lukens panicked. His wife was on her way upstairs and Ruth Zwicker was unconscious. Lukens ran into the hall to prevent his wife from entering the piano room. He returned to the room about fifteen minutes later to find that Ruth still had not moved. Lukens shook her violently. "Snap out of it!" he pleaded, but there was no response. He decided to conceal the crime. Lukens' friends in Akron knew nothing about the thirteen years he spent in the Ohio Reformatory for killing Julia Stiegler.

"I was satisfied in my own mind that she was dead when I carried her down the stairs to the boiler room," Lukens later explained. He placed the corpse in the coal bin, where it remained till the next morning, Easter Sunday. When Ruth did not return home that night, Arthur Zwicker, her father, searched the sixty-two room church building. Lukens led him through the rooms calmly.

The next day Albert Lukens put the corpse into the blast furnace. He got the idea from a magazine article about cremation. Church employees noticed that the furnace was kept going for four days, despite warm, pleasant weather. It seemed strange at the time but nothing was said. For the next week, as the janitor went about his work, teams of Boy Scouts searched the land near the Cuyahoga River. Detectives I.J. Davis and Harry Kimerer focused on the church.

On Apr. 18, the police went back to the boiler room. This time they found charred remains in the ash box of the furnace. Dr. William Sassaman of the Hamann Museum of Human Anatomy and Comparative Anthropology at Western Reserve University Medical School identified 234 bone fragments taken from the ash box as human. Dental porcelain and jewelry were also found.

Lukens confessed to the crime, but insisted Ruth's death was accidental, and that all he wanted from her was a kiss. Indicted for first-degree murder, Albert Lukens pleaded not guilty before a packed courtroom on Apr. 22. Jury selection for what was then described as the "most shocking crime in the history of Summit County" began on Sept. 4 in the Common Pleas Court after the defendant's request for a change of venue was denied. The trial started the next day in the courtroom of Judge Walter B. Wanamaker.

Defense attorneys charged that Lukens was kicked and choked by two detectives during his interrogation. Their claims of police brutality were corroborated by witnesses who noticed bruises on Lukens following his interview with the police. The state maintained that the injuries were self-inflicted with a blunt object, possibly a shoe.

The jury of nine men and three women deliberated Lukens' fate for nearly thirty hours. On Sept. 18, 1941, they returned a verdict of Guilty with a recommendation for mercy. Judge Wanamaker spared Lukens the electric chair, but sentenced him to life in prison at the Ohio Penitentiary. The verdict was a dreadful surprise to Lukens, who expected to be acquitted. For Arthur Zwicker, the decision was equally disappointing. "I think he should be sentenced to the chair," he said.

Lukens' appeal for a new trial was denied. He was taken to prison on Sept. 22, where he remained until his death on July 27, 1956.

Lusk, Grace, b.1878, U.S. There was a venomous streak in Grace Lusk that her married lover, David Roberts, failed to detect when he began his affair with her in the spring of 1917. To Dr. Roberts of Waukesha, Wis., Grace Lusk was just one of his many casual lovers. "I did not deceive her or lead her on," he sobbed. "Other women have thought they cared for me, but I was married and they knew their liking for me would come to nothing permanent. So the affairs usually faded away."

This time, though, the philandering physician got more than he bargained for. One day Mrs. Roberts confronted

Lusk. She told her about an earlier affair that had ended disastrously for the mistress. "I suppose you know about the girl who died in an attic room after an operation, after she had been too interested in my husband?" Mrs. Roberts said. Grace Lusk allowed Mrs. Roberts to have her say, but when she became too personal, Lusk pulled out a .25-caliber handgun and fired two shots into Roberts' chest. Lusk then turned the gun on herself, but managed to inflict only a superficial wound.

Grace Lusk was found Guilty of second-degree murder on May 29, 1918. The insanity defense failed her, and she was sentenced on June 19 to life at the Waupun Penitentiary. As she was led screaming from the courtroom, she tried to attack Prosecutor D.S. Tullar, screaming, "You lied! You lied my life and my love away!" In jail, she reaffirmed her love for Dr. Roberts, and prayed to God to send him back to her. In 1923, the governor of Wisconsin pardoned Lusk.

Lyles, Anjette Donovan, 1917- , U.S. Housewife, mother, and restaurant proprietor Anjette Lyles of Macon, Ga., experimented with black magic. In the spring of 1958, her bizarre hobby implicated her in murder when her young daughter Marcia became ill. Lyles' two previous husbands and one mother-in-law had died under mysterious circumstances. The police were alerted to the possibility that Lyles was a poisoner by an anonymous letter from the Lyles' family cook, Carrie Jackson.

It was too late to save Marcia's life. Arsenic was found in her body and in the exhumed bodies of the two husbands. Lyles suggested that Marcia had ingested the poison while playing doctor and nurse. At the trial, prosecutors maintained she committed the murders for the insurance money. She was found Guilty and sentenced to death but state psychiatrists determined that she was insane. Anjette Lyles was committed to the State Hospital in Milledgeville, Ga.

Poisoner Anjette Lyles with daughters Marcia, whom she murdered, and Carla.

Lyons, Lewis W., 1849-1905, U.S. In 1895, Lewis W.

Lyons was jobless and his wife had left him when he was arrested for stealing a diamond stickpin from Dan S. Carroll. After a week in the New Orleans jail, Lyons was released on $500 bail. Two weeks later when the case came to trial, the plaintiff admitted that Lyons had had nothing to do with the disappearance of the pin and Lyons was discharged. Angered, he then decided to sue Carroll and the two detectives who arrested him, and hired U.S. District Attorney J. Ward Gurley to represent him.

They lost the case as well as a subsequent appeal. Lyons became increasingly incensed at the injustice he perceived had been done to him and developed a persecution complex which now focused on Gurley. In 1901, he sent a second to Gurley's office to challenge him to a duel. Although Gurley apparently considered the request, he later refused it as unreasonable, given Lyons' reason for asking and the fact that duels were seldom fought anymore. Lyons wrote numerous letters to Gurley and confronted him in person on at least one occasion. His resentment and anger grew rather than dissipated over the next few years. On July 20, 1903, he arrived at Gurley's office with a pistol and a quantity of cyanide in his pockets.

After patiently waiting his turn, Lyons went into Gurley's office. Nothing out of the ordinary was heard from the office until Lyons shouted out and fired three shots. He then rushed into an adjoining office where he shot himself in the head. Gurley died immediately but Lyons survived. The trial began in New Orleans on Nov. 11, 1903, and after eight days Lyons was found Guilty of murder. He appealed for a new trial and was retried on Feb. 6, 1904. Again found Guilty, he was hanged at Parish Prison on Mar. 24, 1905.

M

MacArthur, Malcolm, 1947- , Ire. The brutal and unprovoked murder of a nurse by the heir to a wealthy Irish family's fortune caused a crisis in the Irish government in 1982.

In July 1982, Malcolm MacArthur, a University of California graduate in the fine arts and the son of a prominent County Neath family, had run low on funds, having spent about £80,000 in inherited money. He returned to Dublin from a vacation in Tenerife, the Grand Canaries, and decided to become a robber. Seeking to steal a getaway car, the 36-year-old MacArthur walked through Phoenix Park and saw Bridie Gargan, a 25-year-old nurse, sunning herself beside her Renault. Using a fake hand gun, he forced her into the car and when she screamed smashed her over the head with a hammer. Frightening away a gardener from the nearby American ambassador's home, MacArthur drove away with the unconscious Gargan in the car. An ambulance driver mistook the assailant for a doctor with a patient when he saw a hospital sticker on Gargan's car, and sounded his siren to help MacArthur through the traffic to St. James Hospital. MacArthur turned off at an exit and abandoned the car, leaving Gargan inside. The nurse died within four days.

MacArthur had been a house guest at that time of Attorney General Patrick Connolly, and was arrested in Connolly's apartment. Connolly, saying later he was unaware of the murder charges against MacArthur, went ahead with a vacation to the U.S. Quickly recalled by Prime Minister Charles Haughey, who sent a private jet to fly him back, Connolly immediately offered to resign, an offer that was accepted. Haughey's Fianna Fail party, already on shaky ground before the incident, shortly afterward was defeated in a general election. MacArthur pleaded guilty in a Dublin Central Criminal Court and was sentenced to penal servitude for life by Justice McMahon on Jan. 12, 1983. Additional charges of illegal possession of a shotgun and the murder of a farmer were dropped.

McClary, David, 1964- , U.S. An imprisoned drug king reputedly ordered the murder of a police officer because he was angry about his conviction on gun possession charges. The killing led to more drug crackdowns and Tactical Narcotics Teams were created in New York City to put pressure on drug dealers.

Rookie police officer, 22-year-old Edward Byrne, was guarding the house of a drug witness in South Jamaica on the morning of Feb. 26, 1988, when he was shot in the head five times at close range. In a Queens courtroom, prosecutors charged that the killing of Byrne was directed by drug kingpin Howard "Pappy" Mason, who had been convicted on a gun charge and apparently ordered the murder as revenge for his own conviction. He denied any involvement in the slaying.

Convicted on murder and weapons charges instead were Scott Cobb, twenty-five, Todd Scott, twenty, Philip Copeland, twenty-three, and David McClary, twenty-three, with McClary named as the triggerman. All four received the maximum sentence, twenty-five years to life, with a recommendation against parole by New York State Supreme Court justice Thomas A. Demakos. More than one hundred policemen stood in the courtroom, cheering the decision.

McCollum, Ruby, 1915- , U.S. In 1952, Ruby McCollum, thirty-seven, wife of a wealthy black gambler in Live Oak, Fla., shocked the residents of Suwannee County by shooting Dr. Clifford LeRoy Adams, Jr., a prominent local politician. McCollum said at her trial that she had "more than a doctor-patient relationship" with Adams, who was white. In fact, he had fathered one of her children and she was pregnant with another when she killed him. The jury found her Guilty and sentenced her to death.

On appeal, the Florida Supreme Court ruled that Ruby McCollum should be retried. However, Frank Cannon, a white lawyer from the vicinity, knowing that the result would be the same, got her death sentence changed to commitment to a mental asylum, and the second trial was never held. McCollum was later released in the custody of her daughter. The political aspects of the case were exposed in a controversial book by William Bradford Huie, called *Ruby McCollum: Woman in the Suwannee Jail.* Huie was charged with contempt of court for claiming that the judge himself, Circuit Judge Hal W. Adams (not related to Dr. Adams), was a gambler and racially biased. Huie was fined $750.

McCoy, Kid, See: **Selby, Norman.**

McCoy, Russell, 1935- , U.S. On Feb. 9, 1957, Russell McCoy, a 22-year-old factory worker in Zanesville, Ohio, feuded with his half-sister and brother-in-law, Louise and Lloyd See. He shot them to death, doused their bodies and the interior of their house with gasoline, and set everything ablaze. McCoy left the scene and drove to the factory where he worked. There, he approached co-worker Harry Dale Bundy, thirty-nine, and asked him for a loan. McCoy also told Bundy he had murdered the Sees.

Bundy assumed that McCoy had been drinking and was not telling the truth. When he told the younger man to go back home, McCoy pulled a gun on him, warning him not to tell the police of the murders. However, when Bundy saw the story of the Sees' murder in the afternoon newspaper, he called police and repeated the conversation he had had with McCoy that morning. While police issued a warrant for his arrest, McCoy travelled to Columbus where he robbed three stores at gunpoint, boasting to his victims that he had already killed four people and would not hesitate to kill more.

Eight days after the murder, McCoy returned to Zanesville and went to the Bundy residence. After being turned away, McCoy disappeared for two days until local police apprehended him. McCoy freely confessed to the murders of the Sees and to the armed robberies in Columbus. He also confessed to the Uniontown murders of Reynoldo Amodio, a store owner, and Paul Cain, a store clerk. McCoy claimed Bundy had participated in the murders.

Despite Bundy's protests that he had not been involved in the murders—that he had, in fact, been in a tavern in Canton when they were being committed—he was arrested and charged. When Bundy was brought to trial in June 1957, McCoy appeared as the chief witness for the prosecution. In his testimony, McCoy included details about the crime that implicated Bundy. He claimed that Bundy had shot Amodio three times and that the robbery had been Mrs. Bundy's idea—a way of getting money for Christmas presents for their children. The prosecution further enhanced their case by producing a 14-year-old girl who testified that she had seen Bundy in the store just before the robbery and had picked him out of a police line-up before she ever saw a picture of him in a newspaper.

Despite the fact that witnesses in Canton supported Bundy's alibi and a newspaper reporter testified that the 14-year-old witness had told him she had seen Bundy's newspaper photo before identifying him in the police line-up, Bundy was convicted and sentenced to die in the electric chair. After the conviction, a woman who had been in the store prior to the murder came forward and testified that only McCoy had been there. Other witnesses came forward to discredit the testimony of the 14-year-old girl. Despite these new developments, Bundy's motion for a new trial was denied and his execution was set for Nov. 8, 1957. In the meantime, Norma Brajnovic, the owner of a liquor store in Amarillo where McCoy had fled after the Sees murders, saw Bundy's story in a true crime magazine. She recalled a conversation with McCoy in which he told her that he had already killed four people and was going to kill another one,

adding that he was going to have the law commit this murder for him. The comment had seemed cryptic to Brajnovic until she saw the article and recognized McCoy's photo. She immediately contacted the Ohio authorities. Bundy was granted a stay of execution, and after a hearing, his conviction was set aside. At a new trial on June 18, 1958, Bundy was acquitted.

McCracken, Henry, prom. 1954, U.S. A convicted criminal on Death Row in San Quentin prison sat through so many stays of execution, spending extensive time in the death cell, that he eventually lost his mind. An independent panel of psychiatrists examined Henry McCracken and declared him legally insane and thus ineligible to be executed. Prison authorities, informed of this, ordered special electro-shock therapy treatments for McCracken who was then, apparently, jarred back into sanity. When declared legally sane he was rushed to his execution in the gas chamber.

McCue, J. Samuel, d.1905, U.S. In early Autumn 1904, J. Samuel McCue stumbled, bleeding, down the stairs of his Charlottesville, Ky., mansion, hysterical and calling for help. Officer Daniel C. Grady entered the house to find the body of Fannie McCue, the wealthy man's wife, lying in a tub of scalding water. She had been brutally beaten with a heavy object and shot through the breast. The widower explained how an intruder had entered the master bedroom, fired his gun into Mrs. McCue, then turned on him. Struggling with the assailant, McCue had been knocked unconscious and staggered out for help.

With no clues at all to explain the intruder, detectives were called from neighboring areas, including two private detectives who were brothers, Albert Baldwin and W.G. Baldwin, from their agency in Bluefield, W. Va. Asking a number of odd, apparently irrelevant questions, the Baldwins investigated the McCue residence. The City Council posted notice of a $2,000 reward to find the murderer, with Sam McCue adding another $1,000. The day after the funeral, the Baldwins accused McCue of murdering his wife, citing evidence that included a bloodstained baseball bat found in the bedroom, a shirt stained with blood only at the waist (when he had been apparently attacked around the head) and the smashed window through which McCue claimed the intruder had escaped, which was covered with a square foot of cobwebs and sported an undisturbed pot of ferns. The head wounds which McCue claimed had knocked him unconscious were mere scratches. At a forty-day trial which began on Sept. 2, 1904, McCue was found Guilty of first-degree murder and sentenced to be hanged by Judge Morris. He was kept in solitary confinement in the Charlottesville city prison until he was executed on Jan. 20, 1905.

McDonagh, Terence, c.1910-   , Brit. On May 12, 1937, four Irish laborers, Terence McDonagh, his brother, Patrick McDonagh, Peter Connolly, and Pat (or Paddy) McDonagh, were drinking at the Sportsman Club at Huddersfield, England, the same day King George VI and his Queen were crowned in Westminster Abbey. The atmosphere had begun to turn dark at the pub, as Sam Speight, who had gotten on bad terms with the four men, tried to slip away. One of the men struck Speight, knocking him unconscious. In the drunken brawl that ensued, Edith Gertrude Elizabeth Watson was attacked by Terence McDonagh, who beat her first with a jug and then with the leg of a stool, killing her.

The four were indicted for her murder at the Leeds Assizes in July and also charged with wounding five others—Alfred Beardshall, John William Dyson, James Gill, John Samson, and Speight—with intent to commit grievous bodily harm. The defense pleaded that, being drunk, they did not know what they were doing. Justice MacNaghten summed up for the jurors saying that to reduce the charges to manslaughter they would have to consider Terence McDonagh to have been so drunk that he did not realize he was hurting Watson. A verdict of manslaughter was returned against all four defendants. MacNaghten gave Terence McDonagh twelve years of penal servitude for his "savage violence," doling out six years to Patrick McDonagh, and four years each to Peter Connolly and Pat McDonagh.

McDonald, Roland, 1909-   , U.S. On May 25, 1924, the body of 19-year-old schoolteacher Louise Gerrish was found riddled with shotgun wounds in a bed of weeds in Amhurst, Maine. Her handbag had been emptied and a watch she wore on a gold and black ribbon was missing.

Police questioned other teachers at Gerrish's school and learned that several of them had had a slumber party at Gerrish's house four days earlier, during which they danced to a Charleston record. A crude note scrawled on school paper was found among Gerrish's effects, reading, "We wached you dance last night. Thanks for leving the window open. It was real good. We will be watching some more when you dance agin."

Comparing handwritings of her pupils, police arrested

16-year-old Roland McDonald and his brother, Victor McDonald, thirteen. A worker on the farm where Gerrish lived, Roland had spent the extravagant sum of fifty cents on sweets and Victor was found wearing the missing black and gold ribbon. He admitted he followed Gerrish and shot her as she walked toward the post office. When questioned why he had shot her, Roland said, "Dunno."

A dozen psychiatrists pronounced him sane and he was convicted in October 1924 and jailed. Victor, under constant suspicion, shot and killed himself two years later. When doubts about Roland's guilt arose years later, he was given a lie detector test in April 1958 in his cell at the Thomaston (Maine) Penitentiary. The machine registered a falsehood when McDonald hesitated, then responded "No," to the question, "Did you lie to the parole officer yesterday when you said you didn't kill Louise Gerrish?" McDonald remained in jail.

McGannon, William H., 1856-1928, U.S. A prominent judge in Cleveland, Ohio, William H. McGannon, who planned to run for mayor, was accused of murder. On May 8, 1920, just after midnight, three men in a black Cadillac pulled into the busy Hamilton Avenue intersection of bars and night spots that would soon be known as "Death Corner." A shot rang out and one man stumbled and fell near a garage. Police officers Schuld and Perko rushed Harold Kagy to Lakeside Hospital as the other two men disappeared.

The Cadillac was identified as belonging to William H. McGannon, the first chief justice of Cleveland's Municipal Court. When officers asked Kagy who shot him he hesitated, then replied, "Johnny Joyce." Joyce, a bartender and bondsman, was well-known in downtown Cleveland. McGannon explained to officers that he had some car trouble and asked Kagy, a car dealer and old friend, to drive with him to test the repaired engine. Meeting Joyce at a local tavern, the three drank together. When they stopped at the intersection where Kagy was shot, McGannon said he had got out and walked home.

Joyce himself called police, and went with Inspector Sterling and Chief Smith to the hospital where Kagy lay wounded. When Kagy identified Joyce as his assailant, the bondsman became angry, saying, "You know who shot you. Why don't you tell these men who it was? Why don't you tell the truth?" Joyce was released on a $7,500 bail. Kagy, who continued to blame Joyce, died the next day.

A trial began in early Fall 1920 with Joyce accused of murder. Continuing to protest his innocence, Joyce testified that he had got drunk with the judge and the car dealer, and had been pushed out of the car by McGannon when they stopped at the intersection. Aware that the other two men had been arguing over money matters, he heard McGannon ask where the money was, then heard him say he "won't stand for that," followed by a shot or a car backfiring. Joyce had staggered over to a bar, where he passed out and slept until morning. Later, McGannon told him he knew he was innocent, and to keep his mouth shut. Joyce was found Not Guilty.

Within twenty-four hours of this verdict, steps to disbar McGannon went into action and nine days later the judge was indicted for second-degree murder. The trial, assigned to Judge Bernon, began just before Christmas, with Roland Baskin prosecuting. Several witnesses identified McGannon as the man they had seen at the intersection, and Mary Neely, an intimate friend of McGannon's for sixteen years, testified that her lover had offered her $500 "and more later on" to say she had not seen anything when she had been at Hamilton Avenue the night of the shooting. On Dec. 31, 1920, a hopelessly deadlocked jury was discharged by Bernon and the most expensive trial in Cuyahoga County ended in a mistrial.

At McGannon's next trial in February 1921, Neely at first refused to answer questions, then abruptly admitted she had seen McGannon shoot Kagy. Charles Burke, a newspaper reporter, had allowed the judge to use his hotel room for a reconciliation meeting with the estranged Neely, during which she promised to change her testimony, and he coached her on how to answer at the trial. Burke later testified that the judge had paid him $1,025 for his services in preparing for the second trial, and that he had advised McGannon to drop some of the alibi witnesses.

McGannon was found Guilty of perjury and sentenced to from one to ten years in the Ohio State Penitentiary. He invoked the wrath of God on the courtroom as he left. Serving nineteen months of his term as a model prisoner, McGannon was released and moved to Chicago where he worked in a law office. He died in 1928.

McGee, Eddie, c.1951- , U.S. A mentally retarded man declared brain-damaged at seven, probably as the result of repeated beatings by an alcoholic grandfather, was accused at age twenty of murdering two young girls in the city dump.

Eddie McGee, of Shelbyville, Tenn., was seen riding his bicycle into the dump, where Deborah Ray, nine, and Phyllis Seibers, eight, were playing. The next day, the battered, sexually abused bodies of the girls were discovered. Bicycle tracks, and prints that matched McGee's tennis shoes led police to arrest McGee a few days later. Ten months after his arrest, McGee was tried for the murders. With the additional evidence of blood on his jacket matching that of one of the victims, defense attorney Thomas Wiseman pleaded McGee's hopeless childhood, a litany of despair, abuse, and complete incompetence, in an attempt to save his client from the death sentence. Roland Wilson, for the prosecution, presented a possible motive, saying McGee had fought with one of the girls' brothers not long before the murder. McGee denied killing the children. After deliberating for an hour, the jury found him Guilty of first-degree murder, setting his punishment as ninety-nine years in the state penitentiary.

MacGregor, Dr. John, d.1928, U.S. The Sparling family of Huron County, Mich., had a lot of bad luck. First the father, John Wesley Sparling, died in 1909 of a sudden virulent illness that took the farmer within just a few days. He was attended by Dr. John MacGregor, who soon became the family physician. He was at the Sparling house every day for several years, supposedly treating a very persistent eye infection in the widow. He persuaded Mrs. Carrie Sparling to take out life insurance policies on her four children. She purchased them through his father's agency, and Dr. MacGregor did the health reports for the policies. Son Peter, twenty-six, died in 1910 of a condition similar to his father's, followed by Albert in 1911. The solicitous doctor was nearby in both cases. The grateful Mrs. Sparling, using insurance money, bought a house in the town of Ulby, where the doctor and his wife moved.

On Aug. 4, 1911, Scyrel, another Sparling son, became ill. This time Dr. MacGregor realized that the town was talking about him and the Sparlings, and called in other doctors, who suspected arsenic poisoning. One of them notified the county prosecutor, Xenophon A. Boomhower, who had his friend, Dr. MacGregor, arrange for a private nurse to stay with Scyrel. Scyrel died after ten days of illness. MacGregor and an associate did the autopsy, and supposedly found cancer of the liver. But Boomhower had the results checked at the University of Michigan. Arsenic was found, as it was in the exhumed body of Albert Sparling. Dr. MacGregor, Carrie Sparling, and the nurse were all arrested.

MacGregor went to trial in April 1912. The cases against the two women were dismissed, but the physician was found Guilty and sentenced to life in prison. Powerful people were at work behind the scenes, however, and in November 1916, Governor Woodbridge Ferris granted the doctor a full pardon. MacGregor was later appointed prison physician at Jackson State Prison, where he had served his time.

M'Guinness, Thomas, prom. 1917, Scot. Condemned to be hanged for murdering a 5-year-old boy, Thomas M'Guinness was scheduled to die in Glasgow in 1917. Executioner Ellis was called in to do the job, and offered M'Guinness, who looked like he might collapse, some brandy at the last moment. M'Guinness declined firmly, explaining, "I have been a teetotaller all my days, and I'll manage without it now." As the executioner's assistant fastened the straps on M'Guinness' legs, Ellis pulled the lever, almost causing a serious accident. The assistant was saved when Ellis cried out a warning, and the worker jumped clear just as the trap doors gave way beneath him.

MacKay, George (AKA: **John Williams; The Hooded Man**), 1883-1912, Brit. Criminal George MacKay who was tried and generally is written about under the name John Williams, was a well-educated young man from a good family. Despite his upbringing, MacKay became a criminal, specializing in burglary. On the night of Oct. 9, 1912, he was perched on the roof of the home in Eastbourne of Countess Flora Sztaray. As the countess left in a carriage, her driver noticed MacKay on the roof. The countess notified the police. Inspector Arthur Walls appeared and called out to MacKay. MacKay responded by firing two shots at the inspector, killing him.

MacKay escaped and joined Florence Seymour, a young woman with whom he was living and who was pregnant with his child. The pair took the revolver and other incriminating evidence to the beach where they buried it. Another criminal, an acquaintance of MacKay, Edgar Power, discovered that MacKay had shot the policeman and identified MacKay to police as the killer. To obtain evidence against him, Power then went to Seymour and told her that the police knew everything and the only way to save MacKay was to move the buried gun. Unsuspecting, Seymour led Power and the police to the spot where the gun was buried. Confronted with the evidence, Seymour broke down and admitted MacKay's guilt.

MacKay went on trial on Dec. 12, 1912, at the Sussex Assizes in Lewes. Justice Channel presided and Sir Frederick Lowe served as prosecutor. Although no direct evidence linked MacKay to the shooting and the testimony was questionable (Seymour recanted her earlier confession and Power was a known criminal), MacKay was found Guilty and sentenced to death. Despite a debate over MacKay's case in the House of Commons on Jan. 23, 1913, no commutation was forthcoming. The day after MacKay held his newborn child for the first time, he was executed.

M'Kay, James, d.1928, Scot. The dismembered body of Mrs. Agnes Arbuckle was found in a bundle on the banks of the Clyde River in Glasgow, with other parts discovered in a coal bunker near her house. Arrested and charged with murder was her son, James M'Kay, who pleaded insanity when tried in front of Lord Ormidale in a Glasgow circuit court in December 1927. Witness John Russell testified that M'Kay had invited him to his mother's home on Oct. 12, 1927. M'Kay enlisted Russell's help in moving an extremely heavy tin trunk to his place. The trunk was returned empty the next day. M'Kay's neighbor, Mrs. Meiklejohn, said she had come across a dirty, disarrayed M'Kay and surmised a few days later, when she read of the slaying, that he had been disposing of his mother's body.

The jury found the accused Guilty as charged and he was sentenced to death. The case was appealed to the High Court at Edinburgh, with the argument that, though the man had disposed of the body, there was no firm evidence to show he had murdered his mother. The appeal was dismissed and M'Kay was hanged on Jan. 6, 1928.

MacKay, Patrick David (AKA: **Franklin Bollvolt the First**), 1952- , Brit. Patrick MacKay was a violent and dangerous young street thug who tortured animals and beat boys. At an early age, he set fire to the local Catholic church with a candle. The judge at the Dartford juvenile court placed him on probation, to the considerable alarm of neighbors who feared MacKay would commit much worse crimes before he was through.

As a boy, MacKay roasted his pet turtle alive. Later, he became preoccupied with the Nazi regime. He decorated his room with military regalia and began calling himself "Franklin Bollvolt the First," the new world dictator. At age fifteen, MacKay, the son of an alcoholic, had a long record of violent offenses. In 1973 a Catholic priest named Father Anthony Crean took the troubled adolescent under his wing. MacKay rewarded his kindness by breaking into his residence and pilfering a check for £30. He altered the "3" and cashed the check for £80.

On Valentine's Day, 1974, MacKay called on 84-year-old Isabella Griffiths in Chelsea, volunteering to do her grocery shopping. When Griffiths refused, MacKay stran-

British murderer Patrick MacKay.

gled her, plunging a kitchen knife into her stomach. Later that year he committed a string of muggings against elderly women. On Mar. 10 of the following year MacKay followed Adele Price, an elderly widow, to her home in Lowndes Square. Feigning illness, he won the widow's permission to enter her flat where he strangled her. Afterward MacKay paid a call on his widowed mother who lived in Gravesend. Then on Mar. 21, 1975, he decided to drop in on Father Crean, who had attempted to prevent his prosecution on charges of theft two years prior. Finding the priest's residence unoccupied, MacKay stepped inside. When Father Crean returned a short time later the intruder viciously assaulted him. The priest rushed into the bathroom to shield himself from MacKay, but MacKay followed close behind, and killed him.

Two days later the police arrested MacKay. The suspect freely confessed to the three murders, and was considered the prime suspect in at least eight others committed between July 1973 and March 1975. Patrick MacKay was tried at the Old Bailey in November 1975 for the murders of the three elderly people. Judged to be sane at the time the murders were committed, MacKay was convicted and sentenced to life imprisonment. His life formed the basis of a book authored by Tim Clark and John Penycate titled *Psychopath*.

MacKnight, Gladys, 1919-   , and **Wightman, Donald**, 1918- , U.S. Gladys MacKnight, seventeen, and Donald Wightman, eighteen, were high school sweethearts. When they graduated from Bayonne (N.J.) High School in February 1936, they continued their romance despite objections of Helen MacKnight, the girl's 40-year-old mother.

Gladys' rebelliousness caused tension between her and her mother. On July 31, 1936, at 5:30 p.m., Donald dropped by to visit Gladys, who was sitting on the porch with her mother. MacKnight admitted him to the front parlor, where he waited for Gladys to return from the kitchen. Donald sat down at the piano and began to play, while the mother and daughter quarreled in the kitchen about what time the evening meal should be served. Gladys told her mother that she preferred an early supper because she planned to play tennis with Wightman before nightfall. According to Donald, the argument became heated and Mrs. MacKnight advanced on him with a carving knife. He later changed this account, saying that in a fit of temper Gladys picked up a small hatchet and struck her mother repeatedly.

Donald, suspected of stealing $120 from the Robbins Reef Yacht Club where his father worked, tried to intervene in the struggle, but Gladys had inflicted a mortal wound. Next door neighbor Elizabeth Feury heard the screams of the dying woman and demanded to know what the commotion was about. "Nothing," Gladys replied through the open window. When the woman persisted, Gladys told her to "go away. Mother cut her finger a little bit, that's all," she said. She slammed the window shut, locked the doors, and left the house with Donald.

When the girl's father arrived home from work that evening, he found the house locked. Not having a key, Edgar MacKnight borrowed a screwdriver from a neighbor and forced open a window on the back porch. He found his wife lying face down on the floor, beside the bloody hatchet.

Police Chief Cornelius O'Neill was sure that Gladys and Donald were responsible after Feury told him she saw the two of them drive away shortly after the window was slammed in her face. Police picked up the teenagers at 11 p.m., and booked them for second-degree murder. Their trial began on May 24, 1937, and lasted ten days. Donald and Gladys were convicted and sentenced to hard labor at the New Jersey State Prison at Trenton for thirty years. The two were required to complete one-third of the sentence before they would be eligible for parole. Commenting on his decision, Judge Thomas Meaney said: "I believe the jury arrived at the verdict in this case after considering all the evidence and the ages of the defendants." Edgar MacKnight tried to speak to his daughter as she was being led off to jail. If Gladys noticed her father, she pretended not to hear.

In 1950, Gladys was released, and seven years later her story was brought to network television.

McKown, Cora, 1947- , U.S. In Chesapeake, Va., on Jan. 8, 1969, Cora McKown told police that her husband, ex-marine Tim McKown, had been missing since the couple had a fight two days earlier. She also said her husband often beat her with a leather belt before they had sex, and showed them bruises on her thighs. McKown later reported that she had received a statement from a credit-card company that showed someone had signed her husband's name to garage bills, but the owners of the two cars involved in the billing were in possession of their cars and knew nothing of the former soldier.

Two months later, a man noticed a bundle floating in the Elizabeth River at Portsmouth, and realized a human foot stuck out of it. Police fished out a human torso, missing the head and hands, wrapped in a plaid quilt. One police officer working on the McKown case realized that the stabbed, mutilated body was Tim McKown. The body was found opposite a house where the policeman had made inquiries of Judy Clere, a young housewife, and learned that a man matching the description of her husband, Henry Clere, was rumored to be involved with Cora McKown. Clere, with a criminal record, was free on bail for charges of theft and impersonating an officer. Cora McKown came to the police, identifying the quilt as a wedding present, and confirming the identity of the corpse by mentioning a distinguishing mole on her husband's right thigh where a chunk of flesh had been cut out. Confronted with the police information about Clere, McKown confessed, twice. First, she said that she alone had stabbed her husband, dragged his body into the car, and thrown it into the river. In her second confession, McKown claimed Clere had slain her spouse and that she had nothing to do with the murder.

Brought to trial in August 1969 she repeated her charge that her husband was a sexual sadist. She also claimed to have been raped by three of his friends, and said she had an affair with the insurance salesman who sold her a $10,000 policy on her husband's life. Found Guilty of murder, McKown was sentenced to life imprisonment, with a minimum of fifteen years. At Clere's trial, three months later, McKown admitted that her husband beat her because "he knew it excited me." Clere was convicted and sentenced to die in the electric chair.

McManus, Fred Eugene, 1935- , U.S. Described by neighbors as "just about the nicest boy" in Valley Stream, N.Y., 18-year-old Fred Eugene McManus concealed his murderous tendencies. When he graduated from high school in 1953, all thought he would do well. He had an I.Q. of 123 and an average of ninety percent in science. McManus greatly disappointed his father, Mose McManus, however, forsaking college for the Marine Corps. He wanted to "get off the family dole" and away from the elder McManus, a Brooklyn brewery executive.

On Mar. 20, 1953, McManus was granted a ten-day furlough from his desk job at Camp LeJeune, N.C., and hitchhiked to Rochester, N.Y., to visit his girlfriend, 16-year-old Diane Marie Weggeland. On impulse, the two decided to elope, but found that few states allowed a 16-year-old to marry without parental consent. According to an almanac, one state was Minnesota.

Outside a Rochester dime store, on the lookout for a car, McManus flagged down 19-year-old Hobart College student William Braverman driving his 1953 red Plymouth. "After riding awhile I put my gun in my lap and told him to pull over," McManus later related. "I didn't like him at all—he was kind of a snob." So he shot him, buried him in a gravel pit, and marked the grave with a rusty can of anti-freeze

before the two young lovers headed west.

In Keeneyville, Ill., McManus entered a general store owned by 56-year-old George Bloomberg. When the grocer refused to hand over the cash in his drawer, McManus shot him at point blank range and then shot and killed Bloomberg's wife, Florence, because she refused to calm down. "I can't stand screaming," McManus said.

In Spring Valley, Minn., McManus murdered Mrs. David Beaston, owner of an all-night diner, for $49. "When another woman (waitress Harriet Horseman) started hollering and and screaming I shot her too," said McManus. "I was afraid people outside the cafe would hear her." McManus and Weggeland finally arrived in Minneapolis, but discovered that the almanac they had consulted was wrong. The license clerk refused to marry them. "But as far as we're concerned, we are legally married," said Weggeland.

In Iowa, Jack Moore recognized the Plymouth and the license plate and pulled them over at a roadblock near Garnavillo, Iowa. In New York, Mose McManus took the news hard. He said he had never heard his son mention Weggeland's name before. "I can't believe it," he sobbed. "This boy is not my son," he said. "My boy wouldn't do such a thing." The elder McManus nonetheless flew to Iowa, but his son dismissed him after seven minutes. "He said he doesn't want to see me again and doesn't want me to spend any money on his defense."

McManus and Weggeland returned to New York by plane. They played canasta and posed for photographs like newlyweds on their honeymoon—oblivious to death or the consequences of their actions. "I know what is going to happen. The electric chair. I want to die." McManus was eventually tried for murder, but instead of the electric chair received a life sentence. He would serve nearly twenty years before being paroled on Sept. 6, 1973.

McMonigle, Thomas Henry, c.1910-48, U.S. Ex-convict Thomas Henry McMonigle drove a bus in San Mateo, Calif., and according to his wife, Ena, was a "perfect father" to her two children from a previous marriage. The upcoming arrival of their first baby therefore gave this ex-convict from Illinois new hope, and "something to live for."

On Nov. 2, 1945, three days after the child was born, McMonigle murdered 15-year-old Thora Chamberlain. McMonigle, who had a history of sexual assault dating back to his days in Illinois, picked up the San Jose girl, daughter of wealthy building contractor Frank Chamberlain, outside Campbell Union High School shortly after 3:15 p.m. Thora accepted a ride from McMonigle after he asked for directions to Santa Cruz. Offering to direct him in return for a possible babysitting job with his children, she got into the car and they drove south. McMonigle later said that he got lost and ended up near the San Mateo-Santa Cruz county line, where, according to his signed confession to the FBI, he shot the girl and threw her body over a cliff near Devil's Slide, a half-mile north of Half Moon Bay. The high waves and fast undercurrent concealed his crime. Navy divers searched for a body, but the rough water apparently had torn apart the remains. Only a pair of socks believed to be Thora's were found on the craggy coastline.

McMonigle left California Nov. 8 to visit relatives in Illinois, where he once served eight years for attempted rape. But San Mateo police chief Robert O'Brien, recalling that McMonigle was a suspect in a rape case earlier that year in Redwood City, requested round-the-clock surveillance. When McMonigle returned to San Francisco on Dec. 6, he was immediately taken into custody and identified by two high school girls as the man who had attempted to pick them up. McMonigle admitted that he had been drinking heavily, but denied having raped Thora. The FBI disclosed that his confession contained no mention of rape, which led people to wonder what, if any, motive McMonigle had for committing this crime. Complicating matters was the absence of the murder weapon and a body.

McMonigle was convicted in Santa Cruz of kidnapping and murdering Thora and then dropping her body from a 350-foot cliff into the ocean. Upon his conviction, with nothing more to lose, McMonigle confessed to a second murder—that of Dorothy Rose Jones, twenty-three, whose remains were unearthed near the Devil's Slide on Apr. 20, 1946. She had been missing since October.

In his last will and testament, McMonigle refuted his earlier confession, disavowing any involvement in the murder of Thora. As his hopes for a reprieve faded, he contacted Dr. Robert Cornish, a Berkeley physician who experimented with dogs to see if they could be brought back to life after being euthanized. McMonigle volunteered to become a human guinea pig, but the doctor refused. A last-minute appeal to Governor Earl Warren for a stay of execution was denied. McMonigle was put to death in the San Quentin gas chamber on Feb. 20, 1948.

McQuire, George, prom. 1904, Brit. George McQuire, who had been released from the St. Pancras Institution for the mentally insane in August 1904, was, oddly enough, convicted of murder based on the testimony of the man he killed.

During McQuire's stay at the institution he was not viewed as being insane, but possessed of a hatred for superintendent John Skinner. This animosity festered into a marked threat, and McQuire determined to kill Skinner. Upon his release he continually followed the superintendent about, until near the end of October 1904, he shot Skinner in London's Tufnell Park. Before Skinner lost consciousness he told Metropolitan Police Detective Arthur Fowler Neil that McQuire had shot him and even signed the statement he made. Not far from the body lay a Webley revolver from which three bullets had recently been fired.

The next day Neil arrested McQuire, who denied the charge and even resisted arrest before he was finally brought to the police station. A woman witness to the attack hesitatingly picked McQuire from a lineup, and for the next six weeks Justice Fordham at the North London Police Court remanded McQuire to jail seven times. Neil obtained no further evidence, but did have his life threatened by McQuire's daughter. Then Skinner's condition worsened, and with his death imminent, Neil requested that the prisoner be taken before the man he allegedly shot. At the hospital Skinner pointed to McQuire and said, "That man is George McQuire who shot me in Tufnell Park." He died within five minutes of making this damning statement.

The trial began at Central Criminal Court three weeks later before Justice Grantham. There was a dispute raised by the defense that the arrest had been illegal, but the judge found Neil's actions warranted. With the accusation by Skinner, prosecutor Sir Archibald Bodkin had no problem convincing the jury that McQuire was Guilty. Grantham agreed with the defense that McQuire did not have a sound mind, and rather than death, the murderer was sentenced to life imprisonment at Broadmoor Criminal Lunatic Asylum.

Mad Parson, The, See: **Allen, John Edward**.

Madsen, Yvette (Jane Noack), c.1927- , U.S. Yvette Madsen, born Jane Noack, so disliked her Brooklyn, N.Y., background that upon marrying U.S. Air Force Lieutenant Andrew Madsen she was happy to change her name. In October 1949 the Madsens attended a cocktail party near Frankfurt, Ger., where Madsen was stationed. A fellow officer of Madsen's made a comment about the trace of a Brooklyn accent his wife still possessed—following her chiding the Georgian's southern drawl—and she slapped him. She stormed from the party and went home. Madsen, who had refused to join her, left the party half an hour later. When he arrived home his wife shot him in the heart with a .45-caliber gun, killing him instantly.

Yvette Madsen ran to a neighbor's house and screamed

that she had just shot her husband. Not far from the dead body the military police discovered a note in her writing that read, "I know my husband will beat me up. My only defense is to shoot him, the heel, the rat, the low creature."

Madsen's defense at her March 1950 trial for murder was one of insanity and not self-defense. Alfred Noack flew to Frankfurt to defend his daughter at the U.S. District Court there. He claimed his daughter was insane, a claim German psychiatrist Professor Karl Kleist supported. Kleist indicated Madsen suffered from an ingrained persecution complex triggered by jokes about her Brooklyn dialect. He added that "this is the dialect of the common people. Since it revealed her common origin, she felt insulted." In response, the defendant burst out, "Hang me! Hang me if you want, but make him stop." U.S. judges Fred Cohn, Herman Elegant, and John Speight were also convinced that Madsen had "a psychopathic personality" but felt she knew what she was doing and therefore found her Guilty. She was sentenced to fifteen years in the U.S. prison at Alderson, W.Va.

Maggiore, Michele della, d.1928, Italy. In 1927 Fascist dictator Benito Mussolini re-established the death penalty in Italy, which had been abolished in 1888. A year later Michele della Maggiore became the first person to be executed under the new law. The Communist was convicted of killing two Fascists and was shot to death by a Fascist Legionnaires firing squad. Maggiore was also the first to be executed during peace time since abolition of capital punishment.

Mahon, Patrick Herbert, 1890-1924, Brit. Patrick Herbert Mahon became a criminal after he married in 1910. He was soon charged with fraud, embezzlement, and robbery with violence. In 1922, at the age of thirty-two, he appeared to be straightening out his life, for, with his wife's help, he became sales manager of a firm at Sunbury. An ambitious and enterprising worker, he enjoyed an active social life as well. Mahon failed to be satisfied with the apparent successes of his life, however, and began an affair with 37-year-old Emily Beilby Kaye, a typist at the firm where he worked.

Kaye knew he was married, but apparently hoped Mahon would leave his wife and move with her to South Africa. For the plans, she had given him her life savings of several hundred pounds. In the spring of 1924, she began pressing Mahon for a commitment and proposed a "love experiment" in which they would share an isolated beach cottage. Kaye

had a deeper motive for this plan—she was pregnant.

Mahon's wife, apparently unaware of her husband's affair, had become suspicious of his frequent absences. Looking through his suit pockets, she found a cloakroom ticket for the Waterloo station and she asked a friend, a former railway policeman, to investigate. The friend redeemed the ticket and received a suitcase which contained bloodstained clothing, a butcher knife, and a racquet case marked "E.B.K." The friend returned the bag to the coat room and, after having Mahon's wife put the ticket back where she found it, called the police. The following day when Mahon retrieved the bag he was arrested by Scotland Yard.

British murderer Patrick Mahon with his daughter.

Initially he claimed he had been carrying meat for his dog in the suitcase. When confronted with the fact that the blood on the suitcase was human, he admitted to his liaison with Emily Kaye and told police of the cottage they shared on the beach. He said that over the weekend of Apr. 12-13, the two had argued and that during a struggle, the woman had fallen and hit her head on a coal scuttle, causing her death. He left her body in the house until the next Friday, unable to decide how to dispose of it. When he returned to the house he cut off the legs and head and stuffed the now mutilated body into a trunk. With the trunk hidden away in the house, he entertained another young woman in the cottage for the rest of the weekend. After she departed, Mahon returned to the task of butchering the body. At one particularly horrifying moment in his dogged attempt to destroy it he placed her head in the living room fireplace. As a clap of thunder sounded outside, the fire's heat caused the eyes of the severed head to spring open, frightening Mahon.

When police entered the cottage they found hunks of boiled flesh in a saucepan, cut-up pieces of flesh in a hat box, a trunk, and a biscuit tin, and ashes in the fire containing bits of bone. An examination of the remains conducted by the famed pathologist Sir Bernard Spilsbury yielded evidence of Kaye's pregnancy.

Mahon was tried at the Lewis Assizes on July 15, 1924. Sir Henry Curtis Bennett served as the prosecutor and J.D. Cassells defended, and Justice Avory presided. At the trial, it was revealed that Mahon apparently had spent all of Kaye's savings. Spilsbury testified that from medical evidence, he adjudged her to have been pregnant at the time of her death. The piece of evidence, however, that definitely incriminated Mahon was that the knife and saw with which he had done his grisly butchering had been purchased not after Kaye's death, as Mahon originally claimed, but on Apr. 12, before the couple went to the cottage. Mahon was found Guilty of murder and, on Sept. 9, 1924, hanged at Wandsworth Prison.

Mahoney, James, 1916- , Brit. In 1939, Jim Mahoney dreamed of living the good life in the West End of London. When he won £5 from a bookie, the 23-year-old with a cleft palate went to a nightclub where he was enchanted by the singer called "The Black Butterfly," whose real name was Mary Heath. He bravely sent her a drink, and soon had a date to meet her for lunch the next day. When he met her at a restaurant, he bought a bottle of gin, which he carried with him when he saw her home. At her apartment, he opened the bottle while she insisted that he leave. He pulled a knife and stabbed the singer to death.

Robert Fabian, the famous detective from Scotland Yard, found the foil from the gin bottle in Heath's apartment, but did not find any gin. Her sister told him where Mary usually ate lunch, and he quickly found the restaurant where Mahoney had bought the bottle of gin. The waiter said that the man had a cleft palate, at which point Mary's sister was shown the photographs of all the men with cleft palates in the police files. Among them she found young Mahoney. He was tried at the Old Bailey and found Guilty. He was sentenced to hang, but this sentence was later commuted and he spent the rest of his life in Broadmoor Lunatic Asylum.

Maine, Leonard, See: **Braun, Thomas Eugene.**

Major, Ethel Lillie, 1890-1934, Brit. Ethel Lillie Major, one of four children born to Tom Brown, a Lincolnshire gamekeeper, lived comfortably on the estate of Sir Henry Hawley. When she finished school she took up dressmaking. In 1914, the 24-year-old unmarried woman became pregnant but refused to disclose the identity of her child's father. To avoid scandal, the child, Auriel, was raised as Ethel's sister.

In 1918, Ethel fell in love with Arthur Major, a local youth at home in the small Lincolnshire town of Kirkby-on-Bain recuperating from WWI injuries. They married on June 1, 1918, and a year later Ethel gave birth to a son, Lawrence. During sixteen years of marriage, Ethel never confided the truth about Auriel. In 1934, however, Arthur heard some local gossip about the child's birth and demanded to know the truth. Ethel admitted being Auriel's mother, but still refused to tell the father's name.

Arthur was incensed and the couple became quarrelsome. Ethel told neighbors that Arthur had become a drunk and a bully, and accused him of seeing another woman. Finally, she refused to stay in the house at night, and, taking their son, went each evening to her father's home.

On one occasion prior to May 1934 Arthur spat out a mouthful of his sandwich and said to a fellow worker, "That woman is trying to kill me." Arthur's colleague watched as birds pecked at the discarded sandwich and within minutes fell over dead. Similar incidents occurred with neighbor's pets. On May 23, Ethel called in a local physician to attend to her husband who had returned from work ill that day. He was twitching, foaming at the mouth, and convulsing. The doctor, when told by Ethel that he had been having these fits periodically over a couple of years, diagnosed epilepsy and gave him a sedative.

Mrs. Ethel Lillie Major, poisoner.

When Ethel called the doctor the following day to say her husband had died, the doctor pronounced epilepsy as the cause of death.

Just before Arthur's funeral, police received an anonymous note suggesting Arthur was poisoned. They delayed the funeral while an autopsy was performed on Arthur's body and the body of a neighbor's dog that had died after eating scraps fed to it by Ethel. Dr. Robert Lynch, a London pathologist, determined that both had died from strychnine poisoning. When Mrs. Major was brought in for questioning by Scotland Yard's Chief Inspector Hugh Young, she mentioned strychnine before her questioners did. Convinced of Ethel Major's guilt, Young set about collecting evidence. No strychnine could be found anywhere in her home, but Ethel's father admitted to keeping some in a locked box to which he had the only key. He added that the only other key had disappeared ten years earlier. Young searched Ethel Major's household once again, this time finding a key in one of her handbags which unlocked the box holding the poison. Ethel was defended at her trial by defense attorney Norman Birkett, who until that time had never lost a murder trial. Despite her claims of innocence and an attempt to incriminate a neighbor with whom she said her husband was having an affair, Ethel Major was convicted of murdering her husband. Sentenced to hang, she was executed at Hull Jail on Dec. 19, 1934.

Malik, Abdul (Michael de Freitas, AKA: Michael X), 1933-74, Trinidad. Born Michael de Freitas in Trinidad, the Black Power leader who called himself Michael X after Muslim leader Malcolm X, was a pimp and racketeer in London, where he founded the Racial Adjustment Action Society. He was jailed for publicly advocating the killing of any white man seen with a black woman. In 1970, he jumped bail on a charge of robbery, and returned to Trinidad, where he called himself Abdul Malik. He had many famous black supporters in the U.S., some of whom saw him as a powerful leader of the black militant movement. In Trinidad, he tried to turn the strong anti-white sentiment into a rebellion. But when the rebellious movement was suppressed and he needed money, Malik turned to more traditional crimes, such as prostitution and gunrunning.

For a while, Malik's home near Port-of-Spain was a haven for Black Power advocates. In November 1971, Hakim Jamal (born Allen Donaldson) arrived with his girlfriend, Gale Benson, divorced daughter of British writer and member of parliament, Captain Leonard Plugge. She quickly became Malik's devotee and a willing target of his sadistic beatings. Early in 1972, Benson disappeared. Hakim Jamal reported her disappearance to the police, but then left for the U.S. On Feb. 8, 1972, Joseph Skerritt, another follower, was killed by Malik's personal bodyguard, with Malik delivering the final blow, because Skerritt had disobeyed an order.

Trinidad murderer Abdul Malik, alias Michael X, tortured and killed two of his followers.

Skerritt was buried in a ditch he was helping to dig. Ten days later, Malik and his family left for Guyana. That night his house burned to the ground. Malik, hearing of the fire, had his attorney obtain an injunction to keep people away from his property. But on the word of an informant, the police dug up the garden around the burned house and found the bodies of Skerritt and Gale Benson. The woman had suffered numerous superficial stab wounds, just enough to force her into a hole, where she was buried alive.

While the police of Trinidad sought the extradition of Malik from Guyana, they arrested three of his followers: 20-year-old Edward Chadee, 34-year-old Stanley Abbott, and 21-year-old Adolphus Parmasser, who turned state's evidence against the other two. Another participant, Steve Yates, had died while swimming in the ocean. Police finally found Malik in the jungle of South America, and brought him back to Trinidad. Hakim Jamal was shot and killed in Boston, possibly at the orders of Michael X. Abbott and Chadee were each sentenced to life in prison, but Malik was given the death sentence by Mr. Justice Garvin Scott. Abdul Malik was hanged in November 1974.

Maloney, James, 1949-79, U.S. James Maloney, thirty, had long been suspected of having once been a member of the radical Weathermen group, which is why the activist requested permission under the Freedom of Information Act to look at the FBI investigation of himself in the early 1970s. The request was denied, so Maloney, who had recently quit his job as a social worker, visited the El Centro, Calif., FBI office. He had an appointment with one of the agents to discuss his request, but brought with him a shotgun and .38-caliber revolver.

On Aug. 9, 1979, Maloney entered the building carrying a garment bag holding the shotgun. He removed the gun from the bag, and while holding it in his left hand opened fire as an agent answered the door. He got off only one errant shot, which missed and struck no one, before the gun apparently jammed. The gunman then began firing the revolver, which he held in his right hand. Agents Charles W. Elmore, thirty-four, and J. Robert Porter, forty-four, both were killed before Maloney used the sixth and final bullet from his six-gun to kill himself with a shot in the mouth.

Maltby, Cecil, 1876-1923, Brit. Cecil Maltby, forty-seven, kept the body of his dead mistress, Alice Hilda Middleton, with him in his London apartment for a year. In January 1923, police broke down Maltby's apartment door with a search warrant to investigate "unsanitary conditions." As officers entered the apartment, they heard a gunshot. In the search, they found Middleton's putrefied body in a tub and Maltby's bloodied body in bed, shot in the mouth.

Middleton was the wife of a chief in the merchant marine and Maltby's mistress. In early Summer 1922, after her husband had left for the Far East, Middleton moved in with her lover. After Aug. 15, no one saw her. When her husband returned in December, he reported his wife missing to police and thus began the search that led officers to Maltby's home and the hideous discovery.

Police also found seven letters throughout the house written by Maltby in memorial to his live-in mistress. Each letter referred to her suicide, which ostensibly occurred on Aug. 24 the year before. Close examination of the woman's body and the three bullet holes in her back offered proof positive that Maltby had murdered her. Though the defendant was dead, the coroner's jury returned a verdict of Guilty of murder, adding, "He was in a perfectly sound state of health and mind when he took his own life in order to avoid the consequences of his own act."

Mamedzi, Shifulaso, prom. 1929, S. Afri. Shifulaso Mamedzi, midwife for the South African Bawenda tribe, was the victim of changing social mores in 1929 just as surely as the twin newborns she killed were victims of tribal mores. Mamedzi followed a tribal ritual concerning twins when she strangled the identical babies and tied their tiny bodies together for burial, despite pleas by the infants' mother to spare at least one of her children. But the intervening white government called it murder and sentenced her to death.

Mancini, Antonio (AKA: Baby), d.1941, Brit. Seven years after the murder of Violette Kaye by Antonio "Tony" Mancini, the infamous Brighton killer, another young hoodlum with the same name took the life of a London bookmaker at a popular Soho night club.

On a July night in 1941, a terrible fracas broke out at the Wardour Street club where Antonio Mancini worked. At the center of the fight was Harry Distleman, a bookmaker and gambler known to the police as "Scarface" or "Hubby." As German Luftwaffe planes flew overhead dropping bombs on London, Distleman lay dying in the billiards saloon, the victim of a knife-wielding assailant. Chief Inspector Arthur Thorp and his assistant John Sands were summoned to the crime-ridden neighborhood. A "Flying Squad" arrested dozens of underworld figures and took them to the Savile Row Police Station. One name kept coming up in their statements. Tony Mancini had incurred the displeasure of the ruthless Hoxton and King's Cross gangs, and, it seemed, was in fear of his life. For these reasons he had begun

carrying a seven-inch stiletto to protect himself. It was such a weapon that had killed Little Hubby the night of the air raid attack. Sands learned that there had actually been two gang fights that night in Soho. The participants had torn apart the interior of the billiards club, using furniture, pool cues, and knives as weapons. Distleman and his associate Edward Fletcher, who had been wounded during the first fray, were criminal allies of the King's Cross and Hoxton gangs. When they spied Mancini in his club, they drew him into another fight. According to Mancini's version of events, Distleman was stabbed in an act of self-defense. An accurate rendering of everything that happened that night in Soho would not be forthcoming. The gangsters closed ranks and refused to discuss the matter with Scotland Yard. If Antonio "Baby" Mancini had indeed acted in self-defense as he continued to profess, there was no one to corroborate his story.

Mancini was found Guilty of murder following a short trial at the Old Bailey. Mancini fought vigorously to have the verdict overturned; in fact, it became only the third appeal to reach the House of Lords since the passage of the Criminal Appeal Act of 1907. The case was argued before the Lord Chancellor, Viscount Simon, Lord Russell of Killowen, Lord Sankey, Lord Wright, and Lord Porter, on Oct. 2-3. The original decision of Justice MacNaghten was upheld two weeks later on the grounds that there had been no error of law during his summation that would justify the appeal. The defense had argued that the judge had failed to instruct the jury to acquit Mancini of murder if they harbored even a reasonable doubt that he had acted in self-defense. The defendant paid with his life on Oct. 31, 1941, at the Pentonville Prison.

Mancini, Tony (Cecil Lois England, AKA: Babyface; Jack Notyre; Hyman Gold; The Brighton Trunk Murderer), 1908- , Brit. The image of the mysterious Latin lover that women found so irresistible in such screen stars as Rudolf Valentino and Ramon Novarro also appealed to Cecil Lois England, a convicted thief, swindler, ex-soldier, and pimp who lived on the edge of London's criminal underworld. After some consideration, England changed his name to the more romantic-sounding "Tony Mancini."

Following his release from prison in August 1933, Mancini took a job working in a cafe near Leicester Square. There he met a blowzy, 42-year-old vaudeville hoofer named Violette Kaye (also known as Violet Sanders), who had lately turned to prostitution as a means of earning a living. When the cafe was forced to close its doors, Mancini had no funds and dismal prospects of finding a new job. Out of kindness, Violette Kaye offered to put Mancini up at her home in the coastal town of Brighton, on condition that he make himself scarce when she was entertaining clients. The arrangement was an agreeable one until her young charge finally found work as a waiter at the Skylark Cafe. Violette appeared at the dive each day to check up on Mancini. She was a jealous. possessive woman who frowned on the attention that other women showed him. On the afternoon of May 10, 1934, Kaye stormed into the cafe, where she had an angry argument with Mancini and a certain waitress with whom he had been flirting. To Mancini's relief, she was removed from the premises. An eyewitness, Thomas Richard Kerslake, was an associate of Charles Moores, who was forced to break an engagement with Kaye that very afternoon. Kerslake spoke briefly to her, but she disappeared inside her flat, where presumably another man waited, for Kerslake heard the voice of another man in Kaye's apartment. That was the last anyone saw of Violette Kaye.

The next morning Mancini turned up at the cafe. He told his employer that Kaye had gone to Paris in search of a better job. Next, he cabled her sister-in-law in London to say that she had walked out of his life for good. On June 17, the torso of a woman was found in a trunk left at the

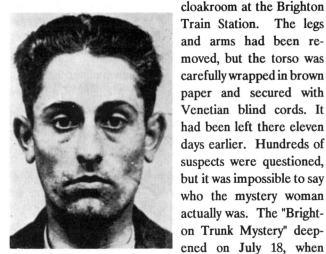

cloakroom at the Brighton Train Station. The legs and arms had been removed, but the torso was carefully wrapped in brown paper and secured with Venetian blind cords. It had been left there eleven days earlier. Hundreds of suspects were questioned, but it was impossible to say who the mystery woman actually was. The "Brighton Trunk Mystery" deepened on July 18, when Brighton Police arrived at

Tony Mancini

Mancini's home on Kemp Street to question him about Kaye's disappearance. The place was deserted, but an examination of Mancini's trunk turned up the decomposing remains of a second woman. This time there was no problem establishing an identity. It was clearly Violette Kaye, the missing prostitute.

Two days later Mancini was arrested on the London-Maidstone Road. He had been sleeping at the Salvation Army Hotel and had taken his meals in cheap restaurants in the East End of London. "Yes, I'm the man," he admitted. "I didn't murder her though. I wouldn't cut off her hand. She has been keeping me for months." Death, according to British pathologist Sir Bernard Spilsbury, was

caused by a severe blow to the head from a blunt object. A hammer was found lying nearby. The police interviewed three men who had spoken to Mancini at a Brighton amusement arcade. "What's the good of knocking a woman about with your fists," Mancini had told them. "You should hit with a hammer, the same as I did." Armed with this evidence, the police secured a murder indictment.

The trial came before Justice Branson at the Lewes Assizes on Dec. 10, 1934. The crown had a strong case against the accused, but Mancini would say, quite simply, "She was a loose woman and I knew it. Strange as it is, I used to love her. We were always on the most affectionate terms. There were no quarrels." His simple denial greatly impressed his lawyer Norman Birkett, whose impassioned plea and relentless cross-examination of Spilsbury won his client an acquittal. The esteemed pathologist was forced to admit on the stand that the fracture in the victim's skull could just as well been caused by a fall down the stairs, especially by someone like Kaye who was known to be frequently intoxicated. "When he went home that night from work and found the woman dead his immediate reaction was one of sheer terror," Birkett explained. "So he went out; he walked about; he turned this dreadful situation in his mind; and when he returned he put the body in the cupboard and nailed the door upon its hideous secret." After five days the jury retired. In his summation, Justice Branson reminded the jury that the court was not concerned with morals, but with the law. The lack of apparent motive, he said, should not impair them from finding the defendant guilty if that was their belief. "But the fact that there is no express evidence of motive called before you makes it necessary for you to scrutinize with all the greater care the other evidence," he said. The jury found Mancini Not Guilty. It was the high point of Birkett's storied career. Tony Mancini retired to live a quiet life, free from the suspicions of his fellow man and the criticisms of the press. In 1976, Mancini made the headlines of the London Sunday tabloids with the startling confession that he had in fact committed Trunk Murder Number 2.

Manson, Charles, 1934- , U.S. The illegitimate son of a teenage prostitute, Charles Manson, who never stood more than five feet, two inches, was an unlikely candidate to lead a criminal commune and a murder cult. He nevertheless became a guru to a pack of psychopathic killers whose murders shocked California and the entire U.S. in 1969. Manson was born in Cincinnati, Ohio, on Nov. 11, 1934. His mother, Kathleen Maddox, of Ashland, Ky., unable to support even herself through prostitution, left her son with his grandmother in McMechen, W. Va. He was later sent to Boys Town in Nebraska, but his incorrigible thieving and truculent manner soon caused him to leave. Living a nomadic life, Manson drifted to Peoria, Ill., where he was arrested for the first time for stealing food. He was sent to the Indiana Boys School in Plainfield, but Manson proved to be as surly and troublesome there as he had been at Boys Town in Nebraska. He escaped eighteen times from the school and finally fled west. He was arrested again in Beaver City, Utah, in 1951 for theft. Over the next four years, Manson spent most of his time in federal reformatories. He served time in the National Training School for Boys in Washington, D.C., and he was finally paroled from the Chillicothe Federal Reformatory in November 1954. In the following year, Manson married Rosalie Jean Willis, and a short time later he was arrested and charged with transporting stolen autos across state lines. For this federal offense, Manson was sent to Terminal Island Prison outside of Los Angeles to serve a three-year prison term.

In 1958, Manson was released and he immediately became a pimp, but again he was arrested, charged with violating the Mann Act for transporting females across state lines for immoral purposes. After several of these arrests, Manson resorted to forging checks and was again arrested, this time drawing a ten-year prison term in the federal penitentiary on McNeil Island, Wash.

Released in March 1967, Manson bummed his way to Los Angeles. By this time he had spent seventeen years behind bars—more than half his life. He was almost illiterate and completely unschooled, yet prison life had turned him into a shifty, cagey, and cunning creature who had learned how to manipulate people in prison to compensate for his diminutive size. He had been used sexually by men in prison and he was bisexual, but by the time he reached California in 1967, Charles Manson had a decided taste for young women, especially the long-legged, long-haired flower children of the turbulent 1960s.

Manson mocked and sneered at convention and authority and he infused his mostly female followers with his own arrogant posture and hatred for the police and law. He labeled everyone opposed to his gypsy lifestyle an enemy of his "family," and he moved from one seamy road camp to another, first living with several young women and a few docile and obedient men outside of San Francisco. Manson complained that the weather was too cold for his delicate body and insisted that his "family" follow him southward to the warmer climate of Los Angeles. There, in 1968, Manson quickly gathered new followers who were mesmerized by his hypnotic stare and monosyllabic pronouncements. He mouthed platitudes and generalities that were about as enlightening as the slogans on calendars in gas stations where he had occasionally worked in earlier years.

Yet his gobbledygook and gibberish appealed to young women seeking excitement and affection.

One such was Patricia Krenwinkel, twenty-one. She had grown up in an untroubled middle-class family and had been a Camp Fire Girl and had a good education. Krenwinkel held a good job with a Los Angeles insurance company but the moment she met Manson on Manhattan Beach, she gave up everything. She even abandoned her car and did not bother to pick up her paycheck. She was typical of the followers Manson led to the Spahn Movie Ranch, a broken down, shack-cluttered dusty area in eastern Simi Valley. Susan Atkins, twenty-one, also joined Manson. Her background rivaled his. She had worked at seamy jobs all her life, including that of a topless dancer and bar hustler. She was unkempt, unschooled, and, like many of her repugnant ilk, proud of her ignorance, defiant to authority. Worse, she had been a practicing satanist for a number of years, an influence which was to infiltrate the deluded, receptive minds of the Manson commune. She quickly became Manson's chief aide.

The group also included tall, pretty Leslie Van Houten, nineteen, a school dropout and LSD addict who had run away from home at an early age and had lived like a tramp in the Los Angeles area until meeting Manson and joining the commune at the Spahn Ranch. In July 1969, Linda Kasabian, twenty, stole $5,000 from the home of a friend to give to Manson so he would accept her as a member of his lunatic commune. Kasabian was married and had small children, but she took her infant daughter Tanya and abandoned the rest of her family to live at the Spahn Ranch. She, like Van Houten, was psychologically addicted to LSD and was usually in a drug daze when cavorting with Manson.

Also among this motley clan was Charles "Tex" Watson, twenty-three, tall, powerfully built, a one-time high school football and track star from Farmersville, Texas. Though he had been a top student, once Watson moved to the Spahn Ranch, he became a mindless robot who slavishly followed Manson's orders. Manson's every waking moment was spent either indoctrinating his followers with his own satanic teachings or by appeasing his insatiable sexual cravings by sleeping with one or two or all of his female followers at the same time. He reveled in the sexual attention and promised each of his fanatical female cohorts that he would make them pregnant with his child as a reward for being loyal to him. As time went on, Manson began to tell his family that he was "Man-son," or "Son-of-Man," which he himself likened to Christ. He grew long hair and a straggily beard and marched about Christ-like on the Spahn Ranch spouting his idiotic philosophy, telling his followers that he was not only Christ but Satan, too.

At this time Manson began to rant against blacks, saying that he had been sent to wreak divine havoc upon the earth, which had allowed blacks to co-mingle with whites. The planet had to be purged of this inferior race, he said, and this could only be brought about by whites who would rise up and slaughter all blacks. This world race war would not begin, Manson pointed out to his followers, until whites themselves had been brutally attacked, especially important white people. His family, Manson proudly stated, had been selected as the instrument of his wrath. They would kill some important whites and blame the slaughter on the blacks. The result would be a general uprising by whites against blacks and the slaughter of blacks would ensue. Manson's hatred for blacks stemmed from his miserable life in prison, where he had been repeatedly raped by black prisoners. He would now take vengeance upon the entire race for this offense to his youthful body.

Meanwhile, Manson began playing the guitar and soon deluded himself into believing that he was one of the most accomplished guitar players in the world and a composer of great talent. He composed a monotonous song that was no more than a few notes strung together and lyrics that consisted of only two words—"You Know"—repeated over and over again. Manson thought that his song would, if he could get it before the public, become the most popular ditty in the U.S. To that end, Manson contacted Gary Hinman, a successful musician, badgering him to make a hit out of his song. Hinman was amused by the dogged Manson and made the mistake of allowing Manson, Susan Atkins, and Robert K. Beausoleil, another fanatical follower of Manson's, to stay in his house. Hinman did little but tolerate Manson, and he enraged the banty cultist by ignoring Manson's composition.

The group moved out of Hinman's house but Manson harbored a deep hatred for the musician, coming to believe that Hinman was jealously ignoring his song. When hearing that Hinman had recently inherited $20,000, Manson sent Atkins and Beausoleil to Hinman's house to steal the money and kill Hinman for snubbing Manson and his brilliant composition. Beausoleil and Atkins held Hinman prisoner, torturing him while they ransacked his house in their desperate search for the inheritance money, naively believing Hinman would keep $20,000 in his home. After two days, Atkins and Beausoleil grew disgusted and simply murdered Hinman; Beausoleil stabbed the musician to death while he was bound hand and foot. Atkins then dipped her fingers in her victim's blood and wrote on the wall of his resplendent home: "Political Piggie." The killers then wiped the house clean of their fingerprints and left, but they were sloppy. Two prints were overlooked, Beausoleil's, and police quickly identified him and tracked him down, finding the killer in his car wearing a shirt stained with Hinman's blood. The knife Beausoleil used to kill the musician was found in the car with him. He was charged with murder and jailed.

Manson ignored the loss of Beausoleil. He was expendable. Manson's only concern was to have his song published, and he approached Terry Melcher, the son of Doris Day, asking Melcher to introduce him to the important people he knew in the music industry so that they could benefit from his musical masterpiece. Melcher apparently did nothing to help Manson, which infuriated the little cult leader. In his demented thinking, Manson came to believe that he would instill terror in the heart of Terry Melcher, so much fear that Melcher would do as Manson asked. To create this terror, Manson would unleash his drugged up followers, instructing them to murder some innocent people. Manson drilled his cultists, making a death squad, telling them to put on black clothes and enter abandoned buildings in grim rehearsals which the cultists called "the Creepie Crawlies." It was all a game to these people who had reduced themselves to moronic obedience. They were cretins, all of them, blindly following the orders of their leader, Charlie Manson.

On Mar. 23, 1969, Manson and Tex Watson went to Melcher's lavish home, a sprawling tree-lined estate in remote Benedict Canyon. Melcher no longer lived at the house on Cielo Drive. Manson saw some glamorous-looking people moving about and he labeled them "movie star types." He did not know their names, but while still brooding about how Melcher had ignored him, Manson decided that everyone now living in the house where Melcher once lived would die. Their deaths would prove to Melcher that Manson meant business, the business of death and that next time Melcher would be more energetic in promoting the little man's long-neglected song. On the night of Aug. 8, 1969, Manson sent his death squad to the house on Cielo Drive. Only Linda Kasabian lost her nerve at the last minute and remained outside the house, according to her later statements.

Those unsuspecting inhabitants of the house included movie star Sharon Tate, eight months pregnant. The beautiful blonde was the wife of Roman Polanski, maker of horror films who was then in London working on a movie. Also residing at the house was Abigail Folger, coffee heiress, who was living at the house with her boyfriend, Polish writer Voyteck Frykowski, a friend of Polanski's. Present in the house that night was Jay Sebring, a celebrated hair stylist to the rich and famous. Sebring was a former boyfriend of Sharon Tate's. Manson had given Tex Watson a rope, a knife, and a .22-caliber revolver, ordering him to take Krenwinkel, Atkins, and Kasabian with him. The cult leader directed Watson to kill everyone in the house adding: "And make it as gruesome as possible."

Mass killer Charles Manson, as a boy of fourteen, at age sixteen, and, last two photos, at the time of the Tate-LaBianca murders in 1969.

Manson as a prisoner in 1970, in 1971 with a swastika on his forehead, Charles "Tex" Watson, and prosecution witness Linda Kasabian.

Left to right, actress Sharon Tate, stabbed to death by Manson's fanatical followers; Polish writer Voyteck Frykowski; Frykowski's fianceé Abigail Folger, heiress to the coffee fortune. All were slain on Aug. 9, 1969.

Manson murderesses Susan Atkins, Patricia Krenwinkel, Leslie Van Houten.   Female Manson followers with shaved heads, protesting his imprisonment.

As the group entered the grounds of the estate, Watson came upon 18-year-old Steven Parent, who had been visiting William Garretson, the 19-year-old caretaker who lived in a small house far removed from the mansion, one completely overlooked by the killers. Watson thrust the revolver into Parent's face and the youth begged for his life. Watson fired four shots into him, killing Parent instantly. Watson then entered the house with Atkins and Krenwinkel. They ordered Tate, Sebring, Frykowski, and Folger into the living room, telling them that they were only robbing the house and would harm no one. Sebring was tied up, but he broke free and started to flee. He was shot to death. Then Frykowski, realizing they would all be killed, leaped forward, attacking the hulking Watson. He was shot, knocked down, and kicked; then Watson beat the Polish writer with the butt of the revolver while the girls stabbed him fifty-one times. Folger made a dash for the back door and managed to reach the lawn before Krenwinkel ran after her and knocked her down. Watson caught up to Folger and stabbed her repeatedly until she was dead.

Only Sharon Tate was left alive. She pleaded for her life, telling Susan Atkins that she was pregnant and begged for the life of her unborn child. "Woman, I have no mercy for you," sneered Atkins who then stabbed Tate sixteen times, killing her. The slaughterhouse killers then tied a rope about Sebring's head and the other end to Tate's mutilated corpse. They spread an American flag on the couch and then wrote the word "pig" on the front door in Sharon Tate's blood. They changed their bloody clothes, gathered their weapons, and drove away, later throwing their clothing and weapons into a ravine in the San Fernando Valley. It was then they realized that they had left Atkins' knife behind at the murder scene. The foursome stopped at a small house and unraveled a hose which they used to wash away the blood on their hands and faces. The homeowner then appeared and chased the killers away.

The next day Manson and his followers, now numbering almost thirty, read the gruesome newspaper accounts of the murders on Cielo Drive. While the country reeled in disgust and shock, Manson and his followers wildly celebrated this "triumph" by having a sex orgy, with Manson at the center of the frenzied love-making, and by smoking endless marijuana cigarettes. Manson then stated it was time to make another terror raid. On the night of Aug. 10, 1969, Manson led his group of killers, including Watson, Atkins, Krenwinkel, Leslie Van Houten, and 23-year-old Steve Grogan to the home of Rosemary and Leno LaBianca, a house Manson randomly selected in the Silver Lake area. The LaBianca home was large and spacious. Rosemary LaBianca, thirty-eight, ran a fashionable dress shop and her husband, 44-year-old Leno LaBianca, owned a grocery store chain.

Manson alone invaded the home by crawling through an open window. He awoke the couple, waving a gun in their faces and tying them up with leather thongs he habitually wore about his neck. He told them that he would not harm them, only rob their house. He took LaBianca's wallet and returned to the car where his cultists sat joking, excited at the prospect of committing more senseless murders. Manson ordered Watson, Van Houten, and Krenwinkel to go into the LaBianca house and murder the man and woman he had tied up and told them he and the others were going into the house next door to murder its occupants. When Watson, Krenwinkel, and Van Houten went into the LaBianca home, Manson and the others drove back to the Spahn Movie Ranch. En route, Manson stopped at a gas station. He handed LaBianca's wallet to Linda Kasabian and ordered her to place it in the women's washroom. He explained that some "greedy bitch" would find the wallet, use the credit cards inside, and then be blamed for the murders. He laughed at the cleverness of his plan.

Watson, meanwhile, was dutifully murdering Leno LaBianca. He dragged the man into the living room of his house and repeatedly stabbed him until he was dead, leaving the knife sticking in his victim's neck. He then covered LaBianca's head with a pillow case. Meanwhile, Van Houten and Krenwinkel had been in the bedroom, repeatedly stabbing the helpless Rosemary LaBianca. They stabbed and chanted at the same time, making forty-one wounds in the woman, a dozen after she was long dead. They tied a cord around her neck and covered her face with a pillowcase. On the living room wall, the slayers wrote on the wall with their victim's blood the words "Death to all pigs" and "Rise." In the kitchen they wrote, also in blood, the words "Healter (sic) Skelter" on the door of the refrigerator. The killers did not flee but enjoyed the home as if it was their own. They took a communal shower to wash away the blood and then helped themselves to a midnight snack by looting the refrigerator. Before the cult killers left the house, Watson took a carving knife and sliced the word "war" on Leno LaBianca's stomach. He then thrust the knife into the man's stomach and left laughing.

Many of Manson's followers left the Spahn Ranch after these incomprehensible slayings, including Atkins, who was arrested and jailed for prostitution. She bragged to a prisoner about the killings and another inmate overheard the boastful confession. She informed police that Charles Manson had been behind the killings. On Aug. 16, 1969, Manson and several of his demented followers were arrested at the Spahn Ranch but later released for lack of evidence. He was rearrested in a sleazy camp with some followers near Death Valley on Oct. 15, 1969. Also in custody at the time were Atkins, Van Houten, Beausoleil,

Grogan, and Kasabian. Police tracked down Krenwinkel in Mobile, Ala., where she was hiding with an aunt. Watson had gone home to Collin County, Texas, where his influential relatives managed to fight off extradition for some time. He was finally returned to California and he, along with Manson, Krenwinkel, Atkins, Van Houten, Grogan, and Beausoleil, were placed on trial for murder.

The trial was often interrupted by the defendants who treated it as a lark. They laughed at the descriptions of their mutilations and murders and posed for newspaper photographers, especially Manson, who delighted in the limelight. He had finally found the attention he had sought all his life. Manson attempted to portray himself as the worst man on earth. He bragged to fellow prisoners that he had murdered at least thirty-five others, in addition to the Tate-LaBianca slayings, another lie from an inveterate liar. All of the repulsive defendants were found Guilty and sentenced to die in the gas chamber. When the death penalty was abolished in California in 1972, the sentences were commuted to life imprisonment, which, by California law, allows prisoners to apply for parole every seven years. Thus far, all appeals for parole by the Manson killer-cultists have been denied. At this writing, the ever-inventive Charles Manson makes extra money to buy cigarettes and candy in the prison commissary at San Quentin by selling to fans his rolled up socks upon which he draws smiling faces and autographs with the flourish of a Pablo Picasso.

Manton, Horace William (AKA: **Bertie Manton**), d.1947, Brit. A fire-truck driver in Luton, England, quarreled with his wife on Nov. 18, 1943, angrily struck her over the head, then grabbed her by the neck and strangled her. He tried to remove all identification from the body, taking out her false teeth and deliberately mutilating her face. Then Bertie Manton wrapped his wife's nude body in sacks, and carried the awkward bundle on his bicycle to the River Lea, where he threw it into the water. Returning home, he polished every item in the house that might bear her fingerprints.

The body was found the next afternoon. Police surgeons reconstructed the face enough to take photographs, which appeared in newspapers and in movie houses. Policemen took the pictures to every house in town, but not even the Manton children recognized the woman.

The following February, Chief Inspector William Chapman of Scotland Yard happened to see a dog digging up some fabric in an empty lot. The rag bore a dyer's tag, which Chapman traced to a coat dyed for Mrs. Caroline "Rene" Manton. He went to the Manton house, and learned that Caroline Manton had left Bertie some months

before, but that she still wrote him letters. Manton showed Chapman some of the letters, on all of which the name "Hampstead" was misspelled. A fingerprint expert who went over the house was startled to discover that everything—even the dirty old bottles in the basement—had been thoroughly cleaned. Finally, one old pickle bottle, standing at the far end of a very dusty shelf, was found to bear a fingerprint. It matched one of the murdered woman's.

Bertie Manton was arrested for the murder of his wife. He said that she had been more interested in having a good time than in taking care of their four children, especially with so many men in uniform around to be entertained. When they had quarreled once again, she threw a cup of hot tea in his face. He responded by striking out with a stool, causing her brain to hemmorage, unintentionally killing her. Cleaning up the blood, he hid her body in the basement until the children went out to a movie that night. He told them that their mother had gone to her mother's in London, and even wrote letters that he mailed in Hampstead, but he spelled the return address "Hamstead." When Chapman asked him to spell the name, Manton misspelled it again. His attorney, Arthur Ward, tried to present a case for manslaughter, but the jury found Manton Guilty of murder. He was sentenced to hang, but that sentence was commuted to life in prison, where he died in 1947.

Manuel, Peter Thomas Anthony, 1927-58, Scot. Peter Thomas Anthony Manuel was born in New York in 1927 to immigrant Scottish parents. During the Depression, Manuel's parents were forced to return to Scotland where they remained. By the time Manuel was sixteen, a probation officer remarked that he had the worst juvenile record he had ever seen. By age thirty, his record included prison sentences for burglary, theft, indecent assault, and rape.

Scottish murderer Peter Manuel, killer of eight people.

In January 1956, Manuel committed a more serious crime. In Glasgow he met 17-year-old Anne Kneilands waiting for her boyfriend. He persuaded her to join him for coffee. As the two walked toward her home later, Manuel dragged the girl into a wooded area where he bashed in her skull with a piece of iron. Manuel was routinely questioned by police, but he did not become a suspect in the murder.

The following summer, Manuel acquired a gun for the first time. In September he and two other men and a woman burglarized an unoccupied home south of Glasgow. After breaking into the first home, Manuel suggested burglarizing a second. When his friends declined, Manuel went alone. The home he selected belonged to the Watt family. Mr. Watt, a master baker, had left that day for a fishing trip to Lochgilphead, eighty miles away. Manuel shot the three people he found there, Mrs. Marion Watt, her sister, Margaret Brown, and 16-year-old Vivienne Brown, at close range. The two older women died immediately and the teenager was mortally wounded. Neighbors and a cleaning lady who discovered the bodies the next day called police. The investigation indicated that although the women's attacker had disarranged their clothing, they had not been sexually assaulted. Some valuables had been stolen.

When the police discovered that Mr. Watt had had affairs, he became a suspect. They soon proved it was possible for him to have driven back to Glasgow, murdered his family, and returned to the small fishing town by the following morning. They also located witnesses who said they had seen Watt on the ferry that night. Watt was then held at Barlinnie Prison, the very place where Peter Manuel was serving an eighteen-month sentence for burglary. On Oct. 8, Watt's attorney received a letter from Manuel offering information about the murders to Watt. As the attorney and

Isabelle Cooke, 17, a Manuel murder victim.

Watt listened to Manuel, they became convinced Manuel was the murderer or had been at least been present. Manuel refused to reveal the identity of the alleged perpetrator, but Watt was released from custody.

A year later, in early December, Manuel traveled to Newcastle-upon-Tyne, England. Although he was never formally charged with the crime, authorities believe he murdered cab driver Stanley Dunn, whose body was found some twenty miles from Newcastle. Dunn had been shot and his throat was slashed. Shortly after Manuel returned to Scotland, on Dec. 28, 1957, 17-year-old Isabelle Cooke disappeared. The girl left her home in a suburb of Glasgow to meet her boyfriend and go with him to a dance in the nearby town of Uddingston. The following day some of her belongings, including a slip and underpants, were found, but no trace of her body was discovered. As police continued the search for her, Manuel struck again. This time, on

Dec. 31, Manuel chose the home of 45-year-old Peter Smart, his wife, Doris, and their 10-year-old son, Michael.

Mrs. Marion Watt, killed by Peter Manuel.

The Smarts had gone to sleep early in preparation for a trip the following day. Apparently as they slept, Manuel broke into their home in Uddingston and shot them to death. Because they were expected to be out of town, no one contacted authorities until Smart failed to return to work on Jan. 6. When police investigated and found the bodies, they also found evidence that the murderer had returned to the scene of the crime: the beds had been walked on with muddy boots, a mattress slashed, food eaten, and the family cat fed.

While conducting the murder investigation, police received information that Manuel, usually without funds, had been seen spending freely. Some of the crisp £5 notes he used were retrieved from a bar he frequented and traced to money Peter Smart had drawn out of his bank for his family's trip. Manuel was arrested on Jan. 13, 1958, and confessed to the murders of the Smarts, the Watts, Isabelle Cooke, and Anne Kneilands. Manuel's trial opened on May 12, 1958, before Lord Cameron.

Mrs. Margaret Brown, killed by Peter Manuel.

Gordon Gillies and Ronald Sutherland conducted the prosecution and Harald Leslie and Malcolm Morrison defended Manuel. On May 22, Manuel dismissed his defense counsel and represented himself. Despite his insistence that Watt had killed his own family and that the police had forced his confession from him, he was convicted on May 26 of all but the Kneilands murder. He was hanged on July 11, 1958, at Barlinnie Prison.

Man With Five Hundred Names, The, See: Edel, Frederick.

Marcelino, Julian, 1902- , U.S. Explaining that he "felt funny in the head" at the time, Julian Marcelino of Seattle decided to kill everyone in sight. Armed with a pair of crudely fashioned knives, the 30-year-old Filipino entered the Midway Hotel on Nov. 24, 1932, in a rage. He proceeded to the room of Pito Gualto, whom he had accused of stealing $300. Without warning, he stabbed Gualto in the heart and then wounded his nephew, Christolo Bayson. "I was sitting in my room with my uncle when Marcelino came in," Bayson said. "They had been quarreling this morning—about what I don't know...Marcelino said nothing. But he had that funny look. All of a sudden he pulled out his knife and stabbed my uncle."

Marcelino fled the hotel, running haywire down the crowded skid row streets. He stabbed grocer W.J. Morris on the sidewalk, and also a bystander who failed to get out of the way in time. He assaulted four more men, throwing the street into confusion as people ran for cover.

The Seattle police arrived on the scene just as Marcelino was about to kill a Japanese man identified as L. Kitamura.

Julian Marcelino, standing, right, in a holding cell with five other murderers, 1932.

Officer Gordon Jensen, driving home from a football game, helped subdue Marcelino. "He fought like a mad wolf," Jensen recounted. "He had more than human strength." The seven-inch razor Marcelino used had been manufactured in the Philippines and was known in the area as a bolo. Sixth Avenue and Jackson Street resembled a combat zone as ambulances rushed fifteen people to nearby hospitals. The six murder victims were taken to the county morgue.

Julian Marcelino was led under heavy guard to the King County Jail. He was declared sane and tried for first-degree murder. Sentenced to life imprisonment, he entered Washington State Penitentiary on Apr. 22, 1933. Three years later, on Mar. 11, 1936, he was transferred to the Eastern State Hospital after examining psychiatrists declared him insane. Sixteen days later he was granted a conditional parole and deported to the Philippines.

Marek, Martha Lowenstein, 1904-38, Aust. Martha Lowenstein was a foundling who, as a teenager, became the ward of an old man named Moritz Fritsch, a department store owner in Vienna. In exchange for her sexual favors, Fritsch dressed the girl well and sent her to an elite finishing school. Soon after Fritsch died, leaving Lowenstein his entire estate, she married Emil Marek, an engineer who helped her spend it all very quickly. They planned an insurance fraud that called for Marek to cut off his own leg. With the cut half made, he had to ask for her help. But the doctor refused to believe that an accidental amputation would produce three separate cuts. The couple ended up in jail for four months for trying to bribe a nurse to testify that the doctor had caused the cuts. They got only enough insurance money to pay their court costs and accepted that amount only when the insurance company threatened to have Fritsch's body exhumed.

In 1932, the couple was close to destitution when Emil died, apparently of tuberculosis, and Martha collected a small insurance payment. Their daughter Ingeborg Marek, soon died as well. But the most profitable death for Martha

Austrian mass murderess Martha Marek, seated left, appearing in court, 1938.

was that of her aunt, who left her a house and small fortune. The money was soon gone, however, and Martha used the house to take in boarders. They, too, died. She stole her own paintings and tried to collect on the insurance, but an investigator found them and Martha was jailed. Upon learning that she was in jail, the son of one of her boarders reported to the police that he thought Martha had killed his mother. The bodies of all the deceased associated with Martha Marek were exhumed and found to contain thallium. Fortunately, an insurance investigator recalled that she had two children, and he located the son just as he was dying of thallium poisoning. The doctors were able to save him. His mother was tried, found Guilty, and beheaded on Dec. 6, 1938.

Marjeram, Albert Edward, 1907-30, Brit. The charged man's mother swore her son was insane and that, as a child, he had to be tied down to be kept from committing acts of violence. As a grown man of twenty-three, Albert Edward Marjeram had committed the ultimate act of violence when he stabbed young Edith May Parker in the back and left her dead on Dartford Heath. But the jury said Marjeram was sane when he killed the woman on Apr. 11, 1930, and found him Guilty of murder. He was subsequently executed at Wandsworth Prison.

Markle, John, 1942-87, U.S. On Nov. 15, 1987, John Markle, son of actress Mercedes McCambridge, killed his two daughters, his wife, and himself, leaving behind a long letter to his mother saying that everything he had done to impress her—including how well he handled her accounts—had been ignored.

It was the handling of her accounts that led Markle to the financial ruin that caused him to lose his job as vice president at Little Rock's Stephens, Inc., the country's fifteenth largest investment banking firm and the largest one off Wall Street. Markle, responsible for the company's in-house investments, allegedly placed his mother's money in an out-of-state account. He would make investments for her and the company at the same time, without distinguishing which money was the company's and which his mother's. If the investment made money he would credit it to his mother's account, and if it lost money he would place the losses on the Stephens' accounts. He was fired on Nov. 13, two days before he committed suicide.

Markle called his lawyer at four in the morning after he had killed his two girls, 13-year-old Amy and 9-year-old Suzanne, and his wife, Chris, forty-five, and told him of his plan to kill himself. Police arrived at the house fifteen minutes later. Strange forewarnings of death were found alongside the slaughtered family of four. An eerie rubber Halloween mask lay next to Markle's body and the horror film *Nightmare on Elm Street* was ready to play on the video screen next to the three guns Markle used for the four murders.

Markle's mother won an Oscar in 1949 for her role in *All the King's Men* and was the voice of the devil in *The Exorcist*. She and Markle's father divorced when the boy was five. She later married Fletcher Markle, an orchestra conductor, and soon afterward sent John to a boarding school in Arizona. Reportedly Markle often told his friends that his childhood had been unhappy and that he wanted a better life for his own children.

Coroner Steve Nawojczyk called the murders-suicide "an act of macabre benevolence. He wanted to spare the girls the publicity."

Marks, Lawrence, 1888-1938, U.S. After thirteen hours of police interrogation, Lawrence Marks, forty-nine, finally confessed to the strangulation of 8-year-old Paula Magagna of Brooklyn. The ex-convict had been out of jail for less than two months when he met Paula at the BMT subway station near DeKalb and Wyckoff avenues on the afternoon of July 31, 1937.

Pretending to be a meter reader, Marks approached the girl. "I asked her where she lived, and she said 'down there,'" pointing to the basement flat of a tenement house. He asked her if she knew where the gas meters might be. Paula said yes, and Marks followed her into the cellar where he reached for a short piece of rope. "I just had an impulse to do it," he said. "I couldn't help it."

Paula's naked body was found a half-hour later on top of a baby carriage. The coroner found signs of sexual assault, which Marks strenuously denied. After wiping the blood from his hands, Marks took a trolley car home, where he was plagued by guilt. "I considered giving myself up to the police," he said. After three days, he attacked another 8-year-old girl. This time Marks was caught in the act by his landlady, Mrs. Miriam Saratkin, who burst into his bedroom and rescued the girl.

Saratkin notified detectives at the Gates Avenue police station. Marks had fled the premises, but returned four days later, on Aug. 8. The detectives were waiting for him. They took Marks to the Wilson Avenue station where he underwent a relentless grilling by Captain George Gallagher and Assistant District Attorney Frederick Kopf. Marks' criminal record revealed that he had spent at least twenty-one of the last twenty-seven years in prison for rape, theft, prison escape, and other offenses dating to 1910. He was twice paroled before receiving a general release from Sing Sing on June 13, 1937.

After Marks confessed to the murder of Paula, homicide detectives tried to link him to the recent deaths of two other

Brooklyn girls, 5-year-old Florence McDonnell on Feb. 4, 1932, and 6-year-old Barbara Wiles on Mar. 28, 1933, whose murders were quite similar to Paula's. "I know I am going to the chair," Marks argued, "Why should I hold back anything? I know nothing at all about those cases!"

Marks was convicted of first-degree murder on Nov. 9, 1937, and executed at Sing Sing on June 2, 1938.

Marshall, Franklin, 1941- , and **Borum, Alfonso**, 1940- , and **Williams, Robert**, prom. 1958, U.S. In May 1958, In Ho Oh, a Korean-born graduate student at the University of Pennsylvania, left his uncle's Philadelphia apartment to mail a letter. The mailbox was little more than a block away, but Oh never made it home. A gang of teenagers accosted the 26-year-old and demanded money from him. They dragged Oh behind a parked car and beat him with their fists and kicked him repeatedly. Oh's pockets and socks were frisked for money and the gang members beat him over the head with a blackjack and a lead pipe. Oh died minutes after the attack.

Within two days, police had arrested eleven youths between the ages of fifteen and nineteen, and they were ordered to stand trial as adults on the charge of murder. Franklin Marshall, seventeen, Alfonso Borum, eighteen, and Robert Williams, nineteen, were convicted of second-degree murder and sentenced to up to twenty years in prison. Of eleven men accused of the slaying, one received the death penalty, three others were sentenced to life imprisonment, and the other four received shorter prison sentences.

Martin, Lee Roy, 1937-72, U.S. The small textile community of Gaffney, S.C., was terrorized by four stranglings in 1967-68. In March 1967, 32-year-old Annie Lucille Dedmond of Rutherford, N.C., disappeared. On May 20, 1967, her nude body was found by the road between Gaffney and Union, N.C. The victim's husband, Robert Zane Dedmond, was convicted of manslaughter. During the last week of January 1968, 14-year-old Nancy Christine Rhinehart was reported missing, and on Feb. 7, 20-year-old Nancy Carol Parris was also reported missing.

Bill Gibbons, managing editor of the Gaffney *Ledger,* received a telephone call during his lunch hour on Feb. 8. The male caller told him to get out three pieces of paper, because he was going to give him three stories, then the mysterious caller gave the newsman detailed directions to the location of the two latest victims, along with details of Dedmond's murder. The sheriff found Rhinehart's and

Parris' bodies just outside Gaffney. Frightened residents purchased guns and escorted their children to and from school.

The murders continued when 15-year-old Opal Dianne Buckson was kidnapped on Feb. 13, 1968. Opal's sister said she saw Opal thrown into the trunk of a black truck. Three days later, officers found the girl's naked, strangled body, but two Gaffney men located the truck and reported the license plate number to police. About 12:15 p.m. on Feb. 16, 31-year-old Lee Roy Martin was arrested at the Musgrove Cotton Mill in Gaffney, where he worked part-time.

Martin pleaded guilty, was convicted for the murders of Buckson and Dedmond, and sentenced to two consecutive life sentences. The latter's husband, who had served ten months of an eighteen-year sentence in the Union County prison camp, was released. In May 1969, Martin again pleaded guilty, was convicted for the murders of Rhinehart and Parris, and was sentenced to two more consecutive life terms. On May 31, 1972, Martin was killed at the Central Correctional Institution in Columbia, S.C. He was stabbed in the chest and back.

Marwood, Ronald Henry, 1933-59, Brit. On the evening of Dec. 14, 1958, 23-year-old London policeman Raymond Henry Summers was called out to break up a fight between two gangs on Seven Sisters Road in North London. Some of the brawlers were armed with knives, bottles, and knucklebusters. While trying to intervene, the unarmed Summers was fatally stabbed in the back. One participant in the fight, Ronald Henry Marwood, wanted for questioning by police, disappeared soon after the murder. On Jan. 27, 1959, he walked into the Caledonian Road police station and confessed to stabbing Summers to death.

Murderer Ronald Henry Marwood.

According to Marwood he had spent the evening, the first anniversary of his wedding, drinking with friends. He estimated that he had consumed twenty half-pints of ale by the time the fight broke out. He told police that he had been carrying a knife in his coat pocket and when Summers grabbed onto a friend of his during the melee, he pulled his hand from his pocket, forgetting that he was holding a knife, and, meaning to push the officer away, stabbed him instead.

Marwood's trial began at the Old Bailey in March 1959 before Justice Gorman. Christmas Humphreys prosecuted and Neil Lawson defended Marwood, who claimed police altered his statement into a confession of murder. The jury was out three hours before returning convicting Marwood of capital murder, requiring the death penalty. The verdict led to some of the largest demonstrations against capital punishment England had ever seen. In some part, demonstrators expressed outrage at the unpopular Homicide Act of 1957 which made the murder of a policeman punishable by a mandatory death sentence, and placed the power of reprieve solely in the hands of the Home Secretary. A petition signed by 10,000 people, including 150 members of Parliament, failed to persuade the Home Secretary, R.A. Butler, to grant Marwood a reprieve. With scenes near riot both within and without Pentonville Prison, Marwood was hanged there on May 8, 1959.

Marymont, Marcus, c.1921- , Brit. U.S. Air Force Master Sergeant Marcus Marymont, along with his wife and three children, was stationed at the U.S. Air Force base at Sculthorpe, Norfolk in January 1956. That July, Marymont met Cynthia Taylor at a club in Maidenhead, and Taylor, who was estranged from her husband, became Marymont's mistress in December. His wife, 43-year-old Mary Helen Marymont, discovered a letter from her husband to the 23-year-old Taylor in April 1958, and confronted him about it. Soon afterward, Marymont began to poison his wife with arsenic, and she began to suffer from gastric pains. Mary Marymont was taken to a hospital on June 9, 1958, where she died the same day. An autopsy was performed over Marymont's objections, revealing arsenic poisoning had been administered for at least a

Marcus Marymont, wife poisoner.

month. Marymont was arrested and tried by a U.S. General Court-Martial. During the trial, several witnesses said the defendant had tried to purchase arsenic or asked them where arsenic could be obtained. Marymont was convicted of murder and unlawful conduct with Taylor. He was sentenced to life and returned to the U.S. to serve his term at Leavenworth Prison in Kansas.

Mason, Alexander Campbell (AKA: Scottie Mason; Scottie Munro), c.1901- , Brit. Alexander Mason was found Guilty of burglary in January 1922 and sentenced to twelve months in prison. After he was released on May 5, 1923, Mason went to London to stay with his friend, James Vivian, another burglar who had been convicted in the same crime. Mason insisted that he wanted a gun, so Vivian bought him a revolver. Within a few days, neither had any money. Vivian was sick on May 9, so Mason went out alone, taking the revolver and Vivian's gold-handled cane. He got into Jacob Dickey's cab near the Trocadero Restaurant in London and asked to be taken to Brixton. When they arrived, Mason shot Dickey several times in the head. He fled, leaving the cane, the gun, a glove, and a crowbar. Police traced the distinctive cane to Vivian, who told them what he knew about the crime and testified against Mason in court. The trial began at the Old Bailey on July 11 and Mason was convicted on July 14, 1923. The sentence was death, but it was later commuted to life imprisonment, and Mason was freed in October 1937.

Mason, Carlton, 1936- , U.S. Located in a small town on the Hudson River twenty-five miles north of Manhattan, the Lakeside Cottage School cared for dependent children. Carlton Mason, sixteen, had lived at the school for two years when he sexually assaulted and murdered 8-year-old Marjorie Boudreau and 5-year-old Esther Nagy, on Mar. 8, 1953, in a stretch of woods near Spring Valley, N.Y.

Carlton lured the girls to an area of the woods that was off-limits to young children. "I told Marjorie that her father was waiting in a house at the corner of the field behind a large pile of brush," he told police investigators who reconstructed the crime.

The boy entertained sexual notions about Marjorie, but the sobs of Esther distracted him. When Esther refused to go away, Carlton strangled the girl and then stabbed her in the back with a butcher knife. When Marjorie saw the bloody knife, she screamed. Carlton strangled her, then hit her over the head with a rock.

Carlton later joined a search party sent out to look for the missing girls. Police became suspicious when he was unable to account for his movements for the half hour before the disappearance of the girls. He also failed to produce the hunting knife known to have been in his possession. The state police grilled Carlton, but his answers were evasive. Then Sheriff J. Henry Mock played upon the boy's love of sports to elicit a confession from him.

Accompanied by Deputy Sheriff Philip Beers, Carlton led the sheriff and a team of cameramen to the murder scene.

When he thought Mock's back was turned, he picked up the murder weapon and flipped it into a nearby pond. "I had been watching him and quickly fished the knife out," the sheriff said. Carlton was driven to New York, where he signed a written confession in the presence of the Rockland County district attorney. School officials could not believe Carlton had committed murder. "It's incredible," said Russell Wight, director of Lakeside. "He never led anyone to believe that he was capable of this kind of thing."

Carlton was arraigned on a charge of first-degree murder and incarcerated at the Rockland County Jail in New York City without bail. When the case went to trial, the judge accepted a plea of guilty to second-degree murder, believing that no jury would convict a boy so young. The 16-year-old received a sixty-year-to-life prison sentence for the murders of Marjorie Boudreau and Esther Nagy. Carlton served twenty years before his parole from the Auburn Correctional and Reception Center on Jan. 30, 1973.

Masset, Louise, 1863-1900, Brit. Louise Masset, a 36-year-old private tutor in London, had a son out of wedlock. Within a few weeks after little Manfred's birth, she had put him into the care of Helen Gentle of Tottenham, paying the fees out of money received from the boy's French father. Masset herself lived with her sister in Stoke Newington. She became involved with her next door neighbor, 19-year-old Eudore Lucas. On Oct. 16, 1899, Masset wrote to Gentle that the boy's father wanted him to be raised with a cousin, and that she would collect him in two weeks. They agreed that Masset would take the boy from outside a pub at Stamford Hill and go straight to London Bridge Station. On Oct. 24th she purchased a black shawl, and the next day she arranged for Lucas to meet her at Brighton on Oct. 28.

On Oct. 27, Gentle turned Manfred over to his mother, who took him to London Bridge Station. Mother and son were seen around the station for several hours before they disappeared. One witness later said that the boy was very fretful and angry at being with the woman. At 6:30 p.m., Manfred's naked body, wrapped in a black shawl, was found in the ladies' room at Dalston Junction Station. He had been struck on the head and then suffocated. Near the body lay a brick made from furnace residue, like the ones used to decorate the garden at Masset's Stoke Newington home. The boy's clothing was found in a brown bag at Brighton Station. Publicity about the dead child brought Gentle to view the body and identify it. Meanwhile, Masset spent the weekend in Brighton with Lucas, then returned to London, but went to another sister's house in Croydon, where she was arrested two days later.

Louise Masset said in court that she had turned Manfred over at London Bridge Station to two women named Browning, who were starting a home for children, and that she had paid them an advance of £12. She said she had met them when playing in the park on one of her weekly visits with her son. She had let Manfred think he was going to his father in order not to hurt her feelings. She said she had not thought to obtain a receipt for the £12. The defense emphasized that Masset had no motive for killing her son, and said that the "baby farmers" had probably done the deed. The jury disagreed, and found Louise Masset Guilty of murder. She was hanged on Jan. 9, 1900, after confessing that she had, indeed, killed her son. Ellen Hayes, an Inspector of Prisons, wrote years later that Masset had told her that she had killed him to spare him the teasing and discrimination that went with being illegitimate, though others were certain she did it in hopes of marrying Lucas.

Massie, Thomas, 1900-44, U.S. In the fall of 1931, Hawaii, then an American Territory, was a wild mixture of cultures—Hawaiian, Japanese, Filipino, Portuguese, Korean, and American. Racial unrest was the norm. In early September, the city of Honolulu began to experience a rash of rapes in which white women were dragged into an old touring car occupied by five "little swarthy men," taken to secluded spots, and sexually attacked. On the night of Sept. 21, 1931, attractive 20-year-old Mrs. Thalia Massie, wife of Navy officer Lieutenant Thomas Massie, left a party at the Ala Wai Inn to cool off by taking a walk alone down the poorly lighted John Edna Road. Suddenly an old Buick drove alongside her and stopped. Five men were inside of it: Horace Ida, a Japanese who owned the large touring car; David Takai, another Japanese; Henry Chang, a Chinese; and Hawaiians Ben Anekuelo and Joe Kahahawai, a tough, well-built young man who was a professional boxer.

Four of the men leaped out of the car and grabbed Mrs. Massie, throwing her into the back seat of the car and speeding off to the Old Animal Quarantine Station which Mrs. Massie recognized. She was dragged out of the car and when she offered resistance Kahahawai sent a powerful punch to her jaw, breaking it. Thalia Massie went limp and the five men pinned her to the ground and then each took turns raping the small woman. After her attackers departed, Mrs. Massie, battered and bleeding, managed to stagger to Ala Moana Drive and flag down a car. She was taken home and Lieutenant Massie, still attending the party, was called. Massie rushed home to find his wife's face battered, her lips cut and bleeding, her eyes swollen and blackened. "I thought at first that she had been hit by a truck," Massie would later recall.

Thalia Massie collapsed into her husband's arms, sobbing: "It's awful, Tommy, the shame! I just want to die!" She then related the story of being raped by five natives of mixed race. She produced a scrap of paper on which she had written the number 58895, the license of the car the men had been driving. Police were summoned and the Buick was tracked down to Ida who quickly involved the others. These same five men had been arrested many times in the past, separately and in a group, for committing a number of sex crimes. All five had been previously accused of raping a Mrs. Peebles, but because of "lack of evidence" had been released. The five men were brought before Mrs. Massie, who identified each one of them as her attackers, adding: "I'd know those savages anywhere."

The news of this rape shocked the island and the story made front-page news in mainland U.S. newspapers. What was doubly shocking was that the Massies were members of the social elite in Hawaii and came from distinguished, upper-class families. Lieutenant Thomas Massie was a quiet, gentle officer who had graduated with honors from the Naval Academy at Annapolis and came from a wealthy, much-respected Kentucky family. Thalia had married Massie when only sixteen, but she had the blessing of her mother, Mrs. Grace Hubbard Bell Granville Fortescue, a wealthy society woman whose husband was a retired army major. Mrs. Fortescue herself came from a prestigious Long Island family and was the niece of inventor Alexander Graham Bell. She and her daughter Thalia were listed in the Social Register.

While the rapists were jailed pending trial, Fortescue flew to Hawaii to be near her daughter. She was infuriated that such a brutal crime could be perpetrated against a white woman and said so publicly and to her friends in Hawaii, all members of the island's social elite. Fortescue also met with Admiral Yates Stirling, commander of the Navy base at Pearl Harbor. Stirling was livid about the attack. He told Fortescue that "our first inclination is to seize these brutes and string them up on trees but we must give the authorities the chance to carry out the law. It will be slow and exasperating, but we must be patient."

On Nov. 19, 1931, the five accused men were brought to trial. Hospital doctors at the trial were of little help to the prosecution, stating that, indeed, Mrs. Massie had been attacked but they had found no real evidence of rape, no presence of sperm in her body. She was not, as popularly thought, pregnant at the time of the attack. Five white men and seven men of mixed races listened to arguments for fifteen days and then decided that there was not sufficient evidence to convict the defendants, even with Thalia Massie's sworn statements that each of the accused had raped her. This travesty of justice inflamed the white

community on Oahu. The rage over the jury decision was centered on the seven jurists of mixed races who, it was said, had freed the rapists because they were of their own race or nationalities. Admiral Stirling summed up the attitude of the white community by later writing: "The criminal assault of a white woman by the five dark-skinned citizens had gone unpunished by the Courts. Sympathies have been aroused in favor of the accused men. Conviction was thus impossible."

The defendants did not help their cause by making sneering remarks about Mrs. Massie and strutting about Honolulu as if they were victors of a boxing match. (These men were later portrayed in a far-from-the-truth TV movie as innocent youths who had been pilloried by a white society. In truth they all had police records as sex offenders.) The conduct of the defendants so enraged a group of Navy officers that, on the night of Dec. 13, 1931, a group of officers seized Horace Ida and drove him to a remote spot where he was beaten and pistol-whipped into unconsciousness and then left to make his way back to Honolulu. Ida had been dealt with in the same manner as had been Mrs. Massie, proper and ironic retribution in the minds of the men who attacked him.

Meanwhile, Mrs. Massie showed the signs of a nervous breakdown. The trial had been a tremendous strain on her and she had been held up to ridicule by defense attorneys whose snide inferences portrayed her as a loose woman—a flirt who invited the advances of white Navy officers. Rumors following the trial had it that Mrs. Massie had not been raped by men of other races but by a group of white Navy men, and that she had put the blame on the hapless Hawaiians. Thomas Massie was also shattered during and after the trial. He was a taciturn young man who said little, keeping his emotional problems to himself. On rare occasions he stated that his wife had been victimized not only by the rapists but by the publicity attending the trial; her reputation was ruined and he sought some sort of justice beyond the court system which had failed them.

Massie enlisted the aid of two sailors, Edward Lord and Albert Jones, who served under his command and held him in great respect. Massie had learned that Joe Kahahawai, the worst offender of the rapist group, reported each day to the court as a condition of his release. On the morning of Jan. 8, 1932, Massie drove up to the courthouse with Jones. Massie was behind the wheel of a rented Buick, disguised as a chauffeur. Jones, in civilian clothes, got out of the car when Kahahawai appeared and stopped him before the Hawaiian entered the court building, showing him a fake summons to appear before a special tribunal. Kahahawai, who understood little English, shrugged and got into the Buick. Massie drove to a bungalow Fortescue had rented in Ala Moana Valley.

Navy officer Thomas H. Massie and wife Thalia at their wedding.

Thalia and Thomas Massie.

Mrs. Grace Fortescue

Sailors Edward J. Lord, left, and Albert O. Jones.

Murder victim Joseph Kahahawai.

Governor Lawrence Judd

TERITORIAL POLICE

MAJOR ROSS, COMMANDING

SUMMONS TO APPEAR

KAHAHAWAI - JOE

Life is a Mysterious and Exciting Affair, and Anything Can Be a Thrill if You Know How to Look for it and What to Do With Opportunity When It Comes

Massie trial defendants with Clarence Darrow at right.

The bogus summons that lured Joe Kahahawai to his death.

Lord posted himself on guard in front of the bungalow while Massie and Jones escorted Kahahawai inside. The Hawaiian stood before a desk behind which Massie sat, acting as inquisitor, while Jones held a gun on the burly boxer. Said Massie: "Okay, we're here to get the truth out of you and to beat it out of you if necessary. If you don't talk before the police get here, we'll beat you to ribbons. Now tell me, who kicked my wife, broke her jaw, and raped her?"

Kahahawai shook his head and said he was innocent.

Massie persisted, stating: "You're a prizefighter. Of course it was you who hit her. Be a man and admit it!"

Kahahawai then broke down, according to the later statements of Massie and Jones, mumbling: "Yeah, I did it all right. We all did it, all right. We attacked your wife."

What happened next has been the subject of courtroom debate and historical argument for decades. Massie went into a blind rage at hearing this offhand admission of a brutal crime against his wife and grabbed a revolver and shot Kahahawai once in the chest, killing him on the spot. Jones was interviewed many years later and claimed that Kahahawai leaned or lurched toward Massie at this point in the questioning while Jones, who was holding a revolver on the man, instinctively squeezed the trigger, shooting the boxer dead. Fortescue and seaman Lord appeared in the living room of the bungalow at the sound of the shot and, after a hurried conference, decided to dump the body in a remote spot. At first Jones and Lord put the body in a bathtub, stripped it, and washed away all the blood. Then they wrapped it in a blanket, and placed the body in the back seat of the Buick. Massie, Fortescue, Jones, and Lord then drove toward Koko Head, thinking to dump the corpse in a canyon there.

Police, however, had already been looking for Massie, Jones, and Kahahawai, who had been seen leaving the courthouse at 8:30 a.m. by Kahahawai's cousin. They intercepted the Massie car and quickly discovered the body of the dead boxer. Fortescue, Massie, Jones, and Lord were taken into custody and charged with murder. The wealthy Fortescue immediately hired the most famous criminal attorney alive, Clarence Darrow, who flew from Chicago to Hawaii to defend the foursome. The Massie case became an overnight sensation, a national *cause célèbre*, with the races violently divided. Riots broke out in Honolulu and in various parts of the U.S. where race tension and strife was high.

Massie made a brief statement: "I'm sorry that this man has been shot, but it was no more than he asked for and deserved." By this statement, Massie established the line of defense in the trial, one which Darrow would vigorously pursue, that of the unwritten law where a man defends his wife's honor at all costs and at all hazards to his own safety

and well-being. The U.S. Navy, rather than disavowing the actions of one of its officers, backed Massie to the hilt. Stated Admiral Stirling: "An Hawaiian rapist had been killed by the family of the tortured girl because they felt that legal justice was impossible." In Washington, D.C., Admiral William Lee Pratt, chief of Naval operations, went even further, issuing the following statement to the press: "American men will not stand for the violation of their women under any circumstances. For this crime they have taken the matter into their own hands repeatedly when they have felt that the law has failed to do justice."

Sympathies were generally with the defendants, although the Honolulu *Star Bulletin* thundered against the killing of Kahahawai, saying: "People who take the law into their own hands always make a mess of it...There is no justification in civilized society for lynch law methods or premeditated killing of any kind." Stated the Honolulu *Advertiser:* "Vengeance which takes the form of private execution cannot be condoned." Most were concerned with how Clarence Darrow would defend his clients who were obviously guilty of murder. The greatest lawyer in the land had been reluctant to take the case, stating privately that he did not like "the smell of it." But his financial difficulties at the time were accute and he accepted Mrs. Fortescue's fee of $25,000 and an all-expenses paid trip to Hawaii for himself and his wife.

On Apr. 5, 1932, Darrow appeared with his clients before Judge Charles Davis, stating that Massie had killed Kahahawai out of "mental illness brought on by extreme provocation." As usual, Darrow's magnetic presence in the courtroom held everyone in fascination. He walked about in his rumpled clothes, his silvery hair falling in front of his forehead. Darrow intoned dramatically the series of events that led up to the killing of Kahahawai, emphasizing the awful ordeal undergone by Mrs. Massie at the hands of savage rapists, depicting how Mrs. Massie had been humiliated by the traumatic experience and how she had been emotionally unstable thereafter.

The same kind of emotional instability seized the mind of Thomas Massie, Darrow pointed out, one which clouded his reason and judgment and led to the shooting of the murder victim.

Throughout Darrow's orations and the court proceedings, Mrs. Fortescue proudly held up her head. She was dressed in the height of fashion, wearing a cloche hat and a red dress. Massie sat immobile, his blank expression interrupted only when he bit his thin lips on occasion. The sailors, Lord and Jones, sat passive, staring ahead. The burning black eyes of Joe Kahahawai's parents were constantly focused upon the defendants as they sat in the spectator's gallery. Across the aisle from them sat Thalia Massie, dressed in black. Darrow's brilliant defense worked only to reduce the status of the charge against the defendants. Prosecutor John Kelley was obviously overwhelmed by Darrow's magical addresses and confined himself to the facts in the case. That was enough for a conviction, although it was not the first-degree conviction Kelley had sought.

All four were convicted of second-degree murder and sentenced to ten years imprisonment. Darrow immediately stated that he would appeal the case to the U.S. Supreme Court but officials had had enough of this case. Riots against blacks, orientals, and Hawaiians had broken out throughout the islands and on the mainland. Further court hearings would only ferment more race riots and unrest, prosecuting attorneys told Darrow after the conviction. They recommended leniency toward the defendants and this plea was acted upon by the much-harrassed Governor Judd who was tired of calling out hundreds of national guardsmen to quell riots taking place over the Massie case. Judd signed an order that commuted the sentences of the four convicted murderers, reducing their time to one hour to be served in the courtroom dock. The defendants were placed in the dock and sat motionless and silent for an hour and then walked free.

Fortescue and Thalia Massie immediately sailed back to the U.S. mainland. Massie and the two seaman remained on duty in the islands. Massie himself would remain in the Navy, later serving on the U.S.S. *New Mexico,* a battleship which saw heavy action in WWII. He later died in obscurity. Thalia did not remain married to Thomas Massie for long. She filed for divorce in Reno, Nev., which was granted on Feb. 23, 1934. At the time, she told reporters that the crime against her had caused so much strain between her and her husband that their marriage disintegrated.

"Do you think you'll marry again soon?" a reporter asked Thalia Massie.

"Sure," she snapped back sullenly. "I'm going to marry Clark Gable, didn't you hear."

That night the despondent woman went to a Reno nightclub and ordered a drink into which she poured poison. She collapsed shortly after drinking the mixture and was rushed to St. Mary's Hospital where she recovered. Thalia Massie then took a train to New York where she booked passage on the *Roma,* a liner sailing to Italy. At sea, Mrs. Massie told other passengers that she did not care to live any longer. She was found hours later bleeding to death in her cabin, her wrists slashed. She was saved by a ship's nurse and Dr. Valliga, the ship's captain. Thalia Massie survived her deep depressions, however, and later moved to Eugene, Ore., living under her maiden name, Thalia Bell. She later married a man many years her junior and died on July 3, 1963. Although it was not listed as such, Thalia's

death may have been a suicide. According to one newspaper account, "she was found in the bathroom of her apartment, barbiturate bottles scattered about her." Her proud and aristocratic mother, Mrs. Grace Fortescue, had already died years earlier.

Mathis, James R., 1970-82, U.S. A 12-year-old honor student about to be named by his grammar school as crosswalk "patrolman of the year" shot and killed his mother, wounded his father and killed himself after being spanked for riding a family motorcycle without permission. The shootings occurred in Hazel Dell, Wash., a small town located north of Vancouver, on May 18, 1982. Armed with two shotguns and a machete, Mathis shot his parents as they arrived on their motorcycles at the driveway of their home. Darlene Mathis, thirty-six, was pronounced dead by Clark County chief civil deputy Robert Songer. James H. Mathis, thirty-two, sustained only superficial wounds. "Jimmie" Mathis disappeared inside after shooting his parents and turned the shotgun on himself.

Mationg, Florencio Lopez, 1934-   , and **Bono, Victor Jerald**, 1939-   , and **Montoya, Alfred**, 1934-   , and **Montoya, Harold**, 1937-   , U.S. On June 17, 1967, two U.S. border patrol officers were stationed at a roadblock and apparently halted four men suspected of smuggling narcotics. The four men, Florencio Mationg, Victor Bono, and Alfred and Harold Montoya abducted the officers and took them to an isolated cabin in the mountains in Riverside County, Calif. Just a few hours after they were kidnapped, 21-year-old George Azrak and 24-year-old Theodore Newton, Jr. were handcuffed to a stove and shot through the head. Both Mationg and Bono were placed on the FBI's Most Wanted list before they were apprehended on July 16, 1967, in an apartment in Los Angeles. The two were tried in Los Angeles along with Alfred and Harold Montoya. On Nov. 6, 1976, Mationg and Bono each received two consecutive life terms, plus a thirty-year term. On Nov. 22, 1967, the Montoya brothers were each sentenced to two thirty-year sentences, to be served concurrently.

Matthews, Rod, 1972-   , U.S. For many weeks, 14-year-old Rod Matthews of Dedham, Mass., wondered what it would be like to kill someone. In Fall 1986, the troubled youth confided his desire to his disbelieving classmates, Rob

Peterson and Jonathan Cash. Matthews became determined to carry out his plan after viewing a bizarre videotape called *Faces of Death*, which graphically depicted actual human and animal tortures and executions.

Matthews considered three possible murder victims, deciding on 14-year-old Shaun Ouillette. On Nov. 20, 1986, he lured Shaun into the woods, supposedly to give him fireworks. Matthews then bludgeoned the boy to death with a Louisville Slugger baseball bat. The body remained in the woods for several days until Matthews decided to share his secret with his two friends. Following a pep rally at Canton High School, the three boys rode their bicycles to the murder site. Matthews allegedly threatened his friends with bodily harm if they told anyone about the dead body.

The boys kept quiet for two weeks, until guilt drove Cash to send an anonymous letter to the Dedham police. Shaun's body was found in the woods on Dec. 15, 1986.

Matthews went to trial on Mar. 7, 1988. Defense attorney John Philip White portrayed him as an unstable child whose actions were influenced by the drug Ritalin. The boy had taken the drug to combat hyperactivity since he was in third grade, and his behavior may have resulted from overdependence. Several child-care specialists refuted the defense claim, however, arguing that Matthews never exhibited the classical signs of psychosis. Psychologist Kenneth Holbert told the jury that, in his opinion, Matthews was able to distinguish between right and wrong. "People were important to the degree they were entertaining," he said. "I don't think doing things to others troubled him."

On Mar. 10, 1988, Matthews was convicted of second-degree murder and sentenced to life in prison. Jeanne Quinn, Shaun's mother, noted that her son's killer would be eligible for parole in fifteen years. "Shaun is not coming home in fifteen years, is he?" she said.

Mattox, Jon, c.1940- , U.S. In the wealthy Columbus, Miss., neighborhood in which he was raised, Jon Mattox began helping neighbor Mrs. Gene Tate by performing odd jobs and running errands during her husband's frequent business trips. In about 1957, the 18-year-old Mattox entered Mississippi State College. When he returned nine months later, the youth began having an affair with Mrs. Tate. The next year he lived at home at Tate's suggestion and they continued their relationship into the next year.

In October 1960, Mrs. Tate ended the romance and Mattox, smarting from his rejection, confided his hurt and anger to a psychology major, Sarah Grayson. He also told Grayson that he wanted to kill Tate. A few months later, near the end of the semester, Mattox attacked Mrs. Tate

in her garage in Columbus, and strangled her with a coat hanger and a scarf. Police arrested the youth as a suspect in the case, but later released him. After two months, Grayson came forward and told Columbus police what Mattox had confided to her. Mattox was brought to trial, and was shocked when Grayson testified against him. He was convicted and sentenced to a life term. During a subsequent appeal, a mistake in the proceedings led to another trial. While still in custody, Mattox tried to persuade two other prisoners to kill Grayson. The prisoners informed the district attorney and Mattox was again convicted and sentenced to life in prison.

Matuschka, Sylvestre, prom. 1931-34, Hung. Hungarian businessman Sylvestre Matuschka prospered after WWI, but was accused of fraud. He was acquitted, but sold his businesses in Budapest and moved to Vienna. There he developed an interest in causing train crashes. His first attempt was on New Year's Day 1931, when he tried unsuccessfully to derail the Vienna-Passau train near

Mad Hungarian train bomber Sylvestre Matuschka, center, under arrest.

Ansbach. His first success came at Juelerboy, Hung., where he managed to overturn several coaches, which then rolled down an embankment, injuring seventy-five people on Aug. 8. Then, on Sept. 12, 1932, he used an explosive device to blow up a Hungarian Railways express as it crossed a viaduct at Bia-Torbagy. Twenty-two people were killed when cars fell off the elevated track. As the dust settled, he bloodied his own face and lay down among the victims.

Matuschka sued the Hungarian Railways over his supposed injuries. But the police could find no one who had seen him on the train. After further investigation, Matuschka was arrested. In his house, police found plans for similar disasters in France, Italy, and the Netherlands. Matuschka soon confessed.

The first of several trials began on June 15, 1932. The only believable motive offered at the trials was that Matuschka derived from the crashes some deep sexual satisfaction that he could not find elsewhere. Matuschka himself blamed his condition on a hypnotist he met at a country fair, or on orders from an invisible spiritual being named Leo. After the second trial, Matuschka was found Guilty and sentenced to hang. However, his sentence was commuted to life imprisonment, and he was reportedly released during WWII by the Soviets, who employed him as an explosives expert.

Maxwell, Edith, 1914-   , U.S. On July 20, 1935, a 21-year-old schoolteacher, Edith Maxwell, returned to her Wise, Va., home after spending the evening with friends. Arriving home about midnight, she was greeted by her 11-year-old sister, Mary Catherine, who cautioned her, "Your bed covers is in Pappy's room but don't go in there. He's drunk and he's going to run Ma out of the house tomorrow." Edith Maxwell did not heed the advice and her father woke up when she entered the room. Taking a carving knife, he chased her out of the bedroom, threatening to whip her. Edith responded by striking out at her father repeatedly with a high-heeled shoe. The elder Maxwell died of his wounds and Edith was charged with his murder.

Edith Maxwell was put on trial in November 1935. Her sister, Mary Catherine, testified on her behalf. Although Edith Maxwell's lawyers argued self-defence, she was found Guilty and sentenced to twenty-five years in prison.

Maynard, William John, 1892-1928, Brit. In southwest England, an elderly man lived in his isolated cottage at Titson, Marhamchurch. Locals speculated that the peculiar 84-year-old Richard Francis Roadley was a rich miser. One of the neighborhood residents, 36-year-old William John Maynard, believed the local tale. Maynard, a rabbit trapper who oversaw more than 1,000 traps, had two helpers. On Feb. 18, 1928, the trapper broke into Roadley's house and struck the old man on the head. After rummaging through Roadley's belongings, he carted away some valuables, and buried them on his father's farm.

Following the discovery of the murder, Maynard was questioned during a routine Scotland Yard investigation. Even before the subject was broached, the trapper volunteered that he would hang himself before he would kill Roadley. He further told police he had been at home with a Mr. and Mrs. Yeo at the time of the murder. Unfortunately for Maynard, the couple had already told police they had visited Maynard, but had not found him at home. The next day Maynard offered yet another alibi, telling police that he and a Mr. Harris had broken into Roadley's house and Harris had killed the old man. The trapper also told police where the stolen goods were hidden. However, Harris had a solid alibi, and in June, Maynard was tried alone. He was convicted, given the death penalty, and hanged on July 27, 1928.

Meade, Thomas, d.1909, Brit. On Nov. 27, 1908, Thomas Meade, a workman in Leeds, England, came home very drunk. He argued with his common-law wife, Clara Howell, and swore to give her "a good hiding." In doing so, he killed her. At the Leeds Assizes in February 1909, his attorney argued that he could not have had any intention of killing Clara because he had been too drunk to form *any* intention. Mr. Justice Coleridge told the jury that if a person is incapable of having the intent to kill, the charge should be reduced to manslaughter. The jury listened carefully, and nevertheless found Meade Guilty of murder.

The decision was appealed to the recently formed Court of Criminal Appeal on the basis that the jury had misunderstood Coleridge's comments to mean that Meade would have to have been "mad with drink" instead of just drunk enough not to be able to form a specific intention to kill. Mr. Justice Darling upheld the decision, saying that the jury had not been misled, that they had believed Meade capable of forming an intention to give Clara "a good hiding" which resulted in her death. Meade was hanged on Mar. 12, 1909.

Melchert, Peter, 1959-   , and **Anstadt, Achim**, 1959-   , Fr. On Feb. 9, 1979, Gerhard Langdoll had a reunion with two college buddies, Peter Melchert and Achim Anstadt, when he accidentally ran into them at a cafe in Pirmasens, Ger. The three had studied together in secondary school. Their friendly visit that evening became a weekend excursion when Melchert recommended the trio take a trip to France, which lay five miles south of Pirmasens. All agreed and they began their journey to Marseilles.

The three young men drove several hours into France

drinking several bottles of wine along the way. Melchert had bought a shotgun en route, which both he and Anstadt used for target practice—shooting at animals, barges, and plate glass windows in houses lining the roadway. When they reached the village of Pirlat, the raucous trio picked up Melinda Park and David Harman, an Australian couple who were hitchhiking across Europe. After traveling several miles, Melchert drove to a secluded gravel pit and demanded that Park and Harman give him their money. When they refused, Anstadt forced them from the car at gunpoint and the couple handed over the sum of 100 francs. Langdoll was shocked by his old friends' actions and argued with them to stop. As they quarreled, Park and Harman ran off into the nearby bushes. Anstadt followed with the gun while Melchert, wielding an axe, trailed behind. Langdoll stood and watched as the couple ran through the woods and the two men hunted the couple down and shot them in cold blood. Horrified by their actions, Langdoll jumped back into the car and drove to Pirmasens where he notified authorities.

Meanwhile at the gravel pit, Melchert and Anstadt, realizing that Park was not dead, raped her, and sexually mutilated her before bludgeoning her to death with the butt of the shotgun. The two men stripped the bodies of their remaining valuables and caught a train back to Pirmasens where they were arrested two days later at the railway station. With the testimony of Langdoll, Anstadt and Melchert were convicted of murder and received the maximum sentence for murder by juveniles—ten years in jail. However, with customary time off for good behavior and the use of German rehabilitation programs, it was expected that the two men would be released within five years.

Mercier, Louis, prom. 1924, U.S. Described as lazy and as a poor provider for his family, Louis Mercier moved his wife and three children to Pittsfield, Mass., in the 1920s. There he led a double-life: by day he stayed home refusing to work, and by night he masqueraded as a bachelor who pursued friendships and love relationships. Just before the death of his wife Eugenie Mercier, one such relationship ended when the woman he had been dating learned that he was a married man with a large family. After she left him, Mercier engineered a plan that would make him single.

Eugenie had been ill for several months and took paregoric to relieve her pain. On the evening of Feb. 13, 1924, she swallowed a dosage of paregoric that her husband had laced with cyanide poison. Pittsfield police officers investigating the case suspected Mercier had killed his wife when her autopsy revealed traces of cyanide in her system.

Investigators uncovered Mercier's secret lifestyle. Following a search of the Mercier home, the cyanide-laced bottle of paregoric was seized along with a jacket belonging to Mercier that contained cyanide stains inside the pockets. The evidence admitted against Mercier proved overwhelming and he was convicted of second-degree murder in May in the Superior Court of Berkshire County. He received a life sentence.

Merrifield, Louisa Highway, 1907-53, Brit. Soon after 45-year-old Louisa Highway married 74-year-old Alfred E. Merrifield, the pair went to work as house servants to the elderly and sick Mrs. Ricketts of Blackpool, England. At approximately the same time that Mrs. Ricketts was complaining to any deliveryman who came to the house that the Merrifields were wasting her money, Mrs. Merrifield was telling friends, neighbors, and even strangers, that her employer had died and left them her house. Mrs. Ricketts did, in fact, die after the servants failed to go out at night and get a doctor. When they tried to have her cremated quickly, the police stopped them and investigated. Mrs. Ricketts was found to have died from phosphorous poison.

British murderer Louisa Merrifield.

Mrs. Merrifield told the police her version of what had happened that evening, down to the detail of giving the old lady a drink of rum the evening of Apr. 14. But in her purse, they found a spoon bearing traces of phosphorous poison and rum. And the stories of her telling about inheriting the house weeks before the woman's death began to surface. The couple was arrested for murder. The bewildered Alfred Merrifield was eventually released, not having been in on the plan. Louisa Merrifield was found Guilty of murder and hanged on Sept. 18, 1953.

Metcalf, Danny, prom. 1956, U.S. On the evening of Feb. 29, 1956, a black De Soto driven by Danny Metcalf was pulled over by Paoli, Pa., police officer Gerald H. Mitchell. As Mitchell approached the car, the driver fired six fatal shots into the patrolman. A report of the shooting sparked a police chase that ended with a spectacular crash as the murderer attempted to ram a roadblock near the town of Gladwyne. The De Soto swerved to avoid patrol cars and crashed into a concrete barrier at the side of a bridge. When officers ran up to the car, the driver had disappeared; he had apparently escaped by jumping over the side of the bridge into the underbrush below.

The next morning, while police continued their search for the murderer, Metcalf forced his way into the home of Margaret Loweth who was alone with her 11-year-old son Billy while her husband was away on business. Metcalf knocked Loweth unconscious with a wrench he had stolen from her garage. From his bedroom, Billy had heard the commotion and after hearing his mother's scream, he entered the kitchen with a loaded .22-caliber rifle. Billy misfired and shot the intruder in the hand. With his one shot gone, Billy surrendered the rifle to Metcalf and ran to his mother's side as she lay bleeding on the floor.

After the woman regained consciousness, Metcalf forced her to drive him safely out of Gladwyne and, while holding a .25-caliber automatic pistol to Billy's head, the trio passed through several roadblocks. Officers followed the hostage vehicle until Loweth drove the automobile off the road in an attempt to facilitate Metcalf's capture. The car came to a stop in a ditch and Metcalf jumped out. Drawing their revolvers, the pursuing officers surrounded Metcalf. Using Billy as a shield, he retreated into a wooded area beside the road. As he backed away from the officers, he stumbled, Billy broke free, and policeman fired, felling him before he could squeeze off one shot. Metcalf was pronounced dead on the scene after having been shot twelve times.

Meurant, Leon (AKA: **Count Vernier de Miraumont**), prom. 1946-52, Fr. In 1946 Leon Meurant, a Belgian steel worker using the *nome de guerre* of Count Vernier de Miraumont, was escorting a Russian countess along the Paris-Brussels Road. Meurant strangled the woman and dumped her nude body in the road to be found several hours later. From descriptions of Count Vernier, police traced Meurant to Germany where he was masquerading as a gynecologist. Meurant immediately confessed to the murder but later withdrew his confession in return for a fascinating story of political espionage. He told police that he was actually a Soviet secret agent—code name Operative B-17—and that the countess had been murdered by fellow agent, Operative B-15, who had secreted himself into the trunk of their automobile and had killed the woman after searching her for classified information. "Brassieres and panties are excellent for hiding microfilm," Meurant told police. A French court later found him Guilty of murder

and sentenced him to death.

Six years later, incarcerated in Amiens prison while awaiting the guillotine, Meurant escaped. Upon his incarceration, he had used his wit to charm the prison guards. By 1952, he had become a source of entertainment and had gained their trust. One day in early January, he asked prison guard Jacques Gauvin if he would like see "how they used to put on silencers in the NKVD." Gauvin took him up on his offer and handed Meurant his revolver, not once but twice, and the second time, Meurant turned it on him forcing the young guard into a prison cell. After rounding up four other guards and locking them up, Meurant and his cellmate, convicted murderer Michel Courtin, dressed in guard uniforms and walked out of the prison. Leon Meurant was captured two days later at an abandoned railway station where he was reading a newspaper report of his escape. Police quickly took him into custody while he complained: "I never had time to get to the end of the article."

Meyer, Alexander, 1917-37, U.S. Alexander Meyer, a farm boy from Chester County, Pa., drove the country backroads in search of a girl. As he later explained in his ten-page confession, sex and murder compelled him. "I took the truck for the sole purpose of running down and killing a girl. About two miles outside Coatesville I saw a girl walking alone..."

In 1935, Alexander Meyer was confined to Huntingdon Reformatory for shooting at two young Philadelphia girls who refused his sexual advances. The 20-year-old Meyer had a history of sex offenses, but the courts and his own father, wealthy Philadelphia coal financier O. Jackson Meyer, seemed to ignore his problems, even after he assaulted Jennie Waterson in January 1937. The 15-year-old girl narrowly escaped injury and death after refusing to have sex with Meyer.

When Meyer saw 16-year-old Helen Moyer walking beside the road two miles from Coatesville, he decided in an instant that she would be his first victim. He slammed down the accelerator pedal of his pick-up truck and ran over her at an estimated speed of forty-five miles per hour. He stopped the truck, placed the still living girl in the back of the cab, and drove to an abandoned farm in Guthrie, fifteen miles from her home in Modena.

Meyer carried the girl over his shoulder into the ramshackle farm house, where he raped her. Thinking she was dead, he threw her into a seventy-five foot well. Meyer then dropped two lit sticks of dynamite into the well, destroying it and burying the remains of Helen Moyer.

On Feb. 21, 1937, ten days after Meyer blew up the well,

he submitted a ten-page confession to Assistant District Attorney Philip J. Reilly after Jennie Waterson identified him as her assailant. The well was excavated and the body identified. O. Jackson Meyer retained attorney J. Paul McElree to represent his son in the upcoming trial, which the local residents privately believed would be a whitewash.

McElree relied on the insanity defense, hoping his client would be spared the death penalty. However, Meyer was convicted of first-degree murder and executed in the electric chair at Rockview Penitentiary on July 12, 1937.

Meyers, Martin, 1964-　, U.S. In the pre-dawn hours of Oct. 18, 1981, 34-year-old Jose Hernandez was asleep in the front seat of his automobile as his wife drove toward their family home in Knox, Ind., after attending a wedding reception in suburban Chicago. Lynn Hernandez was driving down Interstate 65 and as she neared an overpass, a 40-pound concrete block crashed through the windshield of the automobile, instantly killing her sleeping husband. Upon hearing the breaking glass and watching the car come to a screeching halt, 17-year-old Martin Meyers and two teenage companions jumped into their car and fled the site.

Following an investigation into Hernandez's unusually tragic death, Crown Point, Ind., police detectives took Martin and two others into custody. Martin's friends identified him as the one who dropped the block from the overpass onto the Hernandez automobile and explained that it was intended to be a prank. The teenage "prank" ended in death, sent a family into shock, and landed Martin in jail for five years after he pleaded guilty to charges of reckless homicide in Lake County Criminal Court in November 1982.

Michael X, See: Malik, Abdul.

Mikasevich, Gennadiy, 1947-c.1985, U.S.S.R. The trial of Gennadiy Mikasevich of the Soviet Union brought to light corruption within state police agencies charged with investigating the crimes of this mass murderer. Because of the zeal of certain police officials more interested in attaining a promotion than bringing the right man to justice, four pople were wrongly convicted of murders in which they had no part.

The man responsible for the strangulation murders of thirty-six women between 1971-85 was born in Polotsk, Byelorussia, in 1947. Mikasevich worked as the chief of a state-run motor vehicle repair facility in the Soloniki region of the Soviet Union. In his off-hours he was also a volunteer for the local police department, covering the area around Polotsk. For a time he conducted his own investigation of the murders, interviewing suspects and stopping individuals in small red cars—the kind the killer had apparently used—for questioning. Russian authorities later diagnosed Mikasevich as suffering from a "sexual inferiority complex." He lured women into his Russian-made Zaparoshet with the promise of a ride. By his own account, the women accepted his offer willingly. He then strangled them with his scarf or a long weed. In 1984 alone, he claimed fourteen victims. Meanwhile, the Russian courts had already convicted four different men for the Soloniki murders. In 1974, O.P. Glushakov was sentenced to prison for ten years. In 1980, N.S. Tereniv was executed. A third man, V. Gorelov spent six years in prison where he went blind. Oleg Adamov received fifteen years in prison, during which time he attempted to commit suicide. Meanwhile, the killings continued.

The February 1984 murder of a technical school student named Tatianna K. aroused the interest of Detective Nicolai Ivanovich Ignatovich who compared all of the murders to date and found striking similarities. He checked the vehicle registration of 7,000 red Zaparoshets. The search was eventually widened to include 200,000 automobiles of various other makes. Handwriting samples also were compared. The killer had sent a letter to the police stating that his motive was "revenge against adulterous women." It was signed the "Patriot of Vitebsk." This same message was also written on slips of paper found on the bodies of the last two victims in 1985.

Before he narrowed down his list of suspects, Ignatovich personally checked the inner-country passports of some 312,000 citizens. The massive criminal investigation was narrowed down to the village of Soloniki where the detectives found a work receipt Mikasevich had signed. The suspect was taken into custody and interrogated until he finally confessed. Mikasevich then led the police to the well where he had dropped his victims' personal belongings. The confessed murderer was executed sometime between 1985 and 1988.

Miller, Charlotte, 1962-　, Aus. Charlotte Miller of Melbourne, Aus., was raised by her mother and the mother's common-law husband, who had never been able to legally marry Charlotte's mother Hilda because she was still married to another. Hilda Miller believed she was dying of cancer, though doctors insisted otherwise. On Jan. 10, 1980, Mrs. Miller apparently committed suicide by taking two bottles of barbiturates. Police, however, found no fingerprints on the medicine bottles.

Inspector Thomas Hunt of the Melbourne police studied the situation, and soon suspected 40-year-old Arthur Houdson, Hilda Miller's common-law husband. He had been out of town the night she died, but could have sneaked back to carry out a murder. Hunt felt that a 40-year-old man living with an unrelated 18-year-old girl while his wife was in the hospital was likely to seduce the girl. In the following weeks, police noticed that Houdson was deteriorating, as if something was preying on his mind. When he came into the police station, they thought he was going to confess to murder. Instead, he said that Charlotte Miller had seduced him when her mother was in the hospital, and that she had killed her mother so that the two of them could be together.

Charlotte was confronted with a tape of Houdson's statement. She readily confessed to the murder, adding that she had no regrets about killing "her rival." Australian law regarded her as a juvenile, so she was put in the care of the juvenile authorities.

Mills, Herbert Leonard, 1932-51, Brit. Leonard Mills decided to carry out the perfect crime—motiveless and clueless. The 19-year-old Nottingham clerk selected as his victim Mrs. Mabel Tattershaw, the woman sitting next to him in a movie theater on Aug. 2, 1951. Mills asked Tattershaw to meet him the next night. Flattered by his offer, the older woman agreed, and met Mills in Sherwook Vale, where he coldly strangled her. Mills said in a newspaper article that he found the body of the 48-year-old woman when he went to the wooded Sherwood Vale to write a poem. Upon "finding" the body on Aug. 9, Mills called a reporter for *The News of the World,* not the police. He offered the newspaper an exclusive story on the murder for a fee. By the time he called back for their answer, the police had been informed and were tracing the call to a phone booth.

The reporter, under the guidance of the police, encouraged Mills to write his own story. Besides being badly written, the article told the police nothing new. Disturbed by the lack of interest in his story, Mills several days later offered the reporter another sensational story, which again contained nothing of interest. Meanwhile, police were investigating fibers found under Mrs. Tattershaw's fingernails, which proved to be from Mills' coat, and hairs found on her body. Angry at the lack of response to his writing, Mills called *The News of the World* with yet another story. He proudly wrote out a complete confession to the murder. Mills was tried for murder in November. It took the jury

only twenty-five minutes to find him Guilty. He was hanged the next month.

Mills, John H., 1899- , and **Mills, Fred,** 1899- , and **Mills, Ballard,** c.1908- , and **McGinnis, Blaine,** and **Boyd, Thomas,** and **McGinnis, Mollie,** and **Mills, Ora,** and **Mills, Mrs. John,** prom. 1933, U.S. In a dilapidated wooden cabin in the mountains, 72-year-old Lucinda Mills and her children claimed to possess divine powers of healing and the ability to perform miracles. The Mills family truly believed that they could transform rain water to wine and grapevine stalks to living snakes. Curious neighbors told of weird cultish rites in the woods. The Mills family prayed, sang, and chanted in an unknown dialect described by one law enforcement officer as "gibberish."

During a five-day prayer chant on Feb. 8, 1933, Lucinda Mills' eldest son, John, allegedly received divine commands to offer his aged mother as a blood sacrifice. The doors were locked and the shutters of the cabin drawn as John Mills, his in-laws, children, and brothers prepared a ritualistic altar.

Lucinda Mills allegedly agreed to be sacrificed in order to save the life of her son, Leonard, who was confined in a hospital for the insane. "I would willingly give my life for my son Leonard," she had said. After long hours of praying and fasting, John Mills strangled his mother with his bare hands while the family looked on. Blaine McGinnis, Mrs. Mills's son-in-law, wanted to stop the killing but could not. "When I saw John choking his mother to death I tried to grab his arm but I could not. I don't know how to explain it...I couldn't move. I just stood there and watched," he said. Mrs. Mills offered no resistance and went to her death of her own free will. Afterward, metal chains were tied around her neck.

When local residents became suspicious, they called the police in nearby Inez. Just as Lucinda Mills was to be taken to a funeral pyre and set ablaze, the authorities burst on the scene and took the eight family members into custody. The inquest was conducted by Judge T.J. Hardin, who ruled that the old woman's death was brought on by her son. John Mills was charged with murder and the other seven relatives were held as accomplices. The police later learned that four young Kentucky girls were targeted for "virginal" sacrifice by the cult.

While in jail awaiting arraignment, John Mills lapsed into violent seizures, and had to be chained to his cot. Other family members charged him with having "unloosened" the evil spirits as they prayed for salvation. Meanwhile, defense counsel Sam Maynard entered a plea of insanity on behalf of his client. The prosecution requested that Judge Hardin bind John Mills over to the grand jury for indictment.

The Mills family went on trial in March at the Martin Circuit Court in Inez, Ky. Commonwealth attorney J.B. Clark described their crimes as "cold blooded murder," a view the jury carefully considered before returning a Guilty verdict against John Mills, his son Ballard, and Blaine McGinnis. The other participants were acquitted on Apr. 12, 1933. Nine days later, John Mills began serving a life sentence at the Kentucky Prison. He was paroled on Apr. 21, 1941, and was restored to full citizenship by the governor of Kentucky in 1953.

Milone, Richard, 1948-   , U.S. The body of Sally Kandel, a 14-year-old girl from Carol Stream, Ill., was found on Sept. 13, 1972. She had been viciously bludgeoned to death. On circumstantial evidence, 25-year-old Richard Milone was convicted of her murder in 1973 and sentenced to eighty to 175 years in prison. Part of the evidence consisted of a bite mark on Kandel's body. Three dentists testified that the mark matched Milone's teeth, but other dentists disagreed.

In September 1974, Nancy Lossman of McHenry County and her 3-year-old daughter were murdered. A forensic dental specialist attributed a bite mark on Lossman's body to Richard Macek, a convicted murderer who later confessed to the Kandel murder. Governor James Thompson denied Milone's request for a pardon in April 1989. Macek committed suicide in a Wisconsin prison in 1988, and Thompson called his confession "almost incomprehensible." Milone is still serving his time at the Graham Correctional Center in Hillsboro, Ill.

Milosavljeric, Ljubinka, 1917-   , Yug. Ljubinka Milosavljeric and Momcilo Cupic were lovers and Yugoslavian partisan fighters during WWII in the mountains and countryside of their Serbian homeland. Following the war, Milosavljeric and Cupic went their separate routes, each becoming an important official—Milosavljeric working in the Serbian regional government and Cupic working for the national government under President Tito. Milosavljeric did not marry, but she heard that Cupic had, and had started raising a family.

In April 1955, the two met again at a Communist Party congress. They talked eagerly, and Cupic asked if he could walk Milosavljeric to her hotel. As he said goodnight, she pulled a gun from her purse and shot him to death. At her trial, Milosavljeric told of being jilted by her former lover.

She was sentenced to life in a mental asylum.

Minsky, Max (AKA: **Shooey**), prom. 1913, U.S. The murder of Max "Maxie" Levine, a small time gangster, was carried out in the back room of a second floor flat on East Fourteenth Street in New York City in April 1913. Levine had been lured to the building with the promise of a "good time." There were girls waiting for him, he was told. Instead Levine was greeted by four men and two women whose volley of gunfire dropped him dead in his tracks. It was a rude homecoming for this ex-con, who had just been released from prison.

The triggerman was Max Minsky, a rival gangster who once belonged to the Jack Zelig gang. To disguise the crime, Minsky and his associates put a cocked .38-caliber pistol into Levine's hand to make the shooting look like an act of self-defense. Within three days however, the police arrested Moe Horowitz, in whose apartment the shooting took place, his wife Flo, Minsky, and a man named Pennitsky. The gangsters were prosecuted by District Attorney Deacon Murphy who built a case around the testimony of Flo Horowitz, who first had said that Minsky was the murderer, but then changed her story in court.

The jury discounted her story and convicted Minsky of second-degree murder on Jan. 27, 1914, in the Court of General Sessions. Pennitsky, Horowitz, and Levine each received lengthy prison terms for the planning of Levine's murder.

Mitchell, Ray Anthony, 1963-81, U.S. In February 1980, 17-year-old Ray Anthony Mitchell stabbed to death four residents of a wealthy Miami suburb. Tried in July, he pleaded guilty to first-degree murder in the deaths of Albert Skolnick, fifty-nine, stabbed six times; his wife Dorothy, fifty-two, stabbed sixteen times; Paul Klimetz, eighty-three, stabbed twenty-five times; and his wife Charlotte, seventy-seven, stabbed twenty-three times. Mitchell received 100 years in prison for his crimes.

One year after the murders, Mitchell and another convicted murderer, Jerry Rasberry, twenty-seven, entered a prison office, took two secretaries hostage, and demanded a car, guns, and safe passage from the prison. Three prison employees in the office managed to get one of the secretaries away from the prisoners but the other secretary, 22-year-old Terri Rimes, remained a hostage for ten hours. Scared and uncertain, Mitchell telephoned social worker Ms. Ayres once and his mother several times. Authorities ended the kidnapping by storming the office.

According to Ms. Ayres, she was speaking to Rasberry on the phone when he said, "Somebody's coming in." Ayres asked him if he was letting the guards in and then heard three pops and the line went dead. A nine-man attack squad rescued Rimes, shot Rasberry several times, and killed Mitchell. Rasberry lived, though he required surgery. Beatrice Mitchell, Ray's mother, said her son "couldn't face the fact that he was going to live and die in prison."

Mitchell, Timothy, 1947-   , Brit. John Lawson, seventeen, and Timothy Mitchell, fifteen, were friends in Manchester, England. One day, Lawson got into trouble when he attacked another youth. The youth turned the tables and began to beat up Lawson. Mitchell, trying to help his friend, took out his knife to "nick or prick" the youth. Instead, just as he lunged for the other boy's arm, the boy rolled over, and Mitchell stabbed Lawson in the chest and killed him. Panicked and frightened, Mitchell hid the knife. At his trial, Mitchell was found Not Guilty of murder but Guilty of manslaughter because the jury saw no intention of malice. He was sentenced to three years' confinement.

Mitchell, Tyrone, c.1955-84, U.S. On Feb. 24, 1984, armed with an AR-15 assault rifle and a 12-gauge shotgun, Tyrone Mitchell shot thirteen people and killed one 10-year-old girl when he fired upon the children of an elementary school across the street from his home. Police surrounded his Los Angeles home for three hours before firing tear gas and breaking in. They found Mitchell inside, shot in the head with a shotgun—the victim of suicide. Many of the children at the 49th Street Elementary School knew Mitchell as the "crazy man" who lived across the street. Friends and family of the killer said he was despondent and tormented over the mass suicide of the People's Temple at Jonestown, Guyana in 1978, which left 913 people dead, including his parents and several other family members. Although a follower of the Reverend Jim Jones, Mitchell was in nearby Georgetown at a dentist's office at the time of the mass suicide.

Moity, Henry, prom. 1928, U.S. In one of the most brutal crimes of passion in New Orleans history a husband butchered his wife and her sister when his wife announced she was leaving him. Henry Moity, his wife Theresa, and their three children lived in an apartment with his brother,

Joseph Moity, his wife Leonide, and their two children, having recently moved to New Orleans from New Iberia. One evening in 1927, police were called to the Moity apartment where they found a bedroom covered in blood and human limbs in a blood spattered bathtub. Under the bed, police found two trunks, each containing the body of a woman. The women were identified as Theresa Moity and Leonide Moity.

A search for the missing brother ensued. When a sister of the Moity brothers was questioned, she admitted that Joseph was staying with her as Leonide had left him. Henry had visited the previous night and told her Theresa was leaving him as well. Henry also asked her to take care of the children. Police brought Joseph into the police headquarters for questioning the following morning and held him under $10,000 bail though he claimed to know nothing about the murders. Henry was arrested after the chief engineer of a ship notified police that Henry boarded the ship and sold a gun to him.

When questioned, Henry confessed to the two murders and claimed he killed Theresa in a drunken rage when she said she was leaving him. He killed Leonide when she tried to interfere. Charged with murder, Henry Moity exonerated his brother during the trial. On Feb. 28, 1928, Henry was convicted of second-degree murder as the jury felt that extenuating circumstances existed. He was sentenced to life in prison but escaped on Aug. 11, 1945, and was never recaptured.

Molina del Rio, Francisco (AKA: **The Hook**), 1929-   , U.S. In 1960, Francisco Molina del Rio, thirty-one, also known as "The Hook," a pro-Castro gunman, was involved in a shoot-out in a New York restaurant with anti-Castro Cubans during the Cuban dictator's trip to the U.S. During the shooting, Molina accidentally shot and killed Magdalena Urdaneto, a 9-year-old Venezuelan girl. He was convicted of second-degree murder and sentenced to twenty years to life in prison. In 1963, through an agreement masterminded by Attorney General Robert Kennedy, Molina and three other Cuban nationals were swapped for eighteen American citizens and three CIA agents detained on various charges in Cuban prisons. Kennedy asked New York's Governor Nelson Rockefeller, in the nation's interest, to commute Molina's sentence. "The Hook" left the U.S. under the threat that if he set foot on American soil again, he would spend his life behind bars.

Monahan, Annie, prom. 1906-13, U.S. Annie Monahan of New Haven, Conn., poisoned three husbands and her niece for insurance money. Her first husband, Joseph F. Pallman, died on Nov. 20, 1906, of edema and pneumonia—an unusual combination of sicknesses. He died insured for $400. Eighteen months after Pallman was embalmed and buried, Annie married Joseph Monahan who died on Nov. 14, 1909, of apparent alcoholic gastritis. The doctor suspected arsenic poisoning because the symptoms of his gastritis were inconclusive, but chose not to exhume the corpse for an autopsy because the embalming fluid used in those days contained large amounts of arsenic. Five years later, Jennie McNamee, Annie's 17-year-old niece who lived with Monahan after her parents died of tuberculosis, died on Mar. 7, 1913, allegedly of the same illness.

Insurance companies ordered an investigation when they discovered that Monahan not only insured her niece for over $2,000 through several insurance companies, but that she lied on each of the applications. When investigators exhumed McNamee's body, they discovered the presence of arsenic—enough to kill three adult men. Questions asked to family members revealed that when Monahan took care of McNamee while she was ill, Monahan sent Frank, Jennie's younger brother, to get a package of rat poison which contained large quantities of arsenic. Authorities issued a warrant for Monahan's arrest, but later released her when they decided that the evidence uncovered by the investigators was suggestive rather than conclusive. When she was arrested, John T. Monahan, Annie's third husband and the 32-year-old brother of Annie's second husband, became quite distressed and told police that, at his wife's suggestion, he had taken out a life insurance policy of $400.

Three years later, in October 1916, Monahan's third husband became suddenly and violently ill. A doctor was called in but could not properly diagnose the problem. He called another doctor who remembered the police suspicions that Monahan was a poisoner. The second doctor ordered that John Monahan be moved to a hospital where six doctors monitored him. He died on June 12, 1917, after several months of agony. Monahan was again arrested and this time charged with the murder of her third husband. She pleaded not guilty and while the prosecution could not mention the other mysterious deaths in her past, they produced medical and technical evidence that showed Annie had bought arsenic during John's illness, that a small phial of John's medicine contained arsenic, and that an autopsy revealed poisoning as the cause of John's death. On Feb. 13, 1919, the jury found her Guilty as charged and the judge sentenced her to life imprisonment.

Mondolini, Roger, prom. 1952-56, Fr. In Summer

1952 several shots were fired outside Mimi Pinson dance hall, located on Paris' Champs Elysees around 2 a.m., killing a Corsican named Jean Serini. The police eventually arrested another Corsican, Roger Mondolini, a known pimp. Apparently, Serini had stolen one of Mondolini's girls who brought in several million francs a month from one of her regulars, an Indian Maharajah. Though the prosecution asked for the death sentence, the jury felt Mondolini was sufficiently provoked and upheld his right to murder Serini. Judge Jadin sentenced him to four years in prison. Mondolini was released shortly thereafter as he spent nearly four years in prison awaiting his trial. The verdict pleased Mondolini's friends, who had threatened to kill the judge if he imposed the death sentence.

Monster of Dusseldorf, The, See: Kurten, Peter.

Moodie, Duncan, 1935-62, S. Afri. Duncan Moodie holds the distinction of being the only man in South African legal history to be tried twice for the same crime—the murder of his wife, Anita Moodie. Moodie was an alcoholic who was violently abusive to Anita—she had been "rescued" several times by her parents when they feared for her life. After eighteen months of abuse, Anita insisted that she never be left alone with her husband again, and her family agreed to this demand. But Moodie requested that she talk with him, and he vowed never to touch her again if she would just come back. She was not dissuaded, but she agreed to meet him privately one last time at her family's home in Ada May View, Klerksdorp, on Aug. 21, 1960. That meeting proved to be fatal: Moodie shot his wife four times and killed her.

Moodie's ten-day trial began on Apr. 10, 1961, and ended in a unanimous verdict of Guilty. Two of the jurors found extenuating circumstances. But it was soon learned that a deputy sheriff had been present in the jury's quarters during deliberation, a procedure expressly forbidden by South African law. The judge ruled the case a mistrial, and Moodie was freed.

Within hours, however, Moodie was arrested and once again charged with his wife's murder. An appeal found his second arrest unconstitutional, and he was freed. The prosecution continued to press for a retrial, and when the motion was finally approved, Moodie disappeared before police could arrest him a third time.

Although public sympathy swung his way, Moodie eventually surrendered and appeared in court for the second trial on Feb. 12, 1962. He was once again found Guilty, sentenced to death, and was hanged on June 27.

Moon, Norman, 1928- , U.S. Norman Moon, a 26-year-old electrical construction worker from Connellsville, Pa., was convicted of failing to support his divorced wife. As he stood before Judge Ailison Wade on Jan. 13, 1954, District Attorney Myer Kornreich saw Moon pull out a .45-caliber handgun from his coat. Kornreich managed to flee the courtroom, so Moon turned the gun on the judge, who tried to shield himself with a chair. "Don't shoot, I'm not going to sentence you!," Wade cried. It was too late. Moon fired two fatal shots and fled the courthouse.

He reached the outskirts of Warren before state police cornered him. Moon put the gun to his throat and fired, but he shot wildly and only managed to rip out part of his tongue. After he sufficiently recovered from his wounds, Norman Moon was placed on trial for first-degree murder. He was found Guilty and given the death sentence on May 24, 1954.

Moore, Brian Steven, 1952- , and **Dorn, Albert Edward**, 1946- , Brit. Returning from Kent to Shoreham in February 1973, Brian Moore's girlfriend told him she had been raped. Moore believed that Clive Olive, sixteen, had attacked his girlfriend. Moore vowed revenge for the heinous deed that caused emotional problems for his girlfriend and "spoiled" all sexual relations between the couple.

On Feb. 28, 1973, Moore and his brother-in-law Albert Dorn, two Hell's Angels Cougars (a British equivalent to the U.S.'s Hell's Angels), also known as the Sussex Mad Dogs, lured Olive, a member of the same gang, into the back of Dorn's van. As Dorn drove the vehicle, Moore beat his victim with his fists and a truncheon before binding his arms and attaching cement weights to the boy's feet. Dorn drove to Shoreham Harbour, where Moore dragged the unconscious Olive to the edge of the pier and tossed him into the water. Olive revived momentarily when he broke the surface of the water, but the weight pulled him to the bottom. The body was discovered by sailors operating a steamer on Apr. 20.

Both Moore and Dorn were found Guilty, and in December 1973, were sentenced to life imprisonment. Eighteen-year-old Christine Dorn, who was in the van when the murder occurred, was found Guilty of manslaughter and sentenced to ten years' imprisonment.

Moore, Dennis Albert Reginald, prom. 1950s, U.S. Moore strangled his fiancee in Norwich, Conn., three weeks before their wedding. Next to her body lay a note: "I love her—good-bye all." In attempting to prove Moore was insane, the defense produced two psychiatrists who testified that Moore was unstable, saying his behavior was unpredictable and explosive. The courts found no truth in this defense and showed no mercy in his sentence. Dennis Moore was convicted of first-degree murder and hanged.

Moore, Hutchie, c.1929- , U.S. Hutchie Moore was a 55-year-old Chicago policeman, who had been on disability leave from the department since 1978 when his son Michael shot him. After the shooting, he was confined to a wheelchair so that, in 1983 during divorce proceedings, he had to be rolled into the courtroom at the Daley Center in downtown Chicago each day. When Circuit Court Judge Henry Gentile handed down a ruling preventing Moore from firing his attorney during a post-divorce property settlement, Moore became convinced that lawyers, judges, and the entire judicial system were evil and corrupt. The ordeal embittered Moore to the breaking point. On Oct. 21, 1983, he appeared in Gentile's courtroom with a .38-caliber pistol tucked under a blanket on his lap. Moore pulled out the gun and shot 63-year-old Judge Gentile and 34-year-old attorney James Piszczor before court bailiffs could react. Both men died instantly.

Moore's lawyers argued that he was unfit to stand trial for the double murder, but after psychiatrist James Cavanaugh attested to Moore's mental competence, Moore was ordered to stand trial. The murder trial began in the Lake County Courtroom of Judge Harry D. Strouse, Jr. the following July. Before the verdict was read on Aug. 1, Moore said that he would consider it "constitutionally null and void." Defense attorneys argued that James Piszczor's unethical courtroom practices on behalf of the estranged wife understandably brought on Moore's paranoia.

On Sept. 4, 1984, Hutchie Moore was found Guilty. "The judicial system does work," said Jim Gentile, the son of the murdered judge. "You can kill two people and still get a fair trial. My father would be very proud of that. My father did not believe in the death penalty." Moore, however, did. After the verdicts were handed down he turned to the jury and said, "I would appreciate it if you would give me death. This would end everything." He was sentenced to life in prison with no chance for parole.

Moors Murders, The, 1963-64, Brit. Myra Hindley,

a shy, working-class 19-year-old from the Gorton district of Manchester, England, met Ian Brady at Millwards, a local chemical supply firm, in January 1961. Brady, a dark-haired sociopath obsessed with the sadism of the Nazi regime, spent his lunch hours reading *Mein Kampf*. He hardly had time to notice Hindley, whose diary extolled the virtues of this rather sullen young man. "Ian wore a black shirt and looked smashing...I love him," she wrote. Then in December 1961: "Eureka! Today we have our first date. We are going to the cinema." He took her to see *Judgment at Nuremberg*. Brady cemented their courtship in a skillful act of seduction at her grandmother's home that same afternoon. From then on Hindley was his devoted love slave and a willing participant in his sadomasochistic fantasies. They took pornographic pictures of each other and collected them in a scrapbook.

Quickly tiring of this, Brady persuaded Hindley (whom he nicknamed "Myra Hess" in honor of the sadistic Nazi concentration camp guard Irma Grese) to help him procure children and adolescents for a more dangerous game. In July 1963, 16-year-old Pauline Reade of Gorton disappeared. She lived several doors away from David Smith, Hindley's brother-in-law. In November, 12-year-old John Kilbride vanished, and seven months later, another 12-year-old schoolboy named Keith Bennett was abducted and murdered. Although the police never connected the Reade and Bennett killings to this pair, the similarities in the murders were striking.

The murder of 10-year-old Lesley Ann Downey on Dec. 26, 1964, however, was clearly the work of Brady and Hindley. The girl, who was attending a Christmas fair, was

Moors murderers Ian Brady and Myra Hindley.

taken to Brady's house on Wardle Brook Avenue, Hattersley, and forced to pose nude for pornographic photographs. A tape recorder captured the anguished pleas of the schoolgirl shortly before she was strangled. In the background "The Little Drummer Boy" and "Jolly St.

Nicholas" droned on. The macabre recording later became the prosecution's first exhibit during Brady and Hindley's murder trial.

The couple waited ten months before Brady selected his next victim. In October 1965, he met 17-year-old Edward Evans in a Manchester pub and enticed the young man, believed to be a homosexual, to the house on Wardle Brook Avenue. There, in the presence of David Smith, brought there by Hindley on Brady's orders, Evans' skull was bashed with a hatchet. "It's done," chortled Brady. "It's the messiest yet. It normally only takes one blow." The murder of Evans was not done for "kicks" according to Brady's later accounts, but to provide Smith with an "education" in murder. There was little doubt that Brady also desired to implicate Smith in the crime. He handed the hatchet to the startled young man shortly after the murder so that his fingerprints would show up on the handle. The body was wrapped in plastic and taken upstairs amid jokes and derisive laughter from Hindley and Brady.

Sickened by the spectacle, Smith excused himself and went home to tell his wife, Maureen. The teenaged couple decided it was best to call the police, who acted quickly. The officers rushed to Brady's home, where they found the body exactly where Smith said it would be. Two suitcases stuffed with pornographic paraphernalia and the incriminating tape of the murdered Downey were located in a locker at the Manchester Central Station. A photograph of Hindley posing next to the shallow grave of John Kilbride in the Saddleworth Moors tipped off police to the location of the bodies of Downey and Kilbride. The trial of Brady and Hindley began at the Chester Assizes on Apr. 19, 1966, before Justice Fenton Atkinson. Hundreds of television and newspaper reporters crowded the courtroom to glimpse the murderers and hear the sadistic tape. On May 6, the two were found Guilty of killing Evans and Downey. Brady was also found Guilty of murdering Kilbride. They each received life sentences.

Morales, Michael Angelo, 1960-   , and **Ortega, Ricky**, prom. 1980s, U.S. Michael Morales was convicted of the 1981 knife-and-hammer murder of Terri Winchell, whom Morales believed had been having an affair with the male lover of his cousin, Ricky Ortega. Morales and Ortega drove Winchell to a secluded spot in Illinois, where Morales attempted to strangle her with a belt. When this failed, he beat her with a hammer until unconscious, raped her, and then stabbed her to death.

In 1983, Morales received the death penalty because of a special circumstance in Illinois law that allowed for the maximum sentence to be applied to a "lying-in-wait" murder.

The ruling was confirmed on appeal, the state supreme court explained that it was a fair sentence in situations where a person who commits premeditated murder hides his intent and then attacks without warning. Ortega was tried separately, found Guilty, and sentenced to life in prison without parole.

Moreira, Manuel (AKA: **Horseface**), d.1964, Braz. On Aug. 27, 1964, Manuel Moreira shot and killed a policeman in Rio de Janeiro, Brazil. This surprised law enforcement officials—the alleged killer, better known as "Horseface," had a reputation for cowardice and non-violence—but the anger of a fellow officer's death was enough to drive them to revenge. Overnight, Horseface Moreira became the most wanted fugitive in Brazil. Police conducted an extensive manhunt, with many officers leaving their official precincts to conduct their own dedicated manhunts.

Moreira eluded his many captors for more than a month until Oct. 3 when police, acting on a tip, surrounded a cottage in Cabo Frio and ordered Moreira to come out. "Shoot to kill!" he called back to them. "Before dying I will take one more to hell with me!" But this he wasn't able to do. Following a lengthy standoff, he was killed in a flurry of machine gun bullets. The coroner found more than 100 slugs in Moreira's corpse.

Morey, William, 1933- , and **Pell, Max**, 1933- , and **Royal, David**, 1934- , U.S. Known by the media-moniker "The Michigan Murder Trio," William Morey, Max Pell, and David Royal wreaked havoc on the University of Michigan campus in 1951 with a series of violent assaults on female students. The last attack, which occurred around midnight on Sept. 15, 1951, left Pauline Campbell, a 34-year-old nurse, dead from heavy blows to her skull. A week later, the police investigation closed with the arrest of the three teenagers, all from well-off, middle-class homes. It wasn't long before they confessed to the murder, and to some of the other assaults.

It was clear Morey was the "ringleader." The assaults had been his idea, and one of his victims identified him as the attacker. Pell and Royal would stay in their car while Morey would lie in wait for a woman walking alone. The motive for the assaults was usually only robbery, though Morey confessed that the trio was planning on actually abducting Campbell. Of the three, Royal was clearly the least responsible and the one most likely to be easily influenced by peers to commit such acts, and his attorney used this to its greatest advantage in his defense. Pell and Morey both used a defense that they were too drunk to be fully responsible for their actions.

Morey and Pell were found Guilty of first-degree murder and sentenced to life imprisonment without parole. Royal was found Guilty of second-degree murder and received a lighter sentence: twenty-two years to life. Dan Myers, a fourth defendant who had been with the trio during one of their attacks and had testified against them, received a one-to ten-year sentence.

Morgan, Derrick, 1956- , U.S. Derrick Morgan's attorney tried winning the jury's sympathy during his client's 1988 murder trial by pointing out that Morgan grew up in a harsh environment in Chicago's South Side housing projects. Morgan's background did justify his crime, according to Assistant State's Attorney Jack Hynes. "He's not a product of his environment," Hynes said. "He's a manipulator of his environment. The reason people cannot come out of their homes at night is because of the Derrick Morgans who are out there sticking guns in their faces."

Morgan was a "soldier" in the El Rukn street gang, which for many years was involved in gun running, extortion, drug dealing, and contract murder. Chicago police estimate that there are as many as 8,000 El Rukn "associates" in Chicago, and its branch cities of Minneapolis, Milwaukee, St. Paul, and Columbus, Ohio. Morgan was one of many gunmen sent out to kill Jeff Fort, who has led the gang since the mid-1960s, then known as the Blackstone Rangers. Morgan was arrested for the first time in 1974. His record included five convictions for robbery and armed robbery. One conviction involved Morgan and three others, who bound a Hyde Park priest in the church rectory in 1979.

On Dec. 17, 1985, Morgan shot and killed 29-year-old David Smith in the back of the head. Attorney Hynes claimed that the Smith murder was a contract killing. A drug dealer paid Morgan and two other men to eliminate Smith. The details of the crime were repeated to law enforcement officials by an Indiana construction worker who shared a cell with Morgan in the La Porte County (Ind.) Jail. Morgan, jailed on an armed robbery charge, bragged about his exploits to his cell mate, who was serving a 150-day sentence for drunk driving. The man said Morgan planned to escape from the facility and return to Chicago to murder all the eyewitnesses. The plan never got that far, because Derrick Morgan was convicted of murder, and on July 15, 1988, he was sentenced to die by a Chicago jury. At present he resides on Death Row.

Morrison, Steinie (Stinie, AKA: **Morris Stein**), 1880-1921, Brit. The execution-style murder of Leon Beron on Clapham Common on Jan. 1, 1911, suggested to London police that Russian anarchists led by the elusive Peter the Painter were responsible. The "Siege of Sidney Street" and the resulting murders of three policemen by East End anarchists was still a fresh memory. The face of Leon Beron had been carved up by the assassin. The letter "S" was clearly visible on the forehead and cheek, suggesting that he was a police informant. "S" could have stood for the word "spic," or "spiccan," which in Russian and Polish meant spy. Detective-Inspector Frederick Wensley denied that Beron had been helping them locate Peter the Painter and members of his gang. The murderer, whoever he was, carved the "S" as a decoy, he said.

Forty-eight-year-old Leon Beron lived with his brother in a dingy flat on the Mile End Road in Stepney. A Russian Jew, he had emigrated from France in 1894 with his brothers to claim an estate that was temporarily held up in the courts. When Beron was not wrangling with the British solicitors, he spent much of his time in the Warsaw Restaurant, a Whitechapel eatery favored by many Russian emigrés with time on their hands. For hours Beron and his friends would discuss politics in a mixture of both French and Yiddish.

Beron cultivated the friendship of another Russian Jew, the tall, modestly handsome Steinie Morrison, whose charm belied a long criminal record. What these two men had in common could only be surmised. The youthful Morrison contrasted sharply to the squat, overbearing Beron, who was eighteen years his senior. But in the waning days of 1910, they were observed together frequently. On New Year's Eve, Morrison and Beron dropped into the Warsaw Restaurant but left shortly before midnight. A cab driver named Alfred Castlin later told police he had picked up two men speaking a foreign language and had driven them to Clapham Common. Later that morning, Beron's mutilated body was found in a patch of bushes. He had been repeatedly stabbed and beaten.

Morrison was identified and arrested in a restaurant on Jan. 8. He had incriminated himself three ways. First, he had left his room on Newark Street to move in with a prostitute in Lambeth. Second, the waiter at the Warsaw Restaurant recalled that Morrison carried with him a wrapped package on the night of the murder that looked and felt like a heavy iron bar. And third, until New Year's Eve Morrison was poor, but afterward his financial problems vanished. Robbery, and not politics, as previously thought, was the apparent motivation for this murder.

Steinie Morrison was tried for murder at the Old Bailey on Mar. 6, 1911. He was defended by Edward Abinger who argued unsuccessfully that Morrison had gone directly home

the night of the murder, pausing a second to speak with Leon Beron who was standing on the corner of Sidney Street talking to a stranger, presumably the murderer. Abinger's relentless cross-examination of Beron's brother and other witnesses for the prosecution earned him a reputation as one of Britain's most capable defense lawyers. Morrison exhibited a defiant attitude throughout the proceedings. After the jury found him Guilty and Justice Darling passed sentence with the customary hope that God would take mercy on his soul, Morrison shot back: "I decline such mercy. I do not believe there is a God in heaven, either." Before the sentence could be carried out, Home Secretary Winston Churchill commuted the penalty to life imprisonment. Morrison was neither grateful nor relieved. He would have preferred death. On Jan. 24, 1921, he died in the Parkhurst Prison infirmary after refusing to eat.

Mors, Frederick, b.1885, U.S. The murderous work of wealthy Frederick Mors had about it a pattern of the weird, the inexplicable. Arriving in New York from Vienna on June 26, 1914, Mors first appeared at the posh Union Square Hotel. He was attired in a tailored, leather, hunting jacket and leather leggings. Beneath his leather coat, Mors carried in a sheath a large hunting knife. When the curious inquired as to his dress, Mors affably explained that he intended to go bear hunting in the Rocky Mountains. He was a famous hunter in his native Austria, he proclaimed, and had heard much of the game was to be had in the West. He was a tall, slim man with a neatly trimmed black beard, a most impressive figure, the hotel guests concurred.

Six days after his arrival at the Union Square Hotel, the eccentric man appeared at the desk and informed the clerk that he was moving. He was nervous, and his eyes were bloodshot. He had lost all of his money, he mumbled through a grimace. (Reports later stated that he had been the victim of a con ring.) The Austrian removed himself and his few belongings to a cheap rooming house on Lexington Avenue. Guests there suggested he seek work through the Immigrant Free Employment Bureau. Through this agency, Mors was hired as a porter for the German Odd Fellows' Home in Unionport, N.Y., the Bronx. His pay was a meager $18 a week, not much for a man who spoke of growing up on a vast estate outside of Vienna, but it kept him alive. That was certainly not the condition, however, in which Mors left many of the elderly inmates of the home.

Shortly after beginning his work as a porter, Mors demanded that the aging inmates of the home address him as "doctor." He ordered them about as if he were the heir to the Hapsburg throne. He took to wearing a white uniform, giving the appearance of a doctor. A stethoscope usually dangled from one of his pockets. Mors was feared by almost all of the elderly persons in the home, but the many small children housed there, all orphans, seemed to like him.

One couple at the home, later interviewed by police, stated: "We were afraid of Dr. Mors. He had an evil eye. He was so domineering and would not permit anyone to balk him when his will was set upon something." Mors regularly bought special items from druggist H.L. Oxmann, whose store was near the institution. Later, when detectives began to pry into Mors' bewildering background, Oxmann told them, "Oh, he buys face powder, cosmetics and perfume...For himself? Certainly. A most fastidious man. You should notice the care he takes of his beard." Mors also bought large amounts of chloroform from Oxmann. That was not for himself.

From Aug. 9, 1914, to Jan. 4, 1915, the death rate at the Unionport home jumped alarmingly; seventeen in all died while Mors was "on duty." Police were asked to investigate. After talking with several inmates, who all expressed their fear of the porter, Mors was brought into an office for questioning. Detective Cornelius W. Willemse, later a tough, gang-fighting NYPD captain, conducted the interrogation.

As Mors sat down, Willemse thought his manner "was that of a man who has met with friends for a pleasant chat."

"Your name?" detective Willemse inquired.

"Frederick Mors."

"Your real name?"

"I do not care to give it."

"How did you come to be a nurse? What qualifications have you?"

"I studied medicine in Europe and spent some time in a hospital."

"What university?"

"I do not care to give it."

"How about all these deaths up here?" Willemse held his breath at that one, but the reply came from Mors without hesitation.

"Oh, I killed them."

"You killed them. How—how many?"

"Eight." There was no change in Mors's voice; he might have been discussing the weather, Willemse later reflected.

The detective handed Mors a list of those who had died at the home during his employ. The porter placed an X before the names of those he had killed—Christian Hitgers (eighty-two, his death had been attributed to old age), Henry Haensel (sixty-seven, old age), Carl Gass (sixty-five, old age), Catherine Piazza (seventy-seven, old age), Frederick Drey (seventy-five, old age), Elizabeth Hauser

(sixty-nine, dropsy), Henry Horn (sixty-eight, stroke), and Fred Schultz (seventy-seven, no cause listed by Mors). From the list Mors had marked for the detective, it was apparent that he had murdered eight of the inmates inside of four months.

"Why did you kill these poor old people?" Willemse demanded.

"Just to put them out of their misery, and, besides, they really are a nuisance to everyone around them...Take the first one I killed for instance. Christian Hitgers, I mean. I had to change his bed clothes several times a day and I got tired of it. So I said to Hitgers: I'm not going to change any more bed clothes for you...I gave him a glass of beer which contained arsenic. I should have known better. He got convulsions and then became paralyzed. It was several days before he died. I made up my mind that the next one would not cause that much trouble."

Mors became confidential. Leaning forward, he continued his startling revelations as if he were a real doctor discussing the clinical treatment of clients. "Let me explain to you why I killed the other seven. I have a book written by a noted doctor in Austria advocating the right of a physician to kill a person suffering from an incurable disease, or when helpless or suffering from extreme age."

"Does this apply to your own parents?" Willemse put it, still somewhat shocked by Mors' indifferent manner.

"Oh no. My people are well able to take care of themselves. But if old people are without friends or relatives and can't take care of themselves, they certainly are better off dead. What's the use of suffering all of the time without a chance of improving? I killed these people and I believe I did the right thing. All of them were suffering and all of them were great nuisances. So I got rid of them.

"It was a very simple matter—the killing of these useless old people," Mors went on in a monotone. "The only difficulty I had was in devising a way to prevent the fumes of chloroform from escaping into the air of the room and becoming noticeable to anyone who entered. I followed a simple process which I learned abroad while studying medicine. First, I would pour a drop or two of chloroform on a piece of absorbent cotton and hold it to the nostrils of the old person I wanted to assist out of the world. Soon my man would swoon. Then I would close the orifices of the body with cotton, stuffing it in the ears, nostrils, etc. Next I would pour a little chloroform down the throat and prevent the fumes from escaping the same way. It wasn't long before the heart stopped beating."

"Did you kill seven of them just that way?"

Yes, I freed their souls from suffering," Mors said with pride to Willemse. He then added with a sharp bit of anger: "Nuisances, all of them!"

Mors was taken to Bellevue Hospital and placed in the

psychopathic ward for examination. The noted psychiatric authority, Dr. Menas Gregory, examined Mors as the killer stood at a window and stared out into the hospital yard. He watched with great interest the cripples and derelicts of all ages moving about outside.

"I'd like to get a job here, doctor," Mors told Dr. Gregory. "I'd clean up that yard for you quick."

"I'll just bet you would," commented a nearby guard.

It took little time to declare Mors a criminal lunatic. He was committed to Matteawan State Prison for the insane, where millionaire Harry K. Thaw, convicted of killing Stanford White, was a prisoner. Frederick Mors, however, felt his job unfinished, as he so often remarked to fellow inmates at Matteawan. He intended to break free and continue his charitable work with the elderly. He made good his escape in the late 1920s and was never recaptured, leaving many New York authorities thereafter to shudder with apprehension and detectives to conduct hurried investigations whenever an unseemly death occurred in any home for the aged.

Morse, Frederick, prom. 1933, Brit. Frederick Morse, a quarryman, appeared happy as he walked on an outing in February 1933 with Dorothy Winifred Brewer, twelve, who he claimed was his niece. Later in the day, Morse returned alone, explaining that he had left Brewer while he checked rabbit traps. Police found the girl's body in a stream; tests showed that she had been drinking. Morse was convicted of murder following a trial that showed he and his sister were Brewer's parents, and that Brewer was pregnant, apparently with her father's child. Morse was hanged.

Mortensen, Peter, prom. 1901, U.S. A father-in-law's nightmare and a wife's sleeptalking helped lead police to arrest Peter Mortensen for murder. Mortensen, a Salt Lake City, Utah, contractor and builder, owed the Pacific Lumber Company $3,907. On Dec. 16, 1901, he visited the company's Salt Lake City office to settle the difference, and promised to pay company secretary and treasurer James R. Hay at Mortensen's home that night.

At about 9 p.m., Hay left his home for Mortensen's. He never came back. When questioned by Hay's office manager, Romney, Mortensen said he had given Hay the money in gold, and that Hay put it in his outside coat pockets and left. But Romney knew Hay's coat did not have outer pockets. Meanwhile Mortensen was spreading the rumor that Hay, highly regarded for his honesty, had embezzled

the money and run off with a prostitute.

Then, on Dec. 18, Hay's body was discovered buried in the snow. He had been shot in the head with a .44-caliber pistol. Mortensen owned a .38, and this fact may have absolved him had not Hay's father-in-law, James Sharp, kept police on the case. Sharp was obsessed by a recent dream that Mortensen had killed his son-in-law. Then Mortensen's wife, who went to live with her sister when the scandal began, was overheard talking in her sleep about how her husband had left with Hay, returned alone and then begged her for forgiveness. Mortensen was arrested Dec. 18.

During the trial, Sharp testified that he had received a revelation from God that Mortensen murdered his son-in-law. This testimony, coupled with widespread doubt that Mortensen ever had the money for the lumber company in his home, convinced the jury, especially the four Mormon members who believed in divine revelations. Found Guilty, Mortensen was executed by firing squad on Nov. 20, 1903.

Mortimer, Arthur Charles, c.1908- , Brit. A lance corporal in a Welsh regiment, Arthur Charles Mortimer hit four female bicyclists with his car, killing one, in a two-day spree of violence. Mrs. Alice Series was the first to be hit, on Aug. 7, 1935. She was riding her bicycle in Hampshire when Mortimer's car forced her off the road into a ditch. Mortimer then told her that his steering wheel was jammed, but when Series peeked in to look, he punched her in the mouth and continued to hit her as she lay on the ground. Later that day, Mortimer hit bicyclist Nellie Boyes, who memorized his license plate number. The car was later found abandoned.

The next day, 20-year-old Phyllis Oakes sustained fatal injuries when she was knocked from her bicycle. She bounced off the hood of Mortimer's car, and landed on a railway bridge in Winchfield, Hampshire. Her sister, Betty Oakes, and a sign writer saw Oakes get hit by the car, and the sign writer memorized the license plate, AGJ 825. The car, stolen from Farnborough, was later found abandoned at Ash Common; two of the tires were flat and the license plate and bumper were damaged. Lilian Rose Harwood was then knocked unconscious as she rode her bicycle near Knap Hill at Surrey; a neighbor wrote down the plate number.

Police caught up with Mortimer on the road to Guildford, and chased him until he crashed into a parked van. "I have had a drink or two last week," Mortimer explained upon his arrest, "and if I have knocked women about it is through drink and heat. I fell into a quarry when I was young, which made me have fits. I sometimes do things, but why I do them I don't know. I can't say I did not hit the women, but I cannot remember."

Three months later Mortimer was brought to trial at the Winchester Assizes. Although he had fallen into a quarry when he was twelve and was subject to epileptic fits, and was sent to a mental institution for six months when he was seventeen, the jury found him Guilty and sentenced him to die. On Jan. 22, 1936, however, following a medical inquiry required by the Criminal Lunatics Act of 1884, the sentence was commuted to life in prison.

Moseley, Winston, 1935- , U.S. In the early morning hours of Mar. 13, 1964, 28-year-old Kitty Genovese was returning to her apartment in the working-class neighborhood of Kew Gardens, Queens, N.Y., when suddenly a knife-toting man stabbed her from behind. Awakened by Genovese's cries for help, a neighbor in one of the apartment buildings poked his head out the window to see what was happening. "Let that girl alone!" he yelled. But neither he nor any of the other residents came to her aid.

Genovese staggered around the corner toward her home. Her assailant, Winston Moseley, followed close behind in his car, got out, and stabbed her again. "Oh my God! He stabbed me!" she screamed. Her cries awakened other sleeping residents of Kew Gardens, but still no one appeared. She stumbled into the vestibule of the nearest apartment building but Moseley followed her. There, he finished what he had started. The prolonged murder lasted thirty-five minutes. Only after the third attack did someone actually call police. The caller explained that he "did not want to get involved," and had actually phoned a friend in Nassau County for advice on what to do. It was a familiar excuse the police heard from a number of spectators that day. The fact that thirty-eight eyewitnesses stood by and did nothing raised a number of disturbing questions among law enforcement professionals and clinical psychologists. In the next two decades, scholars would ponder the phenomenon that came to be known as the "Genovese Syndrome." In March 1984, experts in sociology, psychology, medicine, and law met on the campus of Fordham University in New York for the first "Catherine Genovese Memorial Conference on Bad Samaritanism." R. Lance Shotland, a psychologist at Pennsylvania State University concluded that a person is less likely to intervene in an emergency if there are a number of other persons present. "They take cues from others," he explained. "A lone bystander may help 70 percent of the time. As a member of a group, that same bystander may help 40 percent of the time."

Moseley, a 29-year-old machine operator, confessed that he had been driving around the neighborhood hoping to "rape and to rob and to kill a girl." He was convicted and sentenced to die in the electric chair, but the sentence was later commuted to life imprisonment. While serving his time at the Attica facility in New York, Moseley attempted to go straight. He earned a college degree and became involved in prison reform movements. In an article published in the New York *Times* on Apr. 16, 1977, he explained his new outlook on life. "The man that killed Kitty Genovese in Queens in 1964 is no more. He was also destroyed in that calamity and its aftermath. Another vastly different individual has emerged, a Winston Moseley intent and determined to do constructive, not destructive things."

Mosley, Wallace Leon, c.1964- , U.S. Raised in the Skid Row area near Miami, Fla., the son of an alcoholic mother who never knew his father, Wallace Leon Mosley confessed to fatally stabbing a 9-year-old playmate, William Greg Billiter, on July 31, 1976.

Mosley became a ward of the Division of Protective Services three months before the stabbing, after telling police his mother's common-law-husband, Charles Whitcomb had beaten him. Despite troubles at home, Mosley ran back to his mother whenever the state attempted to send him to a foster home. He rarely went to school in 1976, preferring instead to repair fishing boats and radios and to operate a fork-lift truck.

The state obtained full custody of Mosley after the killing. William, called Greg by his family, had been dropped off at his grandparents' home by his mother. Wallace Mosley lived next door. Later that day, observers saw the two boys throwing a butcher knife into a tree. The boys went to Whitcomb's apartment, where William apparently called Mosley's mother an alcoholic, and called Mosley a "bastard." William Billiter was then stabbed seven times and his skull was fractured.

A juvenile court judge decided Mosley should be tried as an adult because of the brutal nature of the murder and because he doubted the boy could be rehabilitated. The case was later turned over to juvenile authorities, however. Judge Ralph Ferguson ordered the state to take custody of Mosley. He was sent to the Lancaster Youth Development Center in northern Florida. A guardian was assigned to make reports on Mosley and to protect him from possible harassment from other children at the center, where the average age is sixteen.

Muldowney, Dennis George, 1911-52, Brit. Christine Skarbek was descended from one of Poland's oldest and most noble families. When her country was overrun by the Nazis during WWII, she joined the British secret service, which sent her on many dangerous missions. Posing as "Jacqueline Armand," Christine parachuted into southeastern France. In Italy, a border patrol attempted to arrest her as a spy, but Skarbek raised both hands, revealing two live grenades. The soldiers permitted her to escape. In 1944, with a price already on her head, Skarbek boldly marched into a Nazi prison camp and demanded the release of three allied officers scheduled to be executed by firing squad. Realizing that the American column was quickly advancing, Christine gambled that the sergeant-major would be willing to bargain. "If you shoot them," she said, "I will see to it that you yourself are shot when the Americans reach here." The three men walked out of the prison camp unhurt.

Christine Skarbek was a WWII heroine. For her unusual bravery in the face of dangerous odds, she was awarded the prestigious Croix de Guerre from France, the Order of British Empire, and Britain's George Medal for Special Services. But she refused to advertise this fact when she went job hunting in Kensington after the war. Because she was a foreigner living in England, employers were reluctant to give her a chance. For a time she worked as a salesgirl in Harrods Department Store for $14 a week. In 1951, she found a job as a tourist-class stewardess on board a cruise ship running to Australia and New Zealand. Her supervisor was Dennis George Muldowney, whose infatuation with Skarbek developed into a dangerous obsession. After she resigned from the cruise line, she returned to London, only to be followed by Muldowney, who took a job as a porter at the Reform Club in Westminster.

Time and again she spurned his advances. On June 15, 1952, Muldowney confronted Christine at a hotel in Kensington. She was preparing to rejoin her wartime boyfriend, Major Andrew Kowerski, who lived in Brussels. The demented Muldowney grabbed her on the staircase. "Get him off me!" she screamed. A porter, hearing her cry for help, rushed to the scene but the 37-year-old Countess had fallen to the floor, stabbed in the chest.

Dennis Muldowney refused to be represented by legal counsel when the murder case came before Justice Terence Donovan at the Old Bailey on Sept. 10, 1952. He entered a plea of Guilty, fully aware of the likely consequences. Muldowney said little during the trial, but implied that he had been on intimate terms with Skarbek before the murder – which the prosecution refuted. The murderer was sentenced to die at Pentonville Prison. The home secretary upheld the decision of the court, and Muldowney was executed on Sept. 30, 1952.

Mullin, Herbert William, 1947-   , U.S. In the early 1970s mass killers Ed Kemper and Herbert Mullin terrorized Santa Cruz, Calif. Mullin, the religious-minded, schizophrenic son of a Marine colonel, spent a number of years smoking marijuana and taking LSD. When he was twenty-five, he began to hear voices that told him that if he sacrificed human lives, he would prevent the massive earthquakes predicted for Southern California. Between October 1972 and February 1973, he killed thirteen people: a tramp he met in the mountains, a lone girl whose body he mutilated, a priest in a confessional, four campers, the couple who introduced him to marijuana, a woman and her two children, and finally, on Feb. 13, 1973, an old man working in his backyard. Mullin shot the old man because he heard his father's voice say that he needed to kill someone before coming to his parents' home that day. He committed the murder in broad daylight, and was caught.

At Mullin's trial it was shown that he had voluntarily committed himself to mental hospitals five different times

Left, mass killer Herbert Mullin.

in the preceding years. Each time he was diagnosed as a paranoid schizophrenic with dangerous aggressive tendencies, given some drugs, and sent on his way. The jury, determined he should not be released, found him Guilty on ten counts of murder, and he was sent to prison for life.

Murphy, Frederick George, d.1937, Brit. English prostitute Katherine Peck was found shortly after midnight by police, her throat cut. Frederick George Murphy, an odd job man and her frequent associate, had been seen with her in a pub on the night of her death. Murphy arrived at his rooming house around 1 a.m. that morning, left early and did not return. An acquaintance named Wood said he had met Murphy that afternoon, and that he told him he had slain Peck and was running from the police. Another man testified that Murphy told him the same story. Six weeks later Murphy walked into the Bethnal Green police and said he had heard the police were searching for him. He denied killing Peck, and said he did not spend the night of the murder in his rooming house. Murphy was charged with murder. At his trial, the witness to whom Murphy allegedly confessed was absent. Murphy denied the conversation with Wood, and Eustace Fuller, attorney for the Crown, said it was dangerous to convict the defendant on such slight evidence. Murphy was released, and accused Wood of perjury. He also charged the home secretary, the police, and his member of parliament with bribery. He smashed a window in the home office and spent fourteen days in jail as a result. Murphy found work as a warehouse cleaner in Islington Green and was given his own keys to the establishment. On May 14, 1937, Murphy wrote his employers that there was a dead woman in the cellar, and that he was innocent of the crime. By the time police arrived, Murphy was gone, but he showed up the next day at the Poplar Police Station to explain why he could not have killed the woman, Rosina Field, a prostitute. But police found bloodstains on Murphy's clothes, and he had been seen with Field late at night at the warehouse. Murphy was convicted, and hanged at Pentonville Prison on Aug. 17, 1937.

Murray, Esther del Rosario, prom. 1949, Phil. Kansas City businessman George C. Murray left his wife of two years, Esther del Rosario Murray, at home in Manila, Phil., on the night of Aug. 12, 1949, and went to meet his mistress, actress Carol Varga. But he could not find the gun he usually carried. The maid would later tell police that she saw Mrs. Murray hide the revolver in her sewing basket. At 4 a.m., when Murray returned home, he went to sleep, and was slain by gun shots in the early morning. Calling police, the tearful widow said she heard shots when she was downstairs in the kitchen, and rushed to her husband's bedroom to find him dead. Police photographed the bedroom and examined Murray's papers. They discovered that his yacht, the *Mistress,* was a gun-running boat used to smuggle ammunition, arms, jeeps, and other war materials to Southeast Asian countries. Murray's shady enterprises meant he could have been killed by any one of hundreds of enemies. But the newly developed Philippine Bureau of Investigation (PBI), questioned Esther Murray again. They found a white glove with nitrate stains on it. The family maid, Maria Naral, told PBI Agent Faustos that Mrs. Murray left her youngest child with her around 4:30 a.m., shortly before she heard explosions. According to Naral, Mrs. Murray told her to "tell them the shots you heard were the backfiring of a car and that you also heard the dogs bark." The chauffeur saw a woman emerge from the bedroom just after the shooting, and then saw Esther Murray throw something in the direction of the dogs' pen. Police found the murder weapon in the pen. Tried before Justice Ceferino de Los Santos, Esther Murray was found Guilty of murder and sentenced to life imprisonment. She began serving her sentence on Oct. 26, 1959, after her appeal was denied by the supreme court.

Myrtel, Hera (**Marie-Louise Victorine Grones**), b.1868, Fr. Hera Myrtel was recognized by a handful of fawning admirers in the cafes and art salons of Paris as a writer of romantic fiction. Myrtel (a pen name) was known to her two husbands as a violent and adulterous woman. She later was known as a female Bluebeard, having murdered her husbands.

Born Marie-Louise Victorine Grônes in Lyon, Fr., Myrtel was educated in a convent. She returned to her father's home upon completion of her studies, and worked for a time in the family silk business. In 1892 she went to Mexico to help her father land some new contracts to bolster the failing business. Myrtel attracted attention everywhere she went, most of it unsavory. On one occasion the Mexican federales found her in a remote villa with a wealthy merchant lying dead at her feet. She told the police that a gang of ruthless bandits had entered the hacienda and had shot him dead. The federales were well aware of the presence of bandits in the region, and Myrtel was believed.

While in Mexico City she met fellow Frenchman Paul Jacques, who was many years her senior. Jacques was shy

French murderess Héra Myrtel.

and retiring, but he possessed one quality Myrtel found admirable in a man. He was extremely wealthy. Jacques ran a thriving silk importing business with offices in Europe and Mexico. Following a brief courtship, Jacques and Myrtel were married. They returned to Paris in 1904, and shortly afterward their daughter Paule was born. It was not enough for Myrtel, however, to be the wife of a successful businessman.

Jacques's wife became obsessed with the literary community, and after publishing a novel of some limited commercial success under the name Hera Myrtel, her popularity in literary circles began to spread. Jacques hired a nursemaid for his daughter while his wife cavorted about Paris, very often in the company of lovers. By 1913 Myrtel had had enough of Paris and longed to return to Mexico, but Jacques refused her request. In January 1914 Myrtel slipped a corrosive poison into his soup, but Jacques became suspicious and brought a sample of it to a chemist for analysis. He informed Jacques that there was indeed a deadly poison in the soup. The cuckolded husband seemed strangely unconcerned. He intimated to his friends that he "did not know the woman, never would understand the dark corners of her mind."

Myrtel waited two more months, and then carried her deadly plan forward. On Mar. 5, 1914, the family maid, Georgette Picourla, heard a gunshot from the master bedroom. She came running into the room to find Myrtel standing over the prostrate body of her husband. "Jacques has committed suicide, poor man," she said. The concierge was summoned by the maid. "Madame Chambre," Myrtel said, "my husband is dead, and he was quite alone. Georgette found him dead when she took him his chocolate." When the woman had gone, Myrtel pulled Georgette aside and told her to play along. "When the police come, tell them you found him lying shot in the chair when you brought his chocolate. I don't think I could stand being questioned."

The loyal maid played her part beautifully. The police accepted the story at face value, and ruled Paul Jacques's death a suicide. Myrtel and Paule sailed for Mexico, where she liquidated her husband's assets and renewed her dormant literary career. This time, her romantic interest was a Rumanian national named Charles Bessarabo, who cast a furtive glance toward Myrtel's modest fortune. "Money, fame, and beauty—I shall have them all at the same time," he gushed, not knowing what was in store for him. Bessarabo proposed marriage, Myrtel accepted, and in 1916 they traveled to Paris. They settled in comfortable surroundings at 3 place La Bruyere, and things quickly reverted to the way they were when Jacques was alive. Myrtel reopened her literary salon, which became a clearing house for draft dodgers, pimps, and n'er-do-wells of all types. France was at war, but Myrtel enjoyed life to the fullest, entertaining a plethora of lovers.

Bessarabo accepted all of this rather calmly, for he feared public exposure of his shady private dealings. One night in 1918, Myrtel applied a chokehold to Bessarabo's neck as he lay sleeping. With the greatest effort, the frightened man managed to throw her to the floor. Stunned, Myrtel looked up at her husband and sobbed, "I don't know what came over me." The next attack came on the night of July 8, 1920, when Bessarabo returned home to find his wife preparing herself to entertain one of her lovers. Myrtel grabbed an automatic pistol from the table and told him the matter was of no concern to him. "Get out—or I'll lay you out!" she screamed. She fired an errant bullet as Bessarabo dove for the floor. After this episode, he vowed to leave her, but she snarled, "You walk out on me and I'll expose you."

Fearing for his life, Bessarabo sequestered himself in his private room and had his meals catered. He went so far as to hire a chauffeur named Croix to drive him about the city, but it was still not enough to protect him from Myrtel's wrath. On July 31 the chauffeur presented himself at the door to pick up Bessarabo. "I told you—he's off on a business trip. He'll return on August 2. You're dismissed," Myrtel told him. Croix went to the police with his suspicions when Bessarabo failed to show up on Aug. 2. Myrtel, brought in for questioning, told the police an outrageous story. "He must have gone off to Switzerland with his mistress. Every successful businessman in Paris has a mistress," she added. "Is that not true?" According to Myrtel, she had shipped off a trunk of his belongings to Nancy per her husband's instructions. The trunk was located, but instead of clothing and personal items they found the body of Charles Bessarabo, his head smashed in with a hammer.

Faced with the evidence of the crime, Myrtel confessed. It was a crime of passion, she said; her husband's cheating drove her to murder. Both Myrtel and her daughter Paule went on trial for murder on Feb. 15, 1921, but it was Paule's testimony that convicted her mother. There was no mistress, she explained. Her mother ordered her to drag the trunk down from the attic and place the body inside. The jury acquitted Paule, but returned a verdict of Guilty with "mitigating circumstances" against Myrtel, who was sentenced to twenty years in prison.

N

Nally, William, 1943-   , U.S. It was dark when attorney Timothy McNamee, thirty-four, came out of his Carpentersville, Ill., office on June 8, 1987. Lying in wait in a small wooded area next to the law office's parking lot was William Nally with a 70-year-old, WWI-vintage military rifle. The gun's age did not stop it from accurately sending a bullet into McNamee's abdomen as he came out of his office. The attorney bled to death in the driveway.

Although police continually sought a drug motive in the case, investigations into the law partnership's clients gradually narrowed suspicion down to Nadine Walter, twenty-five, and her quest to keep custody of her son. McNamee's partner, Timothy Mahoney, was the attorney of Walter's ex-husband, Rolando Rodriguez, who had been granted temporary custody. The day before McNamee was shot, Rodriguez had abducted the boy from Tennessee where he had been living with his grandfather, his mother, and her former boyfriend, Nally. Walter, hoping to scare her husband into giving back her son, suggested to Nally that they go after the law partners, whom they blamed for Rodriguez being granted custody.

On Nov. 9, 1988, seventeen months after the killing, Walter agreed to help police convict Nally in exchange for immunity for her role in the murder and an unrelated credit-card fraud. Wearing a concealed tape recorder, she met Nally at O'Hare International Airport. As they walked through the busy airport, Nally's conversation with Walter contained incriminating statements about the murder. Among the things he said was: "I killed him. I shot him dead....Honey, we're killers." He was arrested before leaving the airport.

The tape recording was played in court, and William Nally was found Guilty. On Apr. 27, 1989, Nally was sentenced to life in prison with no opportunity for parole.

Narvaiz, Leo, Jr., 1968-   , U.S. Because Leo Narvaiz, Jr., twenty, had been rejected by his girlfriend, Shannon Mann, he savagely murdered her, her two sisters, and her brother. At 3:27 a.m. on Apr. 16, 1988, a young girl called the 911 emergency number and said, "One of my sister's boyfriends is beating us up and has killed my sister." When police traced the call to the Manns' San Antonio, Texas, mobile home, they found the bodies of the four children. They were stabbed to death with steak knives, some of which had broken off in their necks. Dead were Shannon Mann, seventeen, Martha Mann, fifteen, Jennifer Mann, nineteen, and Ernest Mann, Jr., eleven. Leo Narvaiz, charged with four counts of capital murder, was held in lieu of a $4.05 million bond. He had used five knives in the vicious slayings, attacking the children as they slept in

their five-bedroom trailer. Becky Mann, their mother, was at work. She had recently separated from the children's father, Ernest Mann, Sr., who had filed two complaints against Narvaiz.

Narvaiz was tried, convicted, and sentenced to death. Several months after the slayings, Mann heard on the radio for the first time that his son had been virtually dismembered. Explaining later that "something snapped inside," Ernest Mann, thirty-six, began stealing garden hoses and lawn chairs from front yards, apparently to be jailed in order to confront Narvaiz. Police said Mann seemed "happy and relieved" when caught. He was taken to the Bexar County Jail where, he later told officer Don Marguis, he had hoped to "see the creep face to face." Unknown to Mann, Narvaiz had been transferred to Death Row at Huntsville Prison. Mann was fined $50 on a misdemeanor charge and released.

Nathaniel, Cathy, 1946-   , U.S. "I question whether you have any morals at all," said the judge to prostitute Cathy Nathaniel when he sentenced her to thirty-five years in prison for the murder of a man she picked up in a Chicago bar. On May 3, 1979, Nathaniel and her roommate, Bernice Albright, met attorney Steven Ticho, who invited the two back to his apartment in the John Hancock Building on Michigan Avenue. Albright soon left, but Nathaniel stayed on, and shot Ticho in the back of the head. She then returned to her apartment and got Albright to return with her to the Hancock Building to loot the apartment.

Nathaniel was caught after using Ticho's credit cards. On Oct. 25, 1979, she was convicted of murder in the courtroom of Criminal Court Judge James M. Bailey, who saw no sign of remorse in the murderous prostitute.

Naumoff, Nicolas, and **Tarnowska, Marie Nicolaievna,** and **Prilukoff, Donat,** prom. 1907-10, Italy. From cold Russia to the warmth of Italy came the aristocrats, bringing their passions, hates, and intrigues with them. One of them, young Nicolas Naumoff, had the misfortune to be totally infatuated with Countess Marie Tarnowska. Strange things happened around the countess. First her brother-in-law, and later a doctor, committed suicide over their love for her. Then her husband, who had first taught her the ways of dalliance, simultaneously filed for divorce and shot her current lover, Alexis Borzewski; the court found that homicide to have been justifiable.

The countess' divorce lawyer, Donat Prilukoff, quickly

came under her control and soon was digging deeply into his wealth to pay for her whims. Even when she became involved with a certain Count Kamarovski, he was unable to break away. Whether it was the countess' idea or Prilukoff's, the two persuaded Kamarovski to take out life insurance with Tarnowska as the beneficiary. Tarnowska and Prilukoff then inveigled 21-year-old Naumoff into their scheme after the countess seduced the gullible young man.

The infatuated young man listened intently as, time after time, his love whispered of horrible things the count did to her. He thought to rescue the beautiful woman from the grotesque count. In Venice, she pleaded with him to rid her of Kamarovski. On the morning of Sept. 3, 1907, Naumoff went to the count's villa. Taken to the older man's bedroom, Naumoff gave him no chance to speak. He fired a number of bullets, then left the room by the balcony. Prilukoff, who had arranged to have detectives on hand to take the killer into custody, had left to have coffee, so Naumoff escaped. Actually, Naumoff's badly aimed bullets failed to kill the count; but the doctors, unable to decide what medical treatment to apply, managed to let him die.

All the figures in the plot were quickly arrested and charged, but it was almost three years before they were brought to trial in March 1910. Prilukoff and Naumoff both blamed their problems on their love of the countess. Then the countess herself took the stand. For twelve long weeks she relayed the amorous story of her life. Finally, the jury found Naumoff Guilty of murder, mitigated by the fact that "he was suffering from a partial mental collapse." They found both the countess and Prilukoff Guilty of helping him. The jury said, "We reject the theory that she was mad, but we find that her mental faculties were partially destroyed." Prilukoff, they said, was not impaired, thus the court gave him the strongest sentence, ten years of solitary confinement. Countess Tarnowska was sentenced to eight years and four months. Nicolas Naumoff, the actual killer, received the lightest sentence, three years and four months in prison.

Neal, Tom, 1913-72, U.S. Tom Neal, "The King of the B Pictures," was a violent and often jealous man. A boxer of some note, Neal first appeared as a bit actor in a number of Hollywood films in the early 1940s. His name was listed in the credits along with John Wayne in the war epic *Flying Tigers*. Neal acted in over 180 films, few of them of lasting importance. His first wife, Vicky Lane, divorced him in 1949 because of his obsessive jealousy. He then became involved with Barbara Payton, an aspiring actress of modest talents, who was later arrested for intoxication, passing bad checks, and prostitution. Her

biggest role was that of James Cagney's girlfriend in *Kiss Tomorrow Goodbye*, a 1950 film remembered chiefly for its excessive violence. Payton reappeared in Neal's life at regular intervals. At one time she tried to get him jealous enough to marry her by dating matinee idol Franchot Tone.

On Sept. 14, 1951, Neal cornered Tone outside his residence and beat him badly enough to cause a brain concussion. Franchot Tone went on to marry the sympathetic, adoring Barbara Payton in her Minnesota hometown, a union she said she sought due to the beating he had taken solely because he loved her, but the marriage ended disastrously after only seven weeks. The Tone episode effectively destroyed Tom Neal's film career—as lackluster as it was—so he turned to landscaping, which he had learned from his Japanese gardeners during his more successful days, in order to earn a living. The business he started prospered, and within a few years Tom Neal, the man with the extremely short temper and quick fists, was attending to the lawns and gardens of the Palm Springs elite.

Neal remarried, but his second wife Patricia died of cancer in 1958. That marriage produced a son. He married for a third time in June 1961, this time to a petite brunette named Gail who worked as a receptionist at the Palm Springs Tennis Club. The one-time Hollywood bad boy dutifully attended to his wife and his successful gardening business for the next four years. He managed to keep his name out of the papers until Apr. 2, 1965, when he fired a bullet into his wife's head behind the right ear while she reclined on the couch. During the next several hours he wandered aimlessly around the city, visiting his most intimate friends, to whom he admitted that he had killed his wife.

Neal told a different story to Palm Springs Police. He said that he was making love to Gail when she pulled a gun on him, and during the struggle to take it from her, the weapon accidentally discharged. She had obtained the weapon recently for protection, as she had developed emotional problems and believed she was being followed, but the quarrel had stemmed from Neal's own paranoic jealousy. He had accused his wife of sleeping with other men—a story he later told to the judge and jury. Robert Lawrence Balzer, part owner of the Tyrol Restaurant in Pine Grove and a close friend of Neal's, substantiated these statements by recounting his confession the night of the murder. While visiting Balzer hours after the shooting, Neal complained that Gail "had become my whole life and I could not live without her." Tom Neal had sought out Balzer, a Buddhist monk, the day before for spiritual advice. The two men had discussed Buddhist philosophy for hours, with Balzer advising his friend, "The problems of life are as a tiger at the door," to which he said Neal answered, "I

Actor Franchot Tone leaving a hospital following beating by Neal.

Actress Barbara Payton, later arrested for prostitution, with Neal.

Gail Neal with actor Tom Neal; she was shot to death by Neal.

Tom Neal at the height of his acting career in Hollywood, 1944.

Tom Neal, shown after serving six years in prison at age fifty-eight.

am the tiger, and the walls are all around me."

Some time before Neal reported the murder the gun mysteriously disappeared and was never found. According to police lieutenant Richard Harries, the house was in a shambles when he arrived. Items of clothing belonging to a Steven Peck were found strewn about the rooms. Peck's address was listed as 2481 Cardillo Street, which was Neal's residence, but Peck was never called to testify. The police found the fatal bullet nestled in a plush pillow. Neal was taken into custody and held without bail for four days before being arraigned on a murder charge. No explanation was given for another peculiarity: the fact that all the windows in an adjacent apartment building had been shattered.

Although the prosecution lined up thirty prospective witnesses, they rested their case after calling only eight. No reason was ever given. The nine-woman, three-man jury spent a full day deliberating the evidence before returning their verdict on Nov. 18, 1965. Perhaps more intrigued by the mysteries than by the testimony of the witnesses, the jury found Neal Guilty only of involuntary manslaughter. Tom Neal was sentenced to one to fifteen years at the California Institution for Men at Chino. The courts repeatedly denied Neal's appeals, but he still served less than seven years before being paroled in December 1971. Neal attempted a show business comeback following his release from prison. He produced a morning television show called the *Apartment Hunters,* but it was short lived. The King of the B Pictures died a forgotten man on Aug. 7, 1972.

═══════════════════

Nelson, Dale Merle, 1939-   , Can. Dale Nelson, thirty-one, was a society dropout who kept his wife and three little children in a small shack at the edge of the wilderness near West Creston, British Columbia. He worked occasionally at hard labor in the nearby logging camps, but frequently he sank into bouts of depression that kept him drinking and alone. On the night of Sept. 5, 1970, he had been feeding that depression all day, but instead of going home, he went to the house of his aunt, Shirley Wasyk. She was home alone with her three daughters while her husband was away at a logging camp. He battered the woman to death and strangled her 7-year-old daughter, Tracey Wasyk. Debbie Wasyk, twelve, managed to escape and went running for help. However, a neighbor had already called the police, and Nelson fled as he heard sirens approaching.

Nelson did not get far, racing to a remote house. Ray Phipps opened his front door to a gunshot blast. Nelson stepped over the body and systematically shot Phipps's common-law wife, Isabelle St. Amand, and their four children. He took Cathy St. Amand, eight, with him, and sometime in the next few hours, when the police had left the Wasyk house to search the neighborhood, Nelson crept back in and removed Tracey Wasyk's body. Going farther into the wilderness, Nelson mutilated the bodies of the two young girls.

A day and a half later, after hiding in the woods, Dale

Canadian murderer Dale Merle Nelson, who killed eight people, in the custody of the Royal Mounted Police.

Nelson gave himself up. The first thing he said to the police was, "Must have been the LSD." Nelson was tried at Cranbrook Assizes in March 1971, for the murders of Tracey Wasyk and Cathy St. Amand. The defense admitted all facts, letting them add up to a plea of insanity. The hallucinogen LSD was never introduced as a major factor. The jury found Nelson Guilty, and he was sent to prison for life.

═══════════════════

Nelson, Earle Leonard (AKA: **Roger Wilson; The Gorilla Murderer**), 1897-1928, U.S.-Can. Earle Leonard Nelson was one of the strangest and most evasive mass killers in U.S. history. He killed from coast to coast, selecting only women, and even here, his distinction was that he murdered first and *then* attacked his victims sexually. Nelson's victims were almost always middle-aged landladies, matronly, motherly figures who probably represented the mother he lost early in life, a fantasy figure whom he loved and hated, and an overbearing religious aunt whom he simply hated. Born in Philadelphia, Nelson was orphaned before the age of five and was taken in by his aunt, Mrs. Lillian Fabian. She was kindly, but insisted that Earle follow her each and every dictate, especially when it came to his reading the Bible at least one hour a day. She constantly crowed to friends that Earle "will be a minister some day."

At the age of seven, Nelson was playing on a Philadelphia street with another child and ran into the street to chase a ball. A passing trolley car snared him in its cowcatcher and bounced him fifty feet. His head repeatedly struck the cobblestones. Nelson survived but he developed excruciating headaches, which, he claimed, were so severe, that they made him blind. Although Nelson's brain had not been physically injured, the terrible accident most certainly altered the boy's thinking. He began to conjure one image of horror after another, dwelling upon the crucifixions, suicides, and mass slayings recorded in the Bible. He also became obsessed about the Biblical sirens of the Holy Scripture: Bathsheba, Salome, the Queen of Sheba.

He began to manifest his hatred for females by attacking little girls, including his small cousin. When his aunt scolded him for this behavior, Nelson, clever enough to use Mrs. Fabian's obsession for religion, would drop to his knees and beg his aunt's forgiveness, babbling Biblical phrases, crying and pleading so that Mrs. Fabian only sent him to his room. In his room Nelson passed the time searching his Bible for profiles of evil, of murder, and the darkest deeds of man. He grew up a solitary, sullen youth, graduating from high school without a single friend.

Nelson was a powerful young man with broad shoulders and huge, muscular hands with webbed fingers. He could break solid boards with those hands and also perform amazing feats, like walking on his hands for several blocks without losing his balance. He practiced scaling the sides of buildings and claimed that he could actually use his webbed fingers as suction cups in climbing into second-story windows. On his twenty-first birthday, Nelson dragged a neighbor girl into his basement where he tried to rape her. Her screams brought help and Nelson was arrested.

Mrs. Fabian begged police to release her nephew. He was a misunderstood youth, she said, a recluse who meant no harm. Authorities disagreed. Nelson was convicted of rape and sentenced to two years in a penal farm. He escaped but was recaptured. He escaped again, but police found him a short time later, standing outside a window of his aunt's house in a heavy downpour, watching his cousin Rachel undress for bed. This time Nelson was sent to the penitentiary to serve out his sentence, but on Dec. 4, 1918, he escaped again. Using the alias Roger Wilson, Nelson moved to San Francisco where he met a schoolteacher whom he married on Aug. 12, 1919.

This young woman's life was soon turned into a living nightmare. Whenever they went out together, Nelson accused his wife of flirting with other men. He openly chastised her on public streets and screamed out that she was a slut and a whore. She finally had a nervous breakdown, and while she was recovering in a hospital, Nelson entered her hospital room and raped her. It took several interns and male hospital attendants to drag Nelson from his wife. Nelson ran from the hospital cursing his wife and the hospital staff and vanished for seven years.

On Feb. 20, 1926, Nelson appeared on the doorstep of a boarding house owned by Clara Newman in San Francisco. He told the landlady he was a college student and that he was looking for a nice clean room where he could study in peace. As Mrs. Newman showed Nelson into a third floor room, he attacked her and strangled her to death, and then sexually attacked the dead body. He fled, leaving Newman's naked body on the floor. Richard Newman, Mrs. Newman's nephew, found his aunt's ravaged body a few hours later and called the police, telling detectives that his aunt had last been with a man about five-foot-six with a heavy torso, piercing blue eyes, and ape-like arms.

On Mar. 2, 1926, Nelson struck again, this time strangling Mrs. Laura Beale, another landlady. He raped the dead body repeatedly before fleeing. On June 10, Mrs. Lillian St. Mary was found strangled and ravished, her body hidden under a bed in her rooming house. On June 26, Nelson arrived in Santa Barbara and strangled and raped Mrs. George Russell. By then the press was blaring headlines about a strangler it dubbed "The Gorilla Murderer" because of his long arms and monkey-like face with penetrating blue eyes. On Aug. 16, after strangling and raping Mrs. Mary Nesbit in Oakland, Calif., Nelson was inactive for several months. Police believed he was momentarily seized by an irresistible urge to murder, followed by the sordid acts of necrophilia, but had no clues to the killer's identity or his whereabouts. Warnings were issued that a killer was loose and that unescorted women were in danger.

On Oct. 19, 1926, in Portland, Ore., Nelson tried to rent a room from landlady Beta Withers and strangled and raped her. On Oct. 20, Nelson strangled and raped another Portland landlady, Mrs. Mabel Fluke. A few days later in the same city, he strangled and raped landlady Virginia Grant. He then traveled back to San Francisco, and on Nov. 11, 1926, strangled and raped Mrs. William Edmons. Nelson then took the train back to Portland where he strangled and raped Blanche Myers on Nov. 15, 1926. As the manhunt for the Gorilla Murderer intensified, Nelson began traveling east. On Dec. 23, 1926, he strangled and raped Mrs. John Berard in Council Bluffs, Iowa. He then moved southwest and in Kansas City, Mo., Nelson strangled and raped Mrs. Germania Harpin, another landlady. Before leaving Mrs. Harpin's house, Nelson also strangled her eight-month-old daughter.

Back in his home town of Philadelphia, Nelson strangled and raped Mary McConnell on Apr. 27, 1927. On May 1, he strangled and raped Jennie Randolph in Buffalo, N.Y. By June 1, 1927, Nelson was in Detroit. Here he strangled two sisters at the same time, Minnie May and Mrs. M.C.

Atorthy, raping both corpses. Nelson then moved to Chicago where, on June 3, he strangled and raped Mary Sietsome, his last victim in the U.S. All of Nelson's victims in the U.S., with the exception of Mrs. Harpin, had been landladies. With the entire nation looking for him, Nelson crossed into Canada and took a room in Winnipeg, renting from Mrs. August Hill. He said he was a Bible student. That night, June 8, 1927, Lola Cowan, who supported her family by selling artificial flowers made by her crippled sister, vanished from the streets of Winnipeg.

On June 9, 1927, when William Patterson of Winnipeg returned home, his wife was missing and his small children told him that they had not seen her in hours. Patterson, who knew that a strangler was loose in the city, went into the bedroom where he saw his wife's hand protruding from beneath the bed. When he looked beneath the bed, he saw his wife's naked body. She had been strangled and raped.

A short time later, George Smith, Winnipeg's chief of detectives, gathered his best men and told them: "I think that we must operate on the assumption that the madman who has been killing all those landladies in the States has crossed over into Canada. Mrs. Patterson had been strangled by a man with extremely powerful hands, and then, after death, she had been sexually molested. It is the same pattern."

"But Mrs. Patterson was not a landlady," one of the detectives said.

"The killer has altered his *modus operandi.* But the method of killing and the ravishing of the corpse is in the same manner as that occurring in the States. This time he has stolen things, about $70, Mrs. Patterson's ring and a Bible." Smith also pointed out that the killer left behind his old clothes, and took a shirt, pants, and an old coat from the Patterson house. Detectives began to search every rooming house and hotel in the city, interviewing every boarder and guest. Two detectives arrived at Mrs. Hill's rooming house and she admitted that she had taken in a new boarder, describing him as a serious young man with piercing blue eyes, a dark complexion, and a powerful build.

The officers were shown to the boarder's room, but he was gone. They began to search the place. One of the officers leaned down and looked beneath the bed: "Good God, man!" he shouted to his partner. "Look here!" It was the body of Lola Cowan, the flower girl. She, like the other victims, had been strangled and raped. Nelson had taken her body back to his room and hidden it. He later admitted that he made love to the corpse for two days.

By that time Nelson was heading west, hitching rides and walking. In Regina, 200 miles west of Winnipeg, he rented a room. Only minutes after occupying it, he spotted an attractive female boarder in the hall. He shoved her into his room and began to strip her but she screamed and the landlady and male boarders ran upstairs. Nelson leaped out the window, slid down a drainpipe, and escaped. Police were on his trail within minutes. Nelson headed for the U.S. border but two constables stopped him only a few miles outside of the border town of Kilarney. Nelson stood in the road and talked casually with the officers who sat in their car, studying him.

"My name is Wilson," he told them. "I work as a stock hand on a ranch near here."

Constable Grey then thought to shock the young man into blurting a confession by saying: "We're looking for a man who is responsible for the deaths of twenty women."

Nelson gave him a little grin that was more like a sneer and said: "I only do my lady killing on Saturday night, fellas."

Said Grey: "I think you'd better ride along with us back to Killarney until we can check on your story."

"Fair enough," Nelson said, climbing easily into the back seat of the car. "I guess you fellows have to play it safe when there's a killer on the loose."

In Killarney, Nelson was placed in a small jail and Constables Grey and Sewell went down the street to call Chief Smith in Winnipeg. They described their captive. Smith told them that the killer had used the same name, Roger Wilson, in Winnipeg. Smith then asked where the man was being kept. When he heard that Nelson had been left handcuffed to a cell bar and that his shoes had been taken away, he still cried out: "What! Don't let that man out of your sight! I want one of you with him at all times!" He then said that he and a dozen officers were on their way to Killarney by the next train. When Grey and Sewell returned to the jail fifteen minutes later they found the cell door open and the handcuffs dangling from the bar. Nelson had picked the lock on the handcuffs and the cell door and had fled.

Panic gripped the tiny town of Killarney. All the women and children were taken to the local church where they were guarded by dozens of gun-carrying men. More than 500 men formed a huge posse and they began a desperate search for the mass murderer, going house to house, field by field, through the night, their burning torches sending up eerie shoots of light. Meanwhile, Nelson was sound asleep in the loft of William Allen's barn, which was only a block from the jail. The next morning, wearing a pair of worn-out boots he had found in the barn, Nelson walked to the train station and sat in the waiting room for the next train. When the train pulled into the station, Nelson moved toward it, but suddenly dozens of armed detectives leaped from the cars, Chief Smith in the lead. With two dozen revolvers pointed at him, Nelson surrendered. He was led away handcuffed.

Earle Leonard Nelson in custody in Canada, 1927.

Mrs. Clara Newman, murdered.

Mrs. Blanche Myers, murdered.

Mrs. Mabel Fluke, murdered.

Mrs. Beta Withers (shown with her son), murdered.

Nelson, the Gorilla Murderer.

A banner headline in the Manitoba *Free Press* tells of the terror which mass killer Earle Leonard Nelson spread through Canada in 1927.

Taken to Winnipeg, Nelson was tried and convicted of Mrs. Patterson's murder. He said very little in his defense, except to claim insanity. This plea was not accepted. It was pointed out that because he had changed his clothes and addresses constantly and had made intelligent escapes from dozens of cities in the U.S. and in Canada, he was sane. On Nov. 14, 1927, Nelson was convicted and sentenced to death. He was visited in prison by his aunt and ex-wife on the day of his execution, Jan. 13, 1928. He showed no remorse for his many murders and refused to explain his actions to an alienist who probed the reasons for his sexual attacks on the bodies of his victims.

A few minutes later, wearing a strange smile, Earle Leonard Nelson mounted the thirteen steps to the gallows and stood on the scaffold, saying in a clear voice: "I am innocent. I stand innocent before God and man. I forgive those who have wronged me and ask forgiveness of those I have injured." Just before the black hood was placed about his head, Nelson cried out: "God have mercy!" Five seconds later, one of the worst killers of the twentieth century was sent downward through the trap door, the rope instantly snapping his neck, killing him.

Neilson, Ruth, See: **Ellis, Ruth.**

Nemechek, Francis Donald, prom. 1974-76, U.S. Francis Nemechek was out on bail awaiting trial for firing shots at a car on the highway near Ogallah, Kan. At that time, he also became a suspect in the August 1976 abduction and death of Paula Fabrizius, a 16-year-old girl who was working for the summer as a ranger. She disappeared while on duty at the Cedar Bluff Reservoir. She was not found until the next day when two motorcyclists found her nude body. She had been killed by a knife wound to the heart. In a separate case, the body of 20-year-old Carla Baker of Hays, Kan., was also found dead near the reservoir.

After an FBI investigation, police arrested Nemechek, of Wa Keeney, Kan., for the murder of Fabrizius, and later also charged him with three murders that had puzzled authorities since January 1975 when 3-year-old Guy William Young was found dead of exposure near an abandoned house at Hill City, Kan. In the house were the bodies of two women from Fort Madison, Iowa. Twenty-one-year-old Cheryl Lynn Young, the child's mother, had been shot twice, and 19-year-old Diane Lynn Lovette had been raped and shot once.

Nemechek confessed to the killings but pleaded innocent

by reason of insanity. Public outcry forced a change of venue for the trial, which was held at Salina, Kan. Found Guilty, Nemechek was sentenced by Judge Steven Flood to five consecutive life terms for the five murders.

Nesbitt, Elbert, prom. 1903, U.S. Elbert "Eb" Nesbitt of Trundle County in Kentucky was believed to be part of a continuing inter-family mountain feud when he killed his brother-in-law Thurgood Talbot in the spring of 1903, because he was himself killed soon thereafter. Talbot was sitting in the sun playing with his baby daughter when Nesbitt, sighting Talbot from a clearing some distance away, killed him with a single shot from a powerful Winchester .32-.20-caliber rifle. No one knows why. Then he escaped into the hidden valleys of Brake County.

The family quarrel continued when Thurgood's brother Acie Talbot, traveling with Otis Beary, who may have had some official standing with the local sheriff, began to hunt for Nesbitt. Along Hemp Creek they came across him walking in the woods. He tried to escape by climbing a tree, but their rifles were quicker. Who killed him is uncertain. Acie Talbot went to prison for the deed, but Beary disappeared from the area and was never heard of again.

Nesset, Arnfinn, prom. 1977-80, Nor. "I've killed so many I'm unable to remember them all," said Arnfinn Nesset of Orkdal, Nor., when he finally confessed to killing at least twenty-two, and possibly up to 155, patients in the nursing homes where he had worked. An illegitimate child, he had been raised in a small rural community where he felt isolated and ostracized.

Between May 1977 and November 1980, Nesset obtained large quantities of a derivative of the nerve poison curare by forging prescriptions already signed by the doctors for patients

Norwegian murderer Arnfinn Nesset.

at the home. Although none of the 150 witnesses actually saw Nesset inject a patient, several saw him holding a hypodermic syringe near patients who died minutes later. When a local news reporter heard that the nursing home director was buying curacit, she checked into the story and then notified the police. On Mar. 9, 1981, Nesset was arrested. On different occasions he said that the patients' deaths were mercy killings, that he did it for the pleasure it gave him, that he had an insane need to kill, and that he was driven to it by schizophrenia. His defense attorney, Alf Nordhus, claimed that Nesset felt a god-like power over the elderly patients.

Although investigations were made into the deaths of all patients at the three nursing homes where Nesset had worked, he was actually charged with only twenty-five murders and embezzling funds from patients. He claimed the money was for the use of the Salvation Army. On Mar. 11, 1983, Nesset was found Guilty of murdering twenty-two patients. He was sentenced to twenty-one years in prison, the most allowed under Norwegian law, plus up to ten years of preventive detention.

Neu, Kenneth (AKA: **Louis**), 1910-35, U.S. "I'm Fit As A Fiddle, and Ready To Hang," Kenneth Neu chortled, seconds before the executioner's noose was slipped around his neck. The aspiring nightclub singer performed his last virtuoso performance for assembled reporters and photographers and then went to his death seemingly happier than he had been in many years. Like other unemployed young men during the Depression, Neu dreamed of striking it big. Advertising himself as a singer and dancer, 25-year-old Neu pestered Manhattan's top nightclub owners for a job. He could do it all, he explained, but the few gigs he lined up for himself were barely enough to pay for food or lodging. Worse yet was Neu's history of mental illness. He had been confined to the Georgia State Mental Home at one point in his life.

On Sept. 2, 1933, Neu's fortunes were at a low ebb. He was broke and wandering Times Square when he met a middle-aged man named Lawrence Shead, who introduced himself as the owner of a string of theatres in Paterson, N.J. Shead invited Neu up to his room for drinks, and the implied promise of a job in show business. But Neu soon realized that Shead had deceived him, and tried to entice him into a homosexual tryst.

Realizing that he had been duped, the unemployed crooner knocked Shead to the floor and hit him over the head with an iron and strangled him. Afterward he cleaned himself up in the shower and put on one of Shead's best suits. There was enough money in his wallet to get him to New Orleans, and a new start in life. A week later Neu was pounding the pavement looking for a job as a singer. Always popular with women, he had used his charms to seduce a waitress named Eunice Hotte, promising to take her to New York. "We'll have a big time in the big town,"

he promised. Only one thing was missing—a fresh bankroll to finance the journey. He pawned his watch and bought a blackjack with the proceeds. He used the blackjack on Sheffield Clark, Sr., a Nashville, Tenn., businessman he had earlier attempted to blackmail at the Yung Hotel.

After disposing of Clark, Neu took the dead man's car and $300, which was more than enough to get Eunice Hotte and himself to New York. The singer made a fatal mistake along the way. He removed the license plates from the vehicle and pasted a hand-written sign on the back that read: "New Car In Transit." The New Jersey Police pulled

Nightclub singer Kenneth Neu singing the song he composed for his own execution; he is wearing a suit once owned by the man he murdered.

him over and became immediately suspicious with his confusing stories. Taken to the station, detectives grilled him at length about the Lawrence Shead murder. "Sure I killed him," Neu shot back. "This is his suit I'm wearing now." He also confessed to killing Clark, and was extradited to Louisiana to stand trial. Doubts were expressed about his sanity, but Neu was judged fit to stand trial. Deliberations began on Dec. 12, 1933. He was eventually convicted of first-degree murder and was sentenced to die on the gallows. As he was led out of the courtroom he sang *Sweet Rosie O'Grady*. Neu was hanged on Feb. 1, 1935, after serenading his executioners with a selection of personal favorites from his own musical repertoire.

Newell, Susan, 1893-1923, Scot. A truck driver, observing a woman and her daughter pushing an odd-looking cart down Duke Street, in Glasgow, Scot., stopped his vehicle and offered the two a ride. Near the center of the city, the 30-year-old mother, Susan Newell, asked to be let off. As she stepped down from the truck Mrs. Newell slipped, and the cart containing the bundle spilled into the street. A local resident who happened to be looking out her window thought she noticed a hand and a leg protruding from the bundle. Alarmed by this, the housewife followed the pair down the street, then notified a policeman.

Mrs. Newell and her 8-year-old daughter Janet were stopped and the curious parcel was inspected. Just as the onlooker had expected, a body was found inside. The victim was 13-year-old John Johnston, a Coatbridge newspaper boy who had been collecting fees when he disappeared. Mrs. Newell blamed her husband John, a tube worker, for the horrible murder. The husband and wife were both indicted for murder, although there was no evidence to show that John Newell had anything to do with it. He was acquitted. A verdict of Guilty was returned after the jury sat in stunned silence, listening to the chilling tale of little Janet, who stated that her mother had killed the newsboy for his few coins and that she had been forced to help her mother tie up the body and place it in the sack. Susan Newell became the first woman to be executed in Scotland in fifty years when she was hanged at the Duke Street Prison on Oct. 10, 1923.

Nickell, Stella, 1944-   , U.S. Stella Nickell, a native of Portland, Ore., grew up poor, married young, and had her first child, Cynthia, when she was only sixteen. In her twenties, Nickell was convicted of fraud, child abuse, and forgery. In her early forties, Nickell married Bruce Nickell, a maintenance man who was often unemployed. The couple lived in a trailer in Auburn, Wash. Nickell talked of buying the property the trailer occupied and opening a tropical fish store. According to her daughter, Cynthia, she also spoke often of killing her husband to get the money. For five years Nickell studied books on poisoning, and once gave him what she hoped was a lethal dose of toxic seeds.

Attending a rehabilitation session with her husband, a reformed alcoholic, she learned that he would be vulnerable to other addictive substances, and played with the idea of killing him with cocaine, heroin, or amphetamines. But then she became intrigued with the recent Tylenol poisonings in the Chicago area. In 1984, seven people died after taking cyanide-laced Tylenol capsules.

Late in 1985, Nickell took out an insurance policy on her husband's life for $40,000, naming herself as the sole beneficiary. His state employee's policy would deliver another $31,000, with an additional $105,000 in the case of accidental death. On June 5, 1986, when her husband returned from his job, he took four Excedrin capsules for a headache. A few minutes later, while watching TV on the patio, he collapsed. Nickell called for a paramedic and, when her husband was taken to Harborview Medical Center in Seattle, declined to go with him because she was too upset. Bruce Nickell died within hours. When she called her daughter the next day to inform her, Nickell added, "I know what you're thinking, and the answer is 'no.'" The coroner failed to detect the poison in Bruce Nickell's body and reported the cause of death as pulmonary emphysema. To collect the full value of the insurance, Nickell had to prove that his death was an accident. She opened several containers of Extra-Strength Excedrin and Anacin-3, refilled several capsules with cyanide, clumsily taped or reglued the boxes, and put them on the shelves of three nearby stores.

On June 11, 1986, just six days after Nickell's death, Susan Katherine Snow, a 40-year-old Auburn bank manager, took her daily morning dose of two Extra-Strength Excedrin Capsules. Fifteen minutes later, her 15-year-old daughter found her on the bathroom floor. By noon Susan Snow was dead. Three days later the King County medical examiner announced that Snow had been poisoned with cyanide. Within a week, Stella Nickell called authorities and suggested that her husband had died of the same cause. Tissue tests corroborated her story. When Snow's husband, Paul Webking, filed a wrongful death suit against Bristol-Meyers, manufacturers of Excedrin, Nickell filed too. Three circumstances brought Nickell under suspicion: two of only five contaminated bottles of pills were found in her home, detectives discovered the existence of the insurance policies, and she refused to take a polygraph test. There was still not enough evidence to bring Nickell in for questioning until January 1987, when her daughter Cynthia came forward.

Nickell was charged with five violations of the Consumer Tampering Act passed in response to the Tylenol killings, and two counts of causing death by tampering with a consumer product. She was tried in a federal court in Seattle, in April 1988, and found Guilty on May 9. She was the first person convicted under the new federal law. Judge William Dwyer, citing crimes of "exceptional callousness and cruelty," imposed two 90-year sentences for the murders and three ten-year sentences for tainting the capsules, with all five sentences to run concurrently. Nickell may be eligible for parole in 2018.

Nickols, Kevin, 1963-74, U.S. On Mar. 26, 1974, police in a suburb of Dallas, Texas, were called to the scene of a family murder/suicide. From evidence at the scene of the crime, it appeared that 11-year-old Kevin Nickols, a spelling bee champion, killed his father, mother, and 12-year-old sister before shooting himself with the same .22-caliber revolver. The bodies were discovered in the family's Richardson, Texas, home a week after the slayings.

Nigrisoli, Dr. Carlo, prom. 1963, Italy. The head of the famous family-owned La Casa di Cura, a medical clinic in Bologna, became infatuated with a charming young woman and wished to be rid of his wife of many years, Ombretta Nigrisoli. When he told his wife's doctor of her supposed fatigue and insomnia, the doctor gave her a series of regular injections, which her husband continued to administer. Because everyone knew that his wife's health was precarious, he expected to be believed on Mar. 14, 1963, when he wept over her corpse and said she had died of a coronary thrombosis. But the staff at the clinic and Ombretta's father-in-law thought otherwise. Then the coroner found traces of curare in her body.

Dr. Carlo Nigrisoli was charged with murder. His trial, which began on Oct. 1, 1964, was the first in Italy involving curare and the first filmed by television cameras. Nigrisoli won the right to stay in his cell during the trial and speak over a microphone. The trial lasted 117 days. The younger woman for whom the doctor committed murder, Iris Azzali, testified that she had no intention of marrying the doctor. The jury found Dr. Nigrisoli Guilty and he was sentenced to life in prison.

Nilsen, Dennis Andrew, 1945-   , Brit. Between 1978-83, Dennis Nilsen etched his name in criminal annals as one of Britain's worst mass murderers. In that five-year period he ended the lives of fifteen young men at his two London addresses.

Nilsen was dangerously obsessed with death and dying from an early age. His sense of isolation was fueled by his homosexuality which he was forced to suppress for much of his life. Nilsen was the son of an alcoholic Norwegian sailor named Olav Nilsen, and a Scottish woman named Betty Whyte. When Dennis was four his parents were divorced. The boy was sent to live with his grandparents to whom he became quite attached. His social problems apparently began when his grandfather died in 1952, and the boy was forced to view the corpse. Nilsen lived with his mother and her second husband in Fraserburgh, Scot., until August 1961 when he joined the army. The military life provided him with an identity he had never known before. Nilsen served as an army cook in Aden, Sharjah, and

Cyprus. He remained in the service until 1972 when he retired to take a job with the London Police. The military aspects of the job appealed to Nilsen, but he was quarrelsome and unable to relate to his younger colleagues on the force. He quit the police to become a civil servant at a job center for the unemployed in the Soho district of London.

In 1975, he formed an attachment to a younger man named David Gallichan and moved to his apartment on Teignmouth Road. Though there was no homosexual relationship between them, Nilsen was fond of his roommate who provided the emotional stability previously lacking in his life. When Gallichan moved to the country in 1977, Nilsen was emotionally devastated. The overpowering feeling of rejection continued when a young male prostitute took up residence with Nilsen in his flat. The arrangement proved unsatisfactory and the man moved out. Then, in December 1978, the killings started, co-inciding with the arrest of mass-killer John Wayne Gacy in Chicago. Nilsen, picked up a young Irish laborer in a Soho pub. He brought him back to the flat, strangled him, and concealed the body under the floorboards. Horrified at what he had done, Dennis Nilsen fully expected the police to appear at his door and take him away.

When nothing happened, Nilsen tried to repeat the crime three months later. Like Gacy in Chicago, the British mass murderer cruised the homosexual hangouts for likely victims. Nearly all of the young men Nilsen encountered were drifters, cut off from mainstream society. One of Nilsen's intended victims was a Chinese cook named Andrew Ho, who was fortunate to escape after Nilsen tried to strangle him in the Melrose Avenue apartment. The London police made only a cursory investigation before dropping the case.

The next victim was 23-year-old Canadian Kenneth James Ockendon, who disappeared in the vicinity of High Holborn on Dec. 3, 1979. Ockendon was strangled after he showed more interest in watching TV and listening to the stereo than in Nilsen. His remains were dissected and flushed down the toilet. After the Ockendon disappearance the murder toll climbed with gruesome rapidity. In May 1980, Nilsen lured 16-year-old Martin Duffy back to the apartment and strangled him. The corpse was placed under the floorboards where it was joined by the body of 26-year-old Billy Sutherland a few months later. The seventh victim was an under-fed vagrant that reminded Nilsen of a concentration camp inmate. After eating a sumptuous meal at the apartment, Nilsen strangled the man while he listened to rock music. "You'll have no more troubles now, squire!" he gloated.

The fifteenth and final victim was Stephen Sinclair, a 20-year-old Scotsman with a serious drinking problem. Nilsen met up with Sinclair in the George Pub off Charing Cross and took him back to Nilsen's apartment. After strangling Sinclair, Nilsen disposed of the body in the following manner. "I put the head into a pot, popped the lid on and lit the stove," he said. "Later I listened to music and had a good drink, also watching some TV as the head was simmering." The remaining body parts were wrapped in plastic sacks and thrown into the sewer.

On Feb. 8, 1983, a sanitary engineer named Michael Cattran answered a complaint from Cranley Gardens in the Muswell Hill section of north London where residents were unable to flush their toilets. He removed a manhole cover to discover the gruesome remains. Cattran phoned his supervisor for instructions. They returned the next day to discover that the material had been removed. A tenant told Detective Chief Inspector Peter Jay and Steve McCusker that she had heard a man going up and down the stairs in the middle of the night. When questioned about the remains, Nilsen proved most cooperative. He pointed to his closet and said: "It's in there, in two plastic bags," adding, "it's a long story but I'll tell you everything." The floorboards were torn up and the grisly remains removed. As news of the arrest spread, anxious parents of missing children phoned Scotland Yard for information.

Nilsen was tried for murder on Oct. 24, 1983. Defense attorneys argued unsuccessfully that their client suffered from a personality disorder dating back to childhood when his father abandoned him. Dr. Patrick Gallwey explained that Nilsen suffered from the "False Self Syndrome." The prosecution countered these arguments by testimony from Carl Stotter, Paul Nobbs, and Douglas Stewart, who had been brutally assaulted by Nilsen. On Nov. 4, 1983, the jury found the defendant Guilty by a ten to two vote. Justice Croom-Johnson sentenced Nilsen to life imprisonment.

Nilsson, Richard, 1949- , Brit. Nineteen-year-old construction laborer Richard Nilsson of Buckden, England, had trouble staying away from younger boys. He had already been warned away by the police and was known to have tried to strangle one boy. On May 19, 1968, when most of the village was at home watching the Football Association Cup Final on television, Nilsson met 8-year-old Christopher Sabey, who was riding his bike. When Christopher did not come home that evening, a search began. Early the next morning, his body was found near a sandpit. He had been strangled but not molested.

Police from London investigated every possible clue, but they kept their eyes on Nilsson from the start. Each time they interviewed him, however, he insisted he knew nothing about young Christopher. Police found three fawn-colored dog hairs on the boy's clothing. In the first use of such

evidence, the police gathered hair samples from every light-colored dog in the area. They were sent to the Home Office Central Research Establishment at Aldermaston for analysis by neutron activation procedures. Only three dogs in the area could have shed the hair, and one of them belonged to Richard Nilsson. He was charged with murder, found Guilty, and sentenced to life imprisonment.

Nisby, Marcus (AKA: **Michael Player**), 1960-86, U.S. During a thirty-six-day period in September and October of 1986, ten men, most of them homeless, were found shot in Los Angeles, some attacked as they slept. Then, on Oct. 9, an eleventh victim survived the attack. The next day, 26-year-old Marcus Nisby shot himself in a motel room. The gun he used was the same one he had used to kill the street people. Nisby had been under some suspicion since the discovery of the first murder victim, Rudolfo Roque, fifty-four, on Sept. 4. Nisby had been identified as a possible witness to the shooting.

Nischt, Joseph, 1914- , U.S. Joseph Nischt, a 30-year-old janitor, had been under suspicion since Rose Michaelis, fifty-eight, disappeared in the late afternoon of Feb. 28, 1945, after leaving her Chicago apartment to get some filtered water. Nischt, who worked in the apartment building, was taken into custody after a witness saw him picking up fragments of the bottle Michaelis used to carry the water from a nearby filtration plant. Police gave Nischt a polygraph test, which was inconclusive. He had been questioned by Captain Edward Kelly, Lieutenant Philip Breitzke, and Sergeant Patrick Touhy. The heel of Michaelis' shoe had been found in an alley near the apartment complex, along with pieces of her water bottle and her house key. Nischt said he was out of the building at the time of Michaelis' disappearance, picking up a paycheck, and that he stopped for a few drinks, returning home at around 11 p.m. With no evidence of murder, the police charged Nischt with disorderly conduct and released him on $100 bond. Then, on Mar. 2, Mrs. Matt Werner, wife of another janitor, told police that Nischt had come by, drunk, looking for her husband, and told her that he had killed a woman. Police picked up Nischt a second time and, as they were questioning him in the alley, Breitzke abruptly asked, "What did you do with the body?" Nischt responded, "I put it in the furnace."

Nischt confessed that he had seen Michaelis in the alley, struck her with his fist, dragged her into the basement, and then shoved her body into the furnace. The janitor said he did not know if Michaelis was dead or alive when he pushed her into the fire, explaining that her body was "motionless" on the floor. In the statement he gave to Assistant State's Attorney Blair Varnes, Nischt explained his crime: "When I saw her in the alley I had an urge to hurt or kill someone. I didn't dislike her. I knew her for twelve or fourteen years. I used to play cards with her husband." Police found charred bones in the furnace, including skull and jawbone fragments, a kneecap, and a tooth. Sentenced to life imprisonment for murder, Nischt served twenty-one years of his sentence at Joliet, and was released on Apr. 18, 1966.

Nixon, Robert (AKA: **Thomas Crosby; The Brick Moron**), c.1920-39, U.S. For nearly two years Chicago and Los Angeles police officials puzzled over the identity of the killer called the "Brick Moron" by the media. On June 29, 1936, the body of Florence Thompson Castle, a 24-year-old cocktail hostess, was found in her room at Chicago's Devonshire Hotel. The killer had gained entry from the fire escape and accosted Castle with a brick. The murder was witnessed by the woman's 7-year-old son Jimmy who described the assailant as a "white man painted black." The man picked up a tube of lipstick and scrawled the words "Black Legion Game" on the dresser mirror before fleeing out the window. He left behind a set of fingerprints which later proved useful to the police in both cities.

Mrs. Castle's murderer was an 18-year-old black man named Robert Nixon, who had earlier been picked up by Chicago police for juvenile offenses. Following the Castle murder, Nixon moved to Los Angeles where he was known as Thomas Crosby. He got into trouble with the local police, and was arrested four times in 1937 on charges ranging from purse snatching to suspicion of grand theft. On Mar. 2 of that year, 20-year-old Rose G. Valdez was murdered in her home by a brick-wielding assailant. Several days after that Mrs. Zoe Damrell was beaten in a similar fashion. The brick was found outside the window of her home. On Apr. 4, police were summoned to the home of 48-year-old Edna Worden, wife of a disabled WWI veteran, on Olive Street, Los Angeles. Worden and her 12-year-old daughter Marguerite had been brutally slain in their apartment. As with Rose Valdez and Florence Castle in Chicago, their skulls had been battered by a brick.

Nixon had already been fingerprinted by the Los Angeles police when he made his way back to Chicago. He murdered his final victim, Florence Johnson on May 27, 1938, shortly before being arrested by Chicago police. Nixon named an accomplice, 19-year-old Earl Hicks, but under heavy questioning by State's Attorney Thomas Courtney and Detective Chief John L. Sullivan, the young man broke down and confessed. The story was picked up on the wire services by officials from the Los Angeles Police Department (LAPD), who noted the similarities between the Johnson and Castle murders and those of Mrs. Worden and her daughter. A fingerprint comparison was made, and it was determined that Nixon and Crosby were one and the same. The LAPD requested extradition, but Nixon remained in Chicago where he was convicted of murdering Johnson, wife of a city fireman.

After receiving seven stays of execution, the so-called "Brick Moron" was executed in the electric chair on June 15, 1939, by Cook County Sheriff Thomas J. O'Brien.

Noel, Harrison, 1905-   , U.S. In September 1925, 20-year-old Harrison Noel, a student who had had a nervous breakdown, admitted he kidnapped and murdered 6-year-old Mary Daly of Montclair, N.J. Noel patterned the killing after the murder of Bobby Franks, after reading everything he could find on the killing. A major difference was that Noel kidnapped the child in a taxi, then killed the taxi driver so the driver could not testify against him.

The court tried Noel, not for the murder of Mary Daly, but for the murder of the taxi driver. He was found Guilty but an appeals court reversed the decision, and Noel was committed to a mental hospital.

Noor, Marvin Dean, 1961-   , and **McCarter, James T.**, 1960-   , and **Shope, Dani Lee**, prom. 1979, U.S. Three young people on a hunting trip turned their sights from deer to a black man, saying they found the experience "neat." Marvin Dean Noor, eighteen, James T. McCarter, nineteen, and Noor's 23-year-old girlfriend, Dani Lee Shope, went hunting in the Sierra Nevada mountains not far from their hometown of Oroville, Calif., on Jan. 13, 1979. They smoked marijuana and drank beer. Failing to find a deer to shoot, they shot a black man, Jimmy Lee Campbell, twenty-two, when they saw him walking along a railroad track. They took more random pot shots at other blacks they saw when they returned to town. They bragged to their friends about killing Campbell and an anonymous phone call to the police started an investigation.

The three were charged with first-degree murder. The black community in Oroville wanted a trial so the death penalty could be imposed if they were found Guilty. District Attorney Will Mattly accepted a plea bargain in which McCarter and Noor pleaded guilty—McCarter confessing he pulled the trigger—eliminating the possibility of capital punishment. Mattly believed premeditation could probably not be proved and a trial might open the way for a defense of diminished capacity due to the alcohol and drugs used before the murder.

Shope confessed to the crime and pleaded guilty to second-degree murder. She was sentenced in November 1979 to fifteen years to life in prison. The two men were sentenced the following February to twenty-five years to life in prison. "They forfeited their right to freedom and to live in a free society, as they are a perpetual danger to the lives and safety of others," said Judge Jean Morony.

Nordlund, Herman, prom. 1931, U.S. Two men who ran a small tire shop together in San Francisco had a difference of opinion on how to treat their customers. Bill Oetting, who enjoyed the business and liked helping people with their problems could no longer work with his partner, Herman Nordlund, who was driving the business into the ground with his rudeness, violence, and inefficiency. Police went looking for Nordlund when Oetting, who kept and rebuilt the business himself, was killed by a gunshot to the head.

They found Nordlund lying in his bed behind a door that was boobytrapped so anyone going through would trip the trigger on Nordlund's gun, killing him. In addition, there were cans that looked like explosive powder on the window sill, as well as a knife and a revolver within his reach. Led by Chief of Police William J. Quinn, the police broke into the back door of the house, ran across a room, broke an inner window into the bedroom, and grabbed Nordlund before he could use his lethal weapons. Arrested and tried for murder, Nordlund said he did it because his ex-partner was so annoyingly contented. Found Guilty, Nordlund was sentenced to life in prison but was paroled after less than eight years on July 26, 1939.

Nortje, Jan Christian, 1900- , and **du Plessis, Dirkie Cathrina,** 1903- , S. Afri. Adriaan du Plessis and his sister Anna both married in 1918. After Adriaan died at age twenty-seven, his widow, Dirkie Cathrina du Plessis, twenty-two, moved in with Anna and her husband, Jan Christian Nortje, twenty-five. The problem was that Jan fell in love with Dirkie, and to be together, they decided to murder Anna. They planned to put strychnine in her dinner on Aug. 9, 1925, and claim she had committed suicide.

Several weeks passed before the police began to question whether Anna Nortje committed suicide. Then they learned du Plessis had moved back to her own house, to which Nortje came every night. By December, police had gathered enough evidence to arrest the pair. Their trial took place the following June in the courtroom of Justice Richard Feetham. They denied all accusations, including ones to which they had earlier confessed. The jury found them both Guilty. They were sentenced to hang, but the Executive Council, which had to rule on death sentences, decided that Nortje had controlled du Plessis, and decided she should not hang. She was sentenced to prison and released in 1933. Hours before Nortje's execution, the minister of justice stayed the execution and Nortje's sentence was commuted to life in prison. He served thirteen years before being released in 1939.

Noziere, Violette, 1915- , Fr. When Violette Noziere could not get as much money as she wanted from her doting father, she spent the evenings working as a prostitute to earn money to spend on the young men she fancied. Her parents assumed that she was at one of the Paris nightclubs she favored.

In 1934, when she was nineteen, Noziere promised one young man a sportscar and a holiday abroad, funds for which she planned to take from her father's life savings. On Aug. 23, she drugged her parents' coffee with massive doses of Veronal. When she found them apparently dead, she turned on the gas and waited briefly before calling the neighbors. However, she had not given her mother enough of the tranquilizer, and she survived.

Noziere, realizing that the police suspected her, grabbed what money she could and disappeared. A week later, a man who recognized her from photos in the newspapers turned her in. She was tried, convicted, and sentenced to death. Hers would have been the first execution of a woman in France in fifty years, but at the last minute, President Albert Lebrun, at the pleading of her mother, commuted her sentence to life in prison.

Nuccio, Richard L., prom. 1968, U.S. On June 4, 1968, Chicago police officer Richard Nuccio pursued 19-year-old Ronald Nelson down an alley after a fracas at a drive-in restaurant and fatally shot Nelson in the back as he ran. Charged with murder, Nuccio swore at his trial that Nelson had thrown a knife at him, but witnesses disagreed. Nuccio was found Guilty of murder and sentenced to fourteen years in prison. Illinois Governor Dan Walker later reduced Nuccio's sentence to six to fourteen years, allowing him to be paroled after less than four years.

O

Oates, Reginald Vernon, 1950- , U.S. Explaining that he got his ideas from the Bible, 18-year-old Reginald Oates calmly admitted murdering four young boys, mutilating their bodies, and performing vampire and cannibal rites.

Parents in the southwestern Baltimore, Md., neighborhood where Oates lived had become increasingly concerned over reports of a child molester roaming the Leakin Park-Gwynns Falls Park area in April 1968. On the morning of Apr. 17, three young boys, Dennis Hodge, Benjamin M. Avery, and Clinton Harris, were found near the area, dazed and bleeding. An older youth had enticed them into the park from a nearby playground and forced them to spend the night. The boys suffered severe head wounds from a sharp object and had been sexually molested. The detectives staking out Leakin Park, Southwest District patrolmen Donald Dyson and Harry Richman, spotted a youth lurking in a clearing in the park. When they approached the man he ran into a densely wooded area where the officers captured him. Reginald V. Oates was carrying a lunch bucket and a brown paper bag. The lunch bucket contained a hacksaw, a table knife, an eight-inch strip of iron crudely bent into a claw shape, and several bloody rags. In the paper bag were several body parts of his victims.

After four hours of questioning, Oates led police to the bodies. In a wooded area of the park, two brothers, 5-year-old Mack Jefferson and 9-year-old Larry Jefferson, were lying in a neat row next to the corpse of their cousin, 10-year-old Lester Watson. About 100 yards away lay the body of 10-year-old Lewis R. Hill. All four children had been sexually mutilated, and three of them had their throats cut. Hill's head was cut off and his hands were missing. The liver and the heart of one of the boys was found nearby. After showing police the bodies, Oates gave a series of confessions describing the slayings and the cannibal and vampire rites that followed. Oates lured the boys into the woods by promising to play cowboys and indians with them. He then bound them and slashed their throats. Oates explained that most of his ideas came from the Bible. A Bible with his father's name on the flyleaf and extensive underlined passages was found near the scene of the crimes. The assaults, including the attempted rape of two young girls and the beating and molesting of the three boys who were found alive, took place on Apr. 10, 17, and 18.

Stripped of most of his clothing to prevent a suicide attempt, Oates was held under heavy guard at Central District Headquarters in Baltimore. An unemployed janitor, Oates was described by one Murder Squad veteran as "completely emotionless. He acts as if he is somewhere else." Homicide investigators said he was "well-versed in the Bible." Attorney Fred Weisgal volunteered to defend Oates at the preliminary hearing at Homicide Court in Baltimore. Municipal Court Judge John McGuire then postponed the hearing at the attorney's request so that Weisgal could arrange for extensive mental testing of his client. Eight doctors at the Clifton T. Perkins State Hospital found Oates mentally incompetent to stand trial. He was judged by the same medical staff to have been insane at the time of the alleged crimes, and was committed to a mental institution.

Oberst, Owen, 1911- , U.S. The bodies of seven members of the William F. Oberst family were found in the charred remains of their farmhouse near Florence, Kan., on Apr. 21, 1928, after a fire the night before. Only one family member, 17-year-old Owen Oberst, escaped the fire—because he was attending a movie.

It seemed strange to authorities that all of the bodies were found in the kitchen and that no one escaped.

Murderer Owen Oberst.

Suspicions increased further when it was determined that there had been no explosion. Investigators found it impossible to examine the bodies for clues because they were burned so completely. However, while sifting through the ruins, they found a .22-caliber automatic pistol, which had been recently fired, in the kitchen stove. The barrel and metal pieces of a .22-caliber repeating rifle were found in another corner of the same room. It was determined that Owen bought the suit of clothes he wore to view the remains of his family on the night of the fire. Police grilled Owen daily, but extracted nothing from him. When it was found that Owen's father had won a large amount of money gambling on the day of the incident, speculation arose that the family may have been murdered by his gambling partners.

On May 4, 1928, Owen gave in to the strain of interrogation and confessed to the murders. He testified that he had thought about killing his father for months, because he was a stern taskmaster and had refused to let him drive the family car. He confessed that he had killed his five siblings and his mother with an automatic rifle, and then waited for his father to arrive. When his father walked into the yard, he shot him, then dragged his body inside. Owen then piled the bodies in the kitchen and started a fire.

For days, Owen wavered between agreeing with and recanting his original confession. Before Judge George J. Benson, he pleaded not guilty. Then three days later, before the same judge, he pleaded guilty and demanded to be taken directly to prison. He was sentenced to life imprisonment.

Obreitis, Charles, prom. 1931, U.S. On a spring morning in 1931, a human thigh was found on a New York City bridge. It could not be determined whether it was from a murder victim or was a diseased leg that had been amputated. Perhaps it was part of a medical student's prank. But there were no traces of preservatives or anesthetic. The thigh was wrapped in a six-day-old Brooklyn newspaper, and the bone structure indicated that it was from a man. It was determined by the calcification that his age was between thirty and forty. From the length and thickness, the man was approximately five feet, four inches and weighed 200 pounds. His hair was dark brown, and the presence of alcohol suggested he had been drunk. Apparently the victim of murder, his assailant was skilled in surgery or butchery. The police had no records of missing persons fitting the description. But three days later, the left half of a chest turned up in a Brooklyn lumberyard. Tests indicated that the two parts likely came from the same man. Over the next couple of weeks, the other thigh, the left leg, both arms, and hip were also discovered scattered throughout Brooklyn. Finally, a man digging dirt for his plants found the head, feet, forearms, and hands. The skull had been pierced by a sharp object, probably an ax or a hatchet. Along with the head, police found a dirt-caked shirt. When they washed it, they discovered a laundry mark, and began a search for the shirt's owner.

The police located the man, a small-time bootlegger and speakeasy proprietor, who readily admitted that the laundry mark was his. But he said the shirt belonged to his partner, Andrew Zubresky. When the investigators located the speakeasy, they found Zubresky's wife behind the bar. She said Zubresky had disappeared the day before the first body part was discovered. While living in Cleveland, both Zubreskys had been tried but acquitted for the murder of Mrs. Zubresky's first husband. Mrs. Zubresky denied any involvement in the current case, but the composite parts of the corpse matched perfectly the description of her husband.

Police shadowed Mrs. Zubresky and found her living with another man, Charles Obreitis. He told police he worked as a bartender for Mrs. Zubresky, and then confessed to the

murder of Andrew Zubresky. Obreitis had indeed been a butcher before tending bar, and gave his victim a great deal of alcohol before killing him with a hatchet. He then dismembered the body and scattered the pieces. Obreitis was convicted of the murder, but because he was an epileptic of rather weak mentality, he was sentenced to twenty years instead of death. Twice-widowed Mrs. Zubresky was not even tried for the murder. However, she was caught forging her husband's signature on veterans' benefit checks, and convicted of second-degree forgery. She was sentenced to five to ten years at Westleigh Farms Prison.

O'Brien de Lacy, Patrick, and **Panchenko, Dr.**, prom. 1911, Rus. In 1911, Patrick O'Brien de Lacy, was accused of having arranged for the deaths of three members of his family in Petrograd. He stood to inherit a great deal of money. While married to his first wife, he met a wealthy woman, Mademoiselle Burturlin. After divorcing his wife and marrying Burturlin, he conspired to remove every family member that stood between him and his father-in-law's fortune. He found Dr. Panchenko, a needy practitioner, and offered him 560,000 rubles to help poison the family members through inoculation. On May 16, 1910, the brother-in-law died suspiciously, and an investigation indicated blood-poisoning. Dr. Panchenko was implicated by his mistress, who testified to the Secret Police. He was arrested and sent to prison to await trial. While in prison, he broke down and implicated O'Brien de Lacy.

The trial began in Petrograd in January 1911. Dr. Panchenko confessed that he had substituted diphtheria poison for young Burturlin's anti-cholera medicine. O'Brien de Lacy denied marrying for money. He said his wife's wealth was a mere fraction of the family estate, and that his father-in-law would surely live a long time. Nevertheless, after two weeks on trial, the two men were found Guilty. O'Brien de Lacy was sentenced to life imprisonment, and Dr. Panchenko to fifteen years.

O'Bryan, Ronald, prom. 1974, U.S. Panic swept through Pasadena, Texas, following Halloween 1974, when 8-year-old Tim O'Bryan died from cyanide-laced candy. Tim's father, Ronald O'Bryan, an optometrist, was heavily in debt and held $65,000 life insurance policies on each of his children. He had immediately filed a claim.

The police confiscated Tim's trick-or-treat candy and discovered that several items had enough potassium cyanide to kill as many as twelve adults. O'Bryan had made several inquiries about procuring cyanide, and had asked a fellow church member how much cyanide it took to kill a human being. He was arrested for murdering his son and for the attempted murders of three other children. O'Bryan was convicted on all charges and sentenced to death.

O'Driscoll, James, 1953- , U.S. In the first slaying to take place in Disneyland in its twenty-five-year history, Mel C. Yorda, eighteen, of Riverside, Calif., was killed during a private party in the Tomorrowland section of the Anaheim, Calif., amusement park. James O'Driscoll, twenty-eight, and his girlfriend, Julie Holdener, twenty-five, both of San Diego, were arrested after the Mar. 7, 1981, murder.

In an Orange County Superior Court, O'Driscoll claimed he intended only to scare Yorda but the youth fell on his knife during a scuffle. The incident began when Holdener complained to O'Driscoll that someone had pinched her. Prosecution witnesses testified O'Driscoll had the knife out when he approached Yorda and had been calculating and deliberate in his attack.

The first trial ended in a mistrial on Oct. 25, 1982, when jurors were unable to reach a verdict. At a second trial, the jury returned a second-degree murder verdict against O'Driscoll on May 5, 1983. On May 26, Superior Court Judge Everett Dickey sentenced O'Driscoll to a fifteen-year jail term. The convicted killer was admitted to Soledad Prison on June 15, 1983.

Ogilvie, Adam, 1924- , Brit. On Nov. 6, 1946, Olive Nixon, a 57-year-old widow, was beaten to death with a brick near her home in Regent's Park, England. There was no apparent robbery and police were unable to apprehend the assailant. Ten years later, on Aug. 10, Adam Ogilvie walked into the Albany Street Police Station and confessed to the murder. He had been troubled since the event and felt he might be compelled to kill again. He seemed to know details that had not been released in the newspapers. Ogilvie was charged and brought to trial before Justice Gorman in November 1956.

However, Ogilvie recanted his confession, saying, "I made it to prove my innocence to my wife—to get her back. I pretended to her I did the killing and told her I would murder her, too, if she didn't stop quarreling with me. I thought if I was acquitted she would come back." He claimed that he knew of the intimate details from a stranger. The jury believed his original confession and sentenced him to death. He was reprieved by the Homicide Act of 1957 in which the Home Secretary could exercise the Royal Prerogative. Ogilvie once served a three-year prison sentence. In June 1948, nineteen months after the murder of Mrs. Nixon, he was convicted of hitting a Torquay woman over the head with a brick.

Ogorzov, Paul, 1913-41, Ger. Eight women were murdered between 1939 and 1941 on or near a railway line at Rummelburg, Ger. The women were raped and then beaten with a piece of lead cable. Paul Ogorzov, a 28-year-old railroad worker and Nazi party member, was arrested and brought to trial on July 24, 1941. The Nazis sought a quick trial to avoid embarrassment to the party. The next day he was found Guilty on eight counts of murder. He was executed two days later.

Ogre of Hanover, See: **Haarmann, Fritz.**

O'Laughlin, Pearl, prom. 1930, U.S. On Oct. 15, 1930, near Denver, Colo., 10-year-old Leona O'Laughlin's father and stepmother reported her missing. The next day the parents became ill, apparently from food poisoning. Leona's father, Leo, was a police detective, who had made a few enemies while working on the vice squad. A few days later, the body of the little girl was found near a lake. While she had suffered blows to the head, the cause of death was drowning. A Denver medical examiner also disclosed that ground glass was found in the child's stomach. When Leo O'Laughlin's stomach was pumped, it also contained ground glass. Police searched the O'Laughlin home, found sand from the lake bed and granules of glass, and arrested Pearl O'Laughlin, Leona's stepmother.

Pearl professed her innocence. But it was discovered that her father-in-law, Dennis O'Laughlin, was quite wealthy. When he went to the sugar bowl to indulge his fondness for sugar during a visit to Leo and Pearl's house, he discovered ground glass in the sugar. Both her husband and her father-in-law survived, but their deaths would have made O'Laughlin a very wealthy woman, provided Leona was out of the way. On Nov. 28, 1930, Pearl's trial began. She was convicted of Leona's murder and sentenced to life at hard labor.

Olive, Marlene, 1959- , and **Riley, Charles David**, 1955- , U.S. In 1975, 16-year-old Marlene Olive was a great beauty. Born in South America, she had been adopted by wealthy oil executive James Olive and his wife, Naomi, of San Rafael, Calif. The family had recently moved, and Marlene was having difficulty adjusting. She took an interest in voodoo and claimed to be a witch. She directed her supposed powers toward an anxious, over-weight drug dealer, Charles David Riley, who was four years older than Marlene. The attention had an immediate effect on Riley. He lost fifty pounds, overcame his nervous twitches, and became, literally, Marlene's slave. She made him steal clothes and humiliated him in public. She bit him until he bled, and carved initials on his back with a pocket knife. Marlene's parents tried to break up the pair, claiming that Riley was corrupting Marlene. In June 1975, James Olive failed to appear at a business meeting. Two days later, an anonymous phone call from a friend of Marlene's led police to the charred bodies of James and Naomi Olive near a barbecue pit in San Pablo Bay.

The friend said she visited the Olive home two days after the disappearances and found Marlene cleaning blood stains from the floors and walls. Marlene and Riley admitted battering her mother to death with a hammer and shooting her father four times. They then drove the bodies to the barbecue site, doused them with gasoline and burned them. Police arrested Marlene and Riley.

Riley admitted to killing both parents, but later stated that he had killed only James Olive. He altered his state-ment a third time, saying that Marlene gave him LSD and ordered him to kill her parents. Judge McGuire found Riley Guilty of both murders and sentenced him to the gas chamber. Marlene was found Guilty of first-degree murder in juvenile court. She was given the maximum sentence, four to six years in the California Youth Authority.

=====

Onufrejczyk, Michael, prom. 1953-55, Brit. When WWII ended, former Polish soldier Michael Onufrejczyk decided to stay in Wales and become a farmer. But his farm near Llandilo was never successful, so when his friend Stanislaw Sykut offered to become his partner in March 1953, Onufrejczyk accepted. Within weeks the two men were in conflict about the farm's failure. By May, Sykut had an attorney issue notice to his partner that he would be ending the partnership and would expect his investment back within six months.

The six months passed and Onufrejczyk had not repaid the money, so Sykut continued to live on the farm. Onu-frejczyk knew that he would have to sell the farm to repay Sykut his £600. In December, a routine check on aliens found Sykut missing. Onufrejczyk claimed that he had suddenly gone away on the evening of Dec. 18, but the

police found all his belongings still in the farmhouse. Blood spots were found throughout the kitchen, and there was even a minute bone fragment clinging to one wall. Onu-frejczyk claimed that Sykut had returned to Poland, but he

Michael Onufrejczyk, found Guilty of murder despite the fact that no body was ever found.

was caught in many lies, among them that the two had no major financial problems. Among the many rumors that spread through the region was that Sykut's body had been fed to the pigs.

In September 1954, the authorities gave up trying to find a body and decided to charge Onufrejczyk with murder on the circumstantial evidence. A special panel of magistrates reviewed the evidence and sent him to trial at the Swansea Assizes in November, before Justice Oliver. The jury, willing to accept the circumstantial evidence, found Onu-frejczyk Guilty of murder and sentenced him to death. The home secretary granted him a reprieve on Jan. 23, 1955, and Onufrejczyk was sent to prison for life. His was the first instance in more than three hundred years in which a killer was tried when there was not at least part of a body or a confession at hand.

=====

Osborne, Alberta, and **Osborne, Carl,** and **Weind, James,** prom. 1974-75, U.S. Alberta Osborne, a Columbus, Ohio, barmaid, arranged in December 1974 for the murder of her lover's wife. Osborne worked as a barmaid for a man named Ross before they began an affair that lasted six years. When Ross announced that he was going to end the affair and move to Kentucky with his wife, Alberta planned the murder of Hermalee Ross, his wife. Osborne paid her 20-year-old son, Carl Osborne, and his associate, James Weind, $325 to abduct Mrs. Ross from a parking lot in downtown Columbus. The two men took Mrs. Ross to an abandoned schoolhouse where Weind shot her in the head.

A housewife on a nearby farm witnessed part of the murder and alerted police. Weind was arrested four days later. Police found the murder weapon and identified it as belonging to Mrs. Osborne. She was arrested. Carl Osborne and Weind were arrested shortly thereafter. All three were tried and found Guilty of murder, with Mrs. Osborne's 18-year-old daughter serving as the chief witness. Alberta and Carl Osborne, and Weind were sentenced to die in the electric chair.

Owens, Edgar A., 1932-   , U.S. In October 1952, Brooklyn resident Edgar A. Owens enlisted in the army, but neglected to mention his five arrests for car theft, the years he spent in reform schools, and his five months in a mental hospital for treatment of dementia praecox. Owens was sent to Fort Dix for training, despite the fact that his intelligence rating was three points below the minimum permissible in the service. Although he had a proclivity for going AWOL, Owens was rated a "satisfactory" soldier. At training exercises on Feb. 11, 1953, Owens and 224 other Company L infantry soldiers simulated an attack on a hill, using live ammunition on dummies. Owens aimed his M1 rifle at Lieutenant Richard M. Davenport's back and fired, killing the 22-year-old commanding officer. Investigators assumed that a fragment from a freak artillery burst had killed the officer. An autopsy, however, revealed that Davenport was killed by a rifle bullet. A brass M1 shell was found near the point where the fatal bullet was fired. Recalling the platoon to reenact the attack, investigators found Owens missing. He had gone home to Brooklyn, where he was later arrested by police after speeding through a red light in a stolen car. The chase ended when officers shot at him. Arrested and returned to Fort Dix, Owens confessed on Feb. 18 but could not provide a reason for the killing. Court-martial proceedings were dropped after the neuropsychiatric service at Valley Forge Army Hospital in Phoenixville, Pa., declared Owens mentally incompetent. On Apr. 15, it was ruled that he would be discharged for medical reasons and transferred to a mental hospital for long-term care.

P

Padgett, John, and **Huiel, Henry**, prom. 1970, U.S. On Dec. 4, 1970, John Padgett and his stepdaughter, Linda Padgett, became concerned when Joyce Padgett did not return home for dinner. At about 10:15 p.m., they discovered her at the family-owned gas station in downtown Marietta, Ga. She was slumped over the wheel of her black Cadillac, killed by a .12-gauge shotgun blast. Her purse was missing.

Police searched for several months, turning up no solid clues. In private, John Padgett complained bitterly to his friends about the killer not being found, and suggested that an illiterate, alcoholic employee of his, Henry Huiel, could be a suspect; the shabby man, always in need of money, had been spending money freely and had previously always been short of funds. On Feb. 14, 1971, police received a call from an informer. Howard Kiker, another employee of Padgett's, claimed to be an unwitting ally in the slaying, and told officers to investigate Huiel. In Huiel's house, police found the victim's purse, and the murder weapon. When questioned, Huiel quickly admitted his guilt. When asked why he had murdered Joyce Padgett, Huiel said, "John Padgett asked me to." Police learned that Padgett had collected $53,000 in life insurance policies on his wife, and had been doling out money to Huiel ever since the shooting, hoping the police would become suspicious. Padgett did not, however, consider that Huiel would feel a desperate need to confess his guilt. John Padgett and Henry Huiel were sentenced to life imprisonment. Kiker received a shorter sentence.

Palmer, Inez, 1902-41, and **Stout, Arthur**, 1893-1941, U.S. On Nov. 17, 1926, William Stout, sixty-seven, found his wife, Sarah Stout, forty-two, dead on the kitchen floor of their Vinton County, Ohio, farm house. Strangled, Mrs. Stout's throat bore several small half-moon-shaped marks, and several others on different parts of her body. The corpse had been soaked in kerosene and partially burned. The sheriff, Maude Collins, spotted several small semicircular marks in the ground outside the house, apparently made by a walking stick, the possible murder weapon. Arthur Stout, 32-year old stepson of the murdered woman, worked on a nearby farm, and said he had not been to visit his father that day. A clock key, found close to the corpse, was traced to a local jeweler, Jacob Hauser, who explained he had personally delivered it to Arthur Stout at his father's home on Nov. 17. It was then learned that the dead woman had attempted to have her stepson arrested three weeks earlier on charges of threatening to murder her. Arthur Stout was arrested.

Inez Palmer, Stout's housekeeper, regularly visited the accused in jail. She showed Sheriff Collins a note she said had been written by the elder Stout, in which he declared he would prefer to go away and leave his son everything "for what I've made him suffer" than to testify against his own son. Collins searched Stout's land and found the older man's body in a well. When Palmer refused to give the sheriff a sample of her handwriting, Collins became more suspicious, and finally accused Palmer of the killings when it was found that the half moon marks had been made by the young woman's high heels. Confessing, Palmer said that Mrs. Stout had assailed her morals, and she murdered her; that William Stout was aware of the crime, and that she had soon decided to slay the father as well, procuring his property for her lover, Arthur. Collins was also informed that Arthur Stout had offered Palmer's 18-year-old brother $50 in October 1926 to murder his stepmother. Tried as an accessory before and after the fact, Stout was convicted and sentenced to life imprisonment, as was Palmer. Both died in 1941; Stout in a Columbus, Ohio, prison, and Palmer three years after her release.

Palmer, James Gordon, 1938-   , U.S. A tense hostage situation in the small town of Jerseyville, Ill., (population 7,500) ended happily on Oct. 9, 1959, when a killer was overpowered by his prisoners. Jerseyville, located in southwestern Illinois, was abuzz over the criminal activities committed by one of its own: 21-year-old James Gordon Palmer. In Fall 1959, Palmer blazed a trail of murder and mayhem across three states: Illinois, Tennessee, and Missouri. He shot and killed at close range a bait shop owner, a gas station attendant and a waitress. In each instance the victim had been placed on the floor, bound and gagged, and then shot in the back of the head.

On Oct. 8 Palmer was spotted by local sheriff's deputies as he returned to his Jerseyville apartment. He fled to the outskirts of town and escaped into a cornfield. Later he shot and wounded a railroad brakeman near the spot where he was holed up. A massive police manhunt failed to turn up any signs of the killer as the local residents girded for the worst. That afternoon the supply of guns and ammunition at the local sporting goods store was completely exhausted.

The next morning, Oct. 9, Louis Gorman, owner of a construction company located on Franklin Street, drove down to his office where he was met by two truck drivers in his employ: Robert Cordes and Charles Kroeschel. To his considerable alarm, he noticed that the front door had been opened. Inside there was evidence of an intruder. Shards of glass littered the floor. Gorman entered the washroom when suddenly the shotgun murderer emerged from his hiding place. Palmer ordered Kroeschel and Cordes to sit down on the floor quietly. Gorman, who tried to escape through the washroom window, surrendered meekly. "Open the safe brother," Palmer commanded. But the trick combination was known only to the office manager, Ernie Pohlman, who was scheduled to arrive shortly. So they waited.

In the next few minutes Palmer took three more hostages: truck-driver Edward Fitzgibbons, a railroad engineer named William Kuehnel, equipment operator Herschel Andrews and truck driver Darrell Smith. The men were told to sit on the floor next to their friends. Pohlman appeared a few moments later. But he had trouble opening the safe under such extreme pressure. "I'll give you one more minute. If you don't open that safe, you're a dead man!" Palmer snapped. The tumblers clicked open and the money was stuffed into a paper bag. The killer then ordered Pohlman to bind the seven men together on the floor with a section of rope.

Realizing what was coming next Gorman decided that the only way to escape with their lives was to try to overpower Palmer in a vulnerable moment. But when? Gorman studied Palmer's movements very carefully. He couldn't help but notice that for a bare instant Palmer's shotgun was pointed at the ceiling when he arose from the crouching position. The businessman inched closer to Palmer as he continued to bind the necks of his friends. Then, in a split moment Gorman lunged at Palmer, knocking the shotgun from his hands. "Come on boys!" he yelled, and within an instant the killer was subdued. Gorman and his men, who had come within an inch of death, breathed a long sigh of relief. For his gallantry, he was rewarded with the Silver Medal of the Carnegie Hero Fund Commission. Palmer received a 180 year prison term and will not be eligible for parole until the year 2020.

Pancoast, Marvin, 1950- , U.S. Marvin Pancoast, a hanger-on in Hollywood, became the roommate of Vicki Morgan, Alfred Bloomingdale's long-term mistress and companion in sado-masochistic orgies. Since Morgan had failed to win her "palimony" suit against the late luxury department store owner's estate in 1982, she took in Pancoast, a homosexual whom she had known for several years, to share the rent. When Pancoast failed to pay his rent, the two prepared to move out of the Studio City condominium and go their separate ways. On July 6, the night before they were to move, Pancoast reached some sort of limit with Morgan. "I was tired of being her slave boy," he later said. He waited until she was asleep, then crept into her bedroom, and beat in her head and chest with one of her son's baseball bats.

Pancoast promptly went to the nearest police station and turned himself in. During the coming days, he became the forgotten player in what became a national drama. An attorney in Los Angeles, Robert Steinberg, claimed to have

Vicki Morgan, slain by Marvin Pancoast.

seen videotapes of Bloomingdale-Morgan orgies in which recognizable national figures were involved. Since Bloomingdale had been a close friend of first lady Nancy Reagan, major embarrassment appeared possible. But Steinberg soon said that the tapes had been stolen, and, if they had ever existed, they never turned up again. Pancoast pleaded insanity, but on Sept. 14, 1984, was found Guilty of murder in the first degree and sentenced to twenty-six years to life in prison.

Panconi, Claude, prom. 1949, Fr. In an odd circumstance of exaggeration and pretense that turned lethal, a group of high school students in post WWII France got carried away to the point of murder. A group of male students attending the Parisian high school on the Rue George Sand sought to impress fellow student Nicole Ily with imagined tales of high adventure. Alain Guyader invented a secret double agent life and wrote Ily a letter about his "shady business" and "bad life" in the summer of 1948. The 16-year-old girl wrote back to Guyader, saying she was in love with an "older man," Joe Graziani, twenty-three. Graziani enticed Ily with talk of a mysterious "Superior Intellects" club he had formed in Greece. Ily told Guyader, who told Claude Panconi and others about Graziani. Along with Panconi, who also had a crush on Ily, and several other youths, Guyader and Ily became the leaders in a tangled web of deceit and invention that involved combating an imagined Russian invasion of France, romantic notions about Resistance work in French Morocco, and ideas of theft and disguise for the purpose of higher ideals. When Bernard Petit, a policeman's son, suggested that Guyader was probably a double agent, the idea of murdering him was approved unanimously by seven gang members. Petit plotted the "perfect murder" with the others, borrowing his father's gun, but failing to meet Guyader and Panconi at the appointed time and place.

Panconi later gave three versions of unfolding events, agreeing only on the point that there had been an argument over Nicole, and that he had fired in self-defense when he thought Guyader pulled a gun. On Jan. 11, 1949, Panconi confessed to Guyader's father that, after he had shot his 17-year-old friend, Alain had said to him, "What an idiot you are to do this for a girl," telling him to take everything from his pockets to make it look like a robbery, and promising not to say anything that would make him look suspicious. When Guyader was found by a truck driver and his son in the woods, the young man said he must have stepped into a gunshot trap, and said he had come out to the area to meet his friend Petit, who never showed up. Guyader lay bleeding for two hours in the truck while gendarmes argued over what precinct he had been found in; he died in the hospital before he could be operated on. The defense lawyers claimed that the killing was the direct result of the atmosphere that the children had grown up in, citing WWII, the German occupation, and the rampant post-WWII black market. Panconi was tried and convicted, and sentenced to ten years in jail. Petit and Ily were convicted and given three-year jail terms.

Panzram, Carl (AKA: Jeff Rhoades; John O'Leary),
1891-1930, U.S. Carl Panzram was devoid of all normal human emotions, save one: an obsessive hatred for the human race that bordered on the maniacal. This dislike for himself and his fellow man was manifested in a lifetime of murder and mayhem. "I have no desire to reform myself," he said in his published autobiography. "My only desire is to reform people who try to reform me. And I believe that the only way to reform people is to kill 'em."

Panzram was the son of immigrant Prussian farmers. He was born on a farm near Warren, Minn. His father deserted the family when Panzram was only a boy, leaving a tremendous burden on his over-taxed mother who had precious little time to give her children. Without the nurturing family environment Carl fell into bad ways. In 1899 he was brought before the juvenile court on a drunk and disorderly charge. He was only eight. This led to acts of petty thievery, which convinced the courts to send him to the Minnesota State Training School in Red Wing. The discipline was rigid, if not sadistic. Carl toiled in workshops from dawn to dusk and spent much of his time washing dishes. On the night of July 7, 1905, he set fire to the school warehouse which housed winter blankets and clothing. He later cynically remarked: "That night the whole place burned down at a cost of over $100,000. Nice eh?" Carl Panzram left the guilt to others.

Released in January 1906, Panzram was launched on his

criminal career. On Mar. 29, 1906, he hitched a ride on a west bound freight train at East Grand Forks, N.D. He committed a string of robberies and assaults before winding

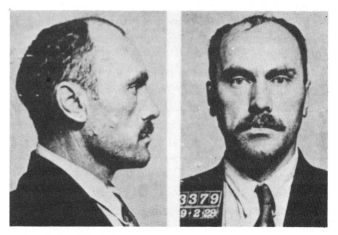

Police photos of Carl Panzram, mass murderer.

up in the Montana State Reformatory. But as future events later showed, there were few jails that could hold this felon. With fellow inmate James Benson, Panzram escaped. In the next few months he robbed and burned down several Montana churches. He joined the army in Helena, Mont., but was court-martialed on Apr. 20, 1907, for insubordination and sentenced to three years in Fort Leavenworth for pilfering government property. He spent the next thirty-seven months breaking rocks under the blazing Kansas sun; an experience that fine-tuned his razor-sharp meanness.

After receiving a discharge in 1910, Panzram went to Mexico to join the rebel leader Pascual Orozco, who served under Venustiano Carranza. Moving about California and the Pacific Northwest, Panzram committed various robberies, assaults, and acts of sodomy. Looking back on his career he would recall: "I have murdered twenty-one human beings. I have committed thousands of burglaries, robberies, larcenies, arson, and last but not least I have committed sodomy on more than 1,000 male human beings."

He was arrested in Chinook, Mont., on a burglary charge and sentenced to a year in the Montana State Prison. He escaped eight months later. Panzram was arrested a year later under the alias of "Jeff Rhoades." He was given a two year sentence in the Montana State Prison on burglary charges, receiving his parole in 1914. Panzram barely had time to enjoy his freedom. In Astoria, Ore., he was arrested on a burglary charge and sent to the state prison at Salem for seven years. An additional seven years was tacked on to his sentence for attempting to lead a prison insurrection. For this he was fed a diet of bread and water, and was beaten and sprayed with a fire hose. Panzram constructed his own tools and hacked his way to freedom in May 1918. He was next seen on the east coast where he robbed a hotel in Frederick, Md., of $1,200. Continuing on to New York, Panzram joined the Marine Firemen's, Oiler's, and Water Tender's Union. He signed on board the *James Whitney*, a merchant vessel bound for South America, but jumped ship in Peru in order to work in a copper mine.

From there he traveled to Chile where he worked as a foreman for the Sinclair Oil Company. In Bocas Del Toro, Panzram senselessly set fire to an oil rig. A $500 reward was posted, but Panzram eluded capture and slipped back undetected into the U.S. In 1920 he broke into a jewelry store in Bridgeport, Conn., making off with $7,000. Later that summer he removed $40,000 in jewels and liberty bonds from the private residence of former president William Howard Taft in New Haven. With this large windfall, Panzram purchased a deluxe yacht under the name of "John O'Leary." He hired ten sailors to refit the boat. After their task had been completed, Panzram invited them to spend the night in the cabin. "When they were asleep I would get my .45 Colt Army Automatic and blow their brains out," he said. The weighted bodies were taken to the middle of the harbor and dropped into the water.

Panzram was later arrested in Bridgeport on a burglary charge. He served his six months in the local jail without incident before heading on to Philadelphia where he was imprisoned for inciting a riot during a labor dispute. After posting bond he fled the country and sailed to Europe on a tramp steamer. Afterward he continued on to Africa. In Portuguese West Africa Panzram got himself a job with the Sinclair Oil Company. By his own admission he murdered a 12-year-old boy. "First I committed sodomy on him and then I killed him," he said. At Lobito Bay Panzram committed yet another atrocity. Deciding that crocodile hunting might pose a challenge, he hired six black porters to guide him through the murky backwater. During the expedition, he shot the six men in the back and tossed them to the crocodiles.

Returning to the U.S. in 1922, Panzram assaulted a 12-year-old Salem, Mass., boy, Henry McMahon, killing him with a rock. "...I tried a little sodomy on him first...I left him laying there with his brains coming out of his ears." In June 1923, while working as a night watchman for the New Haven Yacht Club, Panzram stole a boat and then murdered a would-be robber who climbed aboard in the middle of the night. The body was tossed into the bay at Kingston, N.Y. Later, this one-man crime wave was arrested for attempted robbery and sentenced to five years in Sing Sing. But the guards at this facility were unable to keep him in line. He was transferred to Clinton Prison in Dannemora, considered to be the end of the line for criminal hard cases. Released in 1928 Panzram hit the Baltimore-Washington, D.C., area like a tornado, commit-

ting eleven burglaries and one murder. He was arrested by capital police on Aug. 16, 1928. While in jail Panzram wrote his autobiography and gave it to a sympathetic jailer Henry Lesser. At his trial, Panzram glared at the jurors, chiding them with a deadly threat. "If I live I'll execute some more of you!" Judge Walter McCoy sentenced the defendant to twenty-five years in Leavenworth. "Visit me!" Panzram shot back.

To the deputy warden, Fred Zerbst, Panzram issued a grim warning: "I'll kill the first man who bothers me." Zerbst assigned him to the prison laundry, which was supervised by a civilian employee, Robert G. Warnke, who minded his own business and rarely bothered the prisoners. Warnke maintained a penalty sheet, which he used to record infractions of the rules and then turned over to the warden. Perhaps because of this, Panzram decided to make Warnke his victim—the last as it turned out. On June 20, 1929, Carl Panzram assaulted Warnke with an iron bar. He fell to the floor dead. Panzram surrendered himself to the guard, accepting his fate with weary resignation. He was sentenced to die on the gallows following a hasty trial. When the Society for the Abolishment of Capital Punishment tried to intervene on his behalf, Panzram told them to forget it. Hanging, he said, would be a "real pleasure and a big relief," adding: "the only thanks you or your kind will ever get from me for your efforts on my behalf is that I wish you all had one neck and I had my hands on it...I believe the only way to reform people is to kill 'em...My motto is: 'Rob 'em all, rape 'em all and kill 'em all!'" His last epitaph was signed "Copper John II" in memory of a statue he had seen outside Auburn Prison in New York. Panzram, defiant to the end, was executed in Leavenworth on Sept. 5, 1930.

Papillon, See: **Charriere, Henri-Antoine.**

Pappas, Rosemary (AKA: **Renee Vittorio**), d.1981, U.S. An attractive Greek Chicago couple with a violent and volatile eleven-year marriage and two children had already been divorced and remarried when the husband, Peter Pappas, asked his wife, Rosemary Pappas, for a second divorce. She refused. On the morning of Feb. 16, 1975, the husband arrived home at about 5 a.m. At dawn, police were called to his house and found him in bed, a bullet through his head. Tried for murder, the wife contended that they had wrestled for the gun, and that she had no memory of how the shooting occurred. Assistant District Attorney Joseph Romano charged that Pappas had slain her spouse by shooting him in the back of the head with his own .38-caliber revolver, probably while he was sleeping. Convicted and sentenced to fourteen to twenty years in prison, Pappas remained free on bail for three years until November 1979, when her conviction was affirmed after several appeals, and she disappeared with her two daughters. On Oct. 2, 1981, an East Providence, R.I., mother was killed in a car accident as she drove her daughters to school. Her driver's license identified her as Renee Vittorio, and her children said their last names were "Hall," because their mother had remarried. Police learned that the dead woman was Rosemary Pappas, who had been a fugitive, eluding the FBI, moving through five states as she traversed the country in her flight from the law.

Paprskar, Bonnie, prom. 1970., U.S. Fort Worth, Texas, motorcycle gang queen Bonnie Paprskar, enraged after drug dealers sold her husband impure heroin, ordered the gang to execute the two dealers and one of the dealer's young sons. In exchange for Paprskar's plea of guilty, the judge gave her a twenty-five-year jail sentence, instead of the death penalty that the prosecution had originally intended to demand. Exactly four years after she began serving her sentence, Paprskar was free on parole.

Paris, Richard James, d.1967, U.S. On Jan. 7, 1967, Richard Paris, a two-time deserter from the army, married a woman named Christine. He took her to the luxurious Orbit Inn in Las Vegas, Nev., for a honeymoon. Then he fired a .38-caliber automatic into a bundle of fourteen sticks of dynamite. The bundle exploded, killing Richard Paris, Christine Paris, and five other honeymooners in nearby suites and destroying two floors of the hotel.

Parker, George Henry, c. 1878-1901, Brit. On Jan. 17, 1901, George Parker, an ex-soldier, boarded the train to London from Southampton at Eastleigh with a newly purchased gun in his pocket. Mrs. Rhoda King, on her way to London to visit her sister, was already in the compartment Parker entered. At Winchester, William Pearson, a prosperous farmer, joined them. Parker left the compartment for a moment, and on his return shot Pearson dead and then turned the gun on King, grazing her cheek with a bullet. Stunned, she asked Parker why he did it, and he replied, "I did it for money. I want some money. Have you got any?" The shocked woman handed him a shilling,

which he rejected. He turned to Pearson's body and quickly found some cash, a sovereign which he tried to give to King. She promised not to say anything about him if he left her alone.

"What shall I do with this bloody thing?" he asked, holding up his gun. He suggested putting it in the hand of the corpse so that it would appear he had committed suicide, but King thought he should throw it out the window. He did so, and then, as the train slowed for the platform at Bauzhall, he leaped off. At that time, tickets were collected at the end of a train ride, and Parker thrust Pearson's ticket at the collector and tried to leave the station. But King shouted out that Parker had killed someone, and several men captured him.

Parker was tried for murder and attempted murder. His defense attorney pleaded insanity brought on by alcohol. But the jury found Parker Guilty and sentenced him to death. He was hanged on Mar. 19, 1901.

Parker, Pauline Yvonne, 1938-   , and **Hulme, Juliet Marion,** 1939-   , N. Zea. "I feel keyed up as if I was planning a surprise party. So next time I write in the diary mother will be dead. How odd, yet how pleasing," 16-year-old Pauline Parker wrote in her diary on June 21, 1954.

Teenage Australian killers Pauline Parker and Juliet Hulme.

The next day, she and her best friend and lover, Juliet Hulme, fifteen, walked with Pauline's mother in Victoria Park, Christchurch, N. Zea. They tricked Mrs. Honora Mary Parker into bending down, then beat her over the head with a brick wrapped in a stocking until she was quiet. Then they ran to a nearby tea room for help, assuming people would believe them when they said Mrs. Parker had fallen, and "her head kept bumping, bumping, bumping."

Parker and Hulme had been avid friends for some months. Dr. Hulme, Juliet's father, intended to take her to South Africa because his marriage was breaking up and because he hoped to separate his daughter from Parker. But the girls insisted that they both be allowed to go. Parker readily confessed to the murder and tried to take all the blame, but Hulme admitted hitting Mrs. Parker as well.

The jury had to decide whether or not the girls were sane. Psychiatrists testified that they knew the law, but that they considered themselves "geniuses," above the law. They admitted killing Mrs. Parker to prevent their separation. The jury found Pauline Parker and Juliet Hulme Guilty and sane. They were committed to juvenile prison and released in 1958.

Pascarella, Leo, prom. 1945, U.S. Leo Pascarella was jealous of the attention that 22-year-old Marie Beaver (whose real name was Ethel Marie Berridge) received from other male suitors. His jealousy reached its peak on the afternoon of June 29, 1945. Three days later, Berridge's landlady, who was delivering a dozen roses to the nightclub hostess from an admirer, discovered the body of Berridge under the bed of her Detroit boarding house room. Berridge's throat had been severely bruised, a handkerchief had been stuffed down her throat, and a cut made across her forehead.

Police discovered a large bundle of love letters from a number of men. All of these letters were tracked down, as were the roses, and the victim's former husband who lived in Columbus, Ohio. The former husband and the man who sent the roses had solid alibis, as did the men who sent her love letters. A number of witnesses identified a photo of a sailor who was seen several times with the victim. Though his alibi was beyond question, his photo was used to track the killer. A woman in Saginaw, Mich., spotted the photo in a newspaper and thought it looked like Pascarella. She reported to police that a man she met, Pascarella, looked like the killer. Pascarella was soon arrested and he admitted to the murder. Although described by psychiatrists as having homicidal and suicidal tendencies, Pascarella was sentenced to seven to fifteen years' imprisonment.

Pastorino, Pamela, 1953- , U.S. On Nov. 19, 1977, 15-year-old Debbie Saylor of Chicago wanted to make a pizza, but her stepfather, 53-year-old Leonard Warchol, would not allow it. An argument soon erupted. Warchol was struck over the head with a lead pipe and repeatedly stabbed with a seven-inch long kitchen knife. Debbie, along with her sister, 24-year-old Pamela Pastorino, was charged with the murder on the city's Northwest Side.

Investigators determined that Debbie had attacked Warchol with the knife and stabbed him while Pastorino struck him over the head. The younger sister was convicted of murder in a juvenile court and sent to the Naperville Youth Center. She testified at her sister's three-day trial in 1979. Debbie claimed that Pastorino did not take part in the murder, while the defendant testified that she had attempted to stop Debbie from stabbing Warchol. Assistant State's Attorneys Michael Carey and Michael Shabat argued that Pastorino played a much larger role. The jury agreed. She was found Guilty on Jan. 27, 1979, and sentenced to twenty to sixty years' imprisonment on Mar. 5, 1979, by Criminal Court Judge James M. Bailey.

Pateman, George Baron, prom. 1911, Brit. On the evening of Apr. 29, 1911, 22-year-old Alice Isobel Linfold was leaving her parents' home in Finchley, England, when she was met by George Baron Pateman. As on previous occasions, the woman refused his advances. This time, however, Pateman pulled out a razor and attacked Linfold. He slashed an enormous wound in Linfold's throat, using such force that the razor's handle broke in his grasp. Linfold managed to stagger almost fifty yards down the garden path to the kitchen before she died.

The killer was tried at the Old Bailey in London before Justice Darling. Pateman pleaded that the attack was due to a temporary loss of mind. The judge did not believe him. For the first time in British history, a sample of blood, found on Pateman's jacket, was demonstrated and accepted in court to have come from a human being. Prior to this all blood samples had merely been proven as blood from a mammal. This case also proved to be the first public appearance that Sir Bernard Spilsbury made as a pathologist for the prosecution. Pateman was found Guilty and sentenced to death but was later reprieved.

Pattinson, Joseph Colin, 1935-58, S. Afri. Joseph Colin Pattinson was born in Jeppe, a suburb of Johannesburg, South Africa in 1935. He was a poor student and began smoking hashish-laced cigarettes at the age of nine. The drug use eventually led him to petty theft and eventually to violent arguments with his parents. After one such argument in which he attempted to strangle his father, he was sent to the Rustenberg Industrial School instead of receiving the strict discipline sought by his parents. He nevertheless continued to use drugs and began to associate with a violent group of boys.

When Pattinson graduated from Rustenberg at the age of seventeen, he left the area for Transvaal where he took a job as a fireman on the railway. After becoming dissatisfied with the job, however, he returned to Johannesburg. For the next several years, Pattinson took and lost jobs regularly. His periods of unemployment were filled with drug use, gambling and minor illegal activities. Until 1956, however, Pattinson avoided violent crime.

On May 9 of that year, he met George Winston Thompson near the Johannesburg Railway Station. Thompson, a forty-eight-year old book sales promoter, invited him to his apartment for a drink. According to the story that Pattinson later told police, after several drinks, Thompson made a pass at him. When Pattinson rejected his advance, Thompson went to the kitchen, got a butcher knife and threatened Pattinson with it. Pattinson claimed that he then overpowered the older man, bound him and left him lying on the bed while he made himself a small snack in the kitchen. Once he finished his snack, he returned to find that Thompson, who was lying face down on the bed, had apparently smothered.

Thompson's body was discovered the next day by police. The body was naked and it appeared that Thompson had been strangled with the cord from a dressing gown. A note was found lying next to Thompson's head which said "It was in self-defense. It was him or me. I killed him." The note was signed J.King. Several weeks later, after disappearing from his flat, Pattinson reappeared at the Rustenberg police station and confessed to the murder. He was charged with murder at the Rand Criminal Session on Sept. 26, 1956. Although the court accepted Pattinson's contention that he had not intended to kill Thompson, they found that he had exceeded the limits of self defense and found him Guilty of culpable homicide. He received eighteen months in prison but the sentence was suspended for three years and Pattinson was released.

Earlier, when Pattinson was a student at Rustenberg, he spent a holiday in Johannesburg, where he met and befriended May Diamond. The elderly Diamond lived by herself in a small room and was evidently happy for Pattinson's attention. Pattinson, for his part, came to think of her as a second mother and took to calling her "Auntie May." Once Pattinson was released after the Thompson killing, he took a room in Johannesburg only to discover that "Auntie May" lived just two doors away. The two resumed their earlier friendship. She frequently cooked breakfast for him and listened as he talked about his life. On the morning of Dec. 4, 1957, Diamond invited Pattinson to breakfast. According to Pattinson's later statements, the

two conversed amicably for some time until, for no apparent reason, Diamond became verbally abusive toward him. Pattinson appeared at police headquarters the following afternoon and confessed to killing May Diamond. He stated that after she called him unflattering names, the next thing he remembered was walking into his own room and realizing that his face and clothes were covered in blood and that he was carrying a bread knife with which he apparently had killed Diamond.

Pattinson led police to the building in which he and Diamond lived. After searching a garbage can, he retrieved a bloodstained bread knife which he claimed was the murder weapon. He gave police keys to a padlock on the outside of Diamond's door. When police entered the old woman's apartment, they found blood everywhere. Diamond's naked body was lying on the bed. Her throat had been slit and she had been disembowelled. It was also apparent from her many cuts and bruises that she had been severely beaten before she was killed.

When Pattinson was brought to court at Rand Criminal Sessions on May 14, 1958, his attorney, C.P.Christodolides argued that his client was mentally impaired at the time of the murder and had suffered a blackout so that he could not be held responsible. Regardless of Christodolides' efforts, the jury found Pattinson Guilty of murder without extenuating circumstances. Joseph Pattinson refused to enter an appeal and even threatened to murder a prison guard if they delayed the execution. He was executed on Aug. 18, 1958.

=====

Paul, Rene, c.1927-81, Can. When Rene Paul and his family did not arrive for Sunday dinner as planned on Jan. 4, 1981, their host, and neighbor, stopped by the Pauls' Repentigny, Quebec, home to investigate. The family friend notified police after spying the body of 35-year-old Mrs. Paul through a kitchen window. Inside the home, police found the bodies of the Pauls' 12-year-old twin boy and girl, and their 9-year-old twin sons. Apparently Paul had shot his family to death and then killed himself.

=====

Paul, Sidney George, prom. 1938, Brit. Sidney George Paul, orphaned at the age of ten, went off to fight for England in WWI, but sustained head injuries in the Belgian Congo. He was nursed back to health by a nurse named Claire, whom he married in 1920. The couple returned to England and lived contentedly until 1938 when Paul's sack manufacturing business failed. He went to work in London as a salesman, but lost his job. Unable to tell his wife the unhappy news, Paul pretended to go to work. To save her horrible anxiety he left the house each morning and returned at night, keeping his worsening financial situation to himself. Paul borrowed £150 from his sister to support his family.

Paul brooded over his miserable fate without finding a reasonable solution. On Oct. 3, 1938, Paul inflicted fifteen hatchet blows to Mrs. Paul and then slashed himself with a razor before running out of the family home in Rosebury Vale, Ruislip. "There's a man in my house!" he screamed. A neighbor followed him into the house and found Mrs. Paul's blood-soaked body lying on the floor.

The police questioned Paul about the murder. They were unsure about the intruder, especially after Paul handed the constables a coat button which he claimed to have torn off the assailant during the struggle. The button was found to match four others in a drawer in the Paul home. Moreover, a doctor examined the razor wounds and found them to be self-inflicted. The emotionally troubled murderer was bound over for trial at the Old Bailey in November 1938.

During the deliberations Paul frequently lost his composure, sobbing pitifully that he was innocent. All the time he clutched at a golden crucifix in his hand. "I am not guilty, my lord," he wailed. But a Guilty verdict was returned and the death sentence was handed down by Justice Asquith. Because of the mitigating circumstances of the case, however, the home secretary commuted the sentence to life imprisonment.

Payne, A.D., d.1930, U.S. In March 1930, when the wife of A.D. Payne, a prominent attorney in Amarillo, Texas, opened a closet door, a shotgun blast sent pellets through her hand. Her husband, who had recently taken out large insurance policies on the lives of his wife and children, swore that it was a strange accident. On June 27, 1930, Payne broke his routine and walked to work instead of driving. His wife, glad to have use of the car, planned several errands. Their daughter had decided to walk with

A.D. Payne, who blew up his family.

Payne, and mother and son had just left for the grocery store when the car exploded. Mrs. Payne was killed, and the son was seriously injured by the blast which left him disfigured for life.

Payne himself encouraged outraged newspaper editor Gene Howe to investigate the death. Howe suspected Payne, who specialized in murder cases, but had no proof. Howe called in A.B. MacDonald, an investigative reporter from the Kansas City *Star*, who found that both children were afraid of their father and that they were telling contradictory stories that Payne had concocted for them about the explosion. MacDonald discovered that Payne had had four secretaries in one year, and one of them, Verona Thompson, admitted that she thought her former boss planned to marry her. Payne confessed his guilt when confronted with Thompson's statement. He was convicted of murder and sentenced to die in the electric chair. Payne killed himself in his cell two days before his scheduled execution by detonating a bomb strapped to his chest.

Peakes, Bayard Pfundtner, c.1932- , U.S. Eileen Fahey arrived as usual, just after 9 a.m., on July 14, 1952, for her secretarial position at the American Physical Society on the ninth floor of the Pupin Building of Columbia University in New York City. Fifteen minutes later, she was shot five times with a .22-caliber automatic pistol; three bullets entered her chest directly and two more struck her in the right hand and forearm when she attempted to stop the bullets before they continued on toward her chest. Fahey's killer then quietly left the office and the building. Before leaving he stopped briefly and remarked to another secretary, 32-year-old Mrs. J.V. Lumley, "You better call the police because I just shot somebody. You better call a doctor. I just shot a female."

Deputy Chief Inspector James B. Leggett, who directed the murder investigation, soon discovered that Fahey had neither enemies, nor friends, who met the killer's description. He then decided that the murderer possibly held a grudge against the American Physical Society. Leggett's notion was confirmed after he learned from society treasurer Dr. George B. Pegram of an irate former member named Bayard Pfundtner Peakes. Peakes had written a paper, "So You Love Physics," in which he claimed that the electron did not exist. He had written numerous letters demanding that his work be published. Police found the murder weapon in Peakes's apartment and when the killer returned, he admitted just sixty-three hours after the murder that he had killed Fahey. On Aug. 11 Peakes was examined before a panel of doctors to evaluate his mental state. Psychiatrists Dr. John H. Cassity, Dr. Perry L. Lichtenstein, and Dr. Theodore S. Weiss, were on the panel that declared

Peakes unfit to stand trial, help with his own defense, or even understand the import of the crime or proceedings. He was ordered to be committed to the Matteawan State Hospital for the Criminal Insane on Aug. 18 by General Sessions Judge Edward J. McCullen. The day after Peakes had been judged insane, the parents of Fahey, Mr. and Mrs. Francis Fahey, filed a $250,000 lawsuit against the U.S. on the grounds that the government had acted with carelessness and negligence in allowing a mentally deranged man to be at large. The case was dismissed on Mar. 4, 1954, by Federal Judge Edward J. Dimock.

Pearson, Moses, 1945-76, U.S. A shooting spree which began in Jacksonville, Fla., on Apr. 24, 1976, ended the next day in Jackson, Ga., when the gunman, 31-year-old Moses Pearson, shot himself, bringing the death toll to four. He paved a 250-mile path of blood along Interstate 75 through central Georgia, shooting randomly, wounding thirteen bystanders, taking hostages, and snorting cocaine as he fled.

Pearson, who had previously been convicted of robbery and drug violations, was believed to have been angered over a cocaine deal with his first victim, Horace Fallen, whom he killed in the office of a used car lot. He wounded two more men before fleeing in a 1970 Cadillac. Before thirty minutes had passed, Pearson had shot six more people at two separate locations. At a roadside wig stand, the gunman shot to death 52-year-old George Brownie Quarles and wounded two others before wounding three at a nearby home where Pearson demanded money. The abandoned car was discovered two blocks from the home an hour later. Meanwhile, Pearson had taken another car and headed north toward Georgia. He was next spotted after midnight with three female hostages at a Cordele, Ga., truckstop, about 170 miles northwest of Jacksonville. A hostage informed a waitress they were being held captive and a shoot-out with police soon followed. During the shooting, two bystanders and two Crisp County deputies were injured and two of the hostages escaped.

Pearson continued his northward journey with 25-year-old Susie Critton. Twenty miles later Pearson stopped at a Pinehurst gas station, where Critton escaped while he killed attendant George Griffin, Jr. At Perry he wounded another gas station attendant in an attempted holdup. On the road again, Pearson rammed his car into the back of Leslie Janda's car. Janda and his family were returning to Ohio from Florida. Janda got out of the car and was shot by Pearson, who then jumped in the car and drove off with Mrs. Janda and her two teenage daughters. Police were notified by Janda and a roadblock was set up in Macon.

Pearson eluded the block before crashing the Jandas' car forty miles northwest of that city. He had already fired his gun at Mrs. Janda, who, uninjured, had feigned death. As officers approached the vehicle, Pearson fired twice, killing himself.

Peel, Joseph, Jr., c.1924- , and **Holzapfel, Floyd Albert,** prom. 1955-61, U.S. Circuit Court Judge C.E. Chillingworth of Palm Beach, Fla., and his wife were missing for five years. Their killer was Joseph Peel, Jr., the municipal judge of West Palm Beach. The beneficiary of bribes and illegal scams, Peel had had trouble with the upright Judge Chillingworth, who was threatening to expose him. Peel called a crook named F.A. "Lucky" Holzapfel, who had killed for him before. Holzapfel and his friends abducted the judge and his wife and sank them both with heavy weights into the sea beyond Palm Beach.

Peel prospered for five years after the murders, but then Peel made the mistake of going to James Yenzer, a Brevard County sheriff's aide, to arrange for the murder of Lucky

Holzapfel, who was blackmailing him over the death of a police informer named Lew Harvey. Yenzer contacted Holzapfel and invited him for drinks in a bugged motel room. The more Holzapfel drank, the more he talked, telling all the bloody details of the murder of Judge Chillingworth and his wife, as well as the fact that it was done at the behest of an influential man in Palm Beach.

Joseph Peel, Jr.

Holzapfel and Peel were arrested for the murders of the Chillingworths and Harvey, and both were found Guilty. Peel received two life sentences. Holzapfel was sent to the electric chair.

Peete, Lofie Louise (AKA: **Lofie Louise Preslar; Louise Gould; Anna B. Lee**), 1883-1947, U.S. Louise Peete from Beinville, La., moved to Shreveport, La., and became an expensive call girl after her first husband, Henry Bosely, a traveling salesman, discovered she was unfaithful and committed suicide. Later, she moved to Boston, changed her last name to Gould, and supported herself by stealing valuables from the homes of the rich, in addition to prostitution. Abruptly leaving for Waco, Texas, she met a big spender named Joe Appel, whom she murdered for his diamonds. Arrested and brought before a grand jury, she told a tragic tale of attempted rape, and how she had been forced to shoot him in self defense. The grand jury ordered her released and she was applauded as she left jail. In 1913 she landed in Dallas, penniless, and soon married Harry Faurote, a hotel clerk. Quickly returning to prostitution, headquartered at the hotel where Faurote worked, she lost her second husband to suicide as well; learning of her trade, he hanged himself in the basement. In 1915 she moved to Denver and married Richard Peete, and bore a daughter in 1916. Unhappy with her husband's income, Louise Peete left in May 1920, for Los Angeles.

Louise Peete, who went to the gas chamber in 1947.

There Peete met Jacob Denton, a millionaire businessman, and moved into his mansion as he was preparing for an extended trip east. When Peete proposed marriage to him, he was enraged. By the end of the month, he had disappeared, and Peete, ensconced in his home, ordered a ton of topsoil removed from the garden and placed in the basement, explaining to the gardener that she was going to show Denton how to grow mushrooms. By weaving a convoluted web of lies Peete managed to put off business associates and insurance agents, eventually claiming power of attorney to sell his house and cash forged checks.

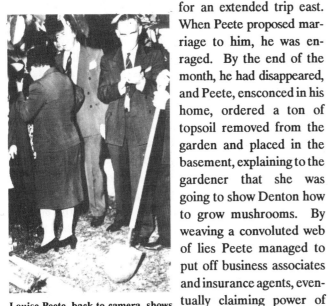

Louise Peete, back to camera, shows officials where she buried the body of Mrs. Margaret Logan.

By August, Peete leased the mansion to a couple named Miller, and returned to Denver to continue fleecing Denton's estate from afar. On Sept. 23, Denton's family hired lawyer Rush Blodgett, who hired private detective A.J. Cody. They found Denton covered with topsoil in the basement. He had been killed with a .32-caliber bullet from his own gun, which still lay in an upstairs drawer. Peete was tried on Jan. 21, 1921. After four hours the jury found her Guilty of first-degree murder, and she was sentenced to life imprisonment. Her current husband swore his loyalty to her, and shot himself in the head three years later when she broke contact with him.

Winning parole in April 1943, Peete, now calling herself Anna B. Lee, stole a revolver and moved into the home of Margaret and Arthur Logan, friends who believed her innocent and had taken care of her daughter while she was in jail. Peete convinced Mrs. Logan to commit her 74-year-old husband to Patton State Hospital; he was later released into his wife's custody. Pretending to have a $100,000 trust fund in Denver she would soon inherit, Peete borrowed $2,000 from Mrs. Logan. After taking Mrs. Logan's jewelry, and forging checks on her account, Peete shot her in the neck, and beat her with the butt of the gun until she died. She buried the body in the backyard and headed for Denver with a new husband, Lee Judson, on May 31. She dumped Arthur Logan back at the hospital; he died there on Dec. 6, 1944. Explaining Mrs. Logan's disappearance with stories of breast cancer and plastic surgery, Peete began to take over the Logans' possessions, cashing checks and selling or giving their personal belongings away.

On Dec. 20, 1944, she and Judson broke open the Logan's home safe and were rifling the contents when Captain Thaddeus Brown of the Los Angeles Police Department arrived and arrested the pair. Judson, being held as a material witness, later killed himself. Tried in April 1944, with Deputy District Attorney John Barnes for the prosecution, Peete tried to blame Logan for his wife's death, but was found Guilty of first-degree murder a second time. She was executed in San Quentin's gas chamber on Apr. 11, 1947.

Pelosi, Giuseppe (AKA: **Pino the Frog**), 1959- , Italy. As a youth, Pier Paolo Pasolini left his home in rural Italy to live in poverty in Rome. There he gathered and absorbed material that he later used as a film director. In 1961, he directed his first film, *Accatone*, or *Beggar*, a movie that depicted prostitutes, pimps, and robbers. On Nov. 2, 1975, the violent life captured in his films became a reality for the 53-year-old Pasolini. After eating dinner with an actor, he drove to the railroad station to pick up 17-year-old Giuseppe Pelosi and the two drove to an empty lot outside of the city. The teenager later said that the director made sexual advances, but Pelosi refused and the two argued. Then the youth, along with unidentified accomplices, beat the director with a board lined with nails before running over him with his own car. Pelosi was found

Guilty on Apr. 26, 1976, and sentenced to nine years, seven months, and ten days imprisonment.

Peltier, Leonard, 1945-   , U.S. On June 26, 1975, members and supporters of the American Indian Movement became involved in a shootout with two FBI agents. Agents Jack Coler and Ronald Williams were shot dead in their cars, which were riddled with about 125 bullet holes, on the Pine Ridge Indian Reservation in South Dakota. Leonard Peltier, the 32-year-old head of the organization, was charged with the murders, tried, and found Guilty on Apr. 18, 1977. He received two consecutive life sentences.

Perry, Arthur, d.1939, U.S. Arthur Perry of Jamaica, N.Y., started the scheme to murder his wife several weeks in advance by collecting samples of the handwriting of his friend, 39-year-old Ulysses Palm. Then, pretending to be Palm, he wrote a letter to his wife, supposedly from Palm, threatening her with death if she did not have sex with him. Phennie Perry, bewildered, showed the letter to her husband, who said he would take care of it. On the evening of July 1, 1937, Phennie played bingo at a movie theater in Jamaica. From there she and her baby were to go to her sister's house.

Perry saw his wife at the theater, then went to Palm's house. He sneaked into Palm's bedroom and stole a shoe and an iron, ripped a pocket off a shirt, and took some papers from Palm's dresser. Perry later met his 20-year-old wife and escorted her through an empty construction lot, where he bludgeoned her to death with the iron. He left Palm's papers under her body, along with the shirt fabric. He abandoned the baby next to his wife's body and spent the night at his sister's.

Phennie Perry's body and the crying baby were found the next morning,

Murderer Arthur Perry.

along with all the evidence neatly pointing to Ulysses Palm. But Captain Henry Flattery ordered both Perry and Palm held. Palm had an alibi until 11:15 p.m., when he arrived home from work. Perry claimed he had seen only his wife

the first time he stopped at the theater, but an usher said he saw Perry come again at 9:50 p.m. Scientists then found a speck of blood on the sole of Perry's sock, matching a hole in the shoe found at the murder site, and another speck inside the rolled-up sleeve of his shirt. Handwriting experts decided that the original letter from Palm was written by Perry. In November 1937, Arthur Perry was brought to trial for murder before Judge Charles S. Cohen. He was found Guilty and sentenced to death. The Court of Appeals called for a new trial, at which time Sidney Cusbeth, a detective who had been planted in prison with Perry before the first trial, testified Perry had confessed to him the killing of his wife. No explanation was offered to explain why this information was not used at the first trial. Perry was again found Guilty and was electrocuted at Sing Sing on Aug. 3, 1939.

Pesce, Ernesto, prom. 1935, Arg. Augusto Okonski, a Polish contractor in Buenos Aires, Arg., generously gave money to charities and helped poor families and beggars. In late August 1935, Okonski met a beggar, Ernesto Pesce, whom the contractor took home, fed, and clothed. Pesce came back the next day, insisting on money, so Okonski gave him money for a hotel. Although the contractor tried to find a job for the poor man, Pesce did not want to work and he continued to badger Okonski for money. He became such a nuisance that after Okonski allowed him to briefly stay in his house, the contractor had to forcibly evict him after three days.

On Sept. 14, 1935, two days before Okonski was to be married, he gave the derelict twenty pesos and told him not to return. However, only a few days after Okonski married Ana Karenski, Pesce came back, and on Sept. 19, 1935, entered Okonski's bedroom where the contractor was taking a nap. Pesce shot and killed him, and when Okonski's wife came into the room, the intruder wiped off the gun and placed it in her hands. Minutes later, police officer Manuel Carrera found her with the gun and she was arrested. A trial was postponed until the matter could be further investigated. Police found that the gun had been stolen about a year previously by a man who fit the same description as the intruder seen by Ana Okonski. Also found was an accounting ledger detailing Okonski's money, which contained an entry for the twenty pesos with the notation, "...he told me his name was Ernesto Pesce." Ana Okonski was released, and in March 1936, Pesce was arrested in Cordoba, north of Buenos Aires. He was tried, convicted, and sentenced to twenty-five years in prison at hard labor.

Peterson, Richard, 1939- , U.S. On April Fool's Day in 1955, Richard Peterson asked his parents for the family car. They refused because he had been drinking. Peterson then went on a thirty-minute shooting spree that ended in the deaths of two men in Pasco, Wash.

Peterson had already shot his father, P.T. Peterson, and his grandfather, Chester Young, with a hunting rifle when policeman Alva M. Jackson arrived on the scene. Jackson cornered the 16-year-old Peterson in an alley and ran toward the youth, his gun still in its holster. Peterson fired six shots at the oncoming officer. While mortally wounded, Jackson managed to take a knife from the youth and hold him until other policemen arrived.

Jackson died that day, and Peterson's father died sixteen days later. Richard Peterson originally pleaded not guilty by reason of insanity to first- and second-degree murder charges. Prosecutor Roger L. Olson later reduced the charges and dismissed a charge for the wounding of the grandfather in exchange for a guilty plea. Peterson was sentenced to a total of sixty-five years in prison. In 1965, Peterson was caught trying to escape from Washington State Penitentiary in Walla Walla, and an additional ten years was tacked onto his sentence.

Petiot, Dr. Marcel Andre Henri Felix (AKA: **Henry John Felix Marcel; Henri Valery**), 1897-1946, Fr. France's worst mass murderer committed his crimes during the German occupation, from 1942 until 1944. Marcel Petiot was born at Auxerre, the son of a postal official. In 1917 he enlisted in the French army but was court-martialed for stealing drugs and then selling them on the black market. Curiously, he was granted a full pension and free ongoing treatment for his condition, which was diagnosed as psychoneurosis.

In 1921 Petiot qualified to become a physician at a time when he was still being treated for a mental disorder. Petiot established his practice in Villeneuve-sur-Yonne and became the town's mayor in 1928. He was accused shortly afterward of fathering a child with his housekeeper. "She told everyone she was having sexual intercourse with me," he said. "In fact I declined this honor." During the time he served as mayor of Villeneuve, the doctor was accused of drug peddling and theft, and actually served time in prison for the latter offense. In 1930 he was implicated in the murder of one his patients, Madame Debauvre, but the principal witness against him died suddenly and the case was forgotten.

In 1933 Petiot turned up in Paris. In 1936 he was arrested there for robbing book shops. The charge was dismissed, but Petiot agreed to submit to psychiatric examinations. He remained on the medical roster though, and re-established his practice at 66 Rue Caumartin. The next few years were very good for Petiot, whose patients numbered 3,000. In 1941 he bought a fifteen-room house at 21 Rue Lesueur to use as his laboratory. Alterations to the building were completed in September of that year. By all accounts it was designed for the peculiar needs of a mass murderer. A triangular "death room" and a massive wall that prevented nosy neighbors from looking in were constructed according to Petiot's specifications.

No one paid much attention to the comings and goings at the Rue Lesueur in the next few years. The residents of the neighborhood were mainly concerned with surviving the ordeal of Nazi occupation until Mar. 11, 1944, when Jacques Marcais complained to the police about a nauseating, smoky odor coming from 21 Rue Lesueur. The police summoned the doctor to his residence to explain the smell, and while awaiting his arrival they ordered a fire brigade to extinguish a fire in the chimney. The firemen forced their way into the house, where they beheld an eerie, disgusting sight. Scattered about the floor of the cellar were the remains of twenty-seven human bodies in various stages of decomposition. Petiot told the police sergeant that the bodies were those of Nazi collaborators executed by the Resistance. Satisfied with this, the sergeant let him go. Petiot, his wife, and their 16-year-old son fled into the countryside and dropped out of sight while speculation mounted that the doctor was not a loyal member of the Resistance, but a Gestapo sympathizer who had carried out the atrocities for the Germans.

In October Petiot wrote a letter to the newspaper *Resistance* stating that he had been cleverly framed by the Gestapo. Because he claimed to be an officer in the Resistance, his handwriting was checked against that of all officers of the Free French forces in Paris. It was found to be that of Captain Henri Valery, a member of the Free Forces for only six weeks. Valery and Petiot were one in the same. Petiot was arrested on Nov. 2, 1944, in a flat at the Rue Faubourg St. Denis, and taken to headquarters for questioning. He declared that the twenty-seven bodies found in the house on Rue Lesueur were mostly German soldiers, but went on to say that he had actually killed sixty-three people while working for the Resistance.

Indicted for murder, Petiot was placed on trial at the Seine Assize Court on Mar. 18, 1946. When asked by Public Prosecutor Pierre Duval about why he refused to mention the names of his former associates in the Resistance, he had a stock answer. "I wouldn't dare name them in this court. There are too many Petainists here." The prosecution charged that Petiot had concocted a scheme to lure wealthy Jews to the mansion, promising to provide them with safe passage out of France in return for all their money and jewels. Introduced into evidence were forty-seven suitcases seized by police in a private residence at Villeneuve. They contained an assortment of clothes that were identified by relatives of some of the victims. Petiot stole in excess of £1 million from the unfortunate French Jews who had solicited his help only to lose their lives. The

French mass murderer Dr. Marcel Petiot at his trial in 1946.

jury returned a Guilty verdict in twenty-four of the twenty-seven murders on Apr. 4, 1946. The president of the court passed the death sentence. As Petiot was led from the court, he screamed to his mortified wife, "You must avenge me!" On May 26, 1946, having exhausted all his appeals, Marcel Petiot was guillotined at Sante Prison in Paris.

Phantom of the Opera Case, See: **Crimmins, Craig.**

Phillips, Ann, 1920- , and **Phillips, Sylvester,** 1932- , U.S. A North Carolina couple was convicted on Feb. 25, 1988, of murdering the 11-year-old girl they were entrusted to care for as foster parents. After being beaten, Tameka Lehmann was pronounced dead and Sylvester Phillips and Ann Phillips, ages fifty-six and sixty-eight respectively, were found Guilty of first-degree murder and sentenced to life imprisonment. The couple must serve at least twenty years of their life sentences plus an additional three years of ten-year sentences for child abuse convictions; each would be eligible for parole in 2011. The girl they killed would have been thirty-four at that time.

Testimony against the Phillips' from their 13-year-old son and two other foster children was instrumental in finding the pair guilty. The children all reported having been beaten regularly with what they called "the batter board," a thirty-inch by three-inch plank found by police with human blood on it. Three days before Tameka died on June 15, 1987, she had been beaten several times with the board after she and the Phillips' son had been chained by their feet upside down. According to the three children, Tameka was also forced to eat soap and hot red pepper on the day she died. An autopsy supported this.

The couple was licensed in Illinois by the Department of Children and Family Services to be foster parents in the early 1970s. They moved to North Carolina in April 1987. Tameka was killed in June.

Phillips, Clara, b.1899, U.S. Attractive 23-year-old former show girl Clara Phillips was happily married to wealthy oil-stock salesman Armour Phillips, when she realized that her husband was seeing another woman. For several weeks she tracked her husband and listened in on his telephone calls, until she was certain he was involved with a widowed 21-year-old, Alberta Meadows.

On July 6, 1922, Phillips and her best friend, Peggy Caffee, also a former show girl, went out drinking. By late afternoon, knowing that Meadows was going to be at her bank, Phillips went there with Caffee. When Meadows came out,

Clara Phillips, known as the Los Angeles "Tiger Woman," savagely murdered her husband's younger lover, Alberta Meadows.

Phillips asked the startled woman for a ride. Meadows agreed. In a little-inhabited area outside Los Angeles, Phillips had Meadows stop the car, ostensibly so they could talk. All three women got out of the car. Phillips then struck Meadows in the face. She then pulled a hammer from her purse and repeatedly struck her rival. The attack was so savage that the head of the hammer broke off and was left embedded in Meadows' skull. A horror-struck Caffee futilely attempted to stop her friend, but fainted from the sight of the bloody attack.

Phillips revived Caffee and drove her home. She then went to her own home where she informed her husband that she had killed his lover. Incredibly, Armour Phillips offered to help his wife leave town. They took Meadows' car and hid it, then Clara took a train to Mexico. Armour then called his lawyers, who promptly informed police about the murder. Clara was arrested before her train reached the border. "The Tiger Woman"—the press' nickname for

Clara because of the way she had stalked her husband's lover—was found Guilty despite an effort to put the blame on her friend Peggy Caffee. On Nov. 16, 1922, she was sentenced to ten years to life in San Quentin.

However, while in Los Angeles County Jail awaiting appeal, an old boyfriend named Jesse Carson brought Phillips a hacksaw. She sawed through the bars on her small window and escaped, climbing down three stories to the ground, then up over a fifty-foot wall. Carson, Phillips, and her sister, Etta Mae Jackson, went to Honduras, but were found. Phillips was extradited to the U.S. the following April. This time she went directly to San Quentin, where she made a feeble suicide attempt. Ten years later, she was moved to Tehachapi Women's Prison. She was paroled in 1935.

Phillips, David Graham, See: **Goldsborough, Fitzhugh Coyle.**

Phillips, John Stanley, 1917- , Brit. John Stanley Phillips' childhood dream of becoming an overseas missionary was indefinitely delayed after he inexplicably murdered a 16-year-old boy.

Having graduated from Selwyn College in Cambridge, England, Phillips, twenty-one, studied for holy orders at Oxford University to fulfill his dream when, for a reason never clearly understood, he killed young Harold Matthews. On Feb. 6, 1938, the boy's body was found on the roof of Wycliffe Hall, where he had worked as a pantry boy. An autopsy revealed that he had suffered grievous injuries before—and after—his death. Phillips immediately pleaded guilty, saying he committed the felony alone and without prior thought.

His Old Bailey trial revealed that Phillips had been insane at the time of the crime. Dr. Henry Yellowlees, after several interviews, described Phillips as showing symptoms of schizophrenic behavior. He was found Guilty but insane and was ordered to be detained in a mental institution.

Phillips, William R., 1931- , U.S. On Dec. 24, 1968, two people were shot to death at point-blank range in a brothel on the East Side of New York. James Smith, a pimp, and Sharon Stango, a prostitute, were killed; Charles Gonzalez, a customer of Stango's, was wounded. In 1971, during the Knapp Commission hearings into police corruption, one of the star witnesses, seventeen-year police veteran, William Phillips, was recognized as the suspect in the brothel murders. He was convicted, but had to be retried when it was learned that one of the jurors had applied for a job as investigator in the District Attorney's office. On Nov. 21, 1974, Phillips was convicted for a second time, and on Jan. 28, 1975, in the New York State Supreme Court before Justice Harold Birns, Phillips was sentenced to twenty-five years to life in the state prison at Attica. On Feb. 23, 1981, the U.S. Supreme Court agreed to hear an appeal, but on Jan 25, 1982, it upheld the murder conviction by a vote of six to three.

Pica, Sean, 1970- , and **Pierson, Cheryl**, 1970- , U.S. Cheryl Pierson's father began sexually molesting her when she was eleven. By 1986, when she was sixteen, he was having intercourse with her up to three times a day. Meanwhile, her mother had died, and Cheryl began to fear for her 9-year-old sister. When Cheryl got pregnant by her boyfriend, she became desperate. She offered her classmate, Sean Pica, also sixteen, $1,000 to kill her father, James Pierson, a 42-year-old Long Island, N.Y., electrician. As Pierson left for work one morning in February 1986, Pica shot him dead with a .22-caliber rifle.

Cheryl Pierson and Sean Pica both pleaded guilty to manslaughter. According to her own testimony, Cheryl's father had threatened to kill her if she reported the abuse. Neighbors and friends testified that they suspected abuse, but were afraid to speak out. "It all fell on the lap of a 16-year-old," defense attorney Paul Gianelli said.

In April 1986, the court sentenced Sean Pica to eight to twenty-four years in prison for manslaughter. Cheryl Pierson received a sentence of six months in prison and five years' probation. She ended up serving 106 days, and on her release, became engaged to her high school boyfriend.

Picchioni, Ernesto (AKA: **Monster of Nerola**), prom. 1944, Italy. Ernesto Picchioni was appropriately known as the "Monster of Nerola." This strange man, a husband and father of two girls and a boy, also was a ruthless killer of an alleged dozen Italians around 1944. He only confessed to two of the homicides, but that was enough to put him away for life.

Picchioni, once described as a loud-mouthed braggart, a chicken thief, and a Fascist-turned-Communist, made his wife and children dig a long family grave in their backyard so "it will be ready when I want to get rid of you." One night in 1944, he murdered a bicyclist unfortunate enough to ask Picchioni for help in repairing his vehicle. Pietro Monni stopped by the Picchioni's lonely stone cottage, asked for help with a leak in his bicycle tire, and spent the last night of his life in the deadly hands of the family's mad patriarch. "I got up and saw my husband carrying out a big bundle—a sheet with a human foot hanging out," Mrs. Picchioni recalled. Three years later, another bicyclist made the same fatal mistake, but this time Mrs. Picchioni called the police. Picchioni was tried, convicted, and sentenced to prison for life.

Pierce, Louis, 1970-   , and **Shanklin, Thomas**, 1970-   , U.S. A mother, attempting to protect her son from a gang of hoodlums, was shot dead on Aug. 5, 1986. Two 18-year-olds, Louis Pierce and Thomas Shanklin, were convicted of the slaying and were each sentenced to thirty-two years in prison.

Illinois Assistant State's Attorney Thomas Hennelly said Magnolia Burton, thirty-five, was acting with the instincts of "a lioness protecting her cubs from the wolves" when she confronted the gang members with a baseball bat. Upon learning that a second son was targeted by the gang as well, Burton ran upstairs with her daughter, Kyica, to warn him. At the men's trials, 19-year-old Kyica testified that she saw Pierce and Shanklin, armed, hiding on both sides of a stairwell in Chicago's Stateway Gardens public housing complex. She then saw their arms reach up the stairwell and heard gunfire.

Pierce, William Joseph, Jr. (AKA: **Junior Pierce**), prom. 1971, U.S. Georgia mental health experts warned the courts against paroling ex-convict William Joseph Pierce, Jr., because the state's diagnostic center said he was emotionally unstable and a corrections department psychologist said he was dangerous. Nonetheless, Pierce won release from Georgia State Prison on May 25, 1970, and a month later the body of 18-year-old Ann Goodwin was found by the couple for whom she had been babysitting. This killing would be followed by seven more over the next seven months. Pierce would be tried and convicted of just one of the slayings.

Perce Hardin was unloading the bread from his truck and was about to take it into Vivian Miles' local grocery on the outskirts of Baxley, Ga., when a tall, thin man rushed out of the store, pointed a gun at him, and fired twice point blank. Miraculously, he missed. Terrified, Hardin ran into the store for protection only to find the proprietor, Miles, sixty, lying on the floor. Miles was rushed to a hospital

where she soon died, but the description Hardin provided police was enough to eventually bring Pierce into custody again.

On Feb. 27, 1971, William "Junior" Pierce was arrested by the deputy sheriff of Summerton, Ga., on a petty larceny charge. Pierce confessed to murdering Miles and Goodwin. He was convicted and sentenced to life in prison.

Pierson, Howard, 1914-   , U.S. While confessing to the murder of his parents in Texas in 1935, Howard Pierson, twenty-one, said he killed them because they were interfering with his plan to save humanity with the help of a "cosmic-ray microscope." Legal and psychiatric issues surrounding the Pierson case caused the courts in 1963 to re-examine their criteria for the mentally unfit and the entire issue of the insanity plea.

Up until that time, courts generally used the so-called M'Naghten Rules as a guide in insanity pleas. This rule, used since 1843 in Scotland, states that an accused person cannot be held accountable for his actions if he is not mentally capable of understanding the nature and quality of his act. Since then, psychiatric medicine has heightened society's understanding of mental illness to the point that the M'Naghten Rules have become outdated. The 1954 Durham Rule, which states a criminal should not be held blameworthy if "his unlawful act is the product of a mental disease or defect," gained popularity as a guideline in several U.S. states including Maine, Vermont, and Illinois. When Pierson was tried in 1935, the court in Austin was determining not whether he was deranged while committing his crime but whether he was mentally competent to defend himself against his murder charge. The court ruled that he was not. Pierson was found Not Guilty by reason of insanity. Under the state's old law, Pierson was forced to be retried after regaining mental competency. Under the state's more recent ruling, he would not have been tried a second time after being found unfit.

Pin, Yong Am, 1933-   , U.S. Yong Am Pin, forty-five, claimed to have endured twenty-five years of abuse before brutally killing his wife, Im Sook Pin, forty-six, in 1978. Convicted of second-degree murder, Pin was sentenced to twenty-five years behind bars.

The Essex, Md., couple had a strange relationship. According to trial testimony covering the murder in which Pin chopped up his wife's body into thirty-five pieces and sealed them in jars and paint cans, Pin claimed his wife had abused him for twenty-five years. The abuse included physical beatings with a wooden meat mallet, taunting of extramarital affairs, limiting him to a 50-cent weekly allowance for personal needs, and forbidding him to have friends. The murder occurred when Pin and his wife fought over her demand that he buy her a cassette tape recorder.

Pin received just five years fewer than the maximum sentence for second-degree murder. Baltimore County Circuit Judge Marvin J. Land said his sentencing was "greatly influenced by Mr. Pin's conduct after the death of his wife," calling it "systematic" because Pin seemed to behave normally for five days after the murder.

Pitchfork, Colin, 1960-   , Brit. At 7 p.m. on Nov. 21, 1983, 15-year-old Lynda Mann of the British midland village of Narborough left her home to visit a girlfriend. She never returned home. The following morning her body was discovered, the victim of a savage rape and strangulation, near a footpath named the Black Pad which abutted the grounds of the Carlton Hayes mental health hospital. The first murder investigation in the history of the quaint village of Narborough convened, led by Inspector Derek Pearce with more than 150 officers at his disposal. Every male became a suspect to the petrified community, even the victim's stepfather who acquitted himself only after a blood sample failed to match a trace of semen taken from the victim. The high sperm count indicated the assailant to be a male between the ages of thirteen and thirty-four, and with the use of computers, police compiled a list of suspects, many of whom were quarantined in the nearby hospital.

Witnesses testified that a girl matching Lynda Mann's description was seen with a young man with a punk haircut at about 8 p.m. on the night of her murder. But they failed to find the suspect and by April 1984 the intense investigation of 150 police men had dwindled to a nominal investigation by only eight men. In August the investigation was curtailed completely, after blood tests administered to 150 suspects had failed to unveil the killer.

Less than ten miles from the murder scene, Alec Jeffreys, a 34-year-old geneticist at Leicester University, was probing the evolution of the human genes through their genetic material called deoxyribonucleic acid—more commonly known as DNA. The research was elusive as Jeffreys discovered a variance in the DNA from each human sample. In September 1984 Jeffreys discovered that by adding enzymes to the fragments of blood cells and separating larger fragments from smaller by exposing them to an electric field, the resultant blotting onto a nylon membrane would reveal a radioactive pattern similar to a supermarket bar-code, that was unique to every individual. Further, he learned that the bands of genetic fingerprints were inherited from both parents, and that the bands were consistent in any bodily material. In March 1985, Jeffreys stated that the chances of two people having the same genetic fingerprint was literally none.

On July 31, 1986, 15-year-old Dawn Ashworth of Enderby, England, was seen alive for the last time at 5 p.m. as she entered the Ten Pound Lane footpath which connected neighboring Narborough. On the morning of Aug. 2, police discovered the girl's body under heavy brush at the side of the path. She had suffered a vicious beating after being raped and strangled to death. As in the case of the man with the punk hairdo, a suspect emerged; this time a motorcyclist wearing a red helmet who was seen beneath a nearby bridge and on Aug. 8, 1986, police arrested 17-year-old Richard Buckland, a kitchen worker at the mental health hospital. After intense interrogation the simple-minded youth confessed to the crime. But, at the suggestion of Buckland's father, samples of semen found in both victims were sent to Dr. Jeffreys.

The police were shocked when Jeffreys stated that Buckland could not have been the murderer, but that the man who had killed Dawn Ashworth was the same man who had killed Lynda Mann three years earlier. On Nov. 21, 1986, on the date his murder trial was to began, and the third anniversary of the death of Lynda Mann, Richard Buckland became the first suspect in history to be released because of evidence refuted by genetic fingerprinting. A squad of fifty officers was assembled to reopen the investigation, headed by Inspector Pearce.

On Jan. 17, 1987, the police announced that all males between seventeen and thirty-four years of age would be required to provide blood and saliva samples. It proved unwieldy as the men were not required by law to provide samples, and those who did submit could easily circumvent the identity process by providing false ID's, as British drivers licenses did not include a photograph. And dozens of the potential perpetrators were incarcerated in a mental hospital. Even though 90 percent of the men readily responded, the laboratory was overtaxed to test the samples.

By May, more than 3,500 men had submitted to the testing, but only half the samples had been tested. One thousand more needed to be tested, but the manpower had been cut to twenty-four officers and soon to only sixteen. Yet the testing continued, often requiring one of the few remaining men to travel hundreds of miles for a single sample. Six months after the second murder, virtually every potential perpetrator in the area had been tested, but no sample matched the indelible evidence left by the killer of the two teenaged girls.

On Aug. 1, 1987, while drinking in a pub, a bakery worker named Ian Kelly casually mentioned to a co-worker that he had taken the blood test for a fellow worker named

Colin Pitchfork. But nothing was reported to authorities until Sept. 18. Pitchfork's folder was pulled and a discrepancy between a signature on Pitchfork's waiver at the blood test and another signature on file was noticed. The following day Ian Kelly was arrested for conspiracy to pervert the course of justice. Kelly stated that Pitchfork had begged him to take the test as he had done the same for another co-worker who had a history of sexual perversion. That same afternoon, Aug. 2, 1987, 27-year-old Colin Pitchfork was arrested on suspicion of murder shortly after he returned to his home. Pitchfork, married and the father of two, was a professional cake decorator who also had a history of sexual perversion. He was a compulsive "flasher" and was also known as a molester of female employees at the bakery. Before arriving at the police station, he had confessed to the two murders. On Sept. 21, Pitchfork was remanded at the Castle Court in Leicester on two counts of murder, two counts of indecent assault, and a count of kidnapping of the girl who had been abducted but was fortunate enough to escape.

The murder trial began on Jan. 22, 1988, at the Castle Court in Leicester before Justice Otton and ended the same afternoon. Ian Kelly was given a suspended eighteen-month sentence for his unwitting cooperation in the cover-up. Pitchfork confessed to both murders and indecent assault charges, as well as conspiracy for involving Ian Kelly. However, he pleaded innocent to the charge of kidnapping the young girl whose life had been spared. He was sentenced to life for the two murders, ten years for both rapes, three years for both sexual assaults, and three years for conspiracy. The sentences were to be served concurrently, but the judge refused to name a minimum term which meant Pitchfork might be eligible for parole after serving a mere ten years. As life returned to normal in the small villages, the conclusiveness of the DNA fingerprinting soothed the usual gnawing doubts after a murder conviction. Many encouraged the reinstitution of the death penalty after seeing how the genetic fingerprint of Colin Pitchfork perfectly matched the grisly evidence that he had left with Lynda Mann and Dawn Ashworth.

Pixley, Andrew, 1943-65, U.S. On Aug. 6, 1964, Robert McAuliffe discovered the bodies of his two oldest daughters in their room at the Wort Hotel in Jackson, Wyo. A vacationing circuit court judge from Maywood, Ill., McAuliffe was in the lobby with his wife when he heard screams. The judge raced to the room his three daughters shared and found 12-year-old Deborah and 8-year-old Cynthia dead in their beds and Andrew Pixley, barefoot and shirtless, on the floor. When policeman James Jensen

arrived on the scene, the 39-year-old judge had the 21-year-old drifter pinned to the floor. He screamed at the officer: "My God, this man has killed my babies!"

Deborah had been struck on the head by a rock. Cynthia had been punched and then strangled. Both girls had been raped after they were killed. In another bed in the same room, 6-year-old Susan McAuliffe had slept through the grisly slayings. It was the first time in twenty years that anyone had been murdered in the tiny resort town located high in the Rocky Mountains. A native of Dallas, Ore., Pixley had been in Jackson less than a week and was already under suspicion for trying to steal a blanket from a local merchant's car. He had climbed a stack of wood at the back of the hotel and removed the screen from the girls' window while they slept. "I didn't do it," Pixley told police after he was arrested.

Thirty to forty people crowded outside Pixley's jail cell in Jackson and talked about lynching the young man. For his own safety, Pixley was transferred some 170 miles east to a Lander jail. He was never tried for Cynthia McAuliffe's murder, but he pleaded guilty to a first-degree murder charge in the death of Deborah McAuliffe. Both the district court and the Wyoming Supreme Court asked for the death penalty.

C. F. Pixley, the killer's stepfather, pleaded with Wyoming governor Clifford Hansen to overturn the death sentence, but Hansen refused to yield. Pixley's stepfather said that Andrew did not remember anything about the slayings. "If I did that, I deserve everything I get," Andrew Pixley told his stepfather. On Dec. 10, 1965, Pixley was executed in the gas chamber at Rawlins, the first execution in Wyoming since 1945.

Poddar, Prosenjit, prom. 1969, U.S. University of California research assistant Prosenjit Poddar confessed to his therapist that he intended to kill a woman named Tarasoff who had rejected him. The therapist wrote a letter to campus security, asking them to apprehend Prosenjit, who suffered from a "severe paranoiac schizophrenic reaction." But Poddar seemed quite rational, and the police did not detain him. On Oct. 27, 1969, Poddar stabbed Tarasoff twenty-two times. The court convicted him of second-degree murder, then reduced the charge to manslaughter. Poddar was deported to India four years later. The Tarasoffs sued the University of California for $200,000 and in 1976, the California Supreme Court ruled that therapists and psychologists were legally obligated to inform all intended victims of any threats made on their lives by a patient during the course of therapy. If such a procedure had been followed in Poddar's case, Tarasoff might have fled her attacker.

Podmore, William Henry (AKA: **William F. Thomas**), d.1930, Brit. William Podmore moved into serious crime after answering a salesman ad for a Southampton oil company. Podmore applied for the job under the alias of William F. Thomas and once hired, began to write up fictitious orders and collect commissions on them. Late in 1928, company representative Vivian Messiter confronted Podmore with this fraud. Rather than face imprisonment, Podmore killed Messiter with a hammer and hid the body behind boxes in a garage.

Messiter's decaying body was found on Jan. 10, 1929, when the Wolf's Head Oil Company sent someone to Southampton to check on their missing employee. In Messiter's apartment, the police found his correspondence with William Thomas. At the address given, they found Podmore, and identified him as a known criminal. The evidence, however, was insufficient for a murder charge, so Podmore was sent to jail for six months for an earlier fraud in Manchester. When he completed the term, he was immediately returned to prison for another six months for robbery. On Dec. 17, 1929, Podmore was charged with Messiter's murder. Among the evidence against him were statements he had made about the murder to fellow inmates in Wandsworth Prison. Podmore was found Guilty and hanged on Apr. 22, 1930.

Poole, Derek Alan, 1931-51, Brit. Derek Poole began his criminal career at fourteen by robbing a shop and then spent two years in reform school. He ran away, broke into another shop, and was sent back to the same school. Apparently Poole blamed his troubles on the police. When the school allowed him out on leave, he threatened a constable with a knife, and his sentence increased by three more years. When he was nineteen, he served in the military but deserted four months later, taking a Sten gun with him. Returning to his hometown of Chatham, England, Poole did not go immediately home but broke into surrounding farms for shelter and food. He met two girls whom he took on his breaking-and-entering escapades.

One night at the Sharstead Farm, two policemen, Sergeant Langford and P.C. Baxter, arrived to investigate a call from a man who claimed he had been shot. Searching one of the farm buildings, Langford surprised Poole and his two girlfriends who rushed out of the hut upon discovery. Poole shot at the officer five times before turning his Sten gun upon Baxter, whom he shot four times in the

abdomen. Baxter died later in the hospital from the shock induced by hemorrhaging. Police learned the identity of the killer and went directly to his parent's home. Once there, they cordoned off the neighborhood and searched the surrounding area. They learned that Poole was hiding in the attic.

Apparently, Poole raced directly to his parents' home after he murdered Baxter and hid in the attic, but notified his parents of his presence only after the police arrived. Police dropped tear gas into the letter slot and fired four shots at the front of the house. After a long silence, Poole fired a quick burst from his Sten gun. Police fired more tear gas into the house then stormed the front under the cover of rifle fire. A minute later, a police officer emerged from the Poole home carrying the dead body of Derek Alan Poole.

Poole, Peter Harold, 1932-60, Kenya. A 28-year-old electrical engineer formerly of Eastwood, Essex, Peter Harold Poole was the first white man hanged in Kenya for the murder of an African. On Oct. 12, 1959, Poole shot Kamawe Musunge in the chest with a Luger pistol in Nairobi, Kenya after Musunge allegedly threw rocks at his dogs. Arrested and tried for murder in Kenya, Poole pleaded not guilty. At his first hearing, the proceedings had barely begun when one of the jurors, a Quaker, upon learning the nature of the trial announced, "I would have a conscientious objection to giving a verdict of guilty." The judge dismissed the jury, the attorney general entered a *nolle prosequi* (will not prosecute), and Poole walked free.

Poole was immediately arrested outside of the courthouse and tried the following week. At the second hearing, the defense counsel pointed out that the crown cannot prosecute the same individual after entering a *nolle prosequi*. The trial judge dismissed this argument and the trial proceeded. On Dec. 10, 1959, the all-white jury found Poole Guilty and sentenced him to be hanged. Poole's attorney filed for an immediate appeal on the grounds that the judge erred in his interpretation of the law concerning *nolle prosequi* and on several other points of the judge's conduct. The appeal went before the Privy Council on Mar. 21, 1960, and Poole's conviction was upheld.

Pople, G.T., d.1932, Brit. On Dec. 19, 1931, two cyclists found Mrs. Mabel Matthews and her bicycle lying on the side of the Oxford-Cheltenham Road near Burford. Her groceries and acetylene cycle lamp were missing. They discovered a duffle bag nearby with sausage sandwiches inside. Farther up the road, police discovered the victim's shopping basket and an electric cycle lamp. Matthews died from a loss of blood from several injuries to her head, face, and neck. Noted pathologist Sir Bernard Spilsbury determined that partial strangulation and kicking caused the injuries.

Investigations revealed that a soldier, Private G.T. Pople, left the place where he was lodging with a duffle bag of sandwiches and an electric lamp. Police traced his movements and discovered that when he stopped for lodging the night following the murder, his bicycle sported an acetylene lamp. Police arrested Pople in Abergavenny in Wales and charged him with murder. At his trial, he testified that he had made up his mind he wanted an acetylene lamp. When he saw one on another bicycle travelling down the road, he "made a grab for the lamp. My trousers caught the pedal of my cycle and I stumbled. I fell on the other machine and tumbled off and rolled down the dip. When I got to the bottom she was unconscious." Pople left her there, taking her groceries and lamp. The jury did not believe his story and deliberated a mere forty minutes before convicting him of murder. Private Pople was hanged at Oxford Gaol on Mar. 10, 1932.

Potter, Bruce, 1899-1946, Can. A former soldier in the U.S. Army, Private Bruce Potter was convicted of murdering Edna Ina Rogers at Dawson Creek, British Columbia, in Summer 1945. He was executed by hanging on Jan. 10, 1946, at the Oakalla Prison in Vancouver. The scaffold was improperly set and Potter was decapitated when the trap fell. Legal action was sought against the executioner.

Power, John Joseph, prom. 1927, Brit. An ex-member of the Birmingham police force, John Joseph Power extorted money from couples at the infamous lover's lane near the canal at Winson Green. Identifying himself as a police officer, he would explain to the couples that they were trespassing, but that he could be bribed to keep quiet. On July 2, 1927, Power confronted Olive Turner and Charles Broomhead. When Power approached, Turner became frightened and fled while Broomhead, trying to protect her, was knocked unconscious by the larger man. Power ran after the woman, whose dead body was found floating in the canal the next day.

Power, already charged with assault and rape, claimed he was home with his wife on the night of the murder, but his alibi was rejected at the December 1927 trial when prosecutor Norman Birkett read a police report from Power's wife that stated he had not arrived home until 11 p.m. Power was found Guilty and presiding Justice Swift sentenced him to death by hanging.

Powers, Harry F. (AKA: **Cornelius O. Pierson**), prom. 1931-32, U.S. On Aug. 29, 1931, the bodies of Mrs. Asta Buick Eicher and her children, Greta, fourteen, Harry, twelve, and Annabel, nine, were found in burlap bags in a shallow grave near Quiet Dell, a suburb of Clarksburg, W.Va. The corpse of Mrs. Dorothy Pressler Lemke was later found at the same location. Charged with the murders was Harry F. Powers, the proprietor of a local delicatessen, who, under a false name, had convinced Asta Eicher, a married woman from Park Ridge, Ill., and Dorothy Lemke, a divorcee from Northboro, Mass., to come to Clarksburg to marry him.

Chief C.O. Duckworth of Clarksburg found the bodies near a garage owned by Powers' legal wife. Powers himself had built the garage just two months before the corpses were discovered. Duckworth investigated after learning that Powers had frequently visited the garage in the middle of the night. On Sept. 20, as Powers awaited trial in the Harrison County jail, a crowd of 4,000 gathered and called for Powers to be released to them. Several deputy sheriffs held back the mob and made three arrests after a bomb went off. Powers, called "the Lothario of the West Virginia hills" by the press, was convicted on Dec. 11, 1931, of the "matrimonial racket" murder of Lemke. The verdict carried a mandatory death sentence. Court evidence showed that Powers had wooed and won dozens of women through the mails, and was alleged to have slain at least five women in the underground death chambers of his soundproof and windowless garage. Powers' trial was held at the Moore Opera House in order to accommodate the huge audiences. Songs, books, and records about the "Bluebeard Slayings at Quiet Dell" circulated for months. On Dec. 12, Judge John G. Southern sentenced Powers to hang at the Moundsville State Penitentiary on Mar. 18, 1932. See: **Landru, Henri Desire.**

Prejean, Dalton, 1960- , U.S. When Dalton Prejean was only thirteen, he was convicted of killing a taxi driver and sentenced to reform school. On July 2, 1977, the 17-year-old and his brother were pulled over by Louisiana State Police trooper Donald Cleveland for a traffic violation in Lafayette in the southern part of the state. The teenager fatally shot 25-year-old Cleveland twice in the face.

Prejean was tried, convicted, and given the death penalty. Though he was scheduled to die on Apr. 15, 1981, the case caused controversy because Prejean was a minor when he committed the crime. A complaint also charged that blacks were eliminated from the jury that tried the black youth. The Louisiana State Supreme Court upheld the death penalty, but Prejean was granted a stay of execution on Apr. 13 by a federal District Court.

Preston, John Trevor, 1941-72, Brit. On Feb. 27, 1966, an Eastbourne landlady, 78-year-old Hilda Couchman, was killed by one of her tenants, 25-year-old John Trevor Preston, and her naked body discovered on a bed in her building. Preston, convicted and sentenced to a life term, was serving his time at Wakefield prison in Yorkshire in 1972 when he was found hanged in his cell, apparently having taken his own life.

Preston, William, 1931- , Brit. On the evening of Sept. 20, 1954, William Preston, twenty-three, had several drinks in Warrington, Lancashire. About 10:30 p.m. he passed 63-year-old Arthur Alan Bentley and Bentley invited the young man into a garage where they played a game. Then, according to Preston, Bentley made indecent advances, began taking his clothes off, and tried to seize him. Preston, a machinist, then strangled the old man, shoved a coat hanger in his throat, stabbed and beat him, and set Bentley's body on fire.

Police were unable to arrest a suspect until 1955. On Oct. 29, 1955, Preston, now twenty-four, was coming home from a dance when he got into a fight with a friend. The incident upset him and he later called the police station at 1:15 a.m., saying he had killed a man. He was taken to the station where he confessed to the Bentley murder, saying, "It's been worrying me. I have got to come clean about it." Preston was found Guilty but insane, and sentenced to be indefinitely confined at Broadmoor.

Price, Albert, prom. c.1950, Brit. A 32-year-old painter, Albert Price, had suffered through years of financial trouble when he and his family received an eviction notice. Price, whose mind apparently snapped, tried to commit suicide but was unable to go through with it. He had murdered his wife with an ax and suffocated their two children in their sleep. Though the jury made a "strong recommendation to mercy," Price was hanged.

Prince, Ernest, 1909- , Brit. Thomas James Bown, forty-nine, caretaker of a large house furnishings company in Chesterfield, was found dead on Mar. 30, 1941, on a bed used by fire-watchers on night duty at the store. He had been killed by hatchet blows and his wallet was missing. About a month later Ernest Prince, a 32-year-old miner, was arrested as he left the mine pit where he worked. Prince confessed the murder to police, explaining that Bown had invited him to the shop to show him around, then made "a suggestion to me which I took offence at" as the two men sat on the bed. Prince said, "I sort of saw red," and detailed how he had stolen the wallet "when I realized what I had done" to try and cover up his crime.

Tried at the Derbyshire Assizes in June, Prince maintained that he had acted under great provocation. He was found Guilty of murder and sentenced to death. A Court of Criminal Appeal later upheld a plea that the trial judge had erred in not making it clear that if the accused had been provoked by an indecent suggestion he was entitled to a manslaughter verdict. The appeal was permitted, and Prince's sentence was reduced to fifteen years of penal servitude. The Homicide Act of 1957 changed the ruling of provocation, which held that mere words could be considered sufficient provocation to reduce the crime of murder to manslaughter. The majority of the provocation cases involved matrimonial relationships.

Prince, Walter, prom. 1934, Brit. Tried at the Nottingham Assizes on June 18, 1934, for murdering 21-year-old Harriet Shaw, Walter Prince had just been convicted when he spoke from the dock and confessed to the 1928 murder of Charles Armstrong of Rusholme, Manchester. He explained that George Fratson had been convicted of his crime. Fratson, Prince said, had been sentenced to death, then reprieved, and was currently doing penal servitude for Prince's crime. Following this confession, Prince was sentenced to death for the murder of Shaw, and soon afterward was found insane and committed to Broadmoor. An intensive investigation followed Prince's courtroom speech, but Fratson's conviction was left to stand. See: **Fratson, George**.

Prong, Keith, 1953- , U.S. By February 1987, Keith Prong's construction business in Hastings, Mich., was floundering. The 34-year-old builder had just started work on a luxury home for Bob and Andrea Main in Middleville. He needed money to continue with the project. He turned to 78-year-old Mary Moynahan, a silent partner in the business, for a loan. Moynahan refused his request, stating that Prong already owed her more than $40,000.

Two bodies were discovered on the construction site of the Mains' Middleville dream house. The bodies of Moynahan and her 70-year-old sister, Dorothy Perkins, were found buried next to the newly-poured basement walls at the five-acre site, twenty miles southeast of Grand Rapids. The women had been tortured before they were murdered. In May 1987, Prong pleaded guilty to two counts of second-degree murder.

Keith Prong apologized for the murders before being sentenced to sixty to ninety years in prison on June 24, 1987. "There is nothing I could really say that could possibly explain what I did," Prong told Judge Hudson Deming.

Prudom, Barry Peter (AKA: **Cop Killer; Clive Jones**), 1944-82, Brit. For seventeen days, Barry Peter Prudom terrorized northeast England, killing two policemen and one resident. Oddly, however, he treated victims who did not resist him with consideration. On June 17, 1982, Police Constable David Haigh stopped the 37-year-old Prudom during a traffic check close to Harrogate in Yorkshire. Prudom pulled out a gun and shot the policeman, who lived long enough to jot down the car's registration number and the suspect's alias and birth date. Another officer recognized the birth date as the same on a warrant for Prudom's arrest, and police began searching for Prudom.

Prudom went to Lincolnshire where he tied up an old woman, stole £5, and left after learning she would be discovered the following morning by her baker. Then he went to Girton, where he tied up George Luckett and his wife and searched for money, food, and a car. When Luckett managed to free himself, Prudom returned, shot him dead, and shot his wife in the head, severely injuring the woman. On June 24, Prudom took the Lucketts' car to north Yorkshire

British cop killer Barry Prudom.

where he injured another police officer, Kenneth Oliver. Not long afterward he walked out of the Old Malton post office, and when an unarmed officer tried to question him

he chased and shot Sergeant David Winter three times at point-blank range. On July 3, Prudom broke into the home of Maurice Johnson and his wife. He held them and their 43-year-old son, Brian Johnson, prisoner, but since they did not struggle he fixed them tea and became friendly with them. He left the house on July 4, entering a hideout he made by stacking wood against a wall. Several hours later he shot at Chief Inspector David Clarkeson and more reinforcements were called. He then shot himself in the head and he was also wounded by police gunfire. An inquiry ruled the death a suicide.

Pruyn, Kenyon W., 1944- , U.S. On Oct. 30, 1976, Kenyon Pruyn, armed with nine rifles, opened fire from his third-floor apartment in Mechanicsville, N.Y., fatally wounding James Marsh, a customer in a bar across the street, and a 21-year-old police officer, Paul Luther. Ten other people were wounded. After a fire started in the 32-year-old gunman's apartment, he surrendered. Pruyn, a warehouse clerk and former Marine, pleaded guilty to two counts of second-degree murder and thirty-five counts of attempted murder and first-degree assault. He received two sentences of twenty-five years for each murder and was given additional terms for injuring nine other people.

Pulliam, Mark, prom. 1942, U.S. Mark Pulliam, a Chatsworth, Ga., farmer apparently found life overly difficult. Despairing over his failing farm and the responsibility of feeding his eight children, Mark Pulliam set fire to his house in November 1942. Five of his eight children and his wife were killed by the fire. Pulliam was tried and found Guilty of murder. He was sentenced to life in prison.

Putt, George Howard, 1946- , U.S. George Howard Putt, previously convicted for assaulting a woman and for molesting young girls, appeared in the Memphis, Tenn., headlines in 1969. On Aug. 14, 1969, the 23-year-old Putt strangled Roy Dumas and his wife, Bernalyn Dumas, and sexually mutilated the woman's body with a knife. On Aug. 25 he killed and mutilated Leila Jackson, an 82-year-old landlady. On Aug. 29, he strangled and stabbed 21-year-old Glenda Sue Hardin in a park, again slashing the body. He struck once more on Sept. 11, when he accosted a 59-year-old nurse, Mary Christine Pickens. When he tried to grab her pocketbook outside her apartment, Pickens screamed, and Putt fatally stabbed her, using a knife he had stolen from the Dumas couple's home. Neighbors heard Pickens cry out and began to chase the assailant, trapping him outside the building. Police arrived and arrested Putt, who was still holding the knife.

In October 1970, Putt was tried and convicted for the murder of Pickens and given the death penalty, but the sentence was later reduced. In April 1973, the killer was tried and found Guilty of the murders of the Dumas couple. He was then sentenced to a total of 497 years in prison.

Q

Queen, Peter, d.1958, Scot. Peter Queen fell in love with Christina Gall, who worked as a maid for his parents until she was fired for a drinking problem. The couple dated for several years, and Gall became increasingly depressed as Queen repeatedly denied her requests to get married. On Nov. 12, 1931, Queen turned to friends for help, saying Gall had threatened to commit suicide and had recently tried to hang herself. On Nov. 21, Queen reported Gall's death to police, noting she had been on a two-day drinking binge and had apparently killed herself. Investigators found Gall's body with a thin rope around her neck. Because one of her arms was covered by the smooth bedclothes lying at her side, they determined she could not have killed herself and arrested Queen for murder.

Queen's murder trial began on Jan. 5, 1932, and featured British pathologist Sir Bernard Spilsbury as a witness for the defense. Spilsbury maintained that a light bruising suffered by Gall before her death contradicted evidence pointing to a murder and that the position of the rope around her neck convinced him that she had, in fact, killed herself. Other witnesses testified that there were no signs of struggle at the crime scene, but prosecutors maintained that at the time of her death, Gall had been too drunk to put up a fight. Police officers also testified that Queen had said: "I think I have killed her." Although no records of his alleged confession existed and all the evidence against him was purely circumstantial, Queen was found Guilty and sentenced to death. His death sentence was commuted and he was later released from prison.

Queripel, Michael, 1938- , Brit. On Apr. 29, 1955, Michael Queripel, a 17-year-old government clerk at Potters Bar, was walking on the golf course, trying to get rid of a migraine headache, when he saw a woman walking her dog nearby. Queripel later said he had a sudden urge to rape the woman. When he grabbed her, she struggled so he hit her on the head with an iron tee marker, killing her. He then fled home where he cut his arm with a razor blade to explain the blood on his clothes. At 11:15 p.m., the woman's husband called police to report her missing. The next morning, her body was found in the rough near the seventeenth hole. The only clue was a small section of a palm print left on the tee marker. After searching their fingerprint archives and taking prints from several thousand men, including the entire population of Potters Bar, Scotland Yard investigators arrested Queripel. He pleaded guilty and, as a juvenile, was to be held for as long as Her Majesty's pleases.

R

Rablen, Eva (AKA: **Mrs. Joe Williams**), 1905-   , U.S. Carroll and Eva Rablen of Tuttleton, Calif., were an unlikely couple. Carroll, an introvert who lost his hearing in an accident during WWI, had married the gregarious, attractive Eva, a woman who liked music, dancing, and drinking. The marriage soured quickly and endured only because Carroll Rablen acquiesced to his wife's wishes.

On Apr. 26, 1929, the couple drove to a Friday night dance at a schoolhouse in Tuttleton. Eva danced with many men, while the resigned Carroll waited dutifully outside. At midnight, Eva brought a cup of coffee to Carroll, the final exchange between husband and wife. Within minutes after drinking the liquid, Carroll died an agonizing death. His final words, witnessed by his father and uncle, were of the extreme bitterness of the coffee.

The coroner's initial probe failed to produce any evidence of poisoning, but Carroll's father, who detested Eva's flirtatious ways, still suspected Eva of poisoning his son to collect $3,000 from two insurance policies. A second examination of the scene of the death uncovered an empty strychnine bottle beneath a staircase in the schoolhouse. The bottle was traced to Bigelow Drug store in neighboring Tuolumne, Calif., where the pharmacist told police that the strychnine was purchased

Carroll Rablen, who got poison in his coffee.

as a rodent poison by a Mrs. Joe Williams, whose description matched that of Eva Rablen. Mrs. Rablen was arrested, but she protested her innocence, saying her father-in-law was simply out to get her. District Attorney C.H. Grayson believed Eva Rablen had committed the murder, but knew that the case was weak because the coroner's report had revealed no traces of the poison.

Criminologist and chemist Dr. Edward Heinrich was asked to examine the dead man's stomach and this time evidence of the suspected poison was found. Traces of strychnine were also found in the cup that Eva had handed to her husband, and on the upholstery of the car seat. When Heinrich appealed to participants of the dance to come forward if they had had a beverage spilled on a garment that night, a woman whom Eva had pushed past in the crowd produced a dress stained with strychnine-laced coffee. Finally, a handwriting analyst matched Eva Rablen's signature to that of the woman who had purchased the strychnine.

C.H. Vance, the defense attorney, entered a not guilty plea for his client, arguing that a woman wishing to commit such a deed would certainly do it in a less public fashion. He also claimed he could prove that she did not purchase the poison. His vehemence polarized the small community, and when the preliminary hearing was held at Columbia, Calif., on May 13, 1929, the event drew hundreds of people from the surrounding communities. Judge J.W. Pitts accommodated their interest by moving the hearing from his tiny courtroom to an open-air pavilion in the center of town. Sheriff Dampacher testified that he had found the fatal bottle, and the pharmacist testified of the matching identities. But the hearing was anticlimactic for the bloodthirsty crowd, for Judge Pitts merely submitted the case to the superior court.

On May 17, 1929, Eva Rablen pleaded innocent before Superior Court judge J.T.B. Warne in Sonora, Calif., and was assigned a trial date of June 10. Before the trial began, however, her attorney learned of Dr. Heinrich's planned testimony, and on June 4, 1929, Eva Rablen changed her plea to guilty. On June 10, the day she was to have stood trial, Eva Rablen began serving a life sentence at San Quentin Prison.

Raffaelo, Roberto, prom. 1921, U.S. In Fall 1920, Salvatore Varotta, a delivery driver, took his eldest son for a ride in the company truck on Long Island. At an intersection, they collided with another truck and little Adolpho Varotta suffered severe cuts, a burned face, and a crushed leg. A wealthy benefactor interceded to help the poor family and pay the boy's hospital bills. Acquaintances also gossiped that Salvatore Varotta had sued the other driver and collected a $50,000 insurance settlement.

On May 24, 1921, another son, Joe Varotta, disappeared after being last seen in front of the family's home. The following day, a ransom note written in Italian was delivered. In it, the kidnapper(s) demanded payment of $2,500. It was signed with a symbol of a black hand next to a dagger dripping in blood. The case was assigned to Sergeant Michael Fiaschetti of the New York Police Italian Squad. He suspected the culprits were neighbors or relatives, because a professional organization would have been more informed and discreet. A policewoman, posing as a relative, moved into the Varotta home.

On June 1, an alleged emissary from the Black Hand visited the household. A sobbing Salvatore Varotta begged for his son's return in exchange for $500. The man, Roberto Raffaelo, returned the following night. As he accepted the money, he was greeted by police officers. Four other people were apprehended nearby, including one of the gossiping neighbors. However, the child was not found until the morning of July 11. The body of the boy was discovered along the Hudson river at Nyack. A coroner determined that the boy had been thrown into the river while alive, and had drowned.

In August, Raffaelo was convicted of murder in the first degree and sentenced to death in Sing Sing. He was reprieved shortly before his execution, when he agreed to testify at the trial of other members of the conspiracy. Due to his testimony, Antonio Marino, James Ruggieri and the neighbor, Santo Cusamano, were all convicted and sentenced to die by electrocution. A fourth man, John Melchione, went mad awaiting trial and was sent to an insane asylum at Matteawan.

Rafferty, Anthony, prom. 1925, U.S. On June 21, 1925, the body of a man was found on Rockaway Beach in New York City. Witnesses had seen the highly intoxicated man shortly before and suspected that he had drowned. However, he had been shot twice in the back. Fingerprints revealed him to be Edward Burke, a man of many aliases and a long criminal record. The previous year, he had escaped from Sing Sing, while serving a three-year sentence for robbery.

A number of unsavory types had been seen near Rockaway Beach the night of the murder. The primary suspect who emerged following an interrogation was Anthony Rafferty. Rafferty had previously been sentenced three times on burglary charges.

On July 15, 1925, Rafferty was charged with first-degree murder for the death of Burke. He killed Burke to keep him from sponging off of a wealthy mutual acquaintance. He was apprehended on Jan. 22, 1926, at a Manhattan restaurant. Before his trial began, several eyewitnesses disappeared because they had received threatening phone calls. But, on May 11, 1926, in the courtroom of Queens County judge Frank Adel, Rafferty was convicted of second-degree murder and received a sentence of twenty years to life.

Ralph, Edward, c.1910-43, U.S. In Autumn 1929, Cleveland, Ohio, was terrorized by a series of attacks against young women. Between October and mid-January, twenty-one women were beaten, raped, or shot. All police department leaves were cancelled. Nine hundred officers worked tirelessly to apprehend the assailant. A break came when the bullets taken from one of the victims, Janet Blood, matched those taken from a gun stolen a month before,

from a local tire store. The proprietor said the only man who had knowledge of the gun's location was former employee Edward Ralph. On Jan. 28, 1930, Ralph was arrested. He was able to plea bargain by pleading guilty to two counts of assault with intent to kill. On Feb. 21, Ralph was sentenced to two consecutive one- to twenty-year terms at the Ohio penitentiary in Columbus. On Nov. 19, 1931, Ralph escaped. He was captured again Feb. 5, after molesting a woman in a Los Angeles movie theater. He was returned to Ohio, and served time until he was paroled on Jan. 27, 1941.

Ralph seemed to be a reformed man. He married the following year and soon he and his wife had a baby. However, in early 1943, Ralph disappeared and his wife filed for divorce. On June 3, 1943, 5-year-old Mary Jane Brady was found strangled to death. Witnesses had last seen her alive next to Ralph's apartment. The following day Ralph was apprehended and confessed to the crime. Later in the month, he was convicted of the murder and sentenced to death, after electing to be tried before a panel of three judges, rather than face a jury trial. He was electrocuted on Oct. 4, 1943.

Ransom, Florence, prom. 1940, Brit. Florence Ransom of Piddington had a lover, Lawrence Fisher, but her lover was married. She moved into a separate establishment with him in 1940. On July 9, Ransom went to Mrs. Fisher's home in Matfield and managed to get her lover's wife and 19-year-old daughter into the garden, where she shot them. When the Fisher maid investigated, Ransom shot her, too. Ransom then ran, but not before inadvertently dropping one of her leather gloves.

Florence Ransom, who had been seen at the house and who possessed the other glove, was tried and found Guilty. Her death sentence was changed to life at Broadmoor, the prison asylum.

Raphael, Sylvia (AKA: **Patricia Roxborough**), 1938- , Nor. Following the slaughter of Israeli athletes at the 1972 Olympic Games in Munich by Arab terrorists, a group of Israeli intelligence agents flew in 1973 to Norway to assassinate Ali Hassan Salemeh, believed to be responsible for the murders of the athletes. The Israelis incorrectly identified an innocent Moroccan as Salemeh and killed him. One of the Israeli agents, Sylvia Raphael, was arrested for the murder. She was tried, convicted, and sentenced to five and half years in prison. Raphael's attorney, Anneaus Schjodt, succeeded in having the killer's sentence reduced to twenty-two months.

Rardon, Gary, c.1944- , U.S. Within five days in mid-November 1974, three seemingly unrelated murders were committed in the Chicago area. On Nov. 14 a man was shot to death in a Prospect Heights real estate office. Three days later, a cab driver was shot and killed in Calumet City. On Nov. 18, a man in a prefabricated garage sales office in Franklin Park was murdered. On Jan. 16, 1975, the FBI arrested Gary Rardon in Louisville, Ky. He had been using one of the victims' credit cards. Rardon had been dishonorably discharged from the Navy in 1962 after he was convicted of manslaughter in Indiana. He served four years, and upon his release a prison psychologist stated that "the likelihood of further violence would be unusual." Rardon was working as a machinist in the Chicago area when he committed the murders. On Feb. 17, 1977, in the Chicago circuit courtroom, Judge James M. Bailey sentenced Rardon to forty to 100 years' imprisonment.

Rasiewicz, William, 1936- , U.S. In early February 1977, a Florida couple was arrested on charges of murdering their 4-year-old son, William, in February 1971 in Howell Township, N.J. William Rasiewicz and his wife, Barbara Rasiewicz, had twelve children. They were arrested in Fort Myers, Fla., on a fugitive warrant. The murder inquiry was initiated when social workers discovered a birth certificate that did not fit any of the twelve children. William Rasiewicz was convicted and sentenced to twenty-eight to thirty years in jail for the slaying. On Nov. 17, 1977, Judge William Huber, of the Toms River Superior Court, accepted William Rasiewicz's plea bargaining agreement when he pleaded no contest in the murder of his 18-month-old son, John, in 1974. He had spanked the child repeatedly because the child cried too much. The body, which the father put in a receptacle that was hauled away by a garbage truck, was never found. On Jan. 25, 1978, Rasiewicz was given a second twenty-eight- to thirty-year term to begin after the earlier sentence is served.

Rees, Melvin David, 1933- , U.S. Melvin David Rees, a student at the University of Maryland in 1953, was taken into custody on Mar. 12, 1955, and charged with assault after he tried to force a 36-year-old woman into his car. The victim later dropped the charges. In the meantime, Rees set up a nook in an abandoned basement in a cinderblock building in the Annapolis, Md., area. He plastered the basement with pornographic pictures and also put up a yearbook picture of Wanda Tipson, a 1955 graduate of the University of Maryland.

On June 26, 1957, Rees was driving a green Chrysler near Annapolis when he passed a car in which Margaret Harold was a passenger. Rees forced the car off the road and, armed with a .38-caliber pistol, forced his way into the back seat of the car. When Harold panicked, Rees shot her in the head. The car's driver, an Army sergeant, quickly jumped from the car and ran down the road, weaving back and forth in an attempt to avoid being shot. Rees did not

Melvin David Rees, shown with dancer Mrs. Patricia Routt.

fire at the sergeant, however. After running a mile, the sergeant saw a farm house, where he stopped and called Annapolis authorities. Police arrived and found Harold's body in the abandoned car.

A year and a half later, Rees was driving in Virginia. He put on his car's high beam lights and closely followed another car. As the other car, driven by truck driver Carroll Jackson, increased speed or slowed, Rees did the same. Then Rees drove beside Jackson's car. Jackson, twenty-nine, slowed and Rees drove in front of Jackson's car, causing Jackson to stop. Jackson got out, leaving his wife, Mildred, and daughters Susan, four, and Janet, eighteen months, in the car. Rees, armed with the pistol, got out of his car and rushed up to Jackson. Rees ordered the rest of the family out of the car, tied Jackson's hands with a necktie, and forced the family into his car trunk. The next day, the Jackson's relative, Mrs. H.M. Ballard, saw the Jackson car and notified Sheriff Willis E. Proffitt. Rees' skid marks, Mildred Jackson's purse, the car keys, and dolls were found.

On Mar. 4, Carroll Jackson's body was found by the side of a road near Fredericksburg, Va., by John Scott and James Beach. Jackson had been shot in the head and his daughter, Janet, had suffocated after Rees put her under her father's body. Shortly afterward, two boys were digging in the dirt not far from the scene of the Howard attack and uncovered some hair. They notified police, who investigated and found 4-year-old Susan Jackson, her skull fractured. Her mother, Mildred Jackson, had been raped and strangled or beaten to death. Police linked the Jackson murders to the basement in the cinderblock building where they found a button like those on Mildred Jackson's dress.

After extensive news coverage, police received many tips from citizens who had noticed a strange man driving a green or blue Ford. Police also received a letter from a Norfolk, Va., man who said Rees, a musician, had killed the Jacksons and Harold and gave a description of Rees, saying he had a thin face, long dark hair, and thick eyebrows. He said he had been with Rees at the time of the Harold murder, and Rees had been taking Benzedrine. When the writer received a letter from Rees postmarked West Memphis, Ark., he notified police. Officials found Rees selling pianos in a music store and arrested him on a charge of flight to avoid prosecution for Harold's murder.

Rees was put in a police lineup and the army sergeant identified him. FBI officials searched Rees's parents' house and found the .38-caliber pistol in a saxophone case in the attic. They also found a picture of Mildred Jackson that had appeared in the newspaper, and attached to the picture was a message that read "Caught on a lonely road...after pulling them over, leveled pistol and ordered them out and into car trunk which was opened by husband and both bound..." Further investigation linked Rees to the slayings of Shelby Jean Venable, sixteen, and Mary Elizabeth Fellers, eighteen, who had been found dead in rivers in Maryland. He was also linked to the sexual assaults and murders of Ann Ryan, fourteen, and Marie Shomette, sixteen, close to the University of Maryland.

After Rees was tried, convicted and sentenced to a life term in prison in 1961 in Baltimore, Md., he was sent to Virginia, where he stood trial for the Jackson family slayings. Once again he was found guilty and sentenced to death. Rees was convicted of federal crimes and managed to evade state death penalties. He is presently confined in the federal detention center in Springfield, Mo.

Remedios, Patricio, prom. 1933, Japan. On Aug. 7, 1933, a foul-smelling trunk was discovered on a wharf in Kobe, Japan. The stench was caused by the corpse of a young oriental girl inside. Police questioned a landlady, who stated that on July 26, a Eurasian man and a Chinese girl had rented a room. On Aug. 3, the couple had a violent quarrel. The next night, the couple again quarreled, and the woman was heard pleading with the man not to hit her. The man, Patricio Remedios, was arrested on Aug. 13, on the charge of murdering Choy Ling. Remedios was convicted and sentenced to twenty years at a penal colony on the Island of Timor in the Dutch East Indies.

Rendleman, Carroll, prom. 1974, U.S. On Apr. 28, 1976, in Chicago, Carroll Rendleman was sentenced to serve between 100 and 300 years in prison for the 1974 strangulation death of a 20-year-old waitress, Anita Duncan. Before the woman's murder, Rendleman was imprisoned for an earlier strangulation death, but was released from prison due to an official blunder. A group of psychiatrists and psychologists had stated that if he was ever set free, he would strangle again. The warnings became prophetic, and after Rendleman's latest crime, Criminal Court judge John F. Hechinger held the Illinois Department of Corrections responsible for the young woman's death.

Rheeder, Margaret Elizabeth, 1922-58, S. Afri. Margaret Elizabeth Rheeder was born on Sept. 6, 1922, in Platbos, S. Afri., one of thirteen children in a poor family. Upon the death of her father when Margaret was twelve, she and her sister were sent to an orphanage where she was trained as a housekeeper. At sixteen she left the orphanage to support herself. She married at the age of twenty-one, but her husband was in jail frequently. Margaret did domestic work to support herself and her two children. She divorced, and on Sept. 6, 1952, she married again to Benjamin Fredenman Rheeder.

Rheeder, whose reputation was that of a stable, dependable man, represented the security that Margaret had missed thus far in her life. Their marriage went well until Rheeder began to object to Margaret's spending habits. Then disputes occurred, reportedly brought on by Margaret's flirting with, or perhaps having sexual relations with, the lodgers in their home. On one occasion, the children, alerted by Margaret's screams, stopped Rheeder from strangling their mother. In 1957, Margaret did take on one of their boarders as a lover, and in the indiscreet fashion that later incriminated her, she repeatedly mentioned to her lover her intention to murder Rheeder. She purchased a bottle of ant poison from a local pharmacy and began administering it to her husband. Rheeder died May 7, 1957. Although the poisoning took only a week, a slow and torturous death for her husband was what Margaret had openly wished for months earlier.

Margaret had no sooner collected her husband's insurance and pension benefits when local suspicion regarding the circumstances of his death instigated a police investigation. Rheeder's body was exhumed June 11. The coroner confirmed Rheeder had died of arsenic poisoning. Although Margaret Rheeder maintained her innocence to the end of the trial, her tendency to incriminate herself through idle comments, and the heavy weight of the evidence in her trial, led to a verdict of Guilty. Although the jury recommended leniency in sentencing in deference to her difficult upbringing and early life, the judge found the premeditated nature of the crime enough to merit the sentence of death by hanging. Just prior to her execution on May 6, 1958, she confessed to the crime, attempting unsuccessfully to implicate her lover.

Richeson, Rev. Clarence V.T., d.1912, U.S. The Reverend Clarence Richeson, a minister at Hyannis on Cape Cod, began an affair with one of his choir singers, Avis Linnell. When he moved to the Baptist church in Cambridge, she moved to a YWCA in Boston, and they continued to see each other quite frequently. Promising to marry the 19-year-old woman, the affair continued to progress, and eventually Linnell became pregnant with Richeson's child. At the same time, however, Richeson was courting Violet Edmands, whose father, the head of the Baptist Missionary Society of America, could have had an important influence on his career. On Oct. 14, 1911, Avis Linnell was found dying in a bathtub at the YWCA. After the police released Richeson, believing that he had had no hand in her death, they learned that he had purchased potassium cyanide, supposedly to kill a dog, at a drugstore in Newton, Mass. He had, it appeared, given Avis pills that he claimed would abort the pregnancy but which instead poisoned her.

The Reverend Richeson, killer.

Richeson was arrested at the home of his fiancée, whose

family continued to support him for some time. On Dec. 20, in a fit of despairing madness, the minister used the jagged lid of a tin can to emasculate himself. As Richeson was recovering, he wrote a confession to the murder. He was sentenced to death and on May 20, 1912, was electrocuted.

Richter, Ursula, 1952- , Ger. Ursula Richter was just a 13-year-old when she became pregnant by Georg Richter. The young resident of Meppen, Ger., married Richter and lived uneventfully with him until 1972, which is when Ursula became romantically involved with a 19-year-old boarder, Kurt Adomeit, and planned Richter's murder with him. The two first tried to kill Richter with rat poison. When that failed, they used a hatchet.

Ursula reported her husband missing in June 1972, a week after his alleged disappearance. Richter had been awaiting trial on a petty theft charge and police assumed that he had skipped across the nearby Dutch border. Gradually, the police began to suspect Ursula of murder, but because there was no body, no charges could be filed. In 1973, Ursula obtained a divorce on the grounds of desertion. Then, in 1975, Adomeit was jailed on a minor charge of selling fake drugs. Police used an informer who played on the young man's jealousy of Ursula to elicit a confession from him. Having confessed to the murder, Adomeit led police to Richter's grave. Because both Ursula Richter and Adomeit were minors when they committed the murder, they were both tried as juveniles and given the maximum ten-year sentence.

Rickard, Christopher, 1941- , U.S. A 39-year-old toy designer, incensed that a former supervisor would not give him a good job reference, shot the supervisor to death. Christopher Rickard, an engineer at Playskool Inc., in Chicago, had worked with 57-year-old Richard Worel at Zenith Corp. until Rickard was laid off in November 1978. Rickard asked Zenith for a reference for an upcoming promotion at Playskool. When it appeared he would not get promoted, Rickard assumed that Worel had given him a bad reference.

With some care, Rickard carved out the pages of a WWII novel and concealed a Walther PPK automatic pistol within the book. On Jan. 31, he lured Worel into his van and shot him three times. One week later, police found Worel's body wrapped in a plastic bag in Rickard's garage. Ironically, Worel had not supplied Playskool with a bad reference and the day after the murder, Rickard got the promotion and a $1,000-a-year salary increase. Because of the pre-meditation and planning that went into the crime, Rickard was sentenced to 100 to 300 years in prison.

Rijke, Sjef, prom. 1972, Neth. Sjef Rijke was a young Dutchman with a penchant for women and poison. In January 1971, his 18-year-old fiancée, Willy Maas, died after suffering stomach pains for more than a week. A little while later, Rijke proposed marriage to Mientje Manders. By the end of March, she also complained of stomach pains. Manders died on Apr. 2, 1971. After both deaths, Rijke seemed suitably grief-stricken. Police were suspicious, but could find no reason for Rijke to murder the young women. Three weeks after Manders' death, Rijke married 18-year-old Maria Haas. Haas left him after six weeks when he proved to be extremely jealous. When the police questioned her, she told them that she had experienced stomach pains while she was living with Rijke but that they had ceased since she left him.

Complaints of stomach pains from Rijke's next girlfriend led to the analysis of some peanut butter that only she had eaten. The peanut butter contained rat poison. What motivation Rijke might have had still seemed unclear to the police; thus, both Rijke and his housekeeper were arrested. When a merchant remembered Rijke had purchased the poison, the investigation focused on him. Rijke soon confessed to poisoning the first two women and attempting to poison the other two. He insisted he did not intend to murder them, however, saying he just enjoyed watching women suffer. Rijke was judged legally sane and tried in January 1972. He was given two life terms in prison.

Riley, Thomas, 1957- , U.S. A alcohol and mari-juana party in a groundskeeper's cottage in the Burr Oak Cemetery in Alsip, Ill., in 1974 ended with three men dead. The prosecution in the case claimed that the defendant, Thomas Riley, had accidentally shot Larry Foster and then to cover-up the first shooting, murdered Marvin Foster (no relation to Larry) and William Todd, all cemetery employees. The defense claimed that Riley's older brother, Ernest, committed the murders and then led Riley to confess because he was a juvenile at the time. Thomas Riley was found Guilty by a jury on May 9. Because of the deliberate nature of the murder of Marvin Foster and William Todd, Judge John Hechinger sentenced Riley to seventy-five to 225 years in prison.

Ritter, Kenneth, d.1971, Ger. U.S. Army private Kenneth Ritter attempted to engage his German-born wife, Inge, in a fantasy game of sexual bondage. She complied on two occasions before refusing and telling him to see a psychiatrist about his obsessive fantasies. For a time, Ritter satisfied himself by dressing in some of his wife's clothes and acting out his fantasy by himself in the back seat of their car.

After a time he sought a partner for his game. Ritter stopped three different women in the German town of Rothenberg, where he was stationed, before he succeeded in his plan. When 18-year-old Helga Harttung accepted a ride from Ritter, he pretended that the motor was not running right and turned into a side road. He began enacting his sexual fantasy in the back seat and invited her to join him. When she refused, he grabbed her. Her screams drove Ritter into a frenzy and he choked her to death. Ritter was tried and found Guilty of unpremeditated murder. He was sentenced to fifteen years in prison and subsequent confinement in a mental institution. On May 11, 1971, Ritter used a belt to hang himself in his cell.

Rivers, Benjamin, d.1938, U.S. On July 13, 1936, two black men, Francis Middleton and Lymus Simmons, re-ported to Charleston, S.C., police that they were being pursued by two other black men, Benjamin Rivers and Isaac Brown after an argument earlier in the evening that had ended with two shots fired at Middleton. Detective Purse A. Wansley accompanied Middleton and Simmons on a search for Rivers and Brown who were apprehended while walking down a nearby street. After Wansley informed the two men that they were under arrest, five gunshots rang out and the police officer slumped to the ground, shot twice in the chest and once in the arm. Rivers and Brown fled, and Wansley died en route to the hospital.

Police began a massive manhunt, and two days later, Brown surrendered and implicated Rivers in Wansley's murder. Rivers was later discovered hiding under a porch, and he was taken to the city jail, only to be transferred shortly afterwards to the county jail following a large demonstration of whites angered by the officer's slaying. Rivers confessed to the murder but claimed he had shot Wansley in self defense. He admitted that he had heard Wansley say, "Consider yourself under arrest," but insisted that Wansley had not identified himself as a police officer. Public sentiment vehemently opposed Rivers's actions, primarily because the white detective had been defending two blacks against two other blacks when he was shot. To ensure his safety, police transferred Rivers to the state penitentiary in Columbia, after a second angry mob of 500 had assembled outside the county jail demanding his release into their custody.

Rivers and Brown were tried separately. In Rivers' trial, the defense claimed that not only had the defendant fired at Wansley without knowing that he was a police officer, but that he shot only after Wansley had fired at him first, shooting him in the hip. The prosecution produced testimony that disputed that Rivers' wound had been caused by Wansley's bullet or by any bullet at all and also used Rivers' African heritage against him, describing him as a "bloodthirsty creature" and depicting him using primitive images. The jury deliberated only two hours before finding Rivers Guilty of murder with no recommendation of mercy. Despite a motion for a mistrial by the defense, Rivers was sentenced to die in the electric chair. The defense appealed the case in the state supreme court on the basis that the verdict of the jury was not at all responsive to testimony and was based on prejudice and bias. The supreme court upheld the lower court's decision, and Rivers was executed on Apr. 29, 1938. When Isaac Brown was brought to trial, he was found Guilty of murder and sentenced to life imprisonment.

<hr>

Roberts, Clarence, 1918-c.1980, U.S. On Nov. 18, 1970, a fire broke out in the barn behind the Nashville, Ind., home of Clarence Roberts and his wife, Geneva Roberts. A prominent businessman, politician, and civic leader, Roberts disappeared either in or after the fire; the burned torso found in the charred house was thought initially to be his corpse. His wife spent the next ten years trying without success to collect about $1.2 million in insurance benefits. In the 1950s, Roberts had been elected county sheriff and had lived as a prosperous member of the small community, but business setbacks left him more than $200,000 in debt when the fire occurred. Disgraced, he told his attorney that he was going to kill himself and make his wife a rich widow. But when county coroner Jack Bond discovered no wound that indicated suicide, he called in a forensic pathologist and the Indiana State Police. None of the X-rays of teeth or bones matched those of the former sheriff, and Donald L. Kuster, head of the investigating team, said the body was not that of Clarence Roberts.

Deserted by her sons and shunned by people who thought her husband had murdered and then fled, Geneva Roberts became withdrawn. Police kept her under surveillance, believing she was a conspirator. She got work as a dishwasher in a restaurant, and "hired" two attorneys, on deferred, speculative payment, to try to collect the insurance. A grand jury was convened, and indicted her husband for the murder of the body found in the barn. In

1977, Geneva Roberts had petitioned to have her spouse declared dead, but the court refused. On May 3, 1979, the trial began. Judge James Dixon of the Monroe Superior Court in Bloomington heard the testimony of Jane Buikstra, a physical anthropologist, who explained how the body in the fire had been dismembered, and of a businessman who said that Roberts had bilked him out of $300,000 during the year before his disappearance. The trial ended on May 25, with Judge Dixon bringing in the judgment a month later, declaring, "Geneva Roberts shall recover nothing." She was ordered to pay the cost of the trial.

Roberts lived alone in a shack with no running water, drawn shades, and an attack dog. On Dec. 2, 1980, a fire raged through the place, killing Geneva Roberts and a man who was soon identified as her missing husband. According to Monroe County forensics pathologist Dr. John Pless, who later identified the corpse as probably that of Roberts, based on teeth and bone X-rays, alcohol "appears to have been a factor." Pless's opinion was corroborated by Dr. Clyde Snow, a physical anthropologist. Bud Allcron, a state police detective, said that a man had been living at Roberts' house for the last six years, but investigators had never actually seen him leaving or entering, and none of the neighbors recognized him as Roberts. Allcron maintained, "If a man wants to hold a private life and remain hidden he can do so."

<hr>

Roberts, Harry Maurice, and **Duddy, John**, and **Witney, John**, prom. 1966, Brit. When Harry Roberts, a man whose police record had been building since he was fifteen, and his two underlings, John Duddy and John Witney, failed to find the specific car they wanted to steal on the night of Aug. 12, 1966, they settled on robbing a rent collector they knew. Before they got to their new destination, they were stopped by a police patrol car. The policemen were only interested in the mufflerless car whose registration appeared to have run out, but Roberts, panicking, pulled out a gun and began to shoot. Within seconds, police officers Christopher Head, David Wombwell, and Geoffrey Fox were dead.

Another driver spotted the car's license number and so the police were quickly able to find the car at a Paddington garage rented by Witney. He was arrested immediately, and Duddy was caught a short time later in Scotland, where he had gone to hide. Roberts, however, had served with the Rifle Brigade in the jungles of Malaya and knew something about hiding. He had set up a bolt hole in a thicket in the middle of Epping Forest. At first Roberts left it only to buy food, but as the weeks passed, he ventured to other neighboring towns. He was away when the police found his hideout, and even though news of the discovery was broadcast, Roberts had failed to listen to the radio at all that day. When the police came, he gave himself up without a fight.

The three men were found Guilty of murder. Justice Glyn-Jones sentenced them to thirty years each in prison with a recommendation that they never be paroled.

Roberts, Roland, 1938-57, S. Afri. In October 1956, on the recommendation of fellow sailors in the South African Navy, 18-year-old Roland Roberts visited a doctor seeking professional help for his often uncontrollable behavior. Roberts stuttered and trembled after drinking alcohol and was known for chewing on his beard. Drunk or sober, he had a penchant for violence, and on several occasions, was observed slamming either his fist or forehead into metal lockers. The Naval doctor prescribed phenobarbital, a mild sedative, for his condition and discouraged the sailor from seeing a psychiatrist.

On Jan. 4, 1957, the body of 47-year-old Clara Arkin was found decaying where she had been murdered one week earlier. Roberts, who had met Arkin in a Cape Town bar around the time of her disappearance, was taken into custody for questioning. Roberts admitted brutalizing and stabbing Arkin, justifying his actions by saying that the woman had refused his sexual advances.

After a month of psychiatric evaluation, Roberts was brought to trial for murder. His attorney entered a guilty but insane plea and attempted to prove that Roberts had been tormented since childhood. As part of the strategy, the defense argued that Roberts was an alcoholic and that the murder was a manifestation of deep-seated hostility and occurred during a "dissociation of consciousness." The jury returned a Guilty verdict, citing extenuating circumstances, but presiding Justice van Wyk sentenced Roberts to death. An appeal was denied, and Roberts was hanged on Nov. 8.

Robertson, James Roland, d.1950, Scot. When Scottish police discovered the body of a 40-year-old woman lying beside Prospecthill Road between Kilmarnock and Glasgow, they figured she had stepped off a curb and been hit by a car. An all points bulletin was issued for an Austin which had been seen in the vicinity and James Roland Robertson was one of the officers to receive the message. Less than twenty-four hours later, Robertson was accused of killing Catherine McCluskey.

When Robertson was brought to trial in November 1950 on murder charges, he told the North Court in Glasgow that while driving a stolen car, he accidentally knocked the woman down, and in a panic to leave the scene, he accidentally ran her over. Robertson confessed that he was supposed to be on duty at the time of the accident and that he was afraid his past liaisons with the woman would become grist for the local newspapers and ruin his career as a policeman. Evidence was also introduced that Robertson may have been the father of one of McCluskey's children and had been giving the murder victim money during their affair. After he was found Guilty of murder by a majority verdict—permitted under Scottish law—Robertson was hanged on Dec. 16, 1950.

Robinson, John, d.1927, Brit. On May 6, 1927, a man checked a large trunk in the baggage claim at Charing Cross Station in London. He told the attendant that he would be traveling later in the day and that the trunk should not be disturbed in the meantime. After four days the man had not returned to claim the trunk and a foul odor had begun to emanate from it. Station officials called police, who forced the trunk open and found four bundles tied in cloth. The bundles contained the remains of a neatly butchered woman.

In addition to the cloth in which the body parts were wrapped, several other articles of women's clothing were found in the trunk. On a piece of underclothing, the police discovered a laundry mark which was traced to a Mrs. Holt. Mrs. Holt obligingly supplied the police with the names of ten different women whom she had employed as maids over the years. Further investigation revealed that only one of these women, Minnie Bonati, could not be located.

Photographs of the trunk were widely circulated in the press. As a result, a luggage dealer in Brixton told police that he had sold a trunk like the one in which the body had been found to a man on May 6. A taxi driver also came forward to say that he had driven a man from an office building in Rochester Row to Charing Cross Station on that date. Police went immediately to the office building where the driver had picked up his passenger with the trunk. The tenant, a John Robinson, however, was no longer there. He had not been there since May 9 when he left a note saying he was "broke" and would not return. Although he had left no forwarding address at his lodgings, police located a woman who said she was his wife (he was actually a bigamist) at the Greyhound Hotel. The woman took police to a meeting she had planned with Robinson for that evening.

Robinson willingly went to Scotland Yard and made a statement in which he denied knowing the dead woman or purchasing a trunk. He was confronted by the three witnesses—the taxi driver, the station porter, and the luggage dealer, but none of them could identify him. Robinson was close to being discounted as a suspect when a Scotland Yard inspector, examining the clothing found in the trunk more closely, discovered the word "Greyhound" on one of the articles. With this additional piece of evidence, John Robinson was recalled to Scotland Yard and confessed his guilt.

Robinson claimed that he met Bonati at Victoria Station and took her back to his office. When he refused her request for money, she attacked him. Robinson claimed that he then struck her in self-defense and she fell backward, striking her head. He then left her alone in the office, assuming she would revive and leave, but he returned the following day to discover that she was dead. In a panic to dispose of the body, he bought a butcher knife and the trunk. Robinson was brought to trial at the Old Bailey in July. The Home Office pathologist Sir Bernard Spilsbury, who had examined Bonati's remains testified that, contrary to Robinson's claims, the victim had been struck on the head and later suffocated. Robinson was found Guilty and sentenced to death. He was hanged at Pentonville Prison on Aug. 12, 1927.

Robinson, Norman Wesley (AKA: John Thompson), 1910-38, U.S.

When Charles Chase started his job as a houseboy at 7:30 a.m., he was not concerned that his boss was still asleep. By 10 a.m., when the early-riser Florence Dougherty Goodwin still had not emerged from her room, a boarder, Mrs. Alphonse Billups became concerned and asked Chase to knock on the door. Chase said Goodwin probably wanted to sleep late, but Billups became concerned and opened the unlocked door to find the landlady lying dead on the couch. The 43-year-old divorcée had been strangled and bludgeoned about the head with a blunt instrument in the second floor bedroom of her Washington, D.C., rooming house. Police were stymied in a search for motives after ruling out robbery and sexual assault.

Officers found the murder weapon in the basement of the rooming house. The killer had tossed a ten-pound iron stove lid into a basement boiler. Despite claims of innocence, Chase was arrested. Officials found a blood spot on his pants and discovered two blue threads matching Goodwin's dressing gown under his fingernails. During the course of their investigation, police found out that a janitor had recently been fired by Goodwin. It took three days, but when officers finally apprehended the janitor, they found out his real name was Norman Wesley Robinson and that he had served time in prison for robbery. Police also found blue threads under Robinson's fingernails and matched the bloodstain on his shirt to the victim's blood type. Robinson

confessed to the crime, citing robbery as the motive. He admitted he had stolen a key to the basement. After having his execution date postponed nine times, Robinson was put to death in the electric chair on Mar. 18, 1938.

Robles, Richard, 1942- , U.S.

In the late afternoon of Aug. 28, 1963, 21-year-old Pat Toller, a researcher for *Time* magazine, returned to the Manhattan apartment she shared with 21-year-old Janice Wylie, employed at *Newsweek*, and 23-year-old Emily Hoffert. Wylie and Hoffert had the day off from work. When Toller entered the

Drug-killer Richard Robles.

apartment, she noticed that objects in the hallway had been disturbed and the bathroom was spattered with blood. Alarmed, Toller retreated from the apartment and called Janice's father, author Max Wylie. Wylie arrived shortly and explored the apartment. In the bedroom he found the bodies of the two young women. Although Janice's body was nude, Hoffert's was fully clothed.

The two bodies bore multiple stab wounds and had been tied together with strips of cloth torn from the sheets. Further investigation revealed that Janice had been eviscerated, and there was evidence that the murderer had intended to rape her.

Little progress was made in the case until the following April, when 19-year-old George Whitmore, Jr. was arrested and charged with a stabbing murder and an assault. Police

Janice Wylie and Emily Hoffert, Robles' victims.

discovered a photo among Whitmore's belongings that they believed to be of Janice Wylie. Whitmore eventually confessed to the Wylie and Hoffert murders but recanted later, claiming the confession had been coerced by police. Regardless, Whitmore was convicted of attempted rape and sentenced to five to ten years in prison. The case might have ended here except that in the fall of that year, Nathan Delaney, a drug addict arrested on a murder charge, told police that he had information regarding the two murders. He told them that 22-year-old Richard Robles had been staying with him and his wife at the time of the murders and had returned home distraught and asking for a fix. He had also told Delaney that he had murdered two young women during a burglary.

Robles was arrested on Jan. 26, 1965, and confessed to the Wylie murders. He was found Guilty on Dec. 1 of first-degree murder and sentenced to life imprisonment.

Robson, Annie, prom. 1931, Brit. When nurse Annie Robson believed that her patient, Mrs. Kate Pochin, was harming her, Robson retaliated by dousing her with boiling water. Pochin's injuries from the scalding led to her death. Robson was indicted for murder at Leicestershire Assizes in October 1931 and entered a plea of insanity in response. On the strength of expert testimony which held that Ms. Robson suffered from delusions and occasional bouts of amnesia, a verdict of Guilty but insane was returned. She was ordered confined for an indefinite period of time.

Rogers, Dayton Leroy, 1953- , U.S. A clearing in the forested hills above the Molalla River at Oregon City, Ore., was the scene of the torture and murder of seven women—all of them known prostitutes—during the summer of 1987. Three of the bodies were found with their feet cut off. These deaths were the extension of violence begun long before. At the 1989 trial of Dayton Rogers, Melody Dahlman Myers testified that in 1972, 19-year-old Rogers had taken her to the woods and stabbed her in the abdomen. Even though he had been married for six weeks, he said he would marry her and take her to the hospital if she would claim to have done the damage herself. He took her for help, but Myers told the truth and Rogers was arrested. He pleaded guilty to second-degree assault and was placed on probation. Thus the violence began, interspersed with a very different life in which Rogers was active in the Seventh-Day Adventist Church and ran his own small-engine repair business.

Rogers was reared in a strict home in which he was severely punished for infractions of various rules. Whenever he or the other six Rogers children made friends with someone, their father would move elsewhere, sometimes three or four times a year. Rogers felt his first wife, Julie Miller Rogers, was physically and mentally cruel. They divorced in 1974 and he later remarried.

As demonstrated with Myers, the knife had become an important tool in Rogers' quest for sexual gratification. One woman testified at his trial that in 1976, she had been picked up by Rogers. They had sat and talked in his truck until she had to leave. At that point, he drew his knife and began to cut her clothes from her. Then he hog-tied her and began to play with her feet, finally threatening to kill her. After releasing the woman, he was charged with kidnapping and returned to prison for violating his parole. Hog-tying became a theme of Rogers in seeking sexual satisfaction. He began taking prostitutes to the woods where he would, usually with their permission, tie them around the wrists and ankles and then fasten the two ties together, so that they were bent over backwards. He then proceeded to cut them on the heels or breasts with a sharp knife. Forty to fifty prostitutes described his similar treatment of them. The eleven who testified at the actual trial said that as long as they protested and fought, he would be in a frenzy and continue to cut them, but once they had given up and become submissive, he lost interest and ultimately took them back to town. A woman whom he picked up in 1986 testified that after they had several vodka drinks, he bit her breasts and feet, drawing blood.

Right, convicted sex murderer Dayton Leroy Rogers, who tortured, killed, and mutilated at least six women.

The increasing violence culminated during the summer of 1987. On Aug. 6, Rogers picked up Portland prostitute Jennifer Lisa Smith in his truck. He spent the next twenty-four hours with her and at some point bound her up in the way that had become his signature. When he drove her back to town, she leapt out of his truck in front of Denny's Restaurant in Oak Grove, where he pursued her. He caught up with Smith and stabbed her to death. Broken shoelaces used to bind her were found on her body. He was arrested and charged with aggravated murder. He called his father-in-law (soon to be ex- because his wife divorced him after he was arrested) to ask if the police had searched the stove in his workshop. They had not, but when they did, they found numerous metal bits of shoes, belts, bra hooks, and other items indicating that women's clothing had been burned. Rogers said that the bits were from Smith's and his own clothing, and the police at that time had no good reason to question the sheer quantity of the metal pieces. Rogers was found Guilty of the murder of Smith and sentenced to life in prison.

In the meantime, however, the nude bodies of seven women, tortured and sexually abused, had been found on an isolated lumbering road back in the forests above the Molalla River. Three of the bodies had had the feet cut off, and a fourth had been severely wounded around the ankles. A leather dog collar bound the wrists of one victim. Broken bits of shoelaces tied in the same knots that had been used on Smith's body, as well as miniature vodka bottles and orange juice containers, were found near each body.

Rogers was charged with the aggravated murder of the six women whose bodies were identified, including Christine Lotus Adams, Lisa Marie Mock, and 16-year-old Reatha Marie Gyles. An all-woman jury found him Guilty on May 4, 1989. According to Oregon law, the death penalty can be imposed only if the jury believes that the killing was completely intentional and that the killer is likely to pose a threat to society if he is not put to death. The penalty phase of Rogers' trial included the testimony of his brother-in-law, Floyd Mohr, various psychiatrists, and the women who could demonstrate that his violent behavior had been going on for a long time. Also testifying, however, were friends who told of his caring and devotion to a prison ministry that he had started while he was an inmate. The deputy district attorney, Andrejs I. Eglitis, said in his closing statement to the jury, "That person is a walking time bomb. That person is an act of criminal violence looking for a place to happen....He's capable of fooling psychologists. He's capable of fooling psychiatrists. I hope to God he's not capable of fooling you." The jury deliberated for seventeen and a half hours over two days before returning a vote in favor of execution by lethal injection.

Rogers, George White, 1898-1958, U.S. On Sept. 8, 1934, the luxury liner *Morro Castle* caught fire on the journey from Havana back to New York. The ship's radioman, George W. Rogers, sent the SOS that brought aid and saved several lives and remained at his post even when flames encroached. One hundred and thirty-four passengers died. Rogers, who suffered superficial but painful burns, was lauded by his hometown of Bayonne, N.J., which greeted him with a brass band, flowers, a $200 gold medal and an embrace from the mayor.

Hired by his hometown police force as assistant to Lieutenant Vincent J. Doyle, radio bureau chief of police, Rogers was imprisoned four years later for severely injuring Doyle when he planted a bomb in a plot to take over Doyle's position. A psychiatrist labeled Rogers a "psycho-pathic personality." The judge who sentenced him to twelve to twenty years accused him of having "the mind of a fiend." Released from jail in 1942 because his services as a radio technician were needed in the armed forces' war effort, Rogers was rejected after the authorities took a look at his record, but was allowed to remain on parole. By 1953, Rogers, living again in Bayonne, owed $7,500 to 83-year-old William Hummel, who was preparing to retire to Florida. Hummel had taken $2,400 in savings out of his bank and had it in his home. When he and Rogers fought over the $7,500 debt, Rogers crushed the old man's head with a footstool, then went upstairs and murdered Hummel's 58-year-old married daughter in a similar fashion.

Deeply in debt prior to the Hummels slayings, Rogers was soon arrested after he began lavishly spending the $2,400. He was convicted and sentenced to life imprisonment at the New Jersey State Prison in Trenton, where he died four years later of a heart attack on Jan. 10, 1958. In 1972, a study of the luxury liner disaster, *Shipwreck: The Strange Fate of the Morro Castle,* by Gordon Thomas and Max Morgan Witts, revealed evidence that indicated that Rogers had set the fire himself with a small bomb after he poisoned the ship's captain. His supposed heroism was presumed to be a cover-up.

Rogers, Irene, prom. 1976, U.S. Irene Rogers, a food service apprentice at the Job Corps Training Center in Excelsior Springs, Mo., often partied with friends on weekends at the apartment of Gloria Jean Sowards in St. Joseph, Mo. On the weekend of Jan. 7, 1976, she and two trainee nursing assistants, Karen Sharp and Sandra Beam, went to party, accompanied by men, liquor, and marijuana. At some point during the first evening, Rogers, who was later determined to be slightly retarded, began picking on Beam. The slightly hostile teasing quickly turned into forcibly getting Beam drunk. Several persons held her down and poured liquor, shampoo, and other noxious liquids down her throat. They encouraged each other's escalating acts of sadism.

It seems that men came and went during that weekend, but none of them did anything to stop the torture of Beam. The girls continually beat her with whatever was handy, including their fists, belts, and chairs. They poured rubbing alcohol down her throat. They broke her nose and knocked out her teeth. Finally, someone in the neighborhood called the police. Beam died of a severe blow to the head and internal burns from the alcohol.

Charged with second-degree murder and manslaughter, the girls were tried and convicted. The court recognized that Rogers played the leading role in the sadistic killing and sentenced her to life in prison.

Rogers, John, 1940- , Brit. "If a wicked, intentional mind, bent on killing or seriously injuring, has accompanied an act which does in fact kill, then in law there is malice aforethought and that is murder," said Queen's Counsel N.R. Fox-Andrews at the trial of John Rogers in October 1960. The 20-year-old brewery clerk in Bristol, England, claimed that he had intended only to rob cab driver William Tripp when he took a stolen sawed-off .22-caliber rifle and got in Tripp's cab late in the evening of July 29, 1960. Nearing the town of Winford, Rogers had Tripp pull to the side. Before the cab stopped, Rogers shot the driver in the back of the head. The cab surged forward into a hedge and overturned. Rogers escaped, took some money, and ran, just as Cyril Farrow arrived and found the cab. Rogers, observed by Farrow when he fled the murder scene, went on to Beaulieu and the August Bank Holiday jazz festival.

The cab's meter had an amount on it that exactly matched the distance to the center of Bristol. Within five days, Rogers had been arrested and tried. He was found Guilty of capital murder and sentenced to death. The Home Secretary later granted Rogers a reprieve and he was sent to prison for life.

Rohart, Armand, prom. 1967, Fr. The mayor of Peuplingues, Fr., a small town near Calais, was a popular figure in the area, though he was notorious for womanizing. Armand Rohart took out life insurance on his wife and discussed ways to murder his wife, without being discovered, with an ex-Foreign Legionnaire, Jacob Kerbahay, who lived in one of his cottages. The soldier recorded the conversation on a small tape recorder.

On June 9, 1967, Rohart and his wife, Jacqueline Rohart, went to a beach on the nearby coast at Escalles. He was found that evening on the front seat of his car in shock and apparently unconscious. His wife's body was found some hours later on the beach. He claimed that they had been picked up by a big wave and he had barely saved himself while his wife drowned. But the coroner found that she had died from asphyxiation. When Kerbahay came forward with his incriminating recording, Rohart was arrested and tried for the murder of his wife. He was found Guilty and sentenced to life in prison.

Rojas, Teofilo (AKA: Sparks), d.1963, Col. From 1945 until 1962 Colombia was plagued by civil disorders and an escalating murder rate that the residents of the South American nation called the period of "La Violencia." There were an estimated 300,000 homicides during this time, which averaged forty-eight a day. The Colombian bandit leader Teofilo Rojas took credit for at least 592 of these murders, committed between 1948 and Jan. 22, 1963, when he was ambushed and shot to death near Armenia. The authorities believe that Rojas may be responsible for up to 3,500 murders, which, if true, would make him the single most prolific killer in history.

Rolle, Randal, 1918-49, U.S. A native of Jackson, Miss., Randal Rolle moved to a farm after WWII and there lived like a hermit. He had been a ranger during the invasion of Europe, where he developed killer instincts that made him the most lethal man in his platoon. Rolle, while fighting in France in 1944, repeatedly volunteered for behind-the-lines missions and was an expert with knife and bayonet, slaying German guards at outposts and guarding ammunition dumps. Once Rolle returned home, he appeared withdrawn and sullen. He refused to marry his childhood sweetheart and worked at odd jobs in Jackson until he inherited a dilapidated farm when a brother died. Few people saw Rolle after that. He raised only the crops he needed to survive and drove off people who accidentally crossed his property, brandishing a long knife and shouting: "Get off! Get off! Unless you want what the others got!"

On Oct. 14, 1949, a towering cloud of black smoke belched skyward from the Rolle farm and officials drove to the place to investigate. The farmhouse was on fire and two deputies braved the flames to find Rolle dead in his bed, part of his head blown away by a shotgun he had used on himself. When the fire was extinguished, lawmen searching the ruins found the bones of several humans. Remains of human bodies, apparently all Rolle's murder victims, were found buried around the farm. One victim was identified through teeth and personal belongings as 17-year-old Frances Callombe, who had vanished on June 8, 1948. Rolle, it was claimed, had been responsible for the deaths of at least nine people, perhaps more. His motive for murdering was never established.

Romer, Richard, 1945-79, U.S. Computer programmer Richard Romer, thirty-four, had been unemployed for a year when his bank foreclosed on his Jacksonville, Fla., home. Seeing no way out of his financial difficulties, he wrote a letter to the Jacksonville police, which they received on Aug. 24, 1979. It said, "Please come to 5069 Brighton Drive. The back door is open. We are all dead." The police called the home and Romer answered. Questioned, he insisted that the letter must have been a hoax. However, the police sent someone to the house anyway. As the letter stated, the officer found the back door open and Romer, his wife, and their two children dead in the living room.

Rose Man of Sing Sing, See: Chapin, Charles.

Ross, Charles Ray, prom. 1945, U.S. Charles Ross and his wife Wilma Ross had been married only a few months when they moved from Knoxville, Tenn., to Bremerton, Wash., to work in the Navy Yard there. But in July 1945, after only a week of working, they decided to vacation in Seattle. After celebrating the Fourth of July, Ross left the hotel to get food and drinks. When he returned he saw Wilma walking off with another man. Ross angrily chased the man away and the newlyweds walked along the waterfront to discuss the situation. Wilma's body was found there later. She had been stabbed in the neck.

Ross blamed an unknown group of four sailors for abducting and killing his wife, but he later confessed to the murder. He pleaded guilty to second-degree murder and on Dec. 10, 1945, was sentenced to thirty years in prison.

Ross, Charles William, 1914-33, Kenya. The son of a big game hunter, 19-year-old Charles Ross had a ferocious, bad-tempered reputation. His neighbors in the small Kenyan town of Nakuru said he sometimes slaughtered game just for the chance to wallow in the blood. On Oct. 6, 1932, he took his girlfriend, Winifred Stevenson, and another friend, Margaret Keppie, out in his car to go to a movie. None were seen again until Oct. 8, when Ross's brother found Charles in his car stuck in a ditch about seven miles from home.

Ross was arrested while the town sent out search parties. Keppie's body was soon found at the bottom of a ravine, with a bullet through her head. On Oct. 14, Ross told authorities where to find Winifred Stevenson. Her body lay camouflaged in the tall grass only a mile from home. She, too, had a bullet through the head. Ross admitted that he had shot them both, though he said he had no particular reason for doing it. Nor would he explain why they found a pile of women's clothing in a small camp with provisions and women's toiletries.

In an attempt to prove him insane, the defense revealed all the horrible joyful killing and strange behaviors Ross had demonstrated in recent months. An X-ray of his brain showed that part of it had not developed properly. An aptitude test suggested he was mildly retarded. Nevertheless, the jury found Ross Guilty of murder and sentenced him to be hanged. He was executed on Jan. 11, 1933.

Ross, Perry Dean, prom. 1957, U.S. On a Saturday night in Spring 1957, at a small cafe in eastern Texas, a bunch of black teenagers danced to the jukebox. Outside, Perry Ross of Tatum was driving by when he got an urge he'd never had before. Holding the steering wheel with his left hand, he laid his automatic rifle across the open window and fired as he drove by at 85 mph. He killed 16-year-old John Earl Reese and wounded two girls.

Fifteen months went by before authorities indicted Ross for murder with malice. At the trial, one of his attorneys asked the jury to just "call it a bad day and let the boy go on in life." The jury found Ross Guilty of murder, but without malice, and recommended that a five-year prison sentence be suspended.

Rossouw, Marthinius, 1939-62, S. Afri. Twenty-three-year-old Marthinius Rossouw, friend and bodyguard to Baron Dietrich Joachim Gunther von Schauroth, a well-to-do dealer in illicit diamonds in South Africa, killed his friend with two shots to the back of the neck. Rossouw, who had known von Schauroth only two months, claimed he committed the murder at von Schauroth's request. He maintained that von Schauroth wanted to die because he was tired of living and not getting along with his wife, and pleaded with him to kill him so that his wife could get almost a half-million dollars in life insurance.

Von Schauroth was found on Mar. 24, 1961, lying dead by the side of a road. A four-carat uncut diamond lay on the ground near the body. According to Rossouw, the baron had asked him, soon after their meeting if he would kill someone for a $14,000 payment. On Mar. 24, von Schauroth gave Rossouw a check for 3,200 rands and announced that the person he wanted Rossouw to kill was himself. Rossouw, who had told a different story when first arrested, claimed that von Schauroth had made him promise that, if caught, he would not to tell the truth for "a day or two." The jury did not believe him and found him Guilty. Rossouw was hanged on June 19, 1962. Although the court had placed no credence in Rossouw's story, the insurance companies found advantage in believing the story and eventually gave the baron's widow only about $28,000 as a settlement of all claims.

Rothschild, Charles Paul (AKA: **Rocky**), prom. 1957-58, U.S. On June 19, 1956, Charles Paul Rothschild and A.D. Allen used William Patterson's car. Rothschild, a former Cairo, Ill., policeman, and Allen, a bootlegger, robbed and murdered 57-year-old Charles Drake, a well-known resident of Jefferson, Ga. When Rothschild returned the car sometime later, he confided the details of the murder. James Foster, a 39-year-old house painter from Gainesville, Ga., was convicted of murdering Drake. The eyewitness testimony of Drake's widow helped convict Foster. After the U.S. Supreme Court refused to consider the case, and it appeared all but certain that Foster was going to be executed, J. Preston Strom of the South Carolina Law Enforcement Division came up with new evidence. Patterson had been arrested and reported Rothschild's confession to police. Allen and Rothschild were found Guilty of murder on Aug. 14, 1958, and sentenced to prison for life.

Rottman, Arthur, 1894-1915, N. Zea. When WWI broke out, 21-year-old Arthur Rottman, a native German, was working aboard a New Zealand ship. He soon became interned and spent the duration of the war working on the farm of Joseph and Mary McCann in Ruahine. On Dec. 27, 1914, he woke up with a hangover and missed his milking stint. When an argry McCann confronted him, Rottman picked up an axe and split his bosses' head open. He then killed Mrs. McCann and their infant son. Next, Rottman delivered the milk to the dairy plant nearby and caught a train to Wellington. At a construction camp, he asked for work. When news of the "Ruahine Ax Murders" reached the camp, Rottman begged one man not to let anyone know where he was.

The entrusted William Kelly, the only man who had volunteered to stay in the camp while the others left for Christmas vacation, called the police and Rottman was arrested. He claimed the ax murders were the result of his drinking so much and that he didn't know what he was doing. Rottman was found Guilty and hanged in March 1915.

Rouse, Alfred Arthur, 1894-1931, Brit. On the evening of Nov. 6, 1930, two young men walking along a country road near Northampton, England, were surprised to see a neatly dressed man carrying a small case emerge from a ditch alongside the road. After the man had passed them and gone a distance ahead, he turned and shouted back to them, "It looks as though someone is having a bonfire up there." Just after he spoke, the men noticed flames on the horizon. When they reached the site of the fire, they discovered an automobile so consumed in flames that it was impossible to tell if there had been any occupants.

British murderer Alfred Arthur Rouse.

When police arrived and extinguished the blaze it was determined that the car had been a Morris Minor. The charred remains of a person were found in the front seat. The flames had all but destroyed the car, but the license plate still was legible. When police traced the number—MU 1468—they discovered that the car was owned by Alfred Arthur Rouse, a traveling salesman who lived in Finchley, North London. Rouse's wife, when contacted, said she had no idea where her husband could be located.

Rouse returned to London on Nov. 7, where he was taken in for questioning by the police. He claimed that he had given a ride to a man and when he had left the car briefly to relieve himself, the man had accidentally set fire to a container of gasoline in the car. Rouse claimed further that he had tried to pull the man from the car, but was prevented by the intensity of the fire.

A police investigation revealed that Rouse was a notorious womanizer and bigamist. They eventually estimated that he had had affairs with more than eighty women over the years he worked as a traveling salesman for a brace-and-garter company. He had fathered several children in several of these unions and had even married one of the mothers (despite the fact that he was already married at the time.) Rouse himself admitted that between Nov. 3 and Nov. 7 he had been with Phyllis Jenkins, a young Welsh woman who was pregnant with his child. Because of his philandering and the increasing financial strain created by orders for child support, police surmised that Rouse had torched the car himself with the unidentified man inside in an attempt to escape his problems, hoping the victim would be mistaken for himself. Police formally arrested Rouse and charged him with murder.

Rouse was tried at Northampton Assizes in January 1931.

The prosecution demonstrated that the car's carburetor had been tampered with, thus enhancing their case that Rouse had planned the murder. He was found Guilty and sentenced to death. He was hanged at Bedford on Mar. 10, 1931.

Roush, Harvey L., prom. 1938, U.S. Conditions during the Depression forced people to take drastic measures to survive. Such was the case when Harvey Roush, a farm employee near Delaware, Ohio, borrowed money from his employer. On Apr. 29, 1938, he went to the farm of Homer T. Meyers, where he worked, and told Meyers that he had the money he owed him. As Meyers wrote "Paid in Full" on the note for $1,500 and signed his name, Roush put his hand in his pocket, and pulled out not the money, but a .38-caliber pistol and shot his benefactor. When Mrs. Meyers came running in, he shot her, too, finishing her off with blows from the butt of a rifle. Hoping to make it appear the work of an anonymous robber, Roush set fire to the house. But the fire failed to hide his work, and police found the signed note near Meyers' charred hand. Once apprehended Roush confessed to the murders. He was tried in the court of Judge Hector S. Young on Aug. 1, 1938. The jury found him Guilty of murder, and he was sentenced to be executed.

Rousseau, Rosella (AKA: **Angele**), prom. 1909, Fr. The use of human hair analysis to solve a 1909 murder in Paris marked a first in this forensic science. Rousseau, the former housekeeper to Albert Oursel, a Parisian employment agent, was finding it difficult to make ends meet in July 1909, even though she shared expenses with a housemate named Martin and his daughter. Knowing that Albert Oursel, the bachelor for whom she had formerly worked, left town every Sunday, the woman sneaked into his office one Saturday afternoon, avoided the receptionist, and waited in the apartment until she left. Oursel had been living with a 15-year-old Breton girl, Germaine Bichon. Before Rousseau could search the apartment, Bichon returned home and locked herself in the bedroom. Convinced that the bedroom was where Oursel kept his money, Rousseau hid the entire night until Bichon woke and unlocked the door again. The would-be burglar started moving around the apartment. When she suddenly ran into Bichon, Rousseau attacked the girl, who ran into the kitchen and grabbed a hatchet. Rousseau took the hatchet from her and beat her to death with it. Bichon managed to grab some of her attacker's hair before she died. For her pains,

Rousseau found only a gold ruble and a watch chain in the apartment. She left, as she would later insist, through the outer apartment door. However, she returned to the main entrance where, calling herself "Angele," she approached the concierge, saying she was looking for a friend, Adele, who was not home.

People in the restaurant below the Oursel suite heard screams that day, but thought only that Germaine was entertaining someone in the bedroom...until drops of blood began leaking from the ceiling above them. The concierge called the police. The medical examiner found a number of hairs clutched in the dead girl's hands. There was no sign of forced entry but the place had clearly been searched, as if by a robber. Eventually the police learned of the woman who had called herself Angele, of the existence of a previous cleaning woman, and that a woman calling herself Bosch had been in the neighborhood the day before the murder. Rousseau told them that her maiden name was Bosch. Further, she had longish, light-brown hair. Finally, the police searched the Martin apartment and found clothes that people in the neighborhood identified as having been worn by Angele. The scientist on the case discovered places on Rousseau's head where hair had been pulled out, hair that matched the microscopic characteristics of the hair found clutched in Germaine's hands.

Rousseau was arrested for murder and tried in February 1910. Found Guilty, she was sentenced to death.

Rowland, Ferrin, d.c.1935, U.S. In the early 1930s, Michigan resident Ferrin Rowland regularly tried to persuade his wife that they should get rid of their two children by giving them up for adoption. She finally agreed, and Rowland took them away—to kill them and drown them in Lake Beebe. After October 1935, Mr. and Mrs. Rowland told people that their children had been adopted by some nice people in Flint. However, their stories did not agree, and the police investigated.

When the authorities came to the farm, Rowland had already fled. When he was captured, he confessed. The children's corpses were found by dragging the lake. Mrs. Rowland was committed to an insane asylum, and Ferrin Rowland hanged himself in his cell before his death sentence could be carried out.

Rowland, Walter Graham, 1907-47, Brit. On Oct. 20, 1946, two children playing on a bombed-out building site in Manchester came across the body of a 40-year-old prostitute, Olive Balchin. The woman had been beaten in the head with a leather-beater's hammer which was found lying near the corpse. After learning that Balchin had been seen the night of her death with a laborer, Walter Graham Rowland, the police located Rowland in a hostel and interviewed him.

Rowland admitted that he had been with Balchin but denied killing her. Police discovered that Rowland had been convicted of the murder of a child some years earlier but had been reprieved. When a forensic investigation revealed dust and plant matter on his clothes which matched the location where the body was found and traces of blood on Rowland's shoes that matched Balchin's type,

Walter Graham Rowland

Rowland was formally charged with murder. He was tried at the Manchester Assizes in December 1946. Despite his vigorous protestations of innocence, he was found Guilty and sentenced to death. Just three weeks before Rowland was scheduled to make his appeal, a 38-year-old prisoner at Liverpool, David John Ware, confessed to Olive Balchin's murder. Rowland's appeal was heard in February 1947 but new evidence, including Ware's statement, was not allowed and the appeal was dismissed. Although an inquiry into this decision was opened by the Home Office, Ware recanted his confession and it was determined there had been no miscarriage of justice as far as Rowland was concerned. Rowland was hanged at Strangeways Prison on Feb. 27, 1947. In November 1951, when Ware was arrested on a charge of attempted murder, he reportedly told police that he had killed a woman. Ware was found Guilty but insane.

Rowles, Snowy, See: Smith, John Thomas.

Rowley, Reginald Walter, 1920- , Brit. "I don't know what made me do it...I knew what I was doing but I couldn't help myself," said Reginald Rowley, a 24-year-old farm laborer who had been discharged from the army in WWII because of epilepsy. Rowley, who worked at a farm

near Arlesey, Bedfordshire, started attacking girls. One of his victims told police that the assailant wore a peaked cap, leading them to suspect military men in the area. In August 1943, Muriel Emery, a nurse from a nearby hospital, was killed. Emery had met her boyfriend in a grove of trees near the hospital. After ten, the two parted and the boyfriend last saw her headed toward the hospital. After the boyfriend turned away, Rowley crept up on Emery and tried to strangle her, then beat her over the head with a thick piece of wood. When the body was found the next morning, there was no evidence of rape or robbery.

The crime remained unsolved and virtually without clues until the following February when an elderly storekeeper, Agnes Ellen Trotter, was attacked in her store in Biggleswade. The woman survived and identified Reginald Rowley as her attacker. Rowley, who wore a peaked railway cap, confessed to the murder. Rowley was tried for Emery's murder, found Guilty but insane, and committed to a mental institution.

Rudloff, Fritz, prom. 1954, Ger. An East German male nurse in 1954 chose to get back at a doctor he hated by killing the doctor's patients. Fritz Rudloff, who resented being a nurse instead of a doctor, had a special dislike for the chief surgeon at Waltershausen Municipal Hospital. His dislike was compounded when the doctor ordered Rudloff to stop an affair he was having with a female nurse. Rudloff complied, but began to arrange for the doctor's patients to take inexplicable turns for the worse when they were apparently on the road to recovery. He took doses of arsenic from the hospital pharmacy and administered it to four of the surgeon's patients. The fourth patient was the last. When it appeared that the patient was about to go home he died suddenly. The man's wife insisted on an autopsy. Arsenic was found, and Rudloff's lethal games were quickly discovered. Rudloff confessed to the killings. Tried and found Guilty, he was sentenced to be executed by guillotine.

Ruhr Hunter, See: Kroll, Joachim.

Ruiz, Luis, 1960- , and **Cabellero, Juan,** 1961- , U.S. In 1980, Luis Ruiz, twenty, and Juan Cabellero, nineteen, met in a restaurant on the Near North side of Chicago with three youths from the suburbs: Michael Salcido and Arthur Salcido, seventeen and nineteen respectively, and 16-year-old Frank Musa. During the course of the conversation about a marijuana deal, the suburbanites made rude comments about the gang to which the two Chicagoans belonged. The youths then left, presumably to complete the drug deal. The three buyers were found later in a car with their throats cut.

Before these murders had occurred, Ruiz had been dismissed on another murder charge in the death of 16-year-old Thomas Griebell, whom he admitted shooting. However, the judge dismissed the charges after the trial had started because two other youths involved in the murder had been allowed to plead guilty to lesser charges in juvenile court.

Ruiz and Caballero were tried for the Salcido and Mura killings at the same time and in the same courtroom with separate juries before Judge James M. Bailey. At various times during the trial, when evidence concerned only one defendant, the other youth's jury would leave the courtroom. On Mar. 24, 1980, Cabellero was found Guilty and sentenced to death. A month later, Ruiz, too, was found Guilty and sentenced to be executed.

Rumbold, Freda, c.1913- , Brit. For twenty years, Freda Rumbold had found it difficult living with her husband, Albert Rumbold. She purchased a gun, and, on Aug. 22, 1956, as he lay sleeping in their bed, shot him through the head. She left him lying in the bed for several days, keeping her 14-year-old daughter out of the bedroom and telling her husband's employees and her mother that her husband had gone on a trip. A few days later, she told her sister and then the police that she had killed her husband when Rumbold had threatened to shoot her and their daughter. Freda claimed she had tried to wrestle the gun away from him and Rumbold was fatally shot in the struggle.

Two shots had been fired in the bedroom, and the gun Rumbold had purchased was a single-shot weapon. Rumbold would have had to open the chamber and insert a bullet while she stood idly by, if her story had been true. At the trial, she blamed part of her problems on the full moon, and the "abnormal" sexual demands her husband was making at that time. Afraid that he would attack his daughter in a like manner, Freda Rumbold had bought the gun and started thinking about murder. The jury disbelieved her impossible story and she was found Guilty and sentenced to death. She later received a reprieve.

Ruopp, Siegfried, 1929- , Ger. Ingeborg Ruopp was killed by her husband but lived to see him tried and convicted for her murder. Her husband Siegfried, a professor of chemistry at the Schubart secondary school in Ulm, W. Ger., learned that his wife had fallen in love with a married doctor. When that affair suddenly ended with the doctor's death in a car accident, Siegfried, in retribution, began to make a practice of having affairs with his attractive female students. One of the affairs, however, became serious, and in 1975 he realized that he wanted to marry the girl. As a chemist, Ruopp knew of and had access to a dangerous chemical which could cause cancer of the liver. He acquired some of the chemical and began putting small amounts in the blackberry jam that he made for his wife, who was fond of it. Gradually, jam pot by jam pot, she acquired cancer of the liver, for which there was no cure. The doctor informed 47-year-old Siegfried of the diagnosis, and he chose not to inform either his children or his wife.

In time, Mrs. Ruopp was hospitalized with her disease. Although the medical staff and her husband were still lying to her, she had begun to suspect that she was dying. She also began to suspect that perhaps there was something more than mere kindness in the way her husband kept urging her to eat his home-made blackberry jam. Finally she asked her doctor to have a pot analyzed. The analyst found the deadly chemical in the jam and said that there was no way it could have gotten in accidentally.

Siegfried Ruopp, on being arrested, professed not to know that the chemical was so deadly, but he had previously demonstrated to a class its ability to kill when he used it on a tank full of fish. On Apr. 13, 1978, he was found Guilty of attempted murder, but the judge, knowing that any day the killer's victim would finally die, sentenced him to life in prison with no possibility of early release. Ingeborg Ruopp died three months after her husband's murder conviction.

Ruppert, James, 1934- , U.S. James Ruppert, forty-one, of Hamilton, Ohio, shared a house with his mother, Charity. On Easter Sunday 1975, she invited the immediate family for dinner, including her other son Leonard, his wife, and their eight children. At dinner time, James, carrying three revolvers and a rifle, walked into the kitchen and began shooting. Those not killed immediately were stunned and made no attempt to escape. Nondescript James Ruppert killed all eleven people with thirty-one shots and then called the police.

Ruppert pleaded not guilty by reason of insanity. Defense psychiatrists presented various motives for the murders. Charity Ruppert had been about to insist that her son move away. He felt that his life was being ruined by a conspiracy among his family, the police, and the FBI. Since childhood, a great rage had been accumulating in him because of his inability to assert himself, and as a result, he was impotent. Prosecution witnesses testified that James Ruppert had long been unemployed, owed large sums of money to his mother and brother, and was now the sole heir to $300,000 in family assets. They suggested that he was willing to spend a short time in a mental institution to get the money.

A panel of three judges determined that Ruppert was sane and should stand trial. He stood trial twice because of a technicality, but was ultimately found Guilty of the murders of his mother and brother, but Not Guilty of the murders of his sister-in-law and the eight children because of insanity. He was sentenced on July 23, 1982, to two consecutive life terms.

Russell, George, d.1948, Brit. On June 1, 1948, a milkman noticed that his delivery of the previous day had not been touched and he reported this to the police. Officers broke into the Maidenhead house of Mrs. Minnie Freeman Lee, finding her stuffed into a large trunk. Her hands were tied behind her back and she had been struck on the head. Mrs. Lee had died of asphyxiation after being placed in the trunk. Her home had been ransacked in what appeared to be a desperate search for money, a futile search, police learned, since Mrs. Lee, the widow of a wealthy barrister, never kept cash on hand, even though it was rumored that she had secreted large sums in her house.

Fingerprints were found on a cardboard box in the house and these were identified as belonging to George Russell, a petty housebreaker and ex-convict. A constable went to Russell's home and told him he was being arrested for the murder of Mrs. Lee. Russell blurted: "Did I murder this poor woman for something she was supposed to have and had not?"

The officer immediately concluded that Russell was guilty in that he knew of the rumor that Lee kept money in her house and that the killer had found none, a fact known only to the murderer and the police. The same conclusion was reached at Russell's trial at the Berkshire Assizes where he was found Guilty. Russell was executed by hanging on Dec. 2, 1948.

Rutherford, Norman, prom. 1919, Brit. On Jan. 13, 1919, Lieutenant Colonel Norman Rutherford came to a Holland Park address in London and asked to see Major Miles Seton, who was visiting his cousin, Sir Malcolm Seton.

Ten minutes after Miles Seton and Rutherford went into the living room, Lady Seton heard several gun shots and ran in to find Major Seton dead. Rutherford, standing at the fireplace holding his gun, said, "I wish I had another bullet for myself." He helped lift the body onto the sofa and made no effort to escape. He was charged with murder. The defense contended that Rutherford was insane, citing proof of family lunacy and of earlier violent behavior by Rutherford, who was apparently angry at Seton for advising his wife's cousin in a divorce matter. After five minutes of deliberation the jury found Rutherford Guilty but insane, and the judge ordered the convicted man to be sent to the Broadmoor Criminal Lunatic Asylum. He was released in 1930.

Rutledge, Dr. Robert C., Jr., prom. 1948, U.S. Just after WWII, Dr. Robert C. Rutledge, Jr., a pediatric resident in St. Louis, married his second wife, Sydney. Because her new husband was frequently away from home, she chose to go to work, where she met Byron Hattman, an aircraft engineer. After a sailing date, of which the doctor approved, Hattman either forced himself on Sydney Rutledge or she readily acquiesced. Rutledge learned of that event the following month when he heard Hattman bragging in a locker room. During the following weeks, the doctor tried to get Hattman to leave his wife alone, and even offered to pay him $2000 to move away. Four months later, on Dec. 15, 1948, a hotel chambermaid found Byron Hattman dead in a Cedar Rapids, Iowa, hotel room that he rented every Monday night while he worked with a firm in that city. The room showed all the signs of a long, bloody struggle.

A hotel maid was able to say that a man—not Hattman—had been in the room the previous afternoon just before Hattman arrived. Then the police learned that Rutledge had also been in Cedar Rapids that night. Determined to question the doctor, Cedar Rapids detectives went to St. Louis. Sydney answered the door and the doctor joined them a few minutes later after taking poison and applying makeup to cover scratches on his face. Although the poisoning was not fatal, further questioning of the doctor was postponed. Later, the doctor said that he had followed Hattman to Cedar Rapids to try to pay him off but instead the man had attacked him. He claimed that he had only knocked Hattman out before leaving for St. Louis. When police learned that at age twelve Rutledge had shot another boy during an argument over a girl, their doubts vanished and they arrested him for murder.

The trial began in Cedar Rapids on May 9, 1949. Sydney Rutledge testified that after the sailing date, Hattman had come into her apartment and raped her. The jury found the doctor Guilty of murder in the second degree, and he was sentenced to seventy years in prison. After serving a year, he was released on bond pending appeal to the Iowa Supreme Court. In April 1951, that court upheld Rutledge's conviction. That evening he committed suicide. In the note he left for his wife he said, "Love is but a fleeting thing at best, and time will cure a lot of grief...Remember that all men are wolves. I love you."

Ruxton, Buck (Bikhtyar Rustomji Ratanji Hakim),
1899-1936, Brit. Dr. Buck Ruxton, who studied medicine at Bombay and London universities, settled in Lancaster in 1930 with his wife, Isabella Ruxton (there is some doubt as to whether they actually married, but she generally was referred to as Mrs. Ruxton) and opened a practice there. The two frequently quarrelled, often on the subject of infidelities Ruxton suspected his wife of committing. The quarrels were violent enough that Mrs. Ruxton sought police protection on two occasions. On Sept. 7, 1935, the couple fought bitterly when Ruxton allegedly accused his wife of having an affair with a young Lancaster Town Hall clerk. Then, on Sept. 14, Isabella Ruxton drove alone in her husband's car to meet her two sisters in Blackpool. After leaving her sisters at 11:30 p.m., she was never seen again.

On the following day, Ruxton altered his normal schedule in a number of ways. He told the cleaning lady not to bother coming in as his wife and the maid Mary Rogerson had gone on vacation to Edinburgh; he turned away tradespeople and patients; he took his three children to a friend's house with the request that she look after them until his wife returned. He also hired another cleaning lady to come in and clean the staircase. This woman reported finding curious, stubborn stains in the bathtub and said that when she went to clean some rugs Ruxton had given her a blood-colored substance had come out of them.

Dr. Buck Ruxton with his daughter.

On Sept. 16, Ruxton rented a car and the following day a minor traffic accident placed him in the Lake District.

Ruxton called in two other cleaning ladies at various times until Sept. 20, both of whom reported finding bloodstains about the house and smelling a foul and persistent odor. On Sept. 29, the dismembered remains of two bodies were discovered in a ravine in Moffat, Scot. Just after Mary Rogerson's mother reported her daughter missing on Oct. 9, Ruxton made a statement to police: "I would like discreet inquiries made by the police with a view to finding my wife." Soon after this request, evidence found with the dismembered bodies suggested a link with the city of Lancaster and suspicion began to focus on Ruxton. On Oct. 13, 1935, he was charged with the murder of Mary Rogerson. On Nov. 5, he was charged with the murder of his wife as well. Ruxton's trial for his wife's murder began on Mar. 2, 1936. The prosecution included J.C. Jackson, K.C., Maxwell Fyfe, K.C., and Hartley Shawcross. Ruxton was defended by Norman Birkett, K.C., and Phillip Kershaw. Evidence in the trial was largely dependent upon the expert testimony of forensic pathologists who had examined the remains. It was discovered when the bodies were reconstructed that all identifying characteristics had been re-

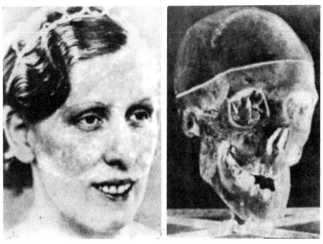

Mrs. Buck Ruxton and her reconstructed skull proved her husband a murderer.

moved. Despite the difficulty this introduced into building a clear-cut case against Ruxton, he was convicted of murder and after losing an attempt at an appeal was hanged at Strangeways Prison in Manchester on May 12, 1936.

Ryan, Bobbie, prom. 1978, U.S. In the days of the "swinging singles" bars, a secretary in Chicago's Loop, Bobbie Ryan, was picked up by Peter Hoban, a Democratic precinct captain. They went to his apartment and continued drinking until Hoban passed out. Ryan waited until she was sure he was unconscious. Then she stripped him of his clothes, explored the apartment, stole everything of value

she could find, and set fire to the apartment. The unconscious Hoban was burned to death. At the bar, people who had seen them leave together identified Bobbie Ryan. She was found Guilty of arson and murder and sentenced to twenty-two years in prison.

Ryan, Michael, 1960-87, Brit. "Dawn came like any other dawn, and by evening it just didn't seem the same day," said Margaret Thatcher, prime minister of England in August 1987, when England saw the worst massacre by an individual in the country's recent history.

Michael Ryan, a 27-year-old, frequently unemployed laborer in the small farming community of Hungerford, west of London, found his only real interest in life in his guns and his ability to shoot them well. To anyone who would listen, he would explain his collection of weapons—all properly licensed—and brag about his marksmanship. Ryan was a member of a rifle and pistol club where he frequently practiced. Gunplay seemed to be the only activity that lifted him out of the deep depression that had plagued him since his father's death in 1985.

On Aug. 19, 1987, Ryan, clad in a military flak jacket and carrying a belt of ammunition, walked through the Savernake Forest where he met a young mother picnicking with her two toddlers. He drew his 9-mm pistol, and shot her through the head. He went to his car and returned to the small house where he lived with his mother. He walked in, shot her, shot the family dog, and set fire to the house. Before leaving, he retrieved his AK-47 automatic assault rifle from the shed where it was stored.

Walking at a leisurely pace through Hungerford, Ryan fired the rifle at random. A motorist en route to the hospital to see his newborn son, a man walking his dog, an elderly immigrant working in his garden, and a woman and her daughter driving past fell victim. Ryan's ten-minute walk left sixteen dead and fourteen wounded.

Police erected roadblocks and a helicopter hovered in the air above. They cornered Ryan in the small elementary school he had attended as a child, and tried to reason with him. He told them nothing as he kept them at bay for several hours. Finally, seven hours after the two toddlers in the woods watched their mother die, a shot rang out from inside the school. Ryan had killed himself. Michael Ryan became his seventeenth victim and no one knew why.

S

Sach, Amelia, 1873-1903, and **Walters, Annie**, d.1903, Brit. Along with an accomplice, Annie Walters, Amelia Sach operated a home in London for unwed mothers. Sach ran advertisements offering their services before and during the birth stating the "baby can remain," leading the mothers to believe Sach and Walters would arrange for adoption.

In addition to paying the basic fees, unwary mothers who did not wish to keep their children were usually charged from £25 to £30 to arrange for adoption. The sad reality was that once the child was born and an "arrangement" agreed upon, Sach turned the baby over to Walters who would poison the infant and then dispose of the body. They would then split the fees.

For an unknown reason, in 1902 Walters took two of the children home with her where each of them unfortunately "died." Her landlord happened to be a policeman whose wife became suspicious when still a third child Walters brought home disappeared. Annie Walters told authorities a "boutful" woman in a coach took the children. Sach's role as "baby farmer" was revealed, and both women were tried and found Guilty of murder. They were hanged in January 1903 in Holloway Prison.

Salabarria, Mario, 1914- , Cuba. As the head of Havana's Police Investigation Bureau, Major Mario Salabarria, thirty-four, was a vain and jealous leader who felt threatened by the presence of the popular young war hero, 29-year-old Emilio Tro, who had fought with distinction on the side of the Loyalists during the Spanish Civil War. In 1947, Tro accused Salabarria's office of malfeasance and running a black market operation, a serious charge that compelled the major to seek an arrest warrant for Tro and his supporters.

With two carloads of armed men, Salabarria descended on Tro's residence in suburban Marianao in late September 1947. Without warning, the uniformed men strafed the house with a seemingly unending barrage of machine gunfire, killing Emilio Tro, four of the hero's supporters, and a pregnant woman. The killing was stopped by a tank crew and an armored personnel carrier. The atrocity had been filmed by army chief Genovevo Perez Damera who submitted it in court as evidence. A roundup of Salabarria partisans was ordered by President Ramon Grau San Martin, who attempted to placate the grieving Tro supporters.

On Mar. 8, 1948, a military court martial sentenced Salabarria to thirty years' imprisonment for murder, and a year for creating a public disorder. Ten other men who participated in the attack received varying terms of six months to twenty-five years.

Salvage, Arthur James Farraday, 1908- , Brit. On July 5, 1931, Arthur Salvage, a poultry farmer from Ruckinge, Kent, murdered an 11-year-old neighbor girl, Ivy Mary Godden, and then buried her in the woods. Salvage joined the search party which was unable to locate the remains of the child for two full days. On the third day Ivy's body was found in a shallow grave. A bloodhound was brought to the scene of the crime, and while Salvage amused himself in a game of cricket, the dog traced a path back to his residence in Sunningdale.

Salvage offered a hasty confession, and was brought before Justice MacNaghten at the Old Bailey the following September. A Guilty verdict was returned after Salvage had recanted his earlier confession on the grounds that the constables had made him certain guarantees. He was given the death sentence, but upon further examination by psychiatrists Salvage was declared insane. Under the terms of the Criminal Lunatics Act of 1884, he was committed to the Broadmoor Asylum for life. The murder might have been avoided if authorities had listened to earlier recommendations by doctors. Prison doctors recommended his committal after Salvage served time in prison for theft in 1927, but authorities released Salvage.

Samples, Duane, 1942- , U.S. Duane Samples was a seemingly normal college student in Salem, Ore., until he left school to serve in Vietnam. In 1975 he viciously attacked two women with a ten-inch knife. One of them died; the other, Diane Ross, narrowly escaped death.

Samples was convicted of murder and sentenced to life imprisonment at the Oregon State Penitentiary. In 1980, Governor Vic Atiyeh commuted the sentence to twenty years in prison after reviewing psychiatric reports that described Samples as suffering from a delayed-stress syndrome caused by his experiences in Vietnam, which compelled him to act out a lurid sexual fantasy involving violence and murder.

A year later, on Sept. 3, 1981, Governor Atiyeh rescinded his commutation order after hearing conflicting opinions about the original prognosis. A previously unpublished 1971 report alleged that Samples had beaten up a woman, which cast some doubts on his "delayed" stress syndrome. In May 1970, Samples had written a letter to his girlfriend, in which he discussed the ways and means of disemboweling women. Marion County district attorney Chris Van Dyke described Samples as a sexual sadist, and a danger to the community.

In his own defense, Samples pointed out that after he returned from Vietnam he had opened a clinic in Salem to help troubled youths. "No one can claim Vietnam takes away their responsibility for what they did, but there were some things in me not strong enough. I reacted poorly to that experience," he said.

Sanders, Lindberg, d.1983, U.S. Lindberg Sanders called himself the "black Jesus." He convinced nine people in the Hollywood section of Memphis, Tenn., that the end of the world was at hand. Sanders and his fellow cult members holed up in a house to await Armageddon. When it did not come, Sanders declared the Antichrist had arrived in its place.

The devil had manifested himself in the form of white policemen, he told his followers. On Jan. 7, 1983, the group placed a call to the police to complain about a purse snatcher. When patrolmen came to their house, the cultists opened fire, severely wounding another officer and Robert Hester, who was dragged into the house and tortured.

After a period of useless negotiations, police stormed the house on Jan. 12 when eavesdropping devices tipped them that Hester had been killed. Inside, they found the bodies of Sanders and his six remaining followers, some of them dead from apparent suicide.

Sangret, August, c.1913-43, Brit. A young woman, Joan Pearl Wolfe, who was living a gypsy-style existence near an army camp in Surrey, England, met and fell in love with August Sangret, a French-Canadian soldier stationed at the nearby camp at Godalming. Sangret helped Wolfe build shelters in the woods near his military post, where she lived and they met frequently as lovers. The wigwam-style huts and Sangret's American Indian heritage caused this case to be known as the "Wigwam Murder."

Wolfe became pregnant, and in September 1942 she insisted that Sangret marry her. He attacked and killed her and buried her body on a ridge in Hankley Common. Two soldiers walking in the vicinity several weeks later discovered the body. She had been stabbed repeatedly with a knife with a peculiar shaped blade and bludgeoned over the head. A log found nearby was determined to be one of the weapons, and a knife, eventually found in the drain of a washroom on the army base, was identified as the other weapon. Sangret, waiting to be interviewed early on in the investigation, had asked permission to go to the washroom and had probably hidden the knife in the drain at the time.

Sangret's clasp knife was missing and bloodstains were found on his clothing. He was found Guilty and was hanged at Wandsworth Prison on Apr. 2, 1943.

August Sangret and his American Indian lover Joan Wolfe, killed by Sangret in 1942.

Sarret, Georges (Georges Alexander Sarrejani), d.1934, and **Schmidt, Catherine** (AKA: Mageli Herbin), and **Schmidt, Philomena**, prom. 1934, Fr. Georges Sarret was a Greek born in Trieste, Italy, who emerged as France's most notorious criminal in the early 1930s. Answering to the name of "Sarret," he prepared for his murderous profession by studying chemistry, medicine and law at the university in Marseilles. Afterward, he selected two vulnerable women to act as confederates in his murder schemes.

Sisters Catherine Schmidt and Philomena Schmidt were suspected of carrying out acts of espionage on behalf of the German government during WWI. They had moved to France from their native Bavaria before the war, and had worked for a time as governesses for a prominent family. While in domestic service, they met the young lawyer Sarret.

After the war, the sisters remained in France, which proved to be a tragic mistake.

Threatened with exposure and arrest, the wily Sarret blackmailed them into marrying a succession of feeble, but wealthy old men. After the ceremonies had been duly performed, Sarret saw to it that the men died premature deaths and that the insurance money wound up in his pocket. The killings continued for some time, and nobody was the wiser. Then Catherine insured herself for the sum of a million francs, taking on the identity of Mageli Herbin who soon died of pneumonia. The insurance companies became suspicious and began investigating Sarret.

A pit of decomposed animal remains that had been saturated with acid was found in the garden of a home that Sarret had rented in Marseilles. Then Sarret made the mistake of doing away with Louis Chambon, a defrocked priest who had acted as a third accomplice to Sarret's many crimes. Chambon and his mistress, Noemie Ballandraux, were shot and the bodies disposed of in a vat of sulfuric acid. Catherine finally confessed to police her knowledge of Sarret's gruesome deed. He was arrested and condemned to die on the guillotine following a lengthy trial in October 1933. The Schmidt sisters each received ten years' hard labor.

The execution was carried out at Aix-en-Provence in April 1934 after some trepidation on the part of Anatole Joseph Deibler, France's notorious master of the guillotine who presided over 300 beheadings. This time, the blade was slow to fall. "Imbeciles!" yelled Sarret, "Be quick can't you!" For ten minutes the condemned man's head rested on the block while Deibler tried to correct the problem. Finally it was done, and the village square was quickly hosed down so the blood would not offend breakfasters.

Saunders, Raymond, prom. 1929, U.S. Elliott Howe of the Virginia State Police was faced with a 16-year-old murder in July 1945 when he was called to investigate the discovery of a skeleton found in an abandoned well near Alexandria, Va. Scattered around the bones were bits of clothing and jewelry. The body was turned over to the coroner who, after calling upon several experts, was able to determine the sex, height, shoe size, and even hat size of the victim. Surmising that a piece of khaki cloth and a button found with the body were military in origin, he checked with the Marine base at Quantico. Their records, along with a dental chart of the skull, identified the remains as those of a missing ex-marine, Brad J. Ellison, who had disappeared sixteen years earlier.

Howe then checked local Quantico police records and found that a police officer, Sergeant Richard Duvall, since deceased, had investigated Ellison's disappearance and suspected two local men of killing Ellison but had lacked the evidence to act. Interviewing neighbors in the area, Howe learned that Ellison had moved in with Frenchy Carney, a local bootlegger, and soon started an affair with Carney's wife, Effie.

Frenchy had later been murdered, but Howe was able to locate Effie Carney. She admitted the relationship with Ellison and that Frenchy had become enraged when she informed him that she was planning to leave him for Ellison and Frenchy had offered $500 to anyone who would kill the latest suitor of his woman. Ellison had moved in with two local fellows named Dooley Dent and Raymond "Scissors" Saunders.

Howe located a man named Robert B. Leitch, a local tramp, who had lived in the area in 1929 and knew all about Ellison's disappearance. He said that he had seen Saunders the day after with a cut on his head. Saunders had said that "he had knocked hell out of Ellison and put him where he wouldn't bother anybody else."

Working on these leads, Howe finally located Scissors Saunders, by then an alcoholic, and arrested him. Saunders was tried for murder on Nov. 25, 1945, and found Guilty. He was sent to prison.

Schaefer, Gerard, prom. 1968-72, U.S. Gerard Schaefer was a serial killer who deceived a number of young Florida girls into accepting rides in his car. Then, he would take them to a secluded spot, usually on Hutchinson's Island near Fort Lauderdale, where he would fashion a noose and tie it to the limb of a tree. Schaefer enjoyed watching his victims expire by the rope. Afterward, he would collect personal artifacts of clothing or jewelry and store them in a trunk at his mother's home. After each murder, Schaefer chronicled his exploits in a diary.

Schaefer began his killing spree a year after his graduation from Florida Atlantic University. His real ambition was to become a police officer, a goal he realized by becoming deputy sheriff of Martin County. Because there were so many teenage runaways, the local police did not bother following up every missing person's report. Schaefer covered his tracks well, and had diverted suspicion from himself by virtue of his position in the police department. In September 1973, however, he made his first mistake. He picked up a girl named Susan Place at her home and then drove off. Worried about her daughter dating a man ten years her senior, Mrs. Place carefully noted the man's appearance and license plate number.

A month passed, and by this time Schaefer had gotten himself arrested on a charge of abduction. Mrs. Place came forward to identify not only Gerard Schaefer, but his Datsun automobile in which she had last seen her daughter. The remains of Susan Place and her friend Georgia Jessup were found in a desolate location on Hutchinson's Island. Doctors decided that Schaefer was sane and he stood trial. Gregarious and outgoing with the press, he became a media darling at his 1972 trial, which masked the darker crimes he was suspected of committing. Police theorized that he was responsible for as many as twenty murders in south central Florida. Schaefer was found Guilty of the Place-Jessup murders and was sentenced to two life terms, to be served concurrently at the Avon Park Correctional Institute in St. Lucie County.

Police photo of deputy sheriff and serial murderer Gerard Schaefer.

Schaft, Hannie, c.1921-45, Neth. In 1945, Hannie Schaft became a martyr of the Dutch resistance movement. After her boyfriend's death, and the imprisonment of her parents at the hands of the Nazis, Schaft engaged in guerrilla tactics against the German occupiers of Holland. She was arrested for murder after pushing a German officer into an Amsterdam canal. She was taken prisoner and locked in a cell with the sign "murderess" tacked on the door. Following a relentless interrogation, Schaft, twenty-four, was taken to the dunes near Haarlem and shot.

Schmid, Charles Howard, Jr. (AKA: **Smitty**), 1942- , and **Saunders, John**, prom. 1964, U.S. Charles Schmid, five feet, three inches tall, was bothered by his short stature. To improve his image, he became a devoted gymnast, winning a state championship in high school. Uncomfortable with his peers in his twenties, he enchanted teenagers in Tucson, Ariz., with fantastic tales. "Smitty" Schmid's fantasies turned to terrible reality in the spring of 1964. Schmid's teenage friends apparently knew when their hero had turned to murder, but they revealed their secret to no one.

Smitty's main female devotee was Mary Rae French, an 18-year-old who worked at his mother's nursing home and turned most of her pay over to him. She never minded when he used his small cottage for orgies, and she often joined in. On the evening of May 31, French, Smitty, and a friend, John Saunders, were talking about Smitty's exploits with girls, when he suddenly announced, "I want to kill a girl...I think I can get away with it." French suggested as their victim 15-year-old Alleen Rowe, whom she knew would be alone because her mother worked late. French

Convicted murderers John Saunders and Charles Schmid.

called the girl and got her to agree to sneak out of her house and meet the threesome.

They drove into the desert where French stayed in the car while the men took Alleen off into the shadows and raped her. Then they killed the girl by bashing in her head with rocks. French and the men dug a shallow grave and buried her. Everyone who knew Alleen Rowe was soon questioned about her disappearance. Schmid said in puzzled tones that he was supposed to have met her that night but that she was not home when he arrived.

Schmid soon started dating 17-year-old Gretchen Fritz, whose wildness seemed to match his own. Schmid was furious, though, when the doctor's daughter told him that she had "gone all the way" with a boy in California. "I really loved that girl! I'll kill her!" he told a friend. On Aug. 16, 1965, Gretchen and her 13-year-old sister, Wendy Fritz, went to a drive-in movie. Schmid met them, enticed them out to the desert, and killed both girls, leaving their bodies along an unfrequented road. He afterward bragged to his friend Richard Bruns that he had killed the two sisters. The two returned to the desert and buried the already-decomposing bodies.

Friends of the Fritzes hired some "Mafia types" to investigate their daughters' disappearances. The men, hearing Schmid's story that the girls had run away to San

Diego, insisted that he go with them to hunt for the girls. Schmid stayed there several months, until he was arrested for impersonating an FBI agent questioning girls on the beach.

Although the police suspected Schmid, they had no direct evidence, and the teenagers who had heard Schmid bragging delighted in protecting their hero. However, Schmid began to crack under the pressure of his murders. He once drove his fist through the wall of his small cottage, then ran outside shouting, "God is going to punish me!" Bruns became apprehensive, then terrified with the thought that Schmid would attack Bruns's girlfriend, Kathy Morath, who had previously been enamored of Schmid. With that possibility preying on his mind, Bruns went to visit his grandmother in Ohio, and from there called the Tucson police and told them everything he knew.

On Nov. 11, 1965, Schmid was arrested for the murders of the Fritz sisters and Alleen Rowe. John Saunders was

Mary French, who, with Saunders and Schmid, killed three teenagers.

arrested for abetting the murder of Rowe. He turned state's evidence against Schmid who was found Guilty and sentenced to death, though the punishment was never carried out because of the 1971 U.S. Supreme Court decision banning capital punishment. Saunders received a sentence of life in prison, and French was sentenced to four to five years. Schmid was later tried for the murder of Rowe. He was convicted and received an additional fifty-five-year sentence on top of his life sentence.

Held in the Arizona State Prison, Schmid escaped on Nov. 11, 1972, along with Raymond Hudgens, a convicted three-time killer. Schmid and Hudgens held four people hostage on a ranch near Tempe, Ariz., before deciding to separate. Both were caught again within days and returned to prison.

Schmidt, Hans (AKA: **Dr. Emil Moliere; George Miller; A. Van Dyke**), 1881-1916, U.S. On the morning of Sept. 5, 1913, a woman spotted a parcel floating in the Hudson River near an abandoned dock on the New Jersey side. The parcel was fished out and unwrapped, revealing the upper torso of a woman's body. The police investigated and discounted several false identifications of the corpse. Then, on Sept. 7, the lower part of the torso washed ashore near Weehawken. Still coming up empty-handed after exhausting other leads, the police pursued a slim clue. The distinctive, hand-crafted pillowcase in which the upper torso had been wrapped bore the name of its manufacturer, the Robinson-Rodgers Company of Newark, N.J. When police inquired at the firm, they found that only a small quantity of the cases had been produced, and the manufacturer, therefore, was able to send them to the sole distributor. The distributor, located in New York City, had sold only two pillowcases and still had the receipt for the sale.

Along with several other household items, the pillowcases had been delivered to an apartment at 68 Bradhurst Avenue rented by a Hans Schmidt. Schmidt, who was the assistant pastor of St. Joseph's Church on West 125th Street, claimed that he had rented and furnished the apartment for a relative, a young woman soon to be married. After watching the apartment for several days and growing suspicious when no one came or went, the police broke in and found considerable evidence that a murder had been committed on the premises. In addition to bloodstains on the bedroom wall and on the floor, police found a newly sharpened butcher knife and saw. Except for a man's coat marked with the name A. Van Dyke, the only clothes in the apartment belonged to a woman. A stack of letters addressed to Anna Aumuller led police to the rectory of St. Boniface Church on 47th Street and Second Avenue where the woman had apparently worked as a housekeeper. There, police gathered information which began to tie the case together. The pastor of St. Boniface said that Aumuller had indeed worked for him for a brief period in 1912. During that time, the pastor informed police investigators, he became suspicious that Aumuller was becoming romantically involved with one of his parish priests, Father Hans Schmidt.

Anna Hirt, a woman who had worked at the St. Boniface rectory with Aumuller, told police she remembered a distinctive birthmark on Aumuller's chest. Police had Hirt view the body, which in fact bore a mark similar to the one she had described. Although unorthodox, the identification was accepted by police. Now armed with a positive identification, the police approached Schmidt at St. Joseph's and questioned him about the crime. Schmidt did not confess immediately although he did display great anxiety. However, when police began to press him with specific details of the murder, Schmidt broke down and admitted killing Aumuller, claiming he had done so "because he loved her." Police thwarted an attempt by Schmidt to kill himself with a razor he had concealed on his person and took him into custody. After his initial confession, Schmidt freely discussed the murder with police. He and Aumuller had obtained a marriage license, and he had performed a ceremony that they both apparently considered a valid marriage. Schmidt said he decided to kill Aumuller on Aug. 31. The only reason he gave for the decision was his love for her, saying that "sacrifices should be consummated in blood." Although it was never proved, evidence uncovered later caused police to suspect that Schmidt's decision to murder his "wife" came when he learned she was pregnant.

Schmidt told police in detail how he had gone to the apartment at night and entered quietly. He turned on only the bathroom light so as not to awaken the sleeping woman. With a butcher knife he had purchased several days earlier, he cut her throat as she slept. In a detailed confession Schmidt gave to police inspector Faurot, he said he then put Aumuller's body in the bathtub and began dismembering it. When questioned about the precision with which the body had been mutilated, Schmidt told Faurot that he had once studied surgery in his native Germany. After dismembering and decapitating the body and cutting the torso in two, Schmidt wrapped the body parts in linens from the apartment, weighted them with rocks, and, in what he recalled to be four or five trips, took them across town to the Fort Lee ferry and dropped them into the river. He also attempted to destroy other evidence of the murder by scrubbing the bloodstained carpet and wall and burning the bloody mattress in a nearby vacant lot.

As word of Schmidt's confession spread, his superiors in the church hinted that Schmidt was an impostor and perhaps had never been ordained. Responses to police inquiries from officials in Schmidt's hometown of Aschaffenburg, Ger., and from church officials in Mainz where Schmidt claimed he was ordained in 1904, confirmed much of what Schmidt had told police. He was born in Aschaffenburg in 1881 and was educated there and in Mayence. He entered the seminary at Mayence on the wishes of his extremely religious mother. Schmidt's own preference for a more secular life was borne out by his fellow seminarians' reports that he led a "notoriously dissolute" life while at the seminary. Shortly before Schmidt was ordained at the age of twenty-four, he forged the documents required for a doctorate and received that title following his ordination. Schmidt used his skills as a forger to produce similar documents for other young priests who wanted titles they had not legitimately earned. In 1907, Catholic authorities who had learned of his "moonlighting" as a forger, deprived Schmidt of his rights as a priest.

In 1909, Schmidt had been arrested for fraud but he had escaped imprisonment on the grounds of insanity. (Further investigation revealed that numerous cases of insanity appeared in Schmidt's ancestry.) As soon as he was able

to obtain his release, Schmidt emigrated to the U.S., where he used his prowess as a forger to obtain an assignment as the temporary pastor of St. Francis Church in Trenton, N.J. From the Trenton parish, Schmidt moved to St. Boniface where he met Aumuller.

During his confession, Schmidt told police that he had frequently posed as a physician under various names, and a search of his room uncovered evidence indicating that he was interested in the sale of substances particular to criminal medical practice. Police also found 500 business cards bearing the inscription: "Dr. Emil Moliere, formerly Assistant Surgeon of the Municipal Women's Hospital, Paris, France. Representative of the Chemical Hygiene Manufacturing Company." Schmidt told Faurot that he had used the name of Dr. Emil Moliere (Moliere being his mother's maiden name) frequently when masquerading as a physician. Also found in Schmidt's room were certificates of stock in companies manufacturing patent medicines.

The already amazing breadth of Schmidt's criminal activity took another leap when receipts police found in his apartment led them to a counterfeiting plant in an apartment on West 134th Street in New York City. In the apartment, rented by Schmidt under the alias of George Miller, police found color printing presses, engraving plates, and cameras. They also found a stack of partially printed ten dollar bills and an unused set of twenty dollar plates. The building superintendent gave police a description of Schmidt's accomplice in the counterfeiting operation that led them to Dr. Ernest Arthur Muret.

Muret, whom police discovered had been practicing dentistry without a license, denied any complicity in the counterfeiting operation. Police learned that Muret had fled England in April 1911 rather that face charges of falsely representing himself as a medical man under the name of Dr. Ernest Stein. Inspector Faurot noted a strong physical resemblance between the two men and began to suspect that they were brothers, a fact which both vehemently denied. However, investigation into the matter revealed that Muret was most likely Adolph Mueller, Schmidt's cousin. Muret was arrested and, along with Schmidt, was charged with counterfeiting.

A continuing police investigation uncovered other evidence suggesting the two men had been jointly engaged in criminal activities. Muret also had apparently used the aliases of Emil Moliere and George Miller, as indicated by business cards and receipts found in his apartment. Schmidt accepted sole responsibility for both the murder and the counterfeiting operation. He told police that he intended to use the counterfeited money to help the poor and unfortunate. When police found forged blank death certificates among his belongings, Schmidt admitted that he had intended to continue murdering people and would have used the certificates to more easily dispose of the bodies. He claimed to believe in euthanasia and intended to put suffering people out of their misery.

Because Schmidt refused to implicate Muret, police were only able to charge him with illegal possession of a firearm. On Sept. 19, a coroner's jury found Hans Schmidt Guilty of the murder of Anna Aumuller. Schmidt was sentenced to die in the electric chair, a fate he said he welcomed. He was electrocuted at Sing Sing in Ossining, N.Y., on Feb. 18, 1916.

Schmidt, Helmuth (AKA: **American Bluebeard; Herman Neugebauer; Carl Ulrich; F. Helmuth; C. Hamann**), d.1918, U.S. Known in the press as the "American Bluebeard," Helmuth Schmidt preyed upon poor immigrant German girls employed as domestic servants. In the years before WWI, Schmidt took out newspaper ads in Missouri, New York, Lakewood, N.J., and Royal Oak, Mich., looking for a "suitable lady to marry soon." The lonely hearts lure attracted several young women seeking to better themselves with the presumably wealthy man. Using various aliases, Schmidt would invite the women to his residence, murder them for what little money they had, and bury the remains under cement.

Schmidt carried out these grisly crimes in New York and Michigan. After moving to Royal Oak, he went to work in a Ford plant outside Detroit. While in Ford's employ, he was arrested for the murder of 38-year-old Augusta Steinbach, who had answered his ad in the New York *Herald.* The police were tipped off by her companion Agnes Dominicki who had immigrated with Steinbach from Europe eleven years earlier.

Schmidt was taken into custody on Apr. 23, 1918, after blood-soaked clothing was found under his porch. Before Schmidt could provide an estimate of just how many women he had lured to their deaths, he killed himself in his prison cell by pulling a heavy iron bed railing down on himself, crushing his skull.

Schmidt, Patricia (AKA: **La Satira**), 1926- , U.S. Patricia Schmidt, an exotic dancer from Toledo, Ohio, used the stage name La Satira. She was touring the Caribbean with five other strippers in 1947 when she abruptly cut short her engagements to rendezvous with John Lester Mee, a philandering former PT boat commander whose long-suffering wife kept house in a posh lakefront suburb of Wilmette, Ill.

Mee had been expelled from Northwestern University in 1933, and then practiced law and learned Spanish, French, and Italian. After their discharge from active combat duty in WWII, Mee and his friend Charles Jackson bought a 75-foot yacht for $750 at a war assets sale. They outfitted the craft for a winter cruise and christened it *La Tirana,* the stage name of one of Mee's numerous girl-friends.

In Panama, Mee and Jackson met Patricia Schmidt during one of her performances. Mee's romance with her had begun in Chicago nearly a year earlier. The men invited Schmidt to join them aboard the yacht, and the three sailed to Havana harbor.

In honor of Patricia Schmidt, the *La Tirana* was re-christened *La Satira.* Jackson moved out of the cabin and Schmidt settled in. It was not until then that Schmidt discovered that Mee was married. During an early morning quarrel on Apr. 8, 1947, Mee ordered Schmidt off the yacht in a threatening manner. Fearing the worst, Schmidt pulled a .22-caliber handgun from the cabin drawer and fired it wildly, shooting Mee in the head. "Then I rushed to Jack's side," she later recalled. Moaning in pain, Mee said to her, "Kill yourself. I'm going to die and I want you to die in my arms."

Jackson then burst into the cabin and seized the gun from Schmidt's hand just as she was about to carry out Mee's request. Jack Mee was taken to the hospital where he hovered near death for the next five days. When his father arrived from Chicago, Patricia Schmidt was identified as the assailant and Cuban police arrested her. Until that time she had posed as Mee's wife so she could stay at his bedside. With Dr. Mee present, Jack finally named La Satira as the one who pulled the trigger.

On Apr. 13, two weeks before he was scheduled to meet his wife in Florida, John Mee died. Patricia Schmidt was charged with homicide on Apr. 15, 1947, and held without bond by order of Judge Santiago Mencia. Her story touched Cuban hotel magnate Amleto Battisti, who paid her legal expenses. Schmidt maintained throughout her long ordeal that the shooting was accidental.

The trial dragged on for nearly eight months. On Dec. 16, 1947, Jackson was acquitted of being an accessory to murder. A week later, on Dec. 22, 1947, Schmidt received fifteen years imprisonment and was assessed a $5,000 fine to be paid to the family of John Mee. Patricia Schmidt remained in the Guanabacoa Woman's Prison until Oct. 7, 1948, when President Ramon Grau San Martin issued a formal pardon.

Schnick, James Eugene, 1951- , U.S. At first, police investigators believed that 14-year-old Kirk Buckner killed seven members of his family and himself in Elkland, Mo., on Sept. 25, 1987. The family's financial hardships troubled Kirk, a sophomore at Marshfield Junior High School.

Shortly before dawn on Sept. 25, a man armed with a .22-caliber pistol shot and killed 8-year-old Dennis Buckner, and his brothers Timothy and Michael, ages seven and two, as they slept in their bedroom. Outside the farmhouse, the gunman killed the parents, Steven Buckner, thirty-five, and his wife Jan, thirty-six. Then he drove to a dairy farm owned by Kirk's aunt Julie Schnick and her husband James Schnick. According to James Schnick, Kirk shot and killed Julie, and before Kirk was able to murder James Schnick, he was hit by an errant bullet during the struggle.

At first police had no reason to doubt Schnick's story. He had suffered severe abdominal wounds during the struggle, and his wife was dead. It seemed like an open and shut case of a troubled teenager on a rampage, until the facts came to light. "Some other evidence surfaced after investigators for the Missouri Highway Patrol were called in, and one lead led to another, and they all had to be followed up," explained Bill Bowers, an officer for the sheriff's department. The murder weapon was found in the dead boy's right hand. Kirk Buckner was left-handed.

On Oct. 5, 1987, James Schnick, a man with no prior criminal record, was arrested by local police and charged with seven counts of first-degree murder. His confession was videotaped at Missouri State Highway Patrol head-quarters.

Six months later, on Apr. 14, 1988, Schnick was convicted. Judge John Parrish imposed the death sentence. Schnick joined fifty-nine other inmates awaiting execution in Missouri. Pending compulsory Supreme Court review, he remains on Death Row.

Schreuder, Frances Bernice, 1939- , and **Schreuder, Marc Francis**, 1961- , U.S. On July 13, 1978, millionaire Franklin Bradshaw, seventy-six, was shot to death in his Salt Lake City, Utah, car parts warehouse. Four years later, his daughter, Frances Bernice Schreuder, was arrested and charged with persuading her then 17-year-old son, Marc Francis Schreuder, to murder his grandfather before the man could cut them out of his will and his estate, estimated at $10.4 million. Marc Schreuder was arrested on Oct. 26, 1981, in Manhattan. His grand-mother posted $100,000 bail which he forfeited in early March 1981, when the young man failed to show up for a lineup scheduled by his attorneys. He was arrested again two weeks later. By the end of April 1982, Frances Schreuder was released on a $500,000 bail.

During a two week non-jury trial, heard by Third Judicial District Court Judge James S. Sawaya, psychiatrists gave conflicting testimony. Dr. Louis G. Moench, University of Utah psychiatrist, painted Marc Schreuder as having an "extremely pathological" relationship with his mother, but Dr. Lee Stewart Coleman contended that psychiatrists had no better tools for assessing a criminal's state of mind than did laymen. On July 7, Marc Schreuder was found Guilty of second-degree murder and was given the maximum sentence of five years to life at the Utah State Prison and was fined $10,000.

Frances Schreuder's trial began in Salt Lake City on Sept. 20, 1983, before Judge James F. Baldwin. Her son testified that he had shot his grandfather because "my mother asked me to" so that she could inherit a great deal of money very quickly. A week later, on Sept. 27, the jury found Frances Schreuder Guilty of first-degree murder. Prosecutor Ernie Jones sought the death penalty, but Judge Baldwin decided that Schreuder would not be sentenced to death. On Nov. 18, 1984, the New York *Times* reported that Schreuder had been moved from Utah State Prison because she was suffering from "culture shock."

In December 1988, a New York State Supreme Court reversed a libel ruling against author Shana Alexander, who had written *Nutcracker: Money, Madness, Murder—A Family Album,* about the Schreuder case. New York psychologist Dr. Herman Weiner had sued because Alexander claimed that Weiner had an intimate affair with Frances Schreuder. Alexander's disclaimer at the beginning of her book said that many of her accounts were from family members who should not be considered "the best sources in any cir-cumstances." The court ruled that this statement gave the author additional leeway that discounted Weiner's defama-tion claim.

Schuetz, Hans, 1933- , Ger. An unemployed house painter on his way to France to look for work murdered 48-year-old Erna Riedel and her 20-year-old daughter Heidrun inside their home in Darmstsdt, W. Ger., on Apr. 19, 1967. Hans Schuetz later told police that he was desperate for sex, and he could not afford to pay a prostitute.

Schuetz had been hired to do some work in the house. Believing that there was sufficient interest on Mrs. Riedel's part, he propositioned her. When she resisted, he bludg-eoned her to death, and then attacked her daughter up-stairs. Arriving on the scene, the police concluded that the motive was sex. The killer had undressed the women after slaying them. Several suspects were arrested, but the trail led back to Schuetz, who had withdrawn fifty marks from the Riedel savings account the day of the murder. Interpol agents located the suspect in Paris where he was working as a laborer. Schuetz was arrested and brought back to Germany where he issued a guarded confession, saying only that "he lost his head" when Mrs. Riedel brushed against him in the cellar.

On the strength of this statement, coupled with the discovery of bloodstained clothing at his home, Hans Schuetz was convicted of murder and sentenced to life imprisonment on Oct. 13, 1968.

Schultz, Raymond T., 1939-77, U.S. After the suicide death of American Nazi Party (ANP) member Raymond Schultz in a police squad car on May 22, 1977, investigators sifted through a tangled web of evidence found in his Calumet City, Ill., home, including Nazi propaganda, human restraint devices, pornography, and what appeared to be a secret torture chamber.

The bizarre aspects of Schultz's private life became a matter of public concern following the cyanide murder of 63-year-old Sydney Cohen on May 22. The elderly Jewish man was murdered by the fanatical Schultz at Cohen's home in Flossmoor. Cohen's son Jeffrey discovered the body of his father on the floor, and he also found Schultz lying unconscious several feet away. Suburban Flossmoor police arrived on the scene to take Schultz away, but in the squad car the killer sniffed a vial of lethal cyanide and died instantly. An autopsy conducted on Cohen showed that his death was also caused by cyanide poisoning.

Schultz's ties to right-wing hate mongers, and white supremacist groups dated back to 1962 when he was arrested for demonstrating against the showing of Soviet travel films at a Chicago hotel. At the time he listed his address as the ANP headquarters. He remained out of the news for the next fifteen years, but operated two Chicago bookstores that were ANP fronts. It was later learned that Schultz had harassed a number of Chicago-area Jews and prepared what appeared to be a "hit list" of potential murder victims. What puzzled investigators was the source of Schultz's income. The 38-year-old drill press operator owned three buildings and had traveled extensively through Third World countries. There was strong evidence to suggest that Schultz may have been involved in a series of unsolved Detroit child murders. A note found in his residence read: "With the help of God and A.H., I can get it done by July 1." The police believed the "A.H." in question here was Adolf Hitler.

Schulz, Duane Allan, 1959- , U.S. After he had

murdered his girlfriend Teresa Kaminski in a jealous rage, Duane Schulz of Bridgeview, Ill., claimed he felt great remorse. While her body lay in state, Schulz slipped into the funeral home undetected in order to place a rose and a note on the registry. It read: "Very much love to my love Teresa from Duane Allan Schulz."

Schulz strangled Kaminski in his home on Feb. 15, 1981, after the 19-year-old girl expressed her intentions to end their relationship. He then dumped the body in a wooded section of Willow Springs Cemetery, in South Suburban Chicago where it was discovered six days later. The police identified Schulz as the killer through the flower, the note, and a discredited alibi. He claimed to have been involved in a tavern fight the day that Kaminski was killed, but the tavern was not open on the night in question.

On May 19, 1984, Criminal Court Judge James M. Bailey sentenced Schulz to forty years in prison. In his remarks to the court, Judge Bailey described the defendant as "smug" and "remorseless."

Schwartz, Charles Henry (Leon Henry Schwartzhof, AKA: **John Doe Stein; Harold Warren**), 1887-1925, U.S. For ten emotionally charged days in the summer of 1925 residents of San Francisco followed the progress of a bizarre murder mystery that was eventually solved by reason, logic, and the resources of modern science.

For several months Bay Area newspapers had been providing considerable coverage to the newly formed Pacific Cellulose Company, the brainchild of Charles Henry Schwartz, an Alsatian chemist born Leon Henry Schwartzhof in Colmar, Fr. After attaining his Ph.D. in chemistry from the University of Heidelberg and various other academic honors, Schwartzhof enlisted in the French Army and was detailed to Algiers where he served in the Red Cross. After completing his military service Schwartzhof (who had shortened his name by this time), settled in Derby, England, went to work for a large textile company and married a young widow named Alice Orchard Warren. For medical reasons the couple emigrated to the U.S., choosing the Bay Area as their new home.

In 1921 Schwartz was hired as a chemist for the California Fibre Company of Berkeley, where he was accused of pilfering 1,800 pounds of scrap iron and a bottling machine. After he threatened the life of a fellow employee, authorities seized his .25-caliber handgun. Schwartz became a familiar figure at the Berkeley police station, advising Chief August Vollmer about police matters. Although dismissed as a harmless eccentric by the police department, financial speculators honestly believed that Schwartz had stumbled on to something when he announced the opening of Pacific

Cellulose, a company which would revolutionize the manufacture of artificial silk from wood fibre. Schwartz's imposing two story factory in Walnut Creek was constructed in great haste with money provided by his wife. The founder shunned all publicity. The only thing he would say about his mysterious process was that he would churn out silk at half the price of other cellulose-spun fabrics. It seemed almost too good to be true.

The inventor's grandiose plans came to an abrupt end on July 30, 1925, when the Walnut Creek factory was rocked by a devastating explosion. By the time the fire department arrived, the building was nearly consumed in flames. Groping firefighters were repelled by a noxious yellow gas as they searched for survivors. The charred remains of a man were pulled from the rubble. Walter Gonzales, an employee of Pacific Cellulose, identified the corpse as that of his employer, Leon Schwartz. "Why, I left him alone here in this room only a little while ago," Gonzales said. "He was working on an experiment and asked me to leave him because he wanted to work alone."

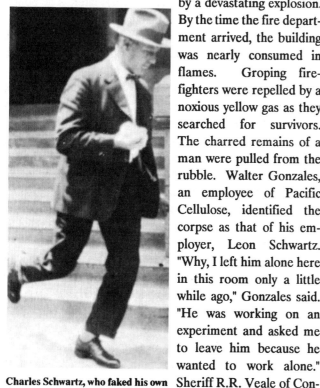

Charles Schwartz, who faked his own death, but later killed himself.

Sheriff R.R. Veale of Contra Costa County went through the building and found nothing to suggest that the explosion was anything other than an industrial accident caused by improperly mixed chemicals. After a preliminary investigation Deputy District Attorney James F. Hoey came to a different opinion. The body found in the factory had been lying neatly on a blanket sandwiched between two benches, an unlikely position after a huge explosion. Sheriff Veale learned that Schwartz had insured his life for $185,000 in the event of accidental death. And finally insurance investigators who examined the corpse found that it was three inches taller than the height Schwartz listed on his policy.

Alice Schwartz demanded that the police allow her to bury the remains of her husband, but Veale stalled as he tried to locate experts to establish positive identification. Dr. Alfred Ruedy, the family physician, positively identified the body as that of Schwartz. In his report the coroner stated that an upper molar was missing from the victim.

Schwartz's dentist claimed he had removed the tooth just recently. In light of these contradictions, Veale chose to bring an expert into the case. He hired Berkeley criminologist Edward Oscar Heinrich to conduct an investigation.

Heinrich compared hair samples taken from Schwartz's brush with that of the dead man, and determined that they were different. Heinrich examined the cavity in the dead man's mouth and determined the tooth had been knocked out by a chisel, not removed by a dentist. Heinrich determined that the man had been murdered—struck on the back of the head with a blunt instrument. He also deduced that the killer made every effort to have the body identified as that of Schwartz—even to knocking out a tooth that was missing in Schwartz's mouth.

Searching through the debris of the burned-out factory the criminologist found faint reddish blood-stains on the walls. Heinrich determined that the yellow gas was carbon disulfide, a highly flammable chemical that would burn through the lungs of the victim if inhaled for a short period of time. Because there was no trace of this substance in the dead man's lungs Heinrich realized the man was murdered before the explosion. Apparently Schwartz had ignited the fire from the outside. The flames ran toward a pool of liquid surrounding the body. "By tracing the flames on the floor I found that the fire had not started in one place but in five different places," Heinrich said. "There was no evidence of a broken chemical tube which would have suggested the likelihood of an accident." The incendiary liquid had been sprinkled over the outer door in order to permit the murderer to escape. Because of Heinrich's methodical work, a murder indictment was secured by District Attorney A.B. Tinning.

While detectives in Northern California looked for Schwartz, possibly in the company of a manicurist named Elizabeth Adam, Heinrich attempted to identify the victim. Among the items pulled out of the laboratory were several charred newspaper fragments and a portion of a letter. Under strong glasses and with the aid of certain chemical processes Heinrich found these were religious tracts, one a passage from St. John. Cecil Barker, an undertaker from Placerville, Calif., saw an excerpt from the letters in a newspaper and recognized the handwriting instantly as that of Gilbert Warren Barbe, a traveling missionary. Barbe, a self-styled chemistry buff, had answered Schwartz's newspaper placement for a lab assistant and had not been seen or heard from since he answered the ad.

The final piece of the puzzle fell into place on Aug. 10. An Oakland resident named N.B. Edmunds opened his Sunday *Tribune* and saw a remarkable likeness of a man he knew as "Harold Warren." Edmunds telephoned Berkeley police to advise Captain Clarence Lee the suspect was living in an apartment building on Forty First Street in Oakland.

Captain Lee, accompanied by building manager C.W. Heywood and Edmunds, battered down the door of the apartment when Warren refused to answer. They found Schwartz lying dead on the floor, clutching a pistol. A suicide note found nearby revealed that Schwartz had killed Barbe in what he described as an act of "self-defense." "He attacked me," Schwartz wrote. "I gave him a blow on his head. He fell. I gave him another. Suddenly I knew he was dead. But I could not make up my mind to go to Bell (his attorney) and tell him." Instead, Schwartz decided to fake his own death and assume a new identity as Harold Warren. Police theorized that Schwartz's creditors were closing in on him and Elizabeth Adam was seeking $50,000 in damages for "alienation of affections." Whatever the actual truth, Schwartz's perfect crime failed and his real motives went to the grave with him.

Schweitzer, William (AKA: **James Taylor**), prom. 1928-35, and **Jackson, Florence**, prom. 1935, and **Jackson, Loretta**, prom. 1935, and **Miller, Jean**, 1914- , U.S. Howard Carter Dickinson, on business in Detroit, met four new friends at the Book-Cadillac Hotel in June 1935. One, William Schweitzer, was an ex-convict with a lengthy record of robbery and attempted murder. On June 27, Schweitzer and his three female companions, Jean Miller, Loretta Jackson, and Florence Jackson, met Dickinson at the Detroiter Hotel. Schweitzer drove them around the city, until arriving at Rouge Park, where one of the Jackson sisters asked to be let out. The car continued down Joy Road, when two shots rang out. Schweitzer had killed Dickinson, taking the $125 in his wallet. The four headed to Chicago where Schweitzer spent the money on new clothes for the girls. Police caught up with them in a roadside hotel in Fort Wayne, Ind. Seven weeks after the murder, Schweitzer, the Jackson sisters, and Jean Miller were all sentenced to life imprisonment.

Schwindt, Werner, prom. 1975, Ger. Estranged from his daughter since her birth, Werner Schwindt picked up Margret Schwindt in Koellerbach, Ger., on Aug. 25, 1975, and raped the girl. Then Schwindt panicked and strangled her, leaving the body in an open field in Pforzheim, where it was found a short time later. On Sept. 4, he attempted suicide with sleeping pills. The incestuous killer was discovered lying on a park bench and was revived by physicians.

With his full confession to the heinous crime, Schwindt was found Guilty of murder and was sentenced to serve a term of life in prison.

Scieri, Antoinette, prom. 1916-24, Fr. Antoinette Scieri was born in Italy but moved with her family to France when she was quite young. During WWI she volunteered for duty as a field nurse but far from an "angel of mercy," Nurse Scieri was actually a thief with her own specialized fraud. Scieri obtained the addresses of her patients and then wrote to their friends and relatives for money. Often the soldiers' families obliged and Scieri pocketed the money. After she stole an officer's paybook and requisitioned a 5,000 franc advance she was arrested and imprisoned in 1915.

A year later she married an Italian soldier named Salmon, but the marriage broke up when the man found out about his wife's extra-marital affairs. The ill-fated union produced two children, who lived with Scieri and her next boyfriend, a bully named Joseph Rossignol who beat her frequently. Despite their less than idyllic living arrangements, Rossignol and Scieri remained together and had one child before moving to St. Gilles in southern France in 1920. There, Rossignol took a job in the local vineyards and Scieri resumed working as a nurse.

In the next few years the tranquil country village was plagued by the mysterious deaths of some its leading citizens. An elderly woman named Drouard died on Dec. 11, 1924, while being cared for by Scieri. The doctor's prognosis was heart seizure. Two weeks later when Lachapelle died shortly after consuming a pork sandwich, the cause of death was listed as ptomaine poisoning. Two days later the woman's husband died. Having devised a seemingly foolproof system to deceive the authorities, Scieri decided to kill Rossignol. She served him a meal of poisoned mussels after one of his drunken outbursts and he died several hours later. Without pause, Scieri returned to caring for the sick and the elderly. Sixty-seven-year-old Marie Martin and her sister Madame Doyer were her next victims. "You must not worry about money," the nurse assured them. "My mission is to heal and help the sick. Fees mean nothing to me." Scieri served Martin a glass of poisoned coffee and watched her die. The sister survived only because she threw her coffee down the drain. "It tasted bitter," she said.

The last victim was the sickly wife of a St. Gilles man named Gouan-Criquet. After the 75-year-old woman passed away the husband contacted her physician, Dr. Clauzel, for an opinion. Before signing the death certificate Clauzel called in the police. The detectives searched the house and came up with a bottle containing a strange-looking green solution which chemical analysis proved to be Pyralion or acetate of lead—commonly used as a weed killer. The dosage used on Madame Gouan-Criquet was potent enough to kill 300 persons. When Rossignol's body was exhumed, traces of pyralion were also found in his system. Antoinette Scieri was arrested and charged with murder. She confessed to the crimes, but attempted to shift much of the blame to a neighbor Rosalie Gire. On Apr. 27, 1926, Scieri stood alone in the docket to answer the charges brought against her. "You have been called a monster," the judge said. "But that expression is not strong enough. You are debauched, you are possessed of all the vices. You are also a drunkard, vicious, and a hypocrite, and you have no shame. I do not believe judicial history contains the records of many criminals of your type." Scieri was sentenced to death but the courts later commuted the penalty to life imprisonment.

Scott, Leonard Ewing, prom. 1955, U.S. In 1949, Leonard Ewing Scott married Evelyn Scott, who had inherited a large amount of money from her four previous husbands. During this marriage, Scott's second, he wrote a handbook for women, *How to Fascinate Men,* a tome that made no money, and for which Scott never paid the printer's bill. On May 16, 1955, his wife sent him out to buy tooth powder; when he returned to their posh Bel Air home, Evelyn Scott was gone. He did not report her missing because, he explained, his hard-drinking spouse often behaved eccentrically. Friends who asked about the woman were told that she had gone to a sanitarium for treatment.

After ten months, police investigators searched the grounds of the Scotts' house, finding metal snaps from a woman's undergarment, false teeth, and eyeglasses buried in a nearby lot; they were identified as Evelyn Scott's. In the ten months since her disappearance, her husband had forged signatures to withdraw money from her bank accounts and safety deposit boxes. Indicted by a Los Angeles jury on thirteen counts of forgery, Scott was arrested in Detroit as he tried to buy a new car. Soon after, his case was reconsidered, and he was indicted for murder. Because there was evidence that the crime had been committed, although neither a murder weapon nor a body was ever found, Scott was found Guilty of murdering his wife in December 1955. Scott was sentenced to life imprisonment.

Scott, Ronald Allen, 1932-   , U.S. Cecelia Arthur, a 50-year-old housewife in East Toledo, Ohio, was a lonely woman who enjoyed socializing with the regulars at the beauty shop and pubs along Starr Avenue. A bartender recalled how Arthur often sat at the bar sipping Diet Coke and conversing about the news of the day with her other customers. Cecelia's husband Terry was an over-the-road truck driver whose work kept him away from home much of the time. During one of his prolonged absences, Arthur met Ronald Allen Scott, an unemployed home-improvements salesman at the local bar. Those who knew him recalled he was a member of the high school football team during its winning days. When Cecilia found out that he had nowhere to stay, she invited him to live at her home on Greenwood Avenue.

At first the arrangement worked out fine. Scott seemed to get along with Terry Arthur, and the rent money he paid for his room came in handy. But as time passed, Scott found it increasingly difficult to meet his obligations. After a full day of drinking at the tavern, he returned to the Arthur residence on Mar. 21, 1988. "I was highly intoxicated," Scott later told the police. "Cecelia started in on me about the rent money I owed." Then, according to sworn statements given to the police, Cecelia hit and kicked him. Scott reached for a .25-caliber pistol to "scare her." But she kept throwing his clothing and other items into the back yard. "That's when I raised the gun and shot her," he said.

Terry Arthur was driving his rig through Pennsylvania, and Scott knew that it was only a matter of time before he would be coming home. After brooding about the matter for a day, he decided to dismember the corpse and dispose of it in the Maumee River in Toledo. It took Scott nearly twenty-four hours to complete the gruesome task. On Mar. 24 he carried the body parts, stuffed into plastic trash bags, to an expressway overpass spanning the river. In full view of passing motorists, he dumped them over the side. The bags floated three miles downstream before three teenage boys found them and notified the police. Scott was taken into custody on Mar. 26 after the owner of the local beauty parlor became concerned when Mrs. Arthur did not answer her phone.

The police were told by the beauty shop owner that the Arthurs were renting a room to a boarder. Scott was grilled by police for two hours before he broke down and confessed. A bloody hacksaw and the .25-caliber handgun used in the murder were recovered from the Arthur home during a police search.

On Sept. 25, 1988, Scott pleaded no contest and was found Guilty of murder and criminal abuse of a corpse in the Lucas County Common Pleas Court. Judge Charles Abood sentenced the defendant to fifteen years to life for murder, and an additional eighteen months for the abuse of the body.

Scott, William Lester, prom. 1931, U.S. On Nov. 9, 1931, engineer Barney McCook and fireman J.E. Bryant, on a passenger train, spotted a stalled car on the tracks near Sasakwa, Okla. Unable to stop, the train smashed into the car. In the crumpled wreckage of the car, they saw the battered body of a young woman, her skin clammy and cold, her limbs set in rigor mortis, and her skull crushed. Local deputy Charles Lyon of Seminole County was called to the scene, along with Jerome Chambers, justice of the peace, and coroner. The car had no license plate, but following the car tracks to an isolated wooded area, investigators found a dental bridge and several teeth which identified the dead woman as Willie Scott, wife of William Lester Scott.

Officers found the young farmer at home the next day at his prosperous establishment. Scott said his wife was visiting her mother and would be back any minute. Lyon found a .38-caliber revolver, and bloodstained pants and shirt in Scott's house. He accused Scott of killing his spouse. The farmer denied the murder, insisting the blood on his trousers came from removing the horns from some steers. He continued to maintain his innocence in the county jail. At a preliminary hearing on Nov. 19, Scott demanded a chemical analysis of the stains on his clothing and gun. When the state chemist ruled that the blood was from an ox, Scott was released on a $15,000 bond. The case was on hold until a newly elected county attorney, Tom Huser, questioned relatives of the Scotts. They admitted that Scott visited them shortly after getting out on bond, and drunk, he responded to a comment that his wife had been killed by a gun saying, "She wasn't killed by a gun. She was killed with a car crank." They told Lyon that Scott then described how he had murdered his spouse. At the trial on Mar. 8, 1933, the jury disagreed over their verdict after lengthy deliberation. Scott was tried a second time on Apr. 16, 1935. After three days of testimony, the jury deliberated for fifteen minutes, finding him Guilty. Sentenced to life imprisonment, Scott entered the state penitentiary at McAlester on Apr. 29, 1935.

Seddon, Frederick Henry, 1871-1912, Brit. Frederick Seddon was an exceptionally vain and greedy individual whose obsession with money led him down a path of ruin in the late summer of 1911. At the time he held down a respectable position with the London and Manchester Industrial Insurance Company, and owned a large, pleasant house at Tollington Park, Islington. Seddon resided there with his wife Margaret Ann, their five children, his aging father, and a servant girl whose mental faculties were suspect. As District Superintendent for Islington, Seddon's income was fairly sizeable. But the bulk

of his earnings were rolled over into real estate investments with only the bare minimum reserved for household expenses. Watching his earnings compound seemed to be Seddon's only pleasure in life.

In July 1910, Eliza Mary Barrow presented herself at Seddon's door seeking lodgings in the Tollington Park home. Seddon agreed to rent out three unfurnished rooms on the upper floor in return for twelve shillings a week. The 49-year-old Barrow agreed to the arrangement, having just departed the home of her cousin, Frank Ernest Vonderahe, on less-than-amicable terms. Barrow moved in on July 25 with her 8-year-old protégé, Ernie Grant, an orphan boy she had taken under her wing and who referred to her as his "Chickie." Joining them in the attic apartment on Tollington Park were Mr. and Mrs. Hook, who had known Barrow for years and were young Ernie's aunt and uncle. A few weeks after the boarders had settled in, Barrow handed Hook a note, presumably written by Seddon, asking them to pack their things at once and leave. A stormy scene followed in which Hook accused Seddon of trying to lay claim to her estate. "I will defy you and a regiment like you to get it!" Hook thundered as he took leave.

The financial holdings that he was referring to were considerable. The spinsterish Barrow owned £1,600 worth of India Stock, as well as the Buck's Head pub and an adjacent

Murderer Frederick Seddon and his wife Margaret on trial at the Old Bailey.

barber shop. In addition, she had £216 deposited in the Finsbury and City of London Savings Bank as well as a sizeable amount of gold and printed notes in her safety deposit box. Eliza Barrow's yearly income was in the neighborhood of £120, and Seddon was fully aware of this when he rented the flat to her.

After the Hooks had departed, the crafty landlord contrived to gain control of Barrow's assets. In October 1910, Seddon persuaded her to assign the India Stock to him in return for his promise that he would pay a life annuity in the amount of £103 and four shillings a year. Three months after this she transferred her leasehold interest in the Buck's Head and the barber shop to Seddon for an additional £1 a week. Barrow closed her account with the Finsbury and City of London Savings Bank for good on June 19, 1911, taking out the entire £216 in gold. His objectives within firm reach, Seddon invited Barrow to accompany the family on a holiday to Southend in early August.

Later that month, Seddon sent his 15-year-old daughter Maggie to a chemist's shop on Crouch Hill to purchase a packet of Mather's Chemical Fly-papers. The label clearly stated that the papers contained arsenic poison, and the buyer was cautioned to beware. On Sept. 1, 1911, Barrow complained of stomach pains and nausea. Dr. Henry George Sworn attended to the sickly woman, whose ailment was diagnosed as "epidemic diarrhea." For the next two weeks, he administered various medicines and cure-alls, but her condition continued to rapidly decline. Early on Sept. 14, Seddon called the doctor to report the death of his tenant.

Burial arrangements were hastily made with a local undertaker friend of Seddon's. The poisoner was awarded a commission of twelve shillings and sixpence for the referral, which was brought up at his trial as an example of the kind of manipulative, insensitive personality Seddon had. Barrow's remains were transported to a common grave and buried before the relatives could intervene. Seddon, his wife, and his father were the only ones to pay their last respects at the Islington Cemetery in East Finchley. Several days later Frank Vonderahe paid a call on his cousin and was surprised to hear from the servant that she was "dead and buried." He returned the next day with his sister-in-law, Mrs. Albert Edward Vonderahe, to inquire into the mystery. Seddon went on the attack, demanding to know why they had not responded to his letter notifying them of Barrow's death. The couple replied that they had received no such correspondence. Seddon pulled out a carbon copy of a letter that he purportedly mailed on Sept. 14 notifying them of what had happened. A second letter addressed to the relatives dated Sept. 21 informed them that Barrow had previously "disposed of her properties and investments" in order to purchase a life annuity, which of course was no good now that she had died. Seddon also showed Vonderahe a black-edged mourning card, bearing the maudlin inscription: "A dear one is missing and with us no more/ That voice so much loved we hear not again/ Yet we think of you now the same as of yore/ And now you are free

from trouble and pain."

Vonderahe demanded to know who the owner of the Buck's Head pub was. "I am, likewise the shop next door," Seddon replied coolly. "I am always open to buy property at a price." When asked about the India Stock, Seddon was elusive. "You will have to write to the governor of the Bank of England and ask him, but everything has been done in a perfectly legal manner through solicitors and stockbrokers. I have nothing to do with it."

Not satisfied with any of this, Vonderahe demanded of the director of public prosecutions that the body be exhumed for a post-mortem. This was done on Nov. 20, and the examination revealed the presence of arsenic in the tissue. Seddon was arrested on Dec. 4, his wife six months later. "Absurd!" the accused murderer screamed. "What a terrible charge—willful murder. It is the first of our family that has ever been charged with such a crime."

The eminent barrister Marshall Hall agreed to defend Seddon, but he was never convinced of his client's innocence. "This is the blackest case I have ever been in!" he said. Margaret Ann Seddon was represented by Gervais Rentoul, who faced the formidable task of trying to convince the jury that his client had not entered into a conspiracy to poison Barrow with arsenic. The prosecution contended that Seddon had diluted the arsenic on the fly-papers in water, then added it to a cup of Valentine's Meat Juice, a prescription administered by Dr. Sworn.

The Seddon's trial opened at the Old Bailey before Justice Bucknill on Mar. 4, 1912. Attorney General Sir Rufus Isaacs established that Maggie Seddon had purchased the fly-papers in question. His key witness was the druggist, Walter Thorley, who recognized the "fair-haired girl." The tactic was roundly criticized by the defense. Marshall Hall told the court that the witness was prejudiced by the pre-trial publicity, including Maggie's photograph appearing in the newspaper. On the eighth day of the trial, the jury retired to consider its verdict. Seddon was found Guilty, but not so much because of the physical evidence against him as for the cool, dispassionate attitude he exhibited on the witness stand. To Filson Young, a courtroom spectator, there was little doubt. "It appeared as if, in fact, Seddon was convicted not because the Crown succeeded in proving his guilt, but because he failed to prove his innocence."

Margaret Seddon was acquitted of murder only because it was shown that her husband kept her in total ignorance of his affairs. Mrs. Seddon was in tears as she was led from the dock. When Justice Bucknill finished passing sentence, Seddon raised his hand and recited words familiar to every member of the Masonic Order. He swore "before the Great Architect of the Universe" that he was innocent of murdering Eliza Barrow. Bucknill, a member of the lodge, was visibly shaken, but was quick-witted enough to say that "our brotherhood does not encourage crime; on the contrary it condemns it. I pray you again to make your peace with the Great Architect of the Universe. Mercy—pray for it. Ask for it." The sentence of death was passed, and on Apr. 18, 1912, Seddon was hanged at Pentonville Prison. A crowd of 7,000 people lingered outside.

Seefeld, Adolf, 1879-1936, Ger. Adolf Seefeld, a 29-year-old watchmaker apparently first raped and killed a boy in 1908. As he journeyed through Germany during the next twenty-eight years, he killed at least eleven other boys by feeding them a concoction he made from poisonous toadstools. He was caught in 1935 and executed on May 23, 1936.

Segee, Robert Dale, 1930- , U.S. Tormented by a recurring nightmare of a scowling woman coming at him out of a fiery grave, Robert Segee confessed to Ohio Fire Marshal Harry Callan that it was he who set fire to a Ringling Brothers Barnum & Bailey Circus tent in Hartford, Conn., on July 6, 1944—a crime that had puzzled police for nearly six years.

Segee was a pyromaniac and murderer whose crimes dated back to Sept. 5, 1938, when he bludgeoned 9-year-old Barbara Driscoll to death on a river bank near the Portsmouth, N.H., railroad yard. He was only eight at the time, and was not considered a prime suspect because of his age. On Mar. 16, 1943, he killed a night watchman who caught him in the act of setting fire to a warehouse in Portland, Maine. That same year Segee assaulted and killed a small boy on a public beach at Cape Cottage, Maine, who had "talked mean" to him. His fourth murder occurred while he served in Japan with the Army of Occupation in 1949. He strangled a Japanese boy, resulting in his expulsion from the armed forces.

Between 1939 and 1946, the year he moved from Portland, Maine, to Ohio, Segee admitted setting at least twenty-five major fires, including the Hartford blaze, which claimed 169 lives in less than six minutes. As a consequence of the fire, James Haley, vice president of Ringling Brothers, and general manager George Smith were sentenced to prison and forced to settle $2 million in damage claims.

Segee claimed to have been plagued by the same horrible nightmares for several years. The face of a woman appeared in one, but worse yet was the Indian riding bareback on a flaming stallion. The mysterious rider commanded Segee to set the fires and then to flee the premises, accord-

ing to his later statements to psychiatrists. Unlike the typical arsonist who lingers at the scene of his crime, Segee avoided police detection by quickly returning home. State fire prevention officials were finally alerted to Segee's possible involvement in the circus fire, and a score of lesser alley fires in Circleville, Ohio, by 28-year-old William Graham, who was held for questioning by police. Segee signed a confession on June 30, 1950. He also confessed to murdering Barbara Driscoll and the other three victims.

Psychiatrists and state medical officers examined Segee for six weeks at the state hospital in Lima. He was declared sane and fit to stand trial. After pleading guilty to setting several smaller fires in Circleville, Segee was sentenced to from four to forty years in prison for arson. He was released from parole supervision on May 1, 1959.

Selby, Joseph Franklyn, c.1907- , and **Collins, Clarence**, c.1935- , and **Morgan, Maggie**, prom. 1959, and **Bounds, Patra Mae**, prom. 1959, U.S. Accountant Joseph Franklyn Selby lived in the Afton Oaks neighborhood of Houston, Texas, with Wilma Selby, his wife of thirty years. The last five years of the marriage, according to Selby, were not so happy, however, so in the fall of 1958 he decided to have his wife killed.

Selby claimed that his wife's treatment of their daughter Marcia was reprehensible. She would hit her and throw things at her, once even scratching him as Selby tried to break up a fight. He maintained that Mrs. Selby had a quick temper and a violent streak of jealousy. Apparently Mrs. Selby would question his faithfulness quite often, checking his shirt collars for lipstick, following him home from work, or asking him who he had just spoken to on the phone. Once she allegedly told him that if she could not have him, no one would because she would kill him. This allegation coupled with Selby's assertion that his wife told him of threatening phone calls she had received concerning his life, led Selby to conclude that since it was apparent his wife planned to kill him, he would have her killed first. He contacted Patra Mae Bounds, a woman at a massage parlor he frequented, who agreed to put Selby in touch with another woman who would procure him a killer. Selby was introduced to Maggie Morgan and an arrangement was made to have his wife killed, by any means except a knife, for $1,500. Selby gave Morgan a picture of his wife and a key to their house and left the rest up to her.

On Nov. 16, 1959, Selby informed Morgan that he and his wife would be home from dinner about 7:30 p.m. After dinner Selby and his wife drove home in separate cars. He made but one stop along the way, just long enough for Clarence Collins to fire two bullets from a .22-caliber pistol and kill Mrs. Selby. Evidence against the four conspirators was almost nonexistent. But police finally arrested and charged all of them with murder after hours of third-degree grilling. Bounds, who became the prosecution's star witness, was taken by two officers down an isolated dirt road near Humble, Texas. The officers intimidated the woman with death threats, twisted handcuff chains around her fingers, and told her what to say on the witness stand. Collins, unaware of his rights, did not realize that the racially driven officers were breaking the law when they incarcerated him for vagrancy under the name of Joe Smith. He was finally taken to a Texas Ranger station and, exhausted from lack of sleep, confessed. The four were found Guilty; Selby and Morgan received life sentences, Collins was sentenced to ninety-nine years in prison, and Bounds was given a ten-year suspended sentence. Even with the admission by Bounds of torture and the obvious illegalities in the treatment of Collins, attorney William F. Walsh could not convince the state that constitutional rights had been denied. The state's attorney argued that Collins was denied his rights because he did not know what his rights were. His conviction and sentence were upheld.

Selby, Norman (AKA: **Kid McCoy; The Real McCoy**), 1873-1940, U.S. Norman Selby, a rough and tumble prize-fighter from the bare-knuckle era, left behind an enduring cliché in American slang—"the real McCoy." Although during Prohibition the phrase meant pure unadulterated alcohol, it originated before the turn of the century when Selby was in his heyday. "I'm in a saloon with a charming lady as usual," the fighter recalled. "A drunk is making passes at her. I try to brush him off without too much fuss. 'Beat it,' I says. 'I'm Kid McCoy.' He laughs and says: 'Yeah? Well I'm George Washington.' I have to clip him a short one and down he goes. He wakes up ten minutes later, rubs his jaw, and says, 'Jeez, it was the real McCoy!'" The oft-told tale was recounted by Damon Runyon and other journalistic lions who wrote of Selby's checkered career in and out of the prize ring.

Selby, calling himself Kid McCoy, won the middleweight and welterweight championships in 1895 and 1897. Selby flattened the reigning champion, Tommy Ryan, in a grueling fifteen-round affair after bluffing his opponent into thinking he was something less than advertised. Selby had sent a letter to Ryan before the bout begging him to "go easy," and carry him for a few rounds. Ryan eased up on his calisthenics and was wholly unprepared for what was to follow in the ring. "The bastard played possum!" cried Ryan after losing the decision.

Selby retired in 1897 at the age of twenty-four. He was

worth half-a-million dollars, part of which was invested in a Broadway cabaret that became the favorite watering hole for celebrities of show business and the sporting world. In 1900 Selby was lured out of retirement for a bout with "Gentleman" Jim Corbett who beat him easily. Within the next two decades Selby married nine different women, each one of whom took a sizeable chunk of his assets in the divorce settlement. In 1924, his fortune all but gone, the out-of-shape ex-fighter moved to Los Angeles to work as

Ex-boxing champ Norman "The Real McCoy" Selby, convicted of manslaughter in the death of his live-in lover.

a Hollywood movie extra. He accepted employment as a security guard in an aircraft factory and became friends with Hub Kittle, a celebrated flyer and a likely suspect in a number of holdups.

Selby began a dangerous affair with Theresa Mors, the wife of Albert Mors, one of Los Angeles' leading art and antique dealers. Mors did not appreciate it when the boozing fighter fell in love with his wife. His rancor only increased when his wife filed for divorce and went to live with the "real McCoy" in an apartment at Hoover and Seventh streets. Happily in love, Selby proposed marriage and Mors readily accepted. Meanwhile, the husband filed a countersuit against his estranged wife naming Selby as corespondent. He advised the U.S. Treasury Department that Theresa Mors was involved in smuggling diamonds. By this time Selby had had enough. He warned Mors to leave her alone. Mors then had the police remove Selby from his home.

The press by now had latched on to the story and everybody had an opinion to offer. Sam Schapp, who owned a millinery store next to the antique dealer, described Selby as a dangerous opportunist bent on securing a $125,000 property settlement bound to come Mrs. Mors's way after her divorce went through. Theresa Mors began to hedge. Albert Mors began acting crazy. He stole from his wife, and then on the night of Aug. 12, 1924, moved out of the family home in the Hollywood Hills to take up residence at the Westgate Hotel. He signed an alias on the guest register.

The room overlooked an alley only a few doors away from the flat Selby and Mrs. Mors had rented. Around midnight the tenant who lived one floor below heard a dull thud coming from Selby's apartment. She then looked out her window and saw a man racing down the stairwell—Albert Mors, there was no denying the fact. Two hours later a drunken Selby appeared in a Hollywood police station asking to see the officer who had forcibly removed him from Mors's home some days earlier. "It's lucky for him he's not here," Selby stammered. "And why was that?" asked one police officer. "Hell, I'll be in the can tomorrow," he said.

The police drove Selby home and told him to sleep it off. At 3 a.m. the following morning Selby appeared at the bedroom window of Jennie Thomas, his sister. Looking haggard and drunk, Selby explained that he had just killed Theresa Mors. He then stumbled from the house and headed toward Mors's antique store where he waited patiently for the owner to arrive. Armed with a .32-caliber pistol, he captured a janitor, Mors, and a clerk, ordering them to sit quietly on one side of the room as the first customers entered. He forced the customers to surrender their cash and valuables and freed only those who appealed to him. Later that morning, Selby shot and wounded a customer who tried to escape. Fleeing from the store, he ran into Sam Schapp and his wife. "My God! What are you doing?" Schapp asked. Before they could make any sense of the situation, Selby turned his gun on them and shot them down.

Selby commandeered a passing car and tried to escape on foot but was brought down by a passing policeman. Investigators later found Theresa Mors lying dead on the floor of her apartment, neatly covered by a bed sheet and a picture of Selby perched at her side. Questioned by Captain Herman Cline of the Los Angeles police, Selby, after he had sobered up, explained that Theresa Mors had committed suicide because of her despondency over her husband's attempt to frame her on smuggling charges. He went on to say that he had struggled with her but the gun had gone off accidentally. Then, believing that he had killed the woman, Selby tried to drink himself to death but had only succeeded in passing out.

Selby was arraigned on murder, armed robbery, and assault charges. The prosecution charged that the defendant had murdered his lover because she had decided not to marry him and planned to return to New York. Defense attorney Jerry Giesler represented Selby. Under cross-examination, he demanded an answer from Mors as to why he had checked into the Westgate Hotel the night of the murder—a perplexing question that went unanswered. Giesler, whose client list would one day be studded with the names of some of Hollywood's biggest celebrities, tried to convince the jury that Theresa Mors stabbed herself with a butcher knife and then inflicted a gunshot wound. However, even he was forced to admit that such a maneuver would be difficult if she had in fact used her left thumb to pull the trigger. The murder charge was reduced to manslaughter and Selby was found Guilty after ninety-nine hours of deliberation. He was sentenced to one to ten years for manslaughter and one to fourteen years on each of the assault charges. Selby served eight years at San Quentin, during which time Governor Al Smith, Sophie Tucker, Douglas MacArthur, and Lionel Barrymore petitioned for his early release. Selby emerged as a tragic but sympathetic figure who had won himself many friends during his incarceration. He was released in 1932 and married for the tenth and last time. In 1940, the year he died, Selby reflected on his times. "It's no fun telling people you're Kid McCoy if they've heard of you before."

Selz, Ralph Jerome Von Braun (AKA: **The Laughing Killer**), 1909-   , U.S. Twenty-seven-year-old Ralph Selz arrived in San Francisco in 1935 and met 58-year-old Ada Franch Rice. Rice, just arrived from Alaska where she had left her husband, the mayor of a small town, moved to Palo Alto, Calif., with Selz and they took a cottage together. Selz killed Rice and took her body into the Santa Cruz Mountains, where he buried it in a shallow pit.

On Feb. 27, 1936, Selz was arrested for auto theft. When the police discovered that the unemployed man apparently had lots of money, they discovered he had forged Ada Rice's signature on checks. After two weeks of intense interrogation, Selz admitted killing the woman and showed the authorities where she was buried, all the time cracking jokes and laughing, thus acquiring the nickname "The Laughing Killer." He was found Guilty on March 13 and sentenced to life in prison. Serving time in the Chino State Prison, he escaped in 1945 and spent a year as a soldier in the Canadian Army before being captured again. In 1962 he escaped from the San Luis Obispo jail, but was found within three days. He was released from prison in 1966, but was returned about a year later on charges of welfare fraud.

Serafima, prom. 1946, U.S.S.R. Serafima, a beautiful woman with eyes "like the clear summer sky," lived with her mother in a two room Moscow apartment in 1946. Entranced by her beauty and her estate, factory worker Udod gave her 20,000 rubles for the privilege of marrying her and he moved into her apartment. He was not happy, however, when Serafima made him sleep in the second room. After the 20,000 rubles were gone Serafima's mother began to long for the time when she and her daughter could again be alone. One morning, as Udod buckled on his boots, his recent bride smashed him over the head with a sharp piece of iron. After disposing of the body, she repainted the room to hide the bloodstains.

Serafima told her neighbors that her husband was a criminal and had gone into hiding. But police inspector Ivan Kudrin grew suspicious when he discovered that Udod had no prior police record, while Serafima's family had previously engaged in several criminal acts. Observing the recent paint job in the apartment, Kudrin continued to investigate until he turned up Udod's body in the cellar.

In early July the newspaper *Vechernaya Moskva* reported the murder to eager Muscovites who get little in the way of news about crime. Though there was no explicit information about what happened to Serafima, she was consistently mentioned in the past tense, as though she had been executed or imprisoned.

Seymour, Henry Daniel (AKA: **Harvey**), c.1879-1931, Brit. Seymour was a convicted criminal who occasionally used more legitimate jobs, such as selling vacuum cleaners door to door, as a means of learning about places that would be worth robbing. On the Friday of an August holiday weekend in 1931, he showed up at the door of one old customer, a Mrs. Andrews of Oxford, and asked for money to take a bus home. She gave him some, which he used to purchase a hammer and chisel. Then he reappeared at Andrews' house, saying he had missed the last bus. She let him sleep there, but before he left the next morning, she saw his parcel containing the new tools. He then walked to the home of Annie Louisa Kempson, about fifty-four years old, where he was seen to enter the house. He attacked the widow with the hammer and chisel and then ransacked the premises, finding a little cash, but missing a box of notes and gold. Kempson was not found

until the following Monday, after she failed to show up for an appointment.

Seymour, in the meantime, had returned to the hotel in Aylesbury where he had stayed on the previous Thursday night, but was not allowed to take his suitcase because he could not pay his bill. Opening the luggage, the proprietor found tools similar to those described by newspaper reports. In the hotel room, police found a Brighton address written backward on the blotting pad, checked the address, and discovered Seymour there, living under the name of Harvey. In October 1931, he was tried and was convicted on circumstantial evidence. He was hanged on Dec. 10, 1931, at Oxford Prison.

Shafer, Russell F., prom. 1960, U.S. On the morning of Apr. 26, 1960, John Muehlenthaler, Jr., discovered the body of 33-year-old Inez Marie Ringgenberg lying in a ditch about a mile north of Ankeny, Iowa. She had been brutally stabbed to death, with at least twenty-two wounds in her neck and chest. Investigators discovered that she had spent the previous evening at the Amvets Club bar with Russell F. Shafer. His white Ford matched the one seen by two men who passed by a parked car at the scene of the murder. Shafer admitted he had been with Ringgenberg the night before and early that morning, and he even confessed to having had an argument with her, but he said she was alive when he left her on the road.

As police still had not found the woman's missing purse or the murder weapon, a search of Shafer's car and home was made. Corwin Johnson, director of the Iowa Forensic-Medical Laboratory discovered no evidence, but did note that the vehicle had recently been thoroughly cleaned.

At first a search of Shafer's house turned up no evidence or clues, but upon searching the premises a second time, a metal bucket containing ashes was unearthed from beneath loose floorboards. Among the ashes was a piece of paper and a cord, both of which were sent to the FBI in Washington, D.C., for analysis. Agents Hilding L. Dahlgreen and Robert E. Duckett learned that the cord was from a plastic purse like that carried by Ringgenberg, and using infrared photography found the charred paper to be the photo of Riggenberg's niece, 9-year-old Jeanette Doolittle, that the girl's mother, Mrs. Clinton Doolittle, said her sister carried.

With this evidence against Shafer he was charged with second-degree murder. In September, County Attorney Ray Hanrahan and his assistant Lawrence F. Scalise had little trouble convincing the jury of the defendant's guilt—despite efforts by defense lawyer J. Blaine Phipps, who argued that the evidence was circumstantial. Shafer was convicted and sentenced to fifty years in prison.

Sharpe, Walter, 1929-50, and **Lannen, George**, 1932- , Brit. A jeweler named Abraham Levine was working in his shop, the Albion Watch Depot, in Leeds, England, when two youths held up his store at 10 a.m. on Nov. 16, 1949. Despite the drawn pistols, the 52-year-old jeweler fought the bandits. He grabbed one, but the other hit Levine over the head with the butt of a revolver. This gunman then fired two shots at Levine and both men ran out the door, shooting wildly as they fled. They escaped through the crowded streets.

Levine was taken to the Leeds General Infirmary, and a massive search using more than 900 police was conducted by Chief Constable J.W. Barnett. The next night Levine gave a brief description of his attackers before dying from his wounds. A bullet recovered from his body proved to have been taken from a Leeds gunsmith during a burglary prior to the murder. On Nov. 18, the murderers were arrested by police in Southport. One of the men, 20-year-old Walter Sharpe, confessed to the shooting. The two criminals then remained silent until they were brought to trial at the Leeds Assizes on Mar. 11, 1950, before Justice Streatfield. At the trial, Sharpe pleaded not guilty, while his co-defendant, 17-year-old George Lannen, pleaded guilty, against the advice of his attorney G.R. Hinchcliffe. Again Sharpe confessed to the shooting. He admitted that he had pulled the trigger while Levine fought with Lannen. But he added that the murder was an accident and that the guns (which he also admitted stealing with Lannen) were only meant to intimidate the jeweller. Regardless of their intent, both men were found Guilty by the jury, which deliberated for only twenty minutes. Lannen was too young to be sentenced to death and was ordered detained for as long as the king desired. Sharpe was sentenced to death and hanged on Mar. 30, 1950, at Armley Jail in Leeds.

Shelfo, Rosary, 1920- , U.S. Rosary Shelfo and her husband, Joseph Shelfo, lived in Los Angeles. When she gave birth to their first child, Ross, in February 1943, her attitude began to change. According to Joseph, a 26-year-old employee of the California Shipyards, Rosary had been "moody...with a faraway look in her eye, ever since we brought her home from the hospital a week ago." Because Ross was a quiet baby, Rosary decided he was not normal. "I even had a priest and the doctor over to examine the baby and they assured her he was a perfect child," her husband said. These assurances did not relieve the new mother's anxieties.

Shortly before noon on Mar. 8, 1943, Rosary Shelfo fed her 2-week-old son for the last time. As Joseph slept in the adjacent bedroom, she killed the baby with a butcher knife. Awakening her husband, Rosary confessed what she had done. Joe Shelfo called his father, Ross, for whom the infant had been named, and in a few minutes the police arrived.

The case went before Judge Charles W. Fricke of the Los Angeles Superior Court, who found Mrs. Shelfo Guilty of second-degree murder. But after reviewing a psychiatrist's report, the judge ruled her Not Guilty by reason of insanity on May 18. Rosary Shelfo was ordered committed to the Mendocino State Hospital for the Insane on June 19, 1943. She was discharged, after only a year, on July 15, 1944.

Sheridan, Andrew (AKA: **Squint; Andrew Thomas**), 1900-1949, U.S. On Jan. 8, 1947, three men, John M."Cock-eye" Dunn, Andrew "Squint" Sheridan, and Daniel Gentile (more commonly known by his former prize ring name of Danny Brooks), ambushed a 43-year-old New York boss stevedore, Anthony Hintz, in the hallway of his Greenwich Village apartment. Hintz, who was in charge of the daily hiring of several hundred longshoremen at New York City's Pier 51, was shot, and died three weeks later of the wounds. When the suspects were tried for the murder, the prosecution contended that the killers were hired by local gangsters who wanted Hintz's position so that they could pick their own men for dock work and collect kickbacks from them.

On Dec. 31, 1947, first-degree murder convictions were returned against all three men. The convictions carried a mandatory sentence of death in the electric chair. The executions were delayed six times in the expectation that Dunn might testify against mob activity on the waterfront in exchange for a commutation of his sentence. Gentile did relent and provided the District Attorney's office with information about waterfront criminal activity. Thirty-six hours after Gentile's sentence was commuted to life imprisonment, Dunn and Sheridan were executed in the electric chair at Sing Sing prison.

Sherrill, Patrick Henry, d.1986, U.S. On Aug. 20, 1986, a disgruntled postal worker in Edmond, Okla., entered the local post office armed with semiautomatic sharpshooting pistols and fifty rounds of ammunition. In the shooting spree that followed, Sherrill killed fourteen coworkers and wounded six more before shooting himself. Sherrill had had several run-ins with his superiors at the post office, including one the day before the shootings. Postal inspectors spent six months investigating the shootings. In February 1987, they published a 5,000-page report which found "considerable evidence of premeditation" by Sherrill.

Shillitoni, Oresto (Shillitano, AKA: **Paper Box Kid**), d.1916, U.S. On the evening of May 3, 1913, two New York policemen, Charles Teare and William Heaney, attempted to break up a fight between two men on Mulberry Street. In the course of the scuffle, both police officers and one of the men, a well-known gangster named John Rizzo, were shot and killed. According to eyewitnesses, the man who shot the other three was Oresto Shillitoni. Shillitoni disappeared after the shootings. More than 100 police officers participated in a country-wide search for Shillitoni. In mid-June, an eyewitness to the crime implicated Shillitoni's father in the shootings, and police arrested the elder Shillitoni. Then, to protect his father, Oresto Shillitoni turned himself in.

Shillitoni was found Guilty of the murders and was sentenced to death. A week before his scheduled execution, Shillitoni shot and killed Daniel McCarthy, a guard at Sing Sing, during an escape attempt. His execution was carried out as planned on June 30, 1916.

Shoaf, Mamie Shey, d.1929, U.S. The day before her desperate act, Mamie Shey Shoaf expressed weariness concerning the financial woes plaguing her husband, Carey Shoaf, and seven children—ages two to seventeen.

On May 24, 1929, Shoaf took three of her children to a cemetery near their home in Lebanon, Ky. In a field she slit the throats of 2-year-old Thomas Shoaf, 7-year-old Ina Shoaf, and 11-year-old Catherine Shoaf. She then cut her own throat. Two boys heard her groans and found her. Just before she died, Shoaf pointed toward the bodies of her dead children.

Shobek, Michael, 1954-76, Bahamas. In January 1974, 21-year-old Michael Shobek, a Milwaukee, Wis., native, fatally stabbed Irwin Bornstein of New York, on the island of Nassau in the Bahamas. When arrested, Shobek confessed to stabbing Ohio lawyer Paul Howell, and to strangling 17-year-old Kate Smith of Detroit, as well as the Bornstein murder. All three victims were tourists in Nassau at the time of the slayings. In his May 1974, trial, Shobek said he "destroyed" his victims because they were "angels of Lucifer."

Shobek was convicted of the Bornstein murder and sentenced to death by hanging. On Sept. 30, 1976, Shobek's last appeal was denied. On Oct. 19, 1976, he was hanged at the Fox Hill Prison just outside Nassau.

Shotton, Edward George, 1880-1958, Brit. A lively and flirtatious ex-chorus girl, Mamie Stuart, twenty-six, met marine engineer Edward George Shotton in 1917. They soon married and rented a place in Swansea. In 1919, they moved to a house called Ty-Llanwydd, outside Swansea. One week after the move, Stuart wrote a letter to her parents. They sent a reply but were surprised when their letter was returned, marked "House Closed." They received a Christmas telegram from their daughter, but then heard nothing more. On Mar. 20, 1920, the Grosvenor Hotel manager in Swansea reported to police that a large suitcase had been left at his hotel. Inside this, police found a second smaller suitcase containing shredded dresses and women's shoes cut into pieces. Two weeks later, a cleaning woman at Ty-Llanwydd found Stuart's mildewed leather purse with her ration card and about £2 in change behind a wash stand. Stuart's parents were contacted as well as Scotland Yard.

In questioning Shotton, it was discovered that he was married to another woman and living with her and their child a few miles from the Swansea hotel. Admitting he knew Stuart, Shotton denied ever marrying her, and said they had broken up after a fight in December 1919. Shotton was tried at Glamorgan Assizes on a bigamy charge for which he received eighteen months of hard labor. In court he said he had left the large suitcase at the hotel, but maintained that someone else, pretending to be him, had married Stuart.

On Nov. 5, 1961, three Welch fishermen found the skeleton of a woman at the bottom of a long abandoned mine shaft. The body had been cut into three pieces; the physical characteristics and clothing matched those of Stuart. A December 1961 coroner's inquest brought in William Symons, an elderly former postman, who testified that he had surprised Shotton, who was carrying a heavy sack, outside Ty-Llanwydd. The startled Shotton was relieved to realize he was looking at a postal worker, and said, "Oh, God, for a minute I thought you were a policeman," before driving away. The murder verdict had no effect on Shotton, who had died three years earlier, at the age of seventy-eight.

Shuck, Douglas Paul, c.1968- , U.S. Patricia Sue "Suzy" Toucheck aspired to be a singer and often sang songs into a tape recorder in her Edgewood, Md., home. During the last week of September 1988, the 14-year-old girl recorded the song *If I Close My Eyes Forever* written by Lita Ford whose lyrics speak about death. On Sept. 28, with the discovery of her nude and strangled body on a wooded hillside less than thirty yards from her house, the lyrics rang eerily prophetic.

Five days earlier, on Sept. 23, Suzy had been drinking with a group of friends. The teenager was reported to have had a problem with alcohol as a result of abuse from her stepfather. That night she apparently became very drunk, and needed help in walking. Douglas Paul Shuck, nineteen, who himself had been drinking heavily, offered to walk Suzy home. She was never seen alive again. Later that night, Shuck was observed with bloodstains on his clothing and shoes. Suzy's body, found beneath a beach blanket, had been severely beaten and raped before she was strangled to death.

When Shuck was arrested and charged with the murder on Nov. 11, 1988, he became the fourth teenager charged with first-degree murder in less than a year in Harford County. The evidence against the youth was provided by FBI laboratory tests of Shuck's blood and semen samples. His samples matched those taken from the dead girl. The case was the first in Harford County in which a DNA "fingerprint" test was used in linking a suspect to a crime. On June 7, 1989, Shuck entered an Alford plea to the first-degree murder charge, in exchange for the prosecution's dropping the rape charge. Under this plea, Shuck did not admit he committed the crime, but realized the state had enough evidence to convict him. In a prepared statement, Shuck told the court he could not "remember what happened on the morning of Sept. 24," and added "after examining all the evidence, it is clear I must be responsible." Circuit Judge William O. Carr sentenced Shuck to life imprisonment, of which the defendant must serve at least fifteen years before he is eligible for parole.

Shutt, Barbara Jean, 1946- , U.S. On May 25, 1969, the teenaged children of psychiatrist Dr. Jane Shutt found her body in her office in the basement of their home in Cincinnati, Ohio. She had been shot once in the chest and twice in the head, and then severely beaten on the head with a fireplace poker. The children were not home when the crime occurred, nor, apparently, were the woman's 75-year-old husband—who was almost twice her age—or her 23-year-old adopted daughter, Barbara Jean Shutt.

Shutt and her adoptive father were soon suspected. Lie-

detector tests were administered, and after two grueling hours, police were certain that the elder Shutt was telling the truth. But after two polygraph tests of the eldest daughter, police believed she had something to hide. Police also discovered that the riding boots Barbara Shutt had worn that morning had dried blood on them. The part-time school teacher then confessed to killing her mother. She explained that her mother had been seeing another man and planned on leaving her husband. Rather than let the family break up, Barbara decided to kill her mother. As police suspected, she fired into the doctor's chest while she was showering. Barbara said her mother then asked her to call for help, which she said she was doing when the wounded woman attacked her. Following a brief struggle, Dr. Shutt collapsed. Then Barbara dragged her mother by the feet into the basement, accounting for the trail of blood from the bathroom. In the office, she grabbed a pillow, placed it over her mother's head and fired two more bullets from her father's .25-caliber pistol. Still not sure that Dr. Shutt was dead, her daughter battered in the woman's head. The day after this confession, Barbara Shutt recanted, claiming she invented the story to protect her father, whom she felt police suspected.

Despite Shutt's retraction of her confession, she was tried for murder. Melvin Rueger prosecuted the case, which opened on Sept. 26 before Judge William Morrissey. Defense Counsel Bernard Gilday disputed the evidence put forth by Rueger and argued that his client had come home early from the Red Fox Stables to find her dead mother, and stained her boots in an attempt to lift the woman. He added that she disposed of the gun in the Ohio River when she realized that her father had probably killed her mother. The jury was given the case, and five hours later they returned a verdict of Guilty of first-degree murder, but with a recommendation for mercy, as the crime carried a mandatory sentence of death. Morrissey sentenced Shutt to life imprisonment. On Oct. 6, the night after the verdict was read, Shutt attempted suicide by swallowing an overdose of sleeping pills she had concealed in her bra. The attempt was discovered and Shutt was saved.

Silvera, Vincent, 1914-53, Jam. Vincent Silvera lived with his wife Martha Silvera in Anchovy, Jam. In 1950, he began an affair with a much younger woman, Princess Campbell. This affair led to a number of fights between husband and wife and in May, Martha Silvera left to live with her mother on the island of St. Elizabeth. She returned in November 1951, and the arguments resumed as Martha Silvera continued to see Campbell. Silvera informed Campbell that his wife would leave him soon, and the two could be together.

On June 15, 1952, Martha Silvera, forty-four, disappeared. Her husband gave friends and neighbors a number of reasons for her departure. He said that her father was ill, she had found employment on St. Elizabeth, she had moved to England, or she had left him. Four days after Martha Silvera's disappearance, a fisherman found a headless, naked body on the cliffs near Anchovy. The next day, clothing was found floating in Bryan's Bay, four miles away. A media campaign to discover the identity of the corpse resulted in the police locating seventy-eight missing women, but not the deceased's name. On June 29, a friend of Martha Silvera's received a letter supposedly from the missing woman, but she did not recognize the handwriting and reported the letter to police.

That same day, a Port Antonio dressmaker identified the corpse's clothing as Martha Silvera's. After his arrest on June 30, Silvera claimed that his wife was visiting her sick father on St. Elizabeth. This soon was proved false. Police quickly uncovered enough information to identify the body as Martha Silvera's, and to establish that her husband killed her. The most telling piece of evidence was obtained from photographs of the missing woman. Police enlarged photographs of Martha Silvera and superimposed these upon photographs of the corpse. The photographs matched perfectly. Later, the letter turned into police was proven to be written by Silvera. Also, the head, which was never recovered, had been skillfully removed from the body. A butcher like Silvera would possess the skill to decapitate a body well.

Silvera's trial opened in Kingston on Dec. 5, 1952, and lasted seventeen days. The prosecution called eighty-two witnesses, while the defendant refused to testify or call any witnesses on his behalf. He was convicted and sentenced to death. On Feb. 16, 1953, his appeal was dismissed, and on Mar. 10, he was executed.

Silverstein, Thomas, 1952- , and **Gometz, Randy**, 1955- , and **Fountain, Clayton**, c.1955- , U.S. On Oct. 22, 1983, at the federal penitentiary in Marion, Ill., 50-year-old prison guard Merle Clutts was stabbed forty times with a knife made from a steel bed frame as he led Thomas Silverstein back to his cell. Ten hours later, another guard, 53-year-old Robert Hoffman, Sr., was killed by inmate Clayton Fountain, who attacked Hoffman and two other guards with a homemade knife. On Dec. 1, 1983, a federal grand jury indicted Randy Gometz, along with Silverstein, for Clutts's death, and Fountain for Hoffman's death. Gometz was serving concurrent sentences, two for fifteen years and one for twenty-five years, all for armed

bank robberies. He was a difficult prisoner, and earned another year on Apr. 23, 1982, for assault, and a few months later on Sept. 2, 1982, he was sentenced to three more years for assault of a correctional officer. Silverstein had been sentenced to twenty years for the 1978 armed robbery of a California bank. Fountain was serving a life sentence for the 1974 murder of a drill sergeant while he was in the Marine Corps.

On Feb. 9, 1984, Gometz and Silverstein were convicted for the murder of Clutts. Silverstein said he killed the guard in self-defense, but he was sentenced to life imprisonment and transferred to the federal penitentiary at Leavenworth, Kan. On May 24, 1984, Gometz was sentenced to 150 years for Clutts's murder. He was resentenced to life imprisonment on Feb. 6, 1986. On July 8, 1988, Gometz was sentenced to an additional fifteen years for assault with a dangerous weapon and possession of contraband at the Marion Correctional Institution, where he is currently being held. Fountain, who had a long and violent criminal history, was sentenced to an additional term of life imprisonment for the murder of Hoffman.

Simececk, James, c.1916- , U.S. In January 1942, lumberjack Joe Holcomb spotted a fire at the farm house of a neighbor near Ellsworth, Wis. Before the roof caved in, he pulled three bodies from the flames. George Petan, ten, was discovered later among the ruins. Investigators discovered that the Petan family had been killed before the house had caught fire. The children, including 6-year-old Neil Petan, and 3-year-old Sylvia Petan, had had their throats slit; their mother, 28-year-old Verna Petan, had been sexually assaulted, stabbed, and shot to death.

A tramp in the area was immediately suspected, as he had once been convicted of rape and had violated his parole. He was cleared by a doctor from Elmswood, Wis., who had given the man a lift on the day of the murders. The doctor had noticed a car in the Petans' driveway, however, and police soon learned that the car belonged to James Simececk. Simececk acknowledged having been at the house earlier. He had stopped by to see if Petan wanted any groceries, an offer he usually extended, as the Petans had no car. Petan, according to Simececk, had not desired any groceries, and he had left. Upon further questioning, Holcomb remembered during his rescue attempt spotting newly purchased groceries on a kitchen chair.

Investigators searched the home of Simececk, whose shirt had already been found to have animal bloodstains, and found a shirt and pants which were heavily covered with human blood. Police also discovered a .32-caliber revolver, which turned out to be the weapon that had fired the bullet lodged in Petan's body, and a hunting knife. The blond hair caught in Petan's wedding ring matched Simececk's. Confronted with the evidence, Simececk confessed. He said that he shot and stabbed Petan when she refused his advances, and then killed the children, who had run into the house from outside when they heard their mother screaming. The murderer was found sane and tried in March 1942. Simececk was found Guilty on four counts of murder and given four life sentences.

Simmons, Beoria, 1954- , U.S. As a social worker in Louisville, Ky., 29-year-old Beoria Simmons was disgusted with the immorality and sinful ways of prostitutes, and he felt it was his duty to cleanse the community of these women. He began in 1984 by murdering a teenager whom he believed to be a prostitute, and then proceeding to kill a 29-year-old woman and a 39-year-old woman before his arrest. Simmons showed no signs of insanity. He was found Guilty and sentenced to death.

Simmons, Ronald Gene, 1941- , U.S. Residents of Cloudcroft, N.M., feared Ronald Simmons. The classmates of his daughter, Loretta, remembered that the retired Air Force master sergeant "had a beer in his hand all the time. He had one little room he would stay in all the time. It was dark and seemed spooky, and it stunk."

In 1981, school officials suspected that Simmons was carrying on an incestuous affair with his 16-year-old daughter, Sheila. School nurse Carol Nix often saw him kissing Sheila good-bye in an illicit and suggestive manner. It was later discovered that Sheila was pregnant with her father's child. Sexual abuse charges were filed against Simmons, whom his wife, Rebecca, described as a violent and abusive father. By this time, the Simmons family had left New Mexico to take up residence in Russellville, Ark., and the charges were dropped when officials were unable to find Simmons. In a safety deposit box at a New Mexico bank, investigators found a five-page letter to Sheila. "You have destroyed me, and you have destroyed my trust in you," Simmons wrote, referring to the allegations of incest that she had made public. He ominously concluded, "I will see you in hell."

Ronald Simmons ruled his large family with an iron fist. His house was described as "fortress-like," and his will was never challenged. For months, his wife considered divorcing him, but she never had the courage. Shortly before Christmas 1987, Simmons decided to kill all fourteen members of his family as a final act of revenge. Prosecuting attorney John Bynum later argued that the decision to murder his family execution style was not the desperate act of a man suddenly possessed by madness. "The family wasn't killed on a sudden impulse," he said. "This was a clear, well-conceived plan."

Simmons purchased a .22-caliber handgun from a local Wal-Mart and shot his wife, forty-six, his seven children, four grandchildren, a son-in-law, and a daughter-in-law on Dec. 23. He strangled one grandchild with a fish stringer and left the body in the trunk of a car. Simmons dug a mass grave behind the mountain home near Dover and soaked the bodies in kerosene. "Why?" Bynum asked rhetorically. "He wanted to keep the smell from coming up out of the ground and attracting animals and people. The top few inches of the ground also had been topped with coils of barbed wire."

Five days later, Simmons drove to Russellville where he shot and killed 24-year-old Kathy Kendrick, who had spurned his romantic overtures, and 33-year-old James D. Chaffin, an employee of a local oil company where Simmons had worked. With a crazed grin on his face, Simmons wounded Roberta Woodley at a mini-mart and Joyce Butts, who had worked with him at Woodline Motors. Both women survived the ordeal and appeared as witnesses in the first of two sensational murder trials, which began in Ozark, but were moved to Clarksville because of publicity. Simmons' murdered family was found by police after the Russellville shootings.

On May 12, 1988, Simmons was convicted of murdering the two Russellville victims after a jury deliberation that lasted an hour-and-a-half. Following the sentencing hearing, the jury handed him a death sentence. "To those who oppose the death penalty (in) my particular case, anything short of death would be cruel and unusual punishment," the convicted man said in a prepared statement.

Simmons went to trial in February 1989 for the mass murder of his family. Before the jury retired, the remorseless killer struck prosecutor Bynum on the chin and then tried to seize a deputy's handgun. This image was fresh in the jurors' minds when they retired on Feb. 10. Four hours passed before they returned a Guilty verdict with a recommendation for death.

As the final plans for Simmons' execution by lethal injection were being made, opponents of capital punishment petitioned Arkansas governor Bill Clinton for a stay and staged a candlelight vigil outside his mansion hours before the execution was to take place on Mar. 16, 1989. Meanwhile, attorney Arthur L. Allen prepared a petition on behalf of another death row inmate, Jonas Hoten Whitmore II, contending that Arkansas' lack of mandatory appeal made capital punishment "arbitrary and capricious."

The written deposition was filed with U.S. Supreme Court Justice Harry Blackmun following the state supreme court's decision not to intervene in the matter. "I felt that our argument was compelling enough that we would receive the stay at some point in the process," Allen said.

At the eleventh hour, the high court granted Simmons a stay of execution. The case could take another six months to a year to be resolved. If the sentence is not overturned, Simmons would become the first Arkansas prisoner executed since 1964. Sheriff Bolin expressed anger and frustration at the decision. "I'm angry that a country such as we live in...can go through this kind of thing," he said. "I had hoped our United States Supreme Court judges would have a little more sense than to listen to some cockeyed death row inmate."

Simpson, Charlie, 1948-72, U.S. Harrisonville, Mo., south of Kansas City, was a quiet farming community on the Kansas border. During the early 1970s, Harrisonville's citizens often complained of the nine long-haired youths who loitered in town. These nine men were natives of Harrisonville, eight of whom received unemployment benefits. Complaints often were filed against the youths, who would sit about daily glaring at passersby. The town council passed an ordinance prohibiting gatherings of three or more people. The nine men claimed police enforced the law only against their group. One night in Spring 1972, the police arrested eight of the nine men. The next day, the ninth, 24-year-old Charlie Simpson, bailed his friends out. He then went on a shooting spree.

Simpson ran through the middle of town firing his M-1 carbine. He killed two police officers outside the bank, then ran inside and wounded two bank clerks. Back outside, he shot to death a laundry deliveryman, then fired two shots through the sheriff's office window. Sheriff Bill Gough was wounded. Finally, the gunman ran to the steps of the Harrisonville Retirement Home, placed the gun's muzzle in his mouth, and fired one last shot.

Simpson, Willie Joe (AKA: **Charlie Smith; Jack Samuels**), 1950-73, U.S. Katherine Cleary lived—and died—on the crime-ridden Upper West Side of Manhattan. She grew up in Holyoke, in northern N.J., a pleasant, middle-class community unlike the teeming sprawl of Manhattan. Cleary had first gone to Newark and then on to New York to teach the deaf. She had a natural rapport with the handicapped because at the age of ten she had developed a serious case of scoliosis that had to be cor-

rected through surgery. For much of her life Cleary bore her physical and emotional scars with quiet dignity. She was well liked by her students at the St. Joseph's School for the Deaf in the Bronx, a sensitive, giving person genuinely perplexed by the subtle nuances of life, particularly the dilemma of understanding good and evil. Her own childhood experiences in the hospital made her question the Catholic piety of her father, an insurance agent who moved his family out of Brooklyn when their neighborhood deteriorated.

By night Cleary frequented the neighborhood taverns in the vicinity of 72nd Street and West End Avenue. Tweed's, the Copper Hatch, and other establishments she dropped into two or three nights a week were not singles bars. There were no dance floors, blaring disco music, or potted palms to suggest these places were favored by the swinging singles.

On New Year's Day 1973, Cleary left her one-room apartment on the west side to partake in some holiday cheer at Tweed's Bar on the south side of 72nd Street near West End. At the opposite end of the crowded bar stood Willie Joe Simpson, a blond, blue-eyed hustler from Clay County, Ill. Years earlier Simpson was diagnosed as suffering from "psychological hysteria" resulting from a childhood injury to his foot. The doctors could find nothing wrong with the bones nor was there any evidence of a physical abnormality. His paralysis had been "psychologically induced," according to physicians' reports. Like Cleary, Simpson's physical problems (real or imagined) clouded his outlook on life. He had few boyhood companions and seemed most at ease playing with animals. In 1964, he stole $10.50 from the local Boy's Club, a first brush with the law which earned him a probationary sentence. At sixteen Simpson ran away from home. He took the bus to California, Arizona, Colorado, New Mexico, and then across country to the East Coast, winding up in seamy Times Square. Like other young runaways with no money or job skills, Willie Joe Simpson hustled for a living. He picked up male homosexuals and charged them anywhere from $20 to $50 for an engagement. He preferred the company of women but put aside his natural inclinations to make more money than he had ever seen in his life.

In 1971, Simpson was living in Miami, Fla., where he met the "true love" of his life, 16-year-old Carole Musty. They were married at the Hotel Vagabond, and for a time Simpson was happier than he had ever been. But in a careless moment he stole a car, was arrested, and sentenced to the county stockade for one year. The lax security afforded Simpson a chance to escape one day. With Carole in tow, Simpson caught the first plane out of Miami and returned to New York. In June 1972, he was keeping constant company with his best friend Danny Murray and living less than three blocks from Katherine Cleary.

On New Year's Day Simpson dined with Murray in a restaurant on Columbus Avenue. Afterward he stopped in Tweed's for a quick drink. In the loud din of the crowded bar Simpson met Cleary. In that last year of her life Cleary's friends—those that knew her—recalled a subtle change. According to one West Sider, "All I know was I saw her around the neighborhood. I used to see her in places I wouldn't want to go and she was with men I wouldn't want to be with." Cleary's promiscuous Manhattan lifestyle became the focus of the 1975 motion picture dealing with the tragedy, titled: *Looking for Mr. Goodbar.*

What passed between Cleary and Simpson that night in the bar could only be surmised. But a short time later the 28-year-old teacher took the cowboy drifter back to her apartment. According to sworn statements Simpson provided the police, they engaged in sex. But Cleary became antagonistic and ordered him out of her room when the act was completed. "She went nuts and started pushing me physically to hurry and get dressed and leave," he said. "She was very nasty, a complete reversal of a few moments before. I have problems with my mines (sic) and I often flip out not knowing whether walls, people, etcetera are real. I hear things, I think sometimes I can fly." Simpson seized her by the throat and started choking her. Afterward he grabbed a paring knife and stabbed her eighteen times. Three days later, the horribly mutilated body of Katherine Cleary was found by a concerned co-worker who prevailed upon the landlord to let him in after the woman failed to show up for work. By this time Willie Joe Simpson had flown back to Miami and from there he continued on to Springfield, Ill., where he visited his brother, Fred. New York police were put on the trail of the murderer by Danny Murray, Simpson's friend and former lover. In return for immunity from prosecution, Murray agreed to appear as a witness for the prosecution. Within days of the murder, Simpson was apprehended in Springfield and extradited to New York to answer charges. Simpson told police of his encounter with Cleary, but neglected to add that his sexual impotence may have been the telling factor of the tragedy.

A neurological examination was scheduled for Simpson by physicians at Bellevue Hospital. He was declared fit to stand trial and was awaiting his day in court when prison guards at the Tombs Prison found him hanging from the ceiling bar of his cell on May 4, 1973. On the day that Simpson was interred in the family plot back in Illinois, Carole Musty delivered his stillborn child in Miami.

Singh, Dalip Lutchmie Persad, d.1955, Trinidad. The son of Hindus who moved to Trinidad as indentured servants, Dalip Singh attended medical school in Scotland, where he acquired a fondness for white women and soon married a beautiful blonde German optician. His appalled parents were barely tolerant of his wife, Inge Singh, when the couple returned to Trinidad to set up practice in the islands. Singh himself became intolerant when his wife turned out to be an alcoholic. His staff members regularly quit because of her drunken abuse. On Apr. 6, 1954, after Inge returned to Port-of-Spain after one of her regular trips to an office on another island, the two had a major argument, and Singh killed his wife. He bundled her body in a sack filled with sand and drove it out to Godinot Bay, about forty miles from his home, where he sank it. But the sand oozed out of the sack, and the body rose to the surface and was found.

While Dr. Russell Barrow was doing the autopsy, Dr. Singh casually chatted with him, although he and Barrow were not friends. Barrow's autopsy showed that Inge Singh's body had been disemboweled and completely drained of blood, by someone who knew surgery. Singh replied to a police request for a visit by hurrying to headquarters. He readily identified some jewelry as his wife's and said that he had last seen her on Apr. 6. The police questioned Singh's servants and former servants, learning of the distaste they had for her and her abusive drunkenness. Finally, from the houseboy, Kramchand Ramsahaye, they learned of the couple's vicious and loud fight on the evening of Apr. 6, a fight that ended with the sound of blows and Singh's disappearing from the house for many hours.

Dr. Dalip Singh was charged with murdering his wife. He was found Guilty and was hanged on June 28, 1955.

Singh Sandhu, Suchnam, prom. 1968, Brit. Suchnam Singh Sandhu said he was following an old Sikh tribal custom dealing with family disgrace when he murdered his daughter and sent her dismembered body parts on trains traveling in opposite directions. Then he claimed he did not do it, but the evidence against the Indian father was overwhelming and a British jury took only ninety minutes to find him Guilty of murder. He was sentenced to life imprisonment.

On Apr. 5, 1968, an abandoned locked olive green suitcase was finally taken off the 10:40 p.m. London train at the Wolverhampton station and opened in hopes of tracing the owner. But the suitcase contained a mutilated upper torso of a woman. Her head, lower torso and legs had been removed. A second suitcase, this one containing the lower torso and legs of a woman, soon was found in the River Roding. British authorities traced the make of the suitcases and the origin of the handmade clothes the woman had been wearing, and examined the victim's remains. They deduced that the body parts found belonged to the same woman, that she was between sixteen and eighteen years old, and of Indian or Pakistani descent. She had been cut with a hacksaw sold near Ilford, England, that was painted blue on one side and yellow on the other. She recently had surgery as evident by suture scars on the inside of one of her legs. Doctors discovered the equivalent of thirty half-grain tablets of phenobarbitone in her stomach but curiously noted that although the woman had ingested a fatal dose, there had not been enough time for the poison to take effect before she was murdered. Recently cut pubic hairs suggested that she was Moslem. On May 8, the severed head was discovered in a blue duffel bag in Wanstead Flats. Wrapped around the head was the Mar. 27, 1968, edition of the *Daily Telegraph*. The victim had sustained two extensive blows to the head. After investigating neighborhoods with high Indian and Pakistani populations and women who had recently undergone gynecological procedures, police learned the victim's name: Sarabjit Kaur. Her father, Suchnam Singh Sandhu, explained his motive for the savage killing, after being identified as the murderer.

Sandhu said Sarabjit had been his favorite child. On Apr. 4, he confessed to having murdered her. Father and daughter had fought about an already-married man in India whom the girl wished to marry. Sarabjit wanted to kill the man's wife to free him for marriage and her father bitterly objected. Sarabjit then allegedly took the poison, and told her father she was killing herself because he would not allow her to marry the man she chose, and that he would be blamed for her suicide and consequently would hang. He lost his temper, smashed her head with a hammer, rushed out to buy a hacksaw, returned and, while his daughter was still alive, began sawing off her head. He spent the next two days disposing of her body.

Despite Sandhu's graphic confession, he pleaded not guilty at his Old Bailey trial held six weeks after the murder. He was sentenced to life in prison.

Sinks, Theodore P., 1939- , U.S. Herbert Jacobson, assistant prosecutor for Montgomery County, Ohio, believed that convicted murderer Ted Sinks derived some personal satisfaction out of having buried his wife in a concrete-covered pit where he worked. "Maybe he got his kicks out of having her there," Jacobson theorized. "He could say 'Good morning Judy,' or when he left, 'Goodbye Judy.'"

Theodore Sinks worked as a plumbing, heating, and air conditioning supervisor for Dayton Newspapers, Inc. (DNI). His wife, Judy Sinks, forty-four, was employed by the same company in the circulation department. The couple seemed

to have a good marriage, but Judy Sinks' coworkers said she was quite often prone to depression, and that Ted Sinks had a "pretty short temper." In September 1986, Judy Sinks apparently tried to kill herself with a gun. Ballistics tests cleared her husband of any involvement in the non-fatal shooting and Judy Sinks sufficiently recovered to get on with her life—until her husband reported her disappearance on Nov. 24, 1987.

Sinks told police that he had returned home from work at 2:30 p.m., to take her to the doctor. When she did not return by the next morning, he notified authorities. Judy Sinks' purse was found in a mailbox on Main Street, leading police to conclude that she had met with foul play.

Four days earlier, on Nov. 20, Kenneth Rice, a DNI employee who worked for Sinks, helped him load a fifty-five-gallon drum allegedly filled with asbestos from Sinks' garage into a pickup truck. Sinks was vague about why he had this material in his garage, but he told Rice that the best way to dispose of it would be to bury the canister in the seventh floor of the DNI building where a water-purifying system was being installed. "It was another way to fill the hole I guess," said Rice. "This way nobody would know and he was the boss. I was just doing what he said."

Rice helped mix the concrete, but Sinks insisted on finishing the job himself. The body of Judy Sinks was buried in the concrete pedestal, and the water filtration unit for the main cooling tower was moved into position over the pit. For the next five months Sinks played the role of the aggrieved husband. When the Dayton *Daily News* offered a $2,000 reward for information about their missing employee, he told them to withdraw the offer and badgered the paper into suppressing news items and follow-up stories about the disappearance. Claiming that his wife had probably taken her own life, he said he feared that continuing publicity would spark a wave of crank phone calls.

The police were stymied in their investigation until they received an anonymous tip on Apr. 26, 1988. With pickaxes and sledgehammers, city workers broke apart the concrete pedestal. The badly decomposed body was exhumed and taken to the Montgomery County Coroner, who ruled that Judy Sinks had been strangled with a nylon-cotton cord, which Sinks had neglected to remove from her throat. Judge Jack Duncan ordered Sinks held at the city-county jail in lieu of a $100,000 bond. The case went to trial on Jan. 4, 1989. Ten days later the jury returned a Guilty verdict, and Sinks was sentenced to fifteen years to life in prison and fined $15,000 by Judge John Kessler of the Montgomery County Common Pleas Court. During the entire proceeding the defendant remained stone cold. "What boils me," said Larry Harmon, a brother of Judy Sinks, "is that all through this, he still didn't show any emotions, and that irritates me. I don't know how anybody can be so damn heartless."

Skid Row Slasher, The, See: **Greenwood, Vaughn Orrin.**

Small, Kenneth B., prom. 1954, U.S. In May 1954, Kenneth B. Small shot Jules Lack in Allegan, Mich., killing him instantly. At his trial for first-degree murder, Small tearfully said that he had killed Lack, forty-five, because his wife wanted to divorce him and marry Lack. With the aid of his wife's testimony, Small was found Not Guilty by reason of insanity and sentenced to a mental hospital.

Edith Small told Kenneth, a dentist, that she wanted to marry Lack because he made more money. She told Small, "You don't know how to live. You're small. I want to live big now." Small showed up at a rendezvous between his wife and Lack at a party. Bursting through the door, he demanded to know which man was Lack. Lack smiled and extended his hand. "I'm Lack," he said. Small fired two shots and Lack fell dead.

Smith, Arthur John, 1946- , Brit. England's Arthur John Smith eventually confessed that on Feb. 23, 1966, he stabbed Phyllis Pearce, forty-eight, six times because she bumped into him and he lost his temper. Smith was sentenced to life imprisonment for what the court superintendent deemed the most meaningless, senseless murder he had ever encountered.

The police interviewed nearly 80,000 people living in the vicinity. In the course of their massive investigation, they discovered that Smith possessed a knife like the murder weapon, and the ominous nickname, "Murder Smith." His father had dumped the knife into Portsmouth Harbor, fearing his son would be suspected in the murder. With that, Smith confessed to the murder and related the tale of his nonsensical attack.

Smith, Clarice, 1964- , U.S. On May 21, 1987, the mummified corpse of a 3-year-old girl was found in a West Philadelphia housing project apartment. Two workers discovered the body of Sylvia Smith after a resident reported smelling gas and hearing running water coming from the sixteenth-floor apartment, according to West Detective Division officer John Yeakel. The tiny corpse,

thirty-eight inches long and weighing only six pounds, was kneeling beside a bed, apparently in the spot where she died three months earlier. Taken into custody after her arrest at the home of a relative was Clarice Smith, twenty-three, the child's mother. Smith initially was charged with the abuse of a corpse, meaning that she knew the child was dead but neglected to report it. After an autopsy, she was charged with murder and endangering the welfare of a child. Acting medical examiner Dr. Robert Catherman listed malnutrition as the cause of death. According to homicide Lieutenant James Hemwood, "The body was mummified, in a sealed-up room, with no air." Sylvia had died around Christmas 1986.

Smith, a cocaine addict, had another daughter, Shantil, six, who had been living with a grandmother for five years. After a three-day non-jury trial at the Common Pleas Court before Judge Michael R. Stiles, Smith was convicted on June 29, 1988, of abuse of a corpse and third-degree murder. Assistant District Attorney James Long and defense attorney Charles Cunningham argued throughout the trial over whether Smith had acted with malice. Long said the defendant had once physically attacked a boyfriend who tried to "show love" to the 3-year-old Sylvia and noted that the doorknob to the bedroom door was found near the body, indicating that the child had tried to escape. Cunningham called the death "a tragic accident" caused by Smith's $1,400-a-week cocaine addiction. After Smith allowed her daughter to starve to death, she left the apartment, fearing that people would think "I was bad person." In September, Stiles sentenced Smith to the maximum ten to twenty years in jail with a concurrent two-year term for the abuse of a corpse. Her daughter's death lead to a state welfare department investigation which faulted the city's human services department for inadequately protecting the child, who had come under its supervision in 1984.

Smith, Edgar Herbert, Jr., 1933- , U.S. In 1957 Victoria Zielinski, a 15-year-old high school cheerleader from Mahwah, N.J., was found bludgeoned with a baseball bat and her skull crushed by a forty-four pound boulder in a gravel pit in Hackensack, N.J. Edgar Herbert Smith, Jr., twenty-three, an acquaintance of Zielinski's, confessed, was tried, and convicted of the crime. Sentenced to die in the electric chair, Smith spent the next fourteen years on death row in a New Jersey prison. Known as "Death Row Smith," he studied the law, and escaped execution nineteen times by appeal. He also became an author, writing *Beyond A Reasonable Doubt* and *Brief Against Death*. Smith wrote a murder mystery and yet another book based on his experiences as a Death Row convict fighting charges he repeatedly claimed were false—he claimed police pressured him to confess. The proceeds from his writings helped finance his many appeals. Smith's best-seller, *Brief Against Death,* attracted the attention of journalist William F. Buckley, Jr., who supported his writing and helped him obtain a release from prison.

In 1971, a federal appeals court ruled Smith's confession came from police pressure and ordered a second trial for him, where he was allowed to plead "no defense" to reduced charges of second-degree murder. Sentenced to twenty-five to thirty years in jail, he was given credit for the time he had already served and received seven years off his sentence for good behavior. He was released on parole on Dec. 6, 1971. On his release from prison, Smith was picked up by a limousine to appear on Buckley's television show, "Firing Line," then spent his first night out of prison in a suite at New York City's elegant St. Regis Hotel. His new-found celebrity status resulted in publication of another book, *Getting Out,* and he wrote several articles about the criminal justice system, meanwhile touring the nation lecturing. Settling in San Diego, Calif., in August 1974, he held a variety of jobs as security guard, public relations consultant, and freelance writer. He married Paige Diana Heimer, nineteen, in 1974. From March 1976 through October 1976 he was often on welfare.

On Oct. 8, 1976, a warrant was issued for Smith's arrest on charges of kidnapping and attempted murder. Lefteriya Lisa Ozbun, a 33-year-old Chula Vista, Calif., clothing factory employee, was walking toward the plant's parking lot to get a ride home from her husband when Smith leaped from his car, put a knife to her throat, and told her, "Keep your mouth shut or I'm going to cut your throat right here." Throwing her in the front seat of his car, Smith taped her wrists together and drove away. Ozbun fought fiercely, explaining later that she was sure he would kill her. "I'd never seen eyes like that. They were so cold and filled with hate." When she said she kicked out the windshield and grabbed the steering wheel, Smith stabbed her with a six-inch butcher knife, missing her heart by a fraction of an inch. The car swerved onto an exit ramp and Ozbun crawled out as Smith raced away. Twelve days later Smith called Buckley from Las Vegas, Nev., leaving his phone and room numbers with Buckley's secretary. Buckley immediately turned Smith in to the FBI. Smith, unarmed and living under an alias, did not resist arrest on Oct. 13. His wife later was arrested on charges of aiding and abetting his flight, and concealing him.

At Smith's San Diego trial in March 1977 he admitted that he had murdered Zielinski and said that his earlier defense—which claimed that police had forced him to confess—was false. He also confessed to all charges of attempted murder, assault, and kidnapping in the Ozbun

case. Smith said he decided to reveal his past lies because he had visited the murder victim's grave in Honesdale, Pa., and there "recognized the devil I'd been looking at in the mirror for forty-three years was me..." Superior Court Judge Gilbert Harelson heard the trial without a jury. Smith's sentencing was delayed when he was hospitalized after a beating by prisoners while in a holding cell. In his Apr. 19, 1977, column, Buckley reiterated statements from a Nov. 20, 1976, column, saying, "I believe now that Smith was guilty of the first crime. There is no mechanism as yet perfected that will establish beyond question a person's guilt or innocence. There will be guilty people freed this year and every year." On April 25, 1977, Smith was sentenced to life imprisonment for kidnapping and attempted murder by Judge Harelson, who rejected his request for a new trial and for an examination to determine whether he was a mentally disordered sex offender. Harelson withheld sentencing on three other charges connected with the Ozbun case until Smith completes his sentence.

First becoming eligible for parole in 1982, Smith was turned down five times. Outraged letters, many from New Jersey, poured in to the parole board, urging that he be kept in prison for the rest of his life. Writing to a Los Angeles *Times* reporter, Smith incomprehensibly blamed his prosecutors in New Jersey for his attack on Ozbun and claimed that he himself was also a victim. "Ask those self-righteous public servants why they gave me the opportunity to do it," he wrote, explaining that there are questions "which need answering, which Lisa Ozbun and I need answered." Smith's wife, who divorced him not long after his second crime, said, "Edgar is a master at manipulating the system. He manipulated his way off death row in New Jersey. He conned Bill Buckley. And now he's doing what he's always done. He's working the system, until the odds are in his favor for parole."

Smith, Frederick D. (AKA: **Curly**), 1908-67, and **Blackstone, David Thomas**, b.1898, and **Oliver, Frank Miles**, 1912- , U.S. When they were boys, Harry Lore and Fred Smith were best friends. They spent hours fishing together in the lakes of the Irish Hill region near Ypsilanti, Mich. In 1927, 19-year-old Fred Smith was arrested for holding up a gas station, and Judge George Sample put him on five years' probation. A year later, on Aug. 25, 1928, Smith was sentenced to five to fifteen years in prison for breaking his parole. Citing a touching letter from Smith's nearly blind mother, Governor Fred Green of Michigan paroled Smith in 1930 after he had served only two years of his sentence. When he was later arrested for the murder of his one-time fishing buddy and three friends, the local press bitterly denounced the decision to release Smith from prison.

On Aug. 11, 1931, Smith left his job at a papermill to meet his two friends, David Blackstone and Frank Oliver, both of whom had a history of petty crime. Blackstone had been released from the Illinois penitentiary a year earlier. They met at Otis Oden's, a saloon near Milan. After drinking whiskey, Smith and Blackstone decided to go out and rob someone. They took Oliver's late-model Pontiac to Peninsula Grove, a popular picnic spot near the County Line Road in Willis, Mich.

As they drove the car slowly through the wooded area and drank, they spotted the car of Thomas Wheatley, a 16-year-old high school student. Smith and Blackstone left their car to "pull the job," according to Frank Oliver. A few minutes later, they returned with $2 and a stolen watch belonging to Anna May Harrison, a 17-year-old guest at the Lore family home. Fearing that Harry Lore would report him to the police, Smith returned to the car and captured its occupants at gunpoint.

Wheatley, Lore, Harrison, and Vivian Gold of Cleveland were driven to Tuttle Hill Road, where they pleaded for their lives. "Yeah," Smith said, "let you go and we'll all go to the jug." Harry Lore struggled with Blackstone, who shot him. Blackstone then shot and killed the other three. Smith first considered burying the victims in a gravel pit near Ypsilanti, but decided that would take too much time. Instead, the killers doused the four bodies with gasoline and placed them in the back seat of Wheatley's car. They set fire to the car and made their way back to Ypsilanti. It was 5:30 a.m.

A farmer in Willis, Mich., soon found the blazing wreck. State police immediately launched an exhaustive manhunt. They took moonshiners Paul Keene and Lawrence Keene into custody, but soon ruled them out as likely suspects.

That morning, David Blackstone drove to Detroit and pawned Anna Harrison's watch for $6. Within seventy-two hours after the discovery of the automobile, Smith, Oliver, and Blackstone were in custody. Blackstone was captured after his gun fell into the hands of an Ypsilanti police informant. Police then traced the weapon to Blackstone.

When news of the shooting spread through Ann Arbor, a crowd of 10,000 descended on the Washtenaw County courthouse and demanded that the police surrender the killers. State militiamen lined the streets as the Lincoln touring car with the three young men inside made its way through the town. Four deputy sheriffs led Smith and his companions through the hostile mob. Police interviewed the three suspects separately. "We know you did the killing, Blackstone told us all!" screamed one of the deputies to the defiant Fred Smith. After two hours of interrogation, Smith

broke down and confessed. He then seized an iron bar from the table and tried to fight his way out of jail, but two deputies quickly overpowered him.

"I don't wonder that the crowd outside is crying for vengeance," exclaimed Judge George Sample. After the full story had been told, the court found each of the defendants Guilty on each of four first-degree murder charges. Judge Sample sentenced them to life imprisonment. Sheriff Henry Bennett was praised for bringing the killers to justice so quickly.

When Smith, Blackstone, and Oliver arrived at the gates of the penitentiary in Jackson, police used tear gas to disperse a crowd of 3,000 spectators. After serving thirty-six years in prison, Frederick Smith died on Feb. 17, 1967. Frank Oliver was paroled on Jan. 16, 1969, and was granted a final discharge from supervision on Jan. 16, 1973. There is no further record of David Blackstone, the man who fired the fatal shots.

Smith, George, Jr., 1907-45, Brit. Twenty-eight-year-old George E. Smith, Jr., of Pittsburgh, a U.S. Army private stationed in England, was arrested in December 1944, and charged with the murder of retired British diplomat, Sir Eric Teichman. Teichman, who lived on a 3,000-acre estate in Norfolk County, heard shots and went outside to discourage what he assumed were poachers. When he did not return, his wife searched the grounds. She found her husband dead, shot in the face with a .30-caliber bullet from a U.S. Army carbine. Nearby police found more spent cartridges and wads of chewing gum.

A few days later, Smith was arrested and charged, along with Private Leonard S. Wijpacha. Smith was charged with murder and Wijpacha with accessory to murder. On Jan. 12, 1945, Smith was convicted by a U.S. Army court-martial and sentenced to be hanged. General Dwight D. Eisenhower did not reprieve Smith, who was executed on May 8, 1945.

Smith, George Joseph (AKA: **George Baker; The Brides of the Bath Murderer; John Lloyd; George Oliver Love; Henry Williams**), 1872-1915, Brit. Everything about this turn-of-the-century mass murderer was prim and proper. Though he murdered for profit, Smith nevertheless had the decorum to marry his victims before sending them swiftly to their watery deaths through a method of his own simple but cunning invention.

Born at 92 Roman Road, Bethal Green, London, on Jan. 11, 1872, according to the birth certificate he was using at the time of his arrest, Smith's family was not well off. His father struggled to pay the bills by selling insurance, a then unpopular field of interest, but one, oddly enough, Smith would later recognize as a source of great income, when coupled with his unique brand of murder. Poorly educated and left mostly to the streets, Smith, at the age of nine, stole some fruit from a vendor and was caught by running into the open arms of a London constable. (His other offenses at this time consisted of similar acts of pilferage and the breaking of a street lamp.)

Being of meager means, his parents did not contest a court action which sent the child to a reformatory for eight years, thrusting him into a brutal environment that certainly helped to create the calculating killer who slowly emerged decades later. Reflecting upon Smith's youthful plight, crime writer Colin Wilson later wrote that "George Joseph Smith is one of the most powerful arguments against judicial savagery in criminal history."

Smith's evolution as a master criminal lacked lightning and thunder. His way toward the gallows involved a plodding series of criminal acts that almost imperceptively, in deepening shades of gray, led to the ultimate murders he committed. And only toward the end of his horrifying career did he truly earn the reputation given to him by one of his biographers as "the most atrocious English criminal since Palmer." (Dr. William Palmer of Rugeley, England, a nineteenth-century killer, poisoned for profit at least a half

"Brides of the Bath Murderer" George Joseph Smith and one of his victims, second wife Alice Burnham.

dozen persons and was hanged in 1856.) Released from the Borstal institution in 1888, Smith busied himself with small larcenies, was sentenced to a week in jail in 1890 for a petty theft, and six months in prison the following year for stealing a bicycle.

The bicycle was in keeping with Smith's athletically inclined young manhood. Though never proven, he reportedly worked for some time as a gymnasium instructor, and, some time during the early 1890s, enlisted in the army,

seeing duty overseas. By 1896, Smith had transformed his once undernourished, bone-thin body into a muscular frame with "unnaturally tough biceps." Also in that year, as he had shed himself of his sickly, unimpressive body, Smith ostensibly did away with George Joseph Smith as a person. Journalist William Bolitho, who studied Smith's life, likened the future killer's transformation to that of "the breaking of the cocoon that frees the full-grown night-moth. The man has separated himself definitely from the caterpillar that was G.J. Smith, to begin a series of lives in other names, each separate in environment, both personal and local, and only joined by the hidden chain of his own identity."

Smith became George Baker, setting himself up in a cheap rooming house in a shabby section of London. He dressed as would any middle-class office worker or government employee, his suits dark and inexpensive, a bowler hat square on his head, the perennial British umbrella hooked on his arm. And there was not only money in his pocket for the first time in his life, but enough for him to start a small savings account. The source of these wondrous new riches were women, several of them, all in love with him, even though he hated all women.

Adorning his hair with gobs of pomade, coating his athletic body with cut-rate cologne, and affecting the manners of a gentleman forced into uncomfortable means, Smith drew the attentions of young, unsophisticated women, mostly domestic servant girls working in the mansions of the rich (which was his plan), who sighed with passion at his slightest nod. Exactly how Smith developed such magnetism is uncertain; perhaps while in the army, or even during his brief stint as a boarding house keeper, imitating the conduct of retired gentlemen in his care. No matter, he was physically handsome in that squarejawed, keen-eyed Victorian tradition made famous by Sidney Paget, who illustrated the first Sherlock Holmes stories for *The Strand* magazine, only a few years before Smith's criminal activities accelerated. Oddly enough, Smith bore a striking resemblance to Holmes as seen by Paget, which may have subconsciously attracted his female admirers. According to Charles Higham, writing in *The Adventures of Conan Doyle*, Paget presented a "sexually attractive, well-fleshed nineties face and figure...His image of Sherlock Holmes had hundreds of thousands of young woman yearn for this fictional character as they might yearn for a stage actor..."

Yet Smith was the antithesis of the great Sherlock. The similarity was only physical; where Holmes struggled to triumph over evil, Smith personified it, commercialized it, made it pay through his bevy of adoring females, a harem he quickly turned into a trained platoon of sneak thieves.

The *modus operandi* of Smith's enterprise was as prosaic as the man himself. Under his direction, these swooning housemaids simply made detailed inventories of the furnishings in the mansions they worked. Smith scrutinized these lists, which catalogued possessions down to the smallest bric-a-brac, then selected the items he thought he might easily sell. The maids then stole the pieces and dutifully returned them to Smith, who in turn sold them. It was during this period that Smith took up the habit of itemizing everything in his life, his true miserly character emerging in exacting ledger books where all income and expenses, down to the last farthing, were detailed, an avaricious trait that led to Smith's downfall years later.

Immediate peril for Smith came in 1896 in the form of jealousy; one of his many working-girl lovers, enraged when he paid too much attention to another, informed on him. Smith was arrested, police finding great quantities of stolen goods in his rooms. He was sent to prison for a year.

Avoiding the London streets, where he figured he might chance upon one of his maidservant cronies, Smith went to Leicester upon his release in 1897, opening a small sweet shop and catering to children. During the day, Smith was the patient and kindly gentleman who peddled penny candies and biscuits to swarms of little ones who had saved for their Saturday spending sprees in his tiny shop. At night, Smith put on his finest linen suit and top hat, and went strolling for bigger commercial game—women. On one of these nocturnal hunts, Smith encountered Caroline Thornhill. Learning that she had a small savings account, he promptly proposed. The couple married in 1898, Smith using the symbolic alias of George Oliver Love. Either out of whimsy or irony, Smith listed his father as a "detective" on the marriage papers. Mr. and Mrs. Love moved into the back rooms of Smith's candy store, which failed a little more each day, until Smith began to eat up his wife's savings. When this meager amount was dissipated, Smith informed his wife that she was useless to him, that he intended to leave her. Caroline Thornhill Love begged Smith to keep her at his side. There must be a way, she pleaded. Well, he admitted, there was—if she was willing to do exactly as he directed. Anything, she agreed. They moved to London.

Mrs. Love's new occupation was one so ably performed by Smith's previous loot-clutching paramours. Her devoted husband meticulously wrote references for her. With these she secured a job as a servant in many handsome homes. Caroline, under Smith's cautious tutorship, became an expert sneak thief, filling Smith's apartment with jewelry, furniture, paintings. Again, Smith made out his niggardly entries into well-kept ledger books, keeping a strict tally on all stolen items received from his wife and their subsequent resales.

With new earnings from his wife's persistent pilferage, Smith suddenly discovered the seaside resorts of England,

traveling through the towns of Hove and Hastings, passing himself off as an antique dealer, searching, as would an archeologist for saleable artifacts, more gullible females to woo, win, and rob. It is not known how many women Smith promised to marry, or even married at this time, in order to obtain their savings and dowries, but it is certain that at this time in his life he had decided on bigamy as a living. He did marry a boarding house owner while still the spouse of Caroline Thornhill Love, absconding with the woman's savings, even her wardrobe. When Caroline returned home one day in 1900, hands full of stolen goods, she discovered these feminine articles and flew into a rage. Smith explained that the brief affair with the landlady was only business, but Caroline became so unnerved that she discarded caution and was caught by one of her employers as she attempted to smuggle a suitcase full of stolen candelabras from his house. She immediately informed on Smith who meekly surrendered to bobbies bounding into his tranquil lodgings. Smith received another prison sentence for receiving stolen goods, this time the maximum of two years. When he emerged from prison in 1902, he searched in earnest for his legitimate wife and meal ticket, Caroline, only to learn that she had fled to Canada a few days before his release.

Smith shrugged at the problem; there were thousands of spinster women available. He began marrying and deserting females in record numbers, spinster after spinster, sucking them dry of their worldly goods and money, then leaving them, most of these hapless females being citizens of the seaside resorts. In Brighton, Smith obtained £90 from an elderly woman, his largest amount in the year 1908. With this money, coupled with his ever-increasing inventory in furnishings taken from previously abandoned wives, Smith opened a second-hand shop in Bristol where he met and married Edith Mabel Pegler, who, like most of his other brides, was "a notch above" him, according to Smith's later statements, referring to her social and educational standing.

Pegler, who was soon drained of her savings by Smith, had the distinction of marrying the *real* Mr. Smith, since he used, for whatever odd reason, his own name at the time. Smith purchased a house, his first home, with £240. He reveled in being a property owner, fondling each night his important papers—title deeds, certificates of transfer. This was the heart of Smith's genuine ambitions, property, and possessions. He loathed females in general, a hatred typical of women exploiters, and was inwardly repelled and disgusted by the sexual performances he was obligated, however briefly, to enact. But George Joseph Smith endured it all. His was a hunt for money through the withered fields of middle-class, middle-aged British womanhood. He would have his possessions at any price, even murder.

The precise time of Smith's decision to commit homicide in his marrying and mulcting schemes has never been pinpointed, but it was most probably caused by his marriage to Edith Pegler. He had actually found himself developing affection for this wife, an emotion that undoubtedly troubled Smith, whose business it was to eliminate all emotions, all feelings, in order that he coldly perform his bigamist-bilking chores. In Summer 1910, Smith got rid of Edith in the same fashion he had abandoned his other wives: he took her to a National Gallery showing, excused himself to go to the men's room, and left her forever as she stared at classics on canvas.

Two months later, in August 1910, while strolling through Bristol, Smith met Beatrice Constance Annie ("Bessie") Mundy, a 33-year-old spinster. Not only was the lovesick Bessie easy prey for the much-marrying Smith, but she held the key to his future in that she was also an heiress to £2,500 left to her by her late father, a bank official. After quickly getting Bessie to accept his hand in marriage (while using the alias Henry Williams), Smith's hot dreams of instant riches were dashed against a hard-willed uncle who controlled Bessie's fortune, and who allowed her only £8 a week to live on. The conniving Smith tried wheedling Bessie's dowry from her executor; he wrote in his groveling manner, a plea to the coffer-clutching uncle from Weymouth, where the couple had wed, on Aug. 29, 1910:

Dear Sir,

My wife and self thank you very much for your letter today with kind expressions. In *re* banks, undoubtedly to transact the business there would be rather awkward. Thus we suggest it would be better if you will be good enough to forward a money order instead of checks—however it will suit the circumstances. Any time we change our address we should let you know beforehand. Bessie hopes you will forward as much money as possible at your earliest (by registered letter). Am pleased to say Bessie is in perfect health, and both looking forward to a bright and happy future.

Believe me, yours faithfully,

H. Williams

As a postscript to this missive, Bessie, at the request of her spouse, added in her own hand: "I am very happy indeed. Bessie Williams."

This appeal from Smith was only the first in a month-long series of notes and letters exchanged between him and the uncle; both men employed solicitors to settle the matter of Bessie's inheritance with the result that £138 was sent to Smith. Thinking that these were the only funds he would

realize from Bessie's estate, the tight-fisted bigamist turned on the cultured, passive Bessie, and, searching for a way to absent himself from their brief union, accused her of infecting him with a venereal disease as a result of being promiscuous! Such a charge was, of course, absurd since

Smith with another wife, Bessie Constance Mundy.

Bessie was a highly moral woman of fine education and propriety, but it served as excuse enough to leave her.

Smith quickly departed into hazy activities, returning to Mrs. Edith Pegler Smith, resuming his "antique" dealings. He moved secretly about for two years, dragging his docile wife with him from London to Bristol. And it was during this period of sketchy migrations that Smith could very well have begun to murder after marrying his victims, for, by the time he again met the hapless Bessie Mundy, his purpose was clear and his ingenious method for resolving relationships was decidedly lethal, a method Smith had undoubtedly pondered and practiced for some time.

On Mar. 14, 1912, Bessie Mundy, having accepted her miserable lot in life as God's will, left the boarding house of one Mrs. Tuckett in Weston-super-Mare, taking her daily constitutional. She returned at 1 p.m. in a nervous state, telling Mrs. Tuckett that she had accidentally met her errant husband, Henry Williams. "He was looking over the sea," said Bessie with trembling lips. "He turned around, stared into my eyes, and said: 'Ah, Bessie, my dove, it's all been a terrible mistake.'" Two years had elapsed since Smith had deserted Bessie, cursing her as he went for afflicting him with syphilis, yet at the moment of their reunion, she forgot and forgave all. Mrs. Tuckett was not of a similar mind, for she had, on instructions of Bessie's uncle, become the woman's ever-watchful guardian.

When Smith showed up at the boarding house two hours later, Mrs. Tuckett showed him to her drawing room. He sat sipping tea with the landlady and Bessie. Mrs. Tuckett, stiff as a ramrod in her rocker, leaned forward and bluntly asked him: "Why did you leave your wife at Weymouth?"

Smith looked at her with a hurt expression. "Why, I've been looking high and low for Bessie for months in every town in England!"

"What was the point of that? You knew very well, Mr. Williams, the addresses of Bessie's relatives. They could have easily told you where to find your wife."

Without hesitation Smith countered: "Exactly—it was through Bessie's uncle—or was it her brother?—that I learned she was living in this area."

The couple were reconciled within the hour, swearing to live forever with each other, Bessie grateful for the return through Providence of her attractive husband, Smith, who was broke, determined this time to obtain all of Bessie's inheritance, no matter what the cost.

That afternoon the pair, at Smith's insistence, visited Baker & Co., solicitors, where he arranged a loan from his adoring wife in the amount of £150 at 4 percent interest, signing a formal note to that affect, making the transaction legal. Smith then queerly talked about the loan from his wife as being "a wonderful investment for her."

They returned to Mrs. Tuckett's establishment to retrieve Bessie's belongings. Mrs. Tuckett did not like the looks of Smith, and it showed on her face when she greeted them at the door.

"I suppose I may go back to my husband?" asked Bessie, seeking the elderly matron's sanction.

"You are over thirty," snapped Mrs. Tuckett. "I cannot hold you back!"

When Bessie was packed, the couple left the house, Mrs. Tuckett glaring at Smith. "We'll return this evening to say our formal goodbyes," Smith told her in a soft voice. They did not return. Smith realized, however, that Mrs. Tuckett's response to him was that of seething suspicion. He penned a clever letter to allay the landlady's fears concerning his wife's fate, having the missive delivered to Mrs. Tuckett that night. It was a perceptive and telling stroke, this letter, one that summed up the attitudes and fears of the British middle-class of that closeted Edwardian era, displaying an intellectual dimension on Smith's part that put him into that rare class of criminal, one that understood the morality, traditions, and apprehensions of a society that worked against him and his sinister plans. It read:

Dear Madam,

In consequence of the past and the heated argument which possibly would have occurred if wife and self had to face you and your friends this evening, thus, for the sake of peace we decided to stop away and remain together as man and wife should do in the apartments which I have chosen temporarily. Later on I will write a long letter to all Bessie's friends clearly purporting all the circumstances on the whole affair solely with the intention of placing all your minds at rest concerning our welfare. All I propose to state at present beside that which has already been stated by Bessie and myself before the solicitors that it is useless as the law stands and in view of all the circumstances together with the affinity existing between my wife and self for any person to try and part us and dangerous to try and do us harm or endeavor to make our lives miserable. It appears that many people would rather stir up strife than try and make peace. As far as Bessie and I are concerned the past is forgiven and forgotten. Bessie has not only stated that on her oath to the solicitors; but has also given it to me in a letter written by herself to me which I shall always prize. Thus my future object and delight will be to prove myself not only a true husband but a gentleman and finally make my peace step by step with all those who have been kind to Bessie. Then why in the name of heaven and Christianity do people so like to constantly interfere and stir up past troubles? It would be more Christian-like and honorable on their part to do their best to make peace. There is time yet to make amends and if people will only let us alone and with the help of the higher powers which has united us twice, Bessie shall have a comfortable settled home and be happy with me. I trust there is many years of happiness before us. I thank with all my heart all those who have been kind to my wife during my absence.

Yours respectfully,
H. Williams

With that, Smith moved his lost bride to Herne Bay where he rented a house on High Street from a wary Miss Rapley. While making arrangements with the proprietor, Smith, in a pleasing voice, became confidential, telling Miss

Rapley that "my wife is a cut above me. Her friends did not at all approve of her marriage. My wife has a private income paid monthly. I have not anything except that I dabble in antiques."

Miss Rapley accepted Smith's volunteered financial confession in lieu of bankers' references, and rented the house to him; her risk was not great since the house itself was rather run-down, and did not even offer an inside public convenience, nor a bath. But that was the exact reason why the sly Mr. Smith so desired to live in it.

Once settled in the house, Smith's waking thoughts concentrated on Bessie's seemingly unattainable inheritance. He knew he would have to move fast; her suspicious in-laws would probably circumvent his move to her money by establishing an annuity with that inheritance. He found his scheming answer in giving over all his worldly possessions to his darling Bessie should he perish, a thoughtful intent echoed by his wife. On July 8, 1912, Smith and Bessie visited a solicitor, lawyer, and parson, the latter a chosen witness to the mutual wills they carefully signed. If Bessie died, her entire estate would be turned over to Smith. If Smith (as Williams) were to die, his estate would be inherited by his wife, which meant she would get absolutely nothing.

The following day, attired in top hat and morning coat, the elegant-looking Smith entered the shop of a man named Hill, an ironmonger by trade. He came to the point abruptly: "The house I have rented with my wife has no bath. She simply will not put up with the lack of such a necessity an hour longer."

Hill showed Smith his iron tubs. The ever-thoughtful husband selected the cheapest model, haggling the ironmonger down to under £2. The bath was delivered on credit that night.

On July 10, the husband and wife paid a surprise call on a Dr. French in Herne Bay, Smith explaining that his cherished one had "suffered some sort of fit." French, thinking Smith meant epilepsy, asked some leading questions, to which Smith, not his wife, replied to the affirmative. "Yes, epileptic fit, that sounds like it," concluded Smith.

Bessie who appeared to Dr. French to be in a drowsy state said: "I don't remember anything so serious. I've always been healthy, but if Mr. Williams says I have had a fit then it must have come and gone outside my consciousness. I *do* remember a headache."

French gave her a bromide and sent the couple home. Two days later, a little past midnight, Smith frantically rang the door to Dr. French's clinic. "My wife has had another fit," Smith told the physician. "Please come at once."

When they reached the Williamses' cottage, Dr. French found Bessie sitting up in bed. It had been a stifling day.

She complained of the heat. She was hot and flushed, that was all. "Keep her quiet," the doctor whispered to Smith. "I can only assume that the intense heat of the day has provoked another epileptic fit." He promised to return later that day, and when he visited Bessie at 3 p.m., Dr. French found Mrs. Williams in astoundingly good health. She felt wonderful, Bessie told him, though she was deeply concerned "about these fits I don't seem to remember." When Dr. French left, Bessie wrote briefly to her uncle a letter, which her dutiful husband was kind enough to get into the mails only minutes after she sealed the envelope. It read in part: "Last Tuesday night I had a bad fit...My whole system is shaken. My husband has provided me with the best medical men, who are...attending me day and night. I have made my will and left all to my husband. That is only natural as I love my husband."

At 7 a.m. on July 13, Smith woke his wife gently from her night's reveries. "I've prepared a nice, hot bath for you, dearest." Bessie rubbed sleep from her eyes with a smile of gratitude. The iron tub, which lacked taps and fittings, and had to be filled and emptied with a bucket, had been placed by Smith in a room without a lock on the door. Bessie entered the room, shed her nightie, and slipped into the tepid water and oblivion. An hour later, Dr. French was handed a note by a schoolboy running an errand for Mr. Williams, who asked in a frantic scrawl: "Can you come at once? I'm afraid my wife is dead."

In minutes, Dr. French was peering down at the naked, cold body of Bessie Mundy Williams, lying on her back in the bathtub, her head submerged, her long legs stretched out stiff, her feet over the end of the tub. In her right hand she clutched a square piece of Castile soap.

French lifted the corpse from the tub, placing it on the floor, trying vainly at artificial respiration. It was no use. The woman was dead. "Where were you, Mr. Williams, when this dreadful thing happened?" quizzed the doctor.

Smith, who had never shown a second's emotion to anyone until that moment, burst into tears, explaining between sobs: "I went out...to fetch some herrings...for our breakfast...When I returned...I found my sweetheart...dead!"

Ordering Smith to sit in the next room and compose himself, Dr. French went for the coroner. A moment later, Smith was himself in the street calling a policeman and a woman neighbor. Through heaving sobs he led the pair into his house and upstairs, pointing at the naked body on the bathroom floor. The policeman thought him temporarily deranged. The woman fainted.

Mrs. Rapley appeared, horrified at the sight. Smith's sorrow was blatantly heaped upon the landlady, though he did manage to murmur: "Lucky thing my wife made her will."

When the coroner arrived, accompanied by Dr. French,

the official asked only a few perfunctory questions. He was informed by the doctor that he had treated the poor Mrs. Williams for epilepsy. A hastily convened coroner's jury, acting on Dr. French's statements, so carefully engineered by the plotting Smith, concluded that Bessie's demise was wholly accidental, an epileptic seizure causing her to drown in her bath. Though Herbert Mundy and other family members protested, wagging fingers in Smith's direction, the coroner and his jury refused to be budged. None of the jury members ever asked themselves how such a tall woman could have drowned in such a small bathtub.

Smith haggled with the undertaker, whittling down his price on his cheapest coffin for his dear departed, and ordered the most inexpensive funeral available. He sent only one short note to Bessie's relatives: "Words cannot describe the great shock, and I am naturally too sad to write more." Two hours after burying his bride, Smith appeared in the ironmonger's store, lugging the lethal bathtub. "This thing is no good," he informed Hill. "It killed my wife." He refused to pay for the iron tub, leaving it in the middle of the floor, and going out with a raging slam of the shop door.

Smith immediately began to wage legal war to obtain his wife's estate from her relatives. The Mundy family entered a caveat against the will but when the family lawyer pointed out the decision of the coroner's jury, and Smith's roaring threats to sue the entire family, the Mundys gave in. Smith was given more than £2,000. He then disappeared.

In late August 1912, George Joseph Smith reappeared at the doorstep of Edith Pegler Smith, the wife that thought him a salesman who traveled the world. He explained that he had been in Canada. When she questioned him about the huge amounts of money he was carrying, Smith gave her a benign smile, saying: "Ah, sweet wife. Fortune stroked the back of my neck. I found an ancient jade idol, and made more than £1,000 on the sale of the Chinese statue. It was a beautiful thing. I hated to part with it, but we must live, my dear, we must live."

But Edith Pegler Smith did not share in this newly acquired wealth. Other than some of Bessie Mundy's stolen clothes, she received only a pittance from her husband with which to purchase necessities. Smith thought of himself as a shrewd businessman; he invested Bessie's estate in the purchase of ten small houses in Bristol, dizzying himself in an orgy of deeds, titles, transfer certificates, ledgers, rents, and receipts, attempting to build a great fortune on Bessie Mundy's stolen money. After many months Smith had succeeded in losing more than £700. It was time to return to his most rewarding profession. Smith again went carousing among the resort towns, meeting Alice Burnham, a fat 26-year-old nurse in Southsea in late October 1913. His courtly manners and quiet advances soon had the fun-loving

nurse crazy for him. Alice took Smith to see her parents in Aston Clinton. He readily accompanied her after learning that, although she herself only possessed £27, her father was holding another £100 for her.

The father, Charles Burnham, a retired coal merchant, took an instant dislike to Smith, later stating that he had "a very evil appearance," and that he "could not sleep while Smith was in the house." Burnham finally asked Smith to leave his home. The distraught Alice went with Smith to the train station on Oct. 31, 1913, feeling her lover persecuted by her family, which was exactly what Smith wanted her to feel. They were married on Nov. 4 in Portsmouth with none of Alice's family members attending. On Dec. 10, Smith and Alice appeared at a boarding house run by a Mrs. Marden in Blackpool, a distant resort. They were shown all the available rooms but Smith, who had married Alice under his real name, sneeringly refused the accommodations. (His confidence had been strengthened by his successful murder of Bessie Mundy; in fact, he was almost carefree now about hiding his identity.)

"None of it will do," Smith told Mrs. Marden. "We are civilized people—you have no baths."

The couple finally found rooms with a bath at Mrs. Crossley's boarding house on Regent's Road. Smith had already insured his wife's life for £500, making himself the sole beneficiary. He had also unleashed a torrent of quasi-legal terms and sharp invective, accusing Charles Burnham of "taking refuge in obdurateness, contempt and remorse," and promising that he, Smith, would "take the matter up without delay" through his lawyers. He advised in another letter that "I am keeping all letters that pass for the purpose of justice." In still another letter he boldly threatened: "I do not know your next move, but take my advice and be careful!" Burnham, fearing a protracted and expensive lawsuit, gave in and sent Alice's savings to Smith who had already set in motion the final stage of his "investment scheme" in Alice Burnham Smith.

The ever-solicitous Smith asked Mrs. Crossley if she could recommend a good doctor. "My wife suffers from severe headaches," he told the woman. The landlady suggested they see Dr. George Billing, who examined Alice a short time later. The physician thought he detected slight heart murmurs. He prescribed a mixture of caffeine and heroin. The couple then went on a long walk. That night, at 6 p.m., Mrs. Smith asked Mrs. Crossley to prepare a bath for her.

Two hours later, while the Crossleys sat at the kitchen table, family members looked up to see a huge stain of water on the ceiling which was dripping onto their dinners. "Go and tell Mrs. Smith not to fill the bath so," Mrs. Crossley instructed her oldest daughter.

The girl started to leave the room, then turned, saying:

"Oh, mother, they will think we are grumbling already, and they are not two days in the house."

Suddenly Smith appeared at the kitchen, placing a package on the table. "I have brought these eggs for our breakfast." He had earlier insisted that Mrs. Crossley prepare their meals, complaining that his wife was a "terrible cook."

Mrs. Crossley pointed to the stain on the ceiling. Smith rushed out and ran up the stairs to his rooms. In a moment he yelled downstairs to the landlady: "My wife will not speak to me!"

"What is it?"

"Get a doctor—get Dr. Billing! He knows her! Hurry!"

When Billing arrived he found Smith in the bathroom, holding his wife's head above high water which covered the rest of her body. Both men struggled to lift the heavy woman from the bath. Dr. Billing could not revive Alice Smith. He spent only a few minutes examining the body, but noted that no signs of violence were present. (Billing later testified that he could not recall whether Mrs. Smith's head was at the foot or head of the bathtub.) The coroner, who was involved with another death at the time, hurriedly arrived, signing a report that Mrs. Smith had suffered "heart failure in the bath. Accidental drowning."

An hour later, Smith stood speechless in Mrs. Crossley's kitchen. The landlady eyed him coldly. He made no signs of sorrow and this time he did not pretend to weep at the death of this bride. Smith's attitude was one of indifference. Mrs. Crossley became incensed with him.

"How dreadful! What an awful thing this is," she finally said to him, thinking him in shock and attempting to urge his emotions to the surface.

Smith was laconic: "I would not be surprised at anything that might happen now."

"What kind of remark is that with your wife lying dead upstairs?"

The husband merely shrugged.

"Now, Smith," Mrs. Crossley said then, "you cannot stay here tonight."

"Why?"

"Because I'll take good care not to have a callous fellow like you in the house."

Smith slowly headed for his rooms to gather up his single brown suitcase. He stopped in the doorway, turning to Mrs. Crossley. "When they're dead, they're dead," he told her matter-of-factly.

That night, Smith stayed in the house next door, writing long letters to his insurance company, putting in the claim for the £500 on his wife's life.

A coroner's jury rendered a verdict of accidental death in the case of Mrs. Alice Smith. Obtaining the insurance money, Smith left Blackpool, but not before leaving a postcard with Mrs. Crossley on which he had written his new address, a bogus address, of course. Mrs. Crossley kept the card, cryptically writing on it: "Wife died in bath. I shall see him again some day."

Again, the world-weary traveling salesman returned to Edith Pegler Smith in Bristol. Again he explained his new riches as the result of some successful sales in Canada.

Not until the following year, in September 1914, could Smith's insidious activities be again known. In that month he hastily wed one Alice Reavil in Woolwich. He did not bother to go through the motions of his bath routine. After discovering that his spinster bride could not be insured because of ill health, he stole the woman's entire wardrobe, leaving her with only the clothes on her back and returned to his wife in Bristol, to whom he gave the clothes as a not-too-welcome gift.

Three months later, Smith, again rooting through the lovelorn ruins of the resort town of Clifton, encountered Margaret Elizabeth Lofty, thirty-eight, daughter of a clergyman, a companion to the elderly by profession, once engaged, and now broken-hearted after learning that her previous lover had been a married man. She was a wounded gazelle to the panther-like Smith, who introduced himself as John Lloyd, a real estate broker from Holloway.

Smith's hasty proposal to the love-starved Miss Lofty was clutched as one would a lifeline in a swirling sea. At Smith-Lloyd's suggestion, the couple took a train to Bath, in Bristol—the selection of the town was undoubtedly Smith's grim little private joke—and were married on Dec. 17, 1914, but not before Smith had insured his wife's life for £700 with the Yorkshire Insurance Company in Bristol.

Immediately following the wedding ceremony, the couple withdrew all of Lofty's savings from her Muswell Hill bank, a total of £20. With this paltry sum they took a train to London. This time Smith wasted no time with his new bride; he would dispose of this new "business" in less than forty-eight hours.

On the afternoon of Dec. 17, Smith appeared at a boarding house on Orchard Road, Highgate, London. Miss Lokker, the proprietor, became alarmed by Smith's manner when he insisted on personally inspecting the bathroom in the rooms he had reserved in advance. He got on his knees, spreading his arms to determine the length of the tub. "It's rather small, isn't it?" Smith reproached the landlady. "I guess someone *could* lie down in it."

Returning downstairs to the reception desk, Miss Lokker timidly asked for Smith's references.

"There's a war on," Smith told her, knowing she was of German ancestry and that, since the outbreak of WWI in recent months, Germans, including herself, had been the subject of abuse and threats. "Persons like you shouldn't make demands of loyal British subjects." He perceived the worry on her face, then contemptuously threw down six shillings on the desk. "Here are my references. I'll return shortly."

Before Smith came back, Miss Lokker called a friendly police officer, Detective Sergeant Dennison. Her new roomer acted queerly, made her nervous, she explained to Dennison. He would handle the situation, the policeman assured her. A half hour later Smith appeared.

Dennison shoved the battered brown suitcase Smith had left toward him, at the same time handing him back his deposit. "There are no rooms here. The place is full up."

"What?" roared Smith, his sharp eyes glaring at the plain-clothesman. "I booked these rooms in advance! Explain yourself! I demand a reason for being turned away!"

Dennison began to gently push Smith out the front door. "You are unable to furnish references, and I am acting on behalf of the landlady. That is an end to the matter."

Pathetically, Smith stood at the entranceway, red-faced, clutching his suitcase. "But I have a banker and plenty of money!"

Dennison slammed the door in his face.

Only a few hours later, Smith and his bride showed up at Mrs. Blatch's rooming house at 14 Bismarck Road, where, after Smith made a point of inspecting the bath ("that will do nicely") the newlyweds rented a sitting room, bedroom, and bath.

Smith's procedure was the same as it had been with his earlier victims. The wife was not well. She asked the landlady if she could suggest a good doctor. A quick trip was made to a Dr. Bates, who found the woman lethargic and "feverish." The husband did all the talking. Perhaps his bride was subject to fits? Perhaps, but Dr. Bates prescribed only a mild sedative. Once again in their rooms, the considerate husband knew just the thing to settle his wife's nerves—a long, hot bath.

Mrs. Blatch drew the bath for Mrs. Lloyd at 7:30 p.m. on Dec. 18, 1914. Minutes later, the landlady heard a faint splashing of water in the tub. Then came the sound of the melodeon in the living room; Mrs. Blatch thought Mr. Lloyd was playing it. Next the front doorbell rang. Mr. Lloyd was outside, explaining that he had forgotten his key. He held up a brown bag. "I've brought some tomatoes for Mrs. Lloyd's dinner." (With Bessie Mundy it had been herrings, with Alice Burnham it was eggs.)

Smith put down the sack of tomatoes, glancing about the living room. "What? My wife isn't down from her bath yet?"

Mrs. Blatch hadn't seen her. Smith suggested that they both fetch her. Going to the bathroom they found the room in darkness. Smith turned on the light. Mrs. Blatch screamed at the sight of Mrs. Lloyd's head submerged under the bath water. Smith yanked the woman out of the tub, pretending to revive her. Of course, it was no use. Dr. Bates was summoned. He quickly concluded that his patient of one day had died "due to asphyxia from drowning. Influenza, together with a hot bath, might have caused an attack of syncope."

Again, missing nothing, Smith called a constable from the streets to view the dead body. The officer was shocked to see the naked body of Mrs. Lloyd exposed on the bathroom floor. "In pity's name," the constable said to Smith, "get something and cover the poor creature. Don't leave her lying like this." Smith shrugged and slowly retrieved a blanket, throwing it over the body. For a bereaved husband, the constable later thought, his lack of outward grief was remarkable.

Following a hasty, cheap funeral, Smith disappeared from the Blatch rooming house, returning to his Bristol wife, Edith Smith. Now there was nothing left to do but collect the £700 of insurance money on Margaret Lofty's death. It was all so simple. Yet, the simplicity of Smith's murder was the very reason for his downfall. Smith had made the mistake most successful criminals make—he had grown comfortable in his *modus operandi*. Repetition would destroy him.

All through the month of January 1915, Smith, through his lawyer, W.T. Davies, badgered the Yorkshire Insurance Company for payment on Margaret's policy. During this time, Charles Burnham, who had never ceased believing Smith was the real cause of his daughter Alice's death, spotted an item published in the popular weekly, *News of the World*, which reported in detail the curious death of Margaret Lloyd, nee Lofty, describing her awkward drowning in a bathtub. Clipping this item to one about his daughter drowning in the same manner the year before, Burnham sent the notices to the police. Joseph Crossley, husband of the suspicious landlady in the Alice Burnham drowning, also noticed the item and sent in two reports of the similar drownings.

Scotland Yard assigned its best man to investigate. Detective Inspector Arthur Fowler Neil, in Kentish Town, was on the case at once. He inspected the bathroom where Margaret Lloyd has died. Measuring the small bathtub, he thought it impossible that a grown person could drown in such a tub. He and his men spread out along the resort towns, piecing together the Burnham and Lofty deaths. When he learned of Bessie Mundy's identical end in Herne Bay, and with descriptions of the three husbands in all the cases, Neil concluded that not only were Williams, Smith, and Lloyd one and the same man but that whomever this man might really be, he had committed murder.

A check of insurance firms revealed that Yorkshire had indeed insured Mrs. Lloyd and was about to settle with Mr. Lloyd's lawyer, W.T. Davies. (Smith had turned over his wife's signed will to Davies only three hours before her death on Dec. 18, 1914.) Neil wasted no time, posting men outside Davies' London offices, watching for a man who had been described in minute detail by three revenge-seeking landladies. Neil had instructed the insurance firm to contact Davies, telling the lawyer they were about ready to pay on Margaret Lloyd's death; the detective knew that Davies would soon be approached by the ubiquitous Mr. Lloyd to collect.

Neil himself, along with two other detectives, was keeping Davies' office under surveillance on Feb. 1, 1915. At 12:30 p.m., Neil spotted a meticulously dressed gentleman walking down the street toward the lawyer's offices. The man hesitated twice, seeming to turn back. Finally, he walked up to the small building and entered. Neil was sure, from the descriptions of Lloyd—the slouching gait, the lean-eyed look, jutting jaw, and peaked nose which seemed to be sniffing for dangerous odors—that he had spotted his man. When the darkly dressed stranger emerged from Davies' offices an hour later, Neil watched him light a cigarette and begin to walk off. Neil and his two men, Page and Reid, moved in on him, crossing the street, and walking along with the man on either side of him. Neil suddenly darted in front of him, blocking his path. The other two men stood so close to him that their coats brushed up against his.

"I am Detective Inspector Neil. Are you John Lloyd?" Smith's manner was nerveless. "Yes, I am."

"The same John Lloyd whose wife was drowned in a bath on the night of Dec. 18, at Bismarck Road, Highgate?"

"Yes, that's me."

"From my investigation, I have reason to believe you are identical with George Smith, whose wife was found drowned in a bath three weeks after marriage in 1913, at Blackpool. You married Miss Lofty, your last bride, at Bath, Bristol, in the name of Lloyd."

Smith was still unperturbed, giving the detective back his own stare. "Yes, that is so," he said slowly, his large, sensual mouth moving from side to side, "but that doesn't prove that my name is Smith." His normally sallow complexion then seemed to flush red. Suddenly he exploded: "Smith! I don't know the name of Smith! My name's not Smith!"

Neil studied the man for some moments; he later concluded that Smith, from his washed-out appearance, was the "sort of fellow a decent man would at once shun as unlikable." Neil was convinced Smith was a murderer, and even though he had no evidence pointing to that conviction, he was determined not to let this most evasive man slip from his grasp. "Very well," said the detective, "I am going to detain you for making a false attestation on oath to a Registrar."

This minor charge jarred Smith into blurting: "Oh, if that's what you're making all the fuss over, I may as well tell you, I am Smith."

"You admit that fact, then?"

"Certainly! My wife died at Blackpool in 1913. But that's only coincidence. It's a man's bad luck! It's the only charge you can prove against me." Smith gave Neil a thin sneer. "Clever as you think you are, Mr. Neil."

The officer thought he saw a dark menace in the man's eyes. Neil could not resist telling Smith: "Yes! And there may be charges of murder against you!"

"You're bloody well mad! You don't know what you're talking about!"

Neil ordered Smith taken away and locked up on a charge of perjury in giving an alias at his marriage with Margaret Lofty. A short time later, the charge of bigamy was added. The charge of murder was withheld. Neil, with the help of the celebrated pathologist Sir Bernard Spilsbury, attempted to discover exactly how Smith had managed to drown at least three of his victims, making all the deaths appear as accidents. The bodies of Bessie Mundy, Alice Burnham, and Margaret Lofty were exhumed and carefully examined by Spilsbury. He found no signs of violence on any of the corpses, and had to admit that they had all died by drowning.

Had Smith attempted to force any of the women's heads under water there would have been a violent struggle that would have left telltale marks on the bodies, Spilsbury and Neil concluded. And the tubs were so small that any other method of murder was inconceivable. G.J. Smith, it appears, *had* baffled the forensic authorities, and would be acquitted for lack of evidence, let alone the absence of any eyewitnesses or confession.

Then Neil had the idea of reenacting the bathtub scenes, using women who were professional swimmers. He positioned these women in several ways inside the very murder tubs, employing females who were the same height and weight as the victims. Yet there seemed to be no way in which he could, without struggle, keep the women submerged. Standing at the foot of the tub, Neil looked over the swimmer sitting in the water which filled the tub to three-quarters. In a flash, the idea came to him. He suddenly grabbed the woman by the ankles, lifting her feet high into the air. She slipped beneath the water, her head wholly submerged. She had been made helpless; the quick lifting of her legs forced her arms, which would have normally gripped the sides of the tub, to slide backward and be rendered useless.

Though the woman had been under water for only a few seconds, when Neil released his hold, the woman remained beneath the water, unconscious. Neil and Spilsbury quickly lifted her from the bathtub and, for a terrible half-hour of fright, worked on the swimmer with artificial respiration and restoratives. She finally came around, explaining to the officials that when her legs were lifted into the air and her head slid under the water, her nostrils and mouth were immediately filled with water and she blacked out. This, then, Neil and Spilsbury triumphantly realized, was the method Smith had employed to kill his "Brides of the Bath," as the press later dubbed the victims. The sudden flow of water into mouth and nostrils caused shock and unconsciousness, Spilsbury later explained in court, but how the inventive Mr. Smith stumbled upon this unique murder method is not known to this day.

Smith was charged with murder, though he stoutly denied any guilt. The case against him was circumstantial but overwhelming. Neil and his detectives had taken more than two thousand statements, the most ever known in any criminal case in England to that time. These, plus mounds of documents, including Smith's own copious and incriminating ledgers, were placed on exhibit in a courtroom at the Old Bailey, where Smith was tried for nine days, between June 22 and July 1, 1915.

"Never before had the venerable old structure been so thronged with women," Jurgen Thorwald was to write in *The Century of the Detective.* "They came by the hundreds—the lonely woman, the physically and mentally deprived, the woman hungering for love—women of the type Smith had chosen for his victims."

Smith stood handsome and collected in the dock. Justice Scrutton presided, while Sir Archibald Bodkin prosecuted and Sir Edward Marshall Hall defended. When the judge cautioned the jury that they were about to hear a murder case, Smith exploded, interrupting the judge with a scream that such a charge was "a disgrace to a Christian country!" He then added in a wounded tone: "I may be a bit peculiar but I am certainly no murderer!"

The testimony of 112 witnesses damned Smith day after day, including the angry statements of the landladies in whose houses he had committed his murders. His first wife, the reformed sneak thief Caroline Thornhill, even returned from Canada to testify against him. His wife in Bristol, Edith Pegler Smith, also testified, trying feebly to help her husband, but her statements only brought more suspicion down on Smith, particularly when she recalled her husband warning her against the use of bathtubs! "I should advise you to be careful of those things," Edith remembered Smith saying to her just before the murder of Margaret Lofty, "as it is known that women often lose their lives through weak hearts and fainting in a bath."

Smith said little in his own behalf, merely shaking his head and saying that the three *known* deaths were all "phenomenal coincidences." His defense counsel, Edward Marshall Hall, could offer only thin rebuttal and wild

speculation. He reminded the jury of the statements of the doctors who had examined the three women before their deaths, that all had been in seemingly dazed conditions. His theory was that Smith never had to enter the bathrooms and that the brides drowned themselves as a result of being hypnotized by his client! Theories on drugs and poisonous vapors in the tub waters were also put forth.

Then Inspector Neil demonstrated before the jury as to

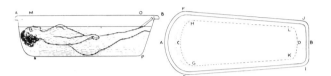

Diagram showing how Smith murdered his wives.

the real method used by Smith to kill his wives by simply yanking their legs high into the air. At the end of the demonstration, the jury gasped open-mouthed. Smith clutched the wooden rail of the dock so tightly that his knuckles went white. He yelled in uncontrollable fury: "That man's a villain!" He shook his fist in Neil's direction. "He ought to be in the dock with me now!"

The jury took only twenty-three minutes to return a verdict of Guilty. Smith was sentenced to death. His appeal was denied. In the early hours of Aug. 13, 1915, Smith sat in his cell at Maidstone Jail, listening to a strange hum of human voices. "Outside the wall," wrote Edmund Pearson in *Murder at Smutty Nose,* "a crowd had collected, many of them women—and the loud chatter of women's voices reached the inside of the prison."

At 8 a.m., Smith was taken from his cell. He refused to make any kind of confession. He began to stagger on his walk into the courtyard and toward the gallows. When he saw the scaffold, his legs failed, and he had to be helped up the stairs. His arms were tied, a bag was put about his head, the heavy rope lowered around his neck. A few seconds before the trap was sprung, George Joseph Smith experienced an emotion he had never allowed his "Brides of Bath."

His solemn, low words, heard at the last by the executioner, came from beneath the dark hood: "I am in terror!"

Smith, Jim (AKA: Gipsy), 1931- , Brit. One thing was certain. Jim Smith, "Gipsy," played an active part in the death of police constable Leslie Meehan. What was not so clear was whether his role constituted murder, manslaughter, or just bad luck. After weeks of legal maneuvering, the court found the 29-year-old Smith Guilty of murder on Apr. 7, 1960.

On Mar. 2, 1960, while Smith and George Artus were driving through Woolwich, England, with several stolen scaffolding clips, their car was stopped by Officer Meehan. When Meehan noticed the clips in the back seat of the car, Smith panicked and sped away. Meehan grabbed onto the car, and after being dragged 200 yards, fell off and was killed by a car traveling in the opposite direction. After removing the stolen metal scraps, Smith returned to the place where Meehan had been hit crying, "Is he dead? I know him. I wouldn't do it for the world. I only wanted to shake him off. I didn't mean to kill him."

According to English law at the time, a crime is murder not only when the killing was intended but also when intent to do bodily harm existed. The prosecuting attorney never suggested that Smith intended to kill Meehan, but maintained that Smith meant to cause bodily harm. The vague law was changed during Smith's case and was rewritten to include no distinction between a person who intends to kill and one who does not.

With this ruling, it no longer made any difference whether or not Smith intended to bring harm to Meehan. The fact was, he had, and he was found Guilty of capital murder and sentenced to death. This conviction was set aside upon appeal and replaced with a manslaughter conviction and a sentence of ten years in prison. An appeal to the House of Lords by the director of prosecutions restored the lower court's decision, but the Home Secretary commuted the sentence.

Smith, John Thomas (AKA: **Snowy Rowles**), d.1933, Aus. George Ritchie spoke to the men who worked for him in the wild Australian bush one night in 1930, quietly detailing the 'perfect murder.' "Supposing I wanted to do you in," he said softly. "I'd kid you into the bush a bit...I'd shoot you dead and burn your body...I'd go through the lot with a sieve, getting out every burnt bone...and toss out the dust for the wind to scatter." Ritchie detailed the gory scenario for the benefit of English novelist Arthur William Upfield, who sought the information for his latest thriller, but John Thomas Smith, alias "Snowy Rowles," was listening in the closest; he would need the information for real life. In two years, three of the men huddled together that night would disappear, and one patch of ashes and bones would be discovered.

One morning in 1930, James Ryan, a short and stocky well-sinker, and young Lloyd, who had come from Adelaide looking for work, accompanied Smith to Mount Magnet. Neither Ryan nor Lloyd were ever seen again. By Dec. 31, 1930, police were searching for Louis J. Carron as well. Carron had set off into the outback with Smith in May 1930,

telling his friend John Lemon that he would write regularly. After months passed without receiving word from his friend, Lemon convinced authorities to investigate. On Feb. 17, 1931, the search party discovered a well-burned fire, ash, bone, a gold ring, a gold dental band, a copper coin marked "1 cent Hong Kong 1904," and a .32-caliber cartridge case and bullet.

Authorities sought the man who had been calling himself Snowy Rowles only to find John Thomas Smith who was wanted for theft, escaping from prison, and now, murder. A search of his residence turned up two loaded .32-caliber Winchester rifles, three shirts, a wrist watch, a white-handled razor, a watch-chain, a pair of scissors, and a razor-hone. Rowles professed to know nothing of the items, but police were unconvinced. On his way to trial for breaking out of jail, Smith made a startling statement in which he unwittingly admitted his guilt of murder. "What a nice fix I'm in," he said. "I'm not worrying about the escape rap but the murder's a different thing. Anyway I'll never have to do the stretch as they'll fit me with the murder charge and I'll swing because I'll never get a reprieve. If they don't swing me I'll find a way to do it myself." During his trial, the items found in his possession were identified by witnesses as belonging to the missing men. Furthermore, Smith's rifles fired the same type of bullets found among the ashes and bones. On June 13, 1932, John Thomas Smith was hanged for murder.

Smith, Matthew, 1925-   , Brit. American soldiers stationed in Great Britain during WWII were there to protect the lives of their allies, not to involve them recklessly in drunken barroom brawls. Nevertheless, in April 1944, 19-year-old U.S. Navy gunner Matthew Smith stabbed to death a 29-year-old Englishman, Charles Gilbey. The defendant was found Guilty of murder by a U.S. court-martial and given a long sentence at Sing Sing Prison.

The tragic night began with revelry, laughing, and a great deal of drinking. The proprietor of London's Railway Tavern, better known as "Charlie Brown's," had emptied his establishment of the drunken mob when a long ebony-handled knife, grasped by a mean hand, thrust through the doorway into the chest of 29-year-old Gilbey. The only clue detectives had to go one was word that the sleeve of the man holding the knife was that of an American soldier.

Detectives had just begun interviewing each of the estimated 4,000 sailors docked in London when a man confided to authorities he owned a knife fitting the description of the murder weapon and that he had loaned it to Matthew Smith, nineteen, the night of the attack. Smith readily admitted to having borrowed the knife and to having stabbed a man, he said, in self defense. An American court later sentenced him to death in the electric chair, but later reduced his sentence to life imprisonment at Sing Sing, due to his young age.

Smith, Perry, See: Hickock, Richard Eugene.

Smith, Russell Lee, 1955-75, U.S. A lovers' quarrel turned into assault, mass murder and suicide on May 24, 1975, when Russell Lee Smith, twenty, ended a dispute between himself and his young girlfriend by shooting her in the head. He then wounded two men with whom he also had been arguing before jumping in his car and continuing his rampage.

Smith took his girlfriend's dead body with him, left it at a Dayton, Ohio, hospital ramp and shot and wounded one passerby as he drove away. He shot and wounded the driver of a car on a highway, then drove into a movie theater parking lot. He approached a family of four, shot each one, and critically wounded the couple's 6-year-old daughter. He entered a residential neighborhood and began knocking on doors. He shot and missed one woman, but shot a neighbor through the neck. Smith then kidnapped a girl from a restaurant and drove off. While driving, he noticed a young couple in a car, approached the girl and dragged her into his car. He then killed the first girl and drove the second one to a wooded area where he raped her. It was at this time that police caught up with the killer, but Smith immediately turned the gun on himself and took his own life. Smith had been on probation after being convicted of a 1971 murder.

Smith, Thomas, 1919-   , U.S. Thomas Smith and Mary Ellen Babcock, both eighteen, lived in the same South Buffalo, N.Y., neighborhood. On the night of Feb. 5, 1937, Smith experienced what he described as an "uncontrollable impulse" that led him to beat and brutally murder the young woman.

Mary Ellen Babcock left her family's home in the early evening to attend a wake with a friend. At about 8:20 p.m. she decided to walk home. At noon the next day, two 8-year-old boys, Donald Hanlon and Edward Murphy, discovered her body in a vacant lot. Medical examiner Rocco N. DeDominicis conducted an autopsy and determined that the girl had not been sexually assaulted. DeDominicis reported that death was the result of a stab wound in the heart, a punctured left lung, fractured skull, and multiple stab wounds in the head and body. A blood-stained four-inch pocket knife with the initials "T.S." was found beneath the corpse. The only other clue was a small scrap of wool found in the girl's left hand. "She must have put up a terrific fight for her life," said DeDominicis, citing numerous cuts on both her hands and a broken fingernail. Babcock's nose was also broken. Detective Chief John J. Whalen said that bloodstains and pieces of Babcock's coat indicated that the body had been dragged across the street and thrown into a slight depression in the field about ten feet from the curb. Although several rewards were offered for information leading to the arrest of the killer, six weeks passed before he was found.

On Mar. 28, 1937, 14-year-old Frances Fitzgerald complained to her mother of a pain in her back. Her mother discovered the five-inch blade of an ice pick embedded under her daughter's left shoulder. Neither the emergency room physician nor the police believed the girl's story that she had tripped on the pick accidentally. She had been seen riding in a car with a man, and she finally admitted to her brother, Pierce Fitzgerald, that she had been picked up by Thomas Smith. Fitzgerald looked up Smith's address in the phone book and went to his house. When the slight 18-year-old Smith answered the door, Fitzgerald recognized him from a high school class and from church. He asked him if he had read about his sister being stabbed. Smith said he had, but denied any involvement at first.

Smith later told Fitzgerald that he had stabbed the girl. Fitzgerald then asked Smith what he knew about the Babcock case, and suggested they go together to the police station. Smith refused, but was willing to talk to a priest. They went to St. Teresa's Church nearby and talked with a clergyman. Smith repeated what he had said to Fitzgerald, adding that he had been provoked by an "uncontrollable impulse," and offered to pay Frances Fitzgerald's hospital bill. Pierce Fitzgerald convinced police to pick up Smith for questioning the next day. After asking to see their badges, Smith went quietly with Acting Captain Glenn H. McClellan, Lieutenant William H. Downey, and Detective Patrick J. Hoar to the South Park station.

Smith admitted attacking the Fitzgerald girl, giving extensive details, including the fact that he "would have killed her with an automobile jack but the handle fell off as I chased her...I grabbed her and took her back to the car. I promised to take her home, but warned her not to talk," Smith explained. After his confession, an officer abruptly asked Smith, "What about the Babcock girl? Where did you meet her?" Smith began, "I've got to get this whole thing off my mind," and then went on to confess to this slaying, as well. He described how the woman had repeatedly begged for mercy, and how this had provoked him to attack her more fiercely. Smith said the impulse to hurt her left him once she lay still. After the slaying, Smith washed his hands in snow and rubbed snow on his clothing to get rid of the bloodstains. Once home, he washed the blood out of his jacket and shirt at a sink in the cellar. Lieutenant Downey, who was present at the confession, said Smith had read all the newspaper stories about the case, but was not worried because he knew the police did not suspect him. Police commissioner James W. Higgins said Smith, "told us that sometimes something seemed to 'click' in his brain. When that happened, he would want to attack and maim." Besides the Babcock murder, Smith admitted attacking another South Buffalo girl, and attempting to lure 8-year-old Marjorie Galvin into his car.

District Attorney Walter C. Newcomb filed a first-degree murder charge against Smith on Mar. 31, 1937. During the murder trial, Smith openly and loudly wept in court when his attorney described him as being on the verge of dementia. Newcomb informed the jurors that it did not make "much difference if he was an imbecile or an idiot," as far as their duty in the matter was concerned. On June 16, 1937, the jury returned from deliberation to find Thomas Smith Guilty of murder and recommended that he be sentenced to life imprisonment.

Snider, Paul, d.1980, U.S. Paul Snider made his living pimping in the streets of Vancouver, British Columbia. In 1977, he told his friends that he was going straight. That summer he met beautiful 18-year-old Dorothy Ruth Hoogstraten, a clerk in a Vancouver Dairy Queen. Snider quickly overwhelmed the girl, who had no ambitions beyond becoming a secretary. Snider suggested that she could be the twenty-fifth anniversary Playmate for *Playboy* magazine.

After gaining her mother's permission, Snider took the young woman to Los Angeles for photographic tests. She lost out as the special anniversary Playmate but was named August 1979 "Playmate of the Month" as Dorothy Stratten. On June 1, before the magazine appeared on the stands, Stratten and Paul Snider were married. He immediately set about procuring small TV and film roles for his wife. Stratten had considerable natural talent for acting, and when Playboy named her the 1980 "Playmate of the Year", bigger studios began to look at her as a potential star.

When Stratten began meeting other men who were more sophisticated than Snider, he resented being left behind. Stratten left Snider and went to New York to appear in a Peter Bogdanovich film, during which Bogdanovich and Stratten became romantically involved. On her return to Hollywood, Stratten asked Snider for a divorce and moved in with Bogdanovich.

On Aug. 12, 1980, Snider telephoned his wife and asked her to meet him at his home to finalize details of their divorce. The next day he bought a 12-gauge shotgun. On Aug. 14, when Stratten came to his home, he shot her and then himself. Later that afternoon, Snider's most recent protégé found the two bodies. Peter Bogdanovich later noted: "Dorothy looked at the world with love, and believed that all people were good down deep. She was mistaken, but it is among the most generous and noble errors we can make."

Snook, James Howard, 1880-1930, U.S. Before he went to the electric chair for the murder of his 24-year-old sweetheart, Professor James Howard Snook asked permission to invite his most intimate friends to join him in a "last supper" at the Ohio Penitentiary. The warden, sympathetic, acquiesced. Four chefs were brought in to prepare a sumptuous feast for Dr. Snook, his long-suffering wife, and two dinner companions. The warden drew the line, however, when Snook asked if he might be permitted to wear his tuxedo for the occasion.

Dr. Snook was a professor of Veterinary Medicine at Ohio State University. He was a distinguished-looking middle-aged man who had participated in the pistol-shooting competition at the 1920 Olympics. He was also a very private man who kept his peccadillos to himself. The professor had a secretary named Theora Hix, who was working her way through medical school on a meager $600 a year allowance from her parents. Hix was the daughter of a retired university professor who lived in Bradenton, Fla. She kept occasional company with William Miller, a 35-year-old instructor from the College of Agriculture, but the relationship was not going anywhere. The one true love of her life was Dr. Snook, the 49-year-old professor she once described as the "nicest man I know!"

Snook conducted his affair with the student with the utmost discretion. He rented a room in downtown Columbus from Margaret Smalley, using the alias "Howard Snook." The professor explained that he was a demonstrator for a salt company, and that his "wife" would be sharing the quarters from time to time. For nearly three years the two led a double life. Snook was revered by the family and was the soul of conformity. They lived in a spacious home on the edge of the campus. Theora Hix was perceived by her classmates to be a demure but earnest student with little time to spare for leisure-time activity. Beneath the facade was an iron-will resolve to control the men in her life, and a strong dependency on cocaine. She forced Dr. Snook to sterilize her so that their lovemaking might continue without complication. At times Hix would diabolically pit Snook against Miller with taunting remarks.

On the night of June 14, 1929, Snook decided to take Hix for an automobile ride. They parked near a local golf course but a tournament was going on and Hix was apprehensive that they might be observed by the police. Snook steered his late model coupe to the nearby New York Central rifle range on the outskirts of Columbus. He stopped the engine and went about his lovemaking with Hix. According to Dr. Snook's statements to police, Hix complained about the cramped confines of his car and made allusions to Miller's superiority as a lover. They quarreled bitterly and Hix struck him in the groin. Snook seized an automobile hammer and inflicted a series of savage wounds to her face and head. After beating her to a bloody pulp he bent over and cut her jugular vein with a pen knife. The prostrate body of the coed was found lying in the weeds shortly after sunrise by two small boys. Coroner Joseph Murphy examined the corpse and determined that the killer had inflicted seventeen separate blows. The corpse was taken to a funeral parlor and it was identified by friends.

The police had little to work with in the way of clues, but had received reports that Hix was riding around with a stockily built man driving a blue Ford coupe. The description did not fit William Miller, who was considered a suspect. The search for the blue car led to the doorstep of the retiring Dr. Snook who told police that the woman had been his mistress for three years. "Neither of us wanted to marry each other," he said. "She was a good companion in a different way than my wife."

Questioned simultaneously by police, Miller proved to be the weaker of the two. He was ill-at-ease and his answers to probing questions were carefully measured. Dr. Snook explained that Miller had also been carrying on an affair with Hix and there was much personal jealousy between the two. The missing pieces were supplied by the landlady Margaret Smalley and an anonymous tipster. Mrs. Smalley readily identified Snook as her tenant and a little brown hat with a rolled brim that Hix had been wearing. A caller who refused to leave a name suggested to the police that they closely examine a suit of clothes Snook had recently taken in for dry-cleaning. The garment was impounded and given to the city chemist for analysis. Bloodstains were found.

Confronted with this evidence, Dr. Snook broke down and confessed to the crime. He said Hix had warned him not to go out of town for the weekend with his wife and daughter as he had originally planned. "She threatened that if I did go she would take the life of my wife and baby," he sobbed. Dr. Snook was indicted for first-degree murder. The trial, which ended on Aug. 14, 1929, was punctuated by sensational details of the adulterous affair, spelled out in graphic detail in a series of lurid letters written by Snook that bordered on the pornographic. Throughout the trial, Helen Snook maintained a stoic attitude. She supported her husband up to the moment he walked into the execution chamber on Feb. 28, 1930.

Snyder, Donald, 1927-53, U.S. In June 1952, after escaping from the New York prison at Stormville, 25-year-old Donald Snyder walked into the home of Marvin and Dorothy Arnold in nearby Lake Mahopac. He told Mrs. Arnold that he was an escaped convict, and that he would kill her children if she did not let him in. Inside the house, he held 9-year-old Betty Jean Arnold hostage with a butcher knife while police surrounded the house. Later, he led Mrs. Arnold and the child out to the family car. He instructed Mrs. Arnold to get behind the wheel while he took the girl and got into the back seat. A police officer entered the garage and tried to convince Snyder to surrender. When he refused, the officer shot Snyder. Before Snyder was subdued, however, he stabbed the child in the abdomen.

Betty Jean Arnold died shortly after being stabbed. Snyder was wounded but recovered and was placed on trial for the girl's murder. He was convicted on Sept. 15, 1952, and was executed in the electric chair at Sing Sing during the week of July 13, 1953.

Snyder, Leroy, 1932- , U.S. In July 1970, 38-year-old Leroy Snyder, a former Camden, N.J., junkyard worker, confessed to murdering six women and a man in an eight-month period in 1969. Snyder claimed that robbery was his motive in six of the slayings, but he could not remember why he had committed the seventh. Two of the women had been raped.

Snyder pleaded no defense to the seven murder charges in his 1970 trial. Under New Jersey law, the death sentence could not be imposed on a self-confessed murderer. Snyder was sentenced on July 16, 1970, to three consecutive life prison terms, making him eligible for parole in 2014, at the age of 82.

Snyder, Ruth May Brown, 1896-1928, and **Gray, Henry Judd**, 1893-1928, U.S. By 1927, Ruth May Brown Snyder was a tall, overage flapper with bobbed blond hair, a voluptuous body, and a ravenous appetite for men of all kinds and sizes. She had an icy stare and a jutting jaw, and she looked upon any male who entered her life as her sexual prey, from doorstep salesmen to delivery boys. The fact that she was married meant little or nothing. Ruth Snyder, in fact, despised her husband and, according to later testimony, had attempted to murder Albert Snyder several times.

Albert and Ruth Snyder lived comfortably in a large three-story house in Long Island, N.Y., on Snyder's $115-a-week salary. He was the art editor of *Motor Boating* magazine and had a power boat of his own. The couple had a 9-year-old daughter, Lorraine, whom Ruth felt was a burden. Forty-four-year-old Albert Snyder busied himself with hunting, fishing, and boating. There was little room for domestic frolic. Ruth Snyder's "dream marriage" had turned into a dull, unpromising routine. She intended to change all that by murdering her husband, whom she had insured for $100,000.

Ruth was born into poverty. By age thirteen she left school to work as a night telephone operator. She studied shorthand and bookkeeping during the day. She later worked as a secretary and, in 1915, met and married the successful Snyder. Within a year, Ruth was referring to her husband as "the old crab." Snyder did little to make his wife happy. He antagonized her by referring to his former lover, Jessie Guishard, as "the finest woman I have ever known." Worse, Snyder placed a picture of Guishard, his first fiancée, above their bed, as a way of honoring her memory; the woman had been dead for ten years by that time.

Ignored by her husband, Ruth Snyder began to have brief affairs with many men. The peroxide blonde dressed as a flapper, wearing short skirts and high heels. Telling her husband she was seeing female friends, she went to dances alone, performing wild *Charleston* dances and picking up men to go to hotels for a few hours of "sexual ecstasy," as one reporter later put it. According to another account, the aggressive Ruth even preyed upon delivery boys who came to her home. At these times, Lorraine was in school and Snyder was busy drawing sketches of motorboats in his Manhattan offices.

One day in June 1925, Ruth and a lady friend went to lunch in Manhattan. The friend introduced the buxom flapper to 33-year-old Henry Judd Gray. Gray was short and myopic and wore thick-lensed glasses. He was nevertheless dapper and wore stylish clothes. Gray was addicted to homburg hats, handmade gloves, tight-fitting three-piece suits, and spats. Gray lived in Orange, N.J., was married and had an 11-year-old daughter. He worked for the Bien Jolie Corset Company, selling corsets. When Ruth heard this news, she excitedly told Gray that she was in Manhattan that day to buy a corset. How ironic. Could he show her some of his merchandise? Gray was delighted and took Ruth to his office after sending Ruth's friend on her way. Said Gray later: "She removed her dress and tried on a

garment to see if it was the right size. She was very badly sunburned and I offered to get some lotion to fix her shoulders." This was the beginning of the Snyder-Gray sex relationship, one which would lead to murder in less than two years. The couple met clandestinely in Manhattan hotels, usually the Waldorf Astoria. On these occasions, Lorraine Snyder would accompany her mother to the hotel and be left in the lobby to read books and while away the hours while her mother and Gray indulged in sexual exploits in a room upstairs. To Ruth Snyder, this was her great romance, this tawdry affair in which she addressed Gray as "Lover Boy," or "Bud." He called her "Momsie," or "Mommie," and was decidedly the weaker of the pair, submitting wholly to the dominant Snyder. The couple baby-talked to each other and sent each other the kind of little love notes usually written by high school sophomores. But beyond this secret affair, Ruth Snyder thought about a future without the hindrance of her cuckolded husband.

In late 1926 she took out the $100,000 life insurance policy on Albert Snyder and began making plans to murder him. According to later statements made by Gray, Ruth Snyder made seven attempts in 1926 to kill her husband by gas, by poison, and even by drowning on one occasion when Ruth "accidentally" bumped her husband overboard from the boat in which they were motoring. Snyder did not grow suspicious, however, blaming the attempts on his life on his wife's "clumsiness, her big-boned awkwardness." Meanwhile, ladies' man Gray began to drink to excess. As Albert Snyder's scheming spouse made each new attempt on her husband's life, Gray became more agitated. Ruth told him that she needed his help to murder Albert, but the corset salesman shook his head and went on another bender. At one point, after Snyder had been haranguing the corset salesman to aid her in her lethal efforts, Gray turned to her and asked: "Do you realize what it would mean in the eyes of God?"

Ruth Snyder by then had nothing to do with such thoughts. She wanted her husband dead and she was impatient for his demise. She cajoled, pleaded and finally ordered Gray to help her kill Albert. On the night of Mar. 19, 1927, Gray appeared in Long Island. According to his later claim, he had agreed to murder Albert Snyder but he kept busy on Mar. 19, hoping that somehow none of this would happen. On the morning of Mar. 19, Gray was selling corsets in Syracuse. That afternoon he took the train to Long Island and arrived at dusk, his two overcoat pockets stuffed with two large bottles of Mountain Dew whiskey. He wandered about the area where the Snyders lived, stopping beneath lampposts to pull out a bottle and take long swigs of the rotgut bootleg liquor. It appeared as if he was seeking to be arrested as a common drunk or for violating the Volstead Act. Neither happened.

Ruth Snyder, sash-weight killer.

Albert Snyder, murdered.

The Snyder home in Queen's Village, Long Island.

Above, Judd Gray, corset salesman gone wrong, shown awaiting trial with his mother.

Below left, Gray being booked for the murder of Arthur Snyder.

Below center, Ruth Snyder, going to the death house in Sing Sing.

Below right, Ruth Snyder being electrocuted; a news photographer smuggled a small camera into the death chamber strapped to his leg and took this sensational shot.

Finally, Gray went to the Snyder home and entered it through a back door Ruth had left unlocked. The family was out, attending a party at a neighbor's house. Gray went to the guest room, following a map of the house Ruth had drawn for him. He looked at the bed, on which his lover had placed the tools for him to commit the murder: A bottle of chloroform, rubber gloves, and a heavy iron sash weight. Gray sat down on the floor, drinking from his bottles, draining one and then going to work on the other.

A little after 2 a.m. the door opened. Ruth Snyder stood in the dimly lit hallway whispering into the dark room: "Are you there, Bud, dear?"

"I'm here, Momsie," Gray replied.

Ruth closed the door and returned a few minutes later wearing only a slip. She and Gray then had sex for more than an hour. Ruth told her half-drunk lover to pick up the sash weight and follow her. He obeyed meekly. Ruth led him into her bedroom, where her husband lay sleeping. She pushed Gray forward and then left the room, standing in the hallway. Gray closed his eyes and then brought the heavy sash weight down on Snyder's head with all his strength. Albert Snyder roared with pain and bolted upright to a sitting position in bed. He reached upward and grabbed the terrified Gray. The corset salesman screamed: "Momsie, Momsie, for God's sake help!"

Ruth Snyder was there within seconds, standing on the other side of the bed. She grabbed the sash weight from Gray's hand as he struggled with Albert Snyder and then brought this down on her husband's head with a powerful blow, knocking her spouse unconscious. As Albert fell, Ruth grabbed the picture of her husband's former fiancée and unwound the wire behind it, looping this around Albert's neck. She twisted it so tightly that the wire became imbedded in the flesh. At the same time, she ordered the quaking Gray to retrieve the bottle of chloroform. Slipping on the rubber gloves, Gray soaked a rag with the chloroform and placed this over Albert Snyder's face, splashing so much onto the rag that it burned the victim's flesh.

Five hours later, at 7:30 a.m., Ruth Snyder, bound and gagged, wiggled her way into her daughter's bedroom, nudging her child awake. The frightened girl removed the gag from her mother's mouth. Ruth told her to run to the neighbors and call the police. Instead the girl brought over the neighbors, who reached down to untie Ruth Snyder. "No, no," she told them. "Leave me be. The police will take care of that. Call them immediately." Her plan, of course, was fixed in her mind and she would not deviate from it; the police, not the neighbors, were to find her bound. When police did arrive, they untied Ruth, but instantly realized that she was so loosely bound that she could have easily freed herself.

The story Ruth Snyder told police that morning was as ridiculous as a plot from a silent film. Snyder said that a burglar wearing a fake mustache like that worn by Bartolomeo Vanzetti, of the Sacco and Vanzetti case, which was much in the news at the time, had barged into her bedroom, tied her and her husband up, and killed her beloved spouse before robbing the place and fleeing.

A medical examiner from the coroner's office, Dr. Howard Neail, looked over the corpse of Albert Snyder in the bedroom. The body was bound loosely with small ropes. There was a picture wire tied around his neck. His head had been crushed on one side and he had been chloroformed. A revolver was found on the bed and three unspent cartridges were on the floor. Dr. Neail determined that Snyder had died of asphyxiation killed by strangulation from the wire.

Police were suspicious of Ruth Snyder from the beginning. She claimed that she too had been knocked unconscious, but Dr. Neail found no evidence of any kind of blow to her head or anything that would render her unconscious for five hours. The house had been ransacked and the money from Albert Snyder's wallet was missing. Ruth said that the burglar had also taken her jewelry. She also stated that all the doors of the house had been locked before she and her family retired that morning, yet police found no signs of forcible entry.

Detectives searched the house and found Ruth's jewelry stuffed inside of a mattress. She suddenly remembered: "Of course, how silly of me. I put it there for safekeeping some nights ago when I thought I heard a burglar prowling outside the house." The detectives went on searching, by this time believing that they were dealing with a killer named Ruth Snyder. After a few hours they were rewarded with the discovery of a bloody sash weight, which had been placed in a tool box in the basement. A bloody pillow slip, which had been used to wipe the blood from the killer's hands, was found in the bathroom laundry hamper. The murderers had been sloppy, indeed. (Broadway columnist and wit Damon Runyon would later term this killing "The Dumb-bell Murder," because, in his words, "it was so dumb.")

Detective Arthur Carey continued to lead the investigation over the next few days. In the bedroom he found a tie clasp with the initials "JG" on it. Inside Ruth's desk he found a cancelled check made out to "H. Judd Gray." Gray's name and address, with his phone number heavily circled in red ink was found in Ruth Snyder's address book, along with the names and addresses of twenty-eight other men whose names were either underscored or circled in red ink. Some of the names had exclamation marks after them.

Two days later, Detective Carey discovered a bank safe deposit box registered under Snyder's maiden name, Ruth Brown. In the box was a $100,000 life insurance policy on her husband; the sole beneficiary was Ruth Brown Snyder.

Judd Gray was tracked to a Syracuse, N.Y., hotel room. When accused of murdering Albert Snyder, the little corset salesman became indignant at such an accusation. "My word, gentlemen," he said with a tone of injured pride, "when you know me better you'll see how ridiculous it is for a man like me to be in the clutches of the law. Why, I've never even been given a ticket for speeding." He was handcuffed and put aboard a train heading for New York City. Detectives grilled him during the trip and Gray finally broke down and confessed to the murder. But he emphasized that he had weakened at the last minute and Snyder had actually murdered her husband.

Snyder was then separately confronted. She was told that Gray had confessed and was already behind bars. Ruth Snyder lifted her lantern jaw and said: "Poor Judd, I promised not to tell." With that she admitted being present when her husband was killed but insisted it was the ruthless Judd Gray who had performed the awful deed. She went on to state that Gray had proposed the murder all along so that he could be with her. She painted herself as one of the most alluring sex goddesses of the age, intimating that her bedroom techniques drove men wild. She could not help it, shrugged Ruth Snyder. It was her animal magnetism.

The pair went to trial in Queens County on Apr. 27, 1927. The defendants were represented by separate lawyers. It was apparent from the beginning that they would each plead cases that incriminated the other. The press dubbed the trial the "Ruth Versus Judd" case. It was a celebrity affair, drawing such distinguished citizens to the spectator gallery as Mary Roberts Rinehart, David Belasco, D.W. Griffith, Peggy Hopkins Joyce, Will Durant, and even evangelists Aimee Semple McPherson and Billy Sunday. McPherson represented the sensation-seeking tabloid, the New York *Evening Graphic*, having received a substantial fee to write about this sordid murder case. To that end, Sister Aimee interviewed several persons outside the courthouse and quoted one young man as saying: "I want to have a wife like mother, not a red-hot cutie."

Edgar F. Hazleton, who represented Snyder, harped on the fact that Albert Snyder "drove love from out that house," by carrying the torch for a fiancée who had been dead a decade, and that it was Judd Gray who had arranged for the insurance policy on Albert Snyder. Thundered Hazleton: "We will prove to you that Ruth Snyder is not the demimondaine that Gray would like to paint her, but that she is a real loving wife, a good wife, and it was not her fault that brought about the condition in that house." Hazleton then put his client on the stand. The 120 reporters present described her every step toward the witness chair, women reporters later stating that she wore a simple black dress that was "not chic but decorous." A black rosary and crucifix hung conspicuously about her neck.

Ruth Snyder acted out the part of the discarded wife, the wronged woman. She said her husband ignored her and never "took me out," except to see an occasional movie. She pointed out that she read the Bible to her daughter Lorraine and took her to Sunday school and church, functions her uncaring husband never attended.

Hundreds of spectators who could not get into the jammed courtroom stood in the corridors and listened to Snyder talk through a microphone clamped to the witness chair. Hazleton then lightly touched upon the Snyder-Gray affair as if it had been only a few brief encounters and not a relationship that had stretched over two years. Snyder said of Gray from the witness stand: "He was in about the same boat I was. He said he was not happy at home." She pointed out that Gray was a hopeless, irresponsible drunk when she met him and that she spent most of her nights going to such hot spots as the Frivolity Club and the Monte Carlo, where she watched Gray drink himself into stupors. Added Snyder: "I rarely took a drink with him and never, ever smoked!"

Snyder went on to claim that Judd Gray urged her to take out the insurance policy and, after the policy had been issued, "he sent me poison and told me to give it to my husband." All of the seamy machinations of the affair and the murder plans, all of the attempts on the life of her husband, said Ruth, were the doing of Henry Judd Gray, the evil genius in her confused, sad life. She was a misdirected pawn in the hands of a ruthless killer. That was all there was to it. *She* was the victim.

Sam Miller, Gray's lawyer, attacked Snyder's statements with heroic bombast and then told the jury: "The tale of my client is the most tragic story that ever gripped the human heart." He described how his client had been almost force-fed twenty shots of whiskey to steel his nerves on the night of murder and to bolster his resolve just to enter the bedroom where Albert Snyder snored away the last few minutes of his life. Gray was a law-abiding citizen until he met the scheming Snyder, said Miller. "He was dominated by a cold, heartless, calculating mastermind and master will," said Miller. "He was a helpless mendicant of a designing, deadly, conscienceless, abnormal woman, a human serpent, a human fiend in the guise of a woman. He became inveigled and drawn into this hopeless chasm when reason was gone, when mind was gone, when manhood was gone, and when his mind was weakened by lust and passion."

Gray next took the witness chair. He was dressed in a well-tailored double-breasted business suit. He wore his glasses and adjusted these as he spoke in a quiet, unassuming voice. He played the love slave to the hilt, describing in detail the many attempts Snyder had made upon her husband's life. "She put poison in his prune whip once," intoned Gray, pretending shock. Then she tried to gas him to death, he added. "I told her I thought she was crazy." He then said that Ruth had given Albert Snyder poison on another occasion when he had the hiccups. "I said to her that was a helluva way to cure the hiccups! I criticized her sorely." Gray then said that Ruth had tried to murder her husband with sleeping powders, but that this had not worked. It was Ruth who thought up and arranged for the insurance policy, said Gray, and he emphasized that it was his ex-lover who had strangled Snyder with the picture wire, describing how powerful she was and that she possessed great upper body strength.

At that moment Ruth Snyder sobbed loudly in court and Judd Gray glanced at her briefly, but for the most part Gray continued to stare ahead during his testimony, his eyes fixed on his mother, who sat nodding at him in the spectator gallery. Next to Mrs. Gray sat the actress and singer Nora Bayes. Gray went on to claim that he had been "hypnotized" by Snyder and was not in his right mind on the night of the murder. He had acted as if he had been sleepwalking, he said.

On May 9, 1927, the trial came to an end. The "Putty Man," and the "Granite Woman" (or "Bloody Blonde" or "Marble Woman") as the press had dubbed the defendants, heard a jury—after only ninety-eight minutes of deliberation—convict them of premeditated murder in the first degree. Both were sentenced to death. While awaiting execution, both Ruth Snyder and Henry Judd Gray wrote their hurried autobiographies, each portraying the other as evil and themselves as good but hapless victims. Snyder wrote a poem which was later published in one of the tabloids, one which attacked the press for painting a dark picture of her. It read:

> You've blackened and besmeared a mother,
> Once a man's plaything—a toy—
> What have you gained by all you've said?
> And has it—brought you joy?
>
> And the hours when 'Babe needed my love,
> You've seen fit to send me away—
> I'm going to God's home in heaven,
> Ne'er more my feet to stray.
>
> Someday—we'll meet together,
> Happy and smiling again,
> Far above this earthly span
> Everlastingly in His reign.

On the cold, wintry night of Jan. 12, 1928, the two ex-lovers were executed at Sing Sing Prison. Judd Gray was the first to go. Warden Lewis E. Lawes found Gray in his Death Row cell smiling. He had received a letter at the last minute from his wife, who had forgiven him, not for killing Albert Snyder, but for sleeping with Ruth. "I am ready to go," Gray told Lawes. "I have nothing to fear." Minutes later Gray sat down calmly in the electric chair. He made no further comments and when the lethal current was sent through his body, Ruth Snyder, still in her death cell, looked up to see the lights dim, indicating that "Lover Boy" was gone.

The "Marble Woman" was next. She had already uttered her last words to Warden Lawes, saying that she knew "God has forgiven me and I hope the world will." She walked steadily into the death chamber and was strapped into the electric chair. A black hood was placed over her head and some reporters later claimed to hear her sobbing, some said praying.

All cameras had been long banned from the room in which the electric chair was located but Thomas Howard, an enterprising cameraman for the New York *Daily News*, had strapped a small camera to his ankle under his trouser leg. Just as the current surged into Ruth Snyder, propelling her body against the head, arm, chest, waist and ankle straps of the chair, Howard, sitting in the first row, crossed his leg, lifted his trouser leg, and squeezed a plunger attached to a cord that ran inside his clothes to the camera. The photo that caught Ruth Snyder at the moment of death took up the entire front page of the morning edition of the *Daily News*. (Because of Howard's crafty photo-taking, all witnesses thereafter were completely searched before entering the execution chamber.) This photo is considered to be the most horrifying in the annals of execution, and it illustrates the desperate measures taken by the yellow journalists of the tabloid era of the 1920s. The execution photo also gave Ruth Snyder undying fame, which outlasted her mawkish memoirs and silly sonnets.

Sodeman, Arnold Karl, 1900-36, Aus. Arnold Sodeman was a quiet man who kept to himself. But after a few drinks, he would experience an uncontrollable need to kill. On Nov. 9, 1930, Sodeman had several drinks at the Orrong Hotel in Armadale, Aus., and decided to go for a walk. Passing through Fawkner Park in Melbourne's inner suburb of South Yarra, Sodeman came across a group of young girls playing. Overcome by one of his disastrous moods, he asked 12-year-old Mena Griffiths to run an errand for him, and went with her, later suggesting that they go on a short trip. They took a tram and then a bus, ending up near an abandoned house on Wheatley Road. By Sodeman's own later confession, "I took her in there...as soon as we got in I seized her by the throat. I then let her go and she fell to the ground. Looking back down on her my memory came back and I said: 'My God, she's dead. I have killed her.'" Sodeman stood wondering what to do, then remembered having read or heard something about "tying people up." He stripped, bound, and gagged the body with the girl's own clothing and left it in a bathroom. Though Sodeman claimed not to have "interfered" with the girl, Coroner Surgeon Dr. Crawford Mollison said that Griffiths had had sexual intercourse on the day she died.

After murdering Griffiths, Sodeman returned to his wife and their 2-year-old daughter, Joan. Police arrested a young man in the Griffiths murder, but released him because he had a perfect alibi. About two months later, on Jan. 9, 1931, Sodeman killed his second victim in the suburb of Ormond. The body of 16-year-old Hazel Wilson was discovered by her brother in a vacant lot in Oakleigh Road. She had been on her way to a dance. The similarities in the crimes led police to intensify their investigation, but they found no clues. Sodeman moved his family to Gippsland in eastern Victoria. It was another four years before he killed again. On New Year's Day 1935, after Sodeman had been drinking, he met 12-year-old Ethel Belshaw at a picnic on the beach at Inverloch. According to Sodeman, Belshaw asked if she could walk with him. He first refused, but then changed his mind. On a back road, he strangled the girl and left her body bound and gagged as he had his other victims. Police questioned many picnickers, including Sodeman, but did not suspect him. He later attended Belshaw's funeral.

Less than a year later, on Dec. 1, 1935, Sodeman, then working at a road camp near Dumbalk, strangled 6-year-old Jane Rushmer, a friend of his daughter. Rushmer had asked the apparently gentle man to give her a ride on his bike. Sodeman, who had been drinking, took the child to a deserted area and killed her. Returning to his camp after the murder, Sodeman became angry when a coworker joked about the slaying. Police knew that the child had been seen with a man on a bike, and the coworker facetiously remarked that Sodeman had been riding his bike on the night of the murder. The worker contacted the police. The next day Sodeman confessed.

Sodeman's trial took place at the Melbourne Open Court, beginning on Feb. 17, 1936, with Justice Gavan Duffy presiding. Sodeman pleaded insanity, explaining that he knew that he had a mania of some kind. His family had a long history of insanity. Two prison doctors and a psychiatrist testified that he was insane when he killed. Government medical officer Dr. Albert Philpott explained that Sodeman was not conscious of what he was doing when he murdered. Philpott testified that Sodeman's condition was, "an obsessional impulse which is there all the time but which does not affect him when he has no liquor." The jury found Sodeman Guilty of murder and Justice Duffy sentenced him to death. Sodeman was hanged at Pentridge on June 1, 1936. A post-mortem examination revealed that Sodeman suffered from leptomeningitis, a brain disease.

Soli, Salvatore, and **Maleno, Steven**, prom. 1975, U.S. Salvatore Soli and his companions in crime, Isais Felix Melendez and Steven Maleno, were vicious criminals, especially Soli, who was a known drug peddler, car thief, and armed robber. He was once accused of attempted murder. Maleno, a homosexual, often robbed his male lovers. The youngest of the trio, Melendez, was a homosexual prostitute. All three, along with others, comprised a murderous gang that entrapped and robbed wealthy homosexuals.

John S. Knight III, heir apparent to the Knight-Ridder newspaper fortune, well-known socialite, a graduate of top schools, and a rising star in the Knight-Ridder newspaper chain, was also a homosexual. Unknown to most of his close associates and friends, he indulged in nefarious and pornographic activities.

Knight did not try to hide his wealth and took pride in showing off his penthouse and collections of art, books, and

Steven Maleno and Salvatore Soli who, with Isiah Melendez, murdered John Knight III, heir apparent to the Knight-Ridder newspaper chain.

erotica to his lovers. He was known as a free spender who paid his lovers well. In doing so, he set himself up for a hit by the Salvatore Soli gang.

On the night of Dec. 7, 1975, Knight entertained guests for dinner at his penthouse. Later, all guests left except for a doctor and his wife, who were spending the night. At about 4 a.m., loud noises were heard from the apartment and the doctor's wife was awakened by an intruder demanding money and jewelry.

The woman was threatened, treated roughly by the three intruders, and then tied up. After the apartment was thoroughly ransacked, two of the thugs left. The one remaining, a young man who was high on drugs, untied the woman, who rushed back to her bedroom to awaken her husband.

The doctor confronted the young invader and, after a brief struggle, was knocked to the floor as the young man fled the apartment. Rushing to Knight's bedroom, the doctor found his friend unconscious, badly beaten, with a dozen or more neckties tied around his head and neck, and firmly bound. He was not breathing and no pulse was found. After attempting CPR, the doctor gave up. Knight had been stabbed to death. In the meantime, the doctor's wife called the police.

During the subsequent investigation, the police found extensive lists of Knight's homosexual contacts and a trunk of related photographs, videos, and paraphernalia. They proceeded to track down the people named on the list and eventually issued warrants for the arrests of Soli, Melendez, and Maleno.

Maleno turned himself in almost immediately, and Melendez's body was found a few days later in New Jersey.

Knight's penthouse, ransacked by his murderers on the night of his death.

He had been murdered. A few days later, Linda Mary Wells, an associate of Soli's, contacted police in Miami, Fla., stating she knew about the murders in Philadelphia. She became the main witness against the gang, providing information leading to the apprehension of Salvatore Soli and implicating Maleno and Melendez. Soli and Maleno were brought to trial, and Maleno confessed to the slayings

of both Knight and Melendez. Maleno received two consecutive life sentences. Soli, the leader of the gang, was convicted and, after losing an appeal, was sentenced to life in prison.

Solis, Magdalena, and **Solis, Eleazor**, and **Hernandez, Santos**, and **Hernandez, Cayetano**, prom. 1963, Mex. In early 1963, two Mexican brothers convinced the villagers of Yerba Buena, Mex., that Inca gods would reward followers with treasure if they sacrificed money and sexual favors. Everyone except for Jesus Rubio was duped by the story, so he was bribed with some of the income. The cult continued for several months, but when no riches appeared, the villagers began to balk. So Santos Hernandez and Cayetano Hernandez went to Monterey, Calif., where they induced a brother and sister, actually a pimp and prostitute, to impersonate the two chief Inca gods. Eleazor Solis and Magdalena Solis agreed and returned to the village where they appeared to the villagers amid a cloud of smoke. Later, when the villagers were still not showered with treasure, two of the doubters were beaten to death. Followers then mixed the victims' blood with chicken blood and drank the mixture.

Six more distrustful villagers were killed during the next two months. Around that time, one teenager, Celina Salvana, Magdalena Solis' personal favorite, began having sex with a male cult member. Solis ordered the girl tied to a cross on May 28, 1963, and the former prostitute knocked her unconscious. Then the other followers attacked her, beat her to death, and burned her body. An awestruck 14-year-old Sebastian Gurrero witnessed the sacrifice and murder of another "unbeliever." The youth ran to police in Villa Gran where a policeman, Luis Martinez, was assigned to go with the boy to investigate the report. Both were slain and police and soldiers arrived at the village where the cult members were hiding in a cave. Three policeman and Santos Hernandez were killed in the shootout and the rest of the cult members were arrested. Cayetano Hernandez had disappeared, and Rubio later admitted to killing him because he planned to take his place as high priest. On June 13, 1963, the Solis brother and sister, along with twelve other cult members, were tried, convicted, and given thirty-year jail terms.

Sommerhalder, Richard (AKA: **Blue**), prom. 1976, U.S. During the 1970s, Richard Sommerhalder operated a store that sold drug paraphernalia in Rio Del Mar. In 1976, the bodies of Mary Gorman and Vickie Bezore were found naked and bludgeoned to death in the mountainous region of Santa Cruz, Calif. Sommerhalder was arrested and charged with their murders. He was convicted and sentenced to two life terms.

Son of Sam, See: **Berkowitz, David.**

Speck, Richard Franklin (AKA: **B. Brian; Richard Franklin Lindbergh; Richard Benjamin Speck**), 1941-91, U.S. When he was nineteen, mass-murderer Richard Speck emblazoned a tattoo into his left forearm which accurately summed up his emotional and mental state at the time. It read: "Born to Raise Hell." Years later, Speck burned the tattoo off using the ember of a lit cigar. From his cell in the Stateville Penitentiary at Joliet, Ill., he dreamed of the day he would be paroled. By his own admission though, the convicted killer of eight student nurses knew that the chances were not good. "If he was ever freed on parole, I'd probably take up arms myself," John Wilkening, father of one of the slain women, once said. "I have a lot of friends and so I would probably have to wait in line."

Richard Franklin Speck was born in Kirkwood, Ill. He was one of eight children belonging to Margaret and Benjamin Speck. In 1947, the family moved to Dallas, Texas, where Speck completed junior high school. It was the only formal education the young man received before he left home. By the time he was twenty, Speck had been arrested ten times on charges ranging from criminal trespass to burglary. He had tallied thirty-seven arrests by Spring 1966, when he returned to Chicago to find work as a merchant seaman. The semi-literate drifter spent his waking hours reading comic books and drinking to excess. He was a habitual pill-popper with a distorted view of reality, evidenced by his total lack of recall concerning his movements the night of July 13, 1966.

Speck shipped out on the cargo vessel the *Randall*, owned and operated by the Inland Steel Company. He was discharged in June 1966 for insubordination and fighting with a superior officer. His sister in Chicago, Martha Thornton, provided him with pocket money and drove him to the National Maritime Union hall, where Speck hoped to find work on a cargo ship heading to New Orleans. But there were no berths available to him on July 10, 1966, the day he made his application. Speck brooded about this for the next three days. He drank heavily in the taverns and skid row dives that dotted the west side of Chicago, plotting ways to earn enough money to pay for his trip to New Orleans. On the night of July 13, the besotted Speck

injected a narcotic into his veins and headed to the South Side to see what he could come up with.

Speck wandered up to a two-story townhouse belonging to the South Chicago Community Hospital on East 100th Street around 11 p.m. He dug into his pockets and pulled out a handgun and a knife. He rapped on the door, and after a few seconds had passed, 23-year-old student nurse Corazon Amurao appeared. "I'm not going to hurt you," he said. "I'm only going to tie you up. I need your money to go to New Orleans." Amurao and two of her companions were directed to the upstairs bedroom where three of their other roommates were sleeping. At gunpoint, the nurses were ordered to lie flat on the floor. The young women complied with Speck's directive. He bound their hands and feet with strips torn from the bed sheets and then waited. At 11:30 p.m., Gloria Davy returned home from a date. Speck seized her at the door and led her upstairs. Then at midnight, Suzanne Farris and Mary Ann Jordan arrived home. Jordan did not live at the address; it was her tragic luck to be Farris' overnight guest.

After Speck had assembled all nine of the women, he demanded their money. He reiterated his peaceable intentions. "Don't be afraid, I'm not going to kill you," he said. A few more minutes passed. Speck chatted with Merlita Gargullo, who was born in the Philippines. "Do you know karate?" he asked. According to the statements of Amurao—the only survivor that night—Speck became increasingly agitated. He led 20-year-old Pamela Wilkening into the adjacent bedroom and stabbed her with his knife. Her muffled scream was stifled when Speck twisted her neck with a strip of sheet. The killer was apparently sexually excited by this and decided to continue killing. Speck returned moments later for Mary Ann Jordan and Suzanne Farris. The two of them were repeatedly slashed in the face, neck, and chest. Farris, the daughter of a Chicago Transit Authority employee, fought him, but was stabbed eighteen times. Afterward, Speck calmly went into the washroom, where he rinsed the blood off his hands. The next victim was 24-year-old Nina Schmale from suburban Wheaton. He stabbed the woman in the neck and then strangled her to death. The remaining student nurses attempted to hide under beds, but Speck tracked them all down but one: Corazon Amurao, who succeeded in pushing herself under the bed and out of the killer's view. Paralyzed with fear, she heard the death cries of her two friends from the Philippines: Valentina Passion and Merlita Gargullo who were stabbed from the next room. Twenty-year-old Patricia Matusek, a former swimming champion, was carried to the bathroom. She begged Speck to untie her ankles before he killed her. He kicked her in the stomach and then strangled her to death. This left Gloria Davy, the only one of the eight that Speck sexually molested.

Richard Speck, mass killer, and his victims, left to right, Mary Ann Jordan, Merlita Gargullo, Valentina Passion.

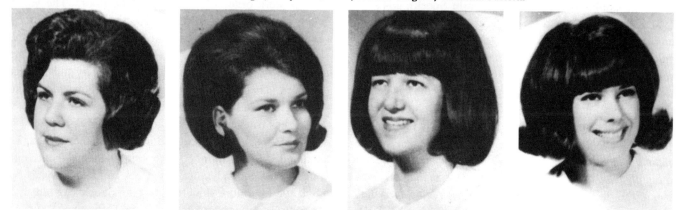

More of Speck's murder victims: left to right, Pamela Wilkening, Gloria Davy, Nina Schmale, Patricia Matusek.

Another victim, Suzanne Farris, and survivor Corazon Amurao.

Two views of the seedy flophouse where Richard Speck spent his last moments of freedom bleeding from self-inflicted wounds.

Amurao remained underneath the bed for hours, fearful that Speck would find her if she attempted to escape. Not until 5 p.m. the next day did she venture out. She stepped out onto a narrow ledge outside her bedroom and called for help. Her cries were heard by two local residents. The police arrived minutes later. What they found shocked and sickened them: eight student nurses, savagely mutilated, were lying dead. Detectives found thirty fingerprints and a man's T-shirt was found beside Davy's body. Police artist Otis Rathel sketched a composite drawing of the suspect from a description provided by Amurao. The Chicago dailies ran the likeness the next day. As it turned out, Rathel's sketch bore an amazing likeness to the killer.

Speck's identity was established when a gas station attendant recognized the suspect from the police sketch. This man told the attendant that he was looking for work at the National Maritime Union. The union retrieved Speck's application from a wastepaper basket. Fingerprints taken at the murder scene were matched to a set of Speck's prints on file with the Dallas police. With a name and a description of their suspect, police prepared to search for Speck. As it turned out, the killer made himself easy to locate.

After the murder spree, Speck had returned to his ninety-cent room at the Starr Hotel on West Madison Street to attempt suicide. On July 16, the gaunt, thin-faced killer slashed his right wrist and left arm with a blade. As the blood poured out. Speck called to the man in the next bunk. Failing to elicit sympathy, Speck stumbled into the hall. A police ambulance was summoned and he was taken to the Cook County Hospital emergency room and attended to by Dr. LeRoy Smith. "What's your name?" Smith asked. He answered, "Richard. Richard Speck."

It took a Cook County jury only forty-nine minutes to convict Richard Franklin Speck of the crime of murder. On June 15, 1967, he was sentenced to die in the electric chair. After the U.S. Supreme Court set aside the death penalty, Speck was resentenced on Nov. 22, 1972, to 400 to 1,200 years at the Stateville Penitentiary—the longest jail term ever given, up to that time. Nevertheless, Speck became eligible for parole in 1976. In 1977 and again in 1981, the convicted killer sent a tersely worded note to the state parole board saying that he was not interested in an early release. He was content to remain behind bars, where he happily pursued his hobby of oil painting. "Why don't you give parole to some of those young guys in here?" he complained. "They don't need to be in here in the first place." In August 1987, Speck had a change of heart and asked that the Illinois Prison Review Board consider granting his application for early release. There was little chance of that occurring, however. The memory of Speck's crime was still fresh in the public's mind. Speck remained

in prison until 1991, when he died at the age of forty-nine of a heart attack.

Spencer, Brenda, 1963- , U.S. In 1979, a 16-year-old high school student opened fire at an elementary school in San Diego, Calif., killing two and injuring several others. The sniper, Brenda Spencer, was a problem child and the product of a broken home. She lived with her father after her parents' divorce several years earlier. Spencer was frequently absent from school, abused drugs, and committed petty thefts. She enjoyed watching violent programs on television and shooting birds. She once used a BB gun to shoot out the windows of Cleveland Elementary School, located across the street from her home. For Christmas 1978, Spencer's father gave her a semi-automatic .22-caliber rifle and about 500 rounds of ammunition.

In early January 1979, apparently preparing for an attack, Spencer moved her weapons to the garage and dug a tunnel as a hideout in her backyard. During the week of Jan. 22, she announced that she planned to "do something big to get on TV." On Monday morning, Jan. 29, she watched the principal of Cleveland Elementary School approach the school's gate. As Principal Burton Wragg opened the gate to the waiting school children, Brenda opened fire. She killed Wragg and janitor Michael Suchar. One of the first police officers to arrive on the scene, 30-year-old Robert Robb, was wounded in the neck as he helped a victim. Nine children from age six to twelve were wounded during the twenty-minute shooting spree, including two 9-year-olds, Christy Burell and Monica Selvig.

For the next several hours, Spencer hid in her house. Talking with police and reporters by telephone, she explained, "I just started shooting. That's it. I just did it for the fun of it. I just don't like Mondays...I did this because it's a way to cheer up the day. Nobody likes Mondays." Six hours after the shooting, Brenda walked out of her house, laid down her rifle, and surrendered to police.

After a change of venue, Spencer was tried in Santa Ana, Calif., and convicted of two counts of murder and one count of assault. She received two concurrent sentences, a twenty-five-year to life term for murder and a forty-eight-year term for assault with a deadly weapon. Spencer's Monday morning shooting spree prompted the song, "I Don't Like Mondays," by the Irish rock group The Boomtown Rats.

Spencer, Brenda, and **Smith, Lucille**, and **Willock, Essie Mae**, prom. 1974, U.S. In 1974, three female convicts at the Kentucky Correctional Institution located near Louisville, escaped from the facility after beating a guard with a broomstick and spraying another with Mace. Brenda Spencer, Lucille Smith, and Essie Mae Willock then hijacked a pickup truck and burgled a house where they stole two pistols and a change of clothing. They drove to Brinkley, Ark., where they robbed a small grocery store of cash and all the beer in stock. After the robbery, policeman Morris Greenwalt pulled their speeding truck over and Spencer shot him once before getting out of the truck and firing seven more bullets into his body with the officer's service revolver. Following the murder, the escapees forced their way into a farmhouse where they held the family hostage. Police officers surrounded the house, but retreated when the women threatened to kill the family. Later that night, after drinking all of the stolen beer, Spencer, Smith, and Willock surrendered. Spencer and Smith were tried, convicted, and sentenced to life terms for the murder of the police officer. Willock received an eleven-year sentence.

Spencer, Verlin, 1902- , U.S. Verlin Spencer, a 38-year-old principal at South Pasadena Junior High School in Pasadena, Calif., had been at the school for seven years. He had served as vice-principal for five years until he was appointed principal in 1938. His perfectionism and intense ambition made him an abrasive and critical leader. Spencer's superiors insisted in 1939 that he take a three-week leave of absence. One year later, in Spring 1940, Spencer was again in conflict with his staff. He disagreed with Ruth Barnett Sturgeon, a long-time teacher, and Verner V. Vanderlip, head of the mechanical arts department. Following an investigation, George C. Bush, superintendent of the South Pasadena city schools, John E. Alman, principal of South Pasadena High School, and Will R. Speer, business manager of the South Pasadena-San Marino School District, decided not to rehire Spencer. Bush informed Spencer of the decision in a letter; Spencer demanded a hearing. The meeting was to be held at 3 p.m. on May 6, 1940.

On that day, Spencer arrived at the school just as the students were leaving for the day. He joined Bush, Alman, and Speer in Bush's second-floor office. Within a few minutes, Spencer's angry voice was heard from the hallway. Then five shots rang out in rapid succession, followed by a short silence, and then another shot. Spencer had shot Alman and Speer in the heart, killing them both instantly. Although Spencer missed Bush's heart, the 62-year-old superintendent died twenty minutes later. Spencer then moved across the hall to find Dorothea Talbert, Bush's secretary, who had heard the shots but remained at her desk. As Spencer aimed his .22-caliber automatic pistol at

her, Talbert ducked and was hit in the shoulder. Spencer fled. Police later timed the first murders at 2:55 p.m.

Spencer drove to the art department of the school, parked his car, and went inside to search for Ruth Sturgeon. He found her alone in the department, and then shot and killed her. Spencer hurried out of the building and reloaded his gun. He found Vanderlip, his next victim, in the schoolyard. Witnesses gave different versions of this encounter. Some said that the two men spoke briefly, then walked together toward the machine shop. Others said Spencer forced Vanderlip to go with him at gunpoint. Inside the machine shop, police found evidence of an intense struggle and chase. Vanderlip apparently fought for his life, and lost to Spencer. Vanderlip's body was found an hour later by two schoolgirls searching for their missing teacher.

Spencer then headed back toward his car, but as he crossed the schoolyard, he noticed that he was being watched. He ran through the cafeteria in an attempt to reach the street. As he entered the building, police officers Clarence Sexton, Clyde Rohyback, and Ray Broadstone, all armed with shotguns, cornered him. As one of the officers took aim, Spencer pressed his own gun against his right side and fired twice, critically wounding himself. He was rushed to Huntington Hospital, where two of his victims lay dead and another was dying. Police found a note from Spencer to his wife, Polly, telling her that he was sane. He left his property to her with the stipulation that she spend no more than $200 on hospital care or funeral expenses for him.

The disgruntled ex-principal survived his wounds and was tried for murder. He pleaded Guilty to all charges and was given five consecutive life terms. He was discharged by California's Department of Corrections in 1977, at the age of seventy-five.

Spenkelink, John A., 1949-79, U.S. In 1973, 24-year-old John Spenkelink, an escapee from a California prison, picked up a hitchhiker, 43-year-old Joseph Syzmanklewicz of Detroit. Syzmanklewicz, an Ohio parole violator, traveled with Spenkelink for about two weeks, assaulting, sodomizing, and robbing the younger convict. Later, Syzmanklewicz was found dead in a motel in Tallahassee, Fla. He had been shot twice.

Spenkelink and another man, Frank Brumm, were arrested for the murder, but Brumm was acquitted. Spenkelink claimed that he and Syzmanklewicz had agreed to part company and Spenkelink had told Brumm, "If you hear a shot, come to room twelve." Spenkelink claimed he retrieved Syzmanklewicz' gun from the car and returned to the hotel room to give it back to him. There, Spenkelink said Syzmanklewicz tried to assault him and he shot him in self defense. He told the jury that his earlier statement to Brumm meant that if gunfire were heard, Brumm should rush to help him. The jury interpreted Spenkelink's statement as premeditation to murder, convicted him in 1974, and he was sentenced to be executed.

Spenkelink's case aroused the indignation of anti-capital punishment groups and his defense lawyer doubted that his guilt had been established beyond a reasonable doubt, but on May 18, 1979, Florida governor Robert Graham signed Spenkelink's death warrant. Six appeals by Spenkelink to the U.S. Supreme Court were unsuccessful. On May 22, about 400 convicts at the Florida State Prison at Starke, Fla., where Spenkelink was held, refused to eat their breakfast to demonstrate their objection to the scheduled executions of Spenkelink and another inmate, Willie Jasper Darden, Jr. On May 25, 1979, yelling, "This is murder! This is murder!" Spenkelink was electrocuted at the Florida prison, the first inmate to be executed in the U.S. since the execution of Gary Gilmore in January 1977.

Spiderman, See: **Coneys, Theodore Edward.**

Spinelli, Evelita Juanita (AKA: **The Duchess**), 1889-1941, U.S. More than three hundred convicts at San Quentin in California petitioned to the governor to prevent the hanging of Juanita Spinelli, more popularly known as "The Duchess." The petition stated that, "After establishing a worthy and universally commendable record, a 100-year record, of never executing a woman, the State should not break that record. If that is done the world at large would declare, in sad disillusionment, that deterioration and retrogression had entered the world's most golden State."

Spinelli was a San Francisco widow who decided on a life of crime when she found herself alone in middle age. She led her new common-law husband, Mike Simeone, in gathering a gang that would follow her commands. She planned the robberies, and she distributed the loot afterwards. On nights when there was no robbery planned, her men were expected to roll drunks.

When the gang held up a barbecue stand and ended up shooting the owner, Leland Cash, Spinelli, Simeone, and three others fled to Sacramento. But when 19-year-old gang member Robert Sherrard showed an inclination to turn himself in to the police, the gang's leader slipped him some chloral hydrate, and the other men took him to the Freeport-Clarksburg Bridge and threw him into the Sacramento River. Another gang member, Albert Ives, arrested for

another crime, turned informer. Spinelli, Simeone, and Gordon Hawkins were all found Guilty of Sherrard's murder and sentenced to death.

Spinelli's execution was reprieved several times, once in response to the convicts' petition, but on Nov. 21, 1941, in front of sixty-six witnesses and with pictures of her children and a grandson strapped under her clothing, the middle-aged crime kingpin became the first woman to be officially executed in California.

Spinelli, William, 1879-1940, U.S. William Spinelli married Rose in 1909. At the time of her murder, they had been married for twenty-nine years and had five children. She had supported the family with her work as a maid in Beverly Hills for ten years while her husband remained unemployed. In the basement of the Spinelli's Los Angeles home, police found a can containing $900 in cash which Spinelli said he had saved out of his wife's wages. The household was apparently not a happy one. Spinelli's parents were both alcoholics, and he became one himself. Psychiatric tests following his arrest revealed that he had had incestuous relations with two of his three daughters over a number of years, and may have fathered one of his own grandchildren. When asked if he thought his wife was aware of the incest, he replied, "We had fights about it, although she never caught me in the act." He was diagnosed as a schizoid personality.

At the request of one of Spinelli's daughters, Helen Angieli, homicide bureau detectives broke into the home on Dec. 20, 1938, and found the bedroom and bathroom heavily stained with blood. Spinelli claimed he had cut his head and hands, adding that his wife had run away with another man on Dec. 12. He showed detectives a letter, supposedly signed by Rose Spinelli, that said she was "eloping to South America." Spinelli and his son, William Spinelli, Jr., were booked on suspicion of murder. The son admitted he suspected that his father killed his mother, but said his father threatened to kill him in his sleep if he did not keep quiet. The son first claimed that his father forced him to forge the letter from his mother, but police later learned that a gas station operator wrote the letter. Police chemist Ray Pinker examined the blood-stained rooms and concluded that no one could lose that much blood and survive. Detective Lieutenants D.R. Patton, Lloyd Hurst, and Aldo Corsini searched the home and ground after learning from neighbors that, on the day Mrs. Spinelli disappeared, her husband had a fire burning in the incinerator for five hours. They discovered bone fragments and a gold ring in the driveway of the home. In the backyard, they found a piece of charred cloth, a purse, and a bloodstained hatchet hidden in a box.

The Spinelli son explained that he had come home around 10 p.m. on Dec. 12 to find his father in the backyard with a fire in the incinerator. "I thought it was funny, but he had threatened me several times so I didn't say anything." Two large suitcases were also missing, the son explained. Neighbors reported seeing the elder Spinelli leave the house several times with packages. Police officers questioned Spinelli for almost seventy-two hours before he confessed. Spinelli explained that, after an angry exchange between the couple, "I laid down on the bed and she hit me. I threw up my hands and grabbed for a hatchet, and I kicked her in the stomach and she fell down, and I got up and hit her two times in the head." After going to the hospital "to get my face fixed up," he wrote a note to the family and left it at the house. The note, supposedly written by his wife, explained to her children that she was going away. Spinelli then went out to a restaurant for supper, and returned home later to dismember his wife's body with a saw, wrap the pieces, and burn them in the backyard incinerator. When his son came home and asked what he was burning, the father replied, "I am burning some trash."

Spinelli was tried and convicted in Los Angeles in December 1938. He was executed in the gas chamber at San Quentin on May 17, 1940.

Splett, Norbert, 1952- , and **Schumacher, Petra**, 1954- , Ger. In June 1972 Kurt Rheiners' wife and 10-year-old son vacationed in the Tyrol, Aust. Left alone in his house in Hanover, Ger., Rheiners, a 36-year-old plumber, invited some friends to go to the Ant Tavern on June 20. He drank beer with Norbert Splett, a 20-year-old apprentice pastry cook, and Splett's girlfriend, 18-year-old Petra Schumacher. They downed more than forty glasses of beer by midnight and left together, tipsy, the girl clinging to both men. They went to Rheiners' house where the host suggested they play strip poker and all agreed, continuing with the game until all were naked by 2 a.m. At this point, Splett later said, he had to go to the bathroom to vomit and when he returned he saw Rheiners on top of his girlfriend. Splett said he thought the woman was struggling and that Rheiners was raping her. Splett grabbed Rheiners' homemade wooden spear, stabbed the man in the back, and then left with his girlfriend.

Rheiners was found the next morning about 9:30 by Hardy Bruggemann, who was at first arrested for the crime. Later that day Splett arrived at the police station to confess. He was charged with murder and Schumacher was charged as an accessory after the fact. Splett's confession, however, did not match the forensic evidence, which indicated that

Rheiners had been participating in unforced sex at the time of his death and his body did not bear any marks from a fighting woman. Additionally, police could find no evidence of vomit in the bathroom and when Rheiners' wife returned she said 1,300 marks were missing. On May 22, 1973, Splett was convicted of murder with extenuating circumstances and received a ten-year sentence. Charges against Schumacher were dismissed.

Stack, Richard, 1956- , U.S. A Southwest Side Chicago man was charged on Mother's Day, May 12, 1980, with murdering his wife and their infant son. Richard Stack, twenty-four, was arrested at Holy Cross Hospital where he was being treated for cuts on his hands and head. Police were called to the scene by neighbors who said Stack had been leaning out a window he had broken, shouting. Family members told officers the Stacks were high school sweethearts who had married in 1978. The victims, Carol Ann Stack, twenty-two, and the infant, Richard Stack, Jr., thirteen months, suffered multiple stab wounds from a broken pool cue.

Tried in April 1982 in a Chicago criminal court before Judge James M. Bailey, Stack had been an unemployed laborer at the time of the murders. Defense attorney Geary Kull presented the testimony of two court-appointed psychiatrists who said Stack was insane when he murdered his wife and child to rid them of demons. Assistant state's attorneys Ernest DiBenedetto and Michael Goggin charged that Stack slashed and stabbed both victims, throwing his child against the wall and cracking the baby's skull. DiBenedetto also said Stack had asked psychiatrists at the Chester Mental Health Center to explain the criteria for being judged insane shortly after he was evaluated as mentally competent to stand trial. On Mar. 30, the jury ruled that Stack was not insane. Calling the murders "brutal and heinous," Bailey sentenced Stack to life imprisonment on Apr. 26, 1982.

Stafford, Roger Dale, 1951- , U.S. Arrested in a North Side Chicago YMCA without incident on Mar. 13, 1979, was Roger Dale Stafford, twenty-seven, implicated by his estranged wife, Vera Stafford, in the slayings of at least nine people.

Stafford was the prime suspect in the first-degree murder of six employees of the Sirloin Stockade Steakhouse in Oklahoma City, Okla., on July 16, 1978, during a robbery that netted $1,300. The body of Terri M. Horst, fifteen, was found in the walk-in freezer. Also murdered were Anthony

Tew, seventeen; David Lindsey, seventeen; David Salsman, fifteen; Issac Freeman, fifty-six; and Louis Zacharias, forty-three. Stafford's brother, Harry Stafford, also a suspect in the murders, was killed in a motorcycle accident in Tulsa, Okla., not long afterward. Stafford was also the main suspect in the killings of air force sergeant Melvin Lorenz, thirty-eight, of San Antonio, Texas; his wife, Linda Lorenz, thirty-one; and their 12-year-old son, Richard. The bodies of the Lorenzes were discovered along Interstate 35 on June 22, 1978, near Purcell, Okla.

Found Guilty in an Oklahoma City courtroom of the shootings of the six steakhouse employees, Stafford was sentenced on Oct. 24, 1979, by Judge Charles Owens to be executed by lethal injection. Stafford proclaimed his innocence, saying, "I wish to God the police department would quit harassing me and find the people who did it." According to Oklahoma law, executions must be carried out by injections of lethal barbiturates. As of this writing, Stafford is still awaiting execution.

Stanciel, Elijah, c.1961- , and Burgos, Violeta, c.1964- , U.S.

A blind couple living on the North Side of Chicago murdered the woman's child and received relatively light sentences because of their handicaps and lack of previous criminal records. In 1984, Eleticia Asbury was born to Violeta Burgos and Andre Asbury. Then the parents separated, Burgos caring for the child. In December 1984, the infant was taken from the mother by the Illinois Department of Children and Family Services because her boyfriend, Elijah Stanciel, allegedly broke the child's arm. The state organization directed Burgos to attend parenting classes, obtain counseling, and avoid Stanciel. Eleticia was reunited with her mother in October 1985. For several months before the toddler's death on Apr. 19, 1986, she was tortured. An autopsy revealed 130 wounds on the body, some of them bites.

The sightless pair stood trial and were convicted. During sentencing, their lawyers pleaded for leniency from Cook County Criminal Court judge James Bailey, claiming a prison sentence would be a difficult ordeal for the killers because they were blind. Stanciel's attorney Sam Adam asserted, "you have before you an individual who has no prior convictions for anything at all...A severely handicapped individual, a man who is legally blind." Judge Bailey sentenced the pair to sixty years in prison each, though the prosecution had argued for the death penalty. Relatives of the child were outraged, including the child's natural father, who contended that blindness should not be used to justify a murder. The child's uncle, William Asbury, commented, "I don't see any more than they do. They didn't have to see

to kill her...These are two individuals that took the life of a child. Sixty years is awful light for taking a life."

Stanley, Arthur Cromwell, d.1923, S. Afri.

Former WWI soldier and hopeful diamond digger in the city of Kimberley, Arthur Stanley was unable to provide for his family. Having decided to turn to crime, he learned that William James Thompson, a diamond buyer, would be making a circuit of various mines the next day, carrying cash to buy stones. Early on Mar. 7, 1923, Thompson's chauffeur picked up the buyer. At a gateway into a farm, two men appeared and at first seemed about to open the gate for the car. Instead, they turned and fired. A bullet went through Thompson's head and five more bullets injured the driver. Stanley and his partner took the money and left, thinking that both men had been killed.

As Stanley and his companion were burying most of the money, investigators were learning Stanley's identity, because the chauffeur, regaining consciousness, named Arthur Stanley as one of the assailants. The killer set off by cab to go to Schmidt's Drift Road where his family was waiting, but the cab drivers already knew that Stanley was wanted by police. Stanley was met at Schmidt's Drift by a policeman and arrested. He was tried and found Guilty. The judge ignored a recommendation of mercy, and Stanley was hanged on June 11, 1923.

Stano, Gerald Eugene, 1951- , U.S.

In 1981, Gerald Eugene Stano was sentenced to three life terms in a Florida prison for strangling and stabbing three women in Florida's Volusia County. Arrested in April 1980 in Daytona Beach, Fla., after slashing a prostitute, Stano was initially saved from the death penalty in a plea agreement that left him ineligible for parole until the age of 103. He confessed to three other murders, including those of Susan Bickrest, twenty-four, and Cathy Muldoon, twenty-three. By mid-August 1982, Stano had confessed to eleven slayings, by October, thirty-three. He may be responsible for as many as forty, a record number for an American murderer in this century, an infamous position formerly held by Chicago's John Wayne Gacy, who was convicted of slaying thirty-three boys and young men.

All of Stano's victims were women. Most were stabbed or shot with a .22-caliber pistol. Most lived in Tampa or in the central Florida area, and many frequented the bars along Tampa's Dale Mabry Highway. According to Stano's confessions, he also killed two women in New Jersey and "four to six" in Pennsylvania. Almost all of the victims had

had to rely on someone else for transportation on the day they were killed, and all were either single, divorced, or separated. Many of the victims were hitchhikers or prostitutes, ranging in age from twelve to the mid-fifties. The victims willingly got into Stano's car after he had charmed them with small talk and offered them beer or marijuana and a relaxing ride.

Stano worked at semi-skilled jobs—cleaning windshields or working as a short-order cook. The bodies of his victims were dumped in desolate areas of Pasco County, with most of the murders occurring in 1976 and 1977.

The killings began in 1973, the year Stano moved from New Jersey to Florida with his adoptive parents. Stano said he killed the women because they argued and "I can't stand a bitchy chick." A psychological profile by Dr. Ann McMillan classified Stano as a multiple killer of the type who "simply enjoys killing." McMillan described Stano as a man who hated women and could probably only obtain sexual release after murdering and mutilating them. Stano frequently mentioned "seeing red" when he described attacking his victims, and often killed women who wore blue, a color he apparently connected with a younger brother on whom he wanted to take revenge. Coming from a background of extreme abuse and neglect, Stano became a juvenile delinquent, damaging property and setting fires. Alcohol triggered his lethal rages. Apparently he never committed murder until he had drunk beer or whiskey. He kept his prized treasure, his car, spotless, scrubbing all bloodstains and evidence of the murders off the seats and upholstery.

By December 1982, authorities had come up with no physical evidence or witnesses to link Stano to the additional murders he claimed to have committed. He had not directed law-enforcement officers to any bodies that had not already been found, according to Florida Department of Law Enforcement agent Ed Williams, who coordinated the investigation for several counties. Sergeant Paul Crow, a Daytona Beach police detective, was the person to whom Stano confessed many of the murders.

In January 1984, Stano was sentenced to death for murder. He was under three death sentences and was serving seven life sentences for ten murders committed in Florida. On May 18, 1988, the eve of his fourth appointment with the electric chair, Stano won an indefinite stay of execution from the Atlanta Circuit Court of Appeals. Stano still resides on Death Row in a Florida state prison as of this writing.

Starkweather, Charles (AKA: **Little Red**), 1940-59, and **Fugate, Caril Ann**, 1945- , U.S. Diminutive Charles Starkweather, also known as Little Red, committed

the first of eleven murders at seventeen and died in Nebraska's electric chair two years later. He and his girlfriend, Caril Ann Fugate, terrorized the plains states for a week in 1958 when they went on a murder rampage.

Charlie Starkweather wanted to be like James Dean. He followed the charismatic actor's career in films like *Rebel Without a Cause* while working as a garbage man. In keeping with the rebel image, he took up with a much younger girl. Where girls of Starkweather's age were put off by his five-foot, two-inch stature, fourteen-year-old Caril Ann Fugate was flattered by his attentions. She was well-developed for her age, rebellious in school, and at home.

On Dec. 1, 1957, Starkweather robbed a service station. He pulled a gun on attendant Robert Colvert, took his money, drove him to a remote spot outside Lincoln, and shot him in the head. Starkweather was seventeen at the time, Colvert twenty-one.

In late January 1958, Starkweather called on Fugate at the home she shared with her mother and stepfather, Marion Bartlett. Fugate was not yet home from school, so Starkweather passed the time quarreling with Fugate's mother, Velda Bartlett.

Starkweather had his prize possession, a hunting rifle, with him—he was rarely without it. The argument heated up and soon Mr. and Mrs. Bartlett were dead. Starkweather later related what happened. "They said they were tired of me hanging around. I told Mrs. Bartlett off and she got so mad that she slapped me. When I hit her back, her husband started to come at me, so I had to let both of them have it with my rifle." In his mind, it was the victims' fault for arguing with him.

Starkweather knew Fugate did not like her parents, so he was not surprised that she did not interfere. She did not stop him when he murdered her sister, either, choking two-year-old Betty Jean Bartlett by shoving the gun barrel down her throat. He hid the baby's body in a cardboard box, put Marion Bartlett's body in a chicken coop behind the house and wrapped it in rags and newspapers, then disposed of Mrs. Bartlett in an abandoned outhouse, covering her with newspapers, too. The two then ate sandwiches and watched TV. To keep away unwanted visitors, Fugate insisted Starkweather put a note on the front door: "Stay Away. Every Body is Sick With the Flu."

The note failed to deter Fugate's older sister when she came to call. She knocked anyway, and Fugate warned her to stay away. The sister told her husband that Caril Ann had refused to let her in. Both of them thought her behavior strange, so they called the police. They, too, were refused entrance. The police went away unsatisfied and were called again two days later when Fugate turned away her grandmother. Assistant police chief Eugene Masters sent two of his officers with the grandmother to check on

Caril Fugate and Charles Starkweather before the murders.

Mr. and Mrs. Bartlett, victims.

Carol King, victim.

Betty Jean Bartlett, victim.

August Meyer, victim.

Robert Jensen, victim.

Lillian Fencl, victim.

Mrs. Ward, victim.

C. Lauer Ward

Caril Fugate, under arrest and unconcerned, drinking pop.

Charles Starkweather, condemned to death, unconcerned.

the Bartlett house. They ignored the warning sign and entered to find the house empty except for the bodies. Police surmised that the couple had made more sandwiches, packed them in Starkweather's car, and left. They swore out arrest warrants and the search began. A short time later, a gas station attendant in nearby Bennet, Neb., told police that the fugitives had stopped to fix a flat, fill their tank, and buy shotgun and rifle ammunition.

Starkweather's next victim was farmer August Meyer. Police received a tip that Starkweather's car was parked outside Meyer's farmhouse. Sheriff Merle Karnopp and his men surrounded the house and called through a bullhorn for Starkweather's surrender. When no answer came, police entered the building to find Meyer dead, his head torn apart by a shotgun blast.

Farmer Evert Broening found two bodies in a storm cellar near Meyer's farm. Seventeen-year-old Robert Jensen and 16-year-old Carol King were shot in the head. Jensen's car was missing, and King had been raped before being killed. The posse seeking Starkweather and Fugate swelled to 200 police officers.

The next victims died at the home of businessman C. Lauer Ward. A car was parked in Ward's driveway, and his own 1956 Packard was gone, although Ward had not gone to work. There was no answer when officers knocked on the Ward's door. When they entered the house, police found Ward, forty-seven, dead in the foyer, shot in the head like the other victims. His wife, Clara, and their maid, Lillian Fenci, were bound and gagged in a bedroom. The women had been stabbed to death and mutilated. To aid in the manhunt the National Guard was called.

Starkweather and Fugate headed west, getting as far as Douglas, Wyo. As they neared Douglas, they noticed a car parked by the side of the road, where shoe salesman Merle Collison was napping. Starkweather woke him up with a gunshot, then fired nine bullets into him as he got out of the car on Starkweather's command. When Starkweather could not release the emergency brake, he flagged Joseph Sprinkle and ordered him to help him with the brake. Sprinkle saw Collison's body and realized that his only chance was to grab Starkweather's rifle as he maneuvered around the brake.

As the two struggled for the firearm, a police car arrived. Fugate ran toward Deputy Sheriff William Rohmer's car. "Help!" she yelled. "It's Starkweather! He's going to kill me! He's crazy! Arrest him!"

Sprinkle wrested the gun away from Starkweather, who drove off in Collison's car at 115 miles per hour. In the ensuing chase, the rear window of Starkweather's getaway car was shot out. He suddenly stopped the car and staggered out, complaining of a superficial cut on his ear from broken glass.

"You're a real tough guy, aren't you?" one of the officers asked the murderer.

Fugate claimed at her trial that she had been an innocent hostage all along. Starkweather was willing to support this until her testimony labeled him a killer. He turned on her and painted a picture of a less-than-innocent hostage. "One time," Starkweather claimed, "she said that some hamburgers were lousy and we ought to go back and shoot all them people in the restaurant."

In Fugate's defense, the warning sign on the Bartlett household's front door was brought out. Her attorney claimed that she refused to let her sister or the police enter to avoid further bloodshed. The jury did not believe it.

Caril Ann Fugate was sentenced to life imprisonment but was paroled in 1981. Charles Starkweather was electrocuted in the Nebraska State Penitentiary at midnight, June 24, 1959. True to his character, he rejected the request that he donate his eyes for transplant after his death, saying, "Hell, no! No one ever did anything for me! Why the hell should I do anything for anyone else?"

Steelman, William, See: **Gretzler, Douglas.**

Stein, Harry, and **Wissner, Nathan,** and **Cooper, Calmen,** d.1955, U.S. A messenger was killed on Apr. 3, 1950, in the offices of *Reader's Digest* near Pleasantville, N.Y. Two months later, three ex-convicts, Harry Stein, Calmen Cooper, and Nathan Wissner, were arrested for the murder, convicted, and sentenced to die in February 1951, but through nine stays of execution, they stayed alive more than four years. However, in July 1955, their luck ran out. After three Supreme Court justices and the governor of New York rejected their last-minute pleas, the three convicts went to the electric chair in Sing Sing Prison.

Steinberg, Joel B., 1941-   , U.S. For more than a decade Joel B. Steinberg, a disbarred lawyer, battered his live-in girlfriend of twelve years and finally beat his illegally adopted daughter to death. In 1976, Hedda Nussbaum, an editor of children's books, met Steinberg and began living with him the same year. Beginning in 1977, Steinberg continually struck and browbeat his lover, and the woman suffered from broken ribs, nose fractures, and chipped teeth. According to Nussbaum, her companion used drugs, humiliation, brainwashing methods, and only allowed her to eat with his permission to coerce her into believing that she was "a worthless person who could be saved only through his wisdom and special powers." If she ate without his consent, she alleged, he made her take an ice-water bath. Countless times neighbors called police to investigate screams coming from the Manhattan, N.Y., apartment, but nothing was found. In 1979, Nussbaum began using drugs, including cocaine and heroin, and Steinberg convinced his lover that many of their friends were cult members attempting to hypnotize him and that she had been involved in sex with numerous people.

The couple illegally adopted two children, Elizabeth (Lisa) in 1981, and Mitchell in 1986. By 1987, Lisa wore dirty clothes, her hair was tangled, and she had no toys. She also had no bed and slept on the couch. Several weeks before her death in November 1987, Steinberg reputedly seized Lisa, shook her, and threw her to the floor. On Oct. 23, 1987, according to one of Steinberg's clients, Mr. Scannapieco, he was driving with Steinberg and Lisa when the father hit the sleeping child on the side of the face for "...staring, just staring," telling his client that Lisa could put herself into a trance. Steinberg then ordered Lisa to smile and blink to stay awake and she obeyed. Steinberg also complained to Nussbaum several weeks before Lisa's death that the child continually stared at him. Said Nussbaum, "He thought the staring was dramatic and important."

On Nov. 1, 1987, Lisa's father struck her three times with his fist at about 6:30 p.m. and left her lying on the bathroom floor. Later, he carried the first-grader out of the bathroom and placed her in Nussbaum's arms, claiming the unconscious child had been "staring at him," and telling Nussbaum to "Relax—go with her. Stay in harmony with her." Steinberg then left to go out to dinner with a friend and Nussbaum considered calling for help but she later explained, "Joel said he would take care of her, he'd get her up when he got back. I didn't want to show disloyalty or distrust for him, so I didn't call. I expected him to get Lisa up because I thought he was a healer." Later that evening, when Steinberg returned, the couple smoked cocaine and Steinberg admitted to Nussbaum that he had hit the child. At 6:35 a.m. the next morning Nussbaum called for emergency help. When officials arrived, they found the unconscious Lisa and 16-month-old Mitchell tied to his playpen and covered with excrement. Police also found burglary tools, drugs, handcuffs, chains, and a gun amid urine and rotting food in the Manhattan apartment. Lisa was taken to the hospital where she was declared brain-dead and died three days later on Nov. 5., one of approximately 1,200 children who died from neglect or abuse in the U.S. in 1987. An autopsy revealed that she had died from a brain hemorrhage as a result of a blow to the head.

Originally both Nussbaum and Steinberg were arrested and charged with murder in November 1987, and the same month their son, Mitchell, was returned to his mother. On Oct. 26, 1988, charges against 46-year-old Nussbaum were dismissed and she became the primary witness against 47-year-old Steinberg. Tapes of Nussbaum, taken about the time of arrest, showed missing hair, open wounds, bruises, and an ulcerated left leg. She also had a broken nose, fractured ribs, a cut lip, and a black eye when she was arrested. In November 1988, Nussbaum filed a $3 million civil suit against her former lover for the violence he had inflicted on her. Steinberg's trial began in late 1988 and, during the proceedings, he contended that the child had vomited, choked, and, after becoming unconscious, had hit her head and her bruises had been caused by his trying to rescue the child. Steinberg was convicted on Jan. 30, 1989, of first-degree manslaughter and sentenced in March 1989 to eight-and-one-third to twenty-five years' in prison.

The case prompted new child abuse laws in New York, the "Lisa Steinberg laws." Though Lisa's injuries had been noticed by teachers and friends of the family, no one had alerted authorities. The laws stipulated that those who notice child abuse but do not report it are subject to criminal prosecution.

Steinheil, Jeanne-Marguerite (Jeanne-Marguerite Japy), 1869-1954, Fr. It was at the time a murder fraught with passion, intrigue, and mystery. The accused killer was Jeanne-Marguerite Steinheil, former mistress of French president Felix Faure, who suffered a heart attack on Feb. 16, 1899, while making love. Faure fell to the floor clutching a lock of her hair. Steinheil, naked and screaming hysterically, had to be taken away from the dying man by the servants. She ran through the garden, leaving behind her corset which an obliging civil servant retrieved as a souvenir. But it was not the death of the aging French president that brought Steinheil, described by one bemused reporter as the "Sarah Bernhardt of the Assize," before the courts. Rather, it was the dual murders of a cuckolded husband and a disapproving mother that led the police to her door.

Steinheil lived on the Impasse Ronsin in Paris, one of four pampered children born to a prosperous businessman in Beaucourt. She was courted by dozens of suitors before settling on Adolphe Steinheil, an unpleasant-looking portrait painter, as her husband. Steinheil was a second-rate painter but his ambitious wife hoped that one day he might become a great master. To this end she took on a series of lovers, requiring each to purchase a painting from her struggling husband. President Faure commissioned the artist to prepare a portrait, one that was bought and paid for at state expense. Steinheil was knighted for his efforts and named to the Legion of Honor. Jeanne-Marguerite had fulfilled her husband's greatest dream.

On the morning of June 1, 1908, her exciting, glamorous life fell apart. At 6 a.m. a servant named Couillard was alarmed by a scream coming from Madame Steinheil's upstairs bedroom. He ran into the room and found his mistress tied to her bed. Nearby the body of her husband lay in the open doorway, a cord wrapped around his neck. The assailant, whoever he was, had strangled not only the artist but Jeanne-Marguerite's mother, Madame Japy, as well. Octave Hamard, chief of the Surete, arrived with the examining magistrate Auguste Leydet, who was another in a long line of lovers who had been welcomed to Jeanne-Marguerite's bed.

Steinheil claimed that three men and a red-headed woman had invaded her bedroom shortly after midnight, demanding money and jewels. She refused to tell the location of the valuables whereby one of the assailants beat her across the face and head. An inventory of the missing items was taken. Steinheil determined that 6,000 francs and several valuable items of jewelry were missing. Coincidentally, the artist was in debt for the same amount at the time of his death.

At first the police accepted her story. A theatrical agent reported that three costumes that closely matched the descriptions given by Madame Steinheil were stolen from his agency. A man and a woman were picked up by the police, but they had a concrete alibi. Nevertheless Steinheil positively identified them as her assailants. Next she accused Couillard of masterminding the murders. By this time her credibility had worn thin. It was completely shattered when the police learned that Steinheil had sent her maid, Mariette Wolff, to a small villa in Bellevue to retrieve a jewel box containing a number of the items claimed to have been taken from her room the night of the murder. The missing jewels were then taken to a specialty shop for alteration. The jeweler, in turn, notified the police. Steinheil was arrested and charged with obstructing justice and lying to the police. She was incarcerated in the Saint Lazare Prison while a murder indictment was drawn up.

The remains of the victims were exhumed but no traces of poison could be found. It was later determined that a swab of cotton wool found at the bedside had not been touched by human hands; this was the same wool that Steinheil said was used to gag her during the assault. The trial was an emotional ordeal for all concerned. Steinheil frequently became hysterical, which greatly taxed the patience of the court. The high point of the trial was reached when a young man named Jean Lefevre appeared to confess to his role in the murder. Lefevre said he had disguised himself as the red-headed woman, but his statements were discounted by the president of the court who saw through the ruse. Lefevre was hopelessly in love with Madame Steinheil and wanted to help her any way he could. The young man was led away to be charged with vagrancy.

To the charge that she had repeatedly lied to the police and the courts, Steinheil said she had only done so to save herself. The lies were, after all, proof-positive that she was innocent, she said. The jury, seeing no other recourse in the matter, acquitted her of murder charges. Steinheil left France for good. She moved to England, married into the British aristocracy, and died as Lady Abinger in Brighton in 1954.

Stewart, Dr. **Glen Gold** (AKA: **Glen Campbell; Dave Burrows; Robert Fennel**), prom. 1970, Can. In 1956, Glen Gold Stewart finished his medical studies at the University of Alberta in Canada and sought a position as a surgeon. After several non-medical jobs, he took a post in Smithers, British Columbia, and there became friendly with Sheila Haupt, the wife of a Canadian soldier serving in Germany. The two appeared in public together, Stewart introducing her as his sister.

In April 1969, Haupt and her child vanished at about the same time Stewart left his current position. Police looked for Stewart to question him about the disappearance. A year later, traveling up and down the Canadian-U.S. coast in the *Gypsy* with an Italian woman, he anchored twice near the Shantyman's Christian Association Bible Camp, located on the west coast of Vancouver Island in British Columbia, where he was charged with stealing a dingy. Stewart also applied for a post as caretaker of the Bible camp, but the post had already been filled by a 24-year-old art student, Gordon Adrian Kralt.

Sometime during the first days of November 1970, Stewart visited Kralt, shot him, stabbed him, crushed his skull with an ax, and apparently carved out Kralt's right lung. Then the murderer dragged the body about half a mile into the woods and stole the young man's car. Authorities in Canada and the U.S. searched for the couple as they zigzagged back and forth between the two countries, finally locating them in a San Francisco hippie community. When police arrived, Stewart refused to let them in and turned on the gas from a stove, but police broke in and saved the couple. Stewart was sent back to Canada and, with the woman's help, police located Stewart's gun, which he had thrown into the water off a ferry dock. The woman, who was not involved in the murder, became a witness for the prosecution and on Mar. 19, 1971, Stewart was found Guilty of the Kralt murder and sentenced to life in prison.

Stinney, George Junius, Jr., 1929-44, U.S. George Stinney met 11-year-old Betty June Binnicker and 8-year-old Mary Emma Thames on Mar. 24, 1944, as they were picking flowers near the Alderman Lumber Company's plant in Alcolu, S.C. When the girls did not return home that evening, their parents notified the police. A search party of 200 looked all night for the children and found their battered bodies in a water-filled ditch at 7:30 the next morning. Thames' skull was fractured and she had five head wounds. Binnicker's head was crushed in

George Stinney, executed at the age of 14 for killing an 11-year-old girl.

several places. Within a few hours, police had arrested Stinney, the 14-year-old son of a sawmill worker. He confessed to Deputy Sheriff H.S. Newman and S.J. Pratt of the governor's office that he killed the girls when Binnicker resisted his advances, beating them to death and hiding their bodies in the ditch. He led police to the spot where he had thrown away the murder weapon, a foot-long railroad spike. Stinney was hidden away to protect him from a lynch mob.

Stinney was returned to Clarendon County for trial on Apr. 24, 1944, exactly one month after the murders. A special court session had been called to try him, and a local lawyer, Charles Plowden, was appointed his defense counsel. Stinney admitted his guilt, and Plowden, who had reluctantly accepted the appointment as counsel and who was preparing to run for elective office, saw no defense. He also decided there was no need for a psychiatric examination of his client. The Clarendon Courthouse was filled to several times its capacity. A crowd of 1,500 spilled over into the hallway, staircases, and grounds. Plowden never asked to move the trial to another county. Testimony started at 2:30 p.m., and the defense had finished presenting its case about an hour and a half later. Stinney's confession was the main evidence. The last evidence presented was his birth certificate, entered to prove that he had attained the traditionally accepted age of responsibility—fourteen. The jury left the courtroom at 4:55 p.m. and returned ten minutes later to pronounce Stinney Guilty as charged with no recommendation of leniency. The 14-year-old bit his finger while facing the judge for sentencing, and showed no response to the verdict. If Plowden had then filed a one-sentence, routine notice of appeal, and then appealed Stinney's case to the state supreme court, the execution would have been automatically delayed for a year. The attorney informed neither Stinney nor his family of his right to appeal, nor did

he ever see his client again after that afternoon. The only possibility of delay, in the absence of an appeal, was an order of clemency from South Carolina governor Olin D. Johnston.

Although Stinney's case received little coverage in South Carolina, and none outside of the state, as the execution date neared, Governor Johnston began to receive letters and telegrams from the NAACP, labor unions, and clergymen, most of them in support of clemency. Johnston, who would also be running for elective office in a few months, apparently never considered a stay of execution. He visited Stinney on June 14 in his small cell a few feet from the death chamber. The day before, prison officials had interviewed Stinney, who repeated his confession and said that he had been finishing the seventh grade when arrested. According to a newspaper report of Johnston's visit, Stinney told the governor that "his mind sometimes went blank." The next day, Johnston announced that he would not grant clemency. On June 16, 1944, thirty witnesses gathered at the Clarendon County State Prison to watch the execution. Stinney told Sheriff Gamble that he was sorry for committing the crime and hoped God and his parents would forgive him. He walked into the death chamber carrying a Bible. The Associated Press reported that "the guards had difficulty strapping the boy's slight form into the wooden chair built for adults," and said that he was so small, "it was difficult to attach the electrode to his right leg." The death mask slipped off after the first 2,400 volt shock, and remained that way as two additional shocks followed. Stinney was the youngest person executed in the U.S. this century.

Most of the countries that still use capital punishment require a minimum age of eighteen. The controversy over executing young people resurfaced recently when Charles F. Rumbaugh was executed in Texas on Sept. 11, 1985, for a murder committed during a robbery when he was seventeen. Prior to Rumbaugh's death by lethal injection, there had been no executions of juveniles since 1964.

Stompanato, Johnny, See: **Crane, Cheryl.**

Stone, Lawrence Clinton, 1910- , U.S. Lawrence Stone, a 24-year-old emergency relief worker, had been drinking on the afternoon of Oct. 14, 1934. A powerfully built man, he was working on a street-widening project on Third Avenue in Mount Vernon, N.Y., in front of the exclusive Pelhutchinson apartments, where he had formerly been employed. In the apartment lobby and on the terrace, 5-year-old Nancy Jean Costigan, who was visiting her aunt,

Mrs. Russell Newhouse, played with a rubber ball. Building superintendent Cyril Gildon and hallmen Carl Hutchinson and James Nash saw her playing there as late as 4:30 that afternoon. At 5 p.m., however, Hutchinson was on his way down to the basement to regulate the furnace when he found his usual entrance locked. He took the elevator down to find a small pool of blood on the floor, then followed a trail of blood to the ping-pong room, where he saw a rubber ball. The trail continued down a metal staircase to a subbasement and the furnace, in front of which was a large bloodstain. On his way out to call the police, Hutchinson glimpsed a figure in the shadowy recesses of the room.

Less than a block from the apartment building, the patrol car answering the call collided with another car. As the injured policemen were climbing into the ambulance, Stone, intoxicated, climbed in, saying he had been injured. Although his shirt and trousers were covered with blood, physicians found no injuries. At Mount Vernon police headquarters, Stone was charged with murder. Although he admitted to having seen the little girl that afternoon, he protested his innocence. A tenant at the apartment building, however, later identified Stone as the man she saw playing with Nancy at about 4 p.m. Police found Nancy's charred body in the oil-burning furnace, burned beyond recognition. She was identified by a small gold ring, her wristwatch, and fragments of clothing. Her purse was found near the basement entrance where she had apparently struggled and dropped it.

Stone pleaded guilty, was convicted of second-degree murder, and sentenced to fifty years to life in prison at Sing Sing by New York Supreme Court justice William F. Bleakley. He was later transferred to a state hospital.

Stone, Leslie George, 1913-37, Brit. During the early 1900s, Ruby Keen, a factory worker, and George Leslie Stone, a sandpit laborer, were lovers until Stone left Leighton Buzzard, England, to join the army. When he returned to his hometown during the week of Apr. 5, 1937, on a medical discharge from the service, the 24-year-old Stone found that his sweetheart was engaged to a police constable.

On Apr. 11, he put on a new suit and went out with 23-year-old Keen to a pub where observers later said that he begged the girl to leave her fiance. After an evening of drinking, the two went for a walk along The Firs, a lover's lane in the town. The couple began arguing and the angered Stone strangled the woman with her scarf. Her body was found the next morning and Scotland Yard was immediately asked for assistance. Stone voluntarily came to police to admit he had been with the girl the previous

night, but said he dropped her off at home. Police took casts of impressions made in the soil by knees and later examined Stone's new suit. They found soil samples that matched the sandy earth at the murder scene and a silk fiber similar to the dead girl's dress was also found on the suit. Stone was tried in June, convicted of murder, and sentenced to death. On Aug. 13 he was hanged at Pentonville Prison.

Stoneley, John William, 1943- , and **Sykes, George Ernest** (AKA: **Bill**), 1941- , Brit. In October 1964, between about 10 p.m. and 11 p.m., two Southampton men robbing a taxi driver beat him to death with an iron pipe. A 21-year-old unemployed cable maker, John William Stoneley, and a 23-year-old dairy worker, George Ernest Sykes, left the cabbie, 60-year-old George Newbery, dying close to a road about seven miles north of Southampton.

Soon after the murder Stoneley used the victim's postal savings account book to withdraw £3 from the post office at Woolston, and the criminal left a distinctive fingerprint on the withdrawal form. When Stoneley was later caught burglarizing a garage, police matched his fingerprints to the print found on the savings book. Stoneley implicated Sykes and though both admitted robbery each blamed the other for the killing. They were tried and Stoneley was convicted of capital murder and sentenced to death, but the sentence was later commuted to a life term in prison. Sykes also was found Guilty, and sentenced to life imprisonment.

Stopa, Wanda (AKA: **Glaskoff**), 1899-1925, U.S. Wanda Stopa, of Chicago's Little Poland section, became an assistant district attorney right out of college. But then

Wanda Stopa and lover Yeremya Kenley Smith.

Stopa, who had always thought she had the soul of a poet,

discovered the Jazz Age and the Bohemian lifestyle. She met an art-minded Russian emigre, Vladimir Glaskoff, whom she quickly married. When reality did not meet Stopa's expectations, she turned her attention to Yeremya Kenley Smith, an advertising executive who enjoyed having the awestruck young woman at his feet while he talked philosophy. While she fell in love, she also became a morphine addict.

Smith gave Stopa money to live in Greenwich Village. But when Smith's payments stopped, she held a party for all her new friends and announced that she was leaving for Chicago "to kill a woman—perhaps a man...I'll probably kill myself afterwards." Her appreciative audience thought she was joking, but she arrived in Chicago on Apr. 24, 1924, and immediately took a cab to Smith's Palos Park country estate. She walked into the house and confronted Mrs. Smith, who called her babblings "ridiculous." Henry Manning, a gardener who had seen Stopa enter, saw her shoot at Mrs. Smith and miss. His employer leaped from her sick bed, flew out the window, and ran to a neighbor's house while Stopa continued to fire after her. One of her bullets hit the old gardener, killing him. Stopa laid down the gun and left the house, going to a train station.

Two days later, a man passing through the lobby of the Hotel Statler in Detroit recognized Wanda Stopa from newspaper photographs. The police found her at the hotel, registered under the name Glaskoff. As they reached her room, she was near death after having taken poison. She died soon afterward.

Stowe, Louis Richard (AKA: Robert Stratton),

prom. c.1940s, U.S. Louis Stowe, a heavyset salesman working as a buyer for a grocery store chain under the name Robert Stratton, became involved with Phyllis Blaine. On a night when Blaine's daughter, Ida, had gone to a movie, Stowe, apparently laughing the whole time, came to the house, killed Blaine with an ax and then put three bullets into her head. Taking the body to his car, he drove onto the highway, where he dropped it alongside the road near a farm. A woman at the farm saw him and came running, so Stowe shot her, too. At the noise, the woman's husband appeared, and killed him.

Stowe sped off at high speed, driving with his gun in his right hand. Passing a car with four young people in it, he shot the driver, Thomas Allen. Viola Burns, sitting next to Allen, took the wheel and slowed the car to a safe stop as Allen bled to death.

Phyllis Blaine's body was seen by people in a passing car. They went to the nearest farm, where young Jean Clay came out, and discovered that both her parents were lying dead in the darkness. Phyllis Blaine was eventually identified, and her daughter, Ida Blaine, described the man she knew as Robert Stratton, who, she said, had been acting strangely. Although Stratton was not at home, the police found a bloodstained suit. They located Stratton at a restaurant, where they were able to capture him.

Stratton, quickly identified as Stowe, was tried and found Guilty but insane. His weird behavior was caused by a brain tumor.

Straffen, John Thomas, 1930- , Brit. At seventeen,

John Straffen had the mind of an 8-year-old. The youth, who had grown up in a school for mentally retarded children, assaulted a 13-year-old girl and the courts sent him to an institution. Released at age twenty-one, he lived in Bath until he strangled two girls, as he said, to annoy the police because he hated them. At his trial at the Taunton Assizes in October 1951, he was found unfit to plead and was committed to Broadmoor Asylum.

Six months later he escaped. He was at large for only a few hours, but in that time he murdered another girl, Linda Bowyer. He told police without being asked, "I did not kill the little girl on the bicycle." His mental condition brought up several questions of how mentally incompetent defendants should be tried in capital cases. In his July 1952 trial for the third murder, he was found Guilty, but his death sentence was commuted to life imprisonment.

Stroud, Robert Franklin (AKA: The Birdman of

Alcatraz), 1887-1963, U.S. Robert Stroud committed his first murder in Alaska at the age of nineteen, killing a bartender who would not pay $10 for Kitty O'Brien, one of Stroud's prostitutes. He was sentenced to twelve years for manslaughter, time he divided between the federal penitentiary on McNeil Island in Puget Sound in the Pacific Northwest and Leavenworth Prison in Kansas. He had a reputation for being quiet and aloof, and the other prisoners found him repulsive.

Stroud had almost served his time when he killed again on Mar. 26, 1916. His victim was Andrew F. Turner, a guard he attacked with a knife in the Leavenworth mess hall. Stroud told another convict, "The guard took sick and died all of a sudden. He died of heart trouble. I guess you would call it a puncture of the heart. Anyhow, there was a knife hole in the guard's heart. I never have given any reason for doing it, so they won't have much to work on; only that I killed him, and that won't do much good. I admit that much."

The gallows on which Stroud was sentenced to die were located in the Leavenworth exercise yard less than 200 feet from his cell, but his mother petitioned President Woodrow Wilson and his wife, Elizabeth Bolling Wilson in 1920, just before the execution was scheduled to take place (Wilson had had a heart attack, so his wife was exercising most of the duties of his office). Elizabeth Stroud impressed the president's wife with her son's studies in ornithology—he had become fascinated with canaries, and his knowledge of how to treat their diseases

The "Birdman of Alcatraz," Robert Stroud.

may already have been the most extensive in the U.S. at the time—so his sentence was commuted to life in solitary confinement eight days before he was to hang.

Prison officials accommodated him with a double cell, tearing down the wall between two standard-sized cells so he would have more room to keep birds for his experiments. In 1943, he published the *Digest of Bird Diseases,* and he wrote an unpublished treatise on prison reform entitled *Looking Outward,* criticizing the U.S. penal system. He was later transferred to Alcatraz, then to Springfield, Mo., where he died of natural causes in 1963.

Sullivan, Robert Austin, 1947-83, U.S. Robert Austin Sullivan, manager of a Homestead, Fla., motel, was charged in August 1972 with stealing from the motel. He pleaded guilty, and was sentenced to five years probation and ordered to repay $6,000. On April 3, 1973, Sullivan and Reid McLaughlin robbed the motel after binding and gagging Donald Schmidt, the assistant manager. They then drove Schmidt to the Everglades where they killed him. Later, Sullivan maintained he was innocent, but McLaughlin testified against him in return for a reduced sentence.

Sentenced to death and imprisoned in Starke, Fla., Sullivan's struggle against execution eventually was supported by Pope John Paul II. On death row for ten years before Florida state governor Bob Graham gave final approval, Sullivan told a reporter, "The hardest thing about all of this is that my life is totally out of my own control...I certainly don't like it. But I haven't much choice." Sullivan was executed on Nov. 30, 1983, the ninth man to be executed since the Supreme Court lifted a ban on capital

punishment in 1976.

Sung Djang Djing, d.1919, Brit. On June 23, 1919, the body of Wu Zee Ming, a Chinese factory worker, was discovered in a wooded area near the Warwickshire-Worcestershire border in England. His head was crushed, his jaw shattered, and two ribs and his breastbone were broken. The next day, another Chinese man brought the dead man's post office savings book to the West Kensington branch and tried to draw cash, but was refused.

A month later, on July 25, 1919, an intruder attacked Dsou Kuo Doung with a hammer as he slept in his room in London. Dsou survived and told police he could not tell if his assailant was Chinese or English, as he wore a handkerchief over his face. The burglar stole £7 and a watch and chain. Police found a bloody hammer, a cap, and a loose button at the site. Dsou told them that Sung Djang Djing, who had lodged at the house some weeks earlier, had written him asking for money. When Dsou refused, Sung wrote another letter, this one abusive and threatening. Dsou reported that Sung now worked in a foundry in Birmingham, near the scene of Wu Zee Ming's murder.

Scotland Yard notified Birmingham authorities, who detained Sung. The physical evidence from Dsou's room matched Sung's belongings, and he was tried for murder, attempted murder, and burglary. He first claimed that another Chinese worker had murdered Wu over an old debt from China and that he had merely witnessed the killing along with several others. But each of the men Sung named produced a provable alibi. Post office employees also identified Sung as the man who tried to draw on Wu's savings. Sung was convicted of murder on Oct. 22, 1919, sentenced to death, and executed.

Sunset Slayer, See: Clark, Douglas Daniel.

Sutcliffe, Peter William (AKA: **Peter Williams, The Yorkshire Ripper**), 1946- , Brit., rape-asslt.-mur. The hunt for the "Yorkshire Ripper" lasted five years and nearly cost Assistant Chief Constable George Oldfield, a man obsessed with capturing the fiend, his life. Oldfield worked around the clock trying to piece together fragmented clues that might bring the killer to justice. Thirteen women were brutally murdered between 1975 and 1980, most of them prostitutes. The British press portrayed this hulking nightstalker as a 1970s reincarnation of Jack the Ripper. Before this latter-day Ripper was apprehended, the British police had questioned 200,000 people, searched 30,000 houses, and checked the registration on some 180,000 motor vehicles. It was without doubt the widest manhunt in British history. But then, the Yorkshire Ripper was the worst mass murderer in twentieth-century England.

The first attack attributed to the Ripper occurred on July 5, 1975, when Anna Rogulskyj was assaulted by a man wielding a hammer. Six weeks later, on Aug. 15, Olive Smelt was struck from behind in a similar manner. Both women recovered after surgery. Not so lucky was Wilma McCann, a 28-year-old Scotswoman who had reverted to prostitution to take care of her four children. McCann was canvassing the pubs of Leeds on the night of Oct. 29-30 in search of customers when the Ripper pounced on her from behind. Struck on the head with a ball-headed hammer, the woman was dragged into an empty field and viciously assaulted with a knife. Her mutilated body was found the next day. The random murder of a prostitute carried little weight in the media. One of the dead woman's neighbors expressed the opinion that "Hotpants" McCann was "no better than she ought to have been."

No one knew at the time that the McCann murder would set into motion a series of these crimes, the next one occurring on Jan. 20, 1976, when 42-year-old Emily Jackson was battered over the head and stabbed to death in a Chapeltown alley in Leeds. Jackson was married to a roofing specialist who did not know that his wife was supplementing the family income by turning "tricks" on the side, By this time the CID and the press were aware that a serial killer might be loose. Chief Superintendent Dennis Hoban expressed concern. "I can't stress strongly enough that it is vital we catch this brutal killer before he brings tragedy to another family." The killer was dubbed the "Yorkshire Ripper" by writer George Hill, who covered the murder for the *Daily Express.*

The Ripper kept a low profile for the next year, resurfacing on Feb. 5, 1977, when he stabbed 28-year-old Irene Richardson to death in Roundhay Park in Leeds. The murder site was scarcely a mile away from Chapeltown, the notorious red-light district where the Ripper cruised for his victims. Richardson, like Emily Jackson before her, was nominally connected to the trade. She had taken to the streets after separating from her husband. The murder count climbed to four on Apr. 23, when Bradford prostitute Patricia Atkinson, thirty-two, was found bludgeoned to death in her apartment on Lumb Lane. This time the killer left behind an important clue: a bloody footprint identical to one found at the scene of the Jackson murder. The scarcity of eyewitnesses however, hampered the investigation.

Sixteen-year-old Jayne MacDonald was certainly no prostitute. She was a fun-loving teenager who had been dancing the night away at the Hofbrauhaus in Leeds. On June 26, 1977, she was grabbed by the Yorkshire Ripper near Roundhay Park and stabbed to death, possibly because he mistook her for a street-walker. The girl lived only a few doors down the lane from Wilma McCann. Maureen Long narrowly avoided a similar fate on July 27. While walking through Bradford, she was accosted by the Ripper and dragged unconscious to a darkened street nearby. Before he could inflict the final fatal blows, something caused him to flee. Long was removed to a local hospital. She provided police with a sketchy description of the suspect and his car, which was proven to be inaccurate when the real killer was arrested several years later.

In the next two years, six more women were murdered, beginning with 21-year-old prostitute Jean Bernadette Jordan on Oct. 1, 1977, in Manchester, and followed by Yvonne Pearson, twenty-two, on Jan. 21, 1978, in Bradford. On Feb. 1, the body of 18-year-old Helen Rytka was found under a railroad viaduct in Huddersfield, West Yorkshire. Next came Vera Millward, a 41-year-old prostitute from Manchester, on May 16, 1978. She was murdered on the grounds of the Manchester Royal Academy. This was followed by the bludgeoning death of Josephine Whitaker, a 19-year-old building society clerk from Halifax, Yorkshire, the night of Apr. 4, 1979.

Following this latest outrage, the Ripper communicated for the first time with the police. On June 26, Constable Oldfield played back a tape-recording he had received from the killer to members of the press. In a slow, recognizable Geordie accent, the killer taunted his pursuers. "I'm Jack," the voice said. "I see you are still having no luck catching me. I have the greatest respect for you, George, but, Lord, you are no nearer catching me than four years ago when I started. I reckon your boys are letting you down, George. You can't be much good, can ya? The only time they came near catching me was a few months back in Chapeltown when I was disturbed. Even then it was a uniform copper, not a detective." The message closed with a chilling warning: "Well, I'll keep on going for quite a while yet. I can't see myself being nicked just yet. Even if you do get near I'll probably top myself first. Well, it's been nice chatting to you, George. Yours, Jack the Ripper."

The next month the emotionally spent constable suffered a heart attack and was forced to temporarily withdraw from the investigation. He was replaced by veteran Leeds detective James Hobson, who seemed to have no better luck than his predecessor. A toll-free number for citizens wanting to hear the voice of the Ripper was provided by the phone company, but after thousands of calls the police were no closer to identifying a suspect.

Even during this major barrage of publicity, the Ripper

was able to kill again. On Sept. 1, 1979, Barbara Leach, twenty, a student at Bradford University, left a Mannville Arms pub and was never seen alive again. Her body was found the following afternoon beside a back-alley dustbin, covered with old carpets. The wounds showed unmistakably the mark of the Yorkshire Ripper: Leach had been stabbed with the same rusty screwdriver used in the Whitaker killing.

Now that the police investigation was becoming so intense, the Ripper laid low for almost a year before his next attack. On Aug. 20, 1980, a 47-year-old civil servant from the Department of Education in Pudsey named Marguerite Walls was assaulted and strangled on her way home to her apartment in Farsley. After two more unsuccessful attacks in Leeds and Huddersfield, the Ripper claimed his final victim, 20-year-old Jacqueline Hill, a literature student at Leeds University. She was taking a bus back to her dormitory on Nov. 17, 1980, when she was assaulted in the "triangle of terror," the familiar stretch of ground that included Leeds, Bradford, and West Yorkshire—the killer's favorite haunt. Hill was the madman's thirteenth victim.

On Nov. 25, West Yorkshire Chief Constable Ronald Gregory announced the formation of a special squad to deal with the Ripper case. Hobson, who superseded Oldfield as the head of the investigation, predicted that the fiend would eventually be captured by the men on patrol. On Jan. 2, 1981, Sergeant Robert Ring and PC Robert Hydes pulled their squad car next to a Rover V-8 parked in an office complex in Sheffield. There they found Peter William Sutcliffe, an over-the-road truck driver from Heaton, engaged in a sex act with a black prostitute named Olivia Rievers. The driver of the car told the officers that his named was Peter Williams, but a quick check of the registration tags showed that they did not belong to the Rover. While the police were deciding what to do with Sutcliffe and Rievers, Sutcliffe asked if he could relieve himself. The officers consented, and he wandered over to some nearby bushes. It would be two days before Sergeant Ring, realizing that the man they had picked up could be the Ripper, would return to the bushes where Sutcliffe had stood and would find the hammer and knife used in several of the murders.

Sutcliffe and Rievers were taken to the police station for further questioning. Again, Sutcliffe asked to go to the bathroom, and again he unloaded another murder weapon: a knife which he deposited in a cistern in the bathroom. When asked to empty his pockets, the suspect pulled out a length of clothesline. On Jan. 4, during an interview with Sergeant Des O'Boyle, the officer produced the hammer and knife found where Sutcliffe had been arrested. "I think you're in trouble," O'Boyle told Sutcliffe, "serious trouble."

Sutcliffe then admitted that he was the Ripper. He confessed to committing eleven murders, but the police charged him with thirteen, and had strong suspicions that he may have killed Joan Harrison, whose body was found in Preston, Lancashire.

Sutcliffe's motive for murdering prostitutes was tied to an incident that occurred in 1969, when he was twenty-two years old. Sutcliffe picked up a streetwalker one night, but was unable to perform. The woman kept the £10 note he handed her, refusing to return the £5 he had coming in change. He ran into her at the same pub several weeks later, and, when asked about the £5, she laughed and rebuked him. "I developed and played up a hatred for prostitutes," Sutcliffe told the West Yorkshire Police in a confession that took seventeen hours to record. He said that he had deliberately arranged the clothes of his victims so that they "would be known for what they were."

In 1974, Peter married Sonia Szurma, a Czech national he had been dating for seven years. The immigrant girl had been previously diagnosed as a schizophrenic. While Sonia took teacher-training courses in London, Peter prowled the red-light districts in search of fresh-faced girls who sold themselves on the street.

For the residents of Yorkshire, the long nightmare was over. Peter Sutcliffe went on trial at the Old Bailey on May 5, 1981, amidst the jeers of a thousand angry spectators who lined the streets outside chanting "Hang him! Hang him!" He pleaded not guilty to the charge of murder on the grounds of diminished responsibility. He told the court about "his mission from God," but a jailer overheard the prisoner tell his wife that he would be let off with a ten-year sentence if he could convince the jurors that he was a prime candidate for the "looney bin." Consequently, the jury found him Guilty of thirteen murders, and seven other assaults. On May 22, 1981, the Yorkshire Ripper was sentenced to life imprisonment with no chance for parole for thirty years by Justice Leslie Boreham.

Swann, Emily, 1861-1903, and **Gallagher, John,** 1874-1903, Brit. One of the few women executed in England, Emily Swann and her lover were hanged for murdering her husband in 1903. A 42-year-old mother of six from Wombwell in Yorkshire, Swann gained a reputation for frequenting the local inns after completing her housework. During one of her trysts, she started an ongoing affair with John Gallagher, thirteen years her junior.

The two lovers decided to kill Swann's husband. Gallagher performed the task, though he had to return a second time with a hatchet to finish the job. Suspicion immediately fell on the couple and Gallagher fled Wombwell. Authorities arrested him in Middlesbrough and returned him to face trial with Swann. The court convicted both of murder and sentenced them to death. When taken to the gallows on Dec. 29, Swann said to her lover who was waiting there, "Good morning, John" to which he replied, "Good morning, love." As the noose slipped around her neck, Emily Swann cried out, "Good-bye. God bless you!"

Swart, Stephen, 1890-1927, S. Afri. In the early 1900s, Stephen Swart operated a farm in South Africa. Over time, he alienated his neighbors and harbored grudges against numerous people. He was annoyed when he lost a civil case and he continually filed petty grievances in court which were dismissed. In 1922, the 32-year-old Swart married a wealthy 58-year-old woman, promptly beating and berating her, and going out with other women. Swart was further irritated when a sexual offense charge was lodged against him in early 1927. Fearing that his wife and farm manager, A.J.C. Visser, would testify against him, in March 1927 he allegedly locked them in a room and threatened to shoot them unless they agreed not to testify.

On Mar. 11, the two hurriedly left the farm, his wife going to live in Charleston, a village on the border of Natal province. During the following weeks, Swart became convinced that at the upcoming trial he would be sent to prison for life and the distraught man did not sleep and scarcely ate. On May 3, 1927, he visited a neighbor's house and shot at the farm manager, but missed his mark. He then went back home. Police issued a warrant for his arrest and on May 5, Swart declared that any trespassers would be shot on sight. That night, Swart summoned his lawyer, dictating a twenty-eight page statement detailing complaints against numerous people and describing how he had set his car on fire on May 3 to prevent any enemies from getting it if he died.

At 4:30 a.m. on May 6, twelve policemen, led by Captain Ashman, set out to capture Swart, arriving at the farm about 6 a.m. They met one of Swart's hands who told them the farmer knew of the planned raid and had armed several of his workers. In the fog, Swart murdered five policemen, including officers Crossman, Mitchell, Grove, van Wyk, and Captain Ashman. Another policeman, Feucht, was injured and sent to the hospital.

Swart rode to a farm owned by neighbor S.J.M. Swanepoel, asked for some coffee, told of the slayings, and said he planned to go to Charleston. Afterward, Swart rode off, and along the road killed Knight, a woman who had previously testified against him, her companion, Roets, and, later, a native. Riding into Charleston, he located the home of the van Vuurens, where his wife was staying. The family

had evacuated the house, but Mrs. Swart remained inside. Swart entered the house, shooting his wife dead, and then he rode off again to commandeer a car. When the first car sped by, he shot at the occupants, injuring the driver and the passenger, but the driver managed to drive away.

Meanwhile, policemen and local townspeople were hunting for the murderer when a railway foreman, Mr. Kriel, spotted Swart, and two more men joined Kriel. They followed Swart along a road, firing at him. A group of policeman soon pulled up and found Swart's body. He had been shot through the head, either by his own hand or by one of the posse.

Sweeney, Dennis, prom. 1980, U.S. At the heart of the political foment and change in the U.S. during the 1960s was Allard Lowenstein, a liberal activist and assistant dean of men at Stanford University in Palo Alto, Calif. Dennis Sweeney, who attended Stanford, idolized Lowenstein, who picked the working-class scholarship student from Portland, Ore., as one of his protégés. Lowenstein got Sweeney to volunteer to work in Mississippi for the Student Nonviolent Coordinating Committee, but the SNCC became militant. Lowenstein withdrew his support, but Sweeney became more involved, readily taking to violent action before he was thrown out of the organization by black-power advocates.

Later, Lowenstein was elected to Congress, while Sweeney turned to drugs. In 1973, Sweeney was admitted to an Oregon mental hospital, but he stayed only a few days, despite his growing belief that he was being controlled by aliens who planted ideas into his head by invisible wires. "I am fairly certain that I have software I wasn't born with," he wrote one friend. He even tore the fillings out of his teeth because he was afraid that the CIA could reach his brain through the metal. In 1975, he called Lowenstein on the phone to accuse him of putting people on his trail.

At the beginning of 1980, Sweeney was living in New London, Conn., working as a carpenter. When he returned from Portland after his stepfather's funeral, he began mumbling that Lowenstein had killed his stepfather. He purchased a .380 semiautomatic pistol, lying on the application about whether he had been in a mental hospital. He made an appointment to see Lowenstein on Mar. 14 at his Layton & Sherman office in New York City. The two of them talked for a few minutes, then Sweeney said, "Al, we've got to put an end to this obsession." He pulled out his gun, killed his mentor, returned to the lobby, and sat waiting for police. He told them, "He's been controlling my life for years. Now I've put an end to it."

Sweeney pleaded guilty and was sent to a mental institution for life.

Taborsky, Joseph, 1923-60, U.S. On Oct. 7, 1955, Joseph Taborsky was released from the Connecticut State Prison's Death Row, where he had been sent in 1951 for murdering Louis Wolfson while robbing his liquor store with his brother, Albert Taborsky. Albert received a life sentence for turning state's evidence. Joseph declared his innocence and called his brother crazy. Granted another trial after Albert's transfer to a state hospital for displaying bizarre behavior, the state was left without a case and Taborsky was released.

Within a year, a wave of murders swept through Connecticut which police called the "Chinese Executions" because all the victims had been kneeling when shot from behind. The slayings began on Dec. 15, 1956, when a 67-year-old Hartford, Conn., tailor was found robbed and shot in the back of the neck. Thirty minutes later, gas station operator Ed Kurpiewski was robbed and forced into the restroom where his murderer shot him through the back of the head. Daniel Janowski, who drove up to the gas station when Kurpiewski was shot, was next. He was found in the storeroom, also shot through the back of the head. Samuel Cohn, a liquor store owner, was similarly killed eleven days later and ten days after that, in North Haven, Bernard Speyer and his wife were killed as they walked into a shoe store. The shoe store owner, who had been knocked unconscious, told police that two men had robbed the store and fatally shot the couple.

Investigations led to the arrest of Arthur Culombe and Joseph Taborsky. The shoe store owner positively identified Taborsky as the killer of the husband and wife. Taborsky confessed to those slayings, as well as to the murder of Louis Wolfson, the murder for which he was initially imprisoned in 1955. Convicted of murder, he was executed in 1960.

Tal, Schlomo, prom. 1977, and **Balabin, Pinhas**, 1949- , U.S. Million-dollar deals are sealed with a handshake and the Yiddish blessing "mazel un brucha" on New York City's Forty-seventh Street between Fifth Avenue and the Avenue of the Americas. This midtown block is the center of the world's diamond industry. Its more than 200 diamond brokers account for more than $1 billion in annual sales. Negotiation is intense, with a profit margin of only 1 or 2 percent. But the area is considered so safe that many brokers conduct their business without insurance. Robbery is extremely rare and murder virtually unheard of.

In late September 1977, the body of 25-year-old diamond cutter Pinchos Jaroslawicz, who had been missing since Sept. 20, was found bound and stuffed into a small box in the Forty-seventh Street office of another diamond cutter,

Schlomo Tal. Jaroslawicz had died of head injuries and asphyxiation after a plastic bag was put over his head. The $1 million in gems he had been carrying in his wallet were missing. Earlier in the week, Tal's wife reported him missing, but he was found sleeping in his wife's car in Queens. Tal said two masked men entered the office and robbed and killed Jaroslawicz, and that he hid the body and did not report the murder for fear of reprisal. Tal said the two men then returned, abducted him, and drove him around Nassau County for three days, finally abandoning him after drugging him. Upon waking, he was found by the police and arrested as a material witness.

The Jaroslawicz case bore a similarity to the unsolved murders of four other diamond merchants. Leo Dershowitz and Howard Block were murdered in Puerto Rico in 1974. In 1977, Abraham Shafizadeh was also murdered in Puerto Rico, and Haskell Kronenberg was murdered in Florida. More than $1.5 million in gems were taken from the four victims. The police questioned Tal's shaky alibi, and when they learned that he had a criminal record in Israel, they arrested him and another diamond cutter, 29-year-old Pinhas Balabin, on Mar. 30, 1978, for the murder of Pinchos Jaroslawicz. Both men were convicted of murder and sentenced to twenty-five years to life in prison.

Talbot, Lug, prom. 1930, U.S. In 1930, a bordello was set up at a sawmill camp in Hemp Hollow, near Brownsville, Ky. On Oct. 4, three men from Brownsville and three men from Rutherford, Ky., visited the brothel. The two groups fought over who would receive the women's services first, and an ensuing brawl ended in a double killing. Oren Baylanch shot and killed Ben Talbot and was then shot to death by Ben's brother, Lug Talbot. Lug was eventually arrested and turned over to Brake County officials. Lug Talbot pleaded guilty to voluntary manslaughter and was sentenced to fifteen years at the Kentucky state penitentiary. After his release, he moved to Owenton County, and in a fit of depression, he committed suicide by hanging himself.

Tansey, John, prom. 1907, U.S. In May 1907, a labor strike shut down the entire San Francisco street-car system. By Sept. 2, Labor Day, no settlement had been reached, but non-union employees kept the system running. Early the following morning, police officers P.J. Mitchell and Edward McCartney heard a ruckus at a nearby saloon. Four men were leaving as the officers approached. Two fled, but the police confronted the other two, shoved them, and warned them that they might be locked up. One of the men drew a gun and shot Officer McCartney in the neck, killing him instantly. During the ensuing manhunt, a railroad inspector stated that the man described was John Tansey, a striking carman. Tansey was arrested when the surviving officer identified him. Tansey's partner, a man named Bell, was apprehended, and also stated that Tansey was the murderer. Tansey countered that Bell had pulled the trigger. But it was Tansey who was convicted of manslaughter and sentenced to ten years in prison. He was paroled on May 10, 1909, because he had consumption.

Tarnower, Dr. Herman, See: **Harris, Jean Struven.**

Tarnowska, Marie Nicolaievna, See: **Naumoff, Nicolas.**

Taylor, Jack S., prom. 1970, U.S. On Feb. 16, 1970, the badly decomposed body of a woman was found in a swampy area near Palm Beach, Fla. A finger had been severed from the body and there was a gaping wound under its left eye. Fingerprints were taken, and the FBI identified the corpse as Judy Ann Vukich of Clarksville, Tenn. Her parents said she had moved to Florida and was living with a man named Jack Taylor. A warrant was issued and he was arrested two weeks later in Oklahoma City. He had killed Vukich for hiding liquor from him. Taylor was tried and convicted for manslaughter and sentenced to twenty years in the Florida State Penitentiary.

Taylor, Perry Alexander, 1967- , U.S. On Oct. 24, 1988, 38-year-old Geraldine Birch was choked and beaten to death on a Tampa, Fla., baseball field by 22-year-old Perry Alexander Taylor. Taylor admitted his guilt, but claimed that he had been provoked. His trial began on May 10, 1989, in the Tampa courtroom of Judge M. William Graybill. Taylor testified that he had paid the woman to have sex with him, and that she injured him during the act, prompting him to choke her and kick her repeatedly. The prosecution countered that Taylor was a habitual criminal. When he was sixteen, he had been convicted of raping a 12-year-old. The prosecution also said that his latest victim had died a slow, agonizing death. The jury agreed, and on May 12, 1989, convicted Taylor of first-degree murder and

sexual battery and sentenced him to die in the electric chair.

Telles, Felix, prom. 1927, Arg. Augustin Martelletti was a partner in the firm of Cores, Martelletti, Hermanosa Cia, one of Argentina's oldest and wealthiest firms. During the night of Jan. 17, 1927, he and his wife were murdered in their apartment above the corporate offices. The two had been beaten unconscious with a blunt instrument and then stabbed. The next morning, employees discovered the gruesome scene, and began a manhunt. The break in the case came on Feb. 12, when the owner of a cleaning establishment notified police that he had received a pair of bloodstained trousers. The owner of the trousers was identified as Felix Telles. Telles was apprehended, and when confronted with the murder weapons, he broke down and confessed. He was a former employee who knew where valuables were hidden. Attempting to burgle the office, he was surprised by the couple. They recognized him, so he killed them. In one of Argentina's speediest trials, the judges unanimously found Telles Guilty and sentenced him to twenty years of hard labor on an island penal colony.

Terpening, Oliver, Jr. (AKA: Jacobowsky), 1930- , U.S. Wondering what it would be like to watch someone die, 16-year-old farm boy Oliver Terpening, Jr., shot his 14-year-old friend, Stanley Smith, while the two boys were searching for crows outside Imlay City, Mich., on May 26, 1947.

Terpening shot Stanley with his father's .22-caliber rifle as he rested beneath a tree. Then, when Stanley's three sisters arrived on the scene, he shot them, too. "I thought the best thing to do was kill them all," he said. The bodies of Barbara Smith, sixteen, Gladys Smith, twelve, and Janet Smith, two, were found several hours later by their sister, Ella Mae Smith, roughly 100 yards from where their brother had been killed. Wildflowers were found in their hands. Terpening went home and ate his dinner, but it "went down pretty hard," as he later recalled. Realizing that the authorities were probably onto him, Terpening stole the family car and drove to Port Huron, Mich., where he abandoned it.

Without a dime in his pocket, Terpening hitchhiked through Detroit and camped out for the night in a filling station on U.S. Highway 24 near the Ohio state line. Concerned for his son's safety, Oliver Terpening, Sr., notified the Michigan State Police, who issued a physical description of the boy on all the local radio stations.

Terpening was spotted by a farmer from Erie, Mich., as he stood on the side of the road, with his thumb out. The farmer's son, Norman Dombrosky, Jr., recognized the hitchhiker from the radio accounts. When asked where he wanted to go, Terpening said: "Any place." "I told him my name was Jacobowsky," he said later, "and that I lived on Flager Street in Toledo. I'd seen that street name in Port Huron and it was the first that came to mind." The elder Dombrosky was suspicious, so he drove to the outskirts of the city and the offices of Justice R.O. Stevens, who had Terpening arrested by local constables.

Terpening was taken back to Erie, where he was questioned about the four murders. "I've always kinda wondered what it would be like to kill somebody," he said in a matter-of-fact way. "I'll tell the truth. I did it. I just wanted to see someone die." Terpening added that he didn't get the kind of thrill he was looking for when he originally decided to murder his friend.

Terpening's father told police that his son had always been a problem child. After he dropped out of the eleventh grade, he ran away to Louisiana because he could not get along with his stepmother. There were times, said the younger Terpening, when he wanted to kill her. His discouraged father sent him $25 for a train ticket when his money ran out.

Circuit Court Judge Albert Perkins signed the warrant accusing Terpening of murder. On June 10, 1947, however, Terpening was declared by three psychiatrists to be mentally unbalanced. At this writing, he remains confined in the G. Robert Cotton Correctional Facility in Jackson, Mich.

Terry, John Victor, 1940-c.1961, Brit. On Nov. 10, 1960, 20-year-old John Victor Terry, upon hearing of the execution of his friend Francis "Flossie" Forsyth, claimed he had become the reincarnation of U.S. gangster "Legs" Diamond. He then walked into a bank in Sussex, England, and shot a bank guard in the head. When apprehended, he defended his actions by saying, "When a person dies his mind leaves him and goes into another body. My mind was from Legs Diamond." The hallucination may have been caused by Terry's drug use. He was found Guilty of the murder, and in the end, he emulated not Legs Diamond, but Flossie Forsyth, when he was hanged from the same gallows at Wandsworth Prison.

Tessnov, Ludwig, d.1904, Ger. At the turn of the century, a German chemist named Paul Uhlenhuth, experimenting with human and animal blood, discovered that if the two samples were mixed together the blood serum of the human would not react in any way to that of the animal's. Uhlenhuth determined that a rabbit injected with a specimen of human blood would develop a natural resistance to it. His research with bloodstains proved invaluable to criminologists and members of the legal profession attempting to use this material as evidence during important murder trials.

The first practical application of Uhlenhuth's theories to a crime involved an itinerant German carpenter named Ludwig Tessnov, implicated in the sex-murders of four German children between 1898 and June 1901. At the same time a farmer in Gohren reported the slaughter of six or seven sheep. The entrails of the animals were scattered across a wide plain. The similarities between the mutilation of the animals and that of the children were so remarkable that the prosecutor of Greifswald asked Uhlenhuth to conduct an analysis. "If we prove the presence of sheep blood, that, along with identification by the shepherd, should make it clear that Tessnov is the killer of the sheep. And considering the way his clothing is spattered, some of it must be human blood, too." Uhlenhuth received two bundles of Tessnov's clothing on July 29, 1901. The scientific community anxiously awaited the results.

The tragedy of the children began in the village of Lechtingen, outside Osnabruck, on Sept. 9, 1898, when two girls, Hannelore Heidemann and Else Langemier, failed to return home from school. A search party that evening found the girls lying dead in a patch of bushes in the surrounding woods, their bodies hacked to pieces. A journeyman carpenter, identified by local authorities as Ludwig Tessnov of Baabe on the island of Rugen, explained that the red spatter marks on his work clothes were wood stains. Unable to conduct a chemical blood analysis, police released Tessnov and the murders entered the books as officially unsolved.

The shocking crime was repeated almost exactly on July 1, 1901, on the Baltic island of Rugen, when Hermann Stubbe, eight, and his brother Peter, six, failed to show up for their evening meal. The boy's father, joined by a policeman and several villagers, searched the adjacent woods with little success. The next morning a neighbor found the mangled bodies in a thicket. The arms and legs had been hacked off and their organs scattered through the woods. Nearby investigators found a bloodstained rock that presumably had been used by the murderer. A local fruit peddler reported to police on July 2 that she observed Tessnov talking to the children shortly before their disappearance.

Tessnov was arrested on suspicion. He claimed that the spots on his hat were cattle blood and other stains resulted from varnish he used in his work. Dr. Uhlenhuth, aided by an assistant, examined nearly 100 stains. He demonstrated through sophisticated blood analysis that there were definite traces of human blood in six areas of Tessnov's trousers, vest, and jacket. Uhlenhuth's evidence not only helped convict Tessnov, but his work with bloodstains greatly advanced forensic science. Tessnov was executed at Greifswald Prison in 1904.

Testro, Angelina, prom. 1912, U.S. During Franklin D. Roosevelt's tenure as governor of New York from 1929 to 1933, he pardoned Angelina Testro, who had served eighteen years of a life sentence at Auburn Prison for murdering her intended on their wedding day.

Testro, a 43-year-old widow, ran a rooming house in the Bronx. A young tenant, Arturo Costello, known throughout the neighborhood as "the Dude," began to pay her attention, which she returned. She also lent him small sums of money to purchase a stylish wardrobe. The widow begged Costello to marry her, and they procured the marriage license. With Testro in her wedding dress and a priest waiting, a friend of Costello entered the home and said that Costello would not go through with the marriage unless he received $400. That evening, she met her lover at a nearby railway bridge. He was found shortly thereafter with a knife protruding from his chest, gasping his last few breaths.

Angelina Testro confessed to the crime, saying, "I killed him because he made a fool of me." She was found Guilty of murder in the first degree and sentenced to death at Sing Sing. But Governor Whitman commuted the sentence to life, and she served eighteen years before being given a full pardon by Governor Roosevelt.

Tevendale, Brian, 1945- , and **Garvie, Sheila W.**, c.1934- , Scot. Maxwell Garvie married Sheila Watson in 1955 and during the next nine years, the couple had three children. In 1967, Sheila Watson Garvie began an affair with 22-year-old Brian Tevendale, while her husband became attracted to Tevendale's married sister, Trudy Birse. The foursome cavorted until May 14, 1968, when Maxwell Garvie left on a trip from which he would not to return. Five days later, Garvie was reported missing and a search began. Mrs. Garvie admitted to her mother that she had killed her husband, and her mother went to the police. In mid-August the body of Garvie, badly bludgeoned and shot through the neck, was found in an underground tunnel.

On Aug. 17, Sheila W. Garvie, Brian Tevendale, and another friend, Alan Peters, were charged with the murder. In November, Mrs. Garvie and Tevendale were found Guilty of murder and sentenced to life. Peters was released when

the court found his participation in the crime Not Proven.

Thacker, William J., d.1903, U.S. William Thacker killed John Gordon and was convicted three times: twice in a court of law, and a third and final time by a vigilante mob. In 1900 Thacker, a man in his early forties, lived in the small hamlet of Noah, in northeastern Kentucky. He owned a general store and doubled as the postmaster. A burly man who liked to drink, Thacker's true passion in life was the Republican Party. The more he drank, the more stoic he became about his party, which had been dominated by the Democrats since the Civil War.

On July 30, 1900, Thacker, accompanied by his 16-year-old son, Robert, left his home on a hunting expedition—not for animals—but for Democrats. He bought a few bottles of liquor, announcing his intended targets to the shopkeeper. Outside the store, he encountered Gordon, a man in his early twenties, who worked at a local sawmill. Asking Gordon if he knew of any local Democrats, Gordon admitted to being one. Thacker goaded Gordon into fighting him with a knife. As Gordon advanced, Thacker drew his gun and shot Gordon in the head. He covered Gordon with brush and left him to die. Thacker was convinced to surrender and he and his son were taken to the Flemingsburg jail. Robert Thacker was later released.

In January 1901, Thacker was convicted of the murder and sentenced to life imprisonment. He appealed, and received the same sentence exactly one year later. He appealed again, but before the third trial, an angry mob gathered outside the Flemingsburg jail. After midnight on July 15, 1903, the mob stormed the jail, and dragged the screaming Thacker from his cell. Shortly after, his clothes shredded and his face gashed by rocks, he was hanged from a honey locust tree. No action was taken against the lynchers. The jury at the coroner's inquest returned a verdict of death by persons unknown.

Thaw, Harry Kendall (AKA: **John Smith**), 1872-1947, U.S. Few murders among America's social elite and super rich rivaled the sensational 1906 murder of architect Stanford White by the demented millionaire Harry K. Thaw. The slaying of White was a public affair, committed in front of hundreds of horrified spectators. Thaw performed this deed with arrogance and disdain, as if dismissing an annoying servant or an unwanted party guest. Harry Thaw was used to having his own way since childhood, and as far as he was concerned, his killing of Stanford White, ostensibly over an affair with Thaw's beautiful wife, Evelyn, was merely a nasty chore he was compelled to perform.

The pampered Thaw was the son of a Pittsburgh magnate who had cornered the coke market in a short time and had accumulated a then staggering fortune of $40 million. Harry Thaw was the profligate heir to this fortune. Terribly spoiled by an over-indulgent mother, Thaw's education was a shambles although he was sent to the finest schools, including Harvard, where he ignored his studies and spent most of his time conducting high-stakes poker games in his suite of rooms off campus. He was finally dismissed for gambling activities. Thaw's father was so vexed at his son's wastrel ways he reduced his allowance to $2,000 a year. Harry wined and carped until his mother awarded him an additional $8,000 a year. Still the headstrong Thaw complained that this was only pin money for a man of his esteem and standing.

Taking a lavish suite of rooms in Manhattan, Thaw attempted to buy his way into several prominent men's clubs, but he was barred because of his eccentricities. Incensed, Thaw rented a horse and tried to ride it into these clubs, knocking down doormen and porters. He was arrested and escorted home. His mother paid his fine. A short time later, Thaw participated in a marathon poker game with New York sharpers and lost $40,000. His mother paid the gambling debt. To vent his wild rages and satiate his sexual perversions, Thaw took another apartment inside of one of New York's fanciest bordellos. There he brought young, gullible women, promising them careers on Broadway or, at least, in the chorus lines of important musicals. After Thaw inveigled the women to his brothel apartment, he fiendishly attacked them, raping them and beating them with sticks and whips.

The bordello madam, Susan Merrill, later stated that she heard a woman screaming in Thaw's apartment and when she could bear it no longer, forced her way inside. She later testified: "I rushed into his rooms. He had tied the girl to the bed, naked, and was whipping her. She was covered with welts. Thaw's eyes protruded and he looked mad."

Merrill ordered Thaw out of the house, and when he refused, she called the police. The millionaire playboy was escorted from the brothel despite his protests that he had paid rent a year in advance. He was barred from the brothel and Madam Merrill was happy to repay him his advance rent. A short time later, Thaw was ejected from one of the finer Fifth Avenue shops. The sales manager refused to have his models show the latest gowns to a bevy of Broadway tarts Thaw paraded into the shop. At this point Thaw had what was later described as a "sort of fit. His eyes bulged and rolled, and he screamed like a child having a tantrum." Police escorted the playboy outside and sent him home; the whores were locked up. In retaliation, Thaw rented a car the next day and drove it through the

shop's display window, almost running over the gaping manager. Thaw was again arrested and fined.

Mrs. Thaw advised her son to leave Manhattan and take a European vacation. Thaw sailed for Paris where he scandalized a city that was weaned on scandal. He rented an entire floor of the Georges V Hotel and invited the city's leading prostitutes to a party that lasted several days and cost him $50,000. He was finally asked to leave the hotel after he was discovered whipping naked women down the hotel corridors.

Another product of Pittsburgh at that time was a 16-year-old sultry brunette, Evelyn Nesbit. She came from poverty and had little formal education, but she had singing and dancing talent and, after being a photographer's model for a short period of time, soon won a spot in the prestigious Floradora Sextette. While performing in the Floradora chorus, she caught the lecherous eye of Stanford White, the most distinguished architect in New York. White, who was tall and heavyset, weighing some 250 pounds, wore a sweeping handlebar mustache and was always sartorially dressed, glittering with a diamond stickpin, gold watch chain, an expensive jewel-encrusted watch fob, and rings.

White was many times a millionaire, having made a fortune designing the resplendent Fifth Avenue mansions of New York's wealthiest movers and shakers. He was a high society architect who catered exclusively to the super rich, although he was known widely for having designed the elegant Washington Square Arch and the Hall of Fame at New York University. He had also designed Madison Square Garden, including its restaurant, arcade, fashionable shops, the amphitheater where prizefights and horse shows were held, and the magnificent roof garden where musicals were performed for open-air audiences who dined while watching the shows.

The tower of Madison Square Garden was reserved by White for himself. There he maintained a lavish home-away-from-home (he was married but seldom saw his wife). This apartment featured a red velvet swing which hung from the ceiling of the tower. According to Evelyn Nesbit's later statements, White was in the habit of bringing his mistresses and one-night stand show girls to the tower where he would swing them high so that he could lasciviously look beneath their billowing skirts. (The portrait of White as a lewd and lustful old man was painted by Nesbit at her husband's trial, certainly a colored, prejudiced view which was designed to vindicate Thaw's murderous actions, although White's skirt-chasing habits were certainly well known long before he ever met Nesbit.)

For three years, Nesbit carried on a relationship with White. He lavished gowns and jewels on the woman, paid for her stylish apartment and chauffeured limousine, and

The rooftop theater at Madison Square Garden, site of Thaw's public execution of Stanford White on June 25, 1906.

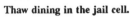
Thaw dining in the jail cell.

Thaw at time of trial.

Mrs. Thaw, Harry's mother.

Evelyn on the witness stand whispering answers to William Travers Jerome.

Thaw with his mother following his conviction.

Evelyn performing years later.

Thaw's attorney, Delphin Delmas.

Evelyn writing her memoirs.

took endless photos of her in seductive poses. When he tired of her, he sent her away to a finishing school.

Harry Thaw had also seen Evelyn Nesbit on the stage briefly and knew that she was White's pampered mistress. While she was in boarding school, he contrived to meet her and then pursued her slavishly until she accepted his marriage proposal. Thaw, however, after the nuptials on Apr. 4, 1905, was more concerned with White than he was with his own wife, persecuting Nesbit for her relationship with the architect. He insisted that she refer to White as "The Beast" or "The Bastard." When she refused, he told her that she must, at least employ the letter "B" whenever she mentioned White. This Nesbit did.

Thaw took his 19-year-old bride to Europe, but it turned out to be a nightmarish honeymoon. Aboard the luxury liner carrying the couple to France, Nesbit later claimed, Thaw tied her to a bed and whipped and beat her until her body was coated with red welts. She finally told her unhinged husband what he wanted to hear—or all she could imagine that was vile and rotten about Stanford White. She told Thaw that White had tricked her into going to The Madison Square Tower apartment on the promise of marriage, but once there, he stripped and raped her, and then forced her to mount the red velvet swing naked while he took obscene photos of her. This story, of course, drove Thaw into blind rages and he forced his wife to repeat this story often so that he could work himself into a frenzy about White, vowing terrible revenge against "The Beast."

On the warm night of June 25, 1906, Harry Thaw took his berserk revenge on Stanford White. Harry and Evelyn Thaw were dining in Rector's with two of Thaw's friends, when White and a party of people left one of the private dining areas. Thaw stiffened as Evelyn passed him a hand-written note which read "The B. is here." She had followed his instructions of informing Thaw any time she saw White in public. Thaw crumpled the note and pocketed it, then patted his wife's hand and said: "Yes dear, I know he's here. I saw him. Thank you for telling me."

A few hours later White was sitting at the best table on the Madison Square Garden rooftop to witness a new, frothy musical, *Mamzelle Champagne*. White was interested in one of the chorus girls to whom the manager promised to introduce him following the performance. Harry, Evelyn, and two of their friends also arrived at the Madison Square Garden rooftop.

Evelyn saw White sitting alone watching the show and, early-on, asked Thaw to take her home, noticing the agitated state he was in. She told her husband that the show bored her and he got up and began to escort her and their friends to the elevator. Suddenly, he was gone. Minutes later he stood glaring down at Stanford White. The architect looked up at Thaw, whom he knew and

disliked. "Yes, Thaw, what is it?" White reportedly asked the staring young man. Without a word, Thaw reached into his pocket and withdrew a revolver, pointing it only a few feet from White's head. He fired one shot and then two more. White, his face a mass of blood, collapsed on the table, then fell sideways, taking the table with him. He sprawled dead on the floor with a bullet in his head and two more in his shoulder.

At first there was a horrible silence. The show stopped completely, performers frozen on the stage. The band did not play a note. The hundreds of customers present stared at the bizarre scene of Thaw standing over the fallen White and then piercing screams came from the women and everyone made a mad dash for the exits, knocking over tables and chairs in a panic to escape what they thought was a madman on the loose.

Thaw, according to some witnesses standing near him, raised the revolver over his head and emptied the remaining three live cartridges from the weapon which fell to the floor. He said something that was later interpreted to mean: "I did it because this man ruined my wife." Some claimed that Thaw said: "This man ruined my life."

Within seconds, Thaw, still holding the weapon above his head, made his way to the elevator where Nesbit and his friends waited in shock. "My God, Harry," Nesbit said. "What have you done?"

The roof garden was by then in pandemonium with women screaming and men shouting for police officers. The manager leaped upon a table and shouted to the band: "Go on playing!" To the stage manager he cried: "Bring on the chorus!" At this moment, a doctor was leaning over White and saw part of White's face blown away, his entire head was blackened by powder burns from bullets fired at close range. The physician pronounced White dead.

In the elevator lobby, Thaw, still clutching the weapon, was confronted by an off-duty fireman who said: "You'd better let me have that gun." Thaw meekly turned it over. A policeman then arrived and Thaw submitted to arrest. He was marched to the Center Street Station where he said his name was John Smith and was a student living at 18 Lafayette Place, New York City. He was searched and his own identification papers quickly revealed his true identity—Harry Kendall Thaw, the millionaire.

"Why did you do this?" a sergeant asked Thaw.

Thaw stared blankly at the policeman for some moments, then replied: "I can't say." He refused to make any more statements until his lawyer arrived. Thaw was charged with murder and placed in a cell in the New York Tombs to await trial. Fifteen months passed before Thaw was brought into court, a stalling tactic designed by Thaw's brilliant defense attorney, California criminal attorney Delphin Delmas, who had defended hundreds of clients in

Top and middle rows: Evelyn Nesbit in various exotic poses, photographed by Stanford White's private photographer; she became White's mistress at age sixteen after briefly appearing in the Floradora Chorus in New York; she would later meet mad millionaire Harry K. Thaw, who would commit the sensational murder of White in 1906.

Evelyn Nesbit performing her ballet act with a hired partner.

Harry K. Thaw, 1905.

Stanford White, 1895.

murder trials and claimed never to have lost a case. Delmas was called "the little Napoleon of the West Coast bar." Hired for an estimated $100,000 by Thaw's mother (the figure was never substantiated), Delmas told the elderly Mrs. Thaw that because her son chose to execute his victim in public, the best they could hope for would be to keep him out of the electric chair. To that end, Delmas mounted a crusade to blacken the name of the victim, a shameless and brazen technique to win Thaw any kind of sympathy.

Press agent Ben Atwell was hired by Mrs. Thaw to destroy the image of Stanford White and a short time later stories appeared in New York newspapers which detailed White's profligate ways. One story dealt with 15-year-old model Susan Johnson, who was inveigled to White's Madison Square Tower apartment, which the *Evening Journal* described as being "furnished in Oriental splendor." The tale was told how Susan Johnson was plied with liquor, seduced, and soon afterward abandoned by the heartless White to make her way penniless through life. The vilification campaign against White went on day after day, month after month, until, it seemed Stanford White had seduced half the female population in New York City.

Mrs. Thaw made no excuses for unleashing the dogs of slander and libel against the dead Stanford White. "I am prepared to spend $1 million to save my son's life," she had announced. The publicity campaign and legal fees for her son's defense, it was later estimated, cost Mrs. Thaw more than $2 million.

Thaw himself was not spared negative publicity. His sordid exploits with prostitutes and his wife were leaked to the press by the prosecution which was headed by the famous William Travers Jerome, New York's district attorney. Said Jerome before the trial: "With all his millions, Thaw is a fiend! No matter how rich a man is, he cannot get away with murder, not in New York!" Jerome's aides unearthed a lawsuit filed against Thaw in 1902 that had been filed by Ethel Thomas. Her story was almost identical to the one later told by Evelyn Nesbit. After meeting Thaw, Thomas had been swept off her feet by Thaw who oozed affection and respect. He had given her flowers, jewels, and clothes. "One day," Thomas stated in her deposition, "I met him by appointment and we were walking toward his apartment at the Bedford, and he stopped at a store and bought a dog whip. I asked him what that was for and he replied laughingly: 'That's for you, dear.' I thought he was joking but no sooner were we in his apartment and the door locked than his entire demeanor changed. A wild expression came into his eyes and he seized me and with his whip beat me until my clothes hung in tatters."

The most bizarre ploys were used by the defense to create hatred for White and glean sympathy for the "befud-dled" Thaw. One story related how a medium had conducted a seance on July 5, 1906, and that a "spirit from beyond appeared to insist that he, a long-departed soul named Johnson, had guided Harry Thaw's hand" and the spirit was the true killer of Stanford White, not Thaw!

Finally, on Jan. 21, 1907, Thaw was brought to trial. Thaw himself took the stand to appear penitent and remorseful, saying: "I never wanted to shoot that man. I never wanted to kill him...Providence took charge of the situation." Apparently Thaw had read the account of the seance and was now pinning the blame on the spirits. Delmas and his battery of lawyers insisted Thaw was not in his right mind when he killed White, that he suffered from "dementia Americana," a neurosis that was singularly American; wherein American males believed that every man's wife was sacred and if she were violated, he would become unbalanced, striking out in a murderous rage.

District Attorney Jerome fought back against this psychological gobbledygook, cross-examining Evelyn Nesbit with dogmatic persistence. He asked about the character of her husband and her replies were so explicit that she insisted on whispering her answers to him. Her responses were later whispered for the court reporter recording the trial transcript and then her sordid stories were shown in printed form to the jury members. By then, however, the jury believed that Stanford White was a beast in human form and deserved to die, that he had ruined the lives of dozens of young women and that Thaw, who was unhinged at the time of the shooting, was merely doing what any noble-minded American male would do, taking vengeance for wronged women all over the U.S.

The jury, on Apr. 11, 1907, could not agree, seven holding for conviction, five others insisting on a not guilty vote. Thaw was tried again, and, on Feb. 1, 1908, he was found Not Guilty "by reason of insanity." This was the verdict Delmas had sought. His client would not face the electric chair. Thaw was sent to the New York State Asylum for the Criminally Insane at Matteawan, N.Y. He was to remain here for life, despite efforts by his mother to free him.

When Mrs. Thaw's millions could not move the courts, she reportedly financed her son's escape on Aug. 17, 1913. Thaw was escorted through unlocked doors to freedom where a limousine was waiting for him. He was driven to Canada and a luxury apartment. The U.S. State Department brought heavy pressure against Canadian officials to have Thaw returned to the U.S. and he was finally turned over, but he was placed in a Concord, N.H., jail where, as had been the case in the New York Tombs while he awaited trial, Thaw dined on catered meals and was offered every convenience and comfort. His lawyers ardently battled extradition to New York until December 1914 when they secured another trial for the murderer.

In the third trial, the same evidence and testimony was examined, but the jury, on July 16, 1915, returned a verdict of Not Guilty and also stated that Thaw was no longer insane and urged his release. He was set free. In 1916, Thaw was back in the news, accused of kidnapping, beating, and sexually molesting 19-year-old Frederick B. Gump. He was arrested, jailed, and went through another trial where he was declared insane. Another hearing was held and Thaw was declared sane and the charges were dropped. It was reported that Thaw's mother had bestowed more than $500,000 on the Gump family to convince them to drop the charges. Thaw then resumed his eccentric lifestyle, buying his way through life. He died in February 1947 of a heart attack, a wizened, shrunken creature of seventy-six.

Evelyn Nesbit had her moment of glory and infamy during the Thaw trial and for some years afterward. She was abandoned by the Thaw family, who reportedly bought her off. She later appeared as a vaudeville attraction, billed as "the girl in the red velvet swing." In 1915, though she had long been divorced by the irresponsible Thaw, Nesbit insisted that her newly born son was Thaw's child, that she had bribed guards at Matteawan to allow her into Thaw's rooms for a night of bliss. Thaw angrily denied this and his parentage. His lawyers reportedly paid her off.

Therrien, Armand R., prom. 1975, U.S. In 1975, Chin Enterprises was a four-man partnership which owned the popular Hawaiian Garden Restaurant in Seabrook, N.H. The corporation sought to borrow $166,000 from a Boston bank to open another restaurant in Marietta, Ga. Three of the four partners were oriental, but the fourth, referred to as Uncle Harry, was a former New Hampshire state policeman named Armand R. Therrien. As a policeman, he specialized in cases involving embezzlement. In 1973, he resigned to become an insurance agent. He had severe financial difficulties after he divorced and began doing odd jobs at the Hawaiian Garden, eventually becoming secretary-treasurer of Chin Enterprises. In January 1975, Therrien left Boston to supervise the construction of the Marietta restaurant.

On Feb. 11, 1975, in the Boston suburb of Westwood, two patrolmen, William Sheehan and Robert P. O'Donnell, approached a car with its emergency lights flashing. The driver appeared to be slumped in his seat. A man exited a passenger-side door and approached the officers, assuring them that the driver was ill but not in need of help. But the officers, suspecting a drunk driver, looked in the driver's window and saw blood. As they turned to confront the passenger, Therrien, he shot them with a .38-caliber snub-nosed pistol. Sheehan died of a bullet wound to his head. O'Donnell survived with two minor wounds, and was able to return fire and wound Therrien. The driver of the car, John Oi, one of Therrien's partners, had been killed before the officers arrived.

Authorities speculated that Therrien, supporting two households since his recent divorce, was financially strapped. A bank loan secured by Chin Enterprises stipulated that corporate officers were limited to annual salaries of $15,000. Chin Enterprises had insurance policies on all partners, which would pay the corporation $200,000, or more than enough to pay back the loan and return a handsome amount to each partner, thus solving Therrien's cash flow problem. Therrien was arraigned and brought to trial at Dedham, Mass. The jury found him Guilty of first-degree murder in the deaths of Oi and Sheehan and sentenced him to two consecutive life terms at the Massachusetts Correctional Institution at Walpole.

Therrien, Joseph W., 1925- , and **St. James, George L.**, 1930- , U.S. Police in Bristol, Conn., received a phone call on Christmas night 1948, telling them about the body of a woman lying in the snow. The caller identified herself as Rose Lombardi, who said she had stumbled over the body on her way to the garbage bin. "Who is she?" Police Chief Edmund S. Crowley wanted to know. The distraught Lombardi, whose Christmas celebration was upset by the tragedy replied, "I never saw her before. I have no idea how she got here—or why." Medical Examiner Fred T. Tirella examined the corpse and determined the woman had been strangled a few hours earlier.

The police searched the immediate vicinity. Entering a locked barn they found a late-model automobile containing a tube of lipstick, a twenty-dollar bill, and several long strands of hair trapped in the screw socket of the rear window frame. The vehicle had been rented to a neighbor who had an unshakable alibi. But the car was somehow linked to the slaying. That much seemed certain when detectives found a woman's handbag lying in the snow near the barn. Inside the purse was a small slip of paper with the word "rich" scrawled in pencil.

No further action was taken and the investigation was stymied until a mortician from Plainville notified police that he knew of a family named Rich in his community. Digging further, the police learned the body was that of Lillian Rich, estranged wife of Harold Brackett. The Plainville police reported that Rich, in her forties, had been evicted from a local cafe with two young men half her age. The three had been drinking and carousing loudly. One of the youths was identified as 23-year-old Joseph W. Therrien, who had been previously arrested for burglary and car theft. Therrien had served six months in prison, but had recently taken up residence at the home of Rose Lombardi in Bristol. When asked about this by Chief Crowley, Lombardi said that she had not seen Therrien for several days. The police obtained a search warrant.

In the Lombardi basement they found a damp, mud-stained dress. A charred, half-burned Social Security card bearing the name of Lillian Rich Brackett was found inside the furnace. "What a Christmas!" wailed Lombardi. "Now you won't believe a word I say!" She went on to say that Therrien, his friend George St. James, and a drunken woman had stumbled into her kitchen on Dec. 24. The young men, chased out of the house, took Brackett to the garage where they raped her in the neighbor's car, and then strangled her to death. A hole was dug in the ground and the body buried. Then they told Lombardi what had happened. Fearing her boarders had buried the woman alive she told them to dig up Brackett and bring her to the kitchen. There they carefully scrubbed the body and changed the clothing, using one of Lombardi's housedresses. It was a snug fit, but she decided it would pass. The corpse was next placed in the snow to make it look like an accident. "But why on earth did you protect these killers?" Crowley asked. "I had to," Lombardi replied. "Therrien is engaged to my daughter and I didn't want anything to happen to postpone the marriage."

Lombardi's hopes for her daughter's marriage were dashed when Therrien and St. James were committed to the state prison for life. As an accessory to murder, Lombardi received three years.

Thomas, Allgen Lars, See: Haerm, Teet.

Thomas, Arthur Alan, prom. 1970, N. Zea. Jeanette and Harvey Crewe were a New Zealand couple living on a farm near the village of Pukekwa. One day in June 1970, Jeanette's father stopped by the farm and found the couple's 18-month-old child, apparently abandoned. Bloodstains were found, and the police, aided by the army, mounted a massive search. On Aug. 16, the body of Jeanette Crewe was found in the Waikato River, wrapped in a sheet. She had been shot in the head with a .22-caliber bullet and bound with wire. Exactly one month later, the body of Harvey Crewe, killed by a bullet of the same caliber and weighted down by a car axle, was found in the same river. Test firings of all .22-caliber weapons in the area led police to suspect Arthur Alan Thomas, a neighboring farmer. Officials later learned that Thomas had once courted Jeanette Crewe. In November 1970, he was charged with the double murder. In February 1971, in the Auckland Supreme Court, Arthur Thomas was found Guilty of the murders and sentenced to life imprisonment.

Thomas, Donald George, c.1925- , Brit. Police constable Nathaniel Edgar stopped a suspicious-looking character while patrolling a crime-ridden area of London on Feb. 13, 1948. People nearby heard three shots, saw a man running from the scene, and found that an officer had been gunned down. The mortally wounded officer had obtained his assailant's name and address and had them written in his notebook—Donald Thomas, 247 Cambridge Road, Enfield.

Thomas was an army deserter who had been on the military's wanted list for many months. The police tracked Thomas down and arrested him as he was trying to hide the gun that had killed Edgar. Police also found rounds of ammunition, a rubber truncheon, and a book on handgun shooting. Furthermore, he had confessed the crime to his landlady.

In April, Thomas was tried, found Guilty of murder, and sentenced to death. The sentence was commuted to life in prison because the courts enacted a temporary suspension of the death penalty.

Thomas, Edward, 1920- , U.S. On Apr. 22, 1941, 73-year-old Addie Gilman was found dead on the floor of her Brooklyn home, an apparent suicide. Gas jets had been left on and there were no signs of a violent struggle. Also, she had been depressed by the departure of her daughter, who had moved upstate. However, no suicide note was found, and upon further examination of the corpse, officials determined she had been strangled.

The murderer had left no clues, but a note indicated that the woman had recently had financial troubles with the upstairs tenant, Jerry Croft. A search of her diary entries uncovered the name of Croft's brother-in-law, Edward Thomas. Also, a friend of Gilman's had stopped by for a visit just before her murder. Gilman was expecting another visitor soon, and mistakenly called out "Hello, Eddie" when he arrived. The friend, however, did not see Gilman's other visitor. This, plus the diary entries, led detectives to Edward Thomas. Thomas, a 21-year-old airport mechanic, was greeted by detectives Harry G. Lavin and William Brennan when he returned home from work. He admitted he had been in the Gilman home, but only to negotiate a settlement of his relative's back rent. Detective Lavin continued to question Thomas, finally accusing him of choking Gilman. The suspect then blurted out information only the killer would have known. Realizing his error, Thomas confessed. On June 3, 1941, Edward Thomas pleaded guilty to first-degree manslaughter, and three weeks later was sentenced to a term of ten to twenty years in Sing Sing.

Thomas, Leonard Jack, 1903- , Brit. In London on Mar. 13, 1949, Leonard Jack Thomas stabbed his estranged wife, Florence Ethel Lavinia, thirteen times with a jackknife. She survived and on May 2, Thomas was sentenced at the Old Bailey to seven years in prison for attempted murder. Then his wife died of her injuries, and Thomas was ordered to be retried for murder. On July 13, the defense moved for dismissal, as Thomas was already serving time for the same attack, and no man could be put in peril twice for the same offense. However, the plea was rejected and Thomas stood trial for murder. He then pleaded temporary insanity stating he and his wife had had an argument over dancing lessons, but that he had blacked out, only to find himself standing with a knife over his wounded wife. The jury was unsympathetic and sentenced him to death. However, more than 12,000 people signed an appeal, begging for mercy, which was sent to the home secretary. The king, on the advice of the secretary, commuted the death sentence.

Thompson, Edith Jessie (Edie), d.1923, and **Bywaters, Frederick**, d.1923. Brit. Edith Thompson and Frederick Bywaters became lovers during Summer 1921. Bywaters, a sailor, was a family friend of Thompson and her husband, Percy, and in June had accompanied the couple on a vacation at the Isle of Wight. The Thompsons began to experience marital discord, and by September Thompson was secretly meeting Bywaters during his extended leaves from sea. The affair continued into the following year until late in the evening of Oct. 4, 1922, when Percy Thompson

Edith Thompson, murderess.

was stabbed to death by an assailant as he and his wife were returning to their London home. Police encountered an hysterical Edith Thompson, who proclaimed that she had done everything within her power to save her husband's life. Authorities might have believed her, but a neighbor stepped forward and told of the relationship with Bywaters.

Searching Bywaters' quarters, police discovered sixty-two letters from Edith proclaiming her love and detailing aborted attempts to poison her husband. The couple was arrested, and Bywaters was charged with the Percy Thompson murder, Edith Thompson charged with being an accessory. They were brought to trial on Dec. 6, 1922, in

Frederick Bywaters, Edith and Percy Thompson, 1922, shortly before Bywaters and Edith killed Perry Thompson.

the Old Bailey courtroom of Justice Shearman. Sir Henry Curtis-Bennett, defending Thompson, and Cecil Whiteley, defending Bywaters, attempted to have the letters dismissed as evidence, but prosecutor Sir Thomas Inskip successfully won their inclusion. Bywaters confessed to the attack but said it was in self-defense and in no way premeditated. He further absolved Edith Thompson of any complicity. But Thompson took the stand and, under intense interrogation, admitted the details of the affair and conversations with Bywaters about eliminating her husband. The jury of eleven men and one woman deliberated for two hours before finding both defendants guilty of murder. Amidst pleas of innocence, both were sentenced to death. They appealed, were denied, and at 9 a.m. on Jan. 9, 1923, Edith Thompson swung from the prison gallows at Holloway, while Bywaters met a similar fate a short distance away at Pentonville.

Thompson, Elizabeth, prom. 1971, and **Fromant, Kenneth Joseph**, 1939- , Brit. On Nov. 5, 1971, the body of 35-year-old Peter Stanswood was found in a parked car on a road near Portsmouth, England. Stanswood, a local businessman, had been stabbed seven times with a Japanese paper knife. The ensuing investigation revealed that Stanswood, a married man with two children, had been involved in an extraordinary number of extramarital affairs. Two of the women bore his children, while a third woman was pregnant. A prime suspect would have been his wife, but it was revealed that Heather Stanswood had had about two dozen lovers of her own. The most recent was Kenneth Fromant, a 39-year-old gas company worker, who had a criminal record. It was further revealed that Peter Stanswood was involved with Elizabeth Thompson, the wife of his business partner.

Nine months after the murder, a Scottish woman stated that her boyfriend had been at the crime scene with Kenneth Fromant. On July 17, 1972, Fromant was interrogated and stated that he had spent the night with Elizabeth Thompson. However, his blood matched the sample taken from the victim's car, and soil samples from Fromant's car tires matched similar samples on the other car. The police waited almost three years, until May 19, 1975, to arraign Fromant and Heather Stanswood on the charge of murder. Stanswood was soon released, and Thompson arrested instead. Thompson stated that she had met Stanswood but they had been surprised by Fromant. A fight ensued and Fromant killed Stanswood. Thompson was formally arrested on Aug. 5, and ordered to stand trial with Fromant.

At the trial on Oct. 21, 1975, at the Winchester Crown courtroom of Justice Talbot, Fromant admitted to being at the murder scene but stated that the killer was Elizabeth Thompson. The jury sentenced them both to life imprisonment.

Thompson, George (AKA: **Buck Jones**), d.1962, S. Afri. Dillie and Koos Scholtz, a happily married young couple, had good jobs, a nice home, and were quite content in Greenways, a suburb of Cape Town, S. Afri. On July 3, 1961, Koos left for work at about 8 a.m. and Dillie twenty minutes later. When Dillie Scholtz failed to arrive at work, the police were called. Soon it became apparent that Dillie Scholtz had disappeared within a few minutes of leaving the house that morning. Her car was still parked in the garage.

When the police arrived, Koos described his wife's usual routine, and they explored the grounds. While they were in the alley, they were greeted by George "Buck Jones" Thompson, a local handyman who was known to the police as an occasional informant. Buck, apparently somewhat drunk, said he had not seen the woman.

On July 9, while excavating a compost heap a short

distance from the garage, the police discovered Dillie Scholtz's body, buried with her purse, keys, a coat, and some work she had been taking to her office. The body, which was burned, was in a sack and had a necktie tied around the throat. One of the constables assigned to the case recognized the necktie as belonging to George Thompson. Investigation determined that on the morning of the murder Thompson was seen by one of his friends standing by a fire near the garage. He had told his friend to wait for him and that he would buy him a drink. He showed up a short while later with a shopping bag and plenty of money.

Thompson was charged with murder. During his trial, he tried to implicate another person, but the chain of evidence was too strong and he was found Guilty of premeditated murder. He was hanged on Mar. 29, 1962.

Thompson, Tilmer Eugene, prom. 1963, and **Mastrian, Norman**, 1924- , and **Anderson, Dick**, prom. 1963, U.S. St. Paul, Minn., attorney Tilmer Thompson and his wife Carol, the parents of four children, had met while attending Macalester College together in the late 1940s. On Mar. 6, 1963, Carol Thompson was attacked in her home, stabbed twenty-five times in the head and face, and clubbed with a blunt object. She died in the hospital after collapsing on a neighbor's doorstep. Cartridges from a luger pistol that had evidently misfired were found on the floor of the victim's home.

A few days after his wife's murder, Tilmer Thompson was seen in a local nightclub with an attractive woman. Investigators also discovered a dozen insurance policies on his wife's life, worth more than $1 million, naming him as the sole beneficiary. And his wife was sole heir to her parents' million-dollar fortune. Three extension phones had recently been removed from the Thompson house, and the family's pet dog, which had served as protection for the family, had been given away.

On Apr. 9, Minneapolis salesman Wayne F. Brandt reported to police that a luger pistol had been stolen from him on Feb. 14. On Apr. 17, two small-time hoods arrested for an attempted hold-up of a St. Paul bar admitted stealing the luger from Brandt's apartment. They gave the gun to Norman Mastrian, who in turn was seen handing it to Dick Anderson. Mastrian, a 39-year-old ex-boxer, had been suspected of a 1961 murder, but was released. He was also a college classmate of the Thompsons. On Apr. 19, he was arrested for his involvement in the Thompson murder and police began to search for Anderson, whom they arrested shortly in a Phoenix motel. Anderson tried to plea bargain, hoping to reduce the first-degree murder charge.

On June 20, he confessed to murder, saying that Mastrian had hired him to kill the woman in a manner that made her death seem accidental.

Tilmer Eugene Thompson was arrested and charged with first-degree murder on June 25, 1963, by the Ramsey County Grand Jury. On Dec. 6, 1963, before Judge Donald Odden, Thompson was found Guilty of instigating the murder plot and sentenced to life imprisonment "at hard labor." Dick Anderson and Norman Mastrian were also found Guilty and sentenced to life.

Thompson, William Paul (AKA: **Bud**), 1938-89, U.S. William Paul "Bud" Thompson spent 28 of his 51 years in prisons or reform schools on various charges, including breaking and entering, counterfeiting, forgery, and murder. In April 1984, Thompson killed a 28-year-old transient, Randy Waldron, in Reno and was sentenced to die by lethal injection. After that sentence, he was also convicted of the murders of two brothers near an Auburn, Calif., campsite. Thompson confessed that he had killed three others and stated that if freed he would likely kill again. On June 18, 1989, the 300-pound Thompson was given a last supper of four double bacon cheeseburgers, two large orders of fries, and a large cola. At 2:01 the following morning, at the Nevada State Penitentiary in Carson City, he was given a lethal injection, and he died eight minutes later.

Thorne, John Norman Holmes, d.1925, Brit. Elsie Cameron, a plain, rather thin, neurotic young secretary fell in love with young John Thorne. Although Thorne, a Sunday school teacher and boys' club supporter, was a most unlikely choice, being a less-than-successful chicken farmer who lived in a shack on his squalid little farm in Sussex, Elsie still wanted him. In November 1924, after a lengthy correspondence in which she falsely claimed she was pregnant, Elsie kept insisting on coming to see him and that they get married. Thorne, in response, informed her that he was involved with another woman and was not interested.

In spite of her erstwhile lover's protestations, Elsie packed her bag and left London to confront John face-to-face on Dec. 5. Six days later Elsie's father sent John Thorne a telegram asking of Elsie's whereabouts. John replied that although he had expected her she had not arrived in Sussex.

John informed the police that he had not seen Elsie, but witnesses came forward to say that they had definitely seen her going to the farm. The police then returned to the farm

to dig up the chicken yard and discovered her dismembered body.

Thorne claimed that while he was out of the house, Elsie had hanged herself. In a panic, he had tried to dispose of the body. However, an autopsy revealed that she had been beaten to death. He was charged with murder and tried at Lewes Assizes in March 1925. He was found Guilty of murder and was executed at Wandsworth on Apr. 22, 1925.

Thorne, Thomas Harold, b.1896, Brit. In early 1921, Harry Blackmore, a 61-year-old man from Hampstead, England, was found dead from twenty stab wounds to the head. His assailant, 25-year-old Thomas Thorne was apprehended, but found insane, and sentenced to a mental institution in Broadmoor. In 1937, Thorn was released with tragic results. After working briefly as a tobacconist in Chester, he attacked a woman Alice Hannah Johnson, who barely survived. Before Justice Singleton at the Chester Assizes, Thorne was sentenced to fifteen years in prison.

Thornhill, Hillary, 1915- , and **McCain, Willie B.**, 1930- , and **Robertson, Eugene**, 1928- , U.S. In 1960, Hillary "Hill" Thornhill was the bootlegging kingpin of rural Columbia, Miss. A local sheriff, J.V. Polk, had recently declared war after years of casual enforcement, and Thornhill brought in two men, Willie McCain and Eugene Robertson, to eliminate the problem. The two men made two unsuccessful attempts on Polk's life, before Robertson withdrew. But on Apr. 22, 1960, McCain succeeded, killing Sheriff Polk with a 12-gauge shotgun at a distance of seventy-five feet. All three conspirators were arrested and all confessed to the plot. Thornhill and McCain were sentenced to life imprisonment, while Robertson was sentenced to ten years.

Tiernan, Helen, 1911- , U.S. Helen Tiernan, a divorced mother of two, loved George Christodulas, a poor Greek immigrant, but she could not marry him—until her children were out of the way. She lived in a two-room tenement flat on West Forty-seventh Street in New York City. Described as quiet and reserved, Tiernan supported her children by working as a stitcher at an Eighth Avenue embroidery firm. The money her boyfriend earned as a steward at the Foltis-Fischer restaurant on Seventh Avenue was not enough to move the four of them into larger quarters. Deciding that the love of this man was more important to her than the lives of her children, Tiernan took her 7-year-old daughter Helen and 3-year-old son James down to the Pennsylvania Railroad Station on May 15, 1937, where she boarded a train bound for Brookhaven.

She told them they were going on a picnic in the woods. But in her suitcase she carried the murder weapons: a carving knife, hatchet, scissors, and a bottle of gasoline. In a dense thicket near busy Yaphank Road, Tiernan cut Helen's throat and then poured gasoline on her. The girl fell to the ground as her mother lit a match. She struck James with the hatchet, but he ran off before the fire could be started. When the 3-year-old was found later that afternoon by Warren Brady and May Savage of Long Island, all he could say was "Mommy! Mommy!" A hundred feet away, Helen's body was found.

The next day, Tiernan told Christodulas at Jones Beach that the final impediment to their marriage had been removed. The children had been turned over to relatives. Emma McGowan of the West Side Nursery School was notified that her services would no longer be needed, but the woman took note of Tiernan's uneasiness. Later she noticed a picture in the paper of a badly injured boy who had been found in the Long Island woods. Irene Roggeveen, a social worker who listened to Helen Tiernan's story, called Detective Frank Naughton at the West Forty-seventh Street police station. Within minutes he arrived on the scene to take the distraught mother into custody. Tiernan changed her story several times. At first she denied any prior knowledge of her children's disappearance, but then admitted that there had been an attack. A strange man attacked them in the brush, she explained. There was little else to do except run away. But Tiernan did not adequately explain why she had failed to notify the police of this.

Homicide charges were filed, and the prisoner was transported to Suffolk County Jail in Riverhead. George Christodulas was held as a material witness, but was later cleared of involvement in the child murders.

Tiernan, whose own mother died in a state sanitarium, was sentenced to twenty years to life by Justice James Hallinan of the Suffolk County Supreme Court on June 21, 1937. Before she was led away, she asked to see her son, who had been placed in the care of the New York City Child Welfare Board. The request was denied pending approval of the social welfare department.

Tiernan served fourteen years in prison before being paroled on Aug. 27, 1951. A final discharge from jurisdiction was granted in 1964.

Tierney, Nora Patricia, 1920- , Brit. Mrs. Basil

Ward left her 3-year-old daughter to play with a neighborhood friend, Stephanie Tierney, while she went to the store. When she returned, her child was missing. Three days later the child's body was found in a nearby bombed-out house with her head crushed. The only clue to the murderer's identity was the imprint of a woman's shoe found near the body.

The playmate's mother, Nora Tierney, was uncooperative while being questioned. Tierney told Scotland Yard inspector James Jamieson she knew nothing about the child's disappearance. Jamieson took several pairs of Tierney's shoes for examination. When he asked for cuttings from her fingernails, she broke down and told Jamieson that her husband had murdered the child with a hammer.

The police soon discovered that James Tierney was elsewhere at the time of the killing. Nora Tierney was charged with the murder and was tried at the Old Bailey in October 1949. She was convicted and condemned to death, but the sentence was commuted to confinement in Broadmoor Criminal Lunatic Asylum.

Nora Patricia Tierney, murderess.

Tinning, Marybeth Roe, 1943- , U.S. Marybeth Tinning and her husband Joseph had lived their entire married life in Schenectady County, N.Y., moving from one two-flat apartment to another. Joseph Tinning worked as a foreman at the General Electric plant in Schenectady. The Tinnings were a nice couple who freely gave of themselves and their time, according to neighbors. But there was something odd behind this facade. In a period of just less than fourteen years, nine of the Tinnings' children died. All died before the age of five.

The daughter of Ruth and Alton L. Roe, Sr., Marybeth Tinning grew up in Duanesburg, a community fourteen miles outside Schenectady. Tinning was the elder of two children and throughout her childhood and adolescence she claimed to have suffered from isolation and her parents' neglect and mistreatment. At twenty-three, she married Mr. Tinning, who, unlike his high-strung and outgoing wife, was overly timid. Together, the Tinnings had eight children of their own and had almost adopted a ninth.

The first of the Tinning children to die was Jennifer Lewis, the couple's third child. Born on the day after Christmas 1971, Jennifer died just eight days later, on Jan.

3, 1972, from respiratory failure and a brain abscess. Her death was the only one attributal to natural causes. On Jan. 20, 2-year-old Joseph "Joey" Tinning, Jr., died. Only days before, Mrs. Tinning had taken him to Ellis Hospital where she told the pediatrician that her son had choked on his own vomit. The doctors could find nothing wrong with the boy and discharged him to his mother's care a few days later. A few hours later Tinning brought him back to the emergency room dead. She explained that she had put him in the crib for a nap and had found him a little while later lying dead, twisted up in the sheets. She claimed Joey had had convulsive fits.

Four-year-old Barbara Ann, the Tinnings' first child and the child who lived the longest of any of the Tinning children, became the third fatality. A hospital autopsy concluded that Barbara had died of Reye's syndrome, partly basing this conclusion on information provided by Tinning. Although no autopsy had been performed on Joey, it was reasoned that he, too, had died of the disease.

The next child born to the Tinnings was also the next to die. Timothy, born on Nov. 21, 1973, died on Dec. 10 of that year. His death and those of the next two children—5-month-old Nathan on Sept. 2, 1975, and 3-month-old Mary Frances on Feb. 22, 1979—were attributed to Sudden Infant Death Syndrome (SIDS). This malady would later be erroneously ascribed to the Tinnings' last three children. As the years passed, the Tinnings' memories of their two sons Timothy and Nathan became blurred.

There were suspicions about Marybeth Tinning, primarily among the nurses at Ellis Hospital who by 1979, when Mary Frances was born, were more attuned to the signs of child abuse than they had been seven years earlier when the first suspicious death occurred. Although people noted that Mrs. Tinning failed to display normal emotions in the face of these appalling events, no one called for an investigation into the children's deaths. The circumstances surrounding the death of Jonathan D. Tinning, on Mar. 24, 1980 were markedly similar to those surrounding Mary Frances' death. The boy was taken to St. Clare's suffering from a lack of oxygen. A genetic consultant had the boy moved to Boston Children's Hospital where he ordered a battery of tests. The test results revealed that Jonathan's birth defects were unrelated to the present difficulty. Before Jonathan was discharged, a Boston physician described him "as wiggly and active a child as you can imagine." He was returned to Mrs. Tinning with an apnea monitor. Three days later the baby was back in the emergency room having suffered permanent brain damage, a sequence of events almost identical to Mary Frances' last few days.

With six children already dead, the Tinnings applied to the state adoption service. They were in the process of adopting 31-month-old Michael, when, on Mar. 2, 1981,

while adoption officials reviewed the Tinnings' petition, the boy died of viral pneumonia. Dr. Robert Sullivan, Schenectady's medical examiner, concurred that the cause of Michael's death, "showed acute Pneumonia," but added, "the family history is bizarre."

On Dec. 20, 1985, another Tinning child, Tami Lynne, died. This last death went beyond the point of coincidence, even for those who still found it difficult to point an accusatory finger at a woman who had suffered so much. An investigation was begun in earnest. No longer were the children's deaths viewed one at a time by investigators. Dr. Thomas F.D. Oram took into account the deaths of all nine children, along with the information supplied by Tinning and medical personnel, and concluded that only Jennifer had died of natural causes. Oram also concluded that the remaining children could very likely have died from suffocation. When Oram called a colleague, who was an expert on SIDS, he was told, "There's only one explanation for all this, and it has to be smothering."

It was not until February 1987, however, that Tinning admitted killing Tami Lynne. In her thirty-six page confession to police she also admitted murdering Nathan and Timothy, but denied having killed any of the others. With regard to Tami Lynne, she told police, "I did not mean to hurt her. I just wanted her to stop crying." Of the three she admitted killing, Mrs. Tinning said, "I smothered them each with a pillow because I'm not a good mother. I'm not a good mother because of what happened to the other children."

At Tinning's trial, which began in June 1987 in the Schenectady County Court before Judge Clifford T. Harrigan, her attorney Paul M. Callahan claimed that the police had coerced a confession out of Tinning, and argued that his client's civil rights had been violated through "trickery and deception." Forensic pathologist Dr. Jack Davies testified that in his view Tami Lynne had died as a result of a rare genetic disorder known as Werdnig-Hoffmann syndrome, akin to amyotrophic lateral sclerosis, or Lou Gehrig's disease. Although mention was made of Tinning's confession to killing Nathan and Timothy, the jury was not allowed to know of the five other suspect deaths. Mr. Tinning was not charged, as it was apparent he knew nothing of his wife's actions. On July 17, 1987, the six-week trial ended with a verdict of Guilty returned against Tinning for committing second-degree murder with a "depraved indifference to human life." Judge Harrigan sentenced her on Oct. 1, 1987, to a term of twenty years to life in prison.

Toal, Gerard, 1909-28, Ire. Eighteen-year-old Gerard

Toal worked as a chauffeur for Father James McKeown. It was a commonly known fact that Toal disliked Mary Callan, McKeown's housekeeper. Questioned about Callan's disappearance on May 16, 1927, Toal denied any knowledge of the woman's whereabouts. No progress was made in the case until months later when a new housekeeper discovered dismantled parts of a woman's bicycle in Toal's room. When confronted, he insisted that he had stolen them. Police continued to be suspicious that the parts belonged to Callan's bicycle which had disappeared on the same day she had.

In April 1928, Toal was dismissed by McKeown. Toal claimed to be headed for Canada but was arrested ten days later for theft in the town of Dundalk. A closer investigation of the priest's home yielded more bicycle parts and women's clothing. When Callan's decomposed body was found in a water-filled quarry nearby, Toal was arrested and charged with murder.

Toal was tried in Dublin in July 1928. The judge advised against a verdict of manslaughter and Gerard Toal was found Guilty of murder. He was hanged on Aug. 29, 1928.

Toole, Otis Elwood, See: **Lucas, Henry Lee.**

Toppan, Jane (Nora Kelley), 1854-1938, U.S. Born Nora Kelley in Boston in 1854, mass murderer Jane Toppan may have had a genetic claim to insanity. Toppan's mother died when she was an infant, and her father cared for her and her siblings until he too went insane. He was found one day trying to sew his eyelids shut and was sent to an insane asylum. The children went first to live with their grandmother but were later sent to an orphanage. Jane was adopted by Mr. and Mrs. Abner Toppan in 1859. She grew up to be an attractive, apparently normal, and bright young lady. However, when she was jilted by her fiance she was devastated, and she tried twice to kill herself. She ended a several-year period of seclusion by attending a Cambridge, Mass., nursing school.

When a patient who was in Jane's care and not seriously ill, suddenly died, she was questioned about the incident and although no report was made, she was discharged from the hospital staff. Without ever finishing her training, Toppan became a private nurse in dozens of New England homes, gaining the confidence of those she cared for.

In 1901, one of Toppan's patients, Mattie Davis, died. Three other members of her family died shortly thereafter. The trusting family insisted each time that she stay to tend the remaining members. However, when Captain Gibbs, a Davis family relative, returned from a sea voyage to find his wife dead, he became suspicious. The police were called, and several autopsies were performed. In each case, it was determined that the death had been caused by morphine poisoning.

Toppan was traced to New Hampshire, but not before she had murdered another Davis relative. Protesting her innocence, she was returned to Massachusetts and charged with murder. As the investigation of her past began, dozens of the bodies of people she had cared for were exhumed and it was discovered that all had died of morphine and atropine poisoning. The atropine counteracted the constriction of the victims pupils so that morphine poisoning would not be suspected. It was also discovered that Toppan had obtained large quantities of the drugs over the years using forged prescriptions.

While Toppan was in jail, a psychologist, Dr. Stedman, visited her. Eventually she told him she had killed over thirty of her patients. (The actual number is probably closer to 100.) On June 25, 1902, Jane Toppan went on trial. When Dr. Stedman testified that she was suffering from an incurable form of insanity, Jane denied his diagnosis, claiming she was completely sane and always knew what she was doing. She was sent to the Taunton State Asylum for the Criminally Insane where she died in 1938 at age eighty-four.

Totterman, Emil, b.c.1875, U.S. Born in Finland and decorated for heroism at the Battle of Santiago during the Spanish-American War, Emil Totterman was convicted of the December 1903 murder of Sarah Martin and spent the next twenty-five years in prison. There was some doubt that Totterman, a sailor at the time, committed the slashing murder, but he was convicted and sentenced to the electric chair on Mar. 2, 1904, because his luggage was found in the dead woman's room. His death sentence was commuted to life imprisonment on July 25, 1905.

Except for an escape from a work farm on Aug. 20, 1916, Totterman was a model prisoner. In his years at Sing Sing, he enthusiastically involved himself in the mechanical trades and iron-working, and was designated the official steeplejack, painting the high chimney whenever needed and placing the flag on a high pole on holidays. On Dec. 24, 1929, Totterman received a Christmas pardon from Governor Franklin Roosevelt. Through the cooperation of the Finnish consulate, he was able to relocate and reestablish himself in his native land.

Tracy, Ann Gibson, 1935- , U.S. On Nov. 14, 1960, cocktail waitress Ann Tracy could no longer stand the infidelities, lies, and torment of her lover, Amos Stricker.

Stricker was a wealthy building contractor who had carried on an affair with Tracy for several years. However, he still saw other women and taunted her with stories of his other affairs. As they were lying in bed together, she shot him dead.

Tracy confessed and was tried and convicted of second-degree murder. Sentenced for life to the Corona Woman's Prison, she still protested that she loved him.

Trebert, Guy, prom. 1959, Fr. Guy Trebert worked as a paint sprayer at a garage in Paris. On the evening of Mar. 15, 1959, he met a young woman by the name of Arlette at a movie theater. Arlette was not particularly interested in Trebert, and when she went to the country on Mar. 26 to visit her two children, she did not inform Trebert of her departure. On her return she found a number of notes from Trebert demanding that she call him immediately. They met once more and Arlette drove with Trebert to the forest of St. Germain. On Apr. 5, her body was found strangled and mutilated.

Trebert was brought to trial for the murder of Arlette in November 1962. Three women testified that Trebert had taken them to the forest at St. Germain also. He had attacked one of the women with a metal tool, and had attempted to strangle two of them while having intercourse with them. Trebert was convicted of murder and sentenced to life imprisonment.

Treffene, Phillip John, d.1926, Aus. In the early part of the twentieth century, stealing gold was prevalent enough on the Kalgoorlie goldfields of western Australia to warrant the formation of a special police squad to combat it. In May 1926, two members of the Goldfields Detection Force, John Joseph Walsh and Alexander Henry Pitman set out on bicycles to investigate reports of an illegal gold treatment plant. The Force acted independently and it wasn't unusual for them to be out of touch on an investigation for days at a time. When Walsh and Pitman did not return by May 10, however, searchers were sent out after them.

On a tip from two Kalgoorlie men, the mutilated bodies of the two police officers were found at the bottom of a mine shaft. Along with the bodies, which had been burned, were a bloody saw, parts of an old gold treatment plant, gold scales, and parts of a furnace. Also in the mine shaft were a pair of specially tailored trousers which had been made in Perth for a Phillip John Treffene. After an intensive investigation, police linked Treffene and two other men, William Coulter and a man named Clarke to the brutal murders of Walsh and Pitman. As police suspected, Pitman and Walsh had come upon the plant where Coulter and Treffene processed stolen gold ore. Rather than sacrifice a highly lucrative enterprise, the two shot the officers. Clarke, who owned the bar where Treffene occasionally worked, aided the pair in covering up the crime and disposing of the bodies. Treffene and Coulter were tried on Aug. 16, 1926, and found Guilty of murder. They both were hanged two months later in Fremantle Jail. Clarke, who had cooperated with the police, was not tried despite a formal statement from the jury in the Treffene-Coulter trial deploring the fact that Clarke did not also stand trial.

Tremamunno, Donato, prom. 1962, Italy. Donato Tremamunno and Antonio Ragone were boyhood friends who parted ways when they became adults. Tremamunno traveled the world with the French Foreign Legion, and Ragone settled in Torrazza, Italy, with his wife and two daughters to work as a foreman at a Genoa factory. In 1961, Tremamunno, tired of travel, married a young woman and moved to Torrazza, where Ragone put the couple and their child up in a small cottage. But Tremamunno was unable to find work and feeling pressured for rent by Ragone, grew depressed.

On Aug. 24, 1962, Tremamunno and Ragone went for a walk. Later the same day, Tremamunno appeared on Ragone's doorstep without Ragone and told Ragone's 13-year-old daughter, Vita, that her father needed help in the orchard. That night, Ragone's wife and older daughter found Ragone's body in the orchard. He had been shot with a 7.65-millimeter pistol through the back of the head. Police later found the bodies of Tremamunno's wife Sebastiana and her infant son, Emilio, in the cottage. Sebastiana had been shot and her throat slit, and the child had been shot in the head.

More than 500 police officers and volunteers combed the countryside looking for the murderer. Late one afternoon, they found the two bodies. Vita Ragone was naked and had been savagely attacked and strangled. Next to her lay the body of Donato Tremamunno, dead from a gunshot wound to the mouth, the gun—a 7.5-millimeter pistol, standard issue for the French Foreign Legion—still clenched in his hand.

"I write this with a calm mind," read the note found in his cottage. "I have grown tired of the struggle for existence in this insane world, and I curse my parents for bringing me into it. I do not want to live anymore. I shall welcome death with open arms."

Trenton Six, See: Cooper, Ralph.

Trolia, John, 1944- , U.S. According to court testimony, on Sept. 1, 1974, John Trolia, a 30-year-old man from Burbank, Ill., and Paula Popik, a 21-year-old cocktail waitress, were seen leaving a South Side Chicago lounge in her car. Later that morning, Popik's car was found burning. Five days later, her body was discovered floating in the Des Plaines River. She had been shot, and her body had been in the river two or three days.

An initial grand jury investigation and hearing implicated no one, then several friends of Trolia said they lied during the hearing and changed their stories. Linda Szilagyi said she saw Trolia and Popik together on Sept. 1. Richard Maskas testified that, on Aug. 30, Trolia borrowed a pistol from him and returned it several days later telling him it could be "hot." Two of Trolia's friends, Thomas O'Neill and Robert Holwell, initially arrested for the murder, testified that Trolia confessed to Popik's murder. After hearing this testimony, the jury convicted Trolia of murder and Justice Louis B. Garippo sentenced him to twenty-five to seventy-five years in prison.

After the trial, a police report surfaced that included a statement by Rebecca Lavin that she had seen Popik on Sept. 3, two days after she was reportedly killed. An appellate court ruled that the new evidence negated the Guilty verdict. After serving five years in prison, Trolia won a new trial. In August 1980, Trolia was again convicted of murder, and Judge Frank Machala sentenced him to twenty-five to seventy-five years in prison.

Trousseau Murderer, The, See: Boyce, Arthur Robert.

True, Ronald, 1891-1951, Brit. Ronald True had difficulty handling reality, and thus indulged in a strong fantasy life. His wealthy Bedfordshire family supported him in his many attempts—becoming a sheep farmer, joining the Royal Canadian Mounted Police, learning to fly. True became a drug addict, divorcing him even further from reality. While living in New York City, he convinced an actress he was a WWI pilot so she would marry him. He eventually left her to run a flying school, though he had never actually learned to fly. Returning to Europe, his family arranged for him to go to Africa for a mining job, but he did not last any longer in that than he had in any other attempt.

True spent the next several years in and out of nursing homes for his addiction. When he was out of them, he frequented questionable nightspots in London. In early 1922, he began to hunt for "the other Ronald True," whom he blamed for the bad things he did, like writing bad checks and stealing money from friends. On Mar. 5, "the other Ronald True" spent the night with a prostitute he had known before, Olive Young (real name: Gertrude Yates). When they rose in the morning, he killed Young with a rolling pin, then dragged her body into the bathroom and nodded politely to the cleaning lady when she arrived, and left.

Murderer Ronald True.

Young's body was found immediately, and the cleaning lady was able to identify True to the police. True pawned Young's jewelry and then dressed to spend an evening at the theater. He was arrested in his box at the Hammersmith Palace. True was found Guilty and sentenced to death, but the home secretary had him examined by psychiatrists and commuted his sentence to life at Broadmoor, where he spent another twenty-eight years.

Truscott, Stephen Murray, 1945- , Can. On summer evenings, large groups of children regularly gathered on the school playground of the Canadian Air Force Station at Clinton, Ontario. On June 9, 1959, 12-year-old Lynne Harper left her home in the non-commissioned officers area after dinner to join some of her friends at the playground. Witnesses who saw Lynne there later told police that she left soon after arriving, riding on the crossbar of the bicycle of 14-year-old Stephen Truscott. Truscott, the son of a noncommissioned officer stationed at the base, reportedly returned approximately an hour after leaving with Lynne. No one who saw him was able to recall anything unusual in his appearance or demeanor. When asked by one of the other children about Lynne, Stephen said that he had taken her, at her request, to a nearby highway where she had accepted a ride in a 1959 grey Chevrolet with yellow license plates. Stephen said that Lynne had told him that she intended to visit a "white house where there were some ponies."

Harper's body was found in a nearby wooded area two days later. She had been raped and strangled. Truscott, described as an amiable, well-adjusted boy with no previous record, was interrogated closely in connection with the murder. A small sore or abrasion on Truscott's genitals, discovered in the course of a physical examination, strengthened the case against him and he was arrested, charged with murder and ordered to stand trial as an adult. The trial, which began on Sept. 16 and lasted for two weeks, included testimony from child witnesses. Both the prosecution and the defense alleged deliberate perjury by the children. Despite obvious omissions and errors in Truscott's defense, the boy was found Guilty and sentenced to death on Sept. 30, 1959. A subsequent appeal was denied but Truscott did receive a reprieve from execution. Truscott remained under the care of the Ontario Department of Reform Institutions until his eighteenth birthday when he was transferred to a prison.

Tucker, Felix, d.1943, U.S. When his wife admitted to having an affair with another man, Felix Tucker flew into a rage and began to choke and beat her. Minnie Margaret Tucker and her husband separated for a couple of weeks, but got back together again. In May 1942, Minnie had exhausted all possible chances for reconciliation and told her husband that she was leaving him to live with Charley Brenner and was taking the couple's 11-month-old baby with her. Tucker beat her up again. The same evening, Tucker ran out of his house screaming for neighbors to call the police because his wife had been murdered.

Tucker said he returned home at 6:10 p.m. to find his wife dead on the bedroom floor of their Nashville, Tenn., home. Tucker first told police that his wife had quarrelled with Brenner. Brenner admitted that he was in love with Minnie and the couple were planning to marry, and said he did not kill her. Only Tucker's fingerprints were found on the crime scene, and authorities found that a footprint left in the soggy grass matched Tucker's. Under intense questioning, Tucker admitted to murdering his wife. He said he would have stabbed her more than twice if the knife had not gotten stuck in her body. Rather than face the pain of losing his wife to another man, he had killed her, Tucker told police. He was electrocuted on July 15, 1943.

Tuer, William Franklin, 1940-73, Can. On Jan. 23, 1974, after weeks of searching, Canadian police discovered the body of Angus McDougall Tuer in a well on his farm just outside of Stratford, Ontario. Tuer had been shot in the head, wrapped in a heavy chain, and dropped down the well weighted with an old truck transmission housing.

Three days after Tuer's body was discovered, the police arrested William Franklin Tuer and charged him with the murder of his younger brother. Tuer's trial began in October 1974, and the prosecution maintained that Tuer had murdered his brother to gain his money. The trial lasted thirteen days, and the jury returned a verdict of Guilty. Tuer was sentenced to life imprisonment.

Turner, Joyce 1928- , and **Noakes, Audrey**, and **Gay, Clestell**, prom. 1956, U.S. The operator of a Columbia, S.C., day-care and mother of six often chatted with Clestell Gay and Audrey Noakes, swearing that some day she was going to kill her bartender husband, Alonzo. In June 1956, Gay asked "Well, are you going to do it or not?" Turner grabbed a .22-caliber pistol gun from Gay, ran to her home, and shot her sleeping husband.

Turner told police that an intruder had killed her husband and complained at his funeral that he saw other women. When the police checked, they found that the man was too lazy even for affairs. They also found out that the gun belonged to Gay. All three women pleaded guilty in separate trials and were sent to prison for life.

Twin-Six Murderer, The, See: **Church, Harvey.**

Tyburski, Leonard, 1944- , U.S. On Oct. 2, 1985, Leonard Tyburski reported the disappearance of his 37-year-old wife to Canton Township police. Tyburski, the head of the attendance department at Detroit's Mackenzie High School, told police that Dorothy Tyburski had been very depressed ever since the death of her sister in 1984. He speculated that she may have left because of emotional problems, and police treated the incident as a missing persons case for more than two years, until they dropped the case due to a lack of progress. For 20-year-old Kelly Tyburski, the disappearance of her mother was manifesting itself in recurring nightmares. Kelly, a student at Michigan State University, could not shake the vision of her mother locked up or tied up somewhere in the family's home in suburban Detroit.

On Jan. 2, 1989, Kelly managed to pry the lock of a basement freezer open and discovered her mother's body. She had been bludgeoned to death. Two days later, Leonard Tyburski was arraigned on murder charges in District Court at Plymouth. The courtroom drama began to unfold in June, when Craig Albright, Kelly's live-in boyfriend, told the courtroom he had been enticed into having sex with Mrs. Tyburski on two occasions. On Sept. 28, 1985, Albright said that he refused the woman's advances. On that same day, Tyburski would testify, Dorothy told her husband of her affair with the teenager and called her husband a "wimp." In a fit of rage, Tyburski attacked his wife, who in trying to defend herself stabbed him with a steak knife. At first, Tyburski told the court his wife had fallen into the freezer, then he admitted he had thrown her into the unit. Subsequently he said he had gone berserk over her confession and smashed her head against a basement beam before depositing her in the freezer. Tyburski testified that even while his wife was wounded in the freezer, she called him a "wimp" and a "punk" and called out for Albright.

In defense of her client, attorney Carole Stanyar portrayed Tyburski as a man emasculated by his wife's taunts and constant humiliation. It was in self-defense that Tyburski acted, Stanyar told the courtroom. Assistant Wayne County Prosecutor Glenn Page argued that Tyburski's story had changed so frequently that the truth might not have been told. Page questioned how Tyburski, in good conscience, could have lied about his wife's whereabouts, filed for divorce, and entertained in his home while Dorothy's body was in the basement. On June 26, it took a jury less than two hours to decide that Tyburski was Guilty of second-degree murder charges. In July, Wayne County Circuit Judge Richard Hathaway sentenced Tyburski to twenty to forty years in prison.

U

Unruh, Howard, 1921-   , U.S. Born and raised in Camden, N.J., Howard Unruh had a normal, uneventful childhood. He was a good student and graduated high school during the early stages of WW II. Unruh was drafted into the army and served with an armored division. In basic training he became a sharpshooter and his fellow GIs noticed that he had a fascination for weapons. He would spend hours each night sitting on his bunk taking apart his rifle and putting it back together again. Unruh never took advantage of weekend passes and was never seen in the company of women. He preferred to remain within the confines of his barracks and occupy himself reading his Bible or cleaning his rifle.

Religion had been deeply rooted in Unruh since childhood. He had attended church regularly, gone to Bible class, and read the Bible each day at home. Unruh continued to carry his Bible with him through battle after battle as his armored unit fought its way up the boot of Italy in 1943. Unruh by this time was a machine gunner in a tank turret. In the following year, Unruh's unit, part of General George Patton's Third Army, helped to liberate Bastogne in the bloody Battle of the Bulge. Throughout these war years, Unruh kept a diary in which he wrote daily his private thoughts. A fellow GI, who later became a New York policeman, sneaked a look at Unruh's diary and was horrified to view its contents. Unruh had recorded the death of every German soldier he had killed, the hour and the place he had killed them, and how they appeared in death after he had shot them.

Yet the Army looked up to Unruh as a hero, and before receiving his honorable discharge at war's end, he was awarded several commendations for his heroic service during battle. There was no hero's welcome for Howard Unruh when he returned to Camden, however. He was just another soldier, among millions, returning to civilian life. Unruh announced to his parents that he intended to become a pharmacist and, to that end, he took some refresher high school courses and then enrolled at Temple University in Philadelphia. Unruh continued his Bible classes and there met the only girl he ever dated. The relationship was only a mild flirtation and quickly ended.

This brief affair left Unruh embittered. By 1949, he was considered the neighborhood recluse. He became more withdrawn and seldom spoke to his parents, keeping to his room. The only preoccupation that made him joyful was maintaining his collection of weapons, which he had begun after his military discharge. Unruh set up targets in the basement of his parents' home and practiced his marksmanship each day.

Unruh then began to take offense at off-handed comments made by neighbors. In his mind these became terrible insults, and he suffered what doctors later termed acute paranoia and schizophrenia. He started another diary, or a hate list, wherein he jotted down every imagined and real insult made by neighbors and friends. No grievance was too small to record. This diary was no less exact than the one he had kept in the service.

His next-door neighbors, the Cohens, were particularly annoying to Unruh. Once, while taking a short-cut through the Cohen backyard, Mrs. Cohen had yelled at him: "Hey, you! Do you have to go through our yard?" When the Cohens gave their 12-year-old son a bugle which he practiced daily, Unruh looked upon this as a personal offense against him, as if the neighbors had purposely awarded their son this noisy instrument to annoy him. The list of names and those who offended Unruh grew and grew, and after each offense Unruh wrote the abbreviation "retal," meaning "retaliate."

At first Unruh tried to shut out the world that offended him, rather than attack it. He built a high wooden fence around the tiny Unruh back yard. With his father's help, he built a huge gate that was locked against the intrusions of the outside. Unruh's room was another haven where he took refuge. Here the young man kept a 9mm German Luger, which he had purchased for $40, several pistols, a large quantity of ammunition, a knife and a machete, both kept razor sharp by their owner.

Unruh's shaky world collapsed on Sept. 9, 1949. He came home at 3 a.m. that morning to find that someone had stolen the massive gate he and his father had labored so long to erect. Local pranksters had done the deed, but to Unruh everyone living was responsible for this unforgivable insult. Unruh was up all night, staring at the ceiling of his room, seething with hatred. He decided to take revenge. At 8 a.m. he sat down to a breakfast prepared by his mother. He stared at her strangely and would later admit that she was to be his first victim. He had to kill her to spare her the grief he would bring upon the family through his homicidal plans. Unruh went to the basement, then returned, eyes glaring at her, walking toward her menacingly. His mother ran from the house to a neighbor where she blurted her fears about her unstable son.

Going to his room, Unruh loaded his Luger and another pistol, pocketing these weapons, along with a knife. He gathered up several clips of ammunition for both guns and filled his pockets. He walked outside and scrambled over the fence instead of going through the gaping area where the gate had been. At 9:20 a.m., Unruh stood in the doorway of a small shoemaker's shop owned by John Pilarchik. The cobbler, who had just recently finished paying off the mortgage for his shop, was busy working on children's shoes. Pilarchik looked up to see Unruh, someone he had known since boyhood. He stared in disbelief as Unruh pulled out the Luger and fired two bullets into his head. Pilarchik pitched forward dead onto his work bench.

Unruh then stepped next door, into the barbershop owned by Clark Hoover who had been cutting Unruh's hair since he was a little boy. Sitting on a small plastic horse in the shop was 6-year-old Edward Smith, whose mother and 11-year-old sister stood nearby. Without a word, Unruh raised his Luger and shot the boy dead and then pumped two more bullets into the startled Hoover. He ignored the screams of Mrs. Smith and her daughter who rushed forward to cradle the dead child. Unruh looked at both of them but strangely did not fire his Luger. With a vacant stare, he wheeled about and headed for the corner drugstore which was owned by the Cohen family, the people he hated most.

James Hutton, Unruh's insurance agent, stepped from the drugstore. "Hello, Howard," he said affably.

"Excuse me," Unruh said in a monotone. He leveled the Luger at Hutton and fired twice. The insurance agent toppled dead to the sidewalk. Cohen, who saw Unruh shoot Hutton through the window of his shop, raced upstairs to warn other members of his family. Unruh entered the drugstore, inserted another clip into the Luger and then plodded up the stairs after his mortal enemy. Upstairs, Unruh saw no one about. He suspected that the Cohens were hiding and when he heard a noise in a closet he fired a bullet through the closet door. He opened this to see Mrs. Cohen sagging to the floor. He sent another bullet into her head. Cohen and his son slipped out a window and walked along the second-story ledge of the building, scrambling to a nearby roof.

Unruh went into another room of the Cohen apartment and saw Cohen's elderly mother desperately calling police on a phone. He fired twice, killing her. Then he spotted Cohen and his son scrambling across a sloping roof and he leaned calmly from a window and fired a bullet that slammed into Cohen's back, causing him to slide off the roof and crash to the pavement below. Unruh carefully leaned further out the window and fired straight down at Cohen, sending another bullet into his back, although the man was already dead. The Cohen boy had by this time slid down to the edge of the roof and was clinging to its edge, screaming. Unruh glanced at him but did not shoot him. He walked back downstairs and went outside.

He found Alvin Day, a passerby, kneeling at the body of James Hutton, trying to help a man who was already dead. Day looked up to see the muzzle of Unruh's Luger poking into his face. Unruh fired twice, killing Day, a man he had never met before this moment. Reloading the Luger, Unruh began to leisurely stroll across the street. A car was idling at the corner, its driver waiting for the light to change. Unruh walked up to the car and stuck the Luger

through the window, shooting the female driver dead. He then fired at and killed the woman's mother who was in the back seat of the car, along with her young son.

Unruh then began walking down the street. He spotted a truck driver getting out of the cab of his truck a block away. Taking careful aim, Unruh shot him in the leg. By then panic had gripped the entire area. The maniac in the streets was shooting anyone he encountered. The manager of a supermarket quickly locked the front doors and told his customers to lie down on the floor. So did the manager of a bar which Unruh approached. As bar customers huddled on the floor, Unruh tried the door and found it locked. He fired twice, trying to blow away the lock but it held. He moved on, seemingly unconcerned.

Going into the tailor's shop next door, Unruh found the place empty. Tom Fegrino, the proprietor, was not present but Unruh heard a noise in the back room. He pushed back a drape to see Mrs. Fegrino cringing behind a chair. "Oh, my God, please don't," she pleaded. Unruh said nothing as he sent two bullets into her, killing her instantly. Stepping outside, Unruh looked about at the now empty street. The only persons present were those whom he had already killed. Neighbors and passersby had rushed into houses and shops and had locked themselves inside against the random rage of the lunatic. Unruh looked up to see 3-year-old Tommy Hamilton staring down at him. He fired once, killing the boy.

Walking to a nearby house, Unruh entered it by the back door which he found unlocked. Inside the kitchen, he found Mrs. Madeleine Harris and her two sons. The older son, a courageous youth, saw the gun in Unruh's hand and dashed forward, driving his shoulder into the body of the tall killer. Unruh fired twice, wounding the youth and his mother. He then stood over these two fallen victims who squirmed in pain. He leveled the Luger at them but, oddly, decided not to end their lives. He turned on his heel and walked once more outside.

Police sirens wailing from squad cars could be heard in the distance. Unruh increased his pace as he walked back to his home where he went to his second-story room, barricading the door and reloading his Luger. He waited patiently as police surrounded his house. He looked out his window at them without firing. His identity was by then known and had been reported to Phillip Buxton, editor of the Camden *Courier Post*. Buxton obtained Unruh's listed phone number and took a chance, calling the killer.

Unruh picked up the phone and one of the strangest phone conversations in the annals of murder then occurred.

"Hello," Unruh said in a calm voice.

"Is this Howard?" Buxton inquired.

"Yes, this is Howard," Unruh replied. "What is the last name of the party you want?"

"Unruh."

"Who are you and what do you want?" Unruh asked politely.

Buxton was diplomatic: "I am a friend and I want to know what they are doing to you."

"Well, they haven't done anything to me yet," Unruh said in an even voice, as if he were chatting with an old friend. "But I am doing plenty to them."

"How many have you killed?"

"I don't know yet—I haven't counted them, but it looks like a pretty good score." (Thirteen persons had been shot to death by Howard Unruh within twelve minutes.)

"Why are you killing people, Howard," Buxton asked, trying to control his own passions while writing down the murderer's every word.

He was greeted by silence. After some moments, Unruh replied in a low voice: "I don't know. I can't answer that yet—I'm too busy. I'll have to talk to you later." He hung up.

At that moment tear gas cannisters fired by police outside smashed through the glass of the bedroom windows and exploded inside, filling the room with eye-searing gas.

Mass murderer Howard Unruh, under arrest.

These were followed by fusilades of bullets that smacked into the walls of Unruh's room, chipping the plaster. After a few minutes, Unruh took down the barricade in front of his door and walked downstairs and outside. He put his hands slowly into the air at a command barked by a police officer. Dozens of guns were trained upon him.

Detectives rushed forward, manhandling him, manacling his large hands. Detective Vince Connelly, sickened at the sight of the bodies in the street nearby, stared at Unruh and

said: "What's the matter with you? Are you a psycho?"

Howard Unruh lifted his head indignantly and snapped: "I am no psycho! I have a good mind!"

More than twenty psychiatrists who examined Howard Unruh disagreed. They believed him to be hopelessly and criminally insane. The mass killer was never brought to trial but sent to the New Jersey State Mental Hospital for life. He had no remorse for his brutal, unthinking murders. In one interview with a psychiatrist, Unruh stated: "I'd have killed a thousand if I'd had bullets enough."

Urich, Dr. **Heinz Karl Gunther** (AKA: **Dr. Henri Urich**), d.1960, Mor. A high-ranking official of the SS in Nazi Germany, Dr. Heinz Karl Gunther Urich, was captured by the French near the end of the war. While serving time in a French prison, Urich was offered the chance of joining the French Foreign Legion in North Africa with the rank of medical major and serving out his sentence. The fact that he would be a commissioned officer in the French forces eliminated the possibility of his being tried for war crimes committed in France. Within months after he arrived in Morocco, Urich managed to get a discharge from the Foreign Legion and became the director of a local hospital owned by a mining company. By the time he married Rose Ascensio in 1948, the doctor had changed his name to Henri Urich. Through the marriage, Urich gained a teenage stepdaughter named Liliane with whom he fell in love.

On June 28, 1960, Police Commissioner Ali Mamoud read an obituary notice in the newspaper concerning the death of 22-year-old Liliane Urich. She had died, the notice read, in Hannover, Ger., following an operation. The commissioner was aware of Mrs. Urich having health problems, but the death of his daughter Liliane caught him by surprise. Upon investigation of the doctor's house, police found that Urich had left town three days ago and requested a three-month leave of absence from the hospital. In investigating the disappearance, police questioned Liliane's boyfriend who said that Urich did not approve of him and discouraged the girl from seeing him. In conversation with a neighbor of the Urichs', police found postcards and a letter from the doctor, detailing his daughter's demise. She had a brain tumor, the doctor wrote, and she died almost immediately following surgery. The neighbor said that she was surprised that Urich had written to her because usually Mrs. Urich did the writing.

Police inquiries to Germany revealed that Liliane had never been admitted to the Hannover hospital and there was no death certificate on file. Unexpectedly, Urich returned to his Moroccan home on July 8 and repeated the story about the tragic tumor for the police. Ali Mamoud also asked him about the houseboy, who had not been seen in a few weeks. The doctor said he had been fired. The Moroccan police received further information from German authorities that contradicted the doctor's story. On Aug. 10, officials sought to question Urich again, but found him dead in a chair. He had shot himself in the head. On a table was a note dated July 15 saying goodbye to his wife and his daughter Monique. Upon further investigation of the house, police discovered the bodies of Mrs. Urich, Liliane, and Monique underneath the garage floor. Police found the houseboy, who said he had been paid by the doctor to keep quiet. He had witnessed the murders, he told police. The shootings occurred after the doctor argued with Liliane, who refused to stop seeing her boyfriend.

V

Vampire Killer, The, See: Haigh, John George.

Vampire of Dusseldorf, The, See: Kurten, Peter.

Van Buuren, Clarence Gordon, 1923-57, S. Afri. On Oct. 2, 1956, Myrna Joy Aken, eighteen, vanished from her home in Durban, S. Afri. A friend reported that she had seen Aken getting into a light-colored car; she had been observed in the company of a man who had come to see her at her office. When the car was traced to a radio shop, the owner of the auto said it had been used by one of his salesmen, Clarence Gordon Van Buuren, thirty-three, who returned it to him the day after Aken vanished, and then disappeared himself. When a search for Aken turned up no clues, her distraught family hired a medium, Nelson Palmer, who went into a trance and said the woman's body would be found sixty miles away, in a drain under the road. Palmer went with the family to the spot he had described, just north of the village of Umtwalumi; the naked corpse was found there. Aken had been raped and shot.

Nine days after the slaying Van Buuren was picked up near Pinetown. His criminal record dated back to when he was seventeen, with charges of theft, forgery, escaping from custody, and passing bad checks. He claimed to have asked Aken out for a drink; she refused, and he went into a bar alone. Returning an hour later, he explained, he found the car parked fifty yards away, and opened the door to find the young woman with blood on her face. Panicking, he got rid of the corpse by throwing it in the culvert, he said. Tried in February 1957, Van Buuren maintained his innocence. But the fact that he had a large supply of .22-caliber ammunition—the type used to kill Aken—weighed against him, as did the fact that he was the last person to be seen with her. He was found Guilty, and hanged at Pretoria Central Prison on June 10, 1957.

van de Corput, Piet (AKA: **John Hendricks**), prom. 1915-16, U.S. In Autumn 1915, Barbara Wright, a widow, was walking with her son from the club where she worked in New York City, heading toward the rooming house where she lived. A man sprang out from behind a car and drove a long-handled dagger into her chest. He ran away as terrified onlookers watched. The detective assigned to the case interviewed the eyewitnesses and other roomers at the boarding house, and became convinced that the killer was John Hendricks, a Dutch man who also lived at the house and had attempted to assault Wright three months earlier. At that time he was arrested and found to be carrying a long-handled dagger. He claimed he was drunk at the time and did not know what he was doing. Convicted and sent to the workhouse, he wrote several letters to Wright while there, attemping to force himself on her again a few days before she was slain.

Thousands of flyers picturing the suspect's face were circulated throughout New York and all major cities in the world, but turned up nothing. A detective went to a home for Dutch sailors in Hoboken, N.J., and learned from a man there that "Hendricks" was really Piet van de Corput, from the town of Breda near the Belgian border. It was a year after the killing when van de Corput was finally arrested in New York City. Not only had he been in New York the entire time, he had been robbed while on a drunken binge in the Bowery, and made a complaint against his assailants, later going before a grand jury and testifying in court.

Eyewitnesses to the Wright murder easily picked van de Corput out of a line-up. Prosecuted by Assistant District Attorney William Edwards, and defended by Bob Moore, who tried to prove that van de Corput's confession was inadmissable because third-degree methods were used to obtain it, van de Corput himself overruled his defense. When Moore said that the line-up was not fair to the defendant, van de Corput himself announced to the court, "They treated me fairly." The jury deliberated only a few minutes before finding him Guilty; he was sentenced to death. While awaiting execution at Sing Sing Prison, van de Corput obtained a picture of the woman he killed, which he carried with him to the electric chair, saying he would "meet Barbara in heaven."

van der Merwe, Dorothea, and **Swatz, Hermanus Lambertus**, prom. 1920, S. Afri. In 1920, a convict named Gibson, also known as Dr. Gibson, who had been employed in a South African prison hospital since the 1918 influenza epidemic, attended a patient named Hermanus Lambertus Swatz. Swatz, who had been convicted of theft and was serving time at the Pretoria Central Prison, confided in Gibson, asking him about the way a body stayed preserved both in and out of a coffin, and what the chances were of fatal wounds being diagnosed after some years. Thinking that this information might lead to a remission of his own sentence, Gibson informed the head warder of their conversations. The body of Louis Tumpowski, a Polish Jew on the Treurfontein farm in the Lichtenburg district of Transvaal, was unearthed. When Tumpowski had disappeared, it was assumed that he had only left the district. Dorothea van der Merwe and Swatz had brutally murdered Tumpowski together. With Gibson's evidence against Swatz, the killers were convicted and hanged.

---

van Heerden, Cornelius Johannes Petrus, 1909-1931, S. Afri. A 22-year-old railway worker who lost his job because of frequent, unexplained absences, Cornelius Johannes Petrus van Heerden lived with his parents in Bethlehem, S. Afri., about one hundred miles from Charleston. On Nov. 4, 1931, van Heerden had his first run-in with the law. Charged on six counts of theft by conversion, his father was the defrauded party who brought charges against him. Although he was found Guilty, the magistrate gave him a suspended sentence, taking his youth and, most probably, his first-time offender status, into consideration. Another charge, that of negligent driving, was still pending. Had van Heerden been found guilty of this offense, his maximum sentence would have been a moderate fine. He had not been arrested, but only summoned to appear in court. But, to avoid another appearance in any court, van Heerden decided to commit suicide, taking several people with him.

On Nov. 25, the unemployed man went to Bethlehem, stayed overnight there, and purchased fifty rounds of rifle ammunition and several revolver cartridges the next day. Looking up T.S. Lessing, an acquaintance, van Heerden informed him he would "be damned if" he would appear in court, and brought a handful of cartridges out of his pocket, warning, "You watch, there is going to be bloodshed..." Returning home to pick up his father's rifle, he told his brother he was going out for "a bit of shooting." During that day, or the night before, van Heerden wrote several letters, including letters to the police, his father, and his girlfriend. He told the police that "though you now contemplate prosecuting me, you will probably have to prosecute my corpse."

Van Heerden's first victim was J.E. Darby, a commercial traveler whom he shot through the head when Darby pulled up on the road. Taking his car, the killer pushed Darby's body down on the seat beside him, and continued on. Coming upon a native woman, he shot at her, continuing to fire on a railway gang as he looked for his father's group, presumably with the intention of murdering his own father. Not finding him, the enraged killer threw a wallet with his farewell letters into the road. An Anglo-Boer war veteran, A.M. Prisloo, a well-known local citizen, was the next of van Heerden's rampage victims; he was shot to death along with two of his native servants. Van Heerden killed five people and wounded six others, before finally turning the gun on himself and taking his own life.

---

van Rensburg, Smartryk Johannes Jacobus Jansen, d.1923, and **Gordon-Lennox, Ellen**, prom. 1923, S. Afri. Arriving in Upington, S. Afri., in January 1921, handsome and flirtatious Barend van Rensburg was popular with the women. He had an affair with Ellen Gordon-Lennox, daughter of George St. Leger Gordon-Lennox, better known as Scotty Smith, the uncrowned "King of the Kalahari" in the late 1870s. When Gordon-Lennox became pregnant, van Rensberg obtained some pills that terminated her pregnancy.

At the same time, van Rensburg was involved with Rachel de Kock, who also became pregnant. When de Kock revealed her condition to her father, and hinted that van Rensburg had offered to marry her, the seducer reluctantly became a bridegroom, even though he had already arranged a date to marry Gordon-Lennox later that year. On Apr. 25, 1922, de Kock and van Rensburg married. A child was born three months later. Unhappy with his marriage, van Rensburg soon resumed his relationship with Gordon-Lennox, and began asking Solomon Gilinsky, an Upington merchant, what grounds were sufficient for divorce. Gordon-Lennox wrote love letters to van Rensburg, and he was often called in at night to go to "work," meeting Gordon-Lennox for clandestine evenings. Their love affair became common knowledge, and soon reached Mr. de Kock, who came to complain. His son-in-law denied anything but friendship with Gordon-Lennox.

Soon after Christmas, van Rensburg obtained some strychnine and added it to one of his wife's headache powders. On Jan. 4, 1923, when Rachael complained of a headache, her husband brought in the box of various powders and she chose one to put in her coffee. She was soon reeling in pain, and Dr. W.M. Brocherds was called in. A neighbor who arrived on the scene, Lena Wylbach, was told by the gasping woman that her husband had given her a headache powder, and that she was sure it contained poison. The doctor arrived to find van Rensburg with his arms around his spouse's neck, begging her to withdraw her accusation. Her last words to him were, "Kiss me. I'm dying."

Through the incriminating evidence of love letters between Gordon-Lennox and van Rensburg, both were arrested for the murder, and tried together on Apr. 18, 1923, in Upington. Justice H.S. van Zyl presided, with E. Wingfield prosecuting along with A.J. Pienaar, and C.G. Hall for the defense. Van Rensburg claimed his wife had lied about his giving her a powder. Gordon-Lennox, pregnant again, was found Guilty along with her lover. Van

Rensberg was executed on May 26, 1923. Gordon-Lennox had her baby in jail, and was released in 1931 after seven years as a model prisoner.

Vaquier, Jean Pierre (Vacquier, AKA: **J. Wanker**), c.1878-1924, Brit. An impassioned French hotel clerk, a British matron on the verge of a nervous breakdown, and a drunken husband who managed an inn in Surrey comprised an unusual love triangle that culminated in murder in early Spring 1924. Jean Pierre Vaquier had served as a telephone operator in the French Army during WWI. After the war his skills with a wireless won him a job at the Hotel Victoria in Biarritz, demonstrating the entertainment potential of the radio to curious vacationers staying at the hotel. Using his own receiver Vaquier beamed musical concerts directly into the hotel salon.

British killer Jean Pierre Vaquier.

In January, Mabel Theresa Jones registered at the Victoria to recover from the emotional shock of a serious business reversal which had left her nearly bankrupt. Jones was attracted to the middle-aged Vaquier and after a week they had begun an affair. Jones was only mildly drawn to Vaquier, and when her husband, Alfred George Poynter Jones, sent a telegram urging her to come home, Mabel broke off her relationship with Vaquier. Although Vaquier begged her not to go she remained firm on her resolve. She did permit Vaquier to accompany her to Paris but from there continued to Surrey alone.

The next day after parting with Jones in Paris, Vaquier headed for London. He dispatched a telegram to Jones from the Russell Hotel in Bloomsbury. "Arrived from Paris on business. Shall be very pleased to see you and to meet Mr. Jones. Perhaps you will inform me which evening." Without waiting for a reply Vaquier turned up at the Joneses' Blue Anchor Inn at Byfleet, Surrey, on Feb. 14, 1924. Although Jones paid his hotel bill and attempted to make him comfortable, it became evident to Vaquier that her ardor had cooled. When Jones refused to go away with him, Vaquier became increasingly desperate and finally decided to kill his rival, in the misguided hope of regaining Jones's affection.

On Mar. 1, Vaquier called on an apothecary on Southampton Row, London. Vaquier told the clerk in French that he required two grains of strychnine—enough poison to kill four healthy men—for a wireless experiment he was conducting. After completing the purchase, Vaquier signed the register under the alias, "J. Wanker." Back in Byfleet he waited for the right moment to administer the poison to the unsuspecting Mr. Jones. The opportunity came on the evening of Mar. 28 when the innkeeper threw a big party.

Guessing that Mr. Jones, an inveterate drunk, would probably wake up with a terrible hangover, Vaquier laced the hotel bar's bromo salts with strychnine. The next morning Mr. Jones did wake up with a hangover and as Vaquier had anticipated, took some of the medicine. Vaquier was actually present at the bar as Mr. Jones took the salts and complained they were bitter. His wife immediately examined the blue bottle and found they had been tampered with. Vaquier obligingly helped carry Mr. Jones up to his bedroom, but the innkeeper was dying. When Dr. Frederick Carle arrived, he was unable to help Mr. Jones who died minutes later. Although Vaquier had removed the bottle, Carle noticed several crystals lying on the floor near the bar. A chemical analysis revealed the presence of strychnine.

Vaquier remained at the Blue Anchor for a few more days. He was about to move to the Railway Hotel when Jones confronted him with her suspicions. The Frenchman moved to Woking on Apr. 4. When a picture of Vaquier was printed in the paper, the Southampton chemist who sold Vaquier the poison, recognized it and notified Scotland Yard. Vaquier was arrested at the Railway Hotel on Apr. 19, and tried at the Guildford Assizes the following July before Justice Horace Avory. He was found Guilty of murder and hanged at Wandsworth Prison on Aug. 12, 1924.

Vasil, George T., 1959- , U.S. In Fort Pierce, Fla., George Vasil, a slight boy of fourteen, tried to rape 12-year-old Pamela Vasser on Sept. 19, 1974. Physically unable to commit the act, Vasil crushed Vasser's skull with a rock, sexually assaulted her with a branch, and hid her corpse in the grass. Because of the "brutal and vicious" nature of the crime, Vasil was tried as an adult in a local circuit court three months later. He was found Guilty by a jury and, on Dec. 12, 1974, was sentenced to death in the electric chair. He had just turned fifteen. On Oct. 10, 1979, Vasil's sentence was changed to life in prison.

Velez, Luis S., 1949- , U.S. On the night of Sept. 16, 1975, Manhattan police officers Sergeant Frederick Reddy and Andrew Glover were checking a car parked in front of one of the tenement buildings on East Fifth Street between avenues A and B. Luis S. Velez pulled out a loaded revolver and shot both officers before they could draw their guns. He later said that he was afraid they would arrest him on bank robbery charges. Manhattan district attorney Robert Morgenthau recommended that Velez be allowed to plead to lesser charges of second-degree murder, rather than face the death penalty if convicted. In requesting that Judge Burton B. Roberts of the State Supreme Court accept the plea, Assistant District Attorney Robert J. Lehner cited a June 1976 U.S. Supreme Court ruling which raised questions about the constitutionality of the mandatory statute in New York which demands execution in cases of the murder of prison guards or police officers.

At a two-hour hearing, during which Velez repeatedly laughed whenever the crime was mentioned, Justice Roberts explained, "...It is in the public's interest to accept the plea." The prosecutor feared that the state's new death penalty law might be invalid or that a first-degree murder conviction would have resulted in a costly retrial. Velez remained standing with his arms folded throughout most of the hearing and told Roberts he shot the officers after they called him racist names. Criticism of the reduced charges plea came from the officers widows and from U.S. Senator James Buckley who called it "an affront to every policeman, every wife of a policeman, and every widow of an officer slain in the line of duty." On Nov. 22, 1976, Justice Roberts sentenced Velez to a 25-year-to-life jail term. When Velez told Roberts in court, "I have no regrets," Roberts called the convicted man a "lying, despicable, cowardly, brutal, thieving human being." Velez maintained that he had been the victim of the inequitable rules of a "police state," adding, "If I don't get dignity, I take it." District Attorney Morgenthau recommended that Velez never be granted parole.

Vernon, Roger (**Robert,** AKA: **Charles Lacroix; Georges Lacroix**), prom. 1936-37, Brit.-Fr. On Jan. 24, 1936, the body of 56-year-old Max Kassel, also known as Red Maxie or Scarface, was discovered by a carpenter riding his bicycle outside St. Albans, Hertfordshire. The maker's labels had been removed from his clothing and, although no money was in his pockets, an expensive ring remained on his finger. Marks on his knuckles and face indicated that he had struggled for his life. Scotland Yard Inspector Sharpe obtained a photograph and fingerprints of the man. He had been both a pimp and a white slave trader in earlier years, and owned a small jewelry shop which served as a front for his fencing. Under the alias of "Allard," Kassel had pretended to be a French Canadian.

Scotland Yard was soon on the trail of Roger Vernon, an ex-convict who had some business dealings with Kassel. The two had fought about the debt on the Jan. 23, 1936. Vernon's girlfriend, Suzanne Bertron, a prostitute, was implicated in the crime; it was later deduced that the murder had taken place in her London apartment in the Soho district. Vernon and Bertron were arrested at a Paris Hotel, where they had gone after they fled Great Newport Street. Both were tried in Paris, because of a French law which prohibited their extradition. On Apr. 29, the Paris jury deliberated for forty minutes before finding Vernon Guilty of premeditated murder but with extenuating circumstances. He was sentenced to ten years hard labor. Bertron was acquitted on charges of being an accessory.

***Veronica* Mutineers,** 1902-03, Brit. In October 1902, the barque *Veronica* set sail on a voyage filled with mutiny and murder. Under the command of Captain Alexander Shaw, the *Veronica,* with a crew of twelve, set sail from Ship Island in the Gulf of Mexico for Montevideo. The captain and his officers were known as rough taskmasters of the old school. The remainder of the crew included Gustav Rau and Otto Monsson, the ringleaders of the impending mutiny. Their intentions were clear when they both brought guns on board. Another rough character, Willem Smith and 19-year-old Harry Flohr, eventually joined the Germans in the mutiny.

Although it definitely was not a happy ship, things went well until they were becalmed in the Atlantic off Brazil. On Dec. 8, 1902, after a minor altercation, First Officer Alexander MacLeod was beaten and thrown overboard. After holding the captain and second mate hostage for several days, the men killed them and put the other four seamen overboard. That left Rau, Monsson, Smith, Flohr and the ship's cook. After setting the ship afire, they set sail in a lifeboat and were picked up by a passing ship which took them to a Brazilian port. From there they boarded a British ship, and on the way back to England Harry Flohr and the ship's cook confessed. The remaining three mutineers were tried for mutiny and found Guilty. Monsson was let off because of his youth, but Rau and Smith were hanged at Liverpool's Walton Prison on June 2, 1903.

Vidal, Ginette, 1931- , Fr. Although Gerard Osselin had signed a contract giving his lover the right to kill him if he was unfaithful, the contract did not keep her from being tried for murder in a court of law. Osselin and a somewhat older neighbor, Ginette Vidal, fell in love and left their families to set up housekeeping together. The pair entered into a contract which provided that if either of them was unfaithful, the aggrieved party could kill the guilty party.

In November 1972, Ginette found evidence that Osselin was seeing his former wife. In keeping with the terms of the contract, she picked up a gun and shot him to death as he slept. After staying alone with the corpse for a number of days, acting as if he were still alive, the police, alerted by the Osselin family, broke in and arrested Vidal. Vidal proudly displayed the contract which she believed was complete justification for her actions. The French courts did not agree. She was convicted and sent to prison.

Vollman, John Jacob, 1938-   , Can. On May 13, 1958, 16-year-old Gaetane Bouchard of Edmundston, New Brunswick, failed to return home after a shopping trip. Her father, Wilfrid Bouchard, contacted his daughter's 20-year-old boyfriend John Vollman. Vollman said he had broken off their relationship, and planned to marry someone else. After notifying police of his daughter's disappearance, Bouchard and his 15-year-old son, Jean Guy Bouchard, went down to the local lover's retreat area, a gravel pit on the outskirts of town. They found a suede slipper, and then the body of the murdered girl. She had been stabbed and her body dragged over the ground. Plaster casts were made of automobile tire tracks found near the pit, and two minuscule chips of green paint were discovered.

A farmer remembered seeing Bouchard and a friend get into a green Pontiac with Maine license plates, and two other witnesses recalled seeing Bouchard sitting next to the driver in the same car. One of Bouchard's schoolmates later claimed that Vollman had a reputation for wanting to "go too far." Questioned by officers, Vollman denied any involvement, but the paint chips found at the scene fit spots on his car, and a strand of his hair was found clutched in Bouchard's fist. Tried on Nov. 4, 1958, in Edmundston, before Judge Arthur L. Anglin, Vollman pleaded not guilty. He was defended by attorney J.A. Pichette. Albany M. Robichaud handled the prosecution. Vollman later claimed a loss of memory resulting from psychic shock as explanation for why he could not remember the events of the day of the girl's death. The jury found him Guilty of murder and he was sentenced to death. On Feb. 14, 1959, the sentence was commuted to life imprisonment.

---

von Sydow, Frederick, prom. 1932, Swed. On Mar. 4, 1932, a triple murder was committed on the small resort island of Mortnas, off the Swedish coast near Stockholm.

The victims, Mr. and Mrs. Zetterberger, and Mrs. Zetterberger's sister, were beaten to death with a piece of iron pipe. Their house had been ransacked and the contents of their safe stolen. Chief Police Inspector Thour soon learned that Zetterberger had loaned money recently, and that several of his investments were failing. A bank guard and a cab driver informed the police inspector that Zetterberger had visited the home of Swedish aristocrat Baron Hjalmar von Sydow not long before he was killed. Von Sydow contributed no new information, but Thour observed that he seemed overwrought and unnerved. A new twist in the case developed when von Sydow was found dead, killed with his housekeeper and a maid. There was evidence of an intense struggle, and a crushed piece of silk from a woman's slip was found under the murdered man's body. The murder weapon, an iron rod, was found in the manager's office of the Tanger restaurant. A cab driver recalled picking up an attractive young couple and taking them to von Sydow's address, where they told him to wait, reappearing a half hour later and ordering him to drive them to the Tanger. Baron von Sydow's son, Frederick von Sydow, a student at Upsala University, came to Stockholm, and talked to police, but was unable to add anything to the investigation.

Inspector Thour went to Commissioner Gustavason and said he believed he knew the identity of the murderers and would need to use the baron's son to capture them. Gustavason agreed, with misgivings, to the plan of having the son stay at the baron's apartment. At 10 p.m., Thour and Gustavason walked to the door of von Sydow's apartment and heard a stifled scream from inside. Thour lunged for the door, broke it open, and watched a young woman felled by a gunshot. Rushing towards the door where the gunfire had come from, Thour was stopped by Frederick von Sydow, who told him he was too late, then turned his gun on himself and fired. With his wife as an accomplice, von Sydow had committed all of the murders. The couple, who had been heavy drinkers and lived wildly in the two years since they met and wed, had turned to Zetterberger to borrow money when the baron, disgusted with their lifestyle, had finally refused to finance them any longer. When Zetterberger went directly to the baron to demand payment, he told the money lender to have his son arrested for the debt. Rejecting the idea of jail, the son had chosen murder, and suicide, as his way out.

Vontsteen, Franciscus Wynand, prom. 1971, S. Afri. A real estate agent in Pretoria, South Africa, Franciscus Wynand Vontsteen met Sonjia Raffanti in 1967, and became her lover. Vontsteen was jealous and possessive of Raffanti, who married police officer Francois Swanepoel two days after meeting Vontsteen. When her husband was posted to official duties on the northern border of South Africa, Vontsteen and Raffanti moved in together, and she became pregnant with his child. When the child was born, Swanepoel accepted it as his own, and Vontsteen became increasingly jealous.

On July 3, 1971, the Swanepoels came back to their house to discover that they had been robbed, and a pistol stolen. Four days later, Raffanti claimed she had been accosted on the street by a native who carried her husband's gun, and threatened to shoot her. On the night of Aug. 2, she was heard shouting that there was a native in the house, just before her husband was found dead from gunshot wounds. A local man soon came forward to say that Vontsteen had asked him to help murder Swanepoel. Told that Sonjia had confessed, Vontsteen admitted stealing the pistol and firing two shots into Swanepoel's head while his wife lay beside him in bed. They were tried together for murder in Pretoria in 1971, a trial that resulted in Sonjia receiving a fifteen-year prison sentence and Vontsteen hanging for his crime in October 1971.

===

Vucetic, Slobodan, 1944- , and **Simic, Slobodan**, 1949- , and **Potkonjac, Vjekoslav**, 1942- , Ger. At the very beginning of 1971, Werner Schmidt and his wife were driving home from a New Year's celebration in Hennef, Ger. To avoid the drunks on the autobahn, the Schmidts took a seldom-used country road that led through the villages of Neunkirchen, Wohlfahrt, and Much. It was a cold, blustery night with temperatures near zero.

Suddenly a naked man appeared before them in the roadway, waving frantically. Mrs. Schmidt, who had been dozing, did not see the figure in the snow and encouraged her husband to keep driving.

At 5 a.m., Hans-Dieter Mueller drove down the same road on his way to work. Although Mueller saw a man lying beside the road, he did not stop. When he later reported the incident to Constable Gunther Weber in Wohlfahrt, police investigated and found the body of a young man dressed in only a pair of briefs with his feet tied together with baling wire.

The victim was 18-year-old Ulrich Nacken, an electrician who had failed to come home the night before after celebrating the new year at the Toeff-Toeff Discotheque in Cologne. His parents told police that he had left his home in the 1966 gray Ford automobile he had purchased a month earlier. It was determined that death was caused by freezing, not by the blows to the face which Nacken had suffered. A trail led 200 yards back into the woods from where the body was found. The evidence indicated that the victim had been tied to a tree, but had managed to extricate himself and hop to the side of the road. A bulletin was issued in the surrounding area for the gray Ford. Two junior patrolmen, Arnold Klein and Leopold Brettweiler, spotted the vehicle between Wohlfahrt and Neunkirchen.

The driver attempted to escape from the pursuing officers, but was trapped on a dead-end road. The operator of the vehicle was a Yugoslav national named Slobodan Vucetic. A quick search of the car uncovered Ulrich Nacken's driver's license in the glove compartment. It was apparent that one or more accomplices had escaped just before the police arrived. Police dog patrols easily tracked down the second man who was identified as Slobodan Simic. Vucetic immediately accused Simic of killing Nacken.

By the time they had reached the police station, a third man, 29-year-old Vjekoslav Potkonjac, was also implicated in the murder. According to the confessions of the three men, they were drinking beer at the Toeff-Toeff when Nacken stopped by. On the spur of the moment they decided to abduct Nacken and steal his car. They forced him to the car at knifepoint, bound him with wire they found in the car, and put him in trunk. After visiting Simic's girlfriend in Siegburg, they stripped Nacken, beat him, and tied him to a tree in the woods. The three Yugoslavians might have slipped through the police dragnet and returned to Yugoslavia undetected, but they became curious and were returning to the scene of the crime when they were spotted by the two officers.

On Nov. 30, 1971, Vucetic, Simic, and Potkonjac were found Guilty of premeditated murder and sentenced to life imprisonment. Werner Schmidt received six months for failing to assist a person in danger, a serious crime under German law.

===

W

Waddingham, Dorothea Nancy, 1899-1936, Brit. Dorothea Waddingham ran an unlicensed nursing home in Nottingham, England, the setting for one of Britain's most celebrated murders in the 1930s. She entered the health care profession later in life. As a young woman she had worked in a factory, and then as a ward-orderly at the Burton-on-Trent Work-house Infirmary. Her criminal record was fairly extensive. It contained several convictions for a string of petty thefts and frauds. While nursing her elderly husband, Thomas Willoughby Leech, through the final stages of throat cancer, she decided to take in

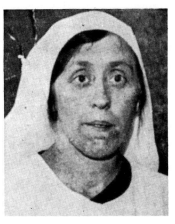

Dorothea Waddingham, the lethal British nurse.

the sick and elderly as a way of providing for the needs of her five children, who ranged in age from eighteen months to nine years. She was assisted by her lover, 39-year-old Ronald Joseph Sullivan, who took on a greater role following the death of the infirm Thomas Leech. Waddingham and Sullivan opened their nursing home on Devon Drive in Nottingham in 1935.

Neither Waddingham nor Sullivan were licensed to care for the sick or the elderly, but this did not dissuade them from operating an increasingly lucrative business. The small, out-of-the-way home received accreditation from the County Nursing Association, which sent them two patients in January 1935: 89-year-old Mrs. Baguley, and her 50-year-old daughter Ada Louisa. Baguley was bedridden and Ada Baguley suffered from creeping paralysis, which had rendered her virtually helpless. The two patients required constant care—more care apparently than Waddingham and Sullivan had anticipated, for they allegedly complained of how little they were paid in return for the care they were required to give the two women. On May 6, 1935, Ada Baguley rewrote her will, leaving her entire estate of £1,600 to Waddingham on the condition that the nurse would care for both her and her mother until their deaths. No one was particularly shocked when the elderly Baguley died on May 12, 1935. Her death was officially attributed to old age. Four months later, however, on Sept. 11, 1935, Ada Baguley also died. The cause of death cited on the death certificate, cerebral hemorrhage, was derived from Waddingham's descriptions rather than from an actual examination of the body. Waddingham allegedly told the doctor that the old woman had consumed too many of the chocolates given to her by her friend, Mrs. Briggs. A coroner's autopsy was not ordered. There was no concrete

evidence at this point to link Baguley's death to Nurse Waddingham.

Immediately following Ada Baguely's death, Waddingham produced a letter dated Aug. 29, 1935. It was purportedly written by the deceased woman and said, "I desire to be cremated at my death, for health's sake. And it is my wish to remain with Nurse and my last wish is my relatives shall not know of my death." In keeping with the law, Waddingham forwarded this letter to Dr. Cyril Banks, the Nottingham medical officer with a request to be allowed to proceed with the cremation. Waddingham's eagerness aroused Dr. Banks's suspicions and he ordered an autopsy. According to Dr. Roche Lynch, who performed the autopsy, there was no evidence that death had been caused by cerebral hemorrhage, as shown on the death certificate. Instead, he found more than three grains of morphine in the corpse, a sufficient amount to suggest morphine poisoning as the cause of death. Because of the results of this autopsy, Mrs. Baguley's remains were exhumed and autopsied. Again, a sufficient amount of morphine was found in the corpse to convince the doctor that Mrs. Baguley too had been poisoned.

Dorothea Waddingham and Joseph Sullivan were jointly charged in Ada Baguley's murder. Their trial began on Feb. 24, 1936, at the Nottingham Assizes before Justice Rayner Goddard. Goddard quickly ruled that because of insufficient evidence, a verdict of Not Guilty should be returned against Joseph Sullivan. This decision left Waddingham to face the murder charges alone. When confronted with the coroner's evidence regarding the amounts of morphine found in the dead women's bodies, Waddingham admitted giving morphine to the Baguleys, but claimed that she had done so on Dr. H.H. Manfield's orders. Manfield denied prescribing morphine for either of the Baguleys but told the court that he had prescribed it for a Mrs. Kemp, another of Nurse Waddingham's patients, who had died at the nursing home in February 1935. He suggested that it was this morphine that Waddingham had given to the Baguleys.

The evidence against Waddingham continued to mount, despite the fact that Ada Baguley was directed to the Waddingham home by the County Nursing Association, and was not coerced by either Waddingham or Sullivan. Dr. Jacob, the long-time family physician, testified that he had visited Ada Baguley just two weeks before she died. She showed no outward signs of approaching death, and her paralysis, in its present form, would have taken several more years to become fatal. Additional evidence introduced during the trial showed that on the day before Baguley's death, Waddingham fed her two rather large meals. "Can you as men of common sense," Justice Goddard asked, "think that anybody in their senses would give a woman suffering from such sharp abdominal pains that morphia had to be given her three nights, two helpings of pork, baked potatoes and fruit pie?"

Nurse Waddingham was found Guilty and hanged at Winson Green Prison in Birmingham on Apr. 16, 1936, despite the jury's urgent plea for mercy. Justice Goddard was less inclined to be charitable because of her sex. "I see no reason why a woman convicted of murder should not hang," he told the royal commission on capital punishment afterward. Nurse Waddingham had the dubious distinction of becoming one of the few women executed in Britain during the twentieth century.

Waite, Arthur Warren (AKA: Dr. Walters), 1889-1917, U.S.

It was hard not to like the personable Dr. Arthur Waite. While it was true that he had committed two fiendishly calculated murders and felt no apparent regrets, the jurors, impressed with his charm, were barely able to stifle their laughter after listening to him tick off one humorous anecdote after another. Dr. Waite was something of anomaly: a physician sworn to uphold the Hippocratic oath, yet scornful of all it stood for, at least in regard to his in-laws.

Arthur Warren Waite was born and raised in Grand Rapids, Mich., his parents struggling farmers who could not provide for their son the life he envisioned for himself. Realizing that his future would be inextricably tied to the soil unless he did something about it, Waite set his eyes on Clara Peck, the pampered daughter of lumber baron John E. Peck, one of the wealthiest men in town. Much attention was given to their courtship, which Clara's father altogether opposed.

Waite attended the University of Michigan before completing his studies at the University of Glasgow in Scotland. He sent back glowing reports to his parents and his thoroughly captivated girlfriend in Grand Rapids, neglecting to mention that he had cheated his way through medical school and had forged false credentials.

With his fresh degree in dentistry, Waite accepted a position with a mining firm in South Africa. While serving as the company's chief dentist, the social-climbing Waite attempted to marry a wealthy young heiress but was thwarted by the woman's father. He was released from his duties before the contract with the mining firm expired, returning to Michigan $20,000 richer and ready to plot new strategy. Clara, happy now that the conquering hero was coming home, decided to make him her husband. On Christmas Day 1914 she proposed against the stern admonishments of 76-year-old John Peck. Nevertheless they were married on Sept. 9, 1915.

As a gesture of reconciliation the elderly Peck gave them a rent-free apartment on Manhattan's fashionable Riverside Drive and a generous allowance of $300 a month. Waite opened a dental practice, but found the work tedious and dull. He spent most of his time on the tennis courts, a throwback to his days in Scotland where he was a reigning court pro. To her concerned parents, Clara wrote, "He's Metropolitan Champion. Isn't that wonderful?"

During these idle times, Waite met a glamorous socialite named Margaret Weaver Horton, wife of an aeronautical engineer of some renown. They began an affair, a costly one no doubt, since Mrs. Horton expected only the best. Their suite at the Plaza Hotel cost Waite a small fortune. The $300 allowance from his father-in-law did not go far enough to meet his mounting expenses. "I expected $50,000 outright!" he thundered to his wife, who received fewer and fewer kind words from him each day. Seeing no other way out of his difficulties, Waite concocted a hare-brained scheme to murder his in-laws and his wife and seize control of the family estate.

He waited until Jan. 10, 1916, when his mother-in-law arrived for a short visit, to put his plan into action. "I started poisoning her from the very first meal after she arrived," Waite would later tell the court. "I gave her six assorted tubes of pneumonia, diphtheria, and influenza germs in her food. When she finally became ill and took to her bed I ground up twelve five-grain veronal tablets and gave her that, too, last thing at night." During her short, unexpected illness, Warren doted on his mother-in-law, bringing her flowers and footwarmers. When she died on Jan. 20, Waite suggested that the only correct thing to do under the circumstances would be to cremate the woman. It was her last wish, he explained.

Peck arrived in town to console himself the first week of February. Within days the old man began feeling ill. As Waite later explained, "I used to insert tubes of typhoid, pneumonia, and diphtheria in his soups and rice pudding. Once I gave him a nasal spray filled with tuberculosis bacteria." Peck was a robust, healthy individual for his age. His system resisted the deadly germs in a way that mystified Waite. "Still nothing happened," he said. I tried to give him pneumonia by putting water in his Wellingtons, damping his sheets, opening his bedroom window and wetting the seat of the automobile before taking him out for a drive." Waite then administered eighteen grains of arsenic, which debilitated the old man but still failed to kill him. Waite ended the ordeal by smothering him with a pillow on Mar. 12.

Waite consoled his wife as best as he could, again suggesting that the body be cremated to spare the family needless torment. Percy Peck, Clara's older brother, drew the line. He insisted that his father be returned to Grand Rapids for proper burial. Warren acquiesced but chose to

Defiant dentist Dr. Warren Waite used poison on his victims.

Waite's father-in-law, John E. Peck, murdered.

A host of germs unleashed by Waite killed Mrs. Peck.

Mrs. Margaret Weaver Horton

Mrs. Peck and Mrs. Warren Waite.

Experts examining Waite's germ lab.

remain behind in New York while the family went to Michigan. Percy Peck received a telegram from a friend, Mrs. Hardwicke, which confirmed his own suspicions about his brother-in-law. "Don't allow cremation until an autopsy as been carried out," it read. The embalmed remains were examined and arsenic and chloroform were found. Advised of these developments, Clara still refused to believe her husband was a murderer. Catherine Peck, Clara's aunt, supported Waite. "I like him so well I gave him a $3,000 wedding present," she added. It was later learned that Aunt Catherine was also on Waite's murder list.

Meanwhile, the New York Police located an atomizer belonging to Waite that contained typhoid and anthrax germs. It was clear by now who the murderer was. The police questioned Oliver Eugene Kane, the embalmer who prepared Peck's body for burial. He told the officers that Waite offered him a $9,000 bribe to inject arsenic in the embalming fluid.

Kane accepted the offer but later reneged and kept the money anyway. "I was so scared I buried it (the arsenic) out in the sand at Orient Point on the tip of Long Island," he said. Waite tried to kill himself with sleeping pills but, having failing badly, blamed the attempt on insanity. "A bad man from Egypt dwells in my body," he said. "He makes me do things! He struggles for possession of my soul."

Waite broke down and confessed the whole sordid affair to the police. He told of his early experiences in the university and how he had forged his postgraduate certificate at Glasgow, as well as the sterling newspaper accounts of his achievements in Europe and South Africa. He secured the deadly poisons and bacteria slides while working at Flower Hospital in New York. "In November 1915, to test my knowledge and to test the effect of germs, I inoculated myself with cultures of anthrax, typhoid, and pneumonia. By the time Mrs. Peck arrived in January 1916 I was ready for her," he told police.

Waite said that he planned to kill his wife because "she was not my equal in anything and I meant to find a more beautiful wife." Experts in psychiatry attempted to show that anyone who killed with such cheerful abandon must be truly crazy. The jury, which had enjoyed listening to the light-hearted antics of the young dentist, nevertheless returned a verdict of Guilty.

Arthur Warren Waite was put to death in the electric chair on May 24, 1917. As his execution time loomed near, the doctor showed remarkable composure. In the hours before his execution, he read passages from the Bible and a selected verse from John Keats.

Walden, Bernard Hugh, d.1959, Brit. "I am not as other men," Bernard Walden told the court at his 1959 murder trial. "I am a cripple and must be armed to put me on fair terms with others...I have an absolute right to kill." His chilling statements were without compassion, yet the jury recommended mercy.

Walden was a lecturer at Rotherham Technical College. Convicted of a homosexual offense in 1949, the dowdy teacher became infatuated with a woman on campus. When she spurned his advances, Walden shot and killed both the girl and her boyfriend. He was diagnosed as suffering from chronic paranoid development, but despite the unsoundness of mind, Walden was hanged at Leeds in August 1959. His execution was controversial in light of the recently enacted Homicide Act which generally limited the death sentence to individuals who killed while in pursuit of criminal activities.

Walker, Ernest Albert, 1905- , Brit. When Ernest Walker of London lost his mother, he appears to have also lost his mind. This was the only explanation he could give for murdering 14-year-old Raymond Charles Davis one night in April 1922. At the time, Walker worked for Colonel Charles Trotter as a personal footman. One night when Trotter was out, Walker summoned a courier from the Sloane Street offices of the District Messenger Company. According to a carefully prepared thirteen-point agenda Walker had prepared, he would torture and murder whomever the company sent over. The unfortunate victim was Davis.

When the vicious act was carried out, Walker fled the house and boarded a train at the Charing Cross station, bound for Kent. There, he cornered a policeman and confessed to what he had done. A court-appointed physician determined that Walker suffered from epileptic automatism, and was not able to fully comprehend what he had done. Consequently, the 17-year-old boy was found Guilty, but insane. He was sent to the Broadmoor Institution. Walker was ordered released in 1937, after the authorities determined that he no longer posed a threat to society.

Walker, Jesse, 1899-1920, U.S. In 1919, at the encouragement of an acquaintance, Henry Rauth, Jesse Walker, twenty, and fellow seaman Guy Nichols, decided to rob a small candy shop in Brooklyn, N.Y. According to Rauth, the owner of the shop, Samuel Wolchak, kept large amounts of cash in a drawer under the counter. While Rauth stood guard outside, Walker and Nichols entered the store. Walker approached the counter and pointed his gun at Wolchak. Instead of surrendering, the shop owner threw a punch at Walker. Without hesitation, Walker shot Wolchak at point blank range, rupturing an artery in Wolchak's chest.

Walker found a two dollar bill in Wolchak's pocket and four more dollars in the cash drawer. In the search for the money, however, Walker managed to get blood on the two dollar bill and on his shirt collar. With the paltry rewards from the crime, the three men left. Walker discarded the blood stained collar and washed off the two dollar bill in a room the three men had previously rented. At a nearby clothing store Walker used the $2 bill to purchase a new collar. Although the officer assigned to investigate Wolchak's murder got as far as finding the bloodstained collar and tracing Walker to the haberdasher's where he got a reasonable description of the murderer, the trail went cold and the case was set aside as one that would most likely remain unsolved.

Walker's crime to this point had little about it of distinction. However, Walker, who was evidently of below average intelligence, had begun keeping a careful diary several years before. Walker's impetus for this effort was a story he had read in the newspapers about a suspect in a murder case who was cleared of the crime because of the discovery of a diary in which he had carefully recorded his activities on the date of the crime. The man in the account that Walker had read was exonerated when the alibi his diary showed checked out. In the simplistic belief that the keeping of the diary was some sort of magic token, Walker from this point on carefully recorded his every activity—including criminal ones. Some months after the Wolchak murder, the Brooklyn police were notified by police in Matoon, Ill., that they had apprehended a man in the theft of a fur coat in whose possession they found a diary which detailed a number of crimes in the New York area. Among the entries for the first week in November was the Wolchak shooting, with all the details of the crime including the names of Walker's accomplices. Carefully inscribed on the inside cover of the diary was the name, Jesse Walker. Walker was returned to New York where he, Nichols and Rauth were tried for first-degree murder. Rauth was acquitted when it was determined that he had remained outside during the commission of the crime. Nichols and Walker, however, were found Guilty. Both men were executed in the electric chair some time later.

Walker, Thomas Ray, Jr., 1944-80, U.S. Thomas Walker placed a call to Dallas television station KDFW from outside a grocery store. He told the switchboard operator on Dec. 1, 1980, that "he had a good story to tell." Walker went on to say that he had shot and killed his wife Linda while she showered, and then called in his four children one by one to murder them. The children, ranging in age from eight to thirteen had been taken out of school for the day. Walker cited emotional despondency and the gnawing fear that his family could not get along without him in the event of his suicide.

The police were able to trace the location of the phone booth after Walker placed a second call to the station. As he stepped from the phone booth, he called to police, "Shoot me! Shoot me!" Walker ran from the scene, but was cut down by police gunfire. At the family home in southeast Dallas, police found the bodies of Linda Walker and her children—Tracie, thirteen; Tammy, eleven; Tommy, nine; and Nicholas, eight—exactly where he said they would be.

Walter, Albert, Jr., c.1908-36, U.S. Albert Walter, Jr., traveled to San Francisco from his home in the fashionable Back Bay section of Boston because, as he explained, he was afraid he might kill his wife Angela. Instead, he murdered a young college student named Blanche Cousins, whom he met on the transcontinental bus after the driver had stopped in Salt Lake City to pick up passengers. Cousins had worked as a bookkeeper at the Latter Day Saints Hospital in Idaho Falls, Idaho, for seven years before striking out for the big city. She was, according to her friend Dorothy Edmonds, "the most lonely person in the world. She always believed that a big city would give her the happiness other people had," Edmonds recalled. "She loved the theater and other things she couldn't get in Idaho Falls." In San Francisco Walter took the woman to an apartment he had rented the night of June 16, 1936. He strangled her after she refused his sexual advances. "I became highly inflamed but she stopped me at a certain point as she had done on previous occasions," he said. "Then I began to hate her. I have hated all women for years and all the hate I felt for women rose up in me right there." The next day he disposed of all his personal belongings before walking into the Bureau of Inspectors at police headquarters where he freely confessed his crime.

Walter explained that at the age of fourteen he had become permanently embittered against women following an unfortunate affair with an older woman who gave him syphilis. "I've tried to lead a normal life, but this hatred and bitterness keeps cropping up in spite of me. I left my wife in New York because I was afraid I'd kill her," he said, adding that his only wish was to be hanged and forgotten.

Angela Walter was located and together with her father-in-law they journeyed west. They told of Albert's erratic life, which included stints in the military, the legal profession, and sales. His fixation against women and his past history of sudden, unprovoked psychotic episodes culminated in murder. Despite his protestations, the defense entered an insanity plea, but state-appointed psychiatrists contended he was sane. Albert Walter was found Guilty of murder. He was executed on the gallows of San Quentin, Dec. 4, 1936.

Walter, Clarence, b.1893, U.S. On Feb. 5, 1934, in Los Angeles radio station KHJ's largest studio, cooking expert Mona Van Dyke was on the air, leading her audience through a recipe—"then add half a cup of sugar, stir well, and let it come to a boil,"—when a scream went out over the air waves. Van Dyke raised her voice and continued her broadcast, but it was not enough to block the screams that followed, a man's curses, the thud of a body falling to the ground, or the general sounds of a scuffle. Over all, station manager C.E. Wylie was heard calling out: "Tell everyone we're just rehearsing a dramatic act for a broadcast tomorrow!" Meanwhile, 21-year-old Edwin Wolverton lay dying from knife wounds to his head.

According to a police reports, 41-year-old Montana rancher Clarence Walter initially approached KHJ receptionist Grace Kane and, pointing to the studio, said, "You have a job waiting for me in there." When Kane asked for his name, Walter pulled a knife. "Never mind my name!" he shouted. "You've got a job for me in there!" He raised the knife, but Wolverton, a vacationing announcer from KFXJ in Grand Junction, Colo., and newsman Warren Fehlman rushed in to disarm him. Walter stabbed Wolverton in the head, however, before being subdued by more than twelve men. "I never saw him before in my life," Wolverton said as he went comatose, never to recover.

"I've been listening to that station," Walter said later, telling what led to the slaying. "I wanted them to let me work there. I wrote them letters asking for work. They answered me in a song they broadcast—('There's a Ring Around the Moon'). I recognized the message telling me to come to work every time I heard the song."

Walter was found Not Guilty by Judge Frank G. Swain after three psychiatrists agreed he was insane at the time of the killing. Committed to Mendocino State Hospital, he appeared again before Judge Swain in June 1935, to seek release on the grounds that he had recovered his sanity. The court ordered Walter to be removed from Mendocino State to a state mental institution in Montana.

Walters, Ann Carol, 1940-   , and **Walters, Wayne**, 1947-   , and **Bean, Harold Walter**, 1940-   , and **Bryon, Robert**, 1949-   , and **Egan, Robert Danny**, prom. 1982, U.S. For Dorothy and George Polulach, an elderly couple from Chicago's Southwest Side Polish neighborhood, their 1969 marriage was only the beginning of what they hoped to be the "golden years" of retirement. A dozen years later it ended tragically in suicide and murder.

Dorothy, a newspaper fashion artist, married George Polulach after his first wife had filed for divorce on the grounds of adultery. The daughter from the first marriage, Ann Carol Walters, harbored deep resentments against her stepmother for many years. At stake was a lavish inheritance and control of the family estate. George Polulach was a prosperous small businessman who owned several retail concerns. Ann Walters later contended that Dorothy had "tricked" her natural mother Frances into signing away the Chicago home, valued at $100,000. In 1979, George Polulach committed suicide. He was in failing health and despondent because of his advancing age. The widow continued to live a comfortable life in the Southwest Side bungalow, while Walters languished in comparative poverty with her husband Wayne and invalid mother in Florida. The tension continued to grow until Ann hired an ex-convict and mobster named Harold Bean to murder Dorothy for $7,500.

Dorothy Polulach, now eighty-one, expressed a feeling of growing apprehension to church officials and close friends. Three days later on Feb. 18, 1981, a man dressed as a priest entered the Polulach home. Dorothy Polulach was tied up and shot through the head twice by Bean. Robert Byron, thirty-three, and Robert Danny Egan, who had been recruited by Bean, rifled through the house overturning furniture and ransacking every room.

Chicago police traced the conspirators through phone company records, which showed a number of long distance calls between the Florida home of Walters, and a female accomplice of Bean in Chicago. Confronted by this evidence, Carol Ann tearfully confessed her role, and that of her husband. Harold Bean and Robert Byron were both convicted of murder and sentenced to death. Wayne Walters received a seven-year prison sentence for conspiracy. In return for his guilty plea on an armed violence charge, Robert Egan was sentenced to seven years. He had driven the getaway car. Ann Walters was handed a twenty-five year prison term on Jan. 18, 1982, by Judge James Bailey in the criminal court. She asked the judge for an early parole in order to care for her infirmed mother in Florida but was denied.

Wanderer, Carl Otto, 1887-1921, U.S. Chicago has had many classic murder cases but one of its most remarkable murders involved a war hero and two colorful newspapermen, Ben Hecht and Charles MacArthur, whose canny sleuthing solved the Ragged Stranger case. The culprit, Carl Otto Wanderer, appeared to be anything but a murderer clever enough to fool the police department and the press in two sensational killings. Born and raised in Chicago, Wanderer attended public schools and, upon graduation from eighth grade, began an apprenticeship as a butcher. His frugal German parents had raised him to be thrifty and law-abiding and nurtured in him a deep love of America. After opening a successful butcher shop in partnership with his father, Wanderer became obsessed with the exploits of Mexican bandit Pancho Villa, incessantly reading about the bloody raids Villa led into Texas border towns.

When volunteers were summoned to fill the ranks of the First Illinois Cavalry in 1916, Wanderer, a patriot to the core, gladly enlisted, telling his startled parents that he was off to fight Villa. He served under General John J. "Black Jack" Pershing and proved to be such an excellent leader of men that Wanderer, at the outbreak of WWI the following year, was promoted to the rank of lieutenant. Wanderer went to France and fought in all the major battles involving American troops. In 1919, he returned a hero, his chest covered with citations. The five-foot-ten-inch, brown-eyed

Carl Otto Wanderer signing his confession.

Wanderer, his brown hair thinning, was given a celebrity welcome in Chicago, the press lauding his overseas heroics. In the fall of that year, Wanderer met and married Ruth Johnson, an attractive 20-year-old. The war veteran and his wife moved into a small apartment with her parents. A few months later Ruth Wanderer proudly announced to her husband that she was pregnant and that the baby was expected the following year.

Unlike most expectant fathers, Carl Otto Wanderer was not delighted by the news. He became withdrawn and moody. He argued with his wife and in-laws constantly and whenever the unborn child was mentioned, he became enraged, slamming his powerful fists against walls before storming out of the apartment. Wanderer spent less time with his wife and was gone from his apartment for long periods of time. Some time later, his spirits seemed to lift and he asked his wife to go to the movies on the night of June 21, 1920. Upon returning to the apartment that night,

the couple entered the small vestibule of the building where they lived. The light in this area was off and Ruth Wanderer ran her hand along the wall, groping for the switch. According to Wanderer's later statement, he heard a voice say: "'Don't turn on the light!' I reached for my gun."

It was not then unusual for men to carry weapons. Chicago laws were lax about such conduct, and in the few years immediately following the war, it was the habit of many former soldiers to carry their service automatics. Wanderer said that the strange man in the dark foyer shouted obscenities at him and his wife and then fired a shot at them. More shots followed and Wanderer returned fire from his Colt .45-caliber automatic, emptying the clip in the direction of the intruder. Fourteen shots were fired by both men, all within a minute's time.

The noisy gunfire brought Ruth Wanderer's mother running. She entered the vestibule, switched on the light, and saw to her horror that her daughter was on the floor, mortally wounded with two bullets in her. Kneeling next to a man dressed in rags, also shot several times and in a dying condition, was Carl Wanderer. Possessed of rage, he was slamming his empty Colt against the dead man's head, screaming: "You've killed my wife, you bastard! You've killed my wife!"

Ruth Wanderer lived for only a few minutes, moaning to her mother: "My baby...my baby is dead." She died en route to the hospital.

The man dressed in shabby clothes, the Ragged Stranger as the press later dubbed him since his identity was unknown, was taken to Ravenswood Hospital. He never came out of a coma and died within a few hours. Police found only $3.80 in his pockets.

The public was shocked to learn of this heinous crime. Carl Otto Wanderer, an admirable war hero, had lost his lovely wife and unborn child to the maniacal whim of a savage killer and thief who struck in the darkness of Wanderer's own home. The war hero was again praised for courageously battling the ruthless murderer, again risking his life to save his pregnant wife. Newspapermen flocked to Wanderer, writing down his every word. These were few. His grief was hard and long and he had little to say after telling police about the attempted robbery and his gun battle with the would-be thief. Chicago newspapers gave front page coverage to the story for many days. Photos of Wanderer, his wife, and relatives stared back at stunned readers. Every aspect of the case was examined, and even the two big .45-caliber automatics, Wanderer's and that of the Ragged Stranger, were photographed side by side.

This photo disturbed Ben Hecht, a veteran crime reporter on the staff of the Chicago *Daily News*. Hecht studied the photo, shaking his head. The Ragged Stranger, he knew, had less than $4 to his name. Why then would he not pawn the automatic he was carrying for $15 or $20, rather than risking a random holdup, particularly one involving Wanderer who was known to carry a gun, and take the chance of being shot? None of it made any sense. Hecht thought about the *type* of weapons both men possessed. Wanderer had held on to his service automatic as a matter of habit. Hecht thought it odd that the Ragged Stranger possessed the same kind of weapon. Perhaps this unknown killer had also been a WWI veteran.

Hecht talked with his good friend Charles MacArthur, a reporter for the Chicago *Herald-Examiner*, who also agreed that the fact that Wanderer and the thief owned the

The great writing team of Charles MacArthur, at typewriter, and Ben Hecht; they solved the Wanderer case in 1920 when both were working as Chicago reporters.

same kind of weapon was odd, perhaps suspicious. MacArthur checked with the Colt Arms Manufacturing Company and learned that the Ragged Stranger's weapon had been sold for the first time in 1913 to a Chicago sporting goods firm. By checking the records of this store, MacArthur discovered that the automatic was sold to a Peter Hoffman, a Chicago telephone repairman.

MacArthur interviewed Hoffman and learned that the repairman had sold the automatic to a mailman some years earlier, one Fred Wanderer, a cousin of Carl Wanderer. MacArthur asked him if he still had the weapon. No, said Fred Wanderer. He had loaned the automatic to Carl on the very day of the shooting. Fred Wanderer believed that the weapon he had given his cousin was the one Carl Wanderer had used to defend himself. When he was told by MacArthur that this was the weapon the Ragged Stranger had fired, Fred Wanderer bolted to his feet, bug-

eyed. He fainted dead away.

Hecht and MacArthur compared notes, and before going to the police with the information about the automatic, decided to give Wanderer the benefit of the doubt. The automatics might have gotten mixed up and Wanderer's weapon wrongly identified as that of the Ragged Stranger. Hecht decided to confront Wanderer. He went to the war hero's apartment, entering by the back porch. He stood for a moment, and through the screen door, heard Wanderer humming and whistling happily. He peered into the kitchen to see Wanderer pressing a pair of pants. The war hero stood barechested performing this domestic chore with the carefree abandon of a man who had miraculously been stripped of grief while his wife and unborn child had been buried only days earlier.

Hecht knocked on the door and asked to come inside. Wanderer cheerfully welcomed him. After a few minutes of idle chatter, Hecht asked to use Wanderer's washroom. Inside the bathroom, Hecht noticed Wanderer's bathrobe hanging on a door hook. A strange object dangled from its pocket. Hecht pulled out a woman's silk stocking. Then he pulled another stocking from the pocket. In the other pocket, he discovered lipstick, mascara, and rouge. From the breast pocket of the bathrobe, the snooping Hecht pulled several letters Wanderer had written, love letters. These had been written to a man. The reporter quickly realized that the virile veteran of a dozen bloody battles on the Western Front was homosexual.

The reporter stepped from the tiny bathroom, quickly explaining to Wanderer that he was working against a deadline and had to rush back to his newspaper. Hecht rushed to join MacArthur and explained his discovery. MacArthur told Hecht that he had checked on the guns and that Wanderer's weapon was, indeed, his service automatic and that the other weapon was the one Fred Wanderer had loaned to Carl. Both men then went to the police. MacArthur explained the discrepancy of the automatic and how the Ragged Stranger's gun belonged to a Wanderer relative. Hecht then told detectives how Wanderer had been acting that morning and how he suspected the war hero of being homosexual. This, Hecht theorized, was the motive for Wanderer's killing *both* the Ragged Stranger and his wife. Ruth Johnson Wanderer was pregnant with Wanderer's child and his homosexuality had so rebelled against the idea of heterosexual love producing a child that he could not bear the thought of it. He had arranged the murder of his wife rather than go on living a sexual double life.

Police lieutenant Mike Loftus listened and nodded. He ordered Wanderer picked up and when the war hero arrived, Loftus interrogated him, pointing out that the automatic used by the Ragged Stranger was the property of Fred Wanderer. "This is some mistake," Wanderer said.

He began a long-winded story about how the automatics had been a part of a large shipment of weapons sent to several training camps during the war and that the weapon used by the Ragged Stranger could not have been his cousin's weapon. He said he did not remember borrowing Fred Wanderer's weapon.

Meanwhile, Hecht checked the bank accounts of Wanderer and his dead wife Ruth. He learned that on the day of her death Ruth Wanderer had withdrawn her life savings of $1,500 from the Second Security Bank. The bold Hecht searched Wanderer's apartment and found $1,500 in bills taped behind a bureau. He took the money to police headquarters and then was allowed to confront Wanderer. He told the war hero that he knew about his love for a man named James, saying that he had read the love letters Wanderer had written but not mailed to James. Hecht decided to bluff his way along, telling Wanderer: "James is coming to see you, Carl. I just talked with him."

The tough-looking war hero began to tremble. "No, not here! Don't let him come here," pleaded Wanderer. "Oh, my God!" Wanderer turned to Lieutenant Loftus and admitted that he was a homosexual and had married Ruth Johnson for her money, even though he hated her. He hated all women, Wanderer said. "The thought that she was going to have my child was repulsive," he said. He said he feared that once the child was born, his affair with James would collapse. He had killed his wife and the Ragged Stranger, he said, to preserve his secret relationship with another man. It had been simple, explained Wanderer. He had spent several nights in skid row bars until he met an ex-Canadian soldier who said his name was Al Watson.

Down on his luck, Watson was looking for a job. Wanderer told him he had an idea that would make Watson some quick money. He explained to Watson that because of his effeminate manners, his wife had doubted his record as a war hero and that he wanted to reaffirm his heroic image. Watson was to stage a fake holdup of the pair when they returned from the movies on June 21, 1920. Watson would wait in the vestibule, and when Wanderer appeared with his wife Watson was to pretend to rob them. Wanderer would hand Watson a gun in the dark and when his wife switched on the light, Watson would point the weapon at the pair and demand their money. Wanderer would then fake throwing a powerful punch that would knock Watson down who would then scramble to his feet and flee. Wanderer would thus become a hero in his wife's eyes.

This was the scenario Wanderer created for Watson, except that when the couple arrived home on the night of the killings, Wanderer did not hand Watson the gun. He fired both automatics at the same time, emptying their clips, firing at his wife and at Watson simultaneously, eliminating a wife he did not want and creating a dead scapegoat for

her murder. He knew that Mrs. Johnson would rush to the vestibule once she heard the firing, and to convince her that he had been defending Ruth, he placed one of the automatics in the hand of the fatally wounded Watson and then leaped upon his victim, striking him in his pretended rage at Watson's ostensible murder of his wife.

Wanderer went through two lengthy trials and was convicted of killing both Ruth Johnson Wanderer and Al Watson. He was sentenced to death. While awaiting execution, Wanderer was visited many times by the very men who had unearthed the evidence that convicted him. They became friends, playing poker together in the Cook County Jail's holding cell. At one point, the penniless Wanderer (his wife's money had been returned to the family), was loaned $5 by MacArthur, an act of kindness that caused Wanderer to ask MacArthur if he could do *him* a favor. MacArthur thought for a moment and then said, yes, there was something the condemned man could do. "Just before you step off the platform, you'll be asked if you have any last words," MacArthur said. "Let me write out a speech for you."

"I'm not good at memorizing," Wanderer said.

"It's okay," MacArthur told him. "You can read it."

MacArthur, with Hecht's help, wrote a long tirade against the editors of both the *Herald-Examiner* and the *Daily News*, the bosses of Hecht and MacArthur. On the day of Wanderer's execution, Mar. 19, 1921, MacArthur gave the speech to the condemned man, who was taken into the courtyard of the old Criminal Courts Building where a high gallows stood. Wanderer mounted the scaffold, with dozens of witnesses standing in the courtyard, including Hecht and MacArthur. He clutched the speech the two scribes had delighted in writing but he never got a chance to read it. The reporters had forgotten that condemned prisoners about to be hanged were tied hand and foot. Wanderer could only look down at the typewritten sheets rolled up in his hand which was pinioned to his side. He shrugged, and as a way of compensating his friend MacArthur, sang an old ballad, "Dear Old Pal of Mine," as the rope was placed around his neck. A black hood was placed over Wanderer's head, but he sang on in a smooth voice until the trapdoor sprang open and Wanderer's singing was cut off by the jerking rope.

The cynical MacArthur turned to his friend Hecht, with whom he would later write the hit play, *The Front Page*, and said: "You know, Ben, that son-of-a-bitch should have been a song plugger!"

Wanka, Alfred, 1927-61, S. Afri. While training to become a miner at the Crown Mines in Johannesburg in

1953, Alfred Wanka, a Czechoslovakian, shot and killed a night watchman who caught him and three of his friends stealing peaches. Wanka later claimed the guard was killed because he had uncovered a bootlegging ring Wanka was operating at the time. The South African courts sentenced him to twelve years, but released Wanka after two. Wanka remained in South Africa, and in the 1950s, joined up with a gang of ex-convicts who committed a string of robberies and thefts in different parts of the country.

While attempting to flee from the police, Alfred Wanka shot and killed Detective Constable Phillipus Johannes Jordaan. The policeman had recognized Wanka on a Durban street on July 26, 1960, and was trying to arrest him when Wanka fled. Before Wanka could flee, he was arrested in Capetown Aug. 2.

He was found Guilty of murder on Oct. 17, 1960, and was sentenced to die on the gallows, despite protests from his lawyer that he was mentally unsound. On Mar. 25, 1961, he attempted to escape from the Pretoria Central Prison. He shot and wounded a prison guard but was executed a short time later.

Ward, Charles William, Jr., 1909-28, Brit. Charles Ward of Ackworth, England, thought he had established a fool-proof alibi for murder. After plunging a pick-ax through the skull of his father shortly after their midday meal on Mar. 28, 1928, young Ward left the house for a business appointment in Barnsley. When the body of his father was found in the easy chair, Charles Ward would simply say that he was in Barnsley at the time of the murder and could not possibly have known about it. Unfortunately for Ward, he had not counted on the wonders of forensic science.

A team of pathologists headed up by the eminent Sir Bernard Spilsbury conducted an autopsy on the remains, and concluded that the elder Ward had died within an hour of completing his meal. This evidence pointed to Charles Ward, the only person who had been present in the cottage at that time. He was convicted at the Leeds Assizes, and was sentenced to die on the gallows by Justice Travers Humphreys.

Wardlaw Sisters, prom. 1900-13, U.S. The three "Sisters in Black," born into a prominent Southern family, chose to lead a weird life of seclusion, regularly moving from town to town. They always dressed in funereal black. The leader of this somewhat strange trio was Virginia Wardlaw, a graduate of Wellesley College who became a

respected educator. Virginia's sisters, Caroline Wardlaw Martin and Mary Wardlaw Snead, went to live with Virginia after leaving their husbands.

The sisters collected $12,000 insurance on Mary's son, John Snead, when he burned to death. Sister Caroline, after being reunited with her husband, Colonel John Martin,

Virginia Wardlaw, left, and her sister Caroline Wardlaw Martin, right.

moved to New York. There, the colonel died from causes never determined, though probably poison, and Caroline collected $10,000 insurance. Caroline, along with her daughter Oscey, joined her two sisters in Tennessee, where Virginia had become the head of Soule College in Murfreesboro.

An insurance policy was taken out on Oscey, who was separated from her husband. While living with the three sisters, she too became ill and died, apparently starved and ultimately drowned in a bathtub. When the three women tried to collect on the insurance policy, they were arrested and charged with the murder of Oscey. Virginia starved herself to

Mary Wardlaw Snead, acquitted of the murders her sisters committed.

death in jail. Caroline was found Guilty of the murder of her daughter, but certified insane. She died in 1913. Mary was acquitted of murder.

Warnock, Stephen, 1946- , Brit. Fifteen-year-old Stephen Warnock was apprenticed to a baker, and attended bakery classes at a technical school in the London suburbs. One day in 1961, two classmates named Gray and Robbins tormented Warnock, teasing and kicking him until a fight broke out in class. Later, Robbins let the air out of Warnock's bicycle tires.

When Warnock saw what had been done, he rushed back into the school building and stabbed Robbins to death with a pastry knife. He was allowed to plead not guilty to murder, but guilty to manslaughter on the grounds that he had been provoked. Various character witnesses appeared on Warnock's behalf. The judge sentenced the boy to three years' probation.

Washington, Allen, 1948- , U.S. In 1969, when 3-year-old Elisa Handy died, her father Allen Washington was a suspect in the case, but the coroner's inquest ruled the death accidental, caused after the child fell off a table. In 1970, Washington, a Chicago garbage collector, beat his 23-month-old daughter, Angela, to death. He was tried in 1971, convicted of involuntary manslaughter, and sentenced to ten years in prison, only to be released after serving two and a half years of the term. On Sept. 7, 1978, Washington hit his 3-year-old son James E. Smith with his hand and left the child lying on the bathroom floor. The next day, he reported his son missing and hired a private detective to search for his son, explaining to the private investigator that he had struck James for wetting his pants and then the boy hit his head on the bathtub. Three weeks later, police officers found the toddler's battered and burned body in a garbage dump. On June 26, 1980, Washington, thirty-two, was convicted of murdering his son, and on July 30 he was sentenced to forty years in prison.

Washington, Leon, 1946- , U.S. Leon Washington, owner of a downtown Chicago executive recruiting firm, left his home on June 6, 1981, dressed in cowboy boots and hat and armed with a semi-automatic handgun and a hunting knife. During the afternoon, the 35-year-old former Davenport, Iowa, police officer drank excessively and accompanied friends to the Marina City bar, where he continued to drink.

First deputy police superintendent James J. Riordan and his date were going to dinner when they met Alice and Martin O'Brien. The O'Briens invited Riordan and his date to Marina City for a drink. There Alice O'Brien apparently told the noisy Washington to "shut up," and Washington walked over to her husband, explaining to him that he would allow him to remain in the bar if O'Brien would buy him a drink. Alice and the bartender both claimed that Washington then held an unloaded gun to her head and pulled the trigger three times. Riordan told the O'Briens

to go to the back of the bar while he quieted Washington. Washington walked into a coat check room and loaded his gun. When he returned to the bar, both he and Riordan walked outside, where Washington shot Riordan three times. Riordan died en route to the hospital.

Pleading self-defense, Washington was tried and convicted on Oct. 30, on murder charges, and on Dec. 2, 1981, he was sentenced to thirty-five years in prison. The death penalty was not invoked because Riordan was off-duty when he was killed. In January 1982, Washington's mother, Hazel Washington, filed a $500,000 suit against two businesses for serving alcohol to her son.

Watkins, Jesse, 1903- , U.S. On Aug. 21, 1927, at the Presidio Army Base in San Francisco, Henry Chambers was bludgeoned to death. Jesse Watkins, a stable hand who had just been fired, had vowed revenge on Chambers, according to a soldier who overheard an argument between the two men.

That night, Chambers, awakened by Watkins breaking into his quarters, fired several shots at the intruder. Watkins, though shot in his cheek, pistol-whipped Chambers to death, took some valuables, and returned home. He cleaned himself of bloodstains and washed his bloody shirt. Later his roommate, believing Watkins had been attacked by robbers, removed the bullet from his cheek.

Watkins was arrested and charged with murder. Criminologist Edward O. Heinrich proved that the bullet that wounded Watkins had been fired from Chambers' gun, that ultraviolet rays detected specks of Chambers' blood on Watkins' shirt, and that a bloody heel print at the murder scene was made by Watkins' boot. Watkins, tried and found Guilty, was sentenced to life imprisonment.

Watson, James P. (AKA: **Joseph Gillam; Laurence Harris**), c.1879-1939, U.S. James P. Watson, a traveling salesman, admitted to marrying twenty-five women for money and murdering many of them. Watson, a native of Eureka Springs, Ark., was first married to a 16-year-old girl in about 1896 when he was seventeen. After their divorce, Watson traveled throughout the nation, placing personal advertisements in newspapers, and after marriage, he convinced his new wife to make him the beneficiary in her will.

He explained his long absences from home by saying that he worked for the U.S. Secret Service. At one time, he was married to four Tacoma, Wash., women, and another time he fled to Canada after he was charged with mail fraud. His final wife, Katharine Wombacker, began to doubt her husband's honesty when he transferred her Liberty Bonds into his name. She hired a private detective and police soon arrested Watson.

After his arrest, Watson led police to the grave of Nina Lee Deloney, whose body he had buried near El Centro, Calif., and he confessed to murdering sixteen wives, among them, Elizabeth Prior, whom Watson said he hit with a hammer near Spokane, Wash. Watson was tried for the Deloney murder, and in 1920 was sentenced to life in San Quentin.

In 1930, still in prison, he apparently convinced Wycliffe A. Hill, a Hollywood scriptwriter, that most of the money stolen from his dead wives was secretly buried. Hill searched for five years and later sued the prisoner, although he received no compensation. Watson, about sixty years old, died in 1939, and left a letter directing the warden to a safe hidden in his cell. The safe, however, contained nothing of value.

Watson, Lionel Rupert Nathan, c.1910-41, Brit.

Lionel Rupert Nathan Watson committed bigamy when he married his second wife, Phyllis Elizabeth Crocker, and later fathered a daughter with the woman. On May 19, 1941, Watson poisoned Phyllis and their 18-month-old daughter, Eileen Alice, with prussic acid. He buried their bodies in the garden in back of their home in Greenford, Middlesex. On May 26, 1941, his digging was noticed and reported to police. In June, the bodies were exhumed and in September, Watson was tried at the Old Bailey where he claimed that he had found his wife and child dead, but was afraid to call for help because he had bigamously married the woman. Watson was convicted, and he was hanged at Pentonville prison on Nov. 12, 1941.

Watt, Miriam, c.1949-   , U.S.

On Jan. 5, 1987, Sandra Ferguson entered a hospital to give birth and left her children, Andrea and Jasmine, with their paternal grandmother, Miriam Watt in Harvey, Ill. On May 3, 1987, 2-year-old Jasmine Ferguson was taken from her grandmother, suffering from head injuries and a large burn and peeling skin on her buttocks caused from immersion in scalding water. The grandmother claimed she thought Jasmine had severe diaper rash and had not taken the child to a doctor because she could not locate a "green card," a state card authorizing the holder to receive free medical care. Two days later, Jasmine was declared brain dead. Her grandmother went on trial for murder in late 1988. On Dec. 15, 1988, Watt was found Guilty of murder and on Jan.

9, 1989, she was sentenced to life in prison with no possibility of parole.

Watts, Coral Eugene, 1953-   , U.S.

Coral Eugene Watts, who killed an estimated forty women, felt that all women were deceitful and unfaithful. In 1974, Watts attended Western Michigan University in Kalamazoo, Mich. There he attempted to strangle a woman but was arrested before he killed her, a "mistake" he did not make again for eight years. Watts was jailed for a few days before the court released him on bond. Six days following the attempt on the woman's life, Watts stalked Gloria Steele, a student at the university. She was found the next morning in her apartment, stabbed thirty-three times, with many jagged incisions made after her death. The police suspected Watts but could not link him to the crime. He was convicted of assault for the earlier attack and sentenced to one year in prison. Upon his release in 1975, he moved to Ann Arbor, Mich.

Watts eventually became a bus mechanic, working during the week and traveling on weekends. During this time, several young women were attacked and killed in Ann Arbor, the victims of multiple stabbings. Many of the bodies were severely mutilated—several with jagged postmortem wounds. Police suspected Watts as the so-called "Sunday Morning Slasher." At that time, Watts was also allegedly killing women in Detroit and Windsor, Ontario, Canada, as well. Not all of his associations with women were violent and fatal, however. In 1980, he married, but his wife found him peculiar and left him within two months. He had a relationship with another woman who gave birth to his child.

In 1981, Watts lost his bus mechanic job and moved to Houston, Texas. There he worked regularly and attended a local Pentecostal church. The Ann Arbor police sent Houston law enforcement officials their suspicions of Watts, and Houston police placed surveillance on him over the weekends for about sixty days. Not finding anything peculiar about his behavior, they discontinued the survey.

In January 1982, two women were killed. Phyllis Tam, a 27-year-old advertising art director was discovered hanged with her

Mass murderer Coral Eugene Watts.

own clothes in a secluded area near Rice University where she jogged every morning. Two weeks later, police found the body of an architecture student stuffed in the trunk of her car. On Jan. 18, student Margaret Fossi had been sideswiped on the road while driving. When she stopped, Watts had pulled her from her car and beaten her to death. In each of the attacks, Watts left no physical evidence and made sure his victims were dead.

On May 23, Watts attacked 20-year-old Lori Ann Lister in her apartment. He twisted a coat hanger around her wrists and throttled her before attempting to drown her in the bathtub. A neighbor called police after rescuing her from the bathtub. Police arrested Watts and charged him with attempted murder, aggravated kidnapping, and burglary. The mass murderer arranged a plea bargain in which he would give the police information on several murders and, in exchange, he would be charged with merely first-degree burglary. In the ensuing months, he took police to the burial sites of many of his victims. He cleared up twenty-two killings in three states and two countries. After reinvestigating other unsolved murders, police concluded that Watts murdered at least forty women. When asked why he killed so many women, Watts replied that women were evil.

The district attorney could not definitely link Watts to any of the murders and proceeded with the plea-bargained charge of first-degree burglary. Facing a sixty-year prison sentence, Judge Doug Shaver sentenced him to the maximum sentence, sixty years in prison. Because the judge ruled that the water-filled bathtub was a deadly weapon, Watts must serve at least twenty years of his sentence before he can become eligible for parole. Shaver asked that the Texas Department of Corrections and the state legislature make sure he completed the entire sentence without a chance for parole. At the sentencing on Sept. 3, 1982, Shaver said to Watts, "I hope you serve each and every minute of the sixty years."

Weber, Jeanne (AKA: **Madame Moulinet; Madame Bouchery**), 1875-1910, Fr. After committing at least eight and perhaps as many as twenty child murders, Jeanne Weber, a Parisian housewife, was caught in the act of strangling her last victim one night in 1908. She had earlier been accused and tried twice for the deaths of children in her care but was acquitted each time.

On Mar. 2, 1905, two children were left in Weber's care, and one of them died. She was not suspected, though there were bruises on the deceased child's neck. Within less than a month, three more children, including Weber's own son, died of strange congestive or convulsive maladies, all with marks on their throats.

A few weeks later, while relatives were visiting, Weber's 10-year-old nephew, Maurice, died. The boy's mother, Weber's sister-in-law, accused her of murder and called the police. The case attracted great attention, and public opinion demanded that she be found Guilty. A brilliant lawyer and some of the best forensic scientists and doctors in France convinced the jury that the children died from various medical problems, not at the hands of Jeanne Weber. She was freed amid great public outcry.

Deserted by her husband and still vilified by many of her neighbors, Weber made an unsuccessful suicide attempt and then left Paris. She next surfaced as Madame Moulinet, living with a man named Bavouzet as his housekeeper and mistress. Bavouzet's son Auguste was found dead in the same manner as the previous victims. Although the police were called in, no charges were brought. Some days later, Auguste's older sister, searching through Moulinet's belongings, found some newspaper clippings about Jeanne Weber and the earlier murder cases. The police were called again. The attending physician attributed Auguste Bavouzet's death to murder by strangulation. Her identity revealed, Jeanne Weber again was brought to trial for murder. The same defense team who got her off in the previous case again got her acquitted.

The director of the Society for Protection of Children, then hired Weber to care for some children. Seen strangling a child, she was fired immediately, but the director made no public charges because of the bad publicity that would result.

Weber returned to Paris, and even confessed to the original murders when she was picked up for vagrancy. After being sent to an asylum, Weber recanted her confession, but a psychiatrist declared her sane and released her. She then became known as Madame Bouchery, and told her landlady that her husband was beating her and asked if one of the landlady's children could sleep with her to keep her husband away. That night, loud noises came from her room. Another guest in the house rushed in to find Weber strangling the boy. This time, Weber was arrested, tried, and found Guilty.

On Oct. 25, 1908, Weber was found insane and sent to a hospital. In 1910, after many months of insane ravings, Jeanne Weber strangled herself to death.

Weger, Chester, 1939- , U.S. On Mar. 14, 1960, Chester Weger, a dishwasher at the Starved Rock Lodge located in Starved Rock Park near Ottawa, Ill., went into the woods, planning to steal purses when he encountered three middle-aged women from the Chicago suburb of Riverside. As Mildred Lindquist, Lillian Oetting, and Frances Murphy, the wives of prominent Chicago businessmen, hiked through the park, Weger threatened them with a broken tree limb and ordered them to lie on the ground. He bound two of them with string that he had stolen from the lodge's kitchen and as he tied up the third woman, one of the others freed herself and hit Weger with a pair of binoculars. Weger then struck the fighting woman with the tree bough, knocked her unconscious, and pulled her into a nearby cave. When the other women struggled Weger hit them, and also dragged them into the cave. Then he pulled up their clothing to make the attack appear to be a sex crime. The three bodies were found two days later on Mar. 16 by a group of boys.

Leading the investigation, La Salle County State's Attorney Harland D. Warren learned that the string used to tie up the women was the same as that used in the kitchen of the Starved Rock Lodge. Initially, Weger passed two polygraph tests and bloodstains found on his jacket were determined to be animal blood. Later, however, Weger failed two additional lie detector tests and a Federal Bureau of Investigation laboratory determined that the blood on his coat was human. Weger confessed several times, but when he was tried, he retracted his statements. He was convicted on his twenty-second birthday, Mar. 4, 1961, and sentenced to life in prison.

Weinger, Mitchell, 1948- , U.S. Twenty-five-year-old drug dealer Mark Demetrius called 28-year-old Mitchell Weinger on May 2, 1976, requesting that Weinger stop by Demetrius' girlfriend's Chicago apartment to buy cocaine. When Weinger arrived, Demetrius' 23-year-old girlfriend, Marigray Jobes, an aspiring actress, was also present. While the two men discussed the price, Weinger stabbed Demetrius and his girlfriend to death. In 1980, Weinger, vice president of Midland Industries, Inc., a family-owned business, stood trial. In May 1980, he was convicted on murder charges, and on July 2, 1980, Weinger received a sentence of thirty to forty years in prison.

Welch, Bernard Charles, Jr., 1940- , U.S. The fifteen-year crime career of Bernard Welch ended in 1980 with his arrest and murder conviction in the death of Washington, D.C., resident Dr. Michael J. Halberstam. Welch began burglarizing luxury homes in 1965 at the age of twenty-five, specializing in the theft of furs, silverware, art objects, and rare coins. He worked alone, making it difficult for law enforcement officials to capture him. Furthermore, he melted down most of the precious metal he stole. However, he was arrested twenty-five times, but

managed to avoid imprisonment either by jumping bail or escaping from prison. It was estimated that between 1965 and 1980, Welch netted between $10 and $20 million.

In 1974, Welch escaped from Dannemora Prison in New York by hiding out on the grounds after a softball game, then scaling a twenty-five-foot-high fence. He became one

Victim, Dr. Michael J. Halberstam, left, and his murderer, Bernard Charles Welch Jr., right.

of the FBI's most-sought-after criminals, and 15,000 circulars with his description and *modus operandi* were distributed to police. After his escape, Welch paid $245,000 cash for a home in Falls Church, Va. He made $750,000 in improvements on the home and lived there with his common law wife and three children. He told neighbors he was a very successful stockbroker, and frequently invited them over to see his private art collection, indoor swimming pool, and environment room. He further equipped his home with an elaborate security system that monitored the grounds with a host of remote control cameras and closed-circuit televisions.

After burglarizing four homes on Dec. 5, 1980, Welch broke into Dr. Halberstam's home. Halberstam, a well-known cardiologist and author, surprised the burglar, and Welch shot him. Halberstam did not die immediately and managed to escape from the house and get into his car. Outside, he saw Welch and ran him over with the auto. Halberstam died on the operating table. With Welch in custody, investigators searched his Virginia home. They found fifty boxes of stolen goods belonging to nearly 2,000 burglary victims who were called to reclaim their property. Welch was sentenced to nine consecutive life terms in prison, making him eligible for parole in 143 years.

Wells, Alfred, d.1942, U.S. The 1941 murder spree of Alfred Wells shocked the citizens of San Bernadino and communities throughout Southern California. The search for Wells, paroled from San Quentin in 1939, touched off a five-county manhunt.

Until Spring 1941 the hunchbacked Wells had been involved in an incestuous relationship with his half-sister, 24-year-old Violet Wells who, on Apr. 26, decided to leave him and return home to her parents. That day, Violet's brother, David Raymond Wells, and his wife, Jean Wells, drove her to her parents' home in Escondido. Upon learning of her disappearance, Alfred Wells threatened David and Jean with bodily injury if they did not tell him where Violet was. The young couple said they knew nothing, but Wells was not convinced.

On May 7, 1941, Wells again arrived at David and Jean's San Bernadino home and convinced Jean and her friend, Rose Destree, to drive him to the desert to a chicken ranch where he had just gotten a job. Jean put her 13-month-old baby, Hester, into the car, and she and Rose drove Alfred Wells to the desert.

After traveling several miles, Wells ordered Jean to pull to the side of the road, and once again accused her of keeping Violet from him. Brandishing a gun, he forced her to write a note to her husband explaining that she, Rose, and the baby were being held hostage until David provided him with Violet's whereabouts.

Wells then shot Jean twice in the chest at close range, killing her instantly. He turned on Rose Destree and shot her twice as well. He laid baby Hester in her mother's arms. Once he had gone, Destree began an arduous crawl toward the road that ended four hours later when her calls for help were answered. Rescuers found Destree slumped in the desert scrub grass and Hester clinging to her mother's dead body.

By the time Destree reached the hospital, Wells had returned to town and had lured David from work with the note. David drove Alfred within two miles of the murder site. There Alfred shot him in the back of the head. David's body was found four days later in a desolate canyon near Cajon Pass in the San Bernadino foothills.

After news of Wells's spree reached the San Bernadino Sheriff's Department, several of his relatives throughout Southern California were taken into protective custody.

Alfred Wells was convicted of the murders of 24-year-old David Wells, 18-year-old Jean Wells, and 17-year-old Rose Destree, who died of her injuries. Wells was sentenced to death.

On Dec. 4, 1942, he was taken to the San Quentin gas chamber that he had helped construct five years before while serving a sentence for robbery. Ten minutes after being strapped into one of the chamber's chairs, Wells was pronounced dead.

Werner, Karl, 1950- , U.S. As a youth, Karl Werner,

a newspaper boy in Marlboro, Mass., had threatened a young housewife with a knife, so police admitted the boy to the children's mental ward of a state hospital for evaluation. There, psychiatrists determined that Werner experienced, "epileptic-like attacks, marked by violence and outrage." His father soon took the family to San Jose, Calif. There, Werner spent time building mechanical devices in the basement of his parents' home.

On Aug. 3, 1969, Werner went for a walk in the park where he met two high school girls from his neighborhood, Debra Gaye Furlong, fourteen, and Kathy Snoozy, fifteen. After talking with them for a few minutes, Werner later said, "This loud bang went off in my head," and he pulled out a pocket knife, first stabbing Kathy, then Debra. He continued to stab one and then the other, knifing Kathy more than 200 times and Debra about 100 times. All of the injuries were above the waist, primarily on the midsection of the bodies, and neither was raped. A motorcyclist found their bodies that evening about 8 p.m. On Apr. 11, 1970, Easter Sunday, Werner attacked 18-year-old Kathy Bilek, while she was reading a book at Villa Montalvo park in Saratoga. Werner stabbed her forty-nine times, leaving knife marks in a pattern similar to those found on the other dead girls.

Police appealed to the public for help, and a 23-year-old woman told police that two weeks prior to Bilek's murder she had been approached by a youth named Karl. The woman said she thought he was going to kill her, and she became even more alarmed when he told her he had lost his keys in the woods and asked her to help him search. She told him her legs were tired and left the trail. A ranger at the Villa Montalvo park also said he had spoken with a youth named Karl on the day of Bilek's murder, and had written down the young man's licence plate number. On Apr. 29, police arrested Werner, a 19-year-old engineering student at San Jose City College. Werner confessed to the murders, re-enacted the crimes, and led police to the murder weapons. During his trial, he pleaded guilty to all three murders, and on Sept. 29, Werner was sentenced to life in prison.

West, Velma, prom. 1928, U.S. In December 1928, Thomas Edward West and his wife, Velma, were invited to a dinner and bridge party. While the Perry, Ohio, couple discussed the matter, Velma West stood on a chair, fixing a broken curtain rod with a hammer, nails, and twine. Her 30-year-old husband did not want to go to the affair because he did not enjoy parties, bridge, or the company of the hostess, Mabel Young. Annoyed, Mrs. West beat her husband on the head with the hammer, put a pillow over his head, and hit him again with a chair leg. To keep her already dead husband from following her to the party in Cleveland, she bound his hands and legs with the twine. Afterward, she dressed, went to the party, played bridge, and danced.

Mrs. West was arrested, and dubbed the "Split-Mind Flapper Slayer" by the newspapers because she had been dropped on her head as a child. She was tried, convicted, and sentenced to a life term in prison.

Westwood, Billy (William), 1948-65, U.S. Although he died not long after his seventeenth birthday, Billy Westwood, who never allowed anyone to call him William, was known throughout the Ozarks of Arkansas as a "bad seed."

At sixteen, Westwood was charged with the death of a classmate, Chad Wilson. Friends of the two boys claimed Westwood shot Wilson because Wilson called Westwood by his given name. The charges were dropped on Dec. 17, 1964, due to lack of evidence. Two days later, Westwood was in a barbershop in Franklin County, Ark., when another classmate kidded Westwood about his disdain for his first name. Five minutes later, four men were dead and one man seriously wounded by gunfire from Westwood's six-gun. For five weeks, a massive hunt was conducted by local authorities for Westwood, who escaped to the mountains.

On Jan. 29, 1965, police found Westwood's body in a ravine. A note was found next to the body which claimed Westwood had been shot by a vigilante who felt justice was best handled with a shotgun.

Wheat, Clarence, d.1980, U.S. In 1979, Clarence Wheat was sentenced to five years in prison at the Mississippi State Penitentiary at Parchman for the shooting death of a Mississippi police officer during a family disturbance. After serving only eight months of his sentence, Wheat, suffering from diabetes, heart disease, and terminal cancer, was pardoned by the governor of Mississippi so that he could return to his home and die there.

Six months later, in June 1980, the ex-convict shot and killed his wife and son before turning the gun on himself. His daughter and her three children escaped. John Watkins, the state corrections commissioner, said that releasing terminally ill convicts was routine practice, and added that it was "...terrible to die in prison."

Whelpton, George, 1916-c.1947, Brit. In 1936, 20-year-old George Whelpton suffered a head injury from a motorcycle accident and afterward, relatives said that the young man sometimes acted peculiarly. Just before going off to war in 1939, Whelpton married. He served in North Africa, and after the war found a job as a bus driver in Doncaster, England. He and his wife had separated when he met Alison Parkin, a widow, in 1947. She lived with her two children, 23-year-old Joyce Parkin and 15-year-old Maurice Parkin.

On Oct. 9, 1947, Whelpton and Parkin went out to a pub together and later the couple went back to Parkin's home, arriving about 11:15 p.m. Parkin's daughter arrived home shortly afterward. After an apparent argument, Whelpton strangled the widow, her daughter, and her son. When a neighbor discovered the bodies the next day, the mother and daughter were naked and all three had been sexually mutilated, their bodies bearing marks similar to those made by North African desert tribesman. Whelpton soon was arrested and he said he remembered a fight with Parkin after she asked for money. Whelpton said he struck the widow, her daughter, and her son. Although Whelpton pleaded insanity at his trial, he was still convicted, sentenced to death, and hanged.

Whitby, Roy, 1948-77, U.S. In May 1976, a married Chicago area couple separated. Shirley Whitby kept their two children, not allowing her husband to see them. In February 1977, Roy Whitby lost his job as a parking lot attendant in downtown Chicago and went to live with his brother. On Mar. 10, the divorce was made final. On the morning of Mar. 22, 1977, 29-year-old Roy Whitby told his brother he was upset because he wanted to see the children, and he thought his ex-wife was dating other men. He blamed one of his wife's co-workers, 25-year-old Tamera Clarke, for the breakup, believing she told his wife to divorce him. After talking with his brother, he went to the securities brokerage company where his 28-year-old ex-wife worked as a clerk. He fatally shot her and Clarke with a .22-caliber handgun and then turned the gun on himself.

White, Daniel James, 1946-85, U.S. Daniel White gave up his job with the San Francisco fire department to run for the post of supervisor, which he won. White ran on a strongly antigay platform, committed "to the confrontation which can no longer be avoided by those who care." In 1978, Supervisor White earned half the salary he had made as a fireman. His wife opened an arcade food stand in the tourist section, which helped financially, but added to other pressures. White began eating junk foods, but the binges solved nothing and ultimately compounded his depression.

On Nov. 10, 1978, White offered his resignation to Mayor George R. Moscone. Supervisor Harvey Milk, the U.S.'s first openly gay elected official, got Moscone's promise to appoint a replacement for White who would support the gay community. White's resignation would change the balance of power in the city council.

San Francisco supervisor Dan White, killer.

Then White's family and friends began to pressure him to recant his resignation and ask Moscone to reinstate him as supervisor. White met with Moscone on Nov. 14 and the mayor agreed to return White's letter of resignation. The next morning, both men announced the news to the press, but Moscone also said they needed to check the legalities of the move and possibly reappoint White instead of just canceling the resignation. However, during the next two days, Moscone was advised that if he renamed White, he would not be re-elected for a second term as mayor.

During the next few days, newspapers speculated about White's replacement. But the story was overshadowed by news of the deaths at Jim Jones' People's Temple in Guyana as most of the victims were former San Franciscans.

Supervisor Harvey Milk and Mayor George Moscone, both killed by White.

Dan White clipped each article concerning his status and read and reread them. On Nov. 27, he heard that the mayor had avoided accepting petitions from more than 1,000 White supporters.

Dan White dressed neatly, put a loaded five-bullet gun in his pocket, and went to City Hall. He waited in Moscone's outer office until the mayor could see him. Moscone took White back to his private office and told him that he would not be reappointing him to the supervisor's position. White pulled his gun and fired at the mayor. When Moscone fell to the floor, White emptied the other four bullets into his back and head. White ran down the hall, reloading the gun, grabbed a key to the back door of the supervisors' office, and went to Harvey Milk's office. White fired five bullets into Milk, then ran down the stairs and out of the building past policemen arriving in response to a phone call from Moscone's secretary. White called his wife and they met at St. Mary's Cathedral, then walked to the local police station where White turned himself in.

Dan White went on trial on May 1, 1979, before Judge Calcagno. His attorney, Douglas Schmidt, concentrated his defense on the periodic depressions White had suffered most of his life. In what came to be known as "the twinkie defense," the testifying psychiatrist, Dr. Donald Lunde, pointed out that a change in eating habits is an important sign of clinical depression. He also said that White had been so depressed that he was incapable of formulating a plan for murder, and thus the killings were not premeditated.

On May 21, 1979, the jury brought in a verdict of Guilty of voluntary manslaughter. Thousands of people, mostly gay, rioted in San Francisco in protest of the lenient verdict. More than 100 people were injured and $1 million in damage was done to City Hall and other public property.

White served five years, one month, and nine days at the Soledad State Prison in California. He was released on Jan. 6, 1984, with a probation requirement that he remain in the Los Angeles area for a year. After his parole expired, he returned to his home in San Francisco. On Oct. 21, 1985, White, reportedly devastated by the trouble he had caused his family and himself, used a rubber hose to pipe exhaust fumes into an automobile in his garage and died of carbon monoxide poisoning.

Whitley, Richard Lee, 1946-87, U.S. Richard Lee Whitley had a long history of sex offenses. He raped his mother, sexually molested his 10-year-old daughter, and sodomized a male hitchhiker before committing one of the most shockingly gruesome murders in the history of Fairfax County, Va.

Born in Chicago, Ill., 34-year-old Whitley lived in Pimmit Hills, Va., a section of the middle-class Washington, D.C., suburb of Falls Church. On the evening of July 25, 1980,

Whitley went to the home of his 63-year-old neighbor, Phoebe Parsons, to use her telephone. He had been on a drinking binge for several days, and his wife had left him two weeks earlier. Parsons knew Whitley well, and had often employed him to do repairs around her home. Whitley later told police that he went to Parsons' house a second time to use the phone. During their visit, Whitley explained, he and Parsons stood talking in her living room. "We just stood around and talked about my wife and going to church and everything, and the next thing I know she was dead," said Whitley.

The next day, Parsons' bloody, mutilated body was found on her bed, covered by clothes and boxes from her bedroom closet. A rope was tied around her neck and she had been stabbed in the throat with a small knife. Once dead, the murderer laid her body on the bed, stripped it naked, and sexually abused it. Whitley was arrested in Tampa, Fla., after he had fled Virginia in Parsons' Volkswagen. He told Tampa Detective Jerry Feltman that Parsons had been praying as he stabbed her with his plastic-handled Boy Scout knife, and that he stabbed Parsons in the jugular vein because "they die quicker when you cut them there." Whitley was returned to Fairfax County and immediately charged with the murder.

He was brought to trial before Circuit Court Judge F. Bruce Bach. After hearing the sordid details of Whitley's violent past and police testimony about his confession, the jury retired to make their decision. On May 13, 1981, after only thirty-two minutes of deliberation, the jury returned a Guilty verdict and recommended the death penalty. Two weeks after the trial, Judge Bach sentenced Whitley to death in the electric chair.

After more than five years of appeals, and an Amnesty International plea for a stay of execution to the governor of Virginia, and a U.S. Supreme Court denial for a stay of execution, Whitley was electrocuted on July 6, 1987, at 11 p.m.

═══════════════════════════════

Whitman, Charles Joseph, 1941-66, U.S. Once an altar boy, Eagle scout, and U.S. Marine, Charles J. Whitman of Lake Worth, Fla., committed one of the most ruthless murder rampages in U.S. history. In July 1966, Whitman, twenty-five, was enrolled as a junior for the summer semester at the University of Texas in Austin. A student in architectural engineering, Whitman was taking an unusually heavy class load of fourteen credit hours. In the early morning of Aug. 1, 1966, Whitman stabbed his 24-year-old wife, Kathleen Leissner Whitman, to death in his Austin apartment, then shot and killed his mother, Mrs. C.A. Whitman. Nothing indicated that the attacks were

provoked. Whitman left three cryptic notes in his apartment. The first, addressed to "Roy," read: "My mother's ill and won't be at work today." The two remaining notes were addressed "To whom it may concern." In one, Whitman professed love for his wife and mother, but confusion about why they had to die, except to "save them the embarrassment" of the action he had planned. Whitman expressed contempt for his father, a plumbing contractor from Lake Worth. He said he hated him "with a mortal passion."

Whitman spent the remainder of the morning assembling an arsenal of weapons and gathering provisions. A mail carrier, Chester Arrington, watched as Whitman retooled his shotgun in the family garage. "I talked to Whitman for about twenty-five minutes on the day he did it," Arrington recalled years later. "I saw him sawing off the shotgun, and I knew that was illegal." Arrington did not call police. "All I had to do was pick up the phone and report him. It could have stopped him. I've always blamed myself." When Whitman was finished with his preparations, his foot locker resembled an arsenal. It contained a 6-mm. rifle with a telescopic sight, a Remington .35-caliber pump rifle, a .357 magnum pistol, a 9-mm. Luger pistol, a 30.06 reconditioned army carbine, a 12-gauge sawed-off shotgun, and a large Bowie knife. The locker was well stocked with food and two bottles of water.

Whitman carried the locker to the tallest building in Austin, a twenty-seven story tower on the university campus. The granite tower housed the university library and administration offices with an observation deck on the top level. In 1966, the deck was open to the public, commanding an expansive view of the entire campus and a significant portion of Austin. Whitman entered the tower, shot and killed the woman at the visitor's registration desk, and proceeded to the elevator. He next killed a mother and her two children who were spending the day sightseeing. Just before noon, Whitman reached the observation deck, and with his cache of weapons he began shooting at random. An office worker on the eighteenth floor of the tower, Ruth Kiykendall, heard gunshots and called a friend in a nearby building. "Somebody's up there shooting from the tower," she said. "There is blood all over the place!" The campus was thrown into an uproar as students, faculty, and visitors scurried for cover. Whitman fired his shots with unerring accuracy. He killed a student riding his bicycle near the Texas Union Building and a police officer standing behind a wood fence. Whitman fired on a small boy and a pregnant woman, Mrs. Claire Wilson, who was taken to a hospital where she gave birth to a stillborn baby.

Police sectioned off the campus, and tried frantically to keep 10,000 students and curiosity seekers out of the line of fire. A police airplane flew over the tower in an attempt

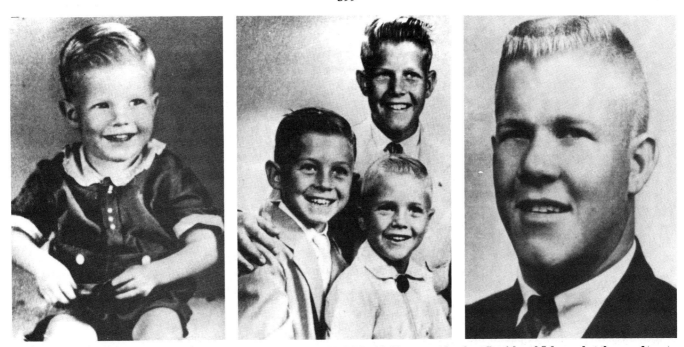

Mass killer Charles Whitman shown, left to right, as a happy 2-year-old child, with his younger brothers Patrick and John, and at the age of twenty-four.

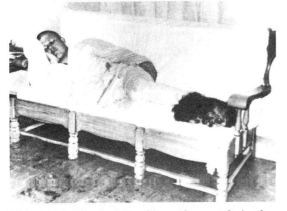

Whitman asleep, a day before his murder spree in Austin.

Whitman's murderous gunfire wounds a man, left, and drives a girl to cover, right.

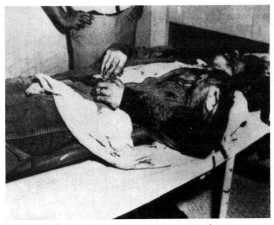

Above, the end of Charles Whitman, shot to pieces, Aug. 1, 1966; right, Austin police officer Romero Martinez, who shot and killed sniper Whitman by inching around a wall on the twenty-seven-story University of Texas Tower and firing six bullets into the beserk Whitman, who traded shots with him; far right, the Texas Tower which haunted Whitman, who, as a student on the Austin campus, stared at it for long periods of time. He later told his psychiatrist that he thought of going to the top and shooting people from it.

to shoot the sniper. Armored cars were called in to rescue the wounded, several of whom lay bleeding in the 98 degree heat for more than an hour.

Whitman sprayed Guadalupe Street with bullets for eighty minutes. Police officers Romero Martinez, Houston McCoy, Jerry Jay, and George Sheppard rode up the tower elevator with civilian Allen Crum to subdue the sniper. Martinez and Crum slowly moved around the observation wall while the others covered exit doorways. Whitman spotted Martinez and fired once at him. Martinez fired six rapid shots while McCoy kicked in a door and emptied his shotgun. Martinez waved a green flag from the top of the tower signaling the all clear. Whitman lay dead on the observation deck, his head covered with blood. "The sniper was on the northwest corner of the roof," Crum told reporters. "We rushed through the door and spread out." Whitman's body was carried out of the tower at 1:40 p.m. Later that day, administration officials allowed reporters up to the tower for a look. A pile of bloody rags was found lying in the corner. The glass face on the massive clock overlooking the campus grounds was chipped and fragmented with three bullet holes. The ex-Marine's murder spree left sixteen dead and thirty-one wounded.

School officials expressed shock over Whitman's actions. They were unable to uncover a motive. According to graduate faculty advisor Leonardt F. Kreisle, Whitman "seemed to be more mature than most people his age." University Chancellor Harry Ransom released Whitman's student records, which showed that he had never been treated at the university for a psychiatric disorder, and was a "B" student. He had received an honorable discharge from the Marine Corps on Dec., 4, 1964, but had gone through court martial proceedings on one occasion for providing gambling loans. Hugo Ley, the owner of a Needville drug store remembered Whitman as a fine young man. "I loved Charlie," he said. "He was the kind of boy you would want for a son."

The residents of Austin were badly shaken by the slayings. Texas governor John Connally cut short a diplomatic visit to Rio de Janeiro to return home to launch a "complete and thorough investigation" into the sniper killings. Connally said that he hoped some good would result, and the inquiry would "shed light on the background and causes and give us some clues on preventing future occurrences of this nature." In 1975, a made-for-television movie adaptation called *The Deadly Tower* starring Kurt Russell and John Forsythe aired on NBC. Martinez sued the network for $1 million, in a breach-of-contract suit, claiming the movie invaded his privacy and misrepresented his character by showing him as a radical. The same year, the University of Texas closed the observation deck, which had also been the site of several suicide attempts. As of this writing, it has not been reopened.

Whittaker, Samuel, 1875-1937, U.S. In 1937, 62-year-old musician Samuel Whittaker was convicted of first-degree murder in the death of his wife, who was killed during a phony robbery that Whittaker arranged to bilk $18,000 from his insurance company. Whittaker, a Los Angeles theatre organist, enlisted the help of 24-year-old James Culver, who later turned state's evidence.

During his trial, Whittaker maintained his innocence and dramatically proclaimed to the court, "May God strike me dead before I get to my cell if I am guilty of this horrible crime." Whittaker was found Guilty of murder, and upon his arrival at California's San Quentin Prison, he complained of chest pains and was immediately transferred into the custody of the prison physician. Whittaker died of a heart attack in the prison infirmary before receiving his cell assignment.

Whittemore, Richard Reese, d.1926, U.S. A delinquent from the age of ten, Richard Whittemore killed a guard while serving his second prison term for armed robbery. Born into an old Maryland family with a reputation for honesty, Whittemore was initially sent to reform school for truancy. He repeatedly ran away from the school and began robbing stores before his teens. He had several conflicts with police, and when WWI broke out, he attempted to enlist in the army, and then the Coast Guard.

In October 1921, Whittemore robbed a Baltimore home of property worth $377 and was sent to the Maryland Penitentiary for fifteen years. Upon his release, he formed a gang of his reformatory and prison companions that "shook down" saloons in Baltimore and Philadelphia while posing as IRS agents. Whittemore was captured in January 1925, convicted of robbery, and sentenced to fifteen years and three months in prison. After being locked up less than a month, he escaped from prison on Feb. 20, killing guard Robert Holtman in the process. He hit Holtman over the head with a pipe because he was convinced the guard would shoot him.

Whittemore escaped to New York where his gang began operations that netted $750,000 in stolen jewelry within a year. He was arrested in connection with a Buffalo, N.Y., bank robbery in which two bank messengers were killed. He was acquitted of those murders but immediately sent to Baltimore where he was tried and convicted of first-degree murder in the slaying of Holtman. He was sentenced to hang. The governor of Maryland denied a stay of execution and U.S. Supreme Court Justice Oliver Wendell Holmes denied a last minute writ of error. On Aug. 13, 1926, Richard Whittemore was hanged in the Maryland State Penitentiary. His last words were, "I wish to say goodbye. That's the best I can wish to any one."

Whitty, Dennis, 1940-63, and **Pascoe, Russell**, d.1963, Brit. William Garfield Rowe was an eccentric 64-year-old WWI deserter who lived on his family's farm near Falmouth, England. By 1963, all of Rowe's family members had either died or moved away, and he lived a reclusive life. On Aug. 15, 1963, a cattle dealer named Henry Pascoe found Rowe's body lying on the floor of his farmhouse. Rowe had been beaten and stabbed to death. Police interviewed known criminals in the area including Russell Pascoe (no relation to Henry Pascoe), who was living with three girls and another man named Dennis Whitty. Rowe's brand of cigarettes were found in the house, and one of the girls told police that they knew Rowe had recently been stabbed although this information had not been made public. Implicated in the crime, the two men admitted to being on Rowe's property and accused each other of the murder. However, it was proven that Rowe had been stabbed and beaten simultaneously, and both men were convicted of the murder. They were executed in December 1963.

Wienchowski, Joseph, prom. 1935, U.S. Joseph Wienchowski lived with his wife and their 17-year-old son Gregory on a farm in northern Michigan. The teenager was headstrong and frequently argued with his parents. In March 1935, Gregory Wienchowski's mutilated body was found in a forest near the farm. While the elder Wienchowski appeared grief stricken, police became suspicious when they discovered bloodstains in the barn. When they found a life insurance policy on Gregory's life which would more than pay for the farm, and a gardening fork whose prongs matched the wounds in the boy's body, they arrested Wienchowski. He confessed that he had killed his son, but only after Gregory had attacked him with a hammer. Wienchowski was convicted of murder and sentenced to life at the state prison in Jackson.

Wilkinson, Alec, prom. 1955, Brit. At the age of twenty-one, Alec Wilkinson married Maureen Farrell, and the newlyweds moved into a house located down the street from Maureen's mother. Wilkinson's mother-in-law was a foul-mouthed, ill-tempered prostitute who wielded great influence over her daughter. Their marriage quickly deteriorated and Maureen moved in with her mother. On Apr. 30, 1955, Wilkinson called on Maureen, but instead encountered her mother. Mrs. Farrell was abusive and threatened Wilkinson with a carving knife. He eluded her charge and knocked her to the floor, kicked her, and set fire to the house. As he was leaving, his estranged wife walked in; Wilkinson also struck her and left her in the burning house. Wilkinson was arrested for murder, and his defense was unable to convince the court to reduce the charge to manslaughter. He was found Guilty and hanged at Armley prison.

Williams, Arnold Jason, 1967- , U.S. On Oct. 3, 1987, in Silver Spring, Md., Shannon Anne McMillan, twenty-two, was found stabbed to death in her apartment. A bloody fingerprint was found on a newspaper page. The print belonged to a neighbor, Arnold Jason Williams, a former Marine guard with a notable record. Williams had been stationed at the presidential retreat at Camp David. He originally was charged with murder and rape, but the rape charge was dropped during plea bargaining in exchange for a guilty plea to the charge of first-degree murder. On July 5, 1989, in the Montgomery County Circuit Courtroom of Judge James S. McAuliffe, Williams was sentenced to life imprisonment.

Williams, Carl, 1954-88, U.S. On Jan. 23, 1988, Dallas police officer John Glenn Chase, twenty-five, was ticketing a motorist for driving without a license when he was accosted by an onlooker who objected to his actions. Carl Williams, a 34-year-old black man, took the white officer's gun during their scuffle. While Chase pleaded for his life, a few members of the gathering crowd implored Williams to shoot the officer. Williams shot Chase in the face, and returned to fire two more shots, killing the policeman. Williams was later shot to death by two off-duty Dallas policemen. The incident galvanized the racially-polarized city. Police chief Billy Prince blamed black politicians for turning the black community against the force, while civil rights leaders blamed the lack of community influence on the department as the problem.

Williams, David Marshall (AKA: Carbine Williams), 1901-75, U.S. On July 21, 1921, a team of federal agents raided a still in the Five Holly Swamp outside Fayetteville, N.C. The still was owned and operated by David M. Williams, a young moonshiner who had been distributing illegal spirits to the county for some time. While trying to escape from the authorities, Williams fired on Deputy Sheriff Al J. Pate of Cumberland County, who was killed instantly. Williams was tracked down in the woods and arrested by local police. Arraigned on a charge of first-degree murder, Williams went on trial before Judge John H. Kerr in Fayetteville on Aug. 31, 1921. Defense attorneys asserted that Williams suffered from paranoia. The jury, upon hearing all the evidence, was unable to reach a verdict and a mistrial was declared on Oct. 17, 1921. The following month the press announced that David Williams would be tried a second time.

Williams withdrew his earlier insanity defense on Nov. 22. He entered a plea of guilty to the lesser charge of second-degree murder. The deal was cut to save Williams from the gallows. Three days later Judge Henry Lane sentenced the defendant to thirty years in jail, the maximum sentence permissible under North Carolina law at the time.

While serving his time in various state prisons, Williams began to tinker with pieces of scrap metal in the blacksmith's shop. With the permission of the prison superintendent, Williams began manufacturing gunmaking tools, which he used to forge a rudimentary design for three innovative weapons that employed the "floating chamber" principle. The Colt Firearms Company heard of his accomplishments and sent a letter of inquiry to George Ross Pou, superintendent of prisons in Raleigh, N.C., in May 1928. The subsequent publicity surrounding Williams' invention of a superior rapid-fire weapon—the carbine rifle—led to his early parole in 1929. Governor Angus W. McLean of North Carolina granted Williams a full and unconditional pardon on Sept. 29 of that year, after the widow of the murdered deputy said Williams might be able to make something of his invention, and his life, if he were released.

David Williams was associated with the carbine, the weapon that helped win WWII, from that day forward. Eight million of these guns were used by U.S. troops in WWII, Korea, and Vietnam. General Douglas MacArthur credited Williams' invention as being "one of the strongest contributing factors to our victory in the Pacific." In his small workshop at the family farm in Camden, S.C., Williams designed the first machine gun capable of firing 2,000 rounds per minute, which brought him one of the seventy weapons patents he held during his lifetime. From his boyhood interest in toy pistols to the time of his death on Jan. 8, 1975, Williams continued to tinker with guns. A Hollywood motion picture titled *Carbine Williams,* starring James Stewart and Jean Hagen, was released in 1952, which profiled the life and times of the inventor.

Williams, Edward, 1872-1924, Aus. Edward Williams, fifty-two, the father of three daughters and the husband of an insane woman, taught music in Sydney, Aus. Depressed about his meager salary and inability to remove his family from hunger and squalor, Williams resorted to drastic means. On Feb. 4, 1924, Williams put his daughters to bed, asked if they wanted to go to heaven, kissed them goodnight, and left the room. As the girls slept, Williams returned to their room and slit their throats. A family friend discovered the bodies of 6-year-old Rosalie, 4-year-old Mary, and 3-year-old Cecilia. The murders were given sensational coverage and Williams became the target of a nationwide manhunt. Six days later, the tired and beleaguered man turned himself in to the police. During his trial, Williams refused to plead insanity, stating calmly that he did not expect to escape punishment. He said, "They went to God with untarnished souls. I was not the callous man they pictured me here today, for when I killed my three children, that was the moment I loved them most intensely." Williams was found Guilty and sentenced to death. He was hanged on Apr. 29, 1924, at the Long Bay jail.

Williams, Lionel Ray, c.1957-   , U.S. On Feb. 13, 1976, 37-year-old Sal Mineo, an actor who had acquired fame and Oscar nominations very young and then disappeared from public view, was returning to his small apartment near the Sunset Strip. Lionel Williams, who made a career of robbery along famous Hollywood streets, waited in the carport and attacked Mineo before he reached the door of his apartment, stabbing him in the chest several times with a hunting knife. But before Williams could grab Mineo's money, a neighbor came running and saw Williams briefly. The witness thought the assailant was a white man rather than a light-skinned black. Mineo died within a few minutes of massive hemorrhaging.

Actor Sal Mineo, the murder victim.

A few days later, Lionel Williams was arrested for robbery, but the police paid no attention when he commented that Sal Mineo had been killed over drugs, because they had found no evidence the actor used drugs. More than a year later, Williams' wife reported to police that her husband had killed Mineo. She said he had come home the night of the murder and told her that he had done it. She described exactly the knife he used, and the medical examiner found that such a knife fit the stab wounds in Mineo's chest.

Williams was, at that time, imprisoned in Michigan for passing bad checks. Prison guards there reported that he often bragged about killing Mineo, but no one had believed it. It took until January 1979 for the authorities to get Wil-

Lionel Williams, the killer, at right, under arrest.

liams back to California for trial. He was tried for eleven robberies and the murder and found Guilty of all but one robbery. Judge Bonnie Lee Martin sentenced Williams to fifty-one years to life in prison.

Williams, Margaret, prom. 1949, Aust. Montague Cyril Williams, a British soldier stationed in Austria in 1949, married that spring while he was home on leave. His wife Margaret later admitted that she did not love him, and she only married him because she was tipsy when she said yes, and because he agreed that they would not have sex until she grew to love him. The couple spent the weekend of July 2 drinking at the Grand Hotel in Anneheim. On their return to their base at Klagenfurt, they had a fight, and Margaret went out for a walk. She met some Austrian friends who took her to a nearby inn to drink, but her husband came after her with two friends who physically removed her from the inn and carried her home. Back in their room, her husband beat her up and she told him she was going to leave him. When he slapped her again, she grabbed a knife from the table and stabbed him. She tried to get help for him, but the knife had penetrated his heart and he bled to death.

Margaret Williams was returned to England for trial, which started at the Old Bailey on Sept. 15. Although Justice Streatfield informed the jury that they could bring in a verdict of manslaughter or self-defense, the jury found Margaret Williams Guilty of murder. She was sentenced to death but was reprieved by the home secretary.

Williams, Matthew, d.1931, U.S. In December 1931, Matthew Williams, a black man, worked in a lumber yard in Salisbury, Md. Angry about his low wages, Williams shot his boss, Daniel Elliott, to death. During an ensuing shootout, Elliott's son wounded Williams in the head, and Williams accidentally shot himself in the chest. Later that day, six men took him from a hospital and delivered him to a throng of 2,000 waiting outside. Williams was blindfolded and hanged from a tree on the courthouse lawn. After twenty minutes, his body was cut down and burned. Nobody was charged with the lynching.

Williams, Norman, prom. 1904, U.S. In February 1904, George Nesbitt appeared near Hood River, Ore., looking for clues in the disappearances four years before of Alma and Louisa Nesbitt, his mother and sister. He suspected Norman Williams, who had known the Nesbitt family when they had lived in Iowa, followed the women to Oregon, and farmed adjoining land. A search of the Nesbitt homestead revealed a gunnysack which may have contained human blood and hair, but this was hardly enough evidence to convict a suspect. However, it was learned that Williams had married Alma Nesbitt, George's sister, while he was married to a woman in neighboring Dufar, Ore. A Portland chemist determined that the hairs in the gunnysack were human hairs pulled violently from the scalp, and a local liveryman recalled that Williams had leased a buggy at about the time of the disappearances. By killing the women, Williams inherited their land. He was arrested for the murders, convicted, and hanged.

Williams, Thomas Joseph, 1923-42, Brit. On Easter 1942, six members of the Irish Republican Army (IRA) shot to death Constable Patrick Murphy. Murphy was shot five times, three times with one weapon, twice with another. IRA members Thomas Joseph Williams, nineteen, Patrick Simpson, eighteen, William J. Perry, Henry Cordner, John T. Oliver, and Joseph Cahill were arrested. Ballistics tests linked them to the weapons. During the trial, Williams confessed to firing one of the weapons. On July 30, 1942, the six men were sentenced to be hanged. On Aug. 30, five of the men were reprieved. Simpson was resentenced to fifteen years in prison and Williams was condemned to die.

Williams, Wayne Bertram, 1958- , U.S. Experience has taught the members of the Atlanta Police Department to expect eight, possibly ten child murders in a calendar year. Frequently the victim dies as a result of senseless domestic violence, be it a quarrel between siblings or the act of an abusive parent. These cases are usually cleared within days, freeing the police for other duties. In 1979, however, the city police force was alerted to the presence of a serial killer within the metropolitan area—one who preyed on young black children between the ages of seven and fourteen. Before the nightmare was over, various experts from across the country would be brought in to lend their special talents to a criminal investigation that dragged on for more than two years, one that sorely tested the resources of the city administration and its police force. In March 1981, President Ronald Reagan committed up to $1.5 million in federal funds to help defray costs of the investigation. At that time the death toll stood at twenty-six. It would climb to twenty-eight before a suspect would be formally charged.

The bodies of the first two victims were found lying adjacent to Niskey Lake on July 28, 1979. A man scavenging for tin cans stumbled across the remains of what he first thought to be a dead animal. Upon further investigation he noticed a pair of boy's pants, a belt, and a human torso. Lying in the underbrush some 150 feet away a second body was found. Forensic investigators identified the sets of remains as 13-year-old James Evans and 14-year-old Edward Smith. Both boys had disappeared from their Atlanta homes earlier in the week. Evans by all indications had been asphyxiated, while Smith was shot. The dual murders did not attract much press attention at the time, and neither did the discovery of the skeletal remains of 14-year-old Milton Harvey on Nov. 5. The youth was first reported missing in October after wandering away from his home in northwest Atlanta. The police were unable to determine the precise cause of death. Three days later a fourth black child was found, 9-year-old Yusef Bell, the son of noted civil rights worker Camille Bell from Mechanicsville. The boy disappeared after he had been sent out on an errand and was found in the maintenance shaft of an abandoned schoolhouse.

Nothing more was heard from the unknown assailant until March 1980, when the killing resumed with sickening regularity. Twelve-year-old Angel Lanier, the first female victim, was found tied to a tree with her panties stuffed in her mouth in early March. The fact that she had been raped puzzled the police who had concluded that the killer was a male homosexual. By July 1980, the death toll had climbed to twelve following the discovery of the bodies of Eric Middlebrooks, Christopher Richardson, Aaron Wyche, and LaTonya Wilson. The black community was convinced that the murders were racially motivated and carried out by a white supremacist. The police did not give much credence to this theory, believing that the presence of a white murderer in the all-black neighborhoods where these children lived would have eventually been detected by the local residents. In July, Camille Bell and the parent of Mary Mapp, one of the victims, called a press conference to announce the formation of the Committee to Stop the Children's Murders. Public Safety Commissioner Lee Brown, the first American black to receive a doctorate in criminology, was taken to task for his department's failure to apprehend a suspect by community activists and officials on the federal level. Former Attorney General Griffin Bell remarked, "I think you ought to be able to catch somebody. If you have more than twenty deaths, why isn't at least one person caught? That's what I hear people saying."

Brown responded by organizing a five-man task force to supplement the police investigation. "I have the utmost confidence in our investigation," Brown said. "I don't believe all knowledge rests in Georgia." By year's end the

Atlanta mass murderer Wayne Williams greeting the press, 1981.

task force had been expanded in the wake of additional killings. Some of the leading figures in criminal investigation were brought in at Brown's behest, including retired Los Angeles Police Department Captain Pierce Brooks, who cracked the Onion Field murders, Lieutenant George Mayer of Stamford, Conn., who had worked on the "Merritt Parkway Bra" murders, and Lieutenant Gilbert Hill of Detroit who brought the Browning Gang to justice after they had murdered fifteen victims. Their presence failed to mollify anxious members of the black community who believed a policeman was responsible for the slayings. Law enforcement officials replied that the killer was in all likelihood a black teenager who was looked up to and trusted by his victims. A $100,000 reward was posted by the city, and additional cash incentives were put up by three recording companies and celebrities from the world of sports and entertainment. And still it continued. By March 1981, twenty bodies had been found. Autopsies showed that none of the victims to date were drugged or given alcohol. Only 23-year-old Michael McIntosh, found floating in the Chattahoochee River on Apr. 20, 1981, was completely disrobed.

The first major break in the case came on May 22 when police officer Fred Jacobs sat in his patrol car near a bridge spanning the river. He heard a resounding splash and then saw a man get into a station wagon. The information was relayed to a second patrol car driving in the vicinity. Before the station wagon could exit the bridge, the second patrol car stopped the driver for questioning. The police searched the vehicle and found some nylon rope, a pair of gloves, and a blood-stain on the front seat. The driver was identified as 23-year-old Wayne Williams, a black man who lived with his parents in a modest brick home in northwest Atlanta. Williams told the police that he was returning from a musical audition. He denied stopping on the bridge and swore he knew nothing about a bundle being dropped in the river. The police warned him that if a body turned up they would be calling him in for further questioning. Williams drove off.

Two days later the remains of Nathanial Cater, the twenty-eighth and final victim, was removed from the Chattahoochee River. An eyewitness told police that Williams and Cater, a 27-year-old homosexual, were seen leaving a movie theater together. A second witness came forward and told police that Williams had also been keeping company with Jimmy Ray Payne, a 21-year-old man pulled out of the muddy waters of the Chattahoochee on Apr. 27. Payne was reported missing after he failed to show up for a job interview.

Convinced that Williams was their man, police detectives sent the car seat containing the bloodstains to the state crime lab in Atlanta for analysis on June 4. It was found that the blood type matched that of Williams and Cater. Additionally, dog hairs found on the body of Cater were identical to those in Williams' car. The dog in question was Williams' German shepherd.

On June 18 Wayne Williams was indicted for the murders of Nathanial Cater and Jimmy Payne. The accused was the only child of Homer and Fay Williams, two retired schoolteachers from Atlanta. Mrs. Williams described her son as a "miracle child" who was born when she was forty-

one. From the time he was a child Wayne's parents encouraged the learning process. They had invested all of their savings into radio equipment Wayne needed to start a radio station. A transmitter was installed in the family home, and it was powerful enough to broadcast a mile in each direction. The project failed and the family suffered financial hardship as a result. Williams was alternately described as a "media junkie" and a frustrated dreamer, obsessed with his own success and failings. He dabbled in photography and promoted himself as a talent scout. Williams printed leaflets offering young black men between the ages of eleven and twenty an opportunity to embark on a musical career through his influence. One of the men answering his ad was Patrick Rogers, an aspiring soul singer who was later murdered. Under heavy security, the murder trial of Wayne B. Williams began at the Fulton County Courthouse on Jan. 5, 1982. Superior Court Judge Clarence Cooper imposed a gag order on district attorney Lewis Slaton and defense attorneys Alvin Binder and Mary Welcome, preventing them from discussing aspects of this highly controversial case with the media. Legal experts conceded that the prosecution faced an uphill battle trying to secure a conviction based solely on forensic evidence and the testimony of police officers. Though inadmissible in court, the most damaging evidence against Williams was the fact that the killing immediately stopped after he was taken into custody.

Williams took the stand on Feb. 22. He denied he was a homosexual and refuted the testimony of a youth who claimed to have been molested by him. "Ain't no way I'm a homosexual," he said. "I have no grudge against (homosexuals) as long as they keep their hands to themselves. I'm scared," he added. The jury, composed of eight blacks and four whites, retired on Feb. 27, 1982, to consider its verdict. After deliberating for less than twelve hours they returned a verdict of Guilty. Judge Cooper sentenced Williams to two consecutive life sentences. The verdict was upheld by the Georgia Supreme Court, amidst growing doubt that Williams was railroaded through unsupported circumstantial evidence. It was alleged that several of the witnesses were more interested in the reward money than securing justice for the defendant. Commented Homer Williams, "It's impossible to find a young man like this guilty." Since 1981, the city of Atlanta has not experienced a similar outbreak of child murder, suggesting that the police and the courts had been right all along.

Williams Farm Murders, 1921, U.S. John Williams, a 58-year-old farmer from Jasper County, Ga., owned a sprawling 2,200-acre plantation thirty-five miles north of

Macon. Over the years Williams and his sons ran the farm, and employed a group of poor black field-hands to harvest the crops and tend to chores. Slavery had ended with the collapse of the Confederacy in 1865, but Williams instituted his own system of peonage and involuntary servitude. "Mr. Johnny never did pay us off and we were all too scared of him to ask for money," one aging black man related to federal authorities. "Once he gave me a dollar but that's all the money I ever got. I worked for him in all about six years. Yes, sir, he always gave us plenty to eat and kept us in clean clothes." He neglected to add that Williams, or one of his boys, kept the field hands shackled in balls and chains and under armed guard in a sweltering stockade by night. The conditions were beyond human endurance. Many of the victims chose death over continued enslavement at the Williams farm.

The bodies of three black men were found weighted down in the murky depths of the Yellow River in early March 1921. From Clyde Manning, a "trusty" on the Williams plantation, the authorities learned that there were other victims, possibly eleven, who had been killed after threatening to escape. Manning's startling confession led to the arrest and indictment of John Williams on Mar. 24. The farmer accused members of the Leverett family of framing these charges against him and his boys. A property dispute dating back nearly seven years was the cause of these present troubles, Williams said. "They also have claimed that I killed some of their live-stock. Last fall the Leverett boys charged my boys with turning up a still to the officers and we almost had a shooting scrape over that," Williams explained.

Manning led a team of federal and state officers to a remote spot in Jasper County where he identified the graves of five farm hands whose skulls had been split open with an axe. "This is the Negro who would rather be shot than whipped," Manning said. "He ain't been buried long." Three other bodies were found weighted down under the Waters Bridge which spanned the Alcovy River. "Me and Mr. Williams took Charlie (Chisholm) to Waters Bridge. Charlie begged hard but Mr. Williams said: 'Throw him over,' so we weighted him pretty good at both ends and splash! That was the end of Charlie," Manning related in gruesome detail.

The coroner's jury believed that both victims were alive when they were thrown into the river. Manning, the self-confessed murderer of blacks, said that he had stood nearby while his victims were forced to dig their own graves. "Why did I do it? Because the boss Mr. Williams said he wanted to get rid of the Negroes and that if I didn't make them disappear he'd kill me." John Williams was convicted by a jury in Covington, Ga., on Apr. 9 for the murder of Lindsay Peterson, one of eighteen victims found in Newton

and Jasper counties. The conviction carried with it an automatic sentence of life imprisonment. Additional indictments were returned against John Williams' three sons, Hayler, Marvin, and Julius, as well as the field-hand "overseer," Clyde Manning. In his instructions to the jury, Judge Parks of the superior court expressed his sorrow. "Lawlessness in this section has now reached the point where it will cause us to be shunned unless we check it," he said. "We will soon reach the stage where no capital will come here and help us to develop our great natural resources." Williams was convicted of additional murders committed in Newton County on Feb. 1, 1922, and was handed a second life sentence. He passed away on Jan. 26, 1932, while serving his time. Manning was later convicted of murder but under appeal to a higher court the verdict was overturned.

Willis, Frances, and **Artegian, Rodney**, prom. 1975, U.S. On Sept. 25, 1975, Frances Willis told Orlando, Fla., police that her husband James had been beaten and murdered by a group of wild-looking strangers. Police found that the man had been shot while asleep, with no signs of a beating. He had also drunk a can of beer laced with horse tranquilizer. His wife held a $17,000 insurance policy on his life.

Investigators found a handicapped cleaning man, Rodney Artegian, who confessed that Willis gave him $5,000 to kill her husband. Who actually fired the fatal shot was never clear, and Artegian and Willis were both tried for the murder. Artegian, who turned state's evidence, received a plea-bargained verdict of second-degree murder and was sentenced to fifteen years in prison. Willis was convicted of first-degree murder and sentenced to life imprisonment.

Wilson, Earl, 1952-   , U.S. On Nov. 18, 1986, on Chicago's South Side, flamboyant drug dealer Willie "Flukey" Stokes, forty-nine, was gunned down, execution-style, while riding in his car. Stokes's driver, 28-year-old Ronald Johnson, was also killed. The three gunmen were not apprehended, but Stokes's bodyguard, 34-year-old Earl Wilson, was arrested for complicity in the murders. He had been in a car following Stokes' on the night of the murder, and was alleged to have communicated with the murderers via car phone. In Wilson's Autumn 1987 trial, the defense claimed that he was working as an informant for the state's attorney and had provided daily information about Stokes. The prosecution countered that Wilson had aspired to Stokes's position as a drug kingpin, noting that he had not released the names of his co-conspirators. On Jan. 7, 1988, in the Cook County criminal courtroom of Judge Ronald Himel, Wilson was convicted of the double murder and sentenced to life imprisonment without the possibility of parole.

Wilson, Edwin, 1928- , U.S. A former secret agent for the CIA, Edwin Wilson smuggled explosives into Libya and used U.S. Special Forces personnel to train Libyan terrorists. In 1976, Libyan dictator Muammar Qaddafi agreed to buy Wilson's expertise on the U.S. military, arms, explosives, and covert operations. Wilson organized, financed, and directed a group of ten men with U.S. Army Special Forces experience to work in Libya training terrorists. Wilson also brought to Libya another group of Americans with expertise in explosives. A grand jury indicted Wilson in 1980 for smuggling twenty tons of explosives and other weapons into Libya. Wilson was a fugitive for a few years, but when he was lured back to the U.S., he was arrested. Wilson was convicted in November 1982 and sentenced on Feb. 18, 1983, to seventeen years in prison for smuggling explosives and fifteen years for smuggling weapons.

While in prison awaiting his trial, Wilson had asked fellow inmate Wayne Trimmer to help him find a hit-man to kill the prosecutors, his former business partner, and several witnesses in his case. He offered a total of $1.25 million for seven or eight killings. The inmate went to the federal authorities and became a key witness against Wilson. Wilson then offered two other inmates money to kill Trimmer and to arrange for another hit-man to kill the people involved in his trial. Those two inmates also went to the federal authorities. An undercover FBI agent met Wilson's son, Erik Wilson, in a hotel room and collected a $9,800 down payment from him. Wilson was charged with attempted murder. Following his trial, which began on Oct. 4, 1983, Wilson was convicted and sentenced to twenty years in prison. He was put in solitary confinement at the federal prison in Marion, Ill.

Wilson, James William, 1969- , U.S. Described as "difficult to manage" and "volatile" by psychiatrists, James William Wilson more than lived up to his description when, in the fall of 1988, he opened fire on the children and staff of an elementary school in South Carolina, leaving nine people wounded and two children dead.

Wilson was nineteen when the shooting took place on Sept. 26, 1988, and had been under psychiatric care from the age of fourteen, being hospitalized six times from May 1983 to April 1988. He lived in Greenwood, S.C., with his paternal grandmother. He had been there ever since his father had asked the boy to move out of the family home—about the time he began psychiatric treatment—because Wilson's father feared for his family's well-being. At seventeen Wilson dropped out of high school and was unable to hold any type of employment.

Between the year he left school, 1986, and the rampage, Wilson's family had twice attempted to have the boy involuntarily committed to a mental institution; each time the court rejected the petition. His grandmother noted that Wilson, who was on medication for his mental state up until two months prior to the killings, would stay awake throughout the night reading, often going to bed at 8 a.m. Wilson would read books and articles on murderers, most notably serial killer John Wayne Gacy (who Wilson read about the night before his shooting spree in Tim Cahill's and Russ Ewing's book, *Buried Dreams: Inside the Mind of a Serial Killer*) and Laurie Dann, whose assault upon a Winnetka, Ill., elementary school was not only similar to Wilson's, but as the killer himself said, in the *People* magazine article on the case, "I read it every day. I had it for a few months. I could understand where she was coming from. I think I may have copied her in a way."

According to forensic psychiatrist Dr. Donald Morgan, Wilson was suffering—and still is—from "borderline personality disorder," which impaired his knowing right from wrong, when he drove to his paternal grandmother's home in nearby Abbeville to arm himself with a nine-shot pistol, his father having removed any guns from the place Wilson currently lived in six months previously on account of his son's disposition.

After purchasing two boxes of ammunition at a discount store, Wilson pulled into the front drive of the Oakland Elementary School in Greenwood where he loaded the .22-caliber handgun, placing extra bullets in his shirt pocket, and entered the building through the front door.

It was shortly after 11 a.m. when Wilson appeared in the school's cafeteria and opened fire, wounding three students and a teacher in a crowd of about 100 first-graders and a third-grade class. The gunman left the lunchroom, having discharged all nine shots, making his way down the hallway to a girls' restroom where he reloaded his weapon. Upon leaving the restroom Wilson was confronted by physical education teacher Kat Finkbiener, who was shot in the mouth and hand while attempting to stop him.

Wilson continued down the hall entering a classroom where one of the twenty-two third-graders said that she laughed at his appearance on first seeing the overweight gunman, but added, "I wasn't laughing when he began shooting."

In that room Wilson shot and wounded four children and killed two others: Shequila Bradley, eight, who was shot once in the forehead, and Tequila Thomas, eight, who died three days later from wounds to her neck and chest. When he had run out of ammunition, Wilson dropped the gun and left the room, surrendering himself to principal Eleanor Rice who asked him to stop and held him until the police arrived.

Following a plea of guilty but mentally ill, Eighth Circuit Court Judge James E. Moore sentenced Wilson, who had waived his right to a jury trial, to death by electrocution.

James William Wilson, who fired on a group of school children, killing two, on Sept. 26, 1988.

The death sentence, which is the first such case involving a plea of guilty but mentally ill, created an enormous judicial controversy over the state's law concerning such a plea.

The defense counsel for Wilson, David G. Belser and William H. Nicholson III, argued that a person declared mentally ill should not be sentenced to death because the penalty is too severe for someone who did not know he was breaking a law. Prosecutor Townes Jones contended that the statute concerning a plea of guilty but mentally ill did allow for a death sentence and added vehemently that "Jamie Wilson decided to act and live in a certain way. He chose to live the way he did. We have a man who chose as his heroes John Wayne Gacy, a serial murderer, and Laurie Dann, a murderer. He didn't choose to save lives. He chose to destroy them."

Along with the death sentence, Wilson was also sentenced to 175 years in prison on various charges stemming from the wounds he inflicted. Wilson is currently awaiting appeal of his sentence on Death Row at the Central Correctional Institution in Columbia, S.C. See: **Dann, Laurie Wasserman; Gacy, John Wayne, Jr.**

Wilson, John Wayne 1949-73, U.S. On Jan. 1, 1973, Roseann Quinn became New York City's first homicide victim of the year. She was strangled, stabbed eleven times, and mutilated beyond recognition. Six days later, 24-year-old John Wayne Wilson was arrested in Indianapolis, Ind., for the murder. He told homicide detectives that he had picked the girl up in a singles' bar, and after sleeping together, the girl severely scratched his back in an effort to throw him out of the apartment. In addition, Wilson told his attorney that he had been mocked by the girl for being impotent. Prison psychologists diagnosed Wilson as schizophrenic with homicidal and suicidal tendencies. He hanged himself in his cell before he could be brought to trial for Quinn's murder. The case served as a model for the book, and subsequent movie, *Looking for Mr. Goodbar.*

Wilson, Mary Elizabeth (AKA: **The Widow of Windy Nook**), b.1891, Brit. If not for a casual remark said in jest Mary Wilson might have slipped through the hands of British authorities and otherwise been forgotten. Instead, she became the first woman sentenced to death under the terms of the recently enacted Homicide Act and the first person to be convicted and sentenced under it for multiple murder.

Mary Elizabeth Wilson, the merry "widow of Windy Nook," disposed of two of her three husbands in a year's time. In Summer 1956 at age sixty-five, when she was a widow for the first time (Mary's first husband, John Knowles, was a retired chimney sweep), Wilson was introduced to 76-year-old Oliver James Leonard, a real-estate agent. "Has the old (man) any money?" she asked her friend, Mrs. Alice Mary Connelly, who owned a lodging house where the man lived. "A little as far as I know," came the reply. The widow Knowles and Leonard were married a short time later. The marriage lasted several months. On Oct. 3, 1956, Leonard died unexpectedly. Two days later a death certificate was signed by Dr. John Hubert Laydon listing the cause of death as "degeneration of the heart with some inflammation of the kidneys." Dr. Laydon, who had prescribed some mild cough medicine just two days earlier, said that Leonard was in good health for his age. Asked how he had known the man was dead, Dr. Laydon replied, "Some person came in and told me Mr. Leonard was dead and I filled in the death certificate." Under British law a physician was permitted to issue a death certificate if he had seen the patient within fourteen days of death.

Several weeks after Leonard's death, his son by a former marriage asked the widow about the will. "There wasn't much," Wilson explained. All that was left was £45 to £75.

Husband number three was Ernest George Lawrence Wilson, a retired engineer who met Mary while seeking out a housekeeper. He intimated that he was seeking a life companion and had £100 in the Cooperative Society to his name. This, coupled with a small insurance policy, enticed Mary into a marriage with the 76-year-old Wilson. At the reception wedding guests asked Mary what she planned to do with the cakes and sandwiches that were in abundance. "Just keep them for the funeral, although I might give this one a week's extension," she laughed. Her whimsy was forgotten until Wilson died on Nov. 11, 1957. Earlier that day Dr. William Proudfoot Wallace was summoned to their home by Mrs. Wilson who reported that her husband had become sick during the night. The physician decided that Wilson was suffering from myocardio degeneration of the heart and prescribed a cough medicine and some pills. The next morning he received a second call from Mary Wilson who said that her husband's condition had worsened. By the time he arrived at the home, Ernest Wilson was dead. Dr. Wallace listed the cause of death as cardio-vascular failure on the death certificate. Three days after the body was interred in the ground Mary Wilson drew out £24 on two of her husband's life insurance policies.

These highly suspicious circumstances came to the attention of pathologist Dr. William Stewart, who ordered that the remains of John Knowles, Ernest Wilson, and Oliver Leonard be exhumed. Stewart arrived at the conclusion that Wilson and Leonard had been poisoned. The presence of elemental phosphorus was found in their systems, a substance used in rat and beetle poisons. When confronted about her flippant remarks at the wedding reception, Mary Wilson shot back, "I know I upset some people by that joke at my wedding. But I think that really people are jealous of me because I have always tried to laugh my way through life. I've had plenty of troubles but I believe in keeping cheerful. My conscience is clear. I have looked after all my men as a good wife should." She added that if the right opportunity came along she would consider marrying again.

Mary was indicted for the double murder of Leonard and Wilson. The trial went before Justice Hinchcliffe at the Leeds Assizes in March 1958. In his opening remarks, Geoffrey Veale, representing the Crown, described Mrs. Wilson as a "wicked woman who in succession married two men and then deliberately poisoned them in order to get the paltry benefits she hoped she might obtain from their deaths." In defense of her client, Attorney Rose Heilbron produced scientific evidence to show that phosphorus was commonly used in prescription medicine to cure rickets, nervous disorders, and on occasion could serve as a sexual stimulant. "What more natural than that these old men, finding a wife in the evening of their lives, should purchase these pills for the purpose for which they are apparently known," she concluded. Druggist Angus Fraser McIntosh explained that it would take 150 of these pills to bring on death.

Acting under the advice of her attorney, Mary Wilson did not appear as a witness on her on behalf. This left many unanswered questions. Why wasn't a doctor called in earlier? On the day of Wilson's death she had attempted to sell an expensive gold watch, which was hardly the rational act of a grieving widow. The jury returned a Guilty verdict after debating the matter for an hour and a half. Justice Hinchcliffe sentenced her to death in his first murder trial. Because of her advanced age however, she was eventually reprieved.

Wilson, Otto Stephen, c.1910-46, U.S. Although outwardly calm and alluring, Otto Stephen Wilson was capable of murder. He choked to death and mutilated the bodies of two women he met for the first time less than seven hours apart.

Before Wilson began his brutal murder spree he got extremely drunk. Still in a drunken stupor two days later, the former Navy man purchased a butcher knife with a nine-inch blade, and, in this same state he met Mrs. Virginia Lee Griffin, his first victim, in one of Los Angeles' seedier bars.

Although married, the 25-year-old Griffin agreed to accompany Wilson to the Barclay Hotel. She told Wilson as the two entered the hotel that her horoscope said Wednesday was her lucky day. Wednesday Nov. 15, 1944, proved anything but lucky for Griffin. By 8 a.m. the next day she was dead.

Wilson claimed that Griffin, after sharing a few drinks in the hotel room, had demanded more money from him. At that point the shipyard commissary fry cook hit Griffin and choked her until she stopped breathing and then mutilated and dismembered the corpse beyond recognition.

On leaving the room Wilson paid the chambermaid $1 "not to disturb his wife." He ended up in another bar and not long after he and Mrs. Lillian Johnson, thirty-eight, were in a room at the nearby Joyce Hotel. After Johnson removed her clothes, Wilson strangled her. By then he realized the butcher knife had been left behind at the Barclay Hotel, so after giving himself a shave with the razor he carried with him, Wilson slashed Johnson's body, cutting his hand in the process.

When Wilson told the hotel desk clerk not to disturb his sleeping wife it was already 3 p.m. on Thursday, and an hour earlier the police had discovered what was left of Griffin; one-half hour later they would learn of Johnson's murder as well.

The Los Angeles Police Department was quick to track down this homicidal maniac. Patrolman Harry E. Donlan noticed a man with a cut on his hand and blood on his mustache talking to woman in a bar not far from the Joyce Hotel. It was Wilson. Just two hours after the discovery of Johnson's body her murderer was in custody.

At first Wilson denied the bloody crimes but later confessed saying Griffin's demand for more money angered him. As for Johnson he said, "for some reason—just pure cussedness, I guess—I hit her."

Authorities in Tulsa, Okla., suspected Wilson in two other murders when they noted similarities between his brutal acts and the killings of Luzila Stewart and her daughter Georgia Green, on Jan. 14, 1943.

Wilson was convicted of the Griffin and Johnson murders and received the death penalty. He was executed in the gas chamber at San Quentin, Sept. 20, 1946.

Wise, Martha Hasel, b.1885, U.S. When 40-year-old Martha Wise of Medina, Ohio, fell in love with Walter Johns, her mother spoke scornfully of the romance. On Jan. 1, 1925, she died of poisoning. Lily and Fred Geinke, Wise's aunt and uncle, also died in February after drinking arsenic-laced coffee. Martha Wise admitted murdering her relatives, but blamed it on the devil, whom she saw following her everywhere. She confessed the devil had also made her burgle houses in the area and set destructive fires.

At Wise's trial, Johns tried to help her defense by testifying that she must be insane, because when they made love she barked. Nevertheless, the jury found Wise Guilty of murder, and she was sentenced to prison for life.

Wise, Olive Catherine, prom. 1931, Brit. Olive Catherine Wise, an unmarried mother, earned money to feed her four childen by peddling chopped wood. Despondent over a fifth pregnancy, she asphyxiated her fourth-born child in an oven. She was apprehended and sentenced to death. However, a sympathetic judge, John Robert Clynes, decreed the penalty too harsh and reduced the sentence to life in prison.

Witherspoon, William, 1925- , U.S. Until Apr. 29, 1959, William Witherspoon's criminal record was limited to petty thievery. But on that date, he shot and killed Chicago police officer Mitchell Stone. Although Wither-

spoon contended that the gun went off accidentally as he handed it to Stone, he was charged with the police officer's murder. Witherspoon was convicted and sentenced to die

Cop killer William Witherspoon; he was paroled in 1979.

in the electric chair. However, in 1986, the U.S. Supreme Court replaced the death sentence with a sentence of 100 years in prison. Witherspoon became eligible for parole in 1970, but parole was not granted until 1979.

Wittman, Manfred (AKA: **The Beast of Oberfranken**), 1945- , Ger. Beginning in 1959, a man known to the local populace as the Beast of Oberfranken had attacked several attractive young women near the small German town of Kaltenbrunn. After forcing his victims to undress and binding them, often with their own undergarments, the attacker then stabbed them repeatedly with a 10-inch serrated knife and, finally, slit their throats. His first victim survived the attack, but the next three victims did not.

Suspicion fell on Manfred Wittman when a resident of Kaltenbrunn told police that she had seen the last victim getting into a car similar to the one driven by Wittman. The description of the attacker, given to police by the surviving victim, suited Wittman, but his popularity in the community initially made him seem less than the perfect suspect. Police ordered a physical examination of Wittman, during which it was discovered that his genitalia were no more developed than that of a 10-year-old. He broke down and confessed to the murders following the examination. In his confession, Wittman claimed that it was frustration over his impotence that led him to murder the women. He was subsequently tried and sentenced to life in prison.

Wolter, Albert W., 1892-1910, U.S. On Mar. 25, 1910, sixteen-year-old Ruth Wheeler, a recent secretarial course graduate, answered a classified ad for a stenographer. When she failed to return home for dinner that evening, her sister Pearl went to the address on the upper east side of Manhattan and found an apartment that belonged to 18-year-old Albert Wolter.

Pearl became suspicious and called police when Wolter claimed he had never seen or heard of Ruth Wheeler. While police questioned Wolter, the building janitor discovered a package containing the charred remains of a human body in the interior courtyard of the building. A more thorough search of Wolter's apartment uncovered clothing and other items belonging to Wheeler. From evidence within the apartment, it became apparent that Wolter had raped and strangled Wheeler shortly after she arrived at the apartment. He then bound her body and stuffed it into the small fireplace. Although Wolter denied committing the crime, he was convicted of Wheeler's murder, and at the age of eighteen, became the youngest person executed in New York state at that time.

Woo Bum Kong, 1955-87, Kor. On Apr. 28, 1982, in an area 170 miles southeast of Seoul, a South Korean police officer went on a rampage killing fifty-eight people before blowing himself up with a hand grenade. The 27-year-old policeman, Woo Bum Kong, reportedly became enraged when his common-law wife, Chun Mal Soon, slapped his chest while trying to kill a fly. Woo became furious, the couple quarrelled, and after several hours of drinking, Woo returned home and beat his wife. When neighbors tried to intercede, Woo began shooting. Chun was shot in the abdomen and was in serious condition after surgery.

After shooting Chun, Woo went on to the police department armory where he equipped himself with two carbine rifles and 180 rounds of ammunition. He also acquired seven hand grenades from a nearby militia station. After leaving the militia station, Woo shot and killed three men in the street. His next stop was the post office where he shot a telephone operator and three other employees. Woo then went to a nearby village where he killed six more people. By this time, police had been alerted and were tracking Woo with orders to shoot to kill. Woo, however, eluded the police and went to yet another village where he killed twelve more people. Woo moved from village to village during the night, randomly killing unsuspecting villagers. After eight hours of attacks, and in his fifth village, Woo exploded a hand grenade, killing himself and three members of a farm family. In addition to the fifty-eight dead, another thirty-seven people were wounded in the rampage.

Woodward, Raymond L. Jr., c.1925- , U.S. Not one of the hundreds of people searching for a missing 15-year-old girl thought to look in the parsonage across the street from the girl's home. If they had, she would have been spared four days of torture and mutilation at the hands of a 15-year-old boy.

Age and the hometown of Reading, Mass., were about all victim Constance Arlene Shipp and perpetrator Raymond L. Woodward, Jr., had in common. Shipp was a nearly straight-A student at Reading High School, where she was a sophomore. Woodward had been expelled for misbehavior from Belmont Junior High School before returning to Reading Junior High School, where he had been under the supervision of the superintendent for the past three years.

Before murdering Shipp, whose body was discovered July 19, 1941, Woodward had already been convicted on a charge of accosting a woman on June 27 of that year, for which he received a $10 fine and a year's probation, and he had been indicted two weeks before he was charged with murder for allegedly attacking another woman, a crime for which he had been released on bail.

Faced with a murder charge, Woodward adamantly professed his innocence, telling investigators he did not have a key to the locked parsonage where Shipp's body was found, but was simply working on the lawn for the vacationing reverend. The youth even claimed he had left his chores and went home at the same time Shipp was last seen alive.

Four days passed before the girl's body was found. The corpse was discovered with twenty-two separate wounds resulting from bludgeoning, cutting, and stabbing. An autopsy revealed that some of the wounds were older than others by as much as a day, which meant her attacker had spent a good deal of time mutilating her. Other injuries had been inflicted while she was alive and she had likely been tortured. There were also a number of wounds to the breasts and Shipp's head had been bashed in.

Evidence against Woodward mounted—the clothes he was wearing when Shipp disappeared were stained with blood, fingerprints were found inside the parsonage, and a witness had seen someone leaving the building during the time the girl's body was inside—when the youth confessed to having killed the girl.

Under Massachusetts law, Woodward's plea of guilty meant that the youth would automatically be sentenced to death, however, at the recommendation of the state's attorney general the governor agreed to commute the boy's sentence to life in prison, thus sparing Woodward from the electric chair in January 1942. He is currently serving his prison sentence at the Southeast Correctional Center in Bridgewater, Mass.

Woolfe, George, 1880-1902, Brit. George Woolfe, twenty-two, had the dubious distinction of being the last man to be hanged at Newgate before the prison was demolished. Woolfe was convicted of the murder of Charlotte Cheeseman, a young woman with whom Woolfe had been involved. Cheeseman resisted Woolfe's attempts to break off their relationship. On the morning of Jan. 26, 1902, Cheeseman's body was found in a ditch, her head battered with a chisel. Woolfe, who had enlisted in the military, was arrested on Feb. 6. In April, he faced trial at the Old Bailey, was found Guilty of murder, and hanged.

Woolmington, Reginald, 1914- , Brit. On Dec. 10, 1934, Violet Woolmington was shot to death in her mother's home. Neighbors reported seeing her husband, Reginald Woolmington, leaving the scene of the crime on his bicycle. Woolmington was arrested and brought to trial for the murder. During the course of the trial, it was revealed that Woolmington had become jealous when he heard reports that his wife, who had moved back to her mother's house after only a few weeks of marriage, had been seen with another man. Woolmington admitted shooting his wife, but insisted that the gun had fired accidentally. The trial ended with a hung jury.

At the end of the second trial, the judge quoted a passage from *Archbold's Criminal Pleading* to the jury which he paraphrased as follows: "If once you find that a person has been guilty of killing another, it is for the person who had been guilty of the killing to satisfy you that the crime is something less than the murder with which he is charged." After these instructions, the jury returned a verdict of Guilty and Woolmington was sentenced to death. Woolmington's counsel appealed the verdict, arguing that the oft-quoted passage offended the very essence of British law—the idea that a person is innocent until the Crown has proved him guilty. After much debate, the Lord Chancellor announced that the jury had been misdirected and the conviction could not stand. Woolmington was released and English legal history was forever amended.

Woomer, Ronald (AKA: Rusty), 1955- , U.S. On Feb. 22, 1979, Ronald Woomer and a companion, Eugene Skaar, went on a crime spree in South Carolina that left four people dead. The two men started off in West Virginia, driving to the South Carolina coast with the intention of robbing some coin dealers. They murdered coin collectors John Turner, Arnie Richardson, Earl Dean Wright, and a convenience store clerk, Mrs. Sellers. In addition to the murders, they also committed armed robbery, attempted murder, and rape.

Skaar shot himself as police surrounded a Myrtle Beach hotel where the two men were hiding. Woomer, who was charged with only one of the murders, remained on Death Row for ten years. The Supreme Court stay of execution that removed him from Death Row came only thirteen hours before Woomer was scheduled to be executed in the electric chair in June 1989. Although the Supreme Court refrained from giving specific reasons for granting the stay, Woomer's attorney indicated that important evidence, withheld during Woomer's trial, had been uncovered.

Shortly after the stay was granted, Senator Strom Thurmond requested that the U.S. Senate introduce legislation to reduce filing of habeas corpus petitions such as the one responsible for Woomer's stay. Using Woomer's case as an example, and citing the statistics that the number of these petitions has increased steadily since 1941, Thurmond requested the legislation as a means of preventing the clogging of the federal courts with petitions used mostly as a delaying tactic. The legislation Thurmond recommended would allow federal courts to deny petitions involving cases that had been fully and fairly adjudicated in state courts, and would permit petitions to be filed only within one year after a defendant exhausted all available state remedies, such as appeals.

Workman, William, 1930-81, U.S. William Workman had a long history of psychiatric disorders before he went on a murder spree in 1973 that left seven people dead. In 1968 Workman, an alcoholic, was readmitted to the Tinley Park, Ill., health center in suburban Chicago for attacking his wife with a butcher knife. On June 27, 1973, after his release from the center, Workman shot and killed seven people: his father, Raymond Workman; his mother, Dena Workman; two neighbors, Henrietta Cliff and her 12-year-old daughter Kimberly; his friend, Paul Clesson, Jr.; and Clesson's parents, Paul Clesson, Sr. and Neta Clesson. After the murders, Workman was committed to the state's maximum security mental institution in Chester without possibility of release or leave. Although Workman requested that he be allowed to stand trial, the state deemed him unfit to stand trial and kept him confined at Chester for most of the next eight years.

Workman was finally brought to trial in 1981. Experts in criminal justice said that he was brought to trial not because of a change in his level of competency, but because society had moved in the intervening years toward demanding greater responsibility of individuals who commit crimes. Workman was convicted of the mass murders and sentenced to three concurrent terms, with a sentence of 100 to 300 years in prison. Workman died in his cell within two weeks of his arrival at the state prison in Joliet, apparently of natural causes.

Wright, Jeanne Anne, 1958- , U.S. A New Jersey mother receiving public assistance drowned her four children because she reportedly thought they would be better off dead. Several times pregnant as a teenager, Jeanne Anne Wright was forced to drop out of high school. Emilio Jaime Andujar fathered three of her four children. Wright lived with her children and her parents in a low-income housing project, but in 1983, she was directed to move because the apartment was occupied by too many people. In October 1983, her food stamps were cut off, and a welfare check arrived two weeks late. Wright, who was later diagnosed as suffering from chronic depression and borderline personality disorders, was also concerned because Andujar, whom she said was abusive, allegedly threatened to take custody of the children.

Late on Nov. 10, 1983, Wright took her four children to the Cooper River, to hide and to think, she later said. She sat on a wooden plank by a railroad trestle for several hours before she dropped the sleeping children into the water. Then she walked to a friend's house, claiming that Andujar had abducted them. On Nov. 27, a gas station attendant spotted the body of 34-month-old Jonathan Wright. On Feb. 21, 1984, Wright pleaded guilty to four counts of murder before a judge. On Apr. 19, 1984, Wright, twenty-six, was sentenced to four concurrent life prison terms.

Wymer, Eugene William, 1927- , U.S. On Apr. 11, 1943, 15-year-old Eugene Wymer and his brother, George, then nine, were climbing the rocks on Table Mountain near Golden, Colo., when they met two other boys. Wymer first forced 11-year-old Milo Flindt to give up his shoes and stockings, explaining that George needed new ones. Then Wymer made Donald James Mattas, eight, hand over his wrist watch. Deciding to leave no witnesses to the thefts, Wymer wrestled Mattas to the edge of a 175-foot cliff and pushed him over the edge, then turned to

Flindt and forced him over, too. On their way back down the Wymer boys came across seven other youths and demanded each pay a 10-cent fee to continue their climb.

The bodies of Flindt and Mattas were found on Apr. 12. Through the testimony of the seven hikers, the Wymers were linked to the crimes, and Eugene Wymer was arrested in a Golden, Colo., hotel. Convicted of first-degree murder, Wymer was sentenced to life imprisonment on July 21, 1943. Except for an escape attempt about a year into his term when he tried to swim through a sewer line but failed, Wymer made, according to Warden Tinsley, "a good adjustment" to prison life. He appealed his conviction in January 1960, and although turned down by then-Governor Steve McNichols, Wymer was commended for his good behavior and urged to try for commutation of his sentence at a later time. Wymer was paroled on July 21, 1968, and was discharged on Mar. 15, 1974.

Wynekoop, Dr. Alice, 1870-1952, U.S. Chicago physician Dr. Alice Wynekoop was widely known for her medical career and her charitable activities. She also adored her youngest son, Earle. In the early 1930s, Earle

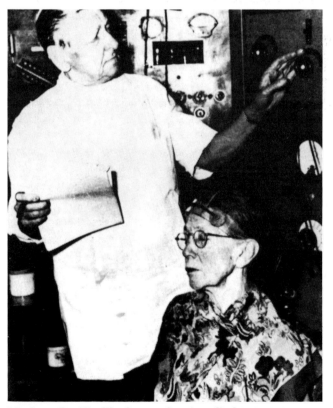

Murderess Dr. Alice Wynekoop, undergoing a lie detector test.

Wynekoop met and married young violinist Rheta Gardner and brought her back to Chicago to live in the family mansion. But Rheta had not turned into the wife Earl expected, and he began to look elsewhere. Dr. Wynekoop, disturbed that her son was unhappy, began to think about how she could fix things. In the early afternoon of Nov. 21, 1933, she took Rheta into the small surgery rooom attached to her home, shot her dead, and left her lying on the table.

After a leisurely evening, at about 10 p.m., Dr. Wynekoop called Cook County Hospital where her daughter, Dr. Catherine Wynekoop, was on staff and told her that Rheta had been shot dead. The daughter sent the police to investigate. They found Rheta lying naked on the operating table, her clothing heaped on the floor nearby, and Dr. Wynekoop muttering, "It must have been a burglar." Earle Wynekoop was on a train to the Grand Canyon with another woman, but he hurried home when he heard of his wife's death.

Dr. Wynekoop was taken to police headquarters and questioned for many hours. She finally wrote a confession in which she said that Rheta had asked to be examined but wanted some anesthetic to be more comfortable. She had used too much chloroform, Wynekoop said, accidentally killing the girl. Realizing Rheta was dead, Wynekoop then put a bullet in her to "ease the situation."

Earle, too, confessed to killing his wife, but there was plenty of evidence that he had been on the train west. Dr. Alice Wynekoop tried to retract her confession at her trial, but she was convicted and sentenced to life in prison. She was paroled in 1949 at age seventy-nine. She died two years later.

Y

Yagoda, Henrikh Gregoryevich, prom. 1938, U.S.S.R. Henrikh Gregoryevich Yagoda began his ascent within the ranks of the Soviet Secret Service in 1920 when he became a member of the Presidium Cheka, the organization that later became the GPU (Government Political Administration), precursor of the KGB. Yagoda served as vice-chief of the GPU in 1924, but due to the poor health of the chief, he virtually controlled the entire police force. Yagoda, although honored and decorated by Lenin, became best known for the accusations of murder levelled against him in his 1938 trial, which began on Mar. 2, in Moscow.

Before the trial ended on Mar. 13, three prominent Soviet doctors testified that Yagoda, a former pharmacist, had forced them to murder patients deemed dangerous to the state. The physicians, D.D. Pletnev, L.G. Levin, and I.N. Kazakov, admitted murdering writer Maxim Gorky, Gorky's son, Yagoda's predecessor as head of the GPU, Menzhinsky, and Kuibyshev, a former friend and assistant of Stalin who had risen to power after Lenin's death. It was implied, though not directly stated, that the deaths of many others, including many Bolsheviks, and even Lenin himself, were attributable to Yagoda.

Yagoda was found Guilty, condemned to death, and executed. It was generally conceded that, although the witnesses at his trial had fabricated parts of their testimony, Yagoda had, on Stalin's instruction, been responsible for the deaths of a number of "enemies of the state."

Yeldham, William James, 1899-1922, Brit. In May 1921, the body of a journeyman printer, George Stanley Grimshaw, was found in Higham's Park, Chingford, a desolate section of Epping Forest. The 54-year-old man had been hit in the head repeatedly with a heavy object and robbed. Police at first surmised that Grimshaw's murder might have been retribution for his spying on couples who frequently came to this secluded part of the woods.

However, when police investigated reports that Grimshaw had been seen recently in the company of a young woman, their appraisal of the motive changed. The young woman, Elsie Yeldham, had married William James Yeldham just three days after Grimshaw's murder. The newlyweds were arrested and quickly confessed to the crime. Elsie lured Grimshaw into the woods, where her fiance ambushed him. Both husband and wife were convicted of murder and sentenced to death. Yeldham was hanged on Sept. 5, 1922, and Elsie's sentence was commuted.

Young, Gig, 1913-78, U.S. At about 2:30 p.m. on Oct. 19, 1978, a resident of the Osborne apartments on Manhattan's upper west side heard what sounded like gunshots. At around 7:30 p.m., visitors to the apartment of actor Gig Young, sixty-four, and Ruth Schmidt, thirty-one, his wife of three weeks, received no answer at the door, and police later discovered the bodies of the newlyweds. According to police sergeant John Murphy, Young had a gun in his hand and had apparently shot his wife and then killed himself. Young had met Schmidt, his fifth wife, in Hong Kong where he was making a movie. The actor's business agent, Ed Traubner, said his client had just recently returned to his New York home from Canada, where he had been performing on stage.

In 1969, Gig Young won an Academy Award for his portrayal of a sadistic dance marathon pitchman in *They Shoot Horses, Don't They?* Critics referred to his performance as "a lifeline for a drowning actor" whose career consisted primarily of "a trail of second leads in second-rate movies." Young described his work in movies prior to winning the coveted award as "thirty years and fifty-five pictures, and there are not more than five that were any good or any good for me." Young had been famous for portraying "the urbane suitor who loses the girl at the end of the picture." Born Byron Barr in St. Cloud, Minn., Young claimed to be a sad and very shy child, saying that he was so grateful to one teacher who liked him, that he used to give her dimes.

In WWII, Young enlisted in the Coast Guard and ferried troops across the Pacific. He returned to Hollywood and received his first Academy Award nomination in 1951 for his role as an alcoholic in *Come Fill The Cup*. He hosted "Warner Brothers Presents," and appeared in the TV series "The Rogues," with David Niven and Charles Boyer in the mid-1960s. Young was again nominated for an Oscar for his work in a Clark Gable and Doris Day movie, *Teacher's Pet*. Three of the actor's five marriages ended in divorce. Young was alleged to have had a serious drinking problem. According to his fourth wife, Elaine Young, his role as an alcoholic in *Come Fill The Cup* was "a terrifying symbol of the years ahead."

Young, Graham, 1948- , Brit. John Hadland, Ltd., a British photographic instrument company, employed seventy people in an attractive building at Bovington, near London. In the summer of 1971, 60-year-old head warehouseman Bob Egle, in robust health and looking forward to retirement, developed a serious illness. He died on July 19, after suffering agonizing back and stomach cramps. Another employee, 56-year-old Fred Biggs, became ill with similar symptoms in October 1971, and within a month he too was dead. When four more employees began suffering similar afflictions, the company sought the aid of Dr. Arthur Anderson. While questioning employees, Anderson encountered 23-year-old Graham Young, who had rapt interest in the fate of his fellow workers, as well as a thorough knowledge of the effects of thallium poisoning. Police discovered that Young had been kept at the Broadmoor Institution for the criminally insane between July 1962 and February 1971 for killing his stepmother with poison and attempting to poison his father, sister, and a friend. He had been released as posing no further threat to society and was hired by John Hadland, whose personnel office had no knowledge of his past. Young was arrested on suspicion of murder, brought to trial in June 1972 at St. Albans, Hertfordshire, and convicted of the murders of Egle and Biggs, as well as the attempted murders of Jethro Batt and David Tilson. Far from contrite, Young said that he could have killed the others but had let them live. He soon began serving a sentence of life imprisonment.

Young, Harry, 1904-32, U.S. In a small farmhouse six miles southwest of Springfield, Mo., Mrs. J.D. Young struggled to feed her children. On Mar. 28, 1927, however, 23-year-old Harry Young went to prison for grand larceny. Paroled in 1928, he murdered Republic, Mo., police constable Mark Noe a year later when Noe tried to arrest him for being drunk and disorderly.

For nearly two-and-a-half years Harry Young was the object of a statewide manhunt. Then on Jan. 2, 1932, police stopped two of Young's sisters, Mrs. Loretta Conlon and Vinita Young, when their vehicle was identified as stolen. The women were taken to police headquarters where they confessed that the car belonged to their brother Harry, who, with two other brothers, was hiding out at the family farmhouse. Greene County sheriff Marcell Hendrix organized a seven-man posse to go after the Young boys, believed to be armed and dangerous.

Deputy Wiley Mashburn, Patrolman Virgil Johnson, and Hendrix slowly advanced on the farmhouse, located in a desolate site and surrounded by scrub oak and barbed wire. They kicked in the kitchen door, but were immediately cut down by gunfire. Mashburn and Hendrix were killed instantly. Johnson ran for the car but was shot in the leg just before he closed the door. He drove to the next house to call for reinforcements. Four other policemen remained pinned down by the hail of gunfire from the house.

Harry Young and his unidentified companions were expert marksmen who picked off the trapped police officers one by one. Chief of detectives Tony Oliver was the third victim. Pinned behind a tree, he got a bullet in the head.

"Run before they kill us all!" he cried just before losing consciousness. Officers Charles Houser and Ollie Crosswhite were next, both hit in the forehead and temple. Detective Owen Brown and patrolman Frank Pike were the last two left alive. "We've killed all but you two, and you had better throw down your pistols and come in here," someone in the house cried out. Pike refused, even though their magazines were empty.

By the time reinforcements arrived on the scene, the siege was over. Brown had escaped unhurt, but Pike sustained a bullet wound. The killers had slipped out of the house and into the rugged Ozark hill country, where detection was all but impossible. An angry mob of 350 farmers was immediately pressed into duty by Constable Scott Curtis. "Alright," Curtis said. "You're all deputized. Go as far as you like to catch them, but don't let them get away!" They dispersed across the farms and fields while ambulances carried away the bodies of the five dead men. Detective Dan Bilyeu believed that two of the gunmen holed up in the Young farmhouse were the notorious bandits Fred Barker and Charles Arthur "Pretty Boy" Floyd.

The 68-year-old widowed mother of the Young brothers was taken in for questioning by police. When the tragedy occurred, she had been visiting another son. She expressed the hope her boys would kill themselves rather than be taken alive.

Two days later, in Houston, Harry and his brother Jennings shot each other in a Magnolia Park rooming house after their landlord, 50-year-old carpenter J.F. Tomlinson, recognized them from photographs in a Houston newspaper. Nine police officers armed with tear gas bombs and shotguns advanced on the house. A dozen shots were fired through the closed doors of the building, but the fugitives did not return fire. "We're dead. C'mon and get us," one of them said. Then there were two quick shots and silence.

Jennings Young lay dead on the bathroom floor. Harry was still breathing, but died soon after at a nearby hospital. Justice of the Peace Campbell Overstreet ruled the shootings a suicide. When the news filtered back to Springfield, Mo., Mrs. Young broke down and cried. "Oh my God, why did they do it?" Reminded of her earlier wish that they not submit to the authorities, she said, "But they're my boys. They're my flesh and blood. Take me away. Take me home God! Father missed all this, why couldn't I?" Paul Young turned himself in to Houston police on Jan. 7, 1932, and was officially charged. It was later revealed that the murder weapons had been supplied by another brother, Oscar Young, a local farmer considered an upstanding member of the community, and thought to be unaware of Harry's murderous tendencies.

Young, John Riley, d.1945, Brit. On June 6, 1945, the 17-year-old daughter of Frederick and Cissie Lucas returned to her home in Leigh-on-Sea, England, to find her parents brutally murdered. Lucas, a jeweler, and his wife had been hit repeatedly on the head with at least two different instruments. Lucas had died shortly after the attack, while Cissie, although dead by the time her daughter discovered the bodies, had lived some seven hours. John Riley Young was arrested in connection with the slayings and was convicted at Chelmsford. When arrested, he attempted suicide by slashing his wrists. Young survived the attempt and was executed at Pentonville.

Young, Robert, d.1980, U.S. In 1974, Robert Young shot and killed a woman who returned home while he was burglarizing her apartment. He then sodomized the dead body. Young was arrested and sentenced to eighteen years in prison for these heinous crimes and for sodomizing an 11-year-old girl in a separate incident. Instead of prison, Young was sent to Matteawan State Hospital for the Criminally Insane. He escaped during a massive prison escape in 1977.

After the breakout, Young teamed up with Blanche Wright. On Jan. 21, 1980, the two approached Felipe Rodriguez, a Colombian drug dealer in the Bedford Park district of the Bronx. Wright convinced Rodriguez to allow the two into his apartment to buy drugs. Young pushed his way inside the door and shot Rodriguez, his common law wife, Maria Navas, and a neighbor, Luis Martin. Wright and Young then ransacked the apartment, stealing $8,000 in cash and narcotics. Only Rodriguez survived the shootings.

Two weeks later, Wright and Young attacked another drug dealer, Marshall Howell, as he left his apartment with bodyguard Sam Nevins. Young shot at Howell, but when his gun jammed, he was himself shot and killed by Nevins. Wright then shot the already wounded Howell in the head, while Nevins escaped. When police visited the home of the woman who had claimed Young's body, they found Wright. She denied any knowledge of the murder. However, when police suggested she had let her partner down by not firing sooner, she became indignant and replied that her bullets had killed Howell. She then confessed that she and Young were contract killers who had been hired to kill Howell for failing to pay a drug debt. She admitted that they were responsible for the attempted murder of Rodriguez, and the murders of Navas and Martin, as well as the contract killing of another drug dealer, Carlos Medina, in November 1979. Wright was sentenced to eighteen years to life in the Howell slaying and fifteen years to life for her part in the Navas and Martin murders.

Young, William Hooper, prom. 1902, U.S. In 1902, the body of Mrs. Joseph P. Pulitzer was found in a ditch in New Jersey. The body was held down by a tie-weight, the piece of iron used to keep livery horses standing in one place. By searching area livery stables for a rented rig returned without its tie-weight, police linked Pulitzer's death to William Hooper Young, grandson of Brigham Young. Suspicion of the Mormon religion encouraged speculation that the murder was part of a secret blood ritual conducted by the Mormons. Mormon leaders strenuously denied any connection between William Hooper Young and the Mormon sect, stating that he had long since been disowned for his immoral lifestyle. Young was captured in upstate New York, masquerading as a hobo. He was charged in the murder, found Guilty, and sent to prison.

Ypsilanti Ripper, The, See: **Collins, John Norman.**

Yukl, Charles (AKA: Mr. Williamson), prom. 1960s-70s, U.S. In July 1974, a Mr. Williamson of Greenwich Village in New York City, ran ads in which he said he was seeking actresses to audition for a role in a film production. Aspiring actress Karin Schlegel applied and while in Williamson's apartment was strangled and raped. Her mutilated body was left in the building.

Police discovered that Williamson was actually Charles Yukl, who had committed an identical crime in October 1966 and had been paroled after serving only five years of his sentence. This time he received a life sentence.

YWCA Murder, The, See: **Byrne, Patrick Joseph.**

Zayas, Fernando, 1962- , U.S. On July 2, 1983, Fernando Zayas, twenty-two, shot and killed Miguel Vargas, twenty, in Chicago, Ill. Four years before, Vargas had pleaded guilty to killing Ramon Vasquez, a friend of Zayas'. Zayas, a reputed gang member, ambushed and killed Vargas and two friends, Juis Cuaresma, seventeen, and Ruben Gutierrez, twenty, as they watched TV on Vargas' porch. The killing was motivated by revenge. Zayas was convicted of murder and sentenced to life in prison on May 18, 1984.

Zebra Killings, 1973-74, U.S. In a period of 179 days between late 1973 and early 1974, five men shot twenty-three people in the San Francisco area. The victims, all of whom were white, were chosen at random. The attacks, which resulted in fifteen deaths and several cases of permanent injury were committed by five black men seeking membership in a Black Muslim-backed organization called the Death Angels. The racial crimes spurred a massive, and controversial, manhunt in which some 600 young black men were stopped on the streets of San Francisco, searched and questioned. The manhunt was halted before the killers were found due to concerns about infringement of civil rights.

The crimes, dubbed by police as the "Zebra killings" because of their interracial nature, were solved when 29-year-old Anthony Harris, one of the original participants, confessed and implicated four other men, Manuel Moore, thirty-one, J.C. Simon, twenty-nine, Larry C. Green, twenty-four, and Jessie Lee Cooks, thirty. The doctrine of the Death Angels dictated that all whites were evil and should be destroyed. The killings, an initiation requirement, were viewed as part of a full-scale war against whites. After a trial that lasted a year and six days in which 181 witnesses were called, Moore, Simon, Green, and Cooks were found Guilty and sentenced to life imprisonment.

Zenge, Mandeville, prom. 1935, U.S. On July 31, 1935, Mandeville Zenge, a carpenter from Missouri, kidnapped 38-year-old Dr. Walter J. Bauer from his Ann Arbor, Mich., hotel. Somewhere between Ann Arbor and Chicago, Zenge sexually mutilated Dr. Bauer with a penknife. Zenge had been engaged to Bauer's wife, Louise Schaffer Bauer until a short time before Bauer married her, and became jealous of the recent marriage. Zenge left Bauer's car with the dying Bauer in it at a Chicago garage. Garage attendants who saw a man leave the car, found the mortally wounded Bauer and called police.

Zenge was arrested in Chicago a short time later and charged in the murder. He was found Guilty by a jury and, in November 1935, was sentenced to life imprisonment.

Zimmerly, Dr. Harry C., prom. 1935, U.S. In March 1935, Dr. Harry C. Zimmerly performed an illegal abortion on Gladys Lawson, who died as result of the operation. Panicking, two of his employees informed the authorities that the doctor had performed an illegal procedure and then had cut up the body and disposed of it on the grounds of his Mechanics Grove, Pa., home. The police found Lawson's body and the bones of several other women in a grave under the floor of a barn. Zimmerly was convicted of performing an illegal operation and sentenced to seven and one half years in prison.

Zinzigk, Perry, prom. 1963, U.S. On Oct. 24, 1963, a Cincinnati woman notified police that her mother, 46-year-old Lillian Greer, had disappeared. Greer worked as a waitress at the Christoph Cafe and lived in an apartment over the restaurant. Beverly Norman, Greer's daughter, told police that her mother was last seen by another daughter on Oct. 13. When police questioned Greer's employer, Perry Zinzigk, he claimed that the woman told him she had become tired of bearing much of the financial responsibility for her children and had moved to Chicago.

When investigations in Chicago yielded no trace of Greer, Norman insisted to Cincinnati police that her mother would not have left town without notifying her children. The case was taken over by Detective Wilbert Stagenhorst, who repeatedly questioned the restaurant owner for further clues. Zinzigk cooperated thoroughly with the investigation and even passed a lie detector test. Stagenhorst's suspicion of Zinzigk deepened, however, when the detective came across a newly poured concrete slab in the basement of the restaurant. Police workers removed the concrete slab, and found Greer's body. Although Zinzigk claimed he had accidentally shot Greer during an argument, he was charged with second-degree murder and brought to trial on May 15, 1964. He was found Guilty and sentenced to fifty years in prison.

Znidar, Thomas F., 1965- , U.S. On the evening of Mar. 31, 1988, in Anne Arundel County, Md., 23-year-old Thomas F. Znidar strangled his girlfriend of four years, 19-year-old Ilka Dibble. After sodomizing her body, Znidar threw it in the trunk of her car and drove to his parents' home in Clay County, Fla., where he buried the body in a shallow grave. Police at first treated the case as a missing person's case, assuming that she had run away. Ilka's mother, Gisela Dibble, persisted in her attempts to have police treat the case with greater urgency. Three days after the murder, police began questioning Znidar. Although he first denied any knowledge of Ilka Dibble's whereabouts, he eventually broke down and detailed the crime to police in a three-hour taped confession.

The prosecutors entered a charge of first-degree murder against Znidar, but no mention was made in the charges of the sexual assault because Maryland law states that it is not a crime to assault a dead body. When the homicide detective investigating the case testified, but skipped over the sexual assault, Dibble's mother stood up and yelled to the jury, "And then he sexually assaulted her!" Although the defense attorney moved for a mistrial on the basis of the outburst, the presiding judge decided, after polling the jurors, that Dibble's actions would not have any impact on the jury's deliberations. However, the prosecuting attorney felt that Dibble's outburst greatly enhanced the chance of a reversal of a guilty verdict in any subsequent appeal. He further reasoned that a subsequent retrial had a far less substantial chance of resulting in a conviction. On the strength of these beliefs, he accepted a plea bargain that enabled Znidar to escape the otherwise virtually certain sentence of life without parole.

On Apr. 26, 1989, Znidar was sentenced to life in prison. The judge who handed down the sentence, which does allow for the possibility of parole, recommended that Znidar be allowed to serve his time at the Paxutent Institution, a prison which offers therapeutic and educational programs.

=====

Zon, Hans von, 1942- , Neth. Hans von Zon, born in Utrecht, Neth., on Apr. 20, 1942, displayed difficulty in distinguishing between fantasy and reality early in life. After he left school, he was dismissed from a succession of jobs for petty dishonesty. At the age of sixteen he went to Amsterdam and claimed to be a student.

In 1964, Zon committed his first murder. His victim, Elly Hager-Segov, allowed Zon to stay the night and make love to her. When she refused to allow him to make love to her a second time, he strangled her and slit her throat. Over the next couple of years, Zon murdered a film director and a long-time lover. While drunk, he boasted about the murders to a convict known as Oude Nol, who blackmailed Zon into committing murders for him. Zon killed two men on Oude Nol's orders and attempted to kill one of Oude Nol's former lovers. The last victim, however, survived the attempt and called police. Both Zon and Oude Nol were arrested and charged with murder. Oude Nol was sentenced to seven years in prison while Zon received a life sentence.

=====

Zowkowski, John, d.1933, U.S. In November 1933, the strangled and badly burned body of a young woman was pulled from a fire in a field near Philadelphia. From personal effects found near the scene of the fire, the woman was identified as Tanka Hetman. Hetman's landlady told police that the young woman had left several days earlier with her boyfriend, a racketeer named John Zowkowski. Zowkowski, apparently alerted to the imminent arrival of the police, had fled only moments earlier. The police traced him to a wooded area where Zowkowski and police exchanged gunfire. When Zowkowski stopped firing, the police closed in. Zowkowski was found dead of a bullet wound in the temple. Powder burns on the skin around the wound indicated that the death was a suicide.

=====

BIBLIOGRAPHY

NOTE: Tens of thousands of sources have been consulted by the author in researching the *World Encyclopedia of 20th Century Murder* over the last twenty-five years. What follows are basic book references which the reader may find helpful in further reading and research. Space does not permit citing the tens of thousands of periodical, newspaper, pamphlet, court document, and transcript sources also consulted by the author.

A

Abbott, Jack Henry. *In the Belly of the Beast: Letters from Prison*. New York: Random House, 1981.

Abrahamsen, David. *Confessions of Son of Sam*. New York: Columbia University Press, 1985.

———. *Crime and the Human Mind*. New York: Columbia University Press, 1949.

———. *The Murdering Mind*. New York: Harper & Row, 1973.

———. *The Psychology of Crime*. New York: Columbia University Press, 1960.

———. *Report on a Study of 102 Sex Offenders at Sing Sing Prison*. Utica, N.Y.: State Hospital Press, 1950.

Adam, Hargrave Lee. *C.I.D.* London: Sampson, Low, 1931.

——— (ed.). *Notable British Trials: Trial of George Chapman*. London: William Hodge, 1930.

———. *Trial of George Chapman*. London: William Hodge, 1930.

———. *Woman and Crime*. London: T.W. Laurie, 1912.

Adams, Samuel Hopkins. *Alexander Woollcott: His Life and His World*. New York: Reynal & Hitchcock, 1945.

Ahearn, Danny. *How to Commit a Murder*. New York: Ives Washburn, 1930.

Alexander, Henry A. *Some Facts About the Murder Notes in the Phagan Case*. Atlanta, Ga.: Published by Author, n.d.

Allen, William. *Starkweather: The Story of a Mass Murderer*. Boston: Houghton Mifflin, 1976.

Alois, Louis. *The Homicidal Maniac, Ten Studies*. Paris: Published by Author, 1967.

Altman, Jack, and Ziporyn, Marvin. *Born to Raise Hell*. New York: Grove Press, 1967.

Ambler, Eric. *The Ability to Kill and Other Pieces*. London: Bodley Head, 1963.

Anatomy of a Murder. London: John Lane, 1936.

Anderson, Clinton H. *Beverly Hills Is My Beat*. New York: Popular Library, 1962.

Apell, George C. *Belle's Castle*. New York: MacMillan Co., 1959.

Ashton-Wolfe, H. *The Cask of Death*. New York: E.P. Dutton, 1932.

———. *Crimes of Love and Hate*. Boston: Houghton Mifflin, 1927.

———. *Crimes of Violence and Revenge*. New York: E.P. Dutton, 1932.

———. *The Forgotten Clue*. Boston: Houghton Mifflin, 1930.

Atwell, Benjamin H. *The Great Harry Thaw Case*. Chicago: Laird & Lee, 1907.

Averbuch, Bernard, and Noble, John Wesley. *Never Plead Guilty*. New York: Straus & Cudahy, 1955.

B

Bacon, James. *Hollywood Is a Four-Letter Town*. New York: Avon Books, 1977.

Bailey, F. Lee. *The Defense Never Rests*. New York: Signet Books, 1972.

———, and Greenya, John. *For the Defense*. New York: Atheneum, 1975.

Bakos, Susan Crain. *Appointment for Murder: The Story of the Killing Dentist*. New York: G.P. Putnam's Sons, 1988.

Balchin, Nigel. *The Anatomy of Villainy*. London: St. James's Place, 1950.

———. *Fatal Fascination*. Boston: Little, Brown, 1964.

Baldwin, Charles C. *Stanford White*. New York: Dodd, Mead, 1938.

Bardens, Dennis. *The Ladykiller*. London: P. Davies, 1972.

———. *Lord Justice Birkett*. London: Robert Hale, 1962.

Barker, Dudley. *Lord Darling's Famous Cases*. London: Hutchinson, 1936.

Barnes, Margaret. *Murder in Coweta County*. New York: Pocketbooks, 1976.

Barr, Jennifer. *Within a Dark Wood*. New York: Doubleday, 1979.

Barthel, Joan. *A Death in Canaan*. New York: E.P. Dutton, 1977.

Barton, George. *The True Stories of Celebrated Crimes*. New York: McKinlay Stone & Mackenzie, 1909.

Basichis, Gordon. *Beautiful Bad Girl*. Santa Barbara, Calif.: Santa Barbara Press, 1985.

Bates, J.C. (ed.). *History of the Bench and Bar of California*. San Francisco: Bench and Bar, 1912.

Bayer, Oliver Weld (ed.). *Cleveland Murders*. New York: Duell, Sloan & Pearce, 1947.

Beach, Sylvia. *Shakespeare and Company*. New York: Harcourt, Brace & World, 1959.

Bear, Robert L. *Delivered Unto Satan*. Carlisle, Pa.: Bear, 1974.

Beard, Ross E., Jr. *Carbine, the Story of David Marshall Williams*. Lexington, S.C.: The Sandlapper Store, 1977.

Beattie, John. *The Yorkshire Ripper Story*. London: Quartet, 1981.

Beaumont, F.A. *The Fifty Most Amazing Crimes of the Last 100 Years*. London: Odhams, 1936.

Bechhofer, Robert. *Famous American Trials*. London: Jarrolds, 1947.

Bechhofer Roberts, C.E. *Lord Mirkenhead*. London: Mills & Boon, 1926.

———. *Sir Travers Humphreys*. London: The Bodley Head, 1936.

Belbenott, Rene. *Dry Guillotine*. New York: Dutton, 1938.

. *Hell on Trial.* New York: Dutton, 1940.

Belin, Jean. *My Work at the Surete.* trans. Eric Whelpton. London: Harrap, 1950.

. *Secrets of the Surete.* New York: Putnam, 1950.

Bell, Arthur. *Kings Don't Mean a Thing.* New York: William Morrow, 1978.

Belli, Melvin. *Blood Money.* New York: Grosset & Dunlap, 1956.

, and Carroll, Maurice C. *Dallas Justice.* New York: David McKay, 1964.

. *The Law Revolution.* Los Angeles: Sherbourne Press, 1968.

, and Kaiser, Robert Blair. *My Life on Trial.* New York: William Morrow, 1976.

Bennett, Benjamin. *The Evil That Men Do.* Cape Town, S. Afri.: Howard B. Timmins, n.d.

. *Famous South African Murders.* London: T. Werner Laurie, 1938.

. *Freedom or the Gallows.* Cape Town, S.Afri.: Howard B. Timmins, 1956.

. *Genius for the Defense, Life of Harry Morris, K.C.* Cape Town, S.Afri.: Howard B. Timmins, 1959.

. *Murder is my Business.* London: Hodder and Stoughton Ltd., 1951.

. *Murder Will Speak.* Cape Town, S.Afri.: Howard B. Timmins, 1962.

. *The Noose Tightens.* Cape Town, S.Afri.: Howard B. Timmins, 1974.

. *This Was a Man.* Cape Town, S.Afri.: H.B. Timmins, 1958.

. *Too Late for Tears.* Cape Town, S.Afri.: Howard B. Timmins, 1948.

. *Up for Murder.* London: Hutchinson, 1934.

. *Was Justice Done?* Cape Town, S.Afri.: Howard B. Timmins, 1975.

. *Why Did They Do It?* Cape Town, S.Afri.: Howard Timmins, 1953.

Benson, Captain L. *The Book of Remarkable Trials.* London: Chatto and Windus, 1924.

Berger, Meyer. *The Eight Million.* New York: Simon & Schuster, 1942.

. *The Story of the New York Times.* New York: Simon & Schuster, 1951.

Berns, Walter. *For Capital Punishment: Crime and the Morality of the Death Penalty.* New York: Basic Books, 1979.

Berrett, James. *When I Was at Scotland Yard.* London: Sampson, Low, Marston, 1932.

Beveridge, Peter. *Inside the C.I.D.* London: Evans, 1957.

Bierstadt, Edward Hale. *Curious Trials and Criminal Cases.* Garden City, N.Y.: Garden City Publishing, 1928.

. *Enter Murderers!* Garden City, N.Y.: Doubleday, Doran, 1934.

. *Satan Was a Man.* New York: Doubleday, Doran, 1935.

Bigelow, L.J. *Bench and Bar.* New York: Harper & Bros., 1871.

Biggs, J., Jr. *The Guilty Mind.* New York: Harcourt, 1955.

Birkenhead, Lord. *Famous Trials of History.* London: Hutchinson, 1926.

. *More Famous Trials.* London: Hutchinson, 1928.

Birmingham, George A. *Murder Most Foul!* London: Chatto & Windus, 1929.

Bishop, C. *Women and Crime.* London: Chatto & Windus, 1931.

Bishop, Jim. *The Murder Trial of Judge Peel.* New York: Simon & Schuster, 1962.

Bixley, William. *The Guilty and the Innocent: My Fifty Years at the Old Bailey.* London: Souvenir Press, 1957.

Black, David. *Murder at the Met.* Garden City, N.Y.: Doubleday, 1984.

Blinder, M. *Lovers, Killers, Husbands and Wives.* New York: St. Martin's Press, 1985.

Block, Eugene B. *Fifteen Clues.* Garden City, N.Y.: Doubleday, 1965.

. *Lie Detectors.* New York: David McKay, 1977.

. *Science Vs. Crime.* New York: Caroline House, 1980.

. *Voiceprinting.* New York: McKay, 1975.

. *The Wizard of Berkeley.* New York: Coward-McCann, 1958.

Boar, Roger, and Blundell, Nigel. *The World's Most Infamous Murders.* New York: Exeter Books, 1983.

Bogdanovich, Peter. *The Killing of the Unicorn: Dorothy Stratten, 1960-1980.* New York: William Morrow, 1984.

Bolitho, William. *Murder for Profit.* New York: Harper & Brothers, 1926.

Bontham, Alan. *Sex Crimes and Sex Criminals.* New York: Wisdom House, 1961.

Bornstein, Joseph. *The Politics of Murder.* New York: William Sloan, 1950.

Borowitz, Albert. *Innocence and Arsenic Studies in Crime and Literature.* New York: Harper & Row, 1977.

Borrell, Clive, and Cashinella, Brian. *Crime in Britain Today.* London: Routledge & Paul, 1975.

Boswell, Charles, and Thompson, Lewis. *Advocates of Murder.* New York: Collier Books, 1962.

. *The Girl in Lovers Lane.* New York: Fawcett, 1953.

. *Practitioners of Murder.* New York: Collier Books, 1962.

Botkin, Benjamin A. *A Treasury of American Folklore.* New York: Crown, 1951.

Boucher, Anthony (ed.). *The Pocket Book of True Crime Stories.* New York: Pocket Books, 1943.

. *Police Intelligence.* New York: AMS Press, 1976.

. *The Quality of Murder.* New York: E.P. Dutton, 1962.

Bowen-Rowlands, Ernest. *In Court and Out of Court.* London: Hutchinson, 1925.

. *In the Light of the Law.* London: Grant Richards, 1931.

. *Seventy-Two Years at the Bar.* London: Macmillan, 1924.

Bowers, William. *Executions in America.* Lexington, Mass.: D.C. Heath, 1974.

Bowker, A.E. *Behind the Bar.* London: Staples Press, 1949.

. *A Lifetime with the Law.* London: W.H. Allen, 1961.

Bradlee, Ben, Jr. *The Ambush Murders.* New York: Dodd, Mead, 1979.

Braly, Malcolm. *On the Yard.* Greenwich, Conn.: Fawcett Publications, 1967.

Branch, Taylor, and Propper, Eugene M. *Labyrinth.* New York: Viking Press, 1982.

Brant, House. *Crimes That Shocked America.* New York: Ace, 1961.

Brantingham, Paul and Patricia. *Patterns in Crime.* New York: Macmillan, 1984.

Brearley, H.C. *Homicide in the United States.* Chapel Hill: University of North Carolina Press, 1932.

Bresler, Fenton. *Reprieve: A Study of a System.* London: Harrap, 1965.

. *Lord Goddard.* London: Harrap, 1971.

. *Scales of Justice.* London: Weidenfeld & Nicholson, 1973.

Brice, A.H.M. *Look Upon the Prisoner: Studies in Crime.* London: Hutchinson, 1933.

Briggs, I. Vernon. *The Manner of Man That Kills: Spencer, Czolgosz, Richeson.* Boston: Richard G. Badger, The Gorman Press, 1921.

Broad, Lewis. *The Innocence of Edith Thompson.* London: Hutchinson, 1952.

Brock, Alan. *A Casebook of Crime.* London: Watmoughs, 1948.

Brodsky, Annette, M. (ed.). *The Female Offender.* Beverly Hills, Calif.: Sage, 1975.

Bronowski, J. *The Face of Violence.* New York: World, 1967.

Brookes, Cannon J.R. *Murder in Fact and Fiction.* London: Hurst & Blackett, 1926.

Brophy, John. *The Meaning of Murder.* London: Ronald Whiting & Wheaton, 1966.

Brown, Michael. *Marked to Die.* New York: Simon & Schuster, 1984.

Brown, Wenzell. *Introduction to Murder: The Unpublished Facts behind the Lonelyhearts Killers, Martha Beck and Raymond Fernandez.* New York: Greenberg, 1952.

Browne, Douglas G., and Tullett, E. V. *Bernard Spilsbury: His Life and Cases.* London: Harrap, 1951.

———, and Brock, Alan. *Fingerprints: Fifty Years of Scientific Crime Detection.* New York: E.P. Dutton, 1954.

———. *The Rise of Scotland Yard.* New York: G.P. Putnam's Sons, 1956.

———. *The Scalpel of Scotland Yard.* New York: E.P. Dutton, 1952.

———. *Sir Travers Humphreys.* London: Harrap, 1960.

Bugliosi, Vincent. *Helter Skelter.* New York: W.W. Norton, 1974.

———. *Till Death Us Do Part.* New York: Norton, 1978.

Buisson, H. *La police, son histoire.* Allier, Fr.: Vichy, 1949.

Buncher, Judith F. (ed.). *Crime and Punishment in America.* New York: Facts on File, 1978.

Bunker, Edward. *No Beast So Fierce.* New York: W.W. Norton, 1973.

Burke, T. *Limehouse Nights.* New York: Robert M. McBride, 1926.

Burnaby, Evelyn. *Memories of Famous Trials.* London: Sisley's, 1907.

Burt, Commander Leonard. *Commander Burt of Scotland Yard.* London: William Heinemann, 1959.

Burt, Olive Woolley. *American Murder Ballads.* New York: Oxford University Press, 1958.

Busch, Francis X. *Casebook of the Curious and True.* Indianapolis, Ind.: Bobbs-Merrill, 1957.

———. *Enemies of the State.* Indianapolis, Ind.: Bobbs-Merrill, 1954.

———. *Guilty or Not Guilty.* Indianapolis, Ind.: Bobbs-Merrill, 1952.

———. *In and Out of Court.* Chicago: De Paul University Press, 1942.

———. *Prisoners at the Bar.* Indianapolis, Ind.: Bobbs-Merrill, 1952.

Butler, Ivan. *Murderers' England.* London: Robert Hale, 1973.

Butler, P.T.T., and Lord Dunboyne (eds.). *The Trial of John George Haigh.* London: Hodge, 1953.

Butterfield, Roger. *The American Past.* New York: Simon & Schuster, 1947.

Bye, Raymond T. *Capital Punishment in the United States.* Philadelphia: Committee on Philanthropic Labor of Philadelphia Yearly Meeting of Friends, 1919.

C

Caesar, Gene. *Incredible Detective: The Biography of William J. Burns.* Englewood Cliffs, N.J.: Prentice-Hall, 1968.

Caldwell, Robert Graham. *Criminology.* New York: Ronald Press, 1965.

Callaghan, Morley. *That Summer in Paris.* New York: Coward-McCann, 1963.

Calvert, Roy. *Capital Punishment in the Twentieth Century.* New York: G.P. Putnam's Sons, 1936.

———. *The Death Penalty Inquiry.* London: Victor Gollancz, 1931.

———. *Executions.* London: National Council for the Abolition of the Death Penalty, 1926.

Campbell, Marjorie Freeman. *A Century of Crime.* Toronto, Can.: McLelland & Stewart, 1970.

Camps, Professor Francis E. *Camps on Crime.* Newton Abbot, Eng.: David & Charles, 1973.

———, and Barber, Richard. *The Investigation of Murder.* London: Michael Joseph, 1966.

———. *Medical and Scientific Investigations in the Christie Case.* London: Medical Publications, 1953.

Cannell, J.C. *When Fleet Street Calls.* London: Jarrolds, 1932.

Canning, John. *50 True Tales of Terror.* New York: Bell, 1972.

Capote, Truman. *In Cold Blood.* New York: Random House, 1965.

Careless, J.M.J., and Brown, R. Craig (eds.). *The Canadians, 1867-1967.* Toronto, Ontario, Can.: Macmillan, 1967.

Carey, Arthur A. *Memoirs of a Murder Man.* Garden City, N.Y.: Doubleday, Doran, 1930.

Cargill, David, and Holland, Julian. *Scenes of Murder: A London Guide.* London: Heinemann, 1964.

Carlen, Pat. (ed.). *Criminal Women.* Oxford, Eng.: Polity Press, 1985.

Carmer, Carl. *Stars Fell on Alabama.* New York: Farrar & Rinehart, 1934.

Carpozi, George Jr. *Ordeal By Trial: The Alice Crimmins Case.* New York: Walker, 1972.

Carr, Harry. *Los Angeles, City of Dreams.* New York: D. Appleton-Century, 1935.

———. *Riding the Tiger: An American Newspaperman in the Orient.* Boston: Houghton Mifflin, 1934.

Carr, John Dickson. *The Life of Sir Arthur Conan Doyle.* New York: Harper, 1949.

Carr, William H.A. *Hollywood Tragedy.* New York: Fawcett-Crest, 1962.

Carrington, Frank G. *Neither Cruel nor Unusual.* New Rochelle, N.Y.: Arlington House, 1978.

———. *The Victims.* New Rochelle, N.Y.: Arlington House, 1977.

Cartel, Michael. *Serial Mass Murder.* Toluca Lake, Cal.: Pepperbox Books, 1985.

Carter, Dyson. *Sin and Society.* New York: Heck Cattell, 1946.

——— (ed.). *The Past as Prelude, New Orleans, 1718-1968.* New Orleans, La.: Tulane University Press, 1968.

Casamayor, Serge Fuster. *Le bras seculier-justice et police.* Paris: Editions de Seuil, 1960.

Casey, Robert J. *Chicago, Medium Rare.* Indianapolis, Ind.: Bobbs-Merrill, 1949.

Cassity, John Holland. *The Quality of Murder.* New York: Julian Press, 1958.

Castle, H.G. *Case for the Prosecution.* London: Naldrett Press, 1956.

Chaiken, J.M. and M.R. *Varieties of Criminal Behavior.* Santa Monica, Calif.: Rand, 1982.

Chalidze, Valery. *Criminal Russia.* New York: Random House, 1977.

Chamberlain, Austin. *Down the Years.* London: Cassell, 1935.

Chambers' Guide to London The Secret City. London: Ocean Books, 1974.

Champion, Pierre. *Splendeurs et Miseres de Paris.* Paris: Calmann-Levy, 1934.

Chapin, Charles. *Charles Chapin's Story.* New York: G.P. Putnam's Sons, 1920.

Chaplain, Ray. *God's Prison Gang.* Old Tappan, N.J.: Fleming H. Revell, 1977.

Chaplin, Ralph. *Wobbly: The Rough-and-Tumble Story of an American Radical.* Chicago: University of Chicago Press, 1948.

Chapman, John. *Incredible Los Angeles.* New York: Harper & Row, 1960.

Chappell, Duncan, and Monahan, John (eds.). *Violence and Criminal Justice.* Lexington, Mass.: Lexington Books, D.C. Heath, 1975.

Charriere, Henri. *Papillon.* trans. June P. Wilson and Walter B. Michaels. New York: Morrow, 1970.

Cherrill, Fred. *Cherrill of the Yard.* London: Popular Book Club, 1955.

Christie, Trevor L. *Etched in Arsenic.* Philadelphia: J.B. Lippincott, 1968.

Churchill, Allen. *A Pictorial History of American Crime 1849-1929.* New York: Holt, Rinehart & Winston, 1964.

_____. *The Year the World Went Mad.* New York: Thomas Y. Crowell, 1960.

Cini, Zelda, and Crane, Bob. *Hollywood, Land & Legend.* New Rochelle, N.Y.: Arlington House, 1980.

Clark, Charles L., and Eubank, Earle E. *Lockstep and Corridor.* Cincinnati, Ohio: University of Cincinnati Press, 1927.

Clark, G. (ed.). *Notable British Trials: Trial of James Camb.* London: William Hodge, 1949.

Clark, Tim, and Penycate, John. *Psychopath.* London: Routledge & Paul, 1976.

Clark, Tom. *The World of Damon Runyon.* New York: Harper & Row, 1978.

Clegg, Eric. *Return Your Verdict.* Sydney, Aus.: Angus & Robertson, 1965.

Clemmer, Donald. *The Prison Community.* Boston: Christopher, 1940.

Clifford, W. *Crime Control in Japan.* Lexington, Mass.: Lexington Books, 1976.

Cobb, Belton. *Critical Years at the Yard.* London: Faber & Faber, 1956.

_____. *The First Detectives.* London: Faber & Faber, 1957.

_____. *Murdered on Duty: A Chronicle of the Killing of Policemen.* London: W.H. Allen, 1961.

Cohen, Louis H. *Murder, Madness and the Law.* New York: World, 1952.

Cohen, Sam. D. *100 True Crime Stories.* New York: World, 1946.

Colby, Robert. *The California Crime Book.* New York: Pyramid Books, 1971.

Collier, R. *Ten Thousand Eyes.* New York: E.P. Dutton, 1958.

Constantine-Quinn, Max. *Doctor Crippen.* London: Duckworth, 1935.

Corbett, James J. *The Roar of the Crowd.* New York: Gosset & Dunlap, 1925.

Corbin, Charles R. *Why News Is News.* New York: Roland Press, 1928.

Corder, Eric (ed.). *Murder My Love.* Chicago: Playboy Press, 1973.

Cornish, G.W. *Cornish of the "Yard".* London: John Lane, 1935.

Cornwell, John. *Earth To Earth.* New York: Ecco Press, 1982.

Cowley, Malcolm. *Exile's Return.* New York: W.W. Norton, 1922.

Crane, Milton (ed.). *Sins of New York.* New York: Boni & Gaer, 1947.

Crane, Stephen. *Maggie.* Gainesville, Fla.: Scholars' Facsimiles and Reprints, 1966.

Crew, Albert. *The Old Bailey.* London: Ivor Nicholson & Watson, 1933.

Critchley, M. (ed.). *The Trial of Neville George Clevely Heath.* London: Hodge, 1951.

Crosby, Caresse. *The Passionate Years.* Carbondale: Southern Illinois University Press, 1968.

Crouse, Russell. *Murder Won't Out.* Garden City, N.Y.: Doubleday, Doran, 1932.

Crowley, Aleister. *The Confessions of Aleister Crowley: An Autobiography.* London: Cape, 1969.

Cullen, Tom. *The Mild Murderer: The True Story of the Dr. Crippen Case.* Boston: Houghton Mifflin, 1977.

Cuthbert, C.R.M. *Science and the Detection of Crime.* New York: Philosophical Lib., 1958.

D

Danforth, Harold R., and Horan, James D. *The D.A.'s Man.* New York: Crown, 1957.

Danto, B.L., et al. *The Human Side of Homicide.* New York: Columbia University Press, 1982.

Darrow, Clarence. *The Story of My Life.* New York: Charles Scribner's Sons, 1932.

Daughen, Joseph R., and Binzen, Peter. *The Cop Who Would Be King.* Boston: Little, Brown, 1977.

David, Andrew. *Famous Criminal Trials.* Minneapolis, Minn.: Lerner Publications, 1979.

David, Jay. *The Scarsdale Murder.* New York: Leisure Books, 1980.

_____ (ed.). *The Weight of the Evidence.* New York: Meredith Press, 1968.

Davis, Bernice Freeman. *Assignment San Quentin.* London: Peter Davies, 1962.

_____, and Hirschberg, Al. *The Desperate and the Damned.* New York: Thomas Y. Crowell, 1961.

Dawson, John D. (ed.). *American State Trials.* St. Louis: Thomas Law, 1923.

Dawson, Robert O. *Sentencing.* Boston: Little, Brown, 1969.

Deale, Kenneth E.L. *Memorable Irish Trials.* London: Constable, 1960.

Dean, John W. *The Indiana Torture Slaying.* Chicago: Beeline Books, 1967.

Deans, R. Story. *Notable Trials: Difficult Cases.* London: Chapman & Hall, 1932.

Dearden, Harold. *Aspects of Murder.* London: Staples Press, 1951.

_____. *Death Under a Microscope.* London: Hutchinson, 1934.

_____. *The Mind of the Murderer.* London: Geoffrey Bles, 1930.

_____. *Queer People.* London: Hutchinson, 1935.

_____. *Some Cases of Sir Bernard Spilsbury and Others.* London: Hutchinson, 1934.

Dedmon, Emmett. *Fabulous Chicago.* New York: Random House, 1953.

Deeley, Peter. *The Manhunters.* London: Hodder & Stoughton, 1970.

_____, and Walker, Christopher. *Murder in the 4th Estate.* New York: McGraw-Hill, 1971.

de Ford, Miriam Allen. *Murderers Sane & Mad!* New York: Abelard-Schuman, Ltd., 1965.

_____. *Stone Walls.* Philadelphia: Chil-ton Books, 1962.

De la Torre, Lilian. *The Truth About Belle Gunness.* New York: Gold Medal Books, 1955.

_____. *Villainy Detected.* London: D. Appleton-Century, 1947.

Deming, Richard. *Women: The New Criminals.* New York: Thomas Nelson, 1977.

deRham, Edith. *How Could She Do That?* New York: Clarkson N. Potter, 1969.

De River, J. Paul. *Crime and the Sexual Psychopath.* Springfield, Ill.: Charles C. Thomas, 1968.

_____. *The Sexual Criminal: A Psychoanalytic Study.* Springfield, Ill.: Charles C. Thomas, 1950.

Derleth, August. *Wisconsin Murders.* Sauk City, Wis.: Mycroft & Moran, 1968.

Dershowitz, Alan M. *The Best Defense.* New York: Vintage Books, 1983.

_____. *Reversal of Fortune.* New York: Random House, 1986.

Desmond, Hugh. *Death Let Loose.* London: Wright & Brown, 1956.

_____. *A Scream in the Night.* London: Wright & Brown, 1955.

Devine, Philip E. *The Ethics of Homicide.* London: Cornell University Press, 1978.

Devlin, Patrick. *Trial by Jury.* London: Stevens, 1956.

Dew, Walter. *I Caught Crippen.* London: Blackie & Son, 1938.

Dewes, Simon. *Doctors of Murder.* London: John Long, 1962.

Dickson, Grierson. *Murder By Numbers.* London: Robert Hale, 1958.

Dillmann, John. *The French Quarter Killers.* New York: Macmillan, 1987.

Dillon, M., and Lehane, D. *Political Murder in Northern Ireland.* London: Penguin Books, 1973.

_____. *Man Hunters: Great Detectives and Their Achievements.* London: Robert Hale, 1937.

_____. *The Real Detective.* London: Geoffrey Bles, 1933.

_____. *Rogues' March.* London: Geoffrey Bles, 1934.

_____. *Scotland Yard: Its History and Organization, 1829-1929.* London: Geoffrey Bles, 1929.

_____. *The Story of Scotland Yard.* Boston: Houghton, Mifflin, 1927.

Dilnot, George. *Celebrated Crimes.* London: Stanley Paul, 1925.

_____. *Great Detectives and Their Methods.* Boston: Houghton Mifflin, 1928.

_____. *Triumphs of Detection.* London: Geoffrey Bles, 1929.

Dobkins, J. Dwight, and Hendricks, Robert J. *Winnie Ruth Judd: The Trunk Murders.* New York: Grosset & Dunlap, 1973.

Domènech, Gabriel. *Lurs Toute L'Affaire Dominici.* Forcalquier: Editions Charles Testanière, 1956.

Dorman, Michael. *King of the Courtroom: Percy Foreman for the Defense.* New York: Delacorte Press, 1969.

Douthwaite, L. C. *Mass Murder.* New York: Holt, 1929.

Down, Thomas. *Murder Man.* New York: Dell, 1984.

Downie, Robert Angus. *Murder in London: A Topographical Guide to Famous Crimes.* London: A. Barker, 1973.

Doyle, Adrian Conan. *The True Conan Doyle.* New York: Coward McCann, 1946.

Drapkin, Israel, and Viano, Emilio (eds.) *Victimology.* Lexington, Mass.: Lexington Books, D.C. Heath, 1974.

_____. *Victimology: A New Focus.* Lexington, Mass.: Lexington Books, D.C. Heath, 1975.

Dreiser, Theodore. *An American Tragedy.* New York: New American Library, 1964.

Droge, Edward. *The Patrolman: A Cop's Story.* New York: New American Library, 1973.

Drummon, A.L. *True Detective Stories.* Chicago: M.A. Donohue, 1909.

Drzazga, John. *Sex Crimes and Their Legal Aspects.* Springfield, Ill.: Charles C. Thomas, 1960.

Dudley, Ernest. *Bywaters and Mrs. Thompson.* London: Odhams Press, 1953.

Duffy, Warden Clinton T. *The San Quentin Story, As Told to Dean Jennings.* Garden City, N.Y.: Doubleday, 1950.

_____, with Hirschberg, Al. *88 Men and Two Women.* Garden City, N.Y.: Doubleday, 1962.

Duke, Thomas S. *Celebrated Criminal Cases of America.* San Francisco: James H. Barry, 1910.

Duke, Winifred (ed.). *Notable British Trials: Trial of Field and Gray.* London: William Hodge, 1939.

_____. *Notable British Trials: Trials of Frederick Nodder.* London: William Hodge, 1950.

_____. *Six Trials.* London: Victor Gollancz, 1934.

_____. *Skin for Skin.* London: Gollancz, 1935.

_____. *The Stroke of Murder.* London: R. Hale, 1937.

Dunbar, Dorothy. *Blood in the Parlor.* New York: A.S. Barnes, 1964.

Dunboyne, Lord (ed.). *Notable British Trials: Trial of J.G. Haigh.* London: William Hodge, 1953.

Dunning, John. *The Arbor House Treasury of True Crime.* New York: Arbor House, 1981.

Dunphy, Thomas, and Cummins, Thomas J. *Remarkable Trials.* New York: Ward & Peloubet, 1878.

Durant, M., et al. *Crime, Criminals and the Law.* London: Office of Population Censuses and Surveys, 1972.

DuRose, John. *Murder Was My Business.* London: W.H. Allen, 1971.

Dyne, D.G. *Famous New Zealand Murders.* London: Collins, 1969.

E

Eames, Hugh. *Sleuths, Inc.* Philadelphia: J.B. Lippincott, 1978.

East, Norwood. *Sexual Offenders.* London: Delisle, 1955.

_____. *Society and the Criminal.* London: H.M. Stationery Office, 1949.

Eaton, Harold. *Famous Poison Trials.* London: W. Collins Sons, 1923.

Edmonds, I.G. *Hollywood R.I.P.* New York: Regency Books, 1963.

Ellenberger, Henri. *Criminologie du Passe et du Present.* Montreal, Can.: Presses de L'Universite de Montreal, 1965.

Elliott, Robert G., and Beatty, Albert R. *Agent of Death: The Memoirs of an Executioner.* New York: E. P. Dutton, 1940.

Ellis, Albert, and Gullo, John. *Murder and Assassination.* New York: Lyle Stuart, 1971.

Ellis, Anthony L. *Prisoner at the Bar.* London: Heath Cranton, 1934.

Ellis, J.C. *Black Fame: Stories of Crime and Criminals.* London: Hutchinson, 1926.

———. *Blackmailers & Co.* London: Selwyn and Blount, 1928.

Erbstein, Charles E. *The Show-Up: Stories Before the Bar.* Chicago: Pascal Covici, 1926.

Erickson, Gladys A. *Warden Ragen of Joliet.* New York: Dutton, 1957.

Eshelman, Byron. *Death Row Chaplain.* Englewood Cliffs, N.J.: Prentice-Hall, 1962.

Every, Edward Van. *Sins of America as 'Exposed' by the Police Gazette.* New York: Frederick A. Stokes, 1931.

F

Fabian, Robert. *Fabian of the Yard.* London: Naldrett Press, 1950.

———. *London After Dark.* London: Naldrett Press, 1954.

Faralicq, Rene. *The French Police from Within.* London: Cassell, 1933.

Feldman, M.P. *Criminal Behaviour.* New York: John Wiley, 1977.

Felstead, Sidney Theodore. *Sir Richard Muir.* London: John Lane, 1927.

———. *Shades of Scotland Yard.* London: John Long, 1950.

Fergusson, Erna. *Murder & Mystery in New Mexico.* Albuquerque, N.M.: Armitage Editions, 1948.

Fethering, Doug. *The Five Lives of Ben Hecht.* London: Lester & Orpen, 1977.

Fetherstonhough, R.C. *The Royal Canadian Mounted Police.* New York: Carrick & Evans, 1938.

Fielding, Cecil. *Justice Triumphant.* London: John Long, 1958.

Fingarette, Herbert. *The Meaning of Criminal Insanity.* Berkeley: University of California Press, 1972.

———, and Hasse, A.F. *Mental Disabilities and Criminal Responsibility.* Berkeley: University of California Press, 1979.

Firmin, Stanley. *Crime Man.* New York: Hutchinson, 1950.

———. *Murderers in Our Midst.* London: Hutchinson, 1955.

———. *Scotland Yard: The Inside Story.* London: Hutchinson, 1948.

Firth, James Brierley. *A Scientist Turns to Crime.* London: W. Kimber, 1960.

Fishman, William J. *The Streets of East London.* London: Duckworth, 1979.

Foner, Philip S. *The Industrial Workers of the World, 1905-1917.* New York: International, 1965.

Fooner, Michael. *A Guide to Interpol.* Washington, D.C.: U.S. Government Printing Office, 1985.

———. *INTERPOL.* Chicago: Henry Regnery, 1973.

Foot, Michael, and Jones, Mervy. *Guilty Men.* London: Victor Gollancz, 1957.

Foot, Paul. *Who Killed Hanratty?* London: Cape, 1971.

Forbes, Ian. *Squad Man.* London: W.H. Allen, 1973.

Fordham, Edward Wilfred. *Notable Cross-Examinations.* London: Constable, 1951.

Forer, Lois G. *Criminals and Victims.* New York: W.W.

Norton, 1980.

Fowler, Gene. *The Great Mouthpiece: The Life Story of William J. Fallon.* New York: Covici-Friede, 1931.

———. *Skyline: A Reporter's Reminiscences of the 1920's.* New York: Macmillan Books, 1962.

Fox, James. *White Mischief.* New York: Random House, 1982.

Fox, James Allen. *Forecasting Crime Data.* Lexington, Mass.: Lexington/D.C. Heath, 1978.

———, and Levin, Jack. *Mass Murder: America's Growing Menace.* New York: Plenum Press, 1985.

Franklin, Charles. *Woman in the Case.* New York: Taplinger, 1968.

———. *The World's Worst Murderers: Exciting and Authentic Accounts of the Great Classics of Murder.* New York: Taplinger, 1965.

Freeman, Lucy, and Hulse, Wilfred C. *Children Who Kill.* New York: Berkley, 1962.

Fricke, Charles W. *California Criminal Evidence.* Los Angeles: O.W. Smith, 1957.

———. *California Criminal Law.* Los Angeles: O.W. Smith, 1956.

———. *California Criminal Procedure.* Los Angeles: O.W. Smith, 1955.

———. *Sentence and Probation: The Imposition of Penalties Upon Convicted Criminals.* Los Angeles: Legal Book, 1950.

Fultz, Hollis B. *Famous Northwest Manhunts and Murder Mysteries.* Elma, Wash.: Elma Chronicle, 1955.

Furneaux, Rupert. *Courtroom USA-1.* Baltimore: Penguin Books, 1963.

———. *Courtroom USA-2.* Baltimore: Penguin Books, 1963.

———. *Famous Criminal Cases, Vols. I - VII.* London: Allan Wingate, 1959.

———. *Guenther Podola.* London: Stevens, 1960.

———. *The Medical Murderer.* London: Elek Books, 1957.

———. *The Murder of Lord Erroll.* London: Stevens, 1961.

———. *Robert Hoolhouse.* London: Stevens, 1960.

———. *They Died By A Gun.* London: Herbert Jenkins, 1962.

———. *The World's Most Intriguing True Mysteries.* New York: Arco, 1966.

G

Gaddis, Thomas E. *The Birdman of Alcatraz.* New York: Random House, 1955.

———, and Long, James O. *Killer, A Journal of Murder.* New York: Macmillan, 1970.

Gale, Edwin O. *Reminiscences of Early Chicago.* Chicago: Revell, 1902.

Gardiner, Muriel. *The Deadly Innocents, Portraits of Children Who Kill.* New York: Basic Books, 1976.

Garrison, Omar V. *The Secret World of Interpol.* New York: Ralston-Pilot, 1976.

Garrity, Donald. *The Prison.* New York: Holt, Rinehart & Winston, 1961.

Garry, Charles, and Goldburg, Art. *Streetfighter in the Courtroom.* New York: Dutton, 1977.

Gaylin, Willard. *The Killing of Bonnie Garland.* New York: Simon & Schuster, 1982.

Geiser, Robert L. *Hidden Victims.* Boston: Beacon Press, 1979.

Gelb, Barbara. *On the Track of Murder.* New York: William Morrow, 1975.

Gibbons, Don C. *Crime and Criminal Careers.* Englewood

Cliffs, N.J.: Prentice-Hall, 1968.

Gibney, B. *The Beauty Queen Killer.* New York: Pinnacle, 1984.

Gifford, Denis. *Chapin.* Garden City, N.Y.: Doubleday, 1974.

Gilbert, Michael F. *Dr. Cripppen.* London: Odhams Press, 1953.

Glaister, John. *Final Diagnosis.* London: Hutchinson, 1964.

_____, and Rentoul, E. *Medical Jurisprudence and Toxicology.* London: Livingstone Press, 1953.

_____. *The Power of Poison.* New York: William Morrow, 1954.

_____, and Smith, S.A. *Recent Advances in Forensic Medicine.* London: Churchill, 1931.

Glaser, Daniel, et al. *The Violent Offender.* Washington, D.C.: U.S. Printing Office, 1968.

Godwin, George. *Peter Kurten, A Study in Sadism.* London: Acorn Press, 1938.

Godwin, John. *Alcatraz 1868-1963.* New York: Doubleday, 1963.

_____. *Killers in Paradise.* London: Herbert Jenkins, 1962.

_____. *Murder U.S.A.: The Ways We Kill Each Other.* New York: Ballantine Books, 1978.

Goldstein, Abraham S., and Joseph (eds.). *Crime, Law and Society.* New York: The Free Press, 1971.

_____. *The Insanity Defense.* New Haven, Conn.: Yale University Press, 1967.

Goldston, Robert. *Satan's Disciples.* New York: Ballantine Books, 1962.

Gollmar, Judge Robert H. *Edward Gein: America's Most Bizarre Murderer.* Delavan, Wis.: Chas. Hallberg, 1981.

Gollomb, Joseph. *Crimes of the Year.* New York: Liveright, 1931.

Goodman, Derick. *Crime of Passion.* New York: Greenberg, 1958.

_____. *Villainy Unlimited.* London: Elek Books, 1957.

Goodman, Ezra. *The Fifty-Year Decline and Fall of Hollywood.* New York: Simon & Schuster, 1961.

Goodman, Jonathon. *The Burning of Evelyn Foster.* New York: Charles Scribner's Sons, 1977.

_____. *The Railway Murders.* London: Allison & Busby, 1984.

_____. *Posts-Mortem: The Correspondence of Murder.* New York: St. Martin's Press, 1971.

Goodwin, John G. *Insanity and the Criminal.* London: Hutchinson, 1923.

Gordeaux, Paul. *Le Docteur Petiot.* Paris: Editions J'ai lu, 1970.

Gordon, Charles. *The Old Bailey and Newgate.* London: T. Fisher Unwin, 1903.

Gottfredson, Don M., Wilkins, Leslie T., and Hoffman, Peter B. *Parole Decision Making.* Washington, D.C.: National Institute of Law Enforcement and Criminal Justice, 1973.

Gottlieb, Gerald H. *Capital Punishment.* Santa Barbara, Calif.: Center for the Study of Democratic Institutions, 1967.

Gough, William Charles. *From Kew Observatory to Scotland Yard.* London: Hurst & Blackett, 1927.

Goulden, Joseph C. *Million Dollar Lawyers.* New York: G.P. Putnam's Sons, 1978.

_____. *The Superlawyers.* New York: Weybright & Talley, 1972.

Graham, Evelyn. *Fifty Years of Famous Judges.* London: John Long, 1930.

_____. *Lord Darling and His Famous Trials.* London:

John Long, 1953.

Graham, Hugh D., and Gurr, Ted Robert. *The History of Violence in America: A Report to the National Commission on the Causes and Prevention of Violence.* New York: Bantam Books, 1969.

Granier, Camille. *La Femme criminelle.* Paris: Doin, 1906.

Great True Stories of Crime, Mystery and Detection. Pleasantville, N.Y.: Reader's Digest Association, 1965.

Greenwall, Harry J. *They Were Murdered in France.* London: Jarrolds, 1957.

Greenwood, William. *Guilty or Not Guilty.* London: Hutchinson, 1931.

Gribble, Leonard. *Adventures in Murder.* London: John Long, 1954.

_____. *The Black Maria or the Criminal's Omnibus.* London: Victor Gollancz, 1935.

_____. *Clues That Spelled Guilty.* London: John Long, 1961.

_____. *Compelled to Kill.* London: John Long, 1977.

_____. *The Dead End Killers.* London: John Long, 1978.

_____. *Detection and Deduction.* Garden City, N.Y.: Doubleday, 1934.

_____. *Famous Feats of Detection and Crime.* Garden City, N.Y.: Doubleday, Doran, 1934.

_____. *Famous Judges and Their Trials.* London: John Long, 1957.

_____. *Famous Manhunts: A Century of Crime.* London: John Long, 1953.

_____. *Famous Stories of the Murder Squad.* London: Barker, 1974.

_____. *Great Detective Exploits.* London: John Long, 1958.

_____. *Great Manhunters of the Yard.* New York: Roy, 1966.

_____. *Hallmark of Horror.* London: John Long, 1973.

_____. *Murders Most Strange.* London: John Long, 1959.

_____. *Queens of Crime.* London: Hurst & Blackett, 1932.

_____. *Sisters of Cain.* London: John Long, 1972.

_____. *Stories of Famous Detectives.* New York: Hill & Wang, 1963.

_____. *Stories of Famous Modern Trials.* London: Barker, 1973.

_____. *Strange Crimes of Passion.* London: John Long, 1970.

_____. *Such Was Their Guilt.* London: John Long, 1974.

_____. *Such Women are Deadly.* London: John Long, 1965.

_____. *They Challenged the Yard.* London: John Long, 1963.

_____. *They Conspired to Kill.* London: John Long, 1975.

_____. *They Had A Way with Women.* London: John Long, 1967.

_____. *Triumphs of Scotland Yard.* London: John Long, 1955.

_____. *When Killers Err.* London: John Long, 1962.

Grier, William H., and Cobbs, Price M. *Black Rage.* New York: Bantam Books, 1969.

Grierson, Francis. *Famous French Crimes.* London: Frederick Muller, 1959.

Gross, Gerald (ed.). *Masterpieces of Murder: An Edmund Pearson True Crime Reader.* Boston: Little, Brown, 1963.

Gross, Hans. *Criminology Psychology.* Boston: Little, Brown, 1915.

Gross, Kenneth. *The Alice Crimmins Case.* New York: Alfred A. Knopf, 1975.

Grosso, Sonny, and Devaney, John. *Murder at the Harlem*

Mosque. New York: Crown, 1977.

Grunhut, Max. Sieverts, Rudolf, and Bemmelen, Jacob M. *Sexual Crime Today.* The Hague, Neth.: Martinus Nijhoff, 1960.

Gurr, Tom, and Cox, H.H. *Famous Australasian Crimes.* London: Frederick Muller, 1957.

Gurwell, John K. *Mass Murder in Houston.* Houston, Texas: Cordovan Press, 1974.

Guttmacher, Manfred. *The Mind of the Murderer.* New York: Farrar, Straus, 1960.

———, and Weihofen, Henry. *Psychiatry and the Law.* New York: W.W. Norton, 1952.

———. *Sex Offenses: The Problem, Causes and Prevention.* New York: W.W. Norton, 1951.

H

Hagemann, Gerard. *Man on the Bench.* Notre Dame, Ind.: Dujarie Press, 1962.

Hahn, Jon K., and McKenney, Harold C. *Legally Sane.* Chicago: Regnery, 1972.

Halper, Albert (ed.). *The Chicago Crime Book.* Cleveland: World, 1967.

Hambrook, Walter. *Hambrook of the Yard.* London: R. Hale, 1937.

Hammer, Richard. *The CBS Murders.* New York: William Morrow, 1987.

Hardwick, Michael. *Doctors on Trial.* London: Herbert Jenkins, 1961.

Hare, R.D., and Schalling, D. (eds.). *Psychopathic Behaviour.* Chichester, Eng.: John Wiley & Sons, 1978.

Harrington, Alan. *Psychopaths.* New York: Simon & Schuster, 1972.

Harrison, Charles Yale. *Clarence Darrow.* New York: Jonathan Cape & Harrison Smith, 1931.

Harrison, Richard. *Criminal Calendar.* London: Jarrolds, 1951.

———. *Criminal Calendar II.* London: Jarrolds, 1952.

———. *Foul Deeds Will Rise.* London: John Long, 1958.

———. *Whitehall 1212: The Story of the Police of London.* London: Jarrolds, 1947.

Hart, J.M. *The British Police.* New York: Macmillan, 1951.

Hartogs, Retanus, and Artzi, Eric. *Violence.* New York: Dell, 1970.

Hastings, Sir Patrick. *The Autobiography of Sir Patrick Hastings.* London: William Heinemann, 1948.

———. *Cases in Court.* London: William Heinemann, 1947.

Hatherill, George H. *A Detective's Story.* New York: McGraw Hill, 1972.

Haupe, Theodore. *Crime and Punishment in Germany.* New York: E.P. Dutton, 1926.

Hawkins, Gordon J., and Zimring, Franklin E. *Deterrance: The Legal Threat in Crime Control.* Chicago: University of Chicago Press, 1973.

Hawley, Lowell S., and Bushnell, Ralph Potts. *Counsel for the Damned.* Philadelphia: J.B. Lippincott, 1953.

Haycraft, Howard. *Murder for Pleasure.* New York: Appleton-Century, 1941.

Heaney, Frank, and Machado, Gay. *Inside the Walls of Alcatraz.* Palo Alto, Calif.: Bull, 1987.

Hecht, Ben. *Charlie: The Improbable Life and Times of Charles MacArthur.* New York: Harper & Bros., 1957.

———. *A Child of the Century.* New York: Simon & Schuster, 1954.

———. *Gaily, Gaily, The Memoirs of a Cub Reporter in Chicago.* New York: Doubleday, 1963.

Heilbron, W.C. *Convict Life at the Minnesota State Prison.* St. Paul, Minn.: W.C. Heilbron, 1909.

Heimer, Mel. *The Cannibal: The Case of Albert Fish.* New York: Lyle Stuart, 1971.

Helpern, Milton, and Knight, Bernard. *Autopsy.* New York: St. Martin's Press, 1977.

Hemm, G. *St. George's Hall, Liverpool.* London: Northern, 1949.

Henderson, Bruce, and Summerlin, Sam. *The Super Sleuths.* New York: Macmillan, 1976.

Henry, E.R. *Classification and Uses of Finger Prints.* London: H.M. Stationery Office, 1937.

Henry, Jack. *Detective-Inspector Henry's Famous Cases.* London: Hutchinson, 1942.

Heppenstall, Rayner. *Bluebeard and After, Three Decades of Murder in France.* London: Peter Owen, 1972.

———. *A Little Pattern of French Crime.* London: Hamish Hamilton, 1969.

———. *The Sex War and Others.* London: Peter Owen, 1973.

Hermann, Donald H.J. *The Insanity Defence.* Springfield, Ill. Charles C. Thomas, 1983.

Hessling, Peter. *Trois monstres.* Paris: Gallimard, 1958.

Heumann, Milton. *Plea Bargaining: The Experience of Prosecutors, Judges and Defense Attorneys.* Chicago: University of Chicago Press, 1978.

Hewart, Lord. *Not Without Prejudice.* London: Hutchinson, 1937.

Hicks, Seymour. *Not Guilty M'Lord.* London: Cassell, 1939.

Higdon, Hal. *The Crime of the Century.* New York: G.P. Putnam's Sons, 1975.

Higgins, Robert. *In the Name of the Law.* London: John Long, 1958.

Higham, Charles. *The Adventures of Conan Doyle: The Life of the Creator of Sherlock Holmes.* New York: W.W. Norton, 1976.

Hill, Paul. *Portrait of a Sadist.* New York: Avon, 1960.

Hirning, L. Clovis. *The Sex Offender in Custody: Handbook of Correctional Psychology.* New York: Philosophical Library, 1947.

Hirsch, Phil. *Death House.* New York: Pyramid Books, 1966.

———. *Hollywood Uncensored.* New York: Pyramid Books, 1965.

———. *The Killers.* New York: Pyramid Books, 1971.

———. *The Law Enforcers.* New York: Pyramid Books, 1969.

———. *Men Behind Bars.* New York: Pyramid Books, 1962.

Hodge, Harry. *The Black Maria, or the Criminal's Omnibus.* London: Victor Gollancz, 1935.

———. (ed.). *Famous Trials.* Baltimore: Penguin Books, 1941.

Hoffman, F.L. *The Homicide Problem.* Newark, N.J.: Prudential Press, 1925.

Hoffman, Paul. *Courthouse.* New York: Hawthorn Books, 1979.

Hogg, Gary. *Cannibalism and Human Sacrifice.* New York: Citadel Press, 1966.

Holbrook, Stewart H. *Murder Out Yonder.* New York: Macmillan, 1941.

Holdredge, Helen. *The Woman in Black.* New York: G.P. Putnam's Sons, 1955.

Hollis, C. *Shadow of the Gallows.* London: Victor Gollancz, 1951.

Holmes, Ronald M., and DeBurger, James. *Serial Murder.* Newbury Park, Calif.: Sage, 1988.

Holroyd, James Edward. *The Gaslight Murders.* London: George Allen & Unwin, 1960.

Holtzoff, H. (ed.). *Encyclopedia of Criminology.* New York: Philosophical Library, 1949.

Honeycombe, Gordon. *The Murders of the Black Museum, 1870-1970.* London: Hutchinson, 1982.

Hood, R.G. *Sentencing in Magistrates' Courts.* London: Stevens, 1962.

Hooper, William Eden. *The History of Newgate and the Old Bailey.* London: Underwood Press, 1935.

Hopkins, R. Thurston. *Life and Death at the Old Bailey.* London: Herbert Jenkins, 1935.

Horowitz, Elinor. *Capital Punishment, U.S.A.* Philadelphia: J.B. Lippincott, 1973.

Horwell, John E. *Horwell of the Yard.* London: Andrew Melrose, 1947.

Hoskins, Percy. *The Sound of Murder.* London: Long, 1973.

———. *They Almost Escaped.* London: Hutchinson, 1938.

House, Brant (ed.). *Crimes That Shocked America.* New York: Ace Books, 1961.

Houts, Marshall. *They Asked for Death.* New York: Cowles, 1970.

———. *Where Death Delights: The Story of Dr. Milton Helpern and Forensic Medicine.* New York: Dell, 1968.

Howe, Cliff. *Scoundrels, Fiends and Human Monsters.* New York: Ace Books, 1958.

Howe, Sir Ronald. *The Pursuit of Crime.* London: A. Barker, 1962.

———. *The Story of Scotland Yard.* London: A. Barker, 1965.

Howgrave-Graham, H.M. *Light and Shade at Scotland Yard.* London: John Murray, 1947.

Hudson, Joe, and Galaway, Burt (eds.). *Considering the Victim.* Springfield, Ill.: Charles C. Thomas, 1975.

Huggett, Renee, and Berry, Paul. *Daughters of Cain.* London: George Allen & Unwin, 1956.

Hughes, Rupert. *The Complete Detective: Being the Life and Strange and Exciting Cases of Raymond Schindler, Master Detective.* New York: Sheridan House, 1950.

Huie, William Bradford. *Three Lives for Mississippi.* New York: Signet, 1968.

Humphreys, Christmas. *Seven Murders.* London: William Heinemann, 1931.

Humphreys, Sir Travers. *A Book of Trials.* London: William Heinemann, 1953.

———. *Criminal Days.* London: Hodder & Stoughton, 1946.

Hunt, William R. *Dictionary of Rogues.* New York: Philosophical Library, 1970.

Huson, Richard (ed.) *Sixty Famous Trials.* London: Daily Express, 1967.

Hyde, H. Montgomery. *Carson: The Life of Sir Edward Carson, Lord Carson of Duncairn.* London: William Heinemann, 1953.

———. *Cases That Changed The Law.* London: William Heinemann, 1951.

———. *Crime Has Its Heroes.* London: Constable, 1976.

———. *An International Casebook of Crime.* London: Barrie & Rockcliff, 1962.

———. *Norman Birkett: The Life of Lord Birkett, of Ulverston.* London: Hamish Hamilton, 1964.

———. *Room 3603.* New York: Farrar, Straus & Giroux, 1962.

———. *Sir Patrick Hastings, His Life and Cases.* London: William Heinemann, 1960.

———. *Their Good Names.* London: Hamish Hamilton, 1970.

Hynd, Alan. *Brutes, Beasts and Human Fiends.* New York: Paperback Library, 1964.

———. *The Giant Killers.* New York: Robert M. McBride, 1945.

———. *Murder, Mayhem and Mystery.* New York: A.S. Barnes, 1958.

———. *Sleuths, Slayers, and Swindlers.* New York: A.S. Barnes, 1959.

———. *Violence in the Night.* New York: Fawcett, 1955.

I

Irving, Henry Brodribb. *A Book of Remarkable Criminals.* New York: George H. Doran, 1918.

Israel, Lee. *Kilgallen.* New York: Delacorte, 1957.

Issel, William, and Cherny, Robert W. *San Francisco, 1865-1932.* Berkeley: University of California Press, 1986.

J

Jackson, Bruce. *Death Row.* Boston: Beacon Press, 1980.

———. *In The Life.* New York: Macmillan, 1972.

———. *Killing Time.* Ithaca, N.Y.: Cornell University Press, 1977.

Jackson, Geoffrey. *People's Prison.* London: Faber & Faber, 1973.

Jackson, Joseph Henry. *The Portable Murder Book.* New York: Viking Press, 1945.

Jackson, R. *The Chief.* London: Harrap, 1959.

Jackson, R.M. *The Machinery of Justice in England.* London: Cambridge University Press, 1964.

Jackson, Sir Richard. *Occupied with Crime.* London: Harrap, 1967.

Jackson, Robert. *Case for the Prosecution: A Biography of Sir Archibald Bodkin, Director of Public Prosecutions, 1920-1930.* London: Arthur Barket, 1962.

———. *The Crime Doctors.* London: Frederick Muller, 1966.

———. *Francis Camps: Famous Case Histories of the Celebrated Pathologist.* London: Hart Davis, 1975.

Jackson, Stanley. *The Life and Cases of Mr. Justice Humphreys.* London: Odhams Press, 1951.

———. *Mr. Justice Avory.* London: Victor Gollancz, 1935.

Jacob, Herbert. *Justice in America: Courts, Lawyers, and the Judicial Process.* Boston: Little, Brown, 1972.

Jacobs, James B. *Stateville: The Penitentiary in Mass Society.* Chicago: University of Chicago Press, 1977.

Jacobs, T.C.H. *Aspects of Murder.* London: Stanley Paul, 1956.

———. *Cavalcade of Murder.* London: Stanley Paul, 1955.

———. *Pageant of Murder.* London: Stanley Paul, 1956.

Jacobson, Lauri. *Hollywood Heartbreak.* New York: Simon & Schuster, 1984.

Jacoby, Joseph E. (ed.). *Classics of Criminology.* Oak Park, Ill.: Moore, 1979.

Jenkins, Elizabeth. *Six Criminal Women.* London: Pan Books, 1949.

Jervis, Eustace. *Twenty-Five Years in Six Prisons.* London: T. Fisher Unwin, 1925.

Jervis, John. *On the Office and Duties of Coroners, with Forms and Procedures.* London: Sweet & Maxwell,

1957.

Jesse, F. Tennyson. *Comments on Cain.* London: William Heinemann, 1948.

――――. *Murder and Its Motives.* New York: Alfred A. Knopf, 1924.

――――. *Trial of Ley and Smith.* London: William Hodge, 1947.

――――. *Trials of Timothy John Evans and John Reginald Halliday Christie.* London: William Hodge, 1957.

Jessor, Richard, et al. *Society, Personality, and Deviant Behavior.* New York: Holt, Rinehart & Winston, 1968.

Johnston, James A. *Alcatraz Island Prison.* New York: Charles Scribner's Sons, 1949.

Jones, Elwyn. *The Last Two to Hang.* New York: Stein-Day, 1966.

Jones, H. *Crime, Race, and Culture.* New York: John Wiley & Sons, 1981.

Jones, Howard. *Crime and Penal System.* London: University Tutorial Press, 1956.

――――. *Open Prisons.* London: RKP, 1979.

Jones, J. Elbert. *The Mysteries of Famous Crimes Solved by St. Louis Policemen.* St. Louis: Moinster, 1924.

Justice, Jean. *Murder vs. Murder: The British Legal System and the A.6 Murder Case.* Paris: Olympia Press, 1964.

K

Kahn, E.J., Jr. *The World of Swope.* New York: Simon & Schuster, 1965.

Kahn, Samuel. *Sing Sing Criminals.* Philadelphia: Dorrance, 1936.

Kalven, Harry, Jr., and Zeisel, Hans. *The American Jury.* Chicago: University of Chicago Press, 1966.

Kandle, George C., and Ronnow, H. Kris. *The Fire in Today's Prisons.* New York: United Presbyterian Church, U.S.A., 1972.

Kanowitz, Leo. *Women and the Law.* Albuquerque: University of New Mexico Press, 1971.

Kates, Brian. *The Murder of a Shopping Bag Lady.* New York: Harcourt Brace Jovanovich, 1985.

Katkin, Daniel. *The Nature of Criminal Law.* Monterey, Calif.: Brooks/Cole, 1982.

Katz, L., Litwin, L., and Bamberger, R. *Justice is the Crime.* Cleveland: Case Western Reserve University Press, 1972.

Kaufman, Beatrice, and Hennessey, Joseph (eds.). *The Letters of Alexander Wollcott.* New York: Viking Press, 1944.

Kaufman, George S., and Hart, Moss. *The Man Who Came to Dinner.* New York: Random House, 1939.

Kaufman, Michael T. *The Gun.* New York: Award Books, 1974.

Keeton, George Williams. *Guilty But Insane.* London: MacDonald, 1961.

――――. *Lord Chancellor Jeffreys and the Stuart Case.* London: MacDonald, 1965.

Keilitz, Ingo, and Fulton, Junius P. *The Insanity Defense.* Williamsburg, Va.: National Center for State Courts, 1984.

Kellogg, Grace. *The Two Lives of Edith Wharton: The Woman and Her Work.* New York: Appleton-Century, 1965.

Kelly, G.G. *The Gun in the Case.* Christchurch, N. Zea.: Whitcombe & Tombs, 1963.

Kelly, Vince. *The Charge is Murder.* London: Angus &

Robertson, 1965.

Kendall, L. *The Phantom Prince: My Life With Ted Bundy.* Seattle, Wash.: Madrona, 1981.

Kennaugh, Robert. *Contemporary Murder.* Johannesburg, S. Afri.: Hugh Keartland, 1968.

Kennedy, Ludovic. *The Airman and the Carpenter.* New York: Viking Penguin, 1985.

――――. *Ten Rillington Place.* New York: Simon & Schuster, 1961.

Kenney, John P. *The California Police.* Springfield, Ill.: Charles C. Thomas, 1964.

Kenny, C.S. *Outlines of Criminal Law.* London: Cambridge University Press, 1947.

Kent, Arthur. *The Death Doctors.* London: New English Library, 1975.

Kentucky Legislative Research Commission. *Capital Punishment.* Frankfort: State of Kentucky, 1965.

Kerner, Dieter, Dalchow, Johannes, and Duda, Gunther. *Mozart's Tod: 1791-1971.* Pahl, Verlag Hohe Warte Bebenberg, 1971.

Kerns, Phil. *People's Temple, People's Tomb.* Plainfield, N.J.: Logos, 1979.

Kershaw, Alister. *A History of the Guillotine.* London: J. Calder, 1958.

――――. *Murder In France.* London: Constable, 1955.

Keve, Paul W. *Prison Life and Human Worth.* Minneapolis: University of Minnesota Press, 1974.

Keyes, Edward. *The Michigan Murders.* New York: Thomas Y. Crowell, 1976.

Keylin, Arleen, and DeMirjian, Arto, Jr. *Crime: As Reported by the New York Times.* New York: Arno Press, 1976.

――――. *The Fabulous Fifties.* New York: Arno Press, 1978.

Kidd, W.R. *Police Interrogation.* New York: Basuino, 1940.

Kidder, T. *The Road to Yuba City: A Journey Into the Juan Corona Murders.* New York: Doubleday, 1974.

Kidner, John. *Crimaldi: Contract Killer.* Washington, D.C.: Acropolis Books, 1976.

Kilgallen, Dorothy. *Murder One.* New York: Random House, 1967.

Kind, Stewart. *Science Against Crime.* New York: Doubleday, 1972.

Kinder, Gary. *Victim: The Other Side of Murder.* New York: Delacorte Press, 1982.

King, Francis. *The Magical World of Aleister Crowley.* New York: Coward, McCann & Geoghegan, 1977.

Kingsmill, Joseph. *A History of the Guillotine.* New York: Taplinger, 1959.

Kingston, Charles. *The Bench & The Dock.* London: Stanley Paul, 1925.

――――. *Dramatic Days At the Old Bailey.* New York: Frederick A. Stokes, 1927.

――――. *Enemies of Society.* London: Stanley Paul, 1927.

――――. *Famous Judges and Famous Trials.* New York: Frederick A. Stokes, 1923.

――――. *A Gallery of Rogues.* London: Stanley Paul, 1924.

――――. *The Judges and the Judged.* London: John Lane, Bodley Head, 1926.

――――. *Law-Breakers.* London: John Lane, Bodley Head, 1930.

――――. *Remarkable Rogues: Some Notable Criminals of Europe and America.* New York: John Lane, 1921.

――――. *Rogues and Adventuresses.* London: John Lane, Bodley Head, 1928.

Kirk, Paul L., and Bradford, L.W. *The Crime Laboratory.* Springfield, Ill.: C.C. Thomas, 1965.

Klare, Hugh J. *Anatomy of Prison.* London: Hutchinson, 1960.

Klasne, William. *Street Cops.* Englewood Cliffs, N.J.: Prentice-Hall, 1980.

Klausner, Lawrence D. *Son of Sam.* New York: McGraw-Hill, 1981.

Klebba, A. Joan. *Homicide Trends in the United States, 1900-1974.* Washington, D.C.: U.S. Government Printing Office, 1975.

Knox, Bill. *Court of Murder: Famous Trials at Glascow High Court.* London: John Long, 1968.

Kobler, John. *Some Like It Gory.* New York: Dodd, Mead, 1940.

Korn, Richard R., and McCorkle, Lloyd W. *Criminology and Penology.* New York: Henry Holt, 1959.

Kraemer, William, et al. *The Normal and Abnormal Love of Children.* Kansas City: Sheed Andrews & McMeel, 1976.

Krafft-Ebing, Richard von. *Psychopathia Sexualis.* New York: G.P. Putnam's Sons, 1965.

Krause, Charles. *Guyana Massacre.* New York: Berkeley, 1978.

Kuhne, F. *The Finger Print Instructor.* New York: Munn, 1942.

Kunstler, William M. *The Case for Courage.* New York: William Morrow, 1962.

_____. *First Degree.* New York: Ocean Press, 1960.

Kurland, Gerald. *Clarence Darrow, Attorney for the Damned.* Charlotteville, N.Y.: SamHar Press, 1972.

Kurth, Ann. *Prescriptions: Murder.* New York: Signet, 1976.

Kuznetsov, Edward. *Prison Diaries.* New York: Stein & Day, 1980.

Kwartler, Richard (ed.). *Behind Bars.* New York: Random House, 1974.

L

La Bern, Arthur. *The Life and Death of a Ladykiller.* London: Published by Author, 1967.

Laborde, Jean. *The Dominici Affair.* New York: William Morrow, 1974.

LaFave, Wayne R. *Arrest.* Boston: Little, Brown, 1965.

_____, and Scott, A.W., Jr. *Handbook on Criminal Law.* St. Paul, Minn.: West, 1972.

Lamb, Ruth DeForest. *American Chamber of Horrors.* New York: Farrar & Rinehart, 1936.

Lambton, Arthur. *Echoes of Causes Celebres.* London: Hurst & Blackett, 1931.

_____. *Thou Shalt Do No Murder.* London: Hurst & Blackett, 1930.

Lamond, John. *Arthur Conan Doyle.* London: John Murray, 1931.

Lampman, Ben Hur. *Centralia Tragedy and Trial.* Tacoma, Wash.: n.p., 1920.

Lane, Margaret. *Edgar Wallace: The Biography of a Phenomenon.* London: William Heinemann, 1938.

Lane, Mark. *The Strongest Poison.* New York: Hawthorn Books, 1980.

Lang, Rev. Gordon. *Mr. Justice Avory.* London: Herbert Jenkins, 1935.

Lange, Johannes. *Crime and Destiny.* New York: Charles Boni, 1930.

Langeluttig, Albert G. *Department of Justice in the United States.* Baltimore: Johns Hopkins University Press, 1927.

Langford, Gerald. *The Murder of Stanford White.* Indianapolis: Bobbs-Merrill, 1962.

Larsen, Richard W. *Bundy, The Deliberate Stranger.* Englewood Cliffs, N.J.: Prentice-Hall, 1980.

Larson, J.A. *A Single Fingerprint System.* New York: D. Appleton, 1924.

Latane, B., and Darley, J.M. *The Unresponsive Bystander.* New York: Appleton, 1970.

Laurence, John. *A History of Capital Punishment.* New York: Citadel Press, 1963.

Laurence, John A. *Extraordinary Crimes.* London: Low, Marston, 1931.

Laurie, Peter. *Scotland Yard: A Study of the Metropolitan Police.* Middlesex, Eng.: Penguin, 1972.

Lavigne, Frank C. *Crimes, Criminals and Detectives.* Helena, Mont.: State, 1921.

Lawes, Warden Lewis Edward. *Cell 202 Sing-Sing.* New York: Farrar & Rinehart, 1935.

_____. *Man's Judgment of Death.* New York: G.P. Putnam's Sons, 1924.

_____. *Meet the Murderer!* New York: Harper & Bros., 1932.

_____. *Twenty Thousand Years In Sing Sing.* New York: R. Long & R. R. Smith, 1932.

Lawson, John D. (ed.). *American State Trials.* 17 vols. St. Louis: Thomas, 1914-1937.

Layman, Richard. *Shadow Man: The Life of Dashiell Hammett.* New York: Harcourt, Brace, Jovanovich, 1981.

LeAveux, William. *Things I Know About Kings, Celebrities and Crooks.* London: Everleigh, Nash & Grayson, 1923.

LeBlanc, Jerry, and Davis, Ivor. *5 to Die.* Los Angeles: Holloway House, 1970.

Le Brun, George P. *Call Me If It's Murder.* New York: William Morrow, 1962.

_____. *It's Time to Tell.* New York: William Morrow, 1962.

Le Clere, Marcel. *Histoire de la police.* Paris: Presses Universitaires de France, 1947.

Lee, Peter G. *Interpol.* New York: Stein and Day, 1976.

Lee, Raymond. *Those Scandalous Sheets of Hollywood.* Venice, Calif.: Venice, 1972.

Leeson, Benjamin. *Lost London: The Memoirs of an East End Detective.* London: S. Paul, 1934.

Lefebure, Molly. *Evidence for the Crown.* London: Heinemann, 1955.

_____. *Murder with a Difference.* London: Heinemann, 1958.

Lefkowitz, Bernard, and Gross, Kenneth G. *The Victims.* New York: G.P. Putnam's Sons, 1969.

Leftkowitz, N.M., et al. *Growing Up to Be Violent.* New York: Pergamon, 1977.

Leighton, Isabel (ed.). *The Aspirin Age, 1919-1941.* New York: Simon and Schuster, 1949.

LeNeve, Ethel. *Ethel LeNeve: Her Life Story.* Manchester, Eng.: Daisy Bank Printing, 1910.

Lenotre, G. *The Guillotine and Its Servants.* trans. Mrs. Rudolph Stawell. London: Hutchinson, 1929.

Leopold, Nathan F. *Life Plus 99 Years.* Garden City, N.Y.: Doubleday, 1958.

Lermolo, Elizabeth. *Face of a Victim.* New York: Harper & Brothers, 1955.

Leslie, Anita. *The Remarkable Mr. Jerome.* New York: M. Holt, 1954.

Lester, David, and Lester, Gene. *Crime of Passion.* Chicago: Nelson-Hall, 1975.

Levin, Jack, and Fox, James Alan. *Mass Murder.* New York: Plenum, 1985.

Levin, Meyer. *Compulsion*. New York: Simon & Schuster, 1956.
_____. *The Obsession*. New York: Simon & Schuster, 1973.
Levine, Richard M. *Bad Blood*. New York: New American Library, 1982.
Levine, Stephen (ed.). *Death Row*. San Francisco: Glide, 1972.
Lewis, Alfred Allan, with Mac Donell, Herbert Leon. *The Evidence Never Lies*. New York: Holt, Rinehart and Winston, 1984.
Lewis, Alfred Henry. *Confessions of a Detective*. New York: A.S. Barnes, 1906.
_____. *Nation-Famous New York Murders*. New York: G.W. Dillingham, 1914.
Lewis, Leonard. *Trunk Crimes Past and Present*. London: Hutchinson, 1934.
Lewis, Mildred and Milton. *Famous Modern Newspaper Writers*. New York: Dodd, Mead, 1962.
Lewis, R.W.B. *Edith Wharton: A Biography*. New York: Harper & Row, 1975.
Limpus, Lowell J. *Honest Cop: Lewis J. Valentine*. New York: Dutton, 1939.
Lindsay, Philip. *The Mainspring of Murder*. London: John Long, 1958.
Linedecker, Clifford L. *The Man Who Killed Boys*. New York: St. Martin's Press, 1980.
Lipsig, Frances. *Murder-Family Style*. New York: Collier Books, 1962.
Liston, Robert H. *Great Detectives*. New York: Platt & Munk, 1966.
Livingston, Armstrong, and Stein, Captain John G. *The Murdered and the Missing*. New York: Stephen-Paul, 1947.
Livingstone, Belle. *Belle Out of Order*. London: Heinemann, 1960.
Livsey, Clara. *The Manson Women*. New York: Marek, 1980.
Locard, E. *L'Enquete Criminelle et les Methodes Scientifiques*. Paris: Flammarion, 1920.
_____. *La Preuve Judiciaire par les Empreintes Digitales*. Lyons, Fr.: A. Rey, 1914.
_____. *Traite de Criminalistique*. Lyons, Fr.: Desvigne, 1931.
Logan, Andy. *Against the Evidence: The Becker-Rosenthal Affair*. New York: McGraw-Hill, 1970.
Logan, Guy. *Dramas of the Dock*. London: Stanley Paul, 1928.
_____. *Great Murder Mysteries*. London: Stanley Paul, 1931.
_____. *Guilty or Not Guilty?* London: Stanley Paul, 1928.
_____. *Masters of Crime: Studies of Multiple Murders*. London: Stanley Paul, 1928.
_____. *Rope, Knife and Chair*. London: Stanley Paul, 1930.
_____. *Verdict and Sentence*. London: Eldon Press, 1935.
_____. *Wilful Murder*. London: Eldon Press, 1935.
Lombroso, Caesar. *Crime, Its Causes and Remedies*. Boston: Little, Brown, 1911.
_____. *Criminal Man According to the Classification of Cesare Lombroso*. New York: Putnam, 1911.
_____, and Ferrero, William. *The Female Offender*. New York: Appleton, 1897.
Longstreth, T. Morris. *In Scarlet and Plain Clothes*. New York: Macmillan, 1933.
_____. *The Silent Force: Scenes From the Life of the Mounted Police of Canada*. New York: Century, 1927.
Loomis, Stanley. *A Crime of Passion*. Philadelphia: Lippincott, 1967.

Lowe, David. *Lost Chicago*. Boston: Houghton Mifflin, 1975.
Lubbock, Percy. *Portrait of Edith Wharton*. New York: D. Appleton-Century, 1947.
Lucas, Norman. *The Child Killers*. London: Barker, 1972.
_____. *Laboratory Detectives*. New York: Taplinger, 1972.
_____. *The Sex Killers*. New York: W. H. Allen, 1974.
Lunde, Donald T. *Murder and Madness*. New York: W.W. Norton, 1975.
Lundsgaarde, Henry P. *Murder in Space City: A Cultural Analysis of Houston Homicide Patterns*. New York: Oxford University Press, 1977.
Lustgarten, Edgar. *The Business of Murder*. New York: Charles Scribner's Sons, 1968.
_____. *A Case to Answer*. London: Eyre and Spottiswoode, 1947.
_____. *A Century of Murders*. London: Eyre Methuen, 1975.
_____. *The Illustrated Story of Crime*. Chicago: Follett, 1976.
_____. *The Judges and the Judged*. London: Odhams, 1961.
_____. *The Murder and the Trial*. New York: Charles Scribner's Sons, 1958.
_____. *Prisoner at the Bar*. London: Andre Deutsch, 1951.
_____. *The Woman in the Case*. London: Andre Deutsch, 1955.

M

McAlmon, Robert. *Being Geniuses Together*. Garden City, N.Y.: Doubleday, 1968.
McCafferty, James A. (ed.). *Capital Punishment*. Chicago: Aldine, Atherton, 1972.
McCallum, John D. *Crime Doctor*. Mercer Island, Wash.: Writing Works, 1978.
McClintock, Frederick H. *Crimes of Violence*. New York: St. Martin's Press, 1963.
_____, and Avison, N.H. *Crime in England and Wales*. London: William Heinemann, 1968.
McComas, J. Francis. *The Graveside Companion*. New York: Obelensky, 1962.
McConnell, Brian. *Found Naked and Dead*. London: New English Library, 1974.
McConnell, Jean. *The Detectives: Turning Points in Criminal Investigation*. Newton Abbot, Eng.: David & Charles, 1976.
McConville, Michael, and Baldwin, John. *Courts, Prosecution and Conviction*. Oxford, Eng.: Clarendon Press, 1981.
McCord, W., and McCord, J. *The Psychopath: An Essay on the Criminal Mind*. Princeton, N.J.: D. Van Nostrand, 1964.
MacDonald, John M. *Homicidal Threats*. Springfield, Ill.: Charles C. Thomas, 1968.
_____. *The Murderer and His Victim*. Springfield, Ill.: Charles C. Thomas, 1961.
MacDonald, Philip. *Mystery of the Dead Police*. New York: Doubleday, 1933.
McGivena, Leo E., et al. (eds.). *The News: The First Fifty Years of New York's Picture Newspaper*. New York: News Syndicate, 1960.
McGrady, Mike. *Crime Scientists*. Philadelphia: J.B. Lippincott, 1961.
Mackaye, Milton. *Dramatic Crimes of 1927*. Garden City, N.Y.: Crime Club, 1928.

Mackenzie, Frederic A. *Landru*. New York: Charles Scribner's Sons, 1928.

———. *The Trial of Harry Thaw*. London: Geoffrey Bles, 1928.

———. *Twentieth Century Crimes*. Boston: Little, Brown, 1927.

———. *World Famous Crimes*. London: Geoffrey Bles, 1927.

McKernan, Maureen. *The Amazing Crime and Trial of Leopold and Loeb*. New York: New American Library, 1957.

McKnight, Gerald. *The Murder Squad*. London: W.H. Allen, 1967.

MacNaghten, Sir Melville. *Days of My Years*. London: Edward Arnold, 1914.

MacNamara, Donald E.J., and Sagarin, Edward. *Sex, Crime and the Law*. New York: Free Press, 1978.

McPhaul, John J. *Deadlines and Monkeyshines: The Fabled World of Chicago Journalism*. Englewood Cliffs, N.J.: Prentice-Hall, 1962.

Madow, Leo, et al. *The Dangerous Sex Offender*. Philadelphia: General Assembly of the Commonwealth of Pennsylvania, 1963.

Maeder, Thomas. *Crime and Madness*. New York: Harper & Row, 1985.

———. *The Unspeakable Crimes of Dr. Petiot*. Toronto, Ontario, Can.: Atlantic, Little, Brown, 1980.

Magee, D. *What Murder Leaves Behind: The Victim's Family*. New York: Dodd, Mead, 1983.

Mailer, Norman. *The Executioner's Song*. Boston: Little, Brown, 1979.

Maine, C.E. (ed.). *The World's Strangest Crimes*. New York: Hart, 1967.

Marjoribanks, Edward. *For The Defence The Life of Sir Edward Marshall Hall*. London: Victor Gollancz, 1926.

———. *The Life of Lord Carson*. Volume one. London: Victor Gollancz, 1932.

———. *The Life of Sir Edward Marshall Hall*. London: Victor Gollancz, 1931.

Marks, Laurence, and Van den Bergh, Tony. *Ruth Ellis: A Case of Diminished Responsibility?* London: Macdonald and Janes, 1977.

Marten, Manuel Edward. *The Doctor Looks at Murder*. Garden City, N.Y.: Doubleday, Doran, 1937.

Martin, John Bartlow. *Butcher's Dozen and Other Murders*. New York: Harper & Row, 1950.

Martinez, Al. *Jigsaw John*. Los Angeles: J.P. Tarcber, 1975.

Marye, George Thomas. *Secrets of the Great City; the Virtues and the Vices, the Mysteries, Miseries and Crimes at New York City*. New York: Published by Author, 1968.

Mason, Alpheus Thomas. *Harlan Fiske Stone: Pillar of the Law*. New York: Viking Press, 1956.

Mason, Philip. *Call the Next Witness*. New York: Harcourt, Brace, 1945.

Masson, Rene. *Number One: A Story of Landru*. trans. Gillian Tindall. London: Hutchinson, 1964.

Masters, Edgar Lee. *The Tale of Chicago*. New York: G.P. Putnam's Sons, 1933.

Masters, R.E.L., and Lea, Eduord. *Perverse Crimes in History*. New York: Julian Press, 1963.

———. *Sex Crimes in History: Evolving Concepts of Sadism, Lust-Murder, and Necrophilia from Ancient to Modern Times*. New York: Julian Press, 1963.

May, Henry John. *Murder by Consent*. London: Hutchinson, 1968.

Maycock, Sir Willoughby. *Celebrated Crimes and Criminals*.

Maidstone, Eng.: George Mann, 1973.

Mayer, Robert. *The Dreams of Ada*. New York: Viking Press, 1987.

Mayo, Katherine. *Justice to All: The Story of the Pennsylvania State Police*. Boston: Houghton Mifflin, 1920.

Meek, Victor. *Cops and Robbers*. London: G. Duckworth, 1962.

———. *Private Enquiries: A Handbook for Detectives*. London: G. Duckworth, 1967.

Meeker, Arthur. *Chicago With Love*. New York: Alfred A. Knopf, 1955.

Melville, Samuel. *Letters from Attica*. New York: William Morrow, 1972.

Merry, S.E. *Urban Danger*. Philadelphia: Temple University Press, 1981.

Meyer, Peter. *The Yale Murder*. New York: Berkley Books, 1983.

Michalowski, Raymond J. *Order, Law, and Crime*. New York: Random House, 1985.

Michaud, Stephen G., and Aynesworth, Hugh. *The Only Living Witness*. New York: Simon and Schuster, 1983.

Millen, Ernest. *Specialist in Crime*. London: Harrap, 1972.

Minot, G.E. *Murder Will Out*. Boston: Marshall Jones, 1928.

Mitchell, C. Ainsworth. *Science and the Criminal*. London: Pitman, 1911.

———. *The Scientific Detective and the Expert Witness*. London: Heffer, 1931.

Moenssens, Andre A. *Fingerprint Techniques*. Radnor, Pa.: Chilton, 1971.

Moiseiwitsch, Maurice. *Five Famous Trials*. Connecticut: New York Graphic Society, 1962.

Moll, A. *Libido Sexualis*. New York: American Ethnological Press, 1933.

———. *Perversions of the Sex Instinct*. trans. M. Popkin. Newark, N.J.: Julian Press, 1931.

Monahan, Florence. *Women in Crime*. New York: Washburn, 1941.

Montarron, Marcel. *Histoire des Crimes Sexuels*. Paris: Plon, 1970.

———. *Histoire du Milieu*. Paris: Plon, 1969.

———. *Les Grande Proces d'Assises*. Paris: Planete, 1967.

———. *Tout Ce Joli Monde*. Paris: La Table Ronde, 1965.

Monteil, Vincent. *Les Officiers*. Paris: Editions du Seuil, 1958.

Moody, Samuel B. *Reprieve From Hell*. New York: Pageant Press, 1961.

Mooney, Michael Macdonald. *Evelyn Nesbit and Stanford White, Love and Death in the Gilded Age*. New York: William Morrow, 1976.

Moore, James and Dahl, Norman. *Famous Lives: Crime and Justice*. London: Hamlyn, 1980.

Mordell, Albert. *Clarence Darrow, Eugene V. Debs and Haldeman-Julius: Incidents in the Career of an Author, Editor and Publisher*. Girard, Kan.: Haldeman-Julius, 1950.

Morland, Nigel. *Background to Murder*. London: Werner Laurie, 1955.

———. *Death for Sale*. London: Hale, 1957.

———. *Hangman's Clutch*. London: Werner Laurie, 1954.

———. *An Outline of Scientific Criminology*. London: Cassell, 1950.

———. *An Outline of Sexual Criminology*. New York: Hart, 1967.

———. *Pattern of Murder*. London: Elek Books, 1966.

———. *Science In Crime Detection*. London: Robert Hale, 1958.

———. *This Friendless Lady.* London: Frederick Muller, 1957.

Morris, Norval, and Tonry, Michael. *Crime and Justice.* Chicago: University of Chicago Press, 1980.

Morris, Terence, and Blom-Cooper, Louis. *A Calendar of Murder.* London: Michael Joseph, 1964.

———. *The Criminal Area.* New York: The Humanities Press, 1958.

———, and Pauline. *Pentonville: A Sociological Study of an English Prison.* London: Routledge & Kegan Paul, 1963.

Moser, Don, and Cohen, Jerry. *The Pied Piper of Tucson.* New York: Signet Books, 1967.

Moulton, H. Fletcher. *The Trial of Steinie Morrison.* London: William Hodge, 1922.

Moylan, John F. *Scotland Yard and the Metropolitan Police.* London: Putnam, 1929.

Mueller, Gerhard O.W. (ed.). *Essays in Criminal Science.* New York: Rothman, 1961.

Mulvihill, Donald J., and Tumin, Melvin M., and Curtis, Lynn A. *Crimes of Violence.* Washington D.C.: U.S. Government Printing Office, 1969.

Munsterberg, H. *On the Witness Stand.* New York: Clark, Boardman, 1908.

Musmanno, Michael A. *Verdict!* Garden City, N.Y.: Doubleday, 1958.

N

Nash, Jay Robert. *Almanac of World Crime.* New York: Doubleday, 1981.

———. *Bloodletters and Badmen, A Narrative Encyclopedia of American Criminals From the Pilgrims to the Present.* New York: M. Evans, 1973.

———. *Crime Chronology.* New York: Facts on File, 1984.

———. *Look for the Woman.* New York: M. Evans, 1981.

———. *Murder, America, Homicide in the United States from the Revolution to the Present.* New York: Simon & Schuster, 1980.

———. *Murder Among the Mighty.* New York: Delacorte Press, 1983.

Needham, Ted and Howard. *Alcatraz.* Millbrae, Calif.: Celestial Arts, 1976.

Neil, Arthur Fowler. *Forty Years of Man-Hunting.* London: Jarrolds, 1932.

———. *Man-Hunters of Scotland Yard.* New York: Doubleday, Doran, 1933.

Nelson, Victor. *Prison Days and Nights.* Boston: Little, Brown, 1933.

Nettler, Gwynn. *Criminal Careers.* Cincinnati, Ohio: Anderson, 1982.

———. *Explaining Crime.* New York: McGraw-Hill, n.d.

———. *Killing One Another.* Cincinnati, Ohio: Anderson, 1982.

Neustatter, W. Lindsay. *The Mind of the Murderer.* London: Christopher Johnson, 1957.

———. *Psychological Disorder and Crime.* London: Christopher Johnson, 1953.

Neutzel, Charles. *Whodunit? Hollywood Style.* Beverly Hills: California Book Company of America, 1965.

Newton, H. Chance. *Crime and the Drama or Dark Deeds Dramatized.* London: Stanley Paul, 1927.

Nice, Richard (ed.). *Crime and Insanity.* New York: Philosophical Library, 1958.

Nicholls, Ernest. *Crime Within the Square Mile.* London: John Long, 1935.

Nicholson, Michael. *The Yorkshire Ripper.* London: W. H. Allen, 1979.

Niles, Blair. *Condemned to Devil's Island.* New York: Grosset & Dunlap, 1928.

Nizer, Louis. *The Jury Returns.* New York: Pocket Books, 1968.

———. *My Life in Court.* New York: Pyramid, 1963.

Nordholt, J.W. Schulte. *The People That Walk in Darkness.* New York: Ballantine Books, 1960.

Nordon, Pierre. *Conan Doyle, A Biography.* New York: Holt, Rinehart & Winston, 1966.

Nott-Bower, Sir William. *Fifty-two Years a Policeman.* London: Edward Arnold, 1926.

O

O'Brien, John T. *Crime and Justice in America.* New York: Pergamon, 1980.

O'Connor, Richard. *Courtroom Warrior: The Combative Career of William Travers Jerome.* Boston: Little, Brown, 1963.

Oddie, S. Ingleby. *Inquest.* London: Hutchinson, 1941.

Odell, Robin. *Exhumation of Murder: The Life and Trial of Major Armstrong.* London: Harrap, 1975.

O'Donnell, Bernard. *Cavalcade of Justice.* London: Clerke & Cockeran, 1951.

———. *Crimes That Made News.* London: Burke, 1954.

———. *The Old Bailey and Its Trials.* London: Clerke & Cockeran, 1950.

———. *Should Women Hang?* London: W.H. Allen, 1956.

———. *The Trials of Mr. Justice Avory.* London: Rich & Cowan, 1935.

———. *The World's Strangest Murders.* London: Frederick Muller, 1957.

———. *The World's Worst Women.* London: W.H. Allen, 1953.

O'Donnell, Elliott. *Haunted Britain.* London: Rider, 1948.

O'Dwyer, Paul. *Counsel for the Defense.* New York: Simon & Schuster, 1979.

Olsen, Jack. *The Man with the Candy: The Story of the Houston Mass Murders.* New York: Simon & Schuster, 1974.

———. *Son: A Psychopath and His Victims.* New York: Dell, 1983.

Orloski, Richard J. *Criminal Law.* Chicago: Nelson-Hall, 1977.

Osterburg, James W. *The Crime Laboratory.* Bloomington: Indiana University Press, 1968.

O'Sullivan, F. Dalton. *Crime Detection.* Chicago: O'Sullivan, 1928.

Owing, Chloe. *Women Police.* Montclair, N.J.: Patterson Smith, 1968.

P

Pakenham, F.A. (assisted by R. Opie). *Causes of Crime.* London: Weidenfeld & Nicholson, 1958.

———. *The Idea of Punishment.* London: Chapman, 1961.

———. *Peace by Ordeal.* London: Jonathan Cape, 1935.

Palmer, Stuart. *The Psychology of Murder.* New York: Thomas Y. Crowell, 1960.

Parkenham, Frank. *Causes of Crime.* London: Weidenfeld, 1948.

Parker, Alfred E. *The Berkeley Police Story.* Springfield, Ill.: Charles C. Thomas, 1972.

Parrish, J.M., and Crossland, J.R. *The Fifty Most Amazing Crimes of the Last Hundred Years.* London: Odhams, 1936.

Parris, John. *Most of My Murders.* London: Frederick Muller, 1960.

Parry, Sir Edward Abbott. *The Drama of the Law.* New York: Charles Scribner's Sons, 1924.

Parsons, Philip Archibald. *Crime and the Criminal.* New York: Alfred A. Knopf, 1926.

Passy, Colonel. *Deuxieme bureau--Londres.* Monte Carlo, Monaco: Solar, 1947.

Pearson, Edmund. *Five Murders.* Garden City, N.Y.: Doubleday, Doran, 1928.

_____. *Instigation of the Devil.* New York: Charles Scribner's Sons, 1930.

_____. *Masterpieces at Murder.* Boston: Little, Brown, 1924.

_____. *More Studies in Murder.* New York: Smith & Haas, 1936.

_____. *Murder at Smutty Nose and Other Murders.* Garden City, N.Y.: Doubleday, 1927.

_____. *Studies in Murder.* New York: Macmillan, 1924.

Perry, J., and Chabert, J. *L'Affaire Petiot.* Paris: Gallimard, 1957.

Peskett, S. John. *Grim, Gruesome, and Grisly.* London: Leslie Frewin, 1974.

Peterson, Mark A. *Doing Crime: A Survey of California Prison Inmates.* Santa Monica, Calif.: The Rand Corporation, 1980.

_____, and Braiker, Harriet B. *Who Commits Crimes.* Cambridge: Oelgeschlager, Gunn & Hain, 1981.

Phillips, Conrad. *Murderer's Moon.* London: Arthur Baker, 1956.

Pike, Luke Owen. *A History of Crime in England.* 2 vols. Montclair, N.J.: Patterson Smith, 1962.

Pinkney, Alphonso. *The American Way of Violence.* New York: Random House, 1972.

Ploscowe, Morris. *Sex and the Law.* New York: Prentice-Hall, 1951.

Pollack, Jack Harrison. *Dr. Sam, an American Tragedy.* Chicago: Henry Regnery, 1972.

Pollack, Otto. *The Criminality of Women.* Philadelphia: University of Pennsylvania Press, 1950.

Pollens, B. *The Sexual Criminal.* New York: Macaulay, 1938.

Porges, Irwin. *The Violent Americans.* Derby, Conn.: Monarch Books, 1963.

Porterfield, Austin L., and Talbert, Robert W. *Crime, Suicide, and Social Well-Being in Your State and City.* Fort Worth: Texas Christian University, 1948.

_____. *Cultures of Violence.* Ft. Worth, Texas: Manney, 1965.

Postgate, Raymond. *Murder, Piracy and Treason.* New York: Houghton Mifflin, 1925.

Poynter, J.W. *Forgotten Crimes.* New York: Macaulay, 1928.

Prendergrass, W. *The Z-Car Detective.* London: John Long, 1964.

Presley, James, and Getty, Gerald W. *Public Defender.* New York: Grosset & Dunlap, 1974.

Prothero, Margaret. *The History of the Criminal Investigation Department of Scotland Yard from Earliest Times until Today.* London: Jenkins, 1931.

Putterman, Jaydie, and Lesur, Rosalyn. *Police.* New York: Holt, Rinehart and Winston, 1983.

Q

Quinby, Ione. *Murder for Love.* New York: Covici-Friede, 1931.

R

Raby, R. Cornelius. *Fifty Famous Trials.* Washington, D.C.: Washington Law Books, 1937.

Radano, Gene. *Walking the Beat.* Cleveland: World, 1968.

Radelet, Louis A., Reed, Hoy, and Reed, Coe. *The Police and the Community.* Encino, Calif.: Glencoe Press, 1977.

Radin, Edward D. *Crimes of Passion.* New York: G.P. Putnam's Sons, 1953.

_____. *Headline Crimes of the Year.* Boston: Little, Brown, 1952.

_____. *The Innocents.* New York: William Morrow, 1964.

_____. *12 Against Crime.* New York: G.P. Putnam's Sons, 1953.

_____. *12 Against the Law.* New York: Duell, Sloan & Pearce, 1942.

Randall, Leslie. *The Famous Cases of Sir Bernard Spilsbury.* London: I. Nicholson & Watson, 1936.

Rao, R. Venugopal. *Facets of Crime in India.* Bombay, India: Allied, 1963.

_____. *Murder: A Pilot Study with Particular Reference to the City of Delhi.* New Delhi: Government of India, 1968.

Ravitz, Abe C. *Clarence Darrow and the American Literary Tradition.* Cleveland: Press of Western Reserve University, 1962.

Ray, Chaplain, with Wagner, Walter. *God's Prison Gang.* Old Tappan, N.J.: Revell, 1976.

Reasons, Charles E. *The Criminologist: Crime and the Criminal.* Pacific Palisades, Calif.: Goodyear, 1974.

_____, and Kuykendall, Jack L. (eds.). *Race, Crime and Justice.* Pacific Palisades, Calif.: Goodyear, 1972.

Reckless, Walter. *American Criminology: New Directions.* New York: Appleton-Century-Crofts, 1973.

Reid, John E., and Inbau, Fred E. *Truth and Deception, the Polygraph.* Baltimore: Williams & Wilkins, 1977.

Reid, Susan Titus. *Crime and Criminology.* New York: Holt, Rinehart, 1976.

Reik, Theodor. *The Compulsion to Confess.* New York: Farrar, Straus, 1959.

_____. *Myth and Guilt.* New York: Braziller, 1957.

Reinhardt, James Melvin. *The Murderous Trail of Charles Starkweather.* Springfield, Ill.: Charles C. Thomas, 1962.

_____. *The Psychology of Strange Killers.* Springfield, Ill.: Charles C. Thomas, 1962.

_____. *Sex Perversions and Sex Crimes.* Springfield, Ill.: Charles C. Thomas, 1957.

Reiter, P.J. *Antisocial or Criminal Acts and Hypnosis.* Springfield, Ill.: Charles C. Thomas, 1958.

Reith, Charles. *The Blind Eye of History.* London: Faber & Faber, 1952.

_____. *A New Study of Police History.* London: Oliver, 1956.

_____. *The Police Idea; its History and Evolution in England in the Eighteenth Century and After.* London: Oxford University Press, 1938.

_____. *A Short History of the British Police.* London: Oxford University Press, 1940.

Reiwald, P. *Society and Its Criminals.* New York: International University Press, 1950.

Renvoize, Jean. *Web of Violence.* London: Rootledge, 1978.

Reppetto, Thomas A. *The Blue Parade.* New York: Free Press, 1978.

———. *Residential Crime.* Cambridge, Mass.: Ballinger Press, 1974.

Reuben, William A. *The Mark Fein Case.* New York: Dial, 1967.

Reynolds, Quentin R. *Courtroom: The Story of Samuel S. Leibowitz.* New York: Farrar, Straus & Cudahy, 1950.

———. *Police Headquarters.* New York: Harper, 1955.

Reynolds, Ruth. *Murder 'Round the World.* New York: Justice Books, 1953.

Rhodes, Henry Taylor-Fowkes. *Clues and Crime.* London: John Murray, 1933.

———. *The Criminals We Deserve.* London: Methuen, 1937.

———. *In the Tracks of Crime.* London: Turnstile Press, 1952.

———. *Science and the Police Officer.* London: Police Chronicle, 1934.

Rhodes, Robert P. *The Insoluble Problem of Crime.* New York: John Wiley & Sons, 1977.

Rice, Craig. *45 Murderers.* New York: Simon & Schuster, 1952.

Rice, Cy. *Defender of the Damned: Gladys Trowles Root.* New York: Citadel Press, 1964.

Rickards, Colin. *The Man from Devil's Island.* London: Dawnay, 1968.

Rignall, Jeff, and Wilder, Ron. *29 Below.* Chicago: Wellington Press, 1979.

Ringel, W. *Identification and Police Line-Ups.* New York: Gould, 1968.

River, J. Paul (ed.). *Crime and the Sexual Psychopath.* Springfield, Ill.: Charles C. Thomas, 1958.

———. *The Sexual Criminal.* Springfield, Ill.: Charles C. Thomas, 1950.

Robbins, Jhan. *Front Page Marriage.* New York: G.P. Putnam's Sons, 1982.

Roberts, C.E.B. *The New World of Crime, Famous American Trials.* London: Burrows, Eyre & Spottiswoode, 1933.

Robins, Natalie, and Aronson, Steven. *Savage Grace.* New York: William Morrow, 1985.

Robinson, E.S. *Law and the Lawyers.* Toronto Ontario, Can.: Macmillan, 1935.

Robinson, Henry Morton. *Science Catches the Criminal.* Indianapolis, Ind.: Bobbs-Merrill, 1935.

Robinson, L.N. *Penology in the United States.* Philadelphia: Winston, 1921.

Robinson, W.W. *Lawyers of Los Angeles.* Los Angeles: Los Angeles Bar Association, 1959.

Roche, Philip Q. *The Criminal Mind.* New York: Farrar, Straus & Cudahy, 1958.

Rodell, Marie F. (ed.). *Boston Murders.* New York: Duell, Sloan & Pearce, 1948.

———. *Charleston Murders.* New York: Duell, Sloan & Pearce, 1947.

———. *Chicago Murders.* New York: Duell, Sloan & Pearce, 1945.

———. *Cleveland Murders.* New York: Duell, Sloan & Pearce, 1947.

———. *Denver Murders.* New York: Duell, Sloan & Pearce, 1946.

———. *Detroit Murders.* New York: Duell, Sloan & Pearce, 1948.

———. *Los Angeles Murders.* New York: Duell, Sloan & Pearce, 1947.

———. *New York Murders.* New York: Duell, Sloan & Pearce, 1944.

———. *San Francisco Murders.* New York: Duell, Sloan & Pearce, 1947.

Rogers, Kenneth Paul. *For One Sweet Grape.* New York: Playboy Press, 1974.

Rogge, O. John. *Why Men Confess.* New York: Nelson, 1959.

Root, Jonathan. *One Night in July.* New York: Coward-McCann, 1961.

Rose, Andrew. *Stinie, Murder on the Common.* London: Bodley Head, 1985.

Rose, T. *Violence in America.* New York: Random House, 1969.

Rosenblatt, Stanley M. *Trial Lawyer.* Secaucus, N.J.: Lyle Stuart, 1984.

Rosenstein, Jaik. *Hollywood Leg Man.* Los Angeles: Madison Press, 1950.

Rosenthal, M.A. *Thirty-Eight Witnesses.* New York: McGraw-Hill, 1964.

Rossner, Judith. *Looking for Mr. Goodbar.* New York: Simon & Schuster, 1975.

Rothblatt, Henry B. *That Damned Lawyer.* New York: Dodd, Mead, 1983.

Roughead, William. *The Art of Murder.* New York: Sheridan House, 1943.

———. *Bad Companions.* New York: Duffield & Green, 1931.

———. *Classic Crimes.* London: Cassell, 1951.

———. *Famous Crimes.* London: Faber & Faber, 1935.

———. *The Fatal Countess.* London: Green, 1924.

———. *In Queer Street.* London: Green, 1924.

———. *Mainly Murder.* London: Cassell, 1937.

———. *Malice Domestic.* New York: Doubleday, Doran, 1929.

———. *The Murderer's Companion.* New York: Readers Club, 1941.

———. *Neck or Nothing.* London: Cassell, 1939.

———. *Reprobates Reviewed.* London: Cassell, 1941.

———. *Rogues Walk Here.* London: Cassell, 1934.

———. *The Seamy Side.* London: Cassell, 1938.

———. *Tales of the Criminous.* London: Cassell, 1956.

———. *Twelve Scots Trials.* London: Green, 1913.

Rowan, David. *Famous American Crimes.* London: Frederick Muller, 1957.

———. *Famous European Crimes.* London: Frederick Muller, 1956.

Rowland, John. *A Century of Murder.* London: Home & Van Thal, 1950.

———. *Criminal Files.* London: Arco, 1957.

———. *More Criminal Files.* London: Arco, 1958.

———. *Poisoner in the Dock.* London: Arco, 1960.

———. *Unfit to Plead?* London: John Long, 1965.

Ruhm, Herbert (ed.). *The Hard-Boiled Detective.* New York: Vintage Books, 1977.

Rule, Ann. *The Stranger Beside Me.* New York: W.W. Norton, 1980.

Runyon, Damon. *A Treasury of Damon Runyon.* New York: Random House, 1958.

———. *Trials and Other Tribulations.* New York: J.B. Lippincott, 1933.

Russell, Charles Edmund. *Adventures of the DCI.* London: Hurst & Blackett, 1924.

Russell, Diana E.H. *Crimes Against Women.* Millbrae, Calif.: Les Femmes, 1977.

Russell, Donn (ed.). *Best Murder Cases.* London: Faber

& Faber, 1958.

Russell, Guy. *Guilty or Not Guilty?* London: Hutchinson, 1931.

Rutledge, Lyman V. *Moonlight at Murder Smuttynose.* Boston: Star King Press, 1958.

S

Samenow, Stanton E. *Inside the Criminal Mind.* New York: Times Books, 1984.

Samuels, Charles. *Death was the Bridegroom.* New York: Fawcett, 1955.

———. and Louise. *The Girl in the House of Hate.* New York: Fawcett, 1953.

———. *The Girl in the Red Velvet Swing.* New York: Fawcett, 1955.

———. and Louise. *Night Fell on Georgia.* New York: Dell, 1956.

Sanders, Bruce. *Murder Behind the Bright Lights.* London: Herbert Jenkins, 1958.

———. *Murder in Big Cities.* New York: Roy, 1962.

———. *Murder in Lonely Places.* London: Jenkins, 1960.

———. *They Caught These Killers.* New York: Roy, 1968.

———. *They Couldn't Lose the Body.* London: Jenkins, 1966.

Sanders, Ed. *The Family.* New York: E.P. Dutton, 1971.

Sanders, William B. *Criminology.* Reading, Mass.: Addison Wesley, 1983.

———. *Detective Work.* New York: Free Press, 1977.

Sandoe, James (ed.). *Murder: Plain & Fanciful.* New York: Sheridan, 1948.

Sands, Bill. *My Shadow Ran Fast.* Englewood Cliffs, N.J.: Prentice-Hall, 1964.

Sanger, Joan. *The Case of the Missing Corpse.* New York: Green Circle Books, 1936.

Sann, Paul. *The Angry Decade: The Sixties.* New York: Crown, 1979.

Santesson, H.S. *The Locked Room Reader: Stories of the Impossible Crimes and Escapes.* New York: Random House, 1968.

Savage, Percy. *Savage of Scotland Yard.* London: Hutchinson, 1934.

Sayer, James Edward. *Clarence Darrow: Public Advocate.* Dayton, Ohio: Wright State University, 1978.

Sayers, Dorothy L. *Tales of Detection, Mystery and Horror.* London: Gollancz, 1928.

Schloss, B., and Giesbrecht, N.A. *Murder in Canada: A Report on Capital and Non-Capital Murder Statistics, 1961-1970.* Toronto, Ontario, Can.: Centre of Criminology, University of Toronto, 1972.

Schreiber, Flora Rheta. *The Shoemaker, Anatomy of a Psychotic.* New York: Simon & Schuster, 1983.

Schudson, Michael. *Discovering the News: A Social History of American Newspapers.* New York: Basic Books, 1978.

Schuessler, Karl (ed.). *Edwin H. Sutherland: On Analyzing Crime.* Chicago: University of Chicago Press, 1973.

Schultz, Gladys Denny. *How Many More Victims, Society and the Sex Criminal.* Philadelphia: J.B. Lippincott, 1966.

Schur, Edwin M. *Our Criminal Society: The Social and Legal Sources of Crime in America.* Englewood Cliffs: Prentice-Hall, 1969.

Schwartz, Ted. *The Hillside Strangler: A Murderer's Mind.* Garden City, N.Y.: Doubleday, 1981.

Scott, Sir Harold (ed.). *Scotland Yard.* London: Andre

Deutsch, 1954.

Scott, J.W. Robertson. *The Life and Death of a Newspaper.* London: Methuen, 1952.

———. *The Story of the Pall Mall Gazette.* London: Oxford University Press, 1950.

Seedman, Albert A., and Hellman, Peter. *Chief!* New York: Avon, 1974.

Sellers, Alvin V. *Classics of the Bar: Stories of the World's Greatest Legal Trials and Forensic Masterpieces.* Washington, D.C.: Washington Law Books, 1942.

Sellin, Thorsten (ed.). *Capital Punishment.* New York: Harper & Row, 1967.

———. *Culture Conflict and Crime.* New York: Social Science Research Council, 1938.

———. *The Death Penalty.* Philadelphia: American Law Institute, 1959.

Seth, Ronald. *Petiot, Victim of Chance.* London: Hutchinson, 1963.

Seymour, W. *Why Justice Fails.* New York: William Morrow, 1973.

Sheridan, Leo W. *I Killed for the Law.* New York: Stackpole Sons, 1938.

Sherman, Michael, and Hawkins, Gordon. *Imprisonment in America.* Chicago: University of Chicago Press, 1982.

Shew, E. Spencer. *A Companion to Murder.* New York: Alfred A. Knopf, 1960.

———. *A Second Companion to Murder.* New York: Knopf, 1961.

Shirer, William L. *20th Century Journey: A Memoir of a Life and the Times of William L. Shirer.* New York: Simon & Schuster, 1976.

Shonle Cavan, Ruth. *Criminology.* New York: Thomas Y. Crowell, 1955.

Shore, W. Teignmouth (ed.). *Crime and It's Detection.* London: Gresham, 1931.

———. *The Trial of Browne and Kennedy.* London: William Hodge, 1930.

Short, James F., Jr. (ed.). *Delinquency, Crime and Society.* Chicago: University of Chicago Press, 1976.

Silberman, Charles E. *Criminal Violence, Criminal Justice.* New York: Random House, 1978.

Simon, Rita James. *The Contemporary Women and Crime.* Rockville, Md.: National Institute of Mental Health, 1975.

———. *Women and Crime.* Lexington, Mass.: D.C. Heath, 1978.

Simpson, Helen (ed.). *The Anatomy of Murder.* New York: Macmillan, 1934.

Simpson, Keith. *Forensic Medicine.* London: Arnold, 1964.

———. *Forty Years of Murder.* New York: Charles Scribner's Sons, 1979.

Singer, Kurt (ed.). *Crime Omnibus.* London: W.H. Allen, 1961.

———, and Sherrod, Jane. *Great Adventures in Crime.* Minneapolis, Minn.: T.S. Denison, 1962.

——— (ed.). *My Greatest Crime Story.* London: W.H. Allen, 1956.

———. *My Strangest Cases.* Garden City, N.Y.: Doubleday, 1958.

Sir Arthur Conan Doyle Centenary: 1859-1959. London: John Murray, 1959.

Slingerland, Peter van. *Something Terrible Has Happened: The Account of the Sensational Thalia Massie Affair which Burst from Prewar Hawaii to Incense the Nation.* New York: Harper & Row, 1966.

Smart, Carol. *Women, Crime and Criminology.* London: RKP, 1977.

Smith, Gibbs M. *Joe Hill.* Salt Lake City: University of Utah Press, 1969.

Smith, Sir Henry. *From Constable to Commissioner: The Story of Sixty Years, Most of Them Misspent.* London: Chatto & Windus, 1910.

Smith, Sir Sydney. *Mostly Murder.* New York: David McKay, 1959.

Smith-Hughes, Jack. *Eight Studies in Justice.* London: Cassell, 1953.

———. *Nine Verdicts on Violence.* London: Cassell, 1956.

———. *Six Ventures in Villainy.* London: Cassell, 1956.

Sparrow, Judge Gerald. *Crimes of Passion.* London: Barker, 1973.

———. *Murder Parade.* London: Robert Hale, 1957.

———. *Satan's Children.* London: Odhams, 1966.

———. *Women Who Murder.* New York: Abelard-Schuman, 1970.

Stack, Andy. *The I-5 Killer.* New York: Signet, 1984.

———. *Lust Killer.* New York: Signet, 1983.

———. *The Want-Ad Killer.* New York: Signet, 1983.

Stead, Philip J. *The Police of Paris.* London: Staples, 1951.

Steiger, Brad. *The Mass Murderer.* New York: Award Books, 1967.

———. *A Roadmap of Time.* Englewood Cliffs, N.J.: Prentice-Hall, 1975.

Steiner, Jesse F., and Brown, Roy M. *The North Carolina Chain Gang.* Chapel Hill: University of North Carolina Press, 1927.

Stekel, Wilhelm. *Compulsion and Doubt.* New York: Liveright, 1950.

———. *Peculiarities of Behavior.* New York: Liveright, 1924.

———. *Sadism and Masochism.* New York: Liveright, 1929.

———. *Sexual Aberrations: The Phenomena of Fetishism in Relation to Sex.* trans. S. Parker. 2 vols. New York: Liveright, 1930.

Stevens, C.L. McCluer. *Famous Crimes and Criminals.* London: Stanley Paul, 1924.

Stevens, Shane. *By Reason of Insanity.* London: Weidenfeld & Nicholson, 1979.

Stewart, C.P., and Stolman, A. *Toxicology: Mechanisms and Analytical Methods.* New York: Academic Press, 1960-1961.

Stinchcombe, A. *Crime and Punishment: Changing Attitudes in American Society.* San Francisco: Jossey-Bass, 1980.

Stone, Irving. *Clarence Darrow for the Defense.* Garden City, N.Y.: Doubleday, 1941.

Stowers, Carlton. *Careless Whispers.* Dallas: Taylor, 1984.

Strange and Mysterious Crimes. New York: MacFadden, 1929.

Strasburg, Paul A. *Violent Delinquents.* New York: Simon & Schuster, 1978.

Straus, M., Gelles, R., and Steinmetz, S. *Behind Closed Doors: Violence in the American Family.* Garden City, N.Y.: Anchor-Doubleday, 1980.

Sullivan, Terry, with Maiken, Peter T. *Killer Clown.* New York: Grosset & Dunlap, 1983.

Sutton, Charles Warden. *The New York Tombs; Its Secrets and Mysteries.* New York: U.S., 1874.

Svensson, Arne, and Wendell, Otto. *Crime Detection.* London: Cleaver-Hume, 1955.

Swanson, C., Chamelin, N., and Territo, L. *Criminal Investigation.* Santa Monica, Calif.: Goodyear, 1977.

Swisher, Carl Brent (ed.). *Selected Papers of Homer Cummings.* New York: Charles Scribner's Sons, 1939.

T

Tabori, Paul. *Crime and the Occult.* New York: Taplinger, 1974.

Taft, Donald R. *Criminology.* New York: J.B. Lippincott, 1954.

Tallant, Robert. *Murder in New Orleans.* London: William Kimber, 1952.

———. *Ready to Hang.* New York: Harper & Brothers, 1952.

Tanay, F. *The Murderers.* Indianapolis, Ind.: Bobbs-Merrill, 1976.

Tanenbaum, Robert, and Rosenberg, Philip. *Badge of the Assassin.* New York: E.P. Dutton, 1979.

———, and Greenberg, Peter S. *The Piano Teacher.* New York: New American Library, 1987.

Tannenbaum, Frank. *Crime and the Community.* New York: Columbia University Press, 1938.

———. *The Habitual Sex Offender.* Trenton: State of New Jersey, 1950.

Taubman, Bryna. *Lady Cop.* New York: Warner Books, 1987.

Taylor, Ian, Walton, Paul, and Young, Jock. *Critical Criminology.* London: Routledge & Kegan Paul, 1975.

———. *The New Criminology.* New York: Harper & Row, 1973.

———. *For a Social Theory of Deviance.* New York: Harper & Row, 1973.

Teeters, Negley K. and Hedblom, Jack H. *"...Hang By the Neck..."* Springfield, Ill.: Charles C. Thomas, 1967.

———. *Scaffold and Chair: A Compilation of Their Use in Pennsylvania, 1682-1962.* Philadelphia: Pennsylvania Prison Society, 1963.

———. *They Were in Prison: A History of the Pennsylvania Prison Society.* Philadelphia: John C. Winston, 1937.

Teichmann, Howard. *Smart Aleck: The Wit, World and Life of Alexander Woollcott.* New York: William Morrow, 1976.

Templewood, Viscount. *The Shadow of the Gallows.* London: Victor Gollancz, 1951.

Thaw, Harry K. *The Traitor.* New York: Dorrance, 1926.

Thomas, Charles W., and Hepburn, John R. *Crime, Criminal Law, and Criminology.* Dubuque, Iowa: William C. Brown, 1983.

———, and Peterson, David M. *Prison Organization and Inmate Subcultures.* Indianapolis, Ind.: Bobbs Merrill, 1977.

Thomas, David. *Seek Out the Guilty.* London: John Long, 1969.

Thomas, Piri. *Down These Mean Streets.* New York: New American Library, 1967.

Thompson, Sir Basil. *The Criminal.* London: Hodder & Stoughton, 1925.

———. *The Story of Scotland Yard.* London: Grayson & Grayson, 1925.

———. *Poisons and Poisoners.* London: Harold Shaylor, 1931.

Thompson, Thomas. *Blood and Money.* Garden City, N.Y.: Doubleday, 1976.

———. *Serpentine.* Garden City, N.Y.: Doubleday, 1979.

Thorp, Arthur. *Calling Scotland Yard.* London: Allan Wingate, 1954.

Thorwald, Jürgen. *The Century of the Detective.* New York: Harcourt, Brace & World, 1964.

———. *Crime and Science.* Orlando, Fla.: Harcourt, Brace & World, 1967.

———. *Dead Men Tell Tales.* London: Thames & Hudson,

1966.
———. *The Marks of Cain.* London: Thames & Hudson, 1965.
———. *Proof of Poison.* London: Thames & Hudson, 1966.
Tierney, Kevin. *Darrow, A Biography.* New York: Thomas Y. Crowell, 1979.
Timewell, James. *Is Stinie Morrison Innocent?* London: Published by Author, 1914.
———. *The Prison Life of Stinie Morrison.* London: Published by Author, 1914.
Toch, Hans, Grant, J. Douglas, and Galvin, Raymond T. *Police, Prisons, and the Problem of Violence.* Rockville, Md.: National Institute of Mental Health Center for Studies of Crime and Delinquency, 1977.
———. *Psychology of Crime and Criminal Justice.* New York: Holt, Rinehart & Winston, 1979.
———. *Violent Men.* Chicago: Aldine, 1969.
Townsend, W., and Townsend, L. *Black Cap: Murder Will Out.* London: Albert E. Marriott, 1930.
Traini, Robert. *Murder for Sex.* London: William Kimber, 1960.
Trasler, G. *The Explanation of Criminality.* London: Routledge & Kegan Paul, 1962.
Traver, Robert. *Anatomy of a Murder.* New York: Saint Martin's Press, 1958.
Treadwell, C.A.L. *Notable New Zealand Trials.* New Plymouth, N.Zea.: T. Avery & Sons, 1936.
Trenery, Walter N. *Murder in Minnesota.* St. Paul: Minnesota Historical Society, 1962.
Trillin, Calvin. *Killings.* New York: Penguin Books, 1984.
Trilling, Diana. *Mrs. Harris, the Death of the Scarsdale Diet Doctor.* New York: Harcourt Brace Jovanovich, 1981.
Tullett, Tom. *Portrait of a Bad Man.* New York: Rinehart, 1956.
———. *Strictly Murder.* New York: St. Martin's Press, 1979.
Tully, Andrew. *The FBI's Most Famous Cases.* New York: William Morrow, 1965.
Turrou, Leon G. *Where My Shadow Falls.* Garden City, N.Y.: Doubleday, 1949.
Tuska, Jon. *The Detective in Hollywood.* Garden City: Doubleday, 1978.
Tyler, Froom. *Gallows Parade.* London: Lorat Dickson, 1933.

U

Underhill, H.C. *Criminal Evidence.* New York: Bobbs-Merrill, 1973.
Unwin, J.D. *Sex and Culture.* London: Oxford University Press, 1934.
———. *Sexual Regulations and Human Behavior.* London: Williams & Norgate, 1933.
Uviller, H. *The Processes of Criminal Justice: Investigation.* St. Paul, Minn.: West, 1979.

V

Van Den Haag, Ernest, and Conrad, John P. *The Death Penalty: A Debate.* New York: Plenum Press, 1983.

———. *Political Violence and Civil Disobedience.* New York: Harper & Row, 1972.
———. *Punishing Criminals: Concerning a Very Old and Painful Question.* New York: Basic Books, 1978.
Van de Water, Frederic F. *The Real McCoy.* Garden City, N.Y.: Doubleday, Doran, 1931.
Van Winkle, Marshall, and Wolff, H. *Sixty Famous Cases.* Summertown, Tenn.: Book Manufacturing, 1956.
Varaut, Jean-Marc. *L'Abominable Dr. Petiot.* Paris: Balland, 1974.
Veheyne, C. *Horror.* London: Brown, Watson, 1962.
Verkko, Veli. *Homicides and Suicides in Finland and Their Dependence on National Character.* Copenhagen: G.E.C. Gads Forlag, 1951.
Vermorel, Auguste-Jean-Marie. *La Police contemporaire.* Paris: Lebigre-Duquesne, 1864.
Villiers, Gerard de. *Papillon Epingle.* Paris: Presses de la Cite, 1970.
Volta, Ornella. *The Vampire.* trans. Raymond Rudorff. London: Tandem, 1965.
von Hentig, Hans. *The Criminal and His Victim.* New York: Schocken Books, 1979.

W

Wagner, Diane. *Corpus Delicti.* New York: St. Martin's/Marek, 1986.
Wagner, Margaret Seaton. *The Monster of Dusseldorf, The Life and Trial of Peter Kurten.* London: Faber & Faber, 1932.
Wakefield, H. Russell. *Landru: The French Bluebeard.* London: Duckworth, 1936.
Walbrook, H.M. *Detective Days.* London: Cassell, 1931.
———. *Murders and Murder Trials, 1812-1912.* London: Constable, 1932.
Walker, Bill. *The Case of Barbara Graham.* New York: Ballantine Books, 1961.
Walker, Nigel. *Crimes, Courts and Figures.* Harmondsworth, Eng.: Penguin Books, 1971.
———. *Crime and Insanity in England.* Edinburgh, Scot.: Edinburgh University Press, 1968.
———. *Crime and Punishment in Britain.* Edinburgh, Scot.: Edinburgh University Press, 1973.
Walker-Smith, Derek. *The Life of Mr. Justice Darling.* London: Cassell, 1938.
———. *Lord Reading and His Cases.* New York: Macmillan, 1934.
Wall, P. *Eyewitness Identification in Criminal Cases.* New York: Thomas, 1965.
Wambaugh, Joseph. *The Blue Knight.* New York: Dell Books, 1972.
———. *The Onion Field.* New York: Delacorte Press, 1973.
Watson, Tex. *Will You Die For Me.* New Jersey: Revell, 1978.
Webb, Duncan. *Crime Is My Business.* London: Muller, 1953.
———. *Deadline for Crime.* London: Muller, 1955.
Webb, Jack. *The Badge.* Englewood Cliffs, N.J.: Prentice-Hall, 1958.
Weinberg, Arthur (ed.). *Attorney for the Damned.* New York: Simon & Schuster, 1957.
———, and Lila. *Clarence Darrow.* New York: G.P. Putnam Sons, 1980.
———, and Lila (eds.). *Verdicts Out of Court.* Chicago: Quadrangle Books, 1963.

Weiner, Ed. *The Damon Runyon Story.* New York: David McKay, 1948.

———. *Let's Go to Press.* New York: G.P. Putnam's Sons, 1955.

Weisberg, Harold. *Post Mortem.* Frederick, Md.: Published by Author, 1971.

Weisberger, Bernard A. (ed.). *The American Newspaperman.* Chicago: University of Chicago Press, 1961.

Wellman, Manly Wade. *Dead and Gone, Classic Crimes of North Carolina.* Chapel Hill: University of North Carolina Press, 1954.

Wensley, Frederick Porter. *Detective Days.* London: Cassell, 1931.

Wertham, Dr. Fredric. *The Circle of Guilt.* New York: Rinehart, 1956.

———. *Dark Legend: A Study in Murder.* London: Victor Gollancz, 1947.

———. *Seduction of the Innocent.* New York: Rinehart, 1954.

———. *The Show of Violence.* New York: Doubleday, 1949.

———. *A Sign for Cain.* New York: Paperback Library, 1969.

West, Donald J. (ed.). *Criminological Implications of Chromosome Abnormalities.* Cambridge, Eng.: University of Cambridge, 1969.

———. *The Habitual Prisoner.* London: Macmillan, 1963.

———. *Murder Followed By Suicide.* London: William Heinemann, 1965.

———. *Sacrifice Unto Me.* New York: Pyramid, 1974.

Weston, Paul B. and Wells, Kenneth M. *Criminal Investigation: Basic Perspectives.* Englewood Cliffs, N.J.: Prentice-Hall, 1974

———. *Criminal Justice: Introduction and Guidelines.* Pacific Palisades, N.J.: Goodyear, 1976.

Whibley, Charles. *A Book of Scoundrels.* New York: Benjamin Blom, 1971.

Whitbread, J.R. *The Railway Policeman.* London: Harrap, 1961.

White, Leslie T. *Me Detective.* New York: Harcourt, Brace, 1936.

White, William Allen. *Crimes and Criminals.* New York: Farrar & Rinehart, 1933.

Whitehead, George G. *Clarence Darrow--the Big Minority Man.* Girard, Kan.: Haldeman-Julius, 1931.

———. *Clarence Darrow: "Evangelist" of Sane Thinking.* Girard, Kan.: Haldeman-Julius, 1931.

Whitelaw, David. *Corpus Delicti.* London: Geoffrey Bles, 1936.

Whittemore, L.H. *Cop.* Greenwich, Conn.: Fawcett, 1969.

———. *The Super Cops.* New York: Bantam, 1973.

Wickman, Peter, and Whitten, Phillip. *Criminology.* Lexington, Mass.: D.C. Heath, 1980.

Wild, Roland. *Crimes and Cases of 1933.* London: Rich & Cowan, 1934.

———. *Crimes and Cases of 1934.* London: Rich & Cowan, 1935.

———, and Curtis-Bennett, D. *Curtis, the Life of Sir Henry Curtis-Bennett.* London: Cassell, 1930.

Wiles, P.N.P., and Carson, W.G. (eds.). *Crime and Delinquency in Britain.* London: Martin Robertson, 1970.

Wilkenson, Fred T. *The Realities of Crime and Punishment.* Springfield, Mo.: Mycroft Press, 1972.

Wilkerson, Michael, and Wilkerson, Dick. *Someone Cry for the Children.* New York: Dial Press, 1981.

Wilkinson, Alec. *Midnights, A Year with the Wellfleet Police.* New York: Random House, 1982.

Wilkinson, Laurence. *Behind the Face of Crime.* London: Frederick Muller, 1957.

Wille, W. *Citizens Who Commit Murder.* St. Louis, Mo.: Warren Greene, 1974.

Willett, T.C. *Criminal on the Road.* London: Tavistock, 1964.

———. *Drivers after Sentence.* London: Heinemann Educational, 1973.

Williams, Brad. *Due Process.* New York: William Morrow, 1960.

Williams, Emlyn. *Beyond Belief.* New York: Random House, 1968.

Williams, Franklin. *Negroes With Guns.* New York: Marzani & Munsell, 1962.

Williams, Glanville. *The Proof of Guilt.* London: Stevens & Sons, 1955.

———. *Salmond on Jurisprudence.* London: Sweet & Maxwell, 1957.

Williams, Guy R. *The Hidden World of Scotland Yard.* London: Hutchinson, 1972.

Williams, Jack K. *Vogues in Villainy.* Columbia: University of South Carolina Press, 1959.

Williams, Jean. *Hume: Portrait of a Couple Murderer.* London: The Windmill Press, 1960.

Williams, Vergil L., and Fish, Mary. *Convicts, Codes, and Contraband: The Prison Life of Men and Women.* Cambridge, Mass.: Ballinger, 1974.

Williamson, W.H. *Annals of Crime: Some Extraordinary Women.* London: George Routledge & Sons, 1930.

Wilson, Colin. *A Casebook of Murder.* New York: Cowles, 1970.

———. *A Criminal History of Mankind.* London: Granada, 1984.

———, and Pitman, Patricia. *The Encyclopedia of Murder.* New York: G.P. Putnam's Sons, 1961.

———, and Seaman, Donald. *Encyclopedia of Modern Murder, 1962-1982.* New York: G.P. Putnam's Sons, 1985.

Wilson, John Gray. *The Trial of Peter Manuel.* London: Secker & Warburg, 1959.

Wilson, Patrick. *Children Who Kill.* London: Michael Joseph, 1973.

———. *Murderesses: A Study of the Women Executed in Britain Since 1843.* London: Michael Joseph, 1971.

Wilton, G.W. *Fingerprints: History, Law and Romance.* London: William Hodge, 1938.

Winn, Steven, and Merrill, David. *Ted Bundy: The Killer Next Door.* New York: Bantam, 1980.

Winslade, William J., and Ross, Judith Wilson. *The Insanity Plea.* New York: Charles Scribner's Sons, 1983.

Winslow, Lyttleton Stewart Forbes. *Recollections of Forty Years: Being an Account at First Hand of Some Famous Criminal Lunacy Cases...* London: John Ousley, 1910.

Wishman, Seymour. *Confessions of a Criminal Lawyer.* New York: Penguin, 1981.

Wolf, Marvin J., and Mader, Katherine. *Fallen Angels.* New York: Facts on File, 1986.

Wolfe, Burton H. *Pileup on Death Row.* Garden City, N.Y.: Doubleday, 1973.

Wolff, Geoffrey. *Black Sun: The Brief Transit and Violent Eclipse of Harry Crosby.* New York: Random House, 1976.

Wolfgang, Marvin E. *Crime and Race.* New York: Institute of Human Relations Press, 1964.

———. *Patterns in Criminal Homicide.* Philadelphia: University of Pennsylvania Press, 1958.

———. *Studies in Homicide.* New York: Harper & Row, 1967.

Wood, Arthur. *Criminal Lawyer.* New Haven, Conn.: College & University Press, 1967.

Wood, Walter (ed.). *Survivor's Tales of Famous Crimes.* London: Cassell, 1916.

Wooden, Kenneth. *The Children of Jonestown.* New York: McGraw-Hill, 1981.

Woodhall, Edwin T. *Crime and the Supernatural.* London: Long, 1935.

_____. *Detective and Secret Service Days.* London: Jarrolds, 1929.

_____. *Secrets of Scotland Yard.* London: The Bodley Head, 1936.

Woodland, W. Lloyd. *Assize Pageant: Fifty Years in the Criminal Courts.* London: George G. Harrap, 1952.

Woollcott, Alexander. *Long, Long Ago.* New York: Viking Press, 1943.

_____. *While Rome Burns.* New York: Grosset & Dunlap, 1934.

Wren, Lassiter. *Masterstrokes of Crime Detection.* Garden City, N.Y.: Doubleday, Doran, 1929.

Wright, Dudley. *Vampires and Vampirism.* London: W. Rider, 1924.

Wright, Gordon. *Between the Guillotine and Liberty.* New York: Oxford University Press, 1983.

Wright, James D., et al. *Under the Gun: Weapons, Crime and Violence in America.* Hawthorne, N.Y.: Aldine, 1983.

Wulffen, Erich. *Woman as Sexual Criminal.* trans. David Berger. New York: American Ethnological Press, 1934.

Wyles, Lilian. *Women at Scotland Yard.* London: Faber & Faber, 1952.

Wyndham, Horace. *Consider Your Verdict.* London: W.H. Allen, 1946.

_____. *Crime on the Continent.* Boston: Little, Brown, 1928.

_____. *Dramas of the Law.* London: Hutchinson, 1936.

_____. *Famous Trials Re-told.* London: Hutchinson, 1925.

_____. *Feminine Frailty.* London: Ernest Benn, 1929.

Y

Yallop, David. *Deliver Us From Evil.* London: MacDonald Futura, 1981.

Yarros, Victor S. *My 11 Years with Clarence Darrow.* Girard, Kan.: Haldeman-Julius Publications, 1950.

Yee, Min S., and Layton, Thomas N. *The Melancholy History of Soledad Prison.* New York: Harper's Magazine Press, 1970.

Young, Filson. *The Trial of Hawley Harvey Crippen.* London: William Hodge, 1920.

Young, Hugh. *My Forty Years at the Yard.* London: W.H. Allen, 1955.

Z

Zalba, Serapio. *Women Prisoners and Their Families.* Sacramento, Calif.: Department of Social Welfare and Department of Corrections, 1964.

Zamora, William. *Trial By Your Peers.* New York: A. Maurice Girodias Associates, 1973.

Zemans, Eugene S. *Held Without Bail.* Chicago: John Howard Association, 1949.

Zerman, Melvyn Bernard. *Call the Final Witness.* New York: Harper & Row, 1977.

Zierold, Norman. *Three Sisters in Black.* Boston: Little, Brown, 1968.

Zimmer, Lucien. *Un Septennat Policier.* Paris: Fayard, 1967.

INDEX

Note: In this comprehensive index the reader and researcher will find that, in addition to all proper names appearing in text, place names are included, as well as sites, organizations, and events. All main text entries are shown in boldface. Murder victims are shown in boldface italic. Alternate names (Bluebeard, The Boston Strangler, The Hillside Strangler, etc.) for the more infamous murderers under which these persons are most commonly identified are shown in cross-reference entries in this index. Photos and illustrations of all those mentioned in text are indicated with page numbers appearing in boldface.

Cleary, Det. Jack, 271
Cleary, Katherine, 505
Clements, Amy Victoria Burnett, 126-127
Clements, Rev. George, 202
Clements, Judge James, 292
Clements, Dr. Robert George, 126-**127**
Clenet, Emile, 72
Clere, Judy, 378
Clere, Henry, 378
Clesson, Neta, 612
Clesson, Paul, Jr., 612
Clesson, Paul, Sr., 612
Cleveland, Off. Donald, 456
Cleveland Elementary School, 533
Cliff, Henrietta, 612
Cliff, Kimberly, 612
Clift, Martha, 131
Clifton T. Perkins State Hospital, 433
Cline, Cap. Herman (LAPD), 497
Clinton, Gov. Bill (Ark.), 503
Clinton Prison, 441
Clutter, Bonnie, 284
Clutter, Herbert W., 284-285
Clutter, Kenyon, 284
Clutter, Nancy, 284-285
Clutts, Merle, 502
Clynes, Judge John Robert, 610
Coast Guard, 244
Cobb, Off. Samuel (Newark P.D.), 55
Cobb, Scott, 372
Cochran, W. Bourke, 53
Cocozza, Lt. Joseph, 205
Codarre, Edwin, 127
Codd, Police Comm. Michael J., 193
Codgo, 35
Cody, A.J., 447
Cody, John Patrick, 210
Coetzee, Jacobus Hendrik, 127
Coffelt, Elijah, 127
Coffin, Betty Lena, 239, 240
Cohen, Judge Charles S., 448
Cohen, Frank, 197
Cohen, Jeffrey, 489
Cohen, Mickey, 138, 140, 141
Cohen, Mr., 571-572
Cohen, Mrs., 571-572
Cohen, Ronald John Vivian, 128
Cohen, Susan, 128
Cohen, Sydney, 489
Cohn, Judge Fred, 380
Cohn, Frederick, 88
Cohn, Samuel, 550
Colanso, Joe, 325
Colavito, Ermina (Big Emma), 321
Colby, Robert A., 128
Colchester, Vt. High School, 179
Coleman, Dr. Lee Stewart, 488
Coleman, Ronald, 166
Coleman, Silas, 168
Coleman, Valerie, 306
Coler, Jack, 448
Coleridge, Justice, 401
Collins, Clarence, 495, 496
Collins, James Thomas, 128
Collins, John Norman (The Ypsilanti Ripper), 128-129
Collins, Loretta, 129
Collins, Sheriff Maude, 438
Collins, Melvin (Bad Boy), 129

Collins, Richard, 33
Collison, Merle, 540
Collomb, Mme., 343-344, **345**
Colonial Hotel (Cleveland, Oh.), 265
Colorado Penitentiary, 249
Colorado Psychopathic Hospital, 248
Colorado Supreme Court, 249, 283
Colt Arms Manufacturing Company, 588, 602
Columbo, Frank, 129
Columbo, Mary, 129
Columbo, Michael, 129
Columbo, Patricia, 129
Colvert, Robert, 538
Combe, Michael, 129-130
Come Fill The Cup, 615
Comet Auto Parts, 279
Committee to Stop the Children's Murders, 604
Common Sense of Drinking, The, 153
Communist Party, 132
Community Hospital of the Valley, 178
Comtesse de Jumilhac, Constance, 158
Cone, Gov. Fred P. (Fla.), 114
Conlon, Loretta, 616
Connelly, Det. Vince, 573
Coneys, Theodore Edward (Spiderman), 130-131
Congdon, Elisabeth, 102
Congdon, Thomas, 102
Congress of Racial Equality, 74
Conlin, Judge John W., 129
Conlon, Sgt. of Det. Luke, 292
Connally, Gov. John (Tex.), 600
Connecticut State Prison, 550
Connelly, Mrs. Alice Mary, 608
Conner, Gov. Martin Sennett (Miss.), 169
Connery, Sean, 138
Connolly, Genevieve, 131
Connolly, Mary, 131
Connolly, Atty. Gen'l. Patrick (Ire.), 372
Connolly, Peter, 374
Connolly, Robert, 131
Connors, Felicity, 324
Conroy, Thomas, 131
Considine Brothers, 47
Constantine, Yvette, 112
Consumer Tampering Act, 428
Convent of Salbris (Fr.), 285
Convin, Judge Morton, 271
Coo, Eva, 131
Cook, Annie, 18
Cook County Circuit Court Psychiatric Institute, 270
Cook County Hospital, 533, 614
Cook County House of Corrections, 272
Cook, Isabelle, 390
Cooks, Asst. Dist. Atty., J. Bernard, 274
Cooks, Jessie Lee, 618
Cooley High, 272
Cooley, Melanie, 92, 94
Coolidge, Constance, 154
Coombs, Walter, 363
Cooney, Judge James H., 105
Cooney, Terence George, 131-132
Cooper, Calmen, 540
Cooper, Judge Clarence, 605
Cooper, Herbert, 132
Cooper, Ralph, 132
Cooper, Ronald Frank, 132-133
Cooper, Ronald John, 133
Coots, Anna Philomena Morgan, 8, 9, 10
Copeland, G.E., 282, 283

Gamble, Sheriff, 543
Gandy, Gene, 331
Garcia, Inez, 226
Garcia, Isabel, 11
Garcia, Joe, Jr., 226-227
Gardner, Deo, 197
Gardner, Dr. Eric, 99
Gardner, Margery, 278
Gareis, William B., 283
Gargan, Bridie, 372
Gargullo, Merlita, 531-(532)-533
Garippo, Judge Louis, 270, 568
Garland, John, 193
Garlick, Edward Donald, 227
Garner, Vance, 227
Garnet, Mark, 132
Garretson, William, 388
Garrity and Prendergast's Saloon (Boston), 312
Garrow, Robert, 227
Garry, Charles, 226, 315
Gartside, John Edward, 228
Garvie, Maxwell, 553
Garvie, Sheila Watson, 553
Garvin, Sandra, 244
Gaskins, Donald Henry (Pee Wee), 228
Gass, Carl, 413
Gauvin, Jacques, 403
Gawthorp John, 190
Gay, Clestell, 569
Gaynor, Mayor William Jay, 47
Gbrurek, Tillie, 228-229
Geale, Eunice Mercel, 295
Geary, Charles Russell, 229
Geary, John, 229
Gedeon, Ethel, 304
Gedeon, Joseph, 304
Gedeon, Mary, 304
Gedeon, Veronica, 304
Gee, David, 198
Gee, Timothy, 198
Gee, Wong, 366
Gein, Edward, i, 229-(230)-231
Gein, Henry, 229
Gein, Mrs., 229
Geinke, Fred, 610
Geinke, Lily, 610
Gelwix, Mrs., 277-278
Gelwix, Catharine, 277-278
Gelwix, Helen, 277-278
General Motors Tech Center, 186
Genovese, Kitty, 415
Gentile, Daniel, 190, 499
Gentile, Jim, 409
Gentile, Judge *Henry*, 409
Gentle, Helen, 395
George II (Gr.), 76
George VI (Brit.), 374
George, Judge Ronald, 62
Georges V Hotel, 554
Georgia State Crime Laboratory, 110
Georgia State Mental Home, 427
Georgia Supreme Court, 605
Georgetown University, 316
Geraghty, Christopher James, 231
German Hospital, 74
Gerrish, Louise, 374
Gestapo, 27, 113, 449
Getting Out, 508
Gettler, Dr. Alexander O., 20, 143

Gewerbe Bank (Switz.), 299
Giaffery, Maitre Moro, **345**, 346
Gianelli, Paul, 451
Gibbons, Bill, 393
Gibbs, Captain, 566
Gibbs, Edward Lester, 231-232
Gibbs, Janie Lou, 232
Giberson, Ivy, 232
Gibons, Benjamin, 233
Gibons, Jacqueline, 232-233
Gibons, Sybil, 233
Giberson, William, 232
Gibson, Dr., 575
Gibson, Gay (Eileen Isabella Ronnie Gibson), 102-103)-104
Gibson, Norman, 272
Gide, Andre, 341
Giese, Petra, 336
Giesler, Jerry **139**, 140, 141, 497
Giffard, Miles, 233
Gilbey, Charles, 520
Gilday, Bernard, 501
Gildon, Cyril, 544
Gilinsky, Solomon, 576
Gill, James, 374
Gillette, Chester, 233-**234**
Gillette, Sheriff Faye, 347
Gillette, Otis, 190
Gilliam, Jackie, 67
Gillies, Gordon, 390
Gillis, Bernard, 34
Gillis, Stephen, 189
Gilly, Annette, 76
Gilly, Paul, 76
Gilman, Addie, 560-561
Gilmore, Gary, 1, 235, 535
Giordano, Gregorio, 235
Giordano, Salvatrice, 235
Giorgio, Jerry, 145
Girard, Henri, 235-236
Gire, Rosalie, 492
Glabe, Karen, 236
Glabe, Kenneth, 236
Glasder, James, 105
Glaskoff, Vladimir, 545
Glass, Jimmy, 236
Gleason, Cap. Frank, 231
Glenmore Hotel (Big Moose Lake, N.Y.), **234**
Glover, Andrew, 578
Glushakov, O.P., 404
Glyn-Jones, Justice, 468
Goddard, Justice Rayner, 169, 581
Godden, Ivy Mary, 481
Godzik, Greg, 226
Goeglein, Richard, 333
Goggin, Asst. St. Atty. Michael, 536
Gohl, Billy, 236-237
Glenwood Memorial Garden Center, 183
Goddard, Lord Chief Justice, 363
Godefroy, Robert, 346
Goff, Judge John W., 39, (49), 52, 53
Goins, Jimmy D., 109
Gold, Vivian, 509
Goldberg, Bernard, 115
Goldberg, Stephen, 115
Golde, Judge Stanley, 77
Goldenberg, Jack, 237-238
Golden Boy, 103
Golden Gate Bridge, 315

Grondkowski, Marian, 252
Gross, Reginald R., 252
Grossmann, George, 252
Grosvenor Hotel, 500
Grove, Officer, 549
Grzechowiak, Stephen, 252-253
Gsellman, George, 266
Guadalajara Cafe, 135
Guanabacoa Woman's Prison, 487
Guay, Albert, 253
Guay, Rita Morel, 253
Guenzel, Guel Sultan, 253
Guerin, Joseph, 253-254
Gufler, Max, 254
Guggenheim Fellowships, 6
Guidroz, Edward, 347
Guillen, Antonio Arias, 254
Guillen, Jose, 254
Guillin, Mme., 343, **345**
Guishard, Jessie, 524
Gump, Frederick B., 559
Gunderman, Stacey, 254-255
Gundlacht, Charles, 83
Gunnell, Bertram Clive, 198
Gunness, Belle, i, 255-(**257**)-261, 342
Gunness, Lucy, 255
Gunness, Myrtle, 255
Gunness, Peter, 255, 260
Gunness, Philip, 255
Gurga, Jeffrey, 261
Gurholdt, Henry, **259**-260
Gurley, U.S. Dist. Atty. J. Ward, 371
Gurrero, Sebastian, 530
Gush, Dr. Howard, 334
Gustavason, Commissioner, 579
Guswelle, Arthur, 200
Guswelle, Barbara, 200
Guswelle, Ron, 200
Guswelle, Vernita, 200
Guszkowski, Joseph, 228
Gutierrez, Ruben, 618
Gutteridge, George W., 89-90
Guyader, Alain, 303
Guyon, Melvin Bay, 261-262
Guyon, Michael, 261
Guys and Dolls, 48
Gyles, Reatha Marie, 471
Gypsy, 542

Haarmann, Fritz (Ogre of Hanover), i, 263
Haas, Rev. Hermann C.A., 289
Haas, Maria, 466
Haase, Judge Herman, 84
Hackett, Mary, 269
Hackett, Off. Thomas J. (Newark P.D.), 55
Haddrell, Det. Basil (Scotland Yard), 56, 98
Hadland, John, 616
Hadley, Det. Sgt. Joseph, 274
Haensel, Henry, 413
Haerm, Ann-Catrine, 264
Haerm, Teet, 263-264
Haga, Eric L., 264
Haga, Mrs. Judith, 264
Haga, Peri Lynn, 264
Hagan, Michael, 264
Hagen, Jean, 602
Hager-Segov, Elly, 619

Haggart, Garnetta Post, 264-265
Haggart, Robert Lee, 264-265
Hagger, Harold, 265
Haggerty, John F., 265-266
Hahn, Anna Marie, 266
Hahn, Maria, 338-339
Hahn, Oscar, 266
Hahn, Phillip, 266
Hahnemann Hospital (N.Y., N.Y.), 145
Haig, Preston, 236
Haigh, David, 458
Haigh, John George (The Acid-Bath Murderer), i,
    266-(**267**)-269
Hailstone, Claude, 217
Halberstam, Dr. Michael J., 594
Haldane, Lord, 36
Haley, James, 495
Halifax Borough Police (Brit.), 121
Hall, Andrea, 67
Hall, C.G., 576
Hall, Chris, 331
Hall, Sir Edward Marshall, 215, 293, 365, 494, 519
Hall, Faye Clements, 269-270
Hall, George Albert, 269
Hall, James W., 269-270
Hall, Leo, 270
Hall, Percival, 178
Hall, Richard, 83
Hall, William, 237
Hallahan, Constable Glen, 29
Haller, Off. John, 292
Hallet, Sara, 330
Hallinan, Justice James, 564
Hallinan, Patrick, 271
Hall of Fame (N.Y. Univ.), 554
Halm, Carmen Miranda, 200
Halm, Peter, 200
Haluka, John J., 136
Hamacher, Gertrude, 338
Hamann, Annie, 352
Hamann Museum of Human Anatomy and Com-
    parative Anthropology, 370
Hamard, Octave, 542
Hamburg, Harry, 325
Hamer, Beatrice, 266
Hamilton, Alexander, 152
Hamilton, Evelyn, 161
Hamilton, Ray, 204
Hamilton, Tommy, 572
Hammersmith Hospital, 33
Hammersmith Palace, 568
Hammond, Geoffrey, 270
Hampton, Melvin, 270
Hancock, Det. Bob, 276
Hand, Dr. W.F., 169
Handy, Elisa, 591
Hanlon, Donald, 521
Hanover Prison (Ger.), 263
Hanrahan, County Atty. Ray, 498
Hansen, Gov. Clifford (Wyo.), 454
Hanson, William P., 270-271
Harborview Medical Center, 428
Hardaker, Betty, 271-272
Hardaker, Charles, 271
Hardaker, Charles, Jr., 272
Hardaker, Dixie Ann, 272
Hardaker, Geraldine, 271-272
Hardin, Andrew, 272
Hardin, Glenda Sue, 458

Malik, Abdul (Michael X), 382
Malin, Jan, 67
Malinowski, Henry K., 252
Malmgren, Camille, 107
Maloney, James, 382
Maloney, Kathleen, 119
Maloney, Judge Thomas, 261
Maloney, Tom, 222
Maltby, Cecil, 382-383
Mamedzi, Shifulaso, 383
Mamoud, Police Commissioner Ali, 573
Mamzelle Champagne, 556
Manchester Crown Court (Eng.), 19
Mancini, Antonio, 383
Mancini, Tony, 383-384
Mandel, Leon, 360
Mandel, Off. Robert W. (NYPD), 193
Manders, Mientje, 466
Mandic, Karen, 61
Mandusa, 118
Manfield, Dr. H.H., 581
Mangin, Dist. Comm., 334
Manhattan House of Detention for Men, 306
Manhattan State Supreme Court, 3
Mann, Becky, 419
Mann, Ernest Mann, Jr., 419
Mann, Ernest Mann, Sr., 419
Mann, Jennifer, 419
Mann, Lynda, 453
Mann, Martha, 419
Mann, Michael, 98
Mann, Shannon, 419
Mann Act, 385
Manning, Clyde, 606
Manning, Henry, 545
Mannis, Larry, 322
Manson, Charles, 185, 220, 250, 384-(387)-389
Manson, Donna Gail, 91, **93**
Manson, Lena, 264
Mantia, Robert, 294
Manton, Mrs. Caroline (Rene), 389
Manton, Horace William, 389
Manuel, Peter Thomas Anthony, 389-390
Man With Five Hundred Names, The, See: Edel, Frederick
Man With the Candy, The, 135
Mapp, Mary, 604
Marcais, Jacques, 449
Marcelino, Julian, 391
Marcette, Louise, 351
Marchadier, Mme., 344
Marchand, Clothilde, 73
Marchand, Henri, 73
Marchese, Judge William J., 111
Marden, Mrs., 515
Marek, Emil, 391
Marek, Ingeborg, 391
Marek, Martha Lowenstein, 391-392
Maremont, Arnold, 360
Margiotti, Atty. Gen'l. Charles J., 254
Marguis, Off. Don, 419
Mariano, Judge Gene, 191
Maricopa County Superior Court (Ariz.), 8
Marina City Bar, 591
Marine Firemen's, Oiler's, and Water Tender's Union, 441
Marino, Antonio, 462
Marion Correctional Institution (Ill.), 502
Marist College (Poughkeepsie, N.Y.), 5

Marjeram, Albert Edward, 392
Markle, Amy, 392
Markle, Chris, 392
Markle, Fletcher, 392
Markle, John, 392
Markle, Suzanne, 392
Markowitz, Rubin, 206
Marks, Jonathan, 116
Marks, Lawrence, 392-393
Marley, Kemper, Sr., 8
Marochel, Father Josef, 186
Marquez, Arturo, 325
Marro, Asst. Dist. Atty. P.F., 205
Mars, Florence, 75
Marsh, James, 458
Marshall, Doreen, 279
Marshall, Franklin, 393
Marshall, Grahame James, 276
Marshall, Janet, 26-27
Mars-Jones, W.L., 110
Martelletti, Augustin, 551
Martin, Aubrey Wayne (Buddy), 76
Martin, Billy, 97-98
Martin, Judge Bonnie Lee, 603
Martin, Caroline Wardlaw, **590**
Martin, Colonel John, 590
Martin, Justice, 331
Martin, Kimberly Diane, 61
Martin, Lee Roy, 393
Martin, Police Supt. LeRoy, 280
Martin, Luis, 617
Martin, Marie, 491
Martin, Oscey, 590
Martin, Oswald Norman, 23-24
Martin, Dep. Sheriff Robert, 167
Martin, Sarah, 566
Martinetti, Paul, 146
Martinetti, Mrs. Paul, 146
Martinez, Gov. Bob (Fla.), 165
Martinez, Luis, 530
Martinez, Off. Romero, **599**, 600
Martinis, Justice Joseph A., 306
Martirosoff, Reuben (Russian Robert), 252
Martland, County Coroner Harrison, 291
Marwood, Ronald Henry, 393-394
Marx, Karl, 1
Maryland Penitentiary, 296, 600
Marymont, Marcus, **394**
Marymont, Mary Helen, 394
Marzek, Sonia, 179
Marshfield Junior High School (Mo.), 488
Mashburn, Dep. Wiley, 616
Maskas, Richard, 568
Mason, Alexander Campbell, 394
Mason, Carlton, 394-395
Mason, Howard (Pappy), 372
Mason, Off. James, 322
Mason General Hospital (Long Island, N.Y.), 59
Massachusetts Supreme Court, 317
Masset, Louise, 395
Masset, Manfred, 395
Massie, Mrs. Thalia, 395-(397)-398
Massie, Thomas, 395-(397)-399
Massie, Judge *Thornton L.*, 16-17
Mast, Harold, 20
Mast, Randi, 20
Masters, Off. Eugene, 538
Masters, Paul, 207
Mastrian, Norman, 562-563

Miller, Ruby, 142
Miller, Sam, 527
Miller, William, 522, 523
Miller, Winifred, 306
Millerand, President Alexandre (Fr.), 163
Mills, Ballard, 405-406
Mills, Fred, 405-406
Mills, Herbert Leonard, 405
Mills, John H., 405-406
Mills, Mrs. John, 405-406
Mills, Leonard, 405
Mills, Lucinda, 405-406
Mills, Ora, 405-406
Mills Hotel (N.Y., N.Y.), 162
Millward, Vera, 547
Milne, Marie, 98
Milone, Richard, 406
Milosavljeric, Ljubinka, 406
Minard, Lt. Aldace, 547
Minasi, Joseph, 54
Mineo, Sal, 602-603
Ming, Wu Zee, 546
Minnesota State Training School, 440
Minsky, Max, 406
Mintiks, Helen Hagnes, 144
Miramar Reservoir (San Diego, Calif.), 274
Mira Mesa High School (San Diego, Calif.), 274
Miranda, Nicholas, 200
Mirecki, Lee, 129-130
Mississippi State College, 400
Mississippi State Penitentiary, 596
Missouri Baptist Hospital (St. Louis), 207-208
Missouri State Highway Patrol, 488
Missouri State Prison, 88
Mistress, 417
Mitchell, Sgt. Arthur, 146
Mitchell, Beatrice, 407
Mitchell, Off. Gerald H., 402
Mitchell, Mrs. Jimmy, 117
Mitchell, Judge John, 364
Mitchell, Lanyon, 129
Mitchell, Lorraine, 249
Mitchell, Off. P.J., 550
Mitchell, Ray Anthony, 406-407
Mitchell, Timothy, 407
Mitchell, Tyrone, 407
Mitchell, Winifred Mary, 99
Mitkiewitz, John, 228
Mixer, Jane, 128
Mock, Sheriff J. Henry, 394
Mock, Lisa Marie, 471
Modoc County *Daily Mail*, 221
Moench, Dr. Louis G., 488
Mohr, Floyd, 471
Moitke, George, 179
Moity, Henry, 407
Moity, Leonide, 407
Moity, Joseph, 407
Moity, Theresa, 407
Moldovsky, Joel, 243
Molina del Rio, Francisco (The Hook), 407
Mollersdorf Jail (Aust.), 291
Mollison, Dr. Crawford, 529
Monaghan, Frank C., 254-256
Monahan, Annie, 407-408
Monahan, John T., 408
Monahan, Joseph, 408
Monckton, Walter, 363
Mondale, Walter, 315

Mondolini, Roger, 408
Monin, Madam, 236
Monni, Pietro, 452
Monohan, Mrs., 243
Monro, James, 70
Monroe, Rev. Jerry C., 332
Monroe, Marck C., 242
Monsson, Otto, 578
Monster of Dusseldorf, The, See: Kurten, Peter
Montana State Prison, 440
Montana State Reformatory, 440
Monte Carlo Club, 527
Montoya, Alfred, 399
Montoya, Harold, 399
Montrose, 148, 149, 150
Moo, John, 255, 260
Moodie, Anita, 408
Moodie, Duncan, 408-409
Moon, Norman, 409
Moor Court (Brit.), 56
Moore, Alvin, Jr., 236
Moore, Bob, 575
Moore, Brian Steven, 409
Moore, Dennis Albert Reginald, 409
Moore, Donald P., 161
Moore, Hutchie, 409
Moore, Off. Jack, 378
Moore, Judge James E., 608
Moore, Manuel, 618
Moore, Roy, 246, 247
Moore Opera House, 456
Moores, Charles, 384
Moors Murders, The, 409-410
Morales, Herberto, 91
Morales, Michael Angelo, 410-411
Moran, Frank, 131
Morath, Kathy, 485
Moreira, Manuel (Horseface), 411
Morey, William, 411
Morgan, Derrick, 411
Morgan, Dr. Donald, 607
Morgan, Harjes & Co., 153
Morgan, J. Pierpont, 152, 153, 158
Morgan, Maggie, 495-496
Morgan, Richard E., 84
Morgan, Vicki, 439
Morgenthau, Dist. Atty. Robert, 578
Moritz, Gerhard, 238
Morman Church, 290
Morman Temple, 290
Morman Murders, The, 291
Morony, Judge Jean, 432
Morris, Ann Orr, 32
Morris, Judge, 374
Morris, Justice, 76
Morris, W.J., 391
Morrison, Arling, 287, 288
Morrison, John, 287, 288
Morrison, Malcolm, 390
Morrison, Merlin, 287
Morrison, Steinie, 412
Morrison Hotel (Chgo.), 305, 354, 360
Morrissey, Judge William, 501
Morro Castle, 471
Mors, Albert, 496-497
Mors, Annika, 263, 264
Mors, Frederick, 412-414
Mors, Theresa, 496-497
Morse, Off. Ernest J., 182

Pershing, General John J (Black Jack), 587
Pesce, Ernesto, 448
Pesce, Mary Anne, 329
Petan, George, 502-503
Petan, Neil, 502-503
Petan, Sylvia, 502-503
Petan, Verna, 502-503
Peter Skene Ogden Park, 220
Peter the Painter, 412
Peters, Alan, 553
Peters, Helen, 130
Peters, Judge Marvin, 226
Peters, Phil, 130-131
Peterson, Evely May, 289
Peterson, James Hodgson, 289
Peterson, J.C., 74
Peterson, Kim, 65
Peterson, Lindsay, 606
Peterson, Phyllis, 289
Peterson, P.T., 449
Peterson, Richard, 449
Peterson, Rob, 399-400
Petiot, Dr. Marcel Andre Henri Felix, i, 449-**450**
Petit, Bernard, 303, 439, 440
Petit, Roland, 285
Petka, State's Atty. Edward, 84
Petrichella, Elsie Keller, 327
Petrone, John P., 63
Petrushansky, Evsle S., 323
Petrzuwalski, Dagmar (Dagmar Peters), 265
Petz, Susan, 227
Peyton Place, 140
Phantom of the Opera Case, See: **Crimmins, Craig**
Pheasant Run Playhouse, 98
Phenix Insurance Company, 236
Phillips, Ann, 450
Phillips, Armour, 450
Phillips, Clara, 450-451
Phillips, David Graham, 237-238
Phillips, James, 76
Phillips, John, 84
Phillips, John Stanley, 451
Phillips, Sylvester, 450
Phillips, William R., 451
Philippine Bureau of Investigation (PBI), 417
Philpott, Dr. Albert, 529
Phipps, J. Blaine, 498
Phipps, Ray, 422
Phoenix Hotel (Phoenix, Ariz.), 7
Piasecny, Doris, 297
Piasecny, Henry, 297-298
Piazza, Catherine, 413
Pica, Sean, 451
Picasso, Pablo, 389
Picchioni, Ernesto (Monster of Nerola), 451-452
Pichette, J.A., 579
Pickens, Mary Christine, 458-459
Pickett, Roosevelt, 296
Pickrel, Judge Mark, 281
Pico, Solomon, 125
Picourla, Georgette, 418
Piddock, Paul, 168
Pienaar, A.J., 576
Pierce, Kathie, 334
Pierce, Louis, 452
Pierce, William Joseph, Jr., 452
Pierson, Cheryl, 451
Pierson, Howard, 452
Pierson, James, 451

Piest, Elizabeth, 225
Piest, Harold, 225
Piest, Ken, 225
Piest, Kerry, 225
Piest, Robert, 225-226
Pierce, Robert, 25
Pike, Off. Frank, 616
Pin, Im Sook, 452-453
Pin, Yong Am, 452-453
Pietila, Velma, 102
Pilarchik, John, 571-572
Pincham, Judge R. Eugene, 205, 272
Pinker, Ray, 535
Pinkerton National Detective Agency, 105, 321
Pioppi, Armando, 304
Pioppi, Gino, 304
Pioppi, John, 304
Pioppi, Marion, 304
Pioppi, Theresa, 304
Pipes, Richard, 88
Pisselli, Vittorio, 321
Piszczor, James, 409
Pitchfork, Colin, 453, 454
Pitcock, Detective, 249-250
Pitman, Alexander Henry, 567
Pitre, Marguerite, 253
Pittman, Jim, 300
Pitts, Judge J.W., 461
Pittsburgh Community Service Center, 362
Pixley, Andrew, 454
Pixley, C.F., 454
Pizza Hut (Tampa, Fla.), 106
Place, Susan, 483-484
Placido, Judy, 58
Plaindealer & Modoc County Times, 221
Platt, Eleanor, 306
Playboy, 522
Playskool, Inc., 465
Pless, Dr. John, 467
Pletnev, D.D., 615
Plitt, Charles, 44
Plotzenee Prison (Ger.), 320
Plowden, Charles, 543
Plugge, Capt. Leonard, 382
Plymouth Brethren, 82, 266, 280
Pochin, Kate, 470
Poddar, Prosenjit, 454-455
Podmore, William Henry, 455
Pohl, Tressin, 133
Pohlman, Ernie, 439
Polanski, Roman, 386
Police Story, 329
Polish Baptist Church, 191
Polk, Sheriff J.V., 563
Pollack, Louis, 55
Pollock, Sir Ernest, 24
Polulach, Dorothy, 35-36, 586
Polulach, George, 586
Pomroy, Karen Ann, 107
Ponder, Judge Andrew, 322
Poniatowski, Michel, 85
Poole, Becky, 167
Poole, Charles, 167
Poole, Derek Alan, 455
Poole, Peter Harold, 455
Pope John Paul II, 546
Popik, Paula, 568
Pople, G.T., 455-456

Popolo, John, 191
Porter, Daniel, 227
Porter, J. Robert, 382
Porter, Kathy, 196
Porter, Lord, 383
Posey, Billy Wayne, 75
Post, George, 265
Post, Vaudrey, 265
Potkonjac, Vjekoslav, 580
Potter, Bruce, 456
Pou, George Ross, 602
Poughkeepsie Middle School (N.Y.), 206
Pound, Ezra, 156
Powell, Brian, 273
Powell, F.J., 90
Powell, Freida (Becky), 367
Powell, Mrs. Irving, 107
Powell, Leonard, 108
Powell First National Bank (Wyo.), 190
Power, Edgar, 376
Power, John Joseph, 456
Power, Terence, 166
Power, Lt. Thomas, 91
Powers, Harry F., 456
Prainito, Salvatore, 308
Prater, William, 76
Pratt, S.J., 543
Pratt, Admiral William Lee, 398
Praun, Dr. Otto, 90
Preacher and the Slave, The, 286
Prejean, Dalton, 456-457
Preston Cemetery (Melbourne, Aus.), 10
Preston, John Trevor, 457
Preston, William, 457
Pretoria Central Prison (S. Afri.), 351, 575, 590
Price, Adele, 377
Price, Albert, 457
Price, Dep. Sher. Cecil R., 74, 75
Price, Police Chief Everett, 32
Priestly, Helen, 182
Priestly, Mrs. 182
Prilukoff, Donat, 419-420
Prince, Ernest, 457
Prince, Katheryn, 97
Prince, Police Chief Billy, 601
Prince, Walter, 219, 457
Prior, Elizabeth, 592
Prisloo, A.M., 576
Procunier, Ray, 172
Proffitt, Sheriff Willis E., 464
Prong, Keith, 457-458
Prudom, Barry Peter (Cop Killer), **458**
Pruyn, Kenyon W., 458
Psycho, 229
Psychopath, 377
Ptak, Tom, 35
Pulitzer, Mrs. Joseph P., 617
Pullen, Constance Anne, 288
Pullen, James, 288
Pulliam, Mark, 458
Purchase, Bentley, 223
Purinton, Kevin, 78
Purnsley, Det. Elery, 129
Putland, William, 209
Putt, George Howard, 458-459
Pyke, Det. James A., 288

Qaddafi, Muammar, 607
Quarles, George Brownie, 446
Quebec Police Dept., 150
Queen City Pure Water Co., 342
Queen of Sheba, 423
Queen, Peter, 460
Queen's University, 240
Queripel, Michael, 460
Quesnel, Bob, 78
Quinlan, Karen Ann, 107
Quinlan, Sergeant, 103
Quinlivan, Asst. State's Atty. Robert, 88
Quinn, Jeanne, 400
Quinn, Robert J., 279
Quinn, Roseann, 608
Quinn, Chief William J., 432

Raab, Selwyn, 111
Rabinowitz, Julius, 55
Rablen, Carroll, **461**
Rablen, Eva, 461
Racial Adjustment Action Society, 382
Raffaelo, Roberto, 461-462
Raffanti, Sonjia, 579-580
Rafferty, Anthony, 462
Raffield, Off. George, 333
Ragone, Antonio, 567-568
Ragone, Vita, 567-568
Rahway State Prison, 62
Raiford Penitentiary (Fla.), 334, 367
Railway Hotel, 577
Railway Police (S. Afri.), 127
Railway Tavern, 520
Rainey, Sheriff Lawrence (Neshoba Cty., Miss.), 75
Rakoczy, Asst. St. Atty. Mark, 203
Ralph, Edward, 462
Ramb, Christine, 289
Ramos Oil Company (Morgan City, La.), 3
Ramsahaye, Kramchand, 505
Ramsperger, Charles, 55
Ranck, Dist. Atty., 232
Rancourt, Susan, 91-**93**
Randall, The, 531
Randazzo, Det. Gaspar, 170
Randolph, Jennie, 423
Random House, 1
Ransom, Florence, 462
Ransom, Chancellor Harry, 600
Raphael, Sylvia, 462-463
Rardon, Gary, 463
Rasberry, Jerry, 406-407
Rasiewicz, Barbara, 463
Rasiewicz, John, 463
Rasiewicz, William, 463
Rasiewicz, William, Jr., 463
Rathel, Otis, 533
Rau, Gustav, 578
Rauth, Henry, 584-585
Ravenswood Hospital (Chicago, Ill.), 587
Ravinia Elementary School (Winnetka, Ill.), 164
Ray, Deborah, 375
Ray, Jean-Michel, 83
Raycroft, Det. Victor, 86
Reade, Pauline, 410
Reader's Digest, 540
Reading High School, 611

Sworn, Dr. Henry George, 494
Sybil, 61
Sykes, George Ernest, 544
Sykut, Stanislaw, 436
Symonds, Yvonne, 278
Symons, William, 500
Syzmanklewicz, Joseph, 534-535
Szabo, Mrs. Ladislaus, 206
Szehsien, Chief Justice Wen, 293
Szendi, Maria, 206
Szilagyi, Linda, 568
Sztaray, Countess Flora, 376
Szurma, Sonia, 548
Szyc, John, 226

Taborsky, Albert, 550
Taborsky, Joseph, 550
Tacklyn, Larry Winfield, **98-99**
Tafel, Monika, 336
Taft, Pres. William Howard, 441
Takai, David, 395, 396
Tal, Schlomo, 550
Talbert, Dorothea, 534
Talbot, Justice, 562
Talbot, Acie, 426
Talbot, Ben, 550
Talbot, Bess, 75
Talbot, Lug, 550
Talbot, Lura Lee, 75
Talbot, Thurgood, 426
Tam, Catherine Morgan, 364-365
Tam, Cecilia, 364-365
Tam, Doris, 364-365
Tam, Phyllis, 592
Tammany (N.Y., N.Y.), 39, 43, 45
Tanguay, Germaine, 293
Tanis, Hazel, 110
Tansey, John, 550-551
Tardy, Mary Louise, 331-332
Tarnower, Dr. Herman, 273-274
Tarnowska, Marie Nicolaievna, 419-420
Tate, Mrs. Gene, 400
Tate, Sharon, 386, **387**, 388
Tattershaw, Mrs. Mable, 405
Taunton State Asylum for the Criminally Insane (Mass.), 566
Taylor, Off. Charles (SFPD), 241
Taylor, Cynthia, 394
Taylor, Edwina, 195
Taylor, Gary, 92
Taylor, Jack S., 551
Taylor, Perry Alexander, 551
Taylor, Richard A., 87
Teacher's Pet, 615
Teare, Charles, 500
Teare, Dr. Donald, 104, 363
Tebourek, Mark, 164
Teddy Boys, 166
Tehachapi Women's Prison, 328, 350, 451
Teichman, Sir Eric, 509
Telles, Felix, 551
Temperance Hotel (Brit.), 67
Temple University, 571
Tenderloin, The, 40

Ten Most Wanted List (FBI), 261
Tereniv, N.S., 404
Terf, Phil, 225
Terminal Island Prison (Calif.), 385
Terpening, Oliver, Jr., 551-552
Terpening, Oliver, Sr., 551, 552
Terry, John Victor, 552
Tesmer, Klara, 336
Tessedre, Serge, 85
Tessier, Dewey, 189
Tessnov, Ludwig, 552-553
Testro, Angelina, 553
Tevendale, Brian, 553
Tevrizzian, Judge Dickran, Jr., 326
Tew, Anthony, 537
Texas Chainsaw Massacre II, 78
Texas Department of Corrections Prison (Huntsville, Texas), 55, 593
Texas Rangers, 244
Thacker, Robert, 553
Thacker, William J., 553
Thames, Mary Emma, 543
Thatcher, Margaret, 480
Thaw, Harry Kendall, i, 22, 414, 553-(**555**, **557**)-559
Thaw, Mrs., **555**
Therrien, Armand R., 559
Therrien, Joseph W., 559-560
They Always Call Us Ladies, 274
They Shoot Horses, Don't They?, 615
Thieben, Ruth, 270
Thief, 98
Thiery, Madeleine, 27
Thomas, Allgen Lars, 263-264
Thomas, Angelina, 251
Thomas, Arthur Alan, 560
Thomas, Cheryl, 94
Thomas, Daniel, 17
Thomas, Donald George, 560
Thomas, Edward, 560-561
Thomas, Elsie, 292
Thomas, Ethel, 558
Thomas, Gordon, 471
Thomas, Jennie, 497
Thomas, Leonard Jack, 561
Thomas, Peter, 84-85
Thomas, Tequila, 608
Thompson, Alvin, 294
Thompson, Edith, 160
Thompson, Edith Jessie, **561**
Thompson, Elizabeth, 561-562
Thompson, George, 562
Thompson, George Winston, 444
Thompson, Judge Howard, 8
Thompson, Gov. James (Ill.), 161, 406
Thompson, Jane, 37
Thompson, Larry, 68
Thompson, Percy, **561**
Thompson, Tilmer Eugene, 562-563
Thompson, Verona, 445
Thompson, William James, 537
Thompson, William Paul, 563
Thomson, Doug, 102
Thomson, Justice Harold F., 249
Thorley, Walter, 494
Thorn, Judge F. Bret, 73
Thorne, John Norman Holmes, 563
Thorne, Thomas Harold, 563
Thornhill, Caroline, 511, 519